D0855447

PERCEPTUAL GAMES AND ACTIVITIES

BY THE SAME AUTHOR:

Educational Games for Fun

Games and Stunts for Schools, Camps, and Playgrounds

Party Fun: For Holidays and Special Occasions

The School Game Book (*with Marian S. Holmes*)

PERCEPTUAL GAMES AND ACTIVITIES

Margaret E. Mulac

Illustrations by Michael S. Paulus

HARPER & ROW, PUBLISHERS

NEW YORK, HAGERSTOWN
SAN FRANCISCO
LONDON

FIRST EDITION

Designed by Sidney Feinberg

Library of Congress Cataloging in Publication Data

Mulac, Margaret Elizabeth, date
Perceptual games and activities.
Bibliography: p. 195
Includes index.
1. Educational games. 2. Perceptual learning.
I. Title.
LB1029.G3M84 1977 371.3 76-5518
ISBN 0-06-013103-9

---

77 78 79 80 10 9 8 7 6 5 4 3 2 1

To Benji
who, at five and one-half, seems always to have
known that learning is fun

Contents

Acknowledgments

How casually one meets an idea which opens up a whole new line of thought. A thought thrown out in a conversation, a line in a book, an accidental pun or "funny" can become the basis for a chapter or a whole book. To those who have supplied such stimuli, knowingly or unknowingly, I am grateful.

Thanks to my favorite "bookies," the librarians, who were patient, courteous, and always helpful no matter how impossible my requests. Special thanks to Jane and Ron Grossman for their above-and-beyond help in the preparation of the manuscript.

As always, my gratitude to family members, Dorothy, John, and Peter Gross, and Carol Hoffmann, and to my friend and colleague Susan P. Mahan, who provided ideas, valuable criticism, and encouragement, that most important ingredient in the writing of any book.

Preface

Learning is a lifetime process. It is an integral part of being alive. Consciously or unconsciously, one or more of our senses is involved in every learning experience. In many such experiences, what we learn is enhanced by the deliberate use of as many senses as possible. We can look at a rose and appreciate its color and shape and perfection. We can enjoy it more if we inhale its fragrance. When we add the sense of touch and feel the prick of a thorn, or the smooth coolness of its petals with our fingers or against our lips or cheeks, our appreciation of it grows with each new sensory stimulation.

This is not a book just for the young. It is for persons of all ages who are still learning new things or learning how to enjoy in new and different ways things they already know. As the book evolved, it became increasingly apparent that it is possible to become excited about something new at any age. It is sometimes even more exciting to learn something new about what has become a familiar and accepted part of one's life. To see a thing in a way you have never seen it before is as exhilarating as seeing it for the first time.

In working on the chapter on mathematics, I fell in love with this marvelous and logical science of learning because I saw it in a way I had never seen it before. In writing about the winds, I discovered fascinating facts about this inescapable part of our lives that we take so matter-of-factly until the winds become wild and jar us out of our complacency. Words, some of my favorite old friends-in-fun, showed me new ways to enjoy them.

To find pleasure in the everyday parts of our lives we take for granted—words, the winds, mathematics—to play with them, enjoy them, to see them in ways other than as parts of our daily routines, is to give our lives new meaning. To see what we have never seen before although we have looked at it thousands of times, to hear what we have never heard before because we have never actually listened, to taste, to smell, to enjoy with all our senses—this is perceptual acuity.

Using all our senses to their fullest capacity in all our learning experiences adds to the value and enjoyment of these experiences. A lesson learned with enjoyment is no less factual than one learned by grim application. Knowledge learned with enjoyment becomes knowledge to enjoy and to share. The more we practice this kind of learning the easier it becomes to learn with enjoyment. Thus what we learn becomes part of everyday living to savor for all our lives.

This has been an exciting book to write. To use all one's senses in learning, enjoying what one learns, is to develop perceptual acuity. That's what this book is all about.

By Way of Introduction

Readers examining this book may say this book is mostly about mathematics, and they will be right. The word "mathematics" stems from two Greek words, *mathēma*, meaning science, and *manthanein*, to learn. Thus mathematics is the science of learning.

How is learning acquired? We learn through our senses, by seeing, hearing, touching, tasting, and smelling. Through our senses we learn to distinguish differences in shapes, sounds, textures, tastes, and odors. In many instances, more than one sense is required to determine the exact identity of the subject being studied. Take, for example, three white powdered substances. They cannot be identified by sight alone, nor by sight and the feel of the textures, nor even with sight, feel, and smell together! They must be tasted to determine which is confectioners sugar, which is cornstarch, and which is baking powder. Granulated sugar and salt must be tasted to determine the difference. Failure of the cook to identify which is which before using one or the other, or both, in a dish could be gastronomically unpleasant or mildly disastrous.

One may be born with the impairment of one or more senses or suffer from the loss of one or more through disease or accident. The teacher sees pupils with partial hearing, impaired sight, dyslexia (the inability to read), or brain damage as pupils with perceptual problems whose needs must be met in special ways. The therapist also works with individuals who are more severely and often multiply handicapped. Both work to help such individuals reach their maximum capabilities and potentials.

We learn through our senses, and the more senses we use the more we learn and the more we enjoy what we learn. Those who are blind can only "see" what their other senses show them. Those who are deaf can only "hear" what their other senses tell them. The blind cannot see flat shapes (as in drawings), printed type, or colors, but by employing their other senses they can learn to "see" many things. They learn shapes by feeling things with their hands. They learn to read by feeling the raised dots of braille. They learn through their ears by listening to instructions or answers to their questions. They learn what food they are eating through their sense of taste, by the smell, and sometimes by the texture or shape of the food in their hands or their mouths. Spaghetti and macaroni may taste the same, but macaroni shapes vary, and a blind person may surprise you by saying, "My, but this shell macaroni salad is delicious."

All of us have known a blind person who has never seen us, as we understand seeing, but who quickly learns to recognize us by the way we walk, or talk, or laugh, or by the scent we wear frequently. Even if we are sighted (not blind) we learn to recognize the voices of our classmates or friends. We do not need to turn around in class to see who is reciting; we learn to recognize friends' voices on the phone and to identify them by their voices before we see them in a crowd. Similarly, we need not see a fire engine, police car, or ambulance to realize that one is clamoring for the right-of-way.

While there are those individuals born with impairment of

one or more senses who must learn to overcome their perceptual handicaps or to compensate in other ways for their lack, there are many, many more individuals who do not have such deficiencies. They may, however, suffer from lack of perceptual acuity, not because they lack the capacity for it, but because they have been deprived of opportunities and stimulation in school or in the home. They may never have been led to understand the importance, the satisfaction, or the sheer fun of enjoying all their senses in the search for knowledge and happiness. As a result they may go through life unnecessarily handicapped perceptually, never fully employing their capabilities or realizing their maximum potential. Nor is this kind of stimulation only necessary for the young. Therapists and recreation leaders who work with older persons need to understand the value of games and activities which stimulate the senses not only of those who have been ill but those who through the normal processes of aging tend to lose mental alertness and perceptual acuity without such stimulation.

The trained eye can view a cloud formation and identify its type and perhaps even the kind of weather it brings. But the one who sees the beauty of its form and feels awed by its size, is stirred by the drama taking place in the atmosphere, sees a humorous form of a person or animal in its shape, and can laugh with pure joy at the discovery, possesses that kind of perceptiveness which gives meaning to each day and richness to a life.

Many sounds become so familiar to us that we need not see what is making the sound to be aware of it or to identify it in our minds. It is the strange sound that makes us prick up our ears. Often we must employ other senses to identify accurately the source of the sound. What sounds like someone tapping at our door may turn out to be the pecking of the bluejay as he cracks a sunflower seed to get at the kernel.

Our senses add to our enjoyment of new experiences and to

the repetition of old and familiar ones. When we suffer from a bad cold and a stuffy nose which impairs our sense of smell temporarily, our sense of taste is also impaired. So, during a cold, food becomes tasteless. We can see it but we cannot smell it. We feel it in our mouths, but the taste is so dulled that eating is less enjoyable. There is no question that the enjoyment of eating is enhanced by the smell and taste as well as by the fact that it satisfies our hunger. We enjoy the texture and coolness of a soft ice cream cone as well as its delicious flavor.

Our five senses have much to do with how we "feel" inside. This kind of feeling, which has nothing—yet everything—to do with the sense of touch, is called an emotional feeling or reaction. What we see or hear, touch, taste, or smell may please us, make us angry, give us a headache, make us sick to our stomachs, or make us laugh aloud.

If we don't really see what we are looking at—the shapes, the color, the movement—if we fail to listen to the sounds around us, we miss much of the beauty around us, and life is not as enjoyable as it might be. Of course, the harder we look, the more we see. We then notice ugliness, dirt, and shocking sights. But if we can see the beauty, we may be stirred to remedying the unbeautiful which need not remain so. There is a saying about those who merely curse the darkness, and those who light a candle. The more we see around us, the more often we ask the why and how of it all. When we seek the answers, we learn more and grow in understanding with each answer.

Enjoyment of life is something we learn. It is not a gift from another. We must train our senses to become more acute, just as the blind must train their fingers and ears to be their eyes and the deaf must train their eyes to be their ears.

Many of the most enjoyable experiences are those made up of many sensory experiences. At a ball game, whether your team wins or loses is only part of the fun. There is the fun of being outside in pleasant weather, the enjoyment of the colorful uniforms, the green turf, the blue sky, the colors of the clothing of those in the stands and bleachers. There is the feeling of hunger satisfied by a hot dog, the aroma and taste of warm popcorn or peanuts, the thirst quenched by a cold drink. The sounds of the game are a great part of it. The sharp, staccato decisions of the umpire, the screams of the spectators, the rhythmic clapping of frantic fans exhorting their team, the crack of the bat when the ball is well hit, all add to the fun of the day. The drama of the game, the suspense on the field, the waiting for the pitch which may spell disaster or triumph for the home team—all these are the sensory reactions that make attending a ball game more enjoyable. If our team wins, that is a bonus. If it loses, we can be philosophical about it; we had fun anyway.

What better science than mathematics to train many of the senses? What science requires so many perceptual decisions, insists upon precision and exactness, demands logic, forces the recognition of relationships, forms, numbers, and arrangements?

Fun with words relies much upon acute hearing and listening. How can one play rhyming games without first hearing a word and then placing it with others which sound like it?

Homophones, the sound-alikes, require listening acuity to enable us to recognize words which sound like, but do not look like, another. Similarly, homographs, the look-alikes which are pronounced differently, require good listening. If one does not actually hear the difference of pronunciation, for whatever reason, he will continue all his life to mispronounce a word and may even completely miss the meaning of a sentence. Wind, for example, may be pronounced to rhyme with find or to rhyme with sinned. The meanings are very different. Language skills are as much a part of hearing as seeing and saying. Playing word games is good training and fun for persons of all ages. There is always something new and fascinating to learn about words.

Take any common factor of life and begin using more senses

than are ordinarily used in considering it, and suddenly a whole new world of excitement will open. The brief chapter on the winds is an example. Any one phase of the study of winds can be a world in itself. Test it for yourself. Along with the fascination of the study comes the realization of how much there is to learn about, and how brief a time we have in which to learn. We view with regret what we have missed along the line which we could have been enjoying, and yet rejoice that it is never too late to learn and enjoy if we will.

Somewhere I came across this statement: "Offer a two-year-old two cookies of the same kind and it will instinctively employ a mathematical principle and reach for the larger one." The child has already entered the magical world of mathematics.

Math is in everyday living,
We use it in all that we do,
It's not just for school and for testing,
It's far more than just two times two.

Counting money is math that is practical,
You must know just how much you own,
If what you want costs more than you have,
You'll just have to leave it alone.

Percentages are math'matical problems,
They're used in all major sports,
How many games won and how many lost,
On diamonds, fields, or courts.

You can measure your height in meters,
Or inches and feet will do, too,
Your weight can be reckoned in kilos or pounds;
Whichever you use, it's still you.

Knowing volume is very important
In so many things that you do.
Pour more in a glass than its limit,
And you'll end up with some spilled on you.

Split seconds and minutes and hours
Are tied into all that you do.
You're slower or faster than others
That's the math part of being just you.

Our universe is truly a math one,
It runs like a well-oiled clock.
The weeks and the months, the moon and the tides,
Run by rules as solid as rock.

The verses may be used as a basis for assignments by having the students bring in pictures from newspapers or magazines, clippings, cartoons, or verses they have written which show math in everyday living. Here are several examples:

1. Tables of statistics and percentages from the sports columns.
2. Bank advertisements showing interest rates.
3. Pictures of sports figures running, skating, swimming, biking, or car racing against time.
4. Pictures of sports contestants jumping for height or distance or throwing a shot or javelin for distance.
5. Pictures of carpenters, bricklayers, or surveyors using measuring instruments.
6. Experimenters using scales, a microscope, recording instruments.
7. Pictures of groups of children or adults showing various sizes and weights.
8. Stock market quotations.

9. Advertisements of sales showing percentage reductions of prices.
10. Pictures of measuring tools, scales, and other calculating devices from tool catalogs.
11. Recipes cut from advertisements or cereal boxes.
12. Someone cutting something from a pattern.

Once the students become accustomed to the idea, the bulletin board will be flooded with materials demonstrating that math is in everything we do.

PERCEPTUAL GAMES AND ACTIVITIES

1

The Winds in Our Lives

No one has ever seen the winds,
Those currents of the air,
Not you, nor I, nor anyone else,
Yet we know the winds are there.

Gentle or killing, friend or foe,
In weather foul or fair,
A vital part of all our lives,
The winds are always there.

THE VARIETY OF WINDS

The most inescapable and talked about part of our lives is the weather. Since they are an important factor in the weather, the winds are an inevitable part of our lives. Learning to know and understand the winds in our lives can be a fascinating and life-long study. It may even save our lives.

Since man's earliest beginnings, the winds have been a source of fascination, wonder, and awe. There have been poems, songs, proverbs, and adventure and horror stories written about the wind. Perhaps you remember that *The Wizard of Oz* began with a cyclone. Later in this chapter, when you read about cyclones and tornadoes, you will learn that it was not a cyclone but a tornado which led to Dorothy's adventures. (In Kansas, tornadoes are called cyclones, and one takes cover in a cyclone cellar until the "cyclone" passes.)

The winds have been given poetic names like breeze and zephyr and romantic sounding names such as maria, chinook, zonda, mistral, and burja. Names that can strike terror to our hearts are those of the killer winds—hurricane, tornado, typhoon, twister, whirlwind, and willy-willies. Once experienced, they can never be recalled without fear.

Then there are the waterspouts, large columns of water-enclosing mist, which travel across large or small bodies of water. And there are the wraith-like, misty veils of water which glide across the Adriatic, blown along by the burja and traveling at 50 to 60 miles per hour. The tourist in Jablanac, Yugoslavia, finding it difficult to stand up in such a wind, is told that this is but a small burja. The big burjas come in the winter and are quite capable of creating waves powerful enough to lift boats out of the water and over the sea wall at Senj, depositing them on the highway which runs along the sea.

Compare these with the dust devils which form when the surface temperature is very hot and the humidity low. Though not of tornado force, they may be strong enough to blow down small buildings or shacks. Dust devils carry sand and debris to altitudes as high as 5000 feet. The dust devils which frequently spin clockwise are similar to waterspouts in that both may occur in clear skies. Both occur where there is high surface temperature and instability of air.

Tornadoes

Tornadoes usually occur after periods of high temperatures. About 53 percent of tornadoes appear between 2:00 P.M. and

8:00 P.M. and about 23 percent between 6:00 P.M. and 8:00 P.M. While we have weather stations with radar which can track tornadoes and give warning, the paths of tornadoes are difficult to predict exactly—so it is wise to heed all warnings and take careful precautions.

When severe thunderstorms show on a radar screen, they are carefully watched; tornadoes form within these storm centers and move downward to the ground. Some tornadoes begin as a hook-shaped cloud, and when such a hook is seen, the presence of a tornado can be definitely established. Since not all tornadoes begin with this hook, they cannot always be predicted. However, once the tornado forms, it can be tracked by radar, and since it moves at 20- to 25-mile-an-hour speeds, communities can be warned in time to prepare.

A tornado funnel may contain winds exceeding 300–400 miles per hour and make a great roaring sound like hundreds of freight trains, or a hissing or buzzing sound like a million bees. This is thought to be caused by the constant lightning flashes within the vortex or center of the funnel. Buildings literally explode when caught in the path of such a storm, and the high winds blow the debris, making it as dangerous as shrapnel. It is the flying pieces of glass, metal, and wood splinters which cause many deaths.

While the path of a tornado may be relatively narrow and its duration only a few seconds, the devastation can be calamitous. When some tornadoes last longer than ten or more minutes, it is believed that more than one funnel is formed and that others may continue to form. When severe thunderstorms and tornado warnings are broadcast, it is wise to take all safety precautions. Learn what these are and take no chances! When you hear the roaring sound, it is too late—the tornado is upon you.

Cyclones

Cyclones, unlike tornadoes, rarely reach wind speeds over 50 miles per hour, but they may last more than a week and be as large as 1000 miles in diameter. In the Northern Hemisphere the movement of cyclones is counterclockwise. In the Southern Hemisphere it is clockwise, as it is with hurricanes and typhoons.

While cyclones are large, they are relatively tame; they may be the largest storm centers, but their winds are not strong enough to do much damage. On weather maps one or more cyclones are usually present. They are called low-pressure systems by weather forecasters. While there is little wind damage in a cyclone, they may bring heavy snows that isolate towns, endanger travelers, and leave cattle stranded without food, causing great losses of livestock. Later, when large accumulations of snow are melted quickly by cyclones bringing high temperatures and heavy rains, the combination of rain and melting snow may cause streams and rivers to flood, resulting in losses of property and even lives.

Anticyclones

Anticyclones are anti-storm regions of high pressure which have the largest vortices in the atmosphere. They may be thousands of miles in diameter and last for long periods of time. The winds in the anticyclones are light ones that blow clockwise (the opposite of those in cyclones). The skies are clear of clouds. Since these are high-pressure areas, the air in them sinks—and dries as it does so. Our barometers show a rise in pressure as the anticyclone approaches; we are in for a period of fair weather.

The Winds and the Ocean Currents

The winds and the rotation of the earth are the two great molders of the ocean currents. The trade winds, blowing constantly in diagonal fashion from east to west, drive the waters ahead of them. The various currents flow through the sea like great rivers. Other factors, such as the tides, radiation, land barriers, heat absorption, and irregular sea bottoms, affect the flow of the currents, but the winds are the major factor.

UNDERSTANDING THE WINDS

Begin your study of the wind as you know it in your life. Put up a small flag and a wind indicator, a little wooden windmill or weathervane which faces into the wind as it turns. From it you can determine the direction from which the wind is blowing. If your indicator swings from one direction to another as you watch, it is a variable wind. If the windmill whirls steadily, you have a steady wind, but if the indicator stops and starts and seems to be going slightly crazy at times, you have winds coming in gusts. If the wind speeds are high in the gusts, thunderstorms are on the way, bringing lightning, rain, or possibly hail.

Winds are named according to the direction from which they are coming. Thus a SW wind is one coming from the southwest and a NW wind is coming from the northwest.

Now you will learn to recognize which winds bring rain. If you have a combination of S to SE winds and a slowly falling barometer, you can expect rain within 24 hours. If the wind is S to SE and the barometer is falling rapidly, you can expect rain within 12 hours. When you learn to recognize which winds may spoil your picnic or help your garden, you can have fun trying to second-guess what the weatherman will have to say in his report. (Even he has to admit that sometimes his reports are guesstimates.)

The Beaufort Wind Scale

The Beaufort Wind Scale was invented by British naval Captain Francis Beaufort (1774–1857), who later was knighted and became an admiral. It was a scale of wind forces that was invaluable to those commanding the big sailing ships. In 1926, the Beaufort Scale was adapted for land use and accepted by the International Meteorological Committee.

Keep a copy of the Beaufort Scale close to where you watch your wind indicator and flag. If you live near a high smokestack, observe it for the degree and direction of smoke drift. If

The Beaufort Wind Scale

Beaufort Number	Wind Speed (miles per hour)	Winds Called	Characteristics
0	Less than 1	calm	Smoke rises vertically
1	1–3	light air	Smoke shows wind direction; weathervanes do not move
2	4–7	slight breeze	Leaves rustle; feel wind on face; vanes move
3	8–12	gentle breeze	Small flag is extended; leaves and twigs move constantly
4	13–18	moderate	Paper and dust are raised; small branches move
5	19–24	fresh breeze	Small trees in leaf begin to sway
6	25–31	strong breeze	Telephone wires whistle; large branches in motion
7	32–38	moderate gale	Whole trees in motion
8	39–46	fresh gale	Difficult to walk; twigs break off
9	47–54	strong gale	Slight damage to houses; chimneys blown off
10	55–63	whole gale	Damage extensive to houses; trees uprooted
11	64–75	storm	Rarely experienced; considerable structural damage
12	Above 75	hurricane	Excessive damage

you have no indicator, try to estimate wind speeds from the movements of leaves and twigs and small trees, then telephone for the weather report and see how close you came to the right speed. Soon you will be able to make fairly accurate estimates on your own.

The Wind-Chill Index

In addition to reading a thermometer to determine how cold it is outside, check your wind indicator for wind speed and then consult a wind-chill index. That will give you the true temperature for which you should dress so that you can properly protect yourself from painful toes, fingers, ears, and nose—or, even worse, from frostbite.

It is interesting to know that scientists have determined that the ideal working temperature is 64 degrees. When the temperature has fallen to 20 degrees, work efficiency has dropped to 75 percent of capacity. At zero degrees, work efficiency has fallen to 50 percent of capacity. At 50 degrees below zero, one's total energy is expended just in staying alive. You may think that a temperature of 50 degrees below zero never happens where you live, but when you check the wind-chill chart you will learn otherwise. If the thermometer reading is 5 degrees above zero Fahrenheit and a 30-mile-an-hour wind is blowing, any uncovered flesh (nose, ears, fingers, face) is being exposed to the equivalent temperature of 41 degrees below zero!

Understanding the winds is important to your comfort and safety. It is good to know which wind is best for kite flying. If you must go out on a rainy, blowy day, don't count on an umbrella to keep you dry; an inside-out umbrella is no protection—and hard on one's umbrella. You will understand the danger to boaters when small craft warnings are sent out. And when the captain on your jet flight talks about bucking head winds or being fortunate to have good tail winds, you will know why one retards your flight and the other hurries it along.

THE WIND-CHILL INDEX*

Equivalent Temperature in Cooling Power on Exposed Flesh (Degrees Fahrenheit)

To read the chart, take the nearest present temperature at the top of the chart. Then find the wind speed at the left of the chart. The Wind-Chill Index temperature is shown where the row and column intersect. For example, if the temperature reading is 25 degrees and the wind is 30 MPH, the equivalent or wind-chill temperature is −11 degrees.

Temperature Readings (Degrees Fahrenheit)

MPH	35	30	25	20	15	10	5	0	−5	−10	−15	−20
10	21	16	9	2	−2	−9	−15	−22	−27	−31	−38	−45
15	16	11	1	−6	−11	−18	−25	−33	−40	−45	−51	−60
20	12	3	−4	−9	−17	−24	−32	−40	−46	−52	−60	−68
25	7	0	−7	−15	−22	−29	−37	−45	−52	−58	−67	−75
30	5	−2	−11	−18	−26	−33	−41	−49	−56	−63	−70	−78
35	3	−4	−13	−20	−27	−35	−43	−52	−60	−67	−72	−83
40	1	−4	−15	−22	−29	−36	−45	−54	−62	−69	−76	−87

Wind speed greater than 40 MPH has little additional chilling effect.

* Wind-Chill Index courtesy of Russ Montgomery, Meteorologist, Station WKYC-TV, Cleveland, Ohio.

THE VERSATILITY OF THE WINDS

Winds as Artists

The winds, driving tiny grains of sand with the force that a sculptor drives his chisel, have shaped the sandstone rocks of the deserts of our West into lifelike figures, chiseled out arches and windows, and have even carved out caves which at one time were used as dwellings by Indian tribes of the Southwest. These cave-homes can be seen still in Mesa Verde and other National Parks.

The constantly blowing wind can shape trees into one-sided

and stunted caricatures of what they might have been. Hot winds blowing against the buds on one side of a tree can cause the buds to dry up and drop off. In winter, cold winds carrying sleet or snow can freeze the buds. A tree subjected to these conditions lives its life bending away from the wind, with all its branches growing only on the less exposed side.

On sand dunes, perhaps a mile from the sea, the wind is an artist that makes little tracks and markings in the sand as it blows a bit of dried sponge or driftwood along. Let the wind find a small clump of grass with one blade bent and it will whirl that blade around like a pinwheel, causing it to inscribe a perfect circle in the sand.

Winds and Sea Creatures

The albatross, known as a glider of the world, lives most of its life at sea and may travel several times around the world in one year. Albatrosses can fly for days without ceasing; no one knows exactly how long an albatross can stay aloft without coming down on the water to rest. Albatrosses have a wing spread of 10 to 12 feet and may weigh as much as 20 pounds, yet they have small flight muscles. In the air, they glide and soar, riding and sailing the winds almost effortlessly. They settle on the water only to rest and feed. It requires great effort for them to get into the air when there is little wind. They must run along the surface for several hundred yards, often hitting the water with their wings before they become airborne. At other times, when the winds are strong and steady, they paddle to the crest of a wave, face into the wind, spread their wings, and let the winds lift them into the air. So for the first few years of their lives, when they live entirely at sea, they live with and depend upon the winds for their very existence. The albatross seeks land only when it is time to breed.

Flying fish, which appear to have wings with which to fly,

actually use their wing-like pectoral fins as gliders. They swim underwater and then break through the surface, spreading their pectoral fins to support the front part of their bodies and propelling themselves with their tails. As they gain speed, they shake their pectoral fins until they look like rapidly beating wings. They shoot into the air and glide rigidly for half a minute or so, over a distance of 200 or 300 yards, and then return to the water to start the process all over again. They could not move through the air in such a fashion without the wind.

Two sea creatures, the deadly Portuguese man-of-war and the smaller sailor-by-the-sea, sail on the surface of the sea, going whichever way the winds blow them.

These are just a few of the strange sea creatures and birds who live in the sea or fly above it, dependent largely on the winds for their existence. The frigate birds, Mother Carey's chickens, the booby birds, and the red-footed booby are others among the fascinating living things whose lives depend as much upon the winds as they do upon the sea.

Winds and Seeds

Many trees and plants depend upon the winds to spread their seed over wide areas. Maple and ash seeds have wings which make them look like tiny helicopters as they whirl and glide on the winds. The dandelion and milkweed seed appear as little parachutes. The dandelion closes up in wet weather, but when the weather conditions are right, it opens up until it is a feathery little ball composed of many seeds which simply wait for the wind to carry them off—as it does, distributing them over a large area. The silver-gray milkweed pod opens at just the right moment and waits for the wind. Cattails, asters, goldenrods, and hawkweeds all have hairlike processes called pappi on their seeds. When the seeds are ripe and the winds come, the air is filled with pappi, and we have a "snowstorm" in summer with the wind playing an important part. Thus green things grow, holding down the soil, wherever the wind blows. Trees spring up here and there, planted not by the hand of man but by the winds.

Caprices and Tricks of the Winds

Do you remember reading earlier in this chapter about the dust devils? What happens to dust that is whirled into the air as high as 5000 feet? During the 1930s, after long and sustained drought, a large area of Oklahoma's once-fertile farmland turned to dust. The Okies, as the residents were called, were forced to leave their homes and try to rebuild their lives elsewhere.

What happened to that Oklahoma land-turned-dust? Some of it was lifted into the air by dust devils. The winds aloft picked it up and moved it eastward. One winter morning, residents of many towns in upper New York state awoke to find a layer of brown dust sifted over the snow. Oklahoma dust had come a long way, carried by the winds before it was set down in a new location. Strange sunsets were seen in many parts of the country due to Oklahoma dust being held or moved about in the upper atmosphere. Perhaps the soil where you live has some Oklahoma dust mixed in it—dust carried there by the winds.

The winds are capable of bringing about many strange occurrences. They have before, and they will again. Many of the strange happenings in your life, those which you will remember always, will be wind-related.

The Wind and Your Senses

Understanding the winds is important to your comfort and safety. It is important to know the right kind of wind in which to fly a kite successfully. As a boater, it is important to know the winds in which it is too dangerous to take out a small craft.

Watching the clouds scurry along the skyways pushed by the wind, or watching the willows dance to the wind's commands or the daffodils and tulips bowing and swaying to the wind minuet can be beautiful fun.

Trees react differently to the winds. The trembling aspen is the one tree which can be identified by the way it moves. This broadleaf poplar with a small oval-round leaf grows from Maine to California. You will see it on hillsides and at the sunny edges of forests. Its leaves are attached to ribbon-like stems at right angles so that the slightest breeze sets the leaves fluttering, wiggling, and waving at the passerby. Because the leaves are lighter on the underside, the trees seem to twinkle in the sunlight as the wind sets their leaves trembling. Watch for this delightful tree next time you are on a drive or a hike. The winds and the aspens are a combination to delight the eye—and the ear as well, for the Indians call this tree the "noisy one" because of the whispering noise it makes. In fall, you will be further delighted to see the aspen's brilliant gold leaves shimmering in the sunlight.

Some poplars, of which the aspen is one, show the whitish undersides of their leaves when the wind is from a certain direction and thereby indicate that rain is coming. So you can see that the wind and the trees sometimes cooperate in predicting weather.

Listening to the Winds

Along with watching the antics of the wind comes the listening. From the Beaufort Wind Scale we learn that the winds make the telephone wires whistle in a strong breeze (25–31 MPH). Sometimes the wind roars, and sometimes high gusts of wind bump the house and shake it. The wind rattles the windows, cries and moans around corners, or blows hail in rat-a-tat-tat sounds against the windows.

Sometimes, when the wind is from a certain direction, we hear sounds which normally we do not notice. The horn of the diesel train, the monotonous drone of its motors, and the clicking of the wheels on the tracks seem close by. At other times the whoo-whooing of the boats or the moaning of the foghorn is heard, not because of the wind, but because of the absence of it in the unnaturally quiet, foggy night.

Winds and Smells

No matter where you live the winds will bring certain fragrant or unpleasant odors with it. Some odors come only with winds from certain directions, so the smell may tell you that rain is coming soon. Perhaps, where you live, the winds may bring the gaseous fumes from the refineries, the appetizing smells of baking bread, the tantalizing odor of coffee roasting, or the nose-wrinkling stench of the fertilizer factory.

The countrysides have their own fragrances. A cabbage or kale field gives off a sewer-like odor. Pig farms have their own special scents, as do the horse barns at the racetrack. Freshly mown hay, a field of clover, a vineyard of ripe grapes—all have their unmistakable fragrances. And if you have ever been downwind of a mint farm when the oil of the plant was being extracted, you will remember how delightful and head-clearing it was.

Fun with the Wind

Have you ever tried using an old umbrella as a sail and let the wind pull you on your roller skates? Surely you have used the wind to fly your kites. If you are running a race, it is better to have the wind pushing you than to have to run against it. On televised football games, the sports announcers are always telling the viewers which team is kicking or passing into or against the wind. The wind can help a well-hit baseball become a home run, it can blow it foul, or it can shorten a long drive to the outfield and cheat the batter of a home run.

You have seen gliders in movies or on television; perhaps you have even had a ride in one. An experienced pilot who knows how to ride the currents can keep his glider in the air for a long time. There is no motor to keep him aloft and the ride is made in silence. It is quite exciting to observe the launching of the glider and even more fun to hear the swishing sound it makes as it glides in for a landing.

Watching such land birds as the hawks swoop, glide, and sail the winds as they circle an area searching for their prey is always a beautiful sight.

Owners of small and large sailboats must know how to use the wind so they can run before the wind, turn safely, and—without losing too much momentum—turn into the wind and sail back in the opposite direction. It is always puzzling to non-sailors how this can be done.

Along the North Sea, where the winds blow hard and steady in stormy weather, one of the favorite sports is to run with the wind and then jump into the air and let the wind carry one along, almost as if one were flying. One writer telling of this experience discovered that his dog knew the trick, too. Both would run and leap into the air and "fly" together for a short distance. The next time you are fighting to keep your feet in a strong wind, pick a clear space and turn and run with the wind and then see if you, too, can "fly."

Wind Story Hour

Ask your parents, grandparents, and friends to tell you true stories about the experiences they have had with the winds. Some will be funny, others frightening, but all will be fun to listen to.

In school, instead of "show and tell," you might tell stories about the winds in your life or stories you have read in which the wind has been a main character.

No matter where you live, inland, near an ocean or lake, along a river, or in a city, the winds will play a constant and important part of your life. Sometimes they may make you uncomfortable or frighten you. At other times, you will be glad for the cooling breezes and delighted at the beautiful sights the winds can create. The terrifying experiences may come rarely in your lifetime, but the delights the winds can create are there constantly. You cannot escape the winds any more than you can escape the weather. While both in their wildest moments may destroy life, for the most part they sustain it. Like every living thing on our planet, you could not live without either one. The more you study the winds in your life and learn to understand them, the more you will find in life to enjoy.

WIND OBSERVATION GAMES

I Know the Wind Was There

Divide the group into teams. Give each player in turn an opportunity to tell what evidence she or he saw, felt, or smelled that the wind was at work. Score a point for each acceptable answer and keep scores by teams. It would be best to give the players some warning that you are going to play this game so that they might be prepared for it. However, to spring this game unannounced will indicate which students are most observing.

Here are some possible answers:

1. The wind ruffled my hair.
2. I saw paper being blown about.
3. I felt the wind on my face.

4. The flag was moving (or hanging limp, or standing straight out from the pole).
5. Leaves and twigs broken off by the wind were lying on the sidewalk.
6. I saw the curtains blowing in the wind.
7. The wind blew the door shut.
8. The wind rattled the windows.
9. I heard the wind making noises in the trees.
10. The waves were high and the wind was blowing spray.
11. The wind blew the rain (or snow) against my face.
12. The wind turned my umbrella inside out.
13. The wind blew my cap off.
14. It was hard walking against the wind.
15. The wind was at my back and made me walk faster.
16. The wind blew dust into my eyes.
17. The swings on the playground were moving in the wind.
18. I saw birds riding the winds.
19. The wind drifted the snow.
20. The wind blew the "head" off the dandelions.
21. The wind made the window shade flap.

The kinds of wind incidents described by the children will differ according to the seasons, the regions in which the students live, and the climate. Each area has its periods of windstorms when conditions may be quite severe. Wherever the participants live, the winds will play an important and sometimes frightening part in their lives.

The Wind in Books and Stories

Announce to the class that, in two days, each student should be prepared to read a short passage from a book in which the winds play an important part. The excerpts may be poems, definitions, descriptive passages, or directions for using the wind in one way or another. The passages may come from a dictionary, encyclopedia, science book, book of poetry, a seafaring story, horror story, detective story, or adventure story.

Make no special assignments; let the participants pick and choose as they will. You will end with a surprising assortment!

Some suggestions are given here in the event students may need a little help. All are wind-related.

1. An account of a sailboat race or how to sail
2. Any seafaring story
3. How to fly a glider
4. The wind and its relation to sea currents
5. The wind in the desert
6. The wind and pollination
7. The wind in *The Wizard of Oz*
8. A description of a tornado, a hurricane, or a dust devil
9. A poem about the wind (there is one in *Winnie the Pooh*)
10. A weather story about a big storm
11. How the wind affects a football or baseball game
12. Wind that brings rain
13. Definitions of such terms as: the winds aloft, a gale, a gentle breeze
14. Definitions of names given certain winds: zonda, maria, mistral
15. The wind in a spooky story or haunted house
16. The wind that caused a shipwreck
17. Winds to fear
18. Winds that destroy crops

2

Magical Magic Squares

Math is puzzles that teach us to think,
Math can be games that are fun,
Playing or working with math is the same,
We learn from the thinking we've done.

Magical squares are fun things to do,
We learn it's important to see
How this one square is different from that.
To see is to think—that's the key.

Magic squares have been a source of recreation and mathematical diversion for hundreds of years. One third-order (nine-cell) square is attributed to Chinese Emperor Yu, who lived about 2200 B.C. The square called Lo Shu (Figure 1) is still considered a magical charm by Oriental peoples.

The Lo Shu uses the numbers 1 through 9 which are arranged in the nine-cell square so that the sum of each row, diagonal, and column is 15.

Fourth-order squares of sixteen cells, fifth-order squares of 25 cells, and even larger ones can be constructed. The larger the square the more possible variations of it there are. While there is one basic pattern in the third-order square, eight variations of it are possible. There are 880 variations of the fourth-order square, of which 384 are pandiagonal squares (explained later in this chapter). When you get to the fifth-order, 3600 are pandiagonal of a number exceeding 13 million!

ODD-NUMBERED MAGIC SQUARES

The Lo Shu Square (Third-Order, Nine-Cell)

TYPE OF GAME: *Individual or Class*
GRADE: *Third and Up*

Prepare work sheets which contain at least six or eight blank nine-cell squares and distribute to the class. Players work lightly with pencil until they have arrived at a solution.

The Lo Shu is a nine-cell, third-order square which uses the numbers from 1 through 9 arranged so as to total 15 (the magic constant) in all columns, rows, and diagonals (Figure 1).

8	3	4
1	5	9
6	7	2

Fig. 1

Present the problem to the players and let them experiment until they have reached a solution. If they seem stymied, suggest they put the 5 in the center cell and proceed from there. A number of solutions may appear, but upon examination they prove to be the same combinations in reverse order or in different row positions. In this way, at least eight solutions are possible.

Formula for Odd-Numbered Squares

There is a formula which can be used to fill any odd-numbered square (9-cell, 25-cell, 49-cell, etc.).

1. Place 1 in the center cell of the bottom row.

2. A number following a number in the bottom row is placed at the top of the next column (with one exception: see rule 5). Here 2 follows the general rule and is placed in the top cell of the column next to 1.

3. Place 3 in the next column to the right, one cell diagonally below the previous number. The following numbers continue down the diagonal as far as that diagonal goes. When the right-hand side is reached, the next number is placed on the continuing diagonal on the left-hand side. For example, if the last number on the right-hand side is the third cell down from the top, the fourth cell down on the left side is the continuing diagonal in which the next number is placed.

4. If in following a diagonal you come to a cell already filled, place the next number above the cell last filled (in this case, 4 would go above 3) and start a new diagonal trend.

5. When the lower right-hand corner cell is filled, the following number is placed directly above it. The next number is placed in the lower left-hand corner, which is the following diagonal.

From this point on, follow the previous rules. If you are correct in your placements, the last number will fall in the center square of the top row directly above the 1. Figure 2 shows how the placement of numbers in a nine-cell square follows the rules. Note how this arrangement differs from the Lo Shu square in Figure 1 and the square in Figure 3.

Variation #1

Ralph Strachey is credited with a formula which is similar to the one given here but in reverse. The 1 is placed in the top

4	9	2
3	5	7
8	1	6

Fig. 2

8	1	6
3	5	7
4	9	2

Fig. 3

11	18	25	2	9
10	12	19	21	3
4	6	13	20	22
23	5	7	14	16
17	24	1	8	15

Fig. 4

13	18	11
12	14	16
17	10	15

Fig. 5

10	15	8
9	11	13
14	7	12

Fig. 6

row center cell. The next number is placed in the bottom cell of the next column. The numbers now move up the diagonals. When a filled cell is reached, the following number goes below the previous number. When the top right-hand cell is filled, the next number is placed below it (see Figure 3).

Compare these two formulae, then note the Lo Shu arrangement. Can you figure out a formula based on that arrangement which can be applied successfully to a fifth-order square?

Fifth-Order, Twenty-five-Cell Squares

Study the diagram of the 25-cell square in Figure 4 to see how the placement of the numbers follows the rules of the formula.

In the nine-cell square, the center number is 5 and the magic constant is 15, exactly three times the center number. In the 25-cell square, the center number is 13. The magic constant is 65 or five times the center number. If the formula is followed correctly, the magic constant will always be the center number times the square root of the number of squares—or, more simply, the center number times the number of cells in any row or column.

Variation #1

Keeping this last fact in mind, fill a nine-cell square using a different sequence of numbers. For example, use a nine-number sequence of 10 through 18. Follow the formula rules and, if you filled the square correctly, the center number will be 14. The magic constant is then 14×3 or 42. Now check to see if all rows, diagonals, and columns add to 42.

Challenge the players to figure out why this happens. In the sequence in Figure 5 each number is nine more than in the first square sequence of numbers 1 through 9. The constant becomes 42, or 27 more than the constant of the first square which uses the numbers 1 through 9. What is 27 but 9 × 3? Nine is the number added to each original number, times the number of squares in one row or column.

Try another sequence (Figure 6) where the numbers are 7 through 15 or where each number is 6 more than in the original square. The center number comes out 11. The magic constant is then 33 or 18 more than the original constant of 15. Eighteen is 6 × 3!

Another interesting way to figure what happens is to total the numbers 1 through 9. The sum is 45. When the sequence is used in a third-order, nine-cell square, the magic constant is 15 or 45 ÷ 3. When the sequence used is numbers 10 through 18, the total of the numbers used is 126. The magic constant is 126 ÷ 3 or 42. Similarly, in the last sequence used, the numbers were 7 through 15, which add to 99. The magic constant then is 99 ÷ 3 or 33.

Guess what the sum of the numbers from 1 through 25 is? If it works one way it should work in reverse. If the constant of the fifth-power square is 5 × 13 (the center square), the total of numbers used should be 65 × 5 or 325. The same answer can be arrived at by adding the sum of the five rows or five columns, each of which is 65.

This is the fun of magic squares. They always present something else to think about, compare, and discover.

Variation #2

Construct a six-power square and divide it into four quadrants of nine cells each (see Figure 7). Number the quadrants in this manner:

#1, upper left
#2, lower right
#3, upper right
#4, lower left

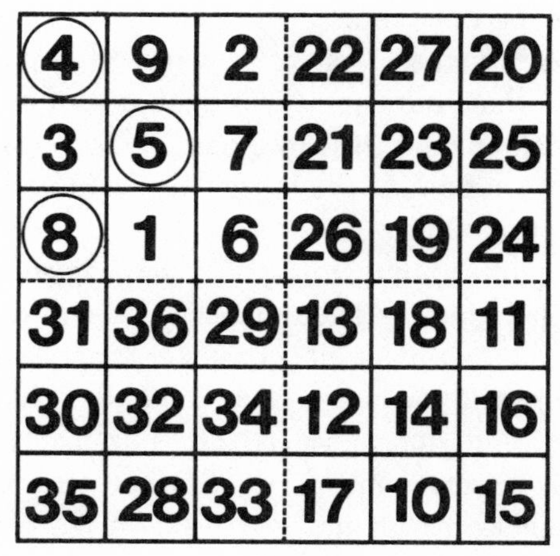

4	9	2	22	27	20
3	5	7	21	23	25
8	1	6	26	19	24
31	36	29	13	18	11
30	32	34	12	14	16
35	28	33	17	10	15

Fig. 7

31	9	2	22	27	20
3	32	7	21	23	25
35	1	6	26	19	24
4	36	29	13	18	11
30	5	34	12	14	16
8	28	33	17	10	15

Fig. 8

Begin in the #1 quadrant. Using the numbers 1 through 9, fill in that square according to the formula for filling odd-numbered squares. Proceed to #2 quadrant and fill with numbers 10 through 18 in the same manner. Now go on to #3 quadrant and fill with numbers 19 through 27. Fill in #4 quadrant with numbers 28 through 36. Check your figures to be sure you have placed them correctly. Again check Figure 7. Note the encircled numbers.

Add the columns, rows, and diagonals. Do you have a magic square? For good reason, you do not. The procedure is not yet complete.

Now interchange the encircled numbers in #1 quadrant with their complement in #4 quadrant (see Figure 8). Change 4 with 31, 5 with 32, and 8 with 35. Now add the rows, columns, and diagonals. Do you have a magic square now? If you do, can you find the answer to why you do?

EVEN-NUMBERED MAGIC SQUARES

Fourth-Order, Sixteen-Cell Squares

TYPE OF GAME: *Individual or Class*
GRADE: *Fifth and Up*

Players try to arrange the numbers from 1 through 16 in a sixteen-cell, fourth-order diagram so that all rows, columns, and diagonals add to 34.

Figure 9 is attributed to Albrecht Dürer, who featured this magic square in an engraving entitled *Melancholie*. If you look it up you can determine for yourself why it was so named. The middle numbers in the bottom row, 15 and 14, give the date of the drawing. Now who can say there is no magic in mathematics? Yet this is only one of 880 possible combinations of numbers in this kind of square. How many can you find?

Note that not only do the rows, columns, and diagonals add

to 34, but each quadrant adds to 34, as do the four corners and the four center squares! Even more magical, the two-cell diagonals when added to their opposite two-cell diagonals total 34!

Figure 10 is another arrangement of the same numbers. The constant remains the same at 34. All the other magical qualities are still present.

Formula for Fourth-Order Squares

One method to arrive at the proper order of numbers in a fourth-order magic square is to draw two diagonal lines lightly from corner to corner of the diagram. Now write the numbers from 1 through 16 in the cells in numerical order beginning in the upper left-hand corner. However, in those cells bisected by the diagonal lines write the numbers in the corner of the cell in small figures. In those cells not bisected by the diagonal lines, write the numbers in large and bold.

When you have filled in all the numbers, note the small numbers in each corner. These are complementary numbers. Each exchanges with its complement. Thus 1 and 16 exchange places (see Figure 11). Similarly, numbers 13 and 4 exchange places. The four center cells are also bisected by the diagonal lines. Following the same rule, 7 and 10 exchange as do 11 and 6. Now the completed square appears in Figure 12.

Remember this is only one of the many different combinations of the fourth-order square. Can you find others?

Diabolic or Panmagic Squares

In Figure 13 not only the columns, rows, diagonals, quadrants, and corners total 34, not only do the four center cells and the two-cell diagonal pairs total 34, but the broken diagonals (a corner number and the three-cell diagonal directly opposite it) also total 34! For example, corner number 1 when added to the

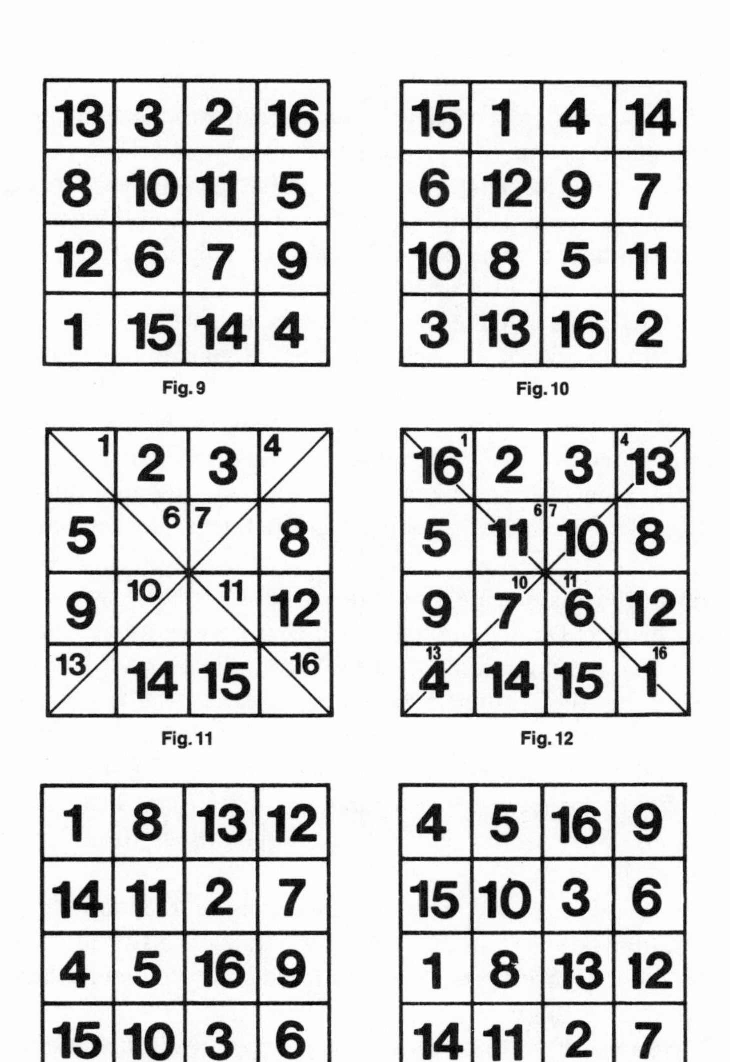

13	3	2	16
8	10	11	5
12	6	7	9
1	15	14	4

Fig. 9

15	1	4	14
6	12	9	7
10	8	5	11
3	13	16	2

Fig. 10

1	2	3	4
5	6	7	8
9	10	11	12
13	14	15	16

Fig. 11

16 (1)	2	3	13 (4)
5	11 (6)	10 (7)	8
9	7 (10)	6 (11)	12
4 (13)	14	15	1 (16)

Fig. 12

1	8	13	12
14	11	2	7
4	5	16	9
15	10	3	6

Fig. 13

4	5	16	9
15	10	3	6
1	8	13	12
14	11	2	7

Fig. 14

three-cell diagonal 8, 2, and 9 totals 34. Can you find the other broken diagonals?

These squares are also called pandiagonal or perfect squares. If you cut this type of square in half either vertically or horizontally and interchange halves, a perfect new panmagic or pandiagonal square is formed. Figure 14 shows how Figure 13 would appear if it were cut in half horizontally and the lower half placed on top of the original top two rows.

Now try interchanging the columns by cutting the square in half vertically. See if all rows, columns, diagonals, and broken diagonals still add to 34. See if all corners still add to 34. Does each pair of two-cell diagonals still total 34? Do the center four cells still total 34?

Is this maneuver possible with the other fourth-order squares discussed earlier in this section? It is left for you to determine that.

Have students prepare a diagram on cardboard and use numbered markers from 1 through 16 so that they can experiment and rearrange more easily. Maybe there will be no new discoveries, but the combinations any player discovers are new and exciting fun for him. It matters little that someone discovered that same combination 2000 years ago—or even 50 years ago. The fascination of magical squares has diminished little over the years. They are magic for anyone who wishes to find out for himself.

Ben Franklin played with magic squares to keep his mind alert during boring sessions of the Pennsylvania Legislature. How many other historic figures have you read about who found these squares fascinating?

Players may want to keep a notebook to record all the varieties they have worked out. There are 880 known variations of the fourth-order squares, 384 of which are the diabolic or panmagic types. Trying to find them all could be a lifetime fun project!

Eighth-Order Squares

Construct an eighth-order, 64-cell diagram. Draw lines bisecting the square from top to bottom and side to side. Now draw two long diagonals from corner to corner. Draw short diagonals in each quadrant which cross the long diagonals. These diagonals form a square within a square (see Figure 15). Proceed as in the fourth-order square and write the numbers from 1 through 64 in numerical order beginning in the top left-hand corner. As in the fourth-order square, write the numbers in those cells crossed by a diagonal in small figures and those in the uncrossed squares in large numerals.

Now proceed to exchange the numbers in the diagonally marked cells with their complements across the square. The tricky numbers to watch are those which are in the diagonally marked cells on either side of a bisecting horizontal or vertical line. Numbers 4 and 5 in the top row exchange with bottom row numbers 61 and 60 respectively. The other tricky numbers are those diagonally marked cells which are on either side of the horizontal bisecting line. These numbers are fourth-row numbers 25 and 32, which exchange with 40 and 33, respectively, in the fifth row. Once over these hurdles, it is relatively easy to make the other changes. See Figure 16 for verification.

If you have been successful in your number arrangements (see Figure 16) you will find that each row, diagonal, and column adds to 260. The numbers in each quadrant total 2 × 260 or 520. The totals of the cells crossed by the diagonals which form the small square also add to 520. (Each pair of opposite four-cell diagonals totals 260.) The center sixteen cells also total 520. Each quadrant of the center square totals 130. Each pair of opposite two-cell diagonals of the center sixteen-cell square totals 130. The four corners of that same square also total 130, as do the four center numbers. The outside four rows

1	2	3	4	5	6	7	8
9	10	11	12	13	14	15	16
17	18	19	20	21	22	23	24
25	26	27	28	29	30	31	32
33	34	35	36	37	38	39	40
41	42	43	44	45	46	47	48
49	50	51	52	53	54	55	56
57	58	59	60	61	62	63	64

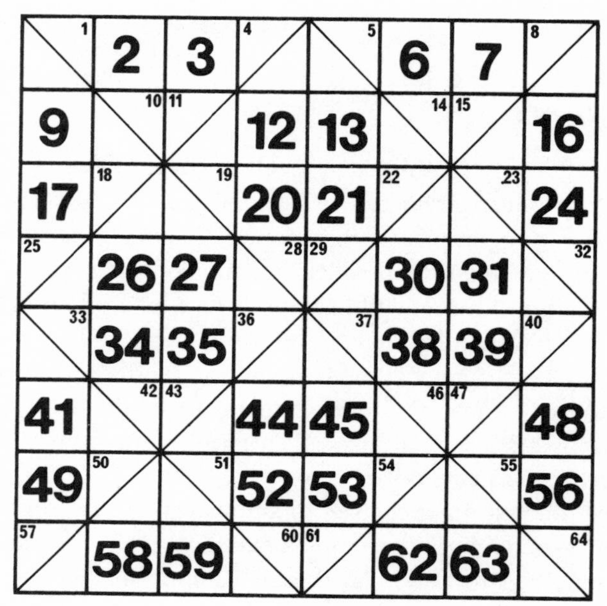

Fig. 15

64	2	3	61	60	6	7	57
9	55	54	12	13	51	50	16
17	47	46	20	21	43	42	24
40	26	27	37	36	30	31	33
32	34	35	29	28	38	39	25
41	23	22	44	45	19	18	48
49	15	14	52	53	11	10	56
8	58	59	5	4	62	63	1

Fig. 16

and columns which border the center square total 3×260 or 780. It is left to the more advanced mathematicians to determine why all these interesting facts work out this way.

As if these are not enough to ponder, there are also Latin squares, explained next. These are in fourth-order squares of which there are a possible 576. When you have exhausted the fourth-order, you can begin on the fifth-order of which there are a mere 161,280; or, if you are looking for a lifetime career, consider working out all of the seventh-order Latin squares of which there are 61.5 trillion!

Perhaps this is why people have found these magic squares irresistible over the centuries. There seems to be no end to their challenges and magic. When one feels the end of fun is in sight, there are actually trillions more to charm and mystify.

LATIN SQUARES

Latin Square (Third-Order, Nine-Cell)

TYPE OF GAME: *Individual or Class*
GRADE: *Third and Up*

Have the players prepare a nine-cell or third-order diagram. Or furnish each with a practice sheet full of such diagrams duplicated on it. Players work lightly with pencil so that mistakes can be easily erased. The object is to place the numbers 1, 2, and 3 in the square so that each number appears only once in each row or column and no number is duplicated in any row or column.

Figures 17, 18, and 19 show three solutions. In all three, each row and column adds to 6. But the sums of the corners differ in each square: In Figure 17 the sum of the corners is 9, in Figure 18 it is 8, and in Figure 19 it is 7. Each figure has one diagonal which adds to 6 and one which is composed of the same numeral. Only in Figure 18 do both diagonals total 6.

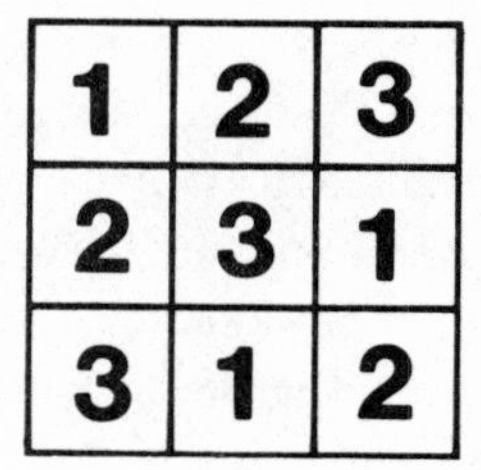

Fig. 17

2	3	1
1	2	3
3	1	2

Fig. 18

1	3	2
2	1	3
3	2	1

Fig. 19

There are twelve possible variations of the third-order square. How many can the players find?

Fourth-Order Latin Squares

Now let players experiment with sixteen-cell fourth-order Latin squares. Numbers 1 through 4 are used in such a manner as to have all four numbers appear in every row and column, with no duplications in any row or column.

In Figure 20, all rows and columns add to 10. Note the diagonals. From left to right running upward each diagonal has only one number, which is repeated two, three, or four times. The two-cell diagonals contain only 1's, an odd number, while the three-cell diagonals contain either all 2's or 4's, an even number. The long diagonal contains only 3's, an odd number.

Now look at the diagonals running upward from right to left. The two-cell diagonals have the even numbers 2 and 4. The three-cell diagonals have odd numbers 1 and 3, and the long diagonal, the even numbers 2 and 4. In other words, the diagonals alternate with either all odd or all even numbers.

Have the players add the totals of each row and column. Each adds to 10. Both long diagonals add to 12, as do the four corners. The upper left and lower right quadrangles are exactly the same and total 8 each, while the duplicate upper right and lower left quadrangles total 12. The four center cells also total 12.

Note that the sequence in each row is repeated in a column. What an exercise in perception this little square is! And there is more to come.

Variation #1

Rearrange the numbers according to the same rules but in a different set of sequences, as in Figure 21. Now look at the diagonals which run upward and downward from left to right.

The whole picture is changed. The diagonals are now a mixture of odd and even numbers. Now there are no column sequences which are duplicated in the rows. But, if you look carefully, you will see that rows 1 and 3 and 2 and 4 are the same numerical sequences in reverse. Counting from left to right, columns 1 and 3 and 2 and 4 are the same sequences in reverse order.

Now all rows, columns, and diagonals add to 10. Add all the corner numbers and the sum is 10! Now divide the square into quadrants. Each quadrant adds to 10. Now look at the four center cells. Those numbers total 10. Magic magical square! Yet there is more! Each two-square diagonal when added to its opposite adds to 10.

Variation #2

Arrange the numbers as in Figure 22. While the number arrangements are different, columns 1 and 2, as in Figure 21, are the same in reverse order, as are columns 3 and 4. Rows 1 and 3 are the same in reverse order, as are rows 2 and 4. All diagonals, columns, and rows total 10. All the corners add to 10. Each quadrant totals 10. The center four squares add to 10. All two-square diagonals when added to their opposites total 10! There are 576 possible fourth-order combinations!

Panmagic Latin Square

Here is still another arrangement of the same numbers following the same rules. In Figure 23, sequences in rows and columns are in reverse-order pairs. All rows, columns, and diagonals total 10. The four corners total 10. Each quadrant adds to 10. The center four cells total 10. Each two-cell diagonal when added to its opposite totals 10. But that's not all. Now we have a diabolic, pandiagonal, or panmagic square. The broken diagonals (a corner number and the three-square diagonal running

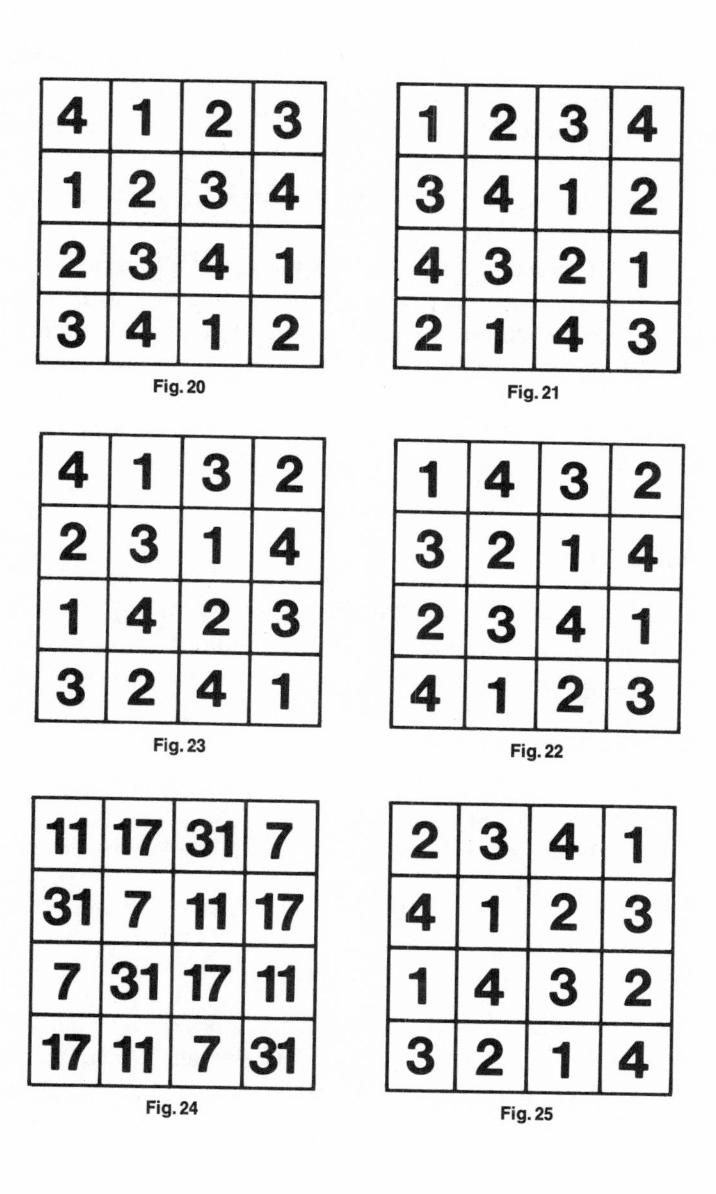

4	1	2	3
1	2	3	4
2	3	4	1
3	4	1	2

Fig. 20

1	2	3	4
3	4	1	2
4	3	2	1
2	1	4	3

Fig. 21

4	1	3	2
2	3	1	4
1	4	2	3
3	2	4	1

Fig. 23

1	4	3	2
3	2	1	4
2	3	4	1
4	1	2	3

Fig. 22

11	17	31	7
31	7	11	17
7	31	17	11
17	11	7	31

Fig. 24

2	3	4	1
4	1	2	3
1	4	3	2
3	2	1	4

Fig. 25

across the opposite corner) also add to 10! In this figure, corner number 2 when added to diagonal, 2, 3, and 3 totals 10. Similarly, corner number 3 and its diagonal of 3, 2, and 2 totals 10. Check the other broken diagonals and see for yourself.

Sharp eyes will perceive that the opposite quadrants are reverse pairs.

Like other such magic squares, this type can be split down the middle and the two left-hand columns moved to the right of the right-hand columns to form a new diabolic or panmagic square. It can also be split horizontally and the top two rows put under the bottom two rows to form still another diabolic or panmagic square. All the magical qualities of the square are retained in spite of the moves.

Variation #4

Any four numbers will work in any of the examples given; they need not be numbers in sequence. Figure 24 takes four random numbers. In this figure, columns, rows, and diagonals each total 66, as do the four corners, each quadrant, and the center four squares. Each two-cell diagonal when added to its opposite totals 66. Since this is the same pattern used in Figure 22, its characteristics are the same.

Try any four numbers and see how many variations are possible with varying results.

Variation #5

Using the original 1, 2, 3, 4 sequence, take each number to the power of 2. What are the results? How many variations can be found? Figure 25, a panmagic square, is carried to the power of 2 in Figure 26. Does it remain a magic square? Does it remain a panmagic square?

Variation #6

Take the panmagic square in Figure 25 and raise it to the power of 3. Does it remain a magic square? Does it remain a panmagic square?

Variation #7

Take any four numbers in a ratio series, such as 5, 10, 15, 20 (Figure 27), or any four numbers in a broken ratio series, such as 3, 9, 15, and 27. How many variations can be found? Which total the same in all rows, columns, and diagonals, but do not total the same in the quadrants, the corners, or the two-cell diagonal pairs?

Which meet all the requirements of a panmagic square?

Game Equipment for Magic Latin Squares

Take a manila folder and draw a third-order square on one half and a fourth-order square on the other half of the folder. Individual cells should be at least 2″ square. Playing pieces can be paper squares about 1½″ square or round discs slightly smaller than the squares. Write the appropriate numbers on one side of the playing pieces and the same number to the power of 2 or 3 on the reverse side.

Keep each set of playing pieces in an envelope and clip to the folder. A student who has completed his work successfully can then play with the magical squares as people have done for hundreds of years.

As a new or different combination is discovered, keep a record and see how many different combinations are presented. An individual playing regularly with the squares may like to keep a notebook record of all the different squares found and the

4	9	16	1
16	1	4	9
1	16	9	4
9	4	1	16

Fig. 26

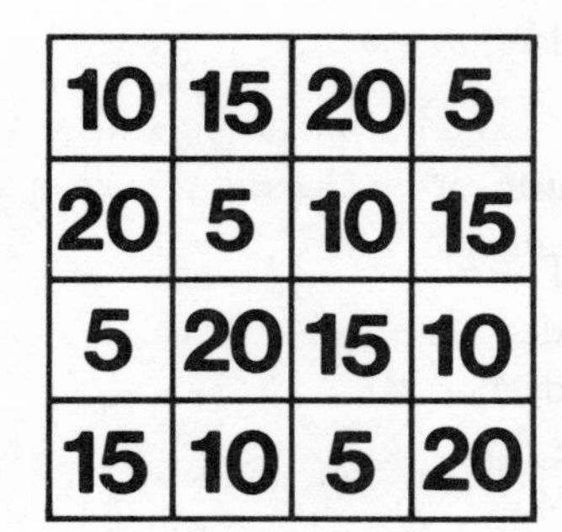

10	15	20	5
20	5	10	15
5	20	15	10
15	10	5	20

Fig. 27

4	3	2	1
3	4	1	2
2	1	4	3
1	2	3	4

Fig. 28

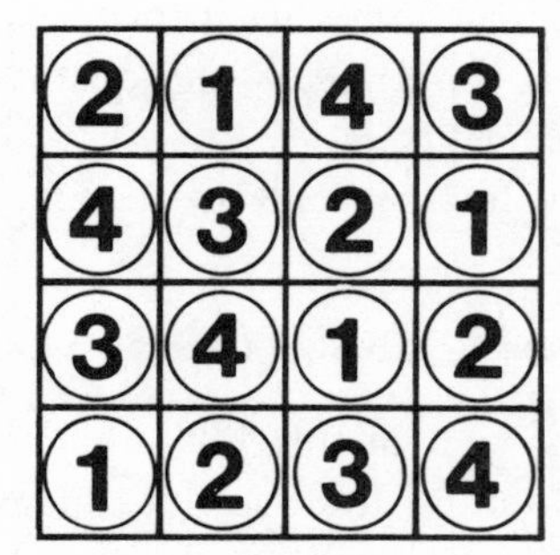

②	①	④	③
④	③	②	①
③	④	①	②
①	②	③	④

Fig. 29

4②	3①	2④	1③
3④	4③	1②	2①
2③	1④	4①	3②
1①	2②	3③	4④

Fig. 30

order in which they were found. Square discovering, like stamp collecting, can be a lifetime diversion.

Fourth-Order Playing Diagram

To construct a durable sixteen-cell diagram, use a manila filing folder. Let the fold be the center line bisecting the diagram. A folder is approximately 9½″ by 12″. Draw a heavy line along the fold. Divide each half of the folder into eight squares 4″ by 4″. Thus you have a completed diagram 12″ by 12″ with the center line on the fold.

Cut eight unlined 3″ by 5″ filing cards in half. The resulting pieces will not be square, of course, but will serve nicely for playing pieces. Number each piece with a single numeral, in the series from 1 through 16. Put the same number on the reverse side of the cards so that the cards will always be right side up and ready to play.

You now have an easily and cheaply made magic square set which is durable, versatile, and easily stored. Simply place the card set in an envelope and store within the closed filing folder when not in use.

The same diagram can be used for a third-order square. Players would use only nine of the sixteen squares and cards from one through 9. If this is confusing to players, a nine-cell diagram can be drawn on the outside of the folder, thus making it usable for either type of square.

Diagrams for Latin Squares

The diagrams for Latin squares are the same, so folders may be used for either type. The envelopes for Latin squares would contain only four sets of cards numbering 1 through 4.

For the third-order, nine-cell Latin square, the players would use three sets of numbers 1 through 3 and the nine-cell diagram.

Graeco-Latin Squares

Graeco-Latin squares are created by taking two Latin squares and joining one with the other and combining the numbers. The squares in Figures 28 and 29 are combined to form Figure 30. In the first two Latin squares all columns, rows, diagonals, corners, and center four cells total 10. In the Graeco-Latin square formed by combining the two Latin squares, the rows, columns, corners, and center cells add to 110.

To combine the two Latin squares, move the numbers from the first square in Figure 28 and write them in front of the numbers of the second square in Figure 29. The numbers are encircled in the second square to show how the final positions appear in the finished Graeco-Latin square shown in Figure 30.

Like other magic squares, the Graeco-Latin squares can be split down the middle and the left two columns moved to the right of the two right columns. And the top two rows can be moved beneath the bottom two rows.

Take each Latin square and move the two left-hand columns to the right of the right-hand columns in each square. Now combine these two newly formed Latin squares to create still another Graeco-Latin square.

Playing Card Latin Squares

Type of Game: *A Puzzler for Classroom or Party*

Remove from a deck of playing cards all the aces, kings, queens, and jacks. Arrange these sixteen cards in a fourth-order sixteen-card magic Latin square so that there is an ace, king, queen, and jack in each row and column. Three of the 576 solutions possible are:

Square A	Square B	Square C
K, J, Q, A	A, K, Q, J	K, A, Q, J
J, Q, A, K	J, A, K, Q	J, Q, K, A
Q, A, K, J	K, Q, J, A	A, K, J, Q
A, K, J, Q	Q, J, A, K	Q, J, A, K

Note that in Square B all four corners are different. So are the four cards in the center square. In Square C the four quadrants each contain a card of each rank.

Variation #1

Another solution arranges the rows and columns so there is no duplication of rank or suit. Here the broken diagonals are composed of all suits and ranks, but the two long diagonals do not qualify, nor do the two-cell diagonals. However, these diagonals are interesting in their own ways.

K spades	Q clubs	A diamonds	J hearts
Q diamonds	K hearts	J spades	A clubs
J clubs	A spades	Q hearts	K diamonds
A hearts	J diamonds	K clubs	Q spades

Variation #2

Now construct a square in which no row, column, or diagonal contains more than one card of any rank or suit! In the solutions below, not only are all these qualifications met, but others as well. The four corner and four center cards are of different ranks and suits. Each quadrant contains a card of each rank and suit. The two-card diagonals when paired with their opposites contain one of each rank and suit.

A spades	K hearts	Q diamonds	J clubs
Q clubs	J diamonds	A hearts	K spades
J hearts	Q spades	K clubs	A diamonds
K diamonds	A clubs	J spades	Q hearts

K diamonds	Q clubs	J hearts	A spades
J spades	A hearts	K clubs	Q diamonds
A clubs	J diamonds	Q spades	K hearts
Q hearts	K spades	A diamonds	J clubs

These are only two of 72 fundamental solutions, each of which can produce seven others by reflections and reversals, for a total of 504 possibilities in all. Care to try for a few hundred, friends?

3

Arithmetic Games and Puzzles

ARITHMAGICS

Magical Nines

Have players write the table of nines from 1 through 10 in the manner shown below. (The answers are given for quick reference for the teacher or leader.)

$1 \times 9 = 9$	$11 \times 9 = 99$	$21 \times 9 = 189$
$2 \times 9 = 18$	$12 \times 9 = 108$	$22 \times 9 = 198$
$3 \times 9 = 27$	$13 \times 9 = 117$	$23 \times 9 = 207$
$4 \times 9 = 36$	$14 \times 9 = 126$	$24 \times 9 = 216$
$5 \times 9 = 45$	$15 \times 9 = 135$	$25 \times 9 = 225$
$6 \times 9 = 54$	$16 \times 9 = 144$	$26 \times 9 = 234$
$7 \times 9 = 63$	$17 \times 9 = 153$	$27 \times 9 = 243$
$8 \times 9 = 72$	$18 \times 9 = 162$	$28 \times 9 = 252$
$9 \times 9 = 81$	$19 \times 9 = 171$	$29 \times 9 = 261$
$10 \times 9 = 90$	$20 \times 9 = 180$	$30 \times 9 = 270$

When the players have completed the multiplication process, have them take each product and make an addition problem of the digits in this manner:

$1 \times 9 = 9 \quad 0 + 9 = 9$
$2 \times 9 = 18 \quad 1 + 8 = 9$
$3 \times 9 = 27 \quad 2 + 7 = 9$

Magical? Yes, arithmagics!

If the players continue the table through 30×9 and again add the digits in the factors, they will get the same results. Three-digit products are added in this manner:

$$12 \times 9 = 108 \quad 1 + 0 + 8 = 9$$

Players examining the columns will find that the top product ends in a 9. From there on the last digits descend down the numerical scale with the last product ending in 0.

Of the 30 problems, only two, $11 \times 9 = 99$ and $21 \times 9 = 189$, have products adding to 18. However, if that sum is taken one step further and those two digits are added, this is what happens:

$$11 \times 9 = 99 \quad 9 + 9 = 18 \quad 1 + 8 = 9$$
$$21 \times 9 = 189 \quad 1 + 8 + 9 = 18 \quad 1 + 8 = 9$$

Or look at it this way. The first product, 99, contains two 9's; the second product, 189, contains an 8 + 1 and a 9.

For the curious who want to pursue the matter further, the following list will serve as a quick reference.

$31 \times 9 = 279$	$41 \times 9 = 369$	$51 \times 9 = 459$
$32 \times 9 = 288$	$42 \times 9 = 378$	$52 \times 9 = 468$
$33 \times 9 = 297$	$43 \times 9 = 387$	$53 \times 9 = 477$
$34 \times 9 = 306$	$44 \times 9 = 396$	$54 \times 9 = 486$
$35 \times 9 = 315$	$45 \times 9 = 405$	$55 \times 9 = 495$
$36 \times 9 = 324$	$46 \times 9 = 414$	$56 \times 9 = 504$
$37 \times 9 = 333$	$47 \times 9 = 423$	$57 \times 9 = 513$
$38 \times 9 = 342$	$48 \times 9 = 432$	$58 \times 9 = 522$
$39 \times 9 = 351$	$49 \times 9 = 441$	$59 \times 9 = 531$
$40 \times 9 = 360$	$50 \times 9 = 450$	$60 \times 9 = 540$

In the 30s sequence, the 18 appears in the first three products; in the 40s sequence it appears in the first four; in the 50s sequence in the first five. From that point on in each sequence the 9 total reappears. Does it follow that in each subsequent sequence there will always be one more 18 answer than in the previous one? The curious are left to discover that for themselves.

The practical application of this magic business is that in any problem in which a number is multiplied by 9, the digits in the product will add to 9 or a multiple of 9. Observe:

$$\begin{array}{r} 456 \\ \times 9 \\ \hline 4104 \end{array} \qquad \begin{array}{r} 2345 \\ \times 9 \\ \hline 21105 \end{array} \qquad \begin{array}{r} 23456 \\ \times 9 \\ \hline 211104 \end{array} \qquad \begin{array}{r} 881 \\ \times 99 \\ \hline 7929 \\ 7929 \\ \hline 87219 \end{array}$$

$4+1+0+4=9$ $2+1+1+0+5=9$

$2+1+1+1+0+4=9$ $8+7+2+1+9=27$ $2+7=9$

or $27=9\times 3$

Thus for a quick check of the accuracy of one's multiplication where a 9 is the factor, one need only to add the digits in the product.

Three-Digit Arithmagics

Take any three-digit number which is not the same in reverse, and reverse it. Subtract the smaller (subtrahend) from the larger (minuend) and add the digits in the remainder. The sum will always be 18:

$$\begin{array}{r} 987 \\ -789 \\ \hline 198 \end{array} = 18 \qquad \begin{array}{r} 663 \\ -366 \\ \hline 297 \end{array} = 18 \qquad \begin{array}{r} 362 \\ -263 \\ \hline 99 \end{array} = 18$$

Any four-, five-, six-, or seven-digit number handled in the same manner will produce either 18 or a multiple of 9 as the sum of the digits in the remainder:

```
  9684          9798          54321
- 4869        - 8979        - 12345
  4815 = 18     819 = 18      41976 = 27

  789654        9876543        99887766
- 456987      - 3456789      - 66778899
  332667 = 27   6419754 = 36   33108867 = 36
```

Can experimenters find exceptions?

It does not follow, however, that the more digits in a number, the larger the sum of the digits of the remainder. Observe these examples:

```
  99887788        87987987        92221
- 88778899      - 78978978      - 12229
  11108889 = 36    9009009 = 27   79992 = 36

  80000091        23333361
- 19000008      - 16333332
  61000083 = 18    7000029 = 18
```

DICE ARITHMETIC GAMES

Dice Arithmetic

TYPE OF GAME: *A Partner or Team Game*
GRADE: *Third and Up*

In the partner game, players are divided into groups of two. Each pair prepares a score sheet to be used by both persons that looks something like this:

1.	1.
2.	2.
3.	3.
4.	4.
5.	5.
6.	6.
7.	7.
8.	8.
9.	9.

This type of score sheet permits the players to keep track of their opponent's score, not only to insure each other's accuracy but to compare scores as the game progresses.

Each player in turn throws two dice. The pips are added and the sum recorded after each number 1. The second turn throws are recorded after each number 2—and so on. After each player has had his nine turns, each adds up his score. The winner is the one with the larger number. Each player checks the addition of his opponent. When a double is thrown, the player gets another throw and thus a second score.

If players choose to keep a running score, the score can be recorded in this manner:

1. 6
2. 6 (the previous score) + 8 = 14
3. 14 + ___ =

In the team game, teams of three to six players prepare a score sheet to record only their own scores. Instead of 9 rolls, the number should be twice or three times the number of players. For a six-player team, the number of rolls could be 12 or 18. For a three-player team, the number could be 9, which would allow three throws for each player. In the event one team is smaller than the others, one player would have an extra turn.

When all teams have completed their turns, the scores are added. Teams could exchange score sheets to check each other for accuracy.

Variation #1

Games may feature subtraction instead of addition. The score would then be the smaller number on the two dice subtracted from the larger. In the event a double is rolled, the player takes another turn. Or a double can be scored as a penalty and the sum recorded as a minus score. The player is still awarded another throw, which may help him wipe out the minus score—unless, of course, he continues to roll doubles.

Variation #2

The pips are now multiplied for scores.

Variation #3

With older players, each numbered roll could present a different type of problem, the teacher stating the type of problem for each number and the players noting these on their score sheets before beginning play. Such score sheets could be printed in advance and handed out to teams to get the game started more quickly.

A suggested list follows. (Each problem score should show the complete problem as well as the answer so it can be checked by the other team for accuracy.)

1. Multiply the two numbers
2. Square both numbers and add together
3. Add the two numbers and square the sum
4. Multiply the two numbers and add the sum of the original numbers
5. Multiply the two numbers, divide by the smaller original number, and add the larger original number

6. Multiply the two numbers and subtract the smaller original number
7. Square the numbers, add the squares together, and divide by the smaller number
8. Square both numbers and multiply the two squares
9. Multiply both numbers and add the sum of the squares of both
10. Multiply both numbers and subtract the smaller original number
11. Square the numbers, add the squares together, and subtract the larger original number
12. Subtract the smaller from the larger and square the remainder
13. Double both numbers and square the sum
14. Add the numbers, square the sum, and subtract the original sum
15. Double the larger number and subtract the smaller number

The experienced mathematics teacher can prepare problems as complex or as simple as necessary for a particular group. However, the problems should always cause the players to stretch toward the higher goal in order to provide challenges and promote growth.

All players on a team should help to solve each problem so that there are no long delays between throws. Or it can be left to each player to solve his own throw-problem while the next player takes his turn.

Variation #4

To make the game more complicated for older players, use three dice instead of two. Some of the suggested types of problems could be augmented to make more difficult problems.

Better still, let the players themselves make up a list of problems before beginning the game.

Additional scores can be awarded when a player rolls three of a kind (a triple). The special score could be three times the answer of that particular throw-problem. Additional throws are awarded whenever a double or a triple is thrown. However, no special score should be awarded for a double other than an extra throw.

Variation #5

Playing cards can be used instead of dice. Remove the picture cards from the deck or count all face cards as ten. The deck is shuffled and each player pulls two cards at random from the deck when his turn comes. Addition, subtraction, and multiplication problems are based on cards drawn. For younger children use only the ace through 6 or 7. Increase the selection to suit the age group playing.

Diceoh

TYPE OF GAME: *A Team or Individual Game*
GRADE: *Third and Up*

As an individual game, one score sheet per player is prepared as shown (for a team game one score sheet is made per team):

—	—	—	—	—	—
D	I	C	E	O	H
4	9	3	5	15	8

Players in turn roll three dice. When the total of pips equals one of the numbers listed above, the corresponding letter is printed on the line. A double rolled entitles a player to another turn. (The number represents the position of the letter in the alphabet, A is 1, B is 2, etc.)

The first player or team to complete the word wins. The difficulty, however, will be with the letter C, which demands a 3 to be rolled. To avoid long delays of the game in rolling for triple 1, the rule can be made that when only the C remains to be filled in, the players may then roll only two dice.

If the game is being played as a team game and the C remains to be placed, require that each player take one more roll with the three dice before the team may reduce the dice to two. Then each player in turn rolls until one rolls a total of 3 points.

Choice Diceoh

Play as the game of DICEOH, but allow each player to choose how he counts his dice. If he can create a problem in which he ends with the answer totaling the number he needs to write in a letter, he may do so. For example, a 9 is needed for the I. A player rolls 2, 4, 1. He can make his 9 by multiplying 2 by 4 and adding the 1. It is wise to have each player record his problem to show how he arrived at the desired number. If the game is played in this manner, it will not be necessary to reduce the number of dice to two to get the C. It could be arrived at with 6, 4, 1 ($6 - 4 + 1 = 3$ or $6 + 1 - 4 = 3$). This will make for some quick and fancy figuring. And the more advanced the student, the more complicated the problems will be.

Phrase Diceoh

A phrase, a greeting, or any word may be used instead of the word DICEOH. It might be a phrase of the day, as St. Valentine's Day, or Hello Spring, or Happy Birthday Charlie. Instead of using the number which corresponds to the letter in the alphabet (if only addition is used), give the letters random numbers which can be rolled with three dice. However, if you permit the players to arrive at a particular number by working out a problem with the pips, there will be no difficulty in rolling for the letters past the letter R, the 18th letter.

MATH PUZZLERS

Chinese Mathematical Puzzle

TYPE OF GAME: *Partner Math Puzzle*
GRADE: *Third and Up*

On an 8½″ by 11″ sheet of paper, have players make a third-order diagram of nine three-inch squares. The center square is used for storage of playing pieces only (paper clips, beans, bottle caps, or can pull rings).

At least 56 playing pieces are required. Twenty-four pieces are placed in the center storage square. The remainder are arranged with 7 in each corner and 1 each in the remaining squares:

7	1	7
1		1
7	1	7

The first player takes a playing piece from the storage square and adds it to any square, thus increasing that row from 15 to 16. If he places it in a corner square, he creates two combinations of 16, one in a row and one in a column. The second player must rearrange the pieces so that they again add to 15 in all rows and columns. For example, if the first player adds his piece to the upper left corner, the numbers have been changed to read:

8	1	7
1		1
7	1	7

Now the top row and left-hand column add to 16 instead of 15. The second player can rearrange the pieces to total 15 in all rows and columns by this arrangement:

8	1	6
1		2
6	2	7

The second player, having been successful in solving the problem, now has his turn to add a piece from the storage pile. He, too, puts his piece in a corner and creates this result:

9	1	6
1		2
6	2	7

The first player can solve this problem by this arrangement:

8	1	6
2		2
5	3	7

He then has the opportunity to add another piece to create another problem.

The game continues in this manner until a stalemate is reached. This will come at the time the pieces are arranged thus:

1	13	1
13		13
1	13	1

All rows and columns still add to 15, but now there are 56 pieces on the diagram, 24 more than at the beginning.

Variation

With younger children, use fewer playing pieces—a total of 16 pieces arranged thus:

```
3   1   3
1       1
3   1   3
```

Eight pieces could be added before a stalemate is reached with the pieces arranged in this manner:

```
1   5   1
5       5
1   5   1
```

Permanent Game Equipment

Construct a nine-cup playing board by cutting an egg carton in half across the width. Overlap the two halves so as to make nine cups out of the twelve and staple together. Or two six-cup muffin tins can be overlapped to make a nine-cup playing board. Playing pieces can be plastic discs, the rings from pop can pulls, bottle caps, or marbles.

Number Spelling

TYPE OF GAME: *An Arithmetic Spelling Game (Team or Individual)*
GRADE: *Second and Up*

In the individual game the teacher prepares and duplicates game sheets for each player. The sheet consists of five or more problems in spelling. The problems are a series of blank lines under which a number is written. The players determine which letter of the alphabet the number under a line represents and then write the letter on that line. While the first player finished would normally be declared the winner, the game is more for accuracy than speed. The winner should be required to read the words, which makes this an exercise in reading as well.

The type of words used depends upon the age of the players. Phrases or short sentences can also be used. Example:

— — — — — — — — — — — — —

3 15 21 14 20 1 14 4 19 16 5 12 12

Answer: COUNT AND SPELL

Alert players will look to see if some numbers are duplicated, fill in those spaces first, and then work from the beginning. Or they will take a quick look after finishing one letter to see if there is a duplicate of it and write that second one in immediately.

Players may write out the alphabet and write the number of each letter under it. Then it is a matter of looking up a number and writing in its corresponding letter quickly.

In the team game the teacher divides the group into teams and writes the number of blanks on the chalkboard as many times as there are teams. The game is run as a relay. The first team with the correct word wins a point.

Arithmetic Problem Spelling

TYPE OF GAME: *Arithmetic Spelling for Individuals or Teams*
GRADE: *Third and Up*

For the individual game the teacher prepares and duplicates game sheets consisting of five or more problems which also spell words. The problems are a series of blank lines under which a number is written which refers to the specific problem the answer of which will be the number of a letter of the alphabet. The players work the problem, determine from the answer which letter of the alphabet is indicated, and then write that letter on the blank. The difficulty of the problem and the word to be spelled is determined by the age and experience of the players.

The winner should be required to read the words, which makes this an exercise in reading as well. The players may also be asked to give the meaning of the words.

Score by giving each player a point for each correct letter. The first player with all correct answers wins an extra five points. If a player recognizes any word as being one of a group of homophones or homographs, give extra points for every one he can name.

A problem example:

__ __ __ __ __ __ __ __   __ __ __ __ __ __ __

1 2 3 4 5 6 7 8   9 10 11 12 13 14 15

1. $2 \times 7 + 5 =$ __
2. $3 \times 5 + 1 =$ __
3. $15 \div 3 =$ __
4. $3 \times 4 =$ __
5. $5 \times 3 - 3 =$ __
6. $2 \times 2 + 5 =$ __
7. $3 \times 4 + 2 =$ __
8. $2 \times 2 + 3 =$ __
9. $4 \times 4 =$ __
10. $7 \times 3 - 3 =$ __
11. $4 \times 4 - 1 =$ __
12. $10 - 8 =$ __
13. $6 \times 2 =$ __
14. $15 \div 3 =$ __
15. $3 \times 3 + 4 =$ __

Answer: SPELLING PROBLEM

For the team game the teacher draws the blanks on the chalkboard and writes the number of the problem under each blank. The set of problems need only be written once for the teams to refer to. Play as a relay.

The problems can be made as difficult as the class is prepared to answer. Since there are many steps which a player must take, the game is not as simple as it might appear. Each player in turn must note the number of the space he is to fill, work the corresponding problem, and then place the answer on the correct blank.

The first team with the correct answer wins five points plus one point for each correct letter. Losing teams score one point for each correct letter. Keep a running score and play the games three or four times.

Dollar Shopping Expedition

TYPE OF GAME: *Team Counting Game*
GRADE: *Third and Up*

This game necessitates knowing the costs of certain items, the value of money, and the ability to subtract. The first player of team A begins: "I had a dollar to spend. I bought a pencil for 5¢. That left 95¢." If he is correct in his figures, a point is scored for his team. The game continues in this manner:

Player 1, team B: "With 95¢ left, I spent 19¢ for a ball-point pen. That left 76¢."
Player 1, team C: "With 76¢ left, I bought a 25-cent ice cream cone. That left 51¢."
Player 2, team A: "With 51¢ left, I bought a tablet for 39¢. That left 12¢."
Player 2, team B: "With 12¢ left, I bought an eraser costing 10¢. That left 2¢."

The next player tries to buy something that costs less than the remainder of the money; to spend all the money will penalize his team a point. He might say: "I bought a penny stamp at the post office and that left 1¢." The next player will surely find something he can spend that last penny on—it might be another stamp—but since he is spending the last bit of money, his team is penalized a point. The game then goes on with the player of the next team starting another shopping expedition with a different amount of spending money.

The amount paid for a specific item must be realistic. Any player can challenge the amount stated, and if the challenge is valid, the team challenging wins a point. If the player stating the price can substantiate his price, the challenged team wins a point and the challenging team is penalized. Players should stick to common purchases that many players have frequently made themselves. Such purchases would be less likely to be challenged. The rule can be made that no player during a particular shopping expedition may duplicate the purchase of a previous player.

Paper and pencil may be used for figuring during the game, but the teacher should set a time limit for each player before the game begins in order to eliminate long pauses. Time limits can be shortened as players begin to sharpen their thinking processes. Time limits would, of course, depend upon the age and the abilities of the players. (With younger players, limit the spending money to 50¢ and allow more time for figuring.)

The teacher may want to keep a list as purchases are made in order to determine whether an article is repeated during one shopping expedition. As the game progresses, it will be difficult to ascertain whether there has been a duplication or not, since after a while all the lists will begin to sound alike.

CLOCK GAMES

Clock Time Confusers

TYPE OF GAME: *Individual or Team Observation Game*
GRADE: *Second and Up*

This is a game of imagination rather than reality since we have made a clock with two hands of the same length. We have also made the rule that the hands move only from one number to another in one move. In a regular clock the small or hour hand takes twelve minutes to move from one minute marker to another between the numbers while the large or hour hand takes only one minute to move the same distance. On a real clock at 12:30 the large hand would be at the 30-minute mark and the small hand halfway between 12:00 and 1:00. Not so on our confusing clock which puts one hand on the 30 minute mark and one hand on the 1:00 to show 1:30. While we know how real clock hands work, in a game we can make the hands do most anything. If someone can invent an animal with a head on each end (do you remember this animal's name?), we can invent a confusing clock which tells confusing time.

Imagine how hard it would be to tell time if both hands were the same length. Some clocks built in the 1300s had only one hand! Try catching the 1:40 plane or bus relying on that clock!

So forget facts and the real way to tell time and play confusing time according to the rules. If fact is often stranger than fiction, then imaginative play can sometimes be more fun than factual and still teach us something important to know. One thing is sure, it will make us appreciate how much thought, study, and experimentation went into the invention of our clocks which can tell time accurately up to the second.

Have each player draw a circle and put in the numbers from 1 through 12 as they appear on a clock face. (Or prepare such a diagram, duplicate it, and give one to each player.) Have each player cut two strips of cardboard or construction paper to serve as hands. Both should be the same length, which will depend upon the size of the clock face. These hands can be held in place at the center of the clock with a pin or a paper fastener so that they can be moved accurately. Now you are ready to begin the game.

Give the players five hand positions, such as 4 and 12, 3 and 5, 11 and 6, 7 and 1, and 9 and 3. See if they can come up with both possibilities for each of the confusing times. The answers are, respectively, 4:00 or 12:20, 3:25 or 5:15, 5:55 (5 minutes to 6) or 11:30, 7:05 or 1:35, and 9:15 or 3:45 (15 minutes to 4).

Once the players understand how to proceed, allow them five minutes to make up their own sets of confusing times by placing the hands on their clocks in various positions and then working out both answers.

Variation #1

Once the players know how the game works, the teacher can call out a combination. The player who answers correctly then gives the next combination.

Variation #2

Even with hands of the same length, there are certain hand positions at which there could be only one time given. How many can the players find? Actually there are twelve positions: 12:00, 1:05, 2:10, 3:15, 4:20, 5:25, 6:30, 7:35, 8:40, 9:45, 10:50, and 11:55.

QUICK REFERENCE LIST

12:00		same	1:00	or	12:05	2:00	or	12:10
12:05	or	1:00	1:05		same	2:05		1:10
12:10		2:00	1:10		2:05	2:10		same
12:15		3:00	1:15		3:05	2:15		3:10
12:20		4:00	1:20		4:05	2:20		4:10
12:25		5:00	1:25		5:05	2:25		5:10
12:30		6:00	1:30		6:05	2:30		6:10
12:35		7:00	1:35		7:05	2:35		7:10
12:40		8:00	1:40		8:05	2:40		8:10
12:45		9:00	1:45		9:05	2:45		9:10
12:50		10:00	1:50		10:05	2:50		10:10
12:55		11:00	1:55		11:05	2:55		11:10

3:00	or	12:15	4:00	or	12:20	5:00	or	12:25
3:05		1:15	4:05		1:20	5:05		1:25
3:10		2:15	4:10		2:20	5:10		2:25
3:15		same	4:15		3:20	5:15		3:25
3:20		4:15	4:20		same	5:20		4:25
3:25		5:15	4:25		5:20	5:25		same
3:30		6:15	4:30		6:20	5:30		6:25
3:35		7:15	4:35		7:20	5:35		7:25
3:40		8:15	4:40		8:20	5:40		8:25
3:45		9:15	4:45		9:20	5:45		9:25
3:50		10:15	4:50		10:20	5:50		10:25
3:55		11:15	4:55		11:20	5:55		11:25

6:00		12:30	7:00		12:35	8:00		12:40
6:05		1:30	7:05		1:35	8:05		1:40
6:10		2:30	7:10		2:35	8:10		2:40
6:15		3:30	7:15		3:35	8:15		3:40
6:20		4:30	7:20		4:35	8:20		4:40
6:25		5:30	7:25		5:35	8:25		5:40
6:30		same	7:30		6:35	8:30		6:40
6:35		7:30	7:35		same	8:35		7:40
6:40		8:30	7:40		8:35	8:40		same
6:45		9:30	7:45		9:35	8:45		9:40
6:50		10:30	7:50		10:35	8:50		10:40
6:55		11:30	7:55		11:35	8:55		11:40

9:00	or	12:45	10:00	or	12:50	11:00	or	12:55
9:05		1:45	10:05		1:50	11:05		1:55
9:10		2:45	10:10		2:50	11:10		2:55
9:15		3:45	10:15		3:50	11:15		3:55
9:20		4:45	10:20		4:50	11:20		4:55
9:25		5:45	10:25		5:50	11:25		5:55
9:30		6:45	10:30		6:50	11:30		6:55
9:35		7:45	10:35		7:50	11:35		7:55
9:40		8:45	10:40		8:50	11:40		8:55
9:45		same	10:45		9:50	11:45		9:55
9:50		10:45	10:50		same	11:50		10:55
9:55		11:45	10:55		11:50	11:55		same

Giving the whole reference list may, at first, seem too obvious, but if one studies the list, there are some interesting things to observe. For example, note how in an hour list, the minutes go up 5 for each number (9:00, 9:05, 9:10) while in the second column the minutes are all at the same time period, in this instance at 45 minutes. Secondly, note the word "same" which indicates that at one period (9:45) the second time is also at 9:45 or the "same." Upon examining the next two columns, the word "same" has moved down one step and is at the 50-minute mark. In each of the subsequent columns, the word "same" is always one step lower or 5 minutes later. Players may want to work out their own time lists and make these discoveries for themselves.

Clock Arithmetic

TYPE OF GAME: *Individual or Team Arithmetic Game*
GRADE: *Third and Up*

Give each player a sheet of paper on which a large clock face has been drawn (or let each player draw his or her own). The game is first played with one hand for the clock. This can be a ruler or any piece of folded paper. The folded paper edge will serve as a straight line.

Have the players place the ruler or folded paper "hand" on the clock face so that it touches the center point and the numbers 12 and 6. Have the players add these two figures together and write the answer on a separate piece of paper. The ruler is then moved around to touch the 1 and the 7. The sum of these figures is written below the first sum. Instruct players to continue around the clock in this manner until they come back to the starting position.

The correct answers will read: 18, 8, 10, 12, 14, 16.

Variation #1

Have the players subtract the smaller number from the larger on each number combination around the dial. The correct answer in each instance will be 6.

Variation #2

Have the players multiply each number combination around the dial. The answers now will read: 72, 7, 16, 27, 40, 55.

Variation #3

Players now divide the larger number by the smaller one to arrive at these answers: 2, 7, 4, 3, 2½, and 2⅕.

To play as a team game, begin with the first game and the first player of team A. That player must give the correct sum of the first two numbers. A point is given to his team for the correct answer. If he misses, the first player of the next team is asked for the correct answer. Play moves from one team to another. When the addition problems are completed, the game proceeds with the subtraction, multiplication, and division problems.

Variation #4

With older players, have them take each number to the power of 2 and add the results together.

Variation #5

With older players, have them square each number and work problems on this basis. Here are the problems and their answers:

ADDITION

$12^2 + 6^2 = 144 + 36 = 180$
$7^2 + 1^2 = 49 + 1 = 50$
$8^2 + 2^2 = 64 + 4 = 68$
$9^2 + 3^2 = 81 + 9 = 90$
$10^2 + 4^2 = 100 + 16 = 116$
$5^2 + 11^2 = 25 + 121 = 146$

MULTIPLICATION

$144 \times 36 = 5184$
$49 \times 1 = 49$
$64 \times 4 = 256$
$81 \times 9 = 729$
$100 \times 16 = 1600$
$25 \times 121 = 3025$

SUBTRACTION

$144 - 36 = 108$
$49 - 1 = 48$
$64 - 4 = 60$
$81 - 9 = 72$
$100 - 16 = 86$
$121 - 25 = 96$

DIVISION

$144 \div 36 = 4$
$49 \div 1 = 49$
$64 \div 4 = 16$
$81 \div 9 = 9$
$100 \div 16 = 6.25$
$121 \div 25 = 4.84$

If the numbers are cubed, the problems and their answers would be:

ADDITION

$12^3 + 6^3 = 1728 + 216 = 1944$
$7^3 + 1^3 = 343 + 1 = 344$
$8^3 + 2^3 = 512 + 8 = 520$
$9^3 + 3^3 = 728 + 27 = 756$
$10^3 + 4^3 = 1000 + 64 = 1064$
$11^3 + 5^3 = 1331 + 125 = 1456$

MULTIPLICATION

$1728 \times 216 = 373{,}248$
$343 \times 1 = 343$
$512 \times 8 = 4096$
$728 \times 27 = 19{,}656$
$1000 \times 64 = 64{,}000$
$1331 \times 125 = 166{,}375$

SUBTRACTION

$1728 - 216 = 1512$
$343 - 1 = 342$
$512 - 8 = 504$
$728 - 27 = 701$
$1000 - 64 = 936$
$1331 - 125 = 1206$

DIVISION

$1728 \div 216 = 8$
$343 \div 1 = 343$
$512 \div 8 = 64$
$728 \div 27 = 26.962962$
$1000 \div 64 = 15.625$
$1331 \div 125 = 10.648$

4

Geometry in the World Around Us

The word geometry comes from the Greek word *geometrein,* meaning to measure the earth. Geometry is a part of mathematics. It deals not only with measurements, but with points, lines, angles, surfaces, and solids and their relationships to each other. Most important, geometry occurs in the world around us. Everywhere we look we see lines, angles, shapes, and solids. Some are man-made, but all are natural in origin.

Man did not invent shapes, he took them from nature. Flowers, sea animals, leaves, patterns we find in natural objects have been spotted by keen-eyed artists and translated into designs for textiles, pictures, pottery, decorations for china—and you can find those same shapes or designs in nature. Which came first? You know the answer to that. Not only did man copy from Nature, but Nature herself repeats her designs. Some flowers are shaped like sea animals (the shrimp plant), others look like birds (and are appropriately named birds of paradise). Jack Frost pictures are of flowers, ferns, geometric designs, birds in flight—all examples of Nature repeating her designs over and over again.

It has not been determined exactly how frost is laid on windowpanes, but what is known is that it follows lines made when windows have been scratched with abrasive window cleaners. Where individuals have scratched their initials or some romantic message on the window, the frost follows along those lines with decorative embellishments. However they are formed, the designs are always delicate and beautiful.

The common pattern of the ice crystal is the hexagon. Snowflakes may be six-sided or they may be six-pointed stars. For sheer delight, examine the book *Snow Crystals*, by W. A. Bentley and W. J. Humphreys. Bentley photographed thousands of crystals in search of knowledge—and found beauty as well. To see the detail of design in these tiny bits of ice crystals is to find new and profound respect for Nature, the greatest artist of them all.

The hexagon is repeated in the crystals of the minerals mica, beryl, quartz, apatite, and many others. But Nature flaunts many different geometric figures in her crystal systems. If you look into any book on minerals, rocks, and precious stones, you will find that there are 32 crystal classes divided into seven crystal systems. The next time you are in a natural science museum, examine the rock and crystal collection and see how many familiar geometric shapes you can identify. Not only will the many geometric shapes astound you, but the colors and beauty of the many specimens will delight you. Be sure to examine the collection of fluorescent rocks which literally spring to life under black light.

Snakes come in a variety of colors, and many snakes are beautifully lined or decorated with geometric designs. Examine a turtle the next time you meet one coming down the path. It won't be in a hurry, so you will have plenty of time to look. You will find that its markings are hexagons, circles, rectangles, and other geometric shapes, all fitting nicely into the convex shape of the shell. If you never see turtles or snakes where you live, except in a zoo, find their pictures in a book. They are a beautiful lesson in geometry.

GEOMETRY GAMES AND ACTIVITIES

Discover and Share Days

Much can be learned and enjoyed about geometry in the world around us from Discover and Share days. School classes and recreation groups can collect either examples of the natural objects themselves or pictures of them which clearly show geometric principles. The natural objects may be fresh or pressed flowers or leaves. Pet snakes and turtles always make exciting exhibitions. Specimens of crystal formations will create interest. Where the actual specimens are not available, books or nature magazines showing photographs in color will serve just as well. Each contributor demonstrates her or his own exhibit, pointing out the geometric forms, the shapes (plane or solid), lines, and angles that she has recognized in her exhibit. A demonstrator may show similarities of design between a Chinese forget-me-not and a starfish, both of which are five-pointed. An apple cut in half horizontally will reveal the same five-pointed star in the seed arrangement.

Keep a place on the chalkboard for listing new articles as students "discover" examples not mentioned before.

Study and Tell Sessions

In the Discover and Share days, examples may be offered about which the participant knows little. Subsequent periods may then become Study and Tell sessions, in which a participant reports on a particular item previously mentioned in a Discover and Share session which aroused his curiosity enough to stimulate him to make a brief study and prepare a report on it. For example, in the discovery of spheres of a man-made variety, a bathysphere might have been mentioned. What is it? Who invented it? How is it used? A study will reveal the fascinating answers.

In either the Discover and Share days or the Study and Tell sessions, the facts may be reported on a team basis, each participant in turn reporting his or her discovery or independent study. It probably won't be possible to cover the whole class in one period, so subsequent sessions will begin with the player whose turn was coming up next. Scores of one point for an acceptable example can be kept for the teams, and items previously discussed can be recorded to see that there are no repetitions. Pictures illustrating the contributions should be welcomed.

Either kind of session encourages an awareness in each participant that can be spread to every other phase of living, helping him see what he has not seen before, thereby enriching his life.

Geometry in What I See Every Day

Players in school classes are divided into teams. Players, in turn, name something they encountered or "discovered" in their everyday lives that demonstrates some phase of geometry. Team scores can be kept. If all players have not had the opportunity to participate in the time allotted for this session, the player whose turn was coming up when the session ended becomes the first to begin the subsequent session. Allow time for a player to explain her or his "discovery" if the object does not at first seem appropriate. A record of "discoveries" should be kept for a period so that no duplication occurs. After all, the possibilities are almost endless.

Here are some of the categories which might be used for this activity:

1. Parallel lines, in streets, sidewalks, crosswalk lines, etc. The children bring in drawings they have made or pic-

tures of examples cut from newspapers or magazines. Just the search for pictures showing such geometric principles in constant use in everyday lives helps to create awareness and recognition. Suggestions following may be treated in the same way.

2. Right angles at cross streets, on edges of desks or books, in the hand positions of a watch or clock, in body positions.
3. Acute and obtuse angles at obliquely intersecting streets, in body angles, in clock hand angles, in printed letters of the alphabet.
4. The hexagon-shaped STOP sign; rectangular and other shapes used in traffic signs.
5. The torus shape: automobile tires, donuts or bagels, a life preserver, Cheerios.
6. Spheres: balls of all kinds, some breakfast cereals, marbles, candies, blueberries.
7. Gas station signs: round, hexagon, oval, rectangular.
8. The ovoid shape of the egg.
9. Shapes of plates, glasses, silverware; and the kinds of designs on them.
10. The rectangular shapes of street name signs and the angles at which they are attached to the poles (which are cylindrical).
11. The shapes of a bed, pillows, sheets, towels, soap.
12. Shapes of certain kinds of tree leaves, the tree shapes themselves; the trunk, the lines on the trunk, the designs of the bark.
13. Shapes of wearing apparel: buttons, watches, belt buckles, eyeglasses, rings, bracelets; and the designs that appear on these objects.
14. Shapes of common school articles: chalk, book, ruler, pen, tablet, protractor.

15. Angles in car and bus designs, the shape of the space a moving windshield wiper creates, the shapes of knobs and steering wheels.
16. Shapes of coins and bills.

As one becomes attuned to the idea, one realizes there is literally no end to the possibilities—and no reason for duplication. Participants cannot help but become acutely conscious of the importance of geometry in their everyday lives. It becomes something more than just a subject in a book one studies in school.

To make this more than just a verbal activity, students might be asked to prepare a scrapbook of pictures depicting geometry in everyday living, or to create a poster collage which can be displayed in the classroom as an open house feature.

Geometric Shapes in Nature

Players in turn are asked to name two of Nature's creations that are similar in shape or design. Some examples:

1. Spheres: sun, moon, planets, stars, fish eggs (roe).
2. Circle designs on snapping turtles, butterflies, moths, some seashells, some snakes, some lizards, ladybirds.
3. Parallel lines on some snakes, on worm lizards and footless lizards, on iguanas, alligators, and crocodiles, on butterflies, on cucumber beetles, on some flower petals.
4. Triangles: shapes of insect wings, designs on reptiles, the triangle form of moths when resting, designs on butterflies.
5. Helix: some seashells are marked with conical helix-shaped designs.
6. Rectangles: turtle-shell designs, some crystals.
7. Hexagons: snow crystals, several crystal formations.
8. Six-pointed or six-parted designs: snow crystals, many flowers such as daylily, blue-eyed grass, some tulips.

9. Five-pointed designs: flowers such as violets, spring beauties, some tulips, clematis, bouncing bet, Chinese forget-me-not cinquefoils.

Lists such as these could go on forever; if a shape has a name, it is one given to some natural object by man. A game or activity such as this can stimulate participants to examine flowers, leaves, nuts, fruits, crystals, shells, turtles, and even snakes. When the specimen itself is not available, pictures of it can be found in magazines and books. Students may be asked to prepare a poster showing geometric shapes and natural objects matching them. Whenever a person is stimulated to see what he has merely glanced at before, a bit more of our magical world is opened to him.

Mix and Match Geometric Exhibit

Have each pupil prepare a small exhibit consisting of a drawing or photograph of some geometric plane or solid shape matched to a picture of that shape in Nature. Actual articles may be used instead of photos wherever possible. Watch geometry come alive!

For players who know geometric shapes, either plane or solid, or are willing to study the shapes shown and identified below, the following games are possible. For those who will consult a dictionary, almost anything is possible.

Sports Geometry

Familiar sports are played on fields of specific shapes and sizes with equipment of specific shapes and sizes. Baseball is certainly not played on a running track with a cube.

The fields are designated by the shapes (planes) and the equipment by the name of the appropriate solid form. For example, a rectangle, parallel lines, an upright barrier, and a small sphere are the shapes and forms of tennis. They might also be those of volleyball if the size of the sphere were not specified.

How many of the following sports puzzlers can you identify? Make some puzzlers of your own and try them on your friends and family.

1. Rectangle, upright parallels, parallel lines, ellipsoid.
2. Square in a quadrant, cylindrical wood, a small sphere.
3. Small sphere, hollow cylinder, slender cylinders with various faces, straight lines, angles.
4. Rectangle with four rectangles and one circle within it, parellel uprights, a sphere.
5. Rectangle, parallel lines, sphere, frustrum of a cone.
6. Rectangle with rounded corners containing four small rectangles and five circles, a slice of cylinder (disc).
7. Narrow cylinders, metal torui (plural of torus).
8. Rectangle, parallel uprights, high barrier, a torus.
9. Two parallel ovals.
10. Rectangle, parallel lines, triangles and frustrums, flat cylinders.

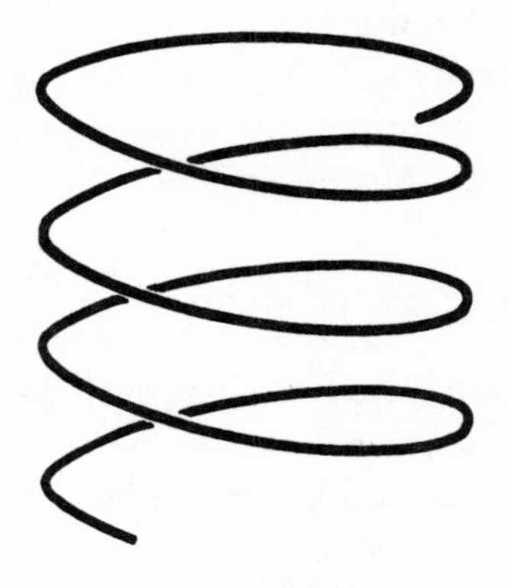

Fig. 31

11. Rectangles, parallel lines, small sphere.
12. Rectangle, sphere, wooden cylindrical pins.
13. Rectangle, parallel uprights, high barrier, frustrum of a cone.
14. Half ovals, small spheres, cylinders with a cylindrical handle, cylindrical stakes.

Answers:

1. Football.
2. Baseball. The "diamond" is actually a square with foul lines making a quadrant of a circle.
3. Golf. The cup is a hollow cylinder, the fairways are straight or angled (doglegs), the clubs are cylinders with club faces.
4. Soccer. Each goal is a rectangle within a rectangle on a rectangular field; there is a face-off circle in the center of the field.
5. Basketball. The hoop with the net is the frustrum of a cone.
6. Ice hockey.
7. Quoits. Played like horseshoes except that quoits are donut (torus) shaped. (Hard to make a ringer!)
8. Deck or ring tennis.
9. Running track.
10. Shuffleboard.
11. Handball.
12. Bowling.
13. Badminton.
14. Croquet.

Geometric Foods

Many common fruits and vegetables are of particular geometric solid shapes. Some may occur in more than one shape; water-

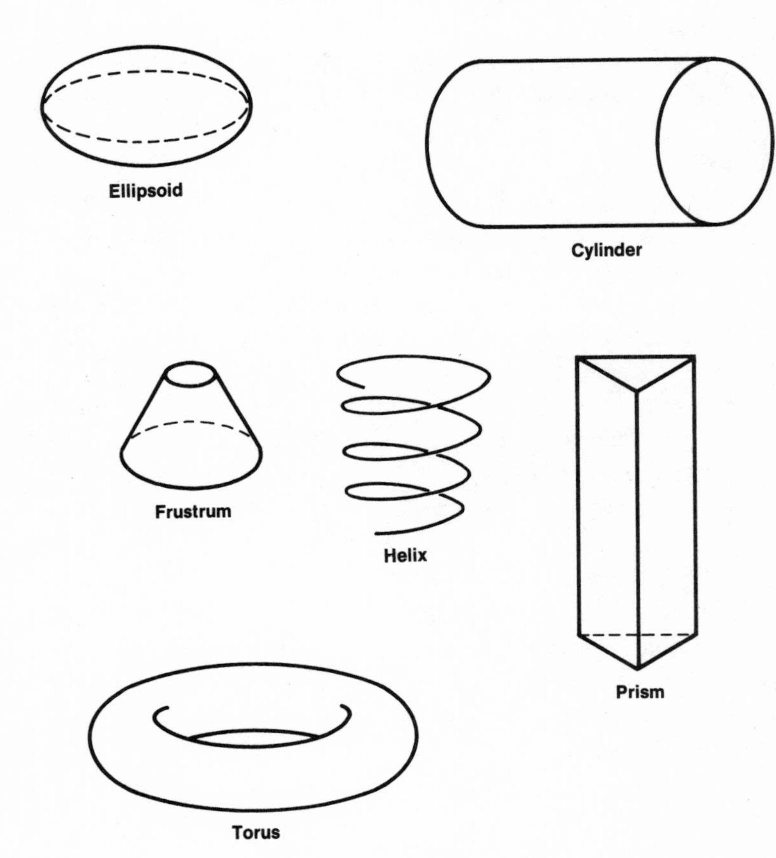

Fig. 32

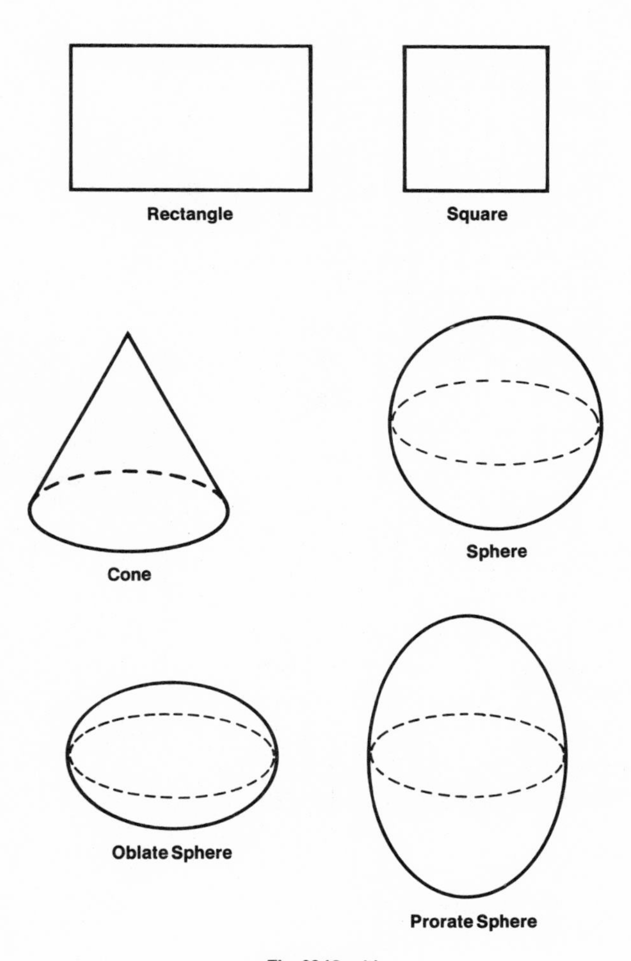
Rectangle
Square
Cone
Sphere
Oblate Sphere
Prorate Sphere

Fig. 32 (Con't)

melons, for example, vary in shape from spheres to prolate and oblate spheroids, depending upon the variety. Consult Figure 32 and your dictionaries. How many fruits and vegetables can you identify by their geometric shapes?

1. Which fruits are large or small spheres?
2. What fruits are ellipsoids?
3. What specific group of fruits are either oblate spheroids, prolate spheroids, or spheres?
4. What fruit is a quadrahedron but a cylinder when peeled?
5. What vegetables are cones?
6. Which vegetables are frustrums of cones?
7. Which vegetables are spheres?
8. What fruits are cones?
9. Which vegetables are small spheres?
10. Which vegetables vary in shape from spheres to oblate and prolate spheroids?
11. Which vegetables are cylinders?
12. What fruit gives its name to a shape?
13. What smaller fruits are oblate spheroids and ellipsoids?
14. What tropical fruits are prolate spheres?
15. What vegetables are cylindroids?

Answers:

1. cherries, oranges, apples, peaches, apricots, blueberries, grapes
2. prune plums, lemons, limes
3. melons: watermelons, honeydews, cantaloupes
4. bananas
5. carrots, long radishes, parsnips, some peppers
6. green or red bell peppers, some apples
7. beets, kohlrabi, some potatoes, some tomatoes, cabbage, head lettuce, pumpkins, onions

8. strawberries
9. peas
10. potatoes, tomatoes
11. corn, cucumbers, zucchini, rhubarb
12. pear (pear-shaped)
13. plums, prune plums
14. pineapples and mangoes
15. string beans, lima beans

Nutty Geometrics

Name the shapes of:

1. peanuts
2. walnuts
3. hazelnuts
4. Brazil nuts
5. pecans
6. cashews
7. pistachios
8. butternuts
9. black walnuts
10. hickory nuts
11. acorns
12. buckeyes or horse chestnuts
13. chestnuts

Geometric Menus

What if you had to order from a menu where the various foods and dishes were given in geometric terms? Can you guess what some of the foods given below are:

1. a cylinder of sphere juice
2. cylinders and cheese
3. a cylinder between two half-cylinders
4. sliced quadrahedron in sphere juice
5. helix and cheese
6. sliced cones and cream
7. cone-flavored sphere in a cone
8. scrambled ellipsoids
9. a slice of prolate spheroid
10. a triangular piece made up of little spheres, topped with a large sphere
11. french fried spheres
12. cheese disk on an almost oblate spheroid
13. green sphere pie and a prism

Answers:

1. glass of orange or tomato juice
2. macaroni and cheese
3. hot dog on a bun
4. sliced banana in orange juice
5. spiral-shaped pasta and cheese
6. sliced strawberries and cream
7. strawberry ice cream cone
8. scrambled eggs
9. slice of watermelon
10. blueberry pie à la mode
11. hush puppies
12. cheeseburger on a bun
13. apple pie and cheese

Challenge your friends and classmates with a few geometric foods you have figured out yourself.

Our Geometric Alphabet

The capital letters of our English alphabet are geometric in shape. Can you identify letters by their geometric descriptions? Math books or dictionaries may be consulted. (Some descriptions will depend upon the particular typeface used as example.)

1. Which letter is composed of one horizontal and two vertical lines?
2. Which letter contains an acute triangle?
3. Which is two vertical parallel lines connected by an oblique line which forms two acute angles in the process?
4. Which letter is an oval or sometimes a circle?
5. Which letters are composed of a vertical line which is touched or crossed by a horizontal one?
6. Which is two horizontal lines connected by an oblique line which forms two acute angles in the process?
7. Which letter is an arc?
8. Which letters are composed of combinations of a vertical line and one or more arcs?
9. Which is composed of a vertical line and two oblique lines which form two obtuse and two acute angles?
10. Which is composed entirely of curves?
11. Which is a partial oval?
12. Which is composed of one vertical line and three parallel lines at right angles to it?
13. Which is composed of two intersecting oblique lines which form two acute and two obtuse angles?
14. Which is composed of two lines which meet to form an acute angle?
15. Which is composed of two pairs of parallel lines arranged so as to form three acute angles?
16. Which is two lines which meet to form an acute angle set upon a vertical line?

17. Which is a vertical line with two parallel lines at right angles to the vertical line?
18. Which is two parallel vertical lines connected by two oblique lines which meet to form three acute angles?
19. Which is a perpendicular line left to stand alone?
20. Which is a vertical line, an arc, and a curved line?
21. Which is an oval or sometimes a circle with a curved line which intersects the perimeter?
22. Which is a horizontal line and an arc?

Answers:

1. H
2. A
3. N
4. O
5. L and T
6. Z
7. C
8. D, B, P, and J
9. K
10. S
11. U
12. E
13. X
14. V
15. W
16. Y
17. F
18. M
19. I
20. R
21. Q
22. G

CLOCK GEOMETRY

Straight Line Time

TYPE OF GAME: *Individual Puzzler*
GRADE: *Third and Up*

The study of lines is part of geometry. A straight line is the shortest distance between two points. Parallel lines—lines curved, wavy, zigzag, or straight—lie in the same position, always an equal distance apart; they may slant to the right or left, lie horizontally or vertically, but so long as they are an equal distance apart they are said to be parallel.

In this game we are talking about the two straight lines which are the hands of the clock. Players study the hands on the wall clock or a picture of a clock they have drawn on paper. Two strips of paper can serve as movable hands, with one end of each "hand" touching the center point of the clock. Two pencils can also be moved about like hands. (See Clock Time Confusers for directions for making a simple clock face.)

At what approximate time positions are the hands in a straight line? (We use the word "approximate" since we are working only with the numbers on the clock face, not the single minutes between. Players who want to be exact may come up with time differences of two or three minutes.) For example, the hands are in a straight line at 6:00. At 9:15 the time would be approximate; more exactly, the hands might be at 9:17, but since we are working with a rather primitive clock face, we need only approximate the time.

Parallel Line Clock Times

At what times are the hands in parallel position, one on top of the other? How many of these times can the players find? There are twelve positions:

12:00	3:15	6:30	9:45
1:05	4:20	7:35	10:50
2:10	5:25	8:40	11:55

Right Angle Time

At what times on the clock (using only the numerals and not the individual minutes) do the hands form a right (90-degree) angle? How many of these times can you find? There are 24 possible times:

12:15	6:45	11:40	5:10
1:20	7:50	10:35	4:05
2:25	8:55	9:30	3:00
3:30	9:00	8:25	2:55
4:35	10:05	7:20	1:50
5:40	11:10	6:15	12:45

Players may soon discover that in any right angle on a clock the hands must point to the first and last numbers of a four-number sequence. In other words, there must be two numbers between the position of one hand and that of the other. Thus at 1:20, one hand is on the 1 and the other is on the 4, with the numbers 2 and 3 between them.

Acute Angle Clock Time

An acute angle being less than 90 degrees, at how many periods do the hands of the clock form an acute angle, using only the numerals and not the individual minutes? There are actually 48 such times:

12:05	6:35	12:55	6:25
12:10	6:40	12:50	6:20
1:10	7:40	11:50	5:20
1:15	7:45	11:45	5:15

2:15	8:45	10:45	4:15
2:20	8:50	10:40	4:10
3:20	9:50	9:40	3:10
3:25	9:55	9:35	3:05
4:25	10:55	8:35	2:05
4:30	10:00	8:30	2:00
5:30	11:00	7:30	1:00
5:35	11:05	7:25	1:55

Players will discover that acute angles are formed with the two hands either on two consecutive numbers or on the first and last numbers in a three-number sequence. The first forms a 30-degree angle, the second a 60-degree angle.

Obtuse Angle Clock Time

An obtuse angle is an angle of more than 90 degrees and less than 180 degrees. At how many times do the clock hands form obtuse angles (at the numbers only and not at the individual minutes)? There are 48 such clock times:

12:20	6:50	12:40	6:10
12:25	6:55	12:35	6:05
1:25	7:55	11:35	5:05
1:30	7:00	11:30	5:00
2:30	8:00	10:30	4:00
2:35	8:05	10:25	4:55
3:35	9:05	9:25	3:55
3:40	9:10	9:20	3:50
4:40	10:10	8:20	2:50
4:45	10:15	8:15	2:45
5:45	11:15	7:15	1:45
5:50	11:20	7:10	1:40

Obtuse angles are formed with the hands on the first and last numbers of a five-number or a six-number sequence. The first forms a 120-degree angle, the second a 150-degree angle. Let the players make this discovery for themselves.

Variation

Play any of the clock angle games in reverse. The teacher calls out a time and the players must name the type of angle. This can be played as a class game or as a team game.

In a team game, the teacher names a time to the first player on team A. A point is given to the team for a correct answer, and the play moves to the first player of the next team. If an incorrect answer is given, the play moves to the player of the next team for a correct answer. Only correct answers win points.

BODY GEOMETRY

Have you ever thought how many geometric forms you can make with parts of your body? The games which follow will help you to find some of them, then you will be on your own. As you sit, stand, move, or exercise, think about the forms you are making. Make a list of some of those not mentioned here and try them on your friends, classmates, and family. Call off your list one by one and see how quickly your friends can respond. Perhaps they can invent a few for you to try.

Body Geometric Exercises

Geometric forms that can be created with various body parts are described in the list below. The teacher might call out a few from each list in a kind of exercise routine. Once the players know how to react geometrically, let the players take turns being leader and calling out forms they have experimented with and listed.

1. Stand in a straight position, feet straight ahead at right angles to your legs.
2. Make parallel lines with your arms above your head, in

front of your body at an acute angle to your body, and at an obtuse angle to the body.

3. Stand with feet parallel to each other, at right angles to each other, at an acute angle with heels together, and at an obtuse angle with toes together.
4. Hold fingers together stiffly in parallel position on each hand and make a right angle to the fingers with each thumb.
5. Spread fingers to form acute angles, with the thumb forming an obtuse angle. With fingers still in acute angle position, move the thumb forward to a right angle position to the forefinger.
6. Make a circle with thumb and forefinger (the okay sign).
7. Hold hands stiff, fingers up. Now bend only the forefinger at the second knuckle into a right angle to the other fingers. At the same time, can you move your thumb forward and into a parallel position to your bent forefinger?
8. Make a large circle with both thumbs and forefingers touching.
9. Make a triangle with both thumbs and forefingers touching.
10. Holding fingers stiff and tightly together, bend hands forward to make right angles at the wrists. Turn your hands toward each other.
11. Hold arm out stiffly to your side at right angles to your body. Bend the hand at right angles to the wrist. Holding all those positions, bend your arm forward at the elbow at right angle to the arm. You now have three right angles on one side. Can you add the three on the left side and make six right angles at the same time? Try other arm positions. (There are many possible ones.)
12. If you sit straight-backed in a chair with your feet flat on the floor you have a right angle at the hips, one at the knees, and your feet are at right angles to your legs.

Fig. 33

Fig. 34

If you add all the arm movements described in exercise 11, you could be making *nine* right angles at the same time.

13. From the positions in exercise 12, change as many angles as you can from right angles to either acute or obtuse.
14. Stand with feet parallel. Put your right foot out to the side, touching your heel to the floor with your foot at right angles to your leg. Don't try this with both feet at the same time!
15. If, while you are standing, you put the heel of your right foot against the arch of the left at right angles, how many right angles is that foot making with the left?
16. Make a circle with your arms out in front of you as if holding a giant round balloon. Move your arms up over your head and make a circle.
17. Lying on the floor in a straight line, can you lift your legs until they are straight up at right angles to your body? Can you keep your feet at right angles to your legs while in this position?
18. Can you sit on the floor with your back straight and at right angles to your legs? Can you keep your feet at right angles to your legs at the same time?
19. When you do a deep knee bend with a straight back, what angles do your legs make?
20. If you kneel with your back straight, you make a right angle. How many more can you make at the same time with your hands and arms?
21. Sit on the floor with back straight at right angles to your legs. Can you spread your legs so that they form a right angle? (It won't be easy, but it is possible.) If you can keep your feet at right angles to your legs while your legs make a right angle and you are sitting with a straight back which is at a right angle to the floor—well, you are quite a contortionist!

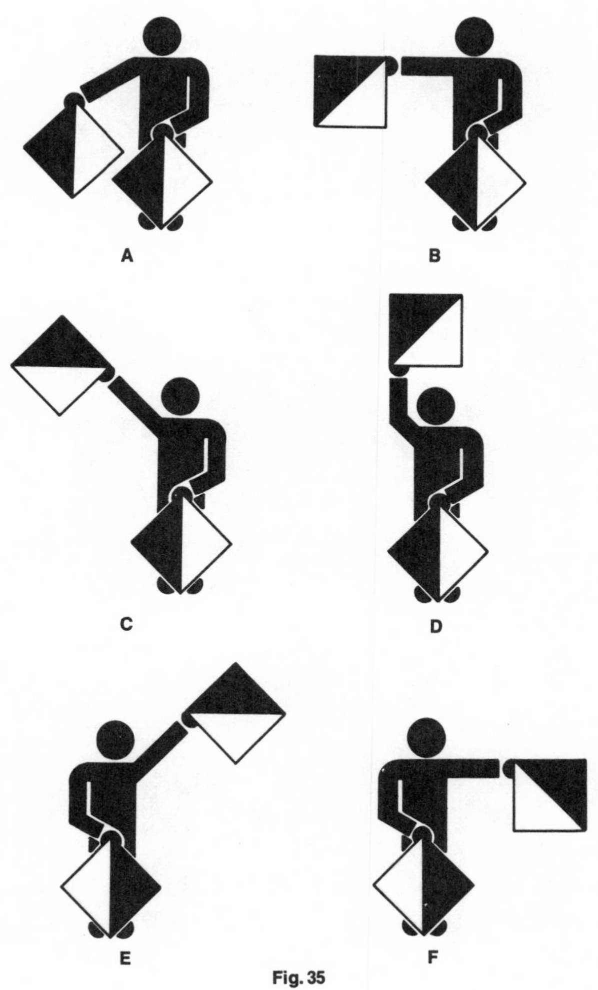

Fig. 35

Fig. 35 (Con't)

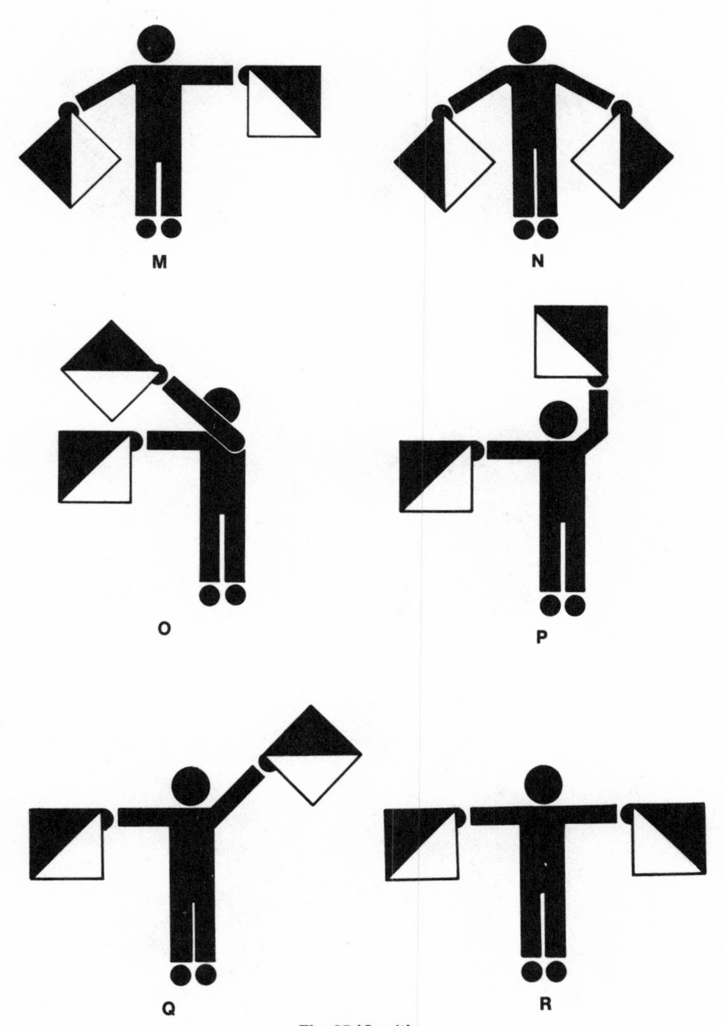

Fig. 35 (Con't)

Fig. 35 (Con't)

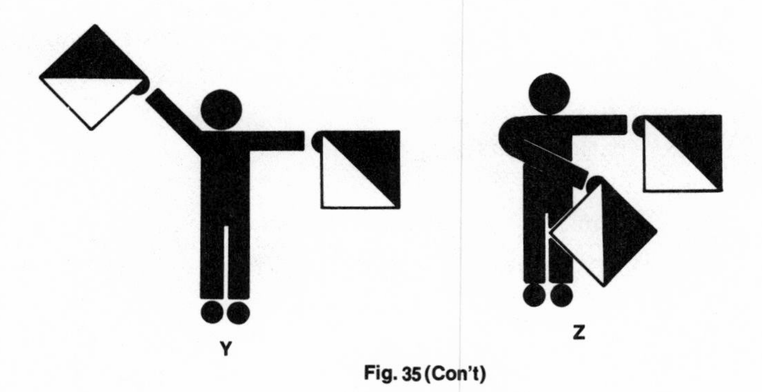

Fig. 35 (Con't)

While these movements may seem silly, take a look at the semaphore system of signaling with two flags from one place to another or one ship to another (Figure 35). It is all a matter of various angles made with the arms holding two flags. The second series shows body signals to aircraft (Figure 36).

Next time you fly, try to watch the signal man with his flashlights signaling a plane to begin taxiing preparatory to take-off. Or watch him signal where the plane is to taxi in and where and when to stop. On city streets, watch the traffic officer when he holds up his hand to signal you to stop. At what angle is his hand to his wrist? Watch the umpire signal a strike, a safe play, or an out. Try imitating the movements and then naming the angles. No matter where you look there are angles, parallel lines, circles, triangles, and all the other geometric forms. We could hardly exist without them.

Geometry is something in a book?
Nonsense! You'll find it everywhere you look!

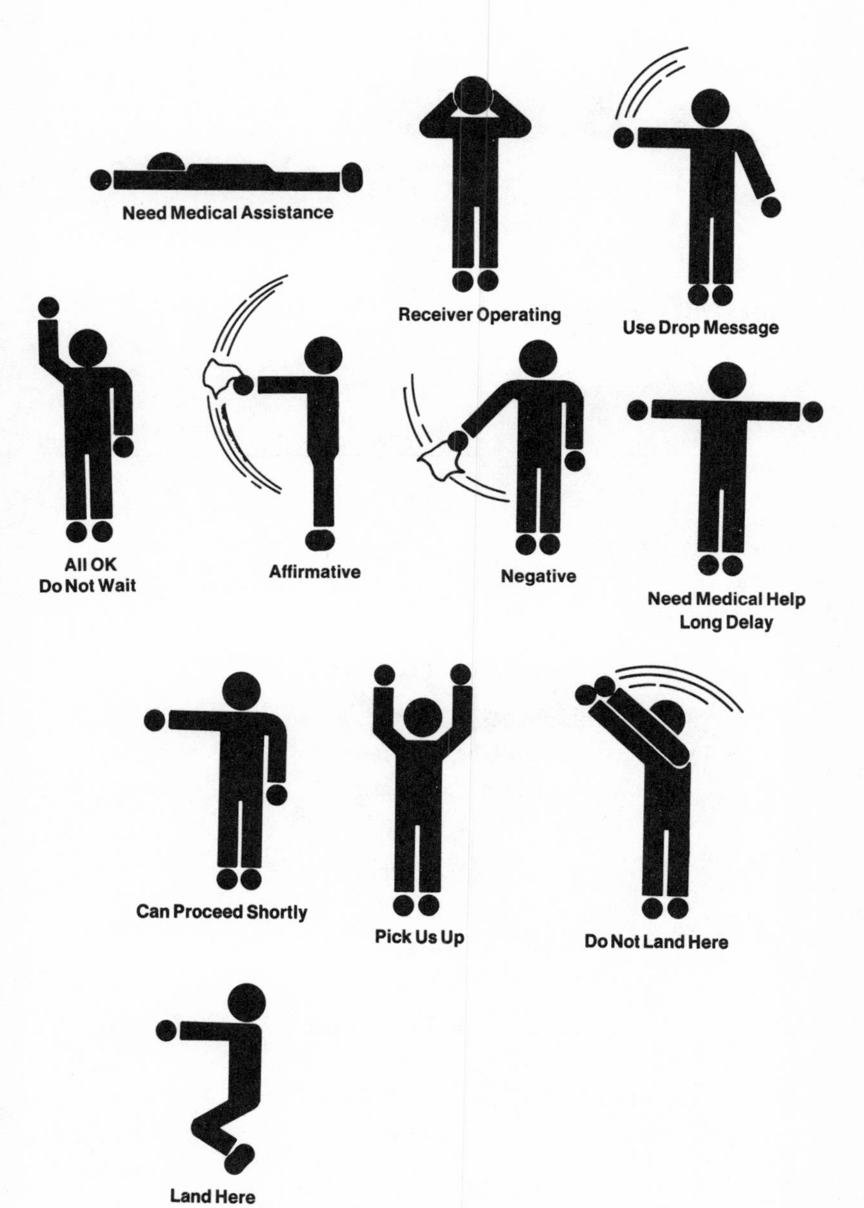
Need Medical Assistance
Receiver Operating
Use Drop Message
All OK
Do Not Wait
Affirmative
Negative
Need Medical Help
Long Delay
Can Proceed Shortly
Pick Us Up
Do Not Land Here
Land Here

Fig. 36

5

Metricmagic

Metric is a decimal system;
We count things in tens or in tenths.
What you will find as you use it is
That it all makes a lot of good sense.

Metric units are easily learned,
We need to remember just four:
Celsius,* meter, liter, and gram,
That's all—there are no more!

Celsius measures heat and cold,
While lengths are told in meters.
For weight and mass there are the grams,
For volume we use liters.

When counting grams, liters, or meters,
Deka is ten of these,
Hecto's a hundred, kilo's a thousand,
And mega's a million, please.

Deci, centi, milli, and micro
Measure things tinier and smaller,

* Also called centigrade.

While deka, hecto, kilo, and mega
Measure things longer, heavier, taller.

Deci is d, it's also one tenth (0.1);
Centi is c, when one hundredth is meant (.01);
Milli is m, when one thousandth is shown (.001);
Micro, Greek letter, is one millionth (.000001).

Deka is ten (10) and written as d,
Hecto's an h, one hundred (100), you see,
Kilo's a thousand (1,000) and written as k,
Mega, next largest, is written as M:
A metrical million (1,000,000) is Mega.

Milligrams weigh the tiniest of things
Used in medicine, science, and such.
A milligram's the weight of a grain of salt;
I think you'll agree that's not much.

An inch is longer than a centimeter (cm),
A meter (m) is longer than a yard,
A mile is longer than a kilometer (km);
I ask you, does that seem so hard?

An ounce weighs more than a gram (g),
Kilos (k) weigh more than pounds,
A quart is less than a liter (1);
It's as simple as it sounds.

THE INTERNATIONAL METRIC SYSTEM

It's here to stay. Don't fight it. Learn it, use it, and you'll wonder why we waited so long to adopt it. It's easy to use and faster to compute. For example, a box of cereal lists the contents as weighing 1 pound, 14 ounces. The price is 96¢. To figure the cost we must first convert the contents to ounces. One pound (16 ounces) plus 14 ounces equals 30 ounces. Divide the cost price 96¢ by 30 and the answer is 3.2¢ per ounce. Two steps.

If the weight of the contents is also listed in grams, it is only necessary to divide the total cost by the number of grams to find the cost per gram. One step!

To compare the costs of the contents of two different sizes of the same product, we must go through the first process two times—four steps. With grams, it would take only two steps.

Computing the price of a square yard of carpeting is even more complicated. For example, we have a piece of carpeting 4 yards, 2 feet, 5 inches by 3 yards, 2 feet, 4 inches. To figure the cost per square yard we must first convert each side to inches. Then we must multiply one side by the other to get square inches. The product of the long side of 173 inches multiplied by the short side of 136 inches is 23,528 square inches. (Are you still there?)

Now we must divide that product by 1296 (the number of square inches in a yard) to determine the number of square yards, which is 18.15. At last we are ready to figure the price of the piece. The cost quoted by the salesman is $89.00. The salesman tells us that the regular cost per yard is $4.95 but he is giving us the piece at a super bargain price. Is he?

If we were buying by the metric system, we would have a different ball game. Here is a piece of carpeting 4 meters and 25 centimers (4.25 meters) on one side by 3 meters and 30 centimeters (3.30 meters) on the short side. The salesman tells you the original price was $5.00 per square meter but he is giving you the special price of $70.00. Is he? Is it a big bargain? One thing is sure: You will learn the answer faster figuring metrically.

Put these two problems side-by-side and have a look.

Your Body as a Ruler

You can use parts of your body for metrics as easily as you did for the U.S. system. We have always used the length of

U.S. SYSTEM
PIECE OF CARPETING

4 yards, 2 feet, 5 inches
by
3 yards, 2 feet, 4 inches

4 yards = 4 × 36 inches = 144 inches
2 feet = 2 × 12 inches = 24
5 inches = 5
173 inches

by

3 yards = 3 × 36 inches = 108 inches
2 feet = 2 × 12 inches = 24
4 inches = 4
136 inches

173 × 136

173
× 136
1038
519
173
23528 square inches

23528 ÷ 1296 = 18.14 square yards

18.14 sq. yards
× $ 4.95 per yard
9070
16326
7256
$89.78 (the $89.00 bargain!)

METRIC SYSTEM
PIECE OF CARPETING

4.25 meters by 3.30 meters

4.25
× 3.30
12750
1275
14.025 sq. meters
× $5 per sq. meter
$70.125 (the $70.00 bargain!)

our foot as a 12-inch measure. For a yard we stretched the material to be measured from the tip of the nose to the tip of an outstretched arm. When we wanted to measure a certain distance, we estimated a stride or long step to be three feet and paced it off for a guesstimated distance.

Under the metric system we use the same methods of measuring, but now we call a pace a meter's length. A foot's length would be figured as one-third of a meter, or 33 centimeters. And there is still one most valuable ruler we have not mentioned

—the hand. Since each individual's hand is a different size, our hand becomes our personal ruler. To make your own, do the following:

1. Place your hand palm down, with fingers stretched as wide as possible, on a clean sheet of paper.

2. Draw around the outline of your hand. This is the outline of your personal ruler (see Figure 37).

3. With a ruler, draw a line from the outside edge of the tip of the little finger to the outside edge of the thumb. Measure this line and write over it the number of centimeters long it is.

4. Draw a straight line from the outside edge of the tip of the little finger to the outside edge of the tip of the forefinger. Measure this line and write in the measurement.

5. With a ruler, draw a line from one outside edge to the other outside edge of the hand just below the base of the fingers. Measure and write in that measurement.

This sketch is your personal metric hand measure. You will want to keep it for ready reference.

Now try the following exercises:

1. Measure the length and width of your desk with your hand. You may have to use a combination of hand measurements to come out even from edge to edge. Once you have the measurements, measure the same distances with a ruler. How close did your hand measurement come to the ruler measurement?

2. Measure the height of your desk at the highest point from the floor, first with your hand and then with your ruler.

3. Measure a book by hand and then by ruler.

4. Measure the length of your shoe with your hand and then with a ruler.

For smaller measurements, measure the width of your forefinger and write the number of mms near that finger in the diagram. Do the same with the middle, ring, and little fingers. Now add all the widths of the fingers together. When you have

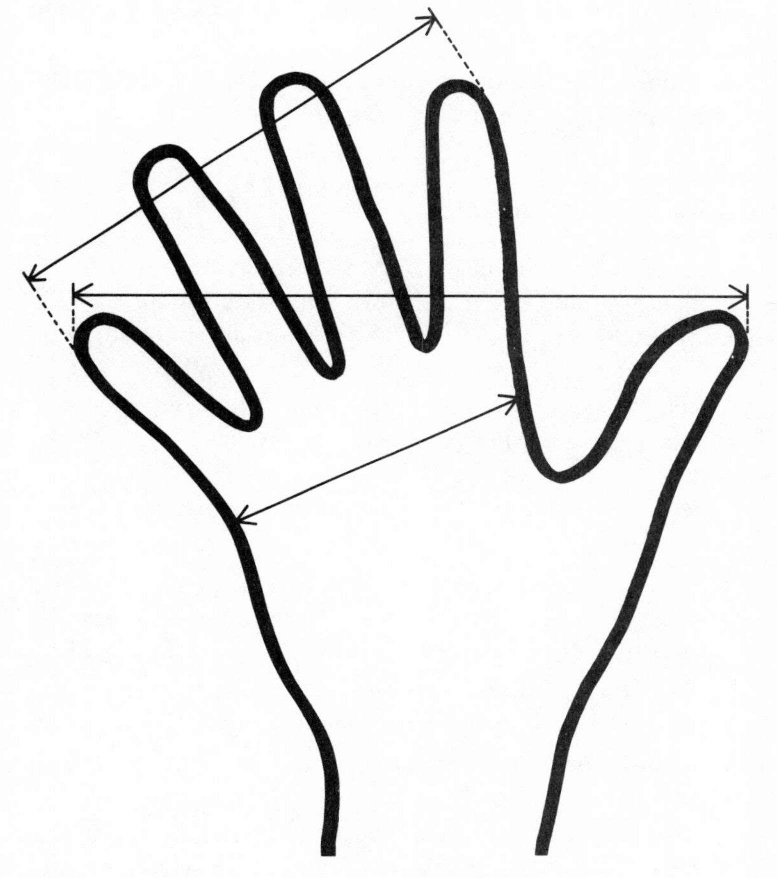

Fig. 37

small areas to measure, you can use one, two, three, or four fingers along with any other measurements you have made with your hand ruler. (It will be fun when you begin measuring with your fingers to write the measurement on each fingernail until you know them by heart.)

Measure, and measure, and measure until it becomes as easy to do as writing your name.

Rule-of-Thumb Conversions

Rule-of-thumb conversions are the quick methods of converting a measurement or weight or temperature from the U.S. Customary System to metrics. The answers are not accurate to the last decimal; they are what you might call the "about" answers or "close, but not quite." However, if someone asks you about how many inches 25 cm is, he is expecting an "about" answer.

There are a couple of rules to remember in conversions:

1. When converting from a larger to a smaller unit, expect a larger number. If you break up a large chocolate bar into smaller units, you will have more pieces than you had before (but not more chocolate).
2. And, in reverse, when converting from a smaller to a larger unit, expect a smaller number.

Listed below are the units you would most often be converting by rule-of-thumb method. As you see measurements, weights, and mile signs, practice converting them from one system to another. When a package carries both measurements, read one, convert it, and check it against the other for accuracy. Make a game of it. You will soon be a metricmagician.

Quick-Change Metrics

In each of the rule-of-thumb conversions that follow, there is a reminder of which unit is larger and which smaller. Remember that the answers are the "about" type; they are not exact to the last decimal.

Inches to Centimeters, Centimeters to Inches

Inches are larger than centimeters, so expect a larger number in centimeters. To convert inches to centimeters, multiply the number of inches by 2 and add one-half the original number. Thus 10 inches times 2 plus 5 (half the original 10) equals 25 centimeters. Or you can multiply the number of inches by 2½ or 2.5, whichever is faster and easier.

To convert centimeters into inches, divide the cm number by 2 and subtract one-tenth of the original number. Or you can divide the cm number by 2.5. Thus 30 centimeters divided by 2 is 15 less 3 (one-tenth of the original 30) equals 12 inches approximately (30 divided by 2.5 equals 12).

Miles to Kilometers, Kilometers to Miles

Miles are longer than kilometers. Expect a larger number of kilometers.

To convert miles to kilometers, multiply the number of miles by 1.6. Thus, 100 miles equals 160 kilometers.

To convert kilometers to miles, multiply the km number by 0.6. Thus, 100 km is equal to 60 miles.

Pounds to Kilos, Kilos to Pounds

A pound is smaller than a kilo, so expect a smaller number of kilos. To convert pounds to kilos divide the number of pounds by 2 and subtract one-tenth of the remainder. Thus:

10 pounds ÷ 2 = 5 − .5 (one-tenth of 5) = 4.5 kilos approximately

To convert kilos into pounds, multiply the number of kilos by 2 and add one-tenth of the product to the answer. Thus:

20 kilos × 2 = 40 + 4 (one-tenth of 40) = 44 pounds

Since a kilo is approximately 2.2 pounds, multiply the number of kilos by 2.2. The answer will come out the same as by the first method.

Ounces to Grams, Grams to Ounces

Since ounces are larger than grams, expect a larger number of grams. To convert ounces to grams, multiply the number of ounces by 30 and subtract one-tenth of the product. Thus:

100 ounces × 30 = 3000 − 300 (one tenth of 3000) = 2700 grams

(The exact number is 2835, a difference of less than five ounces.)

To convert grams into ounces, divide the number of grams by 30 and add one-tenth of the quotient. Thus:

1000 grams ÷ 30 = 33 + 3.3 = 36.3 ounces approximately

(The exact answer is 35.273, close enough for a guesstimate.)

Here are the equivalents of some of the most commonly used measurement units:

LENGTH

U.S. Customary Unit	Metric Equivalent
inch	2.54 centimeters
foot	0.3048 meter
yard	0.9144 meter
rod	5.0292 meters
mile	1.609 kilometers

VOLUME
(*Liquid Measure*)

U.S. Customary Unit	Metric Equivalent
fluid ounce	29.573 milliliters
pint	0.473 liter
quart	0.946 liter
gallon	3.785 liters

VOLUME
(*Dry Measure*)

U.S. Customary Unit	Metric Equivalent
pint	0.551 liter
quart	1.101 liters
peck	8.810 liters
bushel	35.238 liters

WEIGHT
(*Avoirdupois*)

U.S. Customary Unit	Metric Equivalent
ounce	28.350 grams
pound	453.59237 grams
ton (short: 2,000 pounds)	0.907 metric ton (1,000 kilograms)
ton (long: 2,240 pounds)	1.106 metric tons

Fahrenheit to Celsius, Celsius to Fahrenheit

A Fahrenheit reading shows a higher number than a Celsius reading, so expect a lower number with Celsius.

To convert a Fahrenheit reading to Celsius, take half the Fahrenheit reading and subtract 15. Thus:

80°F − 40 − 15 = 23°C approximately
or
32°F − 16 − 15 = 1°C approximately

(Actually, 32°F. is freezing and the exact equivalent in Celsius is 0°C. However, our result is close enough for rapid calculation.)

To convert Celsius to Fahrenheit, add 15 to the Celsius reading and then double the total. Thus:

$$5°C + 15 = 20 \times 2 = 40°F$$

When you listen to weather reports which give the temperature in both Fahrenheit and Celsius, make your own calculations and see how close you come to the actual reading.

The formula for accurate conversions is more complicated. To convert degrees F to degrees C, subtract 32 and multiply by $\frac{5}{9}$ or .555. Thus:

$$212°F - 32 = 180 \times .555 = 99.9°C \text{ (accurate to .1°)}$$

To convert from degrees C to degrees F, multiply the temperature by $\frac{9}{5}$ or 1.8 and add 32. Thus:

$$100°C \times 1.8 = 180 + 32 = 212°F$$

IMPORTANT TEMPERATURE EQUIVALENTS

Fahrenheit		Celsius (*Centigrade*)
212°	boiling water	100°
98.6°	body temperature	37°
32°	freezing	0°

METRIC PRACTICE FUN

Learning the terms which are used to measure quantities in the Metric System—meter for length, gram for weight and mass, liter for volume, and degree Celsius for temperature—is the first step in studying the Metric System. It is equally important to learn the prefixes of measurement: deci-, one tenth (0.1); centi-, one hundredth (0.01); milli-, one thousandth (0.001); and micro-, one millionth (0.000001), all of which make quantities smaller. Those prefixes which make quantities larger are: deca-, ten times (10); hecto-, one hundred times (10^2); kilo-, one thousand times (10^3); and mega-, one million times (10^6).

The next step is to learn to read and write the metric symbols. Here are tables for quick and ready reference of measures and prefixes:

Physical Quantities	Measurement	Symbol
weight and mass	gram	g
volume	liter	l
length	meter	m
temperature	Celsius	°C

Prefix	Make Smaller	Make Larger	Symbol
deci-	one tenth, 0.1		d
centi-	one hundredth, 0.01		c
milli-	one thousandth, 0.001		m
micro-	one millionth, 0.000001		μ
deca-		× ten	da
hecto-		× one hundred	h
kilo-		× one thousand	k
mega-		× one million	M

Writing metric measurements consists of combining the measurement symbol with the prefix symbol. Thus km indicates a kilometer (a thousand meters) and dg signifies a tenth of a gram.

The learning of the symbols of both measurements and prefixes can be done in game form. Having fun while one learns enhances the process!

Metric Symbol Team Game

Divide the group into teams. The teacher takes the #1 players in turn, asking each a specific question. Then the #2 players are taken in turn. Team scores are kept on the board for each correct answer. In the event of an incorrect answer, the question is asked of the next player—and the next, if necessary, until the correct answer is given. The tempo of the game depends on the individual class and where it is in the process of learning. The tempo will be slower for beginners than for more advanced players. The purpose at first is to learn the symbols and terms; later it is to keep players alert and sharp.

Examples of the kinds of problems to be presented in this type of game are:

1. Name the symbol for the given term, as g for gram.
2. Name the term for the given symbol, as gram for g.
3. Name the quantity for the given term (deci- is one tenth).
4. Name the term for the given quantity (one tenth is deci-).
5. What is meant by kl and what is the measurement amount? (kiloliter, 1000 liters)
6. Name the prefix and symbol for a deciliter and state its measurement amount.
7. Give the prefix and symbol for a thousandth of a gram.
8. Name an instrument which measures fine things (micrometer).
9. Name an instrument which magnifies (microscope).
10. What is a millepede? (often called a thousand-legger)
11. How is the word megadeath used? (signifies the number of hypothetical deaths following a nuclear explosion)
12. Which M amplifies? (megaphone)
13. Add a word to M which signifies that a microscope is not needed (megascopic—visible to the naked eye).

14. What unit symbol precedes the word "hertz"? (M)
15. What is the abbreviation of the above? (MH_z)
16. What is a micron? (a millionth of a meter or a thousandth of a millimeter)
17. What is a megaton? (a unit of measure of the power of a thermonuclear weapon, signifying the explosive power of a million tons of TNT)
18. Name insects which have metric prefixes as part of their names (centipede, millepede).

Many of these questions are really multiple questions in that they may be repeated using each of the other prefixes or symbols not specifically named. This is true of questions 1 through 7. Some of the questions, admittedly, are not truly metrical questions but were slipped in just for the fun of it.

Speedy Metric Units Game

Play this as a group game. The teacher begins by naming a term of measurement. The first player must name another, the next player another, and so on. When the fourth term is named, that player has the option of repeating or reversing the order. For example, the game might go like this:

Teacher: Liter
Player 1: Meter
Player 2: Celsius
Player 3: Gram, reverse!
Player 4: (Reversing the order) Gram
Player 5: Celsius
Player 6: Meter
Player 7: Liter, same order!
Player 8: (Back to player 4) Gram

Players will not only need to know the terms of measurement, but they must keep track of the order in which they were given. Players missing their cues are penalized a point. After two misses they are eliminated from the game. However, the disqualified players will help to catch the other players when they miss. Speeding up the play will eliminate players quickly and determine the champ of the day.

Variation

Follow the procedure of the last game and have each player name not only the units of measurement but its symbol as well. The play would then go in this fashion: Liter, l; meter, m; gram, g; Celsius, degree capital C.

Speedy Prefixes

Play as the previous games and use the prefixes in their graduated order. Since there are two sequences, one which makes smaller and one which makes larger, there will be two more possible changes which can be called. As a player names the last measure in one sequence, he can call for a repeat of the same, a reversal, a go-ahead, or a reverse order of the next sequence.

As this game picks up speed, a champion should emerge in a relatively short time.

Variation

After naming the prefix, a player must name its quantity and its symbol, as: deci-, one tenth, d. As before, the player naming the last in a sequence can call the order of the next play.

Since the Metric System's here to stay,
We might as well learn it while we play.

6

Words, Words, Words

Sight and hearing play vital roles in learning to read, spell, and speak correctly. One must be able to hear differences and see differences in order to use one's language fluently and well. Certainly, to learn to spell correctly is more difficult when one does not learn correct pronunciation. If one consistently uses "ast" for "ask" or "pitcher" for "picture" and is not trained to hear the differences or is not corrected consistently, that person will probably misspell the words as he mispronounces them. Incorrect spelling in such instances is a case not so much of poor memorization as it is one of poor perception. The word is spelled as the speller hears his mispronunciation of it.

Word games, as fun approaches to practice with words both spoken and written, are good ways in which to help to establish sound language skills. Not only does practice help to make perfect, but it instills in the players an interest in and a respect for words that will continue as a lifetime concern and fascination.

HOMONYMS, HOMOPHONES, HOMOGRAPHS

Games using homophones, the sound-alike homonyms, stimulate perceptual acuity of both ears and eyes, since these types of words, while sounding alike, are not spelled alike nor do they have the same meanings. Homographs, the look-alikes, while spelled alike, have different meanings, derivations, and often different pronunciations. One must therefore learn to perceive which word is intended in a sentence—and from this intention determine its pronunciation. For example, "He stood in the bow" could refer to the bow of a ship, the word being pronounced to rhyme with "how." However, "He made a neat bow" is confusing and unclear as to meaning. Did he bend at the waist in a neat bow (pronounced "bough") or did he make a neat bow (pronounced "beau") of ribbon? By combining the two sentences and adding a few words, one might clear up the mystery. (But one could not read the following sentence aloud without first having perused it silently to know what meaning was intended.) "He made a neat bow as he presented the neat bow he had made."

It is understood that words are often pronounced differently from one region to another; consequently, what are homophones in one area may not be homophones in another. For example, in the midwest, "pour" and "pore" are considered homophones, but not "pour" and "poor," which were paired by an author from another area. Similarly, rhyming words will differ from one area to another. A teacher from Ohio asked her class to give words which sounded like p-e-n. One child gave the word h-i-n. The teacher corrected the child and said that was a nice word to go with p-i-n, but she wanted a word that went with p-e-n. Finally the child in exasperation said: "Teacher, don't you know what a lady chicken is?" In the child's culture, hen was pronounced as "hin" and therefore hin and pen went together, whereas pin and hen did not.

Differences such as these make our language interesting to study and to play with. A student should learn both pronunciations and accept the fact that if she goes to another region she will have difficulty in making herself understood unless she learns the accepted pronunciation of that area. When it comes to the question of which pronunciation is correct, the dictionary should be the deciding factor. After all, dictionaries don't talk back or listen to arguments; they simply state the facts.

It is easy to see why homonyms, homographs, and homophones are called the confusables. They can also be sources of irritation and frustration relative to the vagaries of the English language. However, through games with words and the use of these confusing types of words in fun and jest, the confusables become the amusables. The lessons are learned, and the frustration turns to enjoyment in exercises of challenges of deliberate confusion.

HOMOPHONE GAMES

Homophones, the sound-alikes,
Are funny, as you'll see.
There's so and sew and even sow,
All different as can be.

What makes it hard—yet makes it fun—
Is to solve the mystery
Of which is witch, and who's is whose,
To be or not to bee.

Alphabetical Homophones

TYPE OF GAME: *Word Game*
GRADE: *Fourth and Up*

In the team game, the teacher prepares a set of alphabet cards large enough to be seen across the room. The cards are shuffled until they are out of alphabetical order. The first card is then shown to the first player of the first team, who must name a set of homophones beginning with the letter shown and define the meaning of each word. If the player can do this successfully, his team wins a point for each word correctly named and defined. If in the homophone group named by the first player there are other words he has not named, and the next player can continue with that group, he may do so. If he cannot, he is not penalized, and he is shown another letter with which to work.

If a player cannot comply, the play moves to the next player, and to the next, if necessary, until a player can comply. Where players are not too familiar with homophones, a reference list supplied to each player can be used (just as a dictionary is permitted in some word games). Such a list supplies only half the answer; the player must also define the words he chooses. This kind of game will not only familiarize the players with many homonyms, but make using them fun as well.

Consult the homophone reference list given in the following pages and make a list suitable for this game. Use unfamiliar words as well as familiar ones, since that is the way the learning process is stimulated.

Homophones and Meanings

TYPE OF GAME: *Team Dictionary Hunt (Written)*
GRADE: *Third–Grade Readers and Older*

The teacher writes a set of homophones on the board (see the homophone reference list). Players then search out meanings and forms of speech for each word they do not already know. When they complete their lists they raise their hands. The players with the first correct lists (the teacher checks the lists of those whose hands were up soonest) win points for their teams. The correct lists are read and discussed briefly. Play continues with a new set of homophones until time runs out. The team with the most points wins. By keeping a running score from day to day, players can watch team standings change —adding to the fun and excitement. (While this game and those to follow can be played as individual games, team games help to develop team spirit and take the pressure off individuals.)

Homophonic Sentences

TYPE OF GAME: *Team Word Game (Oral)*
GRADE: *Third and Up*

Once players become acquainted with homophone groups, this game may be played as an oral mystery sentence game. Any player may start by volunteering a sentence. His team wins a point for his sentence. The player who solves the mystery correctly wins a point for his team and gives the next mystery sentence to solve. Homophones are indicated in mystery sentences by the word "blank." Here are some examples:

The blank (bear) stripped the berry bush blank (bare).

Are you blank (two) going blank (to) the game, blank (too)?

Blank (for) this game you will need blank (four) players before someone can call out "blank" (fore).

The older the group and the more experienced the students become in playing this game, the more difficult the mystery sentences will become. Hopefully, players will seek out books on homonyms (see Bibliography) and make up mystery sentences using more unfamiliar combinations that are really amusable confusables. Try this one: The blank was poor because the blank did not come. (attendance, attendants)

Scoring note: If a team member gives a mystery sentence which players from other teams cannot solve, credit the team giving the sentence an extra point.

Homophones (Sound-Alikes) Reference List

(If some combinations seem questionable, remember that pronunciations differ in various areas.)

A

Abel
able

accept
except

acts
axe

ad
add

addition
edition

adieu
ado

aerie
airy

affect
effect

ah'd
odd

aid
aide

ale
ail

air
heir

'ere
err

aisle
I'll
isle

all
awl

all ready
already

all ways
always

allowed
aloud

alter
altar

ant
aunt

ante
anti
auntie

aural
oral

apprise
apprize

arc
ark

arrant
errant

aureole
oriole

away
aweigh

aye
eye
I

are
our

ascent
assent

ate
eight

attendants
attendance

aught
ought

axil
axle

B

be
Bea
bee

baa
bah

bad
bade

bald
balled
bawled

balm
bomb

band
banned

banns
bans

bard
barred

bare
bear

base
bass

based
baste

baize
bays

bark
barque

bask
Basque

beach
beech

beet
beat

beau
bow

been
bin

beer
bier

bell
belle

berry
bury

berth
birth

bird
burred

better
bettor

beetle
betel

buy
bye
by

bight
bite

billed
build

blessed
blest

blew
blue

bloc
block

blond
blonde

boar
bore

board
bored

boarder
border

bold
bowled
bolled

bole
boll
bowl

bolder
boulder

born
borne

borough
burro
burrow

bough
bow

braid
brayed

braise
brays
braze

breach
breech

bread
bred

brewed
brood

brews
bruise

bridal
bridle

broach
brooch

brood
brewed

brows
browse

bus
buss

bust
bussed

but
butt

C

CCC's
seas
sees
seize

cache
cash

caddie
caddy

Cain
cane

calendar
calender

cannon
canon

can't
cant

canter
cantor

canvas
canvass

capital
capitol

carat
carrot

cast
caste

caster
castor

cause
caws

cede
seed

ceiling
sealing

cell
sell

cellar
seller

cense
cents
sense

censer
censor

chanty
shanty

chased
chaste

cheap
cheep

check
Czech

chews
choose

chic
sheik

Chile
chili
chilly

choir
quire

chorale
corral

choral
coral

chord
cord
cored

chute
shoot

cite
sight
site

clamber
clamor

clause
claws

click
clique

climb
clime

close
clothes

coal
cole
kohl

coat
cote

coax
Cokes

cocky
khaki

coddling
codling

colonel
kernel

complement
compliment

concent
consent

coop
coupe

core
corps

council
counsel

coward
cowered

crape
crepe

creak
creek
crick

crews
cruise

cruel
crewel

currant
current

cygnet
signet

cymbal
symbol

D

dam
damn

days
daze

dear
deer

dense
dents

descent
dissent

desert
dessert

dew
do
due

die
dye

dire
dyer

discreet
discrete

do (syllable)
doe
dough

does (deer)
doze

done
dun

draft
draught

dual
duel

ducked
duct

E

ease
EEE's

earn
urn

eaves
Eve's
eves

eerie
Erie

elicit
illicit

ensure
insure

entrance
entrants

ewe
yew
U
you

ewes
yews
use

exercise
exorcize

F

faint
feint

fair
fare

fairy
ferry

false
faults

fate
fete

faun
fawn

faze
phase

feat
feet

find
fined

finish
Finnish

fir
fur

fisher
fissure

flair
flare

flea
flee

flew
flu
flue

Flo
floe
flow

flocks
phlox

flour
flower

foaled
fold

for
fore
four

forward
foreword

fort
forte

forth
fourth

foul
fowl

franc
frank
Frank

frays
phrase

frees
freeze
frieze

friar
fryer

G

gage
gauge

gait
gate

gamble
gambol

gene
Jean

gib
jib
jibe

gild
guild

gill
Jill

gilt
guilt

gin
ginn

gnu
knew
new

golf
gulf

gored
gourd

grade
grayed

grays
graze

grate
great

Greece
grease

grill
grille

grisly
grizzly

groan
grown

grocer
grosser

guessed
guest

guide
guyed

guise
guys

gym
Jim

H

hail
hale

hair
hare

hall
haul

halve
have

handmade
handmaid

handsome
hansom

hangar
hanger

hart
heart

hay
hey

hays
haze

heal
heel
he'll

hear
here

heard
herd

he'd
heed

hew
hue
Hugh

hi
hie
high

hide
hied

higher
hire

him
hymn

hissed
hist

hoar
whore

hoard
horde

ho
hoe

hoarse
horse

hoes
hose

hole
whole

holey
holy
wholly

hostel
hostile

hour
our

humerus
humorous

I

idle
idol
idyll

in
inn

incidents
incidence

incite
insight

indict
indite

intense
intents

intercession
intersession

islet
eyelet

its
it's

J

jam
jamb

jinks
jinx

K

key
quay

knave
nave

knead
kneed
need

knell
Nell

knew
new

knight
night

knit
nit

knock
nock

knot
not

know
no

knows
noes
nose

L

lacks
lax

lade
laid

lain
lane

Lew
lieu
Lou

Lapps
laps
lapse

ladder
latter

lorry
Laurie

lay
lei

lays
laze

lea
lee

leach
leech

lead
led

leaf
Leif
lief

leak
leek

lean
lien

leased
least

lends
lens

lessen
lesson

licker
liquor

liar
lyre

lie
lye

lightening
lightning

links
lynx

lo
low

load
lode
lowed

loan
lone

locks
lox

loot
lute

lumbar
lumber

M

made
maid

mail
male

main
Maine
mane

maize
May's

mall
maul

mandrel
mandrill

manner
manor

mantel
mantle

marks
Marx

marry
Mary
merry

marten
martin
Martin

marshall
martial

mask
masque

massed
mast

me
mi

mead
meed

mean
mien

meat
meet
mete

meatier
meteor

medal
meddle
mettle

meddler
medlar

mewl
mule

mews
muse

might
mite

missal
missile

missed
mist

misses
missus (Mrs.)

moan
mown

moat
mote

mode
mowed

mood
mooed

moose
mousse

morn
mourn

morning
mourning

muscle
mussel

mussed
must

N

naval
navel

nay
nee
neigh

Nice
niece

none
nun

O

O
oh
owe

oar
or
ore
o'er

odder
otter

ode
oh'd
owed

offal
awful

one
won

overdo
overdue

overseas
oversees

ox-eyed
oxide

P

PPP's
peas

paced
paste

packed
pact

pail
pale

pain
pane

pair
pare
pear

palate
palette
pallet

pall
Paul
pawl

parish
perish

passed
past

patience
patients

pause
paws

peace
piece

peak
peek
pique

peal
peel

paean
peen

pearl
purl

pedal
peddle

peer
pier

pend
penned

pendant
pendent

pencil
pensile

pervade
purveyed

petit
petty

pi
pie

pidgin
pigeon

Pilate
pilot

plane
plain

plaintiff
plaintive

plait
plate

plaiter
plater

pleas
please

plum
plumb

pocks
pox

pole
poll

pommel
pummel

populace
populous

pore
pour

poser
poseur

praise
prays
preys

pray
prey

prayed
preyed

precedent
president

presence
presents

pride
pried

pries
prize

prince
prints

principal
principle

profit
prophet

pros
prose

psalter
salter

Q

QQQ's
cues
queues

quarts
quartz

quean
queen

querist
queerest

R

rabbet
rabbit

rack
wrack

racket
racquet

rain
reign
rein

raid
rayed

raise
rays
raze

raiser
razor

rancor
ranker

rap
wrap

rapped
wrapped

rapper
wrapper

ray
re

read
reed

read
red

real
reel

recover
re-cover

reck
wreck

recede
reseed

residence
residents

rest
wrest

retch
wretch

review
revue

rhyme
rime

rigger
rigor

right
rite
wright
write

ring
wring

rise
ryes

road
rode
rowed

roam
Rome

roe
row

roes
rows
rose
Rose

role
roll

rood
rude
rued

roomer
rumor

root
route

rout
route

rouse
rows

rues
ruse

rung
wrung

rye
wry

S

sac
sack
sacque

sain
sane
seine

sail
sale

sailer
sailor

saver
savor

scene
seen

scent
sent
cent

scull
skull

seam
seem

sear
seer
sere

seas
sees
seize

serf
surf

serge
surge

serial
cereal

sew
so
sow

sewed
sowed

sows
sews

sewer
sower

shear
sheer

shoe
shoo

shone
shown

sic
sick

side
sighed

sighs
size

sign
sine

slay
sleigh
sley

sleight
slight

sloe
slow

soar
sore

soared
sword

sol
sole
soul

sold
soled

some
sum

son
sun

staid
stayed

stair
stare

stake
steak

stationary
stationery

steal
steel

steer
stere

step
steppe

stile
style

straight
strait

straightened
straitened

succor
sucker

suede
swayed

sewer
suer

suite
sweet

sundae
Sunday

T

T-(shaped)
tea
tee
ti

tacked
tact

tacks
tax

tail
tale

tare
tear

taught
taut

team
teem

tear
tier

tease
tees

tense
tents

their
there
they're

theirs
there's

threw
through

throe
throw

throne
thrown

tic
tick

tide
tied

tier (of knots)
tire

to
too
two

toad
toed
towed

toe
tow

told
tolled

ton
tun

tool
tulle

tracked
tract

tri
try

troop
troupe

trussed
trust

tucks
tux

'twill
twill

U

U-(shaped)
ewe

udder
utter

unreal
unreel

urns
earns

V

vain
vane
vein

vail
vale
veil

vial
vile

W

WACS
wax

wade
weighed

wader
waiter

wail
wale
whale

wain
wane
Wayne

waist
waste

wait
weight

waive
wave

wall
waul

ward
warred

ware
wear

waddle
wattle

way
weigh

we
wee

weak
week

weal
we'll
wheel

weave
we've

we'd
weed

weir
we're

weld
welled

who's
whose

wise
YYY's

wood
would

Y

yoke
yolk

yore
you're

you'll
yule

HOMOGRAPH GAMES

The homographs are look-alikes
And often are confusing;
To play with words like these, you'll find,
Is truly quite amusing.

When homographs are found alone
It's difficult to know
If it's the mow which rhymes with cow,
Or the mow which sounds like tow.

The more you play with words like these,
The easier it will be
To know which homophone is meant;
There will be less mystery.

Homographs (Look-Alikes) Reference List

Some homographs differ in pronunciation, as: sow (like (sew) and sow (like how). Others differ more accentually than in sound. In this list, the first type of difference is indicated by rhyming words and the second type by accent marks. Where there is also a difference in sound, rhyming words are added for clarity. For both types, parts of speech are indicated.

A

a'ged (adj.)	old people
aged (vi.)	to grow old
Au'gust (n.)	the month
au gust' (adj.)	dignified, inspiring reverence

B

ba'ses (n.)	foundations
ba'ses (n.)	(rhymes with hey, seize) plural of basis

bass (n.)	(rhymes with face) low male voice, bass viol
bass (n.)	(rhymes with pass) a tree; a fish
blessed (vt.)	(blest) to be endowed with a talent, be blessed by someone
bless'ed (adj.)	bringing comfort or joy
bow (n.)	(rhymes with toe) a knot
bow (v.)	(rhymes with now) to bend; front part of a boat
bowed (adj.)	(rhymes with toad) his legs were bowed
bowed (v.)	(rhymes with cloud) past tense of bow
bo'wer (n.)	(rhymes with blower) he is a good violin bower
bow'er (n.)	(rhymes with flower) arbor of flowers; the heaviest anchor of a ship
buf'fet (n.)	a blow of the hand or fist
buf fet' (n.)	(rhymes with hurray) a piece of furniture, a meal where people serve themselves

C

close (adj.)	(rhymes with dose) near, stuffy, stingy
close (vt.)	(rhymes with doze) shut, bring to a finish, close school for vacation
com'mune (n.)	a small community
com mune' (v.)	come together
com'pact (n.)	a cosmetic case; an agreement
com pact' (adj.)	concentrated in a small area
con duct' (vi.)	lead, act as a conductor
con'duct (n.)	behavior
con'serve (n.)	a thick preserve or jam
con serve' (vt.)	to preserve and save
con'sole (n.)	keyboard of an instrument (organ, piano)
con sole' (vt.)	to give comfort
con'sort (n.)	partner; a queen's husband (if not a king) is known as a prince consort
con sort' (v.)	associate with

con tent' (adj.)	to be happily satisfied
con'tent (n.)	substance inside a bottle or bag or box
con'test (n.)	a struggle for superiority, a race
con test' (vt.)	to challenge a decision or a document's validity
con'tract (n.)	an agreement
con tract' (vi., vt.)	to establish an agreement, to catch a cold, to draw in or together (muscles contract)

D

de sert' (vi.)	(like alert) to abandon; deserving a reward or punishment (he received his just desert)
des'ert (n.)	(like dez-ert) a dry place
di'gest (n.)	shortened version of an article or book
di gest' (v.)	to change food into form easily assimilated; to think over an idea
do (vt.)	(rhymes with to) to perform, to bring about; (n.) a gathering, big party (colloquialism)
do (n.)	(rhymes with sew) syllable in music notation
does (vt.)	(rhymes with fuzz) third person singular of verb to do
does (n.)	(rhymes with toes) plural of female deer (doe)
dove (vt.)	(rhymes with stove) past tense of verb to dive
dove (n.)	(rhymes with shove) a bird

E

en'trance (n.)	(rhymes with fence) a door, opening
en trance' (vt.)	(rhymes with pants) to put into a trance, to delight
ex cuse (n.)	(rhymes with obtuse) a written or verbal explanation for an absence
ex cuse (vt.)	(rhymes with fuse) to apologize for, ask forgiveness for

F

forte (n.)	(rhymes with short) something which one does well
forte (adj.)	(rhymes with forty) musical term signifying loud

G

gill (n.)	(like gil) breathing organ of a fish or other underwater animals
gill (n.)	(sounds like Jill) a fourth of a pint

H

house (n.)	(rhymes with louse) a home, shelter, domicile
house (vt.)	(rhymes with rouse) to give shelter to

I

in'cense (n.)	perfumed material for burning
in cense' (vt.)	to anger, make indignant
in'tern (n.)	advanced student in training
in tern' (vt.)	to confine in a camp; to act as an intern
in'ti mate (vt.)	(rhymes with in a state) to suggest; to imply indirectly
in'ti mate (n.)	(rhymes with in a fit) a close friend; (adj.) close
in'valid (n.)	sick person, chronically ill; (adj.) infirm, sickly
in val'id (adj.)	not in force; without truth or proof

L

learned (vt.)	past tense of to learn
learn'ed (adj.)	having much learning from study usually in a special field
lead (n.)	(rhymes with said) soft gray metal
lead (vt.)	(rhymes with bead) to guide
lead (vt.)	(rhymes with bread) to apply lead when making leaded stained glass windows
live (vi.)	(rhymes with sieve) to be alive, to maintain one's self
live (adj.)	(rhymes with jive) showing life and energy

M

min'ute (n.)	(rhymes with win it) part of an hour; short written record of a meeting

mi nute′ (adj.)	(rhymes with my flute) small, tiny, of little importance
mo′bile (adj.)	(rhymes with noble) movable, capable of being moved
mo′bile (n.)	(rhymes with no feel) an art form that depicts movement or has parts that move freely with air currents
mouth (n.)	(rhymes with south) opening through which a person or animal takes food; entrance to a cave; place where a stream enters a larger body of water
mouth (v.)	(th pronounced hard) to form words soundlessly with the lips
mow (n.)	(rhymes with how) storage place
mow (vt., vi.)	(rhymes with dough) to cut grass or hay
mow (n., vi.)	(rhymes with how) a grimace; to make a face with protruding lips
multiply (vt.)	(rhymes with have some pie) to increase in number; to find the product in multiplication
multiply (adj.)	(rhymes with how to plea) in many or multiple ways

O

ob′ject (n.)	a thing; a part of a sentence toward which the verb is directed
ob ject′ (v., vt.)	to protest, to speak against; to enter a protest or objection

P

pate (n.)	(rhymes with plate) crown of the head
pate (n.)	(rhymes with rot) paste or plastic material used in pottery
pâ′té (n.)	(rhymes with hot day) a paste-like spread of meat, a delicacy
pat′ent (n., adj.)	a protective device to protect rights for inventions
pa′tent (adj.)	(rhymes with say tent) obvious, clear, plain, a patent lie

per'mit (n.)	a certificate of authorization, a license
per mit' (vt.)	to allow, consent, authorize
Po'lish (adj.)	(rhymes with roe fish) pertaining to culture and products from Poland
pol'ish (vt.)	(rhymes with abolish) to shine or rub to a high gloss; (n.) a liquid or paste used to produce a high gloss or shine
pres'ent (n.)	a gift; the immediate time; (adj.) on hand or in attendance
pre sent' (vt.)	to introduce an individual to another; to offer something
prim'er (n.)	(rhymes with dimmer) a first book
pri'mer (n.)	(rhymes with timer) a first coat of paint; the explosive object used to set off a main charge
prog'ress (n.)	forward movement, an advancement
pro gress' (vi.)	(rhymes with duress) to go forward, improve, advance
proj'ect (n.)	a proposal, scheme, undertaking
pro ject' (vt.)	to throw, expel, to think ahead; (vi.) to stick out
pro'test (n.)	an objection
pro test' (vt.)	to object, speak strongly against

R

read (vt.)	(rhymes with seed) to read a book; to find meaning in an incident
read	(rhymes with said) pt. and pp. of verb to read; (adj.) he was a well-read man
re cord' (vt.)	to set down in writing; to make a tape or a disc
rec'ord (n.)	written evidence of an occurrence; a phonograph disc
re fuse' (vt.)	(rhymes with reuse) to decline, to say no
ref' use (n.)	(rhymes with yus) waste, garbage, discards
row (n.)	(rhymes with how) a quarrel, a disturbance
row (vt.)	(rhymes with sew) to propel a boat with oars; (n.) a line of people, etc.; a shallow furrow in which seed is planted

S

seer (n.) — (rhymes with her) an East Indian unit of weight
se'er (n.) — one who sees, a sightseer (also pronounced as "sir" when meaning one who foretells the future

sew'er (n.) — (rhymes with lower) one who sews
sew'er (n.) — (rhymes with doer) a drain carrying waste materials and soiled water; a medieval servant who seated guests and served food

show'er (n.) — (rhymes with blower) a person who shows, an exhibitor
show'er (n.) — (rhymes with flower) a rain squall; a party at which gifts are given

sing'er (n.) — (rhymes with ringer) one who sings
sin'ger (n.) — (rhymes with ginger) one who singes, scorches, or burns

slav'er (n.) — (rhymes with savor) one who deals in slaves
sla'ver (n.) — (rhymes with have her) saliva drooling from the mouth; (vt.) to drool

sow (vt.) — (rhymes with hoe) to scatter seed, to plant seed
sow (n.) — (rhymes with how) a female adult pig or bear; a sluice carrying molten metal from a blast furnace to molds where pig bars are cast

stingy (adj.) — (rhymes with ringy) characteristic of a stinging insect, a wasp or hornet
stingy (adj.) — (rhymes with dingy) characteristic of a close-fisted sort of person; miserly

sub'ject (n.) — a person, thing, or matter under discussion; an individual under control of another (a subject of the king)

sub ject' (vt.) — to control another, to put oneself under the control of another

T

tar'ry (vi.) — (rhymes with fairy) to linger, wait, to hold back
tar'ry (adj.) — (rhymes with starry) covered with tar, sticky with tar

tear (n.)	(rhymes with ear) fluid from eyes; (vi.) to shed tears
tear (vt.)	(rhymes with hair) to split, rip
trans′fer (n.)	a permission slip to make a change from one bus to another; (adj.) one who changes from one school to another (a transfer student)
trans fer′ (vt.)	to cause a person to change from one place to another
U	
use (vt.)	(rhymes with fuse) to utilize, to employ something; to exhaust one's supply; (vi.) to be accustomed to (used to doing it)
use (n.)	(rhymes with moose) to have the use of; a customary practice; to have no use for
W	
wind (vt.)	(rhymes with rind) to roll up; to twist in motion (the pitcher's wind up)
wind (n.)	(rhymes with sinned) a force of nature; (also pronounced as rind in poetic form, as "the wind of the western sea")

Alphabetical Homograph Game

TYPE OF GAME: *Word Game*
GRADE: *Fifth and Up*

For a team game, the teacher prepares a set of alphabet cards large enough to be seen across the room. Shuffling the cards out of alphabetical order, she or he shows the front card to the first player of the first team. That player must name a set or pair of homographs which begin with the letter shown. If he can do so, he scores a point for each word named. The teacher then puts the card just used at the back of the pack, exposing the next letter. The first player of the second team must name homographs beginning with that letter. If a player cannot comply, play moves to the player on the next team, and to the next, if necessary, until a player whose turn it is can comply.

Where players have just studied homographs, a reference list might be used as a dictionary is used in other word games. The player then need only pick a pair of homographs, pronounce each word correctly, and define each. Actually, unless a player knows the words, selecting them from a reference list provides only part of a correct answer. After that, the player is on his own. This kind of game makes players more familiar with homographs and helps them to use such words correctly when they encounter them in reading and spelling exercises.

Consult the homograph reference list to prepare your own list for this game—or use it as is.

WORD GAMES

Ladder Spelling

Arrange a list of vowels, double vowels, and vowel combinations like rungs in a ladder, spaced well apart. To the left of this list make a list of four to six consonants:

	A	table
	E	
T	I	cinder
C	O	
R	U	
M	OA	roaring
B	EE	beer
	OO	
	OU	
	OI	
	EA	
	EI	ceiling

For a team game, make a diagram for each team. The first player of each team comes to the board, selects any consonant, and adds to it any vowel combination and as many letters as he can to form the longest correct word. Score a point for each letter of a correctly spelled word. Each successive player may select any consonant to begin his word, but he may not play a rung (a vowel or vowel combination) already played. In other words, once a word has been written in a particular rung, that rung is out of play until every other rung has been played. Only then can the next player use the rung of his choice. But once he plays a rung, that rung is again out of play for the round.

If a player cannot make a word with the remaining rungs, he forfeits his turn. Before the game is concluded and after all players have had the same number of turns, any unfinished combinations are "up for grabs." Any player may volunteer to fill in any blank rungs; a correct word gives his team an additional score. Allow use of dictionaries throughout the game by players awaiting their turns, but each player must come to the board without delay.

For the individual game, give each player a duplicated sheet with the ladder diagram of vowels, double vowels, and combination of vowels. Then give the entire group a single consonant with which to play. The first player to complete a list correctly is the winner. Scores are added up for each player and recorded. The consonant is then changed and the game begins again on the same sheet. Permit use of dictionaries to help players and to speed up play. (The recognition of a dictionary as a useful tool and ally is important to individual progress and growth.)

Ladder Homophones and Homographs Spelling

In the same game, when a player writes in a word and realizes that she can also supply a homophone at the same time, she underlines the first word and then writes in the homophone or homophones even though the spelling will not fit the combination she is using. For example, a player writes in the word "to" and recognizes it as a homophone. She may then add "too" and "two" and receive credit for all three words. Score double for this effort.

With homographs, of course, the spelling is the same, so the player encircles the homographic word and gives the pronunciation for both. For example, the player has written the word "bow." He encircles it and gives the pronunciations for both "bow" (like how) and "bow" (like toe). Double the score for the effort.

Name a Word

TYPE OF GAME: *Word Game*
GRADE: *Kindergarten and Up*

Organize the group into teams. The leader or teacher selects a letter from the alphabet. The first player of team 1 names a word beginning with that letter. A point is scored if a player names a correct word. Play moves to the first player of the next team. Use the same letter until no one can think of another word. If a player cannot name a word on his turn, play moves to the next player until all the players have had a try for a specific letter. A word may be used only once.

Before beginning a new round, always have the first players on each team move to the ends of their team lines. In this way, each player has a turn to be first in line. Being the last player on the team to find a word is difficult enough without having to be in that position every round.

If players are old enough, permit them to consult their dictionaries providing they are ready to name a word when their turn comes and do not hold up the game. The older the players, the faster the play can be. Think Fast is the name of the game in this instance.

Variation #1

The teacher or leader prepares a set of alphabet cards large enough to be seen across the room. The cards are shuffled out of order. Now each player must name a word beginning with the letter on the card shown him. As a letter is used it is moved to the bottom of the stack. After the first round, the letters are thoroughly reshuffled before beginning the second round.

Variation #2

To make the previous game more difficult, ask each player to give a short sentence in which each word begins with the same letter. Score 2 points for each word.

Alphabet Sentences

Players write the letters of the alphabet down the left side of a sheet of paper. The object is to write a sentence of as many words as possible after each letter, with each word of the sentence beginning with that same letter of the alphabet. A sample set of sentences (if they can be called that) is given below. Remember, a short sentence that makes sense is better than a longer one that makes no sense at all!

For scoring, count each word of a sentence as 1 point.

Alphabet Sentences can be played as a team game with all members contributing ideas. As usual, when stuck consult that good old friend, the dictionary.

Alphabet Sentence List

A. Ann ate apples avidly all autumn.
B. Benji brought buttered banana bread.
C. Carl carried cannel coal carefully.
D. Don drove Dorothy down dangerous, dismal drives.
E. Esther eats expensive Easter eggs endlessly.
F. Frank filleted fresh fish frantically for fast freezing.
G. Good grapes grow gorgeous gradually.
H. How handily Harvey handles his hot hamburger!

I. I imagine Isabel is in Iceland's isolated inn.
J. Jack jogs joyously, jarring joints.
K. Katie kept kissing Kentucky kin keenly.
L. Larry loves lovely ladies.
M. Money may make men murderously mad.
N. Ned's new notebook now needs new notes.
O. Onshore onlookers offered only one oar.
P. Patricia picked pink peonies, purple pansies, patiently.
Q. Quenton quietly questioned quaking, quivering quitters, quickly.
R. Robert, ranting, raving, ran rapidly 'round Robin's room.
S. Sam sat silently, stonily still, staring stupidly.
T. The turtle traveled tardily toward the town.
U. Una usually uses uniquely unusual umbrellas.
V. Vera's various versions vary.
W. When wading, walk with wary watchfulness where weeds will wreck waders.
X. Xmas xylophones.
Y. Yawning, yelling, yowling youths yielded.
Z. Zeb's zoo zebras zipped zanily.

Variations

Players write sentences of only two or three words, playing against time.

Young children who normally play games listing words which begin with a specific letter can play this game making short sentences. The more difficult letters could be eliminated for younger players—but they may surprise you and themselves with sentences for even those hard-to-do letters.

Magic Spelling Squares

Magic spelling squares are somewhat like crossword puzzles except that every space is filled and some words can be used more than once. Using a third-order or nine-cell square, fill it with letters that spell words in each row or column. Here are some examples:

R A N	C O T	R A N	P O T	O N E
A R E	O A R	A R E	E A R	F O G
N E T	T R Y	M E W	T R Y	T W O

In the first example, only three different words appear, they appear only in rows and columns. In the second example, three words are used, but a fourth appears in one diagonal. The third example uses five words, but no word appears in a diagonal. The fourth example hits the jackpot: Five words are used that make another, different word in each diagonal. And the PAY diagonal also spells a different word backwards, for a total of eight different words! The fifth example makes a total of seven words since the diagonal running upward from left to right spells *TOE*.

This game is a mind boggler for persons of every age. Keep your own scores. Can you come up with a square that contains more than eight words? (That would require diagonals with words that spell other words backwards.) Happy hunting!

Fourth- and Fifth-Order Word Squares

When nine-cell squares no longer offer challenges, move up to the fourth-order, sixteen-cell squares. And then go for broke with the fifth-order, 25-cell squares. One of each is presented here. Warning: Word squares, like magic squares, are addictive. If you dare to try, keep your dictionary handy.

16-CELL	25-CELL
M O R E	T R E N D
O K A Y	R A R E R
R A C E	E R A S E
E Y E S	N E S T S
	D R E S S

Magic Square Number Spelling

TYPE OF GAME: *Arithmetic Spelling Game*
GRADE: *Third and Up*

The teacher prepares and duplicates game sheets for each player. The sheets consist of five or six third-order, nine-cell squares in which each cell is at least ¾″ square. In the upper left-hand corner of each square a small number is written to indicate the number of a letter of the alphabet. Players work to fill in the squares with the indicated letters. If the answers are correct, each square will be a magic word square (each row and column will spell a word). In some, one or both diagonals may also contain a word. Have the players count the number of different words in each square and write that number under the square. The players may also be asked to write each of the words in each square along one side of the square. Players must be quite perceptive to find the words in the diagonals.

A selection of magic word squares of the third-order is given below. It is up to the teacher to convert the words to numbers. After a few games, the children may be stimulated to make their own magic squares with which to challenge the rest of the group.

B A N	C U T	L O T	T O N	D O T	H U T
A R E	U S E	A R E	A R E	O R E	U S A
N E T	T E N	P E N	P E T	T E N	T E N

T A M	R A N	A R E	N U T	P E T	S A D
A R E	A R E	T A N	U S E	O A R	O R E
M E T	G E T	E N D	T E N	T R Y	Y E N

T A R	B U S	S A T	O F F
I R E	U S E	O R E	F E E
N E D	T E A	Y E A	F E E

Variation

Use fourth-order, sixteen-cell squares. Prepare game sheets as before, but for squares of sixteen cells, requiring four-letter words. Some examples are given here for quick starters. Let the players work out some themselves with which to challenge each other.

```
A R T S   G N U S   N O O N   S T U N   R O A D
R A R E   N O S E   O T T O   T I R E   O N L Y
T R E E   U S E R   O T T O   U R G E   A L O E
S E E R   S E R F   N O O N   N E E D   D Y E S

D O T E   B R A N   A B L E   A R M S   R A I N
O D O R   R A R E   B O A T   R O I L   A L S O
T O U R   A R T S   L A S T   M I N I   I S L E
E R R S   N E S T   E T T A   S L I D   N O E S

          E D G E   S N O W
          D O O R   N I L E
          G O E S   O L L A
          E R S E   W E A K
```

RHYMING WORD FUN

Rhyming word fun is a good learning technique for children who have not yet learned to read or are just learning. It can be played as a game at the dinner table, in a classroom, or to make a long car ride seem shorter. Adults and children can play it together—and it is no less a challenge to the adult than to the child. It also provides an excellent example that one does not necessarily grow sharper as one grows older. For sharpness of mind is due to usage; wisdom and knowledge are not consequences of aging but the continuation of the education process.

Using sounds that rhyme is easier when done aloud if our ears and listening attention are good. When we look for rhyming words when writing verse, the rhyming is a matter of recognizing words which sound alike, not necessarily those which look alike. Woe to the poet who tries to rhyme "enough" and "bough" without actually sounding them out.

If, as you play the rhyming game, you use some of the suggestions given in the following reference lists, read the words before you begin. In some cases, there is more than one way to pronounce the syllable used.

When playing the game as a written game, clarify the pronunciation of the syllable to be used for the players, as u-s-e as in "loose," not as in "choose."

In the reference lists four syllables are used for each vowel. The more obvious words are omitted to permit room for those which might not come readily to mind. Kudos to the player who names a word that is a homograph or a homophone and recognizes it as one! (Those words which qualify are marked with an asterisk.) If a player names one or more homographs or homophones, count the letters in each correct word for the score for that turn.

When playing as a team game, score each correct word according to the number of letters in it. As usual, permit the use of dictionaries, but stress that a player must be ready with a word when his turn comes. Or let the players know in advance which syllables will be used and let them prepare in advance for the game. After all, players for other games must get in some practice time. For unusual words, insist upon a definition.

When playing with young children, allow any word which rhymes whether or not it is an actual word. Older children must use actual words.

Word games are always proof that one does not need special equipment or a particular place in which to have fun!

VOWEL A

ant	and	ape	air
cant*	bland	cape	are
chant	wonderland	grape	bar
plant	canned	crêpe*	car
scant	gland	drape	gar
instant	grand	escape	scar
elephant	manned	shape	spar
enchant	planned	landscape	star
emigrant	tanned	jape	cigar
fragrant	contraband	nape	feldspar
implant	demand	tape	horsecar
gallivant	disband	gape	jaguar
immigrant	expand	shipshape	memoir
ignorant	overland	seascape	samovar
aunt	secondhand	chape	handlebar
commandant	understand	crape*	registrar

Other syllables in this category: all, arm, aim, ale, ate, ain, and art.

VOWEL E

et	ear	eed	eet
debt	beer*	bead	beet*
fret	gear	velocipede	bleat
alphabet	hear*	greed	meat*
bassinet	revere	cede*	pleat
brunette	reappear	freed	treat
forget	disappear	heed*	concrete
sweat	engineer	keyed	deplete
threat	commandeer	knead*	defeat
wet*	mere	read*	drumbeat
beset	peer*	skied	discreet
bayonet	smear	Swede	mincemeat
cadet	tear*	we'd*	overeat
castinet	adhere	tweed	delete
clarinet	endear	misdeed	parakeet
coverlet	cheer	seaweed	entreat

A few of the many other syllables: est, ent, ert, elt, ew, en, em, and emt.

VOWEL I

itch	ill	ind	ink
ditch	windowsill	blind	blink
hitch	uphill	grind	zinc
pitch	daffodil	lined	bobolink
rich	whippoorwill	pined	countersink
stitch	frill	signed	tiddlywink
twitch	still	twined	unlink
which*	quill	whined	think
bewitch	shrill	assigned	stink
enrich	skill	countersigned	slink
featherstitch	Louisville	intertwined	shrink
sandwich	twill	resigned	clink
fitch	trill	mankind	drink
niche	thrill	mastermind	wink
snitch	drill	womankind	hoodwink
switch	grill	humankind	pink

Some other syllables in this category: inch, ire, ime, ize, ite, ise, ice, ile, ion, and ibe.

VOWEL O

ock	ose	ood	oon
block	blows	brood	moon
clock	grows	crewed*	June
flock	flows	stewed	soon
shock	throws	rood*	loon
smock	snows	intrude	pantaloon
frock	froze	interlude	noon
stock	undertows	mood*	balloon
interlock	rose*	snood	buffoon
peacock	sews*	boohooed	maroon
shamrock	tows*	poohed	croon
unlock	banjos	food	saloon

warlock	buffaloes	cooed	goon
woodcock	bureaus	booed	boon
padlock	impose	shooed*	coon
deadlock	overflows	wooed	tune

Other syllables in this category: ore, one, ote, owl, ole, orn, and ort.

VOWEL U

uck	**ued**	**use**	**use**	**ust**
buck	brewed*	blues	abuse*	bust*
cluck	chewed	booze*	deuce	crust
chuck	clued	choose	juice	cussed
duck	feud	crews*	loose	dust
struck	glued	dues	goose	must
potluck	hewed	gnus	vamoose	trust*
woodchuck	lewd	queues*	caboose	adjust
sawbuck	prude	rues*	excuse	discussed*
thunderstruck	rude*	screws*	misuse	disgust*
stagestruck	strewed	shrews	obtuse	entrust
stuck	sued	who's*	produce*	nonplussed
tuck	viewed	woos	reduce	piecrust
luck	allude	zoos	unloose	sawdust
truck	conclude	snooze	sluice	stardust

Some other syllables in the same category: ure, ute, ule, urn, urt, une, uce, and upe. (This group has an extra column because u-s-e is pronounced in two different ways.)

Letter-Rhyming Alphabet

How many times have we sung our alphabet in its proper order and ended with:

"Now I've said my A-B-C's,
Tell me what you think of me?"

Try setting up the alphabet in the order of its rhyming letters. Begin with A and write after it the other letters of the alphabet which rhyme with it. Then take B and do the same. Continue in this manner until you have written all the letters of the alphabet in this manner. You will now have a peculiar but rhyming arrangement. Had you ever thought how many letters rhyme with others and how many have no rhyming partners?

The letters have been arranged below in the method just described. A few "ands" have been added to make the song come out right. The alphabet now has a new look and is ready for the new sound!

First say the letters in a rhythmic fashion. Then try fitting the new arrangement into the old song. With a little practice, you will soon find the correct rhythm.

A, J, K,
F,
B, C, D, E, G, P, T, V, Z,
H,
I AND Y,
L,
M,
N,
AND
O,
Q, U, W
R,
AND
S,
AND
X

Finish with:

"We've mixed up the alphabet,
Sing and see how silly you get."

Thirty Days

How many times have we repeated the rhyme,

"Thirty days hath September,
April, June, and November . . ."?

Have you ever tried the knuckle count to determine the months which have 31 days and those which have 30 or less? Make a fist of one hand and hold it up in front of you. With the forefinger of your other hand, begin counting the knuckles and the spaces between them in this manner:

First knuckle — January
First space — February
Second knuckle — March
Second space — April
Third knuckle — May
Third space — June
Fourth knuckle — July
And begin again with the first knuckle:
First knuckle — August
First space — September
Second knuckle — October
Second space — November
Third knuckle — December

All the knuckles are 31-day months. The spaces represent the 30-day months and February, which has 28 days, except in leap years when it has 29 days.

7

Tell Me, Please

"Twinkle, twinkle, little star,
How I wonder what you are . . ."

It is man's nature to wonder, to ask questions, to search for answers. It is most likely that there are some questions to which we will never know the answers. No young person today need worry that before she or he grows up there will be nothing left to discover, nothing new to invent, no mysteries left to solve, no contributions for young would-be scientists to pass on to posterity. The trained and inquiring mind that continuously seeks answers to questions often asked yet still unsolved need never worry that all the secrets of the universe will be uncovered and the great division between the known and unknown eliminated.

But before the answers must come the questions, those which only the keen observer can perceive and pose. How? Why? Where? When? What? These are probably the most important words of any language. They are the questions asked by the mind which does not accept the existence of something simply because it is there. The inquiring mind, while it may acknowledge the existence, will still ask: Why is it here? Where did it come from? Is this its natural or evolved state? How did it get here?

The perceptive mind is not just born; it is stimulated and developed through study, creative play, and perceptual activities. It is sometimes led, sometimes gently pushed into situations which demand: Look at me. What do you see? What do you hear? What does this remind you of? Take this idea, play with it, let your imagination run wild. Don't just stand there! *Think!*

The games and activities in this chapter are designed to stimulate the imagination and to make the sight keener. To see a common object in a way you never saw it before, to wonder about the why and what of it, to formulate factual and even fanciful answers—these are the ways to "see" with all your senses.

Both fact and fancy are vital parts of living. A fact is no less a fact because we can have fun with it. A flight into fancy can lead to an undertaking of serious nature. Take astronomy, the science of the study of the universe beyond our own planet Earth. The skies have been described as man's first picture book. Those who studied the stars saw two kinds: stars which remained fixed and stars which moved. (We now know those wandering stars to be planets.) The ancient astronomers saw the fixed stars in patterns which suggested pictures to them. They gave them fanciful names and wrote stories about them. The W they saw in the sky became known as Cassiopeia's Chair. That was a fanciful explanation; the fact is that the W-shaped constellation was there, and astronomers saw it and learned from their study of it. These myths do not diminish the importance of their discoveries; they enhance them.

Who was Cassiopeia? Ah, if you ask the question seriously and really want to know the answer, you must make your own search. Not only will you learn the answer to your question, but you will discover things even more valuable—how to make a search and the thrill of finding the answer for yourself. For one question leads to another, and each answer becomes a link in the individual's golden chain of knowledge that becomes longer with each question asked and each answer discovered. This process might be called the establishment of the habit of learning. It can be sustained throughout a lifetime, enriching and adding joy to it.

The games that follow are intended to stimulate you to see things in new ways, to notice things that have been there always but did not impress you enough to make you think about them or ask questions about them. How fast must the wind be blowing to plaster a piece of old newspaper against your legs as you walk? What geometric shape is a banana before it is peeled? After it is peeled? Geometry in our alphabet? What is so magical about a magic square? What is the math part of being you?

The best part of all is that, once you open the eyes of your mind just a little, all kinds of wonderful thoughts begin to creep in.

> There is so much to see and know,
> So much to do and say,
> Our lives seem hardly long enough
> To learn, to think, to play.

TELL ME, PLEASE

Lister Sinclair states in a book prepared for the Museum of Science and Technology of Canada that the answers to some simple questions cannot be answered simply. They cannot always be found in books or obtained from authorities. So, if you want to know why the grass is green, "You have to ask the grass," writes Sinclair.

We've often heard the expression, If it could talk, what stories it could tell! Well, here is your chance. If you really want to know what something would say if it could talk, ask it! Then listen hard to what it says and let your imagination run free. Wherever you are, in the classroom, in the woods, in a garden, on a playground, just anywhere, pick an object or a living creature as your subject. "See" it as you've never seen it before. Ask it some questions. "Listen" to the answers you imagine. If you get answers you don't understand, then it is up to you to find the answers. Maybe at first you won't get answers—and then again, maybe you will—but the questions you ask will start you thinking in ways you never thought before. Write down your questions and answers and share them with your friends.

A few examples here will get you started—then you are on your own.

Honeybee

Tell me, little bee buzzing in my garden, did you come far? Do my flowers please you? What is your favorite color and flavor? Where will you take the nectar you have collected today? Will I ever taste the honey you are helping to make?

(If you "listened" to the answers, did you "learn" where the nectar is taken, how it is stored, and in what? Did the bee tell you how the honey gets from the hive into the jar that you buy in the store?)

Mother Bird

Busy little mother, do you ever get tired searching for food for your hungry crying babies? What is the best food for them? Where do you find it? Does father bird ever help you? How do you prepare the food for your babies to eat?

Caterpillar

Hi there, Mr. Woolly Bear, where are you going? Have you come far? Does your fur coat seem hot in the warm sunshine? What kind of moth will you be next time I see you?

Weathervane

Tell me, weathervane, poking a hole in the sky, do you know it is the wind that turns you? Do you ever get tired waiting for the wind to turn you in another direction? Does the wind ever make you dizzy turning you one way and then another? Do you get tired sitting on the same roof? Which is your favorite view?

Kite

Hey there, kite, did you have fun up there in the sky? Why were you pulling so hard at the string? Did you hope I would let you go free? Did you enjoy having the wind pushing at your face? Were you as frightened as I when you almost got caught in the tree?

School Desk

Tell me, school desk, what are you made of? How many kids have sat on your seat and kicked you with their feet? Do you get tired of being in school all the time? Do you ever wish you could go out at recess time, too? Do you sleep at night when school is closed? Do desks ever talk together when no people are here?

Cloud

Cloud up there, tell me please, do you enjoy being pushed by the wind? Do you like making shapes for me to look at? Your cheeks are puffy today. Do you have the mumps? Whose hands shape you? Is it the winds? Or are you some magical creature who says magic words and changes from one shape to another?

WORD PICTURES

As you begin to "see" better, try writing word pictures. "Paint" in words the pictures you see in your mind's eye: the cloud that looks like a flying bird, the piece of driftwood that looks like a fish. Unlike a camera, which records *everything* it "sees," you can leave out what does not strike your fancy and put in anything that tickles it.

Take a sketch pad with you when you walk in the woods or go on a long ride. What some might think a long, boring ride can actually offer exciting moving pictures to record along the way.

"Paint" your pictures so clearly that those who read them will see what you saw. Perhaps they will remember your picture when they see the kind of scene you described. Remember, all your word pictures need not be about something beautiful. They may be about funny things or about ugly things that make you angry or want to cry.

Here are examples of scenes you may have passed by without really seeing them. Perhaps they will help you to "see" better—or cause you to remember some things you have seen and had similar thoughts about.

Ballet

The Weeping Willow Ballet danced to the wild strains of the wind.

Harvest

Grotesque, prehistoric monster, growling and spewing out a yellow stream; McCormick called you "threshing machine."

Traffic Light

You are an ill-tempered troll who glares at me with one red eye holding me prisoner until the friendly green-eyed troll releases me from your powers and allows me to go on my way.

Litterbugs

The litterbug calls a dump his home,
From which he loves to roam.

He scatters litter here and there,
Thus feels at home most anywhere.

We find those dreadful litterbugs
In every single state.
The only one I'd like them in
Is the state that's termed as late.

If I could catch a litterbug
Would it really be a sin
To mount that wretched specimen
On a collector's pin?

For litterbugs, it's sad to say,
We've not yet found a lethal spray.

Dig no graves for litterbugs
When no longer they can roam;
Just bury them 'neath tons of junk
—Their spirits will feel at home.

Bay of Fundy Fog

The fog billows in like smoke from some gigantic pipe, enveloping us without ever revealing its source.

Progress

The gigantic road machines tear relentlessly at green hillsides with voracious bites, devouring trees, leaving deep and ugly scars and a trail of concrete called "progress."

Winding Road

The road is a snake asleep in the sun, and I, a shadow, move swiftly along its back.

Poplar Row

The poplars, like strings of a heavenly lute, were gently plucked by the fingers of the wind.

New-mown Hay

The new-mown hay by the roadside expels its last breath in fragrant surrender.

Cattle

Cattle stud the green hills like precious jewels set in a brooch upon the bosom of nature.

Dead Tree

Old dead tree silhouetted against the sky, do birds still nest in your lifeless branches?

Reflection

Fall-tinged trees reflected on serene waters, you are doubly beautiful.

Pine at Sunset

Solitary pine against the flaming sky, you are like the handle of some gigantic torch.

Jet Vapor Trails

Jet plane making patterns in the sky, would you challenge the clouds?

Snow Blanket

The snow fell quietly, gently blanketing the winter-sleeping things beneath the ground, waking neither them nor those who slept in warm houses.

There's No Place Like

Rolling farmlands of New York and Pennsylvania, fir-studded mountains, craggy cliffs of Vermont and New Hampshire, Atlantic-washed coast of Maine—who can say which is most beautiful? But, ah, Ohio, you are the fairest of them all because you are home.

Victorian House

Victorian house of yesteryear, the modern house crouched beside you cannot rob you of your gracious charm.

Winding Road

The road stretched and writhed as if weary of having lain so long in one place.

Police Radar

The seeing eye that dogs our trip.

Star

Unfailing beacon of the night.

Roadside Park

The roadside park was aswarm with hungry winged things and those who came on wheels.

Radio Tower

A needle piercing the atmosphere, binding the seams of the world with gossamer threads of word and melody.

Cloud Shadow

The wind-propelled cloud overhead casts its shadow on the road and challenges us to race to the next hill.

Moon

The only thing that is halved, quartered, and slivered each month and yet can still return to fully delight us.

High Tension Wire System

Long line of marching robots holding their mighty power in upraised hands.

Summer Storm

The rain scratches helplessly at the windshield as we drive snug and dry in our music-filled cocoon.

Electrical Storm

The black storm cloud with fiercely flashing eye marches swiftly across the sky to the wild roll of a thousand giant drums.

Bleak Desert

There are no deserts more bleak and painful to the eye than those strewn with the carcasses of old dead cars.

Tree Cemetery

The sun-bleached skeletons of once stately trees stand like tombstones marking their untimely graves.

Seedlings

The orderly rows of seedling pines give testimony to someone's effort to replace earth's bounty too often rudely snatched with no thought of repayment.

Cadillac Mountain

Mountain, called Cadillac, Atlantic sentinel, first outpost of our eastern shore to greet the sun of each new day, how many times have you witnessed this miracle, yet never failed to glow with pleasure at the touch of first light?

8

Observation Super Sleuth Games

Who has not wanted to be the super sleuth who solves a mystery? The good detective is the one who pays attention to details. Good sleuthing is related to perception. What is missing? What has been added? What is out of place? Which is the unrelated clue in the midst of many related ones? Clues may be related to sound, smell, touch, sight, and taste. In other words, good detecting requires perceptual acuity. Every sense is employed; so is the ability to see relationships. Unless the sleuth understands relationships, how can she or he distinguish between the related and the unrelated?

The games presented here can be used with persons of all ages. Since perceptiveness must be developed through practice, the games and exercises can begin on a simple level and gradually be made more difficult as the players increase their skill. However, even in the first stages, the games should not be so easy as to require little effort. Without challenge, games soon lose their effectiveness.

The test of success is when a player says triumphantly: "Boy, I never would have been able to do *that* two weeks ago!"

ORDER SLEUTHING

Money Changing

Depending upon the age of the players, prepare a row of six to ten coins—nickels, pennies, and dimes—all heads up. Allow players twenty seconds to view the row and then cover it quickly.

Players then write the order as they remember it, using the first letter of the name of the coin for abbreviation. (A capital letter makes for easier reading.) Score a point for each correctly placed coin. Thus a player may get only three or four right and still score some points. Rearrange the coins and continue the game. Shorten the viewing period three seconds each time until a minimum of eight seconds is reached.

As players become more proficient, use more coins.

Variation #1

Arrange the coins so that some are heads up and others tails up. Now players must remember not only the arrangement of the coins but also which side was up. (This seems to be one of the few cases in which we use the plural when only the singular exists. When one flips a coin, the question is always, Heads or tails? But how many heads does a coin have? How many tails?)

Variation #2

Instead of coins, use checker pieces of both colors; this adds the dimension of color to the game. After a few rounds, make some of the pieces into kings. Players now need not only to remember the order of the colors but the rank as well. Again, the answers may be indicated by abbreviations.

Variation #3

Use playing cards as the mystery objects. Use both black suits in one series to see if players make the distinction between suits. The question might be:

1. Total number of cards?
2. How many of each suit?
3. In what order?

When playing with face cards, change occasionally the rank or the suit of some cards. For example, if a queen of hearts is changed to a jack of hearts, or to a queen of diamonds, players must be quite alert to spot such a change.

Quick-Change Playing Cards

When using playing cards, many opportunities for making a quick, simple change are possible. You might begin with all one suit—hearts, for example. Arrange in order from ace through king. The players may see the row for twenty seconds and must then record what they have seen. Then the fast changes begin. Here are some suggestions:

1. Interchange two numbered cards.
2. Remove a card and move other cards over to fill the gap.
3. Replace the missing card and interchange two numbers.
4. Change the queen of hearts for the queen of diamonds.
5. Mix the cards into a random-numbered row.
6. Change the heart ace for a diamond ace, but also make a change in the order.
7. Rearrange so that the face cards are out of order and somewhere in the center of the row as well.

The teacher or leader must be wily and take as much time for a radical change as for a simple one. The players will undoubtedly reason that if the time for the change is short there would be less change in the order than if the changing time were longer.

The black suits can be used, of course. Finding the clubs mixed with the spades requires some perceptual skill, too.

RELATIONSHIP SLEUTHING

In this type of detecting, the players must spot the missing number in a series of one or more numbers that are incorrect.

Number Series Detecting

The series used depends on the age of the players. This type of game can be used with kindergartners up. It is never too soon to begin. For the very young the series would be simple progressions with an omission or an incorrect number, such as:

1,2,3,5,6,7,9

Some suggested series are given for starters. The object is to spot the unrelated number or numbers (they are underlined in the series given here). Can you figure the method of each series?

1. 1,3,5,7,*10*,11,13,15,17
2. 2,4,*5*,8,10,12,*15*,16,18,*21*,22,24
3. 1,2,4,5,6,8,9,10,12,13,*15*,16
4. 3,6,9,*11*,15,*17*,21
5. 3,4,7,11,*19*,29,47,73
6. 1,1,2,4,3,9,4,*14*,5,25,6,*35*,7,49
7. 12,9,3,6,*4*
8. 2,8,3,27,4,64,5,*100*,6,216
9. 3,6,12,*23*,48,96
10. 21,7,24,8,39,*14*,60,20

Alphabet Series Detecting

The letters are arranged in groups of a particular type of letter. The nonconforming letter or letters are underlined. Players must determine why and how they do not conform.

GROUP A	GROUP B
1. A,J,K	1. V,*B*,W,Y,*O*,X
2. B,C,D	2. N,M,W,*T*,Z,E,F
3. E,G,P	3. H,T,F,*N*,E,L
4. T,V,Z	4. V,A,W,Z,N,*F*,M
5. *H,L,M*	5. Q,*B*,O,S,U
6. I,Y	6. B,*M*,D,G,R,P
7. *F,L,N*	7. V,*I*,L,T,*E*,X
8. *R,S*,O	8. H,A,N,Z,F,*X*
9. Q,U,W	

Answers

In Group A, the letters are arranged in rhyming groups; the nonconforming are the groups which do not rhyme.

In Group B, the underlined letters are exceptions in their groups in these ways:

1. All letters are composed of straight lines only
2. All letters contain parallel lines
3. All letters contain right angles
4. All letters contain acute angles
5. All letters are made of curved lines
6. All are made of straight lines and curves
7. All letters contain two straight lines only
8. All are composed of three straight lines

Mystery Words

In each of the lists given below, there is a mystery word which applies to all the words in that particular list. Players are encouraged to make up their own lists with which to challenge their fellow detectives. Remember, one word is common to all the words or phrases in a list; in some instances it may precede the word or phrase and in another follow it. Examples:

1. (horse) feathers
2. get off your high (horse)
3. to (horse)
4. (horse) sense

Remember, if there are doubts, consult your dictionary.

A	B	C
1. aid	1. ball	1. day
2. together	2. bag	2. flower
3. watch	3. navy	3. time
4. marching	4. coffee	4. river
5. Indian	5. vanilla	5. down
6. wagon	6. full of	6. sick
7. shell	7. beetle	7. rail
8. box	8. stalk	8. and board
9. identification	9. string	9. lake
10. head	10. butter	10. asparagus
11. guerrilla	11. lima	11. bunk

D	E	F
1. family	1. common	1. up
2. first	2. head	2. board
3. given	3. polish	3. cheese
4. calling	4. set	4. cold
5. identify by	5. down	5. dress
6. plate	6. up	6. ache
7. greatest	7. brush	7. hunter
8. call by	8. toe	8. the list
9. dropper	9. 20-penny	9. by a
10. tag	10. finger	10. off
11. sake	11. hard as a	11. on

G	H	I
1. take	1. shake	1. fly
2. lose	2. left	2. warden
3. attack	3. hold	3. forest
4. beat	4. glass	4. box
5. burn	5. grenade	5. clay
6. sweet	6. craft	6. trap
7. cherry	7. off	7. wall
8. have a	8. out	8. water
9. strings	9. pick	9. weed
10. suit	10. made	10. works
11. felt	11. on one	11. opal

J	K	L
1. berry	1. end	1. house
2. days	2. center	2. potato
3. biscuit	3. beat	3. seat
4. fish	4. eye	4. spot
5. fight	5. head	5. spring
6. catcher	6. fall	6. plate
7. paddle	7. heat	7. pepper
8. wood	8. lock	8. war
9. cart	9. reckoning	9. water
10. prairie	10. weight	10. shot
11. wild	11. letter	11. dog

Eleven words have been given for each mystery word. Fewer could be used at any one time. When a group or individual has identified the mystery word, have members of the group define the term used in each case. (This should bring out the dictionaries.)

Answers

A—band, B—bean, C—bed, D—name, E—nail, F—head, G—heart, H—hand, I—fire, J—dog, K—dead, L—hot.

Mystery Clues and Ringers

Prepare similar but shorter lists of mystery clues and throw in a false clue to add a new dimension. Not only must the common mystery word be identified, but the "ringer" must be found as well.

To make lists, consult the faithful dictionary. Some lists are given here for starters. Can you spot the "ringer" even before you know the mystery word?

A	B	C	D
about	organ	baked	race
and come	piece	sole	devils
across	wash	pint	loose
down	gill	crab	brake
on	breeder	hour	age
into	watering	moon	note
around	big	note	man
back	part	back	ball

E	F	G	H
gold	business	faced	some
collar	flower	light	paste
paradise	bonnet	quake	hammer
errand	puzzle	cheese	powder
cap	shine	shiner	pick
parsley	suit	set	ache
	jacket	stone	and nail

I	J	K	L
boat	drawing	known	eye
cotton	cloth	bred	faced
blood	bottle	off	elephant
fire	bowl	being	flag
dog	day	foot	bell
man	down	head	fish
metal	board	founded	fox

M	N	O	P
guard	grass	hand	tree
heart	blood	head	maker
jack	baby	up	shine
light	tree	house	flower
list	bottle	trip	string
out	devils	robin	horn
book	chip	egg	horse
in	collar	steak	bill
	bell		

Q	R	S	T
corn	struck	dog	shaft
absorber	hand	coat	squirrel
proof	whisper	cat	wool
shore	sing	minnow	cotton
troops	fright	knot	maple
wave	coach	hat	garden
therapy	craft	boot	fish
		less	hound

U	V	W	X
piece	brain	hale	bread
color	bath	laid	vinegar
quarter	call	let	oil
dime	garage	land	tooth
way	house	pale	talk
ply	man	sect	gum
cornered	cat	sole	heart
fold	dog	come	clover

Answers

The mystery word common to all the words or phrases in each list is given first, followed by the "ringer" thrown in to confuse. As always, when an argument arises, consult the dictionary.

A. come, and come
B. mouth, gill
C. half, crab
D. foot, devils
E. fool's, collar
F. monkey, bonnet
G. moon, cheese
H. tooth, hammer
I. gun, blood
J. wash, bottle
K. well, foot
L. white, bell
M. black, in
N. blue, tree
O. round, egg
P. shoe, flower
Q. shock, shore
R. stage, sing
S. top, cat
T. rock, cotton
U. three, dime
V. bird, garage
W. in, pale
X. sweet, vinegar

Nature's Mysteries

In the following groupings are lists of nature's wonders. In each list there is one ringer. The lists are long enough to be divided for a second go-round, but a new ringer will be needed. Hopefully, the players will be so curious about these intriguing names that they will search out the items to which they apply. Nature reference books should get quite a workout. Better still, make this part of the game; the results will be well worth the effort.

A

ark
butterfly
buttercup
cone
bleeding tooth
fig
Neptune
elephant's snout
marlinspike
Mercury
turkey wing
watering pot
pearl
lima
jewel box

B

spotted queen
monarch
imperial
swallowtail
painted lady
question mark
checkerspot
turtlehead
buckeye
viceroy
parnassus
silver-spotted skipper

C

cohosh
arrow head
blazing star
blue curls
fairy-candles
Dutchman's pipe
marsh mallow
dogbane
rosybells
saxifrage
turtle head
yellow rocket
scullcap
Venus looking glass
rabbitbrushes

D

faded
corn
massasauga
fox
leaf-nosed
rat
coachwhip
cow
yellow-lipped
hog-nosed
ring-necked
rainbow
coral
king
bull

E

leatherback
mud
saw-toothed
Western hawkshead
false map
alligator snapper
gopher
sliders
painted
blanding
diamondback
chicken
spiny soft-shelled
musk
wood
hawksbill
green
loggerhead
saw-toothed

F

wood
spotted
pickerel
leopard
narrow-mouthed
green
spotted-belly
gopher
red-legged
white-lipped
whistling
robber
cricket
bull
tree
squirrel tree
striped chorus
canyon tree
American

G

giant
dusky
spotted
mudpuppy
marbled
red eft
siren
Jefferson
mud cat
hellbenders
red-backed
slimy
worm
newts
Olympic
painted
congo eel
four-toed

H

banyan
hornbeam
chokecherry
London plane
Kentucky coffee
osage orange
pawpaw
staghorn fir
wafer ash
wahoo
live oak
bald cypress
sausage
sweet gum
gumbo limbo
sapodillo
spanish bayonet
poison wood
strangler fig
water tupelo

I

gecko
anole
night
chuckwalla
blue glass-snake
spiny
desert iguana
leopard
Arizona night
ground Utas
earless
zebra-tailed
ground swift
horned
whiptail

Answers

The answers are given in this order: letter, classification, and ringer.

A—sea shells, Mercury
B—butterflies, spotted queen
C—wild flowers, marsh mallow
D—snakes, cow
E—turtles, hawkshead
F—toads and frogs, spotted-belly
G—salamanders, mud cat
H—trees, staghorn fir
I—lizards, blue glass-snake

9

Fun with Nonverbal Communication

Have you ever thought how much you say to others without using words? Or how many commands you respond to which are unspoken? Or how many wordless commands you give to others?

To make a group activity of nonverbal communication, the teacher may name a classification, such as command, greeting, negative, affirmative, or attention-getting gesture, and then call on players in turn to give an appropriate example. When no one can think of another gesture in that category, a new one is introduced and the play continues.

The game may also be played in the same manner with the players divided into teams and points scored for a team when a player gives an acceptable response. The category can be changed for each row of players: the first players of each team will respond with a gesture in one category, the second players will have another category, and so on. Some categories can be repeated after a time, but the answers must not be duplicates of those previously given in that category in any one game.

Here is a list of categories with suggestions for appropriate gestures in each category.

1. Greetings—a hand wave (the silent "hi"), a nod of the head, a slight bow, a two-handed handshake in the direction of the person greeted, a thrown kiss, an eyewink, a puckered-lip kiss gesture.
2. Commands—a "sit-here" point, a "come here" finger wiggle, a snap of the fingers and an imperious point at the culprit, a sharp hand clap for silence, a finger-to-the-lips "hush," the palm-up "stop" of the traffic officer, the wave ahead signal.
3. Approval—the "okay" finger signal, thumbs up, fighter's clasped hand signal, the stomach-rubbing approval of good food, a lip-smacking good food approval, a chop-licking good food approval, a broad grin.
4. Disapproval—thumbs down, a grimace, stuck-out tongue, a sharp open-palm sideways or downward hand movement, a sharp tight-fisted hand movement, an emphatic shaking of the head, any gesture with a tight-lipped mouth, an exaggerated frown, the finger-circling movement at the temple signifying the "you're nuts" appraisal, a turned back.
5. Pensive—tapping of head, the stare into the distance, tapping teeth with thumbnail, elbow on knee and chin cupped in hand, a looking-at-the-ceiling-for-the-answer, wrinkling of eyes or screwing them shut, head scratching, foot wiggling.
6. Derision—tapping-of-temple "you're out of your mind" gesture, thumbs to temples and finger-wiggling, grimace and thumbs down.
7. Absolutely no!—arms crossed on chest and frown, foot stamp, head shaking from side to side with slow and deliberate movements.
8. Sports signals—the various football and ice hockey infraction signals, the umpire's "take a base," the umpire's "out" and "safe" signals, the catcher-to-pitcher hand signals, the coach's signals to the batter or base runner.

9. Calm down—palms down "cool it" signal, finger to lips "shush," lip-pinching, "button your lip," intent look and slow "no" head-turning.
10. Hungry and thirsty—hand-to-mouth eating motion, holding stomach and entreating look, holding throat and swallowing hard, tipping of glass.

Some other categories are:

1. The "hurry up" series
2. Take it easy or simmer down series
3. The "let's-get-out-of-here" series
4. Tired and sleepy series
5. The "I've-had-it" series
6. The too hot or too cold series
7. The "I feel sick" series
8. The So what? series
9. The how-to-look-fascinated-while-being-bored attitudes
10. The defiant gestures

There are many, many more categories of nonverbal expression. Players, once alerted to the concept, will find new ones every day that they were never aware of before. Classes may find it fun to keep a notebook of nonverbal methods of communication by category. As new expressions find their way into the verbal language, someone will find a way of "saying" it nonverbally.

Ask a Verbal Question, Get a Nonverbal Answer

The teacher prepares a set of questions to ask the players. Each student must respond nonverbally.

In a team game player 1 of the first team asks a verbal question of player 1 of the second team, who must respond nonverbally. Player 1 of the third team asks the question of player 1 of the next team, and so on. On the second round, the teacher asks the first question of player 1 of the first team, who responds nonverbally. The next player (who was previously on the nonverbal end) now asks a question of player 1 of the next team. Thus the roles are reversed.

Here are some questions to start the game off:

1. How many inches is it from here to the moon?
2. Do you like spinach?
3. Do you like chocolate sundaes?
4. How do you like the weather we're having?
5. How'd you like the game yesterday? (Name the teams involved.)
6. Do you have all your homework done for today?
7. Did you get enough sleep last night?
8. Is your father going to let you have the car tonight?
9. You know you're in trouble, don't you? What are you going to do about it?
10. I have tickets for the game tonight. Want to go?

Variation #1

The verbal part need not always be questions. It can consist of such statements as:

1. I hear you got a new bike yesterday.
2. I hear you fell off your bike yesterday.
3. The principal wants to see you in his office.
4. You're breaking out in a rash. I think you'd better see the nurse.
5. I've decided to give you a surprise quiz today.
6. For your homework today . . . .
7. I am canceling the quiz for today.
8. Due to poor weather conditions, school will be dismissed in five minutes.

9. We will be having a visit from Board members today. I expect you to . . . .
10. We had the poorest record of any classroom at the paper sale.

Variation #2

Use nonverbal language in a command, a greeting, a question, or any other category, and receive a verbal answer. For example, a point at a real or nonexistent wristwatch is a request for the time. A verbal response is given. (Play as a group or team game.)

Some suggestions to get the game started follow. Remember that any questions or statements given below are to be expressed nonverbally. The individuals giving the verbal answers may not always interpret the gesture accurately—which only adds to the fun.

1. What did I do?
2. Who, me?
3. Oh, no, not again!
4. Why?
5. Look who's coming in the door.
6. I had it here a minute ago.
7. Gosh, my knee hurts.
8. I thought I had enough money with me.
9. What in the world is *that?* (Meaning an article)
10. Who or what is *that?* (Indicating an individual)
11. I know the answer, give me a minute to think.
12. How do I look?
13. That stinks!
14. Boy, it sure is hot in here.
15. I wish she'd hurry up and get it over with.
16. Give me that.
17. Put your gum in the wastebasket.
18. Oh! I just remembered . . .

19. Thumbing a ride.
20. A child holding out arms asking to be picked up.
21. Oooh, that hurts!
22. Who put that there where someone could fall over it?
23. Boy, that smells good!
24. Aha, now I've got you in my power! (The old hand-rubbing routine)
25. What smells in here?

Nonverbal Sounds

There are many nonverbal sounds to which we react in some way, either physically or verbally. When the telephone rings, we move to its command to answer it. An individual sneezes and we respond verbally, God bless you.

In this group game, the first player makes a nonverbal sound or imitates or names a mechanical (nonhuman) sound. The next player responds verbally with an appropriate expression or gives an explanation of a response to that sound. He then turns to the next player and makes or names a sound to which that player responds. Example: The first player coughs. The next player responds by saying, Got a cold?

Some suggested sounds follow. The responses are left to the players. Since some sounds could elicit more than one response, the same sound can be named more than once in any one game.

1. Alarm clock
2. Wolf whistle
3. A finger snap
4. A sneeze
5. Telephone bell
6. Toot of a car horn
7. A horn blast
8. Doorbell

9. Referee's whistle blast
10. A sharp hand clap
11. Rap of a baton on a music stand
12. Police siren, fire engine siren, ambulance siren
13. Applause-type hand-clapping
14. A prolonged coughing spell
15. A door blown shut with a slam
16. A crash of thunder
17. The spinning-wheels sound of a car stuck
18. The whine of a starter when the car doesn't start
19. A moan
20. A sharp indrawn-breath sound
21. A raucous or loud laugh
22. A baby's wail or cry
23. A giggle
24. An under-the-breath, unintelligible mutter
25. A Bronx cheer
26. A sound of a glass or dishes hitting the floor and breaking
27. The sound of an auto crash
28. An airplane flying unusually low
29. The sound of a marching band or a public announcement from a sound truck
30. A scream
31. A lovely bird song
32. A diesel train horn
33. A backfire or gun
34. Dog barking

10

Standing Word Puzzlers

Play with verse long enough and you will find yourself thinking in rhymes—sometimes inspired, sometimes corny, but always fun. When a rhyme slips out unconsciously, corn or not, there is a feeling of minor triumph.

Play with word puzzlers, and after a time the undecipherable, impossible ones become so easy you will wonder why they seemed so difficult. Before long you will be creating your own. Suddenly you'll find yourself stopping in the middle of something and saying, Hey, I just thought of one! When this happens, write it down quickly, or it will get away as fast as a fish wiggling off a hook.

Some puzzlers are done wholly with words; others can be part words and part picture, almost like a rebus. Use them as mixers at parties or banquets. Prepare sheets of them for players to work out together as teams. Use them in small gatherings as conversation stimulators. Write out a few to start the fun. Once the participants know what's what, they will make up their own to challenge each other. Allow drawings and words, or all-word types. Many kinds are demonstrated here in the examples which follow. Children and adults of all ages will want to get into the act. The problem is not so much getting groups started as it is getting them stopped. As the puzzle says:

estimate the power of laughter, or the value of corn
never seriousness erudition.

What does the title to this chapter say? You've surely figured it out by now. It's as clear as the nose on Pinocchio's face. The words "word" and "puzzlers" are under the word "standing," so it reads: Understanding Word Puzzlers.

Now that you know how to read this kind of message, stand
you can
others without your mind if you're not Such exercises will keep
exerting impatient.
your mind sharp. But remember, even if you are it should not
smart all
make you (Even if you are oversmart, it should not, above all,
bearing.
make you overbearing.)

Word Puzzlers

1. an often leads to
   sight reaction
2. a dlihc
3. hurry
   here
4. V O write T E
5. don't come come
   now, later
6. estimate the
   never head costs
7. H O R rock S E
8. written
   the cost was

9. dogs often
———— ————
some react

10. W———H———I———L———E

11. S
  L
    O
      W

12. C H rock A I R

      Y
    R
  R
U
13. H

14. e a V s e, E A peke S E

15. once
————
a time

16. S S
I I
D D
E E

17. S———I———D———E

18. D——I——V——I——S——I——O——N & division

19. T I help M E

20. help
————
time

21. hurry
————
over

      N
    A
  E
L
22. C

23. Gone, gone, gone, gone, end.

24. F I L in T R A T I O N

25.
```
      M
    G   E
  N       S
    I   S
```

Answers to Word Puzzlers (If You Haven't Figured Them Out by Now)

1. An oversight often leads to overreaction
2. A backward child
3. Hurry over here
4. Write-in vote
5. Don't come over now, come over later
6. Never underestimate the overhead costs
7. Rockin' horse
8. The cost was underwritten
9. Some underdogs often overreact
10. A long while
11. Slow down
12. Rockin' chair
13. Hurry up
14. Viennese, Pekingese
15. Once upon a time
16. Side-by-side
17. Along side
18. Long and short division
19. Help in time
20. Overtime help
21. Hurry on over
22. Clean up
23. A foregone conclusion
24. Infiltration
25. Messing around

Puzzlers as Brain Teasers

In the classroom, keep a corner of the chalkboard for the display of word puzzlers. Use the picture types or the word types. Once a pupil has solved the puzzler, erase it and provide another. Give special consideration to the ones the students themselves conjure up. Leave the unsolved ones on the board until someone finds the correct answer.

Puzzlers can be printed nicely on 8½″ by 11″ or 9″ by 12″ paper and hung around the room. These can be prepared by the students themselves. As they are solved, replace the puzzlers with new ones, but keep the solved sheets for future use. They will be fun to show at a parents' open house program. See if parents are as sharp as students at solving the puzzlers or suggesting others!

Short Shorts

1. Knockout

		R		
		I		
$\frac{\text{CHALLENGER}}{\text{RATED}}$	$\frac{\text{THEN}}{\text{MATCHED}}$	R I G H T,	C—O—U—N—T,	$\frac{\text{MATCH}}{\text{QUICK!}}$
		H		
		T		

2. Liberal & Conservative

   1 center & center 1

3. Dessert

   pineapple ǝʞɐɔ

4. Failure

   $\frac{\text{COOK}}{\text{EXCITED}}$ $\frac{\text{CAKE}}{\text{SALTED}}$ $\frac{\text{BAKED}}{\text{THEN}}$ GAR ends BAGE CAN.

5. Scarcity

   few and far few

6. Romance

L O head V E
heels

7. Far East

D in AH

8. Unwelcome Sign

NO
TIME PARKING

9. Pests

T T T T T & t t t t t

10. Sad Miss

HUNTER	* * * *	RABBIT	* * * *	SHOT	* * * *	NOTHING
HERE		THERE		HIGH		THERE

11. Sick, Sick, Sick

R
THE WEATHER U PAR
THEY'RE ALL N AND

12. Good Sense

RAIN THE UMBRELLA!
HEAD? GET

13. Eternally

ever, ever, ever, ever, & ever

14. Expression

RIGHT
BROTHER

15. Quarrel

W S
O D
R
O D
W S

16. Traffic Jam

another one car

17. Inflation

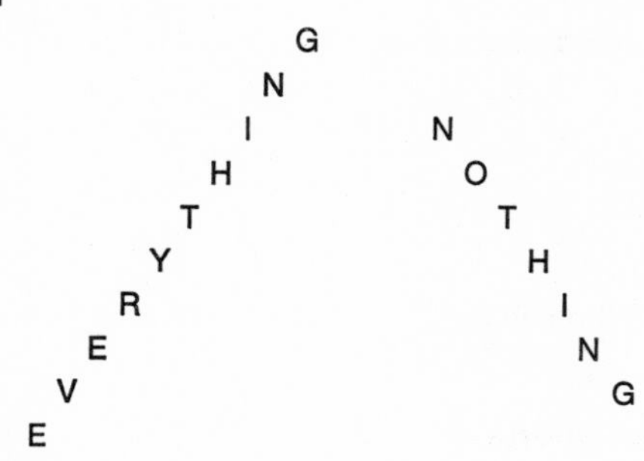

18. Loser

19. Zero

ALL O THERE

20. Persistence

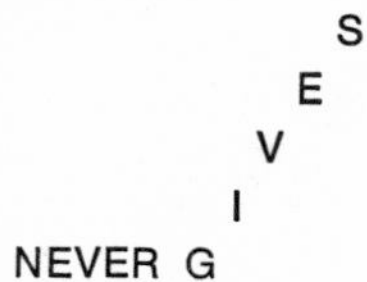

21. Crosses

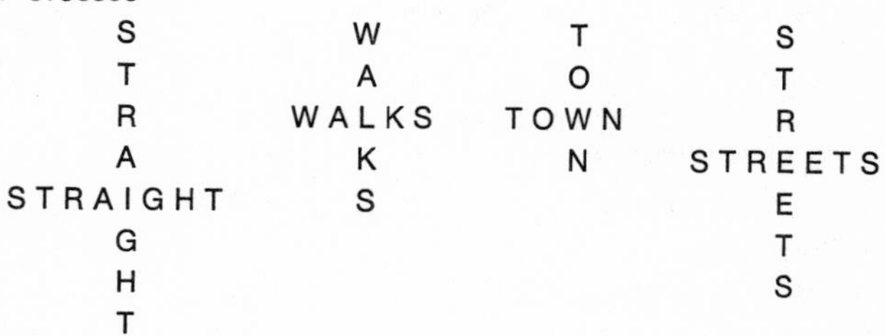

22. Disorganized

H
S E
CIR CLES
E G
O

23. Decision Making

    The matter committee consideration.

    is

24. Do Not Despair

    ALL F U it's all N

25. Curtain

    S I G the end is H T at L——A——S——T !

Answers to Short Shorts

1. Challenger overrated, then overmatched, right cross, long count, match over quick!
2. One to the left of center and one to the right of center
3. Pineapple upside-down cake
4. Cook overexcited, cake oversalted, then underbaked, ends in garbage can
5. Few and far between
6. Head-over-heels in love
7. India
8. No overtime parking
9. Big tease and little tease
10. Hunter over here, rabbit over there, shot over-high, nothing over there
11. They're all under the weather, run down, and under par
12. Rain overhead? Get under the umbrella!
13. Forever and ever
14. Right on, brother
15. Cross words
16. One car right after another
17. Everything going up and nothing coming down
18. Was undertrained, soon overtired, gave up
19. Nothing there after all
20. Never gives up
21. Straight across, cross walks, cross town, cross streets
22. He goes around in circles

23. The matter before the committee is under consideration
24. It's all in fun, after all
25. The end is in sight at long last

Word-and-Picture-Puzzlers

PAID
SHE'S
WORKED

A

HIS·TORY

B

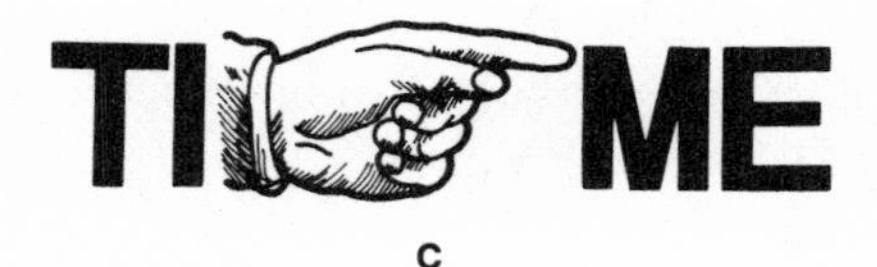

C

HIS **EYES** HIS STOMACH

D

1

E

I BLOW I

F

WIDE SPACES

G

EVERY SHE'S THING

H

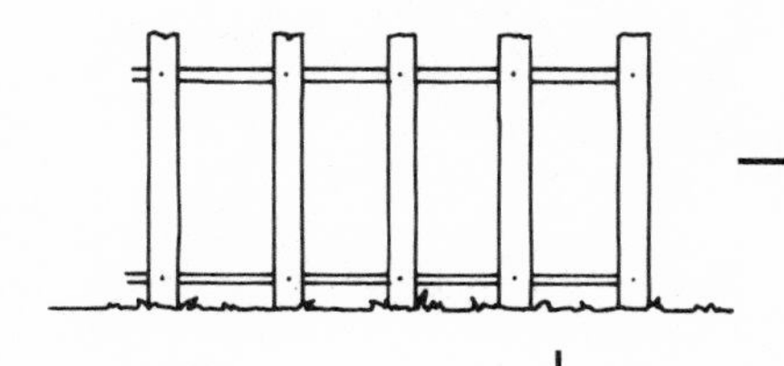

I

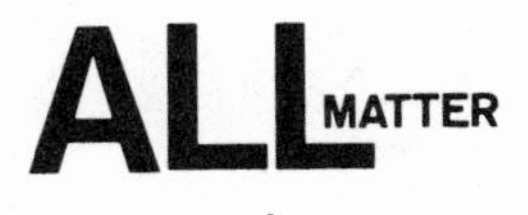

J

O

B.A.
M.A.
B.S.
M.S.
Ph. D.

K

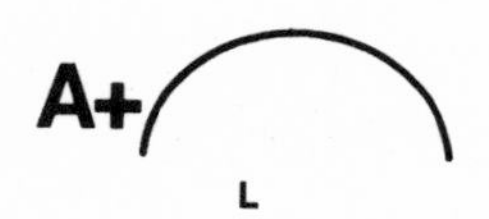

L

TRIUMPH

DIFFICULTIES

M

COFFEE

N

O

P

Q

R

S

MASTERPIEC

T

ONE ANOTHER
ONE ANOTHER
ONE ANOTHER
ONE ANOTHER
ONE ANOTHER
ONE ANOTHER

U

FAR IT

V

BAR OIL GO

W

ALL

THE WORLD

X

HE'S RIGHT

Y

T S
H T
G R
I A
A I
R G
T H
S T

Z

AA

1000

BB

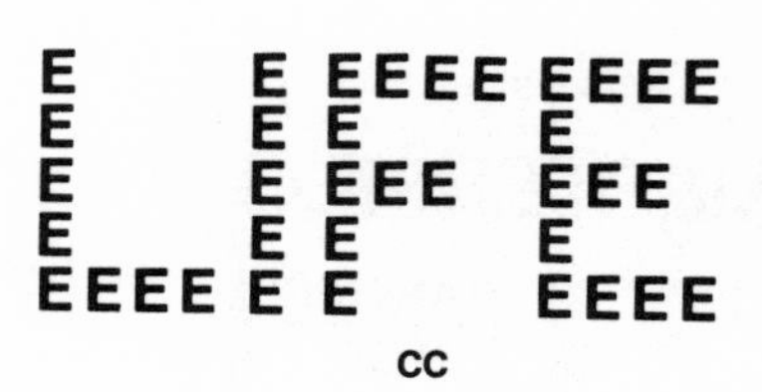

CC

TROALWAYS**UBLE**

DD

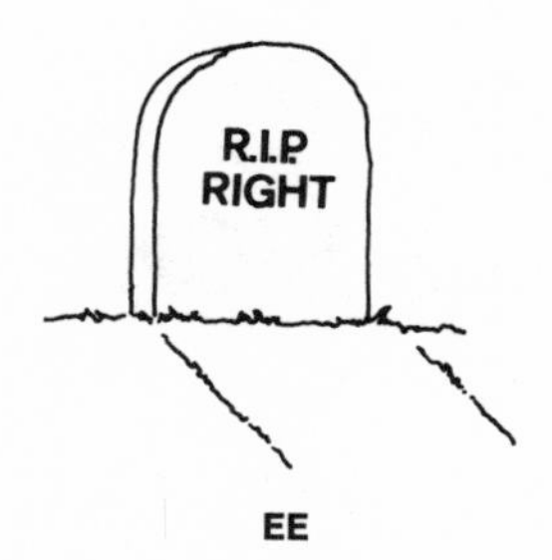

EE

NEVER GIVE A **KOOL**

FF

GG

HH

II

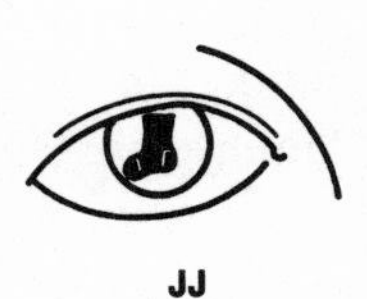

JJ

KK

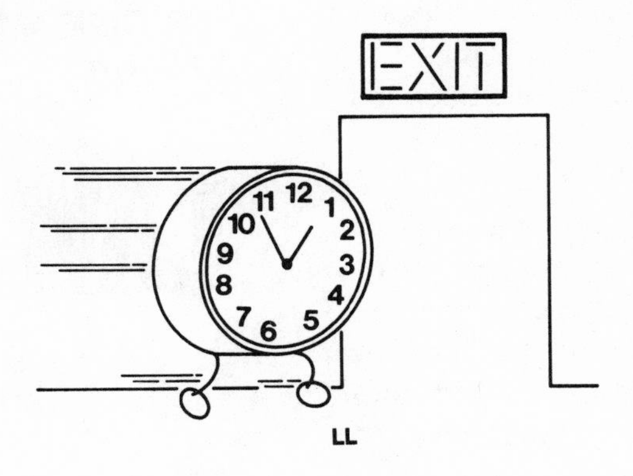

LL

Answers to Word-and-Picture Puzzlers

A. She's overworked and underpaid
B. A period in history
C. A point in time
D. His eyes are bigger than his stomach
E. A hole in one
F. A blow between the eyes
G. Wide open spaces
H. She's in the middle of everything
I. Picket line
J. A small matter after all
K. Five degrees below zero
L. Grade on the curve
M. Triumph over difficulties
N. Coffee break
O. Fast thinking
P. Pocket full of posies
Q. Ring around the rosie
R. The "in" thing
S. All around the world
T. Unfinished masterpiece
U. Six of one and half-dozen of another
V. Far from it
W. Oil embargo
X. All over the world
Y. He's to the left of right
Z. Straight up and down
AA. Two black eyes
BB. One in a thousand
CC. Life of ease
DD. Always in the middle of trouble
EE. Dead right
FF. Never give a backward look

GG. He's up against the law
HH. East and West Indies
II. Misunderstanding between friends
JJ. A sock in the eye
KK. Super bowl
LL. Time running out

Bibliography

Abbott, R. Tucker, *Sea Shells of the World.* New York: Golden Press, 1962.

Ball, W. Rouse, *Mathematical Recreations & Diversions.* Revised by H. M. S. Coxter. London: Macmillan, 1940.

Battan, Louis J., *The Nature of Violent Storms.* Garden City, N.Y.: Doubleday Anchor Books, 1961.

Bauer, Dr. Jaroslav, *Minerals, Rocks, and Precious Stones.* London: Octopus Books, 1974.

Bendick, Jeanne, and Marcia Levin, *Take Shapes, Lines and Letters.* New York: McGraw-Hill, 1962.

Bentley, W. A., and W. J. Humphreys, *Snow Crystals.* New York: Dover, 1962.

Crescimbeni, Joseph, *Arithmetic Enrichment Art for Elementary Schools.* W. Nyack, N.Y.: Parker, 1965.

Davis, Flora, *Inside Intuition (What We Know About Non-Verbal Communication).* New York: McGraw-Hill, 1973.

Evans, I. O., *Rocks, Minerals & Gemstones.* London: Hamlyn, 1972.

Fisher, Robert Moore, *How to Know and Predict the Weather.* A Mentor Book. New York: Harper & Row, 1953.

Freeman, Mae, *Finding Out about Shapes.* New York: McGraw-Hill, 1969.

Hunter, J. A. H., and Joseph S. Madrachy, *Mathematic Diversions.* New York: Dover, 1975.

Kirtland, Elizabeth, *Write It Right: A Handbook of Homonyms.* New York: Golden Press, 1968.

Platt, Rutherford, *A Pocket Guide to Trees.* New York: Dodd, Mead, 1952. (Cardinal Edition, 1953.)

Russell, Solveig Paulson, *Lines and Shapes* (*A First Look at Geometry*). New York: Henry Z. Walck, 1965.

Sinclair, Lister, *To See What Everyone Has Seen and Think What No One Else Has Thought.* Canada: Centennial Centre of Science and Technology, 1969.

Zim, Herbert S., *Insects.* New York: Golden Press, 1956.

———. *Flowers: A Guide to American Wildflowers.* New York: Golden Press, 1950.

———. *Reptiles and Amphibians.* New York: Golden Press, 1956.

The following titles are from the Our Living World of Nature Series, published in cooperation with *The World Book Encyclopedia.* New York: McGraw-Hill, 1966:

Amos, William H., *The Life of the Seashore.*

Berrill, N. J., *The Life of the Ocean.*

Berrill, M., and N. J. Berrill, *The Life of Sea Islands.*

Brooks, Maurice, *The Life of the Mountains.*

Index

PRINCIPLES AND PROCEDURES OF STATISTICS

A Biometrical Approach

Second Edition

Robert G. D. Steel

Professor of Statistics
North Carolina State University

James H. Torrie

Late Emeritus Professor of Agronomy
University of Wisconsin

McGraw-Hill Book Company

New York St. Louis San Francisco Auckland Bogotá Hamburg
Johannesburg London Madrid Mexico Montreal New Delhi
Panama Paris São Paulo Singapore Sydney Tokyo Toronto

PRINCIPLES AND PROCEDURES OF STATISTICS

4 5 6 7 8 9 0 D O D O 8 9 8 7 6 5 4 3 2

Library of Congress Cataloging in Publication Data

Steel, Robert George Douglas, date
Principles and procedures of statistics.

Includes index.
1. Mathematical statistics. 2. Biomathematics.
I. Torrie, James Hiram, date joint author.
II. Title.
QA276.S82 1980 519.5 79-22236
ISBN 0-07-060926-8

This book was set in Times Roman. The editors were Carol Napier
and J. W. Maisel; the cover was designed by Jane Moorman;
the production supervisor was Phil Galea. The drawings were done
by J & R Services, Inc.
R. R. Donnelley & Sons Company was printer and binder.

In memory of James H. Torrie, who was not able to participate in writing the second edition. He had been in failing health for two years and died on May 30, 1976. At that time, he was an Emeritus Professor of Agronomy at the University of Wisconsin in Madison. Jim had a long and productive career, was a friendly and patient teacher and a quiet and unassuming person.

CONTENTS

PREFACE

This second edition of *Principles and Procedures of Statistics* recognizes that statistics is necessary to, and already in use by, an ever-increasing number of disciplines. Statistical principles are independent of subject matter, and procedures used successfully in agriculture and the biological sciences carry over to and work equally well in research areas of industry, government, engineering, medicine, and elsewhere—one might even say everywhere where research is in progress. Universities and colleges now generally recognize this fact and one or more courses in statistics are being required for many advanced degrees. The rapid expansion in the teaching of statistics at the undergraduate level is also associated with a statistical requirement in more and more undergraduate curricula. This extraordinary growth in the use of statistics has been paralleled to some extent by a rapid development in statistical procedures, some of which are dealt with in this edition. Others are beyond its level of teaching. Trends such as expansion in the use of statistics and growth in the body of methods explain why, after a vigorous and successful life of twenty years, the original edition of *Principles and Procedures of Statistics* must yield to an updated, reorganized, and expanded second edition.

Basic tenets of both editions are identical: an essentially nonmathematical approach, because algebraic manipulation seems to engender fears in some students; experimental design and analysis introduced as early as feasible so that students and professional workers in research facilities can apply statistical methods while still in the process of learning them; and incorporation of enough techniques to meet the needs of most research workers.

This edition is approximately 200 pages larger than the first. Obviously, it has more to cover. Among other things, it takes into account comments and suggestions made over the years relative to the first edition. One much-repeated comment was addressed to the language of that text, maintaining that it was difficult because it was too concise. The author has gone over the book word by word and paragraph by paragraph in a concentrated effort to expand the explanatory aspect and thereby simplify the content.

Many new techniques have been added, some of which are discussed briefly and others at greater length. Among new multiple comparisons procedures are Fisher's protected lsd, Scheffé's test, and the Waller-Duncan Bayesian k-ratio t test; the very useful indicator variables are treated briefly but adequately; Satterthwaite's procedure for computing quasi F tests is explained carefully in one place and demonstrated in several others; orthogonal polynomials are used to produce response surface equations in factorial experiments; and Chapter 24, on nonparametric statistics, now includes the Kolmogorov-Smirnov one- and two-sample tests of goodness of fit.

Modernizations of standard techniques have not been neglected. Split-plots in time are considered as examples of split block designs. Chapter 14, on multiple regression, is in matrix notation, the modern approach that necessitates the interpretation of printouts resulting from computer technology. Matrix notation is introduced in the two preceding chapters: Chapter 12, on definitions and operating procedures, is intended to encourage the user of statistical computing packages to acquire greater understanding in working with accompanying printouts; Chapter 13, on linear regression in matrix presentation, parallels the usual approach as developed in a still earlier chapter. This chapter helps the reader make the transition to matrix notation; and the analysis of disproportionate subclass number data is related to multiple regression and computer printouts.

Reorganization of material in the first edition is also an improvement. For instance, discussion of the binomial distribution appears as early as Chapter 2, where it helps to introduce the normal distribution; discussion of a linear function and its mean and variance have been moved forward so that it can be related to the comparison of two means, whether from dependent or independent samples; materials on contrasts and multiple comparisons are gathered together in a new Chapter 8, where error rates are carefully defined and guidelines and warnings provided against the confusion of too much testing; Chapter 9 benefits from an improved discussion of the method for determining the appropriate size of an experiment; and Chapter 24 gives a more orderly presentation of nonparametric statistics.

Consideration has been given to alternative presentations, such as, for example, a more relevant treatment of the use of variance components in planning experiments with relative costs considered; a more adequate handling of intraclass correlations; a better approach—one neglected in the first edition—to contingency tables by making use of models.

Finally, in response to many requests and suggestions, the selection of exercises has been greatly increased and includes data from a much wider range of the biological sciences. In addition, data from a number of sociological studies are included. For one set of before-and-after data, analyses proposed include treatment as two sets of data, as a problem in regression, and as a split block design.

The authors are indebted to Professor Sir Ronald A. Fisher, Cambridge, to Dr. Frank Yates, Rothamsted, and Messrs. Oliver and Boyd, Ltd., Edinburgh, for permission to reprint Table III from their book "Statistical Tables for Biological, Agricultural, and Medical Research."

The authors are also indebted to Fred Gruenberger and the Numerical Analysis Laboratory of the University of Wisconsin for preparing Table A.1; to E. S. Pearson and H. O. Hartley, editors of *Biometrika Tables for Statisticians*, vol. I, and to the *Biometrika* office for permission to reprint Tables A.2, A.6, A.8, and A.15; to C. M. Thompson and the *Biometrika* office for permission to reprint Table A.5; to D. B. Duncan and the editor of *Biometrics* for permission to reprint Table A.7; to C. W. Dunnett and the editor of the *Journal of the American Statistical Association* for permission to reprint Table A.9; to C. I. Bliss for permission to reprint Table A.10; to F. N. David and the *Biometrika* office for permission to reprint Table A.11; to L. M. Milne-Thomson and L. J. Comrie, authors of *Standard Four-figure Mathematical Tables*, and MacMillan and Co. Ltd., London, for permission to reprint Table A.12; to G. W. Snedecor, author of *Statistical Methods*, 4th edition, and the Iowa State College Press for permission to reprint Table A.13; to D. Mainland, L. Herrera, and M. I. Sutcliffe for permission to reprint Table A.14; to F. Mosteller and J. W. Tukey, the editor of the *Journal of the American Statistical Association*, and the Codex Book Company, Inc., for permission to reprint Table A.16; to Prasert Na Nagara for permission to reprint Table A.17; to Frank Wilcoxon and the American Cyanamid Company for permission to reprint Table A.18; to Colin White and the editor of *Biometrics* for permission to reprint Table A.19; to P. S. Olmstead, J. W. Tukey, the Bell Telephone Laboratories, and the editor of the *Annals of Mathematical Statistics* for permission to reprint Table A.20; to D. B. Duncan for permission to reprint Table A.21; to L. H. Miller and the editor of the *Journal of the American Statistical Association* for permission to reprint Table A.22; to Z. W. Birnbaum, R. A. Hall, and the editor of the *Annals of Mathematical Statistics* for permission to reprint Table A.23.

I would particularly like to thank Wyman Nyquist for his valued criticism of the first edition and the manuscript of the revision.

In addition, I am indebted to many colleagues for their suggestions about various topics, to others for their generous permission to use data, and to those individuals who helped with various aspects leading to the preparation of the manuscript. I would have been at a loss without the skills of Dorothy Green who typed, cut, and pasted the final manuscript. Lastly, I wish to thank my wife, Jennie, for her careful proofreading and editing.

Robert G. D. Steel

SELECTED SYMBOLS

$\neq$	not equal to; e.g., $3 \neq 4$
$>$	greater than; e.g., $5 > 2$
$\geq$	greater than or equal to
$<$	less than; e.g., $3 < 7$
$\leq$	less than or equal to
$\vert \ \vert$	absolute value; e.g., $\vert -7 \vert = 7$
$\sum$	sum of
$\ldots$	indicates a set of obvious missing quantities, e.g., $1, 2, \ldots, 10$
$n!$	$n(n-1)\ldots 1$ and called n factorial; e.g., $3! = 3(2)\,1 = 6$
$\bar{\ }$	overbar; used to indicate an arithmetic average or mean
$\hat{\ }$	hat; used to indicate an estimate rather than a true value; most often appears over Greek letters

Greek letters	with few exceptions refer to population parameters
μ	population mean
σ^2, σ	population variance and standard deviation
τ, β, etc.	components of population means; commonly used in conjunction with linear models
ε	a true experimental error
δ	a true sampling error; a true difference
β	population regression coefficient, block effect
ρ	population correlation coefficient
N, S^2	these Latin letters are used as finite population symbols, primarily in Chap. 25

The preceding Greek letters are also used with subscripts where clarity requires. For example:

$\mu_{\bar{Y}}$	mean of a population of $\bar{Y}$'s
$\beta_{YX \cdot Z}$	regression of Y on X for fixed Z
τ_i	a contribution to the mean of the population receiving the ith treatment

Some exceptions to the use of Greek letters for parameters are:

α	probability of a Type I error
$1 - \alpha$	confidence coefficient
β	probability of a Type II error
$1 - \beta$	power of a statistical test
χ^2	common test criterion

Latin letters	used as general symbols, including symbols for sample statistics
Y	a variable
Y_i, Y_{ij}	individual observations
$Y_{i\cdot}$, $Y_{\cdot\cdot}$	totals of observations
D_j	difference between paired observations, $Y_{1j} - Y_{2j}$
n, $n_{\cdot\cdot}$	total sample size
n_{ij}	number of observations in i, jth cell
$\bar{Y}$, $\bar{Y}_{\cdot\cdot}$, $\bar{Y}_{i\cdot}$	sample means, whole or part of sample
$\bar{\bar{Y}}$	mean of sample means
s^2, $s_{\bar{Y}}^2$, $s_{\bar{D}}^2$	sample variances, unbiased estimators of σ^2, $\sigma_{\bar{Y}}^2$, and $\sigma_{\bar{D}}^2$
s, $s_{\bar{Y}}$, $s_{\bar{D}}$	sample standard deviations
$s_{Y \cdot X}^2$, $s_{Y \cdot 1 \cdots k}^2$	sample variances adjusted for regression
CL, CI	confidence limits or interval
l_1, l_2	end points of confidence limits
b	sample regression coefficient
$b_{Y1 \cdot 2 \cdots k}$	sample partial regression coefficient
b'	standard regression coefficient
r	sample total or simple correlation coefficient
$r_{12 \cdot 3 \cdots k}$	sample partial correlation coefficient of X_1 and X_2
$R_{1 \cdot 2 \cdots k}$	multiple correlation coefficient between X_1 and the other variables
df, f	degrees of freedom
C, CT	correction term
SS	$\sum (Y_i - \bar{Y})^2$, sum of squares
MS	mean square
E_a, E_b	error mean squares for split-plot design

E_{YY}, E_{XY}, E_{XX}	error sums of products in covariance (other letters used for other sources of variation)
*	significant, e.g., 2.3*
**	highly significant, e.g., 14.37**
ns	not significant
lsd	least significant difference
RE	relative efficiency
CV	coefficient of variability $(s/\bar{Y})100$
$L = \sum c_i Y_i$	a linear function of observations, c_i is a constant
$Q = \sum c_i Y_i$	a comparison where c_i is a constant, Y_i is often a treatment total, and $\sum c_i = 0$
fpc	finite population correction
psu	primary sampling unit
st	stratified, used as subscript
P	probability
$p, 1 - p$	probabilities in a binomial distribution
H_0	null hypothesis
H_1	alternate hypothesis, usually a set of alternatives
∞	infinity

CHAPTER
ONE
INTRODUCTION

1.1 Statistics Defined

Modern statistics provides research workers with knowledge. It is a young and exciting subject, a product of the twentieth century. For the scientist, particularly the biological scientist, statistics began about 1925 when Fisher's *Statistical Methods for Research Workers* appeared.

Statistics is a rapidly growing subject with much original material still not available in texts. It grows as statisticians find answers to more and more of the problems posed by research workers. Those who were among the earliest contributors to statistics are still productive and newcomers find diverse opportunities for their research talents. In the application of statistics, principles are general even though techniques may differ, and the need for training in statistics grows as increased application is made in the biological and social sciences, engineering, and industry.

This young, vigorous subject affects every aspect of modern living. For example, statistical planning and evaluation of research aid technological advances in growing and processing food; statistical quality control of manufactured products makes automotive and electric equipment reliable. Statistics helps pollsters collect data to determine the entertainment preferences of the public; it furnishes information for environmental impact studies; and it assists in evaluation of governmental requirements that the drug industry prove a product beneficial rather than simply harmless. More and more, research teams have, or have access to, a statistician.

The extent of statistics makes it difficult to define. It was developed to deal with problems in which, for the individual observations, laws of cause and effect are not apparent to the observer and where an objective approach is needed. In such problems, there must always be some uncertainty about any inference based on a limited number of observations. Hence, for our purposes, a reasonably satisfactory definition would be: *Statistics is the science, pure and applied, of creating, developing, and applying techniques such that the uncertainty of inductive inferences may be evaluated.*

To most scientists, statistics is logic or common sense with a strong admixture of arithmetic procedures. The logic supplies the method by which data are to be collected and determines how extensive they are to be; the arithmetic, together with certain numerical tables, yields the material on which to base the inference and measure its uncertainty. The arithmetic is often routine, requiring no special mathematical training for the user. We will not be directly concerned with mathematics although there is hardly an area of this subject which has not provided some usable theory to the statistician.

1.2 Some History of Statistics

A history of statistics throws considerable light on the nature of twentieth-century statistics. Historical perspective is also important in pointing to the needs and pressures which created it.

The term statistics is an old one. Statistics must have started as a state arithmetic to assist a ruler who needed to know the wealth and number of his subjects in order to levy a tax or wage a war. Presumably all cultures that intentionally recorded history also recorded statistics. We know that Caesar Augustus sent out a decree that all the world should be taxed. Consequently he required that all persons report to the nearest statistician—in that day the tax collector. One result of this was that Jesus was born in Bethlehem rather than Nazareth. William the Conqueror ordered a survey of the lands of England for purposes of taxation and military service. This was called the Domesday Book. Such statistics are history.

Several centuries after the Domesday Book, we find an application of empirical probability in ship insurance, which seems to have been available to Flemish shipping in the fourteenth century. This can have been little more than speculation or gambling, but it developed into the very respectable form of statistics called insurance.

Gambling, in the form of games of chance, led to the theory of probability originated by Pascal and Fermat, about the middle of the seventeenth century, because of their interest in the gambling experiences of the Chevalier de Méré. To the statistician and the experimental scientist, the theory contains much of practical use for the processing of data.

The normal curve or normal curve of error has been very important in the development of statistics. The equation of this curve was first published in 1733 by de Moivre. De Moivre had no idea of applying his results to experimental observations and his paper remained unknown until Karl Pearson found it in a library in 1924. However, the same result was later developed by two mathematical astronomers, Laplace, 1749–1827, and Gauss, 1777–1855, independently of one another.

An essentially statistical argument was applied in the nineteenth century by Charles Lyell to a geological problem. In the period 1830–1833, there appeared three volumes of *Principles of Geology* by Lyell, who established the order among the Tertiary rocks and assigned names to them. With M. Deshayes, a French conchologist, he identified and listed fossil species occurring in one or more strata and also ascertained the proportions still living in certain parts of the seas. On the basis of these proportions he assigned the names Pleistocene (most recent), Pliocene (majority recent), Miocene (minority recent), and Eocene (dawn of the recent). Lyell's argument was essentially a statistical one. With the establishment and acceptance of the names, the method was almost immediately forgotten. There were no geological evolutionists to wonder if discrete steps, as implied by the names, were involved or if a continuous process was present and could be used to make predictions.

Other scientific discoveries of the nineteenth century were also made on a statistical basis with little appreciation of the statistical nature of the technique and with the method unfortunately soon forgotten. This is true in both the biological and physical sciences.

Charles Darwin, 1809–1882, biologist, received the second volume of Lyell's book while on the *Beagle*. Darwin formed his theories later and he may have been stimulated by his reading of this book. Darwin's work was largely biometrical or statistical in nature and he certainly renewed enthusiasm in biology. Mendel, too, with his studies of plant hybrids published in 1866, had a biometrical or statistical problem.

In the nineteenth century, the need for a sounder basis for statistics became apparent. Karl Pearson, 1857–1936, initially a mathematical physicist, applied his mathematics to evolution as a result of the enthusiasm in biology engendered by Darwin. Pearson spent nearly half a century in serious statistical research. In addition, he founded the journal *Biometrika* and a school of statistics. The study of statistics gained impetus.

While Pearson was concerned with large samples, large-sample theory was proving somewhat inadequate for experimenters with necessarily small samples. Among these was W. S. Gosset, 1876–1937, a student of Karl Pearson and a scientist of the Guinness firm of brewers. Gosset's mathematics appears to have been insufficient to the task of finding exact distributions of the sample standard deviation, of the ratio of the sample mean to the sample standard deviation, and of the correlation coefficient, statistics with which he was particularly concerned. Consequently he resorted to drawing shuffled cards, computing, and compiling empirical frequency distributions. Papers on the results appeared in *Biometrika* in 1908 under the name of Student, Gosset's pseudonym while with Guinness. Today Student's t is a basic tool of statisticians and experimenters, and studentize is a common expression in statistics. Now that the use of Student's t distribution is so widespread, it is interesting to note that the German astronomer, Helmert, had obtained it mathematically as early as 1875.

R. A. Fisher, 1890–1962, was influenced by Karl Pearson and Student and made numerous and important contributions to statistics. He and his students gave considerable impetus to the use of statistical procedures in many fields, particularly in agriculture, biology, and genetics.

J. Neyman, 1894–   , and E. S. Pearson, 1895–   , presented a theory of testing statistical hypotheses in 1936 and 1938. This theory promoted considerable research and many of the results are of practical use.

In this brief history, we will mention only one other statistician, Abraham Wald, 1902–1950. His two books, *Sequential Analysis* and *Statistical Decision Functions*, are concerned with great statistical achievements not treated in this text, although one application, the minimax solution for a problem in genetics, is illustrated in Chap. 21.

It is in this century then that most of the statistical methods presently used have been developed. The statistics of this text is a part of these methods.

1.3 Statistics and the Scientific Method

It is said that scientists use scientific method. It would be difficult to define scientific method, since scientists use any methods or means which they can conceive. However, most of these methods have essential features in common. Without intending to promote a controversy, let us consider that these are

1. A review of facts, theories, and proposals
2. Formulation of a logical hypothesis subject to testing by experimental methods
3. Objective evaluation of the hypothesis on the basis of the experimental results

Much could be written about these essential features. How does one arrive at a hypothesis? How does one design an experiment? How does one objectively evaluate a hypothesis?

Science is a branch of study which deals with the observation and classification of facts. The scientist must, then, be able to observe an event or set of events as the result of a plan or design. This is the experiment, the substance of the scientific method. Experimental design is a field of statistics.

Objective evaluation of a hypothesis poses problems. It is not possible to observe all conceivable events, and since exact laws of cause and effect are generally unknown, variation will exist among those which are observed. The scientist must then reason from particular cases to wider generalities. This process is one of uncertain inference. It is a process which enables us to disprove hypotheses that are incorrect but does not permit us to prove hypotheses that are correct. The only thing we can muster by way of proof is *proof beyond a reasonable doubt*. Statistical procedures are methods which lead us to this sort of proof.

A part of the possible information necessarily leads only to uncertain inference. Chance is involved in supplying the information and is the cause of the uncertainty. Today's statistician, applying the laws of chance, is able to place a precise and objective measure on the uncertainty of inferences. Actually, this is done for the totality of inferences rather than for the individual inference. In other words, a procedure is followed that assures that 9 inferences out of 10 will be correct, or 99 out of 100, or anything short of all being correct. Why not be right all or very close to all the time? The drawback is one of cost. Cost may rise because of an increase in sample size, the penalty of a wrong decision, or the vagueness of the inference necessary to include the correct answer.

Scientific method is not disjoint hypothesis-experiment-inference sequences which fit into neat compartments. Instead, if a scientist fails to disprove a hypothesis, perhaps the theory may embrace facts beyond the scope of inference of the experiment or, with modification, it may be made to embrace such facts. The cycle is then repeated. On the other hand, all the assumptions involved in the hypothesis may not be necessary; a new hypothesis is formulated with fewer assumptions and the cycle is repeated.

In summary, statistics is a tool applicable in scientific method, for which it was developed. Its particular application lies in the many aspects of the design of an experiment from the initial planning to the collection of the data, and in the analysis of the results from the summarizing of the data to the evaluation of the uncertainty of any statistical inference drawn from them.

1.4 Studying Statistics

No attempt will be made to make professional statisticians of those who read and study this book. Our aims are to promote clear, disciplined thinking, especially where the collection and interpretation of numerical data are concerned, and to present a considerable number of statistical techniques of general applicability and utility in research. Computations are required in statistics but this is arithmetic, not mathematics nor statistics.

Statistics implies, for most students, a new way of thinking—thinking in terms of uncertainties or improbabilities. Here as elsewhere, students vary in ability and when confronted with statistics for the first time, some may find a mental hurdle which can be emotionally upsetting. We believe we have done everything possible, consistent with our aims, to minimize the problems of learning statistics.

Many students will find that they learn statistics best by direct application to their own problems; few will find, in a course of one or two terms, use for all the material presented. Consequently, many students will need considerable reflection and discussion in order to benefit most from a course based on this text. Questions and exercises are provided to provoke reflection and to offer some opportunity to apply and gain familiarity with techniques.

Finally, it is necessary to keep in mind that statistics is intended to be a tool for research. The research will be in genetics, marketing, nutrition, agronomy, and so on. It is the field of research, not the tools, that must supply the "whys" of the research problem. This fact is sometimes overlooked and users are tempted to forget that they have to think, that statistics cannot think for them. Statistics can, however, help research workers design experiments and evaluate objectively the resulting numerical data. It is our intention to supply research workers with statistical tools that will be useful for this purpose.

References

1.1. Box, Joan Fisher: *R. A. Fisher, The life of a scientist*, Wiley, New York, 1978.

1.2. Committee of Presidents of Statistical Societies: *Careers in statistics*, current edition, American Statistical Association, Washington, D.C.

1.3. Eisenhart, Churchill: "Anniversaries in 1965 of interest to statisticians," *Amer. Statist.*, **19:**21–29 (1965).

1.4. Eisenhart, Churchill, and Allan Birnbaum: "Anniversaries in 1966–67 of interest to statisticians," *Amer. Statist.*, **21:**22–29 (1967).

1.5. Fisher, R. A.: "Biometry," *Biom.*, **4:**217–219 (1948).

1.6. Fisher, R. A.: "The expansion of statistics," *J. Roy. Statist. Soc., Ser. A.*, **116:**1–6 (1953).

1.7. Fisher, R. A.: "The expansion of statistics," *Amer. Sci.*, **42:**275–282 and 293 (1954).

1.8. Freeman, Linton C., and Douglas M. More: "Teaching introductory statistics in the liberal arts curriculum," *Amer. Statist.*, **10:**20–21 (1956).

1.9. Hotelling, Harold: "The teaching of statistics," *Ann. Math. Statist.*, **11:**1–14 (1940).

1.10. Hotelling, Harold: "The impact of R. A. Fisher on statistics," *J. Amer. Statist. Ass.*, **46:**35–46 (1951).

1.11. Hotelling, Harold: "Abraham Wald," *Amer. Statist.*, **5:**18–19 (1951).

1.12. Hotelling, Harold: "The statistical method and the philosophy of science," *Amer. Statist.*, **12:**9–14 (1958).

1.13. McMullen, Launce: Foreword, in E. S. Pearson and John Wishart (eds.), "*Student's*" *collected papers, Biometrika* Office, University College, London, 1947.

1.14. Mahalanobis, P. C.: "Professor Ronald Aylmer Fisher," *Sankhya*, **4:**265–272 (1938).

1.15. Mainland, Donald: "Statistics in clinical research; some general principles," *Ann. N.Y. Acad. Sci.*, **52:**922–930 (1950).

1.16. Mather, Kenneth: "R. A. Fisher's *Statistical Methods for Research Workers*, an appreciation," *J. Amer. Statist. Ass.*, **46:**51–54 (1951).

1.17. Menger, Karl: "The formative years of Abraham Wald and his work in geometry," *Ann. Math. Statist.*, **23:** 13–20 (1952).
1.18. Pearson, E. S.: "Karl Pearson, an appreciation of some aspects of his life and work, part I: 1857–1906," *Biometrika*, **28:** 193–257 (1936).
1.19. Pearson, E. S.: "Karl Pearson, an appreciation of some aspects of his life and work, part II: 1906–1936," *Biometrika*, **29:** 161–248 (1938).
1.20. Reid, R. D.: "Statistics in clinical research," *Ann. N.Y. Acad. Sci.*, **52:** 931–934 (1950).
1.21. Tintner, G.: "Abraham Wald's contributions to econometrics," *Ann. Math. Statist.*, **23:** 21–28 (1952).
1.22. Walker, Helen M.: "Bi-centenary of the normal curve," *J. Amer. Statist. Ass.*, **29:** 72–75 (1934).
1.23. Walker, Helen M.: "Statistical literacy in the social sciences," *Amer. Statist.*, **5:** 6–12 (1951).
1.24. Walker, Helen M.: "The contributions of Karl Pearson," *J. Amer. Statist. Ass.*, **53:** 11–27 (1958).
1.25. Wolfowitz, J.: "Abraham Wald, 1902–1950," *Ann. Math. Statist.* **23:** 1–13 (1952).
1.26. Yates, F.: "The influence of *Statistical Methods for Research Workers* on the development of the science of statistics," *J. Amer. Statist. Ass.*, **46:** 19–34 (1951).
1.27. Youden, W. J.: "The Fisherian revolution in methods of experimentation," *J. Amer. Statist. Ass.*, **46:** 47–50 (1951).

CHAPTER

TWO

OBSERVATIONS

2.1 Introduction

Observations are the raw materials with which research workers deal. For statistics to be applicable to these observations, they must be in the form of numbers. In crop improvement, numbers may be plot yields; in medical research, they may be times to recovery under various treatments; in industry, they may be amount of defects in various lots of a product produced on an assembly-line basis. Such numbers constitute *data* and their common characteristic is *variability* or *variation.*

This chapter is concerned with the collection, presentation, summarization, and characterization of data. Populations, samples, a linear model, and a statistical inference are discussed.

2.2 Variables

Statements such as "Marcia is blonde," or "He weighs well over 200 pounds" are common and informative. They refer to characteristics which are not constant but which vary from individual to individual and thus serve to distinguish or describe.

Characteristics which show variability or variation are called *variables*, *chance variables*, or *random variables*.

Since much of our discussion must be general, we employ some symbols. Instead of writing variable each time, let Y denote the variable and let Y_i

(read as Y sub i) denote the ith observation. Here we have no particular observation in mind. When the time comes to refer to a specific observation, we replace i by a number. For example, if three children in a family have weights of 52, 29, and 28 lb and Y denotes weight, $Y_1 = 52$ lb, $Y_2 = 29$ lb, and $Y_3 = 28$ lb. In more general and abstract terms, denote a set of observations by $Y_1, Y_2, \ldots, Y_n$. Here Y_n refers to the last term, the subscript n informs us of the total number, and the three periods between Y_2 and Y_n refer to the other observations, if any. In our example, $n = 3$. The symbols are seen to be a shorthand.

Variables may be either *quantitative* or *qualitative.*

A quantitative variable is one for which the resulting observations can be measured because they possess a natural order or ranking. Examples are heights, weights, and number of heads that appear when 10 coins are tossed.

Observations on quantitative variables may be further classified as *continuous* or *discrete.*

A continuous variable is one for which all values in some range are possible. Height and weight are obvious examples. Height may be measured to the nearest 1/4 in, but this is not to say that heights exist only for 1/4-in values. We are limited by the measuring device in obtaining values of a continuous variable.

A discrete or discontinuous variable is one for which the possible values are not observed on a continuous scale because of the existence of gaps between possible values. Often discrete observations are integers because they arise from counting. Examples are the number of petals on a flower, the number of householders in a city block, and the number of insects caught in the sweep of a net. However, the step between successive possibilities may be other than unity. The average number of dots appearing on two dice is also a discrete variable; here the possible values go from 1 to 6 by increases of one-half.

A qualitative variable is one for which numerical measurement is not possible. An observation is made when an individual is assigned to one of several mutually exclusive (it cannot be in more than one) categories. Observations can be neither meaningfully ordered nor measured, only classified and then enumerated.

Exercise 2.2.1 Classify the following variables as quantitative, qualitative, continuous, discrete: eye color, insect counts, number of errors per pupil in a spelling test, tire-miles to first puncture, times between refills of a fountain pen permitted to run dry under normal use, possible yields of corn from a given field, number of children born in the nearest hospital on New Year's Day, possible outcomes from tossing 50 coins, number of fish in a pond.

Exercise 2.2.2 In 10 tosses of 7 coins, the numbers of heads were 2, 6, 2, 2, 5, 3, 5, 3, 3, 4. If the observations are denoted by $Y_1, Y_2, \ldots, Y_n$, what is the value of n? What is the value of Y_2? Of Y_7? For what values of i does Y equal 2? 3? 4? Distinguish between Y_{i-1} and $Y_i - 1$. What do Y_{i-1} and $Y_i - 1$ equal for $i = 2$?

2.3 Distributions

Values of a variable serve to describe or classify individuals or to distinguish among them. Most of us do more than simply describe, classify, or distinguish because we have ideas about the *relative frequencies* of the values of a variable. Thus, in Minnesota, blondeness is not a rare value for a person's complexion; most people would not put much credence in stories about a 65-lb house cat; a baby that weighed 7 1/2 lb at birth would be considered ordinary to other than his family. One's mind associates a measure with the value of a variable, a measure of its ordinariness or lack of it, or of the probability of the occurrence of such a value. In statistics we say that the variable has a *probability function*, a *probability density function*, or, simply, a *density function*. Thus, for a fair coin, the probability of its falling heads is the same as that for tails, namely, 1/2; this is a statement of the probability density function of a discrete variable. The statement that a certain percentage of adult weights is less than a stated value becomes a *cumulative probability distribution* or, simply, a *distribution function* for a continuous variable when we have the percentages for each and every weight. The terms "chance" and "random variable" are used more particularly for variables possessing probability density functions.

Whereas the closely related terms density function and distribution function are well defined, we tend to use simply the term *distribution* to mean either one or the other as convenience dictates.

The notion of chance or randomness has not been defined. We have merely implied that the laws of chance are applicable. Randomness is discussed further in the next section.

Exercise 2.3.1 From your experience, classify the following events as occurring with high, medium, or low relative frequency: a 2-lb baby; a 6-ft 8-in basketball player; a nighttime low temperature of 0°C at least once in October for your locality; a 115-lb female college freshman; a run of 5 heads in 5 tosses of a coin; a 3,400-lb horse; 27 heads in 50 tosses of a coin.

Exercise 2.3.2 If a thumbtack is tossed, will it land on its head as often as not? In your experience, is a busy signal on the telephone likely to occur as often as 1 time in 10 calls to 10 different people? What percentage of a college freshman class do you expect to be in the sophomore class in the following year? To complete a degree program in the same institution?

(After thinking about Exercises 2.3.1 and 2.3.2, you should realize that the idea of distributions, of their means and of their variability, is not entirely new to you.)

2.4 Populations and Samples

The individual's first concern with a body of data is whether it is to be considered as all possible data or as part of a larger body. It is of great importance and failure to make a clear distinction has resulted in loose thinking and in ambiguous notation in some writings.

A *population* or *universe* consists of all possible values of a variable. These values need not all be different nor finite in number. Examples are the birth weights of pigs in one litter, the number of heads for each of 500 tosses of 10 coins, all possible values of corn yield per acre in Iowa. The variable may be continuous or discrete, observable or unobservable. When all values of a population are known it is possible to describe it without ambiguity since all is known about it.

A *sample* is a part of a population. (In some situations, a sample may include the whole of the population.) Usually, the intention is to use sample information to make an inference about a population. For this reason, it is particularly important to define the population under discussion and to obtain a representative sample from the population defined. This is not a trivial point.

The birth weights of pigs in a litter and the number of heads for each of 500 tosses of 10 coins may both be samples from indefinitely large populations and there is usually more value in considering them as samples than as populations.

A sample must be representative of the population if it is to lead to valid inferences. To obtain a representative sample, we embody in the rules for drawing the sample items the principle of randomness. *Randomness* is the result of a mechanical process intended to ensure that individual biases, either known or unknown in nature, do not influence the selection of sample observations. As a consequence, the laws of probability apply and can be used in drawing inferences. In conducting a public opinion poll, conclusions meant to be applicable to the population of American adults would rarely be valid if the sample were so nonrandom as to include only women or only New Englanders. Throughout this text, the word sample will imply a random sample. Illustrations of the randomization procedure will be given as we proceed.

Exercise 2.4.1 Would you object to regarding the following samples as from possibly infinite populations? A sample of 1,000 herring weights taken from the Grand Banks? A sample of 20 body lengths of killer whales? A sample of 200 households in Madison, Wisconsin? A sample of 25 tins of canned peas from a single shipment to a local supermarket? A sample of 10 cc of blood from an adult person? Explain.

Exercise 2.4.2 Would you regard the following as random samples? A day's trout catch from a moderate-sized lake? A day's catch of squirrels in baited traps. Write-in responses to a political pronouncement as requested by a TV advertisement? A botanist's "authoritative" sample of field vegetation? Explain.

2.5 Random Samples; the Collection of Data

It has been amply demonstrated that the individual cannot draw a random sample without the use of a mechanical process. The mechanical process used to obtain a random sample or to introduce randomness into an experiment or survey usually involves a table of random numbers such as Table A.1. This table consists of the digits 0, 1, 2, ..., 9 arranged in a 100 by 100 table; there are 10,000 random digits. They were turned out by a machine and there was no reason to expect any one number to appear more often than another nor any sequence of numbers more often than another, except by chance. There are 1,015 0s, 1,026 1s, 1,013 2s, 975 3s, 976 4s, 932 5s, 1,067 6s, 1,013 7s, 1,023 8s, 960 9s; 5,094 are even and 4,906 are odd. We will illustrate the use of this table by drawing a random sample of 10 observations from Table 4.1. The data of Table 4.1 have been ranked according to magnitude and assigned item numbers. Ranking is unnecessary for drawing random samples; item numbers could have been assigned in an arbitrary fashion.

To obtain a random sample of 10 weights, draw 20 consecutive digits from Table A.1 and record them as 10 pairs. These will be item numbers corresponding to weights. You may start anywhere in the table, but a more satisfactory way is to poke at one of the pages, read the four numbers most nearly opposite your finger tip, and use these to locate a starting point. Thus,

1. On the first page of Table A.1, my finger finds 1188 (opposite 10 and the first four digits under 20–24).
2. I go to row number 11, column number 88 as starting point.
3. I record the 20 digits, in pairs, that I find by moving to the right. They are 06, 17, 22, 84, 44, 55; for convenience, I drop one line and proceed in reverse to obtain the others, namely, 09, 15, 30, 59.
4. I take these item numbers to Table 4.1 and obtain the corresponding observations: 20, 30, 32, 51, 39, 41, 25, 29, 35, and 42 lb.

This is a random procedure, equivalent to drawing from a bag of 100 beans marked with the 100 butterfat yields, each bean being replaced in the bag and the beans being thoroughly mixed before each draw. For this reason, sampling is said to be *with replacement*. Note that each item may be drawn any number of times from 0 to 10. Sampling is always from the same population and the probability of drawing any item is practically the same. Either procedure gives the same results as if the drawings were made from an infinitely large population.

A sample drawn in this way is a *completely random* sample. In experimental work and in sample surveys there are often valid reasons for restricting randomness to some degree. The use of restrictions will be discussed in later chapters.

Exercise 2.5.1 Suppose that your population has only 50 items. How might you use the random number table to obtain a sample of 10 observations with replacement? Can you suggest an alternate scheme?

Exercise 2.5.2 Suppose that your population has 40 items. How might you draw a sample of 5 observations? Remember that each item should have the same chance of being chosen for the sample.

Exercise 2.5.3 Suppose that your population has 75 items. How might you draw a sample of 10 observations?

Exercise 2.5.4 Suppose that your population has only 40 items and you wish to draw a sample of five observations *without* replacement. How should you proceed?

Exercise 2.5.5 If you have a large field of corn planted in rows and wish to draw a sample of individual plants, how might you go about selection? Can you think of an alternate plan?

Exercise 2.5.6 If you wish to sample the flora in a marsh by looking at areas of one square yard, how might you select your sample?

Exercise 2.5.7 How would you draw a completely random sample of, say, 100 phone numbers from a phone book? Can you think of a two-stage scheme that would involve less effort?

Exercise 2.5.8 In drawing a sample of 100 from a large population containing as many men as women, would you recommend a completely random sample or one with 50 men and 50 women? (What are the objectives of your sampling?)

Exercise 2.5.9 In describing the process of drawing a random sample using Table A.1, it was stated that "the probability of drawing any item is practically the same." Why is the word "practically" used?

2.6 Presentation, Summarization, and Characterization of Data

There are many ways of presenting data, including use of tables, charts, and pictures.

For qualitative data, enumeration is a common way to summarize and present the results. If a small town makes a survey of modes of transportation, the results might be summarized and presented as percentages. To catch the eye, a pie chart (Fig. 2.1) is useful.

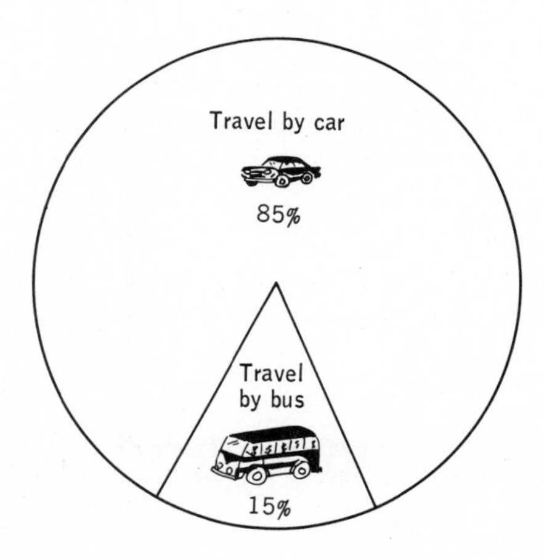

Figure 2.1 Car versus bus, Ourtown, population 17,000.

Such devices as pie and bar charts show information about how you spend your time and your dollar and where your taxes go. They are concise, informative, and easy to read and comprehend, and they often convey information quite dramatically. They are certainly more eye catching than frequency tables listing numbers of people, insects, etc., possessing certain characteristics. Unfortunately, they may not be reliable. For example, Fig. 2.1 may be based on a sample or a census, with respect to miles traveled or number of trips. The possibilities of deceiving the unwary are obvious.

Charts may give actual numbers or percentages. Figure 2.2 illustrates the use of bars and vertical lines. If no scale is indicated, the reader sees relative frequencies and will be unaware of sample size unless specified. When totals are given, both frequencies and relative frequencies are available and can be presented by use of two scales. Relative frequencies or proportions are essentially probabilities, implied by a glance at either the bars or columns as a height or an area.

The histogram and frequency polygon of Fig. 2.3 are common methods of presenting a considerable amount of information collected as quantitative data. The *histogram* pictures the data with *class values*, midpoints of class intervals, along the horizontal axis and with rectangles above the class intervals to represent frequencies. The histogram presents data in a readily understandable form such that one sees at a glance the general nature of the distribution. If it is desired to compare an observed distribution with a theoretical distribution, the theoretical one can be superimposed on the histogram and discrepancies ascertained.

The *frequency polygon* is prepared by locating the midpoint of each class interval and marking a point above it at a height determined by the frequency for the interval. These points are then connected by straight lines. The frequency polygon tends to imply the smooth curve of the population

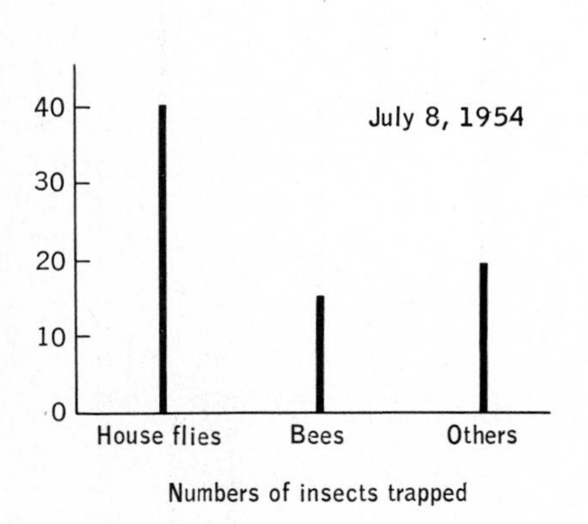

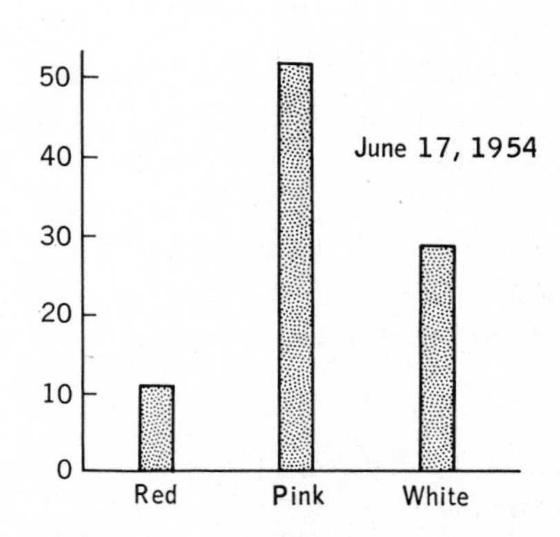

Figure 2.2 Presentation of discrete data.

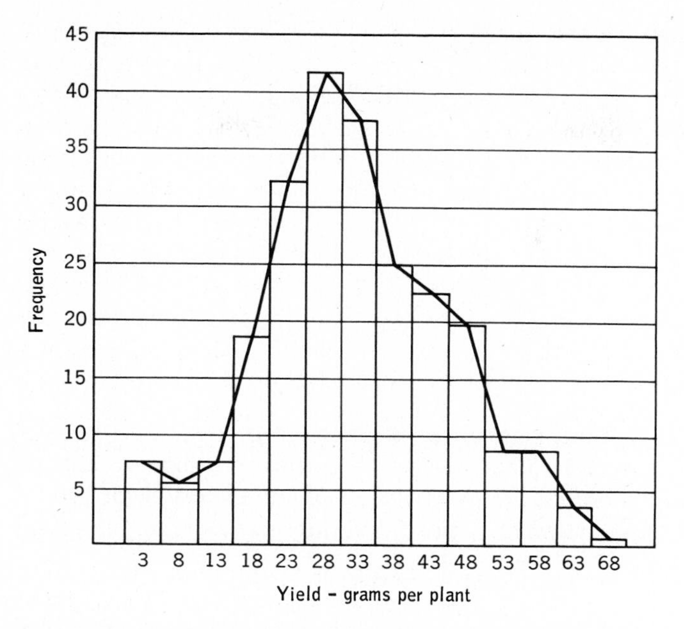

Figure 2.3 Histogram and frequency polygon for the data of Table 2.1.

from which the sample was drawn. The histogram and frequency polygon for the data in Table 2.1 are shown in Fig. 2.3.

It is important in the preparation of both the histogram and frequency polygon that the number of classes be sufficiently large so that the general shape of the distribution can be readily ascertained, yet not so small that too much detail is given.

Finally, data are presented in *frequency tables*. Here there is generally more information for the serious reader but at the expense of a loss in number of readers. Tables 2.1 and 2.2 are examples for continuous and discrete data. Frequency tables are discussed further beginning with Sec. 2.15.

Charts and graphs often summarize and characterize data, but this may also be done by presenting several numbers as a summary and characterization of the data. In particular, we refer to a number locating the center and one measuring the spread of the observations.

Table 2.1 Frequency table for yield of 229 spaced plants of Richland soybeans

Yield in grams	3	8	13	18	23	28	33	38	43	48	53	58	63	68
Frequency	7	5	7	18	32	41	37	25	22	19	6	6	3	1

Table 2.2 Number of heads

Class value	Frequency
5	4
4	15
3	29
2	30
1	17
0	5
Total	100

More generally, some *measure of location* or of *central tendency* is required, that is, a number that locates a central or ordinary value. In addition, a *measure of spread*, of *dispersion*, or of *variation* is needed to tell how far from the central value the more or less extreme values may be found.

Exercise 2.6.1 The "1975 National Survey of Hunting, Fishing and Wildlife-Associated Recreation," conducted by the U.S. Fish and Wildlife Service, surveyed more than 2,000 households by phone and sent questionnaires to at least 1,000 hunters and anglers in every state. Anyone 9 years old or older who hunted or fished on at least one day in 1975 was eligible to participate in the mail survey. Of those residents over 9 years old, 95.9 million participated in some wildlife-related activity. Among the data reported were the following (often approximated from a graphic display):

1. 53 million participated in fishing; 50 million in wildlife observation; 26 million in clamming, crabbing, and shell collecting; 21 million in hunting; 17 million in recreational shooting; 15 million in photography of wild life; and 5 million in archery.
2. In billions of days, the Americans of 1 spent the following time in the same categories, respectively: 1.32, 1.54, .24, .49, .30, .19, .12.
3. Participation by men and women in the same categories was, respectively: 57 percent vs. 43 percent, 48 percent vs. 52 percent, 82 percent vs. 18 percent, 58 percent vs. 42 percent, and 81 percent vs. 19 percent.
4. The average household income of anglers was: Under $5,000, 17 percent; $5,000–$9,999, 17 percent; $10,000–$14,999, 23 percent; $15,000–$24,999, 29 percent; $25,000 or more, 14 percent.
5. The number, in millions, of warm-water anglers by water type, was: 18 in lakes and reservoirs, 17 in lakes and ponds other than the Great Lakes, 14 in streams and rivers, 9 in farm ponds, 3 in tailwaters, and 2 in the Great Lakes.
6. The number in thousands of days of participation in warm water fishing by water type as specified in 5 was, respectively: 279,287, 254,477, 161,427, 93,372, 24,973, and 19,011.
7. The number, in millions, of sea-run anglers by water type was: 2.6 in salt waters, 2.5 in streams and rivers, 2.0 in estuaries, and 1.1 in the Great Lakes.
8. The number in thousands of days participation in sea-run fishing for water type specified in 7 was, respectively: 19,478, 18,606, 16,039, and 6,739.
9. Of big-game hunters hunting in-state, 58.1 percent hunted on private land, 15.9 percent on federal land, 12.5 percent on state wildlife management areas, 2 percent on other state areas, 8 percent on unspecified public lands, and 3.5 percent on lands of unknown ownership.

10. Of big-game hunters hunting out-of-state in the United States, the categories of 9 produced the following percentages, respectively: 37.1 percent, 38.6 percent, 16.6 percent, 1.7 percent, 3.8 percent, and 2.2 percent.

Present each of these 10 sets of data in tabular or graphic form. Try to use a variety of presentations.

Find the 1975 survey and observe the various presentations they have used.

Do you think that the data presented came exclusively from the telephone and questionnaire surveys?

Exercise 2.6.2 Look through a copy of *Fortune*, a company report, an appropriate government publication, and the current volume of a technical journal for ideas on the presentation of data. Is it clear, without reference to the text, whether a sample or a population is involved? Does the presentation involve frequencies or relative frequencies? Is it completely understandable without reference to the text?

Exercise 2.6.3 Compare a copy of a company's annual report with a copy of a technical journal. In which do you find relatively more charts? More tables? Do charts always have a scale on the vertical axis?

Exercise 2.6.4 Prepare a frequency table, relative frequency table, and bar chart for the numbers of integers in Table A.1. See Sect. 2.5.

Exercise 2.6.5 Prepare a frequency table, frequency polygon, and histogram for the data of Table 4.1.

2.7 Measures of Central Tendency

Expressions such as "of average height" are vague but informative. They relate an individual to a central value. When experimenters collect data at some expense in time, energy, and money, they cannot afford to be vague. They want a definite measure of central tendency.

The most common measure of central tendency and the one which is the best in many cases is the *arithmetic mean*, or arithmetic *average*. Since there are other types of means, it must be clear to what mean one refers. The arithmetic mean will be represented by two symbols: μ (the Greek letter *mu*) for a population, and $\bar{Y}$ (read as Y bar) for a sample. It is important to make this distinction, since a population mean is a fixed quantity, not subject to variation, whereas a sample mean is a variable inasmuch as different samples from the same population tend to have different means. Other symbols may be found in statistical writings. The mean is in the same units as the original observations, for example, centimeters, or pounds.

Quantities such as the mean are called *parameters* when they characterize populations and *statistics* in the case of samples.

Consider a die. Its six faces have one, two, three, four, five, and six dots. All possible numbers of dots appearing on the upturned face of a die constitute a finite population. By definition, the parameter

$$\mu = \frac{1 + 2 + 3 + 4 + 5 + 6}{6} = 3\tfrac{1}{2} \text{ dots}$$

If a sample from this population has four observations, say 3, 5, 2, and 2, then by definition, the statistic

$$\bar{Y} = \frac{3 + 5 + 2 + 2}{4} = \frac{12}{4} = 3 \text{ dots}$$

This computation can be symbolized by

$$\bar{Y} = \frac{Y_1 + Y_2 + Y_3 + Y_4}{4}$$

where Y_1 is the value of the first observation, namely, 3; Y_2 is the value of the second; and so on. In the general situation with n observations, Y_i is used to represent the ith and $\bar{Y}$ is given by

$$\bar{Y} = \frac{Y_1 + Y_2 + Y_3 + \cdots + Y_i + \cdots + Y_n}{n}$$

The notation for $\bar{Y}$ is further shortened to

$$\bar{Y} = \frac{\sum_{i=1}^{n} Y_i}{n} \quad \text{or} \quad \frac{\sum_i Y_i}{n} \tag{2.1}$$

This is a sentence with a subject $\bar{Y}$, a verb $=$, and an object $\sum$ (the Greek letter *sigma*, capitalized). The sentence reads "Y bar equals the sum of the Y's divided by n." This is our definition of the sample mean. The letter i, used to tag the ith individual, is called the index of summation and goes from $i = 1$, written under the summation sign $\sum$, to n, written above. The range of summation is from 1 to n. Where all n values are to be summed, 1 and n are usually omitted.

Sample deviations are defined as the signed differences between the observations and the mean, $Y_i - \bar{Y}$. For our example, $Y_1 - \bar{Y} = 3 - 3 = 0$, $Y_2 - \bar{Y} = 2$, $Y_3 - \bar{Y} = -1 = Y_4 - \bar{Y}$.

An interesting property of the arithmetic mean is that the sum of the deviations is zero, that is,

$$\sum (Y_i - \bar{Y}) = 0 \tag{2.2}$$

For the example,

Y_i	$\bar{Y}$	$Y_i - \bar{Y}$
3	3	0
5	3	+2
2	3	−1
2	3	−1

This is a demonstration, not a proof.

Sometimes it is appropriate to weight the observations that are to go into a mean. For example, if there are several means to be averaged and these are based on different numbers of observations, then it is appropriate to use weights that depend on the number of observations in each mean. A *weighted mean* is defined by

$$\bar{Y}_w = \frac{\sum w_i Y_i}{\sum w_i} \tag{2.3}$$

An alternative to the mean as a measure of central tendency is the *median*. It may also be used to supplement the mean. The median is that value for which 50 percent of the observations, when arranged in order of magnitude, lie on each side. If the number of values is even, the median is the average of the two middle values. For example, for the illustration sample 3, 6, 8, and 11, $(6 + 8)/2 = 7$ is the median. Numbers 3, 6, 8, and 30 have the same median. For data distributed more or less symmetrically, the mean and median will differ but slightly. However, where an average of the incomes of a group of individuals is required and most incomes are low, the mean income could be considerably larger than the median income, and quite misleading.

Certain types of data show a tendency to have a pronounced tail to the right or to the left. Such distributions are said to be *skewed* in the direction of the long tail and the arithmetic mean may not be the most informative central value.

Another measure of central tendency is the *mode*, the value of most frequent occurrence.

Other measures of central tendency are averages of certain *quartiles*, *deciles*, and *percentiles*, points which divide distributions of ranked values into quarters, tenths, and hundredths, respectively. For example, 10 percent of the observations are less than the first decile. The median is the 2d quartile, 5th decile, and 50th percentile.

For positive numbers, the geometric mean or harmonic mean may be useful. Their main uses are, respectively, in calculation of relative values such as index numbers and in averaging ratios and rates. They are obtained from equations

$$G = \sqrt[n]{Y_1 Y_2 \cdots Y_n} = (Y_1 Y_2 \cdots Y_n)^{1/n} \tag{2.4}$$

and

$$\frac{1}{H} = \frac{1}{n} \sum_i \left(\frac{1}{Y_i}\right) \tag{2.5}$$

Exercise 2.7.1 A certain instructor asked the girls in his class to estimate his weight. Their responses were: 190, 230, 105, 180, 130, 160, and 170 lb.

Compute the sample mean. What is the sample median?

Exercise 2.7.2 The boys in the class of Exercise 2.7.1 estimated their instructor's weight as: 150, 195, 175, 147, 175, 170, 195, 170, and 190 lb.

Compute the sample mean. What is the sample median?

Exercise 2.7.3 The arithmetic mean may be considered to be a weighted mean where all weights are equal. What are these weights?

Exercise 2.7.4 Suppose that we are given $\bar{Y}_1 = 37$, $\bar{Y}_2 = 41$, and $\bar{Y}_3 = 28$ based on 50, 20, and 10 observations, respectively.

If you are required to choose a single mean as best, what is your choice? Why?

Compute the weighted mean of these means using weights equal to the sample sizes.

What were the three original sample totals? How would you use these to find the arithmetic mean of all 80 observations? Is this the same process as finding the weighted mean with weights equal to sample sizes?

Exercise 2.7.5 One method of sampling fish in a lake is to kill them all by the use of rotenone, collect them in buckets, and then take a random sample of buckets. In one such experiment, a random sample of 2 buckets out of 20 was taken and all fish in each bucket measured for length in inches. The fish were drum. The data were:†

Sample *A* 5 fish of 5 in, 19 of 6, 19 of 7, 8 of 8, and 3 of 9; $n = 54$.

Sample *B* 10 fish of 5 in, 27 of 6, 15 of 7, 6 of 8, and 3 of 9; $n = 61$.

For each sample, compute the mean. What is the modal class for each sample? Did you compute the mean using 54(61) individual observations or as a weighted mean? How many distinct values of the variable are used when computing the weighted mean?

Use the two sample means to compute a weighted mean? Why did you choose the weights you used? Is your weighted mean the same as the arithmetic mean of all 115 lengths?

Exercise 2.7.6 For the sample of Exercise 2.2.2, compute $\bar{Y}$ and all $Y_i - \bar{Y}$'s. Does $\sum (Y_i - \bar{Y}) = 0$?

Exercise 2.7.7 What is the median of the data in Table 2.1? Table 2.2? Table 2.4?

Exercise 2.7.8 Comment on the statement, "Fifty percent of Americans are below-average intelligence."

Exercise 2.7.9 Geometric means are useful in dealing with rates and ratios. If I invest \$100 and have \$120 at the end of the year, and reinvest and have \$144 at the end of the second year, then I have been getting 20 percent on my investment. Clearly the rate of growth is 1.2. The geometric mean is appropriate and is $\sqrt{1.2(1.2)} = 1.2$. Population growth rates, for stable birth and death rates with no migration, give a biological situation where the geometric mean is appropriate. Find an example where the geometric mean is appropriate. Are the values constant or variable? Compute the geometric mean.

Exercise 2.7.10 A company's production of crude oil increased yearly from 1945 to 1955. In 1945, production was 3,250 bbl/day and in 1955, 4,780 bbl/day. What is the geometric mean? For what year would you regard this as an estimate of production?

† Data provided through the courtesy of Don W. Hayne, North Carolina State University.

2.8 Measures of Dispersion

A measure of central tendency provides a partial summary of the information in a set of data. The need for a measure of variation is apparent. Three possible sets of data with a common mean are given here; note how different they are in variability.

8, 8, 9, 10, 11, 12, 12
5, 6, 8, 10, 12, 14, 15
1, 2, 5, 10, 15, 18, 19

The mean, like other measures of central tendency, tells us nothing about variation.

The concept of a measure of spread is a difficult one. How informative is it to say that the three sets of data have spreads 4, 10, and 18, that is, $Y_7 - Y_1$? The second three sets

8, 9, 10, 10, 10, 11, 12
5, 7, 9, 10, 11, 13, 15
1, 5, 8, 10, 12, 15, 19

of data have spreads 4, 10, and 18 also, and the mean is still 10, but the first sets have observations spread more into the tails while in the second three they are concentrated more toward the mean. It seems desirable to have a definition which uses all observations and gives a small value when they cluster closely about a central value and a large one when they are spaced widely.

Consider the numbers

5, 6, 8, 10, 12, 14, 15

By our definition, these are no more variable than the numbers

105, 106, 108, 110, 112, 114, 115

Thus our definition does not depend on the size of the numbers in the sense of relating the measure of dispersion to the mean; it will give the same value for these two sets of numbers.

The resulting numerical measure of spread should admit interpretation in terms of the observations. Hence, it should be in the same unit of measurement. Its function will be to serve as a unit in deciding whether an observation is an ordinary or an unusual value in a specified population. The mean or a hypothesized value will be a starting point for measuring. For example, if a man is many units of spread from the mean of a population, his likeness may be preserved in bronze or he may be committed to an institution, otherwise he's the man in the street; if a male student is 5 ft 4 in, he is not likely to belong to the population of male student basketball players because, in height, he is too many units of spread from the mean of that population.

Finally, the measure should possess mathematical properties with which we need not be concerned at the moment.

The measure which is best on most counts and most common is the *variance* or its square root, the *standard deviation*. The variance will be represented by two symbols: σ^2 (the Greek letter *sigma*) for a population and s^2 for a sample. These are read as sigma square or sigma squared and s square(d). Standard deviations for populations and samples are represented by σ and s, respectively. σ^2 and σ are parameters, constants for a particular population; s^2 and s are statistics, variables which change from sample to sample from the same population. The variance or *mean square* is defined in terms of squared deviations.

Suppose that we have a finite population of N values, each having the same probability, namely $1/N$, of being drawn by a random procedure. It is intended to sample this population with replacement, as discussed in Sec. 2.5. In this case, the population variance is defined as the sum of the squared deviations divided by their total number. The variance is measured in units that are the square of the original, for example, centimeters squared.

Symbolically, the variance is defined by

$$\sigma^2 = \frac{(Y_1 - \mu)^2 + (Y_2 - \mu)^2 + \cdots + (Y_N - \mu)^2}{N}$$

$$= \frac{\sum_i (Y_i - \mu)^2}{N} \tag{2.6}$$

(When the sample values have different probabilities of being drawn, each squared deviation is weighted with its probability and the divisor N is not required. This idea of weighting can be extended quite simply to infinite populations with a discrete variable.)

(The symbol S^2 and definition with divisor $N - 1$ are used for the population variance when sampling is without replacement.)

For the die example of a population,

$$\sigma^2 = \frac{1}{6}[(1 - 3\tfrac{1}{2})^2 + (2 - 3\tfrac{1}{2})^2 + (3 - 3\tfrac{1}{2})^2$$

$$+ (4 - 3\tfrac{1}{2})^2 + (5 - 3\tfrac{1}{2})^2 + (6 - 3\tfrac{1}{2})^2]$$

$$= \frac{35}{12}$$

Note that it is possible to toss a die more than six times. In this case, $n > N$.

For continuous variables, the population variance requires more sophisticated mathematics than this text depends on.

The sample variance or mean square is similarly defined but with divisor $n - 1$.

$$s^2 = \frac{(Y_1 - \bar{Y})^2 + (Y_2 - \bar{Y})^2 + \cdots + (Y_n - \bar{Y})^2}{n - 1}$$

$$= \frac{\sum_i (Y_i - \bar{Y})^2}{n - 1} \tag{2.7}$$

Note that

$$(n - 1)s^2 = \sum_i (Y_i - \bar{Y})^2$$

The numerator of s^2 is referred to as the *sum of squares* and is often denoted by SS. For the numbers 3, 6, 8, and 11, the sum of squares is

$$(3 - 7)^2 + (6 - 7)^2 + (8 - 7)^2 + (11 - 7)^2$$
$$= (-4)^2 + (-1)^2 + (+1)^2 + (+4)^2 = 34,$$

and the variance is $34/3 = 11.33$.

The square root of the sample variance is called the *standard deviation*, denoted by s. *Root-mean-square deviation* is a less-used but descriptive term for s. For our example, $s = \sqrt{34/3} = 3.4$ units of the original observations.

The quantity

$$\text{SS} = \sum_i (Y_i - \bar{Y})^2$$

may be called the *definition formula* for the sum of squares, since it tells us that the sum of squares is the sum of the squared deviations from the arithmetic mean.

The definition formula for the sum of squares reduces to a *working formula* for computation, namely,

$$\sum_i (Y_i - \bar{Y})^2 = \sum_i Y_i^2 - \frac{\left(\sum_i Y_i\right)^2}{n} \tag{2.8}$$

The numbers are squared and added for the first term and added and the total squared for the second. On many computers,

$$\sum_i Y_i^2 \quad \text{and} \quad \sum_i Y_i$$

can be obtained simultaneously. The quantity

$$\frac{\left(\sum_i Y_i\right)^2}{n}$$

is called the *correction term*, or *factor*, or *correction* or *adjustment for the mean*, and is represented by C. The term "correction for the mean" points out that since SS is a measure of variation about $\bar{Y}$, the correction term must be subtracted from

$$\sum_i Y_i^2$$

often called the unadjusted sum of squares. As a correction, the quantity has nothing to do with mistakes. The form $n\bar{Y}^2$, shown in Eq. (2.9), is less desirable computationally since it introduces the necessity of rounding at an earlier stage.

$$\frac{\left(\sum_i Y_i\right)^2}{n} = n\bar{Y}^2 \tag{2.9}$$

The validity of Eq. (2.8) can be demonstrated for an arithmetic example. For our illustration sample,

Y_i	Y_i^2	$Y_i - \bar{Y}$	$(Y_i - \bar{Y})^2$
3	9	−4	16
6	36	−1	1
8	64	+1	1
11	121	+4	16
$\sum_i$: 28	230	0	34

Thus

$$\text{SS} = \sum_i (Y_i - \bar{Y})^2 = 34$$

by the definition formula, and

$$\text{SS} = \sum_i Y_i^2 - \frac{\left(\sum_i Y_i\right)^2}{n} = 230 - \frac{28^2}{4} = 34$$

by the working formula. When the rounding of numbers, such as the mean or the $(Y_i - \bar{Y})$'s, is necessary, there may be minor discrepancies. The computing formula is to be preferred since it is likely to be least affected by rounding errors. Equation (2.9) may also be checked by example.

An important property of the sum of squares is that it is a minimum, that is, if $\bar{Y}$ is replaced by any other value, the sum of squares of the new deviations will be a larger value. It is not feasible to demonstrate this for all possible values.

The quantity $n - 1$ is termed *degrees of freedom*, denoted by df, or f.

Another measure of dispersion is the *range*, the difference between the highest and lowest values. It is not ordinarily a satisfactory statistic for a critical evaluation of data since it is influenced by extreme or unusual values. However, for samples of size 2, it is a multiple of the standard deviation; and for samples of less than 10, it is often satisfactory. Under some conditions, techniques using the range are especially desirable.

A measure of variation with intuitive appeal, because it uses all observations, is the mean of the *absolute values*. The absolute mean deviation or, as it is frequently termed, the *average deviation*, is calculated as

$$\frac{\sum_i |Y_i - \bar{Y}|}{n} \tag{2.10}$$

The vertical bars tell us to take all deviations as positive. For the values 3, 6, 8, and 11, the average deviation is 2.5.

Other measures of dispersion use percentiles. Thus the difference between points cutting off 85 and 15 percent of the ranked observations has appeal; it does not depend on the extremes as does the range.

Exercise 2.8.1 In considering a coin, we may assign the value 1 to a head and 0 to a tail. For a true coin, these values occur with equal probability when the coin is tossed. Thus, we have a finite population of $N = 2$ values. A coin is tossed repeatedly so that we may have a sample as large as we wish. This is sampling with replacement.

What is the variance in this population?

Exercise 2.8.2 When a coin is tossed twice, the outcomes are (H, H), (H, T), (T, H), and (T, T). They occur with equal frequency for a true coin.

Suppose that we add the number of heads to get 2, 1, 1, and 0 and consider these values to constitute a population.

What is the variance in this population?

If we say that we have a random variable with values 2, 1, and 0 but with probabilities of 1/4, 1/2, and 1/4, respectively, can you use only this information to compute the population variance?

Exercise 2.8.3 For the data of Exercise 2.7.1, compute s^2 and s. Find the range.

When the range is multiplied by .370 (for $n = 7$), the result is an unbiased estimate of σ. Do this and compare with s.

Exercise 2.8.4 For the data of Exercise 2.7.2, compute s^2 and s. Find the range.

Multiply the range by .337 (for $n = 9$) to get an unbiased estimate of σ. Compare with s.

Exercise 2.8.5 For the data of sample A in Exercise 2.7.5, compute s^2 and s.

Repeat for sample B.

Exercise 2.8.6 Take any two numbers. Consider them to be a sample and compute s^2. Take the same two numbers, square their difference, and divide by two. The two values just computed should be identical; this result is based on an algebraic identity.

Now read what was said in this section about the use of the range as a measure of dispersion when $n = 2$.

Exercise 2.8.7 Obtain a small set of data from the field most familiar to you or use a set from one of the preceding exercises and compute $\bar{Y}$ and s^2. Check Eqs. (2.8) and (2.9) with your data. Compute the average deviation by Eq. (2.10).

2.9 Standard Deviation of Means

The sampling of populations and characterization of samples have been under discussion. The reader may have been thinking of such characteristics as height and weight, with plants and animals supplying populations of interest. It must also be remembered that sample means and standard deviations are themselves subject to variation and form populations of sample means and sample standard deviations.

In Exercise 2.7.4, you were asked to choose the best mean from among three based on 50, 20, and 10 observations. Presumably you chose the mean based on $n = 50$, but we need some criterion by which to choose. Variability is an obvious choice.

As a matter of observation or intuition, one expects sample means to be less variable than single observations. In other words, means tend to cluster closer about some central value than do single observations. If we take two series of means, each based on a different number of observations, say 10 and 20, we expect the variation among the means of the smaller samples to be greater than that among those of the larger ones. Fortunately, there is a known relation between the variance among individuals and that among means of individuals. This relation and that for standard deviations are

$$\sigma_{\bar{Y}}^2 = \frac{\sigma^2}{n} \quad \text{and} \quad \sigma_{\bar{Y}} = \sqrt{\frac{\sigma^2}{n}} = \frac{\sigma}{\sqrt{n}} \tag{2.11}$$

where $\sigma_{\bar{Y}}^2$ is the variance of the population of $\bar{Y}$'s obtained by sampling the *parent population* of individuals with variance σ^2. Similar relations are used for sample values, namely,

$$s_{\bar{Y}}^2 = \frac{s^2}{n} \quad \text{and} \quad s_{\bar{Y}} = \sqrt{\frac{s^2}{n}} = \frac{s}{\sqrt{n}} \tag{2.12}$$

These relations will be illustrated by sampling in Chap. 4; they are valid for all populations.

The necessity of the subscript $\bar{Y}$ is clear. The subscript Y is also used at times. $\mu_{\bar{Y}}$ is the mean of the population of individuals and $s_{\bar{Y}}^2$ is a variance computed from a sample of individuals.

The value of these relations is apparent. Given σ^2, we can compute the variance of a population of sample means directly and for any sample size. Also, from a single sample yielding a single $\bar{Y}$, we can compute a sample variance which estimates the variance in the population of $\bar{Y}$'s.

The standard deviation of a mean is often called the *standard error* and, less frequently, *standard error of a mean*. In other words, the term standard deviation applies to observations and standard error applies to means, unless otherwise specified. The standard error is seen to be inversely proportional to the square root of the number of observations in the mean. It can be calculated if an s^2 or s is available; more than one $\bar{Y}$ is not required. For sample observations 3, 6, 8, and 11, $s_{\bar{Y}} = s/\sqrt{n} = 3.4/\sqrt{4} = 1.7$. For computational convenience, $s_{\bar{Y}}$ is usually calculated as

$$\sqrt{\frac{s^2}{n}} = \sqrt{\frac{11.33}{4}} = \sqrt{2.8333} = 1.7$$

This is an estimate of σ^2/n, the variance in the population consisting of sample means of four observations from the population of individuals. If we had obtained a number of sample means of four observations and used these means to compute the variance of the means, we would have an estimate of the same quantity; we have a single mean.

Exercise 2.9.1 For the data in Exercises 2.7.1 and 2.7.2, used also in Exercises 2.8.3 and 2.8.4, compute $s_{\bar{Y}}^2$ and $s_{\bar{Y}}$.

Exercise 2.9.2 For samples *A* and *B* in Exercise 2.7.5 and used again in Exercise 2.8.5, compute $s_{\bar{Y}}^2$ and $s_{\bar{Y}}$.

2.10 Coefficient of Variability or of Variation

A quantity of use to the experimenter in evaluating results from different experiments involving the same character, possibly conducted by different persons, is the coefficient of variability. It is defined as the sample standard deviation expressed as a percentage of the sample mean as shown in

$$\text{CV} = \frac{100s}{\bar{Y}} \text{ percent} \tag{2.13}$$

To know whether or not a particular CV is unusually large or small requires experience with similar data. The CV is a relative measure of variation, in contrast to the standard deviation, which is in the same units as the observations. Since it is the ratio of two averages, it is independent of the unit of measurement used, for example, it is the same whether pounds or grams are used to measure weight.

Exercise 2.10.1 For the data first given in Exercises 2.7.1 and 2.7.2, compute the CV.

Exercise 2.10.2 For the data first given in Exercise 2.7.5, compute the CV.

2.11 An Example

To develop a new sanitary engineering technique, amounts of hydrogen sulfide produced from sewage after 42 h at 37°C for nine runs were collected and are presented by Eliassen (2.2). These are given in Table 2.3. The

Table 2.3 Hydrogen sulfide produced in anaerobic fermentation of sewage after 42 h at 37°C

i = run	$Y_i = H_2S$, ppm	$Y_i - \bar{Y}$	
1	210		−8
2	221	+3	
3	218		0
4	228	+10	
5	220	+2	
6	227	+9	
7	223	+5	
8	224	+6	
9	192		−26
Totals	1,963	+35	−34
		+1 (due to rounding)	

$$\bar{Y} = \frac{\sum_i Y_i}{9} = \frac{1{,}963}{9} = 218 \text{ ppm (after rounding)}$$

$$s^2 = \frac{\sum_i Y_i^2 - \left(\sum_i Y_i\right)^2 / 9}{9 - 1} = \frac{429{,}147 - (1{,}963)^2/9}{8} = 124.36$$

$$s = \sqrt{124.36} = 11.1 \text{ ppm}$$

$$s_{\bar{Y}}^2 = \frac{s^2}{9} = \frac{124.36}{9} = 13.82$$

$$s_{\bar{Y}} = \sqrt{13.82} = 3.7 \text{ ppm}$$

$$\text{CV} = \frac{11.1(100)}{218} = 5\% \text{ (approx)}$$

technique was for sweeping hydrogen sulfide from an anaerobic culture medium by means of an inert gas and the trapping of hydrogen sulfide for quantitative analysis with the complete exclusion of air.

These data constitute a sample of nine observations from the population of all possible values obtainable by this technique. The experiment was in the laboratory and various controls had been introduced to lower the CV to this value. Consequently, the population is rather restricted. Variability among observations is presumably caused by such things as the samples of sewage, the samples of the anaerobic culture used, the operator's technique, and a host of other factors both known and unknown. It is clear that we cannot hope to obtain μ and σ for this abstract population, but we can estimate them. This is done by calculating $\bar{Y}$ and s; these values and others are given in Table 2.3.

A $\bar{Y}$ is a sample of one observation from the population of all possible means of samples of the same size, namely, nine. The *derived population* has mean $\mu_{\bar{Y}}(= \mu_Y)$ and $\sigma_{\bar{Y}}^2(= \sigma_Y^2/n)$. From a sample of observations on one population, it has thus been possible to calculate a mean value $\bar{Y}$, an estimate of μ and $\mu_{\bar{Y}}$, and two variances, s^2 and $s_{\bar{Y}}^2$, estimates of σ^2 and $\sigma_{\bar{Y}}^2$.

2.12 The Linear Additive Model

It is common practice in science to try to explain natural phenomena by models. For example, we say the earth is round and turns on a North-South axis. This allows us to explain, from a rudimentary viewpoint, such observations as boats disappearing over the horizon, day and night, and so on. More sophisticated models depend on mathematical statements and, consequently, allow us not only to explain observable facts but also to predict possibly unobserved events. The most important aspect of a mathematical model is that it possesses the intrinsic characteristics of the real-world problem.

In statistics, a common model describing the makeup of an observation states that it consists of a mean plus an error. This is a linear additive model. The mean may involve the single parameter μ or be composed of a sum of parameters. Assumptions about the parameters and the errors depend on the problem. A minimum assumption is that the errors are random, that is, that the population of Y's is sampled at random. This makes the model probabilistic rather than deterministic.

Such a model is applicable to the problem of estimating or making inferences about population means and variances. The simplest linear additive model is given by

$$Y_i = \mu + \varepsilon_i \tag{2.14}$$

together with a definition of the symbols appearing in the equation. It states that the ith observation is one on the mean μ but is subject to a sampling error, ε_i (*epsilon* sub i).

The ε_i's are assumed to be from a population of ε's with mean zero. That the sampling errors be uncorrelated is a theoretical requirement for valid inferences about a population and is assured by drawing the sample in a random manner.

The sample mean is

$$\bar{Y} = \frac{\sum_i Y_i}{n} = \frac{\sum_i (\mu + \varepsilon_i)}{n} = \mu + \frac{\sum_i \varepsilon_i}{n}$$

For random sampling,

$$\frac{\left(\sum_i \varepsilon_i\right)}{n}$$

is expected to be smaller as sample size increases, because positive and negative ε's should tend to cancel and because the divisor n is increasing. This is about the same as saying that the variance of means can be expected to be smaller than that of individuals or that means of large samples are less variable than means of small ones. In summary, the sample mean $\bar{Y}$ is a good estimate of the population mean μ, since $\bar{Y}$ should lie close to μ if the sample is large enough and not unusual.

We still require an estimate of the variance of the epsilons, the real individuals. The model shows that we have a finite sample of ε's, and these lead to an estimate of σ^2. However, we cannot compute the ε's since we do not know μ. On the other hand, we can estimate the ε_i's by corresponding e_i's, calculated as $(Y_i - \bar{Y})$'s, and combine them to give a sample variance computed by Eq. (2.7). The calculable $(Y_i - \bar{Y})$, in preference to a deviation from some other number, has the property, previously stated, that

$$\sum_i (Y_i - \bar{Y})^2$$

is a minimum. It is sometimes stated that $\bar{Y}$ is a *minimum sum of squares* or *least-squares* estimate of μ.

Exercise 2.12.1 Write out a model for the data of Exercise 2.7.1. For Exercise 2.7.2. Suppose that the variances in your two models are equal. Can you write a single equation for a model that covers both sets of data simultaneously?

2.13 An Example

An example will illustrate the calculation and interpretation of the statistics discussed. The data in Table 2.4 are malt-extract values for Kindred barley grown at 14 locations in the Mississippi Valley Barley Nurseries during 1948. The population for which any inference is to be made can be considered as the malt-extract values for Kindred barley grown during 1948 in the region covered by the Mississippi Valley Nurseries. One original value has been modified to facilitate calculations.

The first step in the calculations is to obtain

$$\sum_i Y_i = 1{,}064 \qquad \text{and} \qquad \sum_i Y_i^2 = 80{,}881.38$$

From these, Y and s^2 are obtained from Eqs. (2.1), (2.7), and (2.8). The sample mean is

$$\bar{Y} = \frac{\sum_i Y_i}{n} = \frac{1{,}064}{14} = 76 \text{ percent}$$

Table 2.4 Malt-extract values on malts made from Kindred barley grown at 14 locations in the Mississippi Valley Barley Nurseries during 1948 in percent of dry basis

Malt-extract values			
Original	Y	Deviations from mean $Y - \bar{Y}$	Deviations squared
77.7	77.7	1.7	2.89
76.0	76.0	0	0
76.9	76.9	0.9	0.81
74.6	74.6	−1.4	1.96
74.7	74.7	−1.3	1.69
76.5	76.5	0.5	0.25
74.2	75.0	−1.0	1.00
75.4	75.4	−0.6	0.36
76.0	76.0	0	0
76.0	76.0	0	0
73.9	73.9	−2.1	4.41
77.4	77.4	1.4	1.96
76.6	76.6	0.6	0.36
77.3	77.3	1.3	1.69
Totals 1,063.2	$\sum_i Y = 1{,}064.0$	0	$\sum_i (Y - \bar{Y})^2 = 17.38$

Source: Unpublished data obtained from and used with the permission of A. D. Dickson, U.S. Department Agriculture Barley and Malt Laboratory, Madison, Wisconsin.

and the mean square or variance is

$$s^2 = \frac{\text{SS}}{\text{df}} = \frac{\sum_i Y_i^2 - \left(\sum_i Y_i\right)^2 / n}{n - 1} = \frac{80{,}881.38 - (1{,}064)^2/14}{13} = \frac{17.38}{13} = 1.337$$

The standard deviation or square root of the variance is

$$s = \sqrt{s^2} = \sqrt{1.337} = 1.16 \text{ percent}$$

Calculation of the sum of squares by means of the definition formula is illustrated in the last column of Table 2.4.

The sample mean, $\bar{Y} = 76$ percent, and sample standard deviation, $s = 1.16$ percent, provide us with the best estimates of the corresponding unknown population parameters, namely, μ and σ.

The coefficient of variation is computed using Eq. (2.13).

$$\text{CV} = \frac{s(100)}{\bar{Y}} = \frac{1.16(100)}{76.0} = 1.5 \text{ percent}$$

The single sample mean constitutes a sample of size 1 from a derived population of means, each based on a random sample of 14 observations from the parent population. The mean of the derived population is also estimated by $\bar{Y} = 76$ percent, but the variance and standard deviation must be estimated by Eq. (2.12). We get

$$s_{\bar{Y}}^2 = \frac{s^2}{n} = \frac{1.337}{14} = .0955$$

$$s_{\bar{Y}} = \sqrt{\frac{s^2}{n}} = \sqrt{\frac{1.337}{14}} \quad \text{or} \quad \frac{s}{\sqrt{n}} = \frac{1.16}{\sqrt{14}}$$

$$= 0.31 \text{ percent}$$

in either case. This value is also called the standard error.

2.14 The Use of Coding in the Calculation of Statistics†

Frequently the calculation of statistics can be facilitated and reduced by *coding*. Coding replaces each observation by a number on a new scale by use of one or more of the operations of addition, subtraction, multiplication, and division.

The arithmetic mean is affected by every coding operation. For example, if the observations are coded by multiplying by 10 and then subtracting 100, the mean of the coded numbers must be increased by 100 and divided by 10. The rule is to apply the inverse operation, the inverses of multiplication and subtraction being division and addition, in the reverse order.

The standard deviation is affected by multiplication and division only. Addition or subtraction of a value for each observation does not affect the standard deviation, since a shift in the origin of the observations does not affect their spread. Because both multiplication and division change the unit of measurement, the standard deviation calculated from coded data is decoded by applying the inverse operation to the result.

We illustrate the use of coding in calculating the mean and standard deviation of the data in Table 2.4. The coded values will be obtained by subtracting 70 from each observation and multiplying the result by 10. Since all observations are in the 70s, subtraction of 70 is an obvious choice to give small, positive numbers; multiplication by 10 eliminates the decimal. Thus the first value, $Y_1 = 77.7$, is replaced by its coded value,

† If desired, this section may be omitted without loss of continuity.

$Y'_1 = (77.7 - 70)10 = 77$. The mean and the standard deviation of the coded numbers are then obtained from $\sum_i Y'_i = 840$ and $\sum_i Y'^2_i = 52{,}138$. We obtain

$$\bar{Y}' = \frac{\sum_i Y'_i}{14} = \frac{840}{14} = 60$$

and

$$s' = \sqrt{\frac{\sum_i Y'^2_i - \left(\sum_i Y'_i\right)^2 / n}{n - 1}} = \sqrt{\frac{52{,}138 - (840)^2/14}{13}} = 11.6$$

To decode $\bar{Y}'$, apply the inverse operation in the reverse order. Thus

$$\bar{Y} = \frac{\bar{Y}'}{10} + 70 = \frac{60}{10} + 70 = 76 \text{ percent}$$

as in Sec. 2.13. To decode s',

$$s = \frac{s'}{10} = \frac{11.6}{10} = 1.16 \text{ percent}$$

as in Sec. 2.13. The accuracy of the calculation is in no way affected by the coding process; rather, it is simplified by the use of a more convenient set of numbers.

Exercise 2.14.1 The numbers 10.807, 10.812, ..., were coded as 7, 12, ... The mean of 17 coded observations was 14.6. What was the mean of the original observations? What part of the coding affected the standard deviation? How?

2.15 The Frequency Table†

The frequency table was mentioned in Sec. 2.6. When the sample consists of a large number of observations it is desirable to summarize the data in a table showing the frequency with which each numerical value occurs or each class is represented. Thus both continuous and discrete data can be summarized in frequency tables. This reduces the mass of raw data into a more manageable form and provides a basis for its graphical presentation. Statistics such as the mean and standard deviation can be calculated from frequency tables with much less work than from the original values.

For discrete variables such as the number of heads observed in the toss

† The remainder of the chapter is concerned with large quantities of data, their presentation, and the calculation of $\bar{Y}$ and s. The methods of the preceding sections are applicable but lengthier for such data.

of five coins, the class values to be used are generally obvious. Thus a frequency table for the number of heads occurring in the tossing of five coins one hundred times is given in Table 2.2. Where the number of possible classes is large it may be desirable to reduce their number.

For continuous variables, classes other than observed values have to be chosen in some arbitrary manner. The choice depends on such factors as the number of observations, the range of variation, the precision required for statistics calculated from the table, and the degree of summarization necessary to prevent small irregularities from obscuring general trends. The last two points usually work in opposition; the greater the number of classes, the greater is the precision of any calculations made from the table; but if the number of classes is too great, the data are not summarized sufficiently.

A rule of use in determining the size of the class interval when high precision is required in calculations made from the resulting frequency table is to make the interval not greater than one-quarter of the standard deviation. If this rule is strictly adhered to, the data are sometimes not sufficiently summarized for graphical presentation. If the size of the class interval is increased to one-third to one-half of a standard deviation, the resulting frequency table will usually be a sufficient summary for graphical presentation and adequate for most data; the lack of precision in any statistics calculated from the table will be small enough to be ignored.

Since the standard deviation is not known at the time a frequency table is being prepared, it is necessary to estimate it. Tippett (2.4) prepared detailed tables showing the relation between the sample range and the population standard deviation for normal populations. This has been condensed in a short table by Goulden (2.3) and is reproduced as Table A.2. This table is useful in estimating σ.

Exercise 2.15.1 The range of percentage of dry matter in 48 samples of Grimm alfalfa was 7.6 percent. Estimate the standard deviation.

2.16 An Example

To illustrate the use of Table A.2 and the preparation and use of a frequency table, consider the yields, to the nearest gram, of 229 spaced plants of Richland soybeans, reported by Drapala (2.1). Yields range from 1 to 69 g. From Table A.2 the ratio range/σ for $n = 229$ is about 5.6. Thus σ is estimated as $68/5.6 = 12.2$ g. One-third of the estimate is 4 g; one-half is 6 g. Since 12.2 g is an approximation, the calculated class interval can be adjusted somewhat. It is convenient to make a class interval an odd number rather than an even number since the midpoint of such an interval falls conveniently between two possible values of the variable. Select 5 g as class interval. If greater accuracy in the calculation of the statistics from the table is required, use an interval of 3 g, about one-quarter of the estimated σ. In setting up class values, it is desirable to make the lower limit of the first class slightly less than the smallest value in the sample. Select 3 as the midpoint of the first interval. Table 2.1 is the resulting frequency table.

After the class interval is chosen, set up the necessary classes and sort the observations accordingly. Two methods are commonly used. The first is the tally score method, illustrated below for the first few classes of Table 2.1.

Class range	Class value or midpoint	Tally score	Frequency
1–5	3	~~////~~ //	7
6–10	8	~~////~~	5
11–15	13	~~////~~ //	7

This method consists of making a stroke in the proper class for each observation and summing these for each class to obtain the frequency. It is customary for convenience in counting to place each fifth stroke through the preceding four, as shown. The method has the disadvantage that when there is lack of agreement in checking frequencies, the source is difficult to find.

The second and perhaps safer method is to write the value of each observation on a card of a size convenient for handling. These entries must be carefully checked. Class ranges are then written on other cards and arranged in order on a desk and the observation cards are sorted into classes. Checking is accomplished readily by examining the cards in each class. The frequency in each class is determined by counting cards. If punching and sorting equipment is available, the value of each observation can be punched on a card and the cards mechanically sorted into classes.

If the yields of Table 2.1 were recorded to the nearest tenth of a gram, the class limits would be .5–5.5, 5.5–10.5, 10.5–15.5, etc. When an even number of observations equals a class limit, for example, 5.5, half the observations are assigned to each class; if the number of such observations is odd, the odd observation is assigned to one of the two classes at random.

Effects of grouping can be seen by considering the five values, 6, 7, 7, 9, and 9 g, in the second class of Table 2.1. The arithmetic mean of these values is 7.6 g, but in calculations from Table 2.1, they are given a value of 8 g. If each class were examined for this type of effect, about half would show a negative error and half a positive error, and thus they tend to cancel each other.

2.17 Calculation of the Mean and Standard Deviation from a Frequency Table

These calculations will be illustrated for the data of Table 2.1. Coding is included. First, prepare a table such as Table 2.5. The first column, Y_i, consists of actual class values. The second column, Y'_i, is formed by replacing

Table 2.5 Calculation of $\bar{Y}$ and s from a frequency table

Class value or midpoint of class range				
Actual	Coded	Frequency	Frequency multiplied by coded class value	Frequency multiplied by square of coded class value
Y_i	Y'_i	f_i	$f_i Y'_i$	$f_i Y'^2_i$
3	−6	7	−42	252
8	−5	5	−25	125
13	−4	7	−28	112
18	−3	18	−54	162
23	−2	32	−64	128
28	−1	41	−41	41
33	0	37	0	0
38	+1	25	25	25
43	+2	22	44	88
48	+3	19	57	171
53	+4	6	24	96
58	+5	6	30	150
63	+6	3	18	108
68	+7	1	7	49
		$\sum_i f_i = 229 = n$	$\sum_i f_i Y'_i = -49$	$\sum_i f_i Y'^2_i = 1{,}507$

$$\bar{Y} = a + I \frac{\left(\sum_i f_i Y'_i\right)}{\sum_i f_i} \qquad s'^2 = \frac{\sum_i f_i Y'^2_i - \left(\sum_i f_i Y'_i\right)^2 \Big/ \sum_i f_i}{\sum_i f_i - 1}$$

$$= 33 + 5\frac{(-49)}{229} \qquad = \frac{1{,}507 - (-49)^2/229}{228} = 6.56$$

$$= 31.93 \text{ g} \qquad s = I\sqrt{s'^2} = 5\sqrt{6.56} = 12.80 \text{ g}$$

actual values by coded values. For an odd number of classes, zero is assigned to the middle one to facilitate the arithmetic, and in any case, the new interval is one unit. Column 3 is the frequency; the last two columns are needed in the computations.

The three column totals, $\sum f_i$, $\sum f_i Y'_i$, and $\sum f_i Y'^2_i$, are needed for the calculation of the mean and standard deviation. They correspond to

$$n, \quad \sum_i Y_i \quad \text{and} \quad \sum_i Y_i^2$$

Note that i may refer to the class of the frequency table, $i = 1, \ldots, 14$, or to the observation for the data, $i = 1, \ldots, 229$.

The arithmetic mean $\bar{Y}$ and the standard deviation s in actual rather than coded units are calculated from the coded values by

$$\bar{Y} = a + I \frac{\sum_i (fY')}{\sum_i f_i} \tag{2.15}$$

$$s = I \sqrt{\frac{\sum_i fY'^2 - \left(\sum_i fY_i\right)^2 \Big/ \sum_i f_i}{\sum_i f_i - 1}} \tag{2.16}$$

where I is the class interval and a is the assumed origin, namely, the Y_i value corresponding to the coded class value of 0.

2.18 Graphical Presentation of the Frequency Table

This has been discussed in Sec. 2.6. The histogram and frequency polygon for the data of Table 2.1 are shown in Fig. 2.3.

2.19 Significant Digits

With statistical computations comes the question of accuracy. How many figures are justifiable in the end result of a sequence of computations?

From any observation, two items of information are available: the unit of measurement and the number of units in the measurement. Where a continuous variable is involved, the number of units is clearly the closest value obtainable from the available scale. Thus if a chalkboard measures 3.7 m long, the unit is 1/10 m and the board measures between 36.5 and 37.5 of these units. The number is said to have two significant digits.

Computations carried out by an electronic computer are so simple that it is very possible that the final result of a sequence of calculations will appear more precise than it really is. Rules concerning numbers of significant digits resulting from the application of the arithmetic operations are available but somewhat impractical. In most statistical work, it is best to carry more figures, say not less than two extra, into the final computations than seem necessary and then to round the result to a meaningful number of digits, relative to the accuracy of the original measurements.

References

2.1. Drapala, W. J.: "Early generation parent-progeny relationships in spaced plantings of soybeans, medium red clover, barley, sudan grass, and sudan grass times sorghum segregates," Ph.D. thesis, University of Wisconsin, Madison, 1949.

2.2. Eliassen, Rolf: "Statistical analysis in sanitary engineering laboratory studies," *Biom.*, **6**:117–126 (1950).
2.3. Goulden, C. H.: *Methods of statistical analysis*, 2d ed., Wiley, New York, 1952.
2.4. Tippett, L. H. C.: *Biometrika*, **17**:386 (1926).

A Proposed Laboratory Exercise in Connection with Chap. 2

Purpose (1) To give the student practice in drawing random samples and computing sample statistics. (2) To obtain, on a class basis, empirical evidence about certain sample statistics and to compare this with theoretical results. (To be used in connection with Chaps. 3 and 4.)

1. Draw 10 random samples of size 10 from Table 4.1 using the table of random numbers, Table A.1. Record these in 10 two-digit columns, leaving space below for a dozen or so entries.
2. For each sample, calculate
   (*a*) The sum of the observations
   (*b*) The mean
   (*c*) The correction term
   (*d*) The (adjusted) sum of squares
   (*e*) The mean square or variance
   (*f*) The standard deviation
   (*g*) The coefficient of variation
   (*h*) The standard deviation of the mean
3. Compute the mean of the 10 sample means.
4. Compute $s_{\bar{Y}}^2$ and $s_{\bar{Y}}$ from the 10 $\bar{Y}$'s. In other words, treat the 10 $\bar{Y}$'s as a sample of size $n = 10$ from a derived population of $\bar{Y}$'s, each $\bar{Y}$ being computed from an original set of 10 observations from the parent population.

CHAPTER

THREE

PROBABILITY

3.1 Introduction

Events which are common or unlikely are ones whose probabilities of occurrence are large or small, respectively. The whole range of probabilities is used by most people in one way or another. One says, "The fire might have been caused by carelessness" when not at all sure of the cause; or one says, "The fire was almost certainly caused by carelessness," when feeling strongly about it.

Statisticians replace the informative but imprecise words "might" and "almost certainly" by a number lying between zero and one; they indicate precisely how probable or improbable an event is. Statistics is used to reason from the part to the whole, that is, from the sample to the population. Clearly we cannot with incomplete information expect to be correct in every inference. Chance plays a part and the laws of exact causality do not hold. Statistics supplies us with procedures which permit us to state how often we are right on the average. Such statements are called probability statements. In this chapter, we consider some probability notions and illustrate the use of tables to obtain probabilities associated with the occurrence of statistical events.

3.2 Some Elementary Probability

The use of a ratio or number to represent a probability is not peculiar to statisticians. Sportswriters may predict that a team has, for example, three chances to two of beating the opposing team. The reader may interpret this as meaning a close score is to be expected with the local team in the lead, or as meaning that if this particular game could be played many times, then the local team would win about three-fifths or 60 percent of the games. Expressions such as three to two, often written 3 : 2, are commonly referred to as *odds* and are converted to probabilities by forming fractions with these numbers as numerators and their sum as the common denominator.

Statisticians assign numbers between zero and one as the probabilities of events. These numbers are, basically, relative frequencies. Thus odds of three to two for the local team say that the probability of the local team winning is $3/(3 + 2) = 3/5 = .6$, and of losing, or of the visiting team winning, is $2/5 = .4$. The sum of the probabilities of the complete set of events is one, that is, 1, when the occurrence of one event excludes the occurrence of all others. Only one team can win if we do not permit a tie. The probabilities of zero and one are associated with events that are respectively certain not to and certain to occur.

The illustration is a simple one but with basic features that allow for extension. We have a collection, or *set*, of outcomes. These are *mutually exclusive* in that, if one occurs, the other cannot occur simultaneously. Also, the set includes all permissible or possible outcomes and so is *exhaustive*.

As an extension, consider the outcomes resulting from tossing a coin twice. The set can be represented symbolically as HH, HT, TH, and TT, each an ordered sequence of two letters representing heads H and tails T. If we toss the coin 10 times, then we need a sequence of 10 entries, each being an H or T, presented in order of occurrence. Each entry must be one of two letters, so there are $2 \times 2 \times \cdots \times 2 = 2^{10}$ possible outcomes; all are different and all are needed to complete the set.

In the game illustration, the outcome was the result of a single trial—the game was played to its conclusion. In the second case, a coin was tossed twice so that there were two trials providing an ordered pair as an outcome. In the third case, there were 10 trials resulting in a 10-entry outcome. It is helpful to think of all possible outcomes for any sort of trial or sequence of trials as constituting points in a space. The game would require a space of two points which we could tag L and W; we could show these on a line as in Fig. 3.1. The two coin tosses call for four points and these go conveniently into a two-dimensional space; also see Fig. 3.1. For the 10 coin tosses, we would like to have a 10-dimensional space, one dimension for each toss, but this can exist only in our imaginations.

The ideas above about outcomes of trials being represented by points in various spaces have led to the terms *sample space* as the set of *sample points* used to list the possible outcomes of an experiment. For each outcome, there is exactly one sample point. It is usually most convenient when we first visualize a sample space to think of an outcome as an *indecomposable* result, that is, we cannot visualize another sample space which reduced to the one at hand. A coin tossed twice leads to an ordered sequence rather than

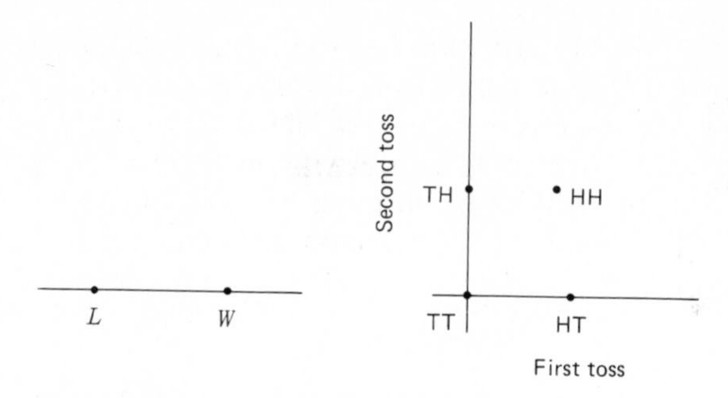

Figure 3.1 Sample points and sample spaces.

directly to the number of heads observed, which is a decomposable result where HT and TH would be the same outcome.

For each of our earlier illustrations, we are able to describe the conduct of an experiment; a game was played by rules—a coin was tossed twice under a set of conditions or a coin was tossed 10 times under these conditions. We can visualize the experiment as being repeated time and time again under essentially the same circumstances. We know that the result must be one of a number of possible outcomes which we can list beforehand but cannot, in advance, predict precisely the particular outcome. Here chance enters to determine which possible outcome is to result and we have a *random experiment*. The observed outcome, that is, the result of the experiment, specifies a particular sample point or outcome in the sample space.

The outcomes of the random experiments we have used for illustrations have not been numbers. Now we need to quantify these outcomes; we need a means of associating a number with the outcome or sample point. For example, we can assign 1 to W and 0 to L in the game; 2 to HH, 1 to HT, 1 to TH, and 0 to TT to tell the number of heads for the twice tossed coin; and 10, 9, . . . , 0, as appropriate, to count the number of heads for each of the 2^{10} outcomes of the coin tossed 10 times.

Any association that assigns a unique, real value to each sample point is called a *chance*, or *random, variable*. The assigned values are the values of the random variable.

Our new definition of a random variable is more formal than that in Sec. 2.2 and is, at the same time, more useful for further development of our subject.

We must assign a probability to each point in the sample space and also to each value of the random variable. This is easily done, when the random variable is discrete rather than continuous, by means of a *probability function*, which is a set of ordered pairs of values of a random variable and the corresponding probability. For the game, we have the probability function

$$(1, 3/5), (0, 2/5)$$

For the twice-tossed coin, if a fair one, we have

$$(2, 1/4), (1, 1/2), (0, 1/4)$$

For the coin tossed 10 times, the probability function is not so obvious. We will consider this subject in the next section.

Meanwhile, we stress two facts about probabilities that were stated earlier:

1. The probability of an event E_i lies between zero and one or may be zero or one. Symbolically,

$$0 \leq P(E_i) \leq 1 \tag{3.1}$$

(The symbol $<$ stands for "less than"; $\leq$ for "less than or equal to"; $>$ for "greater than"; $\geq$ for "greater than or equal to.")

2. The sum of the probabilities of the events in a mutually exclusive set is 1. Symbolically,

$$\sum_i P(E_i) = 1 \tag{3.2}$$

A deck of playing cards contains 26 red and 26 black cards consisting of 13 spades and 13 clubs, all black, and 13 hearts and 13 diamonds, all red; $P(\text{spade}) = P(\text{club}) = P(\text{heart}) = P(\text{diamond}) = 1/4$. Drawing a diamond in a single trial excludes drawing a spade, a club, and a heart. These events are mutually exclusive and $P(\text{spade}) + P(\text{club}) + P(\text{heart}) + P(\text{diamond}) = 1$. On the other hand, drawing a red card in a single draw ($P = 1/2$) does not exclude drawing a diamond, since the former includes the latter; these events are not mutually exclusive, so we cannot add their probabilities.

So far the reader has been presented with nothing strange or new except possibly the use of symbolism, or notation, or new definitions. Even the card probabilities and those for the twice-tossed coin must have been obvious. Yet in their calculation, a classical definition of probability has been used, namely:

> If a chance event can occur in n mutually exclusive and equally likely ways, and if m outcomes have a certain property A, then the probability of A is the fraction m/n, or

$$P = \frac{\text{number of successes}}{\text{total number of events } (= \text{successes} + \text{failures})} \tag{3.3}$$

Probabilities of events associated with discrete variables are involved in many sampling problems, for example, opinion polls, studies of genetic characters, and problems where counts are observed. They are clearly not applicable without modification to problems with continuous variables such as weight.

3.3 The Binomial Distribution

For many trials there are only two possible outcomes; a plant possesses a certain characteristic or it does not, a person registers to vote or fails to do so, a tossed coin falls heads or tails. Such single trials are often called *binomial* or *Bernoulli trials* and an appropriate sample space will consist of two points. The random experiment that generates observations under essentially the same circumstances is easy to describe.

The sample points are represented conveniently, often by E, implying that a certain event has occurred, and by not-E, or $\not{E}$ or $\bar{E}$, for the *complement*. The usual random variable will assign a 1 to E and a 0 to not-E.

In repeated binomial trials, one outcome may have no effect on another, as in coin tossing; such trials are said to be *independent*. In addition, the probability of the occurrence of E may remain constant from trial to trial, again as in coin tossing. When these two properties hold and the number of trials is fixed, we have an underlying binomial distribution. The total outcome of such an experiment is an ordered sequence of E's and $\bar{E}$'s or of 1s and 0s. The usual random variable assigns a value equal to the number of E's or, what is the same thing, the sum of the 1s and 0s. When a probability is associated with each value of the random variable, a binomial probability function or *binomial distribution* results.

It is often possible to present a mathematical formula which in a single statement gives the probability associated with each and every chance event. Thus for a fair coin, if we let $Y = 0$ for a tail and $Y = 1$ for a head, the equation

$$P(Y = Y_i) = 1/2 \qquad Y_i = 0, 1 \tag{3.4}$$

(read as: the probability that the random variable Y takes the particular value Y_i is one-half for Y_i equal to zero and for Y_i equal to one) constitutes a probability distribution.

For tossing a fair die, the probability distribution would be

$$P(Y = Y_i) = 1/6 \qquad Y_i = 1, 2, \ldots, 6 \tag{3.5}$$

Table A.1 is a very large sample for a population with probability distribution

$$P(Y = Y_i) = 1/10 \qquad Y_i = 0, 1, 2, \ldots, 9 \tag{3.6}$$

If we think of only odd and even numbers, we can relate Table A.1 to Eq. (3.4). Equations (3.5) and (3.6) are, of course, not binomial but multinomial.

Let us consider the problem of producing an equation which in a single statement gives all the necessary probabilities of any binomial distribution.

Suppose that a random experiment is to consist of n independent trials. Let $P(E) = P(1) = p$, say; then $P(\bar{E}) = P(0) = 1 - p$, from Eq. (3.2). An outcome of the experiment will be represented as an ordered sequence of 1s and

0s. Thus five tosses of a coin could result in (0, 0, 1, 1, 0), that is, two tails followed by two heads and a final tail. The probability of this outcome is found, because of the independence of the trials, by multiplying the probabilities involved at each stage. Thus, the probability that the event described would occur is $(1 - p)(1 - p)pp(1 - p) = p^2(1 - p)^3$. Of course, the outcome has certainly occurred, so that this probability applied prior to the conduct of the experiment. The probability associated with each sample point is similarly obtained. Of course, when $p = .5$, as when a fair coin is tossed, all points have the same probability, namely, $(.5)^5 = .03125$, about 3 chances in 100. Note that we have required that the heads occur on the third and fourth tosses.

The random variable that associates a unique real value with each sample point will add the entries in the sequence, and so associates 2, the number of 1s, with the sample point of the illustration. This is not the only sample point that has the sample value 2; the two 1s can occur in any of the positions (1, 2), (1, 3), (1, 4), (1, 5), (2, 3), (2, 4), (2, 5), (3, 4), (3, 5), (4, 5), 10 in all. Here we have specified and counted all possibilities; however, Eq. (3.7) allows us to compute this value directly.

$$\binom{n}{Y} = \frac{n!}{Y!\,(n - Y)!} \tag{3.7}$$

We read $n!$ as n factorial; it is defined by $n! = n(n - 1)(n - 2) \cdots 1$. Thus for $Y = 2$, that is, two 1s in $n = 5$ trials, we have

$$\binom{5}{2} = \frac{5 \cdot 4 \cdot 3 \cdot 2 \cdot 1}{2 \cdot 1 \cdot 3 \cdot 2 \cdot 1} = 10$$

Of course, zero is a possible value of Y; if we define $0! = 1$, we have no problem with Eq. (3.7).

With one formula to count sample points with the same Y and another that assigns a probability to each sample point, we can write the binomial probability distribution as

$$P(Y = Y_i \mid n) = \binom{n}{Y_i} p^{Y_i}(1 - p)^{n - Y_i} \tag{3.8}$$

Equation (3.8) is read as "the probability that the random variable Y takes the particular value Y_i in a random experiment with n trials equals...." Recall that $p^0 = 1$.

For the coin illustration, we have

$$P(Y = 2 \mid 5) = \binom{5}{2}\left(\tfrac{1}{2}\right)^2\left(\tfrac{1}{2}\right)^3$$
$$= .3125$$

Now it turns out that the event of two heads in five tosses is not at all unusual, occurring about three times out of ten, on the average.

Table 3.1 gives the binomial distribution for $n = 5$ and several values of

Table 3.1 The binomial distribution, $n = 5$

Y	Probability	$p = .5$	$p = .4$	$p = .25$	$p = .1$	
0	$\binom{5}{0}p^0(1-p)^5$	.03125	.07776	.23730	.59049	5
1	$\binom{5}{1}p^1(1-p)^4$	.15625	.25920	.39551	.32805	4
2	$\binom{5}{2}p^2(1-p)^3$	.31250	.34560	.26367	.07290	3
3	$\binom{5}{3}p^3(1-p)^2$	.31250	.23040	.08789	.00810	2
4	$\binom{5}{4}p^4(1-p)^1$	.15625	.07680	.01465	.00045	1
5	$\binom{5}{5}p^5(1-p)^0$	.03125	.01024	.00098	.00001	0
		$p = .5$	$p = .6$	$p = .75$	$p = .9$	Y

p. Note that the left column is read with p values across the top whereas the right column is read with p values across the bottom. The probabilities in each column add to 1. For $p = .5$, the distribution is symmetric; it becomes increasingly asymmetric as p moves away from this value.

The mean and variance of a random variable with a binomial distribution are given by

Mean: $$\mu = np \tag{3.9}$$

Variance: $$\sigma^2 = np(1-p) \tag{3.10}$$

Notice that the variance is determined by p, so that only one parameter is needed to characterize the binomial distribution; n is an observable parameter, so it is in a different category.

The equation for the mean gives reasonable values; if $p = 1/2$, we would expect about half our coin tosses to fall heads; if $p = .1$ for some other outcome, then we would expect about one-tenth of the trials to result in that outcome.

For the binomial distribution of Table 3.1 with $n = 5$ and $p = .5$, we have $\mu = 2.5$, $\sigma^2 = 1.25$, and $\sigma = 1.12$; for $p = .4$, $\mu = 2$, $\sigma^2 = 1.2$, and $\sigma = 1.10$; for $p = .25$, $\mu = 1.25$, $\sigma^2 = .94$, and $\sigma = .97$; for $p = .1$, $\mu = .5$, $\sigma^2 = .45$, and $\sigma = .67$. Note that the variance of the random variable changes slowly as p begins to move away from .5 but then changes rapidly as it nears 0 and 1.

Tables A.14A through A.17G are based on the binomial distribution and its application; Chaps. 21 to 23 deal with problems where a binomial distribution is in many instances an underlying assumption.

The binomial distribution is also used as an approximation to other discrete variable distributions. For example, sampling is often from finite populations. If the population size is represented by N, then we have a probability of $1/N$ of drawing any particular individual on the first trial. The probability of drawing this particular individual on the second trial is dependent on what happened first, because we are sampling without replacement; it will be zero if the individual has been drawn but $1/(N - 1)$ if not. The probabilities are not constant from trial to trial. However, if the sample size is not too large relative to the population size, the binomial distribution may be a very satisfactory approximation for computing required probabilities. There are still other discrete variable distributions for which the binomial often provides a reasonable approximation.

Exercise 3.3.1 A fair die is rolled twice. How many points are there in the sample space? What probability is to be associated with each sample point?

Sketch the sample space and obtain from it the probability distribution of the sum of the numbers on the two rolls.

Use the definitions of μ and σ^2 from Chap. 2 to find the mean and variance of this sum.

Exercise 3.3.2 Repeat Exercise 3.3.1 using the mean rather than the sum.

Could you have applied Sec. 2.9 to save some effort? Explain.

Exercise 3.3.3 A test has 10 multiple-choice questions, each of which has four options. A student plans to use pure guesswork on this exam and wonders about the probability of success.

What will be the basic Bernoulli trial? What probabilities are to be associated with the sample space for a single trial? How many trials are to be made?

What is the distribution of the number of questions correctly answered? What is the probability that five or more are answered correctly?

Exercise 3.3.4 Investigators frequently compute intervals intended to include population means. Since they are using sample data, they cannot be certain that the intervals will contain the means. However, their techniques are such that they can say with what probability any particular application will be successful in yielding an interval that includes the mean. This probability is often set at .95.

Suppose that an investigator conducts 20 independent investigations, each resulting in a single interval. What is the probability that no more than two intervals will fail to include the population mean they were after?

3.4 Probability Functions for Continuous Variables

Not all probabilities deal with discrete random variables. For continuous variables, frequency tables and histograms can provide approximate probabilities. A probability found from such a device—from computing a relative frequency for each interval, for example—would be an approximation to the true probability of a random variable taking a value in an interval. We must look for a different approach to describing a probability function.

Consider the wheel of fortune in Fig. 3.2. The stopping point is defined as the point opposite the fixed arrow. How many stopping points are there? The wheel could be marked into 10 sectors and the stopping point defined as the number nearest the arrow. But each sector could be further divided into 10 sectors to give 100 stopping points, and so on. Clearly there is not a finite

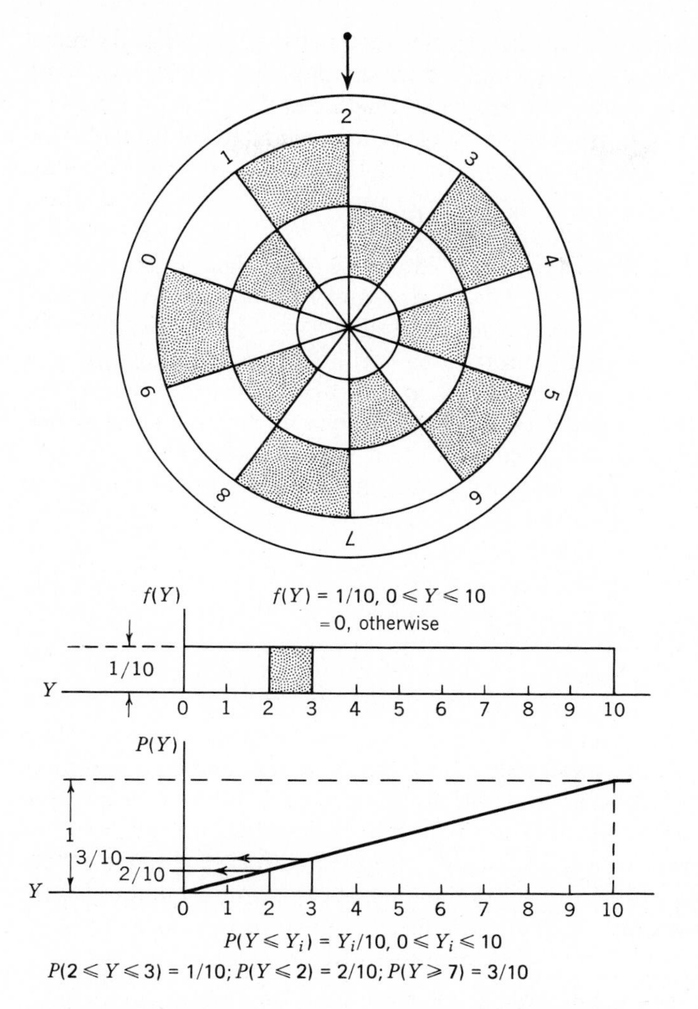

Figure 3.2. A wheel of fortune and associated probability distribution.

number of stopping points and, as a result, our classical definition of probability, Eq. (3.3), fails because we have no number for the denominator.

For a continuous variable with its indefinitely large number of events, one cannot assign a probability to each value. For the wheel of fortune divided into 10 sectors with the numbers 0, 1, 2, ..., 9 marked on successive dividing lines, we talk of probabilities associated with sectors or intervals but not about probabilities associated with points. The pointer must, of course, stop on one of the indefinitely many points. For probabilities associated with such intervals, we conveniently use an expression in Y or a *function* of Y, written $f(Y)$ and called a *probability density function.* The symbol $f(Y)$ is a generic term like "apple"; it requires something additional to fully inform us. For $f(Y)$, we need an equation—for example, Eq. (3.11); for apple, we need a name—for example, MacIntosh.

A probability density function is easily interpreted graphically. Referring to Fig. 3.2, we see that

$$f(Y) = 1/10 \qquad 0 \leq Y \leq 10 \tag{3.11}$$

is a function which describes a probability density. This is the *uniform* distribution. Here, any value of Y between 0 and 10 is possible. Areas under this curve (the term is used to include straight lines) are associated with probabilities. For example, the total area is (1/10)10, or 1; the shaded area between 2 and 3 is one-tenth; there is no area under the curve before 0 or after 10. (The numbers 0 and 10 are the same for this example.) The associated *cumulative distribution function* $P(Y)$ or its graph is used to give *probabilities.* For example, to find the probability that the pointer will stop between 2 and 3, that is, $P(2 \leq Y \leq 3)$, read up from $Y = 3$ to the sloping line, then over to the $P(Y)$ axis to obtain three-tenths. Repeat for $Y = 2$ to obtain two-tenths. Now subtract the probability of obtaining a value less than 2 from that of obtaining a value less than 3 to obtain the probability of a value between 2 and 3, that is,

$$P(2 \leq Y \leq 3) = P(Y \leq 3) - P(Y \leq 2)$$

Probability density functions are characterized in terms of their random variables. The mean and variance, μ and σ^2, are the parameters most used. The calculation of μ and σ^2 for continuous variables is beyond the scope of this text. When unknown, they are estimated by sample statistics.

As we proceed, we will be greatly concerned with cumulative distribution functions, or $P(Y)$'s. For us, this will mean extracting a number from a table. We will have little use for $f(Y)$ density functions except by name.

Exercise 3.4.1 Given $f(Y) = 1/10$, $0 \leq Y \leq 10$, as in Eq. (3.11). Use Fig. 3.2 to determine: $P(2 \leq Y \leq 7)$; $P(1 \leq Y \leq 9)$; $P(2 \leq Y \leq 4$ or $6 \leq Y \leq 8)$; $P(2 \leq Y \leq 4$ and $3 \leq Y \leq 7$, simultaneously).

3.5 The Normal Distribution

Important in the theory and practice of statistics is the *normal distribution.* Many biological phenomena result in data distributed in a manner sufficiently normal that the distribution is the basis of much of the statistical theory used by the biologist. In fact, the same is true in many other fields of application. The graph of the normal distribution, the normal curve, also called laplacian or gaussian, is a bell-shaped curve. Location of the center of this curve is given by μ; the amount of humping or heaping depends on the size of σ^2, a small σ^2 giving a higher hump than would a large σ^2. See Fig. 3.3.

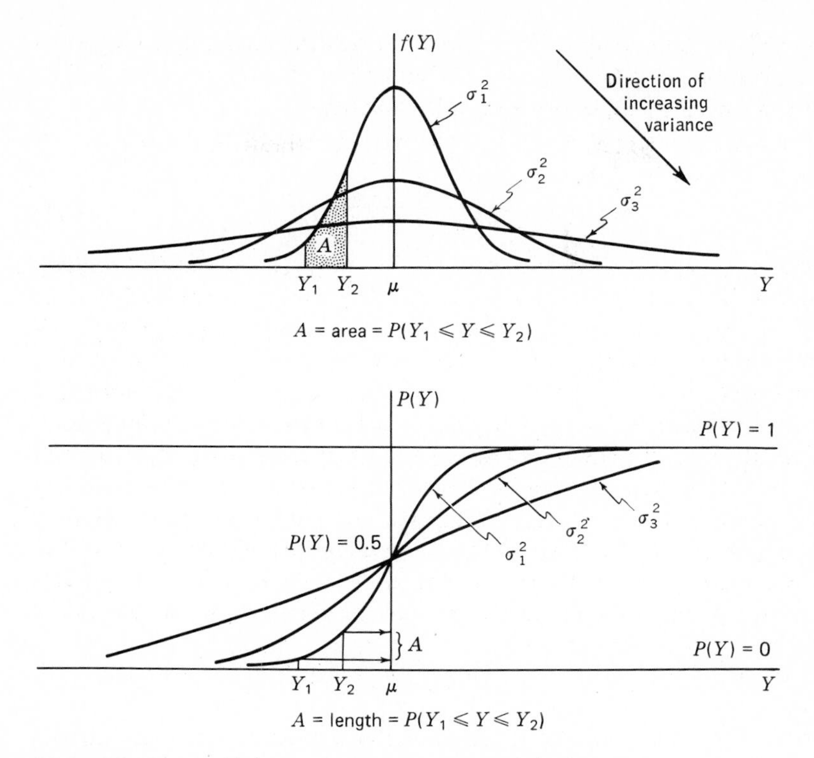

Figure 3.3 Normal, $f(Y)$, and cumulative normal, $P(Y)$, distributions.

For a moment, consider the binomial distribution for $n = 10$ and $p = .5$. Let the random variable be the number of 1s observed, that is the number of heads in 10 tosses of a fair coin, for example. Probabilities for the values are given in Table 3.2 and also shown in Fig. 3.4.

Like the normal distribution, the binomial with $p = .5$ is a symmetric distribution, but it needs only vertical bars to display probabilities. We could make a bar chart look like a histogram with columns of one unit width, as shown by the dotted lines; but a value of the random variable, by implication, now extends one-half unit on either side of the actual value.

Table 3.2 Binomial Probabilities for $n = 10$, $p = .5$

Y	0	1	2	3	4	5†
$\binom{10}{Y}$	1	10	45	120	210	252
$P(Y)$	.00098	.00977	.04395	.11719	.20508	.24609

$\mu = 5$, $\sigma^2 = 2.5$, $\sigma = 1.58$.

† To complete the table, note that $\binom{10}{Y} = \binom{10}{10-Y}$ and $P(Y) = P(10 - Y)$.

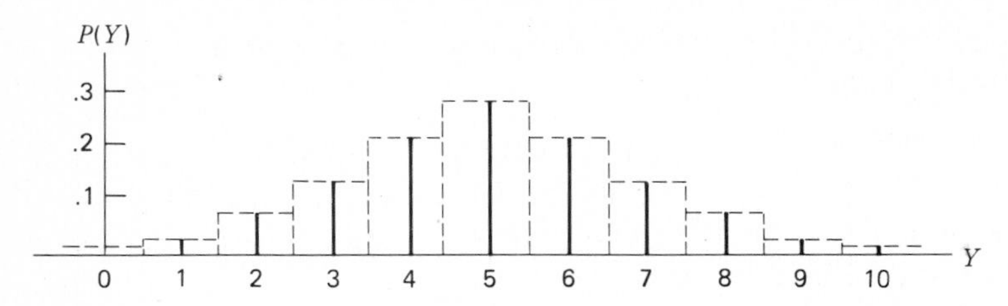

Figure 3.4 Vertical bars, binomial probabilities for $n = 10$, $p = .5$. Dotted lines: histogram representation.

With imagination, we see this histogram as comparable to one of the normal density functions of Fig. 3.3; the histogram simply lacks smoothness. Now imagine that n increases while we continue to draw histograms like that in Fig. 3.4 using the same length base line. It will be necessary to narrow the unit interval and the columns of the histogram. As n increases, more and more probabilities are required. Consequently, they become smaller in corresponding locations like the center or the tails. The steps of the histogram become smaller and the figure begins to look increasingly like a continuous curve, in fact, like the normal curve.

The time comes when the probability of any particular value of the random variable becomes very small because of the large divisor, 2^n, and the number, $n + 1$, of possible values, so it becomes impractical to compute and record probability distributions. We need to know the probability for a set of outcomes, for example, the probability that we will observe between 45 and 55 heads if a coin is tossed 100 times, or for fewer than 25 heads. It was in his search for an approximating distribution that would give such probabilities that de Moivre discovered the normal curve. The curve enables us to compute probabilities for such sets of Y values and is satisfactory for values of p other than .5, providing that n is large enough.

The mathematical formula for the normal probability density function does not give probabilities directly but describes the curves of the upper part of Fig. 3.3; it is completely determined by the two parameters μ and σ^2 or σ. The magnitude of the area A between Y_1 and Y_2 gives the probability that a randomly drawn individual will lie between Y_1 and Y_2, that is, $P(Y_1 \leq Y \leq Y_2) = A$. The total area under the curve and above the Y axis is 1. The curve is symmetric and one-half the area lies on each side of μ.

Cumulative normal distribution functions, curves giving the probability that a random Y will be less than a specified value, that is, $P(Y \leq Y_i)$, are shown in the lower portion of the figure for the curves of the upper part. Read up from Y_i and over to the $P(Y)$ axis to find probabilities. Since cumulative probabilities are given, it is necessary to obtain two values of $P(Y)$ to evaluate expressions such as $P(Y_1 \leq Y \leq Y_2)$. There is no simple mathematical expression for $P(Y)$ for the normal distribution.

3.6 Probabilities for a Normal Distribution; The Use of a Probability Table

Instead of a curve, a table is used to obtain probabilities for a normal distribution. Table A.4 gives probabilities for a normal distribution with $\mu = 0$ and $\sigma^2 = 1$. The variable is denoted by Z. Values of Z are given to one decimal place in the Z column and to a second in the Z row. This table can be used to obtain probabilities associated with any normal distribution provided that the mean and variance are known. Its use will now be illustrated for several problems involving a normal distribution with $\mu = 0$ and $\sigma^2 = 1$.

Case 1 To find the probability that a random value of Z will exceed a positive Z_1, that is, $P(Z \geq Z_1)$. Let us find $P(Z \geq 1.17)$.

Procedure Find 1.1 in the Z column and .07 in the Z row, $1.17 = 1.1 + .07$. The probability is found at the intersection of the row and column, thus $P(Z \geq 1.17) = .1210$. In other words, about 12 times in a hundred, on the average, we can expect to draw a random value of Z greater than 1.17 (see Fig. 3.5*a*).

Case 1a To find the probability that a random value of Z will be less than a positive Z_1, that is, $P(Z \leq Z_1)$. Let us find $P(Z \leq 1.17)$.

Procedure Since the area under the curve is 1,

$$P(Z \leq 1.17) = 1 - .1210 = .8790$$

(see Fig. 3.5*a*).

Case 1b To find the probability that a random value of Z will be less than some negative Z_1, that is, $P(Z \leq Z_1)$ where $Z_1 \leq 0$. Let us find $P(Z \leq -1.17)$.

Procedure The normal curve is symmetric. Since we are discussing a normal curve with zero mean,

$$P(Z \leq -1.17) = P(Z \geq 1.17) = .1210$$

See Fig. 3.5*d* for $Z = -1.05$ and $+1.05$.

Case 2 To find the probability that a random value of Z lies in an interval (Z_1, Z_2), to the right of the origin, that is, $P(Z_1 \leq Z \leq Z_2)$ where both $Z_1 \geq 0$ and $Z_2 > 0$. Let us find $P(.42 \leq Z \leq 1.61)$.

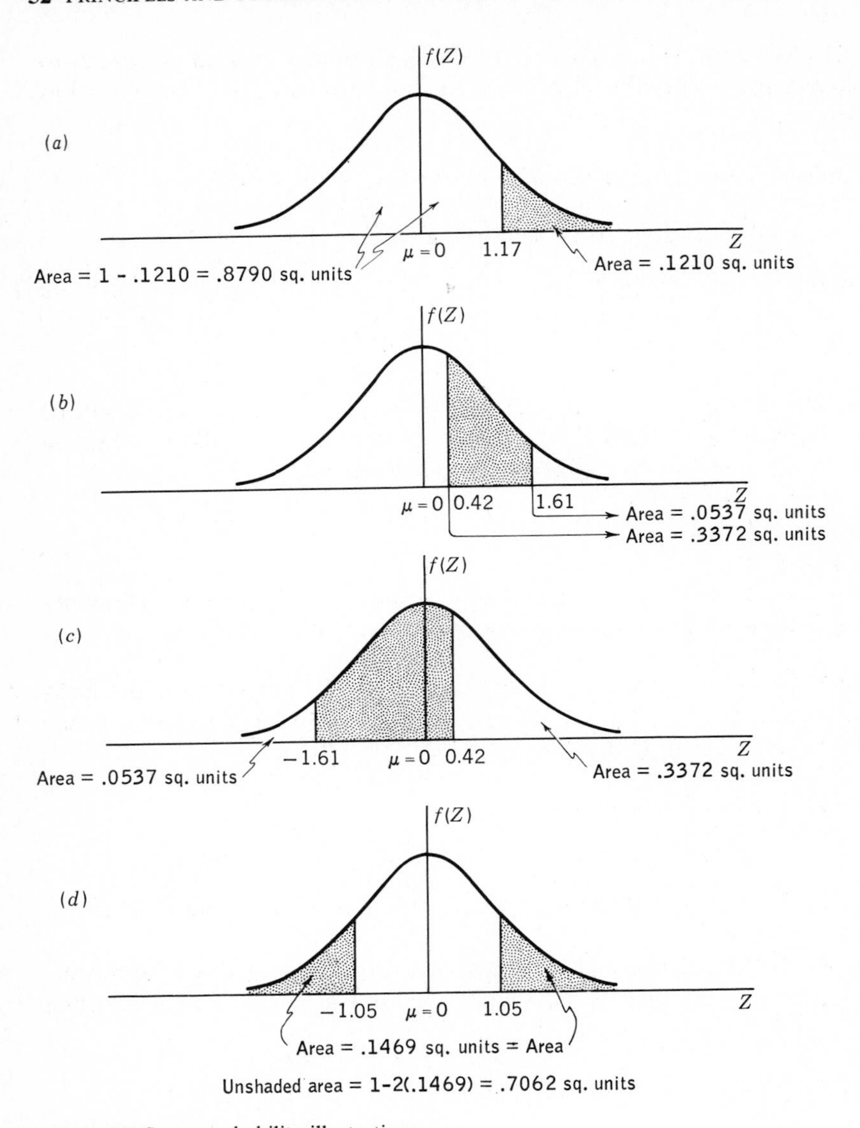

Figure 3.5 Some probability illustrations.

Procedure Find $P(Z \geq .42)$ and $P(Z \geq 1.61)$. Now

$$P(.42 \leq Z \leq 1.61) = P(Z \geq .42) - P(Z \geq 1.61)$$
$$= .3372 - .0537 = .2835$$

(see Fig. 3.5*b*).

Case 2a To find the probability that a random value of Z will lie in an interval to the left of the origin, that is, $P(Z_1 \leq Z \leq Z_2)$ where $Z_1 < 0$ and

$Z_2 \leq 0$. Let us find $P(-1.61 \leq Z \leq -.42)$. (Note that it is not necessary to place any sign before the letter Z unless some special value is being used as illustration.)

Procedure Again because of symmetry and because $\mu = 0$,

$$P(-1.61 \leq Z \leq -.42) = P(.42 \leq Z \leq 1.61) = .2835$$

Case 2b To find the probability that a random value of Z will lie in an interval which includes the origin, that is, $P(Z_1 \leq Z \leq Z_2)$, where $Z_1 < 0$ and $Z_2 > 0$. Let us find $P(-1.61 \leq Z \leq .42)$.

Procedure Since the area under the curve is 1, let us find the areas outside the interval and subtract their sum from one. $P(Z \leq -1.61) = P(Z \geq 1.61) = .0537$ and $P(Z \geq .42) = .3372$. Hence

$$P(-1.61 \leq Z \leq .42) = 1 - (.0537 + .3372) = .6091$$

(see Fig. 3.5*c*).

A probability often required in applications of statistics is that of obtaining a random value numerically greater than some number.

Case 3 To find the probability that a random value of Z will numerically exceed Z_1, that is, lie outside the interval $(-Z_1, Z_1)$, we require $P(|Z| \geq Z_1)$. Let us find $P(|Z| \geq 1.05)$.

Procedure Because of symmetry,

$$P(|Z| \geq 1.05) = 2P(Z \geq 1.05) = 2(.1469) = .2938$$

(see Fig. 3.5*d*). This method is shorter than the one implied in Case 2*b*.

Case 3a To find the probability that a random value of Z will be numerically less than Z_1, that is, lie within the interval $(-Z_1, Z_1)$, we require $P(|Z| \leq Z_1)$. Let us find $P(|Z| \leq 1.05)$.

Procedure Using the fact that the area under the curve is 1,

$$\begin{aligned} P(|Z| \leq 1.05) &= 1 - P(|Z| \geq 1.05) \\ &= 1 - 2(.1469) = .7062 \end{aligned}$$

(see Fig. 3.5*d*). The procedure of Case 2*b* is also available.

In statistics, one is often required to find values of a statistic such that random values will exceed it in a given proportion of cases, that is, with given probability. This amounts to constructing one's own table with desired P values in margins, say, and values of the variable in the body of the table. For example, in dealing with the normal distribution (or any symmetric one), 50 percent of random Z values will exceed the mean on the average.

Case 4 To illustrate, let us find the value of Z that will be exceeded with a given probability (that is, a random value must lie to the right of the required value with specified probability); for example, let us find Z_1 such that $P(Z \geq Z_1) = .25$.

Procedure Look through the body of the table for the probability .2500. It is on line $Z = .6$, approximately halfway between columns .07 and .08. The value of Z is between .67 and .68. Thus $P(Z \geq .67) = .25$ (approx).

A value of Z also often required is that which is exceeded or not exceeded numerically with a stated probability.

Case 5 To find the value of Z, say Z_1, such that $P(|Z| \geq Z_1)$ equals a given value [that is, the random value is to lie outside the interval $(-Z_1, Z_1)$]. Let us find Z_1 such that $P(|Z| \geq Z_1) = .05$.

Procedure Since the curve is symmetric, find Z_1 such that $P(Z \geq Z_1) = .05/2 = .025$. The procedure for Case 4 gives $Z_1 = 1.9 + .06 = 1.96$. Hence $P(|Z| \geq 1.96) = .05$.

Case 5a To find the value of Z, say Z_1, such that $P(-Z_1 \leq Z \leq Z_1)$ equals a stated value [that is, the random value is to lie within the interval $(-Z_1, Z_1)$]. Let us find Z_1 such that $P(-Z_1 \leq Z \leq Z_1) = .99$.

Procedure Since the area under the curve is one, we refer to Case 5 and note that $P(-Z_1 \leq Z \leq Z_1) = 1 - P(|Z| \geq Z_1)$. Hence

$$1 - P(-Z_1 \leq Z \leq Z_1) = P(|Z| \geq Z_1)$$
$$= 1 - .99 = .01$$

As in Case 5, find Z_1 such that $P(Z \geq Z_1) = .005$; Z_1 lies between 2.57 and 2.58. (To three decimal places $Z_1 = 2.576$.) Hence,

$$P(-2.576 \leq Z \leq 2.576) = .99$$

Exercise 3.6.1 Given a normal distribution with zero mean and unit variance, find $P(Z \geq 1.70)$; $P(Z \geq .96)$; $P(Z \leq 1.44)$; $P(Z \leq -1.44)$; $P(-1.01 \leq Z \leq .33)$; $P(-1 \leq Z \leq 1)$; $P(|Z| \leq 1)$; $P(|Z| \geq 1.65)$; $P(.45 \leq Z \leq 2.08)$.

Exercise 3.6.2 Find Z_0 such that $P(Z \geq Z_0) = .3333$; $P(Z \leq Z_0) = .6050$; $P(1.00 \leq Z \leq Z_0) = .1000$; $P(|Z| \geq Z_0) = .0100$; $P(|Z| \leq Z_0) = .9500$.

3.7 The Normal Distribution with Mean μ and Variance σ^2

The normal distribution with $\mu = 0$ and $\sigma^2 = 1$ is one and only one and you may have been wondering about tables for the many possible combinations of values of μ and σ^2. Actually, no further tables are necessary.

Example Suppose that we are sampling from a normal population with $\mu = 12$ and $\sigma^2 = 1$ and require $P(Y \geq 13.15)$.

The distribution is the same as that of the previous section except that it is displaced so that $\mu = 12$ rather than zero. Consequently,

$$P(Y \geq 13.15) = P(Y - \mu \geq 13.15 - 12)$$
$$= P(Z \geq 1.15) = .1251 \qquad \text{from Table A.4.}$$

In general, we wish to find $P(Y_1 \leq Y \leq Y_2)$. For example,

$$\begin{aligned} P(11.20 \leq Y \leq 13.44) &= 1 - P(Y \text{ is outside this interval}) \\ &= 1 - [P(Y \leq 11.20) + P(Y \geq 13.44)] \\ &= 1 - [P(Z \leq -.80) + P(Z \geq 1.44)] \\ &= 1 - [P(Z \geq .80) + P(Z \geq 1.44)] \\ &= 1 - (.2119 + .0749) = .7132 \end{aligned}$$

(see Fig. 3.6). The trick is seen to be the converting of a Y variable with a nonzero mean to a Z variable with a zero mean by subtracting μ.

For the most general case, that is, when $\mu \neq 0$ and $\sigma^2 \neq 1$ (the symbol $\neq$ means "not equal to"), one uses Table A.4 by calculating

$$Z = \frac{Y - \mu}{\sigma} \tag{3.12}$$

a deviation from the mean in units of the standard deviation (see Fig. 3.7). Thus we change any normal variable to another with zero mean and unit variance since σ is the new unit of measurement.

Example If sampling is from a normal distribution with $\mu = 5$ and $\sigma^2 = 4$ or $\sigma = 2$, find the probability of a sample value greater than 7.78.

Enter Table A.4 with

$$Z = \frac{Y - \mu}{\sigma} = \frac{7.78 - 5}{2} = 1.39$$

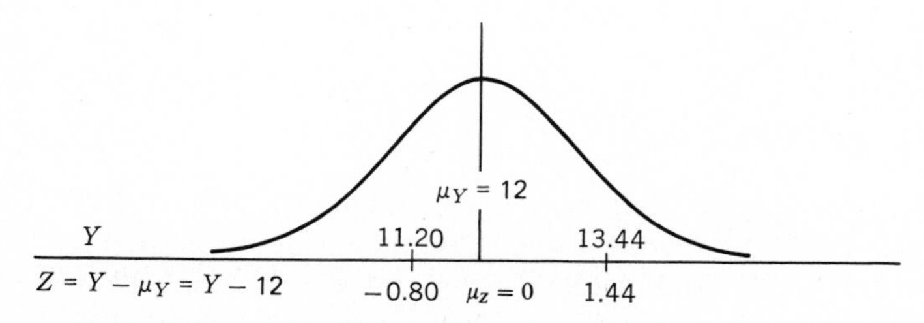

Figure 3.6 Probabilities for a normal distribution with $\mu = 12$, $\sigma^2 = 1$.

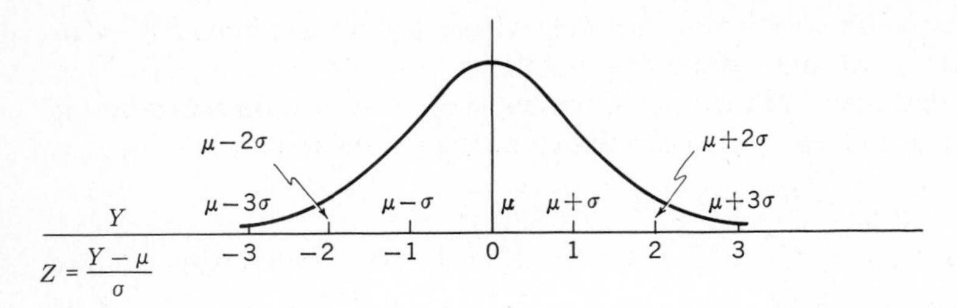

Figure 3.7 Relation between Y and Z for computing probabilities for the normal distribution.

Then
$$P(Y \geq 7.78) = P\left(\frac{Y - \mu}{\sigma} \geq \frac{7.78 - 5}{2}\right)$$
$$= P(Z \geq 1.39) = .0823$$

In this general case, σ is the unit of measurement. The variable Z is a deviation from the mean, namely $Y - \mu$, measured in units of standard deviations, that is, $(Y - \mu)/\sigma$. The preceding probability statement gives the probability of a random value of Z being greater than 1.39, or a random value of Y being farther to the right of μ than 1.39σ. The variable Z is called a *standardized normal* variable. If a distribution is not known to be normal, such a variable is simply a *standardized variable.*

The statement

$$P\left(-1 \leq \frac{Y - \mu}{\sigma} \leq +1\right) = 1 - 2(.1587) = .6826$$

says that the probability of a random value of $(Y - \mu)/\sigma$ lying between -1 and $+1$ is about two-thirds; or that about two-thirds of all values of $(Y - \mu)/\sigma$ lie between -1 and $+1$.

Exercise 3.7.1 Given a normal distribution of Y with mean 5 and variance 16, find $P(Y \leq 10)$; $P(Y \leq 0)$; $P(0 \leq Y \leq 15)$; $P(Y \geq 5)$; $P(Y \geq 15)$.

Exercise 3.7.2 Given a normal distribution of Y with mean 20 and variance 25, find Y_0 such that $P(Y \leq Y_0) = .025$; $P(Y \leq Y_0) = .01$; $P(Y \leq Y_0) = .95$; $P(Y \geq Y_0) = .90$.

3.8 The Distribution of Means

When a population is sampled, it is customary to summarize the results by calculating $\bar{Y}$ and other statistics. Continued sampling generates a population of $\bar{Y}$'s with a mean and variance of its own; and $\bar{Y}$ is a sample of one observation from this new population. The population originally sampled is often called the *parent population* or *parent distribution;* a population of sample means, like other populations of statistics, is called a *derived distribution* since it is derived by sampling a parent distribution. It has already been noted that the mean and variance of a population of means of n observations are the mean and $1/n$th of the variance of the parent population, that is, $\mu_{\bar{Y}} = \mu$ and $\sigma_{\bar{Y}}^2 = \sigma^2/n$. Absence of a subscript indicates a parameter for the parent population.

Consider a type of problem that arises in sampling experiments involving normal populations; namely, what is the probability that the sample mean will exceed a given value?

Example Given a random sample of $n = 16$ observations from a normal population with $\mu = 10$ and $\sigma^2 = 4$. Find $P(\bar{Y} \geq 11)$.

The sample mean is a sample of size 1 from a normal population with

$$\mu_{\bar{Y}} = \mu = 10$$

$$\sigma_{\bar{Y}}^2 = \frac{\sigma^2}{n} = 4/16 = 1/4 \qquad \text{and} \qquad \sigma_{\bar{Y}} = \sqrt{1/4} = 1/2$$

Enter Table A.4 with

$$Z = \frac{\bar{Y} - \mu_{\bar{Y}}}{\sigma_{\bar{Y}}} = \frac{11 - 10}{1/2} = 2$$

Now $P(Z \geq 2) = .0228$, that is, $P(\bar{Y} \geq 11) = .0228$ because 11 is two standard deviations to the right of the mean of the population of $\bar{Y}$'s. Also $P(|Z| \geq 2) = 2(.0228) = .0456$. Hence

$$P(-2 \leq Z \leq 2) = P(9 \leq \bar{Y} \leq 11) = 1 - .0456 = .9544.$$

A sample $\bar{Y}$ less than 9 or greater than 11 would be likely to occur only about 5 times, 100(.0456), in 100 or 1 time in 20, on the average. This is generally regarded as unusual. About 95 times out of 100 or 19 times out of 20, on the average, random $\bar{Y}$'s from this population will lie in the interval (9, 11).

In the previous paragraph, we have defined "unusual" for statistical purposes. If a random event occurs only about 1 time in 20, we agree to label the event unusual. Occasionally we will revise our definition for particular circumstances but this definition is easily the most common.

Exercise 3.8.1 Given that Y is normally distributed with mean 10 and variance 36, a sample of 25 observations is drawn. Find $P(\bar{Y} \geq 12)$; $P(\bar{Y} \leq 9)$; $P(8 \leq \bar{Y} \leq 12)$; $P(\bar{Y} \geq 9)$; $P(\bar{Y} \leq 11.5)$.

Exercise 3.8.2 Given that Y is normally distributed with mean 2 and variance 9. For a sample of 16 observations, find $\bar{Y}_0$ such that $P(\bar{Y} \leq \bar{Y}_0) = .75$; $P(\bar{Y} \leq \bar{Y}_0) = .20$; $P(\bar{Y} \geq \bar{Y}_0) = .66$; $P(\bar{Y} \geq \bar{Y}_0) = .05$.

3.9 The χ^2 Distribution

We now discuss the distribution of χ^2 (Greek *chi*; read as chi-square) because of its relation to s^2 and the very important Student's t distribution, the topic of the next section. Chi-square is defined as the sum of squares of independent, normally distributed variables with zero means and unit variances. Section 3.6 dealt exclusively with a normal variable with zero mean and unit variance, whereas Sec. 3.7 showed how to change any normal variable to one with zero mean and unit variance. Thus we have

$$\chi^2 = \sum_i Z_i^2 = \sum_i \left(\frac{Y_i - \mu_i}{\sigma_i} \right)^2 \tag{3.13}$$

Equation (3.13) is more general than we presently need, since we are discussing sampling a single population with constant σ. In sampling from a normal distribution, the quantity $\text{SS} = (n - 1)s^2$ consists of the sum of squares of $n - 1$ independent deviations as stated in Sec. 2.8. It can be shown that such deviations have zero means; division by the common σ ensures that they have unit variances. Hence

$$\chi^2 = \frac{(n - 1)s^2}{\sigma^2} \tag{3.14}$$

is a particular case of Eq. (3.13) and is the one with which we are to be presently concerned.

The distribution of χ^2 depends on the number of independent deviations, that is, on the degrees of freedom. For each number of degrees of freedom, there is a χ^2 distribution. Some chi-square curves are shown in Fig. 3.8. Obviously χ^2 cannot be negative since it involves a sum of squared numbers. While the peaks are seen to lag to the left of the degrees of freedom, curves begin to look more and more symmetric as the degrees of freedom increase. The mean and variance of a χ^2 variable are df and 2 df, respectively.

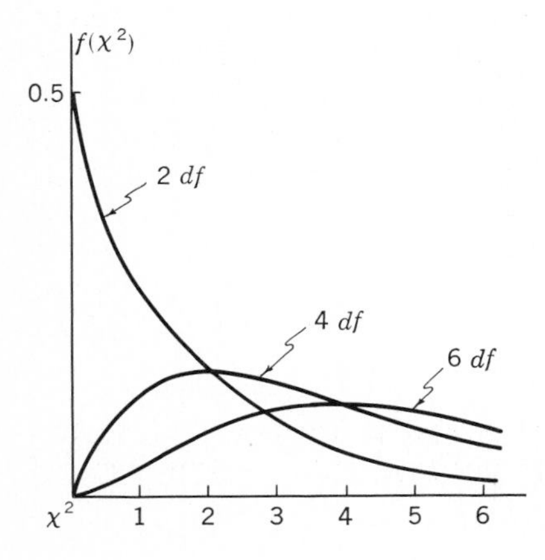

Figure 3.8 Distribution of χ^2, for 2, 4, and 6 degrees of freedom.

It is customary to tabulate only a few values for each of many curves. Thus we have Table A.5. Probabilities are given at the top of the table, degrees of freedom in the left column, and χ^2 values in the body of the table for the stated combinations of P and df.

Example To find the random value of χ^2 with 15 degrees of freedom exceeded with probability .25, that is, to find χ_1^2 such that

$$P(\chi^2 \geq \chi_1^2) = .25$$

Enter Table A.5 for 15 degrees of freedom and read under the column headed .250. Here $\chi^2 = 18.2$ and $P(\chi^2 \geq 18.2) = .25$.

Example To find the probability with which an observed $\chi^2 = 13.1$ with 10 degrees of freedom will be exceeded.

Enter Table A.5 for 10 degrees of freedom and read across for the number 13.1. It lies between 12.5 and 16.0, χ^2 values exceeded with probabilities .25 and .10. Hence $.25 > P(\chi^2 \geq 13.1) > .10$.

These examples illustrate the problems most often met. They involve the use of only the right-hand tail of the distribution, unlike the Z distribution where one may be as interested in both tails as in one.

The distribution of χ^2 with 1 degree of freedom is directly related to the normal distribution. Consider χ^2 with 1 degree of freedom for $P = .10$. In our shorthand, $P(\chi^2 \geq 2.71) = .10$ from Table A.5. Since by definition this χ^2 is the square of a single normal deviation with zero mean and unit variance, $\sqrt{\chi^2}$ must be a normal deviation with zero mean and unit variance. Hence if we enter Table A.4 with $Z = \sqrt{2.71} = 1.645$, we should find the probability of obtaining a greater value at random to be $(1/2)(.10) = .05$. From Table A.4, $P(Z \geq 1.64) = .0505$ and $P(Z \geq 1.65) = .0495$. Thus our whole normal table, Table A.4, is condensed in a single line of Table A.5, that for 1 degree of freedom. Note that Z values from both tails of the normal distribution go into the upper tail of χ^2 for 1 degree of freedom because of the disappearance of the minus sign in squaring, while Z values near zero, either positive or negative, go into χ^2 with 1 degree of freedom at the tail near zero. Values near zero are not generally of special interest, so the χ^2 table is ordinarily used with the emphasis on large values.

Exercise 3.9.1 Find χ_0^2 such that $P(\chi^2 \geq \chi_0^2) = .05$ for 10 degrees of freedom; $P(\chi^2 \geq \chi_0^2) = .01$ for 12 degrees of freedom; $P(\chi^2 \geq \chi_0^2) = .50$ for 25 degrees of freedom; $P(\chi^2 \leq \chi_0^2) = .025$ for 18 degrees of freedom.

Exercise 3.9.2 Find P such that $P(\chi^2 \geq 17.01)$ for 11 degrees of freedom; $P(\chi^2 \geq 6.5)$ for 6 degrees of freedom; $P(\chi^2 \geq 20)$ for 10 degrees of freedom; $P(\chi^2 \leq 3.8)$ for 4 degrees of freedom.

3.10 The Distribution of Student's *t*

William Sealy Gosset, 1876–1937, a brewer or statistician according to your point of view, wrote many statistical papers under the pseudonym of Student. He recognized that the use of s for σ in calculating Z values for use with normal tables was not trustworthy for small samples and that an alternative table was required. He concerned himself with a variable closely related to the variable $t = (\bar{Y} - \mu)/s_{\bar{Y}}$, an expression involving two statistics, $\bar{Y}$ and $s_{\bar{Y}}$, rather than with $Z = (\bar{Y} - \mu)/\sigma_{\bar{Y}}$, with one. Now, the statistic

$$t = \frac{\bar{Y} - \mu}{s_{\bar{Y}}} = \frac{\bar{Y} - \mu}{\sqrt{s^2/n}} \tag{3.15}$$

for samples from a normal distribution, is universally known as Student's t.

Like χ^2, t has a different distribution for each value of the degrees of freedom. Again, we are content with an abbreviated table, Table A.3, with t values rather than probabilities in the body of the table. Table A.3 gives probabilities for larger values of t, sign ignored, at the top. These are often referred to as two-tailed probabilities. For example, for a random sample of size 16, from the line for df $= 16 - 1 = 15$ and in the column headed 0.05, we find that $P(|t| \geq 2.131) = .05$. Table A.3 gives probabilities for larger values of t, sign not ignored, at the bottom. These may be referred to as one-tailed probabilities. Thus, for a random sample of size 16, from the line for df $= 15$ and in the column with .025 at the bottom, we find that $P(t \geq 2.131) = .025 = P(t \leq -2.131)$.

The curve for t is symmetric, as implied by the previous examples. It is somewhat flatter than the distribution of $Z = (\bar{Y} - \mu)/\sigma_{\bar{Y}}$, lying under it at the center and above it in the tails. As the degrees of freedom increase, the t distribution approaches the normal. This can be seen from an examination of the entries in Table A.3, since the last line, df $= \infty$, is that of a normal distribution and the entries in any column are obviously approaching the corresponding value.

An important property of t for samples from normal populations is that its components, essentially $\bar{Y}$ and s, show no sign of varying together. In other words, if many samples of the same size are collected, $\bar{Y}$ and s calculated, and the resulting pairs plotted as points on a graph with axes $\bar{Y}$ and s, then these points will be scattered in a manner giving no suggestion of a relation, such as that large means are associated with large standard deviations. For any distribution other than the normal, some sort of relation exists between sample values of $\bar{Y}$ and s in repeated sampling.

Exercise 3.10.1 Find t_0 such that $P(t \geq t_0) = .025$ for 8 degrees of freedom; $P(t \leq t_0) = .01$ for 15 degrees of freedom; $P(|t| \geq t_0) = .10$ for 12 degrees of freedom; $P(-t_0 \leq t \leq t_0) = .80$ for 22 degrees of freedom.

Exercise 3.10.2 Find $P(t \geq 2.6)$ for 8 degrees of freedom; $P(t \leq 1.7)$ for 15 degrees of freedom; $P(t \leq 1.1)$ for 18 degrees of freedom; $P(-1.1 \leq t \leq 2.1)$ for 5 degrees of freedom; $P(|t| \geq 1.8)$ for 6 degrees of freedom.

3.11 Estimation and Inference

The discussion so far has been concerned with sampling from known populations. In general, population parameters are not known though there may be hypotheses about their values. The subject of statistics deals largely with drawing inferences about population parameters, uncertain inferences since they are based on sample evidence.

Consider the problem of estimating parameters. For example, one might wish to know the average yield at maturity of a wheat variety, or the average length of time to get over a cold. It is fairly obvious that $\bar{Y}$ is an estimate of μ and that s^2 is an estimate of σ^2, especially if we accept the idea, proposed in Sec. 2.12, of the linear additive model. Of course, these are not the only estimates of these parameters. How good are these statistics as estimates of parameters? Unless the parameters are known, one cannot know how well a particular sample statistic estimates a parameter; one must be content in knowing how good a sample statistic is on the average, that is, how well it does in repeated sampling, or, how many sample values can be expected to lie in a stated interval about the parameter. For example, consider three statistics or formulas for estimating the parameter μ. (The median, the mean, and the middle of the range, called the midrange, are three, though not necessarily those of this example.) Denote these by $\hat{\mu}_1$, $\hat{\mu}_2$, and $\hat{\mu}_3$, where the $\wedge$ (call it "hat") indicates an estimate rather than the parameter itself. The formulas are called *estimators* as well as statistics. All possible values of $\hat{\mu}_1$, $\hat{\mu}_2$, and $\hat{\mu}_3$ might generate distributions as in Fig. 3.9 where $\hat{\mu}_1$ gives fairly consistent values, that is, they have a relatively small variance but they are not centered on μ; $\hat{\mu}_2$ gives consistent values that are centered at μ; $\hat{\mu}_3$ gives values centered at μ but spreading rather widely. The problem is now to choose the "best" formula, where best must first be defined.

Instead of defining best, consider a number of desirable properties and try to have as many as possible associated with the choice of an estimator. For example, *unbiasedness* requires that the mean of all possible estimates given by an estimator, that is, the mean of the population of estimates, be the parameter being estimated. The mean of a population of $\bar{Y}$'s is μ, the parameter being estimated for the parent population so that $\bar{Y}$ is an unbiased estimate of μ. The mean of a population of s^2's, namely μ_{s^2}, is σ^2, so s^2 is an unbiased estimate of σ^2. However, if the divisor of the sum of squares had been n rather than $n - 1$, the estimate would not have been unbiased. Bias is not serious if its magnitude is known. This would be the case if n were the divisor in estimating σ^2. Bias may be serious if its magnitude is unknown because no correction for bias is then possible.

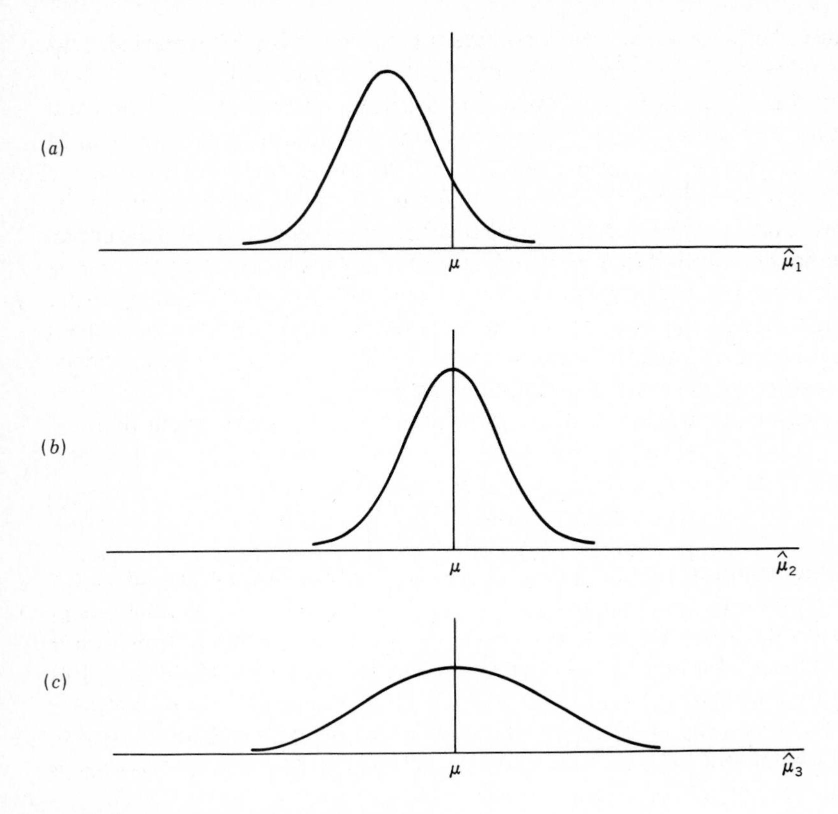

Figure 3.9 Illustration for choice of estimator.

Another desirable property is that of having a small variance. *Minimum variance* is most desirable. In Fig. 3.9, $\hat{\mu}_3$ has too large a variance whereas $\hat{\mu}_1$ and $\hat{\mu}_2$ have comparatively small variances and are preferable on this basis. The estimators $\hat{\mu}_1$ and $\hat{\mu}_2$ are said to be more *efficient* than $\hat{\mu}_3$.

Simplicity of computation is a desirable property. Any estimate found by adding and subtracting multiples of observations is said to be a *linear function* of them. The mean is a linear function requiring one-*n*th of each observation; the variance and standard deviation are not linear functions. Clearly, linear functions are simple to compute.

If for a parameter we can find linear estimators that are unbiased and if among all such estimators there is one with minimum variance, then it is called the *best linear unbiased estimator*, or the *b.l.u.e.* We have already seen that we do not always insist on having such estimators.

Whereas $\bar{Y}$ and s^2 are estimates of μ and σ^2, it would be quite surprising if they were actually μ and σ^2 rather than only in their neighborhoods. This suggests that it might be more appropriate to give an interval about $\bar{Y}$ or s^2

and state that we are reasonably confident that μ or σ^2 is in the interval. This can be done with the help of the t distribution of Sec. 3.10.

For a given μ and σ^2, it is possible to define an interval on the $\bar{Y}$ axis and state the probability of obtaining a random $\bar{Y}$ in the interval; we wish to reverse the process and for a given $\bar{Y}$ and s^2 define an interval and state the probability that μ is in the interval. Since μ will either be or not be in the interval, that is, $P = 0$ or 1, the probability will actually be a measure of the confidence to be placed in the procedure that led to the statement. This is like throwing a ring at a fixed post; the ring doesn't land in the same position or even catch on the post every time. However, we are able to say that we can circle the post nine times out of ten, or whatever the value should be for the measure of our confidence in our proficiency.

To reverse the process, we begin with a probability statement like

$$P\left(-t_{.025} \le \frac{\bar{Y} - \mu}{s_{\bar{Y}}} \le t_{.025}\right) = .95 \tag{3.16}$$

about the random variable $t = (\bar{Y} - \mu)/s_{\bar{Y}}$. It states that the probability P that the random variable $t = (\bar{Y} - \mu)/s_{\bar{Y}}$ will lie between $-t_{.025}$ and $+t_{.025}$ is .95. First, note that t is like Eq. (3.12) but with population standard deviation replaced by its estimate from the sample. This leaves only the one unknown parameter, namely μ, in the random variable. Second, the subscript on t refers to the probability of a random value of t lying to the right of the tabulated value $t_{.025}$; thus the probability of lying to the right of $t_{.025}$ is .025, and to the left of $-t_{.025}$ is .025.

Algebraic manipulation allows us to write Eq. (3.16) as

$$P(\bar{Y} - t_{.025}s_{\bar{Y}} < \mu < \bar{Y} + t_{.025}s_{\bar{Y}}) = .95 \tag{3.17}$$

Now the statement says that the probability that μ will lie in the random interval $(\bar{Y} - t_{.025}s_{\bar{Y}}, \bar{Y} + t_{.025}s_{\bar{Y}})$ is .95. The interval is still in the future; μ continues fixed.

An illustration may make this clearer. A sample, number 1, Table 4.3, was drawn from a known population and the statistics $\bar{Y}$, s^2, and t were calculated. Use of Eq. (3.17) leads to the statement that

$$P(24.77 \le \mu \le 48.03) = .95$$

In fact, $\mu = 40$, so we know with certainty ($P = 1$) that μ lies in this particular interval. Consequently, if we accept the statement as one of probability, then we must interpret it by saying that the probability .95 measures the confidence we place in the process that leads to such intervals. We call .95 the *confidence coefficient*. The practice of writing P_F instead of P when sample results are used calls attention to the nature of the probability involved; the letter F stands for *fiducial*.

In a real situation, an experimenter does not know the mean of the population being sampled; the problem is to estimate the population mean and state the degree of confidence to be associated with the estimate. The confidence interval procedure is a solution to this problem.

Example In a prolactin assay reported by Finney (3.1), response is measured as the crop-gland weight of pigeons, in 0.1 g. For a dose of the test preparation of 0.125 mg, four weights obtained are 28, 65, 35, and 36. The problem is to estimate the population mean.

Assume that the data are a random sample from a normal population with unknown mean and variance, namely, the population of crop-gland weights for all such possible birds that might be housed and kept for assay purposes under the conditions existing at the laboratory and given a dose of 0.125 mg of the test preparation. Sample statistics are $\bar{Y} = 41$ dg, $s^2 = 269$, $s_{\bar{Y}} = 8.2$ dg. Tabulated $t_{.025}$ for 3 degrees of freedom is 3.18. An interval estimate for the population mean is given by $\bar{Y} \pm ts_{\bar{Y}} = 41 \pm (3.18) \times (8.2) = (15, 67)$ dg; we assign .95 as a measure of our confidence in the statement that μ lies in the interval (15, 67) dg. Alternatively, the population mean μ is in the interval (15, 67) dg unless the particular random sample is an unusual one. An unusual sample leads to a false statement about the location of μ; this happens about 1 time in 20 on the average—that is, 5 percent of the time. Consequently, if μ is not in (15, 67) dg, it is because our sample is unusual.

In our example, we have a *confidence coefficient* of .95 and an *error rate* of 5 percent. The choice of error rate will obviously depend on the seriousness of a wrong decision.

If there were a priori reasons to expect the population mean to be 20 dg, this sample would not constitute evidence, at the 5 percent *level of significance*, to throw doubt upon such an expectation. If there were a priori reasons to expect a population mean of 80, this sample would be evidence tending to deny such an expectation at the 5 percent *level of significance.*

When σ^2 is known, it is possible to choose a sample size such that the confidence interval, when obtained, will be of a predetermined length for the chosen error rate. When σ^2 is unknown, it is possible to determine a sample size such that the experimenter can be reasonably confident (the degree of confidence can be set) that the confidence interval to be calculated for a chosen error rate will not be longer than a predetermined value. In addition, a method of sampling, called sequential, can be used to obtain a confidence interval of fixed length.

Exercise 3.11.1 Finney (3.1) also reported crop-gland weights of pigeons, in 0.1 g, for doses of the test preparation of 0.250 and 0.500 mg. The resulting weights were 48, 47, 54, 74 and 60, 130, 83, 60, respectively. Define populations for these two sets of data and estimate the population means using 95 and 99 percent confidence intervals. Note the difference in lengths for each population.

3.12 Prediction of Sample Results

An incorrect statement that one may hear is that a probability statement concerning the population mean tells us something about the distribution of future sample means, for example, that 95 percent of future sample means will be in a stated interval. Most of these statements are misleading and incorrect. However, it is possible to make a statement about a future sample observation that can be very useful.

Consider a problem in hydrologic forecasting. The use and development of water resources have created a serious demand for advance estimates of the flow or runoff supplied by streams in a watershed. In other words, the prediction of a future event or observation is desired. The population of all possible rates of flow supplied by a particular stream in the watershed is obviously unknown, but runoff values for a number of preceding years are a sample from the population. Obviously this is not a random sample of independent observations, but we can begin by assuming that it is. (The experience of checking predictions with results is one method of judging whether the measure of reliability placed on our statements is justified. An alternative method is to use all but the most recent observation in making the prediction, then check the prediction against the unused observation. If this can be done for a sufficient number of similar watersheds, it is possible to pass judgment upon the reliability of the stated error rate before being publicly committed to a probability statement.)

If the population mean is known, we could use this as the predicted value, a point estimate only; there would be no meaning in guessing what the random value itself was going to be. However, an interval estimate or prediction of the next random value can be prepared with the use of normal or t tables. The use of an interval is an attempt to allow for the random ε that is called for in the linear additive model, Eq. (2.13), and is certain to be present.

If μ and σ^2 were known, then the interval and confidence statement could be

$$P(\mu - Z_{.005}\sigma \leq Y \leq \mu + Z_{.005}\sigma) = .99$$

since 99 percent of random observations lie within $Z_{.005}$ standard deviations of the mean (see Sec. 3.7).

In the usual problem, μ and σ^2 are unknown but estimates $\bar{Y}$ and s^2 are available. Prediction of the next Y, for example, next year's runoff, is necessarily $\bar{Y}$. The variance appropriate to this predicted value of Y is the sum of the variances of the observed sample mean and a random component, that is, $(s^2/n) + s^2 = [(n + 1)/n]s^2$. Thus the appropriate confidence statement is

$$P\left[\bar{Y} - t_{.005}\sqrt{s^2\left(\frac{n+1}{n}\right)} \leq Y \leq \bar{Y} + t_{.005}\sqrt{s^2\left(\frac{n+1}{n}\right)}\right] = .99 \quad (3.18)$$

where $t_{.005}$ is the tabulated value of Student's t such that the probability of a larger positive value is .005.

Exercise 3.12.1 In Sec. 3.4, the term *function of Y* is used. Write out six functions of Y used in this chapter that appear to be important in statistics.

Exercise 3.12.2 Distinguish clearly between estimation of a population mean and prediction of a value to be observed. Try to specify situations for which each procedure is more likely to be wanted.

References

3.1. Finney, D. J.: *Statistical method in biological assay*, Hafner, New York, 1952, Table 12.1.

A Proposed Laboratory Exercise in Connection with Chap. 3

Purpose (1) To give the student practice in computing some familiar statistics and using associated tables. (2) To build up more empirical evidence about sample statistics for comparison with theoretical results. (See laboratory exercises for Chaps. 2 and 4.)

For each of your 10 random samples (see laboratory exercises for Chap. 2), compute

(*a*) $Z = \dfrac{\bar{Y} - \mu}{\sigma/\sqrt{n}}$, using $\mu = 40$, $\sigma = 12$

(*b*) $t = \dfrac{\bar{Y} - \mu}{s/\sqrt{n}}$

(*c*) The 95 percent confidence interval for μ

(*d*) The 99 percent confidence interval for μ

(*e*) $\chi^2 = [(n-1)s^2]/\sigma^2$

CHAPTER

FOUR

SAMPLING FROM A NORMAL DISTRIBUTION

4.1 Introduction

Calculation of the common statistics $\bar{Y}$, s^2, and s as measures of central tendency and dispersion has been discussed. When calculated from random samples, $\bar{Y}$ and s^2 are unbiased estimates (Sec. 3.11) of the parent population parameters μ and σ^2 and s is a biased estimate of σ.

The standard deviation of means can be estimated from a sample of observations by the formula $s_{\bar{Y}} = s/\sqrt{n}$, where s is the sample standard deviation. The use of $\bar{Y}$, $s_{\bar{Y}}$, and a tabulated value of Student's t to establish a confidence interval for the population mean was given in Sec. 3.11. The average number as a decimal fraction, of intervals that contain μ, is called the *confidence probability* or *confidence coefficient.*

The results used thus far are based on mathematical theorems and principles. Such results can be demonstrated with a reasonable degree of accuracy by large-scale sampling procedures. This is an *empirical method.* In this chapter, sampling is used as a method of examining the distribution of a number of statistics and the confidence interval procedure.

4.2 A Normally Distributed Population

A normal population has a continuous variable with an infinite range; an observation may consequently assume any real value, positive or negative. Table 4.1 consists of yields in pounds of butterfat for 100 Holstein cows, the

Table 4.1 Array of pounds of butterfat produced during a month by 100 Holstein cows

The original data were modified to approximate a normal distribution with $\mu = 40$ lb and $\sigma = 12$ lb

Item	Pounds	Item	Pounds	Item	Pounds	Item	Pounds
00	10	25	33	50	40	75	47
01	12	26	33	51	40	76	48
02	14	27	34	52	41	77	48
03	15	28	34	53	41	78	48
04	17	29	34	54	41	79	49
05	18	30	35	55	41	80	49
06	20	31	35	56	42	81	49
07	22	32	35	57	42	82	50
08	23	33	36	58	42	83	50
09	25	34	36	59	42	84	51
10	26	35	36	60	43	85	51
11	27	36	37	61	43	86	52
12	28	37	37	62	43	87	52
13	28	38	37	63	43	88	53
14	29	39	37	64	44	89	54
15	29	40	38	65	44	90	55
16	30	41	38	66	44	91	57
17	30	42	38	67	45	92	58
18	31	43	38	68	45	93	60
19	31	44	39	69	45	94	62
20	31	45	39	70	46	95	63
21	32	46	39	71	46	96	65
22	32	47	39	72	46	97	66
23	32	48	40	73	47	98	68
24	33	49	40	74	47	99	70
						Total	4,000

original data having been modified somewhat to form an approximately normal distribution. The resulting data depart from normality in two major respects: the variable has a finite range and is discrete or discontinuous. The effects due to the finite range and discreteness of the data are small in comparison with sampling variation and accordingly will have little effect upon inferences based on samples.

The salient characteristics of the distribution are depicted in Figs. 4.1 and 4.2. Figure 4.1 is a histogram of the data with pounds on the horizontal axis and frequency on the vertical. The values concentrate at the center and thin out symmetrically on both sides, quickly at first and then less rapidly. Figure 4.2 shows the 100 values cumulatively. For example, to find the number of observations (position in array) less than a certain weight in pounds, draw a line vertically from that weight to the smooth curve implied

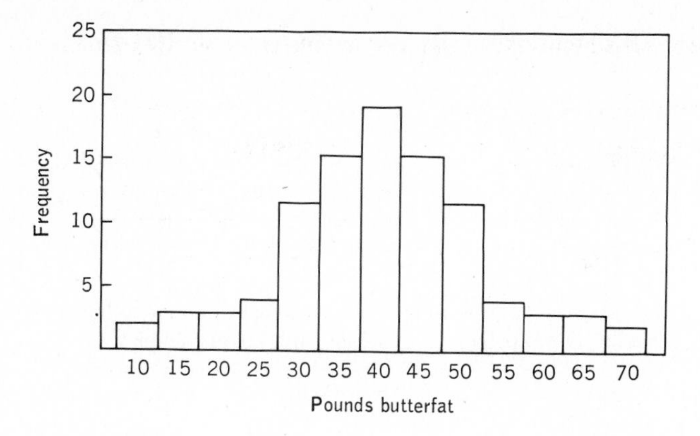

Figure 4.1 Histogram of the distribution of pounds of butterfat from 100 Holstein cows.

by the dots representing the observations, then horizontally to the ordinate axis where the number is read. The relation of the histogram to the array is that the height of the rectangle in any class of the histogram is proportional to the number of dots lying between the corresponding pair of vertical lines of the array.

Table 4.2 is a frequency distribution of pounds of butterfat for the data of Table 4.1. Each class has a range of 5 lb.

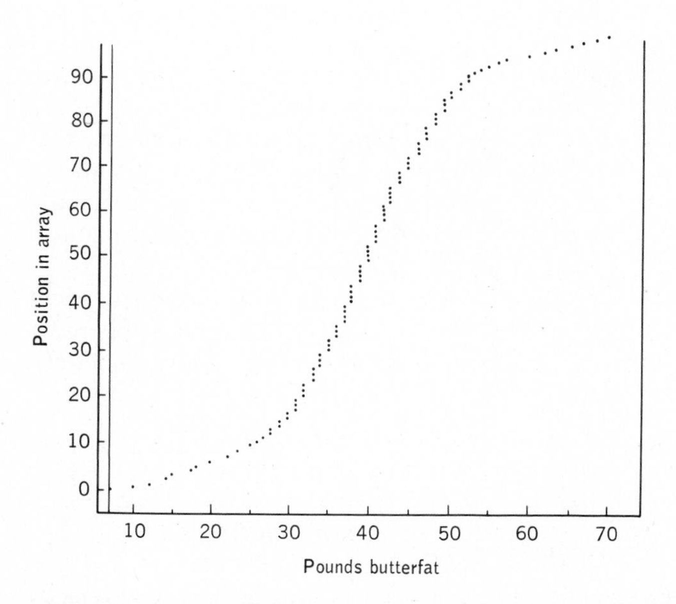

Figure 4.2 Graphical representation of the array of pounds of butterfat of 100 Holstein cows.

Table 4.2 A frequency distribution of pounds of butterfat of 100 Holstein cows

Midpoint, or class mark	10	15	20	25	30	35	40	45	50	55	60	65	70
Frequency	2	3	3	4	12	16	20	16	12	4	3	3	2

Exercise 4.2.1 For a normal distribution, is the variable discrete? Continuous? Qualitative? Quantitative? Finite in range? Is there a minimum value? A maximum?

Exercise 4.2.2 For random samples from normal distributions, do $\bar{Y}$ from Eq. (2.1), s^2 from Eq. (2.7), and $s = \sqrt{s^2}$ give biased estimates of μ, σ^2, and σ?

Exercise 4.2.3 What is the distribution of random $\bar{Y}$'s where Y_i is from a normal distribution? How are the mean and variance of a population of $\bar{Y}$'s related to the mean and variance of the parent population?

4.3 Random Samples from a Normal Distribution

The drawing of random samples cannot be left to subjective discretion but must be the result of objective and preferably mechanical methods. A table of random numbers such as Table A.1 serves to introduce objectivity. To facilitate drawing random samples by use of a table of random numbers, assign consecutive numbers to the individuals in a population. For example, the 100 yields in Table 4.1 have been assigned the numbers 00 to 99, referred to as items.

Use of a random number table was illustrated in Sec. 2.5. For successive samples, the last two pairs of integers may be used to locate the next starting row and column. Applied to Table 4.1, this sampling procedure ensures that each item or yield may be drawn any number of times. Sampling is always from the same population and the probability of drawing any particular item is the same for all items. The procedure is essentially the same as if drawing were from an infinite population.

Table 4.3 gives five random samples, together with certain pertinent calculations, as obtained by the procedure above. These five samples are from 500 random samples of 10 observations from Table 4.1 used for discussion in the remainder of this chapter.

Exercise 4.3.1 The two random sampling procedures given in this section are not precisely equivalent. Why? (*Hint*. See Sec. 2.5 for distribution of digits in Table A.1.)

4.4 The Distribution of Sample Means

From Table 4.1, 500 samples of 10 observations were drawn. The frequency distribution of the 500 means is given in Table 4.4 for a class interval of

Table 4.3 Five random samples of 10 observations from Table 4.1, together with sample statistics

Observation number and formula	Sample number									
	1		2		3		4		5	
	Item	Yield	Item	Yield	Item	Yield	Item	Yield	Item	Yield
1	96	65	39	37	95	63	39	37	94	62
2	37	37	51	40	59	42	63	43	42	38
3	04	17	34	36	54	41	84	51	16	30
4	29	34	81	49	47	39	16	30	08	23
5	84	51	34	36	41	38	17	30	59	42
6	05	18	49	40	81	49	67	45	97	66
7	71	46	47	39	09	25	98	68	98	68
8	35	36	75	47	03	15	97	66	45	39
9	03	15	23	32	15	29	59	42	89	54
10	69	45	96	65	87	52	00	10	50	40
Sum = $\sum Y$		364		421		393		422		462
Mean = $\bar{Y}$		36.4		42.1		39.3		42.2		46.2
$\sum Y^2$		15,626.00		18,541.00		17,175.00		20,488.00		23,498.00
CT = $(\sum Y)^2/10$		13,249.60		17,724.10		15,444.90		17,808.40		21,344.40
SS = $\sum Y^2 - (\sum Y)^2/10$		2,376.40		816.90		1,730.10		2,679.60		2,153.60
$s^2 = \text{SS}/9$		264.04		90.77		192.23		297.73		239.29
$s = \sqrt{s^2}$		16.2		9.5		13.9		17.3		15.5
$s_{\bar{Y}} = \sqrt{s^2/10}$		5.14		3.01		4.38		5.46		4.89
$t = (\bar{Y} - 40)/s_{\bar{Y}}$		−0.70		+0.70		−0.16		+0.40		+1.27
$t_{.025} s_{\bar{Y}} = 2.262 s_{\bar{Y}}$		11.6		6.8		9.9		12.4		11.1
CL (lower) = $\bar{Y} - t_{.025} s_{\bar{Y}}$		24.8		35.3		29.4		29.8		35.1
CL (upper) = $\bar{Y} + t_{.025} s_{\bar{Y}}$		48.0		48.9		49.2		54.6		57.3

For the parent population, $\mu = 40$, $\sigma^2 = 144$.

Table 4.4 Frequency distribution of 500 means of random samples of 10 items from Table 4.1

Class mark,† lb	Observed frequency	Theoretical frequency	Observed cumulative frequency	Theoretical cumulative frequency
26.5	1	0	1	0.2
28.0	0	0.5	1	0.8
29.5	2	2	3	2.6
31.0	2	5	5	7.5
32.5	14	11	19	18.8
34.0	20	23	39	41.9
35.5	47	39	86	80.6
37.0	65	58	151	138.8
38.5	74	72	225	210.4
40.0	71	79	296	289.6
41.5	78	72	374	361.2
43.0	49	58	423	419.4
44.5	40	39	463	458.1
46.0	24	23	487	481.2
47.5	8	11	495	492.5
49.0	4	5	499	497.4
50.5	0	2	499	499.2
52.0	0	0.5	499	499.8
53.5	1	0	500	500.0
Totals	500	500		
	Mean of means: $\bar{\bar{Y}} = 39.79$			

† The center of a class interval.

1.5 lb and illustrates several basic features of sampling. First, the distribution of the means is approximately normal. Theory states that the derived distribution of sample means of random observations from a normal population is also normal. Theory also states that even if the parent distribution is considerably anormal, the distribution of means of random samples approaches the normal distribution as the sample size increases. This is very important in practice, because the form of the parent distribution is rarely known. Second, the average of the 500 means, 39.79 lb, is very close to $\mu = 40$ lb, the parent population mean. This illustrates unbiasedness. The sample mean is said to be unbiased because the mean of all possible sample means is the parent population mean. Third, the variation of the means is much less than that of the individuals, the sample ranges being 27 lb for means and 60 lb for individuals. Theory states that $\sigma_{\bar{Y}}^2 = \sigma^2/n$; here $\sigma_{\bar{Y}}^2 = 14.4$ and $\sigma_{\bar{Y}} = 3.79$ lb. The corresponding sample relation is $s_{\bar{Y}}^2 = s^2/n$. Applying this to the average of the 500 sample variances, that is, $\overline{s^2}$ (see Table 4.5), we obtain $s_{\bar{Y}}^2 = 140.4/10 = 14.04$ and $s_{\bar{Y}} = 3.75$ lb. Computation

Table 4.5 Frequency distribution of 500 variances s^2 for random samples of size 10 from Table 4.1

Class mark	20	40	60	80	100	120	140	160	180	200	220	240	260	280	300	320	340	360	380
Frequency	11	27	40	46	59	62	55	51	43	27	21	16	18	7	5	7	3	1	1

(140.4 marked between class marks 140 and 160)

$\overline{s^2} = 140.4$ lb^2, using df, namely 9, as divisor

($= 126.4$ lb^2, using sample size, namely 10, as divisor)

$\sigma^2 = 144$ lb^2

with the 500 means gives $s_{\bar{Y}} = \sqrt{[\sum \bar{Y}^2 - (\sum \bar{Y})^2/500]/499} = 3.71$ lb. Observed and theoretical frequencies of means are compared in Table 4.4. Theoretical frequencies are for a normal distribution with $\mu = 40$ lb and $\sigma = \sqrt{144/10} = 12/\sqrt{10} = 3.79$ lb, which is $\sigma_{\bar{Y}}$ for our problem. In the theoretical frequency column, one-half was the unit used; in the theoretical cumulative frequency column, one-tenth was the unit. This accounts for the discrepancies between these columns.

Exercise 4.4.1 Given a parent normal distribution and a derived distribution of means of 100 observations, what is the relation between the means of the two populations? Between the variances? Are the ranges of the populations the same? If you had a sample for each population, one of 50 observations, the other 50 means, how would you expect the two ranges to compare?

Exercise 4.4.2 To obtain an estimate of $\sigma_{\bar{Y}}^2$, one procedure above was to average the 500 sample variances and divide by 10. Compare this procedure with that of dividing each s^2 by 10 and averaging the 500 results.

4.5 The Distribution of Sample Variances and Standard Deviations

For each of 500 random samples, the variance and standard deviation were calculated. The procedure and the results are illustrated for five samples in Table 4.3.

The distribution of the 500 sample variances is given in Table 4.5. There is a heaping of the variances to the left of their mean, denoted by $\overline{s^2}$, and an attenuation to the right. The distribution is skewed. Sample quantities $(n-1)s^2/\sigma^2 = 9s^2/144$ are distributed as χ^2 with $n - 1 = 9$ degrees of freedom. The mean variance is $\overline{s^2} = 140.4$ lb^2, closely approximating the population variance $\sigma^2 = 144$. This illustrates the unbiasedness of s^2 as an estimate of σ^2. The individual s^2's range from 20 to 380 lb^2.

Table 4.6 gives the distribution of the standard deviations. Note that the process of taking square roots eliminates much of the skewness exhibited by variances. Examination of equally spaced s's and corresponding s^2's shows

Table 4.6 Frequency distribution of 500 standard deviations s corresponding to the variances of Table 4.5

Class mark	4	5	6	7	8	9	10	11	12	13	14	15	16	17	18	19
Frequency	1	10	14	23	37	42	55	69	66	63	40	26	30	11	11	2

(11.47 marked between class marks 11 and 12)

$\bar{s} = 11.47$ lb

$\sqrt{\overline{s^2}} = 11.85$ lb

$\sigma = 12$ lb

that variances above the mean increase faster than those below, differences between successive s^2's being consecutive odd numbers.

s	10	11	12	13	14
s^2	100	121	144	169	196

(This is an interesting observation in that it suggests the importance of choosing a scale of measurement for any investigation, the distribution of the observations being highly dependent on the scale. If the distribution is normal or can be made so by a transformation, that is, by the choice of a scale of measurement, statistical techniques based on the normal distribution are applicable; otherwise, they are only approximations.)

The average of the 500 standard deviations, denoted by $\bar{s}$, is 11.47 lb as compared with $\sigma = 12$ lb. The square root of the average of the 500 variances, that is, $\sqrt{\overline{s^2}}$, is here $\sqrt{140.4} = 11.85$ lb. It is not surprising that $\bar{s}$ is less than $\sqrt{\overline{s^2}}$ since s underestimates σ. For an unbiased estimate of σ, compute $\{1 + 1/[4(n-1)]\}s$, that is, $(1 + 1/36)s = 1.028s$, for $n = 10$. This is an approximation but quite a good one, even for small n.

Exercise 4.5.1 Draw histograms for the data of Tables 4.5 and 4.6 and observe the resulting skewness in each.

4.6 The Unbiasedness of s^2

It has been stated that $s^2 = \sum (Y_i - \bar{Y})^2/(n-1)$ is an unbiased estimate of σ^2. The average of the 500 s^2's, namely $\overline{s^2}$, is 140.4 lb^2.

If the sample variance is defined as $\sum (Y_i - \bar{Y})^2/n$, we have a biased estimate of σ^2, the average of the population of such values being $(n-1)\sigma^2/n$. We could reconstruct each sum of squares by using $(n-1)s^2 = \sum (Y_i - \bar{Y})^2$. However, since the degrees of freedom are the same for all samples, the average of the 500 variances computed with $n = 10$ as divisor is $9\overline{s^2}/10 = 126.4$ lb^2, a much smaller value than 140.4. The difference between the values obtained using n and $n - 1$ here obviously becomes less as n increases.

4.7 The Standard Deviation of the Mean or the Standard Error

The standard deviation of the mean is one of the most useful statistics. It is calculated as $s_{\bar{Y}} = s/\sqrt{n}$ or $s_{\bar{Y}} = \sqrt{s^2/n}$ and is a biased estimate of $\sigma_{\bar{Y}}$, the standard deviation of means of random samples of size n from a parent population with standard deviation σ. Thus for a sample of size 10 from Table 4.1, $s_{\bar{Y}}$ is an estimate of $\sigma_{\bar{Y}} = \sigma/\sqrt{10} = 12/\sqrt{10} = 3.79$ lb. For an estimate of $\sigma_{\bar{Y}}$ from the 500 samples, extract the square root of the average of the variances divided by $n = 10$. Calling it $(s_{\bar{Y}})'$, we have

$$(s_{\bar{Y}})' = \sqrt{\overline{s^2}/n} = \sqrt{\frac{140.4}{10}} = 3.75 \text{ lb}$$

This is a better procedure for estimating $\sigma_{\bar{Y}}$ from a set of s^2's than that of dividing the average of the 500 standard deviations, an average of biased estimates, by the square root of 10. If the latter is called $(s_{\bar{Y}})''$, then we have

$$(s_{\bar{Y}})'' = \frac{\bar{s}}{\sqrt{n}} = \frac{11.47}{\sqrt{10}} = 3.63 \text{ lb}$$

To further justify obtaining $s_{\bar{Y}}$ from s, we will use the 500 means to estimate $\sigma_{\bar{Y}}$ for comparison. We find

$$s_{\bar{Y}} = \sqrt{\frac{\sum \bar{Y}^2 - (\sum \bar{Y})^2/500}{499}} = 3.71 \text{ lb}$$

The close agreement between this and $(s_{\bar{Y}})' = 3.75$ lb enables us to state with more confidence that the relation $\sigma_{\bar{Y}} = \sigma/\sqrt{n}$ is indeed valid and, accordingly, each random sample provides an estimate $s_{\bar{Y}}$ of the standard error of the mean $\sigma_{\bar{Y}}$.

It is important to realize that the variance, population or sample, of a mean decreases inversely as n whereas the standard deviation of a mean decreases inversely as $\sqrt{n}$. This is clearly shown by example as well as by formula.

n	$\sigma_{\bar{Y}}^2$	$\sigma_{\bar{Y}}$
4	$\dfrac{\sigma^2}{4} = \dfrac{144}{4} = 36$	$\dfrac{\sigma}{\sqrt{4}} = \dfrac{12}{\sqrt{4}} = 6$
8	$\dfrac{\sigma^2}{8} = \dfrac{144}{8} = 18$	$\dfrac{\sigma}{\sqrt{8}} = \dfrac{12}{\sqrt{8}} = 4.24$
16	$\dfrac{\sigma^2}{16} = \dfrac{144}{16} = 9$	$\dfrac{\sigma}{\sqrt{16}} = \dfrac{12}{\sqrt{16}} = 3$

4.8 The Distribution of Student's *t*

Student's t distribution and Student's t were discussed in Sec. 3.10. We are now ready to show that the distribution of our 500 sample t values approximates the theoretical distribution of t for 9 degrees of freedom.

For each of the 500 samples, $t = (\bar{Y} - \mu)/s_{\bar{Y}} = (\bar{Y} - 40)/s_{\bar{Y}}$ was calculated. It is seen that t is the deviation of the sample mean from the population mean in units of sample standard deviations of means, a unit of measurement commonly used for making decisions about the usualness or unusualness of a deviation. Since a population of sample means is distributed symmetrically about μ, approximately one-half the 500 t values should be positive and one-half negative; the mean should be approximately zero. We find 248 are positive, 252 are negative, and the mean is -0.038.

Table 4.7 is a frequency distribution of the observed t values. Unequal class intervals were selected so that the observed frequencies could be compared with the theoretical frequencies tabulated in Table A.3. Thus, the class boundaries are identical with those for tabulated t at the 0.5, 0.3, 0.2, 0.1, 0.05, 0.02, and 0.01 probability levels. Percentage frequencies for sample and theoretical values of t are given to facilitate comparison.

In a population of t values, 2.5 percent are larger than $+2.262$ and 2.5 percent are smaller (numerically larger) than -2.262. This is seen from the theoretical percentage frequency. The last column in Table 4.7 combines both tails of the distribution by ignoring the sign of t. This is the column most often referred to for probability levels. Thus 2.262 is referred to as the value of t at the 5 percent level of significance for 9 degrees of freedom but designated by $t_{.025}$. When only the positive tail of the t distribution is considered, 5 percent of the t's lie beyond 1.833. This value is designated by $t_{.05}$. Again when both tails are considered, 1 percent of the t values lie beyond ± 3.250, the t value at the 1 percent level of significance for 9 degrees of freedom. For the sample values, 20 t's numerically exceed the 5 percent level and 4 t's numerically exceed the 1 percent level as compared with an expected 25 and 5, respectively. This shows reasonable agreement between the sample and theoretical values. A comparison of sample and theoretical values at other probability levels also shows reasonable agreement.

Table 4.7 Sample and theoretical values of t for 9 degrees of freedom

$$t = \frac{\bar{Y} - \mu}{s_{\bar{Y}}}$$

Interval of t		Sample				Theoretical		
				Cumulative			Cumulative	
From	To	Frequency	Percentage frequency	One tail†	Both tails‡	Percentage frequency	One tail†	Both tails‡
—	−3.250	2	0.4	100.0		0.5	100.0	
−3.250	−2.821	2	0.4	99.6		0.5	99.5	
−2.821	−2.262	7	1.4	99.2		1.5	99.0	
−2.262	−1.833	12	2.4	97.8		2.5	97.5	
−1.833	−1.383	29	5.8	95.4		5.0	95.0	
−1.383	−1.100	21	4.2	89.6		5.0	90.0	
−1.100	−0.703	63	12.6	85.4		10.0	85.0	
−0.703	0.0	116	23.2	72.8		25.0	75.0	
0.0	0.703	133	26.6	49.6	100.0	25.0	50.0	100.0
0.703	1.100	38	7.6	23.0	50.2	10.0	25.0	50.0
1.100	1.383	30	6.0	15.4	30.0	5.0	15.0	30.0
1.383	1.833	23	4.6	9.4	19.8	5.0	10.0	20.0
1.833	2.262	15	3.0	4.8	9.4	2.5	5.0	10.0
2.262	2.821	6	1.2	1.8	4.0	1.5	2.5	5.0
2.821	3.250	1	0.2	0.6	1.4	0.5	1.0	2.0
3.250	—	2	0.4	0.4	0.8	0.5	0.5	1.0
		500	100.0					

† Percentage of values larger than the entry in the extreme left column.
‡ Percentage of values larger in absolute value than the entry in the extreme left column.

Exercise 4.8.1 When is a statistic said to be an unbiased estimator of a parameter? Classify the statistics $\bar{Y}$, s^2, s, $s_{\bar{Y}}^2$, $s_{\bar{Y}}$ as biased or unbiased.

Exercise 4.8.2 Given a single sample of 20 random observations from a normal distribution, how can one estimate the variance of the population of sample means of 20 observations? Of 40 observations?

Exercise 4.8.3 Is the relation $\sigma_{\bar{Y}}^2 = \sigma^2/n$ valid if a population is not normal?

Exercise 4.8.4 How does Student's t differ from the corresponding normal Z criterion? Is there more than one t distribution? If one had two random samples of the same size from the same normal distribution and computed $(\bar{Y}_1 - \mu)/\sqrt{s_2^2/n}$, would it be distributed as t? If the samples were of different size, would the criterion be distributed as t? If the samples were from different populations, would the criterion be distributed as t? (*Hint.* See Sec. 3.10.)

4.9 The Confidence Statement

We now check the confidence statements based on the samples to see if the stated confidence is justified. For each random sample and any level of probability, a confidence interval is established about the sample mean. The procedure is to solve the two equations $\pm t = (\bar{Y} - \mu)/s_{\bar{Y}}$ for μ to obtain

$\mu = \bar{Y} \pm ts_{\bar{Y}}$, then a tabulated value of t and the sample $\bar{Y}$ and $s_{\bar{Y}}$ are substituted to give two values of μ, denoted by l_1 and l_2 and called the *limits* of the confidence interval. Thus $l_1 = \bar{Y} - ts_{\bar{Y}}$ and $l_2 = \bar{Y} + ts_{\bar{Y}}$.

For each of the 500 random samples, $l_1 = \bar{Y} - 2.262s_{\bar{Y}}$ and $l_2 = \bar{Y} + 2.262s_{\bar{Y}}$ have been calculated, that is, endpoints for a 95 percent confidence interval. The 1 percent t value, namely $t_{.005}$, for 9 df was also used. Since $\mu = 40$ lb, the number of correct statements regarding μ can be determined. For the 500 samples, the numbers of intervals containing μ were 480 at the 5 percent level and 496 at the 1 percent level. These compare favorably with theoretical values of 475 and 495, respectively. The percentage of intervals not including μ is the same as the percentage of sample t values which exceed the tabulated t's at the 5 percent and the 1 percent levels of significance, namely, $t_{.025}$ and $t_{.005}$.

In actual practice the parameter μ is not known. Accordingly, an experimenter knows only the percentage of correct inferences about μ, never whether μ lies in any particular confidence interval.

An erroneous idea sometimes held is that a 95 percent confidence interval about a sample mean gives the range within which 95 percent of future sample means will fall. This is incorrect because the distribution of sample means is centered on the population mean and not upon a particular sample mean. On the basis of a present sample, a correct statement about a future observation or mean was discussed in Sec. 3.12. To construct an interval that includes a specified proportion of a population with a certain confidence coefficient, one needs a tolerance interval procedure; for example, see Dixon and Massey (4.2).

4.10 The Sampling of Differences

A problem which often confronts an experimenter is that of determining whether there is a real difference in the responses to two treatments or, alternatively, whether the observed difference is small enough to be attributed to chance. An empirical method of approach to this problem is to consider, in the manner of this chapter, the results of a sampling procedure with two dummy treatments, that is, to sample a single population but to consider the resulting data as though from two populations. In this way, we learn what constitutes an ordinary sampling difference and an unusual difference, when no population difference exists.

Signed differences of observations randomly drawn from a normal population will be normally distributed about a mean of zero. The 500 random samples from Table 4.1 were paired at random and signed differences were obtained. Since the original samples were randomly selected, it is sufficient to pair consecutive samples individual by individual; no further randomization is required. For each of the resulting 250 samples of 10 differences D the following statistics were calculated: the mean difference $\bar{D}$, the variance of the differences $s_{\bar{D}}^2$, the standard deviation of the differences s_D, the standard deviation of the mean difference $s_{\bar{D}}$, the t value, and confidence limits for the population mean difference, known to be $\mu_{\bar{D}} = 0$ in this case. This is illustrated in Table 4.8, similar to Table 4.3 for individual values. Table 4.9 is a frequency distribution of the resulting 250 mean differences $\bar{D}$. The observed distribution is approximately symmetrical with 118 of the mean differences greater than zero and 132 less. These numbers were obtained from Table 4.9, along with the additional information that the class with zero class mark has 14 $\bar{D}$'s positive and 19 negative. The mean of the 250 is -0.533, very close to zero.

The notation Y_i, for the ith observation in a sample, is inadequate to distinguish among observations from several samples. Thus, we introduce a second subscript and denote an observation by Y_{ij}. Then Y_{ij} refers to the jth observation in the ith sample. For example Y_{25} (read as Y sub 2, 5; commas are used between numerical subscripts only where required for clarity) is the fifth observation of the second sample; and $Y_{13} - Y_{23}$ is the signed difference resulting from subtracting the third observation in sample 2 from the third in sample 1.

Tables 4.10 and 4.11 are frequency distributions of the 250 sample variances and standard deviations of 10 differences. The forms of these distributions are similar to those of Tables 4.5 and 4.6 for s^2 and s. Compare appropriate tables and note that the ranges are considerably greater for differences than for individuals. The reason is apparent when the possible range of the differences is considered. The possible range is from $(10 - 70) = -60$ lb to $(70 - 10) = +60$ lb, twice that for individuals. The average of the 250 variances, $\overline{s_D^2}$, is 272.7; from Table 4.5, $\overline{2s^2} = 2(140.4) = 280.8$; both are reasonably close to $2\sigma^2 = 2(144) = 288$. The data illustrate an important theorem:

> The variance σ_D^2 of differences of randomly paired observations is twice that of the observations in the parent population.

It then follows that

> The sample variance s_D^2 of differences of randomly paired observations is an unbiased estimate of $2\sigma^2$.

Note that 20 observations have provided 10 differences and as a consequence of differencing, there are only 9 df associated with the estimate s_D^2. In practice, where the variance of a difference between two means is often required, random pairing is not done and differences are not used in calculating $\bar{D}$ or s_D^2. By rearranging the arithmetic, it is apparent that $\bar{D} = \bar{Y}_1 - \bar{Y}_2$. From an s^2, the variance $2\sigma^2$ is estimated by $2s^2 = s_D^2$.

Table 4.8 Three samples of differences between random observations from Table 4.1

Item numbers	Paired observations Y_{1j} Y_{2j}	Differences $D_j = Y_{1j} - Y_{2j}$	Item numbers	Paired observations Y_{3j} Y_{4j}	Differences $D_j = Y_{3j} - Y_{4j}$	Item numbers	Paired observations Y_{5j} Y_{6j}	Differences $D_j = Y_{5j} - Y_{6j}$
97 78	66 48	18	66 72	44 46	−2	21 14	32 29	3
74 69	47 45	2	62 28	43 34	9	63 28	43 34	9
58 81	42 49	−7	15 64	29 44	−15	98 42	68 38	30
48 83	40 50	−10	28 37	34 37	−3	86 05	52 18	34
44 43	39 38	1	00 05	10 18	−8	77 94	48 62	−14
73 15	47 29	18	73 07	47 22	25	79 93	49 60	−11
73 81	47 49	−2	56 57	42 42	0	51 29	40 34	6
93 91	60 57	3	04 25	17 33	−16	99 66	70 44	26
79 46	49 39	10	92 53	58 41	17	39 06	37 20	17
63 21	43 32	11	34 94	36 62	−26	17 62	30 43	−13
Sum = $\sum D$		44			−19			87
Mean = $\bar{D}$		4.4			−1.9			8.7
$\sum D^2$		1,036.00			2,229.00			3,633.00
CT = $(\sum D)^2/10$		193.60			36.10			756.90
SS = $\sum D^2 - (\sum D)^2/10$		842.40			2,192.90			2,876.10
$s_D^2 = \text{SS}/9$		93.6			243.66			319.57
$s_D = \sqrt{s_D^2}$		9.8			15.6			17.9
$s_{\bar{D}} = \sqrt{s_D^2/10}$		3.06			4.94			5.65
$t = (\bar{D} - 0)/s_{\bar{D}}$		1.44			−0.38			1.54
$t_{.025}s_{\bar{D}} = 2.262 s_{\bar{D}}$		6.92			11.15			12.78
CL = $l_1 = \bar{D} - t_{.025}s_{\bar{D}}$		−2.5			−13.1			−4.1
CL = $l_2 = \bar{D} + t_{.025}s_{\bar{D}}$		11.3			9.3			21.5

Table 4.9 Frequency distribution of 250 mean differences $\bar{D}$ for samples of 10 differences

Class mark	−12	−10.5	−9	−7.5	−6	−4.5	−3	−1.5	0	1.5	3	4.5	6	7.5	9	10.5	12	13.5	15
Frequency	4	7	7	8	12	16	30	29	33	21	28	17	13	10	8	4	2	0	1

Table 4.10 Frequency distribution of the variances s_D^2 of 250 random samples of 10 differences based on Table 4.1

Class mark	60	100	140	180	220	260	300	340	380	420	460	500	540	580	620	660	700	740
Frequency	8	14	24	37	40	34	19	16	12	15	13	7	1	4	2	3	0	1

$\overline{s_D^2} = 272.7 \qquad \overline{2s^2} = 2\overline{s^2} = 280.8 \qquad 2\sigma^2 = 288$

Table 4.11 Frequency distribution of the standard deviations s_D of 250 random samples of 10 differences based on Table 4.1

Class mark	7	8	9	10	11	12	13	14	15	16	17	18	19	20	21	22	23	24	25	26	27
Frequency	1	5	4	7	8	17	24	28	29	26	19	13	19	10	16	10	4	4	3	2	1

$\overline{s_D} = 16.04$ lb $\quad \sqrt{\overline{2s^2}} = 16.76$ lb $\quad \sqrt{\overline{s_D^2}} = 16.51$ lb $\quad \sqrt{2\sigma^2} = 16.97$ lb

Averages of standard deviations of differences are $\overline{s_D} = 16.04$ and $\sqrt{\overline{s_D^2}} = \sqrt{272.7} = 16.51$ lb. Again the direct average of standard deviations is less than the square root of the average of the variances but both are reasonably close to $\sigma_D = \sqrt{2\sigma^2} = \sqrt{288} = 16.97$ lb. Standard deviations have a slight bias; variances are unbiased.

It has been stated that $\sigma_{\bar{Y}}^2 = \sigma^2/n$ and that $\sigma_D^2 = 2\sigma^2$. Together, these theorems say that the variance of a difference between two means, denoted by $\sigma_{\bar{D}}^2$, is equal to $2\sigma^2/n$ when each mean contains n observations. Thus $\sigma_{\bar{D}} = \sqrt{288/10} = 5.37$ lb. For the 250 samples, $s_{\bar{D}} = \sqrt{\overline{s_D^2}/n} = \sqrt{272.7/10} = 5.22$ lb or $s_{\bar{D}} = \sqrt{\overline{2s^2}/n} = \sqrt{280.8/10} = 5.30$ lb.

From a single value of s^2, estimates of the following important parameters, $\sigma^2, \sigma_{\bar{Y}}^2, \sigma_D^2, \sigma_{\bar{D}}^2, \sigma, \sigma_{\bar{Y}}, \sigma_D$, and $\sigma_{\bar{D}}$, are obtainable. The interrelations in terms of statistics are shown diagrammatically in Fig. 4.3.

For each of the 250 samples of 10 differences, t was calculated as $(\bar{D} - 0)/s_{\bar{D}}$, a deviation from the population mean in units of standard deviations of $\bar{D}$. Note that $t = \bar{D}/s_{\bar{D}} = (\bar{Y}_1 - \bar{Y}_2)/s_{\bar{Y}_1 - \bar{Y}_2}$ since $\bar{D} = \bar{Y}_1 - \bar{Y}_2$. The distribution of these t values is given in Table 4.12 and is similar to that of Table 4.7 for $t = (\bar{Y} - \mu)/s_{\bar{Y}}$. Of the t values, 118 are positive and 132 are negative; their mean is -0.00013. Fourteen t values exceed the 5 percent

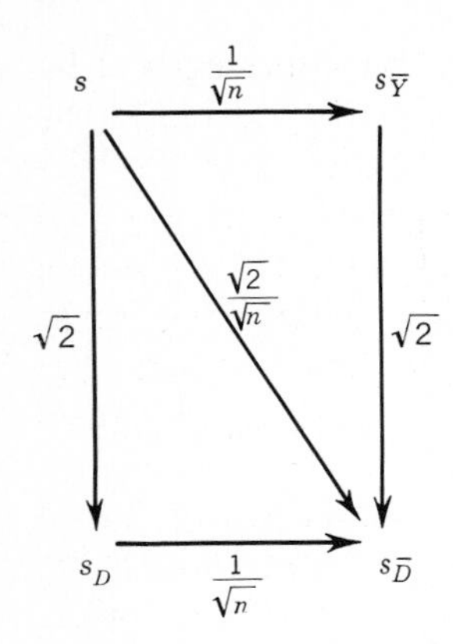

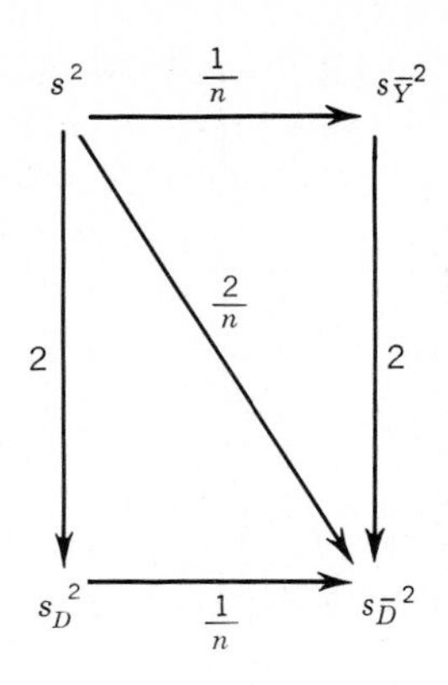

Figure 4.3 Illustration of relations among standard deviations and variances. (This diagram is not meant to imply the theorem of Pythagoras, that is, that the sum of the squares of the lengths of the sides of a right-angled triangle equals the square of length of the hypotenuse.)

level of significance as compared with an expected number of 12.5; four exceed the 1 percent as compared with 2.5.

Returning to the problem of determining whether there is a real difference between the responses to two treatments, we see that the sampling procedure discussed has shown what to expect when there is no real differ-

Table 4.12 Sample and theoretical values of $t = \bar{D}/s_{\bar{D}}$, 9 df, $\mu_{\bar{D}} = 0$

Interval of t		Sample		Theoretical		
					Cumulative	
From	To	Frequency	Percentage frequency	Percentage frequency	One tail	Both tails
—	−3.250	1	0.4	0.5	100.0	
−3.250	−2.821	0	0.0	0.5	99.5	
−2.821	−2.262	7	2.8	1.5	99.0	
−2.262	−1.833	5	2.0	2.5	97.5	
−1.833	−1.383	14	5.6	5.0	95.0	
−1.383	−1.100	13	5.2	5.0	90.0	
−1.100	−0.703	21	8.4	10.0	85.0	
−0.703	0.0	71	28.4	25.0	75.0	
0.0	0.703	62	24.8	25.0	50.0	100.0
0.703	1.100	24	9.6	10.0	25.0	50.0
1.100	1.383	10	4.0	5.0	15.0	30.0
1.383	1.833	7	2.8	5.0	10.0	20.0
1.833	2.262	9	3.6	2.5	5.0	10.0
2.262	2.821	2	0.8	1.5	2.5	5.0
2.821	3.250	1	0.4	0.5	1.0	2.0
3.250	—	3	1.2	0.5	0.5	1.0
		250	100.0			

ence and the results are attributable to chance alone. The values of $t = \bar{Y}/s_{\bar{Y}}$ in Table 4.12 are seen to correspond well with Student's t distribution. In the real situation, it is thus necessary only to calculate the statistic t and find the probability of a value as large as or larger when sampling is random and from a population with zero mean. If the probability of a larger value is small and the experimenter is not sure that sampling is from a population with zero mean, he or she will probably decide that there is a real difference in the responses to the two treatments. The calculation of confidence intervals leads to the same sort of inference, for if the sample t is beyond, say, the 5 percent probability level or $t_{.025}$, then the 95 percent confidence interval will not contain zero. If the confidence interval does not contain zero, the investigator can have little confidence in a statement that there is no difference between the responses to the treatments.

Exercise 4.10.1 Given two samples of paired observations:

I	10,	15,	13,	12,	11
II	12,	14,	14,	15,	13

What is the value of Y_{11}? Y_{22}? Y_{14}? $Y_{12} - Y_{22}$? $\bar{Y}_1 - \bar{Y}_2$?

Exercise 4.10.2

Given $s^2 = 36$. What is s_D^2? $s_{\bar{D}}^2$?

Given $s_{\bar{Y}}^2 = 12$. What is $s_{\bar{D}}^2$? s^2?

Given $s_{\bar{D}}^2 = 50$. What is s^2? $s_{\bar{Y}}^2$? s_D^2?

4.11 Summary of Sampling

A summary of the results obtained from the sampling experiment is given in Table 4.13. This summary clearly shows that by sampling it has been possible to demonstrate a number of important characteristics and theorems concerning normally distributed populations. In particular:

1. Means of random samples of n observations are normally distributed with mean μ and standard deviation $\sigma/\sqrt{n}$. (This theorem is approximately true with respect to the normality of means when sampling is from nonnormal populations and is always true with respect to standard deviation.)
2. Means of differences of random samples of n observations are normally distributed with mean zero and standard deviation $\sqrt{2\sigma^2/n}$.
3. A random sample provides unbiased estimates of μ, σ^2, $\sigma_{\bar{Y}}^2$, σ_D^2, and $\sigma_{\bar{D}}^2$.
4. The statistic $t = (\bar{Y} - \mu)/s_{\bar{Y}}$ or $t = (\bar{D} - 0)/s_{\bar{D}} = (\bar{Y}_1 - \bar{Y}_2)/s_{\bar{Y}_1 - \bar{Y}_2}$ is distributed symmetrically about mean zero and follows the tabulated distribution of Student's t.

Table 4.13 A summary of information from:

1. 500 samples of 10 observations

Sample	Symbol		s^2		s		$s_{\bar{Y}}$		
			Divisor $n-1=9$	Divisor $n=10$	$\sqrt{\overline{s^2}}$	$\bar{s}$	$s_{\bar{Y}}$	$\sqrt{\overline{s^2}/10}$	$\bar{s}/\sqrt{10}$
	Value	39.79	140.42	126.38	11.85	11.47	3.71	3.75	3.63
Population	Value	40.00	144		12		3.79		
	Symbol	μ	σ^2		σ		$\sigma_{\bar{Y}}$		

2. 250 samples of 10 differences

Sample	Symbol	$\bar{D}$	s_D^2		s_D			$s_{\bar{D}}$		
			$\overline{s_D^2}$	$\overline{2s^2}$	$\overline{s_D}$	$\sqrt{\overline{s_D^2}}$	$\sqrt{\overline{2s^2}}$	$s_{\bar{D}}$	$\sqrt{\overline{s_D^2}/10}$	$\sqrt{\overline{2s^2}/10}$
	Value	−0.53	272.71	280.84	16.04	16.51	16.76	5.16	5.22	5.30
Population	Value	0	288		16.97			5.37		
	Symbol	μ	σ_D^2		σ_D			$\sigma_{\bar{D}}$		

3. t values

Number of samples	Mean	Number		Without regard to sign			
				Number beyond $t_{.025} = 2.262$		Number beyond $t_{.005} = 3.250$	
		Plus	Minus	Observed	Expected	Observed	Expected
500	−0.038	248	252	20	25	4	5
250	−0.00013	118	132	14	12.5	4	2.5

A Proposed Laboratory Exercise in Connection with Chap. 4

Purpose To obtain evidence relative to the distribution of randomly paired observations, viz., its mean and variance.

1. Pair the 10 random samples to give five samples of 10 pairs. (Since the 10 samples are random, no further mechanical process is required to assure random pairing. It is sufficient to place consecutive samples adjacent to each other.)
2. For each of the five pairs of samples, compute
   a. The signed differences

b. The mean of the signed differences (This is also the difference between the means.)
c. The variance and standard deviation
d. $t = \bar{D}/s_{\bar{D}}$
e. The 95 and 99 percent confidence intervals for the mean differences

3. Record class data on summary sheets and summarize as in the text.
4. Plot $(\bar{Y}, s)$ pairs as obtained in the laboratory exercise for Chap. 3 to see if any relation is readily apparent (see Sec. 3.10).

References

4.1. Baker, G. A., and R. E. Baker: "Strawberry uniformity yield trials," *Biom.*, **9**:412–421 (1953).
4.2. Dixon, W. J., and F. J. Massey, Jr.: Introduction to statistical analysis, 3d ed., McGraw-Hill, New York, 1969, Sec. 9.8, Table 8*b*.

CHAPTER

FIVE

COMPARISONS INVOLVING TWO SAMPLE MEANS

5.1 Introduction

There are few of us who do not use statistics in some form. Most people make rough confidence statements on many aspects of their daily lives by the choice of an adjective, an adverb, or a phrase. Experimenters use investigation-based confidence statements to each of which is attached a decimal fraction between zero and one as a measure of the confidence to be placed therein. Confidence statements concerning population means were discussed in Sec. 3.11.

Sometimes the problem is changed and one asks whether or not a population mean may have a specific value. For example, we may regularly compute mileage for the family car for each tank of gasoline. Suppose that the average of these values is 12.5 mi/gal and that over a period of time, we have come to think of this value as a parameter. Because of the claimed mileage benefits due to an additive in a competing brand, we later decide to try a few tanks of this brand and to determine if 12.5 mi/gal is still the parameter. Here is a problem of hypothesis testing.

This chapter is devoted to testing hypotheses concerning one and two population means. Student's t is the principal test criterion, although F is introduced in anticipation of a generalization to more than two means and of the analysis of variance. The problem of sample size is considered.

5.2 Tests of Significance

In Sec. 3.11, a confidence interval was constructed for a population mean μ; the procedure is such that a specified long-run percentage of the intervals will contain the parameter. Every value within a confidence interval is acceptable as a candidate for μ; no such value can be ruled out.

It is apparent then that a confidence interval procedure can be used to test a hypothesis concerning the precise location of a parameter. The confidence interval is constructed; if the hypothesized value lies within the interval, then the hypothesis must be acceptable, since for values of μ within the confidence interval, chance and the hypothesis offer an adequate explanation of the data.

In Chap. 4, 500 random samples of 10 observations were drawn and 95 and 99 percent confidence intervals were constructed. It was found that 480, approximately 95 percent, and 495, approximately 99 percent, of the intervals contained μ. Tabulated t values for $t_{.025}$ and $t_{.005}$, with 9 df, were used in the construction, and it was pointed out that the numbers of sample t's, sign ignored, exceeding these were $500 - 480 = 20$ and $500 - 496 = 4$, respectively. In fact, those samples which yielded confidence intervals that did not contain μ were the same ones which provided the sample t values that exceeded $t_{.025}$ and $t_{.005}$, in absolute value. This suggests the possibility of using the sample t directly in hypothesis testing.

The test procedure is then obvious. If the sample t, sign ignored, exceeds the tabulated value, say $t_{.025}$, then random values larger than that observed must occur with probability less than $2(.025) = .05$. Essentially, the observed value is larger than we care to accept as attributable to chance and the hypothesis. We conclude that the hypothesis is false while admitting that this decision can be wrong if we have an unusual random sample, one likely to occur about 5 times in 100 or 1 in 20 if we have selected .05 as our acceptable error rate.

Let us examine the testing problem more closely. We plan to compute a sample t, as *test criterion*, by

$$t = \frac{\bar{Y} - \mu}{s_{\bar{Y}}} \tag{5.1}$$

In this, we measure the distance between our estimate of μ, namely $\bar{Y}$, and the hypothesized value, say μ_0; and as a unit of measurement, we use the standard deviation of $\bar{Y}$. Thus, the sample t is the deviation of a normal variable $\bar{Y}$ from its hypothesized mean measured in standard error units, or it is the number of standard deviations applicable to $\bar{Y}$ that separate $\bar{Y}$ and μ_0. Obviously, we have to specify μ_0 to be able to compute a value of the test criterion even though we may feel that the somewhat vague "in the neighborhood of μ" would have been an adequate hypothesis. When we hypothesize a value of a parameter such that we can compute a test criterion, then we have a *null hypothesis*, written H_0. Now we may simply write H_0: $\mu = \mu_0$.

If the null hypothesis is correct, then the resulting t should not look out of place when compared with ordinary t values, values between $-t_{.025}$ and $+t_{.025}$, say. However, sometimes we will falsely reject the null hypothesis because the sample t happens to be too large numerically. We are reasoning from a sample to a population, making an uncertain inference, and will necessarily get the occasional unusual sample. Fortunately, the long-run percentage of unusual samples with their false inferences can be controlled. This percentage is our *error rate* or *significance level*, generally designated by α; it represents a penalty to be paid because we must make uncertain inferences. Further, if we falsely reject the null hypothesis, then we are said to have made a *Type I error*, or an *error of the first kind*. It follows that we accept H_0, if true, with a probability of $1 - \alpha$.

When we reject the null hypothesis, then we need an *alternative hypothesis*, say H_1 or H_A. This will not usually specify a single value but will simply state that under the alternative μ is not μ_0, that μ is greater than μ_0, or that μ is less than μ_0. Concisely, we use either H_1: $\mu \neq \mu_0$, H_1: $\mu > \mu_0$, or H_1: $\mu < \mu_0$. Note that the choice of alternative affects H_0 to some extent. For these three cases, we might now write H_0: $\mu = \mu_0$, H_0: $\mu \leq \mu_0$, and H_0: $\mu \geq \mu_0$, respectively.

If the null hypothesis is false, then μ is not μ_0 but is some other value. We are still computing t by Eq. (5.1) with $\mu = \mu_0$, but note that $\bar{Y} - \mu_0$ is not the deviation called for by Student's t and is more likely to be larger than if we had used the true μ. This is apparent from Fig. 5.1. Here we see $\bar{Y}$ distributed about μ with variance σ^2/n. Student's t calls for us to compute $\bar{Y} - \mu$ for the numerator. However, we think μ is at μ_0 and so compute $\bar{Y} - \mu_0$. Only if $\bar{Y}$ is fairly well into the left tail of its distribution will the deviation $\bar{Y} - \mu_0$ be small and so give an apparently "ordinary" value of t; for our illustration, this occurs with a small probability. In other words, if

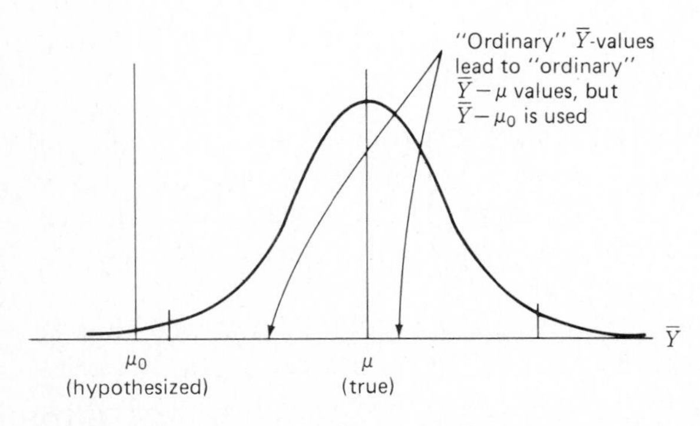

Figure 5.1 Consideration of $\bar{Y} - \mu$ and $\bar{Y} - \mu_0$ for given distribution of $\bar{Y}$.

the true μ is not at μ_0, then the sample t will more likely be large and so we will often reject the null hypothesis, as we would want to do. However, when μ is not at μ_0, that is, when H_1 is true, we will sometimes accept H_0 falsely rather than reject it. In doing so, we will make a *Type II error*, or an *error of the second kind*. The probability of doing so is represented by β. Clearly this probability will be small when μ_0 and the true μ are well separated and will increase as they approach one another.

Finally, we are interested in being able to detect H_1 when H_1 is true. Clearly this involves not making a Type II error, so it has probability $1 - \beta$. This ability to detect H_1 when H_1 is true is called the *power* of the test.

In summary, to test a hypothesis,

1. Have the population of interest clearly in mind and formulate a meaningful hypothesis for which a test statistic can be computed. This is the null hypothesis H_0. Have an alternative hypothesis H_1 in mind in case the evidence to be collected turns out not to support H_0.
2. Choose a probability α based on the seriousness of rejecting H_0 when true; the probability of accepting H_0 when true will be $1 - \alpha$. Simultaneously, keep in mind that it is possible to accept H_0 when H_1 is true. If this has probability β, then the probability of accepting H_1 when true will be $1 - \beta$. How to balance the two types of error is treated in Sec. 5.12.

   Now the experiment is conducted and the data obtained. Probabilities that applied at steps 1 and 2, the planning stage, will not apply when the data are analyzed. The investigator will then draw a conclusion which will be true or false depending on which hypothesis represents the true situation; real probabilities of accepting the true parameter will be zero or one.
3. Compute the sample value of the test statistic and find the probability of obtaining, by chance, a value more extreme than that observed. (So far, we have thought of large values as extreme ones but small ones will be unusual under H_0 for some test criteria.) As an alternative to computing this probability, find the tabulated value of the test criterion such that the probability of a more extreme value occurring by chance will be the α chosen at step 2.
4. If the probability at step 3 is such that chance seems inadequate to explain the result, then conclude that the null hypothesis is incorrect and reject it. Do this if the probability is less than the α chosen at step 2; otherwise, accept H_0. If you find a tabulated value of the test criterion, reject H_0 if the sample value of this criterion is more extreme than the tabulated value; otherwise, accept it.

   Rejection of the null hypothesis is a rather strong statement. We are definitely ruling out the specific value of the parameter chosen for H_0 in favor of some unspecified value included in the set of alternatives. On the other hand, acceptance of H_0 does not mean that the specific value μ_0 is the only one acceptable for the parameter; we have failed to reject H_0 but there are other values, presumably in the neighborhood of μ_0, that could have served equally well as null hypotheses.

At the moment, we are talking more particularly about t as a test criterion. Thus if we wish to compare yields in bushels per acre of a new and a standard cultivar of corn, then at step 1 we could propose the null hypothesis that there is no difference between the population means for the two cultivars: $H_0: \mu = 0$. As an alternative hypothesis, we might propose that the mean of the new cultivar is greater or simply that it is different: $H_1: \mu > 0$ or $H_1: \mu \neq 0$.

At step 2, let us choose $\alpha = .05$. We are prepared to reject the null hypothesis, even if it is true, about 1 time in 20, on the average. Thus we will accept H_0 about 19 times out of 20 when it is true. We are aware that in accepting H_0, we will be wrong if there is a real difference in yield between cultivars; we may not have evaluated this risk.

The experiment is now conducted. We measure a number of differences, say, (yield of new cultivar) − (yield of standard). These differences are random as the result of some procedure and are from a population assumed to be normal with unknown mean μ and unknown standard deviation σ. From the data, we compute a value of t using Eq. (5.1) with μ replaced by the hypothesized value $\mu = 0$. This is a part of step 3.

Since we are not yet using a numerical example, we do not have a sample t for which we can compute the probability of a more extreme value. We will assume that 20 random differences are available and find the critical value when $\alpha = .05$.

What constitutes an extreme value of t will depend on H_1. Thus if H_1 is that $\mu \neq 0$, then any value of t that is numerically large is extreme and gives sufficient reason to reject H_0. From Table A.3 for $20 - 1 = 19$ df, we find that $t = 2.093$ is such that $P(|t| > 2.093) = .05$; this is the tabulated t that qualifies at step 3 as the critical value. Here we have a *two-tailed test*, referring to the alternatives.

On the other hand, if H_1 is that $\mu > 0$, then we are looking for large positive values of t to support H_1 and deny H_0. From Table A.3 for $20 - 1 = 19$ df, we find that $t = 1.729$ is such that $P(t > 1.729) = .05$; this is the tabulated t that qualifies at step 3 if $H_1: \mu > 0$. Here we have a *one-tailed test*.

Finally, we accept or reject H_0 according to the procedure in step 4.

Figure 5.2 shows diagrammatically what is happening in the illustration above. The tabulated value of the test criterion which corresponds to the chosen level of significance divides the possible t values into two classes, the *region of acceptance* and the *region of rejection*, or *critical region*. The t values of ± 2.093 and 1.729 for this illustration are called *critical values*.

In many fields of experimentation, 5 and 1 percent significance levels are customarily used. If by chance a more discrepant value of the test criterion

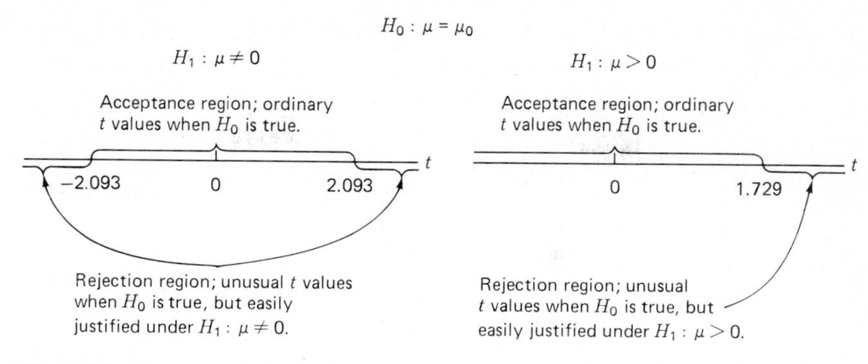

Figure 5.2 Acceptance and rejection regions for text illustration.

than that obtained is likely to occur less than 5 percent of the time but not less than 1 percent of the time when the null hypothesis is true, then the difference is said to be *significant* and the sample value of the test criterion is marked with a single asterisk. If a more discrepant value of the test criterion than that obtained is likely to occur less than 1 percent of the time when the null hypothesis is true, the difference is said to be *highly significant* and the sample value of the test criterion is marked with two asterisks. Acceptance of the null hypothesis may be indicated by the letters *ns*.

The levels of 5 and 1 percent are arbitrary but seem to have been adequate choices in the field of agriculture where they were first used. In the case of small-sized experiments, it is possible that the null hypothesis will not likely be rejected if these levels are required, unless a large real difference exists. This suggests the choice of another level of significance, perhaps 10 percent for small experiments. If an experimenter uses levels other than the 5 and 1 percent, this should be stated clearly.

The outcomes of possible decisions concerning hypotheses are summarized in Table 5.1.

Table 5.1 Decisions and their outcomes

Sample test criterion is in	Decision is to	Data are from a population for which: H_0 is true, H_1 is false	Data are from a population for which: H_0 is false, H_1 is true
Acceptance region, i.e., nonsignificant	Accept H_0 Reject H_1	Correct decision Probability should be high; Symbol: $1 - \alpha$ = confidence coefficient	Incorrect decision Type II error made Probability should be low: Symbol: β
Rejection region, i.e., significant	Reject H_0 Accept H_1	Incorrect decision Type I error made Probability should be low; Symbol: α = significance level	Correct decision Probability should be high; Symbol: $1 - \beta$ = power

5.3 Testing the Hypothesis that a Population Mean Is a Specified Value

Let μ and σ^2 denote the mean and variance of a population. A random sample of size n is drawn and the sample mean and variance, $\bar{Y}$ and s^2, are computed. To test the null hypothesis H_0: $\mu = \mu_0$, assuming that the population is normally distributed, the test criterion is given by Eq. (5.1) as

$$t = \frac{\bar{Y} - \mu_0}{s/\sqrt{n}} \tag{5.2}$$

(A criterion involving an estimate of σ^2 was first studied by Student in 1908. He prepared the distribution of a related statistic which he called z. Later R. A. Fisher worked out the distribution of t, the basis of Table A.3.)

In the first illustration, let us assume that we have a value $\mu = \mu_0$ for our null hypothesis and the alternative is simply that $\mu \neq \mu_0$.

Consider sample 1 from Table 4.3. We know that $\mu = 40$, so let us test H_0: $\mu = 40$ versus H_1: $\mu \neq 40$. We have $\bar{Y} = 36.4$ and $s^2 = 264.04$. Hence,

$$t = \frac{36.4 - 40}{\sqrt{264.04/10}} = -0.701, \text{ 9 df}$$

From Table A.3 for 9 df, we find $P(|t| > .701) > .5$ but very close to .5. Alternatively, observe that -0.701 lies between -2.262 and 2.262. There is no reason to think of -0.701 as an unusual value of t if $\mu = 40$. We accept the null hypothesis and reject the alternative.

In this case, we know we have certainly and correctly accepted the null hypothesis.

Now let us illustrate the one-tailed test using the sheep data in the first column of Table 5.2. These are coefficients of digestibility of dry matter, feed corn silage, that have been measured in percent for seven sheep.

Let us suppose that a second researcher has been working on the same general problem but with another breed of sheep. This researcher was aware that the research was in progress and decided that when the data became available he would test the null hypothesis H_0: $\mu = 54$ percent versus H_1: $\mu > 54$ percent since his extensive experience led him to think of 54 percent as a parameter. Also, evidence had accumulated that there was a good possibility that the breed under investigation had a higher mean value for this coefficient.

Compute

$$t = \frac{56.21 - 54.00}{\sqrt{(54.09/6)/7}} = 1.947, \text{ 6 df}$$

Observe that the difference is in the direction expected under H_1; otherwise, we would accept the null hypothesis immediately. From Table A.3 for

Table 5.2 Coefficients of digestibility of dry matter, feed corn silage, in percent

	Y_1 (sheep)	Y_2 (steers)
	57.8	64.2
	56.2	58.7
	61.9	63.1
	54.4	62.5
	53.6	59.8
	56.4	59.2
	53.2	
$\sum Y$	393.5	367.5
$\sum Y^2$	22,174.41	22,535.87
$\bar{Y}$	56.21 percent	61.25 percent

$$\sum (Y_{1j} - \bar{Y}_1)^2 = \sum Y_1^2 - (\sum Y_1)^2/n_1 = 22{,}174.41 - 22{,}120.32 = 54.09 = (n_1 - 1)s_1^2$$

$$\sum (Y_{2j} - \bar{Y}_2)^2 = \sum Y_2^2 - (\sum Y_2)^2/n_2 = 22{,}535.87 - 22{,}509.37 = 26.50 = (n_2 - 1)s_2^2$$

$$s^2 = \frac{\sum Y_1^2 - (\sum Y_1)^2/n_1 + \sum Y_2^2 - (\sum Y_2)^2/n_2}{(n_1 - 1) + (n_2 - 1)} = \frac{54.09 + 26.50}{6 + 5} = 7.33,$$

an estimate of the common σ^2

$$\text{df} = (n_1 - 1) + (n_2 - 1) = 11$$

$$s_{\bar{Y}_1 - \bar{Y}_2} = \sqrt{s^2 \frac{(n_1 + n_2)}{n_1 n_2}} = \sqrt{7.33 \frac{(7 + 6)}{42}} = \sqrt{2.27} = 1.51 \text{ percent, the standard}$$

deviation appropriate to the difference between the sample means

$$t = \frac{\bar{Y}_1 - \bar{Y}_2}{s_{\bar{Y}_1 - \bar{Y}_2}} = \frac{56.21 - 61.25}{1.51} = \frac{-5.04}{1.51} = -3.33^{**}, \text{ df} = 11$$

For the 95 percent confidence interval for $\mu_2 - \mu_1$, $\bar{Y}_2 - \bar{Y}_1 \pm t_{.025} s_{\bar{Y}_1 - \bar{Y}_2} = 5.04 \pm 2.201(1.51) = 5.04 \pm 3.32$; $l_1 = 1.72$ percent and $l_2 = 8.36$ percent.

6 df, we find $P(t > 1.947) < .05$, although it is almost exactly at the critical value of $t = 1.943$. We reject H_0 and accept H_1.

If a confidence interval is of interest, presumably one wants to know the location of the least acceptable value of μ, since the alternative is $H_1: \mu > 54$ percent.

We begin with the probability statement

$$P\left(\frac{\bar{Y} - \mu}{s_{\bar{Y}}} < t_{.05}\right) = .95 \tag{5.3}$$

Algebraic manipulation of this probability statement about the random variable $(\bar{Y} - \mu)/s_{\bar{Y}}$ leads to

$$P(\mu > \bar{Y} - t_{.05} s_{\bar{Y}}) = .95 \tag{5.4}$$

This is a probability statement about the location of the lower bound,

$\bar{Y} - t_{.05} s_{\bar{Y}}$, for the estimate of the parameter μ. We find this lower bound to be

$$56.21 - 1.943 \sqrt{\frac{(54.09/6)}{7}} = 54.005$$

We say that unless we have an unusual sample, the parameter μ should be no smaller than 54.005.

The linear additive model for the single sample was discussed in Sec. 2.12.

Exercise 5.3.1 Pesticides being sprayed on crops can affect human beings. A symptom of the action of a pesticide is reduction in brain acetylcholinesterase (AChE) activity and a severe reduction can be dangerous in terms of body functions. When cotton is sprayed, one criterion of the existence of such a reduction is whether or not quail in field borders show reduced AChE activity.

In one collection, the following six observations, averages of two determinations, were made in brain AChE activity in quail: 86.03, 83.67, 95.21, 92.94, 83.12, and 80.22.† On the assumption that the quail were a random sample, place an upper bound, using $\alpha = .01$, on the location of the parameter μ.

In another collection, the following four observations were made: 23.76, 34.59, 56.22, and 68.22. Again find an upper bound, using $\alpha = .05$, on the location of the parameter μ.

Exercise 5.3.2 Seven observers were shown, for a brief period, a grill with 161 flies impaled and were asked to estimate the number. The results are given by Cochran (5.2). Based on five estimates, they were 183.2, 149.0, 154.0, 167.2, 187.2, 158.0, and 143.0. Define a reasonable population from which these means might have been obtained.

Test the null hypothesis that the mean of the population is 161 flies, using $\alpha = .05$. Construct a 95 percent confidence interval for μ.

Exercise 5.3.3 Yields of 10 strawberry plants in a uniformity trial are given by Baker and Baker (5.1) as 239, 176, 235, 217, 234, 216, 318, 190, 181, and 225 g. Calculate 95 and 99 percent confidence intervals for the population mean. Test the hypothesis $\mu = 205$ (chosen arbitrarily) against the alternatives $\mu \neq 205$ at the 5 percent level of significance.

Exercise 5.3.4 Suppose that a tire manufacturer measures, in thousands of miles, the life of 10 tires. He finds $\bar{Y} = 26.8$ and $s^2 = 12$.

Test the null hypothesis that $\mu = 25.0$ versus $H_1: \mu > 25.0$. Construct a 95 percent one-sided confidence interval for μ that provides a lower bound on the parameter.

Exercise 5.3.5 Larvae of some monarch butterflies concentrate cardiac glucosides from milkweed plants. This makes the butterflies unpalatable to birds, so the monarchs are avoided after a single encounter.

Assume that butterflies have been collected at one location and their glucoside concentrations measured relative to their dried weight. Suppose that the resulting data are $\bar{Y} = .200$ and $s^2 = .012$ for $n = 75$.

Construct a 95 percent confidence interval on the true population mean. Test the null hypothesis that $\mu = .150$ versus $H_1: \mu \neq .150$; $\mu = .150$ might be considered to be the parameter for another location.

† Data used with permission of P. C. Smithson and O. T. Sanders. See also Ref. 5.11.

5.4 Tests for Two or More Means

Suppose that we have two populations with means μ_1 and μ_2. A random sample is drawn from each population to test the null hypothesis that μ_1 and μ_2 are separated by a specified amount, usually chosen to be zero.

For the null hypothesis of no difference, t is defined by

$$t = \frac{\bar{Y}_1 - \bar{Y}_2}{s_{\bar{Y}_1 - \bar{Y}_2}} \tag{5.5}$$

Here, $s_{\bar{Y}_1 - \bar{Y}_2}$ is the standard deviation appropriate to a difference between two random means from a normal population.

Once again, note that t measures the distance of a random variable from a hypothesized mean, in units of standard deviations of the random variable. When the underlying distributions are normal with a common variance, this statistic will be distributed as the tabulated Student's t, Table A.3, if the hypothesized value is the true value but not if the hypothesis is false. If the sample t cannot reasonably be attributed to chance and the null hypothesis, we conclude that $\bar{Y}_1 - \bar{Y}_2$ is too large because $\mu_1 \neq \mu_2$.

Calculation of $s_{\bar{Y}_1 - \bar{Y}_2}$ depends on whether

1. The two populations have a common variance σ^2
2. The values of the σ^2's, or the common σ^2, are known or estimated
3. The two samples are of the same size and
4. The observations are paired

The choice of a rejection region depends on

1. The level of significance chosen
2. The sample size
3. The test required, that is, whether one- or two-tailed

The test is intended for two means and obviously not suited for generalization to more than two since we have no clear way of defining a numerator for generalization. A new approach is needed which we will now consider.

The variance in a population of sample means is σ^2/n, where σ^2 is the variance of individuals in a parent population and all samples are of size n. This implies that means may be used to estimate σ^2. Thus, using two sample means, we compute an estimate of σ^2/n by $\sum (\bar{Y}_i - \bar{\bar{Y}})^2/(2 - 1)$, which when multiplied by n estimates σ^2. A second estimate of σ^2 may be found directly from the individuals in each sample.

Now when $\mu_1 \neq \mu_2$ but the populations have the same variance, the estimate of σ^2 based on sample means will tend to overestimate σ^2 because the difference between the $\bar{Y}$'s will include a contribution attributable to the difference between population means as well as any random difference.

Thus, in general, if the μ_i's differ, $\bar{Y}$'s are expected to be more variable than when chance alone operates. On the other hand, an estimate based on individuals would be computed within individual samples using deviations from each estimate of a μ_i. In this way, variations among μ_i's could not contribute to the estimate of σ^2.

Hence a test of significance for a difference, that is, a test of H_0: $\mu_1 - \mu_2 = 0$ versus H_1: $\mu_1 - \mu_2 \neq 0$, could involve the ratio of two such estimates of σ^2. In particular, Eq. (5.6) defines a common test criterion.

$$F = \frac{\text{estimate of } \sigma^2 \text{ from means}}{\text{estimate of } \sigma^2 \text{ from individuals}} \tag{5.6}$$

Values of F are given in Table A.6 for five probability values and various pairs of numerator and denominator degrees of freedom. For two means, the estimate of σ^2 for the numerator is based on a single degree of freedom; in this case, the square root of F has Student's t distribution.

5.5 Comparison of Two Sample Means, Independent Samples, and Equal Variances

Let μ_1 and μ_2 be the means of two populations. A random sample is drawn from each. Let $\bar{Y}_1, \bar{Y}_2, s_1^2, s_2^2, n_1$, and n_2 denote the sample means, variances, and sizes. Using these random samples, we are to test the null hypothesis H_0: $\mu_1 = \mu_2$ assuming that the populations are normally distributed and have a common but unknown variance.

The test criterion is

$$t = \frac{(\bar{Y}_1 - \mu_1) - (\bar{Y}_2 - \mu_2)}{s_{\bar{Y}_1 - \bar{Y}_2}} = \frac{(\bar{Y}_1 - \bar{Y}_2) - (\mu_1 - \mu_2)}{s_{\bar{Y}_1 - \bar{Y}_2}} \tag{5.7}$$

which for H_0: $\mu_1 = \mu_2$ becomes Eq. (5.5). In general the difference $\mu_1 - \mu_2$ may be set equal to any value the experimenter may hypothesize.

In the test criterion, $s_{\bar{Y}_1 - \bar{Y}_2}$ is an estimate of $\sigma_{\bar{Y}_1 - \bar{Y}_2}$ and subject to sampling variation. We first estimate σ^2 by pooling the sums of squares of the two samples and dividing by the pooled degrees of freedom:

$$s^2 = \frac{(n_1 - 1)s_1^2 + (n_2 - 1)s_2^2}{(n_1 - 1) + (n_2 - 1)} \tag{5.8}$$

This is a *weighted average* of the sample variances and is superior to the arithmetic average which gives equal weight to the sample variances. The weighted and arithmetic averages are the same when the samples are of the same size. The criterion t, when H_0 is true, is distributed as Student's t for random samples from normal populations, but considerable departures from normality may not seriously affect the distribution, especially near the commonly used critical values for 5 and 1 percent.

Case 1. The test when $n_1 \neq n_2$ Calculate $s_{\bar{Y}_1-\bar{Y}_2}$ by

$$s_{\bar{Y}_1-\bar{Y}_2} = \sqrt{s^2\left(\frac{1}{n_1} + \frac{1}{n_2}\right)} = \sqrt{s^2\left(\frac{n_1 + n_2}{n_1 n_2}\right)} \tag{5.9}$$

Here s^2 is the weighted average of the sample variances, Eq. (5.8).

A numerical example is given in Table 5.2 for data from Watson et al. (5.13). The confidence interval for $\mu_2 - \mu_1$ rather than $\mu_1 - \mu_2$ was calculated only because $\bar{Y}_2 - \bar{Y}_1$ is positive.

When the criterion F is used, the results are generally shown in an *analysis of variance* table where every variance or mean square is an estimate of the same σ^2 if the null hypothesis is true (see Table 5.3). To compute the numerator of F, recall that $(\bar{Y}_1 - \bar{Y}_2)^2$ estimates $2\sigma_{\bar{Y}}^2 = 2\sigma^2/n$. To estimate σ^2, we must multiply by $n/2$.

When the means are for samples of unequal size, the square of the difference is an estimate of $\sigma^2(n_1 + n_2)/n_1 n_2$; hence for an estimate of σ^2, we multiply by $n_1 n_2/(n_1 + n_2)$. Thus $(56.21 - 61.25)^2(6)(7)/(6 + 7) = 81.93$ is an estimate of σ^2, based on means. (The actual computation was made with totals; the one with means differs slightly due to rounding errors.) Note that $n_1 n_2/(n_1 + n_2)$ is the reciprocal of the multiplier of s^2 when t is the criterion and $s_{\bar{Y}_1-\bar{Y}_2}$ is calculated. Now $t^2 = F$ whenever F has 1 degree of freedom associated with the numerator, thus $(3.33)^2$ and 11.19 are equal within rounding errors. Note also that degrees of freedom and sums of squares in the body of the table add to the total. Table A.6 is one of theoretical F values for several probability levels. The first column applies to cases where only two sample means are involved. $F(1, 11) = 4.84$ at the 5 percent level and 9.65 at the 1 percent level. Since sample $F = 11.18$ exceeds 9.65, the difference is declared to be highly significant. The same conclusion is reached using t as the test criterion.

Case 2. The test when $n_1 = n_2 = n$ The procedure given as Case 1 is applicable. The criterion is t as in Eq. (5.7); Eq. (5.9) reduces to

$$s_{\bar{Y}_1-\bar{Y}_2} = \sqrt{\frac{2s^2}{n}} \tag{5.10}$$

Table 5.3 Analysis of variance of data in Table 5.2

Source of variation	df	Sum of squares	Mean square	F
Sheep vs. steers	1	81.93	81.93	11.18**
Among sheep + among steers	6 + 5	54.09 + 26.50	7.33	
Total	12	162.52		

The degrees of freedom are $2(n-1)$. A numerical example is worked in Table 5.4 for data from Ross and Knodt (5.6). Since the observed difference between means is significant at only the 5 percent level, the 95 percent confidence interval does not contain zero but the 99 percent one does.

Table 5.4 Gain in weight of Holstein heifers

	Y_1, control	Y_2, vitamin A
	175	142
	132	311
	218	337
	151	262
	200	302
	219	195
	234	253
	149	199
	187	236
	123	216
	248	211
	206	176
	179	249
	206	214
$\sum Y$	2,627	3,303
$\sum Y^2$	511,807	817,583
$\bar{Y}$	187.6 lb	235.9 lb

$$n_1 = n_2 = n = 14$$

$$\sum (Y_{1j} - \bar{Y}_1)^2 = \sum Y_1^2 - (\sum Y_1)^2/n = 511{,}807 - 492{,}938 = 18{,}869 = (n_1 - 1)s_1^2$$

$$\sum (Y_{2j} - \bar{Y}_2)^2 = \sum Y_2^2 - (\sum Y_2)^2/n = 817{,}583 - 779{,}272 = 38{,}311 = (n_2 - 1)s_2^2$$

$$s^2 = \frac{\sum Y_1^2 - (\sum Y_1)^2/n + \sum Y_2^2 - (\sum Y_2)^2/n}{2(n-1)} = \frac{57{,}180}{26} = 2{,}199,$$

an estimate of the common σ^2

$$\text{df} = 2(n-1) = 26$$

$$s_{\bar{Y}_1 - \bar{Y}_2} = \sqrt{\frac{2s^2}{n}} = \sqrt{\frac{2(2{,}199)}{14}} = 17.7 \text{ lb, the standard deviation}$$

appropriate to the difference between sample means

$$t = \frac{\bar{Y}_1 - \bar{Y}_2}{s_{\bar{Y}_1 - \bar{Y}_2}} = \frac{187.6 - 235.9}{17.7} = \frac{-48.3}{17.7} = -2.73^*; \ (t_{.005} = 2.78)$$

For the 95 percent confidence interval, $\bar{Y}_2 - \bar{Y}_1 \pm t_{.025} s_{\bar{Y}_1 - \bar{Y}_2} = 48.3 \pm 2.056(17.7) = 48.3 \pm 36.4$; $1_1 = 11.9$ and $1_2 = 84.7$ lb.

For the 99 percent confidence interval, $\bar{Y}_2 - \bar{Y}_1 \pm t_{.005} s_{\bar{Y}_1 - \bar{Y}_2} = 48.3 \pm 2.779(17.7) = 48.3 \pm 49.2$; $1_1 = -0.9$ and $1_2 = 97.5$ lb.

When σ^2 is known, the test criterion becomes

$$z = \frac{\bar{Y}_1 - \bar{Y}_2}{\sqrt{\sigma^2(n_1 + n_2)/n_1 n_2}} \tag{5.11}$$

which is compared with tabulated values in the last line of the table of Student's t. These values are taken from tables of the normal distribution.

Exercise 5.5.1 In a running-for-health program, many participants measure their achievement by the time it takes them to run a measured distance. The rate of heart recovery (RHR) after a Harvard step-test is considered to be a predictor of this time.

The following data are times, in minutes and seconds, for a 1.5-mi run by men who had been running for some years and were starting a new season. The men have been categorized as having RHRs of 40–49 or 50–59, RHR1s or RHR2s, respectively.†

RHR1 times: 12 : 24, 12 : 45, 11 : 04, 11 : 22, 11 : 58, 8 : 34, 11 : 16, 11 : 52, 8 : 28, 12 : 01, 11 : 03, 12 : 01, 11 : 31
RHR2 times: 14 : 33, 10 : 35, 12 : 51, 11 : 28, 11 : 48, 14 : 05, 10 : 51, 18 : 50, 18 : 11

Use $\alpha = .05$ and test the hypothesis of no difference in mean running time for the two populations. Compute a 95 percent confidence interval for the difference between population means. How might you have used the confidence interval to draw the same conclusion as with the test of significance?

Exercise 5.5.2 Data similar to that in Exercise 5.5.1 but for participants new to the program are:†

RHR1 times: 10 : 22, 9 : 33, 9 : 16, 11 : 28, 10 : 59, 11 : 46, 13 : 55, 10 : 10
RHR2 times: 10 : 36, 10 : 40, 11 : 31, 12 : 55, 12 : 58, 10 : 54, 11 : 34, 11 : 15, 13 : 43

Use $\alpha = .05$ and test the hypothesis of no difference in mean running time for the two populations where the alternative calls for the mean of RHR2 times to be greater. Estimate the mean difference $\mu_2 - \mu_1$ using a one-sided confidence interval that provides a lower bound for the difference. Can the two procedures give the same information with respect to whether or not the difference is zero?

Exercise 5.5.3 One would expect a more experienced population of runners to have lower running times. Test this hypothesis using the two sets of running times for RHR1 individuals from Exercises 5.5.1 and 5.5.2.

Exercise 5.5.4 Repeat Exercise 5.5.3 for the two sets of RHR2 data.

Exercise 5.5.5 From an area planted in one variety of guayule, 54 plants were selected at random. Of these, 15 were offtypes and 12 were aberrants. Rubber percentages for these plants were:‡

Offtypes: 6.21, 5.70, 6.04, 4.47, 5.22, 4.45, 4.84, 5.88, 5.82, 6.09, 5.59, 6.06, 5.59, 6.74, 5.55
Aberrants: 4.28, 7.71, 6.48, 7.71, 7.37, 7.20, 7.06, 6.40, 8.93, 5.91, 5.51, 6.36

† Data provided through the courtesy of A. C. Linnerud, North Carolina State University.
‡ Data courtesy of W. T. Federer, Cornell University, Ithaca, New York.

Test the hypothesis of no difference between means of populations of rubber percentages. Compute a 95 percent confidence interval for the difference between population means. Present the results in an analysis of variance table. Compare F and t^2.

Exercise 5.5.6 The weights in grams of 10 male and 10 female juvenile ring-necked pheasants trapped one January in the University of Wisconsin arboretum were:†

Males: 1,293, 1,380, 1,614, 1,497, 1,340, 1,643, 1,466, 1,627, 1,383, 1,711
Females: 1,061, 1,065, 1,092, 1,017, 1,021, 1,138, 1,143, 1,094, 1,270, 1,028

Test the hypothesis of a difference of 350 g (chosen for illustrative purposes only) between population means in favor of males against the alternative of a greater difference. This is a one-tailed test.

Exercise 5.5.7 If one had more ($k > 2$) samples, how could one pool the information to estimate a common σ^2? *Hint*. Generalize Eq. (5.8).

5.6 The Linear Additive Model

The linear additive model (see Sec. 2.12) attempts to explain an observation as a mean plus a random element of variation, where the mean may be the sum of a number of components associated with several effects or sources of variation. For samples from two populations with possibly different means but a common variance, the composition of any observation is given by

$$Y_{ij} = \mu + \tau_i + \varepsilon_{ij} \tag{5.12}$$

where $i = 1, 2$ and $j = 1, \ldots, n_1$ for $i = 1$ and $j = 1, \ldots, n_2$ for $i = 2$. (τ is Greek *tau*.) The model explains the jth observation on the ith population as composed of a general mean μ, plus a component τ_i for the population involved, plus a random element of variation. In terms of Sec. 5.5, $\mu + \tau_1 = \mu_1$ and $\mu + \tau_2 = \mu_2$. For convenience when $n_1 = n_2$, we set $\mu = (\mu_1 + \mu_2)/2$ so that $\tau_1 + \tau_2 = 0$ or $\tau_2 = -\tau_1$. In other words, the τ's are measured as deviations. Thus if τ_1 represents an increase, then $\tau_2 = -\tau_1$ represents an equal decrease. While this may not be the truth of the matter, it does not affect the difference between means, that is, 2τ; and the difference is the important aspect of the problem whereas μ is simply a convenient reference point. When $n_1 \neq n_2$, we may set $n_1\tau_1 + n_2\tau_2 = 0$. The ε's are assumed to be from a single population of ε's with mean $\mu = 0$ and variance σ^2. Thus σ^2 may be estimated from either or both samples. The difference between this model and that of Sec. 2.12 is that this is more general; it permits us to describe two populations of individuals simultaneously.

† Data courtesy of Department of Wildlife Management, University of Wisconsin, Madison, Wisconsin.

Let us look at the sample observations, totals, and means. Observe the notation for sums, namely, $Y_{i\cdot}$ and $\varepsilon_{i\cdot}$, and for means, $\bar{Y}_{i\cdot}$ and $\bar{\varepsilon}_{i\cdot}$. The dot notation is an alternative to using $\sum$. Summation is for all values of the subscript for the place occupied by the dot.

Sample 1	Sample 2
$Y_{11} = \mu + \tau_1 + \varepsilon_{11}$	$Y_{21} = \mu + \tau_2 + \varepsilon_{21}$
$Y_{12} = \mu + \tau_1 + \varepsilon_{12}$	$Y_{22} = \mu + \tau_2 + \varepsilon_{22}$
. . . .	. . . .
$Y_{1n_1} = \mu + \tau_1 + \varepsilon_{1n_1}$	$Y_{2n_2} = \mu + \tau_2 + \varepsilon_{2n_2}$
$\sum_j Y_{1j} = Y_{1\cdot} = n_1\mu + n_1\tau_1 + \varepsilon_{1\cdot}$	$\sum_j Y_{2j} = Y_{2\cdot} = n_2\mu + n_2\tau_2 + \varepsilon_{2\cdot}$
$\bar{Y}_{1\cdot} = \mu + \tau_1 + \bar{\varepsilon}_{1\cdot}$	$\bar{Y}_{2\cdot} = \mu + \tau_2 + \bar{\varepsilon}_{2\cdot}$

To obtain s^2,

$$\sum_j (Y_{1j} - \bar{Y}_{1\cdot})^2 = (n_1 - 1)s_1^2$$

is calculated. This sum of squares is associated with ε's only, since $\mu + \tau_1$ is common to all these observations and so does not affect their variation. We also calculate

$$\sum_j (Y_{2j} - \bar{Y}_{2\cdot})^2$$

associated only with ε's. Since the populations have a common σ^2, that is, since there is a single population of ε's, these sums of squares are pooled in estimating σ^2, as seen in Eq. (5.8). No contribution from the τ's enters our estimate of σ^2.

Now consider $(\bar{Y}_{1\cdot} - \bar{Y}_{2\cdot}) = (\tau_1 - \tau_2) + (\bar{\varepsilon}_{1\cdot} - \bar{\varepsilon}_{2\cdot})$. This is the numerator of t; it is used in computing the numerator of F. Under the null hypothesis, the populations have the same mean and $\tau_1 = \tau_2 = 0$; also, $\bar{Y}_{1\cdot} - \bar{Y}_{2\cdot}$ is a difference of two means of observations from the same population and has a variance which is a multiple of σ^2. Thus if the ε's are normally distributed, both t and F are appropriate criteria for testing the null hypothesis.

The quantity $(\bar{\varepsilon}_{1\cdot} - \bar{\varepsilon}_{2\cdot})$ should be small since it is the algebraic sum of two quantities, each with zero mean and with small variance, namely, σ^2/n_i. When the null hypothesis is false, the quantity $(\tau_1 - \tau_2) = 2\tau_1 \neq 0$ since $\tau_2 = -\tau_1 \neq 0$; an alternative is true and the numerator of t or F is enlarged, leading to a larger value of the criterion than would be expected by chance if the null hypothesis were true. Large values of the criterion are thus unusual if the null hypothesis is true, so the probability of detecting a real difference is seen to increase as the real difference increases.

5.7 Comparison of Sample Means; Meaningfully Paired Observations

Observations are often paired. For example, two feed rations may be compared using 2 animals from each of 10 litters of swine by assigning the animals of each litter at random, one to each ration; or the percentage of oil in 2 soybean varieties grown on paired plots at each of 12 locations may be compared. Pairing has been done before the start of the experiment on the basis of expected similar responses when there are no treatment effects. If the members of the pair tend to be positively correlated, that is, if members of a pair tend to be large or small together, an increase in the ability of the experiment to detect a small difference is possible. The information on pairing is used to eliminate a source of extraneous variance, that existing from pair to pair. This is done by calculating the variance of the differences rather than that among the individuals within each sample. The number of degrees of freedom on which the estimate of σ_D^2 is based is one less than the number of pairs. If the ability of the experiment to detect a real difference is to be improved, then the variance of differences must be sufficiently less than that of individuals, that is, σ_D^2 must be less than $2\sigma^2$ to compensate for the loss of degrees of freedom due to pairing; for random pairing, $\sigma_D^2 = 2\sigma^2$.

The test criterion is t, as in Eq. (5.2) with $\bar{D}$ replacing $\bar{Y}$ and s computed as follows:

$$s = \sqrt{\frac{\sum_j (Y_{1j} - Y_{2j})^2 - \left[\sum_j (Y_{1j} - Y_{2j})\right]^2 / n}{(n-1)}} = \sqrt{\frac{\sum_j D_j^2 - \left(\sum_j D_j\right)^2 / n}{(n-1)}} \tag{5.13}$$

In the divisor, $n - 1$ is the degrees of freedom and n is the number of sample differences of pairs.

Tests of hypotheses with meaningfully paired observations are seen to reduce to testing that the mean of differences is a specified number, often zero. An example is worked in Table 5.5 for data from Shuel (5.10).

The null hypothesis tested is that the mean of the population of differences is zero; the alternatives are that the mean is not zero. The test criterion is distributed as t when the assumption that differences are normally distributed is correct and the null hypothesis is true. Tabulated $t_{.005}$ for 9 degrees of freedom and a two-tailed test with $\alpha = .01$ is 3.3. Here the observed difference is hard to explain on the basis of random sampling from the population associated with the null hypothesis. The null hypothesis is rejected on the basis of the evidence presented.

When σ^2 is known, observed t is compared with tabulated t on the last line of the t table. The F criterion for paired observations is discussed in Chap. 8.

Table 5.5 Sugar concentration of nectar in half heads of red clover kept at different vapor pressures for 8 h

	Vapor pressure		
	4.4 mmHg Y_1	9.9 mmHg Y_2	Difference $D = Y_1 - Y_2$
	62.5	51.7	10.8
	65.2	54.2	11.0
	67.6	53.3	14.3
	69.9	57.0	12.9
	69.4	56.4	13.0
	70.1	61.5	8.6
	67.8	57.2	10.6
	67.0	56.2	10.8
	68.5	58.4	10.1
	62.4	55.8	6.6
$\sum Y$	670.4	561.7	108.7
			$1{,}226.07 = \sum_j (Y_{1j} - Y_{2j})^2 = \sum D^2$
$\bar{Y}$	67.0	56.2	10.8

$$s_D^2 = \frac{\sum D^2 - [\sum D]^2/n}{n-1} = \frac{1{,}226.07 - 1{,}181.57}{9} = 4.944$$

$$s_{\bar{D}}^2 = \frac{s_D^2}{n} = \frac{4.944}{10} = 0.4944 \qquad s_{\bar{D}} = .703$$

$$t = \frac{\bar{D}}{s_{\bar{D}}} = \frac{10.8}{.703} = 15.4^{**} \quad \text{for 9 df}$$

The 99 percent confidence interval for the population mean difference is calculated as $\bar{D} \pm t_{.005}\, s_{\bar{D}} = 10.8 \pm 3.3(.703)$. Hence $1_1 = 8.5$ and $1_2 = 13.1$ percent.
Note that $\sum (Y_{1j} - Y_{2j}) = \sum Y_{1j} - \sum Y_{2j}$ and that $\overline{Y_1 - Y_2} = \bar{Y}_1 - \bar{Y}_2$.

Exercise 5.7.1 The cooling constants of freshly killed mice and those of the same mice reheated to body temperature were determined by Hart (5.4) as

Freshly killed: 573, 482, 377, 390, 535, 414, 438, 410, 418, 368, 445, 383, 391, 410, 433, 405, 340, 328, 400

Reheated: 481, 343, 383, 380, 454, 425, 393, 435, 422, 346, 443, 342, 378, 402, 400, 360, 373, 373, 412

Test the hypothesis of no difference between population means.

Exercise 5.7.2 Times for the runners of Exercise 5.5.1 were obtained in September. The times were again recorded in the following May. For the RHR1 group in the same order, May times were: 11 : 16, 12 : 30, 11 : 30, 11 : 06, 11 : 28, 8 : 18, 11 : 44, 12 : 02, 8 : 28, 11 : 55, 11 : 27, 11 : 31, and 11 : 46.†

With $\alpha = .05$, test the null hypothesis that the means of the populations have not changed. Construct a 95 percent confidence interval on the difference between the population means.

Exercise 5.7.3 Times for the RHR2 runners of Exercise 5.5.2 are also for September. For the following May, corresponding times are: 11 : 34, 10 : 39, 11 : 47, 12 : 12, 12 : 48, 10 : 30, 11 : 20, 11 : 11, and 11 : 00.†

Test the hypothesis H_1 that the mean of the May population is lower than that of the corresponding September population. Compute the 95 percent one-sided confidence interval that you think most appropriate for the difference between the two population means.

Exercise 5.7.4 Peterson (5.5) studied the effect of exposure of lucerne flowers to different environmental conditions. He chose 10 vigorous plants with freely exposed flowers at the top and flowers hidden as much as possible at the bottom. Finally, he determined the number of seeds set per two pods at each location. The data were:

Plant	1	2	3	4	5	6	7	8	9	10
Top flowers	4.0	5.2	5.7	4.2	4.8	3.9	4.1	3.0	4.6	6.8
Bottom flowers	4.4	3.7	4.7	2.8	4.2	4.3	3.5	3.7	3.1	1.9

Test the hypothesis of no difference between population means against the alternatives that top flowers set more seeds. Compute a helpful one-sided confidence interval.

5.8 The Linear Additive Model for the Paired Comparison

The linear additive expression for the composition of any observation is given by

$$Y_{ij} = \mu + \tau_i + \rho_j + \varepsilon_{ij} \tag{5.14}$$

Y_{ij} is the observation on the ith sample for the jth pair, $i = 1, 2$ and $j = 1, 2, \ldots, n$. Again we have a general mean μ, a component τ_i peculiar to the sample, and a random element ε_{ij}; in addition, there is a component ρ_j peculiar to the pair of observations. The τ_i's and ρ_j's contribute to the variability of the Y's, provided that they are not all equal to zero. For convenience, we let $\sum \tau_i = 0$ and $\sum \rho_j = 0$. This model admits of a different population mean for each observation, but these means are closely related by construction; Y_{ij} is the only observation from the population with mean

† Data courtesy of A. C. Linnerud, North Carolina State University.

$\mu + \tau_i + \rho_j$, but τ_i is present in $n - 1$ other observations and ρ_j is present in one other observation. The ε's are considered to be from, at most, two populations corresponding to the subscript i but need not be assumed to be from a single population as in the case of the model of Eq. (5.12). Because of the relations among population means, that is, the $(\mu + \tau_i + \rho_j)$'s, it is possible to estimate an appropriate variance for testing the difference of sample means. To see this clearly, set up a table as follows:

	Sample 1 Y_{1j}	Sample 2 Y_{2j}	Difference $D = Y_{1j} - Y_{2j}$
	$Y_{11} = \mu + \tau_1 + \rho_1 + \varepsilon_{11}$	$Y_{21} = \mu + \tau_2 + \rho_1 + \varepsilon_{21}$	$(\tau_1 - \tau_2) + (\varepsilon_{11} - \varepsilon_{21})$
	$\cdots$	$\cdots$	$\cdots$
	$Y_{1n} = \mu + \tau_1 + \rho_n + \varepsilon_{1n}$	$Y_{2n} = \mu + \tau_2 + \rho_n + \varepsilon_{2n}$	$(\tau_1 - \tau_2) + (\varepsilon_{1n} - \varepsilon_{2n})$
Totals:	$Y_{1\cdot} = n\mu + n\tau_1 + \sum \rho_j + \varepsilon_{1\cdot}$	$Y_{2\cdot} = n\mu + n\tau_2 + \sum \rho_j + \varepsilon_{2\cdot}$	$n(\tau_1 - \tau_2) + (\varepsilon_{1\cdot} - \varepsilon_{2\cdot})$
Means:	$\bar{Y}_{1\cdot} = \mu + \tau_1 + \bar{\varepsilon}_{1\cdot}$	$\bar{Y}_{2\cdot} = \mu + \tau_2 + \bar{\varepsilon}_{2\cdot}$	$(\tau_1 - \tau_2) + (\bar{\varepsilon}_{1\cdot} - \bar{\varepsilon}_{2\cdot})$

It is obvious that the differences in the last column have a variation associated only with differences (algebraic sums) of ε's, since $(\tau_1 - \tau_2)$ is a constant in all. The variance of the sample differences is an estimate of $\sigma_1^2 + \sigma_2^2$ if the ε_1's and ε_2's have different variances, or of $2\sigma^2$ if a common variance exists. The numerator of the test criterion, either t or F, involves the mean of the differences and, consequently, has a contribution from the difference between treatment means, namely, $\tau_1 - \tau_2 = 2\tau_1$ if such is present, in addition to a contribution due to the ε's. If then the numerator is much larger than the denominator, the largeness is customarily attributed to a real treatment difference rather than to an unusual chance event. Note that if the ρ_j's are real, they will contribute to any variance computed directly from either sample.

This test has one important property not possessed by the previous tests involving the hypothesis of a difference between population means. Theory tells us that the algebraic sum of normally distributed variables is normally distributed. The application of this to the present case is to the effect that the differences are normally distributed provided that the errors are, *regardless of whether or not the* ε_1's *and the* ε_2's *have a common variance.* Additional discussion is given in Sec. 5.10.

A value in pairing not previously mentioned concerns the scope of inference. It is seen that the variation from pair to pair can be large. If we deliberately make this variation large, we widen the scope of our inference. Thus our pairs of swine can come from many litters involving different sires and dams, and possibly, different breeds; our soybeans may have been grown at quite different locations; our inference is broadened as a result.

5.9 Independent Samples and Unequal Variances

Given a sample from each of two populations with $\sigma_1^2 \neq \sigma_2^2$, that is, with unequal variances, we want to test the hypothesis that $\mu_1 = \mu_2$ using the sample estimates of the variances.

The appropriate $s_{\bar{Y}_1 - \bar{Y}_2}$ is computed as follows:

$$s_{\bar{Y}_1 - \bar{Y}_2} = \sqrt{\frac{s_1^2}{n_1} + \frac{s_2^2}{n_2}} \tag{5.15}$$

Neither the sums of squares nor the degrees of freedom are pooled as when s_1^2 and s_2^2 were estimates of a common σ^2 and the observations were unpaired, as in Eq. (5.8). Now compute t' by Eq. (5.16). The prime indicates that the criterion is not distributed strictly as Student's t but rather as an approximation to it.

$$t' = \frac{\bar{Y}_1 - \bar{Y}_2}{s_{\bar{Y}_1 - \bar{Y}_2}} \tag{5.16}$$

To determine the critical value for t', use a weighted sum of tabulated t's with df $= n_i - 1$ and weights of $w_i = s_i^2/n_i$, $i = 1, 2$, the result to be divided by the sum of the weights [Cochran and Cox (5.3)], or use a tabulated t with "effective df" computed by Eq. (5.17). [See Satterthwaite (5.8) and Searle (5.9).]

$$\text{Effective df} = \frac{(s_1^2/n_1 + s_2^2/n_2)^2}{[(s_1^2/n_1)^2/(n_1 - 1)] + [(s_2^2/n_2)^2/(n_2 - 1)]} \tag{5.17}$$

It is unlikely that the effective df will be an integer, so one can expect to round or interpolate. The resulting test has an error rate, α, approximately equal to that of the tabulated t or t's used in determining the critical value. A confidence interval with a confidence coefficient of approximately $1 - \alpha$ may be computed.

Data in Table 5.6 from Rowles (5.7) are used to exemplify the procedure.

Equation (3.15) appears to define Student's t in a way that can be generalized; t measures a distance between a random variable and its population mean in applicable standard deviations. Why has it been necessary to change from t to t' when $\sigma_1^2 \neq \sigma_2^2$?

A more complete definition of t describes it as the ratio of a Z value to a $\sqrt{\chi^2/\text{df}}$ value. Since Z and χ^2 call for random variables with zero means and unit variances, it appears necessary to use σ^2 in any practical application. When σ^2 is the same for both Z and χ^2, as when $\bar{Y}$ and s^2 are computed from a single sample, this value need not be known since it cancels out of numerator and denominator. In the present problem, the Z of the numerator should be $(\bar{Y}_1 - \bar{Y}_2)/\sqrt{\sigma_1^2/n_1 + \sigma_2^2/n_2}$, whereas the χ^2 in the denominator should be $(n_1 - 1)s_1^2/\sigma_1^2 + (n_2 - 1)s_2^2/\sigma_2^2$. In t, cancellation is not possible except in the unlikely case where the true ratio σ_1^2/σ_2^2 is known. This ratio may be called a nuisance parameter since it creates a considerable problem in devising criteria such as t'.

Table 5.6 Fine gravel in surface soils, percent

	Good soil	Poor soil
	5.9	7.6
	3.8	0.4
	6.5	1.1
	18.3	3.2
	18.2	6.5
	16.1	4.1
	7.6	4.7
$\sum Y$	76.4	27.6
$\sum Y^2$	1,074.60	150.52
$\bar{Y}$	10.91	3.94

$$\sum (Y_1 - \bar{Y}_1)^2 = \sum Y_1^2 - (\sum Y_1)^2/n_1 = 1{,}074.60 - 833.85 = 240.75$$

$$s_1^2 = \frac{\sum (Y_1 - \bar{Y}_1)^2}{n_1 - 1} = \frac{240.75}{6} = 40.12$$

$$\sum (Y_2 - \bar{Y}_2)^2 = \sum Y_2^2 - (\sum Y_2)^2/n_2 = 150.52 - 108.82 = 41.70$$

$$s_2^2 = \frac{\sum (Y_2 - \bar{Y}_2)^2}{n_2 - 1} = \frac{41.70}{6} = 6.95$$

$$s_{\bar{Y}_1 - \bar{Y}_2} = \sqrt{\frac{s_1^2}{n_1} + \frac{s_2^2}{n_2}} = \sqrt{\frac{40.12}{7} + \frac{6.95}{7}} = \sqrt{6.72} = 2.59\%$$

$$t' = \frac{\bar{Y}_1 - \bar{Y}_2}{s_{\bar{Y}_1 - \bar{Y}_2}} = \frac{10.91 - 3.94}{2.59} = \frac{6.97}{2.59} = 2.69^*$$

$$\text{effective df} = \frac{(40.12/7 + 6.95/7)^2}{\dfrac{(40.12/7)^2}{6} + \dfrac{(6.95/7)^2}{6}} \approx 8$$

Compare t' with tabulated t for 8 df (= 2.31 for α = .05). The evidence is that there is a real difference in the percentage of fine gravel.

The 95 percent confidence interval is $\bar{Y}_1 - \bar{Y}_2 \pm t_{.025} s_{\bar{Y}_1 - \bar{Y}_2} = 6.97 \pm 2.306(2.59) = 6.97 \pm 5.97$. Hence $l_1 = 1.00$ percent and $l_2 = 12.94$ percent.

Exercise 5.9.1 In an experiment with oats, the mean was 52.8 bushels per acre and the experimental error variance was 20.31 with 36 df. A similar experiment under somewhat different circumstances might have given $\bar{Y} = 48.4$ and $s^2 = 45.06$ with 24 df.

Test the null hypothesis that the two population means have the same value, assuming the true variances differ.

Exercise 5.9.2 An experiment with guinea pigs gave a mean weight gain of 105.3 g. The experimental error variance was 427.80. In a similar experiment but with a different forage, the mean weight gain was 175.0 g. Let us assume that here $s^2 = 756.20$.

Test the null hypothesis that the two population means have the same value. Assume that population variances differ and here df = 15 and 7, respectively.

5.10 The Mean and Variance of a Linear Function

As we have progressed with sampling problems, the need to know the variance of means, of random differences, and of differences between two sample means under various assumptions has been met by presenting appropriate formulas. These formulas have a common basis which we now examine. The results have further applications in later chapters.

Suppose that we begin to look for this common basis by constructing a linear function of random observations by

$$L = \sum c_i Y_i \tag{5.18}$$

Such functions are common. When $L = \bar{Y} = \sum Y_i/n$, $c_i = 1/n$ for all i. When $L = \bar{Y}_{1\cdot} - \bar{Y}_{2\cdot} = \sum Y_{1j}/n_1 - \sum Y_{2j}/n_2$, $c_i = 1/n_1$ for the Y's of sample 1 and $c_i = -1/n_2$ for the Y's of sample 2, or simply, $c_1 = 1$ and $c_2 = -1$ if we do not define each mean in terms of the Y_{ij}'s.

Consider L as a random variable. It can be generated by repeated sampling from one or more parent populations of Y's and computation of L from each sample. We want to know the mean or *expectation* or *expected value* of this derived population; we write $\mu_L = E(L)$. To write E is to imply that an operation of averaging is to be or has been carried out, much like finding the sum of all possible values and dividing by N, except that we are now talking about averaging a population that does not necessarily have a finite number of observations. If $E(Y_i) = \mu_i$, say, for each Y_i in Eq. (5.18), implying that each Y_i is from a different population, then Eq. (5.19) is a theorem that gives the expectation.

$$\begin{aligned} \mu_L &= E(L) \\ &= E(\textstyle\sum c_i Y_i) = \sum c_i E(Y_i) \\ &= \textstyle\sum c_i \mu_i \end{aligned} \tag{5.19}$$

Note that we are able to interchange the order of expectation and summation. This is possible for the problems with which we have to deal.

Let us apply this to $\bar{Y}$ calculated for a sample from a population with $E(Y) = \mu$.

$$\begin{aligned} \mu_{\bar{Y}} &= E(\bar{Y}) \\ &= E\left(\frac{\sum Y_i}{n}\right) = \frac{1}{n}\sum E(Y_i) \\ &= \frac{1}{n}\sum \mu = \frac{n\mu}{n} = \mu \end{aligned}$$

Here we have simply taken out $1/n$ as a constant; also, $\sum \mu$ requires us to write μ for each of n cases.

Again, for two samples of size n_1 and n_2, each from a possibly different population with $E(Y_{1j}) = \mu_1$ and $E(Y_{2j}) = \mu_2$, we have

$$\begin{aligned} \mu_{\bar{Y}_1 - \bar{Y}_2} &= E(\bar{Y}_{1\cdot} - \bar{Y}_{2\cdot}) \\ &= E(\bar{Y}_{1\cdot}) - E(\bar{Y}_{2\cdot}) \\ &= \mu_1 - \mu_2 \end{aligned}$$

Here we have first changed the order from taking the expectation of a difference to differencing two expectations and then have used the previous result that $E(\bar{Y}) = \mu$. Note that if $\mu_1 = \mu_2$, then $E(\bar{Y}_{1\cdot} - \bar{Y}_{2\cdot}) = 0$, the hypotheses of Secs. 5.5, 5.7, and 5.9.

A variance is defined as an expectation by

$$\begin{aligned} \sigma^2 &= E[Y - E(Y)]^2 \\ &= E(Y - \mu)^2 \end{aligned} \tag{5.20}$$

To determine the variance of L, apply Eq. (5.19) and obtain

$$\begin{aligned} \sigma_L^2 &= E[L - E(L)]^2 \\ &= E(\sum c_i Y_i - \sum c_i \mu_i)^2 = E[\sum c_i(Y_i - \mu_i)]^2 \end{aligned} \tag{5.21}$$

The order of expectation and summation cannot be interchanged here. First we must complete the squaring operation. This leads to cross-products. Now we need a definition of their expectation, called a covariance:

$$\sigma_{12} = E(Y_{1j} - \mu_1)(Y_{2j} - \mu_2) \tag{5.22}$$

If high positive values of Y_1 are associated with high positive values of Y_2, and so on, then the covariance will be positive. The more alike the members of a pair are as compared with members of different pairs, the larger will be the covariance.

Finally we write a very general formula for the variance of L, Eq. (5.23), a theorem about the variance of L.

$$\sigma_L^2 = \sum c_i^2 \sigma_i^2 + 2 \sum_{i<j} c_i c_j \sigma_{ij} \tag{5.23}$$

A common variance is usually involved, that is, $\sigma_i^2 = \sigma^2$ for all i, and the first term becomes $(\sum c_i^2)\sigma^2$. Often, $\sigma_{ij} = 0$ because sampling is random; we say that Y_{1j} and Y_{2j} are independent.

Now suppose that we have a random sample of n observations from a population with mean μ and variance σ^2. Compute $\bar{Y} = \sum Y_i/n$. To find $\sigma_{\bar{Y}}^2$, use Eq. (5.23) with $c_i = 1/n$ for all i, so that $c_i^2 = 1/n^2$. Because we have a single population, $\sigma_i^2 = \sigma^2$, and because random sampling has ensured independence, $\sigma_{ij} = 0$. Consequently, we have

$$\sigma_{\bar{Y}}^2 = \sum \left(\frac{1}{n^2}\right)\sigma^2 = \frac{\sigma^2}{n} \tag{5.24}$$

Again, $\sum$ has required that we write the expression n times; consequently, the final coefficient of σ^2 is $1/n$.

For the difference between two independent sample means, Eq. (5.23) gives

$$\sigma^2_{\bar{Y}_1 - \bar{Y}_2} = \frac{\sigma_1^2}{n_1} + \frac{\sigma_2^2}{n_2} \qquad \text{in general}$$

$$= \sigma^2\left(\frac{1}{n_1} + \frac{1}{n_2}\right) \qquad \text{common } \sigma^2$$

$$= \frac{2\sigma^2}{n} \qquad \text{common } \sigma^2 \text{ and } n_1 = n_2$$

In these cases, the c_i's were $+1$ and -1. Note that since c_i is always squared when a coefficient of σ^2, we can never have σ^2's with negative coefficients. The variance of a difference must always be a sum of variances.

Section 5.7 dealt with meaningfully paired and, consequently, dependent observations. In particular, a positive covariance was expected.

Suppose that we draw random pairs of observations. For example, we might draw an individual randomly and measure both height, Y_1, and weight, Y_2. We have the following, including Eq. (5.25).

$$E(Y_{1j} - Y_{2j}) = \mu_1 - \mu_2$$

$$\sigma^2_{Y_{1j} - Y_{2j}} = \sigma_1^2 + \sigma_2^2 - 2\sigma_{12}$$

$$\sigma^2_{\bar{Y}_{1\cdot} - \bar{Y}_{2\cdot}} = n\left(\frac{\sigma_1^2 + \sigma_2^2 - 2\sigma_{12}}{n^2}\right)$$

$$= \frac{\sigma_1^2}{n} + \frac{\sigma_2^2}{n} - \frac{2\sigma_{12}}{n} \qquad (5.25)$$

If σ_{12} is positive, then $\sigma^2_{\bar{Y}_1 - \bar{Y}_2}$ is smaller than if there were no pairing. This is, of course, the intent of pairing. We are trying to detect a smaller difference between two means than would be possible without pairing. In general, we have two options: we can increase the sample size and so decrease any $\sigma^2_{\bar{Y}} = \sigma^2/n$ or we can control the experiment in a way that reduces the underlying σ^2. The latter approach is possible with meaningful pairing when σ_{12} is positive.

In Sec. 5.8, the model equation for meaningfully paired observations was written as

$$Y_{ij} = \mu + \tau_i + \rho_j + \varepsilon_{ij} \qquad i = 1, 2$$
$$j = 1, \ldots, n$$

with the ε_{ij}'s normally and independently distributed with variance σ_i^2. We see that the covariance is attributable to the "pair" contribution ρ. This contribution is a source of variation in the observations but not one that contributes to differences between treatment means; each treatment mean has $\sum \rho_j/n$, a constant, in it. Consequently, from the unit of measurement that helps us decide whether or not $\bar{Y}_{1.} - \bar{Y}_{2.}$ is a large difference, we must remove any contribution which has to do with the variability among pairs. This may be done by direct use of the covariance or, indirectly, by taking differences. In the latter case, $Y_{1j} - Y_{2j} = (\tau_1 - \tau_2) + (\varepsilon_{1j} - \varepsilon_{2j})$, where both μ and ρ_j disappear. In Sec. 5.7, we chose the latter course.

A sample covariance is defined for n pairs of observations by

$$s_{12} = \frac{\sum (Y_{1j} - \bar{Y}_{1.})(Y_{2j} - \bar{Y}_{2.})}{n - 1} \tag{5.26}$$

It is computed by

$$s_{12} = \frac{\sum Y_{1j} Y_{2j} - (Y_{1.} Y_{2.})/n}{n - 1} \tag{5.27}$$

Note that definition and computing formulas for the variance are particular applications of Eqs. (5.26) and (5.27).

Exercise 5.10.1 Suppose that we have a population of differences $D_j = Y_{1j} - Y_{2j}$ derived from two Y populations with variances σ_1^2 and σ_2^2, respectively, in such a way that the covariance is $\sigma_{12} \neq 0$.

Show that Eq. (5.23) becomes $\sigma_D^2 = \sigma_1^2 + \sigma_2^2 - 2\sigma_{12}$.

Exercise 5.10.2 For the data of Table 5.5, compute s_1^2, s_2^2, and s_{12}, sample estimates of σ_1^2, σ_2^2, and σ_{12}.

Demonstrate that $s_D^2 = s_1^2 + s_2^2 - 2s_{12}$ for these data.

Exercise 5.10.3 Show that totals of n random observations from a single population with variance σ^2 have variance $n\sigma^2$.

5.11 Testing the Hypothesis of Equality of Variances

In Sec. 5.2, the choice of a critical or rejection region was seen to depend, in part, on the set of alternative hypotheses. The tests just discussed have been treated from the point of view of a two-tailed test, the set of alternatives being that a difference existed. For one-tailed tests of such hypotheses, the test criterion is the same but the rejection regions differ.

The test criterion t may be viewed as a comparison of standard deviations, its square as a comparison of two variances. Such a test, the ratio of two variances, can be generalized so that any two independent variances, regardless of the number of degrees of freedom in each, may be compared under the null hypothesis that they are sample variances from populations with a common variance.

Such a test is useful for the purpose of deciding whether or not it is legitimate to pool variances, as was done in Sec. 5.5 when computing a variance for testing the hypothesis of the equality of population means using samples with unpaired observations. An appropriate criterion for testing the hypothesis of homogeneity is denoted by F or $F(m, n)$, where m and n are the degrees of freedom for the estimates of variance in numerator and denominator, respectively.

If we examine F in Eq. (5.6), we realize that large values occur when the set of alternatives $\mu_1 \neq \mu_2$ holds and that the criterion does not distinguish between $\mu_1 < \mu_2$ and $\mu_1 > \mu_2$. Thus our F test is one-tailed relative to F and variances but two-tailed relative to means, that is, $H_1: \sigma^2$ (based on means) $> \sigma^2$ (based on individuals) is equivalent to $H_1: \mu_1 > \mu_2$ or $\mu_2 > \mu_1$, that is, to $H_1: \mu_1 \neq \mu_2$. Near-zero values of t when squared become positive, near-zero values of F; clearly these call for acceptance rather than rejection of the null hypothesis. Thus F could be small, significantly so, if the numerator were small relative to the denominator. For our problem, we must explain such values by attributing them to chance. In some problems of testing the homogeneity of two variances, there may be no reason to assume which variance will be larger, for example, σ_1^2 or σ_2^2 for the populations implied in Table 5.6; thus there is no reason to compute s_1^2/s_2^2 rather than s_2^2/s_1^2. Here is a case where the alternatives are $\sigma_1^2 \neq \sigma_2^2$. This clearly calls for a two-tailed F test.

Consider testing the null hypothesis $\sigma_1^2 = \sigma_2^2$ against the set of alternatives $\sigma_1^2 \neq \sigma_2^2$. Determine s_1^2 and s_2^2 and calculate F by

$$F = \frac{\text{the larger } s^2}{\text{the smaller } s^2} \tag{5.28}$$

This F is compared with tabulated values in Table A.6 where the degrees of freedom for the larger mean square are given across the top of the table and those for the smaller along the side. For the set of alternatives $\sigma_1^2 \neq \sigma_2^2$, the stated significance levels are doubled. If calculated F is larger than $F_{.025}$, we claim significance at the 5 percent level; if larger than $F_{.005}$, at the 1 percent level; and so on. This test is a two-tailed test with respect to F since we do not specify which σ^2 is expected to be larger. Unfortunately, this test is also sensitive to normality.

For the example of Sec. 5.9, compare the two sample variances by $F = 40.12/6.95 = 5.77$ for 6 degrees of freedom in both numerator and denominator. The tabulated F value is 5.82 at the 5 percent level for the desired alternatives ($F_{.025} = 5.82$) and our test just misses significance.

The F tables are tabulated for convenience in making one-tailed tests since the associated alternatives are more common; in the t tests of this chapter, it was seen that the numerator was expected to be larger when the null hypothesis was false, that is, the numerator variance had to be large to deny the null hypothesis. If you square any tabulated value of $t_{.025}$ or $t_{.005}$

you will find this value in the column of the F table headed by 1 degree of freedom, opposite the appropriate number of degrees of freedom and .05 or .01.

Exercise 5.11.1 Test the homogeneity of the variances for the two populations sampled in Table 5.2, Table 5.4, Exercise 5.5.1, and Exercise 5.5.2. Does the assumption of a common variance seem justified in all cases?

Exercise 5.11.2 Test the homogeneity of the variances for the two RHR1 populations of times given in Exercises 5.5.1 and 5.5.2. The two RHR2 populations in Exercises 5.5.1 and 5.5.2.

5.12 Power, Sample Size, and the Detection of Differences

The ideas of Sec. 5.2, namely, Type I and Type II errors and the power of a test, are essential to a clear understanding of the problem of sample size. Figure 5.3 illustrates the ideas when one-tailed alternatives are appropriate. We now consider the matter further.

Let us draw a random sample from a population with unknown μ but known σ^2 for the purpose of testing H_0: $\mu = \mu_0$ versus H_1: $\mu > \mu_0$. An error rate of α will be used and the test criterion will be $Z = (\bar{Y} - \mu_0)/\sigma_{\bar{Y}}$; note that this allows us to look at acceptance and rejection regions on a $\bar{Y}$ axis. The single critical value is computed on the basis that H_0 is true, and is $\mu_0 + Z_\alpha \sigma_{\bar{Y}}$. The upper part of Fig. 5.3 applies.

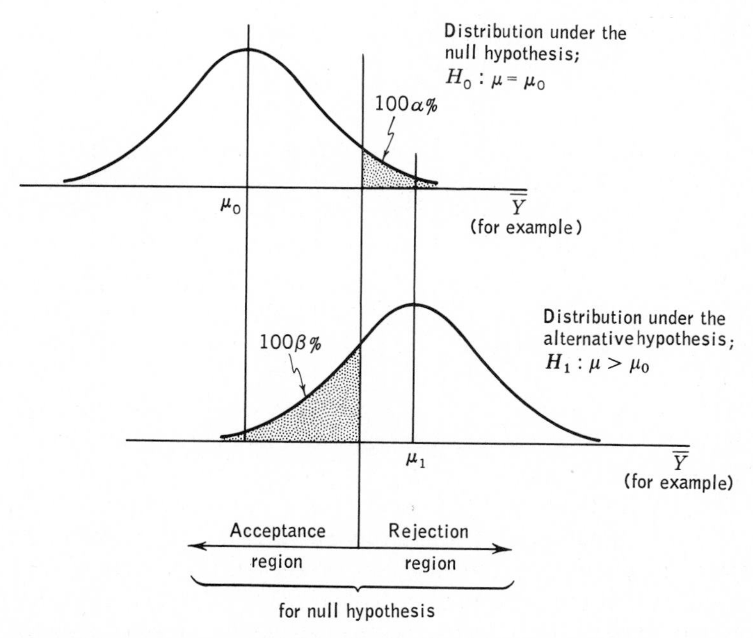

Figure 5.3 An illustration relative to Type I and Type II errors.

Suppose that the true mean is μ_1, as shown in the lower part of Fig. 5.3. If $\bar{Y}$ falls in the acceptance region, then a Type II error is made with probability β and the power of the test is $1 - \beta$. Note that the power against this alternative was determined the moment we settled on the critical value and that this was, in turn, set by α and the one-sided nature of H_1.

Regardless of the true value of μ, Eq. (5.29) holds. If the true $\mu = \mu_0$, then Eq. (5.29) gives the value α.

$$P(\text{rejecting } H_0) = P\left(\frac{\bar{Y} - \mu_0}{\sigma_{\bar{Y}}} > Z_\alpha\right) \tag{5.29}$$

If the true $\mu = \mu_1$, then $(\bar{Y} - \mu_0)/\sigma_{\bar{Y}}$ is not really distributed as Z. However, we can rearrange the equation to give

$$\begin{aligned} P\left(\frac{\bar{Y} - \mu_0}{\sigma_{\bar{Y}}} > Z_\alpha\right) &= P\left(\frac{\bar{Y} - \mu_1}{\sigma_{\bar{Y}}} + \frac{\mu_1 - \mu_0}{\sigma_{\bar{Y}}} > Z_\alpha\right) \\ &= P\left(Z > Z_\alpha - \frac{\mu_1 - \mu_0}{\sigma_{\bar{Y}}}\right) \end{aligned} \tag{5.30}$$

Note that $(\bar{Y} - \mu_1)/\sigma_{\bar{Y}}$ is a true Z value and that $(\mu_1 - \mu_0)/\sigma_{\bar{Y}}$ is a constant, making it possible to compute power from the Z table. Some values, computed without serious interpolation, are presented in Table 5.7 and the power curve, based on these probabilities, is shown in Fig. 5.4.

The power curve is useful in that we can refer to it to get a better impression of the overall picture of the power of the test.

Power against $H_1: \mu \neq \mu_0$ and with a Type I error rate of α is computed by

$$\begin{aligned} P(\text{rejecting } H_0) = &\, P\left(Z > Z_{\alpha/2} - \frac{\mu_1 - \mu_0}{\sigma_{\bar{Y}}}\right) \\ &+ P\left(Z < -Z_{\alpha/2} - \frac{\mu_1 - \mu_0}{\sigma_{\bar{Y}}}\right) \end{aligned} \tag{5.31}$$

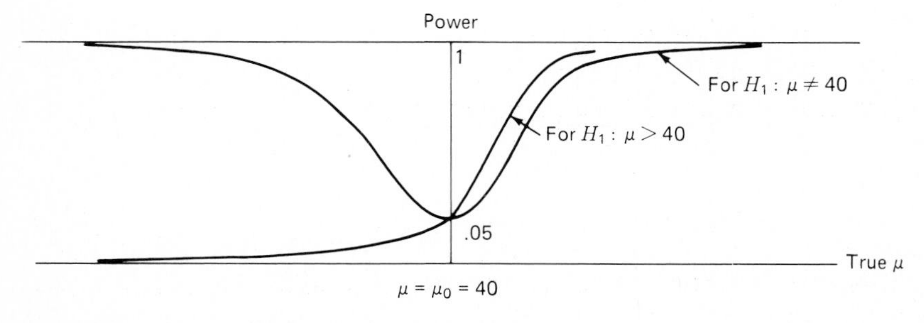

Figure 5.4 Power curves for text illustration.

Table 5.7 Power when $\alpha = .05$ for illustration with $\mu = \mu_0 = 40$

	Power when	
True μ	$H_1: \mu > 40$†	$H_1: \mu \neq 40$†
24		.9881
26		.9582
28		.8845
30		.7517
32	.0000	.5596
32.56		.5000
34	.0006	.3522
36	.0035	.1827
38	.0150	.0828
39	.0281	.0578
40	.0500	.0500
41	.0838	.0578
42	.2061	.0828
44	.2776	.1827
46	.4761	.3522
46.23	.5000	
47.44		.5000
48	.6772	.5596
50	.8389	.7517
52	.9357	.8849
54	.9793	.9582
56	.9945	.9881

† For $H_1: \mu > 40$, critical value is 1.645; for $H_1: \mu \neq 40$, critical value is 1.96.

One of the terms, depending on the sign of $\mu_1 - \mu_0$, will add very little to the required probability, so it is not unreasonable to ignore it. In this case, we use

$$P(\text{rejecting } H_0) = P\left(Z > Z_{\alpha/2} - \frac{|\mu_1 - \mu_0|}{\sigma_{\bar{Y}}}\right) \tag{5.32}$$

Table 5.7 gives some values of power for two-tailed alternatives. These are plotted to give the symmetric power curve of Fig. 5.4.

In many experiments, the experimenter is interested in determining whether a treatment is superior to a control. A one-tailed t test is appro-

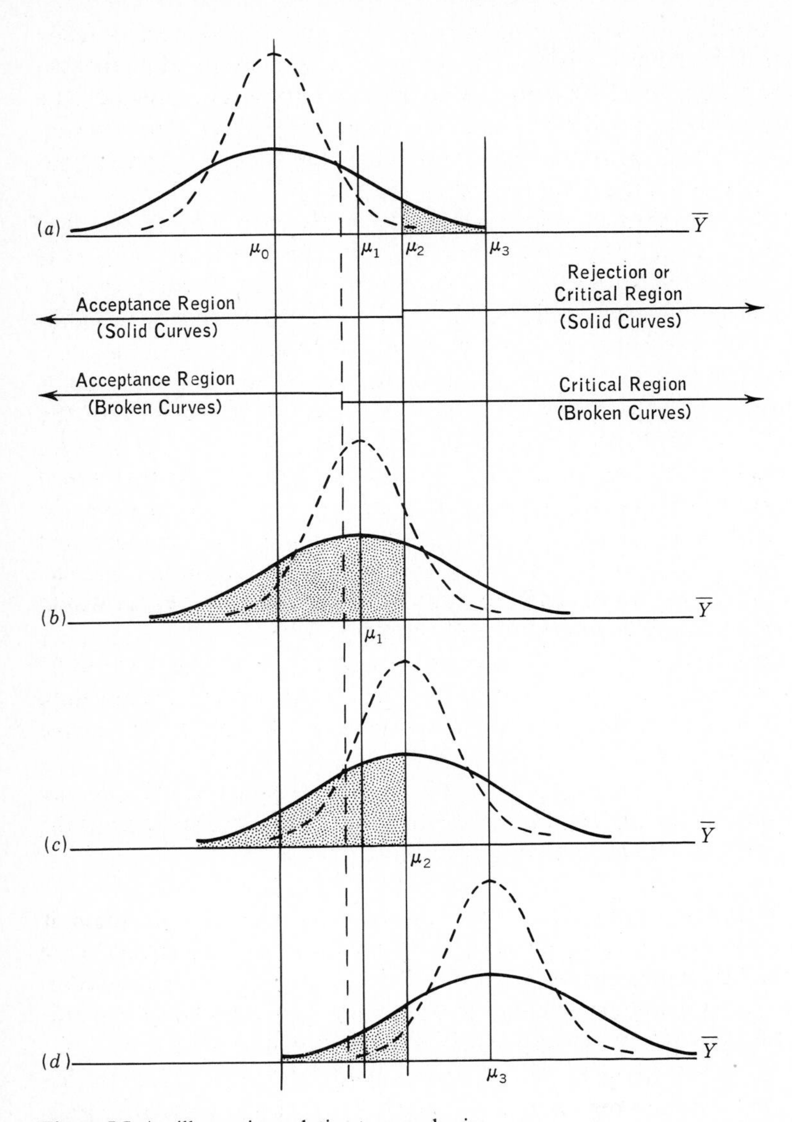

Figure 5.5 An illustration relative to sample size.

priate. The Type I error rate is to be set at α and the Type II error rate at β. Consider Fig. 5.5. Suppose that we have a parent distribution with unknown mean μ and known variance σ^2. Then a, b, c, and d are illustrations of possible derived distributions of $\bar{Y}$'s with different means, $\mu_0, \ldots, \mu_3$ and two possible variances σ^2/n_i, $i = 1$ or 2, depending on the sample size. The shaded areas refer to the population with the larger variance, that is, the smaller sample size. In particular:

a shows the distribution of $\bar{Y}$ when H_0 is true. The shaded area, say 100α percent, gives the probability of a Type I error. The line dividing the two areas separates the $\bar{Y}$ axis into an acceptance and rejection region. The test procedure is based on H_0 regardless of what the true μ is. If we are always presented with data for which H_0 is true, then we wrongly conclude that H_0 is false 100α percent of the time.

b shows the distribution of $\bar{Y}$ when H_0 is false and μ_1 is the true parameter. If we falsely conclude that H_0 is true, we make a Type II error. We do this when $\bar{Y}$ falls in the acceptance region determined by the test criterion used to test H_0. The shaded area of the curve measures β, the probability of a Type II error, over 50 percent in this case.

The power of the test, $1 - \beta$, with respect to the alternative *b* is measured by the unshaded area under *b*. This is associated with the critical region as determined by the test of H_0. When, in fact, $\mu = \mu_1$, this area is a measure of the ability of the test to detect μ_1. In this case, if the experimenter is presented with data for which μ_1 is true, then he will detect μ_1 less than half of the time. If it were important to detect a real difference as large as $\mu_1 - \mu_0$, then we would do better, on the average, to toss a coin to choose between μ_0 and μ_1, for using the coin, we would declare in favor of μ_1 50 percent of the time.

c Now the true μ is μ_2. It is far enough from μ_0 that it will be detected 50 percent of the time. If $\mu = \mu_2$, tossing a coin without collecting any data relative to the experiment is still as satisfactory a test procedure as one based on H_0.

d If $\mu = \mu_3$, we have a good chance of detecting this fact as indicated by the unshaded area under the curve. The power of the test is high and the probability of a Type II error is low.

If we wish reasonable assurance of detecting μ_1 when $\mu = \mu_1$, see *a*, it will be necessary to take a larger sample. This leads to a new distribution of $\bar{Y}$ with a smaller variance since $\sigma_{\bar{Y}}^2 = \sigma^2/n$; for example, one of the distributions shown by the broken curves. The acceptance region no longer extends so far to the right. See the broken curve and vertical line for *a*.

Now the rejection region includes a new portion of the $\bar{Y}$ axis to the left of the original rejection region. Our chances of detecting an alternative to μ_0 when an alternative is true are improved. This can be seen from the broken curves of *b*, *c*, and *d*. Type II error decreases.

In choosing a sample size to detect a particular difference, one must admit the possibility of either a Type I or Type II error and choose the sample size accordingly. Consider Fig. 5.6. Here are two $\bar{D}$ distributions, that for which $H_0\colon \mu = \mu_0$ is true and that for which $H_1\colon \mu = \mu_1$ is true. The sample size has been adjusted to give a variance $\sigma_{\bar{D}}^2$, such that the point $\bar{D}_0$ divides the $\bar{D}$ axis to give an area of 5 percent to the right of $\bar{D}_0$ and under the H_0 distribution and an area of 80 percent to the right of $\bar{D}_0$ and under

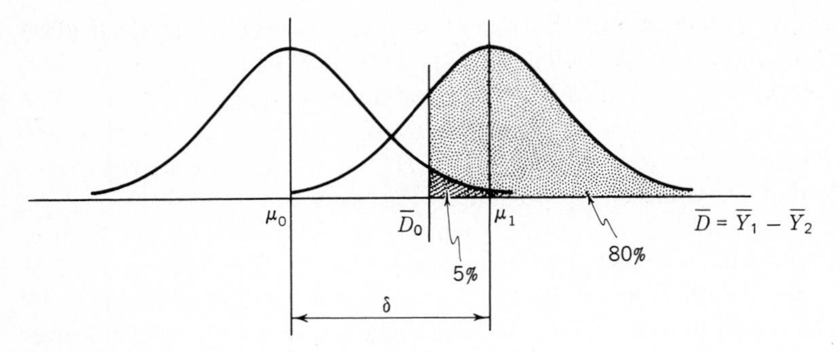

Figure 5.6 Choosing a sample size for desired protection.

the H_1 distribution. In other words, we have a one-tailed test with an error rate of 5 percent associated with H_0 and will accept H_1 80 percent of the time when it is true; the probability of a Type I error is .05, of a Type II error is .20, and the power of the test is .80. The problem is to find a sample size to accomplish our aims. In practice, we rarely know σ^2 so must rely upon an estimate.

When two samples are involved, the random variable usually will be $\bar{Y}_1 - \bar{Y}_2$ and H_0 will call for $\mu_1 - \mu_2 = 0$ while H_1 becomes the size of $\mu_1 - \mu_2 = \delta$ it is desired to detect.

The appropriate formula for computing n, the number of observations on each treatment when the alternatives are one-sided, is given by Eq. (5.33). Since this is likely to give a fraction, use the next higher integer.

$$n = \frac{(Z_\alpha + Z_\beta)^2 \sigma_{\bar{D}}^2}{\delta^2} \tag{5.33}$$

Recall that α and β refer to probabilities associated with a single tail of the normal distribution. For meaningfully paired experimental units, $\sigma_{\bar{D}}^2$ is the variance of differences, while for independent samples, it is $2\sigma^2$.

This solution has several obvious difficulties. The first is that we rarely know σ^2 so must estimate it. If σ^2 is underestimated, n is too small and the power of the test is overestimated; if σ^2 is overestimated, then n is too large and the power of the test is underestimated.

The problem may be obviated by defining δ in terms of σ. For example, we might want to detect a difference of size δ with a specified probability of $1 - \beta$ if δ is one standard deviation in size. We then have $\delta = \sigma$ so that $\sigma/\delta = 1 = \sigma^2/\delta^2$ for use in Eq. (5.33).

Rarely knowing σ^2 also means that we cannot honestly use the Z table. We would like to replace Z_α and Z_β with t values. A reasonable procedure is to use Eq. (5.33) to get an approximate n. Multiply this value by (error df + 3)/(error df + 1). For paired observations, error df will be $n - 1$; for independent samples, error df will be $2(n - 1)$.

When the alternatives are two-tailed, Eq. (5.34) is a satisfactory approximation.

$$n = \frac{(Z_{\alpha/2} + Z_\beta)^2 \sigma_D^2}{\delta^2} \tag{5.34}$$

Again, use the multiplier to adjust this value for the fact that Z values were used.

We now illustrate the procedure.

In Sec. 5.5, data on digestibility of dry matter were presented for independent samples of sheep and steers. It is reasonable to assume that animal researchers might expect steers to have the higher average coefficient of digestibility and so plan on testing against one-sided alternatives. Suppose that in a new experiment, we want to detect with $P = .8$ a real difference between means of one standard deviation when using $\alpha = .05$. It would appear that this might be a real difference of the order of 2.5 to 3 percent since $1(s) = \sqrt{7.33} = 2.7$ percent.

In Eq. (5.33), $\sigma_D^2 = 2\sigma^2$. Hence $\sigma_D^2/\delta^2 = 2\sigma^2/\delta^2 = 2$. For a one-tailed test with $\alpha = .05, Z_\alpha = 1.65$. Since $1 - \beta = .80, Z_\beta = Z_{.20} = .85$. Note that each Z value has been chosen a bit large instead of interpolating in Table A.4. For these conservative Z values $n = (1.65 + .85)^2 2 = 12.5$ and we round to 13.

With 13 observations on each type of animal, there will be $2(12) = 24$ df in error. The required factor is $27/25 = 1.08$ and gives a revised n of $12.5(1.08) = 13.5$. If we use 14 animals of each type, the probability of detecting a real difference of one standard deviation in size between population means should be at least .80.

In Sec. 5.6, the data were sugar concentrations for paired half-heads of clover at different vapor pressures. Let us suppose that in the next experiment, perhaps involving other pressures, the investigator will be satisfied if he or she can detect a true difference of one σ, based on differences, between μ_1 and μ_2 with probability .80. Assume that the test is to be against two-sided alternatives with $\alpha = .05$. Here we use Eq. (5.34).

This time, $\delta/\sigma = 1$, so $\sigma_D^2/\delta^2 = 1$. We also need $Z_{\alpha/2} = Z_{.025} = 1.96$ and $Z_\beta = Z_{.20} = .85$. Now $n = (1.96 + .85)^2 = 7.9$ and we round to 8.

Since we are working with differences, there are only 7 df for error. The required factor is $10/8 = 1.25$ and the revised n is $7.9(1.25) = 9.9$, and we round to 10. The experiment will require 10 clover heads, each split into two.

5.13 Stein's Two-Stage Sample

Where attention is concentrated on estimation rather than testing, a procedure by Stein (5.12) for determining the required number of observations is available for continuous data.

The problem is to determine the necessary sample size to estimate a mean by a confidence interval guaranteed to be no longer than a prescribed length; the procedure is to take a sample, estimate the variance, then compute the total number of observations necessary. The additional observations are then obtained and a new mean based on all observations is computed.

A confidence interval is of length $2t_\alpha s_{\bar{Y}}$. (Where σ^2 is known, no initial sample is required to estimate the sample size. This can be computed as soon as the required confidence interval length is decided upon, by setting the length equal to $2z_{\alpha/2}\,\sigma/\sqrt{n}$ and solving for n.) When σ^2 is unknown, we take a sample and estimate n by

$$n = \frac{t_1^2 s^2}{d^2} \tag{5.35}$$

t_1 is the tabulated t value for the desired confidence level and the degrees of freedom of the initial sample and d is the half-width of the desired confidence interval, which gives the total number of observations required. The additional observations are obtained and a new $\bar{Y}$ is computed. This $\bar{Y}$ will be within distance d of μ unless the total procedure has resulted in an unusual sample, unusual enough that more extreme ones are to be found no more than 100α percent of the time, due to chance. The procedure is made applicable to obtaining sample size for a confidence interval for a difference between population means by multiplying the numerator of Eq. (5.35) by 2.

Example In a field study, R. T. Clausen† wished to obtain a 95 percent confidence interval of not more than 10 mm for leaf length of mature leaves of *Sedum lucidum* on some individual plants. On a plant near Orizaba, Mexico, a sample of five leaves gave lengths 22, 19, 13, 22, and 23 mm, for which $\bar{Y} = 19.8$ and $s = 4.1$ mm. Hence, the total sample size should be

$$n = \frac{(7.71)(16.7)}{25} = 5.2 \text{ observations}$$

where $7.71 = F(1, 4) = t_{.025}^2$, $16.7 = s^2$, and $25 = (10/2)^2$. The confidence interval just misses being within the acceptable standard of length; with one more observation and the new mean of all six, we would simply say that the new $\bar{Y}$ was within 5 mm of μ with confidence .95.

References

5.1. Baker, G. A., and R. E. Baker: "Strawberry uniformity yield trials," *Biom.*, **9**:412–421 (1953).
5.2. Cochran, W. G.: "The combination of estimates from different experiments," *Biom.*, **10**:101–129 (1954).

† Cornell University, Ithaca, New York.

5.3. Cochran, W. G., and G. M. Cox: *Experimental Designs*, 2d ed., Wiley, New York, 1957.
5.4. Hart, J. S.: "Calorimetric determination of average body temperature of small mammals and its variation with environmental conditions." *Can. J. Zool.*, **29:**224–233 (1951).
5.5. Peterson, H. L.: "Pollination and seed set in lucerne," *Roy. Vet. Agr. Coll. Yearb.*, 138–169, (1954).
5.6. Ross, R. H., and C. B. Knodt: "The effect of supplemental vitamin A upon growth, blood plasma, carotene, vitamin A, inorganic calcium, and phosphorus content of Holstein heifers," *J. Dairy Sci.*, **31:**1062–1067 (1948).
5.7. Rowles, W.: "Physical properties of mineral soils of Quebec," *Can. J. Res.*, **16:**277–287 (1938).
5.8. Satterthwaite, F. W.: "An approximate distribution of estimates of variance components," *Biom. Bull.*, **2:**110–114 (1946).
5.9. Searle, S. R.: *Linear models*, Wiley, New York, 1971.
5.10. Shuel, R. W.: "Some factors affecting nectar secretion in red clover," *Plant Physiol.*, **27:**95–110 (1952).
5.11. Smithson, P. C., and O. T. Sanders, Jr.: "Exposure of bobwhite quail and cottontail rabbits to methyl parathion," *32d Ann. Conf., Southeast Ass. Game Fish Comm.* (1978).
5.12. Stein, C.: "A two-sample test for a linear hypothesis whose power is independent of the variance," *Ann. Math. Statist.*, **16:**243–258 (1945).
5.13. Watson, C. J., et al.: "Digestibility studies with ruminants. XII. The comparative digestive powers of sheep and steers," *Sci. Agr.*, **28:**357–374 (1948).

CHAPTER

SIX

PRINCIPLES OF EXPERIMENTAL DESIGN

6.1 Introduction

This chapter is an introduction to the planning and conduct of experiments in relation to aims, analysis, and efficiency.

If we accept the premise that new knowledge is most often obtained by careful analysis and interpretation of data, then it is paramount that considerable thought and effort be given to planning their collection in order that maximum information be obtained for the least expenditure of resources. Probably the most important function of the consulting statistician is providing assistance in designing efficient experiments that will enable the experimenter to obtain unbiased estimates of treatment means and differences and of experimental error.

That the statistician can make a real contribution at the planning stage of an experiment cannot be overemphasized. Frequently the statistician is presented with data that provide only biased estimates of treatment means and differences and experimental error; that do not provide answers to the questions initially posed; for which certain treatments do not provide pertinent information; for which the conclusions drawn do not apply to the population the experimenter had in mind; and such that the precision of the experiment is not sufficiently great to detect important differences. Often by some slight change in the design and with less effort, the experiment would have provided the information desired. The experimenter who contacts the consulting statistician at the planning stage of the experiment rather than after its completion improves the chances of achieving his aims.

6.2 What Is an Experiment?

Different definitions are available for the word *experiment*. For our purposes, we consider an experiment as a planned inquiry to obtain new facts or to confirm or deny the results of previous experiments, where such inquiry will aid in an administrative decision, such as recommending a variety, procedure, or pesticide. Such experiments fall roughly into three categories, namely, preliminary, critical, and demonstrational, one of which may lead to another. In a preliminary experiment, the investigator tries out a large number of treatments in order to obtain leads for future work; most treatments will appear only once. In a critical experiment, the investigator compares responses to different treatments using sufficient observations of the responses to give reasonable assurance of detecting meaningful differences. Demonstrational experiments are performed when extension workers compare a new treatment or treatments with a standard. In this text, we are concerned almost entirely with the critical type of experiment. In such an experiment, it is essential that we define the population to which inferences are to apply, design the experiment accordingly, and make measurements of the variables under study.

Every experiment is set up to provide answers to one or more questions. With this in mind, investigators decide what treatment comparisons provide relevant information. They then conduct an experiment to measure or to test hypotheses concerning treatment differences under comparable conditions. They take measurements and observations on the experimental material. From the information in a successfully completed experiment, they answer the questions initially posed. Sound experimentation consists of asking questions that are of importance in the field of research and in carrying out experimental procedures which answer these questions. In this chapter, we are primarily concerned with the procedures.

To the statistician the experiment is the set of rules used to draw the sample from the population. This makes definition of the population most important. The set of rules is the experimental procedure or experimental design. For example, the use of unpaired observations and the use of paired observations are experimental designs for two-treatment experiments.

6.3 Objectives of an Experiment

In designing an experiment, state objectives clearly as questions to be answered, hypotheses to be tested, and effects to be estimated. It is advisable to classify objectives as major and minor, since certain experimental designs give greater precision for some treatment comparisons than for others.

Precision, *sensitivity*, or *amount of information* is measured as the reciprocal of the variance of a mean. If we let I represent information, then $I = 1/\sigma_{\bar{Y}}^2 = n/\sigma^2$. As σ^2 increases, the amount of information decreases; also, as n increases, the amount of information increases. A comparison of two sample means becomes more sensitive, that is, can detect a smaller difference between population means, as the sample sizes increase.

It is of paramount importance to define the population for which inferences are to be drawn and to sample that population randomly. Suppose that the major objective of an experiment is to compare the values of several rations for swine in a certain area. Suppose also that the farmers in the area handle pigs of different breeds, that some use self-feeders and that others feed by hand. If the experimenter used only one breed of swine in the experiment or fed only by self-feeders, the sample could hardly be considered as representative of the population unless there was previous information that breed and method of feeding had little or no effect on differences due to rations. If no information is available on the effect of breed and method of feeding, it would be extremely hazardous to make inferences from an experiment based upon one breed and one method of feeding to other breeds and methods. To make such recommendations, the experimenter would have to include all local breeds and feeding methods as factors in the experiment. By doing so, the scope of the experiment is increased.

Another example is that of an experiment planned to compare the effectiveness of several fungicides in controlling a disease in oats. Suppose that in the area where these recommendations are to be applied, several cultivars are in common use and that the quality of seed varies. To be able to make adequate recommendations, the experimenter must compare the fungicides on several cultivars and several qualities of seed for each cultivar. This is essential if the experimenter is to determine whether or not a single fungicide can be recommended for all cultivars and qualities of seed used in the area. In general, worthwhile inferences about an extensive population cannot usually be obtained from a single isolated experiment.

6.4 Experimental Unit and Treatment

An *experimental unit* or *experimental plot* is the unit of material to which one application of a treatment is applied; the *treatment* is the procedure whose effect is to be measured and compared with other treatments. These terms are then seen to be very general. The experimental unit may be an animal, 10 birds in a pen, a half-leaf, and so on; the treatment may be a standard ration, a spraying schedule, a temperature–humidity combination, etc. When the effect of a treatment is measured, it is measured on a *sampling unit*, some fraction of the experimental unit. Thus the sampling unit may be the complete experimental unit, such as an animal on a treatment ration, or a random sample of leaves from a sprayed tree, or the harvest from 6 ft of the middle row of a three-row experimental unit. In some cases, the experimental unit will be so large that it is impractical to use it as the sampling unit, whereas a single small sampling unit is inadequate. In such cases, two or more random subdivisions of the experimental unit are measured. For example, in studying cultural practices in stand establishment of forage species, the seedlings in two or more small random areas within every experimental unit are counted separately. Again, where a sampling unit must be destroyed, as when the quality of fruit, vegetables, or a food product is being measured for the marketplace, sampling units are taken within the experimental unit.

In selecting a set of treatments, it is important to define each treatment carefully and to consider it with respect to every other treatment to ensure, as far as possible, that the set provides efficient answers related to the objectives of the experiment.

6.5 Experimental Error

A characteristic of all experimental material is variation. *Experimental error* is a measure of the variation which exists among observations on experimental units treated alike. This statement is more subtle than it may first sound and ties in closely with the definition of the preceding section. For example, if 50 hens are penned together and fed the same ration, the experimental unit consists of the 50 hens. Other pens of 50 hens are needed before we can measure variation among units treated alike. This is true even if a measurement such as body weight is made on an individual hen basis. The point is that if two treatments are to be compared, any observed difference will be in part attributable simply to the difference between pens of 50 hens and this is very likely to be of a larger order of magnitude than differences among hens in the same pen. Again, if 10 mice are housed together as a feeding unit, the same argument applies. However, if half the animals are male and half female, and if we are interested in a possible differential response due to sex, then we have meaningfully paired experimental units for an experiment within an experiment. Here there is a second experimental error to answer a second question. To answer any question about the possible presence of a true treatment difference, we must always deal with the unit to which the treatment was applied at random. These and other questions concerning the choice of an appropriate experimental error are illustrated and discussed in later chapters.

Variation comes from two main sources. First, there is the inherent variability that exists in the experimental material to which treatments are applied. Second, there is the variation which results from any lack in uniformity in the physical conduct of the experiment. In a nutrition experiment with rats as the experimental material, the individuals will have different genetic constitutions unless highly inbred; this is variability inherent in the experimental material. They will be housed in cages subject to differences in heat, light, and other factors; this constitutes a lack of uniformity in the physical conduct of the experiment. The relative magnitudes of the variation from these two sources will be quite different for various fields of research.

The length of a confidence interval and the power of a test ultimately depend on $V(\bar{Y}) = \sigma^2/n$. Thus to obtain short intervals or high power there are only two points of attack. Consequently, it is important that every possible effort be made to reduce the experimental error in order to improve the power of a test, to decrease the size of confidence intervals, or to achieve some other desirable goal. This can be accomplished by attacking the two main sources of experimental error. Thus, we can

1. Handle the experimental material so that the effects of inherent variability are reduced
2. Refine the experimental technique

These methods will be discussed in sections succeeding a discussion of replication and the factors affecting the number of replicates.

6.6 Replication and Its Functions

When a treatment appears more than once in an experiment, it is said to be *replicated*. The functions of replication are

1. To provide an estimate of experimental error
2. To improve the precision of an experiment by reducing the standard deviation of a treatment mean
3. To increase the scope of inference of the experiment by selection and appropriate use of more variable experimental units
4. To effect control of the error variance

An estimate of experimental error is required for tests of significance and for confidence interval estimation. An experiment in which each treatment appears only once is said to consist of a single replicate or replication. From such an experiment, no estimate of experimental error is available. Here it is possible to explain an observed difference as a difference between treatments or between experimental units; it is impossible to have objective assurance about which explanation is correct. In other words, when there is no method of estimating experimental error, there is no way to determine whether observed differences indicate real differences or are due to inherent variation. The experiment is not self-contained, any inference must be based upon prior experience. (*Exception.* A single replication or even a particular fraction of a replicate of an experiment involving a large number of factors or types of treatments may be used and will provide an estimate of error when certain assumptions hold.)

As the number of replicates increases, estimates of population means, namely, the observed treatment means, become more precise. If a difference of five units is detectable using four replicates, an experiment of approximately 16 replicates will detect half this difference or 2.5 units, since the standard deviations are in the ratio of 2 : 1, being $\sigma/\sqrt{4}$ and $\sigma/\sqrt{16}$, respectively. The word "approximate" is used because precision, especially in small experiments, depends in part on the number of degrees of freedom available for estimating experimental error. Also, increased replication may require the use of less homogeneous experimental material or a less careful technique, thus giving a new parent population with a larger experimental error. However, increased replication usually improves precision, decreasing the lengths of confidence intervals and increasing the power of statistical tests.

In certain types of experiments, replication is a means of increasing the scope of inference of an experiment; the sampled population is less restricted in definition and the inference is broadened. For example, suppose that we wish to determine whether there is any real difference in the performance of two varieties of a crop in a given area and that there are two major soil types in this area. If the object of the experiment is to draw inferences for both soil types, it is obvious that both should be in the experiment. It is also important that the area included within each replicate, that is, in each pair of plots on which the pair of varieties is planted, be of one soil type and as uniform as possible; it is not necessary and may be undesirable to have very uniform conditions between or among replicates, especially where rather broad populations are involved.

In many field experiments, the experiment is repeated over a period of years. The reason is obvious, namely, that conditions vary from year to year and make it important to know the effect of years on the differences among treatments, since recommendations are usually made for future years. Likewise, different locations are used to evaluate treatments under the different environmental conditions present in the population, that is, in the area for which recommendations are to be made. Both repetitions in time (years) and space (location) can be considered as broad types of replication. The purpose is to increase the scope of inference. The same principle is frequently used in laboratory experiments, namely, that the entire experiment is repeated several times, possibly by different people, to determine the repeatability of treatments under possibly different conditions which may exist from time to time in the laboratory.

Finally, replication permits us to group experimental units according to expected response in the absence of treatments. The aim is to assign the total variation among experimental units so that it is maximized among groups and, simultaneously, minimized within. Now, if a set of treatments is assigned within any such group, observed differences will measure true treatment differences better than if grouping had been ignored. Clearly, experimental error, our measure for detecting real treatment differences, must not be inflated by differences among groups. Appropriate arithmetic is available for accomplishing this.

6.7 Factors Affecting the Number of Replicates

The number of replications for an experiment depends on several factors, of which the most important is probably the degree of precision required. The smaller the departure from the null hypothesis to be measured or detected, the greater the number of replicates required.

It is important in any experiment to have the correct amount of precision. There is little point in using 10 replicates to detect a difference that 4 will find in most cases; likewise there is little value in performing an experiment where the number of replications is not sufficient to detect important differences except occasionally.

To measure any departure from the null hypothesis, experimental error, that is, variation among observations on experimental units treated alike, must supply the unit of measurement. At times it is not practical to make an observation on the complete experimental unit, for example, in the case of chemical determinations such as that of the protein content of a forage, and the unit is sampled. Usually the variation among experimental units is large in comparison with the variation among samples from a single unit. There is little point in making a large number of chemical determinations on each experimental unit since experimental error must be based on variation among the experimental units, not on variation among samples from within the units.

Certain material is naturally more variable than others. Consider the problem of soil heterogeneity. Certain soils are more uniform than others and, for the same precision, less replication is required on uniform soil than on variable soil. Also, different crops grown at the same location show unequal variabilities.

The number of treatments affects the precision of an experiment, and thus the number of replications required for a stated degree of precision. For example, if we increase the number of treatments while keeping constant the number of replications of each, then we increase the size of the experiment and the number of degrees of freedom for the estimate of σ^2. We still have $s_{\bar{Y}}^2 = s^2/n$, but an improved estimate of σ^2 and, so, improved precision. The number of replications could be decreased if no increase in precision is required. On the other hand, if we keep the size of the experiment constant, then more treatments imply fewer replications of each and fewer degrees of freedom to estimate σ^2. Now $s_{\bar{Y}}^2 = s^2/n$ has a smaller n and a poorer estimate of σ^2. Poorer precision results. The number of replications must be increased to achieve the fixed precision. This whole argument is most appropriate for small experiments with, say, less than 20 df in error.

The experimental design also affects the precision of an experiment and the required number of replications. Where the number of treatments is large and requires the use of more heterogeneous experimental units, the experimental error per unit increases. Appropriate designs can control part of this variation.

Unfortunately the number of replicates is very often determined largely by the funds and time available for the experiment. There is little point in an experiment if the required precision is not obtainable with available funds. The solution is to postpone the experiment until sufficient funds are available or to reduce the number of treatments so that sufficient replication and precision are available for the remaining ones. The practical number of replicates for an experiment is reached when the cost of the experiment in material, time, etc., is no longer offset by an increase in information gained.

Worthy of mention is the fact that replication does not reduce error due to faulty technique. Also, mere statistical significance may give no information about the practical importance of a departure from the null hypothesis. The magnitude of a real departure that is of practical significance can be judged by one with technical knowledge of the subject; this magnitude together with a measure of how desirable it is to detect it serves to determine the required precision and, eventually, the necessary number of replicates.

Since so much has been said about the appropriate amount of replication, the question arises about methods of ascertaining this amount. The problem of determining sample size was discussed in Secs. 5.13 and 5.14. Further discussion is given in Sec. 9.15. With the right kind of information, the experimenter can usually find an available method for determining the replication needed.

6.8 Relative Precision of Designs Involving Few Treatments

The precision of or amount of information in an experiment is measured by $I = n/\sigma^2$. An estimate of the information must then depend on how well s^2 estimates σ^2 and this is affected by the number of degrees of freedom available for the estimation. The degrees of freedom depend on the number of replicates, number of treatments, and experimental design. Increasing the precision may be very worthwhile when fewer than 20 degrees of freedom are involved. Thus observe that $t_{.025}$ for 5 degrees of freedom is 2.57, for 10 degrees of freedom is 2.23, for 20 degrees of freedom is 2.09, and for 60 degrees of freedom is 2.00. The value of t at any probability level decreases noticeably for each additional degree of freedom up to 20; beyond this point the decrease is slow.

To compare two experimental designs, one compares amounts of information. This gives the *relative efficiency*. Fisher's (6.5) procedure, as given by Cochran and Cox (6.2), estimates the efficiency of design 1 relative to design 2 by

$$\mathrm{RE} = \frac{(n_1 + 1)/(n_1 + 3)s_1^2}{(n_2 + 1)/(n_2 + 3)s_2^2} = \frac{(n_1 + 1)(n_2 + 3)s_2^2}{(n_2 + 1)(n_1 + 3)s_1^2} \tag{6.1}$$

where s_1^2 and s_2^2 are the error mean squares of the first and second designs, respectively, and n_1 and n_2 are their degrees of freedom. If the number of observations in a treatment mean differs for the two experiments being compared, replace s_1^2 and s_2^2 by $s_{\bar{Y}_1}^2$ and $s_{\bar{Y}_2}^2$.

Suppose that we wish to compare a design allowing 5 degrees of freedom to estimate σ^2 with one allowing 10 degrees of freedom; this could be a comparison of a paired experiment with a nonpaired one for two treatments and six replications. The paired design is more precise than the nonpaired only if the efficiency of the former relative to the latter is greater than 1, that is, if the relative efficiency

$$\frac{(n_1 + 1)(n_2 + 3)s_2^2}{(n_2 + 1)(n_1 + 3)s_1^2} = \frac{(6)(13)s_2^2}{(11)(8)s_1^2} = \frac{.886\ s_2^2}{s_1^2}$$

is greater than 1. In other words, pairing pays if .886 s_2^2 is greater than s_1^2.

6.9 Error Control

Error control can be accomplished by

1. Experimental design
2. The use of concomitant observations
3. The choice of size and shape of the experimental units

1 ***Experimental design*** The use of experimental design as a means of controlling experimental error has been widely investigated since about the end of the first quarter of the present century. This is an extensive subject and only the basic principles will be discussed here. For more extensive treatment of the subject, the reader is referred to Cox (6.3), Cochran and Cox (6.2), Federer (6.4), John (6.7), Kempthorne (6.8), Youden (6.9), and others.

Control of experimental error consists of designing an experiment so that some of the natural variation among the set of experimental units is physically handled so as to contribute nothing to differences among treatment means. For example, consider a two-treatment experiment that uses a pair of pigs from each of 10 litters. If we apply the treatments, one to each member of a pair, then the mathematical description is $Y_{ij} = \mu + \tau_i + \rho_j + \varepsilon_{ij}$ and the difference between means is $\bar{Y}_{1\cdot} - \bar{Y}_{2\cdot} = (\tau_1 - \tau_2) + (\bar{\varepsilon}_{1\cdot} - \bar{\varepsilon}_{2\cdot})$; there is no contribution due to variation among the pairs, that is, due to the set of ρ's. Alternately if there is no pairing and 10 pigs are simply chosen at random from the 20 and assigned to a specific treatment, then the description is $Y_{ij} = \mu + \tau_i + \varepsilon_{ij}$, where each ε_{ij} now includes a contribution from litters and is an element of a population with a presumably larger variance than that associated with the ε's of the first model. Thus choice of a design with nonrandom pairs has controlled the experimental error σ^2, provided that pairs are an additional source of variation; that is, provided that the natural variation between observations on individuals of the same pair is less than that between observations on individuals of different pairs.

Common sense and acuity in recognizing sources of variation are seen to be basic in choosing a design.

Where the experimental units are grouped into complete blocks, that is, where each contains all treatments, such that the variation among units within a block is less than that among units in different blocks, the precision of the experiment is increased as a result of error control. Such blocks of similar outcome are also called *replications*. The design is known as a *randomized complete block design*. Experimental error is based on the variation among units within a replication after adjustment for any observed, overall treatment effect. In other words, variation among replications and variation among treatments do not enter into experimental error.

As the number of treatments in an experiment increases, the number of experimental units required for a replication increases. In most instances, this results in an increase in the experimental error, that is, in the variance in the parent population. Designs are available where the complete block is subdivided into a number of incomplete blocks such that each incomplete block contains only a portion of the treatments. The subdivision into incomplete blocks is done according to certain rules, so that the experimental error can be estimated among the units within the incomplete blocks. Precision is increased to the extent that the experimental units within an incomplete block are more uniform than the incomplete blocks within a replication. Such designs are called *incomplete block designs*. The reader is referred to Cochran and Cox (6.2) and Federer (6.4).

The *split-plot design* is an incomplete block design where the precision of certain comparisons is increased at the expense of others. The overall precision is the same as the basic design used. Some split-plot designs are considered in Chap. 16.

In experiments where comparisons among all treatments are of essentially the same importance, a different type of incomplete block design is used. The treatments are assigned to the experimental units so that every treatment occurs with every other treatment the same number of times within its set of incomplete blocks. Such designs are known as *balanced incomplete blocks*. Another group, known as *partially balanced lattices*, is available where each treatment occurs only with certain other treatments, not all, in its set of incomplete blocks.

The best design to use in any given situation is the simplest design available which gives the required precision. There is no point in using an involved design if an increase in precision is not obtained.

2 The use of concomitant observations In many experiments, the precision can be increased by the use of accessory observations and an arithmetic technique called the *analysis of covariance*. This analysis is used when the variation among experimental units is, in part, due to variation in some other measurable character or characters not sufficiently controllable to be useful in assigning the experimental units to complete or incomplete blocks on the basis of similar outcome. The analysis of covariance is discussed in Chap. 17.

*3. **Size and shape of experimental units*** As a rule, large experimental units show less variation than small units. This rule holds, in particular, when random errors are truly normal with a common variance, and is a consequence of the relation $\sigma_{\bar{Y}}^2 = \sigma^2/n$. However, an increase in the size of the experimental unit often results in a decrease in the number of replications that can be run since a limited amount of experimental material is usually available for any given experiment. Adequate replication of small plots is generally easier to obtain than is adequate replication of large plots.

In field plot experiments, the size and shape of the experimental unit or plot, as well as that of the complete or incomplete block, are important in relation to precision. *Uniformity trial* studies, that is, studies of data from experiments where there were no treatments, conducted with many crops and in many different countries, have shown that the individual plot should be relatively long and narrow for greatest precision; the block, whether complete or incomplete, should be approximately square. For a given amount of variability among experimental units this tends to maximize the variation among the blocks while minimizing that among plots within blocks. Large variation among blocks indicates that their use has been helpful because this variation is eliminated from experimental error and, also, does not contribute to differences among treatment means. When blocks are square, the differences among blocks tend to be large. It is desirable to have small variation among plots within blocks and, at the same time, have the plot representative of the block. In fields where definite fertility contours apear, the most precision is obtained when the long sides of the plots are perpendicular to the contours or parallel to the direction of the gradient.

For some types of experiment, the experimental units are carefully selected to be as uniform as possible; for example, rats from an inbred line might be the experimental units in a nutrition experiment. As a result, experimental error is reduced, but at the same time, the scope of the inference is also reduced. The response obtained with selected experimental units may differ widely from that with unselected units and inferences must be made with this in mind.

6.10 Choice of Treatments

In certain types of experiment, the treatments have a substantial effect on precision. This is especially true of factorial experiments, discussed in Chap. 15.

In certain types of experiments, the amount or rate of some factor is important. Suppose that the experimenter is measuring the effect of increased levels of some nutrient on the response of a plant. It is important to include several levels to determine if the response is linear or curvilinear in nature. Here, choice of the number of levels and their spacing is important for appropriate answers to the questions asked.

In general, the more the investigator knows about treatments, the better is the statistical test procedure that the statistician can devise. This knowledge often dictates the kind and amount of any particular treatment in a set of treatments. This, in turn, may influence the precision of the experiment. Some aspects of this problem will be seen in Chap. 15.

6.11 Refinement of Technique

The importance of careful technique in the conduct of an experiment is self-evident. It is the responsibility of the experimenter to see that everything possible is done to ensure the use of careful technique because no analysis, statistical or other, can improve data obtained from poorly performed experiments. In general, variation resulting from careless technique is not random variation and not subject to the laws of chance on which statistical inference is based. This variation may be termed *inaccuracy*, in contrast to lack of precision. Unfortunately, accuracy in technique does not always result in high precision because precision is also concerned with the random variability, which may be quite large, among experimental units.

Some points of technique to be considered in conducting an experiment follow. It is important to have uniformity in the application of treatments. This applies equally to the spreading of fertilizer, spraying of fruit trees, cutting of a forage crop to a fixed height for all plots, and the filling of test tubes to a fixed level. Control should be exercised over external influences so that all treatments produce their effects under comparable and desired conditions. For example, to compare the effects of several treatments it may be necessary to create an epidemic by the use of an artificial inoculum. Efforts should be made to have the epidemic as uniform as possible. Again, if it is impossible to have uniform conditions, it may still be possible to have them uniform within each block. For example, in field crop experiments, if a complete experiment cannot be set out or harvested in one day, it is desirable to do complete blocks in any day; in laboratory experiments where it is necessary to use several technicians, it is desirable that each should manage one or more complete sets of treatments.

Suitable and unbiased measures of the effects of the several treatments or of differences among them should be available. Often the required measurements are obvious and easily made; in other instances, considerable research is necessary to secure a reliable measurement to express treatment effects. Thus the sanitary engineering data of Table 2.3 came after repeated trials and revisions of technique because it had been decided that no technique would be used until the coefficient of variation was reduced to the order of 5 percent. Care should always be exercised to prevent gross errors which can occur in experimentation; adequate supervision of assistants and close scrutiny of the data will go far in preventing them.

Faulty technique may increase the experimental error in two ways. It may introduce additional fluctuations of a more or less random nature and possibly subject to the laws of chance. Such fluctuations, if substantial, should reveal themselves in the estimate of the experimental error, possibly by observation of the coefficient of variation. If experimenters find that their estimates of experimental error are consistently higher than those of other workers in the same field, they should carefully scrutinize their technique to determine the origin of the errors. The other way in which faulty technique may increase experimental error is through nonrandom mistakes. These are not subject to the laws of chance and may not always be detected by observation of the individual measurements. Statistical tests are also available for their detection but are not discussed in this text. Faulty technique may also result in measurements that are consistently biased. This does not affect experimental error or differences among treatment means but does affect the values of treatment means. Experimental error cannot detect bias. The experimental error estimates precision or repeatability, not the accuracy, of measurements.

A point sometimes overlooked is that a measurement may be subject to two principal sources of variation, one of which is considerably larger than the other. For illustration, consider the amount of protein per acre produced by a forage crop. The amount is a function of yield per acre and percentage of protein. The variation among measurements of yield of forage is much greater than that among determinations of protein percentage. As a consequence, more effort should be placed in reducing the part of experimental error associated with yield of forage than that associated with protein percentage. In general, where there are several sources of variation, it is most profitable to try to control the greater source.

6.12 Randomization

The function of randomization is to ensure that we have a valid or unbiased estimate of experimental error and of treatment means and differences among them. Randomization is one of the few characteristics of modern experimental design that appears to be really new; the idea may be credited to R. A. Fisher. Randomization generally involves the use of some chance device such as the flipping of a coin or the use of random number tables. Randomness and haphazardness are not equivalent; randomization cannot overcome poor experimental technique.

To avoid bias in comparisons among treatment means, it is necessary to have some way of ensuring that a particular treatment will not be consistently favored or handicapped in successive replications by some extraneous sources of variation, known or unknown. In other words, every treatment should have an equal chance of being assigned to any experimental unit, be it unfavorable or favorable. Randomness provides the equal chance procedure. Cochran and Cox (6.2) state "Randomization is somewhat analogous to insurance, in that it is a precaution against disturbances that may or may not occur, and that may or may not be serious if they do occur."

Systematic designs, where the treatments are applied to the experimental units in a nonrandom but selected fashion, often result in either underestimation or overestimation of experimental error. Also, they can result in inequality of precision in the various comparisons among the treatment means. This is especially obvious in many field experiments. Numerous studies have shown that adjacent plots tend to be more alike in their productivity than plots which are some distance apart. Such plots are said to give correlated error components or residuals. As a result of this fact, if the treatments are arranged in the same systematic order in each replication, then there can be considerable differences in the precision of comparisons involving different treatments. The precision of comparisons among treatments which are physically close is greater than those among treatments which are some distance apart. Randomization tends to destroy the correlation among errors and make valid the usual tests of significance.

6.13 Statistical inference

As we have seen, the object of experiments is to determine if there are real differences among our treatment means and to estimate the magnitude of such differences if they exist. A statistical inference about such differences involves the assignment of a measure of probability to the inference. For this, it is necessary that randomization and replication be introduced into the experiment in appropriate fashion.

Replication assures us the means of computing experimental error.

Randomization ensures us a valid measure of experimental error.

A choice between an experiment with appropriate randomization and a systematic one with apparently greater but unmeasurable precision is like a choice between a road of known length and condition and a road of unknown length and condition which is known only to be shorter. It may be more satisfactory to know how far one has to go and what the going will be like than to start off on a road of unknown condition and length with only the assurance that it is the shorter road. Until further study of systematic designs has been made, it would seem advisable to avoid their use.

References

6.1. Brownlee, K. A.: "The principles of experimental design," *Ind. Qual. Cont.*, **13:** 12–20 (1957).
6.2. Cochran, William G., and Gertrude M. Cox: *Experimental designs*, 2d ed., Wiley, New York, 1957.
6.3. Cox, D. R.: *Planning of experiments*, Wiley, New York, 1958.
6.4. Federer, W. T.: *Experimental design*, Macmillan, New York, 1955.
6.5. Fisher, R. A.: *The design of experiments*, 4th ed., Oliver and Boyd, Edinburgh, 1947.
6.6. Greenberg, B. G.: "Why randomize?" *Biom.*, **7:** 309–322 (1951).
6.7. John, Peter W. M.: *Statistical design and analysis of experiments*, Macmillan, New York, 1971.
6.8. Kempthorne, O.: *The design and analysis of experiments*, Wiley, New York, 1952.
6.9. Youden, W. J.: "Comparative tests in a single laboratory," *ASTM Bull.*, **116:** 48–51 (1950).

CHAPTER

SEVEN

ANALYSIS OF VARIANCE I: THE ONE-WAY CLASSIFICATION

7.1 Introduction

The analysis of variance was introduced by Sir Ronald A. Fisher and is essentially an arithmetic process for partitioning a total sum of squares into components associated with recognized sources of variation. It has been used to advantage in all fields of research where data are measured quantitatively.

In Chap. 7, we consider the analysis of variance where treatment is the only criterion for classifying the data. We discuss the linear additive model and variance components, the assumptions underlying the analysis of variance and tests of significance, residual mean square or experimental error, and sampling error.

In Chaps. 9, 15, 16, and 18, additional designs and aspects of analysis of variance are discussed.

7.2 The Completely Random Design

This design is useful when the experimental units are essentially homogeneous, that is, the variation among them is small, and grouping them in blocks would be little more than a random procedure. This is the case in many types of laboratory experiments where a quantity of material is thoroughly mixed and then divided into small lots to form the experimental units to which treatments are randomly assigned, or in plant and animal experiments where environmental effects are much alike.

Randomization, the process which makes the laws of chance applicable, is accomplished by allocating the treatments to the experimental units entirely at random. No restrictions are placed upon randomization as when a block is required to contain all treatments. The choice of numbers of observations to be made on the various treatments is not considered to be a restriction on randomization. Every experimental unit has the same probability of receiving any treatment, that is, if there are n experimental units then any one of the n treatments, clearly not all different, has the same probability of falling on any experimental unit.

Randomization is carried out by use of a random number table. Suppose 15 experimental units are to receive five replications of each of three treatments. Assign the numbers 1 to 15 to the experimental units in a convenient manner, for instance, consecutively. Locate a starting point in a table of random numbers, for example, row heading 10 and column heading 20 of Table A.1, and select 15 three-digit numbers. Reading vertically, we obtain:

118	701	789	965	688	638	901	841	396	802	687	938	377	392	848
1	8	9	15	7	5	13	11	4	10	6	14	2	3	12

Ranks are then assigned to the numbers; thus 118 is the smallest, rank number 1, and 965 is the largest, rank number 15. These ranks are considered to be a random permutation of the numbers 1 to 15 and the first five are the numbers of the experimental units to which treatment 1 is assigned. Thus units 1, 8, 9, 15, and 7 receive treatment 1, and so on.

The procedure is also applicable when the treatments are replicated unequal numbers of times, say 6, 6, and 3. Three-digit numbers are used since they are less likely to include ties than are two-digit numbers. In any case, ties may be broken by using extra numbers.

Random number tables may be used in alternative fashion. For example, two-digit numbers less than 90 may be divided by 15 and the remainder recorded. This gives the 15 numbers 00, 01, ..., 14 with equal frequency. Duplicates are discarded and other numbers obtained to replace them. The numbers 90, 91, ..., 99 are not used since they would cause 00, 01, ..., 09 to be present in greater frequency than 10, 11, ..., 14.

If, during the course of the experiment, all experimental units are to be treated similarly, for example, hoeing field plots, this should be done in random order if order is likely to affect the results, as when a technique improves as the result of practice.

The analysis for a completely random design is also applicable to data where "treatment" implies simply a variable of classification and when it may even be necessary to assume randomness. For example, one might have weight measurements on the adults of a certain species of fish caught in several lakes (the treatments), and wish to know if adult weight differs from lake to lake.

Advantages The completely random design is flexible in that the number of treatments and replicates is limited only by the number of experimental units available. The number of replicates can vary from treatment to treatment, though it is generally desirable to have the same number per treatment. The statistical analysis is simple even if the number of replicates varies with the treatment and if the various treatments are subject to unequal variances, usually referred to as nonhomogeneity of experimental error. However, tests of significance and confidence interval construction require special attention when there is heterogeneity of variance. Simplicity of analysis is not lost if some experimental units or entire treatments are missing or rejected.

The loss of information due to missing data is small relative to losses with other designs. The number of degrees of freedom for estimating experimental error is maximum; this improves the precision of the experiment and is important with small experiments, that is, with those where degrees of freedom for experimental error are less than 20 (see Sec. 6.8).

Disadvantages The main objection to the completely random design is that it is often inefficient. Since randomization is unrestricted, experimental error includes the entire variation among the experimental units except that due to treatments. In many situations it is possible to group experimental units so that variation among units within groups is less than that among units in different groups. Certain designs take advantage of such grouping, exclude variation among groups from experimental error, and increase the precision of the experiment. Some of these designs are discussed in Chaps. 9, 15, and 16.

7.3 Data with a Single Criterion of Classification. The Analysis of Variance for Any Number of Groups with Equal Replication

Table 7.1 gives the nitrogen content in milligrams of red clover plants inoculated with cultures of *Rhizobium trifolii* plus a composite of five *Rhizobium meliloti* strains, as reported by Erdman (7.9). Each of five red clover cultures, *R. trifolii*, was tested individually with a composite of five alfalfa strains, *R. meliloti*, and a composite of the red clover strains was also tested with the composite of the alfalfa strains, making six treatments in all. The experiment was conducted in the greenhouse using a completely random design with five pots per treatment.

Computations Arrange the data as in Table 7.1. Let Y_{ij} denote the jth observation on the ith treatment, $i = 1, 2, \ldots, t$ and $j = 1, 2, \ldots, r$. Treatment totals require one subscript and the total for the ith treatment may be denoted by $Y_{i\cdot}$, the dot indicating that all observations for the ith treatment have been

Table 7.1 Nitrogen content of red clover plants inoculated with combination cultures of *Rhizobium trifolii* strains and *Rhizobium meliloti* strains, mg

R. trifolii strain

Computation	3DOk1	3DOk5	3DOk4	3DOk7	3DOk13	Composite	Total
	19.4	17.7	17.0	20.7	14.3	17.3	
	32.6	24.8	19.4	21.0	14.4	19.4	
	27.0	27.9	9.1	20.5	11.8	19.1	
	32.1	25.2	11.9	18.8	11.6	16.9	
	33.0	24.3	15.8	18.6	14.2	20.8	
$\sum_j Y_{ij} = Y_{i\cdot}$	144.1	119.9	73.2	99.6	66.3	93.5	$596.6 = Y_{\cdot\cdot}$
$\sum_j Y_{ij}^2$	4,287.53	2,932.27	1,139.42	1,989.14	887.29	1,758.71	12,994.36
$(Y_{i\cdot})^2/r$	4,152.96	2,875.20	1,071.65	1,984.03	879.14	1,748.45	12,711.43
$\sum_j (Y_{ij} - \bar{Y}_{i\cdot})^2$	134.57	57.07	67.77	5.11	8.15	10.26	282.93
$\bar{Y}_{i\cdot}$	28.8	24.0	14.6	19.9	13.3	18.7	

added to give this total. Letters t and r are used for the number of treatments and number of replicates of each treatment; here $t = 6$ and $r = 5$.

For each treatment, obtain $Y_{i\cdot}$ and $\sum_j Y_{ij}^2$ simultaneously on a computing machine as in lines 1 and 2 of the computations of Table 7.1. These values are then totaled; thus

$$\sum_i Y_{i\cdot} = Y_{\cdot\cdot} \qquad \text{and} \qquad \sum_i \left(\sum_j Y_{ij}^2 \right) = \sum_{i,j} Y_{ij}^2$$

In line 3, each treatment total is squared and divided by $r = 5$, the number of replicates per treatment.

Obtain the correction term C of Eq. (7.1) and the total sum of squares (adjusted for the mean) of Eq. (7.2). The correction term is the squared sum of all the observations divided by their number. For these data

$$C = \frac{Y_{\cdot\cdot}^2}{rt} = \frac{\left(\sum_{i,j} Y_{ij}\right)^2}{rt} \tag{7.1}$$

$$= \frac{(596.6)^2}{(5)(6)} = 11,864.38$$

$$\text{Total SS} = \sum_{i,j} Y_{ij}^2 - C \tag{7.2}$$

$$= 12,994.36 - 11,864.38 = 1,129.98$$

The sum of squares attributable to the variable of classification, that is, treatments, usually called the *between* or *among groups sum of squares* or *treatment sum of squares*, is found by

$$\text{Treatment SS} = \frac{Y_{1\cdot}^2 + \cdots + Y_{t\cdot}^2}{r} - C \tag{7.3}$$

$$= \frac{(144.1)^2 + \cdots + (93.5)^2}{5} - 11{,}864.38 = 847.05$$

The sum of squares among individuals treated alike is also called the *within groups sum of squares, residual sum of squares, error sum of squares*, or *discrepance*, and is generally obtained by subtracting the treatment sum of squares from the total, as in Eq. (7.4). This is possible because of the additive property of sums of squares.

$$\text{Error SS} = \text{total SS} - \text{treatment SS} \tag{7.4}$$

$$= 1{,}129.98 - 847.05 = 282.93$$

Error sum of squares may also be found by pooling the within treatments sums of squares as shown in Eq. (7.5). These sums of squares are shown in the second last line of Table 7.1. Each component has $r - 1 = 4$ degrees of freedom. The sum of the components is 282.93. The additive nature of sums of squares is demonstrated. This is an excellent computational check. It also provides information relative to the homogeneity of error variance.

$$\text{Error SS} = \sum_i \left(\sum_j Y_{ij}^2 - \frac{Y_{i\cdot}^2}{r} \right) \tag{7.5}$$

$$= \left(4{,}287.53 - \frac{144.1^2}{5} \right) + \cdots + \left(1{,}758.71 - \frac{93.5^2}{5} \right) = 282.93$$

The numerical results of an analysis of variance are usually presented in an analysis of variance table such as Table 7.2, symbolic, or Table 7.3, example, for the data just discussed.

The error mean square is denoted by s^2 and frequently referred to as a *generalized error term* since it is an average of the components contributed by the several populations or treatments. It is an estimate of a common σ^2, the variation among observations treated alike. That there is a common σ^2 is an assumption and s^2 is a valid estimate of σ^2 only if this assumption is true. The individual components are based on only a few degrees of freedom, so they can vary widely about σ^2 and thus are not as good estimates as is the pooled estimate. The principle is the same as that for means: a mean of 24 observations is a better estimate of μ than one of four observations because the former has a smaller variance. Similarly, a sample variance based on 24 observations is a better estimate of σ^2 than one based on four observations

Table 7.2 Analysis of variance: one-way classification with equal replication
(Symbolic)

Source of variation	df	Sums of squares: Definition	Sums of squares: Working	Mean squares†	F
Treatments	$t-1$	$r\sum_i (\bar{Y}_{i\cdot} - \bar{Y}_{\cdot\cdot})^2$	$\sum_i \frac{Y_{i\cdot}^2}{r} - \frac{Y_{\cdot\cdot}^2}{rt}$	√	√
Error	$t(r-1)$	$\sum_{i,j} (Y_{ij} - \bar{Y}_{i\cdot})^2$	by subtraction	√	
Total	$rt-1$	$\sum_{i,j} (Y_{ij} - \bar{Y}_{\cdot\cdot})^2$	$\sum_{i,j} Y_{ij}^2 - \frac{Y_{\cdot\cdot}^2}{rt}$		

† A mean square is a sum of squares divided by the corresponding degrees of freedom.

because the former variance has a smaller variance. The validity of the assumption that each of the components of error is an estimate of the same σ^2 can be tested by the χ^2 test of homogeneity, discussed in Sec. 17.3.

Treatment mean square is an independent estimate of σ^2 when the null hypothesis is true. Variances among means estimate σ^2/r. Thus the r in the definition formula for treatment sum of squares assures us that the treatment mean square estimates σ^2 rather than σ^2/r. A similar argument applies to the working formula where treatment totals are used. Application of Sec. 5.10 shows that variances among totals (see Exercise 5.10.3) estimate $r\sigma^2$; now a divisor r is required if this computation is to lead to an estimate of σ^2 rather than $r\sigma^2$. Since F is defined as the ratio of two independent estimates of the same σ^2, having the treatment mean square estimate σ^2 is a necessity. We say that both mean squares are on a *per-observation* basis.

The F value is obtained by dividing the treatment mean square by the error mean square, that is, $F = 169.4/11.79 = 14.37^{**}$. Thus the F value gives the treatment mean square as a multiple of the error mean square. These mean squares are on a comparable basis since each estimates the variation among individual observations. The calculated F value is

Table 7.3 Analysis of variance for data of Table 7.1

Source of variation	df	Sum of squares	Mean square	F
Among cultures	5	847.05	169.41	14.37**
Within cultures	24	282.93	11.79	
Total	29	1,129.98		

compared with the tabular F value for 5 and 24 degrees of freedom to decide whether to accept the null hypothesis of no difference between population means or the alternative hypothesis of a difference. The tabular F values for 5 and 24 degrees of freedom are 2.62 and 3.90 at the .05 and .01 probability levels, respectively. Since calculated F exceeds 1 percent tabular F, we conclude that the experiment provides evidence of real differences among treatment means.

The F tables, for the analysis of variance, are entered with the numerator degrees of freedom, that is, treatment degrees of freedom, along the top of the table and the denominator degrees of freedom along the side. This is because the set of alternative hypotheses admits only that treatment differences exist and, consequently, increase the estimate of variance based on treatment means or totals so that only large values of the test criterion are to be judged significant. If the treatment mean square is less than error, the result is declared nonsignificant no matter how small the ratio. A significant F implies that the evidence is sufficiently strong to indicate that all the treatments do not belong to populations with a common μ. However, it does not indicate which differences may be considered statistically significant.

Note that both the degrees of freedom and sums of squares in the body of the table add to the corresponding values in the total line. Mean squares are not additive. The property of additivity of sums of squares is characteristic of well-planned and executed experiments. It leads to certain short cuts in the arithmetic of the analysis of variance, such as finding the error sum of squares by subtracting the treatment sum of squares from the total sum of squares as in Table 7.3 and, in general, as a residual. Experiments not planned and executed so as to possess this property will generally involve far more computations and have a lower precision per observation.

The standard error of a treatment mean and that of a difference between treatment means are given by Eqs. (7.6) and (7.7), respectively. Numerical values are for data of Table 7.1.

$$s_{\bar{Y}} = \sqrt{\frac{s^2}{r}} = \sqrt{\frac{11.79}{5}} = 1.54 \text{ mg} \tag{7.6}$$

$$s_{\bar{Y}_{i\cdot} - \bar{Y}_{i'\cdot}} = \sqrt{\frac{2s^2}{r}} = \sqrt{\frac{2(11.79)}{5}} = 2.17 \text{ mg} \qquad i \neq i' \tag{7.7}$$

These statistics are useful for comparing differences among treatment means as discussed in Chap. 8 and for computing confidence intervals for treatment means and differences among pairs of treatment means. Further applications are discussed in Sec. 3.11 and Chap. 5. The coefficient of variability is given by

$$\text{CV} = \frac{\sqrt{s^2}}{\bar{Y}} 100 = \frac{\sqrt{11.79}}{19.89} 100 = 17.3 \text{ percent} \tag{7.8}$$

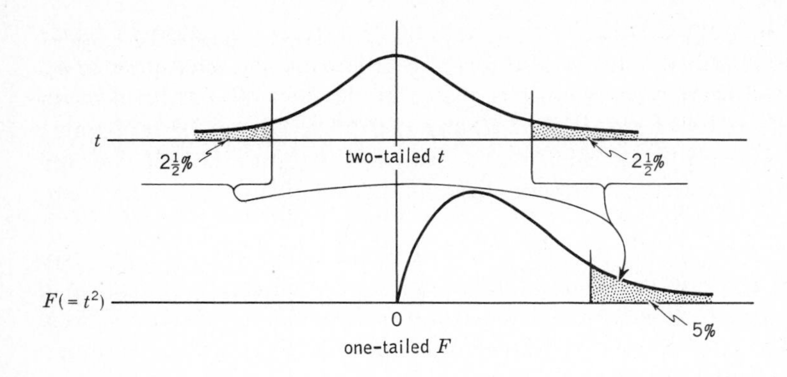

Figure 7.1 Relation between two-tailed t and one-tailed F (curves are only approximate).

It was shown in Sec. 5.5 that the analysis of variance could be used in place of the t test to compare two treatments where the design was completely random.

The one-tailed F test with 1 and n degrees of freedom corresponds to the two-tailed t test with n degrees of freedom. This t test does not specify the direction of the difference between two treatment means for the alternative hypothesis; thus it is like the one-tailed F test that specifies which mean square is to be the larger as the result of differences of unspecified direction between treatments. These tests can be shown to be algebraically equivalent; in particular $t^2 = F$. The relation is shown graphically in Fig. 7.1. Small numerical values of t, when squared, become small values of F, positive quantities. Large numerical values of t, when squared, become large values of F.

Exercise 7.3.1 F. R. Urey, Department of Zoology, University of Wisconsin, made an estrogen assay of several solutions which had been subjected to an in vitro inactivation technique. The uterine weight of the mouse was used as a measure of estrogenic activity. Uterine weights in milligrams of four mice for each of control and six different solutions are shown in the accompanying table.

Control	1	2	3	4	5	6
89.8	84.4	64.4	75.2	88.4	56.4	65.6
93.8	116.0	79.8	62.4	90.2	83.2	79.4
88.4	84.0	88.0	62.4	73.2	90.4	65.6
112.6	68.6	69.4	73.8	87.8	85.6	70.2

Compute the means and the analysis of variance for these data. Compute error sum of squares directly and demonstrate the additivity of sums of squares. Calculate the coefficient of variability.

Exercise 7.3.2 Calculate the sum of squares among treatments 1 through 6, that is, ignoring control. This has 5 degrees of freedom. Calculate the sum of squares for comparing control with the mean of all other observations. (*Clue:* Read Sec. 5.5.) This has 1 degree of freedom. Note that the sum of these two sums of squares is the treatment sum of squares in the analysis of variance. Such comparisons are said to be orthogonal; orthogonality is discussed in Chap. 8.

Exercise 7.3.3 Subjects from the general population of Central Prison, Raleigh, North Carolina, volunteered for an experiment involving an "isolation" experience. (Those convicted of felon offenses are housed in this facility.) This was conducted by Jordan (7.12). The experimental treatment exposed the inmates to combined sensory restriction and suggestion. The intent was to reduce the psychopathic deviant (Pd) scale T scores in the Minnesota Multiphasic Personality Inventory (MMPI) test.

Briefly, treatments consisted of

1. Four hours of sensory restriction plus a 15-min "therapeutic" tape advising that professional help is available
2. Four hours of sensory restriction plus a 15-min "emotionally neutral" tape on training hunting dogs
3. Four hours of sensory restriction but no message.

The MMPI was administered before and after the experiment. Values of Pd T scores are given below for 14 individuals on each treatment.

Compute treatment means and the analysis of variance for the pretest scores. Test the null hypothesis of no differences among groups prior to conducting the experiment. Calculate $s_{\bar{Y}}$, $s_{\bar{Y}_i - \bar{Y}_{i'}}$, and the coefficient of variability.

Treatment					
1		2		3	
Test					
Pre	Post	Pre	Post	Pre	Post
67	74	88	79	86	90
86	50	79	81	53	53
64	64	67	83	81	102
69	76	83	74	69	67
67	64	79	76	81	76
79	81	76	69	76	81
67	74	71	71	74	69
67	50	67	75	60	60
69	60	69	64	67	69
57	57	67	64	86	83
76	62	67	64	86	107
90	76	74	71	74	71
71	71	81	74	71	71
93	76	81	64	71	81

Exercise 7.3.4 Compute treatment means and the analysis of variance for the posttest scores given in Exercise 7.3.3. Test the null hypothesis of no differences among treatment groups following the experiment. Calculate $s_{\bar{Y}}$, $s_{\bar{Y}_i - \bar{Y}_{i'}}$ and the coefficient of variation. Do you think that the F test computed in the analysis of variance will satisfy the investigator's implied test requirement? Explain.

7.4 Data with a Single Criterion of Classification. The Analysis of Variance for Any Number of Groups with Unequal Replication

When the number of observations per treatment varies, we have a general case for which Sec. 7.3 provides a special example.

The analysis of variance will now be illustrated for the data of Table 7.4. The original observations were made on a greenhouse experiment in Ithaca, New York, and were intended to determine whether or not there are genetic differences among plants, either among or within locations, location referring to the place of origin of the plant; the data in Table 7.4 are suitable for among-location (more generally, treatment) comparisons only and are for a single character of many that were checked.

Computations Compute

$$\sum_j Y_{ij} = Y_{i\cdot} \qquad \text{and} \qquad \sum_j Y_{ij}^2,$$

that is, the sum and sum of squares of the observations for each treatment; these are also shown in Table 7.4. Equation (7.9) is the only new computational procedure; Eq. (7.3) arises from this equation when all r_i's are equal.

$$C = \frac{Y_{\cdot\cdot}^2}{\sum r_i} = \frac{(1{,}443)^2}{14} = 148{,}732.07$$

$$\text{Total SS} = \sum_{i,j} Y_{ij}^2 - C = 158{,}731.00 - 148{,}732.07 = 9{,}998.93$$

$$\text{Treatment SS} = \sum_i \frac{Y_{i\cdot}^2}{r_i} - C = \frac{Y_{1\cdot}^2}{r_1} + \cdots + \frac{Y_{t\cdot}^2}{r_t} - C \tag{7.9}$$

$$= 153{,}713.00 - 148{,}732.07 = 4{,}980.93$$

$$\text{Error SS} = \text{total SS} - \text{treatment SS} = 5{,}018.00$$

Table 7.4 Leaf length at time of flowering (sum for three leaves) of *Sedum oxypetalum* from six locations in the trans-Mexican volcanic belt, mm

Location	r_i	$\sum_j Y_{ij}$	$\bar{Y}_{i\cdot}$	$\sum_j Y_{ij}^2$	$Y_{i\cdot}^2/r_i$	$\sum_j (Y_{ij} - \bar{Y}_{i\cdot})^2$
H	1	147	147.00	21,609	21,609.00	
LA	1	70	70.00	4,900	4,900.00	
R	6	634	105.67	71,740	66,992.67	4,747.33
SN	1	75	75.00	5,625	5,625.00	
Tep	3	347	115.67	40,357	40,136.33	220.67
Tis	2	170	85.00	14,500	14,450.00	50.00
Totals	14	1,443	($\bar{Y}_{\cdot\cdot}$ = 103.07)	158,731	153,713.00	5,018.00

Source: Unpublished data used with permission of R. T. Clausen, Cornell University, Ithaca, New York.

Table 7.5 Analysis of variance of the data summarized in Table 7.4

Source of variation	df	SS	MS	F
Among locations	5	4,980.93	996.19	1.59
Within locations	8	5,018.00	627.25	
Total	13	9,998.93		

$s_{\bar{Y}_{i\cdot}-\bar{Y}_{i'\cdot}} = \sqrt{627.25\left(\frac{1}{r_i} + \frac{1}{r_j}\right)}$ mm where r_i and r_j are the numbers of observations in the means for the desired comparison.

Note that $\bar{Y}_{\cdot\cdot} = Y_{\cdot\cdot}/\sum r_i = \sum r_i \bar{Y}_{i\cdot}/\sum r_i$ is a weighted mean of the treatment means.

Also, Eq. (7.9) has a corresponding definition formula given by

$$\sum \frac{Y_{i\cdot}^2}{r_i} - C = \sum r_i(\bar{Y}_{i\cdot} - \bar{Y}_{\cdot\cdot})^2 \tag{7.10}$$

This shows that we are really computing a weighted sum of squares of the deviations of treatment means from the overall mean. The weights are proportional to the information in any mean, as are the reciprocals of the variances, σ^2/r_i, except for the common σ^2.

Finally, error sum of squares may also be found by pooling the within-treatments sums of squares given in the last column of Table 7.4. It is of interest to note that three locations do not contribute anything to the error variance since each supplies only one observation.

The analysis of variance is given in Table 7.5. F is not significant; tabulated $F(.05) = 3.69$ for 5 and 8 degrees of freedom. The evidence is not in favor of location differences.

Exercise 7.4.1 Wexelsen (7.18) studied the effects of inbreeding on plant weight in red clover. Given below is the average plant weight in grams of noninbred (F_1) lines and three groups of inbred families arranged in increasing order of inbreeding.

F_1: 254, 263, 266, 249, 337, 277, 289, 244, 265
Slightly inbred: 236, 191, 209, 252, 212, 224
F_2: 253, 192, 141, 160, 229, 221, 150, 215, 232, 234, 193, 188
F_3: 173, 164, 183, 138, 146, 125, 178, 199, 170, 177, 172, 198

Compute the analysis of variance for these data. Obtain error sum of squares directly and demonstrate the additivity of sums of squares. Calculate the coefficient of variability.

Exercise 7.4.2 The data given in Exercise 7.3.3 are incomplete. The following observations were also obtained.

Treatment					
1		2		3	
Test					
Pre	Post	Pre	Post	Pre	Post
81	83	53	81		
86	88	81	71	No more	
69	60	83	79		
83	74				

(*a*) Carry out the analysis of variance of the pretest scores using all the data. Test the null hypothesis of no difference among the population means. Present the means, s, and the CV.

(*b*) Carry out the analysis of variance of the posttest scores using all the data. Test the null hypothesis of no differencc among the population means. Compute the means, s, and the CV.

Exercise 7.4.3 In an experimental study of the effects of Aroclor 1254, a PCB, Sanders (7.14) incorporated the substance in the diets of random bred, male, albino house mice fed *ad libitum*. Rates were 0, 62.5, 250, 1,000, and 4,000 ppm. After two weeks, the mice were injected with Nembutal and their sleeping times recorded. Sleeping time is a measure of hepatic microsomal enzyme activity.

Sleeping times for the surviving mice follow.

Rates	Sleeping times
0	67, 69, 72, 79
62.5	96, 98, 130, 65
250	74, 24, 15, 33, 17
1000	49, 46

Compute the analysis of variance and test the null hypothesis that there are no differences among population means for the four rates. Compute rate means, s, and the CV.

Exercise 7.4.4 Sanders (7.14) also measured final weight in the experiment of Exercise 7.4.3, as given in the table.

Rates	Final weights
0	55, 47, 46, 53
62.5	47, 51, 40, 44
250	49, 44, 46, 51, 48
1000	36, 41

Repeat Exercise 7.4.3 for these data.

7.5 The Linear Additive Model

An observation has been described as the sum of components, a mean, and a random element, where the mean, in turn, may be a sum of components. A further basic assumption in the analysis of variance, where tests of significance are to be made, is that the random components are independently and normally distributed about zero mean and with a common variance. For the one-way classification, the linear model begins with

$$Y_{ij} = \mu + \tau_i + \varepsilon_{ij} \qquad i = 1, \ldots, t \qquad \text{and} \qquad j = 1, \ldots, r_i \tag{7.11}$$

The ε_{ij}'s are the random components.

Assumptions must also be made about the τ's to clarify the model completely. Thus we have:

The fixed model, or Model I The τ's are fixed and

$$\sum_i \tau_i = 0$$

they constitute a finite population and are the parameters of interest along with σ^2.

The random model, or Model II The τ's are a random sample from a population of τ's for which the mean is zero and the variance is σ_τ^2, the one parameter of interest other than σ^2.

The distinction is that for the fixed model, a repetition of the experiment would bring the same set of τ's into the new experiment; we concentrate our attention on these τ's. A fertilizer experiment will normally illustrate a fixed model. For the random model, a repetition would bring in a new set of τ's but from the same population of τ's, and over time, the whole population of τ's would appear in the ith position; we would be interested in the variability of the τ's since we are not in a position to continue our interest in a specific set. An experiment that examines the genetic effect of dairy cows on milk production illustrates the random model. For the fixed model, we draw inferences about the particular treatments; for the random model, we draw an inference about the population of treatments.

The equation for the linear model could have been written as $Y_{ij} = \mu_i + \varepsilon_{ij}$. In this case, it is clear that all μ_i can be estimated. Now when we write $\mu_i = \mu + \tau_i$, we can estimate $\mu + \tau_i$ but not μ and τ_i. This, too, is clear if we consider sampling a single treated population. How much of the average response are we to assign to the original population and how much to the treatment? We need a bench mark that is not ordinarily available. More generally, we cannot estimate any τ_i or $\sum \tau_i$ when we have t treated populations. The present model is *overparameterized.*

This difficulty is obviated by imposing some condition on the parameters, such as setting $\sum \tau_i = 0$; economists will often set $\tau_1 = 0$.

Conditions imposed solely to get a solution are called *constraints on the solution*, but when they are made an integral part of the model, that is, when they are assumptions, as here, they are called *restrictions on the model.*

Setting $\sum \tau_i = 0$ and, consequently, $\sum \hat{\tau}_i = 0$, is simply measuring treatment effects as deviations from an overall mean. The null hypothesis is then easily stated as H_0: $\tau_i = 0$, $i = 1, \ldots, t$ and the alternative as H_1: some $\tau_i \neq 0$. If $\sum \hat{\tau}_i = 0$ has been a constraint, then H_0 is simply that all treatment effects are equal. Clearly, we have the fixed model in mind in our discussion as we develop the arithmetic of the analysis of variance. However, we later apply it to the random model where we have H_0: $\sigma_\tau^2 = 0$ and H_1: $\sigma_\tau^2 \neq 0$.

Once the particular model has been decided on, it is possible to state what parameters are being estimated when the various mean squares and the F value are computed. For Models I and II, if the experiment were repeated endlessly and the observed mean squares were averaged, we would have the values given in Table 7.6—expected values. For an individual experiment, the mean squares are estimates of the corresponding expected values in Table 7.6.

Consider the *Rhizobium* data of Table 7.1 to be data to which Model I applies. Then, from Table 7.3 and Table 7.6, it is clear that to estimate $\sum \tau_i^2/(t-1)$, we need to subtract the within cultures mean square from the among cultures mean square and divide by $r = 5$. We have

$$\sigma^2 \text{ is estimated by } 11.79$$

$$\frac{\sum \tau_i^2}{t-1} \text{ is estimated by } \frac{169.41 - 11.79}{5} = 31.52$$

The value 31.52 is an estimate of the variability of the fixed set of τ's and any variability in this estimate, from experiment to experiment, comes as the result of variability in the estimate of σ^2; there are no sample-to-sample differences in the τ's.

Table 7.6 Average values of mean squares for Models I and II, equal replication

Source of variation	df	Mean square is an estimate of	
		Model I	Model II
Treatments	$t-1$	$\sigma^2 + r\sum \tau_i^2/(t-1)$	$\sigma^2 + r\sigma_\tau^2$
Individuals within treatments	$t(r-1) = tr - t$	σ^2	σ^2
Total	$tr - 1$		

For an experiment to which Model II applies, variability in the estimate of σ_τ^2 comes as the result of variability in the estimate of σ^2 and sample-to-sample differences in the τ's.

When there is unequal replication of treatments, the coefficient corresponding to r for the average value of the treatment mean square is, for Model II,

$$r_0 = \left(\sum r_i - \frac{\sum r_i^2}{\sum r_i}\right)\frac{1}{t-1} \tag{7.12}$$

For Model I, the average value of the treatment mean square depends on whether the τ's are to be simple deviations from a mean or whether their weighted mean, and consequently weighted sum, is to be zero. The values are given in Table 7.7. The average value of the error mean square is σ^2 regardless of which restriction is placed on the τ's.

That the computed mean squares, for equal replication, have expectations given in Table 7.6 is readily shown. The mean square for individuals within treatments is obtained by pooling estimates like that obtained from $Y_{i1} = \mu + \tau_i + \varepsilon_{i1}, \ldots, Y_{ir} = \mu + \tau_i + \varepsilon_{ir}$, where only the ε's vary. Clearly this will lead us to an estimate of σ^2; the same can be said if r is also a variable. The treatment mean square is based on totals

$$Y_{1\cdot} = r\mu + r\tau_1 + \varepsilon_{1\cdot}, \ldots, Y_{t\cdot} = r\mu + r\tau_t + \varepsilon_{t\cdot}$$

or means

$$\bar{Y}_{1\cdot} = \mu + \tau_1 + \bar{\varepsilon}_{1\cdot}, \ldots, \bar{Y}_{t\cdot} = \mu + \tau_t + \bar{\varepsilon}_{t\cdot}$$

If the null hypothesis is true, then the totals are actually of the form $r\mu + \varepsilon_{i\cdot}$ and their variance is an estimate of $r\sigma^2$. However, the divisor r is used in computing so that the mean square in the analysis of variance table is an estimate of σ^2. If the null hypothesis is false, then the totals are of the form $r\mu + r\tau_i + \varepsilon_{i\cdot}$ and the τ's and ε's contribute to the variability of the totals. The contribution attributable to the ε's is still σ^2. Squaring the totals gives terms like $r^2\tau_i^2$, which yields $r\tau_i^2$ after division by r. Hence the contribution

Table 7.7 Average value of treatment mean square for Model I, unequal replication

Impose condition	Treatment mean square is an estimate of
$\sum \tau_i = 0$	$\sigma^2 + \dfrac{\sum r_i\tau_i^2 - (\sum r_i\tau_i)^2/\sum r_i}{(t-1)}$
$\sum r_i\tau_i = 0$	$\sigma^2 + (\sum r_i\tau_i^2)/(t-1)$

Note that $\sum r_i\tau_i^2 - \dfrac{(\sum r_i\tau_i)^2}{\sum r_i} = \sum r_i(\tau_i - \bar{\tau})^2$ where $\bar{\tau} = (\sum r_i\tau_i)/(\sum r_i)$.

attributable to the τ's is either $r \sum \tau_i^2/(t-1)$ or an estimate of $r\sigma_\tau^2$. Since we assume the τ's and ε's to be independent, there is no contribution that involves products of τ's and ε's.

When there is unequal replication, totals are of the form $r_i \mu + r_i \tau_i + \varepsilon_{i\cdot}$ and means are of the form $\mu + \tau_i + \bar{\varepsilon}_{i\cdot}$. The computation of a treatment mean square directly from totals is clearly not valid since $r_i \mu$ is variable and would introduce a contribution due neither to the τ's nor to the ε's; computation with means would introduce no such difficulty. It can be shown that

$$\sum_i \frac{Y_{i\cdot}^2}{r_i} - \frac{Y_{\cdot\cdot}^2}{\sum_i r_i} = \sum_i r_i(\bar{Y}_{i\cdot} - \bar{Y}_{\cdot\cdot})^2$$

where the left-hand side is the computing formula for the treatment sum of squares. The right-hand side is a weighted sum of squares of the deviations of the treatment means from the overall mean defined as $Y_{\cdot\cdot}/(\sum r_i)$ or its equivalent, $(\sum r_i \bar{Y}_{i\cdot})/(\sum r_i)$. The weights assigned to the squared deviations are seen to be inversely proportional to the variance of each treatment mean, that is, a big variance leads to a small weight and vice versa, as should be the case. It is now clear that if there are no treatment effects, the treatment mean square does lead to an estimate of σ^2; if there are treatment effects, there is also a contribution due to the τ's (see Table 7.7).

When F is the test criterion for testing among treatment means in an analysis of variance, the null hypothesis is one of no differences among population treatment means and the alternative is that differences, most often unspecified with respect to size and direction, exist. True differences may be the result of a particular set of fixed effects or of a random set of effects from a population of effects. The basis of the test criterion is the comparison of two independent variances which are estimates of a common variance when the null hypothesis is true. If real treatment differences exist, we have

$$F = \frac{\widehat{\sigma^2 + r(\sum \tau_i^2)/(t-1)}}{s^2} \quad \text{or} \quad F = \frac{\widehat{\sigma^2 + r\sigma_\tau^2}}{s^2}$$

depending on the model. The $\widehat{\ }$'s, simply called hats, indicate that there is no way to estimate the variance components from the numerator alone. On the average, then, the numerator will be larger than the denominator if real treatment differences exist. We are trying to detect the population quantities $(\sum \tau_i^2)/(t-1)$ or σ_τ^2, depending on the model. Formally, we have H_0: $\tau_i = 0$, $i = 1, \ldots, t$ versus H_1: some $\tau_i \neq 0$ for the fixed model with the restriction $\sum \tau_i = 0$; otherwise H_0 is one of equality of the τ's and H_0: $\sigma_\tau^2 = 0$ versus H_1: $\sigma_\tau^2 > 0$ for the random model. This test is called a one-tailed test, the reference to tails being relative to the F distribution.

Exercise 7.5.1 For the data of Exercise 7.3.1, estimate the contribution of the treatment effects to the variability measured by the treatment mean square. Decide which model applies and define this contribution in terms of the components of the model.

Exercise 7.5.2 Repeat Exercise 7.5.1 for the posttreatment data of Exercise 7.3.3.

Exercise 7.5.3 Repeat Exercise 7.5.1 for the data in Exercise 7.4.1 and the posttreatment data of Exercise 7.4.2.

7.6 Analysis of Variance with Subsamples. Equal Subsample Numbers

In some experimental situations, several observations may be made within the experimental unit, the unit to which the treatment is applied. Such observations are made on *subsamples* or *sampling* units. Differences among subsamples within an experimental unit are observational differences rather than experimental unit differences. For example, consider the data of Table 7.8. A large group of plants were assigned at random to pots, four to a pot, the experimental unit; treatments were assigned at random to pots, three pots per treatment. All pots were completely randomized with respect to location during the time spent in daylight and each group of pots was completely randomized within the low- or high-temperature greenhouse during the time spent in darkness. Observations were made on the individual plants.

Two sources of variation which contribute to the variance applicable to comparisons among treatment means are:

1. The variation among plants treated alike, that is, among plants within pots. Since different treatments are applied to different pots and, consequently, plants, variation among plants will be present in comparisons among treatment means.
2. The variation among plants in different pots treated alike, that is, variation among pots within treatments. This variation may be no greater than that among plants treated alike but usually is. The investigator will generally know whether or not to expect this to be a real source of variation; for example, it may be that the nutrients, light, moisture, etc., vary more from pot to pot than within a pot. A measure of variation computed from pot totals or pot means for the same treatment will, of course, contain both sources of variation.

Mean squares for the two types of variation listed above are generally referred to as *sampling error* and *experimental error*, respectively. If the second source of variation is not real, then the two mean squares will be of the same order of magnitude. Otherwise, the experimental error will be expected to be larger in random sampling since it contains an additional source of variation.

Table 7.8 One-week stem growths of mint plants grown in nutrient solution

Plant number	Hours of daylight at																	
	Low night temperatures									High night temperatures								
	8			12			16			8			12			16		
	Pot number			Pot number			Pot number			Pot number			Pot number			Pot number		
	1	2	3	1	2	3	1	2	3	1	2	3	1	2	3	1	2	3
1	3.5	2.5	3.0	5.0	3.5	4.5	5.0	5.5	5.5	8.5	6.5	7.0	6.0	6.0	6.5	7.0	6.0	11.0
2	4.0	4.5	3.0	5.5	3.5	4.0	4.5	6.0	4.5	6.0	7.0	7.0	5.5	8.5	6.5	9.0	7.0	7.0
3	3.0	5.5	2.5	4.0	3.0	4.0	5.0	5.0	6.5	9.0	8.0	7.0	3.5	4.5	8.5	8.5	7.0	9.0
4	4.5	5.0	3.0	3.5	4.0	5.0	4.5	5.0	5.5	8.5	6.5	7.0	7.0	7.5	7.5	8.5	7.0	8.0
Pot totals = $Y_{ij\cdot}$	15.0	17.5	11.5	18.0	14.0	17.5	19.0	21.5	22.0	32.0	28.0	28.0	22.0	26.5	29.0	33.0	27.0	35.0
Treatment totals = $Y_{i\cdot\cdot}$	44.0			49.5			62.5			88.0			77.5			95.0		
Treatment means = $\bar{Y}_{i\cdot\cdot}$	3.7			4.1			5.2			7.3			6.5			7.9		

Source: These data are a part of a larger set and are available through the courtesy of R. Rabson, Cornell University, Ithaca, New York.

Comparable situations are found in many fields of experimentation. An agronomist may desire to determine the number of plants per unit area in a red clover varietal trial, or an entomologist may wish to determine the number of lice on cattle in an experiment to evaluate insecticides to control lice. In both cases, subsamples can be taken on each experimental unit. In chemical analyses, duplicate or triplicate determinations can be made on each sample. In field and animal experiments the variation among the subsamples or sampling units within an experimental unit is a measure of the homogeneity of the unit, whereas in chemical analyses it is often associated with the repeatability of the technique. This is the variation which leads to the *sampling error.*

In testing a hypothesis about population treatment means, the appropriate divisor for F is the experimental error mean square since it includes variation from all sources that contribute to the variability of treatment means except treatments.

Data that can be classified by a system consisting of a unique order of classification criteria, each criterion being applicable within all categories of the preceding criterion, are said to be in a *hierarchal* or *hierarchical classification*, a *nested classification* or a *within-within-within classification.* Thus, the data of Table 7.8 can be classified according to treatment, the temperature-time combination, then within treatments according to pot, and finally within pots according to plant. There is no other reasonable order. Treatments themselves may be classified in one of two orders, either as hours-within-temperatures or temperatures-within-hours. Treatments form a two-way classification, discussed in Chap. 9.

Computations Let Y_{ijk} be the week's growth for plant k in pot j receiving treatment i, $k = 1, \ldots, 4$, $j = 1, 2, 3$, $i = 1, \ldots, 6$. Thus plant 2 in pot 3 receiving treatment 6 (high night temperature following 16 h of daylight) has a one-week stem growth of 7.0 cm, that is, $Y_{632} = 7.0$ cm. Plant and pot numbers are for convenience in tagging the observations. Thus plants numbered 2 have nothing in common but the number, and pots numbered 3 have nothing in common but the number. On the other hand, plants or pots with the same treatment number received the same treatment so they are expected to respond similarly, whereas plants or pots with a different treatment number may possibly respond differently.

Denote pot totals by $Y_{ij\cdot}$, totals for a particular treatment-pot combination. Thus one-week stem growth of plants in pot 2 receiving treatment 3 (low night temperature following 16 h of daylight) total 21.5 cm, that is, $Y_{32\cdot} = 21.5$ cm. Denote treatment totals by $Y_{i\cdot\cdot}$. The total one-week stem growth of plants on treatment 4 is 88.0 cm, that is, $Y_{4\cdot\cdot} = 88.0$ cm. Denote the grand total by $Y_{\cdot\cdot\cdot}$; $Y_{\cdot\cdot\cdot} = 416.5$ cm.

The dot notation ($Y_{ij\cdot}$, $Y_{i\cdot\cdot}$, $Y_{\cdot\cdot\cdot}$) is a common and useful shorthand that can be generalized easily to many experimental situations. The dot replaces a subscript and indicates that all values covered by the subscript have been added; the particular information formerly supplied by the individuals, as indicated by the subscript, has been discarded in favor of a summary in the form of a total; the subscript is no longer required and is replaced by a dot. Thus

$$Y_{11\cdot} = 3.5 + 4.0 + 3.0 + 4.5 = 15.0 \text{ cm},$$

$$Y_{1\cdot\cdot} = 3.5 + 4.0 + \cdots + 3.0 = 15.0 + 17.5 + 11.5 = 44.0 \text{ cm},$$

and so on.

Obtain the 18 pot totals and sums of squares, that is,

$$\sum_k Y_{ijk} = Y_{ij\cdot} \qquad \text{and} \qquad \sum_k Y_{ijk}^2$$

for the 18 combinations of i and j. From these subtotals obtain the correction term C, the total sum of squares, and the sum of squares for pots. These are, respectively,

$$C = \frac{Y_{\cdots}^2}{srt} = \frac{(416.5)^2}{4(3)6} = 2{,}409.34$$

where s is the number of subsamples per plot, that is, plants per pot, r is the number of replicates of a treatment, that is, pots per treatment, and t is the number of treatments.

$$\text{Total SS} = \sum_{i,j,k} Y_{ijk}^2 - C$$

$$= (3.5)^2 + (4.0)^2 + \cdots + (8.0)^2 - C = 255.91 \qquad \text{with 71 df}$$

$$\text{Pots SS} = \frac{\sum_{i,j} Y_{ij\cdot}^2}{s} - C$$

$$= \frac{(15.0)^2 + \cdots + (35.0)^2}{4} - C = 205.47 \qquad \text{with 17 df}$$

The sum of squares attributable to subsamples (among plants within pots) may be found by subtraction:

$$\text{Within pots SS} = \text{total SS} - \text{pot SS}$$

$$= 255.91 - 205.47$$

$$= 50.44 \text{ with } 71 - 17 = 54 \text{ df}$$

The computations to this point may now be placed in an analysis of variance table (see Table 7.9).

Table 7.9 Analysis of variance of mint plant data, Table 7.8

Source of variation	df	SS	MS	MS is an estimate of
Among pots	17	205.47		
Treatments	5	179.64	35.93	$\sigma^2 + 4\sigma_\varepsilon^2 + \left(12\sigma_\tau^2 \text{ or } 12\frac{\sum \tau^2}{5}\right)$
Among pots within treatments = experimental error	12	25.83	2.15	$\sigma^2 + 4\sigma_\varepsilon^2$
Among plants within pots = sampling error	54	50.44	.93	σ^2
Total	71	255.91		

$s^2 = .93,\ s_\varepsilon^2 = \dfrac{2.15 - .93}{4} = .30,\ \dfrac{\sum t_i^2}{5} = \dfrac{35.93 - 2.15}{12} = 2.82$ (or $= s_\tau^2$ for Model II)

where t_i is an estimate of τ_i.

Pot sum of squares measures variation due to treatments as well as variation among pots treated alike. Partitioning this sum of squares, we obtain

$$\text{Treatments SS} = \frac{\sum_i Y_{i\cdot\cdot}^2}{sr} - C$$

$$= \frac{(44.0)^2 + \cdots + (95.0)^2}{4(3)} - C = 179.64 \qquad \text{with 5 df}$$

Note that there are $sr = 12$ observations in each treatment total, $Y_{i\cdot\cdot}$, hence the divisor in obtaining the treatment sum of squares. Finally,

$$\text{Pots within treatment SS} = \text{pots SS} - \text{treatments SS}$$

$$= 205.47 - 179.64 = 25.83 \qquad \text{with } 17 - 5 = 12 \text{ df}$$

The analysis of variance table is now completed, including mean squares (see Table 7.9). This type of analysis of variance is often presented with the pots line not shown at all or shown as a subtotal below the experimental error line. Note that the various divisors put each mean square on a per-observation, namely, the subsample, basis. Means, too, must be on a per-observation basis when computed.

The sum of squares obtained by subtraction may also be computed directly. The direct procedure indicates very clearly just what source of variation is involved at each stage and how the degrees of freedom arise.

Sampling error concerns the samples from the experimental unit, that is, the plants within pots. Thus the first pot contributes the following sum of squares:

$$\text{Plants SS for pot 1, treatment 1} = (3.5)^2 + \cdots + (4.5)^2 - \frac{(15.0)^2}{4}$$

$$= 1.25 \text{ with 3 df}$$

Similar computations are performed for each of the 18 pots giving 18 sums of squares, each with 3 degrees of freedom. Their total is

$$\text{SS among plants treated alike} = 1.25 + \cdots + 8.75$$

$$= 50.45 \text{ with } 18(3) = 54 \text{ df}$$

The sums of squares and degrees of freedom are pooled to estimate a sampling variance. We assume that there is a common within-pot variance, regardless of the treatment.

Experimental error concerns experimental units treated alike, pots within treatments. Thus, treatment 1 contributes the following sum of squares to experimental error:

Pots SS for treatment 1

$$= \frac{(15.0)^2 + (17.5)^2 + (11.5)^2 - (15.0 + 17.5 + 11.5)^2/3}{4}$$

$$= 4.54 \qquad \text{with 2 df}$$

Similar computations are made for the other five treatments and the results added. We obtain

$$\text{SS (pots treated alike)} = 4.54 + \cdots + 8.67$$

$$= 25.83 \qquad \text{with } 6(2) = 12 \text{ df}$$

Here we assume that the variance among pots is the same for all treatments. The sums of squares and degrees of freedom are pooled to give an estimate of this common variance.

Plant-to-plant variation, used to measure sampling error, is also present in pot-to-pot variation, since the different pots contain different plants, and thus is also present in treatment-to-treatment variation. Therefore, both the treatment variance and the pots-within-treatments variance contain a plant-to-plant variance. Treatment-to-treatment variation has also a contribution attributable to the variation among pots-treated-alike, if such exists, since the effects of different treatments are measured on different pots. It is seen, then, that experimental error is appropriate to comparisons involving different treatments whereas sampling error is not, since the treatment mean square has only one possible additional source of variation not possessed by the experimental error, namely, that due to treatments themselves. A valid test of the null hypothesis of no treatment differences is given by

$$F = \frac{\text{treatment mean square}}{\text{experimental error mean square}}$$

$$= \frac{35.93}{2.15} = 16.7^{**} \qquad \text{with 5 and 12 df}$$

Experimental error may or may not contain variation in addition to that among subsamples. This depends on the environmental differences that exist from unit to unit and whether or not they are greater than those within the unit—the pot in our example. A test is available in

$$F = \frac{\text{experimental error mean square}}{\text{sampling error mean square}}$$

$$= \frac{2.15}{.93} = 2.3^{*} \qquad \text{with 12 and 54 df}$$

The standard error of a treatment mean is $s_{\bar{Y}} = \sqrt{2.15/12} = .42$ cm, and the standard error of a difference between treatment means is $s_{\bar{Y}_i - \bar{Y}_{i'}} = \sqrt{2(2.15)/12} = .60$ cm. The coefficient of variability is $(s/\bar{Y})100 = (1.47/5.78)100 = 25$ percent.

The computations for hierarchal classifications with increasing numbers of classification criteria are the obvious generalization of the computations of this section.

Exercise 7.6.1 Check the computations for the data of Table 7.8. Obtain the sums of squares for sampling error and experimental error directly and thus check the additivity of sums of squares in the analysis of variance.

Exercise 7.6.2 Distinguish between the variability of a pot mean and the variability among pot means (see also Sec. 7.9).

7.7 The Linear Model for Subsampling

The discussion of the mint plant data, Table 7.8, makes it fairly evident that the mathematical expression proposed to explain the data is

$$Y_{ijk} = \mu + \tau_i + \varepsilon_{ij} + \delta_{ijk} \tag{7.13}$$

where each observation is intended to supply information about the mean of the treatment population sampled, namely, $\mu + \tau_i$. If we treat the τ's as fixed effects, as they obviously are, then we measure them as deviations such that $\sum \tau_i = 0$; if we treat them as random, then we may assume that they are from a population with mean zero and variance σ_τ^2. Two random elements are obtained with each observation. The ε_{ij}'s are the experimental unit, that is, pot, contributions and are assumed to be normally and independently distributed with zero mean and variance σ_ε^2; the δ_{ijk}'s are the subsample, that is, plant, contributions and are assumed to be normally and independently distributed with zero mean and variance σ^2. The ε's and δ's are assumed to be unrelated, that is, the drawing of a particular value of δ does not affect the probability of drawing any particular ε.

Now consider the pot totals used in computing experimental error. For our particular set of data, they are given by

$$4\mu + 4\tau_i + 4\varepsilon_{ij} + \sum_k \delta_{ijk}$$

for the 18 combinations of i and j. A variance computed with these sums, considering i fixed, would contain a $4\sigma^2$ and a $(4)^2\sigma_\varepsilon^2$, the first quantity involving the variance of sums of δ's and the second involving the variance of a multiple of each ε, essentially a coding operation. Thus the coefficients are 4 and 4^2, respectively. The computational procedure used requires us to divide any sum of squares by the number of observations in each squared quantity. Hence the computed experimental error mean square estimates $\sigma^2 + 4\sigma_\varepsilon^2$. A similar argument leads to the coefficients of the components of the treatment mean square. The results are presented in Table 7.9. What any F value is intended to detect now becomes clear. From the F value, it appears that both σ_ε^2 and a treatment contribution are present in our data. Since the treatment component is present unless we have a very unusual sample, we conclude that the null hypothesis H_0: $\tau_1 = \tau_2 = \cdots = \tau_6 = 0$, appropriate to the fixed model, is false and that at least one τ differs from the others. (Without the restriction $\sum \tau_i = 0$, we test the equality of all treatment contributions.)

Note that the unit of measurement used was $\frac{1}{2}$ cm and the sampling error was .93, giving a standard deviation of .96 cm. Recall that in Sec. 2.15 a class interval not greater than one-quarter of the standard deviation was recommended to keep the loss in information low. Thus, for an estimate of the sampling error with low loss of information due to the choice of size of unit of measurement, the unit chosen was unsatisfactory. In this case, it is fortunate that we have relatively little use for sampling error. Another point that may be brought out relative to the choice of unit of measurement is this: a treatment such as high night temperature with 8 h of daylight, pot 3, where all observations are identical, contributes nothing to sampling error sum of squares but does contribute 3 degrees of freedom. It is sometimes recommended, in cases like this, that these 3 degrees of freedom be left out of the total.

Exercise 7.7.1 By sampling, construct data for an experiment that includes both experimental and sampling error. For simplicity, have three treatments, two experimental units per treatment and three observations per unit. Sketch a possible physical layout for such an experiment, labeling each unit with an equation describing the makeup of the corresponding observation. Now decide upon a general mean, say $\mu = 80$. Second, choose a set of fixed effects for treatments, say $\tau_1 = -4$, $\tau_2 = -2$, and $\tau_3 = 6$. Third, obtain a set of six random elements for the six experimental units. For these, sample Table 4.1 and compute $\varepsilon_{ij} = (Y - 40)/4$, for Y from the table, so that the population sampled has $\mu_\varepsilon = 0$ and $\sigma_\varepsilon = 3$. Note that the sample of ε's will not likely have $\bar{\varepsilon} = 0$ or $s_\varepsilon = 3$. Finally, obtain 18 random elements for the 18 sampling units. For these, sample Table 4.1 and compute $\delta_{ijk} = (Y - 40)/12$ so that the population sampled has $\mu_\delta = 0$ and $\sigma_\delta = 1$.

Why is it true that ε_{ij} has $\mu = 0$ and $\sigma = 3$?

Write out the analysis of variance showing sources of variation, degrees of freedom, and parameters being estimated. Since all parameters have known values, it is possible to show numerical answers. Compute the analysis of variance and compare all estimates with corresponding parameters. (If convenient, obtain results on a class basis, with each individual doing his own sampling. Average the values of the various estimates obtained and compare them with the parameters.)

Exercise 7.7.2 Repeat Exercise 7.7.1 for the random model. To replace fixed effects, obtain τ_i by sampling Table 4.1 where $\mu = 40$ and $\sigma = 12$.

Arguing as in this section, consider treatment sums and the variance computed from them, and determine what the treatment mean square is estimating.

7.8 Analysis of Variance with Subsamples. Unequal Subsample Numbers

When samples have unequal subsample numbers, the basic analysis is that of Sec. 7.4; in the computations, the square of any total is divided by the number of observations in the total. For example, consider the numbers in Table 7.10. These might be observations on the product of three manufacturing plants in each of two areas, A and B, and of two plants in area C. For the 14 observations, $n = 14$, $\sum Y = 95$, $\sum Y^2 = 659$, $\sum (Y - \bar{Y})^2 = 14.36$, with 13 degrees of freedom.

Proceeding as in Sec. 7.4, we have

$$\text{Plants SS (ignoring areas)} = 6^2 + \frac{(6+8)^2}{2} + \cdots + \frac{(7+9)^2}{2} - \frac{(6+6+8+\cdots+7+9)^2}{14}$$

$$= 5.86 \qquad \text{with 7 df}$$

$$\text{Residual SS} = \text{total SS} - \text{plant SS}$$

$$= 14.36 - 5.86 = 8.50 \qquad \text{with } 13 - 7 = 6 \text{ df}$$

Table 7.10 Observations on the quality of a product made in eight manufacturing plants in three areas

Area	*A*			*B*			*C*	
Plants	I	II	III	I	II	III	I	II
Observations	6	6, 8	6, 7, 8	5, 7	6, 7	6	7	7, 9

Plant sum of squares is further partitioned into a component associated with areas and one associated with plants within areas.

$$\text{Areas SS} = \frac{(6 + 6 + \cdots + 8)^2}{6} + \frac{(5 + \cdots + 6)^2}{5} + \frac{(7 + 7 + 9)^2}{3} - C$$

$$= 4.07 \qquad \text{with 2 df}$$

$$\text{Plants within areas SS} = \text{plants SS} - \text{areas SS}$$

$$= 5.86 - 4.07 = 1.79 \qquad \text{with } 7 - 2 = 5 \text{ df}$$

The resulting analysis of variance is given in Table 7.11.

For these "data," there is no evidence that variation among plants is of a different order of magnitude than that among observations, since $F = 0.36/1.42 < 1$. In such a case, one says $s_\varepsilon^2 = 0$ rather than that it is a negative value, and especially if the degrees of freedom for experimental error are small, one may pool the two errors to obtain a new estimate of a variance suitable for testing areas. Here, the new estimate would be $(1.79 + 8.50)/(5 + 6) = 0.94$, with 11 degrees of freedom.

When unequal numbers of subsamples are involved, computation of the coefficients for the components of variance is far less obvious than when equal numbers prevail. First, let us define r_{ij} as the number of observations at the jth plant in the ith area; for example, $r_{13} = 3$. Now $r_{i\cdot}$ is the total number of observations made in the ith area; for example, $r_{1\cdot} = 1 + 2 + 3 = 6$. Finally, $r_{\cdot\cdot}$ is the total number of observations; here $r_{\cdot\cdot} = 14$. Let k equal the number of areas; here $k = 3$.

The coefficient of σ_ε^2 depends on the line in the analysis of variance. Thus for plants within areas, the coefficient of σ_ε^2 is

$$\frac{\left(r_{\cdot\cdot} - \sum_i \left(\sum_j r_{ij}^2/r_{i\cdot}\right)\right)}{\text{df (experimental error)}} \tag{7.14}$$

$$= \frac{14 - [(1^2 + 2^2 + 3^2)/6 + (2^2 + 2^2 + 1^2)/5 + (1^2 + 2^2)/3]}{5} = 1.64$$

For areas, the coefficient of σ_ε^2 is

$$\frac{\sum_i \left(\sum_j r_{ij}^2/r_{i\cdot}\right) - \left(\sum_{i,j} r_{ij}^2\right)\Big/ r_{\cdot\cdot}}{\text{df (areas)}} \tag{7.15}$$

$$= \frac{(1^2 + 2^2 + 3^2)/6 + (2^2 + 2^2 + 1^2)/5 + (1^2 + 2^2)/3 - (1^2 + \cdots + 2^2)/14}{2}$$

$$= \frac{5.8 - 2}{2} = 1.90$$

Table 7.11 Analysis of variance for "Data" of Table 7.10

Source	df	SS	MS	MS is an estimate of
Areas	2	4.07	2.03	$\sigma^2 + 1.90\sigma_\varepsilon^2 + 4.50\sigma_\tau^2$
Plants within areas = experimental error	5	1.79	0.36	$\sigma^2 + 1.64\sigma_\varepsilon^2$
Observations within plants = sampling error	6	8.50	1.42	σ^2
Total	13	14.36		

$s^2 = 1.42 \qquad s_\varepsilon^2 = \dfrac{0.36 - 1.42}{1.64} < 0$

The coefficient of σ_τ^2 is

$$\frac{r_{..} - \sum_i r_{i.}^2/r_{..}}{\text{df (areas)}} = \frac{14 - (6^2 + 5^2 + 3^2)/14}{2} = 4.50$$

When sampling error is larger than experimental error and chance appears to offer the only explanation of this fact, it is customary to estimate σ_ε^2 as zero, that is, $s_\varepsilon^2 = 0$. In the more general situation, that is, when $s_\varepsilon^2 > 0$, a real problem arises in testing areas for a $\sum \tau_i^2$ or σ_τ^2 component since no line in the analysis of variance differs from the area mean square line by some multiple of $\sum \tau_i^2$ or σ_τ^2 only. This problem arises because of the unequal subsample sizes.

An approximate solution is obtained as follows. Designate the three mean squares in Table 7.11, from the top down, as MS(A), MS(P), and MS(0), where A stands for areas and so on. Then

$$\hat{\sigma}_\varepsilon^2 = \frac{\text{MS(P)} - \text{MS(0)}}{1.64} = \frac{0.36 - 1.42}{1.64}$$

Unfortunately this is negative in our problem and sufficient reason for us not to proceed. We will act as though $\hat{\sigma}_\varepsilon^2$ were positive.

We now construct an "error term" to test areas as

$$\hat{\sigma}^2 + 1.90\hat{\sigma}_\varepsilon^2 = \text{MS(0)} + 1.90\frac{\text{MS(P)} - \text{MS(0)}}{1.64}$$

$$= \left(1 - \frac{1.90}{1.64}\right)\text{MS(0)} + \frac{1.90}{1.64}\text{MS(P)}$$

We test the null hypothesis of no differences among areas using this linear function of independent mean squares as the denominator of a synthesized F

ratio with 2 df for the numerator and an uncertain number for the denominator. This may be estimated as follows.

More generally, let MS be a linear function of independent mean squares, MS_i, with df $= f_i$, $i = 1, \ldots, k$, given by

$$\text{MS} = \sum c_i \text{MS}_i \tag{7.16}$$

An approximate number of df for the approximating χ^2 is given by Satterthwaite (7.15) as

$$\text{Effective df} = \frac{(\sum c_i \text{MS}_i)^2}{\sum [(c_i \text{MS}_i)^2/f_i]} \tag{7.17}$$

Equation (5.17) will be seen to be an application of this equation. The proper equation for the df is given by replacing each MS_i by $E(\text{MS}_i)$, but in practice these will not be available as numerical values.

Exercise 7.8.1 A method of sampling fish was given in Exercise 2.7.5. The sampling, in that case, continued throughout the afternoon. A part of the results follow. The data are frequencies of fish in various length categories. Sample designations A and B have no special significance.

Collection time†	Sample	Length categories, in							n
		3	4	5	6	7	8	9	
1 : 50	A			5	19	19	8	3	54
	B			10	27	15	6	3	61
3 : 20	A		4	11	26	10	11	3	65
	B		3	11	29	13	8	1	65
4 : 40	A	2	8	16	44	15	8		93
	B	1	6	15	35	12	7	2	78

† Data provided through the courtesy of Don Hayne, North Carolina State University.

Compute an analysis of variance of the variable length. (*Sources:* Collection times, samples within times, individuals within samples.) Test the obvious null hypotheses and discuss the results of the experiment. Comment on the unit of measurement.

7.9 Variance Components in Planning Experiments Involving Subsamples

In planning experiments which involve subsampling, the question arises about how to distribute the available time and money—in particular, whether to concentrate on many samples with few subsamples or few samples with more subsamples. The answer depends on the relative magnitude of experimental and sampling errors and on costs. Thus, getting subsamples, where the measurement is made, may involve costly chemical analyses, time-consuming procedures, or destructive tests of expensive items, whereas obtaining samples may be of trivial difficulty. On the other hand, it may be that obtaining samples may involve additional equipment, plots, animals, or expensive travel, while subsampling involves none of these. Probably the true situation will be intermediate.

Where experimental data are available, they can be used in planning future experiments. The data from the mint plant experiment reported in Tables 7.8 and 7.9 will be used to illustrate the procedure. Experimental error, the criterion for judging the significance of comparisons among treatment means, consists of two sources of variation, variation among plants treated alike, σ^2, and variation resulting from differences in the environment of pots treated alike, σ_ε^2. Both sources of variation contribute to the variance among treatment means. The estimates of σ^2 and σ_ε^2 are $s^2 = .93$ and $s_\varepsilon^2 = (2.15 - .93)/4 = .30$. Note that s_ε^2, the variation among means of similarly treated pots over and above that due to plants within pots, is greater than the variance of pot means based on the sampling error, that is, on $s^2/4 = .93/4 = .23$.

Suppose that in place of four plants per pot and three pots per treatment, there were three plants per pot and four pots per treatment, the same number of plants per treatment. Experimental error would be an estimate of $\sigma^2 + 3\sigma_\varepsilon^2$. Such an experiment should lead to an error variance of the order of

$$s^2 + 3s_\varepsilon^2 = .93 + 3(.30) = 1.83$$

with $3 \times 6 = 18$ degrees of freedom as compared with 2.15 with 12 degrees of freedom for the experiment conducted. The variance of a treatment mean is the important value to consider and this is $s_{\bar{Y}}^2 = 1.83/12 = .1525$ as compared with .1792 for the experiment as conducted. Of course, variances are sufficient to consider here where the number of plants per treatment is fixed. At times, we would want to look at plant numbers.

Table 7.12 shows $s_{\bar{Y}}^2$ for alternative allocations of 12 plants per treatment. It is clear that the variance of a treatment mean decreases as we increase the number of pots at the expense of plants within pots. Remember that only one plant per pot will not provide a way to estimate sampling error. Note also the increase in degrees of freedom for estimating experimental error.

Cost was also to be a consideration. Suppose that getting a mint plant for the experiment is inexpensive and costs .1 man-hour but that preparing the pot runs to .5 man-hour. Then the cost of setting up the original experiment is $(12 \times .1) + (3 \times .5) = 2.7$ man-hours per treatment. Clearly the cost must increase if the number of plants per pot decreases and the number of pots increases, because pots involve the greater expense. Costs for other

Table 7.12 Some variances and costs per treatment with 12 observations

Plants per pot	Pots	Experimental error df	$V(\text{Trt } \bar{Y})$	Costs† (.1, .5)	Costs† (.5, .5)	Costs† (1.0, .5)
4	3	$2t$	$2.15/12 = .1792$	2.7	7.5	13.5
3	4	$3t$	$1.83/12 = .1525$	3.2	8.0	14.0
2	6	$5t$	$1.53/12 = .1275$	4.2	9.0	15.0
1	12	$11t$	$1.23/12 = .1025$	7.2	12.0	18.0

† First figure is cost per plant in man-hours; second is cost of pot.

possible experiments with 12 plants per treatment are shown. Remember that the extra cost is accompanied by a decrease in $s_{\bar{Y}}^2$.

Other possible item costs are also considered. When the cost of getting a plant goes up to 1 man-hour, then the increase in the cost of setting up experiments with fewer plants per pot but more pots is relatively slower.

Finally, we can consider other distributions of effort. For example, we might consider two plants per pot with three pots per treatment and increase the number of treatments to twelve. This experiment would have the same number of observations with adequate degrees of freedom for estimating experimental error.

As an additional refinement, we could also introduce the idea of precision of the experiment, as discussed in Sec. 6.8.

In many cases, a fixed budget will determine the permissible amount of effort. Here one will try to allocate this effort between experimental units and sampling units so as to minimize the variance of a treatment mean. Alternatively, one may fix the variance desired and allocate to minimize the cost. (Optimum allocation is discussed in Chap. 25.) The two approaches lead to the same solution.

Cochran (7.4) gives the optimum allocation solution in

$$n_2 = \sqrt{\frac{c_1 s^2}{c_2 s_\varepsilon^2}} \tag{7.18}$$

where n_2 = number of sampling units or plants per plot
c_1 = cost of pot
c_2 = cost per plant
s^2 and s_ε^2 = values as defined in Table 7.11

Note that cost ratios and variance ratios are adequate to solve for n_2.

For $c_1 = .5$ and $c_2 = .1$,

$$n_2 = \sqrt{\frac{.5}{.1}\frac{.93}{.30}} = \sqrt{15.5} \approx 4$$

The number of sampling units used in this experiment was 4.

The investigator will need to compare costs, labor, and aims as well as efficiency in choosing among possible designs.

Exercise 7.9.1 How many degrees of freedom are available for estimating sampling error for each alternative experiment suggested in Table 7.12?

Exercise 7.9.2 Suppose that the mint plant experiment were to be conducted with six plants per pot and two pots per treatment, still the same number of plants per treatment. How many degrees of freedom will be available to estimate experimental error in a t-treatment experiment? To estimate sampling error?

Estimate $V(\text{Trt } \bar{Y})$ for this allocation. Work out costs in man-hours for setting up the experiment for each of the three cost suggestions.

Exercise 7.9.3 Repeat Exercise 7.9.2 for two plants per pot and three pots per treatment. For three plants per pot and three pots per treatment. For two plants per pot and four pots per treatment.

Exercise 7.9.4 Find the efficiencies for all suggested alternatives relative to the experiment conducted.

Exercise 7.9.5 Find n_2 for each of the cost ratios proposed in Table 7.12.

7.10 Assumptions Underlying the Analysis of Variance

In the analysis of variance where tests of significance are made, the basic assumptions are

1. Treatment and environmental effects are additive
2. Experimental errors are random, independently and normally distributed about zero mean and with a common variance

The assumption of normality is not required for estimating components of variance. When the assumption is not made, we require that the errors be uncorrelated rather than independent. In practice, we are never certain that all these assumptions hold; often there is good reason to believe some are false. Excellent discussions of these assumptions, the consequences when they are false, and remedial steps are given by Eisenhart (7.8), Cochran (7.3), and Bartlett (7.2). A brief discussion follows.

Departure from one or more of the assumptions can affect both the level of significance and the sensitivity of F or t to real departures from the null hypothesis. In the case of nonnormality, the true level of significance is usually, but not always, greater than the apparent level. This results in rejection of the null hypothesis when it is true, more often than the probability level calls for; that is, too many nonexistent significant differences are claimed. Experimenters may think they are using the 5 percent level when actually the level may be 7 or 8 percent. In some cases, a test may detect nonnormality rather than a true alternative hypothesis. Loss of sensitivity for tests of significance and estimation of effects occurs since a more powerful test could be constructed if the exact mathematical model were known. In other words, if the true distribution of errors and the nature of the effects, their additivity or nonadditivity, were known, we could construct a test better able to detect or estimate real effects.

For most types of biological data, experience indicates that the usual disturbances resulting from failure of the data to fulfill the above requirements are unimportant. Exceptional cases do occur and procedures to analyze such data will be discussed. In any case, most data do not exactly fulfill the requirements of the mathematical model, and procedures for testing hypotheses and estimating confidence intervals should be considered approximate rather than exact.

Consider the assumption that *treatment and environmental effects are additive.* As illustration, see Eq. (5.14) for meaningfully paired experimental units. A common form of nonadditivity occurs when such effects are multiplicative. Consider a simple case where two environments, called pairs in the illustration that follows, and two treatments have effects that are multiplicative. A comparison of additive and multiplicative models is given in Table 7.13, which ignores experimental errors.

For the additive model, the increase from block 1 to 2 is a fixed amount regardless of the treatment; the same is true for treatments. For the multiplicative model, the increase from block 1 to 2 is a fixed percentage regardless of the treatment; the same is true for treatments. When effects are multiplicative, the logarithms of the data exhibit the effects in additive fashion and an analysis of variance of the logarithms is appropriate. The new data, the logarithms, are called transformed data; the process of changing the data is called a *transformation.* For other types of nonadditivity, other transformations are available. Transforming data implies that experimental errors are independently and normally distributed on the transformed scale if tests of significance are planned. A test of additivity is given in Sec. 15.8.

The presence of nonadditivity in data results in an apparent heterogeneity of error due to false assumptions when no transformation is made before analysis. The components of error variance contributed by the various observations do not supply estimates of a common variance. The resulting pooled error variance may be somewhat inefficient for confidence interval estimates of treatment effects and may give false significance levels for cer-

Table 7.13 Additive and multiplicative models

Model	Additive		Multiplicative		Log (multiplicative becomes additive)	
Pair	1	2	1	2	1	2
Treatment 1	10	20	10	20	1.00	1.30
Treatment 2	30	40	30	60	1.48	1.78

tain specific comparisons of treatment means, whereas the significance level for the F test involving all treatment means may be affected very little.

Our second assumption is not independent of the first, as has been seen, and is really a set of assumptions. Consider the *independence of errors* or more generally, the assumption of zero correlations among them. For field experiments, crop responses on adjacent plots tend to be more alike than responses on nonadjacent plots; the same is also true for laboratory experiment observations made by the same person at about the same time. The result is that tests of significance may be misleading if no attempt is made to overcome the difficulty. In practice, treatments are assigned to the experimental units at random or the order of the observations is determined at random; the effect of the randomization process is to make the errors independent of each other.

In field experiments, convenient systematic designs place the same treatments adjacent to each other in all blocks. Since adjacent plots tend to be more alike, the precision of a comparison is greater for treatments falling on plots close together than for those on plots farther apart. An analysis of variance of such data gives a generalized error term too large for certain comparisons and too small for others. Appropriate error terms for individual comparisons are not available. Cochran and Cox (7.4) summarize the need for randomization very well in the following statement:

> Randomization is somewhat analogous to insurance, in that it is a precaution against disturbances that may or may not occur and that may or may not be serious if they do occur. It is generally advisable to take the trouble to randomize even when it is not expected that there will be any serious bias from failure to randomize. The experimenter is thus protected against unusual events that upset his expectations.

Experimental error must be normally distributed This assumption applies particularly to tests of significance and not to the estimation of components of variance. When the distribution of experimental errors is decidedly skewed, the error component of a treatment tends to be a function of the treatment mean. This again results in heterogeneity of the error term. If the functional relationship is known, a transformation can be found that will give errors that are more nearly normally distributed. Thus an analysis of variance can be made on the transformed data such that the error term will be essentially homogeneous. Common and useful transformations are the logarithmic, square root, and inverse sine; their use is discussed in Sec. 9.16.

Experimental errors must have a common variance For example, in a completely random design, the components of error contributed by the several treatments must all be estimates of a common population variance. Here, heterogeneity of error may result from the erratic behavior of the response to certain treatments. In experiments such as those meant to determine the effectiveness of different insecticides, fungicides, or herbicides, an untreated check may be included to measure the level of infestation and to provide a basis for determining the effectiveness of the treatments. The variation of the individual observations on the check may be considerably greater than that for the other treatments, primarily because the check may have a higher mean and, thus, a greater base for variation. In these situations the error term may not be homogeneous. A remedy is to divide the error term into homogeneous components to test specific treatment comparisons. Sometimes if the means of one or two treatments are much larger than the others and have significantly greater variation, these treatments can be excluded from the analysis.

Violation of any of the other assumptions may result in heterogeneity of experimental error. Suggestions for remedying the situation have been made and depend on the nature of the violation.

References

7.1. Anderson, R. L., and T. A. Bancroft: *Statistical theory in research*, McGraw-Hill, New York, 1952.

7.2. Bartlett, M. S.: "The use of transformations," *Biom.* **3**:39–52 (1947).

7.3. Cochran, William G.: "Some consequences when the assumptions for the analysis of variance are not satisfied," *Biom.* **3**:22–38 (1947).

7.4. Cochran, William G.: *Sampling techniques*, 2d ed., Wiley, New York, 1965.

7.4. Cochran, William G., and Gertrude M. Cox: *Experimental designs*, 2d ed., Wiley, New York, 1957.

7.5. Duncan, D. B.: "A significance test for differences between ranked treatments in an analysis of variance," *Va. J. Sci.*, **2**:171–189 (1951).

7.6. Duncan, D. B.: "Multiple range and multiple *F* tests," *Biom.*, **11**:1–42 (1955).

7.7. Dunnett, C. W.: "A multiple comparisons procedure for comparing several treatments with a control," *J. Amer. Statist. Ass.*, **50**:1096–1121 (1955).

7.8. Eisenhart, C.: "The assumptions underlying the analysis of variance," *Biom.*, **3**:1–21 (1947).

7.9. Erdman, Lewis W.: "Studies to determine if antibiosis occurs among Rhizobia: 1. Between *Rhizobium meliloti* and *Rhizobium trifolii*," *J. Amer. Soc. Agron.*, **38**:251–258 (1946).

7.10. Harter, H. L.: "Error rates and sample sizes for range tests in multiple comparisons," *Biom.*, **13**:511–536 (1957).

7.11. Hartley, H. O.: "Some recent developments in analysis of variance," *Comm. Pure Appl. Math.*, **8**:47–72 (1955).

7.12. Jordan, H. G.: "Sensory restriction and suggestion: A proposed treatment modality for selected prison inmates," Ph.D. thesis, North Carolina State University, Raleigh, NC, 1971.

7.13. Newman, D.: "The distribution of range in samples from a normal population, expressed in terms of an independent estimate of standard deviation," *Biometrika*, **31**:20–30 (1939).

7.14. Sanders, O. T., Jr.: "Effects of a polychlorinated biphenyl in mice caged at different densities and fed at different nutritional levels," Ph.D. thesis, Virginia Polytechnic Institute and State University, Blacksburg, VA, 1974.

7.15. Satterthwaite, F. E.: "An approximate distribution of estimates of variance components," *Biom.*, **2**:110–114 (1946).

7.16. Snedecor, G. W.: *Statistical methods*, 5th ed., Iowa State College Press, Ames, Iowa, 1956.

7.17. Tukey, J. W.: "The problem of multiple comparisons," Princeton University, Princeton, NJ, 1953. (Ditto.)

7.18. Wexelsen, H.: "Studies in fertility, inbreeding, and heterosis in red clover (*Trifolium pratense L.*)," *Norske videnskaps-akad. i Oslo, Mat.-Natur. klasse*, 1945.

CHAPTER

EIGHT

MULTIPLE COMPARISONS

8.1 Introduction

In Chap. 7, the F test is used to test for real treatment differences. When the null hypothesis is not rejected, it may seem that no further questions need be asked. However, consideration of the set of treatments in the mint plant experiment suggests that this is an oversimplification. Six treatments were compared. Suppose that they had been declared not significantly different. Might we not always have wondered if a real difference between temperatures had been lost by being averaged in with the other possible comparisons?

If the null hypothesis is rejected when using F, how well off is the investigator? Where are the real differences? In the mint plant experiment, should he have planned to look for possible differences due to differing night temperatures and differing hours in daylight? If such obvious questions are not suggested, it is reasonably clear that the maximum observed difference can be declared significant since H_0 was rejected. What can be said about any other differences?

With the t test, a Type I error is made in falsely rejecting a simple hypothesis about a single parameter or difference. With the F test, the hypothesis includes many parameters within an experiment; this can be viewed as the simultaneous testing of hypotheses about many differences with overall rejection dependent on one or more unspecified differences. Has our concept of a Type I error changed?

Multiple comparisons procedures and error rates are the subjects of this chapter. The main emphasis is on equal replication, but the problem of unequal replication is considered in Sec. 8.11.

8.2 The Least Significant Difference

Let us suppose that in planning the *Rhizobium* experiment of Sec. 7.3, the investigator had decided to compare treatment means for 3DOk1 and 3DOk5, 3DOk4 and 3DOk7, and 3DOk13 and composite at a 5 percent significance level using three t tests; the means are given at the foot of Table 7.1. Alternatively, the investigator could compute the smallest difference that would be declared significant and compare the absolute value of each observed difference with it. For this, the sample t would have to equal or be larger than the tabulated t value used as critical value; that is, for an α-level test against two-sided alternatives, significance will be declared when

$$\frac{|\bar{Y}_i - \bar{Y}_{i'}|}{s_{\bar{Y}_i - \bar{Y}_{i'}}} \geq t_{\alpha/2}$$

or when $|\bar{Y}_i - \bar{Y}_{i'}| \geq t_{\alpha/2}\, s_{\bar{Y}_i - \bar{Y}_{i'}}$. The test criterion for looking at differences between means directly is called the *least significant difference*, or lsd, given by

$$\begin{aligned} \text{lsd} &= t_{\alpha/2}\, s_{\bar{Y}_i - \bar{Y}_{i'}} \\ &= t_{\alpha/2}\, s\sqrt{\frac{2}{r}} \qquad \text{for equal } r \end{aligned} \tag{8.1}$$

where s is the square root of the pooled error variance. Since the lsd is calculated only once and requires the pooled error variance, its use is a convenience relative to the making of individual t tests.

For the *Rhizobium* data,

$$\text{lsd}(.05) = t_{.025}\, s_{\bar{Y}_{i\cdot} - \bar{Y}_{i'\cdot}} = 2.064\sqrt{\frac{2(11.79)}{5}} = 4.5 \text{ mg}$$

$$\text{lsd}(.01) = t_{.005}\, s_{\bar{Y}_{i\cdot} - \bar{Y}_{i'\cdot}} = 2.797\sqrt{\frac{2(11.79)}{5}} = 6.1 \text{ mg}$$

The observed differences are $\bar{Y}_{1\cdot} - \bar{Y}_{2\cdot} = 28.8 - 24.0 = 4.8$; $\bar{Y}_{3\cdot} - \bar{Y}_{4\cdot} = 14.6 - 19.9 = -5.3$; and $\bar{Y}_{5\cdot} - \bar{Y}_{6\cdot} = 13.3 - 18.7 = -5.4$ mg; all lie between 4.5 and 6.1 in absolute value, so they are significant at the 5 percent level but not at the 1 percent level. Here we have an example of the valid use of the lsd.

Tests against one-sided alternatives as discussed in Chap. 5 can also be made.

Since the lsd can be and often is misused, some statisticians hesitate to recommend it. The most common misuse is to make comparisons suggested by the data, comparisons not initially planned. A planned comparison names treatments in advance; it does not require that we wait for the results, for example, to see which treatment is associated with the largest response. The making of unplanned comparisons is often termed "testing effects suggested by the data" or "arguing after the facts." For the tabulated confidence or significance levels to be valid, the lsd should be used only for comparisons planned before the data have been examined.

Cochran and Cox (8.3) point out that in the extreme situation where the experimenter compares only the difference between the highest and lowest treatment means by use of the t test or the lsd, this difference will likely be substantial even when no effect is present. It can be shown that with three treatments, the observed value of t for the greatest difference will exceed the tabulated 5 percent level about 13 percent of the time; with six treatments the figure is 40 percent, with 10 treatments, 60 percent, and with 20 treatments, 90 percent. Thus, when experimenters think they are making a t test at the 5 percent level, they are actually testing at the 13 percent level for three treatments, the 40 percent level for six treatments, and so on.

However, the tabulated probability level for t is correct when using the lsd to make planned multiple comparisons of paired means. To see this, suppose that all assumptions required by the model are correct, that all responses attributable to treatments are equal, that is, all null hypotheses are true, and that a number of comparisons are planned. Then if the whole experiment is repeated infinitely often and each time A is asked to test only the first hypothesis, she must find that 100α percent of her differences exceed the lsd; and if each time B is asked to test only the second hypothesis, he must find 100α percent of his differences are significant; and so on. Clearly, 100α percent of all comparisons made are falsely declared significant. This would still be true if comparisons of all possible pairs of means were made. Note that no initial F test has been made; each t test within the experiment is made directly as if it were the only test and all are made with the same error variance.

The error rate has been defined by implication; the number of erroneous inferences has been compared with the number of inferences made. This is a *comparisonwise* or a *per-comparison error rate* and is really the value approached by Eq. (8.2) in repeated experimentation.

$$\text{Comparisonwise error rate } (H_0 \text{ true}) = \frac{\text{number of erroneous inferences}}{\text{number of inferences made}} \qquad (8.2)$$

Note in particular that prior to the experiment, we set out the comparisons to be made; none has been suggested by the data. Had A been asked to test the maximum observed difference, this would not have been called a planned comparison between named treatments and significance would have been declared with greater frequency than 100α percent of the time. On the other hand, a person assigned the job of testing the closest pair of means would have declared this difference to be significant with probability lower than that tabulated for t.

Confidence intervals can also be constructed and are often more useful than tests. The probability of a confidence interval containing the difference being estimated is $1 - \alpha$, so that in the long run, $(1 - \alpha)100$ percent of the confidence intervals will contain the true difference. One-sided confidence intervals can also be constructed.

In summary, use of the lsd is a valid test procedure for planned comparisons. The implied error rate is a comparisonwise one and tabulated probability levels for t are appropriate. Since the lsd need be computed only once and takes advantage of the pooled error variance, it can be a convenience relative to using multiple t tests. Many investigators consider it the most appropriate test when the comparisons are meaningfully planned in terms of the nature of the treatments but would not use it to compare all possible pairs of means.

All possible paired comparisons, meaning comparisons of all possible pairs of means, deserve attention in terms of presentation. The following suggestions can also be used with the testing procedures that follow for all possible pairs.

First, rank the means from smallest to largest, or the reverse. It can be helpful to space these in a manner approximating the differences between means.

3DOk13	3DOk4	Composite	3DOk7	3DOk5	3DOk1
13.3(1)	14.6(2)	18.7(3)	19.9(4)	24.0(5)	28.8(6)

Next list all differences and test. We find

$$(6) - (1) = 15.5 > 4.5; \text{ significant}$$
$$(6) - (2) = 14.2 > 4.5; \text{ significant}$$
$$\cdots\cdots\cdots\cdots\cdots\cdots$$
$$(6) - (5) = 4.8 > 4.5; \text{ significant}$$
$$(5) - (1) = 10.7 > 4.5; \text{ significant}$$
$$(5) - (2) = 9.4 > 4.5; \text{ significant}$$
$$\cdots\cdots\cdots\cdots\cdots\cdots$$
$$(2) - (1) = 1.3 < 4.5; \text{ not significant}$$

The pattern should be clear. As an alternative to the words "significant" and "not significant," one could use an "*" and an "ns" to convey the same information.

An obvious space-saving presentation lists the differences as in Table 8.1.

Table 8.1 Differences between nitrogen means in a *Rhizobium* experiment

	(6)	(5)	(4)	(3)	(2)
(1)	15.5*	10.7*	6.6*	5.4*	1.3
(2)	14.2*	9.4*	5.3*	4.1	
(3)	10.1*	5.3*	1.2		
(4)	8.9*	4.1			
(5)	4.8*				

Finally, Duncan (8.6) suggests the following, which may well be the currently most popular method of presentation.

13.3(1) 14.6(2) 18.7(3) 19.9(4) 24.0(5) 28.8(6)

The means are placed approximately to scale. Any two not underscored by the same line are significantly different; any two underscored by the same line are not significantly different. For example, 18.7 and 19.9 have a common underscore, so the evidence is that the two populations involved cannot be distinguished; 14.6 and 19.9 do not have a common underscore, so their populations appear to have different locations; and 28.8 stands alone, so its parent population is distinct from all others.

For this presentation, add 4.5, the lsd, to 13.3. The result is 17.8, so underscore 13.3 and 14.6 but not 18.7. To 14.6 add 4.5 and continue the process. Never use an underscore that lies completely within a longer one; the longer underscore has already declared its means to be homogeneous, that is, from a single population.

For those who wish to use the lsd to make all pairwise comparisons of means, it is sometimes recommended that a measure of conservatism be introduced by first making an F test of treatments and then proceeding only if F is significant. This procedure is often referred to as *Fisher's* (*protected*) lsd. Since F calls for us to accept or reject a hypothesis simultaneously involving all means, the unit for judging the error rate is no longer the comparison but the experiment. Such an error rate is examined in Sec. 8.4.

Carmer and Swanson (8.1 and 8.2) consider the properties of these tests and others introduced in this chapter. Their papers are concerned with the abilities of the tests to detect real differences and other matters.

Exercise 8.2.1 McDonald (8.10) studied the ability of a liberty ship artificial reef to attract and hold macrobenthic epifauna. The variables of most interest were dry weight and density as measured by the number of organisms for 400 cm^2. We look at some density data.

Density data are counts with heterogeneous variance so McDonald considered $Y = \sqrt{\text{count} + 0.5}$, a common transformation for counts (see Sec. 9.16). Eventually, one will want to perform an inverse transformation on the Y means by squaring and subtracting 0.5. These will be somewhat smaller than means of original data and thus conservative estimates of mean density.

The following ranked means were obtained for the transformed data on the family Ostreidae, oysters. Each mean is based on 12 observations; $s^2 = 10.697$ with 66 df.

Locations	Floors of holds	Starboard deck	Starboard side	Port side	Port deck	Sides of holds
Means	4.05	7.76	7.85	10.48	10.54	11.28

Compute the lsd, test all pairs of means, and present your results using Duncan's underscoring technique. Also, prepare a table such as Table 8.1. Compute corresponding inverse transformation means.

Exercise 8.2.2 Repeat Exercise 8.2.1 for the following transformed density data obtained by McDonald (8.10). These are for the family Arbaciidae, sea urchins. Each mean has 12 observations; $s^2 = 0.218$ with 66 df.

Locations	Floors of holds	Sides of holds	Starboard deck	Port deck	Starboard side	Port side
Means	0.79	0.98	1.16	1.30	1.36	1.44

Exercise 8.2.3 For the data of Exercise 7.3.1, compute the lsd, test all pairs of means, and present your results using Duncan's underscoring technique. Also, prepare a table such as Table 8.1.

Exercise 8.2.4 Consider the posttest data of Exercise 7.3.3. Compute the lsd and test all pairs of means.

8.3 Contrasts

In Sec. 8.2, the lsd is recommended for planned comparisons involving pairs of means. A more general recommendation is to use t tests for planned comparisons which involve linear functions of observations.

In Sec. 5.10, the mean and variance of a linear function of observations are given; in particular, see Eqs. (5.18), (5.19), and (5.23), applicable in the following development.

Comparisons or *contrasts*, defined by Eq. (8.3), are a subset of linear functions.

$$Q = \sum c_i Y_i \qquad \text{with } \sum c_i = 0 \tag{8.3}$$

The Y_i's may be treatment totals or means; the former are more convenient for tests, the latter for confidence interval estimation. For convenience, the c_i's are usually integers; the restriction that $\sum c_i = 0$ is essential. A contrast always has a single degree of freedom, so that a t test is appropriate but F may also be used.

Suppose that the Y_i's of Eq. (8.3) are sample means of r observations from populations with possibly different μ_i's but a common variance. Then Eqs. (5.19) and (5.23) give

$$Q = \sum c_i \bar{Y}_{i\cdot} \qquad E(Q) = \sum c_i \mu_i \qquad \sigma_Q^2 = \frac{(\sum c_i^2)\sigma^2}{r}$$

To test $H_0\colon \sum c_i \mu_i = \sum c_i \tau_i = 0$, compute t by

$$t = \frac{Q}{s_Q} = \frac{Q}{s\sqrt{(\sum c_i^2)/r}} \tag{8.4}$$

where s is the square root of the experimental error mean square and r is the number of observations per treatment. When the experimental unit is sampled, r is a multiple of the number of replications. Note that Q is an estimate of $\sum c_i \mu_i = \sum c_i \tau_i$, so that a confidence interval on this is easily constructed as $Q \pm ts_Q$.

For testing null hypotheses, it is generally more convenient to use F and to compute the numerator from treatment totals. Let Eq. (8.5) define a contrast using totals.

$$Q = \sum c_i Y_{i\cdot} \qquad \text{with } \sum c_i = 0 \tag{8.5}$$

Then $E(Q) = r \sum c_i \mu_i$ and $\sigma_Q^2 = r(\sum c_i^2)\sigma^2$. Consequently, the sum of squares and mean square, on a per-observation basis, attributable to the contrast defined in Eq. (8.5) is given by

$$\text{SS}(Q) = \text{MS}(Q) = \frac{Q^2}{r \sum c_i^2} \tag{8.6}$$

This can be used directly as the numerator of an F test with s^2 as the denominator to test $H_0\colon \sum c_i \mu_i = 0$.

Consider again the mint data of Table 7.8. Suppose that prior to the conduct of the experiment, it was decided to look at the following differences between responses:

1. Between high and low night temperatures.
2. Between 8 h and 16 h of daylight exposure. Since these are the extremes, expect the maximum difference for paired exposure means.
3. Between the average of 8 h plus 16 h and 12 h. The mean of 8 plus 16 is 12. If no response is observed in 2, a response at this stage is unlikely; the plants are not showing a differential response due to varying day length in this range. If a response is observed in 2, then a response now indicates that the rate of growth varies within the whole interval.
4. The response in 2, if real, may have components that differ in magnitude with night temperature. Consequently, we look at the difference between two differences, those between 8 h and 16 h for high and for low night temperatures.
5. What is said in 4 about 2 applies also to 3.

Number the treatments of Table 7.8 from left to right as 1[1]6. Then formally the following null hypotheses are proposed to test the above differences for significance.

1. H_0: $(\mu_4 + \mu_5 + \mu_6)/3 = (\mu_1 + \mu_2 + \mu_3)/3$, or
   H_0: $\mu_1 + \mu_2 + \mu_3 - \mu_4 - \mu_5 - \mu_6 = 0$
2. H_0: $(\mu_1 + \mu_4)/2 = (\mu_3 + \mu_6)/2$, or
   H_0: $\mu_1 - \mu_3 + \mu_4 - \mu_6 = 0$
3. H_0: $(\mu_1 + \mu_4 + \mu_3 + \mu_6)/4 = (\mu_2 + \mu_5)/2$, or
   H_0: $\mu_1 - 2\mu_2 + \mu_3 + \mu_4 - 2\mu_5 + \mu_6 = 0$
4. H_0: $\mu_1 - \mu_3 = \mu_4 - \mu_6$, or
   H_0: $\mu_1 - \mu_3 - \mu_4 + \mu_6 = 0$
5. H_0: $(\mu_1 + \mu_3)/2 - \mu_2 = (\mu_4 + \mu_6)/2 - \mu_5$, or
   H_0: $\mu_1 - 2\mu_2 + \mu_3 - \mu_4 + 2\mu_5 - \mu_6 = 0$

In 3, note that $\mu_1 - 2\mu_2 + \mu_3 = (\mu_1 - \mu_2) - (\mu_2 - \mu_3)$ is a comparison between growth in the first 4 h beyond 8, and in the second 4. Consequently it is a measure of the difference between rates of growth under low night temperature. In turn, the linear function of hypothesis 3 pools this response over both temperatures. In hypothesis 5, the difference is examined. Linear functions in hypotheses 2 and 4 are similar but simpler pooled and differential responses, respectively.

Note the linear function of μ_i's given in the second formal statement of each null hypothesis. Each function can be estimated by the same function of the $\bar{Y}_{i.}$'s. Alternatively, we estimate a multiple of each function by $Y_{i.}$'s. Each estimate is seen to be a contrast. If the estimates are denoted by $Q_1, \ldots, Q_5$, then sums of squares attributable to each contrast, on a per-observation basis, are given by Eq. (8.6) as

$$\begin{aligned}\text{SS}(Q_1) &= (44.0 + 49.5 + 62.5 - 88.0 - 77.5 - 95.0)^2/4(3)6 \\ &= (-104.5)^2/72 = 151.67 \qquad F = 70.54^{**}\end{aligned}$$

$$\begin{aligned}\text{SS}(Q_2) &= (44.0 - 62.5 + 88.0 - 95.0)^2/4(3)4 \\ &= (-25.5)^2/48 = 13.55 \qquad F = 6.30^{*}\end{aligned}$$

$$\begin{aligned}\text{SS}(Q_3) &= [44.0 - 2(49.5) + 62.5 + 88.0 - 2(77.5) + 95.0]^2/4(3)12 \\ &= (35.5)^2/144 = 8.75 \qquad F = 4.07\end{aligned}$$

$$\begin{aligned}\text{SS}(Q_4) &= (44.0 - 62.5 - 88.0 + 95.0)^2/4(3)4 \\ &= (-11.5)^2/48 = 2.76 \qquad F = 1.28\end{aligned}$$

$$\begin{aligned}\text{SS}(Q_5) &= [44.0 - 2(49.5) + 62.5 - 88.0 + 2(77.5) - 95.0]^2/4(3)12 \\ &= (-20.5)^2/144 = 2.92 \qquad F = 1.36\end{aligned}$$

Each has been tested by F, using experimental error with 12 df.

Contrast information can be conveniently presented in a table such as Table 8.2. Treatment totals are at the top of the table, contrast coefficients

Table 8.2 Contrast information for the mint data of Table 7.8

	Treatment names and totals									
	L8	L12	L16	H8	H12	H16			SS(Q) =	
Contrast	44.0	49.5	62.5	88.0	77.5	95.0	Q	$r \sum c_i^2$	$Q^2/r \sum c_i^2$	F
1	1	1	1	−1	−1	−1	−104.5	12(6)	151.67	70.54**
2	1	0	−1	1	0	−1	−25.5	12(4)	13.55	6.30**
3	1	−2	1	1	−2	1	35.5	12(12)	8.75	4.07
4	1	0	−1	−1	0	1	−11.5	12(4)	2.76	1.28
5	1	−2	1	−1	2	−1	−20.5	12(12)	2.92	1.36

Tab $F(1, 12)$: $F_{.05} = 4.75$, $F_{.01} = 9.33$

are in the body, and computations are completed at the right. Note that the only effect of a complete change of signs for any contrast is a change in the sign of Q.

It is now clear that most of the variation among treatment means is associated with high vs. low night temperatures; observation of the means or of the sign of the contrast shows growth to be greatest with the high temperature. There is also a significant difference in growth due to hours of daylight, with greater growth in the longer day. The third contrast suggests that the rate of growth is not constant as day length increases, since $F_{1,12}(.05) = 4.75$. Because there were only 12 df in error, this might be worthwhile pursuing in a future investigation.

Questions often asked at this stage are: How closely related are these meaningful comparisons? There seems to be a lot of overlap with some means used in all. Has all the available information about treatments been extracted?

Orthogonality is defined for any two contrasts in terms of the coefficients. If $Q_1 = \sum c_{1i} Y_{i\cdot}$ and $Q_2 = \sum c_{2i} Y_{i\cdot}$, then they are orthogonal if Eq. (8.7) holds.

$$\sum c_{1i} c_{2i} = 0 \tag{8.7}$$

For comparisons 1 and 2 on the mint data, we have

$$1(1) + 1(0) + 1(-1) + (-1)1 + (-1)0 + (-1)(-1) = 0$$

These comparisons are orthogonal, as are all pairs in the chosen set. Note how convenient Table 8.2 is for checking orthogonality.

In general, t treatments call for $t - 1$ df and the treatment sum of squares can be partitioned into $t - 1$ single degree of freedom components which add to this sum of squares. However, the $t - 1$ components must be derived from a set of $t - 1$ orthogonal contrasts. Such a set of contrasts may be considered to include all the information available in the data. This statement is further supported if we observe that since $\sum c_{1i} = 0 = \sum c_{2i}$, Eq. (8.7) is nothing more than the numerator of a covariance as defined in Eq. (5.27). However, it is up to the investigator to decide if the contrasts are meaningful in terms of the nature of the treatments, and if this is what is wanted from the data.

Many statisticians recommend that tests with a comparisonwise error rate be used for orthogonal contrasts.

When $\sum c_{1i} c_{2i} \neq 0$, the contrasts are not orthogonal. A nonorthogonal set of $t - 1$ single degree of freedom contrasts will not give sums of squares that add to the treatment sum of squares.

Exercise 8.3.1 Show that the five contrasts used in analyzing the mint data are pairwise orthogonal.

Exercise 8.3.2 Show that the sums of squares for the orthogonal set of contrasts illustrated do add to the treatment sum of squares.

Exercise 8.3.3 For Exercise 7.3.1, write out the coefficients required to compare "control" with each treatment. How many degrees of freedom are involved in the set? How many degrees of freedom are there for treatments? Are the contrasts orthogonal? Compute the sum of squares for each contrast. Compare the sum of the six contrast sums of squares with the treatment sum of squares.

Exercise 8.3.4 For Exercise 7.3.2, write out the coefficients for the contrast that compares "control" with the mean of all other observations. Use these coefficients in computing a sum of squares for the contrast. Compare this result with that obtained in Exercise 7.3.2.

Exercise 8.3.5 Contrasts 1, 2, and 3 when first written as formal hypotheses are clearly comparisons of two means. In 3, these do not involve equal numbers. The general procedure for finding sums of squares on a per-observation basis for unequal replication is given in Sec. 7.8. Use this procedure to show that it gives the same results as does the method of the present section.

Exercise 8.3.6 In Exercise 8.2.1, McDonald (8.10) set out to find likenesses and differences in response at various locations. Suppose he had planned to make the following contrasts:

1. Floors vs. sides of hold
2. Port vs. starboard
3. Deck vs. sides, except for holds
4. The difference between the port-vs.-starboard components, namely, those for sides and decks
5. The difference between the sides-vs.-deck components, namely, those for port and starboard

Set up a table like Table 8.2 and test the null hypothesis that the population mean for each contrast is zero. Do these contrasts constitute an orthogonal set?

Exercise 8.3.7 Repeat Exercise 8.3.6 for the sea urchin data of Exercise 8.2.2.

Exercise 8.3.8 In Exercise 7.3.3, the "treatment" is defined as combined sensory restriction and suggestion. Hence treatments 2 and 3 must be considered to be controls.

For the posttest data, two contrasts of interest might have been planned as (1) a comparison of the two controls and (2) a comparison of the "treatment" vs. the mean of the controls.

Test the null hypothesis that the population mean of each contrast is zero. Are the contrasts orthogonal? Does $SS(Q_1) + SS(Q_2) = SS(\text{Trts})$?

8.4 Testing Effects Suggested by the Data

When so little is known about the nature of treatments that one hesitates to propose meaningful comparisons, then techniques for testing effects suggested by the data are needed. Such techniques are much used in comparing all possible pairs of means, although this set can be considered a planned one. In any case, when null hypotheses are to be suggested by the data or are so inclusive as to involve many more than the number of degrees of freedom for treatments, it is recommended that considerable caution be built into the test procedure.

Perhaps the most obvious comparison suggested by the data is of the maximum vs. the minimum mean. For this, the required distribution is the range of t means, a range that has been Studentized to take care of any standard deviation. See Table A.8 heading.

Of course, if the maximum difference is found significant and other ranges within the set are seen to exceed the critical value used, they too can be cited as evidence that the corresponding population means are not homogeneous.

A comparison suggested by the data involves the experiment as the natural or conceptual base unit. This leads to an *experimentwise error rate* defined as the value approached by Eq. (8.8) in repeated experimentation.

Experimentwise error rate (H_0 true)

$$= \frac{\text{number of experiments with at least one erroneous inference}}{\text{number of experiments conducted}} \tag{8.8}$$

For an experiment in which a significant difference is declared, no matter how many additional differences are also found, a count of exactly one goes into the numerator of Eq. (8.8).

This is not the only definition of error rate alternative to comparisonwise. In particular, it must not be confused with a per-experiment error rate for which the definition is

$$\text{Per-experiment error rate } (H_0 \text{ true}) = \frac{\text{number of erroneous inferences}}{\text{number of experiments}}$$

We will not use this error rate.

For a fixed experimentwise error rate, for example, with $\alpha = .05$, the critical value must increase as the number of treatments increases. This makes it conservative or cautious when the null hypothesis is true. It also reduces its ability to detect real differences, and some investigators suggest that the 5 percent error rate, common with comparisonwise error rate tests, is too cautious. Later sections show how one test or another meets this criticism to some degree.

A true experimentwise error rate must clearly allow any and all possible hypotheses to be tested. Generally, it is desired to test only a subset or *family* of null hypotheses; the set of all possible paired comparisons is really a family, each treatment vs. control is another, and a meaningful set of contrasts such as that proposed for the mint data is also one. Usually, a single family is associated with any experiment.

If we restrict ourselves to a family of hypotheses within all those possible, a smaller critical value should be adequate. It is important, then, to have one more definition. A *familywise error rate* is defined as the value approached by

$$\text{Familywise error rate } (H_0 \text{ true}) = \frac{\text{number of families with at least one erroneous inference}}{\text{number of families tested}} \tag{8.9}$$

Again note that a per-family error rate would be defined differently.

In general, multiple comparisons procedures also have related confidence interval construction techniques. These call for all statements to be simultaneously correct with a stated family or experiment confidence coefficient. Again, the error rate is seen to be the probability that at least one component statement will be false.

8.5 Scheffé's Test

Scheffé's (8.12) method is very general in that all possible contrasts can be tested for significance or confidence intervals constructed for the corresponding linear functions of parameters. This means that infinitely many simultaneous tests are permitted, although a finite number must be made, resulting in an error rate no larger than planned; the set of confidence intervals will have a confidence coefficient at least as large as stated.

Necessarily, the test must have a large critical value for any contrast. Consequently, it is conservative in this sense, and the power may be low. Its use seems most appropriate for "data dredging"—looking at contrasts suggested by the data—as is often done in survey analyses.

The critical value for a contrast, Q, requires computation of S

$$S = \sqrt{f_t F_\alpha(f_t, f_e)} \tag{8.10}$$

where f_t and f_e are treatment and error df and F is the tabulated value for an error rate of α.

The critical value is computed by

$$\text{Scheffé's value} = Ss_Q \tag{8.11}$$

To illustrate the use of this test, consider Q_1 of Sec. 8.3. $Q_1 = -104.5$, based on totals. Each total has 12 observations, $f_t = 5, f_e = 12, s^2 = 2.15$, and $\sum c_i^2 = 6$. Consequently, $s_Q = \sqrt{6(12)2.15}$; for $\alpha = .05$, $F = 3.11$. Using Eqs. (8.10) and (8.11), we find

$$\begin{aligned}\text{Scheffé's value} &= \sqrt{5(3.11)6(12)2.15} \\ &= 49.06\end{aligned}$$

Since the observed value is numerically larger, the evidence is that the null hypothesis is false.

We may also proceed to test at $\alpha = .05$, null hypotheses about $Q_2, \ldots, Q_5$, and any other linear functions we choose, possibly only because the data themselves suggest these functions. The α level of .05 applies to the totality of hypotheses tested. In other words, if the null hypotheses are true, then all will be accepted with probability $1 - \alpha = .95$, or at least one will be falsely rejected with probability $\alpha = .05$.

Many statisticians feel that this technique overprotects against Type I errors when making orthogonal comparisons and do not recommend it in this case.

To construct a confidence interval for $\mu_1 + \mu_2 + \mu_3 - \mu_4 - \mu_5 - \mu_6$, means are appropriate so that this linear function is estimated by $-104.5/12 = -8.71$; its variance is $(\sum c_i^2)s_{\bar{Y}}^2 = 6(2.15)/12$; and the confidence interval is

$$Q(\text{using means}) \pm Ss_Q = -8.71 \pm \sqrt{\frac{5(3.11)6(2.15)}{12}} = (-12.80, -4.62)$$

Again, this and all possible confidence intervals constructed by this technique should simultaneously include the corresponding linear functions of parameters with probability at least $1 - \alpha = .95$ since there will be only a finite number constructed.

As a second and possibly more appropriate illustration, compare all possible pairs of means of the red clover nitrogen data, Table 7.1, by computing the critical value $Ss_{\bar{Y}_{i\cdot} - \bar{Y}_{i'\cdot}}$, applicable directly to differences between means. For this, $f_t = t - 1 = 5, f_e = 24, r = 5$, and $s^2 = 11.79$.

$$\begin{aligned}Ss_{\bar{Y}_{i\cdot} - \bar{Y}_{i'\cdot}} &= \sqrt{f_t F_\alpha(5, 24) s^2_{\bar{Y}_{i\cdot} - \bar{Y}_{i'\cdot}}} \\ &= \sqrt{5(2.62)2(11.79)/5} \\ &= 7.9 \text{ for } \alpha = .05\end{aligned}$$

The lsd was only 4.5.

Presentation of the test results by underscoring follows.

13.3 14.6 18.7 19.9 24.0 28.8

For $\alpha = .01$, Scheffé's critical value is 9.6 and the lsd is 6.1.

Exercise 8.5.1 For each of the remaining Q's constructed from treatment totals for the mint data, Tables 7.8 and 8.2, compute Scheffé's critical value to test the corresponding null hypothesis.

Exercise 8.5.2 For each of the linear functions of μ's constructed using the coefficients in Table 8.2, compute a confidence interval by Scheffé's method using $1 - \alpha = .95$ and also $1 - \alpha = .99$. To what does the confidence coefficient apply? When all assumptions necessary to the model are true and the five confidence intervals are correctly computed, is the confidence coefficient precisely .95 or .99?

Exercise 8.5.3 Apply both test and confidence interval procedures to the data of Exercise 7.3.1. Use $1 - \alpha = .95$.

Exercise 8.5.4 Refer to the contrasts of Exercise 8.3.6. Test the null hypotheses that the population means of the given contrasts are zero. Construct confidence intervals on the population means for these contrasts. Use Scheffé's technique with $\alpha = .05$.

Exercise 8.5.5 Repeat Exercise 8.5.4 for the sea urchin data of Exercise 8.2.2.

8.6 Tukey's *w* Procedure

Tukey's procedure (8.13) makes use of the *Studentized range* and is applicable to pairwise comparisons of means. It requires a single value for judging the significance of all differences and is thus quick and easy to use. Since only pairwise comparisons are made, the critical value is smaller than that required by Scheffé's method. All pairs of means constitute a family and error rate is familywise, as is the confidence coefficient when constructing interval estimates of differences.

The procedure consists of computing a critical value by Eq. (8.12) and applying it to differences between all pairs of means.

$$w = q_\alpha(p, f_e)s_{\bar{Y}} \tag{8.12}$$

where q_α is obtained from Table A.8, $p = t$ is the number of treatments, and f_e is error df.

For the *Rhizobium* data, $p = 6$, $f_e = 24$, $q_{.05} = 4.37$, and $s_{\bar{Y}} = \sqrt{11.79/5} = 1.54$. Consequently $w = 4.37(1.54) = 6.7$ mg. Summarizing the test results by underscoring follows.

13.3 14.6 18.7 19.9 24.0 28.8

For Scheffé's method, the critical value is 7.9 mg, but the summary is the same. In general, this will not be so.

The error rate of $\alpha = .05$ applies to the family of all paired comparisons. Thus, in repeated experimentation when all population means are equal, 5 percent of the families or sets of differences would have one or more false declarations of significance and in 95 percent of the families, no declarations of any significant difference would be made.

Tukey's w may also be used to compute a set of confidence intervals for differences. The true difference between population means estimated by $\bar{Y}_{i\cdot}$ and $\bar{Y}_{i'\cdot}$ is estimated by

$$\text{CI} = \bar{Y}_{i\cdot} - \bar{Y}_{i'\cdot} \pm w \qquad \text{for } w \text{ as in Eq. (8.12)} \tag{8.13}$$

The confidence coefficient applies to the family of intervals. With probability $1 - \alpha$, all intervals contain the $\mu_i - \mu_{i'}$ being estimated; with probability α, at least one fails to do so.

The procedure can also be generalized for linear contrasts.

Exercise 8.6.1 Compute confidence intervals for pairwise differences between means for the *Rhizobium* data. Use $1 - \alpha = .95$ and $.99$ with Tukey's w procedure.

Exercise 8.6.2 Test all pairs of means for the mint data, Table 7.8, using Tukey's w procedure and $\alpha = .05$.

When it comes to extracting information from the data, what do you think of this set of comparisons vs. the meaningful set proposed in Sec. 8.3?

Exercise 8.6.3 Using the oyster data of Exercise 8.2.1, apply Tukey's procedure to the problem of testing all pairs of means. Construct confidence intervals on the differences between all population means.

Exercise 8.6.4 Repeat Exercise 8.6.3 for the sea urchin data of Exercise 8.2.2.

8.7 Student-Newman-Keuls' or S-N-K Test

Each of the three persons named contributed to this test, but it is also referred to as the Newman-Keuls' (8.11) test, or simply Keuls' method. It is not as conservative as Tukey's test; it uses multiple ranges for testing. However, this makes it a result-guided procedure, so that it is difficult to describe the error rate. The interested reader is referred to other sources, for example, Hartley (8.15). Confidence intervals are not appropriate.

Label a set of treatment means by magnitude as $\bar{Y}_{(1)}, \ldots, \bar{Y}_{(t)}$ where $\bar{Y}_{(1)}$ is the smallest. The S-N-K test procedure begins like Tukey's test, comparing the maximum and minimum means. If the range is not significant, no further testing is done and the set of means is declared homogeneous. If this maximum difference is declared significant, it is concluded that $\mu_{(1)} \neq \mu_{(t)}$ and testing continues as though this were fact. In other words, at the next stage, test $\bar{Y}_{(1)}$ vs. $\bar{Y}_{(t-1)}$ and $\bar{Y}_{(2)}$ vs. $\bar{Y}_{(t)}$ using a test criterion for $t - 1$ means. At any stage, where a difference is not significant, testing stops and the set is declared homogeneous. Otherwise, testing continues.

The procedure is to compute a set of critical values by

$$W_p = q_\alpha(p, f_e)s_{\bar{Y}} \qquad p = t, t-1, \ldots, 2 \tag{8.14}$$

using q_α from Table A.8, $p = t =$ the full number of treatments, and $f_e =$ error df. For the *Rhizobium* data, these values follow.

p	2	3	4	5	6
$q_{.05}(p, 24)$	2.92	3.53	3.90	4.17	4.37
W_p	4.5	5.4	6.0	6.4	6.7

Note that W_6 is the single value required for Tukey's method.

A summary of the test results, using underscores, follows.

```
13.3   14.6        18.7   19.9      24.0      28.8
_______________________
       ______________________
                   ______________________
```

More declarations of significance are made than when Tukey's test is used but fewer than with the lsd.

Exercise 8.7.1 Apply the S-N-K procedure to the problem of testing all pairs of means for the oyster data of Exercise 8.2.1.

Exercise 8.7.2 Repeat Exercise 8.7.1 for the sea urchin data of Exercise 8.2.2.

Exercise 8.7.3 Apply the S-N-K method to the mint data, Table 7.8. For these treatments, do you think that testing means pairwise is as informative as testing the meaningful set of orthogonal comparisons given in Sec. 8.3?

8.8 Duncan's New Multiple-Range Test

In 1955, Duncan (8.6) developed a *new multiple range test*. This test, while not as powerful as an earlier test (8.5), has the advantage of simplicity.

It resembles the S-N-K test in that it uses multiple ranges and is result-guided. However, it is less conservative. Confidence intervals are not appropriate; the notion of confidence is replaced by that of *protection levels* against finding false significant differences at various stages of testing. Pursuit of this idea is left to the reader. The test is quite popular. Unfortunately, it has been used when planned comparisons seemed more appropriate.

The test departs from the S-N-K procedure where a constant significance level is used at all testing stages. It uses a variable level dependent on the number of means involved at any stage. The idea is that as the number of means under test increases, the smaller is the probability that they will all be alike. If $t = 2$ means, then use some generally acceptable α such as .05. However, for three means, $1 - (1 - \alpha)^2 = .0975$ for $\alpha = .05$ is suggested; for four means, use $1 - (1 - \alpha)^3 = .14$; ...; for t means, use $1 - (1 - \alpha)^{t-1}$.

Table A.7 is accordingly constructed from the Studentized range distribution.

The test procedure is illustrated for the *Rhizobium* data, Table 7.1, and proceeds like the S-N-K test but uses Table A.7. Begin by computing *least significant ranges* R_p by

$$R_p = q_{\alpha'} s_{\bar{Y}} \qquad \alpha' = 1 - (1 - \alpha)^{p-1} \qquad p = 2, 3, \ldots, t \tag{8.15}$$

p	2	3	4	5	6
$q_{\alpha'}(p, 24)$	2.92	3.07	3.15	3.22	3.28
R_p	4.5	4.7	4.9	5.0	5.1

A summary of the test results, using underscores, follows.

13.3 14.6 18.7 19.7 24.0 28.8

The results are seen to be the same as when the lsd is used, although this will not always be so. Note that for $p = 2$, the critical value is the same as for the lsd and for the S-N-K test.

Exercise 8.8.1 Apply Duncan's new multiple range test to the problem of testing all pairs of means for the oyster data of Exercise 8.2.1.

Exercise 8.8.2 Repeat Exercise 8.8.1 for the sea urchin data of Exercise 8.2.2.

Exercise 8.8.3 Apply Duncan's test to the means for the mint data, Table 7.8. For these treatments, do you think Duncan's procedure is as informative as making the set of meaningful comparisons in Sec. 8.3?

Exercise 8.8.4 Apply Duncan's test, making pairwise comparison of the means computed in Exercise 7.3.1.

8.9 Comparing All Means with a Control

The objective of an experiment is sometimes to locate treatments which are different or better than some standard, but not to compare them; comparison is left for a later experiment. Such a family of comparisons, that is, control against each treatment, is not an independent set but one worthy of special consideration. By restricting comparisons to this family, the resulting technique should call for a smaller critical value than Tukey's test.

Dunnett's (8.8) procedure requires a single value for judging the significance of observed differences between each treatment and control. Table A.9 is available for comparisons against one- and two-sided alternatives. Error rate is familywise and confidence intervals can be constructed.

The procedure is now applied to the *Rhizobium* data with the composite as a standard or control.

Consider the *Rhizobium* data means as p treatment means and a control with p comparisons to be made. Enter Table A.9 for the appropriate set of alternatives and error rate, with the number of treatments, p, and error degrees of freedom f_e, and extract a Dunnett t value. For the illustration, each comparison is to be two-tailed with $\alpha = .05$, $p = 5$, and $f_e = 24$. The critical value is given by

$$\begin{aligned} d' &= t(\text{Dunnett})s_{\bar{Y}_{i\cdot} - \bar{Y}_{i'\cdot}} \\ &= 2.76\sqrt{2(11.79)/5} = 5.99 \text{ mg}, \end{aligned} \tag{8.16}$$

for the example. The only difference to be declared significant is that between 3DOk1 and the composite. The procedures of Tukey, S-N-K, and Duncan also declared this difference to be significant, although each required a different value for judging significance. The S-N-K method has the difference between 3DOk13 and the composite significant when only one decimal point is used. Duncan's method also declares the differences between 3DOk13 and the composite and between 3DOk5 and the composite to be significant; they are close to being significant by Dunnett's procedure. Dunnett's critical value is smaller than that for Tukey's procedure where the family contains more contrasts.

Note that Eq. (8.16) calls for $s_{\bar{Y}_{i} - \bar{Y}_{i'}}$, so that a $\sqrt{2}$ is required. Tests based on the distribution of the range call for $s_{\bar{Y}}$.

Simultaneous confidence intervals, that is, intervals included simultaneously under a single confidence coefficient, for true differences, $\mu_i - \mu_0$, are given by Eqs. (8.17) and (8.18).

$$\text{CI} = (\bar{Y}_{i\cdot} - \bar{Y}_{0\cdot}) \pm ts\sqrt{\frac{2}{r}} \tag{8.17}$$

where $\bar{Y}_{0\cdot}$ is the control mean and t is from Dunnett's two-sided comparisons table, for a two-sided interval.

$$\text{CI} = (\bar{Y}_{i\cdot} - \bar{Y}_{0\cdot}) - ts\sqrt{\frac{2}{r}},\ \infty \tag{8.18}$$

where t is from the one-sided comparisons table, Table A.9A. For a one-sided interval, we state that the true $\mu_i - \mu_0$ is at least as large as the value computed by Eq. (8.18). The symbol ∞ indicates that there is no finite endpoint on the right. When values smaller than the control represent better performance, replace $\bar{Y}_{i\cdot} - \bar{Y}_{0\cdot}$ by $\bar{Y}_{0\cdot} - \bar{Y}_{i\cdot}$ for a more appealing presentation of the results.

The confidence coefficient covers the family of statements. All intervals contain the corresponding true differences simultaneously with probability $1 - \alpha$.

Exercise 8.9.1 Apply Dunnett's test procedure to the data of Exercise 7.3.1. Test against two-sided alternatives. Construct a set of simultaneous confidence intervals by Eq. (8.17).

Exercise 8.9.2 Presuming that the investigator might have expected decreased response due to treatments in Exercise 7.3.1, apply Dunnett's test procedure against one-sided alternatives. Construct a set of simultaneous confidence intervals for all differences between treatments and control. For your construction, what do you state about where the true differences lie with respect to the values you have computed?

Exercise 8.9.3 Apply Dunnett's test procedure to the data of Exercise 7.3.3. Use treatment 1 as Dunnett's "control." Treatment 1 is being compared with two treatments, 2 and 3, described by Jordan (7.12) as controls. Since treatment 1 was intended to reduce the T scores, carry out an appropriate one-sided test and construct one-sided confidence intervals. Use $\alpha = .05$, $1 - \alpha = .95$.

Exercise 8.9.4 Apply Dunnett's test procedure to the mint data, Table 7.8. Use "low temperature, 8 h" as control. Presumably, an investigator familiar with the material would expect this treatment to give the least response. Make one-sided tests with $\alpha = .05$ and construct confidence intervals with $1 - \alpha = .95$.

8.10 Waller-Duncan's Bayesian *k*-ratio *t* Test

Duncan's (8.7) interest in multiple comparisons procedures has continued through several approaches. The test in this section is the one he hopes will replace others intended for pairwise comparisons. A thorough presentation of this approach and solution requires considerable effort, so we can give it only scant treatment. Interval estimates can be computed but are not illustrated here; see Ref. 8.4.

First, a significance level is not involved. Instead, a *Type I to Type II error seriousness* or *error weight* is chosen. This would be difficult for most of us; we are advised that k ratios of 50 : 1, 100 : 1, and 500 : 1 may be considered, in a loose sense, to take the place of $\alpha = .10, .05$, and $.01$. Table A.21 contains minimum-average risk t values for $k = 100$. These are the only such values presented here.

The table is entered on the basis of the value for the F test of treatments. For illustration, refer to the *Rhizobium* data of Table 7.1 where the F value is 14.37. Almost certainly, interpolation will be required; here, tabulated F's of 10.00 and 25.0 are given. These parts of the table are entered with $q = f_t =$ treatment df and $f = f_e =$ error df; $q = 5$ and $f = 24$. Tabulated *minimum average risk t values* are 1.96 for $F = 10.0$ and 1.88 for $F = 25.0$. The footnote tells us to interpolate on b, a value given with F; for $F = 10.0$, $b = 1.054$ and for $F = 25.0$, $b = 1.021$. The sample or experiment b is $b = [F/(F - 1)]^{1/2} = (14.37/13.37)^{1/2} = 1.037$. Interpolation to obtain the required t calls for $1.96 - 1.88$ to be to $1.054 - 1.021$ as $1.96 - t$ is to $1.054 - 1.037$; or

$$t = 1.96 - \frac{1.96 - 1.88}{1.054 - 1.021}(1.054 - 1.037) = 1.92$$

The critical value or LSD is given by Eq. (8.19). Note the use of capitals to distinguish from the lsd of Sec. 8.2.

$$\begin{aligned} \text{LSD} &= ts_{\bar{Y}_{i\cdot}-\bar{Y}_{i'\cdot}} \\ &= 1.92\sqrt{2(11.79)/5} = 4.2 \text{ mg} \end{aligned} \qquad (8.19)$$

for the example. The lsd (.05) was found to be 4.5 mg.

Summarizing the test results by underscoring gives

```
13.3   14.6          18.7   19.9          24.0          28.8
-------------
       --------------------
                     -------------
                            --------------------
```

The results are seen to be the same as when the lsd and Duncan's new multiple range test are used. This need not have been so. No significance level applies in this Waller-Duncan procedure (8.14).

Exercise 8.10.1 Apply the Waller-Duncan procedure for testing paired means to the oyster data of Exercise 8.2.1.

Exercise 8.10.2 Apply the Waller-Duncan procedure for testing paired means to the sea urchin data of Exercise 8.2.2.

Exercise 8.10.3 Apply the Waller-Duncan procedure for testing paired means to the weight data of Exercise 7.3.1.

Exercise 8.10.4 Apply the Waller-Duncan procedure for testing paired means to the mint data, Table 7.8.

Exercise 8.10.5 Review all multiple comparisons test procedures for comparing all pairs of means. Compare conclusions for those sets of data where you have used more than one procedure.

8.11 Testing Unequally Replicated Means

The problem of testing single degree of freedom contrasts can become inconvenient when there is variable replication. If it is desired to make such tests, the following procedures, primarily for paired means, are suggested.

For the lsd Compute $s_{\bar{Y}_{i\cdot}-\bar{Y}_{i'\cdot}}$ as

$$s_{\bar{Y}_{i\cdot}-\bar{Y}_{i'\cdot}} = \sqrt{s^2\left(\frac{1}{r_i}+\frac{1}{r_{i'}}\right)} = \sqrt{s^2\frac{r_i+r_{i'}}{r_i r_{i'}}} \qquad (8.20)$$

Now lsd $= ts_{\bar{Y}_{i\cdot}-\bar{Y}_{i'\cdot}}$, where t is Student's t for the chosen significance level and error degrees of freedom and r_i and $r_{i'}$ are the numbers of observations in the two means being compared. Also $s_{\bar{Y}_{i\cdot}-\bar{Y}_{i'\cdot}}$ may be used for computing confidence intervals. This procedure is statistically sound.

For contrasts Let $Y_{i\cdot}$ be the total of the ith treatment with r_i observations. A contrast, using totals, is defined by

$$Q = \sum c_i Y_{i\cdot} = \sum r_i c_i \bar{Y}_{i\cdot} \qquad \text{with } \sum r_i c_i = 0 \tag{8.21}$$

Now $E(Q) = \sum r_i c_i \mu_i$ and $\sigma_Q^2 = (\sum r_i c_i^2)\sigma^2$. To test $H_0\colon \sum r_i c_i \mu_i = 0$, use

$$t = \frac{Q}{s_Q} = \frac{Q}{s\sqrt{\sum r_i c_i^2}} \tag{8.22}$$

When using F, Q^2 requires a divisor of $\sum r_i c_i^2$ to be on a per-observation basis.

Any two contrasts, $\sum c_{1i} Y_{i\cdot}$ and $\sum c_{2i} Y_{i\cdot}$, are said to be orthogonal when

$$\sum r_i c_{1i} c_{2i} = 0 \tag{8.23}$$

Otherwise they are not orthogonal.

For Scheffé's test No special treatment is needed because it was defined for contrasts and these have just been generalized.

For Tukey's w procedure Obtain a value $w' = q_\alpha(p, f_e)s$ similar to Eq. (8.12) but with s replacing $s_{\bar{Y}}$. For any desired comparison, multiply w' by the value

$$\sqrt{\frac{1}{2}\left(\frac{1}{r_i} + \frac{1}{r_j}\right)} \tag{8.24}$$

The validity of this procedure has not been verified.

For the S-N-K test Obtain values $W'_p = q_\alpha(p, f_e)s$ similar to Eq. (8.14). For any desired comparison, multiply by the appropriate value given by Eq. (8.24). The validity of this procedure has not been verified.

For Duncan's new multiple range test Obtain significant Studentized ranges and multiply by s rather than $s_{\bar{Y}}$ to give a set of intermediate significant ranges. For any desired comparison, multiply the appropriate intermediate value by the necessary quantity computed by Eq. (8.24).

Kramer (8.9) has proposed this procedure for unequally replicated treatments; its validity has not been verified.

For Dunnett's procedure Obtain t's where t is from Dunnett's table. For any desired comparison, multiply by

$$\sqrt{\frac{1}{r_i}+\frac{1}{r_{i'}}}$$

The validity of this procedure has not been verified.

Exercise 8.11.1 Make pairwise comparisons of the means for the posttest data in Exercise 7.4.2 (including data of Exercise 7.3.3) using
(*a*) The lsd
(*b*) Scheffé's test
(*c*) Tukey's w test
(*d*) The S-N-K test
(*e*) Duncan's test
(*f*) Dunnett's test (using treatment 1 as control and test against the appropriate one-sided alternatives, which call for a reduced score with 1)

Exercise 8.11.2 Make pairwise comparisons of the means for the data of Exercise 7.4.1 using the procedures listed in Exercise 8.11.1.

For Dunnett's test, use F_1 as control and test against the appropriate one-sided alternatives.

Exercise 8.11.3 Suppose that we can take 20 observations to test the null hypothesis of no difference between the means of two populations with a common variance.

What will be the variance of the difference between the means if we take 10 observations from each population? If you take 12 from the first and 8 from the second? 15 and 5, respectively? 18 and 2, respectively? How many df do you have to estimate σ^2 in each case?

What conclusion can you draw from your computations? [This argument concerning optimum allocation of observations does not apply to the treatment-vs.-control problem. See Dunnett (8.8).]

References

8.1. Carmer, S. G., and M. R. Swanson: "An evaluation of ten pairwise multiple comparison procedures by Monte Carlo methods," *J. Amer. Statist. Ass.*, **68:**66–74 (1973).
8.2. Carmer, S. G., and M. R. Swanson: "Detection of differences between means: A Monte Carlo study of five pairwise multiple comparison procedures," *Agron. J.* **63:**940–945 (1971).
8.3. Cochran, William G., and Gertrude M. Cox: *Experimental designs*, 2d ed., Wiley, New York, 1957.
8.4. Dixon, Dennis O., and David B. Duncan: "Minimum Bayes risk t-intervals for multiple comparisons," *J. Amer. Statist. Ass.*, **70:**822–831 (1975).
8.5. Duncan, D. B.: "A significance test for differences between ranked treatments in an analysis of variance," *Va. J. Sci.*, **2:**171–189 (1951).
8.6. Duncan, D. B.: "Multiple range and multiple F tests," *Biom.*, **11:**1–42 (1955).
8.7. Duncan, D. B.: "t tests and intervals for comparisons suggested by the data," *Biom.*, **31:**339–359 (1975).
8.8. Dunnett, C. W.: "A multiple comparisons procedure for comparing several treatments with a control," *J. Amer. Statist. Ass.*, **50:**1096–1121 (1955).

8.9. Kramer, C. Y.: "Extension of multiple range tests to group means with unequal numbers of replication," *Biom.*, **12**:307–310 (1956).
8.10. McDonald, Michael E.: "The standing crop, distribution, and production of the macrobenthic epifauna on an artificial reef off the coast of North Carolina," M.S. thesis, North Carolina State University, Raleigh, NC, 1978.
8.11. Newman, D.: "The distribution of range in samples from a normal population, expressed in terms of an independent estimate of standard deviation," *Biometrika*, **31**:20–30 (1939).
8.12. Scheffé, Henry: *The analysis of variance*, Wiley, New York, 1959.
8.13. Tukey, J. W.: "The problem of multiple comparisons," Princeton University, Princeton, NJ, 1953. (Ditto.)
8.14. Waller, Roy A., and David B. Duncan: "A Bayes rule for the symmetric multiple comparisons problem," *J. Amer. Statist. Ass.*, **64**:1484–1503 (1969).
8.15. Hartley, H. O.: "Some recent developments in analysis of variance," *Comm. Pure Appl. Math.*, **8**:47–72 (1955).

CHAPTER
NINE
ANALYSIS OF VARIANCE II: MULTIWAY CLASSIFICATIONS

9.1 Introduction

The completely random design is appropriate when no sources of variation, other than treatment effects, are known or can be anticipated. In many situations it is known beforehand that certain experimental units, if treated alike, will behave differently. For example, in field experiments, adjacent plots usually are more alike in response than those some distance apart; likewise, heavier animals in a group of the same age may exhibit a different rate of gain than lighter animals; also, observations made on a particular day or using a certain piece of equipment may resemble each other more than those made on different days or using different equipment. In such situations, where the behavior of individual units may be anticipated in part and the units classified accordingly, designs or layouts can be constructed such that the portion of the variability attributable to the recognized source can be measured and thus excluded from the experimental error; at the same time, differences among treatment means will contain no contribution attributable to the recognized source. In Chap. 5, this principle was used in the comparison of two treatments with paired observations.

This chapter deals with the analysis of variance where two or more criteria of classification are used. Analyses for the randomized complete block and Latin square designs are given. In addition, interaction is defined and the use of transformations is discussed.

9.2 The Randomized Complete Block Design

This design may be used when the experimental units can be meaningfully grouped, the number of units in a group being equal to the number of treatments generally. Such a group is called a *block* or *replication*. The object of grouping is to have the units in a block as uniform as possible so that observed differences will be largely due to treatments. Variability among units in different blocks will be greater, on the average, than variability among units in the same block if no treatments are to be applied. Ideally, the variability among experimental units is controlled so that the variation among blocks is maximized while the variation within is minimized. Variability among blocks clearly does not affect differences among treatment means, since each treatment appears the same number of times in every block.

In field experiments, each block usually consists of a compact, nearly square, group of plots. Likewise, in many animal experiments the individual animals are placed in outcome groups or blocks on the basis of such characteristics as initial weight, condition of the animal, breed, sex, or age, as stage of lactation and milk production in dairy cattle, and as litter in hogs.

During the course of the experiment all units in a block must be treated as uniformly as possible in every respect other than treatment. Any changes in technique or other condition that might affect results should be made on the complete block. For example, if harvesting of field plots is spread over a period of time, all plots of any one block should be harvested the same day. Also, if different individuals make observations on the experimental material and if there is any likelihood that observations made on the same plot will differ from individual to individual, and if only one observation is to be made on each experimental unit, then one individual should make all the observations in a block. Again, if the number of observations per unit equals the number of observers, then each observer should make one observation per unit. These practices help control variation within blocks, and thus experimental error; at the same time, they contribute nothing to differences among treatment means. Variation among blocks is arithmetically removed from experimental error.

Note the balance that exists in this design. Each observation is classified according to the block containing the experimental unit and the treatment applied, giving a two-way classification. Each treatment appears an equal number of times, usually once, in each block and each block contains all treatments. Blocks and treatments are orthogonal to one another. It is this property that leads to the very simple arithmetic involved in the analysis of the resulting data. This design is used more frequently than any other design and if it gives satisfactory precision, there is no point in using an alternative.

Randomization When the experimental units have been assigned to blocks, they are numbered in some convenient manner. Treatments are also numbered and then randomly assigned to the units within any block. A new randomization is carried out for each block.

The actual procedure may be one of those given in Sec. 7.2. For example, if we have eight treatments, we obtain 8 three-digit numbers and observe their ranks. The ranks are considered to be a random permutation of the numbers 1, ..., 8. For example, we might obtain 1, 8, 7, 5, 4, 6, 2, 3 as the random permutation. Now treatment 1 is applied to unit 1, treatment 8 to unit 2, ..., treatment 3 to unit 8. Alternatively, we could apply treatment 1 to unit 1, treatment 2 to unit 8, ..., treatment 8 to unit 3. The other randomization procedures of Sec. 7.2 are as easily generalized.

The randomized complete block design has many advantages over other designs. It is usually possible to group experimental units into blocks so that more precision is obtained than with the completely random design. There is no restriction on the number of treatments or blocks. If extra replication is desired for certain treatments, these may be applied to two or more units per block with appropriate randomization to give a generalized randomized block design. Designs that include unreplicated treatments are also possible; see Federer (9.26). The statistical analysis of the data is simple. If, as a result of mishap, the data from a complete block or for certain treatments are unusable, these data may be omitted without complicating the analysis. If data from individual units are missing, they can be estimated easily so that arithmetic convenience is not lost. If the experimental error is heterogeneous, unbiased components applicable to testing specific comparisons can be obtained.

The chief disadvantage of randomized complete blocks is that when the variation among experimental units within a block is large, a large error term results. This frequently occurs when the number of treatments is large; thus it may not be possible to secure sufficiently uniform groups of units for blocks. In such situations, other designs to control a greater proportion of the variation are available.

9.3 Analysis of Variance for any Number of Treatments; Randomized Complete Block Design

A symbolic summary of the working and definition formulas for the sums of squares and degrees of freedom in the analysis of variance of data from the randomized complete block design is given in Table 9.1.

Let Y_{ij} be the observation from the jth block on the ith treatment, $i = 1$, ..., t treatments and $j = 1, \ldots, r$ blocks. Dot notation is used wherever possible. Thus $\sum_j Y_{.j}^2$ means obtain sums

$$Y_{.j} = \sum_i Y_{ij}$$

for each value of j, square them, and add them for all values of j. Represent the grand mean by $\bar{Y}_{..}$. Since the variance of means of n observations is σ^2/n,

Table 9.1 Formulas for the analysis of variance for t treatments arranged in a randomized complete block design of r blocks

Source of variation	df	Sums of squares: Definition	Sums of squares: Working
Blocks	$r - 1$	$t \sum_j (\bar{Y}_{.j} - \bar{Y}_{..})^2 =$	$\dfrac{\sum_j Y_{.j}^2}{t} - C$
Treatments	$t - 1$	$r \sum_i (\bar{Y}_{i.} - \bar{Y}_{..})^2 =$	$\dfrac{\sum_i Y_{i.}^2}{r} - C$
Error	$(r - 1)(t - 1)$	$\sum_{i,j} (Y_{ij} - \bar{Y}_{.j} - \bar{Y}_{i.} + \bar{Y}_{..})^2 =$	SS(Total) − SS(Blocks) − SS(Treatments)
Total	$rt - 1$	$\sum_{i,j} (Y_{ij} - \bar{Y}_{..})^2 =$	$\sum_{i,j} Y_{ij}^2 - C$

multipliers of t and r shown in the definition SS column result in all mean squares being estimates of the same σ^2 when there are no block or treatment effects. The same reasoning, based on totals, accounts for the divisors t and r in the working SS column.

Table 9.2 gives the oil content of Redwing flaxseed in percent for plots located at Winnipeg and inoculated, using several techniques, with spore suspensions of *Septoria linicola*, the organism causing pasmo in flax. The data were reported by Sackston and Carson (9.16). The original data have been coded by subtracting 30 from each observation. One might further code by multiplying each number by 10 to eliminate decimal points; however, coding without multiplication requires no decoding of variances or standard deviations. Note that sums of squares computed in two directions provide a check on the computation of the total sum of squares.

In detail, the computations proceed as follows.

Step 1 Arrange the raw data as in Table 9.2. Obtain treatment totals $Y_{i.}$, block totals $Y_{.j}$, and the grand total $Y_{..}$. Simultaneously obtain $\sum Y^2$ for each treatment and block, that is,

$$\sum_j Y_{ij}^2 \qquad i = 1, \ldots, t$$

$$\sum_i Y_{ij}^2 \qquad j = 1, \ldots, r$$

Obtain the grand total by summing treatment totals and block totals

Table 9.2 Oil content of Redwing flaxseed inoculated at different stages of growth with *S. linicola*, Winnipeg, 1947, in percent

Original observation = 30 + tabled observation

Treatment (stage when inoculated)	Block 1	2	3	4	Treatment totals $Y_{i\cdot}$	$\sum_j Y_{ij}^2$	Decoded treatment means
Seedling	4.4	5.9	6.0	4.1	20.4	106.98	35.1
Early bloom	3.3	1.9	4.9	7.1	17.2	88.92	34.3
Full bloom	4.4	4.0	4.5	3.1	16.0	65.22	34.0
Full bloom (1/100)	6.8	6.6	7.0	6.4	26.8	179.76	36.7
Ripening	6.3	4.9	5.9	7.1	24.2	148.92	36.0
Uninoculated	6.4	7.3	7.7	6.7	28.1	198.43	37.0
Block totals $Y_{\cdot j}$	31.6	30.6	36.0	34.5	132.7		35.5
Block totals $\sum_i Y_{ij}^2$	176.50	175.28	223.36	213.09		788.23	

Analysis of variance

Source of variation	df	SS	MS	F
Blocks	$r - 1 = 3$	3.14	1.05	
Treatments	$t - 1 = 5$	31.65	6.33	4.83**
Error	$(r - 1)(t - 1) = 15$	19.72	1.31	
Total	$rt - 1 = 23$	54.51		

separately. Simultaneously obtain the sum of squares of these totals. These are not shown in Table 9.2, with 788.23 being

$$\sum_{i,j} Y_{ij}^2$$

Step 2 Obtain (adjusted) sums of squares as follows.

$$\text{Correction term} = C = \frac{Y_{\cdot\cdot}^2}{rt} \tag{9.1}$$

$$= \frac{(132.7)^2}{24} = 733.72$$

$$\text{Total SS} = \sum_{i,j} Y_{ij}^2 - C \tag{9.2}$$

$$= 106.98 + \cdots + 198.43 - 733.72 = 54.51$$

or $$= 176.50 + \cdots + 213.09 - 733.72 = 54.51$$

$$\text{Block SS} = \frac{\sum_j Y_{\cdot j}^2}{t} - C \tag{9.3}$$

$$= \frac{31.6^2 + \cdots + 34.5^2}{6} - 733.72 = 3.14$$

$$\text{Treatment SS} = \frac{\sum_i Y_{i\cdot}^2}{r} - C \tag{9.4}$$

$$= \frac{20.4^2 + \cdots + 28.1^2}{4} - 733.72 = 31.65$$

$$\text{Error SS} = \text{total SS} - \text{block SS} - \text{treatment SS} \tag{9.5}$$

$$= 54.51 - 3.14 - 31.65 = 19.72$$

The F value for testing the null hypothesis of no treatment differences is $6.33/1.31 = 4.83^{**}$ with 5 and 15 degrees of freedom. It is significant at the 1 percent level. This is evidence that there are real differences among the treatment means. To determine where the differences lie, general procedures such as discussed in Chap. 8 can be used. The appropriate procedure will be determined by the questions initially posed by the experimenter. Other procedures are discussed in Chap. 15.

The sample standard error of the difference between two equally replicated treatment means is given by $s_{\bar{Y}_{i\cdot} - \bar{Y}_{i'\cdot}} = \sqrt{2s^2/r}$. In this formula, s^2 is error mean square and r is the number of blocks. For the data of Table 9.2, $s_{Y_{i\cdot} - Y_{i'\cdot}} = \sqrt{2(1.31)/4} = 0.81$ percent oil where percent of oil is the unit of measurement. The coefficient of variability is $\text{CV} = s(100)/\bar{Y}_{\cdot\cdot} = 1.14(100)/35.5 = 3.2$ percent, where percent no longer refers to the unit of measurement. If certain treatments receive extra replication, the formula is given by $s_{\bar{Y}_{1\cdot} - \bar{Y}_{2\cdot}} = \sqrt{s^2(1/r_1 + 1/r_2)}$. Extra replication in a randomized complete block experiment implies that any treatment appears an equal number of times in all replications, the number varying from treatment to treatment; r_1 and r_2 will be multiples of r.

The variation among blocks may also be tested. It is not significant in our example. The F test of blocks is valid but requires care in its interpretation. In most experiments, the null hypothesis of no differences among blocks is of no particular concern since blocks are an acknowledged source of variation—often, on the basis of past experience, expected to be large. In some experiments, blocks may measure differences in the order of performing a set of operations, in pieces of equipment, in individuals, etc. In such cases, the F test of blocks may have special meaning.

If block effects are significant, it indicates that the precision of the experiment has been increased by use of this design relative to the use of the completely random design. In fact, gain in efficiency may be of more interest than the result of a test of significance; efficiency is discussed in Sec. 9.7.

Also, the scope of an experiment may have been increased when blocks are significantly different since the treatments have been tested over a wider range of experimental conditions. A word of caution should be injected here: if block differences are very large, the problem of heterogeneity of error may exist. This problem is discussed in Secs. 7.10, 9.5, and 9.16. If block effects are small, it indicates either that the experimenter was not successful in reducing error variance by grouping of the individual units or that the units were essentially homogeneous to start.

Exercise 9.3.1 Tucker et al. (9.18) determined the effect of washing and removing excess moisture by wiping or by air current on the ascorbic acid content of turnip greens. The data in milligrams per 100 g dry weight are shown in the accompanying table.

Treatment	Block				
	1	2	3	4	5
Control	950	887	897	850	975
Washed and blotted dry	857	1,189	918	968	909
Washed and dried in air current	917	1,072	975	930	954

Carry out an analysis of variance of these data. Use Dunnett's procedure to test differences between the control and treatment means. What error rate applies?

As an alternative to Dunnett's procedure, the investigator might wish to compare

1. Control vs. the mean of the other two treatments
2. The two washing treatments

Set up the necessary contrasts. Write out formally the implied null hypotheses. Are the contrasts orthogonal? Test the null hypotheses. What sort of error rate applies? Compare the sum of the sums of squares with the treatment sum of squares. Be sure sums of squares are on a per-observation basis.

Another alternative would be to test the two preceding hypotheses simultaneously. Make these tests using Scheffé's procedure. What sort of error rate applies? Construct joint confidence intervals for the two linear functions implied by the tests; what are these linear functions? To what does the confidence coefficient apply?

Exercise 9.3.2 Bing (9.4) compared the effect of several herbicides on the spike weight of gladiolus. The average weight per spike in ounces is given below for four treatments.

Treatment	Block			
	1	2	3	4
Check	1.25	1.73	1.82	1.31
2.4-D TCA	2.05	1.56	1.68	1.69
DN/Cr	1.95	2.00	1.83	1.81
Sesin	1.75	1.93	1.70	1.59

Analyze the data. Use Dunnett's procedure to test differences between check and each treatment mean. Construct a set of confidence intervals for these three differences. To what does the $1 - \alpha$ apply?

Suppose that the investigator wishes to compare check with the mean of the other three treatments. What is the necessary contrast? Write formally the null hypothesis that is to be tested. What is the sum of squares, on a per-observation basis, attributable to this contrast? Test the null hypothesis.

Test the null hypothesis that the three treatment means other than check are a homogeneous set. To do this, compute the sum of squares among these three treatments; it will have 2 df and must be on a per-observation basis. Experimental error mean square is an appropriate divisor for the F test.

Sum the sums of squares and degrees of freedom for the check-vs.-non-check and among-non-checks comparisons. Compare this sum with the treatment sum of squares.

Exercise 9.3.3 The data of Table 5.5 are in a two-way classification with each line being a block involving two halves of the same red clover head.

Analyze these data by the procedures of this chapter. Do you reach the same conclusion about the null hypothesis? Is MS(Error) the same as in the Chap. 5 illustration? Is one error an integral multiple of the other? How do you account for this?

Note that the error term in the illustration was measured as the variability among the differences in response to the two treatments in the same block or as the failure of the differential responses to treatments to be alike. Keep this in mind when reading Sec. 9.4.

Exercise 9.3.4 Repeat Exercise 9.3.3 with the data of Exercise 5.7.1. With the data of Exercise 5.7.2.

Exercise 9.3.5 Linthurst conducted a greenhouse experiment on the growth of *Spartina alterniflora*, an ecologically important salt marsh plant species, to evaluate the effects of salinity, nitrogen, and aeration. The variable reported here is biomass, the dried weight of all aerial plant material.

	Treatment											
Block	1	2	3	4	5	6	7	8	9	10	11	12
1	11.8	18.8	21.3	83.3	8.8	26.2	20.4	50.2	2.2	8.8	1.4	25.8
2	8.1	15.8	22.3	25.3	8.1	19.5	8.5	47.7	3.3	7.6	15.3	22.6
3	22.6	37.1	19.8	55.1	2.1	17.8	8.2	16.4	11.1	6.0	10.2	17.9
4	4.1	22.1	49.0	47.6	10.0	20.3	4.8	25.8	2.7	7.4	0.0	14.0

Source: Unpublished data courtesy of R. A. Linthurst and E. D. Seneca, North Carolina State University, Raleigh, NC. Planned title: Aeration, nitrogen, and salinity as determinants of *Spartina alterniflora* growth response.

	Treatment code											
Number	1	2	3	4	5	6	7	8	9	10	11	12
Salinity, parts/thousand	15	15	15	15	30	30	30	30	45	45	45	45
Nitrogen, kg/hectare	0	0	168	168	0	0	168	168	0	0	168	168
Aeration (0 = none, 1 = saturation)	0	1	0	1	0	1	0	1	0	1	0	1

Present an analysis of variance for these data. Compute the coefficient of variation.

Test the null hypothesis that there are no differences in response attributable to differences in salinity. How much of the data are usable for this test?

Test the null hypothesis that there are no differences in response attributable to nitrogen treatments. How much of the data are usable for this test? What is the probability of obtaining a larger value of the test criterion, under the null hypothesis, than that observed?

Test the null hypothesis that there are no differences in response attributable to aeration treatments. How much of the data are usable in this test? What is the probability of obtaining a larger value of the test criterion, under the null hypothesis, than that observed?

Is the nitrogen contrast orthogonal to the aeration contrast?

Have the proposed meaningful comparisons accounted for all the treatment df? Comment.

9.4 The Nature of the Error Term

In the analysis of variance for a randomized complete block design, the error sum of squares is found by subtracting the block and treatment sums of squares from the total sum of squares. This is possible since the sums of squares are additive. The error sum of squares can be obtained directly from

$$\text{Error SS} = \sum_{i,\,j} (Y_{ij} - \bar{Y}_{i\cdot} - \bar{Y}_{\cdot j} + \bar{Y}_{\cdot\cdot})^2 \qquad (9.6)$$

This definition formula arises from the model that defines the means of the various populations sampled. There are rt means in the case of the randomized complete block design, one per cell, with only one observation necessarily made on each population. A mean or expected value is defined in terms of a general mean μ, a treatment contribution τ_i, and a block contribution β_j; that is, the mean of the i, jth cell is $\mu + \tau_i + \beta_j$. An observation is subject to a random error, errors being from a single population with zero mean and fixed but unknown variance. Thus

$$Y_{ij} = \mu + \tau_i + \beta_j + \varepsilon_{ij}$$

Using t and b to indicate estimates, we require that $\sum t_i = 0 = \sum b_j$ as a consequence of a similar restriction on the model (see Sec. 7.5), that is, that treatment and block effects be measured as deviations. We obtain

$$t_i = \bar{Y}_{i\cdot} - \bar{Y}_{\cdot\cdot} \qquad \text{and} \qquad b_j = \bar{Y}_{\cdot j} - \bar{Y}_{\cdot\cdot}$$

Actually, these are the least-square estimates with μ being estimated by $\bar{Y}_{\cdot\cdot}$. In other words, our estimate of the cell mean $\mu_{ij} = \mu + \tau_i + \beta_j$ is given by

$$\hat{\mu}_{ij} = \bar{Y}_{\cdot\cdot} + (\bar{Y}_{i\cdot} - \bar{Y}_{\cdot\cdot}) + (\bar{Y}_{\cdot j} - \bar{Y}_{\cdot\cdot}) = \bar{Y}_{i\cdot} + \bar{Y}_{\cdot j} - \bar{Y}_{\cdot\cdot}$$

and

$$\sum [Y_{ij} - (\bar{Y}_{i\cdot} + \bar{Y}_{\cdot j} - \bar{Y}_{\cdot\cdot})]^2 = \sum (Y_{ij} - \bar{Y}_{i\cdot} - \bar{Y}_{\cdot j} + \bar{Y}_{\cdot\cdot})^2$$

is the smallest possible sum of squares, given complete freedom to choose estimates of μ, the τ_i's and β_j's with the restriction that $\sum \tau_i = 0 = \sum \beta_j$.

Table 9.3 Nature of error term in analysis of variance

Treatment	Observed values, Y_{ij} Block 1	2	3	Totals	Means	Estimates of the means, $\hat{\mu}_{ij}$ Block 1	2	3	Means
1	5	4	3	12	4	4	3	5	4
2	4	5	6	15	5	5	4	6	5
3	6	3	9	18	6	6	5	7	6
4	7	6	8	21	7	7	6	8	7
5	3	2	4	9	3	3	2	4	3
Totals	25	20	30	75					
Means	5	4	6		5	5	4	6	5

Treatment	Residuals = differences = $Y_{ij} - \hat{\mu}_{ij}$ Block 1	2	3	Total	SS
1	1	1	−2	0	6
2	−1	1	0	0	2
3	0	−2	2	0	8
4	0	0	0	0	
5	0	0	0	0	
Total	0	0	0		
SS	2	6	8		16

Analysis of variance

Source of variation	df	SS
Blocks	2	10
Treatment	4	30
Error	8	16
Total	14	56

Table 9.3 shows the computation of estimates of the rt means and residuals for synthetic data. An estimated cell mean is denoted by $\hat{\mu}_{ij}$, where

$$\hat{\mu}_{ij} = \bar{Y}_{i.} + \bar{Y}_{.j} - \bar{Y}_{..} \tag{9.7}$$

The sum of squares for residuals

$$\sum_{i,j} (Y_{ij} - \hat{\mu}_{ij})^2$$

is seen to be identical with that obtained from the analysis of variance. Finally, $Y_{ij} - \hat{\mu}_{ij} = e_{ij}$ is an estimate of ε_{ij}. The resulting error term measures the failure of the treatment differences to be the same in all blocks; note that for treatments 4 and 5, differences are the same in all blocks so that nothing is contributed to error here. The error term is also seen to measure the failure of the observations to equal the estimates of their expected values.

Note that the sums of residuals are zero for every row and column. This indicates why we have 8 degrees of freedom in error. If one fixes the row and column totals of the residuals, then the table of residuals cannot be filled completely at will. It is necessary to reserve all spaces in the last row and column, for example, for whatever values are necessary to give row and column totals of zero. Essentially this means that we are free to choose only $(r - 1)(t - 1)$ residuals; we have only $(r - 1)(t - 1)$ degrees of freedom.

9.5 Partitioning Experimental Error

Random errors have been assumed to be from a single population. At times, this assumption will be false and error variance will be larger for some treatments than for others. This can create a problem in hypothesis testing, for example, like that with unpaired observations and unequal variances, discussed in Sec. 5.9. At times, a simple solution to the problem is available as when differences are used for meaningfully paired observations regardless of whether or not the variance is treatment-related (see Secs. 5.7 and 5.8). This latter solution can be generalized to apply to contrasts for this type of heterogeneity of variance.

Hoppe recorded observations intended to compare seven seed fungicides and an untreated check for emergence of corn seedlings infected with *Diplodia spp.* The experiment was conducted in a greenhouse with six blocks in a randomized complete block design. Each experimental unit consisted of 25 seeds. The data and a treatment code are given in Table 9.4 along with the conventional analysis of variance.

It is desired to partition the sum of squares and 7 degrees of freedom for treatments to give an orthogonal set of comparisons. The comparisons of interest are between the means of: the check and the 7 fungicides, mercuric and nonmercuric fungicides, the two mercuric fungicides, fungicides of companies I and II, fungicides of company I, the original and the new formulations of company II, and the new formulations of company II.

Table 9.4 Greenhouse stand from corn seed infected with *Diplodia spp.* following seed treatment with various fungicides

Block	Treatment								Block totals
	A	*B*	*C*	*D*	*E*	*F*	*G*	*H*	
1	8	16	14	10	8	8	7	12	83
2	8	19	16	11	7	8	6	19	94
3	9	24	14	12	1	3	6	9	78
4	7	22	13	8	1	3	6	11	71
5	7	19	14	7	3	3	4	9	66
6	5	19	13	3	2	7	4	5	58
Treatment totals	44	119	84	51	22	32	33	65	$G = 450$

Symbol	Treatment
A	untreated check
B and *C*	mercuric fungicides
D and *H*	nonmercuric fungicides, company I
E, *F*, and *G*	nonmercuric fungicides, company II, where *F* and *G* are newer formulations of *E*

Analysis of variance

Source	df	SS	Mean square	*F*
Blocks	5	102.50	20.50	
Treatments	7	1,210.58	172.94	29.92**
Error	35	202.17	5.78	
Total	47	1,515.25		

Source: Data used with permission of P. E. Hoppe, University of Wisconsin, Madison, Wisconsin.

Table 9.5 shows the treatment comparisons, coefficients, divisors, and sums of squares. Integers, rather than the fractions called for by means, are used as coefficients for the comparisons. The sum of coefficients in any row is zero and the sum of cross products of the coefficients in any two rows is zero; thus we have comparisons according to our definition and they are orthogonal.

With regard to the coefficients of Table 9.5, all signs in any line or lines can be changed without affecting any sum of squares. For comparison 1, we have

$$-7(44) + 1(119 + 84 + 51 + 22 + 32 + 33 + 65) = (-308 + 406) = 98,$$

the difference between seven times the total of treatment *A* and the total of the other seven treatment totals or, alternatively, $7r$ times the difference

Table 9.5 Pertinent information for seven orthogonal comparisons

Treatment	*A*	*B*	*C*	*D*	*E*	*F*	*G*	*H*			
Treatment total, T_i	44	119	84	51	22	32	33	65	Q	$(\sum c_i^2)r$	SS
Comparison and no.:											
1 *A* vs. rest	−7	+1	+1	+1	+1	+1	+1	+1	98	56(6)	28.58*
2 *BC* vs. *DEFGH*	0	+5	+5	−2	−2	−2	−2	−2	609	70(6)	883.05**
3 *B* vs. *C*	0	+1	−1	0	0	0	0	0	35	2(6)	102.08**
4 *DH* vs. *EFG*	0	0	0	+3	−2	−2	−2	+3	174	30(6)	168.20**
5 *D* vs. *H*	0	0	0	+1	0	0	0	−1	−14	2(6)	16.33
6 *E* vs. *FG*	0	0	0	0	+2	−1	−1	0	−21	6(6)	12.25
7 *F* vs. *G*	0	0	0	0	0	+1	−1	0	−1	2(6)	0.08
Total											1,210.57

between the mean of the check and the mean of the seven fungicides. For this comparison, $\sum c_i^2 = (-7)^2 + (1)^2 + \cdots + (1)^2 = 56$.

Each sum of squares has a single degree of freedom and the sum of the sums of squares equals the treatment sum of squares because we have an orthogonal set of comparisons. Each sum of squares is tested against experimental error and compared with $F(1, f_e)$ where f_e is the number of degrees of freedom in error.

The sum of squares for error, with 35 degrees of freedom, can be partitioned into seven components with 5 degrees of freedom each, one component for each of the seven orthogonal comparisons. The procedure is to obtain Q's for each of the comparisons of Table 9.5, for each block, just as differences were obtained by pairs or blocks in Table 5.5. These are shown in Table 9.6. For comparison 1, block 1, $Q = -7(8) + 1(16 + 14 + 10 + 8 + 8 + 7 + 12) = 19$; for comparison 2, block 1, $Q = 5(16 + 14) - 2(10 + 8 + 8 + 7 + 12) = 60$; and so on. The totals for each comparison within blocks are given in Table 9.6. The total, over blocks, of any of these comparisons is the total given in Table 9.5 for the same comparison; we have simply rearranged the arithmetic.

Any comparison within a block is unaffected by the general level of the block if the randomized complete block model is valid. Thus, if we add 10 to every observation in a block, the comparison for that block is unchanged. This is so because we have simply added $(\sum c_i)10 = 0$, because $\sum c_i = 0$, to each comparison. Consequently, the variance among the six block values of any comparison should be a suitable variance for testing a hypothesis about the mean of the comparison, that is, about the total. For example, for comparison 1, we have the sum of squares

$$\frac{19^2 + 30^2 + \cdots + 18^2}{56} - \frac{98^2}{6(56)} = 34.75 - 28.58 = 6.17 \qquad \text{with 5 df}$$

Table 9.6 Differences for seven comparisons by blocks, and error sums of squares for these comparisons

	Comparison						
Block	1	2	3	4	5	6	7
1	19	60	2	20	−2	1	1
2	30	73	3	48	−8	0	2
3	6	128	10	43	3	−7	−3
4	15	117	9	37	−3	−7	−3
5	10	113	5	28	−2	−1	−1
6	18	118	6	−2	−2	−7	3
Total	98	609	35	174	−14	−21	−1
Divisor	56	70	2	30	2	6	2

	Error components (as sums of squares)						
Comparison no.	1	2	3	4	5	6	7
Sum of squares among blocks	34.75	938.50	127.50	223.67	47.00	24.83	16.50
Correction term = $Q^2/(\sum c_i^2)r$	28.58	883.05	102.08	168.20	16.33	12.25	0.08
Error component	6.17	55.45	25.42	55.47	30.67	12.58	16.42

Thus for any comparison that is to be tested by its own component of error, we begin by synthesizing six observations as linear combinations of the observations in any block. Block differences are not a source of variation among the synthesized observations. We then compute a variance among the six observations and use it to test the null hypothesis that the mean of the population of such observations is zero.

These component sums of squares are all computed similarly, as shown in Table 9.6. The divisor $\sum c_i^2$ is used throughout to give components on a per-observation basis. The sum of the seven components is 202.18 as compared with an error term of 202.17 obtained by subtraction in the initial analysis. The small difference is due to rounding. Bartlett's chi-square test of homogeneity, Sec. 20.3, gives a value of 7.95 with 6 degrees of freedom. This value will be exceeded in the random sampling of variances when the null hypothesis of homogeneous variance is true, with probability between .30 and .20. It is concluded that the components of error variance are not heterogeneous. Partitioning error to test the proposed contrasts seems unwarranted.

Exercise 9.5.1 How many sums of products of coefficients in Table 9.5 must be checked to be sure the seven comparisons are orthogonal?

Exercise 9.5.2 Check several pairs of the comparisons in Table 9.5 for orthogonality.

Exercise 9.5.3 Compute the sum of squares among the six values given in Table 9.6 under comparison 2. Test the null hypothesis that the mean of the population from which these observations come is zero, that is, treat column 2 as if it were all the data available.

Compute F for testing the null hypothesis for comparison 2 by dividing the mean square (Table 9.5 or appropriate correction term in Table 9.6) by the mean square of the corresponding error component. Use a t test to test the same null hypothesis. (F and t^2 should differ by rounding errors only.)

Exercise 9.5.4 Consider the alternative to Dunnett's procedure, Exercise 9.3.1. Partition the error as described in this section and test the two proposed contrasts. What kind of error rate applies now? Does partitioning seem to have been appropriate?

Exercise 9.5.5 Consider the data of Exercise 9.3.5. Find a component of experimental error strictly applicable to the nitrogen contrast. To the aeration contrast. How many df does each component have? Are these components homogeneous? Under the null hypothesis what is the probability of finding a more extreme value of the test criterion than that observed?

9.6 Missing Data

Sometimes data for certain units are missing or unusable, as when an animal becomes sick or dies but not as a result of the treatment, when rodents destroy a plot in a field trial, when a flask breaks in the laboratory, or when there has been an obvious recording error. A method developed by Yates (9.20) is available for estimating such missing data. An estimate of a missing value does not supply additional information to the experimenter; it only facilitates the analysis of the remaining data.

Where a *single value* is missing in a randomized complete block experiment, calculate an estimate of the missing value by

$$Y = \frac{rB + tT - G}{(r-1)(t-1)} \tag{9.8}$$

where r and t = number of blocks and treatments
B and T = totals of observed observations in block and treatment containing the missing unit
G = grand total of the observed observations

The estimated value is entered in the table with the observed values and the analysis of variance is performed as usual with one degree of freedom being subtracted from both total and error degrees of freedom. The estimated value is such that the error sum of squares in the analysis of variance is a minimum. The treatment sum of squares is biased upward by an amount

$$\text{Bias} = \frac{[B - (t-1)Y]^2}{t(t-1)} \tag{9.9}$$

where Y is determined from Eq. (9.8).

The standard error of a difference between the mean of the treatment with a missing value and that of any other treatment is

$$s_{\bar{Y}_{i\cdot}-\bar{Y}_{i'\cdot}} = \sqrt{s^2\left[\frac{2}{r} + \frac{t}{r(r-1)(t-1)}\right]} \tag{9.10}$$

To illustrate the procedure, suppose that the data are the last three treatments of Table 9.2 with the missing observation that on "Ripening" in the second block; we delete the observation 4.9 and proceed.

Observed block totals become 19.5, 13.9, 20.6, and 20.2; observed treatment totals become 26.8, 19.3, and 28.1; the new grand total is 74.2. Use Eq. (9.8) to obtain

$$Y = \frac{4(13.9) + 3(19.3) - 74.2}{3(2)} = 6.55$$

The computed value 6.55 is treated as an observed value for the analysis of variance. The block total 13.9 becomes 20.45, the treatment total 19.3 becomes 25.85, and the grand total becomes 80.75. The resulting analysis of variance is given in Table 9.7.

The upward bias in the treatment sum of squares is computed using Eq. (9.9) as $[13.9 - 2(6.55)]^2/3(2) = .1067$, so the unbiased estimate is .53125.

These data, with an observation missing, have lost the balance expected in a randomized complete block experiment. The three treatment means are seen to be estimates of

$$\mu + \tau_1 + \sum_1^4 \beta_j \qquad \mu + \tau_2 + \sum_{j \neq 2} \beta_j \qquad \text{and} \qquad \mu + \tau_3 + \sum_1^4 \beta_j$$

Variation among the observed means is not solely due to τ's and random components, because treatment 2 mean does not have a full set of β's. Blocks and treatments are not orthogonal. The missing-plot procedure has estimated a cell mean, $\mu + \tau_2 + \beta_2$, by the least-squares method and the

Table 9.7 Analysis of variance for partial set of data with missing observation

Source	df	SS	MS
Blocks	3	.2373	.0791
Treatments	2	.6379†	.3190
Error	6 − 1	1.7471	.3494
Total	11 − 1	2.6223	

† Bias = .1067; unbiased SS(trts) = .6379 − .1067 = .53125.

Table 9.8 Analysis of variance alternative to that of Table 9.7

Source	df	SS	MS
Blocks and Trts	5	.8402	
Blocks, ignoring trts	(3)	.3089	
Trts, adjusted for blocks = Trts | blocks	(2)	.5313	.2656
Error	5	1.7471	.3494
Total	10	2.5873	

analysis has proceeded with this value. The estimate had no random component, so degrees of freedom in total and error were reduced by 1.

A possibly more informative analysis is given in Table 9.8. The SS(Total) is computed from the 11 observations, so it differs from that of Table 9.7. The SS(Error) is taken from Table 9.7 and is an unbiased estimate of $f_e \sigma^2$, where $f_e = 5$; alternative computing procedures are given in Chaps. 14 and 18. The difference, SS(Total) − SS(Error), must be the sum of squares associated with having block and treatment effects in the model. These effects are not orthogonal, so we next compute a block sum of squares ignoring treatments, as though this were a one-way classification with blocks providing the categories; each squared sum must have its own divisor. This SS(Blocks ignoring trts) subtracted from SS(Blocks and trts) tells how much of the latter can be attributed to treatment effects after blocks have been accounted for. It is called the sum of squares for *treatments adjusted for blocks*, or SS(Trts | blocks), and is the same as the unbiased treatment sum of squares computed previously.

When there are *several missing values*, values are first approximated for all units except one. Reasonable approximations of these may be obtained by computing $(\bar{Y}_{i\cdot} + \bar{Y}_{\cdot j})/2$, where $\bar{Y}_{i\cdot}$ and $\bar{Y}_{\cdot j}$ are the means of the known values for the treatment and block, respectively, containing any one of the missing values. Values may also be obtained by inspection. Equation (9.8) is then used to obtain an approximation for the remaining value. With this approximation and the values previously assigned to all but one of the remaining missing plots, again use Eq. (9.8) to approximate this one.

After making a complete cycle, a second approximation is found for all values in the order previously used. This is continued until the new approximations are not materially different from those found in the previous cycle. Usually two cycles are sufficient. The estimated values are entered in the table with the observed values, and the analysis of variance is completed. For each missing value, one degree of freedom is subtracted from total and error degrees of freedom. This is because the estimated values make no contribution to the error sum of squares.

Table 9.9 Missing plot technique

	Blocks				Treatment totals	
Treatment	1	2	3	4	Observed values	All values
1	4.4	5.9	6.0	4.1	20.4	
2	(a = 4.5)	1.9	4.9	7.1	13.9	18.4
3	4.4	4.0	4.5	3.1	16.0	
4	6.8	6.6	(b = 7.2)	6.4	19.8	27.0
5	6.3	4.9	5.9	7.1	24.2	
6	6.4	7.3	7.7	6.7	28.1	
Block totals: Observed values	28.3	30.6	29.0	34.5	122.4	
Block totals: All values	32.8		36.2			134.1

To illustrate the procedure, suppose that two values, a and b, are missing from the data of Table 9.2 (see Table 9.9).

Computations proceed as follows.

1. Estimate b as

$$b = \frac{\bar{Y}_{i\cdot} + \bar{Y}_{\cdot j}}{2} = \frac{19.8/3 + 29.0/5}{2} = 6.2$$

2. Estimate a, first cycle, by Eq. (9.8)

$$a_1 = \frac{rB + tT - G}{(r-1)(t-1)} = \frac{4(28.3) + 6(13.9) - (122.4 + 6.2)}{(4-1)(6-1)} = 4.5$$

3. Estimate b, first cycle, as

$$b_1 = \frac{4(29.0) + 6(19.8) - (122.4 + 4.5)}{(4-1)(6-1)} = 7.2$$

4. Estimate a, second cycle, as

$$a_2 = \frac{4(28.3) + 6(13.9) - (122.4 + 7.2)}{(4-1)(6-1)} = 4.5$$

5. Estimate b, second cycle, as

$$b_2 = \frac{4(29.0) + 6(19.8) - (122.4 + 4.5)}{(4-1)(6-1)} = 7.2$$

Here $G = 122.4 + 4.5 = 126.9$ as in the first cycle, since a_1 and a_2 are the same when rounded to one decimal place.

The estimated values of the population means for the missing cells are given by Eq. (9.7). For missing value cells a and b, these estimates are

$32.8/6 + 18.4/4 - 134.1/24 = 4.5$ and $36.2/6 + 27.0/4 - 134.1/24 = 7.2$, the same as the missing values to one decimal place. Missing value formulas supply estimates of population means, and thus the estimates do not contribute to error. In turn, there is no reason for the estimates to contribute to error degrees of freedom.

The analysis of variance is computed as usual after the estimated values have been entered. Total and error degrees of freedom are 21 and 13. Block, treatment, and error mean squares are 0.96, 5.89, and 1.45. Error mean square is an unbiased estimate of σ^2; treatment mean square is biased upward. The F test of the null hypothesis of no differences among treatment means is unlikely to be much in error unless a substantial number of values are missing. This approximate procedure and a little common sense are satisfactory for most problems. An exact method is given by Yates (9.20). An easy and exact method is also given by covariance in Sec. 17.11. Chapter 18 deals with this problem in the general case.

To obtain a standard error for the comparison of two treatment means, each with a missing plot, we use an approximation due to Taylor (9.24). In

$$s_{\bar{Y}_i - \bar{Y}_{i'}} = s\sqrt{\frac{1}{r_i} + \frac{1}{r_{i'}}}$$

replace r_i and $r_{i'}$ with an "effective number of replicates" computed as follows: for r_i, count 1 if both treatments are present, count $(t-2)/(t-1)$ if treatment i is present but i' is absent, and count 0 if treatment i is absent.

Let a and b in Table 9.9 be missing. Suppose that $s_{\bar{Y}_{2\cdot} - \bar{Y}_{4\cdot}}$ is required, so r_2 and r_4 have to be computed. For r_2: in block 1, assign 0; in blocks 2 and 4, assign 1; in block 3, assign $(6-2)/(6-1) = .8$. Then $r_2 = 2.8$. For r_4: in block 1, assign $(6-2)/(6-1) = .8$; in blocks 2 and 4, assign 1; in block 3, assign 0. Then $r_4 = 2.8$ and

$$s_{\bar{Y}_{2\cdot} - \bar{Y}_{4\cdot}} = \sqrt{s^2\left(\frac{1}{2.8} + \frac{1}{2.8}\right)}$$

Again, $s_{\bar{Y}_{2\cdot} - \bar{Y}_{3\cdot}}$ is required as are r_2 and r_3. For r_2: in block 1, assign 0; in blocks 2, 3, and 4, assign 1. Then $r_2 = 3$. For r_3: in block 1, assign $(6-2)/(6-1) = .8$; in blocks 2, 3, and 4, assign 1. Then $r_3 = 3.8$ and

$$s_{\bar{Y}_{2\cdot} - \bar{Y}_{3\cdot}} = \sqrt{s^2\left(\frac{1}{3} + \frac{1}{3.8}\right)}$$

Exercise 9.6.1 From the data of Table 9.2, discard the value on ripening in the second block and regard the resulting data as having one missing plot. Compute a value for the missing plot and complete the analysis of variance. Compute the bias in and adjust the treatment sum of squares. Compare your results with those in this section where only three treatments were used.

Exercise 9.6.2 From the data of Exercise 9.3.1 or 9.3.2, discard two or three values to be regarded as missing plots. Compute missing plot values and complete the analysis of variance. Compute the effective number of replicates for comparing two treatment means, each with a missing plot; for two treatment means, only one of which has a missing plot.

Take SS(Error) from this analysis and generalize the exact method of analysis described for a single missing observation for finding SS(Treatments, adjusted for blocks). This requires SS(Total) from the incomplete data, SS(Blocks + treatments) by subtraction, and SS(Blocks, ignoring treatments), also from the incomplete data.

Exercise 9.6.3 In the data of Exercise 9.3.5, the observation for treatment 11 in block 4 is zero. This suggests that something went wrong in handling the experimental material. Treat this "observation" as though it were missing. Compute a missing plot value and recompute the analysis of variance. Compute the standard error of the difference between the two nitrogen means. Between the two aeration means.

Test the null hypothesis that there is no real difference in response to nitrogen levels. What is the probability of a more extreme value of the test criterion, under the null hypothesis, than that observed? Compare this result with that observed for the same question in Exercise 9.3.5.

Repeat the above for aeration levels.

9.7 Estimation of Gain in Efficiency

Whenever a randomized complete block design is used, it is possible to estimate the efficiency relative to that expected from a completely random design. Begin by estimating what the experimental error, MSE(CR), might have been had a completely random design been used. MSE(CR) is estimated by

$$\widehat{\text{MSE(CR)}} = \frac{f_b\text{MSB} + (f_t + f_e)\text{MSE}}{f_b + f_t + f_e} \qquad (9.11)$$

where MSB and MSE are the block and error mean squares, and f_b, f_t, and f_e are the block, treatment, and error degrees of freedom. Note that the weight assigned to MSE is the degrees of freedom that would have applied had there been no treatments. The argument comes from a consideration of the properties of randomization and uniformity trials, where there are no treatments. If the degrees of freedom for the randomized complete block error are under 20, it is important to consider the loss in precision resulting from fewer degrees of freedom with which to estimate the error mean square of the randomized blocks experiment as compared with the completely random design. This is accomplished by multiplying the precision factor, when obtained, by $(f_1 + 1)(f_2 + 3)/(f_2 + 1)(f_1 + 3)$ (discussed in Sec. 6.8), where f_1 and f_2 are the degrees of freedom associated with error for the randomized complete block and the completely random design, respectively.

Applying Eq. (9.11) to the data of Table 9.2, we have

$$\widehat{\text{MSE(CR)}} = \frac{3(1.05) + (5 + 15)1.31}{3 + 5 + 15} = 1.28$$

Using Eq. (6.1), we find the efficiency of the block design relative to the completely random design, RE(RCB to CRD).

$$\text{RE(RCB to CRD)} = \frac{(f_1 + 1)(f_2 + 3)\,\widehat{\text{MSE(CR)}}}{(f_2 + 1)(f_1 + 3)\,\text{MSE(RB)}}\,100$$

$$= \frac{(15 + 1)(18 + 3)\,1.28}{(18 + 1)(15 + 3)\,1.31}\,100 = 96 \text{ percent}$$

where $f_2 = f_b + f_e = 18$.

In this case, information is sacrificed, in theory, by using the randomized block design, since 96 replicates in a completely random design give as much information as 100 blocks or replications for a randomized complete block design. A proof of Eq. (9.11) is given by Cochran and Cox (9.8).

Exercise 9.7.1 Compute the efficiency of the randomized complete block design relative to the completely random design for the data used in Exercises 9.3.1 and 9.3.2.

Exercise 9.7.2 The use of blocks in greenhouse experiments does not always control the variance. Compute the efficiency of the randomized complete block design relative to the completely random design for the experiment described in Exercise 9.3.5.

9.8 The Randomized Complete Block Design: More Than One Observation per Treatment per Block

Two-way classifications with multiple observations in the cells are common. They arise in two ways. In one case, each observation is made on an experimental unit where the full set was involved in the random assignment of treatments. Clearly, there were more than t experimental units per block, so some or all treatments appear more than once in any block. When there are r_i experimental units per treatment in the ith block, the experiment is a *generalized randomized (complete) block design*. Chapter 18 includes a discussion of the case where r_i depends on the block, the case of proportional subclass numbers. A recommendation for greater use of the generalized randomized block design, along with additional references, is given by Addelman (9.27).

In the other case, there are usually only rt experimental units with all t treatments randomly assigned within each block. However, the complete experimental unit is not the unit measured, nor is there a single sampling unit (see Sec. 7.6) per experimental unit. Instead, there is more than one sampling unit per experimental unit; now it is necessary to have both sampling error and experimental error. *Observational* or *sampling units* are selected at random within the experimental unit. For the most information per observation and for greatest computational convenience, an equal number of observations per experimental unit is required where possible. This is the case we consider.

Let Y_{ijk} represent the kth observation made in the jth block on the ith treatment, $i = 1, \ldots, t, j = 1, \ldots, r$, and $k = 1, \ldots, s$ observations. Here i and j refer to criteria of classification whereas k is a necessary label but does not serve as such a criterion. In other words, the kth observation in the i, jth unit is no more like the kth in another unit than it is like the $(k + 1)$st or any other observation. Hence the only meaningful totals are the grand total $Y_{\ldots}$, the experimental unit or cell totals $Y_{ij\cdot}$, the block totals $Y_{\cdot j\cdot}$, and the treatment totals $Y_{i\ldots}$.

The computations required for the sums of squares in the analysis of variance are shown symbolically in Table 9.10. Compare the definition formulas with those in Table 9.1; those of Table 9.10 are s times those in Table 9.1. If we were to compute either totals or means of experimental units and analyze these without reference to s, then the first three lines would be multiples of the per-observation analysis of Table 9.10, s times for totals, $1/s$ times for means, and sampling error could not be estimated. However, this analysis would be sufficient for tests of hypotheses concerning treatments and blocks because F values would be identical.

Sampling error sum of squares may be found by subtracting the sums of squares for blocks, treatments, and experimental error from the total sum of

Table 9.10 The computation of sums of squares for a randomized complete block design with several observations per experimental unit

		Sums of squares	
Source	df	Definition	Working
Blocks	$r - 1$	$ts \sum_j (\bar{Y}_{\cdot j\cdot} - \bar{Y}_{\ldots})^2$	$\frac{\sum_j Y_{\cdot j\cdot}^2}{ts} - \frac{Y_{\ldots}^2}{rts}$
Treatments	$t - 1$	$rs \sum_i (\bar{Y}_{i\ldots} - \bar{Y}_{\ldots})^2$	$\frac{\sum_i Y_{i\ldots}^2}{rs} - \frac{Y_{\ldots}^2}{rts}$
Experimental error	$(r - 1)(t - 1)$	$s \sum_{i,j} (\bar{Y}_{ij\cdot} - \bar{Y}_{\ldots})^2$ $-$SS(Blocks) $-$ SS(Trts)	$\frac{\sum_{i,j} Y_{ij\cdot}^2}{s} - \frac{Y_{\ldots}^2}{rts}$ $-$SS(Blocks) $-$ SS(Trts)
Sampling error	$rt(s - 1)$	$\sum_{i,j} \sum_k (Y_{ijk} - \bar{Y}_{ij\cdot})^2$	$\sum_{i,j} \left(\sum_k Y_{ijk}^2 - \frac{Y_{ij\cdot}^2}{s} \right)$
Total	$rts - 1$	$\sum_{i,j,k} (Y_{ijk} - \bar{Y}_{\ldots})^2$	$\sum_{i,j,k} Y_{ijk}^2 - \frac{Y_{\ldots}^2}{rts}$

squares or as shown in Table 9.10. The method shown is to obtain the sum of squares among observations within each cell and sum; for the i, jth cell, the sum of squares among observations is

$$\sum_k Y_{ijk}^2 - \frac{Y_{ij\cdot}^2}{s}$$

Sampling error measures the failure of the observations made in any experimental unit to be precisely alike.

Experimental error is often expected to be larger than sampling error; in other words, variation among experimental units is often expected to be larger than variation among subsamples of the same unit. When both sources of variation are assumed to be random, experimental error is the appropriate error for testing hypotheses concerning treatments and blocks.

When block and treatment effects are assumed to be fixed, one does not necessarily assume that the so-called experimental error line is, in fact, based only on random components. When some nonrandomness is assumed, we say essentially that there are fixed effects, fixed because block and treatment effects are fixed, for each block-treatment combination over and above the additive treatment and block contributions. This can also be stated by saying that the differences in responses to the various treatments are not of the same order of magnitude from block to block. These additional responses, then, are added to the random components. Such situations are not uncommon. They are discussed as *interactions* in Chap. 15. (Although the term was not used, interactions were considered in Sec. 8.3 when discussing some mint data.) For example, suppose that a field experiment is being conducted, by choice, on a hillside with the top quite dry and the bottom reasonably moist. Blocks are chosen accordingly with block effects being considered as fixed. The experiment is a varietal trial of several locally grown cultivars of a forage crop, one of which is considered to be drought-resistant. Treatment effects are also considered to be fixed. Now the drought-resistant variety should be outstanding in the dry block relative to its performance in the moist block. In other words, the size of the difference in response between this and any other variety depends on the block. This cannot be called a random effect. Hence, what we have been calling experimental error is not purely random; we relabel it as interaction plus error. No line in the analysis of variance provides an appropriate error term for testing hypotheses concerning interaction or hypotheses concerning treatment and block effects.

Exercise 9.8.1 The data in the following two-way classification are times, in seconds, for various runners to complete a 1.5-mi course. These men fall in three age groups and three fitness categories, the latter being functions of a number of variables.†

† Data courtesy of A. C. Linnerud, North Carolina State University.

	Fitness		
	Low	Medium	High
Age: 40	669	602	527
	671	603	547
50	775	684	571
	821	687	573
60	1009	824	688
	1060	828	713

In what way does the design of this experiment differ from that of an animal nutrition experiment where animals are housed or penned together in pairs and treatments are assigned at random to the penned pairs? What is the experimental unit in the animal experiment? For the runner data?

For the analysis of variance of the runner data, how should the lines in Table 9.10 be relabeled? Complete the analysis of variance. Test the null hypothesis that the running time population means are the same for these three age groups. That running time population means do not depend on the fitness categories.

What information is available in the line originally labeled "experimental error?" (Consider how this was computed.)

9.9 Linear Models and the Analysis of Variance

For a proper evaluation of experimental data, the model must be specifically stated. Two common models are the *fixed effects* model, or *Model* I, and the *random effects* model, or *Model* II (see Sec. 7.5).

Another common model is the *mixed model*, which calls for at least one criterion of classification to involve fixed effects and another to involve random effects. Other models are also possible.

From Table 9.11, it is evident what sorts of conclusions can be drawn from tests of significance, in the form of ratios of mean squares. In referring to Table 9.11, keep in mind that expected values are averages of the results one would obtain in repeated experimentation under the particular model. Thus for fixed effects, the same effects would be repeated in the same positions in successive experiments. For random effects, a new sample is taken each time, and while the same effects will eventually appear again, they may appear in any position.

For the *random model* without interaction, both treatments and blocks are drawn at random from populations of treatment and block effects. Inferences are drawn about the populations rather than about the particular treatments and blocks. Very often it is desirable to have blocks random when generalizations concerning treatment effects are to be made for some

Table 9.11 Expected values of mean squares for a randomized complete block analysis

		Random model	
		No sampling	Sampling†
Source	df	$Y_{ij} = \mu + \tau_i + \beta_j + \varepsilon_{ij}$	$Y_{ijk} = \mu + \tau_i + \beta_j + \varepsilon_{ij} + \delta_{ijk}$
Blocks	$r - 1$	$\sigma_\varepsilon^2 + t\sigma_\beta^2$	$\sigma^2 + s\sigma_\varepsilon^2 + ts\sigma_\beta^2$
Treatments	$t - 1$	$\sigma_\varepsilon^2 + r\sigma_\tau^2$	$\sigma^2 + s\sigma_\varepsilon^2 + rs\sigma_\tau^2$
Residual	$(r - 1)(t - 1)$	σ_ε^2	$\sigma^2 + s\sigma_\varepsilon^2$
Sampling error	$rt(s - 1)$		σ^2
Fixed model, no interaction		Fixed model, interaction	
No sampling	Sampling†	No sampling	Sampling†
$Y_{ij} = \mu + \tau_i + \beta_j + \varepsilon_{ij}$	$Y_{ijk} = \mu + \tau_i + \beta_j + \varepsilon_{ij} + \delta_{ijk}$	$Y_{ij} = \mu + \tau_i + \beta_j + (\tau\beta)_{ij} + \varepsilon_{ij}$	$Y_{ijk} = \mu + \tau_i + \beta_j + (\tau\beta)_{ij} + \varepsilon_{ij} + \delta_{ijk}$
$\sigma_\varepsilon^2 + t \sum \beta_j^2/(r - 1)$	$\sigma^2 + s\sigma_\varepsilon^2 + st \sum \beta_j^2/(r - 1)$	$\sigma_\varepsilon^2 + t \sum \beta_j^2/(r - 1)$	$\sigma^2 + s\sigma_\varepsilon^2 + st \sum \beta_j^2/(r - 1)$
$\sigma_\varepsilon^2 + r \sum \tau_i^2/(t - 1)$	$\sigma^2 + s\sigma_\varepsilon^2 + sr \sum \tau_i^2/(t - 1)$	$\sigma_\varepsilon^2 + r \sum \tau_i^2/(t - 1)$	$\sigma^2 + s\sigma_\varepsilon^2 + sr \sum \tau_i^2/(t - 1)$
σ_ε^2	$\sigma^2 + s\sigma_\varepsilon^2$	$\sigma_\varepsilon^2 + \sum_{i,j} (\tau\beta)_{ij}^2/(r - 1)(t - 1)$	$\sigma^2 + s\sigma_\varepsilon^2 + s \sum_{i,j} (\tau\beta)_{ij}^2/(r - 1)(t - 1)$
	σ^2		σ^2
Mixed model, no interaction		Mixed model, interaction	
No sampling	Sampling†	No sampling	Sampling†
$Y_{ij} = \mu + \tau_i + \beta_j + \varepsilon_{ij}$	$Y_{ijk} = \mu + \tau_i + \beta_j + \varepsilon_{ij} + \delta_{ijk}$	$Y_{ij} = \mu + \tau_i + \beta_j + (\tau\beta)_{ij} + \varepsilon_{ij}$	$Y_{ijk} = \mu + \tau_i + \beta_j + (\tau\beta)_{ij} + \varepsilon_{ij} + \delta_{ijk}$
$\sigma_\varepsilon^2 + t\sigma_\beta^2$	$\sigma^2 + s\sigma_\varepsilon^2 + st\sigma_\beta^2$	$\sigma_\varepsilon^2 + t\sigma_\beta^2$	$\sigma^2 + s\sigma_\varepsilon^2 + st\sigma_\beta^2$
$\sigma_\varepsilon^2 + r \sum \tau_i^2/(t - 1)$	$\sigma^2 + s\sigma_\varepsilon^2 + rs \sum \tau_i^2/(t - 1)$	$\sigma_\varepsilon^2 + t\sigma_{\tau\beta}^2/(t - 1) + r \sum \tau_i^2/(t - 1)$	$\sigma^2 + s\sigma_\varepsilon^2 + st\sigma_{\tau\beta}^2/(t - 1) + sr \sum \tau_i^2/(t - 1)$
σ_ε^2	$\sigma^2 + s\sigma_\varepsilon^2$	$\sigma_\varepsilon^2 + t\sigma_{\tau\beta}^2/(t - 1)$	$\sigma^2 + s\sigma_\varepsilon^2 + st\sigma_{\tau\beta}^2/(t - 1)$
	σ^2		σ^2

† Keep in mind that s may equal 1, in which case σ^2 cannot be estimated.

variable set of conditions such as a county or state. An assumption of randomness may thus be made if the claim that blocks are representative of the population can be reasonably justified. Random treatment effects are appropriate in many plant and animal experiments and in production studies where there may be batch-to-batch or day-to-day variation. Residual mean square is the appropriate error mean square for testing block and treatment effects, whether or not there is sampling. Tests can be made even though only one sample observation is made on the experimental unit; however, σ_δ^2 cannot be estimated when $s = 1$.

For the random model with interaction, an additional component, $(\tau\beta)_{ij}$, is assumed. The symbol $(\tau\beta)$ calls attention to the source of the component; the subscript outside the parentheses avoids labeling the interaction as a multiplicative effect without ruling out this possibility. For a model with random block and treatment effects, one would also assume interaction effects to be random with zero mean and variance, $\sigma_{\tau\beta}^2$. This would add $\sigma_{\tau\beta}^2$ to the no-sampling model and $s\sigma_{\tau\beta}^2$ to the sampling model in all lines except sampling error. Tests of hypotheses can be made although σ^2 and $\sigma_{\tau\beta}^2$ cannot be estimated separately. This model with interaction is not often needed.

Where the *fixed effects model* without interaction is appropriate, all treatments about which inferences are to be drawn are included in the experiment. The same is true for blocks. Inferences about treatments or blocks are not intended to apply to treatments or blocks not included in the experiment. Testing is straightforward with or without sampling. This model is not uncommon, owing to the very nature of categories in a classification system.

For a fixed effects model with interaction effects, the latter will be fixed because both treatment and block effects are fixed. No satisfactory testing can be done with or without sampling, so it is important to try to learn more about the nature of interaction.

The *mixed model* is certainly a common one. Blocks most often supply the random effects and are presumably representative of a population of blocks that cover a range of conditions over which inferences about treatments are to apply. The treatments are the only ones of interest with respect to inferences, so they are considered fixed in repeated experimentation. In the model with no interaction, testing is seen to offer no special problems with or without sampling.

For the mixed model with interaction, consider the interaction effects to be in t endless rows, where each column is a finite population of t elements that sum to zero while the expectation of a row is zero. The elements that get into an experiment are a random sample of r columns, one for each block. The expectations of the mean squares under these assumptions are as shown. There is no problem in testing treatments using experimental error, regardless of whether or not there is sampling. Not all statisticians require that a column of elements sum to zero. In this case, the coefficient $t/(t - 1)$ for $\sigma^2_{\tau\beta}$ will be replaced by 1. Testing procedures will not be affected but estimates of $\sigma^2_{\tau\beta}$ will be.

9.10 Double Grouping: Latin Squares

In the Latin square design, we arrange the treatments in blocks in two different ways, namely, by rows and columns. For four treatments, the arrangement might be

A	*D*	*C*	*B*
B	*C*	*A*	*D*
D	*A*	*B*	*C*
C	*B*	*D*	*A*

Each treatment occurs once and only once in each row and column; each row, like each column, is a complete block. By appropriate analysis, it is possible to remove from error the variability due to differences in both rows and columns.

This design has been used to advantage in many fields of research where two major sources of variation are present in the conduct of an experiment. In field experiments, the layout is usually a square, thus allowing the removal of variation resulting from soil differences in two directions. In the greenhouse or field, if there is a gradient all in one direction, the experiment can be laid out as follows:

A D C B	*B C A D*	*D A B C*	*C B D A*

Here rows are blocks and columns are positions in the blocks. Marketing experiments lend themselves to this arrangement, with days being rows and stores being columns.

Since rows and columns are general terms for referring to criteria of classification, they may be a kind of treatment. When there is interaction between any two or among all of the criteria—rows, columns, and treatments—computed F is not distributed as tabulated F and no valid tests of significance are possible. In cases where the experimenter is not prepared to assume the absence of interaction, the Latin square should not be used.

Babcock (9.2) used a Latin square design in an experiment to determine if there were any differences among the amounts of milk produced by the four quarters of cow udders, quarters being the treatments or letters of the square. In this experiment four times of milking were the rows of the Latin square, and the orders of milking were the columns of the square—order meaning position in time. The Latin square has also been used to advantage in the laboratory, in industry, and in the social sciences.

The chief disadvantage of the Latin square is that the number of rows, columns, and treatments must be equal. Thus, if there are many treatments, the number of plots required soon becomes impractical. The most common square is in the range 5×5 to 8×8, and squares larger than 12×12 are rarely used. Latin squares, like randomized blocks, suffer in that as the block size increases, the experimental error per unit is likely to increase. Small squares provide few degrees of freedom for estimation of experimental error and thus must give a substantial decrease in experimental error to compensate for the small number of degrees of freedom. However, more than one square may be used in the same experiment; for example, two 4×4 squares will give 15 degrees of freedom for error if the treatments respond similarly in both squares. The degrees of freedom for the analysis of s, $r \times r$ squares are as shown in the table.

Source	df
Squares	$s - 1 = 1$
Rows within squares	$s(r - 1) = 6$
Columns within squares	$s(r - 1) = 6$
Treatments	$r - 1 = 3$
Error	$s(r - 1)(r - 2) + (s - 1)(r - 1) = 15$
Total	$sr^2 - 1 = 31$

Randomization in the Latin square consists of choosing a square at random from among all possible Latin squares. Fisher and Yates (9.11) give the complete set of Latin squares for 4×4 through 6×6 squares, and sample squares up to size 12×12. Cochran and Cox (9.8) give sample Latin squares from 3×3 through 12×12. A method of randomization suggested by Cochran and Cox follows.

The 3×3 *square* Assign letters to the treatments; this need not be random. Write out a 3×3 square and randomize the arrangement of the three columns and then that of the last two rows.

The 4×4 *square* Here there are four squares such that one cannot be obtained from another simply by rearranging rows and columns. Hence we randomly select one of the four possible squares and arrange at random all columns and the last three rows.

The 5×5 *and higher squares* By now there are many squares such that one cannot be obtained from another by rearranging rows and columns. Assign letters to the treatments at random. Randomize all columns and all rows.

Table 9.12 Analysis of variance for an $r \times r$ Latin square

Source of variation	df	Sums of squares: Definition formulas	Sums of squares: Computing formulas
Rows	$r-1$	$r\sum_i (\bar{Y}_{i\cdot} - \bar{Y}_{\cdot\cdot})^2$	$\frac{\sum_i Y_{i\cdot}^2}{r} - C$
Columns	$r-1$	$r\sum_j (\bar{Y}_{\cdot j} - \bar{Y}_{\cdot\cdot})^2$	$\frac{\sum_j Y_{\cdot j}^2}{r} - C$
Treatments	$r-1$	$r\sum_t (\bar{Y}_t - \bar{Y}_{\cdot\cdot})^2$	$\frac{\sum_t Y_t^2}{r} - C$
Error	$(r-1)(r-2)$	$\sum (Y_{ij} - \bar{Y}_{i\cdot} - \bar{Y}_{\cdot j} - \bar{Y}_t + 2\bar{Y}_{\cdot\cdot})^2$	By subtraction
Total	r^2-1	$\sum_{i,j} (Y_{ij} - \bar{Y}_{\cdot\cdot})^2$	$\sum_{i,j} Y_{ij}^2 - C$

9.11 Analysis of Variance of the Latin Square

The degrees of freedom and formulas for sums of squares for an $r \times r$ Latin square are given in Table 9.12. Here Y_{ij} represents the observation at the intersection of the ith row and jth column. Row sums and means are given by $Y_{i\cdot}$ and $\bar{Y}_{i\cdot}$ for $i = 1, \ldots, r$ and column sums and means by $Y_{\cdot j}$ and $\bar{Y}_{\cdot j}$, $j = 1, \ldots, r$. While this notation is adequate to locate an observation, it tells nothing about the treatment received. We have used Y_t and $\bar{Y}_t$ to denote treatment totals and means, $t = 1, \ldots, r$.

The statistical analysis of a 4×4 Latin square is illustrated with yield data from a wheat varietal evaluation trial conducted by Ali A. El Khishen, College of Agriculture, Alexandria University, Alexandria, Egypt. The data, analysis, and actual field layout are shown in Table 9.13. The varieties are represented by letters: $A =$ Baladi 16, $B =$ Mokhtar, $C =$ Giza 139, and $D =$ Thatcher. Yields are in kilograms per plot of size 42 m^2. The computational procedure follows.

Step 1 Obtain row totals $Y_{i\cdot}$, column totals $Y_{\cdot j}$, treatment totals Y_t, and the grand total $Y_{\cdot\cdot}$. Simultaneously find

$$\sum_j Y_{ij}^2 \qquad \text{and} \qquad \sum_i Y_{ij}^2$$

for each value of i and j, respectively. The sum of the four resulting quantities for the i's will equal that for the j's and provides a computational check. This is the total unadjusted sum of squares.

Table 9.13 Field layout showing yields, in kilograms per plot, of wheat arranged in a 4 × 4 Latin square

Row	Column 1	Column 2	Column 3	Column 4	Row totals $Y_{i\cdot}$	Row totals $\sum_j Y_{ij}^2$
1	$C = 10.5$	$D = 7.7$	$B = 12.0$	$A = 13.2$	43.4	487.78
2	$B = 11.1$	$A = 12.0$	$C = 10.3$	$D = 7.5$	40.9	429.55
3	$D = 5.8$	$C = 12.2$	$A = 11.2$	$B = 13.7$	42.9	495.61
4	$A = 11.6$	$B = 12.3$	$D = 5.9$	$C = 10.2$	40.0	424.70
Column totals $Y_{\cdot j}$	39.0	44.2	39.4	44.6	$\sum_{i,j} Y_{ij} = 167.2$	$\sum_{i,j} Y_{ij}^2 = 1{,}837.64$
Column totals $\sum_i Y_{ij}^2$	401.66	503.42	410.34	522.22		

Variety totals and means

	A	B	C	D
Totals = Y_t	48.0	49.1	43.2	26.9
Means = $\bar{Y}_t$	12.0	12.3	10.8	6.8

Analysis of variance

Source of variation	df	SS	MS	F
Rows	$(r-1) = 3$	1.95	0.65	1.44
Columns	$(r-1) = 3$	6.80	2.27	5.04
Varieties	$(r-1) = 3$	78.93	26.31	58.47**
Error	$(r-1)(r-2) = 6$	2.72	0.45	
Total	$(r^2-1) = 15$	90.40		

$s = 0.67$ kg $s_{\bar{Y}} = 0.34$ kg $s_{\bar{Y}_{i\cdot} - \bar{Y}_{i'\cdot}} = 0.47$ kg CV = 6.4 percent

Step 2 Find the correction term and (adjusted) sums of squares.

$$\text{Correction term} = C = \frac{Y_{\cdot\cdot}^2}{r^2} = \frac{167.2^2}{4^2} = 1{,}747.24$$

$$\text{Total SS} = \sum_{i,j} Y_{ij}^2 - C = 1{,}837.64 - 1{,}747.24 = 90.40$$

$$\text{Row SS} = \frac{\sum_i Y_{i\cdot}^2}{r} - C = \frac{43.4^2 + \cdots + 40.0^2}{4} - 1{,}747.24$$

$$= 1.95$$

$$\text{Column SS} = \frac{\sum_j Y_{\cdot j}^2}{r} - C = \frac{39.0^2 + \cdots + 44.6^2}{4} - 1{,}747.24$$

$$= 6.80$$

$$\text{Treatment SS} = \frac{\sum_t Y_t^2}{r} - C = \frac{48.0^2 + \cdots + 26.9^2}{4} - 1{,}747.24$$

$$= 78.93$$

$$\text{Error SS} = \text{SS(total)} - \text{SS(rows)} - \text{SS(cols)} - \text{SS(trts)}$$

$$= 90.40 - (1.95 + 6.80 + 78.93) = 2.72$$

Sums of squares are entered in an analysis of variance table and mean squares found. The F value for varieties (treatments) is $26.31/0.45 = 58.47^{**}$, with 3 and 6 degrees of freedom; it greatly exceeds the tabulated 1 percent value of 9.78. Highly significant differences are said to exist among yields for varieties.

The sample standard error of a treatment mean is $s_{\bar{Y}} = \sqrt{s^2/r} = 0.34$ kg, where s^2 is the error mean square and r is the number of experimental units per treatment. The sample standard error of a difference between two treatment means is $s_{\bar{Y}_i - \bar{Y}_{i'}} = \sqrt{2s^2/r} = 0.47$ kg. If heterogeneity of error is suspected, the error cannot be subdivided as readily as in the case of the randomized complete block design. The procedure is illustrated by Cochran and Cox (9.8).

The method for determining how varieties differ depends on the aims of the experiment and knowledge of the varieties, for example, genetic background. Valid methods have been discussed in Chap. 8.

Exercise 9.11.1 Peterson et al. (9.15) present moisture content of turnip greens and other data for an experiment conducted as a Latin square. The data are shown in the accompanying table for (moisture content − 80) percent. Treatments are times of weighing since moisture losses might be anticipated in a 70°F laboratory as the experiment progressed.

	Leaf size (A = smallest, E = largest)				
Plant	A	B	C	D	E
1	6.67(V)	7.15(IV)	8.29(I)	8.95(III)	9.62(II)
2	5.40(II)	4.77(V)	5.40(IV)	7.54(I)	6.93(III)
3	7.32(III)	8.53(II)	8.50(V)	9.99(IV)	9.68(I)
4	4.92(I)	5.00(III)	7.29(II)	7.85(V)	7.08(IV)
5	4.88(IV)	6.16(I)	7.83(III)	5.83(II)	8.51(V)

Compute the analysis of variance. What is the standard deviation applicable to a difference between treatment means? Between leaf-size means?

Exercise 9.11.2 An experiment with six yearling dairy heifers was conducted as two Latin squares. Treatments were three rations selected on the basis of diverse quality and physical characteristics and fed *ad libitum*. Each animal ate the three rations sequentially, one week on each. The variable given here is $Y =$ pounds dry matter consumed per 100 lb body weight. The data follow; numbers in ( ) indicate treatments. Treatments were (1) alfalfa hay, (2) corn silage, (3) blue-grass straw pellets.

Square	1			2		
Heifer	1	2	3	4	5	6
Week						
1	2.7(1)	2.6(2)	1.9(3)	3.3(1)	2.3(2)	0.1(3)
2	2.1(2)	0.2(3)	2.3(1)	1.7(3)	2.8(1)	1.8(2)
3	1.9(3)	2.1(1)	2.4(2)	2.1(2)	1.7(3)	2.7(1)

Source: Data courtesy of A. C. Linnerud, North Carolina State University Raleigh, NC.

Compute an analysis of variance for each square separately.

Are the ration means significantly different for each square? Heifer means for each square? Week means for each square?

Exercise 9.11.3 A 3×3 Latin square has only 2 df to estimate error. One way to improve the situation is to pool the results from similar experiments.

It is clear that pooling can be done by lines from the individual analyses. For example, for the two preceding squares, add the SS(weeks) to get SS(weeks within squares) with 4 df. Proceed similarly with heifers, treatments, and error. The missing df is that for "squares," which is easily computed. This analysis is not very imaginative and misses some points.

Instead of the above, pool the information from the two Latin squares of the preceding exercise as follows:

1. Compute SS(squares) using the two square totals. This was suggested above.
2. Compute SS(weeks) using the three week totals over both squares. This is different from the previous suggestion. It makes sense if the weeks are the same. Otherwise, the previous suggestion is satisfactory.
3. Compute SS(heifers within squares) by pooling the SS(heifers) from the two squares. This has 4 df. This procedure is that suggested in the preceding paragraph. (There are 5 df among heifers. The missing df is for "differences between heifers in different squares" or, simply, "squares.")
4. Compute SS(treatments) using the three treatment totals over squares. This is clearly the meaningful way to go after treatment differences.
5. Prepare a 3×2 table of week totals by squares. Analyze this on a per-observation basis as a two-way classification. SS(squares) and SS(weeks) are already in your analysis. The SS(residuals) with 2 df is a candidate for error.
6. Repeat step 5 for treatments. The SS(residuals) here is also a candidate for error.
7. Complete the analysis of variance table. Sum the df and SS columns. Your analysis is complete.
8. Find SS(total). How many df does it have? Does it equal the total in the SS column of 7?

9.12 Missing Plots in the Latin Square

The principle involved in the estimation of *missing values* is illustrated in Sec. 9.6 for the randomized complete block design. The formula for a *single missing observation* is

$$Y = \frac{r(R + C + T) - 2G}{(r-1)(r-2)} \tag{9.12}$$

where R, C, and T are the totals of the observed values for the row, column, and treatment containing the missing value, and G is the grand total of the observed values. The analysis of variance is performed in the usual manner with one degree of freedom being subtracted from total and error degrees of freedom for each missing value.

As in the case of the randomized complete block design, the treatment sum of squares is biased upward, this time by an amount given by

$$\text{Bias} = \frac{[G - R - C - (r-1)T]^2}{[(r-1)(r-2)]^2} \tag{9.13}$$

The sample standard error of the difference between the treatment mean, A, with the missing unit and a treatment mean, B, with all units present is

$$s_{\bar{Y}_A - \bar{Y}_B} = \sqrt{s^2\left[\frac{2}{r} + \frac{1}{(r-1)(r-2)}\right]} \tag{9.14}$$

The procedure suggested as more informative for a randomized block experiment with a missing plot can be adapted to the Latin square; however, it is quite lengthy.

If *several units*, not constituting a whole row, column, or treatment, are missing, the procedure is to make repeated applications of Eq. (9.12) as with Eq. (9.8). When all missing units have been estimated, the analysis of variance is performed in the usual manner, with degrees of freedom subtracted from total and error. The exact procedure for obtaining the standard error between two means is complicated. A useful approximation by Yates (9.20) can be used to determine the number of "effective replicates" for the two treatment means being compared. The effective number of replicates for one treatment being compared with another is determined by summing values assigned as follows:

1 if the other treatment is present in the corresponding row and column
2/3 if the other is missing in either row or column but not both
1/3 if the other is missing in both the row and column
0 when the treatment in question is missing

This is illustrated for the 5 × 5 Latin square given below with three units missing, one for each of treatments A, B, and C. The missing units are indicated by parentheses.

B	(A)	C	E	D
D	B	E	A	(C)
E	D	A	C	B
C	E	B	D	A
A	C	D	(B)	E

The effective number of replicates for treatments A and B in the comparison of their means is as follows. Starting with column 1, find A. B is in the same column but not the same row with A; assign value $\frac{2}{3}$. For column 2, A is missing; assign value 0. For column 3, B is present in both row and column with A; assign value 1. For column 4, B is absent in the column but present in the row with A; assign value $\frac{2}{3}$. For column 5, B is present in both column and row with A; assign value 1. Similarly for B. The assigned values and effective numbers of replicates are

For A: $\frac{2}{3} + 0 + 1 + \frac{2}{3} + 1 = \frac{10}{3}$

For B: $\frac{2}{3} + \frac{2}{3} + 1 + 0 + 1 = \frac{10}{3}$

The standard error of the difference between the means for treatments A and B is then $\sqrt{s^2(1/r_A + 1/r_B)} = \sqrt{s^2(\frac{3}{10} + \frac{3}{10})}$ where r_A and r_B refer to effective replication. The effective number of replications for a treatment can differ with the comparison being made.

When all values of one or more rows, columns, or treatments are missing, the analysis is usually more involved. The procedure when one row, column, or treatment is missing is given by Yates (9.21); if two or more are missing, see Yates and Hale (9.22). DeLury (9.9) also gives these procedures. Youden (9.23) discusses the construction of incomplete Latin squares as experimental designs.

At times investigators may have new materials they wish to include among their treatments but in insufficient amounts for replication. It is possible to replace a treatment in a Latin square by r unreplicated treatments and still provide an analysis of the data. Also, Latin squares are the basis of augmented designs in which each plot is split so that the experiment accommodates an additional r^2 unreplicated treatments. Finally, appropriately chosen rows may be added to a Latin square to provide designs where carry-over effects can be measured when it has been necessary to use each experimental unit for a sequence of treatments. Dairy cattle experiments often use such designs. For illustration, see Lucas (9.25).

Exercise 9.12.1 Discard one of the observations given in Exercise 9.11.1. Compute a missing value for the discarded observation and complete the analysis of variance. Compute the bias in treatment sum of squares. What is the standard deviation applicable to the difference between two treatment means, one having the missing observation?

Exercise 9.12.2 For the preceding exercise, find the total sum of squares of the 24 observations not discarded. Use this and the error sum of squares previously determined to find SS(rows, columns and treatments) with 12 df.

Now consider that the 24 observations are from a block design with rows and columns corresponding to blocks and treatments. Compute a missing value by Eq. (9.8). Complete the analysis of variance. Use the procedure recommended as informative to compute SS(rows and columns) = SS(rows and columns, ignoring treatments).

Now SS(rows, columns and treatments) − SS(rows and columns, ignoring treatments) = SS(treatments adjusted for rows and columns). This SS should equal SS(trts) from the Exercise 9.12.1 analysis when reduced by the bias. It may also be described as the additional reduction in total SS attributable to treatment effects in a model that previously included rows and columns only.

9.13 Estimation of Gain in Efficiency

The precision of a Latin square relative to a randomized complete block experiment can be estimated. Two estimates of the relative efficiency can be made, one when rows are considered as blocks and the other when columns are considered as blocks. We estimate the randomized complete blocks error mean square, if rows are the only blocks, as

$$\widehat{\text{MSE(RB)}} = \frac{f_c\text{MSC} + (f_t + f_e)\text{MSE}}{f_c + f_t + f_e} \tag{9.15}$$

where MSC and MSE are the mean squares for columns and error in the Latin square, and f_c, f_t, and f_e are the degrees of freedom for columns, treatments, and error in the Latin square. This means that columns are to be ignored as a source of variation. If columns are the only blocks, and rows are to be ignored, replace f_c and MSC in Eq. (9.15) by f_r and MSR, the degrees of freedom and mean square for rows in the Latin square.

Since more degrees of freedom are available for estimating the error mean square of randomized blocks than of Latin squares, this must be considered when computing the relative efficiency of the two designs if less than 20 degrees of freedom are involved in the Latin square error. This is accomplished by incorporating $(f_1 + 1)(f_2 + 3)/(f_2 + 1)(f_1 + 3)$ into the formula for the efficiency factor, where f_1 and f_2 are degrees of freedom for the Latin square and randomized complete block design error terms.

The data in Table 9.13 will be used to illustrate the procedure. The estimated error mean square with rows as blocks and columns eliminated is $3(2.27) + (3 + 6)(0.45)/(3 + 3 + 6) = 0.91$; with columns as blocks and rows eliminated it is $3(0.65) + (3 + 6)(0.45)/(3 + 3 + 6) = 0.50$. The adjustment for differences in degrees of freedom for the two designs is $(6 + 1) \times (9 + 3)/(9 + 1)(6 + 3) = 0.933$. Thus, the estimated relative precision using rows as blocks, so that we are comparing designs with and without columns in the presence of rows, is

$$\text{RE(LS to RCB)} = \frac{(f_1 + 1)(f_2 + 3)}{(f_2 + 1)(f_1 + 3)} \frac{\widehat{\text{MSE(RCB)}}}{\text{MSE(LS)}} 100$$

$$= .933 \frac{0.91}{0.45} 100 = 189 \text{ percent}$$

Columns are clearly a source of variation an experimenter would want to control.

If columns were blocks, so that designs with and without rows can be compared,

$$\text{RE(LS to RCB)} = .933 \frac{0.50}{0.45} 100 = 104 \text{ percent}$$

The row grouping has not controlled variation appreciably and the investigator might wish to ignore it when designing a new experiment for similar circumstances.

The column grouping increased the precision by an estimated 89 percent and rows by an estimated 4 percent. Thus, if the randomized complete block design had been used with the rows of the Latin square as blocks and if columns had been ignored, an estimated 89 percent more replicates would have been required to detect differences of the same magnitude as detected by the Latin square, whereas 4 percent more would have been required if columns had been blocks and rows had been ignored. Rows appear to be inefficient as blocks, whereas columns seem reasonably efficient. In any field of research, a number of such comparisons are generally needed before it can be concluded that Latin squares are likely to be more precise, on the average, than randomized blocks.

Exercise 9.13.1 Compute the efficiency of the Latin square relative to the randomized complete block design for the data in Exercise 9.11.1, using leaf size as blocks. Repeat, using plants as blocks.

9.14 The Linear Model for the Latin Square

Let Y_{ij} represent the observation at the intersection of the ith row and jth column. This locates any observation but tells nothing of the treatment applied. A third subscript could be misleading, implying r^3 rather than r^2 observations. For example, treatment 1 appears once in each of the r rows, once in each of the r columns, but only r times in all; hence, $t = 1$ implies a set of i, j values, r in number. Similarly for the other values of t.

Table 9.14 Average values of mean squares for a Latin square analysis

Source	df	Average values of mean squares	
		Model I (fixed)	Model II (random)
Rows	$r-1$	$\sigma^2 + r(\sum \beta_i^2)/(r-1)$	$\sigma^2 + r\sigma_\beta^2$
Columns	$r-1$	$\sigma^2 + r(\sum \kappa_j^2)/(r-1)$	$\sigma^2 + r\sigma_\kappa^2$
Treatments	$r-1$	$\sigma^2 + r(\sum \tau_t^2)/(r-1)$	$\sigma^2 + r\sigma_\tau^2$
Residual	$(r-1)(r-2)$	σ^2	σ^2

We express any observation by

$$Y_{ij(t)} = \mu + \beta_i + \kappa_j + \tau_{(t)} + \varepsilon_{ij} \tag{9.16}$$

This implies, by the use of (t), that an ordinary three-way classification is not involved.

For valid conclusions, the ε's must be random and uncorrelated, and if tests of significance or confidence statements are to be made using procedures already discussed, they must also be normally distributed. A model with interactions does not lead to a valid error for testing hypotheses and the Latin square is not a suitable design if interactions are present.

Various assumptions may be made about the components of the means, that is, the β's, κ's, and τ's. Average values of the various mean squares are given in Table 9.14 according to the model assumed.

The mixed model is not shown, but average values of mean squares are obtained by replacing the appropriate contribution by the corresponding contribution as one changes from fixed to random effects, for example, replacing $(\sum \beta_i^2)/(r-1)$ by σ_β^2.

9.15 The Size of an Experiment

Sample size is discussed in Secs. 5.13, 5.14, and 6.7. These sections deal with obtaining confidence intervals not larger than some stated length and with detecting differences of stated size; problems involving more than two treatments are not considered, although most experiments include more than two treatments.

Approaches to the general problem of size of an experiment include those of Cochran and Cox (9.8), Harris et al. (9.12), Harter (9.13), Tang (9.17), and Tukey (9.19). Two of these will be discussed.

Calculation of the number of replicates required depends on

1. An estimate of σ^2
2. The size of the difference to be detected

3. The assurance with which it is desired to detect the difference (Power of the test = $1 - \beta$)
4. The level of significance to be used in the actual experiment (Type I error)
5. The test required, whether one- or two-tailed

Section 5.13 gives a reasonable solution to the problem and illustrates the procedure. This solution calls for a comparisonwise error rate.

In practice, one may obtain an estimate of σ^2 from previous experiments or circumvent the need by expressing δ as a multiple of the true standard deviation, σ. For a block design with t treatments, $\sigma_{\bar{D}}^2$ of Chap. 5 will be $2\sigma^2$. Thus, for two-tailed alternatives, Eq. (5.33) may be rewritten as

$$r \geq 2(Z_{\alpha/2} + Z_\beta)^2 \left(\frac{\sigma}{\delta}\right)^2 \tag{9.17}$$

Subscripts on each Z are based on acceptable Type I and Type II errors but refer specifically to the amount of probability in a single tail of the Z distribution.

To illustrate the use of Eq. (9.17), suppose that we wish to conduct an experiment like that which gave rise to the data of Table 9.2, again using six treatments. We desire to detect differences, regardless of direction, of not more than 2.5 percent of oil at the 95 percent level with 90 percent assurance of detecting a true difference of this size; thus $\alpha = .05$ and $\beta = .10$.

Table 9.2 gives $s^2 = 1.31$, which is an estimate of σ^2; $Z_{\alpha/2} = Z_{.025} = 1.96$ and $Z_\beta = Z_{.10} = 1.28$. Consequently,

$$r \geq \frac{2(1.96 + 1.28)^2 1.31}{2.5^2} = 4.4, \text{ or } 5, \text{ blocks}$$

The experiment with 6 treatments and 5 blocks will have $(6 - 1) \times (5 - 1) = 20$ df. The required adjustment factor is $(20 + 3)/(20 + 1)$ and the adjusted number of blocks becomes $4.4(23)/21 = 4.8$ to give 5 blocks.

Tukey's (9.19) procedure gives the sample size necessary to give a set of confidence intervals not larger than a specified size for all possible differences between true treatment means. The level of significance is chosen by the investigator and the error rate applies to a Type I error on an experimentwise basis.

Since an experiment is a sample, it is impossible to give complete assurance that, for example, 95 percent confidence intervals will be invariably less than the specified size. Hence it becomes necessary to state how frequently, or with what assurance, it is desired to have the confidence intervals less than the specified length.

Tukey gives the following formula for computing experiment size.

$$r = \frac{s_1^2 q_\alpha^2(p, f_2) F_\beta(f_2, f_1)}{d^2} \tag{9.18}$$

where s_1^2 is an available estimate of σ^2 based on f_1 degrees of freedom; q is obtained from Table A.8 for the desired confidence coefficient and the degrees of freedom, f_2, for the error mean square in the experiment being planned; F_β is obtained from Table A.6 (one-tailed) for the indicated pair of degrees of freedom; and β is defined such that $1 - \beta$ is the assurance we wish to have that the confidence intervals for differences will be less than $2d$. In other words, d is defined as the half-length semiconfidence interval desired. Note that q and F depend on the value being sought. This implies that we may have to apply the formula several times.

To illustrate the use of Eq. (9.18) suppose that we again use the data of Table 9.2. It is decided to use a set of confidence intervals at the 95 percent level and to include the same six treatments; the number of treatments is necessary when obtaining q. We wish all the 95 percent semiconfidence intervals to be of length not more than 2.5 percent oil with assurance of .90.

From Table 9.2, $s_1^2 = 1.31$ and $f_1 = 15$ degrees of freedom. To obtain q, we must guess f_2. If we guess β will be five replicates and are planning a randomized complete block design, then $f_2 = (5 - 1)(6 - 1) = 20$ degrees of freedom and $q_\alpha(p, f_2) = 4.45$. We find $F_{.10}(20, 15) = 1.92$ and have set $d = 2.5$ percent oil. Hence

$$r = 1.31(4.45)^2(1.92)/(2.5)^2 = 8.0 \text{ blocks}$$

Since 8 blocks are considerably more than expected, we underestimated f_2. It is then worthwhile to estimate r again, using 7 or 8 blocks to determine f_2. For 7 blocks, $f_2 = (7 - 1)(6 - 1) = 30$ degrees of freedom. Now

$$r = 1.31(4.30)^2(1.87)/(2.5)^2 = 7.2 \text{ blocks}$$

It now appears that 7 blocks are not quite sufficient, but 8 blocks are somewhat more than adequate for the desired purpose.

Stein's two-sample procedure (Sec. 5.14) has been generalized by Healy (9.14) for obtaining joint confidence intervals of fixed length and confidence coefficient for all possible differences between population means. The procedure is applicable when the investigator is able to continue the same experiment and does not need to worry about heterogeneity of variance for the two stages of the experiment.

9.16 Transformations

The valid application of tests of significance in the analysis of variance requires that the experimental errors be independently and normally distributed with a common variance. In addition, the scale of measurement should be one for which the linear additive model holds. It is customary to rely upon randomization to break up any correlation of experimental errors whenever it is possible to incorporate a randomization procedure into the investigation. Additivity may be tested by a method given in Sec. 15.8. The other condition which has been given much attention by statisticians is that of stabilizing the variance.

Heterogeneity of error, or heteroscedasticity, may be classified as irregular or regular. The *irregular* type is characterized by certain treatments possessing considerably more variability than others, with no necessarily apparent relation between means and variances. Differences in variability may or may not be expected in advance. For example, in comparing insecticides, untreated or check experimental units are often included. The numbers of insects in the check units are likely to be considerably larger and more variable than those in units where an insecticide offers considerable control. Thus, the check units contribute to the error mean square to a greater degree than do the treated units. Consequently, the standard deviations, based on the pooled error mean square, will be too large for comparison among insecticides and may fail to detect real differences. In other cases, certain treatments may exhibit considerably more variation than others for no apparent reason. This part of the experiment is not under statistical control.

When heterogeneity of error is of the irregular type, the best procedure is to omit certain portions of the data from the analysis or to subdivide the error mean square into components applicable to the various comparisons of interest. The latter procedure is discussed to some extent in Sec. 9.5.

The *regular* type of heterogeneity usually arises from some type of nonnormality in the data, the variability within the several treatments being related to the treatment means in some reasonable fashion. If the parent distribution is known, then the relation between the treatment means and the treatment variances, computed on an individual treatment basis, is known. The data can be transformed or measured on a new scale of measurement so that the transformed data are approximately normally distributed. Such transformations are also intended to make the means and variances independent, with the resulting variances homogeneous. This result is not always attained. When it is impossible to find a transformation that will make the means and variances independent and the variance stable, other methods of analysis, such as weighted analyses, must be used.

The more common transformations are the square root, logarithm, and angular or arcsin transformation. These are discussed briefly below.

Square root transformation, $\sqrt{Y}$ When data consist of small whole numbers, for example, number of bacterial colonies in a plate count, number of plants or insects of a stated species in a given area, etc., they often follow the Poisson distribution for which the mean and variance are equal. (See Sec. 23.6.) The analysis of such enumeration data is often best accomplished by first taking the square root of each observation before proceeding with the analysis of variance.

Percentage data based on counts and a common denominator, where the range of percentages is 0 to 20 percent or 80 to 100 percent but not both, may also be analyzed by using the square root transformation. Percentages between 80 and 100 should be subtracted from 100 before the transformation is made. The same transformation is useful for percentages in the same ranges where the observations are clearly on a continuous scale, since means and variances may be approximately equal.

When very small values are involved, $\sqrt{Y}$ tends to overcorrect so that the range of transformed values giving a small mean may be larger than the range of transformed values giving a larger mean. For this reason, $\sqrt{Y + \frac{1}{2}}$ is recommended as an appropriate transformation when some of the values are under 10 or even under 15 and especially when zeros are present.

The appropriate means for a table of treatment means are found by squaring the treatment means computed from the $\sqrt{Y}$ values. These will be lower than means of the original data, a situation roughly corrected by addition of the unconverted error mean square to each. It must also be remembered that the additive model should hold on the transformed rather than the original scale. A test of additivity is given in Sec. 15.8.

Logarithmic transformation, log Y When variances are proportional to the squares of the treatment means or standard deviations are proportional to means, the logarithmic transformation equalizes the variances. The base 10 is used for convenience, though any base is satisfactory. Effects which are multiplicative on the original scale of measurement become additive on the logarithmic scale, for example, where one treatment gives a response consistently 20 percent higher than another; see Table 7.13. Means obtained by transforming back to the original scale using antilogs of means of log Y values are geometric means of the original data. When tests like the lsd are used on the transformed data, they are the equivalent of *least significant ratios* on means that have been transformed back to the original scale. This provides an appropriate method of presenting the experimental results.

The logarithmic transformation is used with positive integers which cover a wide range. It cannot be used directly for zero values and when some of the values are less than 10, it is desirable to have a transformation which acts like the square root for small values and like the logarithmic for large values. Addition of 1 to each number prior to taking logarithms has the desired effect. That is, $\log(Y + 1)$ behaves like the square root transformation for numbers up to 10 and differs little from log Y thereafter.

In some experimental work, it is desired to conduct an analysis of variance where the variable is the variance. The logarithmic transformation of the variances prior to analysis is appropriate, that is, we analyze $\log s^2$. Such variances should have 10 df or more for an analysis of variance of the transformed data to be appropriate. Also Bartlett's test of the homogeneity of a set of variances, Sec. 20.3, requires the use of $\log s^2$.

Angular or inverse sine transformation, arcsin $\sqrt{Y}$ *or* $\sin^{-1}\sqrt{Y}$ This transformation is applicable to binomial data expressed as decimal fractions or percentages, and is especially recommended when the percentages cover a wide range of values. The mechanics of the transformation require decimal fractions, but tables of the arcsin transformation are usually entered with percentages (see Table A.10). The tabled values or arcsin values are expressed in either degrees or radians. The variance of the resulting observations is approximately constant, being $821/n$ when the transformed data are expressed in degrees and $1/(4n) = 0.25/n$ when in radians, n being the common denominator of all fractions. This variance makes it clear that all percentages are intended to be based on an equal number of observations. However, the transformation is often used when the denominators are unequal, especially if they are approximately equal; otherwise, a weighted analysis is necessary. Bartlett (9.3) suggests that $25/n$ be substituted for 0 percent, and $100 - 25/n$ for 100 percent (n being the divisor).

The square root transformation has already been recommended for percentages between 0 and 20 or 80 and 100, the latter being subtracted from 100 before transformation. If the range of percentages is 30 to 70, it is doubtful if any transformation is needed.

Some general considerations It is always helpful to examine discrete data to ascertain whether or not there is a correlation between the treatment means and their within-treatment variances. Unfortunately, this is not possible for most designs. If the variation shows little change, the value of any transformation is doubtful. Where there is change in the variation, it is not always clear which transformation is best.

When the appropriate transformation is in doubt, it is sometimes helpful to transform the data for several treatments, including some with small, intermediate, and large means on the original scale, and again examine means and variances for the possibility of a relationship on the transformed scale. The transformation for which the relation is minimum is likely the most appropriate.

When a transformation is made, all comparisons or confidence interval estimates are made on the transformed scale. If it is not desired to present findings on the transformed scale, then means should be transformed back to the original scale. When the results of an analysis of transformed data are presented using the original scale of measurement, this should be made clear to the reader. It is not appropriate to transform standard deviations or variances, arising from transformed data, back to the original scale.

The experimenter who is interested in further information on the assumptions underlying the analysis of variance and on transformations is referred to papers by Eisenhart (9.10), Cochran (9.5, 9.6, 9.7), and Bartlett (9.3). These papers give many additional references.

Exercise 9.16.1 In evaluating insecticides, the numbers of living adult plum curculios emerging from separate caged areas of treated soil were observed. The results shown in the accompanying table are available through the courtesy of C. B. McIntyre, Entomology Department, University of Wisconsin. Note that this is a randomized complete block design and we cannot directly measure the within-treatment variances.

	Treatment					
Block	Lindane	Dieldrin	Aldrin	EPN	Chlordane	Check
1	14	7	6	95	37	212
2	6	1	1	133	31	172
3	8	0	1	86	13	202
4	36	15	4	115	69	217

What transformation would you recommend for these data? Analyze the data using log $(Y + 1)$ as the transformation. Use both of Duncan's procedures to test all possible pairs of treatment means exclusive of that for check.

Exercise 9.16.2 Aughtry (9.1) presents the following data on the symbiosis of *Medicago sativa* (53)–*M. falcata* (50) cross with strain *B*. Data are percentages of plants with nodules out of 20 plants per cell. The experiment was conducted as a randomized complete block design.

	Parents		F_1	F_2 lots from each F_1			
Block	53	50	53 × 50	114–1	114–2	114–3	114–4
1	11	65	47	31	22	16	70
2	16	67	32	40	16	19	63
3	6	76	40	27	20	20	52

What transformation would you recommend for the analysis of these data? Use the angular transformation and conduct the analysis of variance. How does the observed variance compare with the theoretical variance?

References

9.1. Aughtry, J. D.: "The effects of genetic factors in Medicago on symbiosis with Rhizobium," *Cornell Univ. Agr. Exper. Sta. Memo.* 280, 1948.

9.2. Babcock, S. M.: "Variations in yield and quality of milk," *6th Ann. Rep. Wis. Agr. Exper. Sta.*, **6**:42–67 (1889).

9.3. Bartlett, M. S.: "The use of transformations," *Biom.*, **3**:39–52 (1947).

9.4. Bing, A.: "Gladiolus control experiments, 1953," *Gladiolus* 1954, New England Gladiolus Society, Inc.

9.5. Cochran, W. G.: "Some difficulties in the statistical analysis of replicated experiments," *Empire J. Exper. Agr.*, **6**:157–175 (1938).

9.6. Cochran, W. G.: "Analysis of variance for percentages based on unequal numbers," *J. Amer. Statist. Ass.*, **38**:287–301 (1943).
9.7. Cochran, W. G.: "Some consequences when the assumptions for the analysis of variance are not satisfied," *Biom.*, **3**:22–38 (1947).
9.8. Cochran, W. G., and G. M. Cox: *Experimental designs*, 2d ed., Wiley, New York, 1957.
9.9. DeLury, D. B.: "The analysis of latin squares when some observations are missing," *J. Amer. Statist. Ass.*, **41**:370–389 (1946).
9.10. Eisenhart, C.: "The assumptions underlying the analysis of variance," *Biom.*, **3**:1–21 (1947).
9.11. Fisher, R. A., and F. Yates: *Statistical tables for biological, agricultural and medical research*, 5th ed., Hafner, New York, 1957.
9.12. Harris, M., D. G. Horvitz, and A. M. Mood: "On the determination of sample sizes in designing experiments," *J. Amer. Statist. Ass.*, **43**:391–402 (1948).
9.13. Harter, H. L.: "Error rates and sample sizes for range tests in multiple comparisons," *Biom.*, **13**:511–536 (1957).
9.14. Healy, W. C., Jr.: "Two-sample procedures in simultaneous estimation," *Ann. Math. Statist.*, **27**:687–702 (1956).
9.15. Peterson, W. J., H. P. Tucker, J. T. Wakeley, R. E. Comstock, and F. D. Cochran: "Variation in moisture and ascorbic acid content from leaf to leaf and plant to plant in turnip greens," No. 2 in *Southern Coop. Ser. Bull.* 10, pp. 13–17 (1951).
9.16. Sackston, W. E., and R. B. Carson: "Effect of pasmo disease of flax on the yield and quality of linseed oil," *Can. J. Bot.*, **29**:339–351 (1951).
9.17. Tang, P. C.: "The power function of the analysis of variance tests with tables and illustrations of their use." *Statist. Res. Mem.*, **2**:126–157 (1938).
9.18. Tucker, H. P., J. T. Wakeley, and F. D. Cochran: "Effect of washing and removing excess moisture by wiping or by air current on the ascorbic acid content of turnip greens," No. 10 in *Southern Coop. Ser. Bull.* 10, pp. 54–56 (1951).
9.19. Tukey, J. W.: "The problem of multiple comparisons," Ditto, Princeton University, Princeton, NJ, 1953.
9.20. Yates, F.: "The analysis of replicated experiments when the field results are incomplete," *Empire J. Exper. Agr.*, **1**:129–142 (1933).
9.21. Yates, F.: "Incomplete latin squares," *J. Agr. Sci.*, **26**:301–315 (1936).
9.22. Yates, F., and R. W. Hale: "The analysis of latin squares when two or more rows, columns, or treatments are missing," *J. Roy. Statist. Soc. Suppl.*, **6**:67–69 (1939).
9.23. Youden, W. J.: *Statistical methods for chemists*, Wiley, New York, 1951.
9.24. Taylor, J.: "Errors of treatment comparisons, when observations are missing," *Nature*, **162**:262–263 (1948).
9.25. Lucas, H. L.: "Extra-period latin square change-over designs," *J. Dairy Sci.*, **40**:225–239 (1957).
9.26. Federer, W. T.: "Augmented designs with one-way elimination of heterogeneity," *Biom.*, **17**:447–473 (1961).
9.27. Addelman, Sidney: "The generalized randomized block design," *Amer. Statist.*, **23**(4):35–36 (1969).

CHAPTER

TEN

LINEAR REGRESSION

10.1 Introduction

In previous chapters, we developed the idea that an observation is the sum of a population mean and a random component. A further set of components was available for means and each component was either present in or absent from any particular mean. For example, in a completely random design every population mean contained μ, whereas the ith contained τ_i but no other τ. We now consider population means with one component a fixed multiple of some measurable and variable quantity, called a *concomitant variable.*

In this chapter, we discuss the uses of a concomitant observation, with the assumptions involved in the various uses, and with the necessary computations. Chapters 11, 14, 17, and 19 also deal with these general problems.

10.2 The Linear Regression of Y on X

In linear regression, Y values are obtained from several populations, each population being determined by a corresponding X value. Randomness of Y is essential for probability theory to apply. Also, it is assumed the Y populations are normal and have a common variance.

The Y variable is termed the *dependent* variable since any Y value depends on the population sampled. The X variable is called the *independent* variable or *argument.*

The data in Table 10.1, pen records from the 1953–1954 New York random sample test, are used for illustration. The dependent variable is feed

Table 10.1 Average body weight X and food consumption Y for 50 hens from each of 10 White Leghorn strains

350-day period

Body weight		Food consumption	
X	$X' = X - 4.0$	Y	$Y' = Y - 80$
4.6	0.6	87.1	7.1
5.1	1.1	93.1	13.1
4.8	0.8	89.8	9.8
4.4	0.4	91.4	11.4
5.9	1.9	99.5	19.5
4.7	0.7	92.1	12.1
5.1	1.1	95.5	15.5
5.2	1.2	99.3	19.3
4.9	0.9	93.4	13.4
5.1	1.1	94.4	14.4
$\sum (X - \bar{X})^2 = 1.536$		$\sum (Y - \bar{Y})^2 = 135.604$	
9 df each			

Source: Data courtesy of S. C. King, now at Purdue University, Lafayette, Indiana.

consumed Y; it depends on the variable body weight X. The 10 pairs of values from Table 10.1 are plotted in Fig. 10.1. A fairly definite relation exists between the two variables. In particular, a straight line such as has been drawn among these points could serve as a moving average of the Y values. It is always a good idea to plot such data to get an indication of the sharpness of any relation, of departure from linearity, and of outlying or

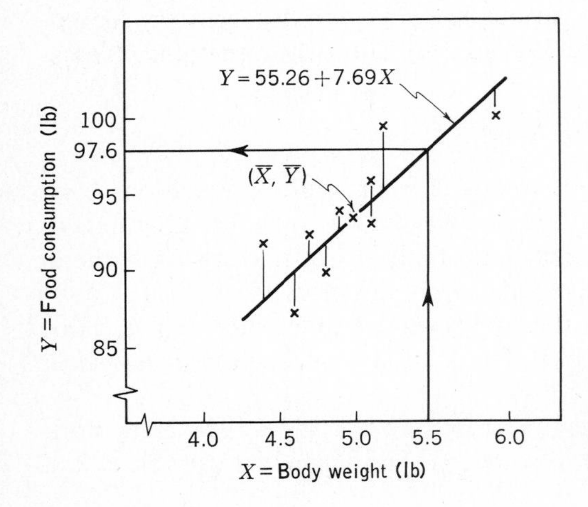

Figure 10.1 Regression of food consumption Y on body weight X for 10 White Leghorn strains (averages for 50 birds).

unusual observations. Let us now consider a straight-line graph and its equation.

The equation of any straight line may be written in the form $Y = a + bX$ (see Fig. 10.2). Any point (X, Y) on this line has an X coordinate, or *abscissa*, and a Y coordinate, or *ordinate*, whose values satisfy the equation. Coordinates of points not on the line do not satisfy the equation. When $X = 0$, $Y = a$ so that a is the point where the line crosses the Y axis, that is, a is the Y *intercept*. When a is zero, the line goes through the origin. A unit change in X results in a change of b units in Y so that b is a measure of the *slope* of the line. When b is positive, both variables increase or decrease together; when b is negative, one variable increases as the other decreases. For a straight line, any two points or the slope and the Y intercept uniquely determine the position of the line. Mathematicians call relations such as $Y = a + bX$ *functional relations*. For a value of X, a functional relation assigns a value to Y; an exact mathematical formula relates the two variables. This sort of relation has been used in Chap. 3 to assign probabilities, as in Eqs. (3.4) to (3.6), and determine ordinates of a curve, as in Eq. (3.11).

The research scientist dealing with bivariate observations will not have data that fall on a straight line. Even when temperatures are being measured on Fahrenheit and Celsius scales, there will be random variation attributable to measurement error; this will negate a perfect relation, even though an underlying functional relation between the variables exists. More often, bivariate data will follow a *statistical law*, one that holds on the average. This is the case for the data in Table 10.1. Clearly, for a particular body weight X, there is no single established value of food consumption Y; rather there is a population of Y's and random observations are drawn from this population.

When a straight line is to be fitted to data consisting of more than two pairs of values, one chooses that line which best fits the data, that is, the one which is the best moving average. Our criterion of best is the least-squares criterion. This requires that the sum of the squares of the deviations of the observed points from the straight-line moving average for the same X be a

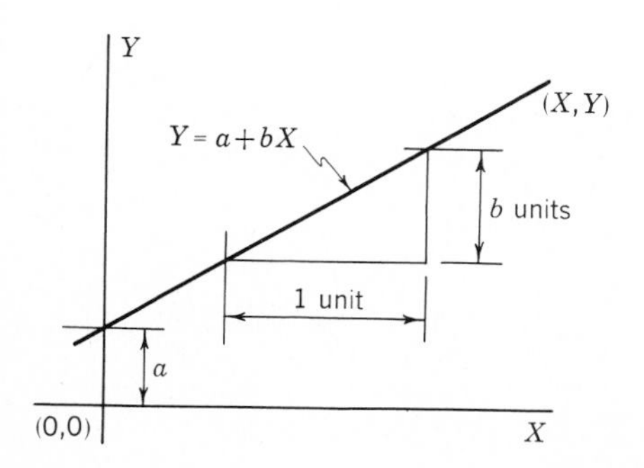

Figure 10.2 Straight-line graph.

minimum. For such a "fitted" line, b is called the *regression coefficient*; the line is called a regression line; its equation is called a *regression equation.*

To determine the regression coefficient b, we need the sum of *cross products* of the deviations of the observations from their corresponding means, and the sum of squares of X. Definition and computing formulas for a sum of cross products are given in Eqs. (10.1) and (10.2), respectively.

$$\text{SP} = \sum_i (X_i - \bar{X})(Y_i - \bar{Y}) \qquad \text{definition} \qquad (10.1)$$

$$= \sum_i X_i Y_i - \frac{\sum_i X_i \sum_i Y_i}{n} \qquad \text{computing} \qquad (10.2)$$

For coded X and Y, that is, X' and Y', we obtain

$$\sum (X - \bar{X})(Y - \bar{Y}) = 144.70 - \frac{(9.8)(135.6)}{10} = 11.812$$

Coding by addition or subtraction of a constant for each variable does not affect sums of cross products. The following relations are also useful:

$$\sum (X_i - \bar{X})(Y_i - \bar{Y}) = \sum X_i(Y_i - \bar{Y}) = \sum (X_i - \bar{X})Y_i$$

The similarity between a sum of cross products and a sum of squares, for both definition and working formulas, is obvious when Y_i and $\bar{Y}$ are replaced by X and $\bar{X}$ in the cross-product formula. Sums of squares and cross products are often referred to simply as *sums of products.*

When $\sum (X - \bar{X})(Y - \bar{Y})$ is divided by the degrees of freedom, it is called a *covariance* (see Sec. 5.10). We have $\sum (X - \bar{X})(Y - \bar{Y})/(n - 1) = 11.812/9 = 1.312$. A covariance is a measure of the joint variation of two variables and may be either positive or negative. It is symmetrical in X and Y, and the variables need not be specified as dependent and independent.

The regression coefficient is determined from

$$b = \frac{\sum (X - \bar{X})(Y - \bar{Y})}{\sum (X - \bar{X})^2} \qquad (10.3)$$

$$= \frac{11.812}{1.536} = 7.69 \text{ lb of feed per pound of bird}$$

For an increase of 1 lb in body weight, food consumption is 7.69 lb.

The regression equation may be written as Eq. (10.4) since the regression line passes through the sample mean.

$$\hat{Y} - \bar{Y} = b(X - \bar{X}) \qquad \text{or} \qquad \hat{Y} = \bar{Y} + b(X - \bar{X}) \qquad (10.4)$$

The ^ simply indicates that this is the sample regression line, not an observed Y.

$$\hat{Y} - 93.56 = 7.69(X - 4.98)$$

or

$$\hat{Y} = 93.56 + 7.69(X - 4.98) \qquad \text{or} \qquad \hat{Y} = 55.26 + 7.69X$$

(see Fig. 10.1). The Y intercept a is $\bar{Y} - b\bar{X} = 55.26$.

Lines computed in regression problems are lines about which the pairs of values cluster; they are not lines upon which the points fall. A point on a regression line is an estimate of a mean of a population of Y's, those Y's having the corresponding X value.

Exercise 10.2.1 The pen records shown below for White Leghorns in the California Random Sample Test† are similar to the data of Table 10.1.

Y(350-day food consumption, lb)	87.8, 93.2, 98.0, 89.8, 94.0, 83.0, 88.3, 82.4, 84.8, 80.2
X(Average body weight of 50 birds, lb)	4.15, 4.76, 5.23, 4.75, 5.13, 4.24, 4.66, 4.41, 4.50, 4.23

Compute the sample regression equation of consumption Y on body weight X. What is the regression coefficient and what unit applies to it? What is the interpretation of this regression coefficient?

Exercise 10.2.2 Show algebraically that $\sum (X - \bar{X})(Y - \bar{Y}) = \sum (X - \bar{X})Y$. (*Hint:* Show that each equals the computing formula.)

Exercise 10.2.3 In a running-for-health program, measurements were made toward the end of a running year on X_1 = rate of heart recovery after a Harvard step test, X_2 = number of jumps to exhaustion, X_3 = a blood cholesterol measurement, X_4 = a blood uric acid measurement, and Y = time in min : sec to run 1.5 mi for a number of males. Some of the data follow.

X_1	52	39	39	51	49	45	54	54
X_2	45	60	40	101	60	51	50	99
X_3	269	279	248	318	318	254	263	320
X_4	43	65	78	73	71	69	67	45
Y	11 : 16	12 : 30	11 : 30	10 : 17	11 : 48	11 : 06	12 : 02	11 : 52

X_1	47	69	35	33	45	39	61	46	42
X_2	34	41	251	125	105	40	42	113	25
X_3	228	306	303	264	253	281	346	223	266
X_4	69	60	65	59	76	40	70	72	60
Y	11 : 28	13 : 45	8 : 18	10 : 23	12 : 02	13 : 45	13 : 41	10 : 30	23 : 11

Source: Data courtesy of Ardell Linnerud, North Carolina State University, Raleigh, NC.

Compute the sample regression equation of running time Y on each of the X variables separately. Write each equation in intercept form and in the form of Eq. (10.4). What is the interpretation of the regression coefficient in each case?

† Data courtesy of S. C. King, Purdue University, Lafayette, Indiana.

Exercise 10.2.4 In a study of forest floor accumulations, plots of $\frac{1}{10}$ acre of lodgepole pine on a watershed in Wyoming were used. The response variable recorded here is Y = weight of humus in pounds per acre. Various predictor variables were used, including X_1 = basal area in square inches measured at waist height and X_2 = tree density. Some of the data follow.

X_1	3,062	2,347	1,948	3,075	2,899	2,138	2,316	1,968	2,827	1,072
X_2	280	203	307	148	79	71	97	51	192	44
Y	51,916	47,022	29,945	42,649	43,557	34,964	57,129	21,633	68,620	51,417
X_1	2,804	2,358	2,526	2,400	2,507	3,009	3,764	4,070	3,038	3,116
X_2	122	136	97	124	404	270	55	88	82	33
Y	34,008	52,667	48,575	30,793	29,242	38,174	61,653	71,410	61,625	54,180

Source: Data courtesy of James Reynolds, North Carolina State University, Raleigh, NC. See also J. I. Reynolds and O. H. Knight (10.9).

Compute the sample regression equation of weight of humus on each of the X variables. Write each equation in intercept and in deviations-from-means form. What is the interpretation of the regression coefficient in each case?

Exercise 10.2.5 Reynolds et al. (10.8) studied Y = (photosynthesis rate)10^4 of *Larrea tridentata* and its relation to X_1 = irradiance, X_2 = ambient CO_2 concentration, $X_3 = 10^6/X_1$, and X_4 = leaf resistance to water vapor among other independent variables. The data were collected in the Duke University phytotron; some of these data follow.

X_1	294	190	294	550	550	2,000	550	550	550	550	2,000	2,000
X_2	665	671	664	577	577	576	682	614	605	605	545	502
X_3	3,401	5,263	3,401	1,818	1,818	500	1,818	1,818	1,818	1,818	500	500
X_4	990	968	1,868	1,814	2,521	1,516	4,707	1,935	4,675	2,234	1,158	985
Y	348	131	402	731	526	1,346	4,767	655	360	618	1,385	1,550

X_1	2,000	2,000	800	800	1,200	1,200	1,200	1,600	1,600	400	400	800	800
X_2	502	521	536	536	556	570	547	582	553	576	568	553	557
X_3	500	500	1,250	1,250	833	833	833	625	625	2,500	2,500	1,250	1,250
X_4	1,697	646	1,086	998	911	765	1,284	915	1,410	4,111	1,802	801	983
Y	1,415	1,467	842	927	1,099	1,086	910	1,055	937	349	498	989	829

Compute the sample regression equation of photosynthesis rate ($\times 10^4$) on each of the X variables. Write each equation in intercept form and as in Eq. (10.4). What is the interpretation of the regression coefficient in each case?

10.3 The Linear Regression Model and Equation

By definition, the true regression of Y on X consists of the means of populations of Y values, where a population is determined by the X value. A regression line need not be straight. In sampling, it is necessary to assume the form of the line of the means; otherwise it would not be possible to develop a computation procedure. We have assumed a straight line, or *linear regression.* Such assumptions are usually made on the basis of theory or experience, or even after looking at the plotted data. Because of computational ease, the straight line is often chosen as an approximation when it fits reasonably well over the range of X involved, even when the true form is known to be nonlinear.

The mathematical description of an observation is given by

$$Y_i = \mu_{Y \cdot X} + \varepsilon_i = \alpha + \beta X_i + \varepsilon_i$$
$$= \mu + \beta(X_i - \bar{X}) + \varepsilon_i \tag{10.5}$$

α and β are parameters to be estimated and X is an observable parameter; α represents the population Y intercept, the value of μ_Y at $X = 0$, that is $\mu_{Y \cdot 0}$; β is the slope of the line through the means of the Y populations. In the last form of the model given by Eq. (10.5), with the X's measured from their mean, μ is estimated by $\bar{Y}$. The ε's are assumed to be from a single population with zero mean and variance σ^2. This variance is another parameter to be estimated.

The regression model may be Model I with fixed X's, or Model II with random X's.

For Model I, the X's are selected by the investigator; there is no random sampling variation associated with them. The Y values must be random. Selection of the X's may involve a specific set of values or values that are simply within a desired range. Response to an insecticide might thus be measured for a specific series of dilutions, whereas human body weight might be for a range of heights restricted by a job description. When expected values are being considered, the same X's are to be used in defining the repeated sampling that is their basis. These X's must be measured without error.

Values of the independent variable, for example, hours of artificial sunlight, levels of temperatures, amounts of treatments, and distances between seedlings, may be equally or otherwise conveniently spaced for efficiency in the conduct of an experiment.

Measurement of Y without error is not a theoretical requirement provided that the error of measurement has a distribution with known mean, generally zero. The observed variance of Y is, then, the sum of the biological or other variance in Y and the variance of the error of measurement. It is, of course, important to keep errors in measurements to a minimum.

If one makes a random observation on Y for a correctly identified $X = X_i$, then the observer may proceed to use this information meaningfully. However, if one records the value of X_i incorrectly as X_i', then the subsequent computations may result in misleading conclusions because the population of Y's is incorrectly identified. Figure 10.3 should make this clear.

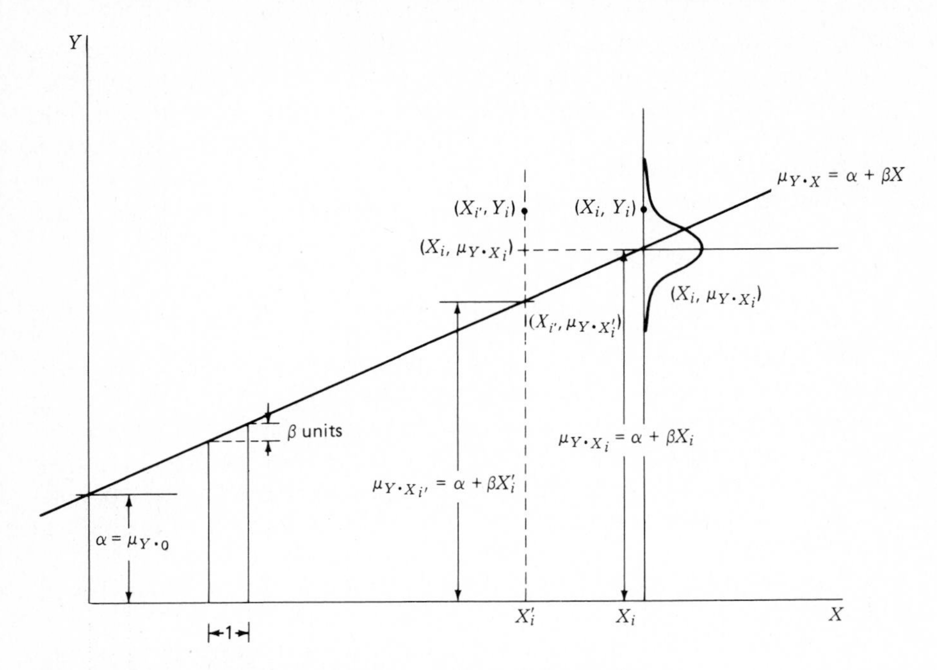

Figure 10.3 True regression of Y on X; error of measurement in X_i.

Suppose that Model I is appropriate and the problem is further specified as follows.

First, assume that an underlying functional or mathematical relation exists between X and Y but that observational errors are possible. The problem is to estimate the relation. If the X's only are measured without error as in Fig. 10.4*a*, then the computing procedures already discussed are applicable. There is a single regression line, that of Y on X.

Second, if the X's are also measured with error as in Fig. 10.4*b*, then one must visualize a bivariate distribution at each point on the true line. To estimate this underlying functional relationship, an alternative computing procedure should be used; see Bartlett (10.6) or Natrella (10.7).

Third, a statistical relation or association exists between X and Y. Initially, a single bivariate distribution over the X, Y plane is appropriate. However, X is restricted rather than random, as in Fig. 10.4*c*. Consequently, there is only one meaningful regression line to estimate, that of Y on X. Measurement error in X or Y is likely to be negligible relative to the range of X's chosen or to the random variation in Y. The methods of this chapter are appropriate.

For Model II, both the X's and Y's are random, as in Fig. 10.4*d*. This is the classical bivariate regression problem with normality assumed. Random sampling is of individuals on which pairs of measurements are made. The

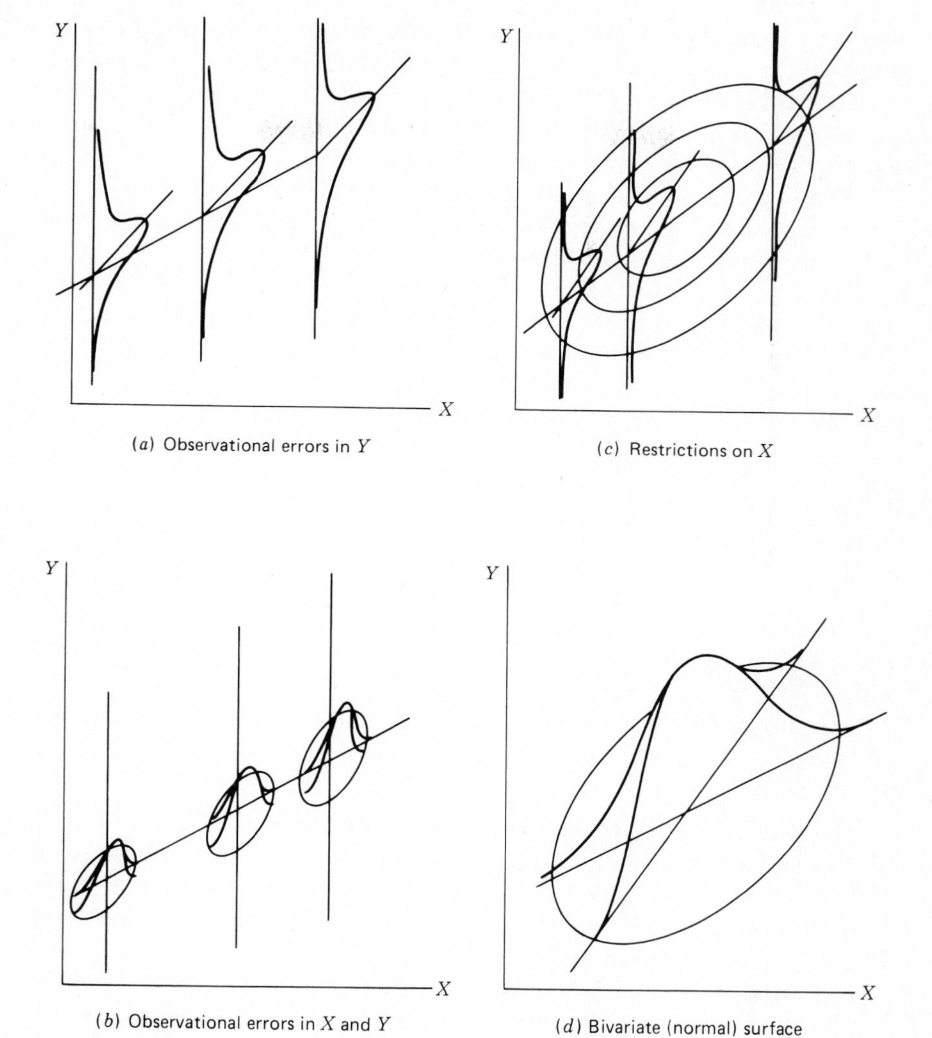

Figure 10.4 Graphic models for regression problems.

choice of which variable is to be the dependent one is determined by the problem. Two regression lines are possible, that of Y on X and that of X on Y.

For linear regression, it is assumed that the ε's are normally and independently distributed with a common variance. When the assumption of a common variance is valid, residual error mean square is applicable to making valid probability inferences about a population mean regardless of the value of X. This mean square is computed from deviations from the regression line, also called residuals. If variances are not homogeneous, a weighted regression or a transformation of the data so that the variances are homogeneous is necessary. For instance, when entomologists compute probit analyses based on percentage of kill, where the variance is binomial in nature, they use both transformation and weighting.

The Leghorn data could be from either a fixed or a random model, the latter being a real possibility. We need to know whether body weight was restricted in any way for these data.

Once α and β have been estimated, it is possible to estimate the mean of a population of Y's without ever having observed a single one of the individuals. For example, we observed no Y's for $X = 5.5$ lb for the White Leghorn data. However, we estimate the mean of the population of Y's for $X = 5.5$-lb body weight, using Eq. (10.4) as

$$\hat{Y}_{5.5} = 55.26 + 7.69(5.5) = 97.6 \text{ lb of feed}$$

Since the notation $\bar{Y}_{5.5}$ might easily lead one to believe that a sample of Y's with $X = 5.5$ lb had been observed, it is customary to use an alternative to denote an estimate of a population mean. We use $\hat{Y}_X$ or simply $\hat{Y}$, or $\hat{\mu}_{Y \cdot X}$.

Estimates of α and β are written as $\hat{\alpha}$ and $\hat{\beta}$ or as a and b; $\hat{\alpha} = a = 55.26$ lb of feed and $\hat{\beta} = b = 7.69$ lb of feed per pound of body weight.

The solution of the linear regression problem possesses the following properties:

1. The point $(\bar{X}, \bar{Y})$ is on the sample regression line.
2. The sum of the deviations from the sample regression line is zero, that is, $\sum (Y_i - \hat{Y}_i) = 0$. A deviation or residual is the signed difference between the observed value and the corresponding estimate of the population mean. Also, the following weighted sum equals zero: $\sum X_i(Y_i - \hat{Y}_i) = 0$.
3. The sum of the squares of the residuals is a minimum. That is, if we replace the sample regression line as computed in Sec. 10.2 with any other straight line, the sum of squares of the new set of residuals will be a larger value.

Exercise 10.3.1 What model applies to the data of Exercise 10.2.1?

Exercise 10.3.2 For the data in Exercise 10.2.1, which is the dependent variable? The independent variable? Discuss the requirement that "X be measured without error" as it applies to these data.

Exercise 10.3.3 Compute the 10 deviations from the sample regression line, Exercise 10.2.1. Show that the sum of these 10 residuals is zero (within rounding errors). Find the sum of squares of the 10 deviations from the regression line. Show that the point $(\bar{X}, \bar{Y})$ is on the sample regression line.

Exercise 10.3.4 What model would apply to the data of Exercise 10.2.3 when Y is regressed on X_1? X_2? X_3? X_4? In each case, give some justification for your choice of a model.

Exercise 10.3.5 Repeat Exercise 10.3.4 for the data of Exercise 10.2.4.

Exercise 10.3.6 Repeat Exercise 10.3.4 for the data of Exercise 10.2.5.

10.4 Sources of Variation in Linear Regression

The linear regression model, Eq. (10.5), considers an observation as the sum of a mean $\mu_{Y \cdot X} = \alpha + \beta X$ and a random component ε. Since by chance or by intent different X values are observed, different population means are involved and contribute to the total variance. Thus, the two sources of variation in observations are means and random components. Variation attributable to the means may be considered as attributable to X, since X determines the mean.

In terms of the sample regression, an observation Y is composed of a sample mean $\hat{Y}$ determined from the regression line and a sample deviation or residual $e = Y - \hat{Y}$ from this mean (see Fig. 10.5). In itself, $\hat{Y}$ consists of the sample mean $\bar{Y}$, and another deviation $\hat{Y} - \bar{Y} = b(X - \bar{X})$, this one attributable to regression. The residual $e = Y - \hat{Y}$ is an estimate of the chance deviation ε and may also be written $e_{Y \cdot X}$. Thus Eq. (10.4) becomes

$$Y - \bar{Y} = (\hat{Y} - \bar{Y}) + (Y - \hat{Y}) = b(X - \bar{X}) + e_{Y \cdot X} \tag{10.6}$$

The total unadjusted sum of squares of the Y's can be partitioned according to these sources. The sum of squares attributable to the mean is

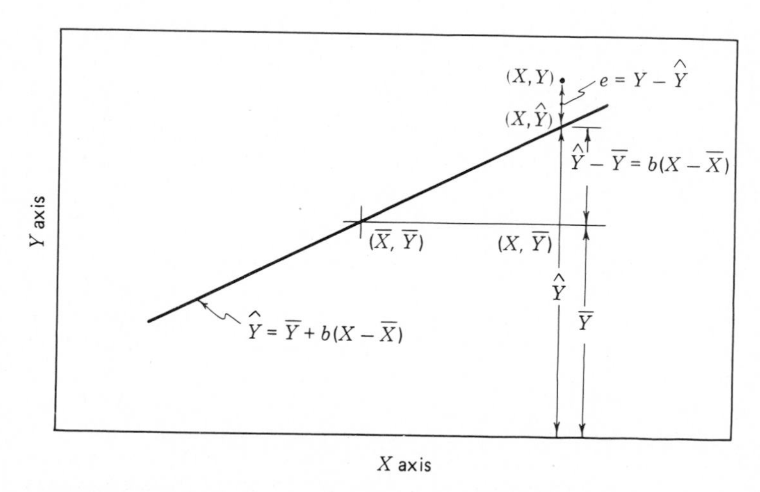

Figure 10.5 Regression of Y on X; sources of variation in Y.

$n\bar{Y}^2 = (\sum Y)^2/n$; that attributable to regression is $b^2 \sum (X - \bar{X})^2 = [\sum (X - \bar{X})(Y - \bar{Y})]^2/\sum (X - \bar{X})^2$; and that attributable to chance is $\sum e^2_{Y \cdot X}$, which is found as a residual sum of squares.

Equation (10.7) is derived from Eq. (10.6) and is comparable to its population counterpart, Eq. (10.5).

$$Y = \bar{Y} + b(X - \bar{X}) + e_{Y \cdot X} \qquad (10.7)$$

From Eq. (10.7) it can be shown that

$$\sum Y^2 = n\bar{Y}^2 + b^2 \sum (X - \bar{X})^2 + \sum e^2_{Y \cdot X}$$

This gives

$$\sum Y^2 - \frac{(\sum Y)^2}{n} = \frac{[\sum (X - \bar{X})(Y - \bar{Y})]^2}{\sum (X - \bar{X})^2} + \text{residual SS}$$

The residual SS is found by subtraction. For the example, 135.604 = 90.836 + 44.768. The total sum of squares of Y, $\sum (Y - \bar{Y})^2 = 135.604$, has been partitioned into a sum of squares attributable to regression and an unexplained portion, the residual sum of squares.

The sum of squares attributable to regression on X may be written in any one of the following forms

$$\text{SS(b|a)} = \frac{[\sum (X - \bar{X})(Y - \bar{Y})]^2}{\sum (X - \bar{X})^2}$$

$$= b \sum (X - \bar{X})(Y - \bar{Y}) = b^2 \sum (X - \bar{X})^2 = \sum (\hat{Y} - \bar{Y})^2$$

of which the first (read as sum of squares of b given a) states that we are dealing with a sum of squares of Y attributable to variation in X; the second is the most common for calculations; the third and fourth are interesting but likely to produce rounding errors if used for computing; and the last is not at all practical. This quantity has a single degree of freedom.

The residual sum of squares is found by subtraction and has $n - 2$ degrees of freedom; the residual mean square or *variance about regression* is an estimate of experimental error, the common σ^2.

Exercise 10.4.1 Compute SS(b|a) = MS(b|a) and the residual mean square for the data in

(*a*) Exercise 10.2.1
(*b*) Exercise 10.2.3, four regressions.
(*c*) Exercise 10.2.4, two regressions.
(*d*) Exercise 10.2.5, four regressions.

10.5 Regressed and Adjusted Values

Values determined by the regression equation, *regression* or *regressed values*, $\hat{Y}$'s, are estimates of population parameters, that is, of $\mu_{Y \cdot X} = \alpha + \beta X_i$'s. Differences between these and the observed values are estimates of the varia-

Table 10.2 Regressed consumptions, residuals, and adjusted consumptions, White Leghorn Data†

X Body weight, lb	Y Food consumption, lb	$\hat{Y}$ Regressed consumption, lb	$e_{Y \cdot X} = Y - \hat{Y}$ Deviation from regression, lb	$e^2_{Y \cdot X}$ Squared residuals	$93.56 + e_{Y \cdot X}$ Adjusted consumption, lb
4.6	87.1	90.6	−3.5	12.25	90.0
5.1	93.1	94.5	−1.4	1.96	92.2
4.8	89.8	92.2	−2.4	5.76	91.2
4.4	91.4	89.1	+2.3	5.29	95.9
5.9	99.5	100.6	−1.1	1.21	92.4
4.7	92.1	91.4	+0.7	0.49	94.3
5.1	95.5	94.5	+1.0	1.00	94.6
5.2	99.3	95.3	+4.0	16.00	97.6
4.9	93.4	92.9	+0.5	0.25	94.0
5.1	94.4	94.5	−0.1	.01	93.5
	935.6	935.6	0.0	44.22	935.7

† Computations for this table were made with more decimals than indicated and the results rounded.

tion in Y that is not accounted for by variation in X. Observed residuals are shown in Table 10.2 for the White Leghorn data of Table 10.1. The sum of their squares is 44.22, which differs due to rounding errors from the value 44.768, found in the preceding section.

The careful investigator always looks at the individual observations. In a nonregression problem, he will be particularly conscious of observations which show greatest deviation from the mean. In a regression problem, one looks to deviations from regression for comparable information.

Residuals can be particularly helpful when plotted against X. If they tend to be of the same sign at both ends of the plot and of opposite sign in the middle, then this is evidence that the response is nonlinear. If their magnitude changes in a regular manner, say by increasing with X, there is evidence of heterogeneity of variance and, possibly, even of its nature. Outliers or extreme values may be detected without a plot. Plotting against other variables, such as time, may be helpful in elaborating on the nature of the response.

Adjusted values, Eq. (10.9), have the regression contribution removed. It is as though each Y were moved parallel to the sample regression line until above X, and then measured as a new or adjusted Y. The last column of Table 10.2 contains adjusted consumptions, to be expected if all birds have a body weight of $\bar{X} = 4.98$ lb. These are obtained by adding the residuals to $\bar{Y} = 93.56$ lb.

$$\text{Adjusted } Y = \bar{Y} + e_{Y \cdot X} = Y - b(X - \bar{X}) \qquad (10.9)$$

The latter form is convenient if one does not care to compute the residuals; subtract that part of the observation attributable to regression, namely, $b(X - \bar{X})$. The mean of the Y's and the chance deviation are left (see Fig. 10.5). Differences among adjusted values are identical with those among the residuals; we have simply changed their location. The use of adjusted values replaces the moving standard, the regression value, with a fixed standard, the mean value.

Comparisons among adjusted means are very useful. Suppose that two groups of observations are available, for example, data for each of two years, two locations, or two types of housing. It may be pertinent to compare the group means if they are adjusted to a common X value. It will be necessary to assume a common regression coefficient, an assumption which can be tested as the hypothesis of homogeneous regression coefficients. Procedures for comparing adjusted means are given in Chap. 17 on covariance.

Exercise 10.5.1 D. Kuesel, University of Wisconsin, determined the average percentage of alcohol-insoluble solids Y and the tenderometer reading X for 26 samples of sieved-size Alaska peas. The observations follow.

Y, X: 7.64, 72; 8.08, 78; 7.39, 81; 7.45, 81; 9.56, 81; 7.96, 82; 10.81, 83; 10.70, 83; 10.56, 89; 11.75, 93; 11.56, 96; 11.74, 97; 13.72, 99; 15.08, 103; 16.26, 112; 16.79, 115; 15.40, 118; 15.90, 122; 16.30, 122; 17.56, 133; 17.38, 135; 17.90, 139; 18.80, 143; 19.90, 145; 20.10, 161; 22.01, 165

$$\sum (X - \bar{X})^2 = 18{,}774.62 \qquad \sum (X - \bar{X})(Y - \bar{Y}) = 2{,}924.50 \qquad \sum (Y - \bar{Y})^2 = 489.58$$

Plot the 26 pairs of points. Compute the sample regression equation of Y on X. What unit of measurement applies to b? Draw this line on your plot. Obtain information on how a tenderometer reading is made and comment on the assumption concerning X being measured without error. How do you think you would test the null hypothesis that no variation in Y is attributable to variation in X?

Exercise 10.5.2 Compute two regressed values of alcohol-insoluble solids (for $X = 78$ and $X = 112$) and the deviations from regression or residuals. Compute adjusted values of Y for these two X's and compare them.

Exercise 10.5.3 Plot the pairs of observations given in Exercise 10.2.1. Draw the computed regression line through your plot. Compute regressed values for $X = 4.50$ and $X = 5.13$. Find the corresponding $b(X - \bar{X})$ values and the deviations from regression or residuals.

Exercise 10.5.4 Repeat Exercise 10.5.3 using the data in Exercise 10.2.3. For X_1, use $X_1 = 35$ and $X_1 = 54$. For X_2, use $X_2 = 60$ and $X_2 = 125$. For X_3, use $X_3 = 248$ and $X_3 = 303$. For X_4, use $X_4 = 60$ and $X_4 = 70$.

Exercise 10.5.5 Repeat Exercise 10.5.3 using the data in Exercise 10.2.4. For X_1, use $X_1 = 2{,}400$ and $X_1 = 3{,}075$. For X_2, use $X_2 = 79$ and $X_2 = 270$.

Exercise 10.5.6 Repeat Exercise 10.5.3 using the data in Exercise 10.2.5. For X_1, use $X_1 = 1{,}200$ and $X_1 = 2{,}000$. For X_2, use $X_2 = 545$ and $X_2 = 605$. For X_4, use $X_4 = 1{,}935$ and $X_4 = 2{,}521$.

10.6 Standard Deviations, Confidence Intervals, and Tests of Hypotheses

An unbiased estimate of the true variance about regression is given by the residual mean square with $n - 2$ degrees of freedom. It is denoted by $s^2_{Y \cdot X}$ and defined as

$$s^2_{Y \cdot X} = \frac{\sum (Y - \hat{Y})^2}{n - 2} = \frac{\sum (Y - \bar{Y})^2 - [\sum (X - \bar{X})(Y - \bar{Y})]^2 / \sum (X - \bar{X})^2}{n - 2}$$

$$= \frac{44.77}{8} = 5.60 \text{ lb}^2 \qquad (10.10)$$

for the White Leghorn data. Its square root is called the *standard error of estimate* or the *standard deviation of Y for fixed X* or the *standard deviation of Y holding X constant.*

Figure 10.6 shows that a single standard deviation does not apply to all $\hat{Y}$'s but must depend on the X value that determines the Y population. If we consider samples of Y values for a fixed set of X values, then $\bar{X}$ is a constant while $\bar{Y}$ and b are variables. Variation in $\bar{Y}$ raises or lowers the regression line parallel to itself; the effect is to increase or decrease all estimates of means by a fixed value. Variation in b rotates the regression line about the point $\bar{X}$, $\bar{Y}$ and the effect on an estimate depends on the magnitude of the

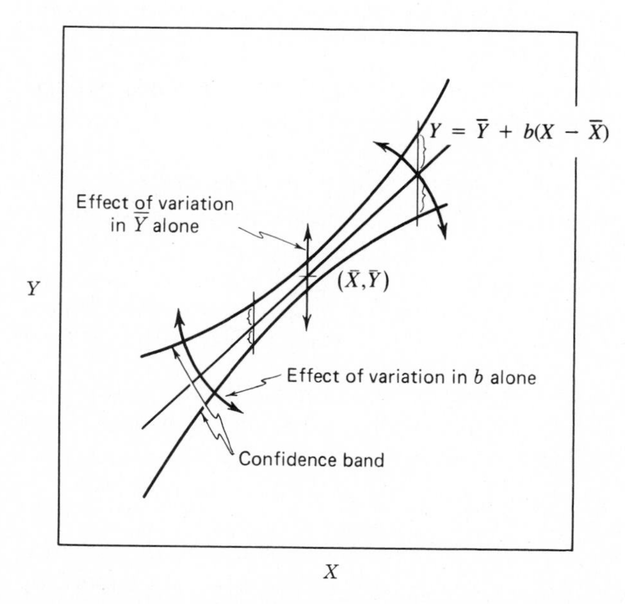

Figure 10.6 Effect of sampling variation on regression estimates of population means; fixed set of X's.

$X - \bar{X}$ that determines the Y population. Variation in b has no effect on the estimate of the mean if $X = \bar{X}$ but otherwise increases it in proportion to the size of $X - \bar{X}$. This is readily seen from the equation that estimates the population mean, that is, $\hat{Y} = \bar{Y} + b(X - \bar{X})$.

A standard deviation applicable to an estimate of a mean must allow for variation in both $\bar{Y}$ and b for the distance $X - \bar{X}$. The variance of $\bar{Y}$ is simply an estimate of $\sigma^2_{Y \cdot X}/n$, namely, $s^2_{Y \cdot X}/n$. The regression coefficient b is a linear function of Y's. In particular, $\sum (X_i - \bar{X})(Y_i - \bar{Y}) = \sum (X_i - \bar{X})Y_i$ allows us to write

$$b = \frac{\sum (X_i - \bar{X})(Y_i - \bar{Y})}{\sum (X_i - \bar{X})^2} = \frac{\sum (X_i - \bar{X})Y_i}{\sum (X_i - \bar{X})^2}$$

$$= \sum \frac{(X_i - \bar{X})}{\sum (X_i - \bar{X})^2} Y_i \qquad (10.11)$$

Now b is expressed as a linear function L, as defined by Eq. (5.18), with $c_i = (X_i - \bar{X})/\sum (X_i - \bar{X})^2$; b is also a contrast as defined by Eq. (8.3). Distinguish the two uses of i. In the numerator, it specifies the ith observation; in the denominator, it is an index of summation, $i = 1, \ldots, n$. The variance now follows from Eq. (5.23); all $\sigma_{ij} = 0$, $i \neq j$, because sampling is random. The variance of b is the variance $\sigma^2_{Y \cdot X}$ multiplied by the sum of the squares of the coefficients of the Y's. Thus we estimate the variance of b by

$$s_b^2 = \frac{s^2_{Y \cdot X}}{\sum (X - \bar{X})^2} \qquad (10.12)$$

The required variance of an estimate, $\hat{Y} = \bar{Y} + b(X - \bar{X})$, of a population mean is given by the sum of the variances of $\bar{Y}$ and $b(X - \bar{X})$, since the covariance between $\bar{Y}$ and b is zero. [The latter fact is not immediately obvious but can be deduced by noting the coefficients of the Y's in $\bar{Y}$ and b. For $\bar{Y}$, all equal the constant $1/n$ and for b they vary but have a sum equal to zero. Use Eq. (8.7) to check orthogonality.] This variance is given by

$$s^2_{\hat{Y}} = s^2_{Y \cdot X}\left[\frac{1}{n} + \frac{(X - \bar{X})^2}{\sum (X - \bar{X})^2}\right] \qquad (10.13)$$

This variance increases as $X - \bar{X}$ increases. If tabular t times the standard deviation were plotted in conjunction with the regression line, it would form a band as in Fig. 10.6. This band is applicable point by point, and the associated error rate and confidence coefficient are comparisonwise or pointwise.

A *confidence band* for the regression line, one in which the entire regression line will be said to lie, requires that the standard deviation implied by Eq. (10.13) be multiplied by $\sqrt{2F_{2,n-2}}$ for tabular F. In this case, an experimentwise error rate and confidence coefficient are applicable.

To set a confidence interval for the population mean, the variance given in Eq. (10.13) is applicable and the 95 percent confidence interval is

$$CI(\mu_{Y \cdot X}) = \bar{Y} + b(X - \bar{X}) \pm t_{.025} s_{Y \cdot X} \sqrt{\frac{1}{n} + \frac{(X - \bar{X})^2}{\sum (X - \bar{X})^2}} \tag{10.14}$$

where t is Student's t for $n - 2$ degrees of freedom. Note that $\bar{Y} + b(X - \bar{X})$ may be replaced by $a + bX$.

For the White Leghorn data, a confidence interval of the population mean for $X = 5.5$ lb is

$$CI(\mu_{Y \cdot X=5.5}) = 93.56 + 7.69(5.5 - 4.98) \pm 2.306(2.37)\sqrt{\frac{1}{10} + \frac{(0.52)^2}{1.536}}$$

$$= 97.6 \pm 2.9$$

$$= (94.7, 100.5) \text{ lb}$$

For a 95 percent confidence band on the whole regression line, the multiplier $\sqrt{2F_{.05}(2, 8)} = \sqrt{2(4.46)} = 2.99$ is required. Note that this one-tailed F value does lead to a band. Limits on the band when $X = 5.5$ lb are

$$93.56 + 7.69(5.5 - 4.98) \pm 2.99(2.37)\sqrt{\frac{1}{10} + \frac{(0.52)^2}{1.536}}$$

$$= 97.6 \pm 3.7 = (93.9, 101.3) \text{ lb}$$

These limits are only slightly farther from the regression line than are those of the point estimate of $\mu_{Y \cdot X=5.5}$. However, width of the band has gone from $2(2.9) = 5.8$ to $2(3.7) = 7.4$ lb. On the average, 95 percent of such bands will contain the whole true regression line.

Sometimes it is desirable to construct a confidence interval for β, the population regression parameter being estimated by b. This interval depends on s_b^2 as given in Eq. (10.12) and is given by

$$CI(\beta) = b \pm \frac{t_{.025} s_{Y \cdot X}}{\sqrt{\sum (X - \bar{X})^2}} \tag{10.15}$$

For the White Leghorn data, we have

$$CI(\beta) = 7.69 \pm \frac{2.306(2.37)}{\sqrt{1.536}} = 7.69 \pm 4.41$$

$$= 3.28, 12.10$$

We conclude that β lies between 3.28 and 12.10 lb of feed per pound of bird. Note the effect of the small $\sum (X - \bar{X})^2$ on the limits of β. The procedure which leads us to this conclusion is such that, on the average, 95 percent of such conclusions will be correct.

Any relevant null hypothesis about a mean may be tested. To test the null hypothesis that the mean of the population of Y's, for which $X = X_0$, is $\mu_{Y \cdot X_0}$, compute t as

$$t = \frac{\hat{Y}_{X_0} - \mu_{Y \cdot X_0}}{\sqrt{s_{Y \cdot X}^2[(1/n + (X_0 - \bar{X})^2/\sum (X - \bar{X})^2]}} \tag{10.16}$$

This is distributed as Student's t with $n - 2$ degrees of freedom.

To test the null hypothesis that $\beta = \beta_0$, compute t as

$$t = \frac{b - \beta_0}{\sqrt{s_{Y \cdot X}^2/\sum (X - \bar{X})^2}} \tag{10.17}$$

This is distributed as Student's t with $n - 2$ degrees of freedom. The F test of Table 10.3 is a test of the null hypothesis $\beta = 0$ or of the null hypothesis that variation in X does not contribute to variation in Y.

Exercise 10.6.1 For the data of Exercise 10.2.1, find $s_{Y \cdot X}$, $s_{\bar{Y}}^2$, s_b^2, $\hat{Y}$ at $X = 5.00$, $s_{\hat{Y}}$ at $X = 5.00$, the 95 percent confidence interval for the population mean at $X = 5.00$, and limits for the 95 percent confidence band on the true regression line at $X = 5.00$. (Remember that confidence intervals have a comparisonwise or pointwise error rate whereas confidence bands have experimentwise error rates.) Compute and compare the lengths of the confidence interval and confidence band at $X = 5.00$. Test the null hypothesis that $\beta = 0$.

Exercise 10.6.2 Repeat Exercise 10.6.1 for the data of Exercise 10.2.3. For X, use $X_1 = 35$. Use $X_2 = 60$. Use $X_3 = 248$. Use $X_4 = 60$.

Exercise 10.6.3 Repeat Exercise 10.6.1 for the data of Exercise 10.2.4. For X, use $X_1 = 2{,}400$. Use $X_2 = 79$.

Exercise 10.6.4 Repeat Exercise 10.6.1 for the data of Exercise 10.2.5. For X, use $X_1 = 1{,}200$. Use $X_2 = 545$. Use $X_3 = 1{,}250$. Use $X_4 = 1{,}935$.

Exercise 10.6.5 Repeat Exercise 10.6.1 for the data of Exercise 10.5.1. For X, use $X = 78$.

10.7 Control of Variation by Concomitant Observations

The sources of variation which affect a variable are not always controllable by an experimental layout. When layout cannot effect control, it may be possible to measure some characteristic of the source of variation. For example, the amount of feed consumed by hens is a variable of economic importance. One would expect it to be affected by other measurable variables such as body weight and number and weight of eggs laid. For the data of Table 10.1, body weight easily accounts for the greatest amount of variability in feed consumed. The economic importance is obvious.

We now use the data of Table 10.1 to illustrate statistical control of a source of variation by use of a concomitant observation. The standard deviation of Y prior to adjustment for variation in X is $\sqrt{\sum (Y - \bar{Y})^2/(n-1)} = \sqrt{135.604/9} = 3.88$ lb. We have seen that after adjustment it is $s_{Y \cdot X} = 2.37$ lb.

That part of the Y sum of squares attributable to variation in X is given by Eq. (10.18); see also Eq. (10.8).

$$\text{Reduction in SS} = \text{Regression SS} = \text{SS}(\text{b}|\text{a}) = \frac{[\sum (X - \bar{X})(Y - \bar{Y})]^2}{\sum (X - \bar{X})^2}$$

$$= \frac{(11.812)^2}{1.536} = 90.836 \qquad (10.18)$$

for our example. It has 1 degree of freedom. We may also note that the proportion of the Y sum of squares attributable to variation in X is

$$\frac{[\sum (X - \bar{X})(Y - \bar{Y})]^2/\sum (X - \bar{X})^2}{\sum (Y - \bar{Y})^2} = \frac{90.836}{135.604} = .67 \text{ (or 67 percent)}$$

The reduced or residual Y sum of squares is found by subtraction and has $n - 2$ degrees of freedom.

$$\text{Residual SS for } Y = 135.604 - 90.836 = 44.768 \qquad \text{with 8 df}$$

An analysis of variance table may be used to present the results. Table 10.3 shows two possibilities. The first of these is comparable to the tables of Chap. 7; the second is more complete and serves as a basis for generalization to tables for partial and multiple regression (Chap. 14) and covariance (Chap. 17).

Table 10.3 Analysis of variance for data of Table 10.1

			Example			
Source	df	Symbolic SS	df	SS	MS	F
X	1	$[\sum (X - \bar{X})(Y - \bar{Y})]^2/\sum (X - \bar{X})^2$	1	90.836	90.836	16.22**
Residual	$n - 2$	by subtraction	8	44.768	5.60	
Total	$n - 1$	$\sum (Y - \bar{Y})^2$	9	135.604		

Alternative presentation (example only)

						Residual		
Source	df	$\sum (X - \bar{X})^2$	$\sum (X - \bar{X}) \times (Y - \bar{Y})$	$\sum (Y - \bar{Y})^2$	Regression SS = SS($Y \mid X$)	SS	MS	F
Total	$n - 1 = 9$	1.536	11.812	135.604	90.836	44.768	5.60	16.22**

Exercise 10.7.1 Present an analysis of variance of the data in Exercise 10.2.1; use the form given in the upper part of Table 10.3. Is there a significant reduction in the variation in Y attributable to variation in X? Compare the F value here with t^2 for the test of H_0: $\beta = 0$ as computed in Exercise 10.6.1.

Exercise 10.7.2 Repeat Exercise 10.7.1 for the data in Exercise 10.2.3. For t^2, see Exercise 10.6.2.

Exercise 10.7.3 Repeat Exercise 10.7.1 for the data in Exercise 10.2.4. For t^2, see Exercise 10.6.3.

Exercise 10.7.4 Repeat Exercise 10.7.1 for the data in Exercise 10.2.5. For t^2, see Exercise 10.6.4.

Exercise 10.7.5 Repeat Exercise 10.7.1 for the data in Exercise 10.5.1. For t^2, see Exercise 10.6.5.

10.8 Difference between Two Independent Regressions

It may be desired to test the homogeneity of two b's, that is, to determine whether or not they can be considered to be estimates of a common β. For this, t as in Eq. (10.19) is distributed as Student's t with $n_1 + n_2 - 4$ degrees of freedom.

$$t = \frac{b_1 - b_2}{\sqrt{s_p^2[1/\sum (X_{1j} - \bar{X}_{1\cdot})^2 + 1/\sum (X_{2j} - \bar{X}_{2\cdot})^2]}} \qquad (10.19)$$

Quantities

$$b_1 \qquad \text{and} \qquad \sum_j (X_{1j} - \bar{X}_{1\cdot})^2$$

are the regression coefficient and sum of squares for X from the first sample, and similarly for the second sample and

$$s_p^2 = \frac{\begin{array}{c}\{\sum (Y_{1j} - \bar{Y}_{1\cdot})^2 - [\sum (X_{1j} - \bar{X}_{1\cdot})(Y_{1j} - \bar{Y}_{1\cdot})]^2/\sum (X_{1j} - \bar{X}_{1\cdot})^2\} \\ + \{\sum (Y_{2j} - \bar{Y}_{2\cdot})^2 - [\sum (X_{2j} - \bar{X}_{2\cdot})(Y_{2j} - \bar{Y}_{2\cdot})]^2/\sum (X_{2j} - \bar{X}_{2\cdot})^2\}\end{array}}{n_1 - 2 + n_2 - 2}$$

is the best estimate of the variation about regression. It is seen to be the pooled residual sums of squares from the two independent regressions divided by the pooled degrees of freedom.

Homogeneity of regression says that the two lines have the same slope but not that they are the same line. To decide about this, it is necessary to test adjusted means. This is dealt with in Chap. 17.

Homogeneity of regression may also be tested by F. Briefly, find the reduction in sum of squares attributable to X when a single regression coefficient is assumed, and the reduction when two coefficients are assumed. The latter cannot be smaller than the former. The difference in the two sums

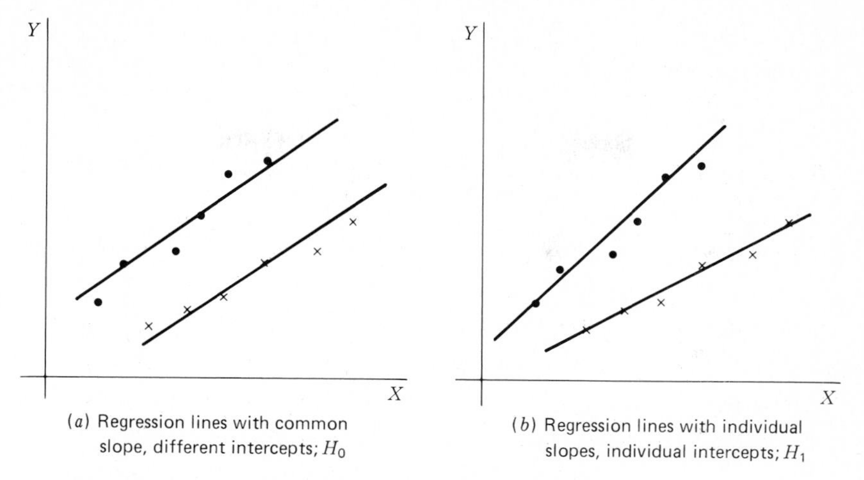

(a) Regression lines with common slope, different intercepts; H_0

(b) Regression lines with individual slopes, individual intercepts; H_1

Figure 10.7 Testing independent regressions for homogeneity.

of squares is an additional reduction that will ordinarily be attributable to chance if there is a single β, but will be larger, on the average, if there are two β's. Figure 10.7 illustrates the underlying approach.

The procedure is indicated in Table 10.4. Checked spaces are filled by the usual computational procedures. In line 6, column 8, the difference (line 5 minus line 4) will give the same answer as in column 6. The extension of this procedure to test differences among more than two β's is presented in Chap. 17.

Exercise 10.8.1 H. L. Self (Ph.D. thesis, University of Wisconsin, 1954) reported the back-fat thickness Y and slaughter weight X for four lots of Poland China pigs fed different rations. Data for treatment 3 are:

Y, mm 42, 38, 53, 34, 35, 31, 45, 43
X, lb 206, 261, 279, 221, 216, 198, 277, 250

and, for treatment 4:

Y 33, 34, 38, 33, 26, 28, 37, 31
X 167, 192, 204, 197, 181, 178, 236, 204

Compute the two regression coefficients and test the null hypothesis that they are estimates of a common β.

What percentage of the SS(within samples) with $n_1 + n_2 - 2$ df can be attributed to a single regression coefficient in the model under H_0, the null hypothesis? To two regression coefficients under H_1, the alternative hypothesis?

Exercise 10.8.2 In assuming a common variance, it is the variance about regression that is referred to. Test the null hypothesis of a common variance about regression.

Table 10.4 Analysis of variance table for testing difference between two β's

Line \ Column	Computations use	1	2	3	4	5	6	7	8	9
1		Source of variation	df	$\sum (X - \bar{X})^2$	$\sum (X - \bar{X})(Y - \bar{Y})$	$\sum (Y - \bar{Y})^2$	$\frac{[\sum (X - \bar{X})(Y - \bar{Y})]^2}{\sum (X - \bar{X})^2}$	df	Residual SS = col 5 − col 6	df
2	H_1	Within sample 1	$n_1 - 1$	✓	✓	✓	✓	1	✓	$n_1 - 2$
3	H_1	Within sample 2	$n_2 - 1$	✓	✓	✓	✓	1	✓	$n_2 - 2$
4	H_1	(Two regressions)					Subtotal	2	Subtotal	$n_1 + n_2 - 4$
5	H_0	Within 1 + within 2 (one regression)	$n_1 + n_2 - 2$	✓	✓	✓	✓	1	✓	$n_1 + n_2 - 3$
6	H_1 vs. H_0	Regression coefficients (two regressions vs. one)					Line 4 − line 5	1		

$$F = \frac{\text{line 6, col 6 entry}}{(\text{Line 4, col 8 entry})/(n_1 + n_2 - 4)}, \ 1 \text{ and } n_1 + n_2 - 4 \text{ df}$$

Exercise 10.8.3 The accompanying data are Y = running times in minutes and seconds and X = number of jumps to exhaustion. The first set is for men who have been in a running program for 10 years and are near the end of a running season.†

Y	11 : 16	12 : 30	11 : 30	10 : 17	11 : 48	9 : 29	11 : 06	12 : 02	11 : 52	11 : 28
X	45	60	40	101	60	80	51	50	99	34

The second set is for men who joined this particular running program later but are at the same stage in the running season.

Y	11 : 34	13 : 21	10 : 39	10 : 14	9 : 27	9 : 56	11 : 47	12 : 12	12 : 20	11 : 03	11 : 24	10 : 21
X	125	40	123	92	93	100	70	57	67	101	70	85

Compute the two regression coefficients for Y on X and test H_0: $\beta_1 = \beta_2$.

Presumably you assumed a common variance when making the preceding test. Do the data support this assumption?

10.9 A Prediction and Its Variance

Among the uses of regression, there is prediction as first suggested in Sec. 3.12. There are times when one wishes to say something about a particular future value such as a time of first frost, maximum rainfall, etc. Or it may be possible to observe an X value and impossible or impractical to observe the corresponding Y. In fact, it is not so much desired to say something about a mean as about how far from it the future observation may be. We would really like to predict the random component and this is, of course, not predictable by definition.

If the population mean were known, this would be the prediction. However, we would associate with this some multiple of the standard deviation of observations to give an interval; the multiple would depend on what assurance we want of having the interval contain the future observation. More likely, the population mean is unknown and the prediction will be an estimate of it. This is a variable and its variation must also be allowed for as well as that of the random component we are really trying to account for. Thus the variance of a predicted Y is given by

$$V(\text{pred } Y) = \sigma^2_{Y \cdot X} + \frac{\sigma^2_{Y \cdot X}}{n} + (X - \bar{X})^2 \frac{\sigma^2_{Y \cdot X}}{\sum (X - \bar{X})^2}$$

$$= \sigma^2_{Y \cdot X}\left(1 + \frac{1}{n} + \frac{(X - \bar{X})^2}{\sum (X - \bar{X})^2}\right) \tag{10.20}$$

† Data courtesy of A. C. Linnerud, North Carolina State University.

It is estimated by

$$s^2(\text{pred } Y) = s^2_{Y \cdot X}\left(1 + \frac{1}{n} + \frac{(X - \bar{X})^2}{\sum (X - \bar{X})^2}\right) \tag{10.21}$$

This variance applies to the following situation: take a random sample of Y's for a set of X's, compute the regression equation, and then take a single $\hat{Y}$ from this line at a particular X. Also, randomly select a new Y with the same X. Our interest is in the variability of differences, $(Y - \hat{Y})$'s, when the whole process is repeated indefinitely, that is, in $V(Y - \hat{Y})$.

A confidence interval for a predicted Y is of interest. Whereas we usually construct confidence intervals for parameters, many practical situations make them appropriate for predictions. To set a 95 percent confidence interval on a predicted value, compute

$$\text{CI(pred } Y) = \bar{Y} + b(X - \bar{X}) \pm t_{.025}\, s_{Y \cdot X}\sqrt{1 + \frac{1}{n} + \frac{(X - \bar{X})^2}{\sum (X - \bar{X})^2}} \tag{10.22}$$

where $t_{.025}$ is tabulated t for $n - 2$ degrees of freedom. Keep in mind that this Y is still to be obtained and was not used in finding the regression equation

Table 10.5 Horses on Canadian farms, June, 1944–1948

X = year	$(X - \bar{X})$	Y = number of horses on Canadian farms, thousands
1944	−2	2,735
1945	−1	2,585
1946	0	2,200
1947	+1	2,032
1948	+2	1,904

$\sum (X - \bar{X})^2 = 10 \qquad \sum (X - \bar{X})(Y - \bar{Y}) = -2{,}215$

$\sum (Y - \bar{Y})^2 = 508{,}702.8$

$\bar{Y} = 2{,}291.2$ horses

$b = -221.5$ horses per year

$$\text{SS}(b|a) = \frac{[\sum (X - \bar{X})(Y - \bar{Y})]^2}{\sum (X - \bar{X})^2} = 490{,}622.5$$

$$\text{Residual MS} = \frac{18{,}080.3}{3} = 6{,}026.8$$

Source: Data from *Canada*, 1950, p. 127.

that gave $\hat{Y}$. For any other confidence coefficient, replace $t_{.025}$ by t for the appropriate probability level.

Consider the data in Table 10.5. It is desired to predict the number of horses for 1949 on the assumption that the decrease in numbers is linear over years.

The regression equation is

$$\hat{Y} = 2{,}291.2 - 221.5(X - 1946) \tag{10.23}$$

and $s_{Y \cdot X} = 77.6$ horses. The data and regression equation are shown in Fig. 10.8.

To predict the number of thousands of horses for 1949, substitute $X = 1949$ in Eq. (10.23). We find $\hat{Y}_{1949} = 1{,}627$ horses. The standard deviation applicable to this result is

$$s_{Y \cdot X}\sqrt{1 + \frac{1}{n} + \frac{(X - \bar{X})^2}{\sum (X - \bar{X})^2}} = 77.6\sqrt{1 + \frac{1}{5} + \frac{3^2}{10}} = 112.5 \text{ horses}$$

The 95 percent confidence interval is

$$1{,}627 \pm 3.182(112.5) = (1{,}269,\ 1{,}985)$$

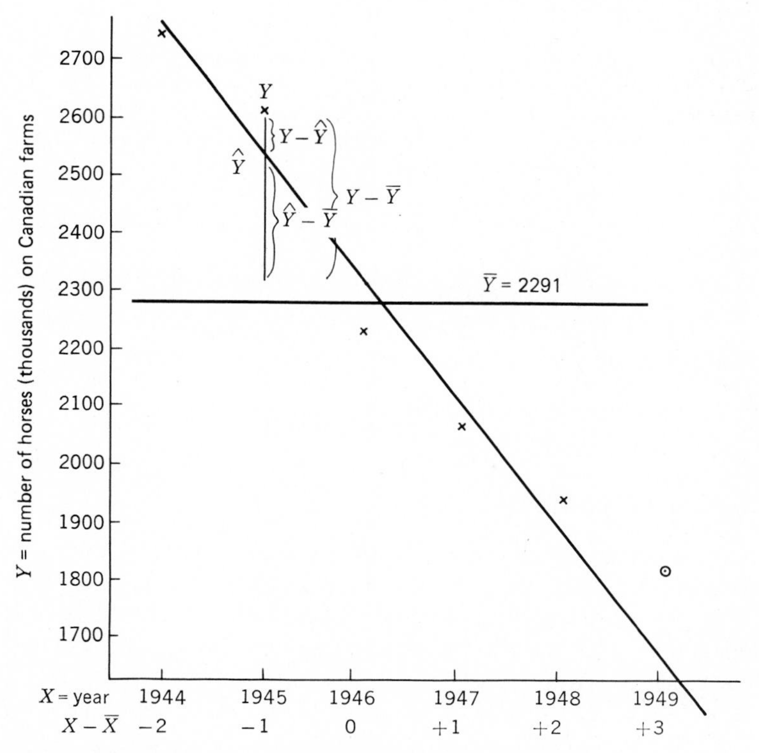

Figure 10.8 Data and regression line for data of Table 10.5.

In 1949, the number of thousands of horses was 1,796, well within the confidence interval but 1,796 − 1,627 = 169 thousand horses more than the point estimate.

If our sample is an unusual one and we predict many observations, it may be that none of the actual future observations will lie in the predicted interval. This points out the fallacy of using one regression line with a comparisonwise or pointwise error rate to make predictions time after time. If random sampling is not repeated, the least one can do is revise the regression line as experience accumulates.

To predict a future mean for n_1 observations, the regression value is used for the predicted mean. The variance appropriate to the prediction is given by replacing the 1 in the parentheses of Eqs. (10.20) and (10.21) by $1/n_1$.

In predicting a value or estimating a mean for an X outside the observed range, that is, in extrapolating as opposed to interpolating, one assumes that the relationship will continue to be linear. This assumption may not be sound, especially if a straight line is being used as an approximation and if one extrapolates very far outside the range. In the case at hand, interpolation would not be very informative, since the data were likely collected throughout the year rather than at a fixed date.

Exercise 10.9.1 Suppose that a lot of 50 hens on the New York random sample test (Table 10.1) has an average weight of 5.3 lb. What is the 95 percent confidence interval for the prediction of the 350-day food consumption for this particular lot of birds? What is the 95 percent confidence interval for the mean food consumption for lots with an average weight of 5.3 lb?

Exercise 10.9.2 What is the standard deviation of a predicted Y at $X = 5.00$ for the data of Exercise 10.2.1?

Of a predicted Y at each of $X_1 = 35$, $X_2 = 60$, $X_3 = 248$, and $X_4 = 60$ for the data in Exercise 10.2.3?

Of a predicted Y at each of $X_1 = 2{,}400$ and $X_2 = 79$ for the data in Exercise 10.2.4?

Of a predicted Y at each of $X_1 = 1{,}200$, $X_2 = 545$, $X_3 = 1{,}250$, and $X_4 = 1{,}935$ for the data of Exercise 10.2.5?

Of a predicted Y at $X = 78$ for the data of Exercise 10.5.1?

10.10 Prediction of X, Model I

At times it is required to predict an X or estimate the mean of a population of X's even though X is a fixed variable in the available data. This is a common situation in biological assay and dosage-mortality problems. In such circumstances one predicts or estimates by solving the regression equation of Y on X, for X. Thus

$$X - \bar{X} = \frac{Y - \bar{Y}}{b} \quad \text{or} \quad X = \bar{X} + \frac{Y - \bar{Y}}{b}$$

This gives a point estimate of X where one usually prefers a confidence interval estimate. Computation of an interval is possible, straightforward, but more lengthy than for a value of the dependent variable. The reader interested in additional explanations is referred to Bliss (10.1), Eisenhart (10.2), Finney (10.3), Irwin (10.4) and Natrella (10.7).

10.11 Bivariate Distributions, Model II

In many instances, (X, Y) pairs are observed at random; that is, no control over X is exercised. For example, consider height and weight of adult American males, the individuals being drawn at random and a pair of measurements made; or consider an experiment to determine potato yields under a variety of field conditions, where one also observes the rate of nematode infestation. In such cases, sampling is from a bivariate distribution.

Consider the pairs of observations of Table 10.6 on a single strain of guayule, a plant from which rubber is obtained. The variables are oven dry shrub weight and crown circumference; the data are a portion of the original. As dependent variable, choose the one for which means are to be estimated, values are to be predicted, or statistical control by use of the other variable is desired. Thus when circumference is the dependent variable, we have

$$\text{Regression SS} = \text{SS}(\text{b}\,|\,\text{a}) = \frac{(176.84)^2}{8{,}120.9} = 3.851$$

$$\text{Residual SS} = 7.764 - 3.851 = 3.913$$

$$\text{Percent reduction} = \frac{3.851}{7.764}\,100 = 49.6 \text{ percent}$$

$$b = \frac{176.84}{8{,}120.9} = .022 \text{ cm/g}$$

When weight is the dependent variable

$$\text{Regression SS} = \text{SS}(\text{b}\,|\,\text{a}) = \frac{(176.84)^2}{7.764} = 4{,}027.9$$

$$\text{Residual SS} = 8{,}120.9 - 4{,}027.9 = 4{,}093.0$$

$$\text{Percent reduction} = \frac{4{,}027.9}{8{,}120.9}\,100 = 49.6 \text{ percent}$$

$$b = \frac{176.84}{7.764} = 22.78 \text{ g/cm}$$

It is clear, then, that in random sampling of pairs from a bivariate distribution, there are two regression equations. The two residual sums of

Table 10.6 Oven dry weight and circumference of crown for a random sample of guayule plants

Oven dry weight, g	Circumference of crown, cm
65	6.5
100	6.3
82	5.9
133	6.3
133	7.3
165	8.0
116	6.9
120	8.1
150	8.7
117	6.6
$\bar{X}$: 118.1	7.06
$\sum (X - \bar{X})^2$: 8,120.9	7.764
$\sum (X_1 - \bar{X}_1)(X_2 - \bar{X}_2) = 176.84$	

Source: Data courtesy of W. T. Federer, Cornell University, Ithaca, New York.

squares are measured in terms of perpendiculars to different axes. The lines do not coincide, as can be seen from the fact that the two b's are not reciprocals of each other. The product of the b's is the reduction in sum of squares as a decimal fraction. Thus, $(22.78)(.022)100 = 50.1$ percent, differing from 49.6 percent by rounding errors. Both lines pass through the sample mean $(\bar{X}, \bar{Y})$.

The proportion of the sum of squares of the dependent variable that can be attributed to the independent variable is always the same regardless of which variable is independent. This is seen by comparing formulas; we have

$$\frac{[\sum (X - \bar{X})(Y - \bar{Y})]^2/\sum (X - \bar{X})^2}{\sum (Y - \bar{Y})^2} = \frac{[\sum (X - \bar{X})(Y - \bar{Y})]^2/\sum (Y - \bar{Y})^2}{\sum(X - \bar{X})^2}$$

This quantity, often denoted by r^2 and called the *coefficient of determination*, is considered in more detail in the next chapter.

When random sampling is not from a bivariate distribution, it is still possible to estimate means and predict values for either the dependent or the independent variable. This is done with a single regression line, the regression of the dependent variable upon the independent variable. References at the end of Sec. 10.10 deal with the problem of a confidence interval for estimation or prediction of values of the independent variable.

Exercise 10.11.1 Compute the coefficient of determination for the data of Exercise 10.8.1. Interpret this coefficient.

10.12 Regression through the Origin

In some situations, theory calls for a straight line that passes through the origin. In such cases, we are given a point on the line, a point for which there is no sampling variation. Clearly such a point must be treated differently from an observed point.

As an example of regression through the origin, consider the data of Table 10.7. Since the regression line must pass through the origin, the required equation may be written $Y = bX$. The regression coefficient is given by

$$b = \frac{\sum XY}{\sum X^2} \tag{10.24}$$

$$= 3.67 \text{ induced reversions per dose}$$

The regression line is

$$\hat{Y} = 3.67X$$

Table 10.7 Induced reversions to independence per 10^7 surviving cells Y per dose (ergs/bacterium) $10^{-5}X$ of streptomycin dependent *Escherichia coli* subjected to monochromatic ultraviolet radiation of 2,967 = Å wavelength

X	Y
13.6	52
13.9	48
21.1	72
25.6	89
26.4	80
39.8	130
40.1	139
43.9	173
51.9	208
53.2	225
65.2	259
66.4	199
67.7	255
$\sum X =$ 528.8	$\sum Y =$ 1,929
$\sum X^2 =$ 26,062.10	$\sum Y^2 =$ 356,259
$\sum (X - \bar{X})^2 =$ 4,552.14	$\sum (Y - \bar{Y})^2 =$ 70,025
$\sum XY =$ 95,755.7	$\sum (X - \bar{X})(Y - \bar{Y}) =$ 17,289.9

$t = a/s_a = .468$ ns

Source: Data courtesy of M. R. Zelle, Cornell University, Ithaca, N.Y.

The sum of the deviations from this line is not zero. The reduction in sum of squares attributable to regression is $(\sum XY)^2/\sum X^2 = 351{,}819$. The residual sum of squares is 4,440 with 12 degrees of freedom and the residual mean square for Y is 370. Since no adjustment has been made for the mean, $\sum Y^2$ has 13 degrees of freedom = number of observations, and the residual mean square has 12 degrees of freedom.

Any relevant hypothesis about the value estimated by b may be tested by Student's t test. A test of the hypothesis $\beta = 0$ is also given by $F = (\text{Regression SS})/\text{residual MS}$.

When there are reservations about the assumption that regression is through the origin, it may be desirable to test this as a hypothesis. To do this, compute the regression line $\hat{Y} = \bar{Y} + b(X - \bar{X})$. This is given by

$$\hat{Y} - 148.4 = 3.80(X - 40.68) \tag{10.25}$$

The reduction attributable to the mean is $(\sum Y)^2/n = 286{,}234$ and to b is $[\sum (X - \bar{X})(Y - \bar{Y})]^2/\sum (X - \bar{X})^2 = 65{,}670$. The total reduction is $(286{,}234 + 65{,}670) = 351{,}904$; the residual sum of squares is 4,355 with 11 degrees of freedom and the residual mean square for Y is 396. This is actually higher than the mean square for regression through the origin, though the sum of squares is necessarily lower.

To test the hypothesis that regression is through the origin, compute the additional reduction due to fitting the mean. This is $(286{,}234 + 65{,}670) - (351{,}819) = 85$ or $4{,}440 - 4{,}355 = 85$ with a single degree of freedom and is clearly not significant. (The latter computation is the difference between the two residual sums of squares.) The appropriate error mean square is $4{,}355/11 = 396$.

The analysis of variance of Table 10.8 is a summary of the computations. Note that SS(Total) has 13 df since no initial adjustment for the mean is made. The top line gives the sum of squares associated with fitting the regression equation; computation consists of adding the lower pair of bracketed lines, those we associate with the usual regression problem as contributions attributable to the mean and slope sequentially. The upper

Table 10.8 Analysis of variance for Table 10.7 data. Is intercept 0?

Source	Model equation	df	SS	MS	F
Slope and intercept	$Y = \alpha + \beta X + \varepsilon$	2	351,904		
Slope ignoring intercept	$Y = \beta X + \varepsilon$	1	351,819		
Intercept after slope		1	85	85	.215 ns
Intercept ignoring slope	$Y = \mu + \varepsilon$	1	286,234		
Slope after intercept		1	65,670	65,670	165.8**
Residual		$n - 2 = 11$	4,355	396	
Total		$n = 13$	356,259		

pair of bracketed lines has to do with the problem at hand; first we account for the slope only, by having regression through the origin and then follow this by seeing how much the addition of a nonzero intercept can improve the model.

This procedure is the general one introduced in Sec. 9.6 as an exact method of wide applicability and used again in Sec. 10.8. It calls for the fitting of two models, one under H_0, the other under H_1. One then looks for the improvement by observing the additional sum of squares attributable to introducing an extra parameter, or set, into the model. This general procedure is informative though not necessary here. Instead, we may use Eqs. (10.4), (10.13), and (10.14) with $\bar{X} = 0$, as appropriate.

As in the general regression case, it is assumed that deviations from the regression line are normally distributed with a common variance. More extensive data than those presented here indicate that the variance is probably a function of the dose and the wavelength. In this case, a weighted regression analysis is appropriate.

Exercise 10.12.1 Complete the F test of H_0: $\alpha = 0$ using Table 10.8.

Compute the intercept from Eq. (10.25) and use Student's t to test the null hypothesis that it differs from zero because of sampling error. Square t and compare with the F value previously computed.

Exercise 10.12.2 In Exercise 5.5.1, data included running times for experienced runners falling into two categories, RHR1s and RHR2s, at the beginning of a new season. In Exercise 5.7.2, times for the same individuals were given after a season of running. In the latter exercise, the alternative hypothesis implied that all runners improved equally, within random sampling.

Now, regression allows us to propose an alternative model. Under H_0, times should be equal when regression is through the origin, that is $Y = X + \varepsilon$. Under H_1, regression should still be through the origin but now $Y = \beta X + \varepsilon$ where $\beta < 1$.

Test H_0: $\beta = 1$ vs. H_1: $\beta < 1$.

Make no assumption about the value of β but test H_0: $\alpha = 0$ vs. H_1: $\alpha \neq 0$.

Exercise 10.12.3 Repeat Exercise 10.12.2 using the RHR2s from Exercises 5.5.2 and 5.7.3.

10.13 Weighted Regression Analysis

At times data are available where the observations have unequal variances. For example, we might require the regression of treatment means on a concomitant variable, when treatment means are based on differing sample sizes, the variances being $\sigma^2/n_1, \ldots, \sigma^2/n_k$. The assumption of homogeneous variance is not justified and a weighted regression analysis must be performed.

In most weighted regression analyses, the weights depend upon the amounts of information in or the precision of the observations. They are the reciprocals of the variances, that is, $w_i = 1/\sigma_i^2$ where w_i represents the weight for the ith observation. If the observations are means, then $w_i = n_i/\sigma^2$.

It is the relative rather than the actual weights that are important. Hence, when observations have a common variance and we are computing the regression of means on another variable, the weights are the numbers of observations.

For a weighted regression, the total sum of squares of the Y's is a weighted one. In particular,

$$SS(Y) = \sum w_i(Y_i - \bar{Y})^2 \qquad \text{definition}$$

$$= \sum w_i Y_i^2 - \frac{(\sum w_i Y_i)^2}{\sum w_i} \qquad \text{computing,}$$

where $\bar{Y} = (\sum w_i Y_i)/\sum w_i$, a weighted mean. The regression coefficient is

$$b = \frac{\sum w_i(X_i - \bar{X})(Y_i - \bar{Y})}{\sum w_i(X_i - \bar{X})^2} \qquad \text{definition}$$

$$= \frac{\sum w_i X_i Y_i - [(\sum w_i X_i)(\sum w_i Y_i)/\sum w_i]}{\sum w_i X_i^2 - [(\sum w_i X_i)^2/\sum w_i]} \qquad \text{computing}$$

where $\bar{X} = (\sum w_i X_i)/\sum w_i$. The regression equation is

$$Y = \bar{Y} + b(X - \bar{X})$$

The reduction in sum of squares attributable to regression is

$$\text{Regression SS} = \text{SS}(\text{b}|\text{a})$$

$$= \frac{\{\sum w_i X_i Y_i - [(\sum w_i X_i)(\sum w_i Y_i)/\sum w_i]\}^2}{\sum w_i X_i^2 - [(\sum w_i X_i)^2/\sum w_i]} \qquad \text{1 df}$$

and the residual sum of squares is found by subtracting the reduction from the total. The weighted sum of deviations from regression is zero. That is,

$$\sum w_i[Y_i - \bar{Y} - b(X_i - \bar{X})] = 0$$

Also, the weighted sum of squares,

$$\sum w_i[Y_i - \bar{Y} - b(X_i - \bar{X})]^2$$

is a minimum; there is no other regression line giving a smaller weighted sum of squares.

Computations are seen to be lengthier than for the usual regression. However, if columns of $w_i X_i$ and $w_i Y_i$ are used, the weighted sums of products, $\sum w_i X_i^2$, $\sum w_i Y_i^2$, and $\sum w_i X_i Y_i$, are easily obtained from pairs of columns $w_i X_i$ and X_i, $w_i Y_i$ and Y_i, and $w_i X_i$ and Y_i or $w_i Y_i$ and X_i, respectively.

In the special case where the regression is one of means of differing numbers of observations on an independent variable, we have $w_i Y_i = n_i \bar{Y}_i$ the total of the observations in the ith mean, a quantity already available. Consequently, entries for the column $w_i Y_i$ have already been computed.

References

10.1. Bliss, C. I.: *The statistics of bioassay*, Academic, New York, 1952.

10.2. Eisenhart, C.: "The interpretation of certain regression methods and their use in biological and industrial research," *Ann. Math. Statist.*, **10:**162–186 (1939).

10.3. Finney, D. J.: *Probit analysis*, 2d ed., Cambridge University Press, Cambridge, 1951.

10.4. Irwin, J. O.: "Statistical methods applied to biological assays," *J. Roy. Statist. Soc. Suppl.*, **4:**1–48 (1937).

10.5. Winsor, C. P.: "Which regression?" *Biom. Bull.*, **2:**101–109 (1946).

10.6. Bartlett, M. S.: "Fitting a straight line when both variables are subject to error," *Biom.*, **5:**207–212 (1949).

10.7. Natrella, G.: *Experimental statistics*, Nat. Bur. Stand. Handb. 91, 1963, chap. 5.

10.8. Reynolds, J., G. Cunningham and J. Syvertsen: "A net Co_2 exchange model for *Larrea tridentata*," *Photosyn.*, **13**(3)**:** (1979).

10.9. Reynolds, J., and D. H. Knight: "The magnitude of snowfall and rainfall interception by litter in lodgepole and spruce-fir forests in Wyoming," Northwest Sci., **47**(1)**:**50–60 (1973).

CHAPTER

ELEVEN

LINEAR CORRELATION

11.1 Introduction

Bivariate distributions were discussed briefly in Sec. 10.11. In sampling from a bivariate population, an observation consists of a random pair of measurements. Here, two regressions are possible and valid, although ordinarily only one regression is desired. A summary of the data in a sample from a bivariate distribution consists of two means, two variances, and the covariance. The covariance may be replaced without loss of information by the coefficient of determination or its square root, the coefficient of linear correlation. This chapter deals with linear correlation.

11.2 Correlation and the Correlation Coefficient

Correlation, like covariance, is a measure of the degree to which variables vary together or a measure of the intensity of association. As such, it must be symmetric in the two variables. The sample linear correlation coefficient, also called the simple correlation, the total correlation, and the product-moment correlation, is used for descriptive purposes and is defined by

$$r = \frac{\sum (X - \bar{X})(Y - \bar{Y})/(n-1)}{\sqrt{\sum (X - \bar{X})^2/(n-1)}\sqrt{\sum (Y - \bar{Y})^2/(n-1)}}$$

$$= \frac{\sum (X - \bar{X})(Y - \bar{Y})}{\sqrt{\sum (X - \bar{X})^2 \sum (Y - \bar{Y})^2}} \qquad (11.1)$$

It is assumed that in the population, a linear relation exists between the variables. This is a valid assumption when sampling is from a bivariate normal distribution. The correlation coefficient r is an unbiased estimate of the corresponding population correlation coefficient ρ (Greek *rho*) only when the population parameter ρ is zero. Unlike a variance or a regression coefficient, the correlation coefficient is independent of the units of measurement; it is an absolute or dimensionless quantity. The use of X and Y is no longer intended to imply an independent and a dependent variable.

Some insight for the interpretation of linear correlation may be gained from the *scatter diagrams* of Fig. 11.1 for which the data have been especially manufactured. In part *a* of the figure, the points cluster about a line through $(\bar{X}, \bar{Y})$ and parallel to the X axis simply because the variance of X is larger than that of Y. The lack of a tendency to cluster about any line other than one through $(\bar{X}, \bar{Y})$ and parallel to an axis is typical of data where there is little or no linear correlation. In such cases, each regression line is close to a line through $(\bar{X}, \bar{Y})$ and parallel to the axis of the independent variable. Lack of linear correlation is more noticeable where the scatter diagram uses standard deviations as units of measurement, as in part *b*. Each datum of part *a* has been divided by its standard deviation, that is, $(X - \bar{X})/s_X = (X - \bar{X})/6$ and $(Y - \bar{Y})/s_Y = (Y - \bar{Y})/2$, so that each variable has unit variance. Variables with zero means and unit variances are called *standard variables*. The points no longer show a tendency to cluster about any axis. The covariance equals the correlation.

Where linear correlation is small, r is near zero. Reference to Fig. 11.2*a* shows this. The sample points would be approximately equally distributed in each of the four quadrants so that $(X - \bar{X})(Y - \bar{Y})$ cross products of the same magnitude occur about equally often in each. Hence $\sum (X - \bar{X}) \times (Y - \bar{Y})$, the numerator of r, tends to be near zero.

Figure 11.1*c* and *d* make use of the same numbers as do *a* and *b* but they are differently paired. For *c*, $\sum (X - \bar{X})(Y - \bar{Y}) = 83$ but the means and variances are unchanged. Now the points tend to cluster about a line other than an axis. This is typical of data where a high correlation is present. The regression lines are nearly coincident and are tipped toward the X axis because of the large variance of X. Near coincidence of regression lines is typical of data which exhibit high correlation.

High linear correlation, r near $+1$ or -1, is more readily recognized on scatter diagrams where the variables are standardized, as in Fig. 11.1*d*. Here the points cluster about a line approximately halfway between the axes. Both regression lines are near this line and the regression coefficients equal the correlation coefficient and are near $+1$ or -1. A unit change in one variable implies approximately a unit change in the other for regression lines in this near-midway position. Reference to Fig. 11.2*b* and *c* shows why r will be numerically large. Here, large cross products appear more frequently in the upper right and lower left or upper left and lower right corners.

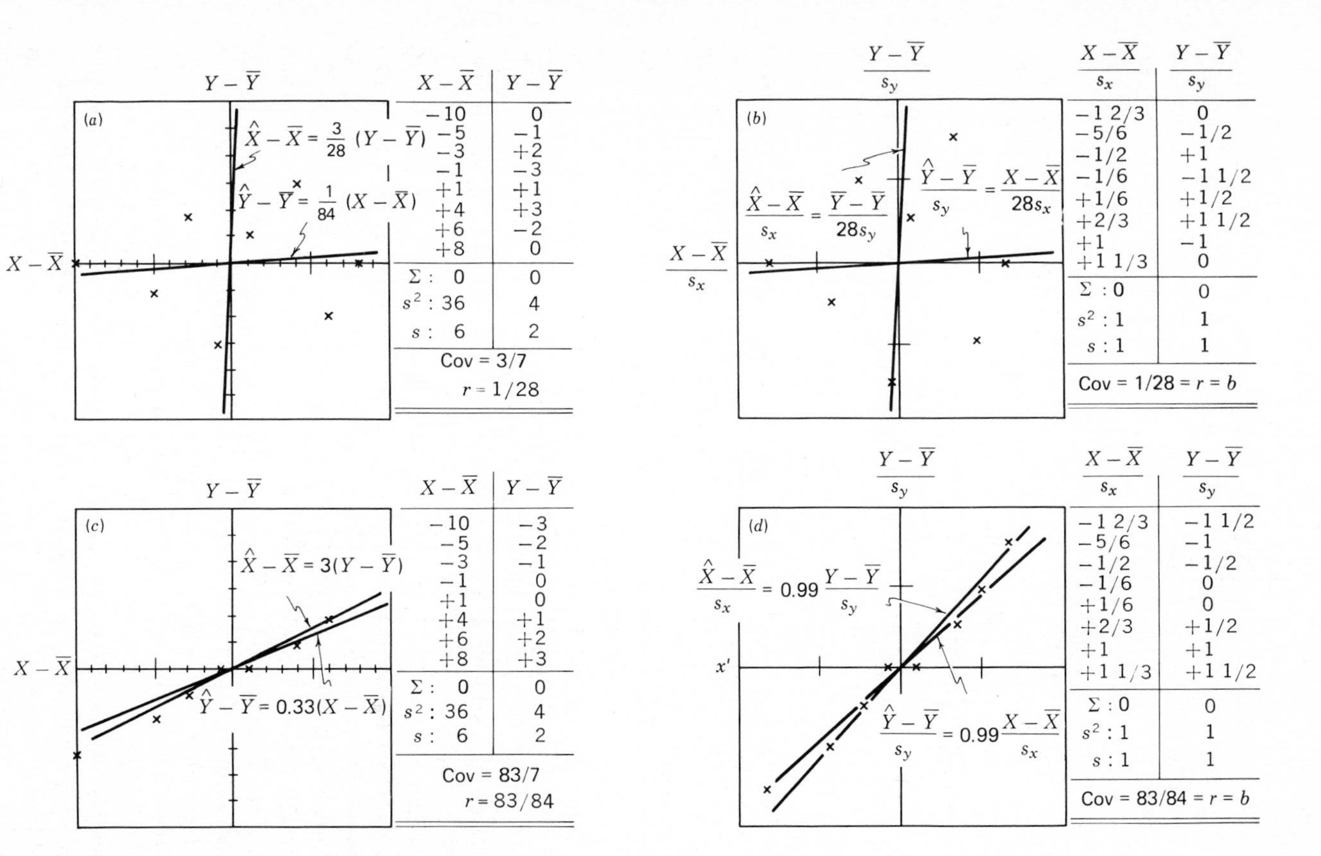

(a)

$X-\overline{X}$	$Y-\overline{Y}$
−10	0
−5	−1
−3	+2
−1	−3
+1	+1
+4	+3
+6	−2
+8	0
Σ : 0	0
s^2 : 36	4
s : 6	2
Cov = 3/7	
r = 1/28	

(b)

$\frac{X-\overline{X}}{s_x}$	$\frac{Y-\overline{Y}}{s_y}$
−1 2/3	0
−5/6	−1/2
−1/2	+1
−1/6	−1 1/2
+1/6	+1/2
+2/3	+1 1/2
+1	−1
+1 1/3	0
Σ : 0	0
s^2 : 1	1
s : 1	1
Cov = 1/28 = r = b	

(c)

$X-\overline{X}$	$Y-\overline{Y}$
−10	−3
−5	−2
−3	−1
−1	0
+1	0
+4	+1
+6	+2
+8	+3
Σ : 0	0
s^2 : 36	4
s : 6	2
Cov = 83/7	
r = 83/84	

(d)

$\frac{X-\overline{X}}{s_x}$	$\frac{Y-\overline{Y}}{s_y}$
−1 2/3	−1 1/2
−5/6	−1
−1/2	−1/2
−1/6	0
+1/6	0
+2/3	+1/2
+1	+1
+1 1/3	+1 1/2
Σ : 0	0
s^2 : 1	1
s : 1	1
Cov = 83/84 = r = b	

Figure 11.1 Scatter diagrams to illustrate correlation.

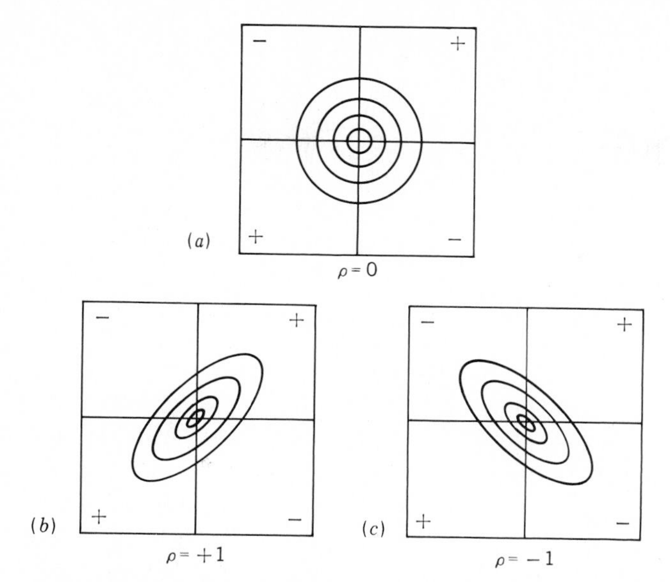

Figure 11.2 Diagrams to illustrate correlation. Corner signs ($\pm$) refer to the sign of the cross products for that quadrant. The probability of a point lying in an area between successive circles or ellipses is intended to be the same for each area. Thus, the three-dimensional frequency distribution would show a heaping up over the intersection of the axes and a gradual lowering as one moved away from this point. This presentation is in lieu of a three-dimensional figure such as Fig. 10.4*b* and *d*.

This tends to give a numerically large $\sum (X - \bar{X})(Y - \bar{Y})$. In Fig. 11.2*b*, $\sum (X - \bar{X})(Y - \bar{Y})$ will be positive and lead to a positive correlation; in Fig. 11.2*c*, $\sum (X - \bar{X})(Y - \bar{Y})$ will be negative and give a negative correlation.

Detecting linear correlation visually from plotted points can be difficult. An unfortunate choice of scale may tend to hide a real correlation or indicate a real one when none is present. A change of scale will change the apparent slope of the regression line. If a scatter diagram does not actually use standard deviations as units, at least the standard deviations should be available with the diagram to help prevent false conclusions.

In addition to difficulties due to an unfortunate choice of scale, visual detection is further hindered by the fact that the relation between r and the proportion of the total sum of squares explained by regression is not a linear one. Figure 11.3 shows this graphically. For $r = .1$, only 1 percent of the variation in a dependent variable is explained by the independent variable; for $r = .2$, the percentage is only 4; for $r = .5$, it is only 25. For $r > .5$, the explained percentage increases more rapidly. Apart from actual computation of r, detection is most likely by selecting large or small values of one variable and seeing if the corresponding values of the other variable tend to be at one end of the scale for that variable. Counts of the numbers of points in each of the quadrants are also informative.

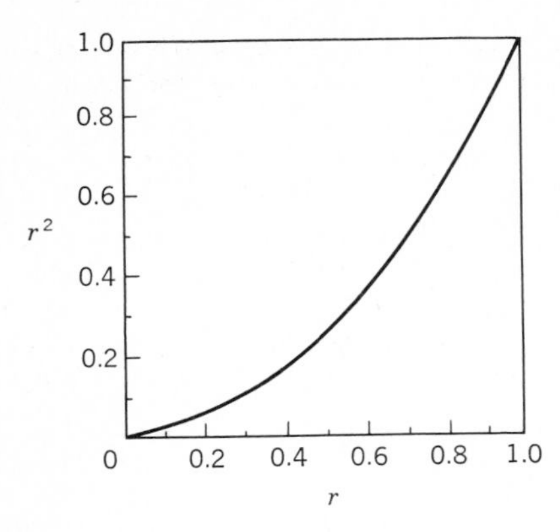

Figure 11.3 Relation between r and r^2.

Finally, the sampling variation in r is quite large for small-size samples.

It can be shown that r lies between -1 and $+1$, that is, $-1 \leq r \leq 1$. The values $+1$ and -1 indicate perfect linear correlation or a functional relation between the two variables. This places the observations outside the province of statistics. Barring rounding errors, one finds perfect correlation only in moments of carelessness as one might if correlating height with shoulder height plus height from shoulder to top of head. Extremely high correlations exist but when observed should always be closely scrutinized since the above form of carelessness may have been involved and perfect correlation missed only because of rounding errors in the computations.

Two quantities closely related to r are the coefficients of determination and alienation. The *coefficient of determination* is r^2, the square of the correlation coefficient. This term may also be used in connection with regression analysis, where the correlation coefficient is not applicable. In such cases, r^2 is the proportion of a total sum of squares that is attributable to another source of variation, the independent variable.

The *coefficient of nondetermination* is given by $1 - r^2 = k^2$ and is the unexplained proportion of a total sum of squares. Usually, this makes it the basis of an error term. Its square root k is called the *coefficient of alienation;* $k' = 1 - k$ has been called the *improvement factor*. These are not very common terms.

Exercise 11.2.1 H. H. Smith collected the following data on flowers of a Nicotiana cross. T = tube length, L = limb length, and N = tube base length.†

T: 49, 44, 32, 42, 32, 53, 36, 39, 37, 45, 41, 48, 45, 39, 40, 34, 37, 35
L: 27, 24, 12, 22, 13, 29, 14, 20, 16, 21, 22, 25, 23, 18, 20, 15, 20, 13
N: 19, 16, 12, 17, 10, 19, 15, 14, 15, 21, 14, 22, 22, 15, 14, 15, 15, 16

Compute the correlation coefficients between T and L, T and N, L and N. What are the coefficients of determination in each case?

† Published with permission of H. H. Smith, Brookhaven National Laboratories.

Exercise 11.2.2 In studying the use of ovulated follicles in determining eggs laid by ring-necked pheasant, C. Kabat et al. (11.3) present the following data on 14 captive hens.

Eggs laid:	39, 29, 46, 28, 31, 25, 49, 57, 51, 21, 42, 38, 34, 47
Ovulated follicles:	37, 34, 52, 26, 32, 25, 55, 65, 44, 25, 45, 26, 29, 30

Compute the correlation coefficient and coefficient of determination.

Exercise 11.2.3 In Exercise 10.2.3, measurements were given for X_3 = a blood cholesterol measurement and X_4 = a blood uric acid measurement. Compute the correlation coefficient between these two variables.

11.3 Correlation and Regression

We now have three methods for treating random pairs of observations:

1. Ignore any relation between variables and analyze them separately.
2. Use a regression analysis.
3. Examine the correlation.

Here we are concerned only with the second and third methods.

Correlation measures a co-relation, a joint property of two variables. Where variables are jointly affected because of external influences, correlation may offer the most logical approach to an analysis of the data. Regression deals primarily with the means of one variable and how their location changes with another variable. For correlation, random pairs of observations are obtained from a bivariate normal distribution, not too common a distribution; for regression, only the dependent member of each pair need be random and normally distributed. Correlation is associated with descriptive techniques; regression has to do with a relation between population means and values of a concomitant variable. Thus, whereas a correlation coefficient tells us something about a joint relationship between variables, a regression coefficient tells us that if we alter the value of the independent variable then we can expect the dependent variable to alter by a certain amount on the average, sampling variation making it unlikely that precisely the stated amount of change will be observed.

It has already been noted that

$$r^2 = \frac{[\sum (X - \bar{X})(Y - \bar{Y})]^2}{\sum (X - \bar{X})^2 \sum (Y - \bar{Y})^2} \quad \text{i.e., square of definition } r$$

$$= \frac{[\sum (X - \bar{X})(Y - \bar{Y})]^2/\sum (X - \bar{X})^2}{\sum (Y - \bar{Y})^2} = \frac{\text{SS(due to } X)}{\text{Total SS}(Y)}$$

$$= \frac{[\sum (X - \bar{X})(Y - \bar{Y})]^2/\sum (Y - \bar{Y})^2}{\sum (X - \bar{X})^2} = \frac{\text{SS(due to } Y)}{\text{Total SS}(X)}$$

In addition,

$$r^2 = \left(\frac{\sum (X - \bar{X})(Y - \bar{Y})}{\sum (X - \bar{X})^2}\right)\left(\frac{\sum (X - \bar{X})(Y - \bar{Y})}{\sum (Y - \bar{Y})^2}\right) = b_{YX} b_{XY} \quad (11.2)$$

where b_{YX} and b_{XY} are the regression coefficients for the regression of Y on X and of X on Y. Thus, the product of the regression coefficients is the square of the correlation coefficient; or the correlation coefficient is the square root of the product of the regression coefficients, or their geometric mean. These results are always algebraically correct; *they have meaning only when the sample consists of random pairs.*

If we standardize our variables, then the regression equation for Y on X becomes

$$\frac{Y - \bar{Y}}{s_Y} = r\frac{X - \bar{X}}{s_X} \qquad \text{or} \qquad Y' = rX'$$

as stated in Sec. 11.2. Similarly,

$$\frac{X - \bar{X}}{s_X} = r\frac{Y - \bar{Y}}{s_Y} \qquad \text{or} \qquad X' = rY'$$

Here r is a regression coefficient. Note that neither of these equations can be obtained by solving the other; a regression coefficient is not a symmetric statement about the relation between two variables.

11.4 Sampling Distributions, Confidence Intervals, and Tests of Hypotheses

Since $-1 \leq r \leq 1$, one cannot expect the sampling distribution of r to be symmetric when the population parameter ρ is different from zero. Symmetry occurs only for $\rho = 0$ and lack of symmetry or asymmetry increases as ρ approaches $+1$ or -1. This means that for small samples, a normal approximation is not generally suitable for computing a confidence interval for ρ and the confidence interval should not be centered on r. The failure to center on r will increase as observed values approach $+1$ or -1, since these values are the limits of possible values.

Sample r's are quite variable for small samples, particularly for ρ at or near zero. A single pair of values can make a lot of difference to the value of r. This makes it difficult to detect small but real values of ρ using small samples. Fortunately small values of ρ are of little practical use as was pointed out in Sec. 11.2 concerning the relation between r and r^2.

Possibly the simplest method of setting a confidence interval for ρ is to use the charts prepared by David (11.1). These charts are given as Table A.11. To set a confidence interval on ρ, draw a vertical line through the observed value of r on the "scale of r." At the points of intersection of this line with the two curved lines corresponding to the sample size, draw lines that cut the "scale of ρ" at right angles. The two ρ values on this scale are the limits of the confidence interval. These easy-to-use charts are sufficiently accurate for most purposes.

A convenient alternative is given by Fisher (11.2). For this, compute the transformation

$$Z' = .5 \ln \frac{1 + r}{1 - r} \tag{11.3}$$

which is approximately normally distributed with approximate mean and standard deviation of $.5 \ln [(1 + \rho)/(1 - \rho)]$ and $1/\sqrt{n - 3}$, regardless of the value of ρ. (ln is the natural logarithm, base e.) Values of Z' for r from .00 [.01] .99, are given in Table A.12. For a confidence interval for ρ, first determine one for the population mean of Z' and then convert for ρ. The conversion formula is $r = (e^{2Z'} - 1)/(e^{2Z'} + 1)$, but Table A.12 can be used quite satisfactorily.

To illustrate, the correlation of percent of resin and percent of rubber content in guayule was observed to be $r = .527$ for 50 plants of strain 416. We find

$$n - 3 = 47 \qquad \sigma_{Z'} = \sqrt{\frac{1}{47}} = .146$$

$$Z' = .5 \ln \frac{1 + r}{1 - r} = .5 \ln \frac{1.527}{.473} = .5 \ln 3.23$$

$$= .5(1.172) = .586$$

$$\text{CI}(\mu_{Z'}) = .586 \pm 1.96(.146)$$

$$= .300, .872$$

A rough interpolation in Table A.12 yields the 95 percent confidence interval for ρ of (.290, .703).

To test the null hypothesis that ρ equals some specified value other than zero, transform to approximate normality as in the previous paragraph and use the normal test. The hypothesized mean will also have to be transformed.

If the hypothesis is that $\rho = 0$, it is simpler and correct to compute

$$t = \frac{r}{\sqrt{(1 - r^2)/(n - 2)}}$$

and compare with Student's t for $n - 2$ degrees of freedom. The square of t equals F from the analysis of variance for regression, and consequently, the procedure is equivalent to testing the hypothesis that $\beta = 0$. This test cannot be used for testing the hypothesis $\rho = \rho_0 \neq 0$, that is, ρ equals a constant other than zero.

Table A.13, under one independent variable, gives values of r at the 95 and 99 percent levels of significance for a number of values of the degrees of freedom.

The distinction between significance and meaningfulness is not a serious problem with small samples but can be so with large samples. This is especially true of correlation, since many large bivariate samples are collected in certain types of studies. In large samples, small values of r may be significant. However, if the percentage reduction in total sum of squares is small for either variable considered as dependent, then the correlation may be quite useless.

Exercise 11.4.1 Set a confidence interval on one of the correlation coefficients computed in Exercise 11.2.1. Use the chart by David (Table A.11) and a transformation to Z' and back to r. Do the results differ appreciably?

Exercise 11.4.2 For the correlation coefficient obtained in Exercise 11.2.2, test the null hypothesis that $\rho = 0$.

Exercise 11.4.3 Construct a confidence interval for the parameter estimated by the correlation coefficient in Exercise 11.2.3. Test the null hypothesis that $\rho = 0$.

11.5 Homogeneity of Correlation Coefficients

The test of a difference between two population values of ρ is simple. The two r's are converted to Z''s and the appropriate large sample normal test of Chap. 5 is applied. For tests of hypotheses about one or two ρ's, Z' values must be found but no reconversion is required; reconversion is required only in the case of confidence intervals. An example of the test of homogeneity of two r's is given in Table 11.1.

Table 11.1 Test of the hypothesis $\rho_1 = \rho_2$ for the correlation of rubber content of branch on diameter of wood in guayule

Strain	Number of plants	r	Z'	$1/(n-3)$
109	22	0.310	0.32055	0.0526
130	21	0.542	0.60699	0.0556

Difference = 0.28644, sum = 0.1082

$$Z^* = \frac{0.28644}{\sqrt{0.1082}} = \frac{0.28644}{0.329} = 0.87 \text{ ns}$$

* This Z is a standard normal variable with $\mu = 0$ and $\sigma = 1$ under H_0.

Source: Data from U.S. Dept. Agr. Tech. Bull. 919, 1946, by W. T. Federer.

Table 11.2 Homogeneity and pooling of r's for the correlation of percent of resin content and percent of rubber content in guayule

Strain	n_i	r_i	Z'_i	$Z'_i - \bar{Z}'_w$	$(n_i - 3)(Z'_i - \bar{Z}'_w)^2$
405	50	0.362	0.379	−0.0913	0.392
407	50	0.419	0.446	−0.0243	0.028
416	50	0.527	0.586	+0.1157	0.629
	150				$\chi^2 = 1.049$, 2 df

$$\bar{Z}'_w = \frac{\sum (n_i - 3)Z'_i}{\sum (n_i - 3)} = 0.4703$$

Source: Data from U.S. Dept. Agr. Tech. Bull. 919, 1946, by W. T. Federer.

For the test shown in Table 11.1, a difference is compared with its standard deviation, the square root of the sum of the variances, and the result compared with values tabulated in a normal table. The probability of a larger difference arising by chance when there is no difference is about 38 percent for these two r values. Note that $r = 0.310$ is not significant whereas $r = 0.542$ is highly significant. However, the direct comparison is the appropriate one.

It is sometimes desired to test the homogeneity of several correlation coefficients and obtain a single coefficient if they seem to be homogeneous. For example, measurements on two characteristics of a crop or type of animal may be available for several strains or breeds. The strain or breed variances may not be homogeneous, so that pooling sums of products and calculating a single correlation coefficient is not valid. The test of homogeneity and the method of pooling are illustrated in Table 11.2.

The Z''s are approximately normally distributed. Since the variances, $1/(n_i - 3)$, will generally be unequal, a weighted mean $\bar{Z}'_w$ is used in the computations. The test criterion is χ^2, with degrees of freedom equal to one less than the number, say k, of r's. The criterion χ^2 was originally defined by Eq. (3.13). In our present example, $Z'_i - \bar{Z}'_w$ replaces Y_i; and zero, the mean of the population of all possible deviations, replaces μ_i. The standard deviation σ_i is replaced by $1/\sqrt{n_i - 3}$. Hence Eq. (3.13) becomes

$$\chi^2 = \sum_i \left(\frac{Z'_i - \bar{Z}'_w}{1/\sqrt{n_i - 3}} \right)^2 = \sum_i (n_i - 3)(Z'_i - \bar{Z}'_w)^2$$

Since only $k - 1$ deviations are independent, χ^2 has $k - 1$ degrees of freedom only. Here χ^2 is not significant, so we conclude that the correlation coefficients are homogeneous. Converting $\bar{Z}'_w$ back to r gives a pooled value of the several coefficients; pooled $r = 0.438$. To set confidence limits on the common ρ, place an interval about $\bar{Z}'_w$ and convert to values of r. The appropriate standard deviation is $1/\sqrt{\sum (n_i - 3)}$. Since $n_i - 3$ is the amount of information in Z'_i, the amount of information in $\bar{Z}'_w$ is $\sum (n_i - 3)$ and the reciprocal of this is the variance appropriate to $\bar{Z}'_w$.

There is a small bias in Z' which may be serious if many correlations are averaged. Since only three are involved here, we convert without hesitation. This bias equals

$$\frac{\rho}{2(n-1)}$$

and is positive. Since ρ is unknown, the bias cannot be eliminated. It has been suggested that the average r obtained from $\bar{Z}'_w$ be used for ρ to compute the bias for each Z'. These biases are subtracted from their respective Z''s and a new $\bar{Z}'_w$ computed. This is converted to an adjusted r which should be more accurate than the unadjusted. It is not appropriate to compute a new χ^2.

Exercise 11.5.1 To show the effect of skewness on the distribution of r, assume that three sample r's of Table 11.2 are increased by 0.4 to 0.762, 0.819, and 0.927. Test the homogeneity and compare the two χ^2 values and the two probabilities of getting a larger χ^2.

11.6 Intraclass Correlation

Sometimes a correlation coefficient is desired where there is no meaningful criterion for assigning one member of the pair to one variable rather than the other. This could be so when measuring the correlation of a characteristic in twins. In many such cases, we may obtain a value of the coefficient from the calculation of certain variances. The resulting coefficient is called an *intraclass correlation* and is computed by Eq. (11.4) when there are n observations per class.

$$r_I = \frac{\text{MS(among classes)} - \text{MS(within classes)}}{\text{MS(among classes)} + (n-1)\text{MS(within classes)}} \qquad (11.4)$$

The same result is also obtained from

$$r_I = \frac{\widehat{\sigma_\tau^2}}{\widehat{\sigma_\tau^2} + \widehat{\sigma^2}} \qquad (11.5)$$

where $\widehat{\sigma^2}$ and $\widehat{\sigma_\tau^2}$ are estimates of the corresponding components of variance in an among- and within-classes analysis. This definition of a sample quantity is based on the definition of the population *intraclass correlation*, namely,

$$\rho_I = \frac{\sigma_\tau^2}{\sigma_\tau^2 + \sigma^2}$$

where σ_τ^2 is the variation in the population of class means.

The first paragraph of this section constitutes a justification of or need for the term intraclass correlation rather than a definition. The definition is applicable even when the number of observations varies from class to class. It is of interest to note that this is the second time variances have been used in determining correlation. The ratio of a regression sum of squares to a total sum of squares is the square of a correlation coefficient; hence, the ratio of variances is a multiple of r^2 dependent on the degrees of freedom for the total sum of squares.

On occasion, it is known that responses by individuals within a group are not independent. For example, a number of randomly selected animals may be penned together as an experimental unit. Within each pen, they will compete for a fixed amount of food and the stronger ones will get the larger shares. Consequently, responses within pens are negatively correlated; they are more variable than would be the case if competition were not present. Here, an estimate of ρ_I should be negative, and if estimated from an analysis of variance, this can happen only if MS(among classes) $<$ MS(within classes), an unexpected result. Or, children within a classroom may respond similarly to some test procedure to the point where the responses are positively correlated relative to a purely random sample. This could happen because they attend a neighborhood or a private school where selection has created an unusually close homogeneity.

Suppose that we have a completely random design, ordinarily Model II, but now with an intraclass correlation appropriate. A reasonable alternative to Model II would be $Y_{ij} = \mu + \tau_i + \varepsilon_{ij}$, where μ is fixed, the τ_i are randomly drawn from a population with mean $\mu_\tau = 0$ and variance $\sigma_\tau^2 > 0$, and the ε_{ij} are normally distributed with mean $\mu_\varepsilon = 0$, common variance $\sigma^2 > 0$, but $\sigma_{jj'} = \rho_I \neq 0$ for $j \neq j'$; zero correlations among the ε's are not assumed. For this model,

$$E[\text{MS(within classes)}] = \sigma^2(1 - \rho_I)$$

$$E[\text{MS(among classes)}] = \sigma^2[1 + (n - 1)\rho_I]$$

Equations (11.4) and (11.5) are now seen to be reasonable.

The value of r_I may go as high as $+1$ but can never fall below $-1/(n - 1)$, the case when MS(among classes) $= 0$. The product-moment correlation is an *interclass correlation.* The intraclass correlation is a measure of fraternal resemblance when this term is meaningful.

For the data of Table 11.3,

$$r_I = \frac{16{,}320.5 - 2{,}199.2}{16{,}320.5 + 13(2{,}199.2)} = .314$$

$$= \frac{1{,}008.7}{1{,}008.7 + 2{,}199.2} = .314$$

Table 11.3 Analysis of variance of gain in weight of two lots of Holstein heifers

Source	df	MS	MS estimates (usual model)	Component
Treatments	1	16,320.5	$\sigma^2 + 14\sigma_\tau^2$	$\sigma_\tau^2 = 1{,}008.7$
Error	26	2,199.2	σ^2	$\sigma^2 = 2{,}199.2$

A test of significance of an intraclass correlation is now obvious. Test for the presence of σ_τ^2 in the analysis of variance; the criterion is F and the numerator and the denominator are the among- and within-classes variances. One usually performs a test of significance before computing r_I.

When the data are simply paired observations (Y, Y'), as in the first paragraph, one can compute the intraclass correlation coefficient by

$$r'_I = \frac{2\sum(Y-\bar{Y})(Y'-\bar{Y}')}{\sum(Y-\bar{Y})^2 + \sum(Y'-\bar{Y}')^2} \tag{11.6}$$

No special technique assigns one member of a pair to be Y and the other Y'. Equation (11.6) is equivalent to including each pair twice, once as (Y, Y') and then as (Y', Y); this also applies when $Y = Y'$. Snedecor and Cochran (11.5) illustrate this procedure using data on the number of finger ridges of identical twins; they also use the analysis of variance.

The procedures of Secs. 11.4 and 11.5 may be used for r'_I with a change in the approximate variance to $\sigma_{Z'}^2 = 1/(n - \frac{3}{2})$, where n is the number of pairs before doubling. Estimates of ρ are biased. For a close approximation to an unbiased value, add $1/(2n - 1)$ to Z' before transforming back to r.

Fisher (11.4, Chap. 7) discusses the intraclass correlation coefficient at greater length.

References

11.1. David, F. N.: *Tables of the Ordinates and Probability Integral of the Distribution of the Correlation Coefficient in Small Samples*, Cambridge, New York, 1938.

11.2. Fisher, R. A.: "On the 'probable error' of a coefficient of correlation deduced from a small sample," *Metron*, **1**:3–32 (1921).

11.3. Kabat, C., I. O. Buss, and R. K. Meyer: "The use of ovulated follicles in determining eggs laid by ring-necked pheasant," *J. Wildlife Manage.*, **12**:399–416 (1948).

11.4. Fisher, R. A.: *Statistical Methods for Research Workers*, 11th ed., rev., Hafner, New York, 1950.

11.5. Snedecor, G. W., and W. G. Cochran: *Statistical Methods*, 6th ed., Iowa State University Press, Ames, Iowa, 1967.

CHAPTER

TWELVE

MATRIX NOTATION

12.1 Introduction

A research worker who collects quantitative data will likely use statistical calculations which are the outgrowth of mathematical approaches to the analysis of data. For example, various estimators are said to be unbiased, to have minimum variance, or to be least-squares estimators; mathematics has often been necessary to develop the computational procedures, some of which are quite complex.

To interpret and gain understanding of complex procedures, the investigator may seek the cooperation of a statistician. When such aid is sought, the investigation should know some mathematical language. Among the mathematical tools that are often used, matrices rank high. These are used a great deal in preparing data for high-speed machine calculation and presenting results.

This chapter is intended to provide some understanding of and manipulative skills with matrices. It is hoped that the presentation of problems in matrix notation will help to clarify them and also help the reader visualize the nature of the solution.

For those not inclined to let anything impede their progress through the statistical methodology, it may be sufficient to proceed with the following as background:

1. The illustrations of matrices given in Sec. 12.2 through Eq. (12.2)
2. The example of matrix multiplication preceding Eq. (12.6)

3. The example of the presentation of a set of equations in matrix notation, Eq. (12.7)
4. The definition of the identity matrix, Eq. (12.8)
5. Section 12.4 on inverses until the term "inconsistent" is defined

If a need for more familiarity with matrices is felt, students can return to the chapter or seek alternative sources. Searle's (12.1) text is certainly appropriate for biologists.

12.2 Matrices

A *matrix* is a rectangular array of numbers, also called scalars. For example,

$$\begin{pmatrix} 2 & 3 & -1 \\ 3 & -8 & 2 \end{pmatrix}$$

is a matrix. This might be the matrix of coefficients for a pair of linear equations in unknowns x, y, and z. The equations could be

$$\begin{aligned} 2x + 3y - z &= 8 \\ 3x - 8y + 2z &= 3 \end{aligned} \qquad (12.1)$$

The variance-covariance matrix for the data in Table 10.1 is

$$\begin{pmatrix} 1.536/9 & 11.812/9 \\ 11.812/9 & 135.604/9 \end{pmatrix}$$

Boldface capital letters usually symbolize matrices. Equation (12.2) defines a general matrix.

$$\mathbf{A} = \begin{pmatrix} a_{11} & a_{12} & \cdots & a_{1j} & \cdots & a_{1c} \\ a_{21} & a_{22} & \cdots & a_{2j} & \cdots & a_{2c} \\ \cdots & \cdots & \cdots & \cdots & \cdots & \cdots \\ a_{i1} & a_{i2} & \cdots & a_{ij} & \cdots & a_{ic} \\ \cdots & \cdots & \cdots & \cdots & \cdots & \cdots \\ a_{r1} & a_{r2} & \cdots & a_{rj} & \cdots & a_{rc} \end{pmatrix} \qquad (12.2)$$

This is an $r \times c$ matrix, or a matrix of *order* or *dimensions* r by c. It has r rows and c columns. The element a_{ij} is at the intersection of the ith row and jth column; it is sometimes called the ijth element. The letter i is the *row index* and j is the *column index*.

The elements in a row will have something in common, as will the elements in a column. In the first illustration, the elements in the first row were coefficients in the first equation, and the elements in the first column were all coefficients of x. Thus matrices are *two-way ordered* arrays of numbers.

Finally, matrices must obey certain rules about combining with one another. This allows us to have a *matrix algebra*, with each matrix treated as an entity although the elements within will be involved.

The *transpose* of a matrix is one in which the first row is the first column of the original, the second row is the second column, and so on. The transpose is symbolized by $\mathbf{A}'$. Equation (12.3) holds.

$$\mathbf{A}' = \begin{pmatrix} a_{11} & a_{21} & \cdots & a_{r1} \\ a_{12} & a_{22} & \cdots & a_{r2} \\ \cdot & \cdot & \cdot & \cdot \\ a_{1j} & a_{2j} & \cdots & a_{rj} \\ \cdot & \cdot & \cdot & \cdot \\ a_{1c} & a_{2c} & \cdots & a_{rc} \end{pmatrix} \tag{12.3}$$

If $\mathbf{A}$ is an $r \times c$ matrix, then $\mathbf{A}'$ is $c \times r$.

When $r = c$, $\mathbf{A}$ is a *square matrix*. The elements a_{ii} lie on the *main* or *principal diagonal*. If $a_{ij} = a_{ji}$, then $\mathbf{A}$ is *symmetric* and $\mathbf{A} = \mathbf{A}'$.

A matrix of one column is a *vector* or a *column vector*. For example,

$$\begin{pmatrix} 8 \\ 3 \end{pmatrix} \qquad \begin{pmatrix} 3 \\ 1 \\ 1 \end{pmatrix} \qquad \text{and} \qquad \begin{pmatrix} x \\ y \\ z \end{pmatrix}$$

are vectors. The first is a vector of the constant terms in the two equations, the second is a solution of the equations, and the last is a list, or vector, of the unknowns.

A matrix that is a single row is called a *row vector*.

Exercise 12.2.1 See Table 2.3. The Y_i column is a vector of observations. The $Y_i - \bar{Y}$ column is a vector of signed deviations.

Find five other tables that present vectors of observations.

Exercise 12.2.2 See Table 5.5, columns headed 4.4 mm and 9.9 mm Hg. These data are a matrix of observations. What are the values of r and c? What do the elements in a row have in common? What do the elements in a column have in common?

Exercise 12.2.3 The observations in Table 10.2 are presented as a data matrix. What are its dimensions? What do the elements in a row have in common? The elements in a column?

Write out the transpose of the data matrix. In the transpose, what do the elements in a row have in common? The elements in a column? What is the dimension of the transposed matrix?

Exercise 12.2.4 What matrix given in this section is a square matrix? Name one class of matrices which must always be square.

12.3 Matrix Operations

Matrix algebra requires us to combine matrices by operations of the sort customarily used in arithmetic, namely addition, subtraction, multiplication, and division. Definitions are required.

Matrix *addition* is defined in a natural way as an element-by-element operation carried out by adding entries in corresponding positions. Equation (12.4) defines addition.

$$\mathbf{A} + \mathbf{B} = \begin{pmatrix} a_{11} + b_{11} & \cdots & a_{1c} + b_{1c} \\ \cdots & \cdots & \cdots \\ \cdots & a_{ij} + b_{ij} & \cdots \\ \cdots & \cdots & \cdots \\ a_{r1} + b_{r1} & \cdots & a_{rc} + b_{rc} \end{pmatrix} \tag{12.4}$$

Clearly, addition requires that the matrices be of the same order or be *conformable for addition.*

Suppose that a sales manager records car sales according to whether the cars are compact, standard, or deluxe models and by period of the week, say Monday through Thursday and the weekend. He has collected data on a new salesperson for each of two weeks. He will want to add the data to give the sales for the period.

$$\begin{pmatrix} 2 & 3 & 1 \\ 5 & 4 & 3 \end{pmatrix} + \begin{pmatrix} 4 & 3 & 2 \\ 7 & 6 & 3 \end{pmatrix} = \begin{pmatrix} 6 & 6 & 3 \\ 12 & 10 & 6 \end{pmatrix}$$

In this presentation, a row represents a period; one could just as conveniently present the data transposed so that columns were periods.

The poultryman who measures food intake, egg production by number, and egg production by weight per bird on a daily basis obtains an $n \times 3$ data matrix daily. Presumably he will add these matrices to get totals over some time period of interest.

It is easy to visualize data matrices for laboratory animals, plants, and so on. Many of these will be for short time intervals with the data to be accumulated over a longer period of study.

Application of the definition of addition to k identical matrices leads to the definition of *multiplication of a matrix by a scalar, k*; see Eq. (12.5).

$$k\mathbf{A} = \underbrace{\mathbf{A} + \cdots + \mathbf{A}}_{k \text{ times}} = \begin{pmatrix} ka_{11} & \cdots & ka_{1c} \\ \cdots & \cdots & \cdots \\ ka_{r1} & \cdots & ka_{rc} \end{pmatrix} \tag{12.5}$$

This definition also applies when k is not an integer.

Subtraction of matrices follows directly.

Suppose that an investigator assigns 10 male and 10 female mice to each of a number of treatments, measuring both initial and final weights. Her first data set consists of initial weights for each mouse recorded by sex of mouse and treatment to be given. These may be summarized conveniently by totals in a $2 \times t =$ sex $\times$ treatment matrix. Multiplication by $\frac{1}{10}$ gives means. Her final data set summary consists of final weights. The difference between the two data matrices measures mean weight gains.

Construction of any linear function of matrices now follows naturally.

Multiplication of matrices is defined in, perhaps, an unexpected manner. It might be described as a row-by-column operation. For example,

$$\mathbf{AB} = \begin{pmatrix} 2 & 5 \\ 3 & 8 \end{pmatrix}\begin{pmatrix} 1 & 6 \\ 4 & 7 \end{pmatrix} = \begin{pmatrix} 2(1)+5(4) & 2(6)+5(7) \\ 3(1)+8(4) & 3(6)+8(7) \end{pmatrix} = \begin{pmatrix} 22 & 47 \\ 35 & 74 \end{pmatrix} = \mathbf{C}$$

Note that elements of the first row of **A** multiply corresponding elements of the first column of **B** and are added to give c_{11}. Elements of the first row of **A** multiply corresponding elements of the second column of **B** to give c_{12}. For elements in the second row of **C**, elements in the second row of **A** multiply those of the appropriate column of **B**.

Equation (12.6) defines matrix multiplication.

$$_r\mathbf{A}_s\,{}_s\mathbf{B}_t = \begin{pmatrix} \sum_l a_{1l}b_{l1} & \sum a_{1l}b_{l2} & \cdots & \sum a_{1l}b_{lt} \\ \cdots & \cdots & \cdots & \cdots \\ \sum a_{rl}b_{l1} & \sum a_{rl}b_{l2} & \cdots & \sum a_{rl}b_{lt} \end{pmatrix} \tag{12.6}$$

Subscripts on **A** and **B** give the number of rows and columns in each. Note that **A** needs as many columns as **B** has rows for the two to be conformable for multiplication. Also, the dimensions of the product matrix are given by the number of rows in **A** and the number of columns in **B**; that is, if **A** is $r \times s$ and **B** is $s \times t$, then $\mathbf{AB} = \mathbf{C}$ is $r \times t$.

It is clear that the order of matrices cannot generally be reversed in multiplication; in fact, they will not be conformable if $r \neq t$ in Eq. (12.6). For the example, where both **AB** and **BA** exist,

$$\mathbf{BA} = \begin{pmatrix} 1 & 6 \\ 4 & 7 \end{pmatrix}\begin{pmatrix} 2 & 5 \\ 3 & 8 \end{pmatrix}$$

$$= \begin{pmatrix} 1(2)+6(3) & 1(5)+6(8) \\ 4(2)+7(3) & 4(5)+7(8) \end{pmatrix} = \begin{pmatrix} 20 & 53 \\ 29 & 76 \end{pmatrix}$$

None of the elements in the **BA** product matrix correspond to any of those in $\mathbf{AB} = \mathbf{C}$.

In the case of **AB**, we say that **B** is *premultiplied* by **A** and **A** is *postmultiplied* by **B**.

We now see that Eqs. (12.1) may be written in matrix notation as

$$\begin{pmatrix} 2 & 3 & -1 \\ 3 & -8 & 2 \end{pmatrix}\begin{pmatrix} x \\ y \\ z \end{pmatrix} = \begin{pmatrix} 8 \\ 3 \end{pmatrix} \tag{12.7}$$

Here we have multiplication of a 2×3 matrix of coefficients and a 3×1 matrix of unknowns, the latter being also a vector. The result is a 2×1 matrix that equals a 2×1 matrix or vector of scalars.

Again, we may write the expected values of the treatment means in a completely randomized design as follows.

$$\begin{pmatrix} 1 & 1 & 0 & 0 \\ 1 & 0 & 1 & 0 \\ 1 & 0 & 0 & 1 \end{pmatrix} \begin{pmatrix} \mu \\ \tau_1 \\ \tau_2 \\ \tau_3 \end{pmatrix} = \begin{pmatrix} \mu + \tau_1 \\ \mu + \tau_2 \\ \mu + \tau_3 \end{pmatrix}$$

The important *identity matrix* **I** is defined by

$$\mathbf{I} = \begin{pmatrix} 1 & 0 & 0 & \cdots & 0 \\ 0 & 1 & 0 & \cdots & 0 \\ \cdot & \cdot & \cdot & \cdots & \cdot \\ 0 & 0 & 0 & \cdots & 1 \end{pmatrix} \tag{12.8}$$

This square matrix consists of 1s on the main diagonal and 0s elsewhere. If an $r \times r$ matrix is premultiplied or postmultiplied by an $r \times r$ identity matrix, the original matrix remains unchanged. That is,

$$\mathbf{AI} = \mathbf{A} = \mathbf{IA} \qquad \text{for } \mathbf{I}_r \text{ and } {}_r\mathbf{A}_r$$

One needs only one subscript on **I** to indicate its order since, by definition, it is square.

I is an identity matrix for multiplication because it does not change the matrix it multiplies. It is like the 1 of ordinary arithmetic or algebra; $1 \times 4 = 4 = 4 \times 1$.

Finally, an analog of division is needed as a matrix operation. This is provided by use of inverse matrices (Sec. 12.4), and the identity matrix is needed in the definition.

Exercise 12.3.1 In the following matrices, rows represent three groups or blocks of guinea pigs. Successive columns give initial weights, forage consumed, and gains in weight, all in grams, for the guinea pigs. The matrices are for unfertilized and fertilized soil, the source of the forage. (See Table 17.12.)

$$\begin{pmatrix} 220 & 1{,}155 & 224 \\ 246 & 1{,}423 & 289 \\ 262 & 1{,}576 & 280 \end{pmatrix} \qquad \begin{pmatrix} 222 & 1{,}326 & 237 \\ 268 & 1{,}559 & 265 \\ 314 & 1{,}528 & 256 \end{pmatrix}$$

Add the two matrices.

Exercise 12.3.2 These matrices are similar to those of Exercise 12.3.1 but for a different soil source.

$$\begin{pmatrix} 198 & 1{,}092 & 118 \\ 266 & 1{,}703 & 191 \\ 335 & 1{,}546 & 115 \end{pmatrix} \qquad \begin{pmatrix} 205 & 1{,}154 & 82 \\ 236 & 1{,}250 & 117 \\ 268 & 1{,}667 & 117 \end{pmatrix}$$

Add these matrices.

Exercise 12.3.3 The following data matrices are initial weights and weight gains for various groups (rows) of guinea pigs assigned to rations derived from various combinations of fertilizer and soils (columns). (See Table 17.12.)

$$\begin{pmatrix} 220 & 222 & 198 & 205 \\ 246 & 268 & 266 & 236 \\ 262 & 314 & 335 & 268 \end{pmatrix} \quad \begin{pmatrix} 224 & 237 & 118 & 82 \\ 289 & 265 & 191 & 117 \\ 280 & 256 & 115 & 117 \end{pmatrix}$$

Add these matrices. What is the variable measured by the result?

Exercise 12.3.4 The following data matrices are weight gains in pounds for male and female bacon pigs according to the pen (rows) in which they were kept and the ration (column) they were fed. (See Table 17.7.)

$$\begin{pmatrix} 9.52 & 8.51 & 9.11 \\ 8.21 & 9.95 & 8.50 \\ 9.32 & 8.43 & 8.90 \\ 10.56 & 8.86 & 9.51 \\ 10.42 & 9.20 & 8.76 \end{pmatrix} \quad \begin{pmatrix} 9.94 & 10.00 & 9.75 \\ 9.48 & 9.24 & 8.66 \\ 9.32 & 9.34 & 7.63 \\ 10.90 & 9.68 & 10.37 \\ 8.82 & 9.67 & 8.57 \end{pmatrix}$$

Subtract the first matrix from the second. In how many cases did the weight gain for females exceed or equal that for males?

Exercise 12.3.5 Multiply the matrices found in Exercises 12.3.1 and 12.3.2 by the scalar $\frac{1}{2}$. Note that the results are averages for the two rations in each case.

Exercise 12.3.6 Perform the following matrix multiplications.

$$\begin{pmatrix} 1 & 2 \\ 3 & 4 \end{pmatrix}\begin{pmatrix} 1 & 2 \\ 3 & 4 \end{pmatrix} \quad \begin{pmatrix} 1 & 3 \\ 2 & 4 \end{pmatrix}\begin{pmatrix} 1 & 3 \\ 2 & 4 \end{pmatrix} \quad \begin{pmatrix} 1 & 2 \\ 3 & 4 \end{pmatrix}\begin{pmatrix} 1 & 3 \\ 2 & 4 \end{pmatrix} \quad \begin{pmatrix} 1 & 3 \\ 2 & 4 \end{pmatrix}\begin{pmatrix} 1 & 2 \\ 3 & 4 \end{pmatrix}$$

Exercise 12.3.7 Perform the following matrix multiplication.

$$\mathbf{AB} = \begin{pmatrix} 1 & 2 & 3 \\ 3 & 2 & 1 \end{pmatrix}\begin{pmatrix} 3 & 2 \\ 2 & 3 \\ 1 & 1 \end{pmatrix}$$

Can we add more rows to **A** and still carry out matrix multiplication? More columns?

Can we add more rows to **B** and still carry out matrix multiplication? More columns?

Exercise 12.3.8 The following data come from Exercise 7.3.1. Complete the indicated matrix operation.

$$\begin{pmatrix} 1 & 1 & 1 & 1 \\ 89.8 & 93.8 & 88.4 & 112.6 \end{pmatrix}\begin{pmatrix} 1 & 89.8 \\ 1 & 93.8 \\ 1 & 88.4 \\ 1 & 112.6 \end{pmatrix}$$

In general terms, what are the four numbers you now have?

Exercise 12.3.9 Find $\mathbf{X}'\mathbf{X}$, where

$$\mathbf{X}' = \begin{pmatrix} 1 & 1 & \cdots & 1 \\ X_1 & X_2 & \cdots & X_n \end{pmatrix}$$

Find $\mathbf{X}\boldsymbol{\beta}$, where

$$\boldsymbol{\beta} = \begin{pmatrix} \alpha \\ \beta \end{pmatrix}$$

Find $\mathbf{X}'\mathbf{Y}$, where $\mathbf{Y}' = (Y_1, \ldots, Y_n)$.

The equations $(\mathbf{X}'\mathbf{X})\hat{\boldsymbol{\beta}} = \mathbf{X}'\mathbf{Y}$ are those that were solved to give estimates of α and β in the regression problem, Chap. 10.

12.4 Inverses, Linear Dependence, and Rank

Consider Eq. (12.7), a matrix equation involving a vector of unknowns. If it were possible to divide both sides by the matrix of coefficients, the equation would be solved and, hopefully, numerical values would be equated to the unknowns.

In arithmetic or algebra, multiplication by the reciprocal of a number is the equivalent of division by that number; any number, other than zero, times its reciprocal equals unity. This idea provides the clue to developing the needed analog of division.

The *inverse* of a matrix is like a reciprocal in that a matrix multiplied by its inverse gives the identity matrix.

In arithmetic, division by zero is not defined, so that a usable definition of its reciprocal is also not defined. Similarly, there are square matrices for which inverses are not defined. Thus, inverses are defined only for some square matrices.

When an inverse of a square matrix $\mathbf{A}$ exists, the symbol $\mathbf{A}^{-1}$, called *A* inverse, is used. Such a matrix is unique and is both a right and a left inverse, so Eq. (12.9) holds.

$$\mathbf{A}\mathbf{A}^{-1} = \mathbf{I} = \mathbf{A}^{-1}\mathbf{A} \qquad (12.9)$$

Equation (12.9) defines *A* inverse.

From Eq. (12.9), the nature of the problem of finding an inverse becomes apparent. Assume that $\mathbf{A}$ is known but that the elements of $\mathbf{A}^{-1}$ are unknown. From Eq. (12.9), we construct the following illustration.

$$\begin{pmatrix} 1 & 2 \\ 3 & -1 \end{pmatrix}\begin{pmatrix} a & b \\ c & d \end{pmatrix} = \begin{pmatrix} 1 & 0 \\ 0 & 1 \end{pmatrix}$$

The matrix of letters represents $\mathbf{A}^{-1}$. Completing the multiplications, we have, element by element,

$$a + 2c = 1 \qquad 3a - c = 0 \qquad b + 2d = 0 \qquad 3b - d = 1$$

These simultaneous equations are easily solved pairwise to yield $a = \frac{1}{7}$, $b = \frac{2}{7}$, $c = \frac{3}{7}$, and $d = -\frac{1}{7}$. Now

$$\begin{pmatrix} 1 & 2 \\ 3 & -1 \end{pmatrix}\begin{pmatrix} \frac{1}{7} & \frac{2}{7} \\ \frac{3}{7} & -\frac{1}{7} \end{pmatrix} = \begin{pmatrix} 1 & 0 \\ 0 & 1 \end{pmatrix} = \begin{pmatrix} \frac{1}{7} & \frac{2}{7} \\ \frac{3}{7} & -\frac{1}{7} \end{pmatrix}\begin{pmatrix} 1 & 2 \\ 3 & -1 \end{pmatrix}$$

On the other hand, if we choose

$$\mathbf{A} = \begin{pmatrix} 1 & 2 \\ 4 & 8 \end{pmatrix}$$

the implied equations cannot be solved. In particular, $a + 2c = 1$ says that $a = 1 - 2c$. Substitution in $4a + 8c = 0$ gives $4 - 8c + 8c = 4 \neq 0$. The two equations have no solution and are said to be *inconsistent*. Another contradiction is found if we set up the equations with b and d. This matrix has no inverse.

In the second **A** matrix, the second column is a multiple of the first. We can write

$$2\begin{pmatrix} 1 \\ 4 \end{pmatrix} - \begin{pmatrix} 2 \\ 8 \end{pmatrix} = \begin{pmatrix} 0 \\ 0 \end{pmatrix}$$

If we think of **A** as two column vectors of two elements each, then $\mathbf{A} = (\mathbf{C}_1\mathbf{C}_2)$ and

$$2\mathbf{C}_1 - \mathbf{C}_2 = 0$$

Note that

$$\mathbf{0} = \begin{pmatrix} 0 \\ 0 \end{pmatrix}$$

This is called the *null*, or *zero, vector*.

In general, whenever a linear function of the column vectors that make up a matrix equals zero, the vectors are *linearly dependent*. Some vector in the system consists of information already available from other vectors; it is redundant.

More particularly, for $\mathbf{A} = (\mathbf{C}_1, \ldots, \mathbf{C}_c)$, where $\mathbf{C}_i$ is a column of r elements, the columns of **A** are *linearly dependent* if there are c scalars, $\lambda_1, \ldots, \lambda_c$ not all zero, such that

$$\sum \lambda_i \mathbf{C}_i = 0 \tag{12.10}$$

If Eq. (12.10) holds only when all $\lambda_i = 0$, then the vectors are said to be *linearly independent*.

From a set of linearly dependent vectors, eliminate one with a nonzero coefficient. The eliminated vector is a linear combination of the others, so it has no information that is not in the other vectors. Examine the remaining vectors for linear dependence and continue the process until a linearly independent set is found. This set contains the maximum number of linearly independent columns in **A**. This maximum is called the *rank* of the matrix; it is designated by $r(\mathbf{A})$. In practice, the procedure for finding the rank of a matrix uses elementary operators which are not discussed here. This procedure is programmed for computer application.

The column rank of a matrix is also the row rank, since the same value would have been reached if we had started with the rows as vectors. Thus the rank of a matrix is unique and cannot exceed $\min(r, c)$.

Recall that a matrix must be square to have an inverse and that not all square matrices have inverses. The inverse of a matrix exists only when the matrix is of full rank, then $r(\mathbf{A}) = r = c$. Such a matrix is said to be *nonsingular*. When a matrix is not of full rank, it is said to be *singular* or to have one or more singularities.

A method for determining whether a square matrix has an inverse or is nonsingular is to evaluate its *determinant*. The determinant of a matrix is a number or scalar, symbolized by $|\mathbf{A}|$. For a 2×2 matrix, the determinant is defined by

$$|\mathbf{A}| = \begin{pmatrix} a & b \\ c & d \end{pmatrix} = ad - bc \qquad (12.11)$$

For the 2×2 **A** matrices used earlier in this section, the determinants are

$$\begin{vmatrix} 1 & 2 \\ 3 & -1 \end{vmatrix} = 1(-1) - 2(3) = -7$$

and

$$\begin{vmatrix} 1 & 2 \\ 4 & 8 \end{vmatrix} = 1(8) - 2(4) = 0$$

A matrix with a nonzero determinant is nonsingular and has an inverse; otherwise it is singular and the inverse is not defined.

For a 3×3 matrix, evaluate the determinant by

$$|\mathbf{A}| = \begin{vmatrix} a & b & c \\ d & e & f \\ g & h & i \end{vmatrix} = aei + bfg + cdh - ceg - afh - bdi \qquad (12.12)$$

Evaluation is easy if columns 1 and 2 are first written after **A** in a 3×5 arrangement. The products of the elements in each of the three left-to-right diagonals provide the positive terms, whereas those in the three right-to-left diagonals provide the negative terms.

We will not be directly concerned with evaluation of determinants for larger matrices, assuming that this will be done electronically. However, definition of the determinant of an $r \times r$ matrix is given by

$$|\mathbf{A}| = \begin{cases} \sum_{j=1}^{r} a_{ij}(-1)^{i+j}|\mathbf{M}_{ij}| & \text{any } i \\ \sum_{i=1}^{r} a_{ij}(-1)^{i+j}|\mathbf{M}_{ij}| & \text{any } j \end{cases} \tag{12.13}$$

This definition calls for *expansion by the elements of the ith row*, the first case, or by the *elements of the jth column*, the second case.

$\mathbf{M}_{ij}$ is called a *minor* of $\mathbf{A}$. It is found by striking out the ith row and jth column of $\mathbf{A}$ to give an $(r-1) \times (r-1)$ matrix and then taking its determinant. The minor, together with its sign, is called the *cofactor* of a_{ij} in $|\mathbf{A}|$.

Equations (12.13) and (12.12) enable us to evaluate a 4×4 matrix. This evaluation and Eq. (12.13) let us proceed to 5×5 matrices, and so on.

In general, the expansion of any matrix is presented as a polynomial in the elements of the matrix. Each term of the final expansion will be an appropriately signed product of a single element from each row and column of the matrix, that is, a product of r elements.

Finally, the *inverse* of a 2×2 matrix is given by

$$\mathbf{A}^{-1} = \frac{1}{|\mathbf{A}|}\begin{pmatrix} d & -b \\ -c & a \end{pmatrix} \tag{12.14}$$

In general, we have

$$\mathbf{A}^{-1} = \frac{1}{|\mathbf{A}|}\begin{pmatrix} \mathbf{M}_{11} & -\mathbf{M}_{21} & \mathbf{M}_{31} & \cdots & (-1)^{r+1}\mathbf{M}_{r1} \\ -\mathbf{M}_{12} & \mathbf{M}_{22} & -\mathbf{M}_{32} & \cdots & (-1)^{r+2}\mathbf{M}_{r2} \\ \cdots & \cdots & \cdots & \cdots & \cdots \\ (-1)^{r+1}\mathbf{M}_{1r} & (-1)^{r+2}\mathbf{M}_{2r} & (-1)^{r+3}\mathbf{M}_{3r} & \cdots & \mathbf{M}_{rr} \end{pmatrix} \tag{12.15}$$

It is assumed that determination of this inverse, if required, will be done by an electronic computer. The actual method of computation will not likely be that implied by Eq. (12.15).

Exercise 12.4.1 Find inverses for the matrices

$$\begin{pmatrix} 1 & 2 \\ 3 & 4 \end{pmatrix} \quad \text{and} \quad \begin{pmatrix} 1 & 3 \\ 2 & 4 \end{pmatrix}$$

Check that these are both right and left inverses.

Exercise 12.4.2 Find the inverse of **AB**, computed in Exercise 12.3.7.

Exercise 12.4.3 Show that the determinant of

$$\mathbf{A} = \begin{pmatrix} 1 & 2 \\ 4 & 8 \end{pmatrix}$$

is zero.

Exercise 12.4.4 For $(\mathbf{X}'\mathbf{X})$ from Exercise 12.3.9, find the inverse. Multiply both sides of the matrix equation given there, to find a solution for $\hat{\boldsymbol{\beta}}$. Show that this solution is the same as that given in Chap. 10.

Compute $\hat{\boldsymbol{\beta}}'(\mathbf{X}'\mathbf{Y})$. What familiar quantity does this equal?

References

12.1. Searle, S. R.: *Matrix Algebra for the Biological Sciences*, Wiley, New York, 1966.

CHAPTER

THIRTEEN

LINEAR REGRESSION IN MATRIX NOTATION

13.1 Introduction

In upcoming chapters, we discuss multiple regression and disproportionate subclass number problems. The arithmetic of the analyses is quite tedious, so it will be left to high-speed computers. However, the underlying statistical concepts must remain clear and the limitations of computer programs and printouts must be fully understood. For help here, we rely on matrix notation. Although the problems are complex, their presentation in this form is concise. The same is true of the solutions.

In this chapter, the simple linear regression problem is presented in matrix notation and related to Chap. 10. Thus the material is familiar. In addition, the solutions developed in matrix form are easily generalized to the more complex problems of later chapters. Equations of special importance are so noted.

13.2 The Model and Least-Squares Estimates

The equation for the linear regression model is given in Eq. (10.5) as

$$Y_i = \beta_0 + \beta_1 X_i + \varepsilon_i \qquad i = 1, \ldots, n$$

We can then write the set of observations as

$$\begin{aligned} Y_1 &= \beta_0 + \beta_1 X_1 + \varepsilon_1 \\ Y_2 &= \beta_0 + \beta_1 X_2 + \varepsilon_2 \\ &\cdots\cdots\cdots\cdots\cdots \\ Y_n &= \beta_0 + \beta_1 X_n + \varepsilon_n \end{aligned} \tag{13.1}$$

These n equations have elements that fall naturally into categories. On the left of the equalities are the observations themselves; on the right are the coefficients of the parameters, the parameters, and the error components. In vector and matrix notation, they may be written, respectively, as

$$\mathbf{Y} = \begin{pmatrix} Y_1 \\ Y_2 \\ \vdots \\ Y_n \end{pmatrix} \quad \mathbf{X} = \begin{pmatrix} 1 & X_1 \\ 1 & X_2 \\ \vdots & \vdots \\ 1 & X_n \end{pmatrix} \quad \boldsymbol{\beta} = \begin{pmatrix} \beta_0 \\ \beta_1 \end{pmatrix} \quad \boldsymbol{\varepsilon} = \begin{pmatrix} \varepsilon_1 \\ \varepsilon_2 \\ \vdots \\ \varepsilon_n \end{pmatrix}$$

The vector $\mathbf{Y}$ is the random observation vector. The $\mathbf{X}$ *matrix*, also called the *design matrix*, is one of observable parameters. Here the column of 1s may be considered to be values of a *dummy variable* $X_{0i} = 1$, $i = 1, \ldots, n$. The vector $\boldsymbol{\beta}$ is a vector of unknown parameters and $\boldsymbol{\varepsilon}$ is a vector of unknown random components.

Equations (13.1) may now be written as

$$\begin{pmatrix} Y_1 \\ Y_2 \\ \vdots \\ Y_n \end{pmatrix} = \begin{pmatrix} 1 & X_1 \\ 1 & X_2 \\ \vdots & \vdots \\ 1 & X_n \end{pmatrix} \begin{pmatrix} \beta_0 \\ \beta_1 \end{pmatrix} + \begin{pmatrix} \varepsilon_1 \\ \varepsilon_2 \\ \vdots \\ \varepsilon_n \end{pmatrix}$$

or, compactly, as matrix Eq. (13.2).

$$\mathbf{Y} = \mathbf{X}\boldsymbol{\beta} + \boldsymbol{\varepsilon} \tag{13.2}$$

This important statement of the model equation should be thoroughly understood.

In terms of the data in Table 10.1,

$$\mathbf{Y} = \begin{pmatrix} 87.1 \\ 93.1 \\ \vdots \\ 94.4 \end{pmatrix} \quad \mathbf{X} = \begin{pmatrix} 1 & 4.6 \\ 1 & 5.1 \\ \vdots & \vdots \\ 1 & 5.1 \end{pmatrix} \quad \boldsymbol{\beta} = \begin{pmatrix} \beta_0 \\ \beta_1 \end{pmatrix}$$

For the model, we assume that the ε's have zero population mean and a common population variance σ^2 and are uncorrelated. When tests of significance are to be made, the ε's must also be from a normal population.

Most aspects of the model may be presented in matrix notation. For the assumption that the ε's have zero mean, write $E(\boldsymbol{\varepsilon}) = {}_n0_1$, the null vector. E is for expectation or mean, an idea first introduced in Sec. 5.10 and used repeatedly in talking about expected values of mean squares. Then Eq. (13.2) implies $E(\mathbf{Y}) = \mathbf{X}\beta$; this is the required statement about the mean. Finally, note that

$$\boldsymbol{\varepsilon\varepsilon}' = \begin{pmatrix} \varepsilon_1^2 & \varepsilon_1\varepsilon_2 & \varepsilon_1\varepsilon_3 & \cdots & \varepsilon_1\varepsilon_n \\ \varepsilon_2\varepsilon_1 & \varepsilon_2^2 & \varepsilon_2\varepsilon_3 & \cdots & \varepsilon_2\varepsilon_n \\ \cdots & \cdots & \cdots & \cdots & \cdots \\ \varepsilon_n\varepsilon_1 & \varepsilon_n\varepsilon_2 & \varepsilon_n\varepsilon_3 & \cdots & \varepsilon_n^2 \end{pmatrix}$$

Squares on the diagonal suggest variances; off-diagonal cross products suggest covariances. Consequently, assumptions concerning homogeneous variance and uncorrelated errors may be stated as follows.

$$E(\boldsymbol{\varepsilon\varepsilon}') = \begin{pmatrix} \sigma^2 & 0 & 0 & \cdots & 0 \\ 0 & \sigma^2 & 0 & \cdots & 0 \\ \cdots & \cdots & \cdots & \cdots & \cdots \\ 0 & 0 & 0 & \cdots & \sigma^2 \end{pmatrix}$$

$$= \mathbf{I}\sigma^2 \qquad \text{or} \qquad \mathbf{I}\sigma^2_{Y \cdot X}$$

From the sample, $\boldsymbol{\beta}$ is estimated by $\hat{\boldsymbol{\beta}}$, say, or $\mathbf{b}$. To estimate the population mean when $\mathbf{X} = \mathbf{X}_0$, we write $\mathbf{X}_0' = (1 \quad X_0)$ and then the sample regression equation as

$$\hat{\mu}_Y = \mathbf{X}_0' \hat{\boldsymbol{\beta}} \qquad \text{or} \qquad \hat{Y} = \mathbf{X}_0' \hat{\boldsymbol{\beta}} \tag{13.3}$$

When $X_0 = X_i$, one of the observed X's, then $\hat{Y}$ is called a *regressed* or *fitted value* and $e = Y - \hat{Y}$ is a deviation of the observation from the regression line, or a residual. The sum of squares of the residuals is a measure of the overall failure of the model to fit the data, that is, it is the error sum of squares. This, too, may be written in the new notation as

$$\mathbf{e}'\mathbf{e} = (e_1, e_2, \ldots, e_n) \begin{pmatrix} e_1 \\ e_2 \\ \vdots \\ e_n \end{pmatrix} = \sum e_i^2$$

Ordinarily, we choose $\hat{\boldsymbol{\beta}}$ or $\mathbf{b}$ so that $\sum e^2$ is minimized; that is, we obtain *least-squares estimates* of the parameters in the model. The least-squares equations or *normal equations* that provide these estimates are

$$({}_2\mathbf{X}'_n\,{}_n\mathbf{X}_2)\,{}_2\hat{\boldsymbol{\beta}}_1 = {}_2\mathbf{X}'_n\,{}_n\mathbf{Y}_1 \tag{13.4}$$

This matrix equation is the standard one for normal equations.

The $\mathbf{X}'\mathbf{X}$ matrix for our problem is of dimension 2×2 and that of $\mathbf{X}'\mathbf{Y}$ is 2×1. For the uncoded data of Table 10.1,

$$\mathbf{X}'\mathbf{X} = \begin{pmatrix} 1 & 1 & \cdots & 1 \\ 4.6 & 5.1 & \cdots & 5.1 \end{pmatrix} \begin{pmatrix} 1 & 4.6 \\ 1 & 5.1 \\ \vdots & \vdots \\ 1 & 5.1 \end{pmatrix}$$

$$= \begin{pmatrix} 10 & 49.8 \\ 49.8 & 249.54 \end{pmatrix}$$

These numbers are $10 = n$, $49.8 = \sum X_i$, and $249.54 = \sum X_i^2$. Thus Eq. (13.5) holds for linear regression.

$$\mathbf{X}'\mathbf{X} = \begin{pmatrix} n & \sum X_i \\ \sum X_i & \sum X_i^2 \end{pmatrix} \tag{13.5}$$

For the same data,

$$\mathbf{X'Y} = \begin{pmatrix} 1 & 1 & \cdots & 1 \\ 4.6 & 5.1 & \cdots & 5.1 \end{pmatrix} \begin{pmatrix} 87.1 \\ 93.1 \\ \vdots \\ 94.4 \end{pmatrix}$$

$$= \begin{pmatrix} 935.6 \\ 4671.10 \end{pmatrix}$$

These numbers are $935.6 = \sum Y_i$ and $4{,}671.1 = \sum X_i Y_i$. Equation (13.6) holds.

$$\mathbf{X'Y} = \begin{pmatrix} \sum Y_i \\ \sum X_i Y_i \end{pmatrix} \tag{13.6}$$

If $\mathbf{X'X}$ is nonsingular, then its inverse exists and the solution to the matrix Eq. (13.4) is given by

$${}_2\mathbf{b}_1 = {}_2\hat{\boldsymbol{\beta}}_1 = {}_2(\mathbf{X'X})_2^{-1}\,{}_2\mathbf{X}'_n\,{}_n\mathbf{Y}_1 \tag{13.7}$$

This equation should be completely understood and memorized as the solution of a set of normal equations when $\mathbf{X'X}$ is nonsingular.

The inverse of $(\mathbf{X'X})$ can be computed using Eq. (12.14) to give

$$(\mathbf{X'X})^{-1} = \frac{1}{n \sum X_i^2 - (\sum X_i)^2} \begin{pmatrix} \sum X_i^2 & -\sum X_i \\ -\sum X_i & n \end{pmatrix} \tag{13.8}$$

For the numerical illustration,

$$(\mathbf{X'X})^{-1} = \frac{1}{2{,}495.4 - 2{,}480.04} \begin{pmatrix} 249.54 & -49.8 \\ -49.8 & 10 \end{pmatrix}$$

$$= \begin{pmatrix} 16.24609375 & -3.2421875 \\ -3.2421875 & 0.65104167 \end{pmatrix}$$

Finally, Eq. (13.7) and some algebraic manipulation give

$$\mathbf{b} = \hat{\boldsymbol{\beta}} = \begin{pmatrix} \bar{Y} - \hat{\beta}_1 \bar{X} \\ \dfrac{\sum X_i Y_i - (\sum X_i)(\sum Y_i)/n}{\sum X_i^2 - (\sum X_i)^2/n} \end{pmatrix} \tag{13.9}$$

These are the familiar expressions of Chap. 10. For the numerical problem,

$$(\mathbf{X'X})^{-1}(\mathbf{X'Y}) = \begin{pmatrix} 16.24609375 & -3.2421875 \\ -3.2421875 & 0.65104167 \end{pmatrix} \begin{pmatrix} 935.6 \\ 4671.10 \end{pmatrix}$$

$$= \begin{pmatrix} 55.26 \\ 7.69 \end{pmatrix}$$

These estimates are the same as those found in Chap. 10.

Exercise 13.2.1 By direct multiplication, show that $(\mathbf{X}'\mathbf{X})^{-1}$ as found for the Leghorn data is both a right and left inverse.

Exercise 13.2.2 Round the elements in the inverse matrix above to two decimal places and compute the **b** or $\hat{\boldsymbol{\beta}}$ vector. Note the discrepancy between this and the result given in the text. (*Note*: In regression computations, carry as many figures as possible or rounding errors may create serious difficulties.)

Exercise 13.2.3 For Exercise 10.2.1, what is the **Y** vector? The **X** matrix? The $\hat{\boldsymbol{\beta}}$ vector? Compute $\mathbf{X}'\mathbf{X}$ and $\mathbf{X}'\mathbf{Y}$. Find $(\mathbf{X}'\mathbf{X})^{-1}$. Compute $\hat{\boldsymbol{\beta}} = (\mathbf{X}'\mathbf{X})^{-1}\mathbf{X}'\mathbf{Y}$.
Compare $\hat{\boldsymbol{\beta}}$ with the intercept and slope for the equation found in Exercise 10.2.1.

Exercise 13.2.4 Repeat Exercise 13.2.3 for Exercise 10.2.3.

Exercise 13.2.5 Repeat Exercise 13.2.3 for Exercise 10.2.4.

Exercise 13.2.6 Repeat Exercise 13.2.3 for Exercise 10.2.5.

Exercise 13.2.7 Repeat Exercise 13.2.3 for each set of data in Exercise 10.8.1.

Exercise 13.2.8 Repeat Exercise 13.2.3 for each set of data in Exercise 10.8.3.

13.3 The Analysis of Variance

To estimate σ^2, the sample residual sum of squares is required; it is given by

$$\begin{aligned} \text{SS(residuals)} &= \mathbf{e}'\mathbf{e} = (\mathbf{Y} - \mathbf{X}\hat{\boldsymbol{\beta}})'(\mathbf{Y} - \mathbf{X}\hat{\boldsymbol{\beta}}) \\ &= \mathbf{Y}'\mathbf{Y} - \hat{\boldsymbol{\beta}}'\mathbf{X}'\mathbf{Y} \qquad n - 2 \text{ df} \end{aligned} \tag{13.10}$$

The importance of this equation will become even more apparent as we proceed. It should be thoroughly understood at an operational level.

The first right-hand expression for $\mathbf{e}'\mathbf{e} = \sum e_i^2$ may be inferred from Eq. (13.2); the final expression calls for somewhat more algebraic expertise than is provided in Chap. 12.

Equation (13.10) gives the residual sum of squares as the difference between the sum of squares of the observations, $\mathbf{Y}'\mathbf{Y}$, and a component that has to do with fitting the model, that is, with the parameters in $\boldsymbol{\beta}$. For the White Leghorn data,

$$\text{SS(total, unadjusted)} = \mathbf{Y}'\mathbf{Y} = \sum Y_i^2 = 87{,}670.34 \qquad n = 10 \text{ df}$$

and

$$\begin{aligned} \text{SS(model)} &= \hat{\boldsymbol{\beta}}'\mathbf{X}'\mathbf{Y} = (55.26 \quad 7.69)\begin{pmatrix} 935.6 \\ 4671.1 \end{pmatrix} \\ &= 87{,}625.644 \qquad 2 \text{ df} \end{aligned}$$

More decimal places than are shown were used in these computations.

Table 13.1 Analysis of variance for regression

Source	df	SS	MS	F
Regression, X	1	$\hat{\boldsymbol{\beta}}'\mathbf{X}'\mathbf{Y} - (\sum Y)^2/n = 90.908$	90.908	16.3**
Residual	$n - 2 = 8$	$\mathbf{Y}'\mathbf{Y} - \hat{\boldsymbol{\beta}}'\mathbf{X}'\mathbf{Y} = 44.696$	5.587	
Total	$n - 1 = 9$	$\mathbf{Y}'\mathbf{Y} - (\sum Y)^2/n = 135.604$		

Observe Eq. (13.11).

$$\text{SS(model)} = \hat{\boldsymbol{\beta}}'\mathbf{X}'\mathbf{Y} \qquad 2 \text{ df} \tag{13.11}$$

This sum of squares has 2 df, the rank of $\mathbf{X}'\mathbf{X}$.

To find the contribution attributable to regression, subtract the correction term from Eq. (13.11).

$$\text{SS(regression)} = \hat{\boldsymbol{\beta}}'\mathbf{X}'\mathbf{Y} - \frac{(\sum Y)^2}{n} \qquad 1 \text{ df}$$

$$= 87{,}625.644 - 87{,}534.736 = 90.908$$

Finally, the analysis of variance is presented as in Table 13.1. The F test is of H_0: $\beta_1 = 0$ versus H_1: $\beta_1 \neq 0$, a test against two-tailed alternatives; it is a test of whether or not variation in X contributes to variation in Y. Table 13.1 is essentially the same as Table 10.3. More decimal points have been used than are indicated, which is necessary when uncoded data are used.

Exercise 13.3.1 Using the procedures given in this chapter, complete an analysis of variance of the data in Table 10.5. Show the regression equation.

Exercise 13.3.2 Compute $\hat{\boldsymbol{\beta}}'\mathbf{X}'\mathbf{Y}$, $\mathbf{Y}'\mathbf{Y}$, $(\sum Y)^2/n$, and present the analysis of variance for the data in Exercise 10.2.1. Make use of computations from Exercise 13.2.3.

Exercise 13.3.3 Repeat Exercise 13.3.2 using Exercises 10.2.3 and 13.2.4.

Exercise 13.3.4 Repeat Exercise 13.3.2 using Exercises 10.2.4 and 13.2.5.

Exercise 13.3.5 Repeat Exercise 13.3.2 using Exercises 10.2.5 and 13.2.6.

Exercise 13.3.6 Repeat Exercise 13.3.2 using Exercises 10.8.1 and 13.2.7.

Exercise 13.3.7 Repeat Exercise 13.3.2 using Exercises 10.8.3 and 13.2.8.

13.4 Standard Deviations, Confidence Intervals, and Tests of Hypotheses

While the analysis of variance provides a test of H_0: $\beta_1 = 0$, it does not provide standard deviations of $\hat{\beta}_0$ and $\hat{\beta}_1$ directly. An estimate of σ^2 is available and variances and standard deviations can be found, tediously, by considering each $\hat{\beta}$ or b as a linear combination of Y's. However, with a matrix approach, the variance-covariance matrix for $\hat{\boldsymbol{\beta}}$ is given by

$$\begin{aligned}\mathbf{V}(\hat{\boldsymbol{\beta}}) &= \begin{pmatrix} \sigma^2(b_0) & \sigma(b_0, b_1) \\ \sigma(b_1, b_0) & \sigma^2(b_1) \end{pmatrix} \\ &= (\mathbf{X}'\mathbf{X})^{-1}\sigma^2_{Y \cdot X} \\ &= \begin{pmatrix} \left(\dfrac{1}{n} + \dfrac{\bar{X}^2}{\sum (X - \bar{X})^2}\right)\sigma^2_{Y \cdot X} & \dfrac{-\bar{X}\sigma^2_{Y \cdot X}}{\sum (X - \bar{X})^2} \\ \dfrac{-\bar{X}\sigma^2_{Y \cdot X}}{\sum (X - \bar{X})^2} & \dfrac{\sigma^2_{Y \cdot X}}{\sum (X - \bar{X})^2} \end{pmatrix}\end{aligned}$$

The first two lines of Eq. (13.12) are another essential equation in the matrix presentation.

Variances are in the principal diagonal and covariances are off-diagonal elements. In a real data problem, $\sigma^2_{Y \cdot X}$ will be replaced by its estimate, $s^2_{Y \cdot X}$. Note that $\sigma^2(b_1)$ in the last form of Eq. (13.12) is the parameter corresponding to the sample estimate in Eq. (10.12) and $\sigma^2(b_0)$ is the parameter corresponding to the estimate in Eq. (10.13) when $X = 0$.

The expression $\sigma(b_0, b_1) = \sigma(b_1, b_0)$ is the covariance between b_0 and b_1. It is not zero unless $\bar{X} = 0$. When the covariance is not zero, sums of squares are not additive. Hence, we compute

$$\begin{aligned}\text{SS(regression)} &= \text{SS}(b_1 | b_0) \\ &= \text{SS(model)} - \text{SS}(b_0 \text{ ignoring regression}) \\ &= \text{SS(model)} - \left(\sum Y\right)^2/n\end{aligned}$$

In other words, we compute SS(regression) as an additional sum of squares after fitting the mean while *ignoring regression* or *unadjusted* for regression. Also, we compute SS(intercept) by fitting regression through the origin and then finding an additional sum of squares due to including an intercept in the model. That is,

$$\begin{aligned}\text{SS(intercept)} &= \text{SS}(b_0 | b_1) \\ &= \text{SS(model)} - \text{SS}(b_1 \text{ unadjusted}) \\ &= \text{SS(model)} - \frac{\left(\sum XY\right)^2}{\sum X^2}\end{aligned}$$

The motivation was outlined in the last paragraph of Sec. 10.12.

For the White Leghorn data, the sample variance-covariance matrix follows.

$$\begin{aligned}\hat{\mathbf{V}}(\hat{\boldsymbol{\beta}}) &= \begin{pmatrix} 16.24609375 & -3.2421875 \\ -3.2421875 & 0.65104167 \end{pmatrix} 5.587 \\ &= \begin{pmatrix} 90.76643637 & -18.11400389 \\ -18.11400389 & 3.63734611 \end{pmatrix}\end{aligned}$$

To test H_0: $\beta_1 = 0$ versus H_1: $\beta_1 \neq 0$, we are able to write directly from $\hat{\boldsymbol{\beta}}$ and $\hat{\mathbf{V}}(\hat{\boldsymbol{\beta}})$,

$$t = \frac{7.69}{\sqrt{3.6373}} = 4.03^{**} \qquad 8 \text{ df}$$

The null hypothesis is rejected; the evidence does not support the hypothesis that the slope of the regression line is zero.

To construct a 95 percent confidence interval, compute the limits as follows:

$$\text{CI}(\beta_1) = 7.69 \pm 2.306\sqrt{3.6373} = (3.29, 12.09)$$

Unless a sample has been obtained that is as unusual as to occur only 1 time in 20, on the average, the true slope of the regression line should lie in this interval. It differs by only one unit in the second decimal place from that obtained in Chap. 10.

To test H_0: $\beta_0 = 0$ versus H_1: $\beta_0 \neq 0$, the hypothesis that the linear regression is through the origin, compute

$$t = \frac{55.26}{\sqrt{90.7664}} = 5.80^{**} \qquad 8 \text{ df}$$

We conclude that regression is not through the origin. This hypothesis would not be of much interest in this problem; it is presented only for illustration of the technique. A confidence interval for the intercept is easily constructed and more appropriate.

$$\text{CI}(\beta_0) = 55.26 \pm 2.306\sqrt{90.7664} = (33.29, 77.23)$$

Exercise 13.4.1 For the data of Table 10.5, find the variance-covariance matrix for the vector $\hat{\boldsymbol{\beta}}$. Construct 95 percent confidence interval estimates for both β_0 and β_1. From the confidence interval for β_1, what can be said about the null hypothesis H_0: $\beta_1 = 0$?

Exercise 13.4.2 Repeat Exercise 13.4.1 as a continuation of Exercises 13.2.3 and 13.3.2.

Exercise 13.4.3 Repeat Exercise 13.4.1 as a continuation of Exercises 13.2.4 and 13.3.3.

Exercise 13.4.4 Repeat Exercise 13.4.1 as a continuation of Exercises 13.2.5 and 13.3.4.

Exercise 13.4.5 Repeat Exercise 13.4.1 as a continuation of Exercises 13.2.6 and 13.3.5.

Exercise 13.4.6 Repeat Exercise 13.4.1 as a continuation of Exercises 13.2.7 and 13.3.6.

Exercise 13.4.7 Repeat Exercise 13.4.1 as a continuation of Exercises 13.2.8 and 13.3.7.

13.5 Estimation and Prediction

To estimate the population mean at $\mathbf{X}_0$, say $\hat{\mu}_Y$, $\hat{\mu}_{Y \cdot X}$, $\hat{Y}$, or $\hat{Y}_X$, set $\mathbf{X}_0' = (1 \; X_0)$ and compute $\hat{\mu}_Y = \mathbf{X}_0' \hat{\boldsymbol{\beta}}$, given earlier as Eq. (13.3). The variance of this estimate is given by

$$V(\hat{\mu}_{Y \cdot X}) = \mathbf{X}_0' \mathbf{V}(\hat{\boldsymbol{\beta}})\mathbf{X}_0$$
$$= \mathbf{X}_0'(\mathbf{X}'\mathbf{X})^{-1}\mathbf{X}_0 \sigma^2_{Y \cdot X} \qquad (13.13)$$

In practice, $\sigma^2_{Y \cdot X}$ will be replaced by $s^2_{Y \cdot X}$ to provide an estimate of the variance.

When $X_0 = 5.5$ lb,

$$\hat{\mu}_Y = (1 \quad 5.5)\begin{pmatrix} 55.26 \\ 7.69 \end{pmatrix} = 97.56 \text{ lb}$$

as obtained in Sec. 10.6. The variance of this estimate is

$$s^2_{\hat{Y}} = (1 \quad 5.5)\begin{pmatrix} 90.7664 & -18.1140 \\ -18.1140 & 3.6373 \end{pmatrix}\begin{pmatrix} 1 \\ 5.5 \end{pmatrix}$$
$$= 1.5407$$

and $s_{\hat{Y}} = 1.2418$ lb.

The 95 percent confidence interval estimate for μ_Y at $X = 5.5$ is computed as

$$\text{CI}(\mu_Y | X = 5.5) = \hat{\mu}_Y \pm t_{.025}(8 \text{ df})s_{\hat{Y}}$$
$$= 97.56 \pm 2.306(1.2418)$$
$$= (94.70, 100.42)$$

Any difference between this and the corresponding result obtained in Sec. 10.6 should be attributable to rounding errors.

When a problem calls for prediction rather than estimation, that is, when we are trying to say something about a future observation, the predicted value must be the same as the estimate of the mean, but its variance will be larger. To begin with, this variance must be that of observations and to it must be added the variance of the estimate that is also the predicted value. This variance is given by

$$V[Y(\text{predicted for } \mathbf{X} = \mathbf{X}_0)] = [1 + \mathbf{X}_0'(\mathbf{X}'\mathbf{X})^{-1}\mathbf{X}_0]\sigma^2_{Y \cdot X} \qquad (13.14)$$

Again, $s^2_{Y \cdot X}$ replaces $\sigma^2_{Y \cdot X}$ to give an estimate of this variance.

Exercise 13.5.1 Using the notation of Eqs. (13.3) and (13.13), estimate for the data of Exercise 10.2.1 the mean of the population of Y's for which $X = 5.00$. Estimate the variance. Construct a 95 percent confidence interval for the population mean. Refer to Exercise 13.4.2.

Exercise 13.5.2 Repeat Exercise 13.5.1 referring to Exercises 10.6.2 and 13.4.3.

Exercise 13.5.3 Repeat Exercise 13.5.1 referring to Exercises 10.6.3 and 13.4.4.

Exercise 13.5.4 Repeat Exercise 13.5.1 referring to Exercises 10.6.4 and 13.4.5.

Exercise 13.5.5 Using the notation of Eqs. (13.3) and (13.13) and data from treatment 3, Exercise 10.8.1, estimate the mean of the population of Y's at $X = 235$ and its variance. Construct a 95 percent confidence interval for the population mean. Refer to Exercise 13.4.6.

Repeat for the data from treatment 4.

Exercise 13.5.6 Repeat Exercise 13.5.5 for the data on the 10-yr runners in Exercise 10.8.3; use $X = 80$. Refer to Exercise 13.4.7.

13.6 Indicator or Binary Variables

(This section can be omitted without loss of continuity. It introduces binary variables, which extend the use of regression techniques to the analysis of variance. A singular matrix is dealt with. The section could be covered as appropriately at the end of Chap. 14.)

The regression variables of this chapter have been primarily quantitative, although a dummy variable, taking the value 1 only, was introduced for convenience or consistency of notation. However, many variables of interest are categorical, for example, sex and treatment—sex with two categories and treatments with $t \geq 2$. By introducing *indicator* or *binary variables*, variables which take on only the values 0 and 1, we can extend matrix regression techniques to handle categorical variables and mixtures of the two.

Consider two independent samples with homogeneous variance and a null hypothesis of a common mean. For example, see the data in Table 5.2. The usual equation for the model under H_1 is

$$Y_{ij} = \mu + \tau_i + \varepsilon_{ij} \qquad i = 1, 2, \qquad j = 1, \ldots, n_i \tag{13.15}$$

Let us rewrite the observations with changed subscripts as $Y_1, \ldots, Y_{n_1}$ for the first sample and $Y_{n_1+1}, \ldots, Y_{n_1+n_2}$ for the second. Next consider

$$Y_i = \beta_0 X_i + \beta_1 X_{1i} + \beta_2 X_{2i} + \varepsilon_i \qquad i = 1, \ldots, n_1 + n_2 \tag{13.16}$$

where

$$X_i = 1 \quad \text{for all } i \qquad X_{1i} = \begin{cases} 1 & i = 1, \ldots, n_1 \\ 0 & i = n_1 + 1, \ldots, n_1 + n_2 \end{cases}$$

$$X_{2i} = \begin{cases} 0 & i = 1, \ldots, n_1 \\ 1 & i = n_1 + 1, \ldots, n_1 + n_2 \end{cases}$$

The variable X_{1i} indicates when we are dealing with sample 1, X_{2i} when we have sample 2. Equation (13.16) is seen to provide the same information as Eq. (13.15). In particular, note the following expectations.

$$E(Y_i | X_1 = 1, X_2 = 0) = \beta_0 + \beta_1 \qquad E(Y_i | X_1 = 0, X_2 = 1) = \beta_0 + \beta_2$$

We have exchanged β_0 for μ, β_1 for τ_1, and β_2 for τ_2. Nothing has really changed.

The data described by Eq. (13.16) are presented in matrix notation as follows. Compare Eq. (13.2).

$$\begin{pmatrix} Y_1 \\ \vdots \\ Y_{n_1} \\ Y_{n_1+1} \\ \vdots \\ Y_{n_1+n_2} \end{pmatrix} = \begin{pmatrix} 1 & 1 & 0 \\ \vdots & \vdots & \vdots \\ 1 & 1 & 0 \\ 1 & 0 & 1 \\ \vdots & \vdots & \vdots \\ 1 & 0 & 1 \end{pmatrix} \begin{pmatrix} \beta_0 \\ \beta_1 \\ \beta_2 \end{pmatrix} + \begin{pmatrix} \varepsilon_1 \\ \vdots \\ \varepsilon_{n_1} \\ \varepsilon_{n_1+1} \\ \vdots \\ \varepsilon_{n_1+n_2} \end{pmatrix}$$

The normal equations $\mathbf{X'X\hat{\beta}} = \mathbf{X'Y}$ follow.

$$\begin{pmatrix} n_1 + n_2 & n_1 & n_2 \\ n_1 & n_1 & 0 \\ n_2 & 0 & n_2 \end{pmatrix} \begin{pmatrix} \hat{\beta}_0 \\ \hat{\beta}_1 \\ \hat{\beta}_2 \end{pmatrix} = \begin{pmatrix} \sum_1^{n_1+n_2} Y_i \\ \sum_1^{n_1} Y_i \\ \sum_{n_1+1}^{n_1+n_2} Y_i \end{pmatrix}$$

If we add rows 2 and 3 in this $\mathbf{X'X}$, we obtain row 1 and learn that $\mathbf{X'X}$ is singular and thus does not have an inverse. Also, if we add elements 2 and 3 in $\mathbf{X'Y}$, we obtain the first. This confirms that the first equation is the sum of the other two. In turn, we can conclude that the three equations in three unknowns do not really provide three different bits of information. We can not solve for all three unknowns in $\hat{\boldsymbol{\beta}}$.

Let us drop X_2 and thus β_2 and the third one of the original three normal equations. Remember that the first equation included this information. We now have $Y_i = \beta_0 X_{0i} + \beta_1 X_{1i} + \varepsilon_i$, or

$$\begin{pmatrix} Y_1 \\ \vdots \\ Y_{n_1} \\ Y_{n_1+1} \\ \vdots \\ Y_{n_1+n_2} \end{pmatrix} = \begin{pmatrix} 1 & 1 \\ \vdots & \vdots \\ 1 & 1 \\ 1 & 0 \\ \vdots & \vdots \\ 1 & 0 \end{pmatrix} \begin{pmatrix} \beta_0 \\ \beta_1 \end{pmatrix} + \begin{pmatrix} \varepsilon_1 \\ \vdots \\ \varepsilon_{n_1} \\ \varepsilon_{n_1+1} \\ \vdots \\ \varepsilon_{n_1+n_2} \end{pmatrix}$$

Here $E(Y_i | X_1 = 1) = \beta_0 + \beta_1$ and $E(Y_i | X_1 = 0) = \beta_0$. These expectations are not the same as those following Eq. (13.16). Originally, we defined elements of a three-parameter $\boldsymbol{\beta}$ vector but did not have enough information to estimate them. The system of equations was overparametrized. Now we have a two-parameter $\boldsymbol{\beta}$ vector and, hopefully, can solve the equations. However, the solution is for β's differently defined from those in the earlier $\boldsymbol{\beta}$ vector; this is apparent from the changed expected values.

The normal equations in matrix form are now

$$\begin{pmatrix} n_1 + n_2 & n_1 \\ n_1 & n_1 \end{pmatrix} \begin{pmatrix} \hat{\beta}_0 \\ \hat{\beta}_1 \end{pmatrix} = \begin{pmatrix} \sum_1^{n_1+n_2} Y_i \\ \sum_1^{n_1} Y_i \end{pmatrix} \tag{13.17}$$

This $\mathbf{X}'\mathbf{X}$ matrix is nonsingular and we can solve the equations.

$$(X'X)^{-1} = \begin{pmatrix} \frac{1}{n_2} & -\frac{1}{n_2} \\ -\frac{1}{n_2} & \frac{n_1 + n_2}{n_1 n_2} \end{pmatrix}$$

The solution of Eq. (13.17) is given by $\hat{\boldsymbol{\beta}} = (\mathbf{X}'\mathbf{X})^{-1}\mathbf{X}'\mathbf{Y}$ or

$$\hat{\boldsymbol{\beta}} = \begin{pmatrix} \hat{\beta}_0 \\ \hat{\beta}_1 \end{pmatrix} = \begin{pmatrix} \frac{1}{n_2} & -\frac{1}{n_2} \\ -\frac{1}{n_2} & \frac{n_1 + n_2}{n_1 n_2} \end{pmatrix} \begin{pmatrix} \sum_1^{n_1+n_2} Y_i \\ \sum_1^{n_1} Y_i \end{pmatrix}$$

$$= \begin{pmatrix} \sum_{n_1+1}^{n_1+n_2} Y_i/n_2 \\ \frac{\sum_1^{n_1} Y_i}{n_1} - \frac{\sum_{n_1+1}^{n_1+n_2} Y_i}{n_2} \end{pmatrix} \quad \text{or} \quad \begin{pmatrix} \bar{Y}_{2\cdot} \\ \bar{Y}_{1\cdot} - \bar{Y}_{2\cdot} \end{pmatrix} \quad \text{in earlier notation} \tag{13.18}$$

It is now clear that $\hat{\beta}_0 = \bar{Y}_{2\cdot}$ and $\hat{\beta}_1 = \bar{Y}_{1\cdot} - \bar{Y}_{2\cdot}$. Moreover, it is $\hat{\beta}_1$ that is needed to test the null hypothesis of no difference between the means of the populations from which the samples were drawn.

For the data of Table 5.2,

$$\mathbf{Y} = \begin{pmatrix} 57.8 \\ \vdots \\ 53.2 \\ 64.2 \\ \vdots \\ 59.2 \end{pmatrix} \qquad \mathbf{X} = \begin{pmatrix} 1 & 1 \\ \vdots & \vdots \\ 1 & 1 \\ 1 & 0 \\ \vdots & \vdots \\ 1 & 0 \end{pmatrix} \qquad \text{after } X_2 \text{ is discarded}$$

$$\mathbf{X'X} = \begin{pmatrix} 13 & 7 \\ 7 & 7 \end{pmatrix} \qquad \mathbf{X'Y} = \begin{pmatrix} 761.0 \\ 393.5 \end{pmatrix} \qquad (\mathbf{X'X})^{-1} = \begin{pmatrix} \frac{1}{6} & -\frac{1}{6} \\ -\frac{1}{6} & \frac{7+6}{7(6)} \end{pmatrix}$$

$$\hat{\boldsymbol{\beta}} = \begin{pmatrix} \hat{\beta}_0 \\ \hat{\beta}_1 \end{pmatrix} = (\mathbf{X'X})^{-1}\mathbf{X'Y} = \begin{pmatrix} \frac{1}{6}(761.0) - \frac{1}{6}(393.5) \\ -\frac{1}{6}(761.0) + \frac{13}{7(6)}(393.5) \end{pmatrix} = \begin{pmatrix} 61.25 \\ -5.04 \end{pmatrix}$$

For tests and confidence intervals, sample variances are required. Begin with SS(total, unadjusted) = $\mathbf{Y'Y}$, and the SS(model) = $\hat{\boldsymbol{\beta}}'\mathbf{X'Y}$.

$$\mathbf{Y'Y} = (57.8)^2 + \cdots + (59.2)^2 = 44{,}710.28$$

$$\hat{\boldsymbol{\beta}}'\mathbf{X'Y} = (61.25 \quad -5.04)\begin{pmatrix} 761.0 \\ 393.5 \end{pmatrix} = 44{,}629.70$$

Next

$$\text{SS(residuals)} = \mathbf{Y'Y} - \hat{\boldsymbol{\beta}}'\mathbf{X'Y} = 80.58 \qquad \text{with 11 df}$$

$$s^2 = 7.3258 \qquad \text{and} \qquad s = 2.71 \text{ percent}$$

We are now able to compute $\hat{\mathbf{V}}(\hat{\boldsymbol{\beta}})$.

$$\begin{aligned} \hat{\mathbf{V}}(\hat{\boldsymbol{\beta}}) &= (\mathbf{X'X})^{-1}s^2 \\ &= \begin{pmatrix} \frac{1}{6} & -\frac{1}{6} \\ -\frac{1}{6} & \frac{13}{42} \end{pmatrix} 7.3258 \\ &= \begin{pmatrix} 1.2210 & -1.2210 \\ -1.2210 & 2.2675 \end{pmatrix} \end{aligned}$$

The variance of $\hat{\beta}_1$ is seen to be 2.2675 and $s_{\hat{\beta}_1} = 1.5058$ percent. Finally, to test $H_0\colon \beta_1 = 0$ versus $H_1\colon \beta_1 \neq 0$, a test of whether or not there are real differences in coefficients of digestibility, we have

$$t = \frac{-5.04}{1.51} = 3.34^{**} \qquad \text{with 11 df}$$

Since $t_{.005}$ (11 df) = 3.106, we conclude that there is a real difference in population means. The same result was obtained and presented in Table 5.2. A confidence interval for the population difference is easily constructed.

The investigator might also want confidence intervals for the two population means. Note that $\bar{Y}_{2\cdot} = \hat{\beta}_0$ from Eq. (13.18). Also $\hat{V}(\hat{\beta}_0 = \bar{Y}_{2\cdot}) = 7.3258/6 = 1.2210$ from $\hat{\mathbf{V}}(\hat{\boldsymbol{\beta}})$. A confidence interval for the mean of the second population is now easily computed.

From Eq. (13.18), observe that $\bar{Y}_{1\cdot} = \hat{\beta}_0 + \hat{\beta}_1 = (1 \quad 1)\hat{\boldsymbol{\beta}}$. In turn, $V(\bar{Y}_{1\cdot}) = V(\hat{\beta}_0 + \hat{\beta}_1) = V[(1 \quad 1)\hat{\boldsymbol{\beta}}]$ is given by Eq. (13.19), an application of Eq. (13.13).

$$\hat{V}(\hat{\beta}_0 + \hat{\beta}_1) = (1 \quad 1)\hat{\mathbf{V}}(\hat{\boldsymbol{\beta}})\begin{pmatrix}1\\1\end{pmatrix}$$

$$= (1 \quad 1)\begin{pmatrix}\dfrac{1}{n_2} & -\dfrac{1}{n_2}\\ -\dfrac{1}{n_2} & \dfrac{n_1+n_2}{n_1 n_2}\end{pmatrix}\begin{pmatrix}1\\1\end{pmatrix}s^2 \qquad (13.19)$$

$$= \frac{s^2}{n_1}$$

For the data, $\bar{Y}_{1\cdot} = \hat{\beta}_0 + \hat{\beta}_1 = 56.21$ percent, and

$$\hat{V}(\bar{Y}_{1\cdot}) = (1 \quad 1)\begin{pmatrix}1.2210 & -1.2210\\ -1.2210 & 2.2675\end{pmatrix}\begin{pmatrix}1\\1\end{pmatrix}$$

$$= 1.0465$$

Compare this with $s^2/7 = 1.0465$. The arithmetic has simply been rearranged. A confidence interval for this population mean can now be constructed.

It is fairly easy to see how the use of indicator variables can be extended to cover t treatments. Again, it becomes necessary to delete one variable if we are to avoid a singular matrix. After this, it is necessary to look at expected values for an understanding of what information is available in the $\hat{\boldsymbol{\beta}}$ vector.

Exercise 13.6.1 Using indicator variables, carry out Exercise 5.5.1. Continue with the matrix methods of this chapter to find variances for the means of both samples.

Exercise 13.6.2 Repeat the preceding exercise but use the data of Exercise 5.5.2.

CHAPTER

FOURTEEN

MULTIPLE AND PARTIAL REGRESSION AND CORRELATION

14.1 Introduction

Chapters 10 and 13 dealt with straight-line regression where values of the dependent variable must be drawn at random. Chapter 11 was concerned with the measurement of the strength of the linear association or the *total* or *simple correlation* between two variables where pairs of observations must be drawn at random. Multiple regression and correlation, discussed in this chapter, involve linear relations among more than two variables.

Simple correlations may not be what is wanted in situations where the dependent variable is influenced by several independent variables. Consider the data reported by Drapala (14.6), where the following correlations are for 152 F_2 plants of Sudan grass and Sudan grass-sorghum hybrids.

Green yield and coarseness	$r_{YC} = +0.554$
Green yield and height	$r_{YH} = +0.636$
Coarseness and height	$r_{CH} = +0.786$

Simple correlations are computed while ignoring values of all other variables. Consequently, we cannot conclude from r_{YC}, for example, that the relation between yield and coarseness will be the same if a different set of values of height is considered. In fact, it can be shown that the correlation between Y and C at a single value of height, called a *partial correlation*, is $+0.113$ and is not significant. Thus when all plants are selected to have some specified height, then there is no apparent relation between yield and coarseness. The simple correlation between coarseness and yield appears to be largely a reflection of the close relation between coarseness and height, which is also closely related to yield. That is, most of the causes producing correlation between height and coarseness appear to be the same as those producing correlation between height and yield. Partial linear correlation and regression are discussed within the framework of multiple linear correlation and regression.

When interest is primarily in estimation or prediction of values of one characteristic from knowledge of several other characteristics, we need a single equation that relates the dependent variable and the independent ones. Such an equation need only be useful for prediction or estimation; it need not describe a complicated physical relation between changes in the independent variable and responses in the dependent one. *Multiple regression* techniques provide the necessary equation; *multiple correlation* measures the degree of relation between the dependent variable and the set of independent ones. For the data referred to, the multiple correlation of height and coarseness with yield is 0.642.

14.2 The Linear Equation and Its Interpretation in More than Two Dimensions

Some of the statements of the introduction will be clearer if related to Fig. 14.1, which shows a plane in three-dimensional space.

Equation (14.1) is that of a plane in three dimensions.

$$Y = b_0 + b_1 X_1 + b_2 X_2 \qquad (14.1)$$

The plotted points in Fig. 14.1 have the coordinates given below.

Point no.	X_1	X_2	Y
1	10	2	11
2	10	4	7
3	10	6	3
4	20	2	14
5	20	4	10
6	20	6	6
7	30	2	17
8	30	4	13
9	30	6	9

To construct a physical model of such a surface, cut two identical right-angled triangles and place them parallel to the X_1, Y plane, and with the

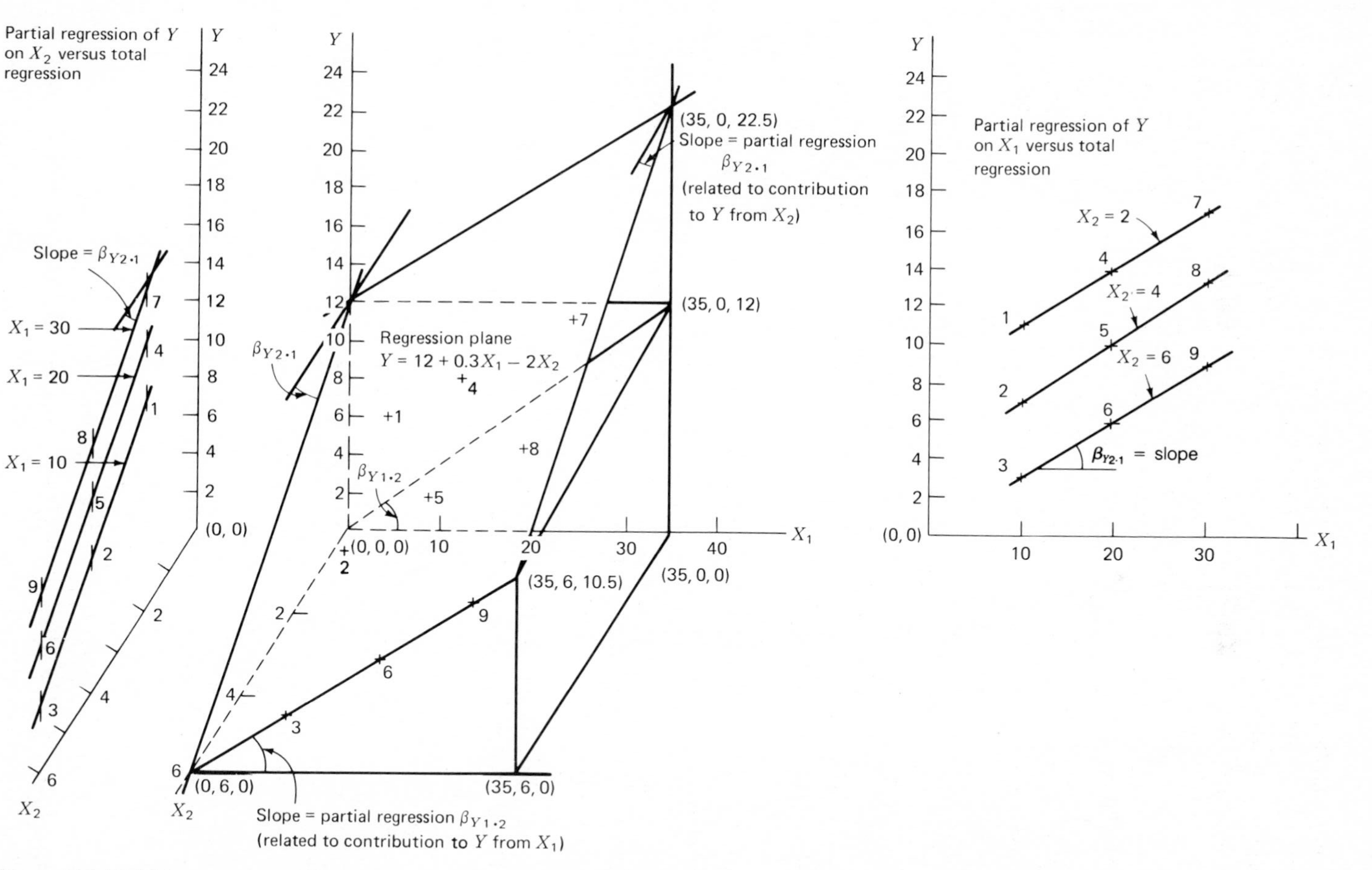

Figure 14.1 Multiple regression surface.

right angles at the same X_1 value, here $X_1 = 35$; see one at the front of the figure with an angle at $X_2 = 6$ and base perpendicular to the X_2 axis, and the other in the X_1, Y plane with an angle at $X_2 = 0$. (There is a third identical triangle, used later, in the X_1, Y plane and with an angle at $Y = 12$.) Now cut two other identical right-angled triangles, not necessarily the same as the first pair, and place them parallel to the X_2, Y plane, resting on the previous two triangles and with their right angles at the same X_2 value, here $X_2 = 0$; see one on the X_2, Y plane and the other resting on the rectangle parallel to the X_2, Y plane at $X_1 = 35$. The plane resting on the latter triangles is the desired plane. It slopes toward the X_1, X_2 plane because b_2 is negative. In Fig. 14.1, the equation of the plane is $Y = 12 + 0.3X_1 - 2X_2$. In general, one would now expect to have to raise or lower this plane to have the proper intercept, but this is not necessary in our illustration.

From the method of constructing this plane, it is clear that all lines on it parallel to the X_1, Y plane have the same slope, that of the first pair of triangles. Similarly, all lines on the constructed plane parallel to the X_2, Y plane have the same slope, that of the second pair of triangles, and probably different from that of the other pair. These properties are associated with partial regression coefficients.

A point on the plane has three components. We illustrate for the point at (35, 6, 10.5).

1. A base value equal to the intercept a of Eq. (14.1). In the illustration, $a = 12$. This is the value of Y on the regression plane above $(X_1, X_2) = (0, 0)$.
2. A contribution due to X_1 alone. To see this, keep X_2 fixed at $X_2 = 0$ and move X_1 out to $X_1 = 35$. As X_1 increases, Y moves up an amount $b_1 X_1 = 0.3(35) = 10.5$ to $Y = 12 + 10.5 = 22.5$. The slope b_1 or $b_{Y1 \cdot 2}$ is a partial regression coefficient and $b_{Y1 \cdot 2}$ times the change in X_1 measures the increase in Y for that change at any fixed value of X_2. That is, this change is independent of the value of X_2.
3. A contribution due to X_2 alone. Finally, let us keep X_1 fixed at $X_1 = 35$ while X_2 moves forward to $X_2 = 6$. Now Y moves an amount $b_2 X_2 = -2(6) = -12$ to $Y = 22.5 - 12 = 10.5$. Again, b_2 or $b_{Y2 \cdot 1}$ times the change in X_2 measures the increase in Y for that change at any fixed value of X_1. Here $b_{Y2 \cdot 1}$ is negative and X_2 changes from 0 to 6 so that the resultant change is to decrease Y. This change is independent of the value of X_1.

14.3 Partial, Total, and Multiple Linear Regression

Any sample regression equation determines or supplies an estimate of a population mean. A multiple linear regression equation has more than one independent variable. For a population, parameters are concerned and a regression equation can be written in the following form:

$$E(Y|X_1, \ldots, X_k) = \mu_{Y \cdot X_1 \ldots X_k} = \beta_0 X_0 + \beta_1 X_1 + \cdots + \beta_k X_k \quad (14.2)$$

$E(Y|X_1, \ldots, X_k)$ is the expected value or mean of the population of Y's for a specified set of values of the X's, say, $(X_1, \ldots, X_k)$. $X_0 = 1$ always and β_0 represents the Y intercept or the mean of the population of Y's when $(X_1, \ldots, X_k) = (0, \ldots, 0)$. For clarity, β_i is written as $\beta_{YX_i \cdot X_1 \ldots X_{i-1}, X_{i+1} \ldots X_k}$ and may be read as the *regression of Y on X_i for fixed values of the other X's* or as the *partial regression of Y on X_i*. When such an equation arises from a sample, we write

$$\hat{Y} = \hat{\mu}_{Y \cdot X_1 \ldots X_k} = b_0 + b_1 X_1 + \cdots + b_k X_k \quad (14.3)$$

where $b_i = b_{YX_i \cdot X_1 \ldots X_{i-1}, X_{i+1} \ldots X_k}$. The estimate of β_0 is $\bar{Y} - b_1 \bar{X}_1 - \cdots - b_k \bar{X}_k$. Consequently, we sometimes replace Eq. (14.3) with

$$\hat{Y} = \bar{Y} + b_1(X_1 - \bar{X}_{1\cdot}) + \cdots + b_k(X_k - \bar{X}_{k\cdot}) \quad (14.4)$$

Equation (14.2) may be written as follows:

$$E(Y|X_1, \ldots, X_k) = \mu_{Y \cdot X_1 \ldots X_k} = \mu_{Y \cdot \bar{X}_1 \ldots \bar{X}_k} + \beta_1(X_1 - \bar{X}_{1\cdot}) + \cdots + \beta_k(X_k - \bar{X}_{k\cdot})$$

For a sample, an observed point will rarely lie on the regression plane but will be above or below it. Thus to the components of any point on a plane as listed in Sec. 14.2, add a random component to give a sample point. In other words, the illustration used there gives values of $\mu_{Y \cdot X_1 \ldots X_k}$ whereas the description of an observation is given by

$$Y_i = \beta_0 X_0 + \beta_1 X_{1i} + \cdots + \beta_k X_{ki} + \varepsilon_i \quad (14.5)$$

In Fig. 14.1, $b_{y1 \cdot 2}$ and $b_{y2 \cdot 1}$ are slopes or angles of the triangles used to construct the regression plane. As a slope, $b_{y1 \cdot 2}$ measures the increase in Y per unit of X_1 for any value of X_2. This contribution is independent of X_2 because of the nature of a plane. This independence can be seen in the right-hand portion of Fig. 14.1 where X_1, Y values are plotted for the different values of X_2. The same applies to $b_{y2 \cdot 1}$ and the left-hand portion of Fig. 14.1. Values of $b_{y1 \cdot 2}$ and $b_{y2 \cdot 1}$ are called *partial regression coefficients*.

From the right-hand part of Fig. 14.1, the distinction between total or simple and partial regression is evident. The figure was constructed so that all points fell on the regression plane. A total regression, say, of Y on X_1, ignores the observed X_2 and is concerned with the nine points in the X_1, Y plane. Clearly the total regression of Y on X_1 does not account for much variation in Y. Also this regression can be greatly changed without affecting the partial regression. For example, if $X_2 = 4$ had been observed for $X_1 = 20$, 30, and 40, and $X_2 = 2$ for $X_1 = 30$, 40, and 50, and if the Y's were still on the given regression plane, the total regression of Y on X_1 would seem quite different. The right-hand part of Fig. 14.1 may be altered to illustrate this point.

Similar comments apply to total and partial correlation. The *partial correlation* of Y on X_1, denoted by $r_{y1 \cdot 2}$, is a measure of the association of Y and X_1 at $X_2 = 2$, at $X_2 = 4$, and at $X_2 = 6$. Clearly this is perfect correlation. The total or simple correlation between Y and X_1 ignores X_2 and is seen, from the right-hand part of Fig. 14.1, to be rather low. The example in the introduction was of the opposite type, with a high total correlation masking a low partial correlation between yield and coarseness for fixed height.

A *multiple correlation* coefficient measures the closeness of association between the observed Y values and a function of the independent values, namely, the regressed or *fitted values*. These values are on the sample regression plane for $(X_1, \ldots, X_k)$ values corresponding to those observed. The multiple correlation coefficient is denoted by $R_{y \cdot 12 \ldots k}$.

14.4 The Sample Multiple Linear Regression Equation

By definition, a sample regression equation supplies estimates of population means. In practice, it may also be used to predict events.

Estimation of the parameters in the regression equation is by least squares. Essentially, we consider all possible values for each of the entries in $\boldsymbol{\beta}' = (\beta_0, \beta_1, \ldots, \beta_k)$ and choose that set for which the sum of the squares of the residuals is minimum. Finally, Eq. (14.6) holds.

$$\sum (Y - \hat{Y})^2 = \text{minimum} \tag{14.6}$$

It is also true that these deviations sum to zero, that is, $\sum (Y - \hat{Y}) = 0$ when β_0, an intercept, is included in the model.

To find the appropriate estimate of $\boldsymbol{\beta}$, consider, in matrix notation, the observations as given by Eq. 14.5.

$$\begin{pmatrix} Y_1 \\ \vdots \\ Y_n \end{pmatrix} = \begin{pmatrix} X_0 & X_{11} & X_{21} & \cdots & X_{k1} \\ \vdots & \vdots & \vdots & & \vdots \\ X_0 & X_{1n} & X_{2n} & \cdots & X_{kn} \end{pmatrix} \begin{pmatrix} \beta_0 \\ \vdots \\ \beta_k \end{pmatrix} + \begin{pmatrix} \varepsilon_1 \\ \vdots \\ \varepsilon_n \end{pmatrix}$$

or

$$\mathbf{Y} = \mathbf{X} \boldsymbol{\beta} + \boldsymbol{\varepsilon}$$

Following the procedure of Sec. 13.2, we see that the normal equations become matrix Eq. (14.7).

$$\mathbf{X}'\mathbf{X}\hat{\boldsymbol{\beta}} = \mathbf{X}'\mathbf{Y} \tag{14.7}$$

Now, $\mathbf{X'X}$ is $(k + 1) \times (k + 1)$ and since $X_0 = 1$ always,

$$\mathbf{X'X} = \begin{pmatrix} n & \sum X_{1i} & \sum X_{2i} & \cdots & \sum X_{ki} \\ \sum X_{1i} & \sum X_{1i}^2 & \sum X_{1i}X_{2i} & \cdots & \sum X_{1i}X_{ki} \\ \cdots & \cdots & \cdots & \cdots & \cdots \\ \sum X_{ki} & \sum X_{ki}X_{1i} & \sum X_{ki}X_{2i} & \cdots & \sum X_{ki}^2 \end{pmatrix}$$

and

$$\mathbf{X'Y} = \begin{pmatrix} \sum Y_i \\ \sum X_{1i} Y_i \\ \vdots \\ \sum X_{ki} Y_i \end{pmatrix}$$

Nothing has really changed since Sec. 13.2 except the dimensions of the matrix equation and the arithmetic difficulties. If $\mathbf{X'X}$ is nonsingular, we can even write the solution as

$$_{k+1}\mathbf{b}_1 = {}_{k+1}\hat{\boldsymbol{\beta}}_1 = {}_{k+1}(\mathbf{X'X})^{-1}_{k+1}\ {}_{k+1}\mathbf{X'}_{nn}\mathbf{Y}_1 \tag{14.8}$$

Let us assume that this solution will ordinarily be provided by a computing facility.

It is easy to show that $b_0 = \bar{Y} - b_1 \bar{X}_{1\cdot} - \cdots - b_k \bar{X}_{k\cdot}$, to substitute this in the last k normal equations and to reduce these to matrix Eq. (14.9).

$$\begin{pmatrix} \sum (X_{1i} - \bar{X}_{1\cdot})^2 & \sum (X_{1i} - \bar{X}_{1\cdot})(X_{2i} - \bar{X}_{2\cdot}) & \cdots & \sum (X_{1i} - \bar{X}_{1\cdot})(X_{ki} - \bar{X}_{k\cdot}) \\ \sum (X_{2i} - \bar{X}_{2\cdot})(X_{1i} - \bar{X}_{1\cdot}) & \sum (X_{2i} - \bar{X}_{2\cdot})^2 & \cdots & \sum (X_{2i} - \bar{X}_{2\cdot})(X_{ki} - \bar{X}_{k\cdot}) \\ \cdots & \cdots & \cdots & \cdots \\ \sum (X_{ki} - \bar{X}_{k\cdot})(X_{1i} - \bar{X}_{1\cdot}) & \sum (X_{ki} - \bar{X}_{k\cdot})(X_{2i} - \bar{X}_{2\cdot}) & \cdots & \sum (X_{ki} - \bar{X}_{k\cdot})^2 \end{pmatrix}$$

$$\times \begin{pmatrix} b_1 \\ b_2 \\ \vdots \\ b_k \end{pmatrix} = \begin{pmatrix} \sum (X_{1i} - \bar{X}_{1\cdot})(Y_i - \bar{Y}) \\ \sum (X_{2i} - \bar{X}_{2\cdot})(Y_i - \bar{Y}) \\ \vdots \\ \sum (X_{ki} - \bar{X}_{k\cdot})(Y_i - \bar{Y}) \end{pmatrix} \tag{14.9}$$

These equations are also referred to at times as the normal equations. We will use these equations with $k = 2$ in the next section to illustrate some general aspects of multiple regression which can be easily generalized to $k > 2$ independent variables. Since each sum of squares or products has been *adjusted* for the means, and b_0 has been deleted from $\hat{\boldsymbol{\beta}}$, let us write these equations as matrix Eq. (14.10).

$$\mathbf{X}'_A \mathbf{X}_A \hat{\boldsymbol{\beta}}_A = \mathbf{X}'_A \mathbf{Y}_A \tag{14.10}$$

Keep in mind that $\sum (X - \bar{X})(Y - \bar{Y}) = \sum (X - \bar{X})Y$ so that $\mathbf{X}'_A \mathbf{Y}_A = \mathbf{X}'_A \mathbf{Y}$.

Exercise 14.4.1 Compute $\sum (X_1 - \bar{X}_{1\cdot})(X_2 - \bar{X}_{2\cdot})$, $\sum (X_1 - \bar{X}_{1\cdot})(Y - \bar{Y})$, $\sum (X_2 - \bar{X}_{2\cdot}) \times (Y - \bar{Y})$ for the illustration in Sec. 14.2. Note the value of $\sum (X_1 - \bar{X}_{1\cdot})(X_2 - \bar{X}_{2\cdot})$. It is this property of orthogonality that can make the solution of Eq. (14.9) or (14.10) simple and will permit us to compute independent contributions directly as in the case of orthogonal contrasts.

14.5 Multiple Linear Regression; Two Independent Variables

Table 14.1 gives percentages of nitrogen X_1, chlorine X_2, and potassium X_3, and log of leaf burn in seconds, Y, for 30 samples of tobacco taken from farmers' fields. Of these four variables, the first two independent variables and the dependent one will be used in this section to determine a regression equation. The data for all four variables will be used to illustrate the procedure for any number of independent variables starting in Sec. 14.7.

The raw data are entered into computing equipment programmed to do the following:

1. Compute sums, sums of squares, and sums of cross products for the raw data. These are given at the foot of Table 14.1.
2. Construct the **X** matrix, **X′X**, **X′Y**, and, in turn, the normal equations with $\hat{\boldsymbol{\beta}}' = (\hat{\beta}_0, \hat{\beta}_1, \hat{\beta}_2) = (b_0, b_1, b_2)$.

$$\mathbf{X} = \begin{pmatrix} 1 & 3.05 & 1.45 \\ 1 & 4.22 & 1.35 \\ \cdots & \cdots & \cdots \\ 1 & 2.94 & 2.22 \end{pmatrix} \qquad \mathbf{X'X} = \begin{pmatrix} 30 & 98.36 & 24.23 \\ 98.36 & 332.3352 & 81.5834 \\ 24.23 & 81.5834 & 30.1907 \end{pmatrix}$$

$$\mathbf{X'Y} = \begin{pmatrix} 20.58 \\ 61.6502 \\ 12.4103 \end{pmatrix}$$

The normal equations follow in matrix form.

$$\begin{pmatrix} 30 & 98.36 & 24.23 \\ 98.36 & 332.3352 & 81.5834 \\ 24.23 & 81.5834 & 30.1907 \end{pmatrix} \hat{\boldsymbol{\beta}} = \begin{pmatrix} 20.58 \\ 61.6502 \\ 12.4103 \end{pmatrix}$$

3. Solve the normal equations. Coding is likely done, at some stage, so that the arithmetic is as efficient as possible. The printed solution will consist of some or all of the following: $(\mathbf{X'X})^{-1}$, $\hat{\boldsymbol{\beta}}$, the regression equation,

$$\text{SS(model)} = \text{SS}(b_0, b_1, b_2) = \hat{\boldsymbol{\beta}}'\mathbf{X'Y}$$

$$\text{SS(regression)} = \text{SS}(b_1, b_2 | b_0) = \text{SS}(X_1, X_2 | X_0) = \hat{\boldsymbol{\beta}}'\mathbf{X'Y} - \frac{(\sum Y)^2}{n}$$

$$\text{SS(residuals)} = \mathbf{Y'Y} - \hat{\boldsymbol{\beta}}'\mathbf{X'Y}, \qquad \hat{\mathbf{V}}(\hat{\boldsymbol{\beta}}) = (\mathbf{X'X})^{-1}s^2$$

the analysis of variance, tests of $H_0\colon \beta_1 = \beta_2 = 0$ simultaneously, and of $H_0\colon \beta_1 = 0$ and $H_0\colon \beta_2 = 0$, where β_1 and β_2 are partial regression coefficients. Other information may also be included.

Note that SS(regression) is a difference; $\hat{\boldsymbol{\beta}}'\mathbf{X'Y}$ measures how much of the total variation $\mathbf{Y'Y}$ can be associated with fitting the parameters in the full linear model $Y = \beta_0 + \beta_1 X_1 + \beta_2 X_2 + \varepsilon$, whereas $(\sum Y)^2/n$ measures that for the reduced model $Y = \beta_0 + \varepsilon$. This difference in sums

Table 14.1 Percentages of nitrogen X_1, chlorine X_2, potassium X_3, and log of leaf burn in seconds Y, in samples of tobacco from farmers' fields

Sample no.	Nitrogen % X_1	Chlorine % X_2	Potassium % X_3	Log of leaf burn Y, s
1	3.05	1.45	5.67	0.34
2	4.22	1.35	4.86	0.11
3	3.34	0.26	4.19	0.38
4	3.77	0.23	4.42	0.68
5	3.52	1.10	3.17	0.18
6	3.54	0.76	2.76	0.00
7	3.74	1.59	3.81	0.08
8	3.78	0.39	3.23	0.11
9	2.92	0.39	5.44	1.53
10	3.10	0.64	6.16	0.77
11	2.86	0.82	5.48	1.17
12	2.78	0.64	4.62	1.01
13	2.22	0.85	4.49	0.89
14	2.67	0.90	5.59	1.40
15	3.12	0.92	5.86	1.05
16	3.03	0.97	6.60	1.15
17	2.45	0.18	4.51	1.49
18	4.12	0.62	5.31	0.51
19	4.61	0.51	5.16	0.18
20	3.94	0.45	4.45	0.34
21	4.12	1.79	6.17	0.36
22	2.93	0.25	3.38	0.89
23	2.66	0.31	3.51	0.91
24	3.17	0.20	3.08	0.92
25	2.79	0.24	3.98	1.35
26	2.61	0.20	3.64	1.33
27	3.74	2.27	6.50	0.23
28	3.13	1.48	4.28	0.26
29	3.49	0.25	4.71	0.73
30	2.94	2.22	4.58	0.23
$\sum X_i$	98.36	24.23	139.61	20.58
$\bar{X}$	3.2787	0.8077	4.6537	0.6860
$\sum X_i^2$	332.3352	30.1907	682.7813	20.8074
$\sum X_i X_j$	$\sum X_1X_2 = 81.5834$	$\sum X_1X_3 = 459.4052$	$\sum X_1 Y = 61.6502$	
	$\sum X_2 X_3 = 120.3950$	$\sum X_2 Y = 12.4103$	$\sum X_3 Y = 98.4408$	

Source: Data obtained through the courtesy of O. J. Attoe, University of Wisconsin, Madison, Wisconsin.

of squares measures the additional reduction attributable to adding the linear terms $\beta_1 X_1$ and $\beta_2 X_2$ to the model with only a constant and a random component. In other words, we are computing additive or orthogonal sums of squares, as discussed in Sec. 8.3 for contrasts.

Also, note that β_0 in the vector $\boldsymbol{\beta}$ does not have the same estimator as in the reduced model. In the full model, $\hat{\beta}_0 = b_0 = \bar{Y} - b_1 \bar{X}_{1\cdot} - b_2 \bar{X}_{2\cdot}$, whereas in the reduced model, $\hat{\beta}_0 = b_0 = \bar{Y}$. In other words, when terms are added to a model, estimators of the common parameters can be expected to change.

3a. Item 3 might be described as a modern approach to the solution of the regression problem. However, many texts still treat matrix Eq. (14.10) as the normal equations; we will look at its use with two independent variables.

The model equation is the same, namely, $E(Y) = \beta_0 + \beta_1 X_1 + \cdots + \beta_k X_k$, but it is also written as $E(Y) = \beta_0 + \beta_1(X_1 - \bar{X}_{1\cdot}) + \cdots + \beta_k(X_k - \bar{X}_{k\cdot})$. Here $\beta_1, \ldots, \beta_k$ remain the same but β_0 is the Y intercept in the former case, that is, β_0 (first form) $= E(Y \mid X_1 = 0, \ldots, X_k = 0)$, whereas it is the population mean at $(\bar{X}_{1\cdot}, \ldots, \bar{X}_{k\cdot})$ in the latter, or β_0(latter form) $= E(Y \mid X_1 = \bar{X}_{1\cdot}, \ldots, X_k = \bar{X}_{k\cdot})$.

The sample regression equation estimating population means in the second form may be written as

$$\hat{\mu}_Y = \hat{Y} = \bar{Y} + b_1(X_1 - \bar{X}_{1\cdot}) + \cdots + b_k(X_k - \bar{X}_{k\cdot}) \qquad (14.11)$$

We must know in advance the general form of the estimate of the Y intercept without being specific about the estimates of β_i, $i = 1, \ldots, k$. Equation (14.10) must still be solved.

Table 14.2 gives adjusted sums of squares and products to construct $\mathbf{X}'_A \mathbf{X}_A$ and $\mathbf{X}'_A \mathbf{Y}_A$, $(\mathbf{X}'_A \mathbf{Y} = \mathbf{X}'_A \mathbf{Y}_A)$. For our data, Eq. (14.10) is

$$\begin{pmatrix} 9.845547 & 2.141307 \\ 2.141307 & 10.620937 \end{pmatrix} \begin{pmatrix} b_1 \\ b_2 \end{pmatrix} = \begin{pmatrix} -5.82476 \\ -4.21148 \end{pmatrix}$$

Table 14.2 Adjusted sums of squares and products and simple correlations for data of Table 14.1

	X_1	X_2	Y
X_1	$\sum (X_1 - \bar{X}_1)^2 = 9.845547$	$\sum (X_1 - \bar{X}_1)(X_2 - \bar{X}_2) = 2.141307$ $r_{12} = 0.209400$	$\sum (X_1 - \bar{X}_1)(Y - \bar{Y}) = -5.82476$ $r_{Y1} = -0.717729$
X_2		$\sum (X_2 - \bar{X}_2)^2 = 10.620937$	$\sum (X_2 - \bar{X}_2)(Y - \bar{Y}) = -4.21148$ $r_{Y2} = -0.499638$
Y			$\sum (Y - \bar{Y})^2 = 6.68952$

These equations may be solved by substitution or by computing $(\mathbf{X}_A'\mathbf{X}_A)^{-1}$.

$$(\mathbf{X}_A'\mathbf{X}_A)^{-1} = \begin{pmatrix} 0.106227 & -0.021417 \\ -0.021417 & 0.098471 \end{pmatrix}$$

Next, estimate

$$\boldsymbol{\beta}_A = \begin{pmatrix} \beta_1 \\ \beta_2 \end{pmatrix}$$

This calls for $\mathbf{X}_A'\mathbf{Y}_A$.

$$\hat{\boldsymbol{\beta}}_A = \begin{pmatrix} b_1 \\ b_2 \end{pmatrix} = (\mathbf{X}_A'\mathbf{X}_A)^{-1}\mathbf{X}_A'\mathbf{Y}_A = \begin{pmatrix} -.52855 \\ -.28996 \end{pmatrix}$$

If the intercept form of the equation is to be used, $b_0 = \bar{Y} - b_1\bar{X}_{1\cdot} - b_2\bar{X}_{2\cdot} = 2.65313$. The regression equation is determined from Eq. (14.11) or Eq. (14.3).

$$\begin{aligned} \hat{Y} &= 0.6860 - .5285(X_1 - 3.2787) - .2900(X_2 - 4.6537) \\ &= 2.6531 - .5285X_1 - .2900X_2 \\ &= (1 \quad X_1 \quad X_2)\begin{pmatrix} 2.6531 \\ -0.5285 \\ -0.2900 \end{pmatrix} \end{aligned}$$

Table 14.3 gives the analysis of variance; a discussion of the partitioning of the regression sum of squares follows the t-tests below.

Computer output can include the variance-covariance matrix and will almost certainly include tests of hypotheses about β_1 and β_2.

$$\hat{\mathbf{V}}(\hat{\boldsymbol{\beta}}_A) = (\mathbf{X}_A'\mathbf{X}_A)^{-1}s^2 = \begin{pmatrix} .009401717 & -.001895498 \\ -.001895498 & .008715337 \end{pmatrix}$$

It is apparent that partial regression coefficients are not independent; their covariances are off-diagonal elements in $\hat{\mathbf{V}}(\hat{\boldsymbol{\beta}}_A)$, when given. In turn, sums of squares for F-tests for testing these coefficients are not additive.

To test H_0: $\beta_1 = 0$,

$$t = \frac{b_1}{s_{b_1}} = \frac{-.52855}{\sqrt{.009401717}} = -5.45^{**}$$

Similarly, to test H_0: $\beta_2 = 0$,

$$t = \frac{b_2}{s_{b_2}} = \frac{-.28996}{\sqrt{.008715337}} = -3.11^{**}$$

Table 14.3 Analysis of variance for Y regressed on X_1 and X_2 from Table 14.1

Source of variation			df	SS	MS	F
Regression $\|b_0$	or	$b_1, b_2 \| b_0$	$k = 2$	$\hat{\boldsymbol{\beta}}'_A \mathbf{X}'_A \mathbf{Y}_A = 4.29985$	2.14992	24.3**
X_1 ignoring X_2	or	$b_1 \| b_0$ only	1	$\dfrac{(\mathbf{X}'_{1A} \mathbf{Y}_A)^2}{\mathbf{X}'_{1A} \mathbf{X}_{1A}} = 3.44601$		
$X_2 \| X_0, X_1$	or	$b_2 \| b_0, b_1$	1	$\hat{\boldsymbol{\beta}}'_A \mathbf{X}'_A \mathbf{Y}_A - \text{SS}(X_1 \| X_0) = .85384$	.85384	9.6**
X_2 ignoring X_1	or	$b_2 \| b_0$ only	1	$\dfrac{(\mathbf{X}'_{2A} \mathbf{Y}_A)^2}{\mathbf{X}'_{2A} \mathbf{X}_{2A}} = 1.66996$		
$X_1 \| X_0, X_2$	or	$b_1 \| b_0, b_2$	1	$\hat{\boldsymbol{\beta}}'_A \mathbf{X}'_A \mathbf{Y}_A - \text{SS}(X_2 \| X_0) = 2.62989$	2.62989	29.7**
Error = residual			$n - k - 1 = 27$	$\mathbf{Y}'_A \mathbf{Y}_A - \hat{\boldsymbol{\beta}}'_A \mathbf{X}'_A \mathbf{Y}_A = 2.38967$	.08851	
Total			$n - 1 = 29$	$\mathbf{Y}'_A \mathbf{Y}_A = 6.68952$		

Both null hypotheses are rejected using a t-test with a comparisonwise error rate.

Confidence interval construction is also direct. For $1 - \alpha = .95$,

$$\begin{aligned}
\text{CI}(\beta_1) &= b_1 \pm t_{.025} s_{b_1} = -.52855 \pm 2.052\sqrt{.009401717} \\
&= (-.7275, -.3296) \\
\text{CI}(\beta_2) &= b_2 \pm t_{.025} s_{b_2} = -.28996 \pm 2.052\sqrt{.008715337} \\
&= (-.4815, -.0984)
\end{aligned}$$

To test the null hypothesis H_0: $\hat{\boldsymbol{\beta}}_A = {}_2\mathbf{O}_1$, a simultaneous testing, use the F-test at the top of Table 14.3; $= 2.14992/.08851 = 24.3^{**}$. Construction of a joint confidence region for β_1 and β_2, either rectangular or elliptical, is possible. The confidence coefficient would apply to joint estimation; that is, in repeated simultaneous estimation, the confidence region will contain both parameters $100(1 - \alpha)$ percent of the time and will contain neither or only one 100α percent of the time.

The individual tests above are of hypotheses concerning partial regression coefficients, tests about the regression of Y on an independent variable when the other independent ones are held constant, or tests of the value of introducing an independent variable into a model where others have already been included. Computationally, we may partition SS(regression $| b_0) =$ SS(regression) as in Table 14.3. First compute SS(X_1 ignoring X_2) as in Chap. 10. For this, introduce $\mathbf{X}_{iA}$. By implication, Eq. (14.9) defines $\mathbf{X}_A$ as a matrix with ith column composed of n deviations, $X_{ij} - \bar{X}_{i\cdot}, j = 1, \ldots, n$. Let $\mathbf{X}_{iA}$ represent the ith column or vector of deviations in $\mathbf{X}_A$; i labels the vector in $\mathbf{X}_A$; and A tells us that each X has been adjusted for the appropriate mean. Equation (14.12) follows.

$$\mathbf{X}'_{iA} = (X_{i1} - \bar{X}_{i\cdot}, X_{i2} - \bar{X}_{i\cdot}, \ldots, X_{in} - \bar{X}_{i\cdot}) \tag{14.12}$$

It is clear that $\mathbf{X}'_{iA}\mathbf{X}_{iA} = \sum_j (X_{ij} - \bar{X}_{i\cdot})^2$; similarly $\mathbf{Y}'_A\mathbf{Y}_A = \sum (Y_j - \bar{Y})^2$ and $\mathbf{X}'_{iA}\mathbf{Y}_A = \sum (X_{ij} - \bar{X}_{i\cdot})(Y_j - \bar{Y})$. In turn, we write $\text{SS}(X_1 | X_0) = \text{SS}(b_1 | b_0) = (\mathbf{X}'_{1A}\mathbf{Y}_A)^2/\mathbf{X}'_{1A}\mathbf{X}_{1A}$. This is the sum of squares, over and above the correction term, that is attributable to X_1.

In the analysis of variance, $\text{SS}(X_1 | X_0) = \text{SS}(b_1 | b_0)$ is subtracted from $\text{SS(regression} | b_0) = \text{SS}(b_1, b_2 | b_0)$ to give $\text{SS}(b_2 | b_0, b_1)$; that is, compute $\text{SS}(b_1, b_2 | b_0) - \text{SS}(b_1 | b_0) = \text{SS}(b_2 | b_0, b_1)$. This is the sum of squares, over and above the correction term and variation attributable to X_1, that can be attributed to X_2. Note that $(-3.11)^2 = t^2 = F = 9.65$ within rounding errors, in testing H_0: $\beta_2 = 0$.

Computation of $\text{SS}(X_2 | X_0)$ is similar and, in turn,

$$\text{SS}(X_1 | X_2, X_0) = \text{SS}(b_1 | b_0, b_2) = \text{SS}(b_1, b_2 | b_0) - \text{SS}(b_2 | b_0).$$

Exercise 14.5.1 Solve the equations referred to in Exercise 14.4.1 and show that the regression equation of Sec. 14.2 is correct. Compare the total and partial regression coefficients. Explain this particular result.

Exercise 14.5.2 Birch (14.2) collected the accompanying data on maize in a study of phosphate response, base saturation, and silica relationship in acid soils. Percentage of response is measured as the difference between yield on plots receiving P and those not receiving P, divided by yield on plots receiving no P, and multiplied by 100. Hence, a correlation between Y and X_1 has been introduced by the computing procedure. BEC refers to base exchange capacity.

Y = response to phosphate, percent	X_1 = Control yield, lb grain/acre	X_2 = saturation of BEC, percent	X_3 = pH of soil
88	844	67	5.75
80	1,678	57	6.05
42	1,573	39	5.45
37	3,025	54	5.70
37	653	46	5.55
20	1,991	62	5.00
20	2,187	69	6.40
18	1,262	74	6.10
18	4,624	69	6.05
4	5,249	76	6.15
2	4,258	80	5.55
2	2,943	79	6.40
−2	5,092	82	6.55
−7	4,496	85	6.50

Consider this as a regression problem with X_1 and X_3 as the only independent variables. What are $\mathbf{Y}$, $\mathbf{X}$, $\boldsymbol{\beta}$? Compute $\mathbf{X'X}$ and $\mathbf{X'Y}$. Write the least-squares equations in matrix notation. Compute $\mathbf{X'X}$ and find $\hat{\boldsymbol{\beta}}$. Write the regression equation.

Compute $\mathbf{Y'Y}$, SS(model), SS(regression) and SS(residuals), and present the numerical results in an analysis of variance similar to that in Table 14.3. Using $\alpha = .05$, test H_0: $\beta_1 = 0 = \beta_2$; H_0: $\beta_1 = 0$; H_0: $\beta_2 = 0$. To what does $\alpha = .05$ apply in these tests?

Find $\hat{\mathbf{V}}(\hat{\boldsymbol{\beta}})$. Compute $\hat{Y}$ for $\mathbf{X}_0' = (1, 2{,}000, 6.00)$. Find $\hat{V}(\hat{Y})$ and construct a 95 percent confidence interval for the population mean just estimated.

Exercise 14.5.3 Repeat Exercise 14.5.2 using the data of Exercise 10.2.3. For independent variables, use X_1 and X_2, two measures of fitness. For $\hat{Y}$, use $\mathbf{X}_0' = (1, 50, 100)$. Does this $\mathbf{X}_0'$ look like a vector that might apply to a real person?

Repeat the exercise using X_3 and X_4, two blood measurements. For $\hat{Y}$, use $\mathbf{X}_0' = (1, 280, 50)$. Does this $\mathbf{X}_0'$ look like a vector that might apply to a real person?

Repeat the exercise using X_1 and X_3. For $\hat{Y}$, use $\mathbf{X}_0' = (1, 50, 280)$. Does this $\mathbf{X}_0'$ look like a vector that might apply to a real person?

Exercise 14.5.4 Repeat Exercise 14.5.2 using the data of Exercise 10.2.4. For $\hat{Y}$, use $\mathbf{X}_0' = (1, 2{,}400, 150)$.

Exercise 14.5.5 Repeat Exercise 14.5.2 using the data of Exercise 10.2.5. For independent variables, use X_1 and X_2. For $\hat{Y}$, use $\mathbf{X}_0' = (1, 1{,}200, 550)$.

14.6 Partial and Multiple Correlations

Multiple and partial correlation coefficients are strictly applicable only when the total observation, that is, $(Y_i, X_{1i}, \ldots, X_{ki})$, is random. However, regardless of the randomness of the observations, these correlation coefficients may be useful for computing and other reasons.

Partial correlations are defined as correlations between two variables when all others are fixed. The symbol $r_{Y1 \cdot 23}$ is used for the sample correlation between Y and X_1 when X_2 and X_3 are constant or "adjusted for." Since the total observation should be random and the coefficient is primarily a descriptive one, there is no need to refer to a particular variable as the dependent one or to denote it by Y.

To compute partial correlation coefficients, first define $\mathbf{R}$ as the symmetric matrix of simple correlations among a set of k variables $X_1, \ldots, X_k$, none being labeled as dependent. In general, $\mathbf{R}$ is given by

$$\mathbf{R} = \begin{pmatrix} 1 & r_{12} & r_{13} & \cdots & r_{1k} \\ r_{21} & 1 & r_{23} & \cdots & r_{2k} \\ \cdots & \cdots & \cdots & \cdots & \cdots \\ r_{k1} & r_{k2} & r_{k3} & \cdots & 1 \end{pmatrix} \tag{14.13}$$

The inverse of $\mathbf{R}$ is determined by Eq. (12.15) and is also symmetric; let us write it as

$$\mathbf{R}^{-1} = C = \begin{pmatrix} C_{11} & C_{12} & \cdots & C_{1k} \\ C_{21} & C_{22} & \cdots & C_{2k} \\ \cdots & \cdots & \cdots & \cdots \\ C_{k1} & C_{k2} & \cdots & C_{kk} \end{pmatrix} \tag{14.14}$$

Now Eq. (14.15) defines the partial correlation between X_i and X_j.

$$r_{ij \cdot 1 \cdots i-1, i+1 \cdots j-1, j+1 \cdots k} = \frac{-C_{ij}}{\sqrt{C_{ii}C_{jj}}} \tag{14.15}$$

In Eq. (14.15), the inverse matrix elements may be replaced by the signed minors or cofactors of $\mathbf{R}$. See Eq. (12.13) and (12.15). Inverse elements are simply cofactors divided by the determinant of the matrix.

The correlation matrix for X_1, X_2, and Y is obtained from Table 14.2; X_1, X_2, and Y are given for identification.

$$\mathbf{R} = \begin{matrix} X_1 \\ X_2 \\ Y \end{matrix} \begin{pmatrix} 1.000000 & 0.209400 & -0.717729 \\ 0.209400 & 1.000000 & -0.499638 \\ -0.717729 & -0.499638 & 1.000000 \end{pmatrix}$$

(columns: X_1, X_2, Y)

The matrix of cofactors is easily computed.

$$\begin{pmatrix} 1 - r_{Y2}^2 & -r_{12} + r_{1Y}r_{Y2} & -r_{1Y} + r_{12}r_{2Y} \\ -r_{21} + r_{Y1}r_{2Y} & 1 - r_{Y1}^2 & -r_{2Y} + r_{21}r_{1Y} \\ -r_{Y1} + r_{21}r_{Y2} & -r_{Y2} + r_{12}r_{Y1} & 1 - r_{12}^2 \end{pmatrix}$$

$$= \begin{pmatrix} .750361 & .149205 & .613105 \\ .149205 & .484865 & .349346 \\ .613105 & .349346 & .956151 \end{pmatrix}$$

We now compute

$$r_{Y1\cdot 2} = \frac{-.613105}{\sqrt{.750361(.956151)}} = -.723829$$

$$r_{Y2\cdot 1} = \frac{-.349346}{\sqrt{.484865(.956151)}} = -.513076$$

Again, we have used all the decimal points our desk computer provided. In general, to test H_0: $\rho_{ij\cdot 1\ldots i-1,\,i+1\ldots j-1,\,j+1\ldots k} = 0$ compute t by

$$t = \frac{r\sqrt{n-k}}{\sqrt{1-r^2}} \tag{14.16}$$

For the data, to test H_0: $\rho_{Y2\cdot 1} = 0$ against H_1: $\rho_{Y2\cdot 1} \neq 0$, compute

$$t = \frac{r_{Y2\cdot 1}\sqrt{n-3}}{\sqrt{1-r_{Y2\cdot 1}^2}}$$

$$= \frac{-.513076\sqrt{27}}{\sqrt{1-(-.513076)^2}} = -3.11^{**} \qquad \text{with 27 df}$$

The test may also be made against one-sided alternatives. The t-test against two-sided alternatives is seen to be equivalent to the F-test of the same null hypothesis; $t^2 = (-3.11)^2 = 9.65$ compares with $F = 9.6$ in the analysis of variance.

Confidence intervals may also be constructed.

The multiple correlation coefficient, denoted by $R_{Y\cdot 1\ldots k}$, measures the closeness with which the regression plane fits the observed points. That is, it is the correlation between the observed Y's and the regressed Y's, that is, the $\hat{Y}$'s. Thus $R_{Y\cdot 1\ldots k}$ measures the combined effect of all independent variables on the dependent variable Y. This coefficient is defined by

$$R_{Y\cdot 1\ldots k} = \sqrt{\frac{\text{SS(regression)}}{\text{SS(total, adjusted)}}}$$

$$= \sqrt{\frac{\hat{\boldsymbol{\beta}}'\mathbf{X}'\mathbf{Y} - (\sum Y)^2/n}{\mathbf{Y}'\mathbf{Y} - (\sum Y)^2/n}} = \sqrt{\frac{\hat{\boldsymbol{\beta}}'_A\mathbf{X}'_A\mathbf{Y}_A}{\mathbf{Y}'_A\mathbf{Y}_A}} \tag{14.17}$$

The square of this coefficient is also called the *coefficient of (multiple) determination.*

Equation (14.17) can be manipulated to give Eqs. (14.18) and (14.19), which are often useful.

$$\text{SS(regression)} = \hat{\boldsymbol{\beta}}_A' \mathbf{X}_A' \mathbf{Y}_A = R_{Y\cdot 1\ldots k}^2 \mathbf{Y}_A' \mathbf{Y}_A \qquad k \text{ df} \tag{14.18}$$

$$\begin{aligned} \text{SS(error)} &= \mathbf{Y}'\mathbf{Y} - \hat{\boldsymbol{\beta}}'\mathbf{X}'\mathbf{Y} = \mathbf{Y}_A'\mathbf{Y}_A - \hat{\boldsymbol{\beta}}_A'\mathbf{X}_A'\mathbf{Y}_A \\ &= (1 - R_{Y\cdot 1\ldots k}^2)\mathbf{Y}_A'\mathbf{Y}_A \qquad n - k - 1 \text{ df} \end{aligned} \tag{14.19}$$

Equation (14.20) implies a sequential computing procedure.

$$1 - R_{Y\cdot 1\ldots k}^2 = (1 - r_{Y1}^2)(1 - r_{Y2\cdot 1}^2) \cdots (1 - r_{Yk\cdot 1\ldots k-1}^2) \tag{14.20}$$

For the tobacco data with X_1 and X_2 only,

$$R_{Y\cdot 12} = \sqrt{\frac{4.29985}{6.68952}} = .8017 \qquad \text{by Eq. (14.17)}$$

From Eq. (14.20),

$$\begin{aligned} 1 - R_{Y\cdot 12}^2 &= [1 - (-.7177)^2][1 - (-.5131)^2] \\ &= .3572 \qquad \text{and} \qquad R_{Y\cdot 12} = .8017 \end{aligned}$$

Significant values of R are given in Table A13.

Exercise 14.6.1 Compute $r_{Y1\cdot 2}$, $r_{Y2\cdot 1}$, $r_{12\cdot Y}$, and $R_{Y\cdot 12}$ for the data of Exercise 14.5.2.

Exercise 14.6.2 Construct 95 percent confidence intervals for the parameters $\rho_{Y1\cdot 2}$ and $\rho_{Y2\cdot 1}$, estimated in Exercise 14.6.1. Do these intervals include zero? What conclusion can be drawn from this?

Exercise 14.6.3 Test the null hypothesis that the population parameter estimated by $R_{Y\cdot 12}$ in Exercise 14.6.1 is zero. (See Table A.13.)

Exercise 14.6.4 Show that the F-test of H_0: $\beta_1 = 0 = \beta_2$ in the analysis of variance can be reduced to

$$F = \frac{R_{Y\cdot 12}^2}{1 - R_{Y\cdot 12}^2} \frac{n - k - 1}{k}$$

Exercise 14.6.5 Exercises 14.6.1 to 14.6.4 may be repeated for Exercises 14.5.3 to 14.5.5.

14.7 Multiple Linear Regression; Printouts for k Independent Variables

In multiple linear regression, the first step in obtaining estimates of the $\boldsymbol{\beta}$ vector is to set up the normal equations $\mathbf{X}'\mathbf{X}\hat{\boldsymbol{\beta}} = \mathbf{X}'\mathbf{Y}$. These may be solved by the straightforward technique of gaussian elimination, multiplying an equation by a constant and adding this multiple to another equation so as to reduce the number of variables. An early attempt to structure this technique for use in statistics was made by Doolittle. The basic Doolittle method was introduced in 1878 while Doolittle was an engineer with the United States Coast and Geodetic Survey. The result was a sequential procedure where each step offered some information but the problem was not solved until $(\mathbf{X}'\mathbf{X})^{-1}$ was finally obtained. Today's computer methods do not generally let us see all that is going on but they still provide results from various stages in obtaining the solution.

First, the data are made available to the computing equipment. Let these be the data of Table 14.1, 30 multivariate observations of 4 entries each. A program tells the computer what to do and what to print.

From the data, **X** is constructed. The equation is to include an intercept, so **X** will consist of a column of thirty 1's and three more columns of thirty each, the X_1's, the X_2's, and the X_3's from Table 14.1. The column headed Y gives the **Y** matrix. In turn, **X'X** and **X'Y** are obtained and other computations completed.

The printout can include a table similar to Table 14.1. This allows a check for transcription errors. The **X'X** matrix and $(\mathbf{X}'\mathbf{X})^{-1}$ may be printed. These are shown in Table 14.4. If the model equation includes the intercept, as here, the upper left entry of **X'X** will be $n = 30$.

Table 14.5 is from an SAS printout; see A. J. Barr et al. (14.13). In the analysis of variance opposite MODEL, we find df = 3. This gives SS(regression) in our notation since it clearly refers to the three X variables only and is $\hat{\boldsymbol{\beta}}'\mathbf{X}'\mathbf{Y} - (\sum Y)^2/n = \hat{\boldsymbol{\beta}}'_A\mathbf{X}'_A\mathbf{Y}_A$. The column headed PR > F gives the probability that a random value of F will be greater than that observed. Here, the statement is that $P(F > 40.27) \leq .0001$. This test is of H_0: $\beta_1 = \beta_2 = \beta_3 = 0$ simultaneously versus H_1: at least one $\beta_i \neq 0$, where all β's are

Table 14.4 The X'X and $(\mathbf{X}'\mathbf{X})^{-1}$ matrices for the tobacco data
Leaf burn in seconds in samples of tobacco from farmers' fields

THE X'X MATRIX

DEPENDENT VARIABLE: Y

	INTERCEPT	X1	X2	X3
INTERCEPT	30.00000000	98.36000000	24.23000000	139.61000000
X1	98.36000000	332.33520000	81.58340000	459.40520000
X2	24.23000000	81.58340000	30.19070000	120.39500000
X3	139.61000000	459.40520000	120.39500000	682.78130000

X'X INVERSE MATRIX

	INTERCEPT	X1	X2	X3
INTERCEPT	1.71457789	−0.32895337	0.09529059	−0.14605239
X1	−0.32895337	0.10623365	−0.02105557	−0.00050401
X2	0.09529059	−0.02105557	0.11706378	−0.02595908
X3	−0.14605239	−0.00050401	−0.02595908	0.03624479

Table 14.5 Regression analysis of tobacco data

LEAF BURN IN SECONDS IN SAMPLES OF TOBACCO FROM FARMERS' FIELDS

DEPENDENT VARIABLE: Y LOG OF LEAF BURN

SOURCE	DF	SUM OF SQUARES	MEAN SQUARE	F VALUE	PR > F	R-SQUARE	C.V.
MODEL	3	5.50473408	1.83491136	40.27	0.0001	0.822889	31.1178
ERROR	26	1.18478592	0.04556869		STD DEV		Y MEAN
CORRECTED TOTAL	29	6.68952000			0.21346824		0.68600000

SOURCE	DF	SEQUENTIAL SS	F VALUE	PR > F	DF	PARTIAL SS	F VALUE	PR > F
X1	1	3.44600764	75.62	0.0001	1	2.65871240	58.35	0.0001
X2	1	0.85384481	18.74	0.0002	1	1.65106256	36.23	0.0001
X3	1	1.20488163	26.44	0.0001	1	1.20488163	26.44	0.0001

PARAMETER	ESTIMATE	T FOR HO: PARAMETER = 0	PR > |T|	STD ERROR OF ESTIMATE
INTERCEPT	1.81104253	6.48	0.0001	0.27951935
X1	−0.53145530	−7.64	0.0001	0.06957678
X2	−0.43963579	−6.02	0.0001	0.07303727
X3	0.20897531	5.14	0.0001	0.04064022

partial regression coefficients. The error rate is clearly experimentwise. R-SQUARE is the square of the multiple correlation coefficient, that is, $R^2 = [\hat{\boldsymbol{\beta}}'\mathbf{X}'\mathbf{Y} - (\sum Y)^2/n]/[\mathbf{Y}'\mathbf{Y} - (\sum Y)^2/n] = 5.504734/6.689520 = .822889$.

The second part of the table includes tests of the X's as sources of variation, equivalent to tests of the associated β's. Under SOURCE, we have the sequence in which the X's are added into the model after the mean. Sums of squares obtained in this sequence are under SEQUENTIAL SS. First is X_1, which accounts for an additional sum of squares of 3.4460; for this, $F = 75.62^{**}$. We know that this equals

$$[\sum (X_1 - \bar{X}_1)(Y - \bar{Y})]^2/\sum (X_1 - \bar{X}_1)^2.$$

Next X_2 is included in the equation and accounts for an additional sum of squares of .8538; for this, $F = 18.74^{**}$. This computation is not obvious to us, since both Y and X_2 had to be regressed on X_1 first. In turn, Y deviations from regression on X_1 are regressed on X_2 deviations from regression on X_1 in this sequential procedure. Finally, X_3 is included and accounts for an additional sum of squares of 1.2049; $F = 26.44^{**}$. The F values, in fact, test H_0: $\beta_{Y1} = 0$, H_0: $\beta_{Y2 \cdot 1} = 0$, and H_0: $\beta_{Y3 \cdot 12} = 0$, sequentially.

The last X to be included, X_3, has a sequential sum of squares which allows a test of X_3 adjusted for both X_1 and X_2. This sum of squares must also be a partial sum of squares and so tests H_0: $\beta_{Y3 \cdot 12} = 0$. So far, this is the only test of a partial regression coefficient that actually appears in the required regression equation.

In the PARTIAL SS column are computations which have been repeated so that X_1 can be last in the equation and, again, so that X_2 can be last. These lead to the usual tests of partial regression coefficients. The F-tests given are equivalent to t-tests and thus have comparisonwise error rates.

Finally, estimates of the parameters in $\boldsymbol{\beta}$ are given. Tests of significance are t-tests and equivalent to F-tests for partial sums of squares. This can be checked by squaring the t values. Also PR > F and PR > $|T|$ will be identical opposite corresponding X's. Standard deviations or standard errors are the final entries. These can be computed directly from $(\mathbf{X}'\mathbf{X})^{-1}$ and s^2. For example, to find s_{b_1}, obtain the appropriate entry in $(\mathbf{X}'\mathbf{X})^{-1}$ and s^2 from the analysis of variance; $s_{b_1} = \sqrt{.106234(.045569)} = .069577$ as in the standard error column. Standard errors are needed to set confidence intervals on these parameters.

F values following PARTIAL SS's indicate that all X's are important to this regression equation; there is no need to consider dropping one. Such will not always be the case.

It is possible to find data where some of the independent variables will be significant in the sequential procedure and none of the partial regression coefficients will be. This will generally indicate fairly high correlations among all variables. This is *intercorrelation* or *multicollinearity*, the latter term applying to a perfect or near-perfect relationship. As a result, any single independent variable can be dropped; others are closely enough related to overcome the loss. Thus, if we are regressing weight on height and leg length, the latter two are likely to be sufficiently highly correlated so that we can leave one out but not both; both partial correlation coefficients could fail to be significant.

Printouts may include regressed values corresponding to all observed values. The SAS printout calls these predicted values. They are not given here. Residuals are also computed, squared, and summed for comparison with the error sum of squares. These sums should differ by rounding errors only.

Since $(\mathbf{X}'\mathbf{X})^{-1}$ and s^2 are given, tests of hypotheses concerning parameters and confidence intervals at specified sets of X values can be computed.

Exercise 14.7.1 Obtain the regression equation for the regression of Y on X_1, X_2, and X_3, data of Exercise 14.5.2. Be sure to obtain $\mathbf{X}'\mathbf{X}$ and $(\mathbf{X}'\mathbf{X})^{-1}$ or $\mathbf{X}'_A\mathbf{X}_A$ and $(\mathbf{X}'_A\mathbf{X}_A)^{-1}$.

Exercise 14.7.2 Present an analysis of variance for Exercise 14.7.1. Test H_0: $\beta_1 = \beta_2 = \beta_3 = 0$ simultaneously. What is the probability of observing a random value of F that is larger than that observed. What are $\bar{Y}$, s, CV, and $R^2_{Y\cdot123}$?

Exercise 14.7.3 The variable X_3 is considered to be an alternative to X_2 for assessing phosphate responses. Does X_3 give information about Y that is not already available from X_1 and X_2? Which of the X's would you certainly not want to eliminate from the regression equation?

Exercise 14.7.4 Estimate the population mean at (3,000, 80, 6.40). Construct a confidence interval for the parameter.

Repeat for (1,500, 60, 6.00).

Exercise 14.7.5 Suppose that the values in Exercise 14.7.4 are to be predictions of future Y's. What will be their standard errors?

Exercise 14.7.6 Repeat Exercises 14.7.1 and 14.7.2 for the data in Exercise 10.2.3 using all X's.

Which variable seems least valuable in estimating population means?

Estimate the population mean for $\mathbf{X}' = (1, 50, 75, 280, 70)$. What is the variance of this estimate?

Exercise 14.7.7 Repeat Exercise 14.7.6 for the data in Exercise 10.2.5. For $\mathbf{X}$, use $\mathbf{X}' = (12{,}000, 500, 500, 1{,}600)$.

14.8 Miscellaneous

The problem of selecting the "best" regression equation is not one we consider although it was hinted at in referring to multicollinearity. A number of procedures are available. Draper and Smith (14.11) discuss the problem at some length.

If the independent variables are ordered so that those known to be important are first and these are followed by others of unknown importance, then the latter subset can be tested simultaneously. This is clear from the SEQUENTIAL SS column. We simply add the sums of squares for those in the doubtful set, which is last in the sequential procedure, find the mean square, and use this as the numerator in an F-test.

Joint estimation of the parameters in the $\boldsymbol{\beta}$ vector by a confidence region is possible. The boundary will likely be an extension of the idea of an ellipse and ellipsoid.

A *confidence region* for the entire regression surface can be computed. This is an extension of the procedure for construction of a confidence band as given in Sec. 10.6.

Extrapolation outside the applicable region defined by the observed set of $(X_1, \ldots, X_k)$ values should be avoided or done with care. It is not sufficient to look at the ranges of the X's to determine this region. For example, ranges imply a rectangle in two dimensions, but the observed (X_1, X_2)'s may fall in an ellipse. Generally, a regression surface is an approximation to the true situation, and extrapolation implies that the approximation will still be valid outside the region determined by the observed set of $\mathbf{X}$ vectors.

Printouts can also include *plots of residuals* against different variables, for example, each of the X's separately. These could help determine whether an equation linear in each X was adequate. Draper and Smith (14.11) give a good discussion of such plots. Other plots may be available.

Prediction of a single future observation, rather than estimation of a parameter, is also possible. Here we need to add 1 to the coefficient of the error mean square of an estimate of a parameter. In other words, $\hat{V}(\text{predicted } Y) = [1 + \mathbf{X}_0'(\mathbf{X}'\mathbf{X})^{-1}\mathbf{X}_0]s^2$. For a new mean of m observations, add $1/m$ rather than 1.

Clearly, the techniques of this chapter are appropriate to *polynomial models*, models still linear in the parameters but nonlinear in the independent variable or variables. The model equation

$$Y_i = \beta_0 + \beta_1 X_i + \beta_2 X_i^2 + \cdots + \beta_k X_i^k + \varepsilon_i$$

is called a kth *order* model with one independent variable. An illustration for $k = 2$ is given in Sec. 19.4. For a second-order model in two variables, the equation is

$$Y_i = \beta_0 + \beta_1 X_{1i} + \beta_{11} X_{1i}^2 + \beta_2 X_{2i} + \beta_{22} X_{2i}^2 + \beta_{12} X_{1i} X_{2i} + \varepsilon_i$$

The $X_{1i} X_{2i}$ term looks after the possibility that the linear change in Y for unit change in X_1 may depend on the value of X_2. This failure of the linear response to be constant is an example of *interaction*. The statement is symmetric in X_1 and X_2.

The warning concerning extrapolation is obvious for polynomials; we would simply not want an estimate of a population mean where $X_1 = 3$ and $X_1^2 = 16$, since $3^2 \neq 16$.

Finally, no intercept will be called for in the model when regression is to be through the origin.

14.9 Standard Partial Regression Coefficients

Standard partial regression coefficients are those in equations where all variables have been standardized, that is, measured from their means in units of standard deviations. Standard partial regression coefficients may be denoted by b'_i or $b'_{Yi \cdot 1 \ldots i-1, i+1 \ldots k}$. The standard regression equation is

$$\frac{\hat{Y} - \bar{Y}}{s_Y} = b'_1 \frac{X_1 - \bar{X}_1}{s_1} + \cdots + b'_k \frac{X_k - \bar{X}_k}{s_k} \tag{14.21}$$

or

$$\hat{Y}' = b'_1 X'_1 + \cdots + b'_k X'_k$$

A comparison of Eq. (14.3) or (14.4) with Eq. (14.21) gives Eq. (14.22), relating b's and b''s.

$$b'_i = b_i \frac{s_i}{s_y} \qquad \text{and} \qquad b_i = b'_i \frac{s_y}{s_i} \tag{14.22}$$

Since each b'_i is now dimensionless, a comparison of any two gives a measure of the relative importance of the two X's involved. If b'_1 is twice as large as b'_2, then X_1 is approximately twice as important as X_2 in estimating or predicting Y in that a unit change in X_1 results in double the change in Y for a unit change in X_2. Some warning is appropriate in that the standard deviations of the b''s are not equal and they must be considered in the context of the other X's in the model.

For the example of Sec. 14.5,

$$b'_1 = b_1 \frac{s_1}{s_Y} = -0.5285 \sqrt{\frac{9.845547/29}{6.68952/29}}$$

$$= -0.6412$$

$$b'_2 = b_2 \frac{s_2}{s_Y} = -0.2900 \sqrt{\frac{10.620937/29}{6.68952/29}}$$

$$= -0.3654$$

When the standard equation is found from the original data by going directly to standardized variables, the $\mathbf{X}'_A \mathbf{X}_A$ matrix consists of 1s down the main diagonal and r_{ij}'s as off-diagonal elements.

Again, if we consider the correlation matrix of all variables, including the dependent one, so that there are $k + 1$ variables and use the notation

R and $\mathbf{R}^{-1} = \mathbf{C}$ as in Eqs. (14.13) and (14.14), then the standard partial regression coefficients are easily found by

$$b'_{ij \cdot 1 \ldots i-1, i+1 \ldots j-1, j+1 \ldots k+1} = \frac{-C'_{ij}}{C'_{ii}} \tag{14.23}$$

Note that these coefficients are not symmetric in i and j; in fact, Eq. (14.24) holds.

$$r_{12 \cdot 3 \ldots k+1} = \pm\sqrt{b'_{12 \cdot 3 \ldots k+1} b'_{21 \cdot 3 \ldots k+1}} \tag{14.24}$$

Both b''s will have the same sign and the common sign is given to the square root. This equation is also valid for b's.

Exercise 14.9.1 Compute the three standard partial regression coefficients for the data of Exercise 14.5.2.

Exercise 14.9.2 Johnson and Hasler (14.10) studied several factors influencing rainbow trout production in three dystrophic lakes. The following simple correlation coefficients were obtained.

	X_2	X_3	X_4	X_5
X_1	0.2206	−0.3284	−0.0910	−0.2160
X_2		0.6448	−0.1566	−0.1079
X_3			0.0240	−0.2010
X_4				−0.7698

X_1 = instantaneous growth rate of age group I trout for the interval concerned

X_2 = index of zooplankton density (availability of food)

X_3 = total standing crop of trout (competition)

X_4 = temperature of water

X_5 = size of age group I trout

If your computer has an inverse matrix program, invert the correlation matrix above. Compute $r_{12 \cdot 345}$, $r_{13 \cdot 245}$, $r_{14 \cdot 235}$, and $r_{15 \cdot 234}$.

Compute all standard partial regression coefficients and write the standard partial regression equation with X_1 as the dependent variable.

References

14.1. Anderson, R. L., and T. A. Bancroft: *Statistical Theory in Research*, McGraw-Hill, New York, 1952.

14.2. Birch, H. F.: "Phosphate response, base saturation and silica relationships in acid soils," *J. Agr. Sci.*, **43**:229–235 (1953).

14.3. Cochran, W. G.: "The omission or addition of an independent variate in multiple linear regression," *J. Roy. Statist. Soc. Suppl.*, **5**:171–176 (1938).

14.4. Cowden, D. J.: "A procedure for computing regression coefficients," *J. Amer. Statist. Ass.*, **53:** 144–150 (1958).
14.5. Cramer, C. Y.: "Simplified computations for multiple regression," *Ind. Qual. Contr.*, **8:** 8–11 (1957).
14.6. Drapala, W. J.: "Early generation parent-progeny relationships in spaced plantings of soybeans, medium red clover, barley, Sudan grass, and Sudan grass times sorghum segregates," Ph.D. thesis, University of Wisconsin, Madison, 1949.
14.7. Durand, D.: "Joint confidence regions for multiple regression coefficients," *J. Amer. Statist. Ass.*, **49:** 130–146 (1954).
14.8. Dwyer, P. S.: *Linear Computations*, Wiley, New York, 1951.
14.9. Friedman, J., and R. J. Foote: "Computational methods for handling systems of simultaneous equations," *U.S. Dep. Agr. Handb. 94*, 1957.
14.10. Johnson, W. E., and A. D. Hasler: "Rainbow trout production in dystrophic lakes," *J. Wildlife Manag.*, **18:** 113–134 (1954).
14.11. Draper, N., and H. Smith: *Applied Regression Analysis*, Wiley, New York, 1966.
14.12. Reynolds, J., G. Cunningham and J. Syvertsen: "A net CO_2 exchange model for *Larrea tridentata*," *Photosyn.*, **13**(3): In press (1979).
14.13. Barr, A. J., J. H. Goodnight, J. P. Sall, and J. T. Helwig: *A User's Guide to SAS 76*, SAS Institute, Raleigh, N.C., 1976.

CHAPTER

FIFTEEN

ANALYSIS OF VARIANCE III: FACTORIAL EXPERIMENTS

15.1 Introduction

In this chapter, we deal with factorial experiments. Here there are a number of treatments in each of several categories and they define a treatment grid. This choice of treatment design leads to a logical partitioning of the treatment sum of squares into additive components with corresponding tests of hypotheses.

The topic of independent comparisons, introduced in Sec. 8.3, is discussed further, with special attention given to equally spaced treatments and regression. Tukey's test for nonadditivity is also given.

15.2 Factorial Experiments

A *factor* is a kind of treatment, and in factorial experiments, any factor will supply several treatments. For example, if diet is a factor in an experiment, then several diets will be used; if baking temperature is a factor, then baking will be done at several temperatures.

The concept of the factorial experiment can be illustrated by an example. Consider an experiment to evaluate the yielding abilities of several soybean cultivars. In a single-factor approach, all variables other than cultivar are held as uniform as possible, that is, one particular level of each of the other factors is chosen. Suppose that a second factor, distance between rows, is of interest. A two-factor experiment can be planned in which the treatments consist of all combinations of cultivars and the chosen row spacings, that is, each cultivar is present at all row spacings. In a single-factor experiment, all cultivars would be planted at only one row spacing or one cultivar would be planted for all row spacings. In soils, an experiment could be designed to compare all combinations of several rates of phosphorus and potassium fertilizers. In an animal feeding experiment, factors under consideration might be amounts and kinds of protein supplement.

The term *level* refers to the several treatments within any factor. It is derived from some of the earliest factorial experiments. These dealt with soil fertility where combinations of several amounts, or levels, of different fertilizers were the treatments. Today the word has a more general meaning, implying a particular amount or state of a factor. Thus, if five cultivars of a crop are compared using three different management practices, the experiment is called a 5×3 factorial experiment with five levels of the cultivar factor and three levels of the management factor. The number of factors and levels which may be compared in a single experiment is limited only by practical considerations.

Thus, a *factorial experiment* is one in which the set of treatments consists of all possible combinations of the levels of several factors. A treatment design is implied in the word "factorial."

Factorial experiments are used in practically all fields of research. They are of great value in exploratory work where little is known concerning the optimum levels of the factors, or even which ones are important. Consider a new crop for which several promising cultivars are available but little is known regarding a suitable date and rate of planting. A three-factor experiment is indicated. If the single-factor approach is used, one date and rate of planting are selected and a cultivar experiment is conducted. However, the cultivar that does best at the chosen date and rate may not be the best for some other date and rate. Any other single factor must involve only one cultivar. At other times, the experimenter may be primarily interested in the interaction between factors, that is, she may wish to know if the differences in response to the levels of one factor are similar or different at different levels of another factor or factors. Where considerable information is available, the best approach may be to compare only a very limited number of combinations of several factors at specific levels.

Thus, we see that the scope of an experiment, or the population concerning which inferences can be made, can often be increased by the use of a factorial experiment. It is particularly important to do this where information is wanted on some factor for which recommendations are to be made over a wide range of conditions.

Notation and definitions Systems of notation used with factorial experiments are generally similar but differ enough that the reader has to check carefully when using any new reference. We follow a notation similar in most respects to that suggested by Yates (15.18). Capital letters are used to refer to *factors*; for example, if an experiment involves several sprays to control insects and these are applied by several methods, we can denote a spray factor by A and the method factor by B. Combinations of lowercase letters and numerical subscripts, or simply the subscripts, are used to denote *treatment combinations* and *means*; for example, $a_1 b_3$ may refer to the treatment combination consisting of the first level of A and the third level of B, and to the corresponding treatment mean. Often, zero is used for the first level of a subscript.

For a two-factor experiment with two levels of each factor, that is, for a 2×2 or 2^2 factorial, any of the following notations is adequate. The first and third are readily extended to many factors and levels; the second is readily extended to many factors but to only two levels of each.

Factor	A						
	Complete form			Abbreviated forms			
	Level	a_1	a_2	a_1	a_2	a_1	a_2
B	b_1	$a_1 b_1$	$a_2 b_1$	(1)	a	00	10
	b_2	$a_1 b_2$	$a_2 b_2$	b	ab	01	11

The three degrees of freedom and sum of squares for the variance among the four treatment means in a 2^2 factorial can be partitioned into single independent degrees of freedom and corresponding sums of squares whose general interpretation is meaningful and relatively simple. For the general factorial experiment, degrees of freedom and sums of squares are partitioned into additive subsets or components not necessarily with single degrees of freedom. The principles involved in the partitioning are best illustrated by the use of a table. Table 15.1 is an illustration for a 2^2 factorial.

In Table 15.1, let the numbers be averages or means of measured responses to treatment combinations indicated by row and column headings; the means are for all replications.

The four differences, $a_2 - a_1$ at each level of B and $b_2 - b_1$ at each level of A, are termed *simple effects*. They are not included in the usual summarization of a factorial experiment but are useful in interpreting the summary as well as in themselves. For the data under I, the simple effect of A at the first level of B is 2; under II, the simple effect of B at the second level of A is -6.

When simple effects are averaged, the results are termed *main effects*. These are denoted by capital letters, as are factors. The main effect of factor

Table 15.1 Illustration of simple effects, main effects, and interactions

Factor	I				
	A = kind				
	Level	a_1	a_2	Mean	$a_2 - a_1$
B = rate	b_1	30	32	31	2
	b_2	36	44	40	8
	Mean	33	38	35.5	5
	$b_2 - b_1$	6	12	9	

Factor	II				
	A = kind				
	Level	a_1	a_2	Mean	$a_2 - a_1$
B = rate	b_1	30	32	31	2
	b_2	36	26	31	−10
	Mean	33	29	31	−4
	$b_2 - b_1$	6	−6	0	

Factor	III				
	A = kind				
	Level	a_1	a_2	Mean	$a_2 - a_1$
B = rate	b_1	30	32	31	2
	b_2	36	38	37	2
	Mean	33	35	34	2
	$b_2 - b_1$	6	6	6	

A for the data under I is 5; the main effect of factor B for the data under III is 6. In general for the 2^2 factorial, A and B are given by Eqs. (15.1) and (15.2).

$$A = \tfrac{1}{2}[(a_2 b_2 - a_1 b_2) + (a_2 b_1 - a_1 b_1)]$$
$$= \tfrac{1}{2}[(a_2 b_2 + a_2 b_1) - (a_1 b_2 + a_1 b_1)] \tag{15.1}$$
$$B = \tfrac{1}{2}[(a_2 b_2 - a_2 b_1) + (a_1 b_2 - a_1 b_1)]$$
$$= \tfrac{1}{2}[(a_2 b_2 + a_1 b_2) - (a_2 b_1 + a_1 b_1)] \tag{15.2}$$

Main effects are seen to be computed on a per-unit basis. Equations (15.1) and (15.2) are easily extended to 2^n factorials.

Main effects are averages over a variety of conditions just as are any other treatment means. For a factorial experiment in a randomized complete block or Latin square design, the variety of conditions exists within blocks as well as among blocks; thus factor A is replicated within every block since it is present at both levels for each level of factor B. This is *hidden replication.* Averaging implies that the differences, that is, the simple effects, vary only because of chance from level to level of the other factor or factors. This is, in fact, a hypothesis that is usually subjected to a test of significance when treatments are factorially arranged; the hypothesis is that of no interaction between factors.

For the data under I and II, the simple effects for both kind and rate differ. Under III, the simple effects for A are the same, as are the simple effects for B; here, they also equal the corresponding main effect. When simple effects for a factor differ by more than can be attributed to chance, this differential response is termed an *interaction* of the two factors. The relation is a symmetric one; that is, the interaction of A with B is the same as that of B with A. From Table 15.1 you will see that the difference between the simple effects of A equals that for B in all three cases; it would be impossible to construct a table otherwise. In our notation, the interaction of A and B is defined in

$$\begin{aligned} AB &= \tfrac{1}{2}[(a_2b_2 - a_1b_2) - (a_2b_1 - a_1b_1)] \\ &= \tfrac{1}{2}[(a_2b_2 + a_1b_1) - (a_1b_2 + a_2b_1)] \end{aligned} \tag{15.3}$$

The value $\frac{1}{2}$ is used so that interaction, like the main effects, is on a per-unit basis. For the data under I,

$$\begin{aligned} AB &= \tfrac{1}{2}(8 - 2) \qquad \text{in terms of simple effects of } A \\ &= \tfrac{1}{2}(12 - 6) \qquad \text{in terms of simple effects of } B \\ &= 3 \end{aligned}$$

For the data under II, we find

$$AB = \tfrac{1}{2}(26 - 36 - 32 + 30) = -6$$

and under III,

$$AB = \tfrac{1}{2}(38 - 36 - 32 + 30) = 0$$

Note that the interaction is also one-half the difference between the sums of the two diagonals of the 2×2 table, which is one-half the difference between the sums of the treatments where both A and B are present at the higher and lower levels and of the treatments where only one is present at the higher level. This is always true of the 2^2 factorial.

Interaction measures the failure of the A effect, or the response to A, to be the same for each level of B or, conversely, the failure of the B effect to be the same for each level of A. Under I, the simple effects for kind are 2 and 8 whereas the main effect is 5. Interaction may be defined as a measure of the departure of the simple effects from an additive law or model based on main effects only.

Under I, Table 15.1, the response to A or the increase from a_1 to a_2 is greater for b_2 than for b_1, that is, there has been a change in the magnitude of the increase. Under II, the response to A is an increase in the presence of b_1 and a decrease in the presence of b_2; there has been a change in the direction of the increase. In terms of treatment means presented in a two-way table, sufficiently large changes in the magnitudes of the differences between treatment means in a column (or row), as one goes from column to column (or row to row), constitute an interaction. Also, changes in the rank of any treatment mean for a column (or row), as one changes columns (or rows), may constitute an interaction.

Figure 15.1 illustrates graphically what is meant by an interaction. The presence or absence of main effects tells us nothing about the presence or

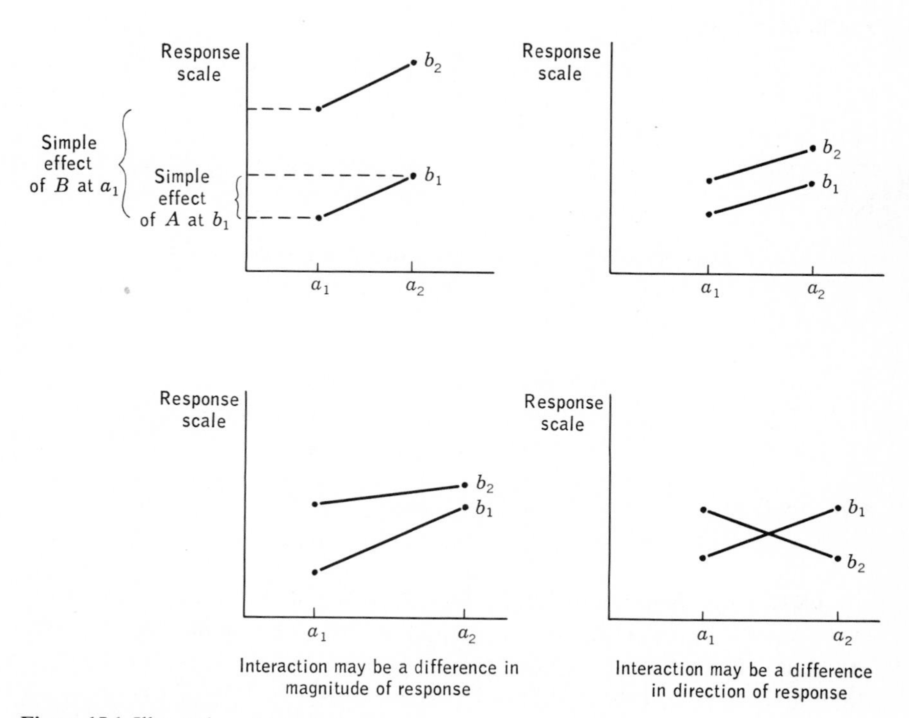

Figure 15.1 Illustration of interaction.

absence of interaction. The presence or absence of interaction tells us nothing about the presence or absence of main effects but does tell us something about the homogeneity of simple effects.

A significant interaction is one that is too large to be explained on the basis of chance and the null hypothesis of no interaction. With a significant interaction, the factors are not independent of one another; the simple effects of a factor differ and the magnitude of any simple effect depends on the level of the other factor of the interaction term. Where factors interact, a single-factor experiment will lead to disconnected and possibly misleading information.

If the interaction is nonsignificant, it is concluded that the factors under consideration act independently of each other; the simple effects of a factor are the same for all levels of the other factors, within chance variation as measured by experimental error. The average of simple effects, namely, the main effect, is appropriate and the best estimate of the common difference. The evidence is that there is no departure from a simple additive model with components due to the levels of the factors only. Where factors are independent, the factorial experiment saves considerable time and effort. This is so since the simple effects are equal to the corresponding main effects and a main effect, in a factorial experiment, is estimated as accurately as it would be if the entire experiment had been devoted to that factor.

In the analysis of a factorial experiment, it is correct to partitition the treatment degrees of freedom and sum of squares into the components attributable to main effects and interactions even when the overall F-test of no differences among treatments is not significant; main effects and interaction comparisons are planned comparisons. It is easy to visualize a situation where one factor, say B, does neither good nor harm in itself nor has any effect on A and hence contributes no more to the treatment sum of squares than can be attributed to chance; a significant response to A might well be lost in an overall test of significance such as F. Thus in a 2^2 factorial with 3 degrees of freedom for treatments, the sum of squares for the real A effect with its 1 degree of freedom may easily be lost when averaged with the sums of squares for the nonreal B and AB with their 2 degrees of freedom. Calculation of the sum of squares for treatments is more often used as part of a computational procedure than to supply the numerator of an F-test.

All units of the factorial experiment are involved in measuring any one main effect or interaction. This is apparent from Eqs. (15.1) to (15.3). Thus it appears that in a factorial experiment as opposed to several single-factor experiments, all units are devoted to measuring A, and in turn to B, and to AB, and so on, when there are more factors; nothing is lost either in replication or in measuring main effects; something is gained in that we do measure any one factor at various levels of other factors and, in terms of treatment comparisons, we are also able to measure interactions and test hypotheses concerning them.

The results of a factorial experiment lend themselves to a relatively simple explanation because of the variety and nature of treatment comparisons. If the factors are largely independent, the table of treatment means and analysis of variance summarize the data well. When the factors are not independent, the data require a detailed study with the possibility of further experimentation. Here the difficulty lies in the complex nature of the situation and not in the factorial approach to it. The factorial experiment has indicated the complexity, a fact that might well have been missed had a single-factor approach been used.

15.3 The 2 × 2 Factorial Experiment: An Example

Wilkinson (15.17) reports the results of an experiment to study the influence of time of bleeding, factor A, and diethylstilbestrol (an estrogenic compound), factor B, on plasma phospholipid in lambs. Five lambs were assigned at random to each of four treatment groups; treatment combinations are for morning and afternoon times of bleeding with and without diethylstilbestrol treatment. The data are shown in Table 15.2.

Table 15.2 The influence of time of bleeding and diethylstilbestrol on phospholipid in lambs

Treatment groups

	a_1 = A.M.		a_2 = P.M.		Totals
	a_1b_1 = control 1	a_1b_2 = treated 1	a_2b_1 = control 2	a_2b_2 = treated 2	
	8.53	17.53	39.14	32.00	
	20.53	21.07	26.20	23.80	
	12.53	20.80	31.33	28.87	
	14.00	17.33	45.80	25.06	
	10.80	20.07	40.20	29.33	
$\sum Y$	66.39	96.80	182.67	139.06	484.92
$\sum Y^2$	963.88	1,887.02	6,913.63	3,912.17	13,676.70
$\bar{Y}$	13.28	19.36	36.53	27.81	24.25

Treatment totals

Factor		A = time		
	Level	(a_1) = A.M.	(a_2) = P.M.	Totals
	(b_1) = control	66.39	182.67	249.06
B = estrogen	(b_2) = treated	96.80	139.06	235.86
	Totals	163.19	321.73	484.92

The table of treatment totals can be used in computing sums of squares for testing hypotheses concerning main effects and interactions. Treatment totals are distinguished from treatment means by parentheses around the treatment combination symbol. Thus $(a_2 b_2)$ is the sum over all replications of the observations made on treatment combination $a_2 b_2$, whereas (a_1) is the sum over all replications of observations made on treatment combinations $a_1 b_1$ and $a_1 b_2$. For example, for the main effect of A, we have

$$(A) = [(a_2 b_2) - (a_1 b_2) + (a_2 b_1) - (a_1 b_1)] \tag{15.4}$$

Treatment totals may also be presented as in Table 15.3. Here we stress contrasts, discussed in Sec. 8.3. Observe how easy it is to check orthogonality and, in turn, additivity of sums of squares. This table is especially convenient for computation of main effects and interactions.

The computing proceeds as follows. Let r, a, and b represent the number of replications (number of observations per treatment combination), levels of A, and levels of B. Then the number of treatments is ab. The design is completely random.

Step 1 Compute the analysis of variance without regard to the factorial arrangement of treatments for the experimental design used. We obtain

$$\begin{aligned} &\text{Correction term} = C = 11{,}757.37 \\ &\text{Total SS} \qquad\qquad = \ \ 1{,}919.33 \\ &\text{Treatment SS} \qquad = \ \ 1{,}539.41 \\ &\text{Error SS} \qquad\qquad = \quad\ 379.92 \end{aligned}$$

Step 2 From treatment totals in Table 15.2 compute the sums of squares for main effects and interaction as follows:

$$\text{SS}(A) = \frac{\sum_i (a_i)^2}{rb} - C$$

$$= \frac{163.19^2 + 321.73^2}{5(2)} - \frac{(484.92)^2}{5(4)} = 1{,}256.75$$

Table 15.3 Treatment totals and factorial effects

Effect symbol	Treatment totals and coefficients, c_i: $(a_1 b_1) = 66.39$	$(a_1 b_2) = 96.80$	$(a_2 b_1) = 182.67$	$(a_2 b_2) = 139.06$	Effect totals	$r \sum c_i^2$
A	−1	−1	+1	+1	158.54	5(4) = 20
B	−1	+1	−1	+1	−13.20	5(4) = 20
AB	+1	−1	−1	+1	−74.02	5(4) = 20

or, use Eq. (15.5), a repetition of Eq. (8.6), and Table 15.3.

$$\text{SS}(A) = \frac{(A)^2}{r \sum c_i^2} \tag{15.5}$$

$$= \frac{(158.54)^2}{20} = 1{,}256.75$$

$$\text{SS}(B) = \frac{\sum_j (b_j)^2}{ra} - C$$

$$= \frac{249.06^2 + 235.86^2}{5(2)} - C = 8.71$$

or, use Eq. (15.6) and Table 15.3.

$$\text{SS}(B) = \frac{(B)^2}{r \sum c_i^2} \tag{15.6}$$

$$= \frac{(-13.20)^2}{20} = 8.71.$$

$$\text{SS}(AB) = \text{SS(trts)} - \text{SS}(A) - \text{SS}(B)$$

$$= 1{,}539.41 - 1{,}256.75 - 8.71 = 273.95$$

or, use Eq. (15.7) and Table 15.3.

$$\text{SS}(AB) = \frac{(AB)^2}{r \sum c_i^2} \tag{15.7}$$

$$= \frac{(-74.02)^2}{20} = 273.95$$

The results are transferred to an analysis of variance table such as Table 15.4, where the degrees of freedom for the general case are also shown.

The significant interaction indicates that the factors are not independent; the difference between simple effects of A for the two levels of B is

Table 15.4 Analysis of variance for data of Table 15.2

Source	df	SS	Mean square	F
Treatments	$(ab - 1 = 3)$	(1,539.41)		
A	$a - 1 = 1$	1,256.75	1,256.75	53**
B	$b - 1 = 1$	8.71	8.71	<1
AB	$(a - 1)(b - 1) = 1$	273.95	273.95	11.5**
Error	$ab(r - 1) = 16$	379.92	23.75	
Total	$rab - 1 = 19$	1,919.33		

significant and, conversely, the difference in simple effects of B at the two levels of A is significant. In other words, the difference in measurements between times of bleeding differs for the control and treated groups or, the same thing, the difference in measurements between the treated and control animals differs for the two times of bleedings. Thus, any simple effect is dependent on the level of the other factor in the experiment. We have

$$\begin{aligned}(AB) &= [(a_2 b_2) - (a_1 b_2)] - [(a_2 b_1) - (a_1 b_1)] \\ &= [139.06 - 96.80] - [182.67 - 66.39] = -74.02 \\ &= [(a_2 b_2) - (a_2 b_1)] - [(a_1 b_2) - (a_1 b_1)] \\ &= [139.06 - 182.67] - [96.80 - 66.39] = -74.02\end{aligned}$$

where parentheses indicate a total over replications and brackets simply call attention to the simple effects referred to in the text. Figure 15.2 shows the nature of the interaction.

As a result of the significant AB interaction, the investigator may decide to examine the simple effects, since they have been declared heterogeneous. Sums of squares for the simple effects are calculated as follows:

$$\text{SS}(A \text{ within } b_1) = \frac{(182.67 - 66.39)^2}{2 \times 5} = 1{,}352.10$$

$$\text{SS}(A \text{ within } b_2) = \frac{(139.06 - 96.80)^2}{2 \times 5} = 178.59$$

Note that the sum of these equals that for A and AB, that is,

$$1{,}352.10 + 178.59 = 1{,}530.69 \text{ against } 1{,}530.70 = 1{,}256.75 + 273.95$$

In the case of A and AB, the information in the two simple effects has been differently arranged in terms of their mean and variance. Recall that

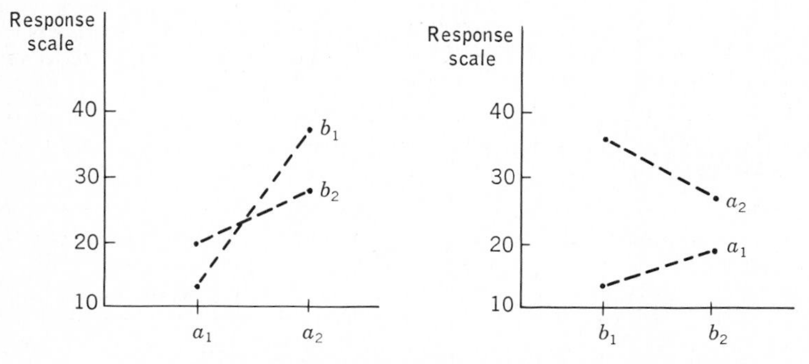

Figure 15.2 Interaction for the data of Table 15.2.

$(Y_1 - Y_2)^2/2 = \sum (Y - \bar{Y})^2$ and that variance measures spread, heterogeneity or homogeneity of observations. Also

$$SS(B \text{ within } a_1) = \frac{(96.80 - 66.39)^2}{2 \times 5} = 92.48$$

$$SS(B \text{ within } a_2) = \frac{(139.06 - 182.67)^2}{2 \times 5} = 190.18$$

Here the sum equals that for B and AB, that is,

$$92.48 + 190.18 = 282.66 = 8.71 + 273.95$$

The results may be presented in an auxiliary treatment sums of squares table. For example,

Treatment comparison	df	Mean square	F
Between times within control	$a - 1 = 1$	1,352.10	57**
Between times within treated	$a - 1 = 1$	178.59	7.5*
Between estrogen levels, AM	$b - 1 = 1$	92.48	3.9
Between estrogen levels, PM	$b - 1 = 1$	190.18	8.0*

Where there is only one degree of freedom for each comparison, there seems little point in presenting sums of squares unless they are made part of a table such as Table 15.4. Note that the auxiliary table contains 4 degrees of freedom for treatment comparisons whereas there are only 3 degrees of freedom among treatment means. Our four comparisons cannot be orthogonal as are the main effects and interaction comparisons of Table 15.4. These F-tests are essentially *lsd* comparisons but made after the significant interaction showed evidence of real differences among simple effects. They are result-guided as a consequence of a test of significance. Severe criticism of these tests would seem unjustified.

Exercise 15.3.1 A. Wojta of the Departments of Agricultural Engineering and Soils, University of Wisconsin, determined the draft, in 10-lb units, required to plow wet mud where the tractor traveled at 2 mi/h. The data follow for each of three positions of the right wheel. Two tire sizes of the left wheel and two hitches give a 2 × 2 factorial for each of three right-wheel positions. (The original experiment was a 3 × 2 × 2 factorial in a completely random design with three observations per treatment.)

	Right wheel straight		Right wheel toe in 1.29°		Right wheel castered	
	Left-wheel tire		Left-wheel tire		Left-wheel tire	
Hitch, in	6.50 × 16	7.50 × 16	6.50 × 16	7.50 × 16	6.50 × 16	7.50 × 16
2	76, 76, 81	76, 76, 75	65, 78, 68	42, 56, 35	74, 85, 79	74, 69, 74
4	69, 74, 79	50, 63, 62	77, 60, 82	48, 50, 48	60, 88, 88	66, 62, 57

Consider these data as being from three different experiments. Analyze each set of data separately. Prepare a table like Table 15.3 to compute main effects and interaction and their sums of squares.

What hypotheses are tested by the various entries in the F column of the analyses of variance? Interpret your results.

Exercise 15.3.2 Exercise 9.3.5 has data for a $3 \times 2 \times 2$ factorial experiment. Compute the nitrogen, aeration, and nitrogen $\times$ aeration interaction effects and sums of squares for each salinity level. Use the experimental error term from the whole experiment to test the various null hypotheses. What are these null hypotheses?

Exercise 15.3.3 For the visually handicapped, listening is considered a reading activity, called "listening-reading." Rawls (15.21) studied some techniques intended to improve efficiency with this skill. Her subjects were students from the Governor Morehead School, Raleigh, North Carolina in grades 10 to 12. All were severely visually impaired; all read braille. However, some of the students did read print by preference.

Two of the treatments included in the study were: (1) Instruction in listening techniques plus practice listening to selected readings; (2) The same as 1 but with copies of the selected readings in their choice of braille or ink print to be followed as they listened.

A number of performance measures were used that provided the posttest data. These are for accuracy as measured by the Gilmore Oral Reading Test. A limited set of data is given so that balance can be maintained and also so that the methods of the chapter can be applicable. Pretest data are provided to establish whether there are any differences in the groups prior to the experiment.

	Pretest data		Posttest data	
	Treatment 1	Treatment 2	Treatment 1	Treatment 2
Braille	89, 82, 88, 94	89, 90, 91, 92	87, 86, 94, 96	84, 94, 97, 93
Print	71, 88, 96, 96	89, 99, 84, 87	58, 82, 97, 93	96, 97, 75, 77

Analyze the pre- and posttest data separately. Compute main effect and interaction sums of squares for each data set. What hypotheses can now be tested? What conclusions do you draw from your analyses?

15.4 The $3 \times 3 \times 2$ or $3^2 \times 2$ Factorial: An Example

The data in Table 15.5 are the results of a greenhouse experiment conducted by Wagner (15.15) to determine the rate of emergence of seed of three species of legumes, treated and not treated with a fungicide, and planted in three soil types. (These data are from an experiment with a fourth factor, depth of planting, at three levels.) The layout was a randomized complete block design. The data of Table 15.5 are in a $3 \times 3 \times 2$ or $3^2 \times 2$ factorial, each datum being a sum over blocks.

The raw data are arranged in a two-way table similar to Table 9.2 with treatments listed down the side and blocks across the top. The initial analysis of variance is then carried out as described in Sec. 9.3. In addition,

Table 15.5 Number† of plants emerged for three legume species A, planted $\frac{1}{2}$ in deep in three soil types B, with seed treated and not treated with a fungicide C

Species = A	Fungicide = C	Soil type = B: Silt loam = b_1	Sand = b_2	Clay = b_3	Total = $b_1 + b_2 + b_3$
Alfalfa = a_1	None = c_1	266 = $(a_1 b_1 c_1)$	286 = $(a_1 b_2 c_1)$	66 = $(a_1 b_3 c_1)$	618 = $(a_1 c_1)$
	Treated = c_2	276 = $(a_1 b_1 c_2)$	271 = $(a_1 b_2 c_2)$	215 = $(a_1 b_3 c_2)$	762 = $(a_1 c_2)$
	Total = $c_1 + c_2$	542 = $(a_1 b_1)$	557 = $(a_1 b_2)$	281 = $(a_1 b_3)$	1,380 = (a_1)
Red clover = a_2	None = c_1	252 = $(a_2 b_1 c_1)$	289 = $(a_2 b_2 c_1)$	167 = $(a_2 b_3 c_1)$	708 = $(a_2 c_1)$
	Treated = c_2	275 = $(a_2 b_1 c_2)$	292 = $(a_2 b_2 c_2)$	203 = $(a_2 b_3 c_2)$	770 = $(a_2 c_2)$
	Total = $c_1 + c_2$	527 = $(a_2 b_1)$	581 = $(a_2 b_2)$	370 = $(a_2 b_3)$	1,478 = (a_2)
Sweet clover = a_3	None = c_1	152 = $(a_3 b_1 c_1)$	197 = $(a_3 b_2 c_1)$	52 = $(a_3 b_3 c_1)$	401 = $(a_3 c_1)$
	Treated = c_2	178 = $(a_3 b_1 c_2)$	219 = $(a_3 b_2 c_2)$	121 = $(a_3 b_3 c_2)$	518 = $(a_3 c_2)$
	Total = $c_1 + c_2$	330 = $(a_3 b_1)$	416 = $(a_3 b_2)$	173 = $(a_3 b_3)$	919 = (a_3)
Total = $a_1 + a_2 + a_3$	None = c_1	670 = $(b_1 c_1)$	772 = $(b_2 c_1)$	285 = $(b_3 c_1)$	1,727 = (c_1)
	Treated = c_2	729 = $(b_1 c_2)$	782 = $(b_2 c_2)$	539 = $(b_3 c_2)$	2,050 = (c_2)
	Total = $c_1 + c_2$	1,399 = (b_1)	1,554 = (b_2)	824 = (b_3)	3,777 = G

† Each value is a total of three replications of 100 seeds each.

the 18 treatment totals are entered in Table 15.5 and various subtotals are obtained. This table is necessary for the computation of the sums of squares of the main effects and interactions.

In the computations that follow, a, b, c, and r represent the number of levels of factors A, B, C, and the number of blocks or replications. Previously described symbols are generalized. Thus in a three-factor experiment, $(a_1 b_2 c_1)$ is the total of the r observations on the treatment combination with A and C at their lowest levels and B at its second level; $(a_1 b_2)$ is the total of the rc observations made on units for which A was at the lowest level and B at the second level; and so on.

Step 1 Compute

$$\begin{aligned} \text{Correction term} = C &= 264{,}180.17 \\ \text{Total SS} &= 35{,}597.67 \\ \text{Block SS} &= 356.77 \\ \text{Treatment SS} &= 32{,}041.50 \\ \text{Error SS} &= 3{,}199.40 \end{aligned}$$

Step 2 The treatment sum of squares is partitioned into components attributable to main effects and interactions. In most cases, these will involve more than single degrees of freedom. Definitions such as those of Eqs. (15.1) to (15.3) will not be applicable, nor will the computing formulas given as Eqs. (15.5) to (15.7). We must use standard sums of squares formulas. Thus,

$$SS(A) = \frac{\sum_i (a_i)^2}{rbc} - C \tag{15.8}$$

$$= \frac{1{,}380^2 + 1{,}478^2 + 919^2}{3(3)2} - C = 9{,}900.11$$

$$SS(B) = \frac{\sum_j (b_j)^2}{rac} - C$$

$$= \frac{1{,}399^2 + 1{,}554^2 + 824^2}{3(3)2} - C = 16{,}436.11$$

$$SS(C) = \frac{\sum_k (c_k)^2}{rab} - C = \frac{[(c_2) - (c_1)]^2}{2rab}$$

$$= \frac{1{,}727^2 + 2{,}050^2}{3(3)3} - C = \frac{(2{,}050 - 1{,}727)^2}{2(3)3(3)} = 1{,}932.02$$

$$\mathrm{SS}(AB) = \frac{\sum_{i,j} (a_i b_j)^2}{rc} - C - \mathrm{SS}(A) - \mathrm{SS}(B) \tag{15.9}$$

$$= \frac{542^2 + \cdots + 173^2}{3(2)} - C - (9{,}900.11 + 16{,}436.11) = 658.44$$

$$\mathrm{SS}(AC) = \frac{\sum_{i,k} (a_i c_k)^2}{rb} - C - \mathrm{SS}(A) - \mathrm{SS}(C)$$

$$= \frac{618^2 + \cdots + 518^2}{3(3)} - C - (9{,}900.11 + 1{,}932.02) = 194.03$$

$$\mathrm{SS}(BC) = \frac{\sum_{j,k} (b_j c_k)^2}{ra} - C - \mathrm{SS}(B) - \mathrm{SS}(C)$$

$$= \frac{670^2 + \cdots + 539^2}{3(3)} - C - (16{,}436.11 + 1{,}932.02) = 1{,}851.14$$

$$\mathrm{SS}(ABC) = \frac{\sum_{i,j,k} (a_i b_j c_k)^2}{r} - C - \mathrm{SS}(A) - \mathrm{SS}(B) - \mathrm{SS}(C) - \mathrm{SS}(AB)$$

$$- \mathrm{SS}(AC) - \mathrm{SS}(BC) \tag{15.10}$$

$$= \frac{266^2 + \cdots + 121^2}{3} - C - (9{,}900.11 + 16{,}436.11 + 1{,}932.02$$

$$+ 658.44 + 194.03 + 1{,}851.14) = 1{,}069.65$$

Observe that sums of squares for interactions AB, AC, and BC are no more than residuals from two-way tables. Similarly, SS(ABC) is a residual from a three-way table. You may decide to construct the two-way tables or to mark appropriate totals distinctively, as with colored pencils. Note also that this example permits an easy generalization to a factorial experiment of any dimensions.

The results are presented in an analysis of variance table such as Table 15.6. Here we have not shown the total sum of squares for treatments although this would have been quite correct. Often this is done and the partitioning into main effects and interactions is, then, inset below "Treatments" in the analysis of variance. See Table 15.4.

Interactions involving two factors are called *two-factor*, or *first-order*, *interactions*, for example, AB, AC, BC. Interactions with three factors are *three-factor*, or *second-order*, *interactions*.

For these data, the analysis of variance shows that all three main effects and interactions BC and ABC are significant. The significant BC interaction implies that the differences between responses to C vary with the level of B,

Table 15.6 Analysis of variance of data in Table 15.5

Source	df	SS	Mean square	F
Blocks	$(r - 1) = 2$	356.77	178.39	1.90
A = species	$a - 1 = 2$	9,900.11	4,950.06	52.60**
B = soil type	$b - 1 = 2$	16,436.11	8,218.06	87.33**
C = fungicide	$c - 1 = 1$	1,932.02	1,932.02	20.53**
AB	$(a - 1)(b - 1) = 4$	658.44	164.61	1.75
AC	$(a - 1)(c - 1) = 2$	194.03	97.02	1.03
BC	$(b - 1)(c - 1) = 2$	1,851.14	925.57	9.84**
ABC	$(a - 1)(b - 1)(c - 1) = 4$	1,069.65	267.41	2.84*
Error	$(r - 1)(abc - 1) = 34$	3,199.40	94.10	
Total	$abcr - 1 = 53$	35,597.67		

where responses are measured over all levels of A. Alternately, the differences among responses to levels of B vary for the two levels of C, where responses are again measured as totals or means over all levels of A. Specifically, the differences in emergence rates, when averaged over all species, between treated and untreated seed are not the same for the three soil types; or the differences among emergence rates of seed grown in three soil types are not the same for treated as for untreated seed.

Interactions of the second or higher orders are sometimes difficult to interpret. The significant ABC interaction can be considered in three ways; namely, as an interaction of the interaction AB with factor C, of the interaction AC with factor B, or of the interaction BC with factor A. Here the BC interaction is not consistent for the levels of A, and so on. The way to handle this will depend on which approach is most meaningful and possibly on the significance of the two-factor interactions.

For these data, since the BC and ABC interactions are significant, it seems logical to begin by examining the BC interaction. Since C is at two levels only, let us start by considering the simple effects of C at the various levels of B. Apparently, the simple effects of C are not homogeneous for the three soil types. Hence let us examine the two-way table, contained in Table 15.5, and used in computing the BC interaction. This is presented as Table 15.7 where the responses to fungicide are compared for the various soil types. The difference 254 stands out immediately. Now we will propose a test of a contrast suggested by the data. However, a test of significance has already alerted us to the presence of real differences.

Each sum of squares has a single degree of freedom and their sum is the same as the sum for C and BC, that is, $193.39 + 5.56 + 3{,}584.22 = 3{,}783.17 = 1{,}932.02 + 1{,}851.14$.

The sums of squares for C and BC represent a common partitioning of a sum of squares of $n = 3$ observations into a correction term (the overall

Table 15.7 Examination of the BC interaction for the data of Table 15.5

	Fungicide		
	c_1	c_2	$c_2 - c_1$
Soil type:			
b_1	670	729	59
b_2	772	782	10
b_3	285	539	254
$b_1 + b_2 + b_3$	1,727	2,050	

$$C \text{ within } b_1 \text{ SS} = \frac{[(b_1c_2) - (b_1c_1)]^2}{2ra} = \frac{(729 - 670)^2}{2(3)3} = 193.39\ ns$$

$$C \text{ within } b_2 \text{ SS} = \frac{[(b_2c_2) - (b_2c_1)]^2}{2ra} = \frac{(782 - 772)^2}{2(3)3} = 5.56\ ns$$

$$C \text{ within } b_3 \text{ SS} = \frac{[(b_3c_2) - (b_3c_1)]^2}{2ra} = \frac{(539 - 285)^2}{2(3)3} = 3{,}584.22^{**}$$

C effect) and a variance or measure of homogeneity or heterogeneity (the BC interaction). Since there is a BC interaction and the simple effects of C are not homogeneous, we choose to look at the information presented by individual sums of squares for simple effects.

We find that the difference in emergence rates of treated and untreated seed, averaged over three species, is not significant for silt loam or for sand but is for clay.

Because of the problems of interpreting significant interactions in the analysis of variance, we have chosen to examine certain simple effects at the expense of a loss of replication; each of the simple effects of C is measured at only a single level of B.

The significant ABC interaction implies that the BC interaction differs with the level of A. We take this point of view in looking at ABC, since BC is significant. Having looked at the BC interaction, we find it reasonable to conclude that the difficulty is tied to C on clay soil and we proceed directly

Table 15.8 Examination of an *AC* interaction, that for b_3, for the data of Table 15.5

	Clay = b_3		
	c_1	c_2	$c_2 - c_1$
Alfalfa = a_1	66	215	149
Red clover = a_2	167	203	36
Sweet clover = a_3	52	121	69

$$C \text{ within } a_1 \text{ for } b_3 \text{ SS} = \frac{[(a_1 b_3 c_2) - (a_1 b_3 c_1)]^2}{2r} = \frac{(215 - 66)^2}{2(3)} = 3{,}700.17^{**}$$

$$C \text{ within } a_2 \text{ for } b_3 \text{ SS} = \frac{[(a_2 b_3 c_2) - (a_2 b_3 c_1)]^2}{2r} = \frac{(203 - 167)^2}{2(3)} = 216.00 \text{ } ns$$

$$C \text{ within } a_3 \text{ for } b_3 \text{ SS} = \frac{[(a_3 b_3 c_2) - (a_3 b_3 c_1)]^2}{2r} = \frac{(121 - 52)^2}{2(3)} = 793.50^{**}$$

to an examination of the simple effects of C for the clay soil type b_3 at the various levels of A. A glance at the three tables of soil type times fungicide totals contained within Table 15.5 seems to justify this approach. Thus, we look at the AC interaction on clay soil. The appropriate two-way table and computations are shown in Table 15.8.

Some of the more important conclusions to be drawn from this experiment follow. No difference was found between the emergence rates of treated seed c_2 and untreated seed c_1, when averaged over all species for silt loam b_1, and sand soils b_2; however, the difference was significant in favor of treated seed for the clay soil b_3. Since the three-factor interaction was significant, a further analysis was made and indicated that for clay soil, treated seed of alfalfa a_1 and sweet clover a_3 emerged better than untreated seed, whereas no difference was found for red clover a_2. The differences between emergence rates for treated and untreated seed, for each of the three species, were not significant for silt loam and sand soils.

Exercise 15.4.1 Sketch the BC interaction of Table 15.7 and the BC interactions for each level of A. This will add to your appreciation of the nature of a three-factor interaction.

Exercise 15.4.2 The data of Exercise 9.3.5 are for a $3 \times 2 \times 2$ factorial experiment. Analyze these data using this information. What hypotheses are tested by the various F-tests? What are the important conclusions?

In Exercise 15.3.2, you examined three 2×2 interactions. The information on these should be in the present analysis. Where does it appear? Does the present analysis add to your understanding of the nature of the nitrogen $\times$ aeration interaction?

Exercise 15.4.3 In the light of your new knowledge of main effects and interactions, reconsider the analysis of variance done in Exercise 9.8.1. To what conclusions do the various F-tests lead you?

Exercise 15.4.4 Analyze the data of Exercise 15.3.1 as though from a single completely random design, which was the case. Is the experimental error found by pooling the original error terms? What has become of the three interactions computed earlier?

Exercise 15.4.5 Partition the treatment sum of squares of Table 7.9 into sums of squares for main effects and interactions. What new hypotheses can you now test?

15.5 Linear Models for Factorial Experiments

Linear models have been discussed throughout the text. If we look upon the randomized complete block design as a two-factor experiment, then the linear model has been discussed for some factorial experiments. In fact, these two situations are different, as is clear from the randomization. Anderson (15.23) and Anderson and McLean (15.24) consider this difference carefully.

Two fundamentally different classes of problems have been raised. Class I problems involve the *fixed effects model, Model I*. Class II problems involve the *random effects model, Model II*.

Many sets of data present a mixture of the two classes of problems, so we have the *mixed model*. Still other models are possible. In any case, the computations will be the same regardless of the model, though the choice of error terms and the type of inference will vary. See also Scheffé (15.10) and Wilk and Kempthorne (15.16).

The average or expected values of the mean squares in a three-factor experiment, in a randomized complete block design, are given in Table 15.9. Capital letters refer to effects, that is, main effects or interactions; lowercase letters refer to the numbers of levels of the effects designated by the corresponding capital letters. The error variance is σ^2; other variances have subscripts which relate them to the effect concerned. Greek letters refer to the individual components used to describe any particular observation; these are used in expected values where effects are fixed, since the ones in the experiment constitute the complete population. Subscripts on Greek letters or combinations of letters are omitted as a matter of convenience in presenting the table. However, the complete mathematical description for any observation is as follows.

$$Y_{ijkl} = \mu + \rho_i + \alpha_j + \beta_k + \gamma_l + (\alpha\beta)_{jk} + (\alpha\gamma)_{jl} + (\beta\gamma)_{kl} + (\alpha\beta\gamma)_{jkl} + \varepsilon_{ijkl}$$

Table 15.9 Expected values of mean squares for factorial experiments: the three-factor experiment

		Expected value of mean square	
Source	df	Model I (fixed)	Model II (random)
Blocks	$r-1$	$\sigma^2 + abc \sum \rho^2/(r-1)$	$\sigma^2 + abc\sigma^2_\rho$
A	$a-1$	$\sigma^2 + rbc \sum \alpha^2/(a-1)$	$\sigma^2 + r\sigma^2_{\alpha\beta\gamma} + rc\sigma^2_{\alpha\beta} + rb\sigma^2_{\alpha\gamma} + rbc\sigma^2_\alpha$
B	$b-1$	$\sigma^2 + rac \sum \beta^2/(b-1)$	$\sigma^2 + r\sigma^2_{\alpha\beta\gamma} + rc\sigma^2_{\alpha\beta} + ra\sigma^2_{\beta\gamma} + rac\sigma^2_\beta$
C	$c-1$	$\sigma^2 + rab \sum \gamma^2/(c-1)$	$\sigma^2 + r\sigma^2_{\alpha\beta\gamma} + rb\sigma^2_{\alpha\gamma} + ra\sigma^2_{\beta\gamma} + rab\sigma^2_\gamma$
AB	$(a-1)(b-1)$	$\sigma^2 + rc \sum (\alpha\beta)^2/(a-1)(b-1)$	$\sigma^2 + r\sigma^2_{\alpha\beta\gamma} + rc\sigma^2_{\alpha\beta}$
AC	$(a-1)(c-1)$	$\sigma^2 + rb \sum (\alpha\gamma)^2/(a-1)(c-1)$	$\sigma^2 + r\sigma^2_{\alpha\beta\gamma} + rb\sigma^2_{\alpha\gamma}$
BC	$(b-1)(c-1)$	$\sigma^2 + ra \sum (\beta\gamma)^2/(b-1)(c-1)$	$\sigma^2 + r\sigma^2_{\alpha\beta\gamma} + ra\sigma^2_{\beta\gamma}$
ABC	$(a-1)(b-1)(c-1)$	$\sigma^2 + r \sum (\alpha\beta\gamma)^2/(a-1)(b-1)(c-1)$	$\sigma^2 + r\sigma^2_{\alpha\beta\gamma}$
Error	$(r-1)(abc-1)$	σ^2	σ^2

Source	Mixed model; A and B fixed, C random
Blocks	$\sigma^2 + abc\sigma^2_\rho$
A	$\sigma^2 + rb\frac{a}{a-1}\sigma^2_{\alpha\gamma} + rbc \sum \alpha^2/(a-1)$
B	$\sigma^2 + ra\frac{b}{b-1}\sigma^2_{\beta\gamma} + rac \sum \beta^2/(b-1)$
C	$\sigma^2 + rab\sigma^2_\gamma$
AB	$\sigma^2 + r\frac{a}{a-1}\frac{b}{b-1}\sigma^2_{\alpha\beta\gamma} + rc \sum (\alpha\beta)^2/(a-1)(b-1)$
AC	$\sigma^2 + rb\frac{a}{a-1}\sigma^2_{\alpha\gamma}$
BC	$\sigma^2 + ra\frac{b}{b-1}\sigma^2_{\beta\gamma}$
ABC	$\sigma^2 + r\frac{a}{a-1}\frac{b}{b-1}\sigma^2_{\alpha\beta\gamma}$
Error	σ^2

It is readily seen from Table 15.9 that for the fixed model, the error variance is an appropriate term for testing hypotheses about any source of variation in the analysis of variance. However, as we have seen in our examples, a significant interaction may cause us to lose interest in tests of hypotheses concerning main effects and to become interested in other tests such as those of simple effects. Thus in a fixed effects model, we have selected all treatment combinations and are interested in these only. Consequently, we will almost certainly be interested in simple effects when there is interaction. Such a shift in emphasis is more likely to lead to a satisfactory interpretation of the data. However, for a mixed model, we may not be at all interested in simple effects for a fixed effect, since they will be measured at randomly selected levels of another factor and thus will be values of a random variable.

For the random model the choice of a suitable error term, when all sources of variation are real, is more difficult when hypotheses concerning main effects are to be tested. Table 15.9 shows that error is appropriate for testing the three-factor interaction; if $\sigma^2_{\alpha\beta\gamma}$ is real, the ABC mean square is appropriate for testing the two-factor interactions. For tests of main effects, some pooling of mean squares is necessary. For example, to test H_0: $\sigma^2_\gamma = 0$, we might use an F-like test criterion with MS(C) as the numerator and MS(AC) + MS(BC) − MS(ABC) as the denominator. Because negative signs in such linear functions can lead to difficulties, it has been proposed that MS(C) + MS(ABC) be used as the numerator and MS(AC) + MS(BC) as the denominator. Satterthwaite (15.9) suggested this latter criterion and Cochran (15.3) has also considered it. Test criteria where mean squares are subtracted have been studied. The reader is referred to Gaylor and Hopper (15.20).

More generally, Satterthwaite (15.9) has given us Eqs. (15.11) and (15.12), where each M_i represents a mean square and any M_i must not appear in both numerator and denominator of F or F', as it is often designated. Such ratios are also called *quasi* F ratios. The test criterion is distributed approximately as F.

$$F_{p,q} = \frac{M_r + \cdots + M_s}{M_u + \cdots + M_v} \tag{15.11}$$

where

$$p = \frac{(M_r + \cdots + M_s)^2}{M_r^2/f_r + \cdots + M_s^2/f_s} \tag{15.12}$$

f_i is the df for M_i; q is defined similarly to p. Here, p and q are "effective" degrees of freedom.

It is this test criterion that is used in Sec. 5.9 for testing two means where variances are unequal.

Let us consider how expected values are obtained for the random model. A convenient rule for doing so is given by Crump (15.4) and rules for more general situations, including mixed models, are given by Schultz (15.11).

Rule 1 For the random model, any effect will have, in the expected value of its mean square, a linear combination of σ^2 and those variances, but no others, whose subscripts contain all the letters of the effect. For example, the expected value of the mean square for AC will include σ^2, $\sigma^2_{\alpha\beta\gamma}$, and $\sigma^2_{\alpha\gamma}$. The coefficients of the variances are: 1 for σ^2 and, for any other variance, the product of the number of replications (blocks in Table 15.9) and all the small letters corresponding to the capital letters not in the subscript. For example, for AC we have σ^2, $r\sigma^2_{\alpha\beta\gamma}$, and $rb\sigma^2_{\alpha\gamma}$. Note that the complete set of letters used for factors appears with each variance other than σ^2, either as a coefficient (lowercase) or a subscript (corresponding lowercase Greek).

Rule 2 For the mixed model, begin by finding expected values of mean squares for the random model and then delete certain variances and replace others by mean squares of population effects. The component with the same subscript as the name of the effect is always present in the effect mean square. In the mean square for any effect, consider any other component. In any subscript, ignore any letter which is used in naming the effect; if any other letter of a subscript corresponds to a fixed effect, cross out the variance component. For example, in Table 15.9 for the mixed model and opposite A, we have to consider $\sigma^2_{\alpha\beta\gamma}$, $\sigma^2_{\alpha\beta}$, and $\sigma^2_{\alpha\gamma}$; in each subscript, ignore A; for $\sigma^2_{\alpha\beta\gamma}$ and $\sigma^2_{\alpha\beta}$, B is fixed so both variances are crossed out; for $\sigma^2_{\alpha\gamma}$, C is random so $\sigma^2_{\alpha\gamma}$ is not crossed out; finally, since A is fixed, σ^2_α is replaced by $\sum \alpha^2/(a-1)$. Again, for AC, we look at B only; B is fixed so we cross out $\sigma^2_{\alpha\beta\gamma}$; since C is random, AC is also random and $\sigma^2_{\alpha\gamma}$ is left as a variance.

Rule 3 (Mixed model only) After application of rule 2, if any variance left in an expected value has, in its subscript, one or more letters corresponding to fixed effects, then the coefficient of the variance requires a factor for each fixed effect. The factor is the ratio of the number of levels of the fixed effect to one less than the number of levels. For example, in Table 15.9 for the mixed model and opposite A, $\sigma^2_{\alpha\gamma}$ has A as a fixed effect. Consequently, the coefficient requires the factor $a/(a-1)$. [Most workers do not use this factor; for example, Schultz (15.11)].

A word of explanation may help in remembering these rules, especially as they apply to interactions. Consider a set of $(\alpha\gamma)$'s in an experiment.

$$\begin{matrix} (\alpha\gamma)_{11} & (\alpha\gamma)_{12} & \cdots & (\alpha\gamma)_{1c} \\ (\alpha\gamma)_{21} & (\alpha\gamma)_{22} & \cdots & (\alpha\gamma)_{2c} \\ \cdots & \cdots & \cdots & \cdots \\ (\alpha\gamma)_{a1} & (\alpha\gamma)_{a2} & \cdots & (\alpha\gamma)_{ac} \end{matrix}$$

For the fixed model, this is the population of interest and

$$\sum_i (\alpha\gamma)_{ij} = 0 \qquad \text{all } j$$

and

$$\sum_j (\alpha\gamma)_{ij} = 0 \qquad \text{all } i$$

In words, row and column sums equal zero.

Consider MS(A). The computations require A totals. In these totals, the table above is summed over levels of C for each level of A; these sums are zero. Consequently, E[MS(A)] does not contain any $(\alpha\gamma)$ component.

For the random model, consider a parent $(\alpha\gamma)$ table that is an infinitely large two-way table. Here the mean or expected value for any row or column is zero. This table is sampled by the random selection of levels of A and of C. The elements at the intersections of these rows and columns become the $(\alpha\gamma)$'s of the experiment. The sum of the elements in any row or column of this table is a random value distributed about zero.

Consider MS(A). Now when we sum the sampled $(\alpha\gamma)$'s over levels of C, they have a sum that varies from experiment to experiment in repeated sampling. Consequently, $E[\text{MS}(A)]$ will have a $\sigma^2_{\alpha\gamma}$ term.

For the mixed model with A fixed and C random, a parent $(\alpha\gamma)$ table will have only a rows but an infinite number of columns. Here, the $(\alpha\gamma)$'s sum to zero over the a elements in any column whereas the population mean or expectation for any row is zero. The $(\alpha\gamma)$'s in any experiment are obtained by taking a random sample of c columns. The sum for any column is zero; for a row, the sum is that of a random sample of c elements and so is only distributed about zero.

Consider MS(A). Since it is over levels of C, an A sum is a random value with respect to $(\alpha\gamma)$ components. Hence $\sigma^2_{\alpha\gamma}$ is a component of $E[\text{MS}(A)]$. Consider MS(C). Now the sum is over the a levels of A and the $(\alpha\gamma)$'s sum to zero. No $\sigma^2_{\alpha\gamma}$ will appear in $E[\text{MS}(C)]$.

Finally, consider the A totals needed in the computing formula for SS(A). Expressed in terms of the model, this includes the sum of a squared $(\alpha\gamma)$ totals. The expectation of SS(A) must then have a term that is a multiple of $a\sigma^2_{\alpha\gamma}$. To get MS(A), we divide by df $= a - 1$. Consequently, $a/(a-1)$ must be part of the coefficient of $\sigma^2_{\alpha\gamma}$.

In general, when a model component does not sum to zero in the totals used to compute the mean square for a source of variation, the coefficient of the variance corresponding to the model component will have a multiplier like $a/(a-1)$ for every fixed effect named in its subscript, provided there is also a random effect named there.

The rules given in this section are also applicable when a factorial experiment includes sampling, that is, when we have both a factorial and a nested or sampling experiment. Table 15.10 consists of an example. New notation has been introduced to handle this new situation: a subscript for a variance may contain letters in and letters not in parentheses; letters in parentheses indicate the position in the hierarchy at which the component arises. For example, $\sigma^2_{\delta(\gamma)(\alpha\beta)}$ is the variance of D within C within AB. Letters in parentheses are not involved in the application of rule 2, because it applies to deletions.

To illustrate the use of the rules with a nested classification, consider the expected value of the mean square for A in Table 15.10 for the random model. An A total includes variation due to subsamples and thus has the component $\sigma^2_{\delta(\gamma)(\alpha\beta)}$, variation due to samples and thus has $\sigma^2_{\gamma(\alpha\beta)}$, variation due to AB and thus has $\sigma^2_{\alpha\beta}$, variation due to A and thus has σ^2_{α}, but no variation due to B since every level of B appears in each A total. The appropriate coefficient of any σ^2 is composed of the letters (lowercase) that do not appear in the subscript of the component. Hence, the expected value is $\sigma^2_{\delta(\gamma)(\alpha\beta)} + d\sigma^2_{\gamma(\alpha\beta)} + cd\sigma^2_{\alpha\beta} + bcd\sigma^2_{\alpha}$. Thus far, only rule 1 has been used.

If the model calls for only A to be fixed, then all other letters refer to random effects so that no component in the expected value of the mean square for A will be deleted and the only change will be to replace σ^2_{α} by $\sum \alpha^2/(a-1)$.

If the model calls for both A and B fixed, then in the expected value of the mean square for A, we delete $\sigma^2_{\alpha\beta}$, because B refers to a fixed effect and is not in parentheses. We obtain the value given in Table 15.10.

If the model calls for A fixed and B random, then there will be a $\sigma^2_{\alpha\beta}$ in the expected value for A, since B is random and its Greek counterpart appears in the subscript $\alpha\beta$. Rule 3 also applies.

Table 15.10 Expected values of mean squares for a factorial experiment involving sampling

Source	df	Expected value of mean square, random model
A	$a-1$	$\sigma^2_{\delta(\gamma)(\alpha\beta)} + d\sigma^2_{\gamma(\alpha\beta)} + cd\sigma^2_{\alpha\beta} + bcd\sigma^2_{\alpha}$
B	$b-1$	$\sigma^2_{\delta(\gamma)(\alpha\beta)} + d\sigma^2_{\gamma(\alpha\beta)} + cd\sigma^2_{\alpha\beta} + acd\sigma^2_{\beta}$
AB	$(a-1)(b-1)$	$\sigma^2_{\delta(\gamma)(\alpha\beta)} + d\sigma^2_{\gamma(\alpha\beta)} + cd\sigma^2_{\alpha\beta}$
C in AB	$(c-1)ab$	$\sigma^2_{\delta(\gamma)(\alpha\beta)} + d\sigma^2_{\gamma(\alpha\beta)}$
D in C in AB	$(d-1)abc$	$\sigma^2_{\delta(\gamma)(\alpha\beta)}$

Mixed model

Source	A fixed	A and B fixed
A	$\sigma^2_{\delta(\gamma)(\alpha\beta)} + d\sigma^2_{\gamma(\alpha\beta)} + cd\dfrac{a}{a-1}\sigma^2_{\alpha\beta} + bcd\sum \alpha^2/(a-1)$	$\sigma^2_{\delta(\gamma)(\alpha\beta)} + d\sigma^2_{\gamma(\alpha\beta)} + bcd\sum \alpha^2/(a-1)$
B	$\sigma^2_{\delta(\gamma)(\alpha\beta)} + d\sigma^2_{\gamma(\alpha\beta)} + acd\sigma^2_{\beta}$	$\sigma^2_{\delta(\gamma)(\alpha\beta)} + d\sigma^2_{\gamma(\alpha\beta)} + acd\sum \beta^2/(b-1)$
AB	$\sigma^2_{\delta(\gamma)(\alpha\beta)} + d\sigma^2_{\gamma(\alpha\beta)} + cd\dfrac{a}{a-1}\sigma^2_{\alpha\beta}$	$\sigma^2_{\delta(\gamma)(\alpha\beta)} + d\sigma^2_{\gamma(\alpha\beta)} + cd\sum (\alpha\beta)^2/(a-1)(b-1)$
C in AB	$\sigma^2_{\delta(\gamma)(\alpha\beta)} + d\sigma^2_{\gamma(\alpha\beta)}$	$\sigma^2_{\delta(\gamma)(\alpha\beta)} + d\sigma^2_{\gamma(\alpha\beta)}$
D in C in AB	$\sigma^2_{\delta(\gamma)(\alpha\beta)}$	$\sigma^2_{\delta(\gamma)(\alpha\beta)}$

For example, A might refer to treatment and B to observer. Each observer is required to make an observation at each of a number of times C. (There is to be no learning process or trend in time that would imply that first observations are more alike than any other set, for example, than would be a set involving several times.) Finally, D might imply a set of subsamples observed within each time.

In some areas of investigation, equal subclass numbers are the exception rather than the rule. Methods for obtaining average values of mean squares in such cases are given by Henderson (15.8), Searle (15.22), and others.

Exercise 15.5.1 Decide upon an appropriate model for the data of Tables 7.8, 15.2, and 15.5, and Exercise 15.4.2. Make out a table of the expected values of the mean squares as called for by your models.

Exercise 15.5.2 In a 2 × 2 factorial experiment, let an observation be described by $Y_{ijk} = \mu + \alpha_i + \beta_j + (\alpha\beta)_{ij} + \varepsilon_{ijk}$. In terms of this equation, write the sum of each treatment combination. Continue and write A, B, and AB as defined by Eqs. (15.1) to (15.3). What is the main effect A in terms of treatment contributions? Main effect B? Interaction AB?

15.6 *n*-Way Classifications and Factorial Experiments; Response Surfaces

Table 15.5 contains sums classified in a three-way system. They provide all the necessary material for computing sums of squares for main effects and interactions (Table 15.6). To compute block and error sums of squares, the individual observations are required.

In general, n-way classifications of data, not necessarily sums as in Table 15.5, are common. We now see that they may be analyzed, from a purely computational point of view, as we analyzed the treatment totals of Table 15.5. The question of tests of significance is another matter. For example, an investigator of seed emergence rates who must work in the field will not be able to randomize all 3 × 3 × 2 experiment combinations but only 3 × 2 of them; his soils will be at different locations. If he regards soils as blocks so that each treatment combination appears only once on each soil type, there is no replication of soil types and he cannot test any hypotheses about them.

Suppose that the following analysis is proposed:

Source of variation		df
Blocks (soil types, B)		2
Treatments:		5
Species, A	2	
Fungicides, C	1	
Species × fungicides, AC	2	
Residual (= error)		10
Total		17

We have already seen that the 10 degrees of freedom for residual are those associated with interactions AB, BC, and ABC with 4, 2, and 4 degrees of freedom; also, AB is not significant, BC is highly significant, and ABC is significant. In other words, the residual or error variance would be an average of nonhomogeneous components and not truly appropriate to test hypotheses about A, C, and AC. The conclusions drawn from the analysis above would be questionable. A different experimental design is needed.

This illustrates that the choice of regarding data in an n-way classification as an n-factor experiment with one block or as a randomized complete block experiment with fewer than n factors is not always as simple as looking at the randomization scheme. Essentially, it is a problem of recognizing potential sources of variation and including them in the model. In many instances, such data are analyzed using the factorial approach since, at worst, the partitioning of the total sum of squares is excessive and, consequently, somewhat meaningless. It is also at the expense of degrees of freedom in error which leads to a less precise estimate of error variance. Here, the n-factor interaction is likely to be used as the error term, especially if it seems to have no meaningful interpretation. In any case, its significance cannot be tested. In the species-soil-fungicide experiment, the three-factor interaction had a clear explanation.

Often, n-way classifications and factorial experiments, in which the levels of any factor refer to measured amounts of a treatment such as fertilizer, insecticide, cooking temperature, or diet component, may be considered as experiments planned to determine the nature of a *response surface*. In particular, one is presumably looking for a value at or near a maximum since most responses are not purely linear. Main effects and interactions can be fairly easily interpreted in terms of such surfaces. Much of today's interest in response surfaces centers about the research of Box and Hunter (15.2) and others.

Consider Fig. 15.3, which represents the results of a 4×3 factorial experiment. Plotted points are for the means of the 12 treatment combina-

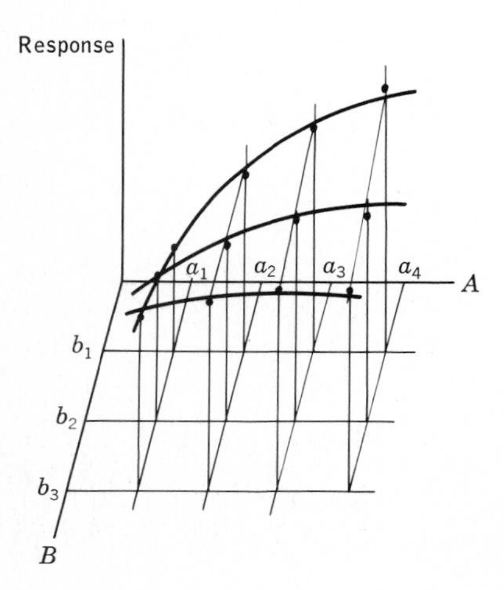

Figure 15.3 Possible response surface for a two-factor experiment.

tions and the indicated surface is intended to fit these points reasonably well. Four lines indicate the responses to three amounts of B at four levels of A; these are comparable to simple effects. Here they are shown to be straight but with slopes that vary according to the level of A. It would appear that the response to B is real and mostly linear, and that this linear response is not homogeneous over the different levels of A; the slopes of the regression lines vary. Computationally, it is possible to examine the linear regression of response on B or the *linear component* of B at each level of A and to test the hypothesis of homogeneity. The latter would be a test of the interaction between the linear component of B and factor A. Such an interaction would seem to exist for the surface in Fig. 15.3. If the first of the four lines tipped up, the fourth tipped down, and the other two were intermediate, then we might find that the main effect B showed no significance, since it is based on B averages over all levels of A; at the same time the interaction of the linear component of B and factor A could be significant, since an interaction measures homogeneity of response.

Factor A shows a tendency toward curvilinearity which a test of significance might detect. Since the curvatures are fairly slight, the linear component of A would likely be significant also for a response like that in Fig. 15.3. Neither of these components appears to be unaffected by the level of B, so we might expect the interactions of the linear component of A with B and of the curvilinear component of A with B to be significant, since neither component appears to be homogeneous over levels of B. Further partitioning of the six degrees of freedom and sum of squares for this interaction is possible; six single, independent degrees of freedom and sums of squares can be obtained, tested, and interpreted.

Since a set of meaningful comparisons is to involve regression, the next section deals with regression components of a treatment sum of squares and with their homogeneity. Some illustrations of response surfaces will be given in later sections.

15.7 Individual Degrees of Freedom; Equally Spaced Treatments

Many experiments are planned to determine the nature of a response curve or surface where the levels of a factor refer to increasing amounts of the factor. The standard regression analysis of Chaps. 10 and 13 is applicable. However, when there are equal increments between successive levels of a factor, a simple coding device may be used to accomplish the analysis with much less effort. In addition, simple methods have been developed for dealing with polynomial regression and the homogeneity of the various components of regression. We refer, in particular, to the use of values of *orthogonal polynomials* or coefficients for orthogonal comparisons in regression. Orthogonal polynomials are equations such that each is associated with a power of the independent variable, for example, with X, X^2, or X^3, and all are pairwise uncorrelated or orthogonal. This permits an independent computation of any contribution according to the degree of the independent variable and an independent test of the contribution. Each sum of squares is the additional reduction due to fitting a curve of one degree higher. In other words, fitting is sequential. A general discussion of the construction of orthogonal polynomials is given in Sec. 19.5.

Orthogonal polynomials for equally spaced X's are defined by

$$\xi_0 = 1, \text{ all } X; \quad \xi_1 = \frac{X_i - \bar{X}}{d}; \quad \xi_2 = \left\{\left(\frac{X_i - \bar{X}}{d}\right)^2 - \frac{n^2 - 1}{12}\right\};$$

$$\cdots; \xi_{k+1} = \xi_1 \xi_k - \frac{k^2(n^2 - k^2)}{4(4k^2 - 1)} \xi_{k-1} \qquad (15.13)$$

where d is the spacing between consecutive X's, k is the degree of the polynomial, and n is the number of levels of the factor.

The first polynomial is of degree zero and clearly concerns the mean. The second is of first degree, measures each X from the mean in units of the X spacing, and concerns linear regression; if there are three X's, ξ_1 takes values $-1, 0, +1$; if there are four X's, ξ_1 takes $-3/2$, $-1/2$, $+1/2$, $+3/2$; and so on. The values of the polynomials, found by substituting values of X, are multiplied by a coefficient λ to give integers; these are then tabulated.

Table 15.11 contains values for up to six equally spaced treatments of the polynomials times the λ values, sums of squares of these integers, and λ values. Coefficients and divisors for up to $n = 75$ and $n = 104$ treatments are given by Fisher and Yates (15.6) and by Anderson and Houseman (15.1), respectively. These go as far as the fifth-degree polynomial. The orthogonal polynomials are not applicable to unequally spaced treatments. For unequally spaced treatments, see Sec. 19.7 and Robson (19.8).

With three levels of a factor, there are two degrees of freedom which can be partitioned into one associated with the linear response and one for the quadratic or second-degree response. Since a second- or higher-degree curve will always go through three points, it may be more appropriate to refer to the latter as being associated with nonlinear response or with *lack of fit* to a linear response. For four levels, an additional degree of freedom is available for estimating the cubic response; again, it might be better to refer to the latter as deviations from quadratic response or *lack of fit*; and so on. If more than four levels are present, usually only the linear and quadratic and, sometimes, the cubic responses are of interest. It may be desirable to calculate the sum of squares for each comparison of the set in order to check the work.

Since the individual comparisons are orthogonal, the sum of their sums of squares equals the sum of squares for the factor concerned. Each of the individual sums of squares is tested by means of the error term, the null

Table 15.11 Coefficients and divisors for orthogonal comparisons in regression: equally spaced treatments

Number of treatments	Degree of polynomial	Treatment totals						Divisor	
		T_1	T_2	T_3	T_4	T_5	T_6	$= \sum c_i^2$	λ
2	1	−1	+1					2	2
3	1	−1	0	+1				2	1
	2	+1	−2	+1				6	3
	1	−3	−1	+1	+3			20	2
4	2	+1	−1	−1	+1			4	1
	3	−1	+3	−3	+1			20	10/3
	1	−2	−1	0	+1	+2		10	1
5	2	+2	−1	−2	−1	+2		14	1
	3	−1	+2	0	−2	+1		10	5/6
	4	+1	−4	+6	−4	+1		70	35/12
	1	−5	−3	−1	+1	+3	+5	70	2
	2	+5	−1	−4	−4	−1	+5	84	3/2
6	3	−5	+7	+4	−4	−7	+5	180	5/3
	4	+1	−3	+2	+2	−3	+1	28	7/12
	5	−1	+5	−10	+10	−5	+1	252	21/10

hypothesis being that the population mean for the comparison is zero or that β for the particular orthogonal polynomial is zero. If the linear effect only is significant, we conclude that the increase in response between successive levels of the factor is constant within random variation of the order of experimental error. The response may be negative or positive, depending on whether it decreases or increases with additional increments of the factor. A significant quadratic effect indicates that a parabola fits the data better, that is, accounts for significantly more variation among treatment means, than does a straight line; in other words, the increase or decrease for each additional increment is not constant but changes progressively. In planning experiments in which the levels of one or more factors involve equally spaced increments, it is desirable to have the highest level beyond that value for which the maximum response is anticipated.

The use of orthogonal polynomials will be illustrated with an experiment on soybeans performed by Lambert. The effect on seed yield of five row spacings differing by increments of 6 in was studied using Ottawa Mandarin soybeans in six blocks of a randomized complete block design. The data, analysis of variance, and application of orthogonal regression comparisons are given in Table 15.12.

The last part of Table 15.12 illustrates the use of orthogonal polynomials in partitioning the treatment (row spacings) sum of squares into linear, quadratic, cubic, and quartic components. In terms of Chap. 14, the SS

Table 15.12 Yield of Ottawa Mandarin soybeans grown at Rosemount, Minnesota, 1951, in bushels per acre

Block	Row spacing, in					Block totals
	18	24	30	36	42	
1	33.6	31.1	33.0	28.4	31.4	157.5
2	37.1	34.5	29.5	29.9	28.3	159.3
3	34.1	30.5	29.2	31.6	28.9	154.3
4	34.6	32.7	30.7	32.3	28.6	158.9
5	35.4	30.7	30.7	28.1	29.6†	154.5
6	36.1	30.3	27.9	26.9	33.4	154.6
Treatment totals	210.9	189.8	181.0	177.2	180.2	939.1
Means	35.15	31.63	30.17	29.53	30.03	31.30

† Estimated value. See also degrees of freedom for error and total.

Analysis of variance

Source	df	SS	MS
Block	5	5.41	
Row spacing	4	125.66	31.42**
Error	19	73.92	3.89
Total	28	204.99	

Partition of row spacings SS by use of orthogonal polynomials

Effect	Row spacing, inches, and yields, bushels per acre: 18 210.9	24 189.8	30 181.0	36 177.2	42 180.2	Q	$r \sum c_i^2$	SS	F
Linear	−2	−1	0	+1	+2	−74.0	6(10)	91.27	23.46**
Quadratic	+2	−1	−2	−1	+2	53.2	6(14)	33.69	8.66**
Cubic	−1	+2	0	−2	+1	−5.5	6(10)	0.50	< 1
Quartic	+1	−4	+6	−4	+1	9.1	6(70)	0.20	< 1
Total								125.66	

SOURCE: Data used with permission of J. W. Lambert, University of Minnesota, St. Paul, Minnesota.

column gives $SS(X \mid X^0)$, $SS(X^2 \mid X^0, X)$, $SS(X^3 \mid X^0, X, X^2)$ and $SS(X^4 \mid X^0, X, X^2, X^3)$. The procedure is a particular application of single-degree-of-freedom orthogonal comparisons as discussed in Sec. 8.3. Thus, for the linear component, Eq. (8.3) gives

$$Q = -2(210.9) - 1(189.8) + 0(181.0) + 1(177.2) + 2(180.2) = -74.0$$

The sum of squares for this comparison is, from Eq. (8.6),

$$SS(X \mid X^0) = \frac{Q^2}{r \sum c_i^2} = \frac{(-74.0)^2}{6[(-2)^2 + (-1)^2 + 0^2 + 1^2 + 2^2]} = 91.27$$

Values of $\sum c_i^2$ are given in Table 15.11 for each comparison. Each sum of squares has one degree of freedom, so it is also a mean square; F values are obtained by dividing each mean square by the error mean square.

The analysis shows highly significant linear and quadratic effects for the row spacing treatments. On the average, yield decreases as distance between rows increases. The linear component is the portion of the sum of squares attributable to the linear regression of yield on spacing. The quadratic component measures the additional improvement due to fitting the second-order polynomial. It shows that the decrease in yield becomes less for each increment or increase in row spacing. The relation between row spacing and average yield in bushels per acre is depicted in Fig. 15.4.

With the results above in mind, one might decide to fit a second-degree curve through the means. This can be done by multiple regression techniques, but orthogonal polynomials provide a convenient alternative. We require Eq. (15.14).

$$\hat{\bar{Y}} = \bar{Y} + b_1 \lambda_1 \xi_1 + b_2 \lambda_2 \xi_2 \tag{15.14}$$

For b_1 and b_2, we need appropriate $\sum (X - \bar{X})(Y - \bar{Y})/\sum (X - \bar{X})^2$ quantities. The numerators are the Q's of Table 15.12 and denominators are the corresponding $(r \sum c_i^2)$'s. λ_1 and λ_2 are found in Table 15.11 for five

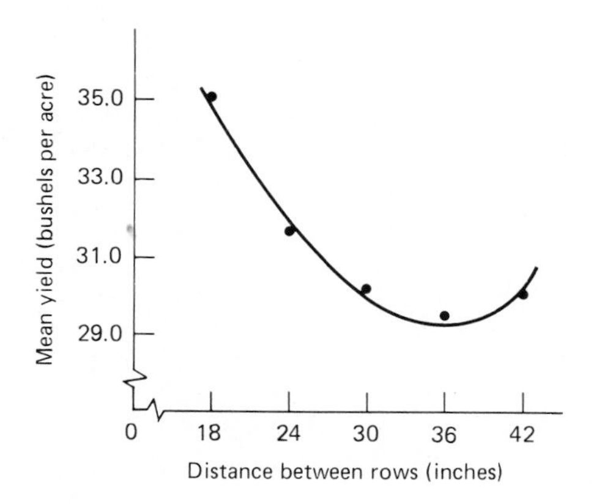

Figure 15.4 Relation between seed yield and row spacing of Ottawa Mandarin soybeans.

treatments and first- and second-degree polynomials. The spacing, d, is 6 in and $n = 5$, the number of levels. Equation (15.14) becomes

$$\hat{\hat{Y}} = 31.30 + \frac{(-74.0)}{10(6)}(1)\left(\frac{X - 30}{6}\right) + \frac{53.2}{14(6)}(1)\left[\left(\frac{X - 30}{6}\right)^2 - \frac{5^2 - 1}{12}\right]$$

This is a convenient form when the equation is to be used for estimation. We may also present it as the usual polynomial.

$$\hat{\hat{Y}} = 52.03333 - 1.26111X + .01759X^2$$

In this latter form, rounding errors may be more of a problem.

Another application of orthogonal polynomials is now shown for the data of Table 15.13. These are square roots of the number of quack-grass shoots per square foot, 52 days after spraying with maleic hydrazide. The experiment was conducted by Zick (15.19) at Madison, Wisconsin, and involved two factors, namely, maleic hydrazide in applications of 0, 4, and 8 lb/acre, called rates R, and days delay in cultivation after spraying, referred to as days D. The data are used to illustrate how orthogonal polynomial values can be used in partitioning the sums of squares for rates and rates times days into linear and quadratic components. In these data, since the interaction sum of squares is less than error, there is little point in partitioning it for other than illustrative purposes.

The underlying logic says to compute simple effects as new observations and then consider their sum or mean as the main effect and their variance or differences as lack of homogeneity or interaction. The actual computing procedure does not always make the logic apparent.

Observe the bottom part of Table 15.13. For D, there are three simple effects, namely, $64.9 - 61.5 = 3.4$, $49.3 - 48.7 = 0.6$, and $39.5 - 37.5 = 2.0$ in terms of totals. These are differences between sums of observations; the variance of each is $4(2)\sigma^2$. The sum of the three simple effects, a multiple of main effect D, is 6.0 with variance $4(3)2\sigma^2$. It is shown conveniently as contrast 1. On a per-observation basis, $SS(D) = 6.0^2/4(3)2 = 1.5$.

The variance, a measure of homogeneity or heterogeneity, among these simple effects is $3.4^2 + 0.6^2 + 2.0^2 - 6.0^2/3 = 3.92$. On a per-observation basis, this becomes $3.92/4(2) = .49$ with 2 df. This is the *rates times days* interaction. Recall that interaction is the failure of simple effects to be alike. Prior to this, we have found interaction as a residual in a two-way table, but when one factor has only two levels, a variance provides an alternative.

If we let W represent a difference, for example, a simple effect, then we have used the following equation: $\sum W_i^2 = (\sum W)^2/n + \sum (W_i - \bar{W})^2$, an equation we usually see with $(\sum W)^2/n$ on the left side of the equality and thus equating a definition and a computing formula for a variance.

Contrasts 2 and 3 are essentially those of linear regressions of the response on rate R within each of three- and ten-day delays. Call them

Table 15.13 Square root of the number of quack-grass shoots per square foot 52 days after spraying with maleic hydrazide

Days delay in cultivation, D	Maleic hydrazide per acre, lb, R	Blocks 1	2	3	4	Total
	0	15.7	14.6	16.5	14.7	61.5
3	4	9.8	14.6	11.9	12.4	48.7
	8	7.9	10.3	9.7	9.6	37.5
	0	18.0	17.4	15.1	14.4	64.9
10	4	13.6	10.6	11.8	13.3	49.3
	8	8.8	8.2	11.3	11.2	39.5
Totals		73.8	75.7	76.3	75.6	301.4

Analysis of variance

Source	df	SS	Mean square
Blocks	3	0.58	0.19
Rates, R	2	153.66	76.83**
Days, D	1	1.50	1.50
Rates × days, RD	2	0.49	0.25
Error	15	39.38	2.63
Total	23		

		3 days			10 days					
		0	4	8	0	4	8			
No.	Contrast	61.5	48.7	37.5	64.9	49.3	39.5	Sum	Divisor	SS
1	$**D$	−1	−1	−1	+1	+1	+1	6.0	4(6)	1.5
2	$*R_L\|(d_1 = 3)$	−1	0	+1				−24.0	4(2)	72.0
3	$*R_L\|(d_2 = 10)$				−1	0	+1	−25.4	4(2)	80.645
4	$**R_L$	−1	0	+1	−1	0	+1	−49.4	4(4)	152.5225
5	$R_L D$	+1	0	−1	−1	0	+1	−1.4	4(4)	.1225
6	$*R_Q\|(d_1 = 3)$	+1	−2	+1				1.6	4(6)	.1067
7	$*R_Q\|(d_2 = 10)$				+1	−2	+1	5.8	4(6)	1.4017
8	$**R_Q$	+1	−2	+1	+1	−2	+1	7.4	4(12)	1.1408
9	$R_Q D$	−1	+2	−1	+1	−2	+1	4.2	4(12)	.3675

* Simple effects
** Main effects.

$R_L|(d_1 = 3)$ and $R_L|(d_2 = 10)$. The divisors make them regression coefficients on a per-observation basis but for a 4 lb/acre unit rather than a 1-lb one. At this point, we have fitted a model with two regression coefficients. They are seen to be negative, as one would expect for a herbicide. The computed sums of squares are reductions attributable to the regression within each value of D.

Contrasts 2 and 3 may be considered as extensions of the idea of simple effects. Pooling gives a main effect, in this case, main effect R_L, the overall linear regression on rates pooled over days delay. Contrast 4 is the result.

Pooling tacitly assumes homogeneity. To measure the lack of homogeneity of R_L, or interaction with D, look at the difference between regression coefficients. Contrast 5 is seen to do this. It gives the *rates-linear times days* interaction, $R_L D$, and it is to be noted that the coefficients of the contrast can be obtained by multiplying those for R_L and D. This is the method of choice.

Contrasts 6 and 7 are similar to 2 and 3 but are quadratic rather than linear effects. The contrasts or sums divided by the appropriate number in the divisor column and multiplied by the λ value of Table 15.11 give regression coefficients. These are for the quadratic polynomial defined by Eq. (15.13). Computed sums of squares imply that two coefficients have been computed, one for each level of D.

Alternatively, we sum the information to give the main effect R_Q, contrast 8, and take the difference to measure the interaction $R_Q D$, contrast 9.

Note that the sums of squares for main effect R_L and interaction $R_L D$ and the sums of squares for the two R_L simple effects are alternative partitionings of a part of the treatment sum of squares; $152.5225 + .1225 = 72.0 + 80.645$. A similar relation holds for the quadratic effect: $1.14083 + .3675 = .10667 + 1.40167$.

In general, the main effect and interaction partitioning is more informative. We establish whether there is homogeneity of the regression coefficients involved and provide a pooled value. The contrast coefficients show that all the information is used in every comparison. If the data turn out to be heterogeneous, we can compute separate coefficients using appropriate subsets of the data. This latter procedure would, of course, be result-guided as a consequence of a test of significance.

Since no interaction is significant, interest lies only in the main effects. The sum of squares for the linear effect of rates is highly significant whereas that for the quadratic effect is less than error. Days do not appear to be a source of variation. It can be concluded that the decrease in the square root of the number of quack-grass shoots is the same for an increment of maleic hydrazide whether cultivation is delayed 3 or 10 days. Had the linear component of interaction been significant, it would indicate that the decrease in the square root of shoot number for each increment in rate differed for the 2 days; in other words, two regression coefficients of response on rate would differ. It would then be necessary to examine the simple effects, that is, the linear components or linear regression coefficients, within each of the 2 days.

With two or more measured independent variables, one can construct a response surface through the treatment means. This is an extension of the idea of a polynomial, as for the soybean data. Again, multiple regression techniques are available but we illustrate with orthogonal polynomials. Also, we ignore the fact that the only significant treatment effect is R_L and include all possible components. In this case, our surface will fit the means perfectly, within rounding errors.

The desired equation is

$$\hat{\hat{Y}} = \bar{Y} + b_1\lambda_1\xi_1 + b_2\lambda_2\xi_2 + b_3\lambda_3\xi_3 + b_4\lambda_1\xi_1\lambda_3\xi_3 + b_5\lambda_2\xi_2\lambda_3\xi_3 \tag{15.15}$$

where ξ_1 and ξ_2 are linear and quadratic orthogonal polynomials for R, and ξ_3 is the linear orthogonal and only polynomial for D. Note that $\xi_1\xi_3$ and $\xi_2\xi_3$ are concerned with $R_L D$ and $R_Q D$ interactions. These are one of two quadratic terms and the cubic term in the equation.

From Table 15.13, $b_1 = -49.4/4(4)$, $b_2 = 7.4/12(4)$, $b_3 = 6.0/6(4)$, $b_4 = -1.4/4(4)$, and $b_5 = 4.2/12(4)$. The orthogonal polynomials and λ values are obtained from Eq. (15.13) and Table 15.11. Equation (15.15) becomes

$$\begin{aligned}\hat{\hat{Y}} = 12.5583 &+ \left(\frac{-49.4}{16}\right)1\left(\frac{X_1-4}{4}\right) + \frac{7.4}{48}(3)\left\{\left(\frac{X_1-4}{4}\right)^2 - \frac{3^2-1}{12}\right\} \\ &+ \frac{6.0}{24}(2)\left(\frac{X_2-6.5}{7}\right) + \frac{(-1.4)}{16}\left(\frac{X_1-4}{4}\right)2\left(\frac{X_2-6.5}{7}\right) \\ &+ \frac{4.2}{48}(3)\left\{\left(\frac{X_1-4}{4}\right)^2 - \frac{3^2-1}{12}\right\}2\left(\frac{X_2-6.5}{7}\right)\end{aligned}$$

This is a convenient form in which to substitute (X_1, X_2) values. The polynomial form follows.

$$\begin{aligned}\hat{\hat{Y}} &= 15.0107114 - .71875X_1 - .0015625X_1^2 \\ &\quad + .1214286X_2 - .04375X_1X_2 + .0046875X_1^2X_2\end{aligned}$$

When yield shows a linear response to a factor A and when this response is not homogeneous over levels of another factor B, then we have an A-linear times B or $A_L B$ interaction. It is sometimes desired to examine the nature of this interaction by determining whether the linear regression coefficients show a linear response to B, and so on. This component of interaction would be labeled an A-linear times B-linear or $A_L B_L$ interaction. Like other interactions, this one is symmetrical in A_L and B_L; that is, we can consider this interaction as dealing with the linear regression coefficients of response to B and their linearity over levels of A. Similarly, we might consider $A_Q B_L$, $A_L B_Q$, $A_Q B_Q$, and other such interactions.

The computation of sums of squares for such interactions is straightforward. For the $A_L B_L$ interaction contrast we simply multiply the coefficients for the A_L and B_L contrasts. These are applied to the treatment totals and the resulting quantity is squared and divided by the number of observations in each total times the sum of squares of the coefficients just found. In the next section, we work an example of such an interaction where the spacing is not equal and the interaction has a special meaning.

Exercise 15.7.1 From Table 15.12, obtain treatment means and row spacings. Using this information, compute the regression coefficient of yield on row spacing by the methods of Chaps. 10 or 13. Observe that your value is the same as that found shortly after Eq. (15.14).

Exercise 15.7.2 Use one of the realizations of Eq. (15.14) to find fitted values for the five soybean means. Find the five deviations $\bar{Y} - \hat{Y}$, square, and sum. This will measure lack of fit to a quadratic equation. On a per-observation basis, it should equal the sum of the cubic and quartic sums of squares. The variance of a mean of six observations is $\sigma^2/6$, so six is the appropriate multiplier.

Do your deviations sum satisfactorily close to zero, as they should?

$$\text{Does } 6\,[\text{SS(deviations)}] = \text{SS(cubic)} + \text{SS(quartic)?}$$

Exercise 15.7.3 Use one of the realizations of Eq. (15.15) to find fitted values for the six quack-grass means. Observe deviations of the observed means from the fitted values. All should be zero.

Use the latter realization and round all regression coefficients, including b_0, to four decimal places. Repeat the exercise just completed.

Would you be satisfied with a computing procedure that provided only four decimal places?

Exercise 15.7.4 For the data of Exercise 9.3.5 as analyzed in Exercise 15.4.2, examine the linear and lack of fit components for salinity. Are these homogeneous over nitrogen levels? Over aeration levels?

Exercise 15.7.5 For the data of Exercise 9.8.1 as analyzed in Exercise 15.4.3, partition the response to age into linear and nonlinear components. Are these homogeneous over fitness categories?

15.8 A Single Degree of Freedom for Nonadditivity

Tukey (15.13) gives a method for isolating a sum of squares from error for the purpose of testing nonadditivity; this has one degree of freedom. The method originally proposed is applicable to the two-way classification or randomized complete block design and is illustrated below. A method (15.14) has also been given for Latin square designs.

We now compute a sum of squares for nonadditivity with one degree of freedom for the data of Table 9.2. The data and computations are shown in Table 15.14. The first step is to measure deviations of treatment and block

Table 15.14 One degree of freedom for nonadditivity: an example
(See also Table 9.2)

Treatment (stage when inoculated)	Block 1	2	3	4	Decoded treatment means	$\bar{Y}_{i\cdot} - \bar{Y}_{\cdot\cdot}$
Seedling	4.4	5.9	6.0	4.1	35.10	−0.43
Early bloom	3.3	1.9	4.9	7.1	34.30	−1.23
Full bloom	4.4	4.0	4.5	3.1	34.00	−1.53
Full bloom (1/100)	6.8	6.6	7.0	6.4	36.70	1.17
Ripening	6.3	4.9	5.9	7.1	36.05	0.52
Uninoculated	6.4	7.3	7.7	6.7	37.03	1.50
Decoded block means	35.27	35.10	36.00	35.75	35.53	
$\bar{Y}_{\cdot j} - \bar{Y}_{\cdot\cdot}$	−0.26	−0.43	0.47	0.22		0.00
$Q_j = \sum_j (\bar{Y}_{i\cdot} - \bar{Y}_{\cdot\cdot})Y_{ij}$	8.149	10.226	7.316	5.991		

$$Q = \sum_j (\bar{Y}_{\cdot j} - \bar{Y}_{\cdot\cdot})Q_j = \sum_j (\bar{Y}_{\cdot j} - \bar{Y}_{\cdot\cdot}) \sum_i (\bar{Y}_{i\cdot} - \bar{Y}_{\cdot\cdot})Y_{ij}$$

$$= \sum_{i,j} (\bar{Y}_{\cdot j} - \bar{Y}_{\cdot\cdot})(\bar{Y}_{i\cdot} - \bar{Y}_{\cdot\cdot})Y_{ij}$$

$$= -1.759$$

$$\frac{Q^2}{r \sum c_i^2} = \frac{Q^2}{\sum_i (\bar{Y}_{i\cdot} - \bar{Y}_{\cdot\cdot})^2 \sum_j (\bar{Y}_{\cdot j} - \bar{Y}_{\cdot\cdot})^2} \quad \text{since } r = 1$$

$$= \frac{(-1.759)^2}{7.928(.5218)} = .7483 \quad \text{with 1 df}$$

Analysis of variance

Source of variation	df	SS	MS	F
Blocks	$r - 1 = 3$	3.14	1.05	
Treatments	$t - 1 = 5$	31.65	6.33	4.83**
Error	$(r - 1)(t - 1) = 15$	19.72	1.31	
Additivity	1	.75	.75	<1
Residual	14	18.97	1.36	
Total	$rt - 1 = 23$	54.51		

means from the overall mean. Next we compute the Q_j values, defined by Eq. (15.16), at the bottom of the first part of the table. Thus

$$Q_j = \sum_i (\bar{Y}_{i\cdot} - \bar{Y}_{\cdot\cdot})Y_{ij} \qquad j = 1, \ldots, b\ (=4) \tag{15.16}$$

That is, multiply each deviation of a treatment mean from the overall mean by the corresponding value in block 1 and add. Note that Eq. (15.16) is the same as Eq. (8.3) with the data supplying the c_i as $c_i = (\bar{Y}_{i\cdot} - \bar{Y}_{\cdot\cdot})$; Y_{ij} is a total of one observation. Repeat for all blocks and thereby obtain the Q_j's. Note that each computation is equivalent to computing the numerator of a regression coefficient; we compute the regression of the response of the individuals in any block on the deviations of the treatment means from the overall mean. We need only square each Q_j and divide by

$$\sum c_i^2 = \sum_i (\bar{Y}_{i\cdot} - \bar{Y}_{\cdot\cdot})^2$$

to have four treatment-linear or T_L sums of squares.

The next computation involves measuring the homogeneity of regression coefficients; in particular, we see if they show a linear trend. The result may be looked upon as a treatment-linear times block-linear or $T_L B_L$ interaction. For coefficients, we use the deviations of the block means from the overall mean, that is, the $(\bar{Y}_{\cdot j} - \bar{Y}_{\cdot\cdot})$'s. The computation is

$$Q = \sum_j (\bar{Y}_{\cdot j} - \bar{Y}_{\cdot\cdot}) Q_j \tag{15.17}$$

Finally,

$$Q = \sum_{i,j} (\bar{Y}_{i\cdot} - \bar{Y}_{\cdot\cdot})(\bar{Y}_{\cdot j} - \bar{Y}_{\cdot\cdot}) Y_{ij} \tag{15.18}$$

The equation is seen to be symmetric in i and j.

Now we compute the sum of squares attributable to nonadditivity by

$$\frac{Q^2}{\sum c_i^2} = \frac{Q^2}{\sum (\bar{Y}_{i\cdot} - \bar{Y}_{\cdot\cdot})^2 \sum (\bar{Y}_{\cdot j} - \bar{Y}_{\cdot\cdot})^2} \quad \text{with 1 df} \tag{15.19}$$

We have seen that this may be interpreted as a $T_L B_L$ interaction where the data supply the coefficients; ordinarily, in a two-factor experiment, we would arrange for equal spacing of the factors and rely on a table of orthogonal polynomial values.

The nature of the nonadditivity being investigated may be seen by rewriting Eq. (15.18) in an equivalent form, namely, as

$$Q = \sum_{i,j} (\bar{Y}_{i\cdot} - \bar{Y}_{\cdot\cdot})(\bar{Y}_{\cdot j} - \bar{Y}_{\cdot\cdot})(Y_{ij} - \bar{Y}_{i\cdot} - \bar{Y}_{\cdot j} + \bar{Y}_{\cdot\cdot}) \tag{15.20}$$

Now $\bar{Y}_{i\cdot} - \bar{Y}_{\cdot\cdot}$ and $\bar{Y}_{\cdot j} - \bar{Y}_{\cdot\cdot}$ are estimates of τ_i and β_j, respectively. Hence $(\bar{Y}_{i\cdot} - \bar{Y}_{\cdot\cdot})(\bar{Y}_{\cdot j} - \bar{Y}_{\cdot\cdot})$ is an estimate of the block treatment contribution to be expected in the i, jth cell if block and treatment effects, that is, main effects, are multiplicative instead of additive. Also, $Y_{ij} - \bar{Y}_{i\cdot} - \bar{Y}_{\cdot j} + \bar{Y}_{\cdot\cdot}$ is an estimate of the error component in the i, jth cell when the assumption of a linear additive model is valid. Hence, Q is the numerator of the sample coefficient of regression of error from an additive model on the product of effects. Now

$$\sum_i (\bar{Y}_{i\cdot} - \bar{Y}_{\cdot\cdot})^2 \sum_j (\bar{Y}_{\cdot j} - \bar{Y}_{\cdot\cdot})^2 = \sum_{i,j} [(\bar{Y}_{i\cdot} - \bar{Y}_{\cdot\cdot})(\bar{Y}_{ij} - \bar{Y}_{\cdot\cdot})]^2$$

so that finally the sum of squares for nonadditivity is that part of the customary residual sum of squares which can be attributed to this regression. When the mean square for nonadditivity is significant and not due to a few aberrant observations, a transformation is required. Harter and Lum (15.7) present the idea of regression and nonadditivity for a two-factor experiment.

Exercise 15.8.1 The data of Table 15.13 are transformed data. Compute the sum of squares attributable to nonadditivity with one degree of freedom. Has the transformation resulted in data for which the additive model still does not apply?

Exercise 15.8.2 In Exercise 9.16.1, the data were to be transformed for analysis. Check the data for nonadditivity. Check the transformed data for nonadditivity.
What was the purpose of the transformation?

Exercise 15.8.3 In Exercise 9.16.2, the data were to be transformed prior to analysis. Check the data for nonadditivity before and after the transformation.
What was the purpose of the transformation?

References

15.1. Anderson, R. L., and E. E. Houseman: "Tables of orthogonal polynomial values extended to $N = 104$," *Iowa Agr. Exp. Sta. Res. Bull.* 297, 1942.

15.2. Box, G. E. P., and J. S. Hunter: "Experimental designs for exploring response surfaces," in V. Chew (ed.), *Experimental Designs in Industry*, pp. 138–190, Wiley, New York, 1958.

15.3. Cochran, W. G.: "Testing a linear relation among variances," *Biom.*, **7:**17–32 (1951).

15.4. Crump, S. L.: "The estimation of variance components in analysis of variance," *Biom. Bull.*, **2:**7–11 (1946).

15.5. Federer, W. T.: *Experimental Design*, Macmillan, New York, 1955.

15.6. Fisher, R. A., and F. Yates: *Statistical Tables for Biological, Agricultural and Medical Research*, 5th ed., Hafner, New York, 1957.

15.7. Harter, H. L., and M. D. Lum: "A note on Tukey's one degree of freedom for non-additivity," Abstract 474, *Biom.*, **14:**136–137 (1958).

15.8. Henderson, C. R.: "Estimation of variance and covariance components," *Biom.*, **9:**226–252 (1953).

15.9. Satterthwaite, F. E.: "An approximate distribution of estimates of variance components," *Biom. Bull.*, **2:**110–114 (1946).

15.10. Scheffé, H.: "Statistical methods for evaluation of several sets of constants and several sources of variability," *Chem. Eng. Progr.*, **50:**200–205 (1950).

15.11. Schultz, E. F., Jr.: "Rules of thumb for determining expectations of mean squares in analysis of variance," *Biom.*, **11:**123–135 (1955).

15.12. Snedecor, G. W.: *Statistical Methods*, 5th ed., Iowa State College Press, Ames, Iowa, 1956.

15.13. Tukey, J. W.: "One degree of freedom for non-additivity," *Biom.*, **5:**232–242 (1949).

15.14. Tukey, J. W.: "Reply to 'Query 113,'" *Biom.*, **11:**111–113 (1955).

15.15. Wagner, R. E.: "Effects of depth of planting and type of soil on the emergence of small-seeded grasses and legumes," M.Sc. thesis, University of Wisconsin, Madison, 1943.

15.16. Wilk, M. B., and O. Kempthorne, "Fixed, mixed, and random models," *J. Amer. Statist. Ass.*, **50:**1144–1167 (1955).

15.17. Wilkinson, W. S.: "Influence of diethylstilbestrol on feed digestibility and on blood and liver composition of lambs," Ph.D. thesis, University of Wisconsin, Madison, 1954.

15.18. Yates, F.: "The principles of orthogonality and confounding in replicated experiments," *J. Agr. Sci.*, **23:**108–145 (1933).

15.19. Zick, W.: "The influence of various factors upon the effectiveness of maleic hydrazide in controlling quack grass, *Agropyron repens*," Ph.D. thesis, University of Wisconsin, Madison, 1956.

15.20. Gaylor, D. W., and F. N. Hopper: "Estimating the degrees of freedom for linear combinations of mean squares by Satterthwaite's formula," *Technometrics*, **11**:691–706 (1969).

15.21. Rawls, R. F.: "Training for increased comprehension with accelerated word rates in auditory reading media (compressed speech)," Ph.D. thesis, North Carolina State University, Raleigh, N.C., 1970.

15.22. Searle, S. R.: *Linear Models*, Wiley, New York, 1976.

15.23. Anderson, V. L.: "Restriction errors for linear models (an aid to develop models for designed experiments)," *Biom.*, **26**:255–268 (1970).

15.24. Anderson, V. L., and R. A. McLean: *Design of Experiments: A Realistic Approach*, Marcel Dekker, New York, 1974.

CHAPTER

SIXTEEN

ANALYSIS OF VARIANCE IV: SPLIT-PLOT DESIGNS AND ANALYSIS

16.1 Introduction

In our previous discussion of factorial experiments (Chap. 15), it was assumed that the set of all treatment combinations was to be applied to the experimental units according to the randomization procedure appropriate to the completely random, randomized complete block, or Latin square design. However, other randomization procedures are possible. One of the alternate randomizations gives rise to the split-plot design, which is a special kind of incomplete block design. The split-plot design and some of its applications are the subject of this chapter.

16.2 Split-plot Designs

Split-plot designs are frequently used for factorial experiments. Such designs may incorporate one or more of the completely random, randomized complete block, or Latin square designs. The underlying principle is this: *whole plots* or *whole units*, to which levels of one or more factors are applied, are divided into *subplots* or *subunits* to which levels of one or more additional factors are applied. Thus each whole unit becomes a block for the subunit treatments. For example, consider an experiment to test factor A at four levels in three blocks of a randomized complete block design. A second factor B, at two levels, can be superimposed by dividing each A unit into two subunits and assigning the two B treatments to these subunits. Here the A units are the whole units and the B units are the subunits.

After randomization, the layout may be as follows.

Block 1				Block 2				Block 3			
a_4b_2	a_1b_2	a_2b_1	a_3b_2	a_2b_1	a_1b_2	a_4b_1	a_3b_1	a_1b_1	a_2b_2	a_4b_2	a_3b_1
a_4b_1	a_1b_1	a_2b_2	a_3b_1	a_2b_2	a_1b_1	a_4b_2	a_3b_2	a_1b_2	a_2b_1	a_4b_1	a_3b_2

Note that the randomization is a *two-stage* one. We first randomize levels of factor A over the whole units; we then randomize levels of factor B over the subunits, two per whole unit. Each whole unit plot may be considered as a block as far as factor B is concerned but only as an *incomplete block* as far as the full set of treatments is concerned. For this reason, split-plot designs may be called incomplete block designs.

The split-plot design is desirable in the following situations.

1. It may be used when the treatments associated with the levels of one or more of the factors require larger amounts of experimental material in an experimental unit than do treatments for other factors. This is common in field, laboratory, industrial, and social experimentation. For example, in a field experiment one of the factors could be methods of land preparation or application of a fertilizer, both usually requiring large experimental units or plots. The other factor could be varieties, which can be compared using smaller plots. Another example is the experiment designed to compare the keeping qualities of ice cream made from different formulas and stored at different temperatures. The procedure for a single replication would be to manufacture a large batch by each formula, whole units, and then divide each batch for separate storage at the different temperatures, the subunits.
2. The design may be used when an additional factor is to be incorporated in an experiment to increase its scope. For example, suppose that the major purpose of an experiment is to compare the effect of several fungicides as protectants against infection from a disease. To increase the scope of the experiment, several varieties are included which are known to differ in their resistance to the disease. Here, the varieties could be arranged in whole units and the seed protectants in subunits.
3. From previous information, it may be known that larger differences can be expected among the levels of certain factors than among the levels of others. In this case, treatment combinations for the factors where large differences are expected could be assigned at random to the whole units simply as a matter of convenience.
4. The design is used where greater precision is desired for comparisons among certain factors than for others. This is essentially the same as the third situation, but the reasons can be different.

In summary, since in split-plot experiments variation among subunits is expected to be less than among whole units, the factors which require smaller amounts of experimental material, or which are of major importance, or which are expected to exhibit smaller differences, or for which greater precision is desired for any reason, are assigned to the subunits.

The form of the analysis of variance for a two-factor split-plot experiment will now be discussed for a randomized complete block design. Let r equal the number of blocks, a the number of levels of A or whole units per block, and b the number of levels of B or subunits per whole unit. Suppose $r = 3$, $a = 4$, and $b = 2$. The whole units constitute $ar = 12$ units. The 11 degrees of freedom *among whole units* are partitioned into 2 degrees of freedom for blocks, 3 degrees of freedom for the main effect A, and 6 degrees of freedom for an experimental error applicable to whole unit comparisons. Within each whole unit there is 1 degree of freedom associated with the variation among subunits within a whole unit, giving a total of 12 degrees of freedom *within whole units* for the experiment. These 12 degrees of freedom are partitioned into 1 degree of freedom for the main effect B, 3 degrees of freedom for the interaction AB, and 8 degrees of freedom for an experimental error applicable to subunit comparisons.

The partition of the degrees of freedom for a split-plot design in which the whole units are arranged completely at random, in randomized complete blocks, and in a Latin square is given in Table 16.1. Factor A, applied to whole units, has a levels; and factor B, applied to subunits, has b levels. Factor B may be applied to the subunits in arrangements other than that used here.

Since each whole unit is to be split to accommodate all levels of B, a whole unit is a block as far as B is concerned. Consequently, a two-way analysis applies with sources: blocks, B, and residual or blocks $\times$ B. If blocks is partitioned, as it is to give the whole unit analysis, then residual can also be partitioned as each component times B. Clearly, we will want to examine the AB interaction. On the other hand, we are prepared to include blocks $\times$ B in error (b) for the randomized complete block design, and rows $\times$ B and columns $\times$ B in error (b) for the Latin square. All this implies that for the randomized complete block design, blocks do not interact with factor B; and that for the Latin square design, neither rows nor columns interact with factor B. If there is reason to doubt this assumption, error (b) should be further partitioned into components according to a more complete model. Any doubt as to the model must be examined in the light of the nature of the experimental material and past experience with it. Note that each error (b) has the same number of degrees of freedom.

The whole unit error, conveniently designated as E_a, is usually larger than the subunit error, designated as E_b. This is because the observations on subunits of the same whole unit tend to be positively correlated and thus react more alike than subunits from different whole units. E_a cannot be less

Table 16.1 Partition of degrees of freedom for a split-plot design with different whole unit arrangements

Completely random (r replications)		Randomized complete blocks (r replications = blocks)		Latin square ($r = a$ replications = side of square)	
Source	df	Source	df	Source	df
Whole unit analyses					
				Rows	$a - 1$
		Blocks	$r - 1$	Columns	$a - 1$
A	$a - 1$	A	$a - 1$	A	$a - 1$
Error (a)	$a(r - 1)$	Error (a)	$(a - 1)(r - 1)$	Error (a)	$(a - 1)(a - 2)$
Whole unit total	$ar - 1$	Whole unit total	$ar - 1$	Whole unit total	$a^2 - 1$
Subunit analyses					
B	$b - 1$	B	$b - 1$	B	$b - 1$
AB	$(a - 1)(b - 1)$	AB	$(a - 1)(b - 1)$	AB	$(a - 1)(b - 1)$
Error (b)	$a(r - 1)(b - 1)$	Error (b)	$a(r - 1)(b - 1)$	Error (b)	$a(a - 1)(b - 1)$
Subtotal	$ar(b - 1)$	Subtotal	$ar(b - 1)$	Subtotal	$a^2(b - 1)$
Total	$abr - 1$	Total	$abr - 1$	Total	$a^2b - 1$

than E_b except by chance; and if this happens, it is proper to consider both E_a and E_b as estimates of the same σ^2 and consequently the two sums of squares can be pooled and divided by the pooled degrees of freedom to obtain an estimate of σ^2.

On occasion, E_a may be much less than E_b. In field experiments, whole units may be on a single axis perpendicular to a fertility gradient and thus much alike, whereas the subunits may be samples along a fertility gradient and thus quite different. Consequently, variation among subunits has been maximized at the expense of variation among whole units, contrary to what was anticipated for the experiment.

If a factorial experiment is not laid out in a split-plot design, then the design that is used has a certain overall precision applicable to treatment means. Relative to this experiment, the split-plot design should give increased precision for subunit comparisons but at the cost of lower precision for the whole unit comparisons, since the overall precision is not likely to be changed. Standard deviations or standard errors appropriate for comparisons among different means are given in Table 16.2. In the first three cases, divisors are the numbers of subunits in a mean; in the last case, r is the number of subunits in a treatment mean but rb is the correct divisor.

Comparisons of two A means, at the same or different levels of B, involve both main effect A and interaction AB. This is apparent from the treatment symbols. They are both whole and subunit comparisons; it is appropriate to use a weighted average of E_a and E_b as given in Table 16.2. The weights are $b - 1$ and 1, their sum is b, so b appears in the divisor. For

Table 16.2 Standard errors for a split-plot design

Difference between	Measured as†	Example	Standard error of difference
Two A means	$a_i - a_j$	$a_1 - a_2$	$\sqrt{\frac{2E_a}{rb}}$
Two B means	$b_i - b_j$	$b_1 - b_2$	$\sqrt{\frac{2E_b}{ra}}$
Two B means at the same level of A	$a_i b_j - a_i b_k$	$a_1 b_1 - a_1 b_2$	$\sqrt{\frac{2E_b}{r}}$
Two A means at the			
1. Same level of B or	$a_i b_j - a_k b_j$	$a_1 b_1 - a_2 b_1$	$\sqrt{\frac{2[(b-1)E_b + E_a]}{rb}}$
2. Different levels of B (any two treatment means)	$a_i b_j - a_k b_l$	$a_1 b_2 - a_2 b_1$	

† All means are measured on a subunit basis. This is implied in the computational procedures.

such comparisons, the ratio of the treatment difference to its standard error does not follow Student's t distribution. The approximation of Sec. 5.9 may be adapted to obtain a value for any significance level. Let t_a and t_b be the tabulated t values, at the chosen level of significance, corresponding to the degrees of freedom in E_a and E_b. Then

$$t' = \frac{(b-1)E_b t_b + E_a t_a}{(b-1)E_b + E_a} \tag{16.1}$$

is the value, at the chosen level of significance, with which we compare our sample t. Thus t' corresponds to a tabulated t. It will lie between t_a and t_b.

Many variants of the split-plot design are in common use. One of these involves dividing each subunit into c sub-subunits for the inclusion of a third factor C at c levels. Levels of the C factor are assigned at random to the sub-subunits. Partition of the degrees of freedom is exactly as in Table 16.1 with the addition of a sub-subunit analysis. This is

Source	df
C	$c-1$
AC	$(a-1)(c-1)$
BC	$(b-1)(c-1)$
ABC	$(a-1)(b-1)(c-1)$
Error (c)	$ab(r-1)(c-1)$
Subtotal	$abr(c-1)$
Total (sub-subunits)	$abcr-1$

Calculation of sums of squares is on a sub-subunit basis. Divisors are the numbers of sub-subunits in any total being squared. The sum of squares for error (c), E_c, is obtained by subtracting from the total sum of squares for the sub-subunits, the sum of all other sums of squares. This design is commonly referred to as a split-split-plot design. For other variants of the split-plot design, the reader is referred to Cochran and Cox (16.2) and Federer (16.3).

It is not necessary to have an additional split for each factor. If three factors are involved the AB combinations may be assigned to the whole units and the levels of the C factor to the subunits, or the levels of A to the whole units and the BC combinations to the subunits.

Exercise 16.2.1 Consider a 2 × 2 factorial experiment with A randomized over whole plots and B within whole plots. Assume a randomized complete block design with two blocks.

Prepare a table with eight columns representing the four treatment symbols for each of the two blocks so that each column heading represents an observation. Be sure that observations in the same whole plot are adjacent.

In the table, write coefficients for single df contrasts representing: (1) Blocks, (2) A, (3) Blocks $\times$ A = error (a), (4) B, (5) AB, (6) Blocks $\times$ B, and (7) Blocks $\times$ AB. Note that contrasts (6) and (7) together constitute error (b).

Observe that each of the contrasts (1), (2), and (3) has the same coefficient in any whole plot. Differences, involving changes in sign, exist between whole plots only. There are no split-plot contrasts in this part of the analysis.

Observe also that the remaining contrasts have a $+1$ and a -1 within each whole plot. These are all within whole-plot or split-plot comparisons.

The reasons for the split-plot analysis should now be more obvious. We might also say that main effect A is confounded with whole plots.

16.3 An Example of a Split-Plot

An experiment performed by D. C. Arny at the University of Wisconsin compared the yields of four lots of oats for three chemical seed treatments and an untreated check. Two of the seed lots were Vicland, designated by Vicland (1) when infected with *H. Victoriae* and by Vicland (2) when not. The other two seed lots were samples of Clinton and Branch oats which are resistant to *H. Victoriae*. The seed lots, factor A, were assigned at random to the whole plots within each block; the seed protectants, factor B, were assigned at random to the subplots within each whole plot. The whole-plot design was a randomized complete block design of four blocks. Yields in bushels per acre are given in Table 16.3.

The analysis of variance of the data is computed on a subunit basis, the unit on which response is measured. It proceeds as follows. Let Y_{ijk} denote the yield in the ith block from the subunit receiving the jth level of factor A and the kth level of factor B. Then $Y_{i\cdot\cdot}$ is the total for the ith block, the sum of ab subunit observations; $Y_{\cdot j\cdot}$ is the total for all subunits receiving factor A at the jth level, the sum of rb observations; $Y_{\cdot\cdot k}$ is the total for all subunits receiving factor B at the kth level, the sum of ra observations; $Y_{ij\cdot}$ is a whole unit total, the sum of b observations; etc.

Step 1 Find the correction term and total sum of squares.

$$\text{Correction term} = \frac{Y_{\cdots}^2}{rab} = \frac{3{,}379.8^2}{64} = 178{,}485.13$$

$$\text{SS(total)} = \sum_{i,j,k} Y_{ijk}^2 - C$$

$$= 42.9^2 + \cdots + 47.4^2 - C = 7{,}797.39$$

Step 2 Complete the whole-unit analysis.

$$\text{SS(whole units)} = \frac{\sum_{i,j} Y_{ij\cdot}^2}{b} - C$$

$$= \frac{190.6^2 + \cdots + 209.6^2}{4} - C = 6{,}309.19$$

Table 16.3 Yields of oats, in bushels per acre

		Treatment, B				
Seed lot, A	Blocks	Check	Ceresan M	Panogen	Agrox	Totals
Vicland (1)	1	42.9	53.8	49.5	44.4	190.6
	2	41.6	58.5	53.8	41.8	195.7
	3	28.9	43.9	40.7	28.3	141.8
	4	30.8	46.3	39.4	34.7	151.2
Totals		144.2	202.5	183.4	149.2	679.3
Vicland (2)	1	53.3	57.6	59.8	64.1	234.8
	2	69.6	69.6	65.8	57.4	262.4
	3	45.4	42.4	41.4	44.1	173.3
	4	35.1	51.9	45.4	51.6	184.0
Totals		203.4	221.5	212.4	217.2	854.5
Clinton	1	62.3	63.4	64.5	63.6	253.8
	2	58.5	50.4	46.1	56.1	211.1
	3	44.6	45.0	62.6	52.7	204.9
	4	50.3	46.7	50.3	51.8	199.1
Totals		215.7	205.5	223.5	224.2	868.9
Branch	1	75.4	70.3	68.8	71.6	286.1
	2	65.6	67.3	65.3	69.4	267.6
	3	54.0	57.6	45.6	56.6	213.8
	4	52.7	58.5	51.0	47.4	209.6
Totals		247.7	253.7	230.7	245.0	977.1
Treatment totals		811.0	883.2	850.0	835.6	3,379.8

Block	1	2	3	4
Totals	965.3	936.8	733.8	743.9

Source: Data used with permission of D. C. Arny, University of Wisconsin, Madison, Wisconsin.

$$\text{SS(blocks)} = \frac{\sum_i Y_{i..}^2}{ab} - C$$

$$= \frac{965.3^2 + \cdots + 743.9^2}{4(4)} - C = 2{,}842.87$$

$$\text{SS}(A = \text{seed lots}) = \frac{\sum_j Y_{.j.}^2}{rb} - C$$

$$= \frac{679.3^2 + \cdots + 977.1^2}{4(4)} - C = 2{,}848.02$$

$$\text{SS[error }(a)] = \text{SS(whole units)} - \text{SS(blocks)} - \text{SS}(A)$$
$$= 6{,}309.19 - (2{,}842.87 + 2{,}848.02) = 618.30$$

Step 3 Complete the subunit analysis.

$$\text{SS}(B = \text{seed treatments}) = \frac{\sum_k Y_{\cdot\cdot k}^2}{ra} - C$$
$$= \frac{811.0^2 + \cdots + 835.6^2}{4(4)} - C = 170.53$$

$$\text{SS}(AB) = \frac{\sum_{j,k} Y_{\cdot jk}^2}{r} - C - \text{SS}(A) - SS(B)$$
$$= \frac{144.2^2 + \cdots + 245.0^2}{4} - C - (2{,}848.02 + 170.53)$$
$$= 586.47$$

$$\text{SS[error }(b)] = \text{SS(total)} - \text{SS(whole units)} - \text{SS}(B) - \text{SS}(AB)$$
$$= 7{,}797.39 - 6{,}309.19 - 170.53 - 586.47 = 731.20$$

The sums of squares are entered in an analysis of variance table such as Table 16.4, which is for the data under discussion. Two coefficients of variation are given. For whole plots, define $\text{CV} = (\sqrt{E_a/b}/\bar{Y}_{\cdots})100$. This is the equivalent of ignoring the subplot division and analyzing whole-plot values only. For the fixed model, the F value for seed lots requires E_a in the

Table 16.4 Analysis of variance for data of Table 16.3
(On a subunit basis)

Source of variation	df	SS	Mean square	F
Blocks	3	2,842.87	947.62	
Seed lots, factor A	3	2,848.02	949.34	13.82**
Error (a)	9	618.30	68.70	
Seed treatments, factor B	3	170.53	56.84	2.80
Interaction, AB	9	586.47	65.16	3.21**
Error (b)	36	731.20	20.31	
Total	63	7,797.39		

Coeff. of variability: $\text{CV}(a) = \frac{\sqrt{68.70/4}}{52.8}(100) = 7.8\%$;

$\text{CV}(b) = \frac{\sqrt{20.31}}{52.8}(100) = 8.5\%$

denominator; those for seed treatments and interaction require E_b. The F value for seed lots is highly significant, that for seed treatments is just short of the 5 percent level, and that for interaction is highly significant. For the random model, the choice of denominator for the several F-tests may not be as straightforward. The reader is referred to Table 16.9.

Since interaction is significant, differences in the responses among seed lots vary over seed treatments in a way that chance and the null hypothesis cannot easily explain; it is important to examine the simple effects. The simple effects of most interest are those among the four seed treatments within each seed lot. For the desired comparisons, treatment means and standard errors, as in Table 16.2, are given in Table 16.5.

To compute a t value, corresponding to a tabulated $t_{.025}$ for comparing two seed lots means with the same seed treatment, we use Eq. (16.1). Tabulated t's for 9 and 36 degrees of freedom are 2.262 and 2.028, respectively. Hence, $t_{.025}$ for the comparison is

$$t' = \frac{3(20.31)2.028 + 68.70(2.262)}{3(20.31) + 68.70} = 2.152$$

Table 16.5 Mean yields and standard errors
Mean yields of oats, in bushels per acre, for data of Table 16.3

Seed lots	Seed treatment				Seed lot means
	Check	Ceresan M	Panogen	Agrox	
Vicland (1)	36.1	50.6	45.9	37.3	42.5
Vicland (2)	50.9	55.4	53.1	54.3	53.4
Clinton	53.9	51.4	55.9	56.1	54.3
Branch	61.9	63.4	57.7	61.3	61.1
Seed treatment means	50.7	55.2	53.1	52.2	52.8

Standard errors

Difference between	Standard error as bushels per acre	df
Two seed lot means, factor A	$\sqrt{\frac{2(68.70)}{4(4)}} = 2.93$	9
Two seed treatment means, factor B	$\sqrt{\frac{2(20.31)}{4(4)}} = 1.59$	36
Two seed treatment means in same seed lot	$\sqrt{\frac{2(20.31)}{4}} = 3.19$	36
Two seed lot means for same seed treatment	$\sqrt{\frac{2[(3)20.31 + 68.70]}{4(4)}} = 4.02$	—

Such a t' value always lies between the two t values used in computing it, since it is a weighted mean of these tabulated t's. Knowing this will often obviate the necessity for computing t'. This test is against two-sided alternatives with $\alpha = .05$.

For comparisons involving the check with each of the seed protectants within lots, Dunnett's procedure gives

$$t_{.05}(36 \text{ df})s_{\bar{Y}_c - \bar{Y}_i} = 2.14(3.19) = 6.8 \text{ bushels per acre} \qquad \text{one-sided test}$$

$$t_{.01}(36 \text{ df})s_{\bar{Y}_c - \bar{Y}_i} = 2.84(3.19) = 9.1 \text{ bushels per acre} \qquad \text{one-sided test}$$

where t is from Dunnett's tables, Table A.9. A one-sided test is used here because a protectant is expected to be beneficial. The probability applies to the joint set of statements, that is, a set of three, rather than to each individual statement.

We conclude that for Vicland (1) the increase in yield over check is highly significant for Ceresan M and Panogen but not for Agrox. No significant differences are found for the other seed lots.

Exercise 16.3.1 In 1951, J. W. Lambert, at the University of Minnesota, compared the effect of five row spacings on the yield of two soybean varieties. The design was a split-plot with varieties as whole-plot treatments in a randomized complete block design; row spacings were applied to subplots. The yield in bushels per acre for six blocks is given in the accompanying table.

Variety	Row spacing, in	Block					
		1	2	3	4	5	6
	18	33.6	37.1	34.1	34.6	35.4	36.1
	24	31.1	34.5	30.5	32.7	30.7	30.3
OM†	30	33.0	29.5	29.2	30.7	30.7	27.9
	36	28.4	29.9	31.6	32.3	28.1	26.9
	42	31.4	28.3	28.9	28.6	18.5	33.4
	18	28.0	25.5	28.3	29.4	27.3	28.3
	24	23.7	26.2	27.0	25.8	26.8	23.8
B	30	23.5	26.8	24.9	23.3	21.4	22.0
	36	25.0	25.3	25.6	26.4	24.6	24.5
	42	25.7	23.2	23.4	25.6	24.5	22.9

† OM = Ottawa Mandarin; B = Blackhawk.

Write out the analysis of variance. Perform the computations. Interpret the data. Calculate the CV's for whole units and subunits.

Exercise 16.3.2 Partition the sum of squares for row spacings and the variety times row-spacing interaction into linear, quadratic, and deviations from quadratic = lack of fit components. Use orthogonal polynomial values where possible. Interpret the data further.

Exercise 16.3.3 The entries in the "Totals" column of Table 16.3 are whole-plot yields. Analyze these 16 values as though they were the entire experimental results. How do your mean squares compare with those in Table 16.4? How does your CV compare?

Exercise 16.3.4 Repeated measurements such as pre- and posttreatment data are sometimes analyzed as though from a split-plot experiment.

Let us consider that $3 \times 14 = 42$ individuals are randomly assigned in equal numbers to three treatments. Two observations are now made over time. Although we clearly cannot randomize the pre and post as treatments, we will analyze the data as though from a split-plot experiment. Let Exercise 7.3.3 provide the data.

The analysis is the first of those in Table 16.1. Error (a) may be described as "among subjects within treatments" and error (b) as "(pre vs. post) $\times$ subjects within treatments." Error (a) is computed from responses pooled over both tests; error (b) looks at the homogeneity of this kind of variability over the two tests.

Complete the analysis of variance. Where do you look for a test of an overall response to treatments? Where is the evidence that looks at the problem of determining whether there is a differential response to treatments?

Exercises 7.3.3 and 7.3.4 gave analyses of the same data. If the present analyses had pooled all previously computed error terms, there would now be $6 \times 13 = 78$ df to estimate error. What has become of this information? (*Hint:* Reread the previous paragraph.)

Exercise 16.3.5 The pre and post data of Exercise 15.3.3 may be analyzed as suggested in Exercise 16.3.4. The whole-plot analysis will involve a 2×2 factorial while the split plots will introduce a third factor at two levels.

Analyze the complete set of data. Where is the information relative to the differences between the methods of instruction?

16.4 Missing Data in Split-plot Designs

Formulas for estimating missing observations in the split-plot design are given by Anderson (16.1). Consider the case where a single subunit is missing and the treatment is $a_j b_k$. Let Y represent the missing subunit observation, W be the total of the observed subunits in the whole unit from which the observation is missing, $(a_j b_k)$ be the total of observed subunits that received the same treatment $a_j b_k$, and (a_j) be the total of observed subunits that received the jth level of A. Then the estimate of the missing value is given by Eq. (16.2). Note that this is Eq. (9.8) where blocks are those whole plots where A is at the jth level.

$$Y = \frac{rW + b(a_j b_k) - (a_j)}{(r-1)(b-1)} \qquad (16.2)$$

For example, suppose that in Table 16.3, the value of the check in block 1 for Vicland (1), namely, 42.9, is missing. Then

$$W = 190.6 - 42.9 = 147.7$$

$$(a_j b_k) = 144.2 - 42.9 = 101.3$$

$$(a_j) = 679.3 - 42.9 = 636.4$$

and

$$Y = \frac{4(147.7) + 4(101.3) - 636.4}{3(3)} = \frac{359.6}{9} = 40.0$$

If several values are missing, each in different whole unit treatments, estimate the missing values within each whole unit treatment as described above. If more than one subunit is missing in a whole unit treatment, make repeated use of the equation above.

The computation of sums of squares for the analysis of variance is carried out in the usual way after the missing value or values have been inserted. One degree of freedom is subtracted from error (b) for each missing subunit. The estimate of E_b is unbiased; however, the mean squares for treatments and E_a are biased upward. If only a few values are missing, these biases can be ignored. Procedures for obtaining unbiased estimates are given by Anderson (16.1), as are procedures for estimating a missing whole unit. The reader is also referred to Khargonkar (16.4).

Formulas for estimating the standard errors of differences between two means where missing values are involved are given by Cochran and Cox (16.2) and are reproduced in Table 16.6.

Where only one missing value occurs, the factor f in Table 16.6 is $1/[2(r-1)(b-1)]$ for comparisons involving a mean with the missing value and another mean. However, if more than one observation is missing, f depends on the location of the missing subunits. The following approximation is correct for certain cases but tends to be slightly large for others.

$$f = \frac{k}{2(r-d)(b-k+c-1)}$$

Table 16.6 Standard errors for the split-plot design with missing data

Comparison	Measured as	Standard error of difference
Difference between two A means	$a_i - a_j$	$\sqrt{\frac{2(E_a + fE_b)}{rb}}$
Difference between two B means	$b_i - b_j$	$\sqrt{\frac{2E_b(1 + fb/a)}{ra}}$
Difference between two B means at the same level of A	$a_i b_j - a_i b_k$	$\sqrt{\frac{2E_b(1 + fb/a)}{r}}$
Difference between two A means		
1. At the same level of B	$a_i b_j - a_k b_j$	$\sqrt{\frac{2E_a + 2E_b[(b-1) + fb^2]}{rb}}$
2. At different levels of B	$a_i b_j - a_k b_l$	

where k, c, and d refer only to missing observations for the two means being compared; in particular

k = number of missing observations
c = number of blocks containing missing observations
d = number of observations in the subunit treatment $a_j b_k$ that is affected most

Exercise 16.4.1 For the data of Exercise 16.3.1, assume that the values for variety OM, row spacing 18, block 1, and for variety B, row spacing 30, block 5, and for variety OM, row spacing 42, block 5 are missing.

Compute missing values for these observations. Set up a table such as Table 16.6, putting in numerical values except for E_a and E_b, which should come from a new analysis.

16.5 Split-block Designs

The split-plot designs previously discussed are frequently referred to as split plots in space, since each whole unit is subdivided into distinct subunits. In some experiments, successive observations are made on the same whole unit over a period of time. For example, with a forage crop such as alfalfa, data on forage yield are usually obtained two or more times a year over a period of years. Such data are somewhat analogous to those from a split-plot design in many respects, and their analysis is sometimes conducted as such and referred to as a split plot in time.

However, an interesting feature of such experiments is that there are no split plots within whole plots in the physical sense of the initial discussion and illustration. Each cutting is of the whole plot. This implies a certain symmetry of the two factors so that one seems as likely a choice as the other to be named the whole-plot treatment. Such designs, including those where the plots of each factor physically cross one another, are called *split-block* designs or designs with *both factors in strips.*

When plots physically cross one another, a randomized layout might be as follows.

Block 1

	a_3	a_1	a_2
b_1			
b_2			

Block 2

	a_2	a_1	a_3
b_2			
b_1			

Block 3

	a_1	a_3	a_2
b_2			
b_1			

With a randomization in mind, the alternative analysis that follows is often used. Three error terms are provided. One expects that these might be relatively high for main effects but relatively low for interaction. This analysis seems particularly appropriate in that experience tells us that blocks times A, blocks times B, and blocks times AB are often not homogeneous. This is not too difficult to foresee. For example, let blocks be different areas on a sloping field. Any differential responses to cultivars, A, may be fairly homogeneous over blocks so that blocks times A is of reasonable magnitude. On the other hand, differences between cuttings, B, may depend upon the block where one with adequate moisture gives noticeable differences while one with inadequate moisture between cuttings results in little second growth and thus larger differences. Consequently, blocks times B as a source of variation is of different order of magnitude than blocks times A. Finally, this latter pattern of differences may depend on the cultivars, since they are likely to differ in their ability to resist drought. The blocks times AB component may be of a still different order of magnitude. This partitioning amounts to recognizing possible sources of variation and putting a term for each into the model, and computing the analysis accordingly.

Suppose that yields are obtained on each plot for b cuttings of a alfalfa cultivars in a randomized complete block design of r blocks. Let Y_{ijk} represent the observation in the ith block on the jth variety where the kth cutting was made.

Step 1 Conduct an analysis of variance for each cutting, that is, an analysis for the Y_{ij1}'s, for the Y_{ij2}'s, and so on. (This step applies only to experiments where multiple harvests make up the data.)

Step 2 Prepare a two-way table of block times variety totals over all cuttings, that is, a table of $Y_{ij\cdot}$'s (see Table 16.7). These correspond to whole-unit totals in the split-plot design.

Step 3 From the table of totals, compute the whole-unit analysis on a subunit basis as in Table 16.8, that is, use divisors based on number of subunits.

Table 16.7 Whole-plot totals for the analysis of a split plot in time

Block	Variety 1	⋯	j	⋯	a	Block totals
1	$Y_{11\cdot}$	⋯	$Y_{1j\cdot}$	⋯	$Y_{1a\cdot}$	$Y_{1\cdot\cdot}$
⋮	⋯	⋯	⋯	⋯	⋯	⋮
i	$Y_{i1\cdot}$	⋯	$Y_{ij\cdot}$	⋯	$Y_{ia\cdot}$	$Y_{i\cdot\cdot}$
⋮	⋯	⋯	⋯	⋯	⋯	⋮
r	$Y_{r1\cdot}$	⋯	$Y_{rj\cdot}$	⋯	$Y_{ra\cdot}$	$Y_{r\cdot\cdot}$
Variety totals	$Y_{\cdot 1\cdot}$	⋯	$Y_{\cdot j\cdot}$	⋯	$Y_{\cdot a\cdot}$	$Y_{\cdot\cdot\cdot}$

Table 16.8 Analysis of variance for the split-block design

Source	df	SS
Blocks, R	$r - 1$	$\sum_{i} Y_{i..}^2/ab - C$
Varieties, A	$a - 1$	$\sum_{j} Y_{.j.}^2/rb - C$
Error (a), RA	$(r - 1)(a - 1)$	$\sum_{i,j} Y_{ij.}^2/b - C - SS(R) - SS(A)$
Whole units for A	$ra - 1$	$\sum_{i,j} Y_{ij.}^2/b - C$
Cuttings, B	$b - 1$	$\sum_{k} Y_{..k}^2/ra - C$
Error (b), RB	$(r - 1)(b - 1)$	$\sum_{i,k} Y_{i.k}^2/a - C - SS(R) - SS(B)$
Whole units for B	$rb - 1$	$\sum_{i,k} Y_{i.k}^2/a - C$
Varieties × cuttings, AB	$(a - 1)(b - 1)$	$\sum_{j,k} Y_{.jk}^2/r - C - SS(A) - SS(B)$
Error (c), RAB	$(r - 1)(a - 1)(b - 1)$	$\sum_{i,j,k} Y_{ijk}^2 - C - SS(\text{whole units for } A)$ $- SS(B) - SS[\text{error } (b)] - SS(AB)$
Total (subunits)	$rab - 1$	$\sum_{i,j,k} Y_{ijk}^2 - C$

Step 4 Prepare a similar two-way table of blocks times cuttings totals over all varieties; that is, a table of $Y_{i.k}$'s. Compute a two-way analysis on a subunit basis as in the second part of Table 16.8. Since SS(blocks) is already in the analysis of variance table, it is not repeated.

Step 5 Complete the subunit analysis as in Table 16.8. An AB table is required and a total SS on a per-subunit basis.

The totals necessary for the calculation of the sums of squares for B, AB, and RB are contained in the individual analyses of cuttings. Thus, SS(B) requires the grand totals from the individual cuttings analyses, SS(AB) requires the variety totals from the individual cuttings analyses, and SS(RB) requires the block totals from the individual cuttings analyses.

Certain relationships exist between the individual cuttings analyses and the combined analysis. These serve as checks on the computations or as computing procedures. SS(B) is the sum of the individual correction terms less C, the overall correction term. The sums of the degrees of freedom and sums of squares for A and AB equal those for A in the individual cuttings.

This implies that SS(AB) can be obtained by subtracting SS(A) in the combined analysis from the sum of the SS(A)'s in the individual cuttings analyses. Similarly, the sums of the degrees of freedom and sums of squares for R and RB in the combined analysis equal those for R in the individual cuttings. Also, the total SS equals the sum of the total SS's for the individual analyses plus SS(B).

If several years' results involving several cuttings each year for a number of varieties are to be analyzed, the problem of heterogeneity and correlation of error variance is very likely to arise. Other methods of analysis have been proposed. Steel (16.5) has proposed a multivariate analysis, a procedure which has also been used by Tukey (16.6) in pooling the results of a group of experiments.

16.6 Split-plot and Split-block Models

Let

$$Y_{ijk} = \mu + \rho_i + \alpha_j + \gamma_{ij} + \beta_k + (\alpha\beta)_{jk} + \varepsilon_{ijk} \tag{16.3}$$

represent the observation in the ith block of a randomized complete block design, on the jth whole-unit treatment with the kth subunit treatment. Let $i = 1, \ldots, r$ blocks, $j = 1, \ldots, a$ whole-unit treatments, and $k = 1, \ldots, b$ subunit treatments. Let γ_{ij} and ε_{ijk} be normally and independently distributed about zero means with σ_γ^2 as the common variance of the γ's, the whole-unit random components, and with σ_ε^2 as the common variance of the ε's, the subunit random components. This representation serves for the analysis of variance of the randomized complete block design of Table 16.1 and for the example of Sec. 16.3.

The model may be fixed, random, or mixed. If either the α's or the β's are random, then the $(\alpha\beta)$'s are random. Expected values of the mean squares are given in Table 16.9. From this table it is clear what null hypotheses can be tested by errors (a) and (b). For the random and mixed models where interactions are real, it is necessary to synthesize an error in several cases. For the procedure, see Sec. 15.5.

In Sec. 16.5, an observation was represented by

$$Y_{ijk} = \mu + \rho_i + \alpha_j + \gamma_{ij} + \beta_k + \theta_{ik} + (\alpha\beta)_{jk} + \varepsilon_{ijk} \tag{16.4}$$

A component for blocks times cuttings has been included. Let us assume that the ρ's and α's are random and that the β's are fixed. This is a mixed model. Expected values of mean squares are given in Table 16.10. To test cuttings, an error must be synthesized.

Exercise 16.6.1 For the experiment that led to Table 16.10, assume that both A and B are fixed. Use the rules of Chap. 15 to obtain expected values for the mean squares in this case. (Note that AB will also be fixed.)

Table 16.9 Expected values of the mean squares for a split-plot model in a randomized complete block design

Source of variation	df	Model I Fixed effects	Model II Random effects
Blocks	$r - 1$	$\sigma_\varepsilon^2 + b\sigma_\gamma^2 + ab\sigma_\rho^2$	$\sigma_\varepsilon^2 + b\sigma_\gamma^2 + ab\sigma_\rho^2$
A	$a - 1$	$\sigma^2_\varepsilon + b\sigma^2_\gamma + rb\dfrac{\sum_j \alpha_j^2}{a-1}$	$\sigma^2_\varepsilon + b\sigma^2_\gamma + r\sigma^2_{\alpha\beta} + rb\sigma^2_\alpha$
Error (a)	$(r-1)(a-1)$	$\sigma_\varepsilon^2 + b\sigma_\gamma^2$	$\sigma_\varepsilon^2 + b\sigma_\gamma^2$
B	$b - 1$	$\sigma_\varepsilon^2 + ra\dfrac{\sum_k \beta_k^2}{b-1}$	$\sigma_\varepsilon^2 + r\sigma^2_{\alpha\beta} + ra\sigma_\beta^2$
AB	$(a-1)(b-1)$	$\sigma_\varepsilon^2 + r\dfrac{\sum_{j,k} (\alpha\beta)_{jk}^2}{(a-1)(b-1)}$	$\sigma_\varepsilon^2 + r\sigma^2_{\alpha\beta}$
Error (b)	$a(b-1)(r-1)$	σ_ε^2	σ_ε^2

Mixed model

A random, B fixed	A fixed, B random
$\sigma_\varepsilon^2 + b\sigma_\gamma^2 + ab\sigma_\rho^2$	$\sigma_\varepsilon^2 + b\sigma_\gamma^2 + ab\sigma_\rho^2$
$\sigma^2_\varepsilon + b\sigma^2_\gamma + rb\sigma^2_\alpha$	$\sigma_\varepsilon^2 + b\sigma_\gamma^2 + r\dfrac{a}{a-1}\sigma^2_{\alpha\beta} + rb\dfrac{\sum \alpha^2}{a-1}$
$\sigma_\varepsilon^2 + b\sigma_\gamma^2$	$\sigma_\varepsilon^2 + b\sigma_\gamma^2$
$\sigma_\varepsilon^2 + r\dfrac{b}{b-1}\sigma^2_{\alpha\beta} + ra\dfrac{\sum \beta^2}{b-1}$	$\sigma_\varepsilon^2 + ra\sigma_\beta^2$
$\sigma^2_\varepsilon + r\dfrac{b}{b-1}\sigma^2_{\alpha\beta}$	$\sigma_\varepsilon^2 + r\dfrac{a}{a-1}\sigma^2_{\alpha\beta}$
σ_ε^2	σ_ε^2

Exercise 16.6.2 For an experiment similar to that which led to Table 16.8, suppose that A had been fixed and B random. What will be the expected values of the mean squares for this experiment?

16.7 Split Plots in Space and Time

An example of a split plot in both space and time is an experiment with a perennial crop laid out in a split-plot design. Consider a pasture experiment to evaluate different fertilizer treatments, (factor A), arranged in whole units

Table 16.10 Expected values of the mean squares for a possible model for the data of Table 16.8

Model: ρ's and α's random, β's fixed

Sources of variation	df	Expected values
Blocks, R	$r-1$	$\sigma_\varepsilon^2 + a\sigma_\theta^2 + b\sigma_\gamma^2 + ab\sigma_\rho^2$
Varieties, A	$a-1$	$\sigma_\varepsilon^2 + b\sigma_\gamma^2 + rb\sigma_\alpha^2$
Error (a), RA	$(r-1)(a-1)$	$\sigma_\varepsilon^2 + b\sigma_\gamma^2$
Cuttings, B	$b-1$	$\sigma_\varepsilon^2 + a\sigma_\theta^2 + r\dfrac{b}{b-1}\sigma_{\alpha\beta}^2 + ra\dfrac{\sum_k \beta_k^2}{b-1}$
Error (b), RB	$(r-1)(b-1)$	$\sigma_\varepsilon^2 + a\sigma_\theta^2$
AB	$(a-1)(b-1)$	$\sigma_\varepsilon^2 + r\dfrac{b}{b-1}\sigma_{\alpha\beta}^2$
Error (c), RAB	$(r-1)(a-1)(b-1)$	σ_ε^2

with several management practices, (factor B), as subunits, and conducted without re-randomization for a number of years, (factor C). Data from such analyses are usually analyzed each year as described for the split block in Sec. 16.5. A combined analysis of the data can be made to determine the average treatment responses over all years and whether these responses are consistent from year to year. The form of the analysis is given in Table 16.11, where Y_{ijkm} represents the observation made in the ith block on the subunit receiving the treatment consisting of the jth level of factor A and the kth level of factor B in the mth year, factor C. Then $Y_{i\cdots}$ is a block total over all subunits and years; it is a total of abc observations. Also $Y_{\cdot jk\cdot}$ is the total for the j,kth treatment combination over all blocks and years; it is a total of rc observations. Other totals are given similarly.

Parts I and II in Table 16.11 give the partition of the degrees of freedom and sums of squares for the portion of the analysis concerned with the average treatment responses over all years. The procedure is identical with that described for a split-plot design in Secs. 16.2 and 16.3 except for the additional constant c in the divisors; totals used in the calculations are for c years. Parts III to V are extensions of the analyses described in Sec. 16.5.

Standard errors for comparisons between treatment means for all years are the same as those in Table 16.2 except that c is included in the divisor since the means to be compared cover c years. The same precautions which are discussed in Sec. 16.5 apply to comparisons among treatments within and between individual years. Since the complete analysis and interpretation of experiments involving split units in both space and time may be complex, it is suggested that the reader seek advice.

Table 16.11 Analysis of variance for a split plot in space and time

Reference no.	Source	df	SS
	Blocks, R	$r-1$	$\sum_i Y_{i\cdots}^2/abc - C$
I	Fertilizers, A	$a-1$	$\sum_j Y_{\cdot j\cdot\cdot}^2/rbc - C$
	Error (a), RA	$(r-1)(a-1)$	$\sum_{i,j} Y_{ij\cdot\cdot}^2/bc - C - \text{SS}(R) - \text{SS}(A)$
	Subtotal I	$ra-1$	$\sum_{i,j} Y_{ij\cdot\cdot}^2/bc - C$
	Management practices, B	$b-1$	$\sum_k Y_{\cdot\cdot k\cdot}^2/rac - C$
II	AB	$(a-1)(b-1)$	$\sum_{j,k} Y_{\cdot jk\cdot}^2/rc - C - \text{SS}(A) - \text{SS}(B)$
	$E(b)$, $RB + RAB$	$(r-1)a(b-1)$	$\sum_{i,j,k} Y_{ijk\cdot}^2/c - C - \text{SS}(I) - \text{SS}(B) - \text{SS}(AB)$
	Subtotal I + II	$rab-1$	$\sum_{i,j,k} Y_{ijk\cdot}^2/c - C$

	Years, C	$c - 1$	$\sum_{m} Y^2_{\cdot\cdot\cdot m}/rab - C$
III	$E(c)$, RC	$(r - 1)(c - 1)$	$\sum_{i,m} Y^2_{i\cdot\cdot m}/ab - C - \mathrm{SS}(R) - \mathrm{SS}(C)$
	Subtotal III	$rc - 1$	$\sum_{i,m} Y^2_{i\cdot\cdot m}/ab - C$
	AC	$(a - 1)(c - 1)$	$\sum_{j,m} Y^2_{\cdot j\cdot m}/rb - C - \mathrm{SS}(A) - \mathrm{SS}(C)$
IV	$E(d)$, RAC	$(r - 1)(a - 1)(c - 1)$	$\sum_{i,j,m} Y^2_{ij\cdot m}/b - C - \mathrm{SS}(I) - \mathrm{SS}(C) - \mathrm{SS}(E_c) - \mathrm{SS}(AC)$
	Subtotal I + III + IV	$rac - 1$	$\sum_{i,j,m} Y^2_{ij\cdot m}/b - C$
	BC	$(b - 1)(c - 1)$	$\sum_{k,m} Y^2_{\cdot\cdot km}/ra - C - \mathrm{SS}(B) - \mathrm{SS}(C)$
V	ABC	$(a - 1)(b - 1)(c - 1)$	$\sum_{j,k,m} Y^2_{\cdot jkm}/r - C - \mathrm{SS}(A) - \mathrm{SS}(B)$ $- \mathrm{SS}(C) - \mathrm{SS}(AB) - \mathrm{SS}(AC) - \mathrm{SS}(BC)$
	$E(e)$, $RBC + RABC$	$(r - 1)a(b - 1)(c - 1)$	$\sum_{i,j,k,m} Y^2_{ijkm} - C - \mathrm{SS}(I + II + III + IV)$ $- \mathrm{SS}(BC) - \mathrm{SS}(ABC)$
	Grand total	$rabc - 1$	$\sum_{i,j,k,m} Y^2_{ijkm} - C$

16.8 Series of Similar Experiments

Many agricultural experiments are conducted at more than one location and for several years. This practice is very common in varietal evaluation of different crops. The purpose is to obtain information that permits recommendations for future years over a wide area. Both locations and years can be considered as broad types of replication, locations being replications or samples of the area for which information is desired and years being replications or samples of future years.

A series of similar experiments may be conducted to determine the effect of different external environmental conditions, such as different day lengths, on a response such as the growth of plants or the iodine number of flax; or to determine whether differently manufactured tires behave similarly under varying driving conditions. The repetition of similar experiments under different conditions is essential to provide variation in the external conditions under study. Again, an experiment to evaluate a product by biologic assay or a procedure for chemical determinations may be conducted at several laboratories; the object might be to ascertain the accuracy at the several laboratories and whether or not the same conclusions are reached.

The procedure for the analysis of such data varies with the objectives. Preliminary analyses are usually the same. However, the final analyses differ and are often quite complex, the details being beyond the scope of this text. The reader is referred to Cochran and Cox (16.2), Federer (16.3), Steel (16.5), and Tukey (16.6), where other references may also be found. Some of the more important points that concern the analyses of a series of agricultural experiments will be discussed here.

Treatment effects, in agricultural experiments repeated at several locations over a period of years, are usually fixed; that is, they are not a random set of treatments but are selected in advance by the experimenter as those most likely to succeed. Location and year effects are usually considered to be random, locations being a random set of possible locations and years being a random set of future years. In actual practice, these assumptions are rarely, if ever, fulfilled. In most situations, the locations used are not selected at random but are experimental stations or fields permanently located in the area for which information is desired. Such locations are assumed to be at least representative of particular soil types or areas. The same locations are used year after year for the duration of the experiment. With annual crops, different fields at the selected experiment stations are generally used. Finally, a sample of several successive years will not always be representative of future years.

Error variances often differ considerably from test to test. When the pooled error term is used in the denominator of F, such heterogeneity tends to invalidate the F-test for comparisons involving the interaction of treatments with locations and with years. The result is that the F-test may produce too many significant results, and in any one experiment, the stated probability level may be quite incorrect if the heterogeneity is extreme. A conservative approach in testing interactions involving treatments is to compare the calculated F with tabulated F for $(t - 1)$ and n degrees of freedom where t is the number of treatments and n is the number of degrees of freedom for error in a single test, rather than with tabulated F for the degrees of freedom in the interaction and pooled error. The true numbers of degrees of freedom for the distribution of such a ratio lie somewhere between the two extremes. If this test indicates significance there need be few doubts; the difficulty comes in deciding about F values that are between the extremes.

Heterogeneity of interaction frequently complicates the interpretation of data from similar experiments. This results when certain treatments differ widely from trial to trial while others do not. Such heterogeneity invalidates the F-test of treatments against interaction in a way similar to that described for testing interaction against pooled error. In some cases, a subdivision of the treatment comparisons and interactions into components of special interest may be helpful.

In the interpretation of data from varietal trials conducted at several places for a period of years, it is very helpful to study carefully the varietal means at the different locations. That is, analyses should be made for each station for each year and for each station over the several years. An interaction of varieties times locations is usually expected, especially if the locations or varieties differ widely. Such an interaction does not mean that all varieties react differently at all stations but usually that only certain varieties at certain stations do so. Even then, it may be only that the magnitudes of differences change and not that the order or ranking changes. A particular variety could be at or near the top for all locations in spite of a very large variety times location interaction. In this case, other things being equal, the single variety could be recommended over the area covered by the test. If, however, a variety is good in performance at certain locations but not at others, different recommendations could be made for different parts of the area.

Another point concerns the variability that exists within varieties from test to test. Two varieties may give about the same performance at each of several locations. However, one may vary considerably from year to year whereas the other may be quite consistent. If it were possible to predict, in advance of a year and with reasonable accuracy, the weather conditions likely to be encountered, then specific recommendations could be made about what variety to plant. Since this is not fully possible at present, the grower who is interested in reasonably uniform yield each season is to be advised to plant the consistent variety.

Exercise 16.8.1 Twelve strains of soybeans were compared in a randomized complete block experiment with three blocks at each of three locations in North Carolina. Yields given here are in grams per plot.

	Plymouth			Clayton			Clinton		
Variety	1	2	3	1	2	3	1	2	3
Tracy	1,307	1,365	1,542	1,178	1,089	960	1,583	1,841	1,464
Centennial	1,425	1,475	1,276	1,187	1,180	1,235	1,713	1,684	1,378
N72-137	1,289	1,671	1,420	1,451	1,177	1,723	1,369	1,608	1,647
N72-3058	1,250	1,202	1,407	1,318	1,012	990	1,547	1,647	1,603
N72-3148	1,546	1,489	1,724	1,345	1,335	1,303	1,622	1,801	1,929
R73-81	1,344	1,197	1,319	1,175	1,064	1,158	1,800	1,787	1,520
D74-7741	1,280	1,260	1,605	1,111	1,111	1,099	1,820	1,521	1,851
N73-693	1,583	1,503	1,303	1,388	1,214	1,222	1,464	1,607	1,642
N73-877	1,656	1,371	1,107	1,254	1,249	1,135	1,775	1,513	1,570
N73-882	1,398	1,497	1,583	1,179	1,247	1,096	1,673	1,507	1,390
N73-1102	1,586	1,423	1,524	1,345	1,265	1,178	1,894	1,547	1,751
R75-12	911	1,202	1,012	1,136	1,161	1,004	1,422	1,393	1,342

Source: Data courtesy of C. A. Brim, North Carolina State University, Raleigh, North Carolina.

Prepare an analysis of variance for each location.

Combine the analyses. You will now have SS(locations) and SS(blocks within locations) accounting for variation among the nine blocks. SS(locations) is new. The three SS(strains) within locations should be partitioned more informatively into SS(strains) with 11 df and SS(locations × strains) with 22 df. The three SS(error) components are pooled as are their degrees of freedom.

What useful conclusions can you draw from your combined analysis?

Exercise 16.8.2 Suppose that the data in Exercise 7.3.3 had been presented from the following point of view: Each pre and post set of data is an individual experiment concerned with evaluating a single isolation experience.

Analyze each set of data.

Combine the three analyses into a single analysis. What additional information is now available that could not be found in the original analyses? Compare your combined analysis with that of Exercise 16.3.4.

References

16.1. Anderson, R. L.: "Missing-plot techniques," *Biom. Bull.*, **2**:41–47 (1946).
16.2. Cochran, W. G., and G. M. Cox: *Experimental Designs*, 2d ed., Wiley, New York, 1957.
16.3. Federer, W. T.: *Experimental Design*, Macmillan, New York, 1955.
16.4. Khargonkar, S. A.: "The estimation of missing plot values in split-plot and strip trials," *J. Ind. Soc. Agr. Statist.*, **1**:147–161 (1948).
16.5. Steel, R. G. D.: "An analysis of perennial crop data," *Biom.*, **11**:201–212 (1955).
16.6. Tukey, J. W.: "Diadic anova," *Hum. Biol.*, **21**:65–110 (1949).

CHAPTER

SEVENTEEN

ANALYSIS OF COVARIANCE

17.1 Introduction

The analysis of covariance is concerned with two or more measured variables where any measurable independent variable is not at predetermined levels as in a factorial experiment. It makes use of the concepts of both analysis of variance and of regression. This chapter deals with linear covariance. A linear relation is often a reasonably good approximation for a nonlinear relation provided the values of the independent variables do not cover too wide a range.

17.2 Uses of Covariance Analysis

The most important uses of covariance analysis are

1. To control error and increase precision
2. To adjust treatment means of the dependent variable for differences in sets of values of corresponding independent variables
3. To assist in the interpretation of data, especially with regard to the nature of treatment effects
4. To partition a total covariance or sum of cross products into component parts
5. To estimate missing data

These will now be covered in more detail.

1 ***Error control*** The variance of a treatment mean is $\sigma_{\bar{Y}}^2 = \sigma^2/n$. Hence, to lower this variance, we have only two approaches: increase the sample size or control the variance in the sampled population.

Control of σ^2 is accomplished by experimental design or by means of one or more covariates. Both methods may be used simultaneously. When covariance is used as a method of reducing error, that is, of controlling σ^2, it is in recognition of the fact that observed variation in the dependent variable Y is partly attributable to variation in the independent variable X. The use of covariates calls for the regression techniques of Chaps. 10, 13, and 14.

The use of covariance to control error is a means of increasing the precision with which treatment effects can be measured by removing, by regression, certain recognized effects that cannot be or have not been controlled effectively by experimental design. For example, in a cattle feeding experiment to compare the effects of several rations on gain in weight, animals assigned to any one block will vary in initial weight. Now if initial weight is correlated with gain in weight, a portion of the experimental error for gain can be the result of differences in initial weight. By covariance analysis, this portion, a contribution which can be attributed to differences in initial weight, may be computed and eliminated from experimental error for gain.

Forester (17.6) illustrates the application of covariance to error control on data from fields where the variability has been increased by previous experiments. Federer and Schlottfeldt (17.4) use covariance as a substitute for the use of blocks to control gradients in experimental material. Outhwaite and Rutherford (17.9) extend Federer and Schlottfeldt's results.

2 ***To adjust treatment means*** When observed variation in Y is partly attributable to variation in X, variation in treatment $\bar{Y}$'s must also be affected by variation among treatment $\bar{X}$'s. To be comparable, treatment $\bar{Y}$'s should be adjusted to make them the best estimates of what they would have been if all treatment $\bar{X}$'s had been the same. If the prime object of covariance is to adjust treatment $\bar{Y}$'s, it is also in recognition of a regression situation which calls for a corresponding adjustment of error. In any case, it is necessary to measure the appropriate regression, independent of other sources of variation that may be called for by the model.

The general idea is apparent from Fig. 17.1 for two treatments. For each treatment, variation in X is seen to contribute to variation in Y. Hence a need to control error variance by use of the covariate is seen. At the same time, the distance between $\bar{X}_1$ and $\bar{X}_2$ can contribute greatly to the difference between $\bar{Y}_1$ and $\bar{Y}_2$. If the treatment $\bar{Y}$'s had been observed from some common $\bar{X}$, say X_0, then they would be comparable. Thus the need for adjusting treatment means is apparent.

For illustration, consider canning peas. This crop increases rapidly in yield with increase in maturity. In a trial to evaluate yields of different

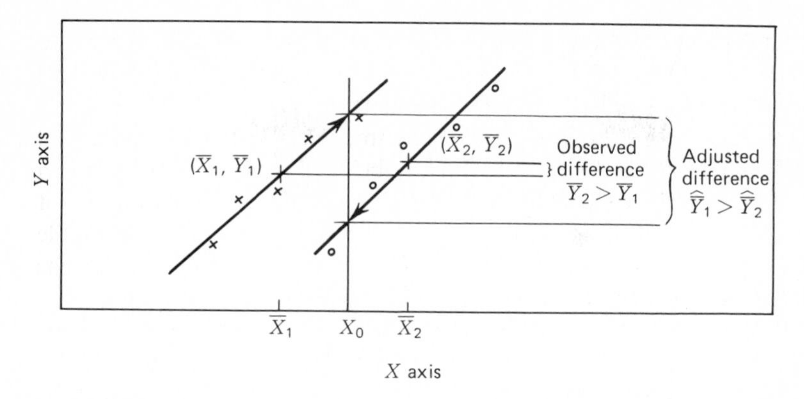

Figure 17.1 Error control and adjustment of treatment means by covariance.

varieties, it is difficult to harvest all at the same state of maturity. An analysis of yields unadjusted for differences in maturity may have little value. However, maturity can be used as a covariate when measured by a mechanical device, the tenderometer, which measures the pressure required to puncture the peas. A comparison of yields adjusted for maturity differences would be more meaningful than a comparison among unadjusted yields.

In field experiments, yields can be adjusted for differences in plot productivity as determined by uniformity trials. A uniformity trial measures yields from plots handled in a uniform manner prior to the performance of the main experiment. Love (17.7) concludes that with annual crops, the increased precision resulting from the use of uniformity data rarely pays; however, with long-lived perennials such as tree crops, there is often much to be gained.

In animal feeding experiments, differences among unadjusted treatment means may be due to differences in the nutritive value of the rations, to differences in the amounts consumed, or to both. If differences among mean gains in weight for the different rations are adjusted to a common food intake, the adjusted means indicate whether or not the rations differ in nutritive value. Here covariance is getting at the principles underlying the results of the investigation by supplying information on the way in which the treatments produce effects.

3 Interpretation of data Any arithmetical procedure and associated statistical technique are meant to assist in the interpretation of data. Thus uses 1 and 2 are definitely involved with data interpretation. However, use 3 is intended to be more specific in that covariance analysis often aids the experimenter in understanding the principles underlying the results of an investigation. For example, it may be well known that certain treatments produce real effects on both the dependent and independent variables. Covariance as a means of controlling error and adjusting treatment means is intended for use primarily when the independent variable measures environmental effects and is not influenced by treatments. If the independent variable is so influenced, the interpretation of the data is changed. This is so because the adjusted treatment means estimate the values expected when the treatment means for the independent variable are the same. Adjustment removes part of the treatment effects when means of the independent variable are affected by treatments. Covariance must be used with caution.

In a fertilizer trial on sugar beets, the treatments may cause differences in stand. When stand, the independent variable, is influenced by treatments, the analysis of yield adjusted for stand differences removes part of the treatment effect and the experimenter may be misled in the interpretation of the data. An analysis of covariance can still supply useful information. Total yield is a function of average weight per beet and of stand. Now if stand is influenced by treatments, the analysis of covariance of yield adjusted for stand measures essentially the effects of the treatments on the average weight of the beets. A significant F value for yields adjusted for stand differences would indicate that treatments affect individual beet weights on the average.

For space-planted crops such as sugar beets, where variation in number of plants per plot is random and there is a correlation between number and yield, experimental error for yield will be increased by the random variation of the covariate. To counter this increase and adjust yield means, an adjustment in proportion to the number of plants is sometimes practiced. This procedure is not recommended, because it usually results in an overcorrection for the plots with smallest stand since yields are rarely proportional to the number of plants per plot. In other words, the true regression of yield on stand for any treatment rarely goes through the origin. The analysis of covariance provides a more satisfactory and appropriate method of adjusting the experimental data.

In situations where real differences among treatments for the independent variable do occur but are not the direct effect of the treatments, adjustment is warranted. For example, consider a variety trial for which seed of the various varieties or strains has been produced in different areas. Such seed may differ widely in germination, not because of inherent differences but as a result of the environment in which it was grown. Consequently, differences in stand may occur even if planting rate is controlled. In this situation, the use of covariance for both error control and yield adjustment is warranted.

The problem of whether or not covariance is applicable is one for which the experimenter must use careful judgment. Extreme care is also required in the interpretation of the differences among adjusted treatment means. A discussion of a case where an independent variable is influenced by treatments is given by DeLury (17.3).

4 Partition of a total covariance As in the analysis of variance, a sum of products is partitioned. While this use supplies the title for our chapter, it is often an incidental, although necessary, part of an analysis of covariance.

A covariance from a replicated experiment is partitioned when we want to determine the relation between two or more measured variables when the relation is uninfluenced by other sources of variation. For example, consider the data from a randomized complete block design with four blocks of 25 random lines of soybeans, where it is desired to determine the relationship between oil and protein content. The total sum of products of the 100 observations can be partitioned into components according to the sources of variation, namely blocks, lines, and error. The components have 3, 24, and 72 degrees of freedom, respectively. If the several regression and correlation coefficients corresponding to these sources differ significantly, the total regression and correlation are heterogeneous and not interpretable. For this experiment, interest would be in the relationships for the line means and for the residual, the latter measuring the average relation between the two observed variables, within lines, after overall block effects have been removed. There is often every reason to assume that these two regressions will be different.

5 Estimation of missing data Formulas given previously for estimating missing data result in a minimum residual sum of squares. However, the treatment sum of squares is biased upward. The use of covariance to estimate missing plots results in a minimum residual sum of squares and an unbiased treatment sum of squares. The covariance procedure is simple to carry out though more difficult to describe than previous procedures which required little more than a formula.

17.3 The Model and Assumptions for Covariance

The assumptions for covariance are a combination of those for the analysis of variance and linear regression. The linear additive model for any given design is that for the analysis of variance plus an additional term for the concomitant or independent variable. Thus, for the randomized complete block design with one observation per cell, the mathematical description is given by

$$Y_{ij} = \mu + \tau_i + \rho_j + \beta(X_{ij} - \bar{X}_{..}) + \varepsilon_{ij} \qquad (17.1)$$

The variable being analyzed, the dependent variable, is generally denoted by Y, whereas the variable used in the control of error and adjustment of means, the independent variable or covariate, is denoted by X.

It is of interest to rewrite this expression in the following forms:

$$Y_{ij} - \beta(X_{ij} - \bar{X}_{..}) = \mu + \tau_i + \rho_j + \varepsilon_{ij}$$

$$Y_{ij} - \tau_i - \rho_j = \mu + \beta(X_{ij} - \bar{X}_{..}) + \varepsilon_{ij}$$

In the first case, we are stressing the experimental design aspects of the problem. We wish to carry out an analysis of variance of values which have been adjusted for regression on an independent variable. We are stressing use 2 (Sec. 17.2), though we obviously have uses 1 and 3 in mind.

In the second case, we are stressing the regression approach. We wish to measure the regression of Y on X without the interference of treatment and block effects. Use 4 is now uppermost. Note that if X were not measured, then $\beta(X_{ij} - \bar{X}_{..})$ could not be determined and would thus be included in the residual or error term.

The assumptions necessary for the valid use of covariance are:

1. The X's are fixed, measured without error, and independent of treatments.
2. The regression of Y on X after removal of block and treatment differences is linear and independent of treatments and blocks.
3. The residuals are normally and independently distributed with zero mean and a common variance.

Assumption 1 states that the X's are fixed. This means that, in finding expected values, the same set of X's is repeated. In turn, inferences apply only for the set of X's actually observed. Whereas the X's will not be chosen exactly or visualized as identical in real repeated sampling, inferences will be for interpolated rather than extrapolated values. Also, the X's must be measured exactly so that the population means are properly identified. In reality, measurement error is simply to be trivial relative to observed variation. Assumption 1 also implies as well as states that for the standard use of covariance, the treatments will not affect the X values, because being fixed, they may be chosen or restricted for reasons of convenience. It has already been pointed out that covariance can be used where the X values are so affected, but it must be used with caution.

Assumption 2 states that the effect of X on Y is to increase or decrease any Y, on the average, by a constant multiple of the deviation of the corresponding X from the $\bar{X}_{..}$ for the whole experiment, that is, by $\beta(X_{ij} - \bar{X}_{..})$. The regression is assumed to be stable or homogeneous. Thus, no subscript is required on β to relate it to either blocks or treatments. A case of such a relationship is discussed in Sec. 17.9.

Assumption 3 is the one on which the validity of the usual tests, t and F, depends. An analysis, as determined by the model, supplies a valid estimate of the common variance when there has been randomization of treatments within blocks. The assumption of normality is not necessary for estimating components of the variance of Y; randomization is necessary.

The residual variance is estimated on the basis of least-squares estimators for μ, the τ_i's, the ρ_j's and β, indicated by hats. Equation (17.2) holds.

$$\sum_{i,j} [Y_{ij} - \hat{\mu} - \hat{\tau}_i - \hat{\rho}_j - \hat{\beta}(X_{ij} - \bar{X}_{..})]^2 = \text{minimum} \tag{17.2}$$

Here we fit the full model, which is called for when all implied alternative hypotheses are true. For the least-squares estimates, Eq. (17.3) is correct.

$$\sum_{i,j} [Y_{ij} - \hat{\mu} - \hat{\tau}_i - \hat{\rho}_j - \hat{\beta}(X_{ij} - \bar{X}_{..})] = 0 \tag{17.3}$$

The sum of all the deviations is zero. It is not necessary to obtain and use estimates of the parameters in Eq. (17.2) any more than it was for the randomized complete block analysis without covariance. However, Eqs. (17.4) to (17.6) define the estimates and give the residual variance.

$$\begin{aligned} \hat{\mu} &= \bar{Y} \\ \hat{\tau}_i &= t_i = \bar{Y}_{i.} - \bar{Y}_{..} - b(\bar{X}_{i.} - \bar{X}_{..}) \\ \hat{\rho}_j &= r_j = \bar{Y}_{.j} - \bar{Y}_{..} - b(\bar{X}_{.j} - \bar{X}_{..}) \end{aligned} \tag{17.4}$$

$$\hat{\beta} = b = \frac{E_{XY}}{E_{XX}} \tag{17.5}$$

$$\hat{\sigma}^2_{Y \cdot X} = s^2_{Y \cdot X} = \frac{E_{YY} - (E_{XY})^2/E_{XX}}{f_e} \tag{17.6}$$

where E_{XX}, E_{XY}, and E_{YY} are adjusted sums of products for error; for example, E_{XX} is the error sum of squares for X, and f_e is error degrees of freedom. It can be seen from the second of Eqs. (17.4) that in order to estimate the treatment effect τ_i, the deviation of any treatment mean from the general mean must be adjusted by the quantity $b(\bar{X}_{i.} - \bar{X}_{..})$. This adjustment removes any effect that is attributable to the variable X. It is the adjusted treatment means that are comparable. All estimates are partial regression coefficients as in Chap. 14. Dummy variables would have to be introduced for $\hat{\mu}$, the $\hat{\tau}$'s, and $\hat{\rho}$'s to make the analogy complete. Equation (17.6) is the computing formula for what amounts to the definition formula, given as Eq. (17.2).

17.4 Testing Adjusted Treatment Means

Table 17.1 gives the analysis of covariance for a randomized complete block design and, at the same time, illustrates the general procedure. Note the new notation with capital letters and paired subscripts to denote sums of products; a square is a particular kind of product.

Table 17.1 Testing adjusted treatment means
The analysis of covariance for the randomized complete block design

		Sums of products of					
Source	df	X, X	X, Y	Y, Y	df	$\sum (Y - \hat{Y})^2$	MS
Total	$rt - 1$	$\sum (X - \bar{X})^2$	$\sum (X - \bar{X})(Y - \bar{Y})$	$\sum (Y - \bar{Y})^2$			
Blocks	$r - 1$	R_{XX}	R_{XY}	R_{YY}			
Treatments	$t - 1$	T_{XX}	T_{XY}	T_{YY}			
Error	$(r - 1)(t - 1)$	E_{XX}	E_{XY}	E_{YY}	$(r - 1)(t - 1) - 1$	$E_{YY} - \frac{(E_{XY})^2}{E_{XX}}$	$s_{Y \cdot X}^2$
Treatments + error	$r(t - 1)$	S_{XX}	S_{XY}	S_{YY}	$r(t - 1) - 1$	$S_{YY} - \frac{(S_{XY})^2}{S_{XX}}$	
Treatments adjusted					$t - 1$	$\left[S_{YY} - \frac{(S_{XY})^2}{S_{XX}}\right] - \left[E_{YY} - \frac{(E_{XY})^2}{E_{XX}}\right]$	MS(T, adjusted)

The logic of the procedure depends on fitting models by multiple regression techniques. A strict analogy requires the inclusion of $r - 1$ and $t - 1$ dummy variables for block and treatment effects, respectively, as well as all measured covariates. Our interest is in that aspect of regression where SS(total, adjusted) is partitioned into components attributable to regression and to error or residual. This must be done for the *full model*, that under H_1, and again for the *reduced model*, that under H_0. The additional reduction attributable to introducing, into the model, the set of parameters under test is measured by

$$\begin{aligned} &\text{SS(regression} \mid H_1) - \text{SS(regression} \mid H_0) \\ &\qquad = \text{SS(residuals} \mid H_0) - \text{SS(residuals} \mid H_1) \end{aligned}$$

Remember that

$$\text{SS(regression} \mid H_1) = \text{SS}(\{\tau_i\}, \{\rho_j\}, \beta)$$

The "additional reduction" as a mean square is tested against MS(residuals $\mid H_1$).

Table 17.1 sketches the process. First, the full model is fitted. A sequential process, as discussed in Sec. 14.7 on printouts, is used. The sequence followed adjusts for block and treatment effects first. This is convenient because of orthogonality. The Y, Y column is computed with the residual

$$E_{YY} = \text{SS(total, adjusted)} - \text{SS}(\{\tau_i\}, \{\rho_j\})$$

still unadjusted for regression on X. To do this, residuals E_{XX} and E_{XY} are also needed. The idea was discussed in Sec. 14.7 when considering the second part of Table 14.5. Now use the "Error" line to compute the contribution attributable to regression adjusted for blocks and treatments, namely

$$\frac{E_{XY}^2}{E_{XX}} = \text{SS}(\beta \mid \{\tau_i\}, \{\rho_j\}).$$

Compare Eq. (10.18). The final residual or error sum of squares is

$$\sum (Y - \hat{Y})^2 = \text{SS(total, adjusted)} - \text{SS}(\{\tau_i\}, \{\rho_j\}, \beta)$$

where

$$\text{SS}(\{\tau_i\}, \{\rho_j\}, \beta) = T_{YY} + R_{YY} + \frac{E_{XY}^2}{E_{XX}}.$$

Finally, we have MSE $= s_{Y \cdot X}^2$ for the full model. The partial regression coefficient of Y on X is given by $b = E_{XY}/E_{XX}$; it estimates the β of Eq. (17.1).

Second, the reduced model is fitted. Here, there are no treatment effects; the model calls for only block effects and regression on X. Begin by fitting blocks but not treatments, since the latter are no longer in the model.

$R_{YY} = \text{SS}(\{\rho_j\})$ and a new SS(residuals) $= \sum (Y - \bar{Y})^2 - R_{YY}$ are needed. As we have seen, R_{XX}, R_{XY} and corresponding new SS(residuals) will be required when fitting β. Clearly SS(residuals) for Y is $T_{YY} + E_{YY} = S_{YY}$ and would be so regardless of the experimental design. The other residuals are similar. Now fit β and obtain $\text{SS}(\beta | \{\rho_j\}) = S_{XY}^2/S_{XX}$. In turn, compute

$$\sum (Y - \hat{Y})^2 = \text{SS(total, adjusted)} - \text{SS}(\{\rho_j\}, \beta) = S_{YY} - \frac{S_{XY}^2}{S_{XX}},$$

where

$$\text{SS}(\{\rho_j\}, \beta) = R_{XX} + \frac{S_{XY}^2}{S_{XX}},$$

Finally, the difference between the residual sums of squares for the two models is the amount attributable to including treatment effects as the last set of components in the model, that is, after block effects and the regression term. It is $\text{SS}(\{\tau_i\} | \{\rho_j\}, \beta)$. We have done the equivalent of finding a sum of squares attributable to fitting partial regression coefficients for the treatment effects.

To test the mean square for adjusted treatments, the appropriate error mean square is $s_{Y \cdot X}^2$. When it is desired to make a number of tests, as when a treatment sum of squares is partitioned into components, exact tests require a separate computation of treatment plus error and adjusted treatments for each comparison. An approximation to shorten the computations is illustrated in Sec. 17.10.

Exercise 17.4.1 Matrone et al. (17.8) compared the effect of three factors, each at two levels, on gain in weight of lambs. The factors were soybean hay A, from plots fertilized with either KCa or PKCa, urea supplement B, and dicalcium supplement C. A randomized complete block design of two replicates was used and food intake was determined for each lamb. The data are given in the accompanying table.

	Block 1 Ewe lambs		Block 2 Wether lambs	
Ration	X = intake	Y = gain	X = intake	Y = gain
000	209.3	11.2	286.9	27.2
100	252.4	26.1	302.1	30.6
010	241.5	13.2	246.8	15.4
001	259.1	24.4	273.2	24.0
110	201.1	18.8	274.6	20.1
101	287.5	31.0	276.3	24.4
011	286.6	27.9	270.7	29.9
111	255.7	20.8	253.0	20.8

Ignore the factorial nature of the experiment and carry out the computations outlined in Table 17.1. Compute b and $s^2_{Y \cdot X}$. (Computational procedures are given in detail in the next section.) In terms of a statistical analysis of the data, how valuable are the decimal points?

Exercise 17.4.2 The data of Exercise 7.3.3 have been analyzed as two completely random experiments and, in Exercise 16.3.4, as a split-plot experiment. In the latter case, the model calls for a fixed increase attributable to each and every treatment, to be tested by the pre-vs.-post contrast, and for a heterogeneity over treatments component, to be tested by means of the (pre-vs.-post) × treatments interaction.

However, increases may be linearly related to the pretest scores so that the gain is greater (or less) depending on where one starts on the scale. This implies that the pretest measurement can be a satisfactory covariate.

Carry out the computations as suggested by Table 17.1 and the accompanying discussion. What modification of Table 17.1 is required? Compute b and $s^2_{Y \cdot X}$.

Exercise 17.4.3 The data of Exercise 7.3.3 are incomplete and should include observations in Exercise 7.4.2. Include these observations and consider how to analyze the complete set of data. Is it any more complicated than that used in Exercise 17.4.2? Carry out the required computations. Compute b and $s^2_{Y \cdot X}$.

Exercise 17.4.4 Consider the data in Exercise 15.3.3. Let the pretest scores be values of a covariate and the posttest data be values of a dependent variable. Ignore the factorial nature of the treatments and carry out the computations needed to test adjusted treatment means.

17.5 Covariance in the Randomized Complete Block Design

The form of the analysis of covariance in a randomized complete block design is shown in Table 17.1. The procedure will be illustrated using the data of Table 17.2 from an experiment by J. L. Bowers and L. B. Permenter, Mississippi State College, in which 11 varieties of lima beans were compared for ascorbic acid content. From previous experience it was known that increase in maturity resulted in decrease in vitamin C content. Since all varieties were not of the same maturity at harvest and since all plots of a given variety did not reach the same level of maturity on the same day, it was not possible to harvest all plots at the same stage of maturity. Hence the percentage of dry matter based on 100 g of freshly harvested beans was observed as an index of maturity and used as a covariate.

The calculation of sums of products for the randomized complete block design is basically given in Eqs. (9.1) to (9.5) and (10.2). For the data of Table 17.2, the computations follow. Sums of products for total are

$$\sum (X_{ij} - \bar{X}_{..})^2 = \sum X_{ij}^2 - \frac{X_{..}^2}{rt} = 2{,}916.22$$

$$\sum (Y_{ij} - \bar{Y}_{..})^2 = 61{,}934.42$$

$$\sum (X_{ij} - \bar{X}_{..})(Y_{ij} - \bar{Y}_{..}) = \sum X_{ij} Y_{ij} - \frac{X_{..} Y_{..}}{rt} = -12{,}226.14$$

Table 17.2 Ascorbic acid content† Y and percentage of dry matter‡ X for lima beans

	Replication										Variety totals	
	1		2		3		4		5			
	X	Y	X	Y	X	Y	X	Y	X	Y	$X_{i\cdot}$	$Y_{i\cdot}$
1	34.0	93.0	33.4	94.8	34.7	91.7	38.9	80.8	36.1	80.2	177.1	440.5
2	39.6	47.3	39.8	51.5	51.2	33.3	52.0	27.2	56.2	20.6	238.8	179.9
3	31.7	81.4	30.1	109.0	33.8	71.6	39.6	57.5	47.8	30.1	183.0	349.6
4	37.7	66.9	38.2	74.1	40.3	64.7	39.4	69.3	41.3	63.2	196.9	338.2
5	24.9	119.5	24.0	128.5	24.9	125.6	23.5	129.0	25.1	126.2	122.4	628.8
6	30.3	106.6	29.1	111.4	31.7	99.0	28.3	126.1	34.2	95.6	153.6	538.7
7	32.7	106.1	33.8	107.2	34.8	97.5	35.4	86.0	37.8	88.8	174.5	485.6
8	34.5	61.5	31.5	83.4	31.1	93.9	36.1	69.0	38.5	46.9	171.7	354.7
9	31.4	80.5	30.5	106.5	34.6	76.7	30.9	91.8	36.8	68.2	164.2	423.7
10	21.2	149.2	25.3	151.6	23.5	170.1	24.8	155.2	24.6	146.1	119.4	772.2
11	30.8	78.7	26.4	116.9	33.2	71.8	33.5	70.3	43.8	40.9	167.7	378.6
Block totals $X_{\cdot j}$ and $Y_{\cdot j}$	348.8	990.7	342.1	1,134.9	373.8	995.9	382.4	962.2	422.2	806.8	1,869.3	4,890.5

† In milligrams per 100 g dry weight.
‡ Based on 100 g of freshly harvested beans.
Source: Data used with permission of Bowers and Permenter, Mississippi State College, State College, Mississippi.

Sums of products for blocks are

$$R_{XX} = \frac{\sum_j X_{\cdot j}^2}{t} - \frac{X_{\cdot\cdot}^2}{rt} = 367.85$$

$$R_{YY} = 4{,}968.94$$

$$R_{XY} = \frac{\sum_j X_{\cdot j} Y_{\cdot j}}{t} - \frac{X_{\cdot\cdot} Y_{\cdot\cdot}}{rt} = -1{,}246.66$$

Sums of products for treatments (varieties) are

$$T_{XX} = \frac{\sum_i X_{i\cdot}^2}{r} - \frac{X_{\cdot\cdot}^2}{rt} = 2{,}166.71$$

$$T_{YY} = 51{,}018.18$$

$$T_{XY} = \frac{\sum_i X_{i\cdot} Y_{i\cdot}}{r} - \frac{X_{\cdot\cdot} Y_{\cdot\cdot}}{rt} = -9{,}784.14$$

Sums of products for error are found by subtraction and are

$$E_{XX} = \sum (X_{ij} - \bar{X}_{..})^2 - R_{XX} - T_{XX}$$
$$= 2{,}916.22 - 367.85 - 2{,}166.71 = 381.66$$
$$E_{YY} = \sum (Y_{ij} - \bar{Y}_{..})^2 - R_{YY} - T_{YY} = 5{,}947.30$$
$$E_{XY} = \sum (X_{ij} - \bar{X}_{..})(Y_{ij} - \bar{Y}_{..}) - R_{XY} - T_{XY}$$
$$= -12{,}226.14 - (-1{,}246.66) - (-9{,}784.14)$$
$$= -1{,}195.34$$

These results are entered in Table 17.3.

These sums of products contain the material for the analyses of variance of X and Y as well as the analysis of covariance. Thus, to test the hypothesis of no differences among unadjusted variety means for ascorbic acid content Y,

$$F = \frac{T_{YY}/(t-1)}{E_{YY}/(r-1)(t-1)} = \frac{51{,}018.18/10}{5{,}947.30/40} = 34.31^{**} \qquad 10 \text{ and } 40 \text{ df}$$

We conclude that real differences exist among unadjusted variety means for ascorbic acid content.

To test the hypothesis of no differences among variety means for percentage of dry matter X at harvest,

$$F = \frac{T_{XX}/(t-1)}{E_{XX}/(r-1)(t-1)} = \frac{2{,}166.71/10}{381.66/40} = 22.71^{**} \qquad 10 \text{ and } 40 \text{ df}$$

We conclude that real differences exist among variety means for percentage dry matter in the beans at harvest.

Table 17.3 Analysis of covariance of data in Table 17.2

Source of variation	Sum of products				Y adjusted for X			
	df	X, X	X, Y	Y, Y	df	SS	MS	F
Total	54	2,916.22	−12,226.14	61,934.42				
Blocks	4	367.85	−1,246.66	4,968.94				
Treatments	10	2,166.71	−9,784.14	51,018.18				
Error	40	381.66	−1,195.34	5,947.30	39	2,203.45	56.50	
Treatments + error	50	2,548.37	−10,979.48	56,965.48	49	9,661.13		
Treatments adjusted					10	7,457.62	745.76	13.20**

The latter significant F illustrates a situation mentioned in Sec. 17.2, namely, significant differences may exist among treatment means for the independent variable and yet adjustment of the treatment means of the dependent variable is warranted. Differences in maturity as measured by percentage of dry matter are not necessarily treatment effects. They occur in part because all varieties were not harvested at the same stage of maturity. In any case, we want to adjust variety ascorbic acid means to the same percentage of dry matter or maturity since this is the logical stage at which to compare varieties.

To test the hypothesis that no differences exist among the adjusted treatment means, it is necessary to calculate the error and treatment plus error sums of squares of Y adjusted for their respective regressions on the covariate X. The sum of squares for testing the hypothesis of no differences among adjusted treatment means is the difference between these adjusted sums of squares. The procedure was outlined in Table 17.1 and is illustrated in Table 17.3.

For error, the regression coefficient is given by Eq. (17.5) as

$$b_{YX} = \frac{E_{XY}}{E_{XX}} = \frac{-1{,}195.34}{381.66}$$

$$= -3.13 \text{ mg ascorbic acid per } 1\% \text{ of dry matter}$$

The sum of squares of Y attributable to regression on X is

$$b_{YX}E_{XY} = \frac{(E_{XY})^2}{E_{XX}} = \frac{(-1{,}195.34)^2}{381.66} = 3{,}743.85 \qquad \text{with 1 df}$$

The adjusted sum of squares is implied in Eq. (17.6) as

$$E_{YY} - \frac{(E_{XY})^2}{E_{XX}} = 5{,}947.30 - 3{,}743.74$$

$$= 2{,}203.45 \qquad \text{with } (r-1)(t-1) - 1 = 39 \text{ df}$$

and the residual variance is

$$s^2_{Y \cdot X} = \frac{2{,}203.45}{39} = 56.50$$

For treatment plus error, the adjusted sum of squares is

$$S_{YY} - \frac{(S_{XY})^2}{S_{XX}} = 56{,}965.48 - \frac{(10{,}979.48)^2}{2{,}548.37}$$

$$= 9{,}661.13 \qquad \text{with } r(t-1) - 1 = 49 \text{ df}$$

For adjusted treatment means, the sum of squares is the difference between the treatments plus error and the error sums of squares, that is,

$$\text{Adjusted } T_{YY} = 9{,}661.13 - 2{,}203.45 = 7{,}457.62 \qquad \text{with } t - 1 = 10 \text{ df}$$

The adjusted sum of squares for error is used to estimate the variance within each and all populations of Y values. Homogeneity of variance is assumed. The adjusted sum of squares for treatments plus error is an estimate of the sum of squares to be expected for the two combined sources if all treatment $\bar{X}$'s were equal.

For the given adjustments to be both valid and useful, it is necessary for the linear regression of Y on X to be homogeneous for all treatments adjusted for block differences. Homogeneity of regression is, then, an assumption, as is homogeneity of error variance after adjustment for regression. There is no simple way of testing the homogeneity assumptions.

To test the hypothesis of no differences among treatment means for Y adjusted for the regression of Y on X,

$$F = \frac{\text{MS(adjusted treatment means)}}{s_{Y \cdot X}^2}$$

$$= \frac{745.76}{56.50} = 13.20^{**} \qquad \text{with 10 and 39 df}$$

The highly significant F is evidence that real differences exist among the treatment means for Y when adjusted for X. If the unadjusted but not the adjusted treatment means had been significant, it would indicate that differences among the unadjusted means merely reflected differences in maturity and not in ascorbic acid content at a common maturity.

Exercise 17.5.1 Test adjusted treatment means for Exercise 17.4.1. Test the null hypothesis that $\beta = 0$.

Exercise 17.5.2 Test adjusted treatment means for Exercise 17.4.2. Test $H_0: \beta = 0$.

Exercise 17.5.3 Test adjusted treatment means for Exercise 17.4.3. Test $H_0: \beta = 0$.

Exercise 17.5.4 Test adjusted treatment means for Exercise 17.4.4. Test $H_0: \beta = 0$.

17.6 Adjustment of Treatment Means

The formula for adjusting treatment means is essentially given by Eq. (17.4), and is an application of the procedure given as Eq. (10.9). The basic idea is also illustrated in Fig. 17.1. In familiar notation, the equation for an adjusted treatment mean is given by

$$\hat{\bar{Y}}_{i\cdot} = \bar{Y}_{i\cdot} - b_{YX}(\bar{X}_{i\cdot} - \bar{X}_{\cdot\cdot}) \tag{17.7}$$

$b_{YX} = b$ is the error regression coefficient. Adjusted treatment means are estimates of what the treatment means would be if all $\bar{X}_{i\cdot}$'s were at $\bar{X}_{\cdot\cdot}$. Adjusted treatment means are given in Table 17.4 for the data of Table 17.2.

Table 17.4 Adjustment of treatment means; data of Table 17.2

Variety no.	Mean percentage of dry matter $\bar{X}_{i\cdot}$	Deviation $\bar{X}_{i\cdot} - \bar{X}_{\cdot\cdot}$	Adjustment $b_{YX}(\bar{X}_{i\cdot} - \bar{X}_{\cdot\cdot})$	Observed mean ascorbic acid content $\bar{Y}_{i\cdot}$	Adjusted mean ascorbic acid content $\hat{\bar{Y}}_{i\cdot} = \bar{Y}_{i\cdot} - b_{YX} \times (\bar{X}_{i\cdot} - \bar{X}_{\cdot\cdot})$
1	35.42	1.43	−4.48	88.10 (5)†	92.59 (5)
2	47.76	13.77	−43.10	35.98(11)	79.12 (8)
3	36.60	2.61	−8.17	69.92 (9)	78.10 (9)
4	39.38	5.39	−16.87	67.64(10)	84.53 (6)
5	24.48	−9.51	29.77	125.76 (2)	95.98 (4)
6	30.72	−3.27	10.24	107.74 (3)	97.51 (3)
7	34.90	0.91	−2.85	97.12 (4)	99.98 (2)
8	34.34	0.35	−1.10	70.94 (8)	72.04(11)
9	32.84	−1.15	3.60	84.74 (6)	81.15 (7)
10	23.88	−10.11	31.64	154.44 (1)	122.78 (1)
11	33.54	−0.45	1.41	75.72 (7)	74.32(10)
	$\bar{X} = 33.99$	$\sum = -0.03$‡	$\sum = +0.09$‡	$\bar{Y}_{\cdot\cdot} = 88.92$‡	Mean = 88.92‡

† Ranks.
‡ Theoretically $\sum (\bar{X}_{i\cdot} - \bar{X}_{\cdot\cdot}) = 0$. Hence $\sum b_{YX}(\bar{X}_{i\cdot} - \bar{X}_{\cdot\cdot}) = 0$ and $\sum \bar{Y}_{i\cdot} = \sum \hat{\bar{Y}}_{i\cdot}$. In practice, rounding errors may appear.

The standard error of an adjusted treatment mean is simply a modified Eq. (10.13). That is,

$$s_{\hat{\bar{Y}}_{i\cdot}} = s_{Y\cdot X}\sqrt{\frac{1}{r} + \frac{(\bar{X}_{i\cdot} - \bar{X}_{\cdot\cdot})^2}{E_{XX}}}$$

The standard error of the difference between two adjusted treatment means is given by Wishart (17.12) as

$$s_{\hat{\bar{Y}}_{i\cdot} - \hat{\bar{Y}}_{i'\cdot}} = \sqrt{s^2_{Y\cdot X}\left[\frac{2}{r} + \frac{(\bar{X}_{i\cdot} - \bar{X}_{i'\cdot})^2}{E_{XX}}\right]} \tag{17.8}$$

For example, to compare varieties 7 and 10 (assuming a legitimate reason), we require

$$s_{\hat{\bar{Y}}_{7\cdot} - \hat{\bar{Y}}_{10\cdot}} = \sqrt{56.50\left[\frac{2}{5} + \frac{(34.90 - 23.88)^2}{381.66}\right]} = 6.38 \text{ mg ascorbic acid}$$

The comparison is of the adjusted means $\hat{\bar{Y}}_{7\cdot} = 99.97$ and $\hat{\bar{Y}}_{10\cdot} = 122.78$, the difference obviously being significant.

Equation (17.8) necessitates a separate calculation for each comparison. This is probably justified if the experiment took an appreciable amount of time or was more than a preliminary experiment. However, Finney (17.5) suggests the following approximate $s_{\hat{Y}_{i\cdot}-\hat{Y}_{i'\cdot}}$, which utilizes an average in place of the separate $(\bar{X}_{i\cdot} - \bar{X}_{i'\cdot})$'s required by Eq. (17.8). The formula is

$$s_{\hat{Y}_{i\cdot}-\hat{Y}_{i'\cdot}} = \sqrt{\frac{2s^2_{Y\cdot X}}{r}\left[1 + \frac{T_{XX}}{(t-1)E_{XX}}\right]} \tag{17.9}$$

From Table 17.3,

$$s_{\hat{Y}_{i\cdot}-\hat{Y}_{i'\cdot}} = \sqrt{\frac{2(56.50)}{5}\left[1 + \frac{2{,}166.71}{10(381.66)}\right]} = 5.95 \text{ mg ascorbic acid}$$

for our example. For treatment means with unequal numbers, replace $2/r$ in Eqs. (17.8) and (17.9) by $(1/r_1 + 1/r_2)$. Cochran and Cox (17.2) state that Finney's approximation is usually close enough if error degrees of freedom exceed 20, since the contribution from sampling errors in b_{YX}, the adjustment factor, is small.

If variation among the $\bar{X}_{i\cdot}$'s is significant, for example, due to treatments, the approximation formula may lead to serious errors and should not be used. This would apply here also, since there were significant differences among treatment means for dry matter X.

Exercise 17.6.1 Compute adjusted treatment means for the eight treatments of Exercise 17.4.1. Compute the standard deviation of the mean for ration 111. Compute the standard deviation of the difference between means for treatments 000 and 111.

Compute the adjusted treatment means for the two means used to measure main effect A. Compute the standard deviation of the difference between these means. Test the null hypothesis of no A main effect.

Use Eq. (17.9) to compute an approximate standard deviation between A means. Compare this with the exact standard deviation. Were there significant differences among treatment means for the covariate?

Exercise 17.6.2 Compute the three adjusted treatment means for Exercise 17.4.2. Find standard deviations for the three differences.

Use Finney's proposal, Eq. (17.9), to find a single standard deviation approximating those just computed. Were there significant differences among the treatment means for the covariate?

Exercise 17.6.3 Consider Exercise 17.4.3. What formula will you use to compare two adjusted treatment means based on different numbers of observations?

Exercise 17.6.4 Compute the four adjusted treatment means for the four treatments of Exercise 17.4.4.

Compute the two adjusted means for braille and print. For treatment 1 and treatment 2. Compute the standard deviation for the difference between braille and print means. Between means for treatment 1 and treatment 2. Test the null hypothesis of no difference between adjusted population means for braille and print. For treatment 1 and treatment 2.

17.7 Increase in Precision due to Covariance

To test the effectiveness of covariance as a means of error control, a comparison is made of the variance of a treatment mean before and after adjustment for the independent variable X. The error mean square before adjustment is $5{,}947.30/40 = 148.68$ with 40 degrees of freedom and after adjustment is 56.50 with 39 degrees of freedom. It is necessary to adjust the latter value to allow for sampling error in the regression coefficient used in adjusting. The *effective error mean square* after adjustment for X is given by

$$s^2_{Y \cdot X}\left[1 + \frac{T_{XX}}{(t-1)E_{XX}}\right] = 56.50\left[1 + \frac{2{,}166.71}{10(381.66)}\right] = 88.58 \qquad (17.10)$$

An estimate of the relative precision is $(148.68/88.58)100 = 168$ percent. This indicates that 100 replicates with covariance are as effective as 168 without, a ratio of approximately 3 : 5.

Exercise 17.7.1 Compute the effective mean square for Exercise 17.4.1. From the relative precision, conclude how many blocks would be required to give the same precision without using the covariate.

Exercise 17.7.2 Compute the effective mean square for Exercise 17.4.2. From the relative precision, conclude how many replications would be required to give the same precision without using the covariate.

Exercise 17.7.3 Compute the effective mean square for Exercise 17.4.4. From the relative precision, conclude how many replications would be required to give the same precision without using the covariate.

17.8 Partition of Covariance

The term analysis of covariance implies a use not generally stressed, namely, the partitioning carried out in the cross-products column. This is extended in Table 17.5 to include regression and correlation coefficients.

When the null hypothesis of no treatment differences among adjusted treatment means is true, treatments and error provide independent estimates

Table 17.5 Partitioning for a covariance; data of Table 17.2

Source of covariation	df	Sum of products	b_{YX}	r
Total	54	−12,226.14	−4.19	−0.910
Blocks	4	−1,246.66	−3.39	−0.922
Treatments	10	−9,784.14	−4.52	−0.931
Error	40	−1,195.34	−3.13	−0.793

of common regression and correlation coefficients. If a test of adjusted treatment means shows significance, then it may be presumed that treatment and error regressions differ. If the test does not show significance, then there may or may not be a treatment regression. If there is a treatment regression, then it is the same as error regression. In rare instances, it may be desired to test the homogeneity of the regression coefficients. The appropriate numerator sum of squares is given by

Treatment versus error regression SS

$$= \frac{T_{XY}^2}{T_{XX}} + \frac{E_{XY}^2}{E_{XX}} - \frac{(T_{XY} + E_{XY})^2}{T_{XX} + E_{XX}}$$

$$= \frac{(-9{,}784.14)^2}{2{,}166.71} + \frac{(-1{,}195.34)^2}{381.66} - \frac{(-10{,}979.48)^2}{2{,}548.37} \qquad (17.11)$$

$$= 621.31$$

Observe that each term is a sum of squares; the first for a regression using treatment means; the second for a regression using residuals; the third for a pooled regression. Together they are a variance between two regression coefficients with appropriate weights, as discussed in Sec. 10.13.

The appropriate variance for testing the null hypothesis of homogeneity is generally considered to be the error variance. [The use of deviations from treatment regression for estimating the variance of the treatment regression coefficient and of error variance for the error regression coefficient has been suggested. These variances will often differ and require a test procedure like that of Sec. 5.9; divisors for Eqs. (5.15) will be T_{XX} and E_{XX} rather than n_1 and n_2.] For our example,

$$F = \frac{621.31}{56.50} = 11.00^{**} \qquad \text{with 1 and 39 df}$$

This test is equivalent to using the t-test of Eq. (10.19).

The test of homogeneity of treatment and error regressions is sometimes presented in an alternate form. The following argument may be used to explain and justify the procedure.

1. Compute the sum of squares for adjusted treatment means. This may be considered to be the sum of squares of deviations of treatment means from a common regression line, a moving average. Since the slope of the regression line is obtained from error, a degree of freedom is not partitioned from those available for treatment means.

2. Compute the sum of squares of deviations of treatment means from their own regression. This will have $t - 2$ degrees of freedom since the means supply the estimate of the regression coefficient.
3. Subtract the latter sum of squares from the former. If the regressions are the same, the result should be no larger than one would expect from random sampling. If the result cannot reasonably be attributed to chance and the null hypothesis, then we conclude that the regressions are not homogeneous.

For our example,

$$\text{Deviations from treatment regression} = T_{YY} - \frac{T_{XY}^2}{T_{XX}}$$

$$= 51{,}018.08 - \frac{(-9{,}784.14)^2}{2{,}166.71} = 6{,}836.27 \qquad \text{with } t - 2 = 9 \text{ df}$$

Treatment versus error regression SS

$$= \text{adj } T_{YY} - \text{deviations from treatment regression}$$

$$= 7{,}457.57 \text{ (10 df)} - 6{,}836.27 \text{ (9 df)} = 621.30 \qquad \text{with 1 df}$$

Again, $F = 621.30/56.50 = 11.00^{**}$ with 1 and 39 degrees of freedom. Since differences among adjusted treatment means were significant, this result was to be expected and the test would not normally be made.

A comparison of correlation coefficients may be made using the appropriate procedure of Sec. 11.5. This procedure indicates no difference between correlation coefficients. That this can happen, that is, that regression coefficients may be very different while correlation coefficients are the same, can be seen from the relation

$$r = b_{YX}\frac{s_X}{s_Y}$$

Two r's may be very much alike in spite of very different b_{YX}'s provided that the ratio s_X/s_Y counters these differences.

17.9 Homogeneity of Regression Coefficients

Where the experimental design is a completely random one, the regression of Y on X can be computed for each treatment. In this case, the usual assumption of homogeneity of the regression coefficients can be posed as a null hypothesis and tested by an appropriate F-test in an analysis of covariance. (For other designs, we are not aware of methods presently available for testing homogeneity of regression coefficients.)

The procedure follows and is summarized in Table 17.6.

Table 17.6 Homogeneity of within-treatment regressions for a completely random design

Treatment	df	$\sum (X - \bar{X})^2$	$\sum (X - \bar{X})(Y - \bar{Y})$	$\sum (Y - \bar{Y})^2$	df	Residual SS
1	$n_1 - 1$	$E_{XX}(1)$	$E_{XY}(1)$	$E_{YY}(1)$	$n_1 - 2$	SS_1(residuals)
2	$n_2 - 1$	$E_{XX}(2)$	$E_{XY}(2)$	$E_{YY}(2)$	$n_2 - 2$	SS_2(residuals)
⋮	⋮	⋮	⋮	⋮	⋮	⋮
t	$n_t - 1$	$E_{XX}(t)$	$E_{XY}(t)$	$E_{YY}(t)$	$n_t - 2$	SS_t(residuals)
Residuals from individual regressions					$\sum n_i - 2t$	$\sum SS_i$(residuals) = pooled error = A
Totals for single regression	$\sum n_i - t$	$\sum_i E_{XX}(i)$	$\sum_i E_{XY}(i)$	$\sum_i E_{YY}(i)$	$\sum n_i - t - 1$	$\sum E_{YY}(i) - \frac{[\sum E_{XY}(i)]^2}{\sum E_{XX}(i)} = B$
Difference for homogeneity of regressions					$t - 1$	$B - A$

To test homogeneity of regression, $F = [(B - A)/(t - 1)]/[A/(\sum n_i - 2t)]$, with $t - 1$ and $\sum n_i - 2t$ df.

1. Compute

$$\sum_j (X_{ij} - \bar{X}_{i\cdot})^2 \qquad \sum_j (X_{ij} - \bar{X}_{i\cdot})(Y_{ij} - \bar{Y}_{i\cdot}) \qquad \text{and} \qquad \sum_j (Y_{ij} - \bar{Y}_{i\cdot})^2$$

for each treatment.

For the ith treatment, call these $E_{XX}(i)$, $E_{XY}(i)$, and $E_{YY}(i)$, respectively.

2. From the above and for each treatment, compute

$$\text{SS}_i(\text{regression}) = \frac{E_{XY}^2(i)}{E_{XX}(i)}$$

(not shown in Table 17.6), and the residual sum of squares

$$\text{SS}_i(\text{residuals}) = E_{YY}(i) - \frac{E_{XY}^2(i)}{E_{XX}(i)}, \qquad i = 1, \ldots, t.$$

See Table 17.6. Fitting of t means and t regression coefficients has now been done.

3. Total the sums of squares of residuals to give the residual sum of squares of deviations from individual regression lines. This is the residual after the fittings in 2 and is denoted by A in Table 17.6. It has $\sum (n_i - 2) = \sum n_i - 2t$ degrees of freedom.
4. Total the $E_{XX}(i)$, $E_{XY}(i)$, and $E_{YY}(i)$ over all treatments.
5. From the results in step 4, compute the sum of squares of Y attributable to regression on X, and the residual sum of squares. This residual sum of squares is of deviations from individual regression lines, each passing through its own $(\bar{X}, \bar{Y})$ but all having a common regression coefficient. Here t means and one regression have been fitted. The residual is denoted by B in Table 17.6 and has $\sum (n_i - 1) - 1 = \sum n_i - t - 1$ degrees of freedom.
6. Compute $B - A$. This is the amount of the total sum of squares for Y that can be attributed to differences among the regression coefficients. It is necessarily positive, since we can always do better by fitting several coefficients rather than one.

The quantity $B - A$ can also be found by computing $\sum \text{SS}_i(\text{regression})$ with t df and, from this total, subtracting $[\sum E_{XY}(i)]^2/\sum E_{XX}(i)$ with 1 df. The difference $B - A$ has $t - 1$ degrees of freedom. The appropriate error term is the mean square of the deviations from the individual regressions.

Exercise 17.9.1 Test the null hypothesis of homogeneity of regression coefficients for the data of Exercise 10.8.1. Compare the resulting F with the value t^2, where t is that obtained in Exercise 10.8.1.

Exercise 17.9.2 In Exercise 17.4.2, the data of Exercise 7.3.3 were analyzed as a covariance problem. What does the evidence tell us about the homogeneity of the three regression coefficients that might be computed?

Exercise 17.9.3 Repeat Exercise 17.9.2 referring to Exercises 7.4.2 and 17.4.3.

Exercise 17.9.4 In Exercise 17.4.4, the data of Exercise 15.3.3 were analyzed as a covariance problem. Test the homogeneity of the four regression coefficients assumed to be homogeneous at that time. How many df were available to estimate each regression coefficient?

17.10 Covariance Where the Treatment Sum of Squares Is Partitioned

The application of covariance analysis to a factorial experiment is illustrated for the data in Table 17.7, from Wishart (17.13). The experiment was a 3×2 factorial in a randomized complete block design of five replications. The treatments were three rations, factor A, and two sexes, factor B. The procedure is applicable whenever a treatment sum of squares is to be partitioned.

The analysis is presented in Table 17.8. The computational procedure is the same as in Sec. 17.5 except that the treatment sum of squares is partitioned into main effects and interaction components as in Chap. 15. For easy reference, write $T_{XY} = A_{XY} + B_{XY} + AB_{XY}$ to denote the partitioning of the sum of cross products for treatments into components for rations A, sex

Table 17.7 Initial weights X and gains in weight Y in pounds for bacon pigs in a feeding trial

		Rations						Totals	
		a_1		a_2		a_3			
Pens (blocks)	Sex	X	Y	X	Y	X	Y	X	Y
1	M = b_1	38	9.52	39	8.51	48	9.11		
	F = b_2	48	9.94	48	10.00	48	9.75	269	56.83
2	M	35	8.21	38	9.95	37	8.50		
	F	32	9.48	32	9.24	28	8.66	202	54.04
3	M	41	9.32	46	8.43	42	8.90		
	F	35	9.32	41	9.34	33	7.63	238	52.94
4	M	48	10.56	40	8.86	42	9.51		
	F	46	10.90	46	9.68	50	10.37	272	59.88
5	M	43	10.42	40	9.20	40	8.76		
	F	32	8.82	37	9.67	30	8.57	222	55.44
Totals	M	205	48.03	203	44.95	209	44.78	617	137.76
	F	193	48.46	204	47.93	189	44.98	586	141.37
	M + F	398	96.49	407	92.88	398	89.76	1,203	279.13

Table 17.8 Analysis of covariance for the data in Table 17.7

		Sums of products			Y adjusted for X			
Source of variation	df	X, X	X, Y	Y, Y	df	SS	MS	F
Total	29	1,108.70	78.507	16.3453				
Blocks (pens)	4	605.87	39.905	4.8518				
Rations	2	5.40	−0.147	2.2686				
Sex	1	32.03	−3.730	0.4344				
Rations × sex	2	22.47	3.112	0.4761				
Error	20	442.93	39.367	8.3144	19	4.8156	0.2535	
Rations + error	22	448.33	39.220	10.5830	21	7.1520		
Difference for testing adjusted ration means					2	2.3366	1.1683	4.61*
Sex + error	21	474.96	35.637	8.7488	20	6.0749		
Difference for testing adjusted sex means					1	1.2594	1.2594	4.97*
Ration × sex + error	22	465.40	42.479	8.7905	21	4.9133		
Difference for testing adjusted ration × sex interaction					2	0.0977	0.0489	0.19

B, and interaction AB. A similar notation is used with T_{XX} and T_{YY}. To partition the treatment sum of cross products, compute

$$A_{XY} = \frac{\sum_i (a_i)_X(a_i)_Y}{rb} - \frac{(\sum X_{ij})(\sum Y_{ij})}{rt}$$

$$= \frac{398(96.49) + 407(92.88) + 398(89.76)}{5(2)} - \frac{1{,}203(279.13)}{5(6)}$$

$$= -0.147$$

$$B_{XY} = \frac{\sum (b_j)_X(b_j)_Y}{ra} - \frac{(\sum X_{ij})(\sum Y_{ij})}{rt}$$

$$= \frac{617(137.76) + 586(141.37)}{5(3)} - \frac{1{,}203(279.13)}{5(6)} = -3.730$$

$$AB_{XY} = T_{XY} - A_{XY} - B_{XY}$$

$$= \frac{205(48.03) + \cdots + 189(44.98)}{5} - \frac{1{,}203(279.13)}{5(6)} - (-0.147)$$

$$- (-3.730) = 3.112$$

where $(a_i)_X$ is the total of X values for level i of factor A, and so on, with $t = ab$. The directly computed sums of products are entered in Table 17.8 and the residuals obtained by subtracting the block, sex, ration, and ration times sex components from the total sum of products. To test the null hypotheses of no differences among levels of factor A, levels of factor B, and of no AB interaction, after adjustment for the concomitant variable, the procedure is basically that of Tables 17.1 and 17.3. However, each hypothesis is tested separately, as shown in Table 17.8. Thus, the adjusted sum of squares for testing the null hypothesis about rations is the difference between the adjusted sum of squares for rations plus error and the adjusted sum of squares for error. For example, the adjusted sum of squares for error is

$$E_{YY} - \frac{(E_{XY})^2}{E_{XX}} = 8.3144 - \frac{(39.367)^2}{442.93}$$

$$= 4.8156 \qquad \text{with } (r-1)(t-1) - 1 = 19 \text{ df}$$

The adjusted sum of squares for rations plus error is

$$(A_{YY} + E_{YY}) - \frac{(A_{XY} + E_{XY})^2}{A_{XX} + E_{XX}}$$

$$= 2.2686 + 8.3144 - \frac{[(-0.147) + (39.367)]^2}{[5.40 + 442.93]}$$

$$= 7.1520 \qquad \text{with } (a-1) + (r-1)(t-1) - 1 = 21 \text{ df}$$

The difference

$$\left[A_{YY} + E_{YY} - \frac{(A_{XY} + E_{XY})^2}{A_{XX} + E_{XX}}\right] - \left[E_{YY} - \frac{(E_{XY})^2}{E_{XX}}\right] = 7.1520 - 4.8155$$

$$= 2.3366 \qquad \text{with } a - 1 = 2 \text{ df}$$

is the adjusted sum of squares for rations.

Adjusted sums of squares for sex and rations times sex are obtained similarly.

F-tests of the three null hypotheses are made with the adjusted error mean square in the denominator. For example, to test the null hypothesis that there are no differences among ration means after adjustment to a common $\bar{X}$, $F = 1.1683/0.2534$ with 2 and 19 degrees of freedom.

In an experiment where the treatment sum of squares is partitioned to test several null hypotheses, the procedure above is time-consuming but justifiable for most experiments. Cochran and Cox (17.2) give the following time-saving approximation. Prepare an analysis of adjusted Y's, that is, of $[Y - b(X - \bar{X})]$'s where $b = E_{XY}/E_{XX}$, from the preliminary analysis of covariance. This is illustrated in Table 17.9, using the covariance analysis in Table 17.8. The analysis of $Y - b(X - \bar{X})$ is accomplished by computing

Table 17.9 Analysis of variance of $[Y - b(X - \bar{X})]$ for the data of Tables 17.7 and 17.8

Source of variation	df	Sum of squares	Mean square	F	F†
Rations	2	2.3374	1.1687	4.61*	4.61*
Sex	1	1.3507	1.3507	5.33*	4.97*
Rations × sex	2	0.1004	0.0502	0.20	0.19
Error	19	4.8156	0.2535		

† F from Table 17.8.

$E_{YY} - 2bE_{XY} + b^2E_{XX}$ for error and corresponding quantities for each source of variation for which it is desired to test a null hypothesis; in all cases, $b = E_{XY}/E_{XX} = 39.367/442.93 = 0.0889$ lb of gain per pound of initial weight. For example, for sex,

$$0.4344 - 2(0.0889)(-3.730) + (0.0889)^2(32.03) = 1.3507$$

This approximate method gives the correct residual mean square within rounding errors; sums of squares for main effects and interactions, and consequently F values, are larger than those obtained using the exact method of Table 17.8. Overestimation of F is seldom great when variation in X is random and should be checked by the exact procedure only when just significant. The approximate procedure should not be used when X is influenced by treatments or is otherwise larger than such as is due to chance, since the F values may be considerably in error in such cases.

Adjusted treatment means are obtained as in Table 17.4.

Exercise 17.10.1 Compute exact tests of adjusted treatment means for each of the main effects and interactions for the data of Exercise 17.4.1. State what the null hypothesis is, in each case. Compare the results of your test for main effect A with the t-test of the same hypothesis in Exercise 17.6.1.

Exercise 17.10.2 Compute tests of main effects and interactions using Cochran and Cox's approximate procedure. Compare the resulting F values with those found for Exercise 17.10.1.

Exercise 17.10.3 Compute exact tests of adjusted treatment means for the two main effects and the interaction of Exercise 17.4.4. Compare the results with corresponding ones for Exercise 17.6.4.

17.11 Estimation of Missing Observations by Covariance

To illustrate this use of covariance, consider the data of Table 17.10, from Tucker et al. (17.11). Although all observations are available, assume that the one in the upper left corner is missing.

Table 17.10 Mean ascorbic acid content of three 2-g samples of turnip greens, in milligrams per 100 g dry weight

Block (day)	1	2	3	4	5	Totals
Treatment:						
A		887	897	850	975	3,609
B	857	1,189	918	968	909	4,841
C	917	1,072	975	930	954	4,848
Totals	1,774	3,148	2,790	2,748	2,838	13,298

The procedure, which gives an unbiased estimate of both treatment and error sums of squares, is:

1. Set $Y = 0$ for the missing plot.
2. Define a covariate as $X = 0$ for an observed Y, $X = +1$ (or -1) for $Y = 0$.
3. Carry out the analysis of covariance (see Table 17.11).
4. Compute $b = E_{XY}/E_{XX}$ and change sign to estimate the missing value.

Table 17.11 Analysis of covariance as an alternative to missing plot equation for data of Table 17.10

		Sums of products					
Source	df	X, X	X, Y	Y, Y	df	Adjusted SS(Y)	MS
Total	14	$1 - \frac{1}{15} = \frac{14}{15} = \frac{\text{df}}{n}$	-886.53	945,296			
Blocks	4	$\frac{1}{3} - \frac{1}{15} = \frac{4}{15} = \frac{\text{df}}{n}$	-295.20	359,823			
Treatments	2	$\frac{1}{5} - \frac{1}{15} = \frac{2}{15} = \frac{\text{df}}{n}$	-164.73	203,533			
Residual	8	By subtraction $= \frac{8}{15} = \frac{\text{df}}{n}$	-426.60	381,940	7	40,713	5,816
Treatments + residual	10	$\frac{10}{15} = \frac{\text{df}}{n}$	-591.33	585,473	9	60,966	
Treatments adjusted					2	20,253	10,126

$$\text{Missing plot} = -b = \frac{426.60}{8/15} = 800 \text{ (approx.)}$$

The missing plot value, $-b$, is essentially an adjustment to the so-called observation $Y = 0$, to give an estimate of the Y that would have been obtained if X had been 0 instead of 1.

Missing plot Eq. (9.8) gives a value of 800 for a residual mean square of 5,816 (the same results as given by the covariance procedure) and an adjusted treatment sum of squares of 25,293, which is biased. Equation (9.9) may be used to compute the bias when Eq. (9.8) is used. The analysis of covariance procedure leads directly to an unbiased test of adjusted treatment means.

On application, the covariance method for missing plots is seen to be convenient and simple. The technique can be extended to handle several missing plots by introducing a new independent variate for each missing plot and using multiple covariance, as illustrated in the next section. An example of the use of covariance for a missing plot along with the usual type of covariate is given by Bartlett (17.1).

Exercise 17.11.1 Apply the covariance technique to the missing plot problem given as Exercise 9.6.1. Obtain the missing plot value, error mean square, and treatment mean square. Compare these results with those of Exercise 9.6.1.

Exercise 17.11.2 If there had been missing observations in the data used in Exercises 17.4.2 and 17.4.4, would a missing observation technique be needed? Why?

17.12 Covariance with Two Independent Variables

Sometimes a dependent variable is affected by two or more independent variables. Multiple covariance analysis is a method of analyzing such data. An example of such data is given in Table 17.12 with two independent variables X_1 and X_2 measuring initial weight of and forage (Ladino clover) consumed by guinea pigs and a dependent variable Y measuring gain in weight. {It can be shown [see Steel (17.10)] that when initial weight is a covariate, final weight as an alternative to gain in weight leads to the same covariance analysis, in that adjusted sums of squares for the two analyses are identical.}

Initial weight is unaffected by the treatments but is included to give error control and to adjust treatment means. Initial weight was largely the basis for assigning the animals to the three blocks, but there was still enough variation remaining to advise its measurement. The amount of forage consumed is affected by treatments. It was introduced to assist in interpreting the data. Differences among unadjusted treatment means for gain in weight could be due to differences in palatability and thus consumption of forage, or in nutritive value or both. Thus the comparison among treatment means for gain adjusted for consumption gives information on the nutritive values of the treatments and thereby aids in the interpretation of the data.

Table 17.12 Initial weight X_1, forage consumed X_2, and gain in weight Y, all in grams, from a feeding trial with guinea pigs

Soil treatment	Unfertilized			Fertilized		
Block	X_1	X_2	Y	X_1	X_2	Y
			Miami silt loam			
1	220	1,155	224	222	1,326	237
2	246	1,423	289	268	1,559	265
3	262	1,576	280	314	1,528	256
Total	728	4,154	793	804	4,413	758
Mean	242.7	1,384.7	264.3	268.0	1,471.0	252.7
			Plainfield fine sand			
1	198	1,092	118	205	1,154	82
2	266	1,703	191	236	1,250	117
3	335	1,546	115	268	1,667	117
Total	799	4,341	424	709	4,071	316
Mean	266.3	1,447.0	141.3	236.3	1,357.0	105.3
			Almena silt loam			
1	213	1,573	242	188	1,381	184
2	236	1,730	270	259	1,363	129
3	288	1,593	198	300	1,564	212
Total	737	4,896	710	747	4,308	525
Mean	245.7	1,632.0	236.7	249.0	1,436.0	175.0
			Carlisle peat			
1	256	1,532	241	202	1,375	239
2	278	1,220	185	216	1,170	207
3	283	1,232	185	225	1,273	227
Total	817	3,984	611	643	3,818	673
Mean	272.3	1,328.0	203.7	214.3	1,272.7	224.3

$\sum X_1 = 5{,}984$ $\qquad \sum X_2 = 33{,}985$ $\qquad \sum Y = 4{,}810$

$\bar{X}_1 = 249.3$ $\qquad \bar{X}_2 = 1{,}416.0$ $\qquad \bar{Y} = 200.4$

$\sum X_1^2 = 1{,}526{,}422$ $\qquad \sum X_2^2 = 48{,}971{,}371$ $\qquad \sum Y^2 = 1{,}045{,}898$

$\sum X_1 X_2 = 8{,}555{,}357$ $\qquad \sum X_1 Y = 1{,}199{,}664$ $\qquad \sum X_2 Y = 6{,}904{,}945$

Source: Data obtained through the courtesy of W. Wedin, formerly of University of Wisconsin, Madison, Wisconsin.

The computational procedure follows:

1. Obtain sums of products as in Secs. 17.5 and 17.10. (This is a factorial experiment with fertilizers and soil types as factors.) The results are given in Table 17.13.
2. Calculate the necessary sets of partial regression coefficients and the corresponding sums of squares attributable to regression. By definition, partials have been adjusted for all other components in the model. Thus for the full model, we now need to solve Eqs. (17.12), where the E_{ij} are sums of squares or products of residuals after block and treatment effects have been removed. Compare with the error line in Table 17.1. Subscripts 1, 2, and Y refer to variables X_1, X_2, and Y.

$$E_{11}b_{Y1\cdot 2} + E_{12}b_{Y2\cdot 1} = E_{1Y}$$

$$E_{12}b_{Y1\cdot 2} + E_{22}b_{Y2\cdot 1} = E_{2Y} \qquad (17.12)$$

Relate these equations to matrix Eq. (14.10) and the numerical one following shortly after Eq. (14.11).

For each model associated with a null hypothesis, the corresponding treatment T_{ij}'s must be added to the error E_{ij}'s to give S_{ij}'s as in Table 17.1. Thus we have

2a. For *error* the equations are

$$6{,}159b_{Y1\cdot 2} + 17{,}778b_{Y2\cdot 1} = -229$$

$$17{,}778b_{Y1\cdot 2} + 473{,}377b_{Y2\cdot 1} = 66{,}179$$

Their solution is $b_{Y1\cdot 2} = -0.4944$ and $b_{Y2\cdot 1} = 0.1584$ for the full model.

2b. For *soil types plus error*, the equations are

$$6{,}639b_{Y1\cdot 2} + 20{,}784b_{Y2\cdot 1} = 383$$

$$20{,}784b_{Y1\cdot 2} + 639{,}210b_{Y2\cdot 1} = 71{,}187$$

Table 17.13 Sum of products for the multiple covariance analysis of the data in Table 17.12

Source of variation	df	Sums of products					
		X_1, X_1	X_2, X_2	X_1, X_2	X_1, Y	X_2, Y	Y, Y
Total	23	34,411	847,195	81,764	371	93,785	81,894
Blocks	2	20,397	122,438	49,815	917	2,835	496
Soil types	3	480	165,833	3,006	612	5,008	57,176
Fertilizers	1	1,320	24,384	5,674	1,973	8,479	2,948
Interaction	3	6,055	61,163	5,491	−2,902	11,284	5,545
Error	14	6,159	473,377	17,778	−229	66,179	15,729

Their solution is $b_{Y1\cdot 2} = -0.3240$ and $b_{Y2\cdot 1} = 0.1219$ for this reduced model. And so on.

3. Compute the sum of squares of Y adjusted for X_1 and X_2 from formula (17.13). This is the residual or error sum of squares.

$$E_{YY} - b_{Y1\cdot 2}E_{1Y} - b_{Y2\cdot 1}E_{2Y} \tag{17.13}$$

Note that the two terms with negative signs constitute SS(regression) = $\hat{\boldsymbol{\beta}}'_A \mathbf{X}'_A \mathbf{Y}_A$. We have

$$15{,}729 - (-0.4944)(.229) - 0.1584(66{,}179) = 5{,}133.0$$

with $14 - 2 = 12$ df

The adjusted sums of squares for soil types plus error, fertilizers plus error, and interaction plus error are similarly computed using S_{ij}'s. These values are shown in Table 17.14.

4. Compute sums of squares for adjusted treatment means as differences between the adjusted sum of squares for error computed at step 3 and the appropriate error plus treatment sum of squares computed at the same step.

For example, the adjusted sum of squares for *soil types* is

$$64{,}351.4 - 5{,}133.0 = 59{,}218.4 \qquad \text{with } 15 - 12 = 3 \text{ df}$$

The other adjusted sums of squares for use in testing the various null hypotheses are also given in Table 17.14.

Table 17.14 Computation of adjusted treatment sums of squares for the multiple covariance analysis begun in Table 17.13

		Sums of squares			Y adjusted for X_1 and X_2			
Source of variation	df	$S^{\dagger}_{YY}$	$b_{Y1\cdot 2}S^{\dagger}_{1Y}$	$b_{Y2\cdot 1}S^{\dagger}_{2Y}$	df	SS	MS	F
Error	14	15,729	113.2	10,482.8	12	5,133.0	427.8	
Soil types + error	17	72,905	−124.1	8,677.7	15	64,351.4		
Difference for testing adjusted soil types SS					3	59,218.4	19,739.5	46.14**
Fertilizers + error	15	18,677	−485.2	12,176.7	13	6,985.5		
Difference for testing adjusted fertilizer SS					1	1,852.5	1,852.5	4.33
Interaction + error	17	21,274	1,817.9	13,184.2	15	6,271.9		
Difference for testing adjusted interaction SS					3	1,138.9	379.6	0.89

† This S_{ij} notation is intended to include E_{ij}.

5. Compute F values as required. To test adjusted soil-type means

$$F = \frac{19{,}739.5}{427.8} = 46.14^{**} \qquad \text{with 3 and 12 df}$$

The other F values are also shown in Table 17.14.

Adjusted treatment means for gain in weight are computed from

$$\hat{\bar{Y}}_{i\cdot} = \bar{Y}_{i\cdot} - b_{Y1\cdot 2}(\bar{X}_{1i\cdot} - \bar{X}_{1\cdot\cdot}) - b_{Y2\cdot 1}(\bar{X}_{2i\cdot} - \bar{X}_{2\cdot\cdot}) \qquad (17.14)$$

where i refers to treatment for the $4(2) = 8$ treatment combinations, the numerical subscript refers to the corresponding independent variable, and $\bar{X}_{1\cdot\cdot}$ and $\bar{X}_{2\cdot\cdot}$ refer to general means. For example, the adjusted mean for gain in weight of animals fed forage from fertilized Miami silt loam is

$$252.7 - (-0.4944)(268.0 - 249.3) - (0.1584)(1{,}471 - 1{,}416) = 253.2 \text{ g}$$

All adjusted treatment means for gain in weight are given in Table 17.15. The feeding trial lasted 55 days and the *average* daily gains for both adjusted and unadjusted means are also given.

The standard error of a difference between two adjusted treatment means is given in Eq. (17.15) for treatments i and i'

$$s_{\hat{\bar{Y}}_{i\cdot} - \hat{\bar{Y}}_{i'\cdot}} = \sqrt{s^2_{Y\cdot 12}\left[\frac{2}{r} + \frac{(\bar{X}_{1i\cdot} - \bar{X}_{1i'\cdot})^2 E_{22} - 2(\bar{X}_{1i\cdot} - \bar{X}_{1i'\cdot}) \times (\bar{X}_{2i\cdot} - \bar{X}_{2i'\cdot})E_{12} + (\bar{X}_{2i\cdot} - \bar{X}_{2i'\cdot})^2 E_{11}}{E_{11}E_{22} - E_{12}^2}\right]} \qquad (17.15)$$

Table 17.15 Adjusted treatment means for data of Table 15.12

Treatment		$\bar{Y}_{i\cdot}$	$b_{Y1\cdot 2}(\bar{X}_{1i\cdot} - \bar{X}_{1\cdot\cdot})$	$b_{Y2\cdot 1}(\bar{X}_{2i\cdot} - \bar{X}_{2\cdot\cdot})$	$\hat{\bar{Y}}_{i\cdot}$†	Average daily gain‡ Adjusted	Average daily gain‡ Unadjusted
Miami silt loam	F	252.7	−9.2	+8.7	253.2	4.60	4.59
	Not F	264.3	+3.3	−5.0	266.0	4.84	4.81
Plainfield fine sand	F	105.3	+6.4	−9.3	108.2	1.97	1.92
	Not F	141.3	−8.4	+4.9	144.8	2.63	2.57
Almena silt loam	F	175.0	+0.1	+3.2	171.7	3.12	3.18
	Not F	236.7	+1.8	+34.2	200.7	3.65	4.30
Carlisle peat	F	224.3	+17.3	−22.7	229.7	4.18	4.08
	Not F	203.7	−11.4	−13.9	229.0	4.16	3.70
Total		1,603.3	0.1	0.1	1,603.3		

† $\hat{\bar{Y}}_{i\cdot} = \bar{Y}_{i\cdot} - b_{Y1\cdot 2}(\bar{X}_{1i\cdot} - \bar{X}_{1\cdot\cdot}) - b_{Y2\cdot 1}(\bar{X}_{2i\cdot} - \bar{X}_{2\cdot\cdot})$.

‡ The adjusted and unadjusted daily gains are obtained by dividing columns $\hat{\bar{Y}}_{i\cdot}$ and $\bar{Y}_{i\cdot}$ by 55, the number of days the animals were on trial.

Equation (17.15) is an application of Eq. (13.13). The $2/r$ looks after the variance of $\bar{Y}$ in Eq. (17.14). The remaining terms, E_{22}, $-E_{12}$, and E_{11}, with their common divisor $E_{11}E_{22} - E_{12}^2$, are elements in the variance-covariance matrix of the b's.

An approximate formula corresponding to Eq. (17.9) for a single covariate is given by

$$s_{\hat{\bar{Y}}_{i\cdot}-\hat{\bar{Y}}_{i'\cdot}} = \sqrt{\frac{2}{r} s_{Y\cdot 12}^2 \left[1 + \frac{T_{11}E_{22} - 2T_{12}E_{12} + T_{22}E_{11}}{(t-1)(E_{11}E_{22} - E_{12}^2)}\right]} \qquad (17.16)$$

As illustration of Eq. (17.15), the standard deviation of the difference in response to fertilized and unfertilized forage grown on Plainfield sand is

$$s_{\hat{\bar{Y}}_{i\cdot}-\hat{\bar{Y}}_{i'\cdot}} = \sqrt{427.8\left[\frac{2}{3} + \frac{(236.3 - 266.3)^2 473{,}377 - 2(236.3 - 266.3)(1{,}357.0 - 1{,}447.0)17{,}778 + (1{,}357.0 - 1{,}447.0)^2 6{,}159}{6{,}159(473{,}377) - (17{,}778)^2}\right]}$$

$$= 18.65 \text{ g}$$

By Eq. (17.16) we obtain an approximate standard deviation of

$$s_{\hat{\bar{Y}}_{i\cdot}-\hat{\bar{Y}}_{i'\cdot}} = \sqrt{\frac{2(427.7)}{3}\left\{1 + \frac{7{,}855(473{,}377) - 2(14{,}171)(17{,}778) + 251{,}380(6{,}159)}{(8-1)[(6{,}159)(473{,}377) - (17{,}778)^2]}\right\}}$$

$$= 18.97 \text{ g}$$

Equation (17.15) gives a different standard deviation for each comparison, whereas (17.16) gives the same, a compromise which yields too large a value for some comparisons and too small a value for others. When variation among the treatment means for one or more of the independent variables is larger than normally attributable to chance, as when influenced by treatments, serious error may result from applying Eq. (17.16).

Exercise 17.12.1 The accompanying table, furnished through the courtesy of C. R. Weber, Iowa State College, is a randomized complete block experiment with four replications. Eleven strains of soybeans were planted. The data and definition of the variables follow:

X_1 = maturity, measured in days later than the variety Hawkeye.

X_2 = lodging, measured on a scale from 1 to 5.

Y = infection by stem canker measured as a percentage of stalks infected.

	Block 1			Block 2			Block 3			Block 4		
Strain	X_1	X_2	Y	X_1	X_2	Y	X_1	X_2	Y	X_1	X_2	Y
Lincoln	9	3.0	19.3	10	2.0	29.2	12	3.0	1.0	9	2.5	6.4
A7-6102	10	3.0	10.1	10	2.0	34.7	9	2.0	14.0	9	3.0	5.6
A7-6323	10	2.5	13.1	9	1.5	59.3	12	2.5	1.1	10	2.5	8.1
A7-6520	8	2.0	15.6	5	2.0	49.0	8	2.0	17.4	6	2.0	11.7
A7-6905	12	2.5	4.3	11	1.0	48.2	13	3.0	6.3	10	2.5	6.7
C-739	4	2.0	25.2	2	1.5	36.5	2	2.0	23.4	1	2.0	12.9
C-776	3	1.5	67.6	4	1.0	79.3	6	2.0	13.6	2	1.5	39.4
H-6150	7	2.0	35.1	8	2.0	40.0	7	2.0	24.7	7	2.0	4.8
L6-8477	8	2.0	14.0	8	1.5	30.2	10	1.5	7.2	7	2.0	8.9
L7-1287	9	2.5	3.3	9	2.0	35.8	13	3.0	1.1	9	3.0	2.0
Bav. Sp.	10	3.5	3.1	10	3.0	9.6	11	3.0	1.0	10	3.5	0.1

The principal objective was to learn whether maturity or lodging is more closely related to infection. This will be determined from the error multiple regression. Incidentally, test the hypothesis of no differences among adjusted means for the varieties.

What is the appropriate test to attain the principal objective?

Exercise 17.12.2 What is the appropriate equation for computing adjusted treatment means?

Exercise 17.12.3 Compute an approximate standard deviation for the difference between any pair of adjusted treatment means. Is there any reason to believe this standard deviation might not be applicable in this case?

17.13 High-speed Computation and Computer Printouts

It is not likely that many investigators will compute their own analyses of covariance with two or more covariates. High-speed computers will do this and provide various printouts. Table 17.16 is a SAS (14.13) printout.

Table 17.16 gives a covariance analysis for the data of Table 17.12. The first partitioning of the adjusted total sum of squares is for MODEL AND ERROR; the former does not include the mean. Recall that 100R-SQUARE measures the percentage of SS(CORRECTED TOTAL) attributable to the model. The SS(error) and MS(error) are approximately the same as in Table 17.14, done on a desk computer. Presumably the computations in Table 17.16 are more accurate.

Type I sums of squares are computed sequentially. These are orthogonal for blocks and treatments as a consequence of the experimental design and the same as in the Y, Y column of Table 17.13. For X_1 and X_2, the sum is $8.49 + 10{,}585.05 = 10{,}593.54$, essentially the same as $113.2 + 10{,}482.8 = 10{,}596.0$ from Table 17.14. In Table 17.16, the sequential sums of squares can be interpreted individually, whereas the individual regression terms $b_{Y1\cdot 2}E_{1Y}$ and $b_{Y2\cdot 1}E_{2Y}$ have no meaning but are only parts of a whole.

Table 17.16 Multiple covariance analysis
GENERAL LINEAR MODELS PROCEDURE

DEPENDENT VARIABLE: Y

SOURCE	DF	SUM OF SQUARES	MEAN SQUARE	F VALUE	PR > F
MODEL	11	76758.29697647	6978.02699786	16.31	0.0001
ERROR	12	5135.53635686	427.96136307		
CORRECTED TOTAL	23	81893.83333333			

R-SQUARE	C.V.	STD DEV	Y MEAN
0.937290	10.3221	20.68722705	200.41666667

SOURCE	DF	TYPE I SS	F VALUE	PR > F
BLOCK	2	495.58333333	0.58	0.5754
SOIL	3	57176.16666667	44.53	0.0001
FERTLZER	1	2948.16666667	6.89	0.0222
SOIL*FERTLZER	3	5544.83333333	4.32	0.0278
X1	1	8.49366072	0.02	0.8903
X2	1	10585.05331575	24.73	0.0003

SOURCE	DF	TYPE IV SS	F VALUE	PR > F
BLOCK	2	395.40120649	0.46	0.6408
SOIL	3	59216.44313232	46.12	0.0001
FERTLZER	1	1850.62488503	4.32	0.0597
SOIL*FERTLZER	3	1136.58247353	0.89	0.4764
X1	1	1341.58895597	3.13	0.1020
X2	1	10585.05331575	24.73	0.0003

Each Type IV sum of squares in Table 17.16 is a sum of squares adjusted for other components in the model. Each corresponds to a "difference for testing an adjusted SS" in Table 17.14. Mean squares are not provided. Presumably the primary interest in this analysis is in the main effects and interaction. Note that we can test null hypotheses about the separate partial regression coefficients. These provide information on the value of X_1 and X_2 in controlling error.

Table 17.17 consists of parts from another printout. It gives least squares or adjusted treatment means for each level of both main effects and for all treatment combinations. The coding for soils is for the sequence in Table 17.12. For fertilizers, 1 is for unfertilized and 2 is for fertilized. The standard error for each adjusted mean is given; these are unequal because of the adjustments.

The individual hypotheses that each population mean is zero are not realistic here, although tested. Testing the difference between fertilizer means was already done using F, in Table 17.16; note that the probability of a

Table 17.17 Multiple covariance analysis
GENERAL LINEAR MODELS PROCEDURE

LEAST SQUARES MEANS

SOIL	Y LSMEAN	STD ERR LSMEAN	PROB > |T| HO: LSMEAN = 0
1	259.598426	8.594161	0.0001
2	126.545658	8.485458	0.0001
3	186.164174	9.334271	0.0001
4	229.368408	9.145719	0.0001

NOTE: TO ENSURE OVERALL PROTECTION LEVEL, ONLY PROBABILITIES ASSOCIATED WITH PRE-PLANNED COMPARISONS SHOULD BE USED.

FERTLZER	Y LSMEAN	STD ERR LSMEAN	PROB > |T| HO: LSMEAN = 0	PROB > |T| HO: LSMEAN1 = LSMEAN2
1	210.118178	6.292618	0.0001	0.0597
2	190.715155	6.292618	0.0001	

SOIL	FERTLZER	Y LSMEAN	STD ERR LSMEAN	PROB > |T| HO: LSMEAN = 0
1	1	266.006700	12.078556	0.0001
1	2	253.190151	12.917782	0.0001
2	1	144.833755	12.769879	0.0001
2	2	108.257562	12.444568	0.0001
3	1	200.653832	13.986703	0.0001
3	2	171.674517	11.962663	0.0001
4	1	228.978425	14.268837	0.0001
4	2	229.738391	15.152531	0.0001

larger value of the test criterion is the same for F as for $|t|$. Also note the warning about unplanned comparisons. This is important here since the program calls for a pairwise comparison of all means (comparisons deleted from this printout).

Exercise 17.13.1 Prepare the data of Exercise 17.12.1 for high-speed machine computation. Compare your printout results with your earlier computations.

Compare your printout with that given in Tables 17.16 and 17.17.

References

17.1. Bartlett, M. S.: "Some examples of statistical methods of research in agriculture and applied biology," *J. Roy. Statist. Soc. Suppl.*, **4:**137–183 (1937).

17.2. Cochran, W. G., and G. M. Cox: *Experimental Designs*, 2d ed., Wiley, New York, 1957.

17.3. DeLury, D. B.: "The analysis of covariance," *Biom.*, **4:**153–170 (1948).

17.4. Federer, W. T., and C. S. Schlottfeldt: "The use of covariance to control gradients in experiments," *Biom.*, **10:**282–290 (1954).

17.5. Finney, D. J.: "Standard errors of yields adjusted for regression on an independent measurement," *Biom. Bull.*, **2:**53–55 (1946).

17.6. Forester, H. C.: "Design of agronomic experiments for plots differentiated in fertility by past treatments," *Iowa Agr. Exp. Sta. Res. Bull.* 226, 1937.

17.7. Love, H. H.: "Are uniformity trials useful?" *J. Amer. Soc. Agron.*, **28:**234–245 (1936).

17.8. Matrone, G., F. H. Smith, V. B. Weldon, W. W. Woodhouse, Jr., W. J. Peterson, and K. C. Beeson: "Effects of phosphate fertilization on the nutritive value of soybean forage for sheep and rabbits," *U.S. Dep. Agr. Tech. Bull.* 1086, 1954.

17.9. Outhwaite, A. D., and A. Rutherford: "Covariance analysis as alternative to stratification in the control of gradients," *Biom.*, **11:**431–440 (1955).

17.10. Steel, R. G. D.: "Which dependent variate? Y or $Y - X$?" *Mimeo Series* BU-54-M, Biometrics Unit, Cornell University, Ithaca, N.Y., 1954.

17.11. Tucker, H. P., J. T. Wakeley, and F. D. Cochran: "Effect of washing and removing excess moisture by wiping or by air current on the ascorbic acid content of turnip greens," *S. Coop. Ser. Bull.*, 10, 54–56 (1951).

17.12. Wishart, J.: "Tests of significance in the analysis of covariance," *J. Roy. Statist. Soc. Suppl.*, **3:**79–82 (1936).

17.13. Wishart, J.: "Growth-rate determinations in nutrition studies with the bacon pig and their analysis," *Biometrika*, **30:**16–28 (1938).

17.14. *Biom.*, **13:**261–405, No. 3 (1957). (This issue consists of seven papers devoted to covariance.)

CHAPTER
EIGHTEEN

ANALYSIS OF VARIANCE V: UNEQUAL SUBCLASS NUMBERS

18.1 Introduction

Chapter 9 dealt with the randomized complete block design. Data from such a design are normally presented in a two-way classification—blocks by treatments. In some instances, more than one observation may be made per treatment within any block. These may be made on separate parts of a single experimental unit; this is sampling and the appropriate analysis was given in Table 9.10. Alternatively, they may be on separate experimental units; this case was also discussed as a generalized block design in Sec. 9.8. In this chapter, we take a further look at the generalized block design with proportional subclass numbers but spend most of our time on the analysis of disproportionate subclass number data.

18.2 Multiple Observations within Subclasses

Data are often presented in a two-way classification where the *cells* or *subclasses* contain observations on more than one experimental unit. This would be the case for the generalized randomized block design discussed in Sec. 9.8. Here, each of t treatments appears n_i times in the ith block and the treatments are randomized over the $n_i t$ experimental units forming the block.

In some cases, as in Exercise 9.8.1, blocks may be a classification system other than that for a purely physical blocking of experimental units. In practice, randomization may be an assumption, provided that it is not unreasonable. Finally, the number of observations per cell need be neither equal nor proportional.

A great deal of data fall in this general category. One source is experiments with domestic and wild animals and birds. For example, an investigator might be interested in average brood size of pheasants at different locations for wild and spring-released hens. Clearly, the numbers observable in the wild are not under control and sampling possibilities may be limited; the numbers released must depend on availability of habitat. Such data almost certainly involve disproportionate subclass numbers.

When the observations are on experimental units rather than sampling units, variation among units within a cell measures true experimental error or pure error. Consequently, the mathematical description of an observation is

$$Y_{ijk} = \mu + \alpha_i + \beta_j + (\alpha\beta)_{ij} + \varepsilon_{ijk} \tag{18.1}$$

We have used α and β here rather than τ and ρ to stress the fact that for disproportionate subclass number data, so-called blocks will often be a classification system. In this case, the possibility of a blocks times treatments interaction needs to be proposed as a hypothesis. The assumptions for the model are that the ε's are normally and independently distributed with zero mean and common variance; the α's and β's may be fixed or random; the $(\alpha\beta)$'s are interaction components. This model is in contrast to that in which observations are on sampling units.

18.3 Proportionate Subclass Number Analysis

An illustration of proportional subclass numbers is given in Table 18.1. The analysis presents no particular difficulties. The error sum of squares is the sum of the within-cells sums of squares. The sum of squares for a main effect is computed from appropriate marginal totals, as for a single-factor experiment with unequal numbers; this is a weighted sum of squares of deviations.

Table 18.1 Proportional subclass numbers analysis
Model: $Y_{ijk} = \mu + \alpha_i + \beta_j + (\alpha\beta)_{ij} + \varepsilon_{ijk}$

Number of observations						Analysis of variance	
Factor		*B*			*A* totals	Source	df
	Level	b_1	b_2	b_3		*A*	1
						B	2
A	a_1	3	4	6	13	*AB*	2
	a_2	6	8	12	26	Error	33
B totals		9	12	18	39	Total	38

The interaction sum of squares is obtained by subtracting the main effects sums of squares from the weighted sum of squares among cell totals, that is, as

$$\sum_{i,j} \frac{Y_{ij.}^2}{n_{ij}} - \frac{Y_{...}^2}{n_{..}} - \text{SS}(A) - \text{SS}(B) \tag{18.2}$$

where $Y_{ij.}$ represents a cell total of n_{ij} observations, or as

$$\frac{(a_1 b_1)^2}{3} + \cdots + \frac{(a_2 b_3)^2}{12} - \frac{Y_{...}^2}{39} - \text{SS}(A) - \text{SS}(B)$$

for the illustration.

Tests of hypotheses depend on the assumptions for the model components.

In developing an analysis for any set of data, it is necessary to estimate the various unknown parameters in the model. Recall that SS(model) = $\hat{\boldsymbol{\beta}}'\mathbf{X}'\mathbf{Y}$. This is as true for balanced data, such as those which come from a randomized complete block experiment, as it is for unbalanced data, those with disproportionate subclass numbers. (Once the analysis has been developed, we may never consciously use the estimates.) In order to obtain a unique set of estimates, it is generally necessary to impose restrictions on the model or constraints on the solution, the latter being solely for the purpose of getting a solution, as discussed in Sec. 7.5. Suppose that restrictions are imposed. For the randomized complete block design with one observation per cell, the mathematical expression for an observation is $Y_{ij} = \mu + \tau_i + \rho_j + \varepsilon_{ij}$. In the population, either $\sum \tau_i = 0$ (fixed effects) or $\mu_\tau = 0$ (random effects), so we require that $\sum \hat{\tau}_i = 0$ where $\hat{\tau}_i$ is our estimate of τ_i, since it follows naturally from the model. We also require that $\sum \hat{\rho}_j = 0$.

For the illustration of Table 18.1, where interaction is assumed, the analysis outlined imposes the restrictions that weighted sums of $\hat{\alpha}$'s, of $\hat{\beta}$'s, and of $\widehat{(\alpha\beta)}$'s be zero, the weights being essentially the proportions. Here,

$$\hat{\alpha}_1 + 2\hat{\alpha}_2 = 0$$

$$3\hat{\beta}_1 + 4\hat{\beta}_2 + 6\hat{\beta}_3 = 0$$

$$\widehat{(\alpha\beta)}_{11} + 2\widehat{(\alpha\beta)}_{21} = 0$$

$$\widehat{(\alpha\beta)}_{12} + 2\widehat{(\alpha\beta)}_{22} = 0$$

$$\widehat{(\alpha\beta)}_{13} + 2\widehat{(\alpha\beta)}_{23} = 0$$

$$3\widehat{(\alpha\beta)}_{11} + 4\widehat{(\alpha\beta)}_{12} + 6\widehat{(\alpha\beta)}_{13} = 0$$

and

$$3\widehat{(\alpha\beta)}_{21} + 4\widehat{(\alpha\beta)}_{22} + 6\widehat{(\alpha\beta)}_{23} = 0$$

Table 18.2 Treatment totals and means for illustration of Table 18.1

Factor	Level	B: b_1	b_2	b_3	A totals	A means
A	a_1	$3\mu + 3\alpha_1 + 3\beta_1 + 3(\alpha\beta)_{11} + \varepsilon_{11\cdot}$	$4\mu + 4\alpha_1 + 4\beta_2 + 4(\alpha\beta)_{12} + \varepsilon_{12\cdot}$	$6\mu + 6\alpha_1 + 6\beta_3 + 6(\alpha\beta)_{13} + \varepsilon_{13\cdot}$	$13\mu + 13\alpha_1 + 3\beta_1 + 4\beta_2 + 6\beta_3 + 3(\alpha\beta)_{11} + 4(\alpha\beta)_{12} + 6(\alpha\beta)_{13} + \varepsilon_{1\cdot\cdot}$	$\mu + \alpha_1 + \frac{3}{13}\beta_1 + \frac{4}{13}\beta_2 + \frac{6}{13}\beta_3 + \frac{3}{13}(\alpha\beta)_{11} + \frac{4}{13}(\alpha\beta)_{12} + \frac{6}{13}(\alpha\beta)_{13} + \bar{\varepsilon}_{1\cdot\cdot}$
	a_2	$6\mu + 6\alpha_2 + 6\beta_1 + 6(\alpha\beta)_{21} + \varepsilon_{21\cdot}$	$8\mu + 8\alpha_2 + 8\beta_2 + 8(\alpha\beta)_{22} + \varepsilon_{22\cdot}$	$12\mu + 12\alpha_2 + 12\beta_3 + 12(\alpha\beta)_{23} + \varepsilon_{23\cdot}$	$26\mu + 26\alpha_2 + 6\beta_1 + 8\beta_2 + 12\beta_3 + 6(\alpha\beta)_{21} + 8(\alpha\beta)_{22} + 12(\alpha\beta)_{23} + \varepsilon_{2\cdot\cdot}$	$\mu + \alpha_2 + \frac{3}{13}\beta_1 + \frac{4}{13}\beta_2 + \frac{6}{13}\beta_3 + \frac{3}{13}(\alpha\beta)_{21} + \frac{4}{13}(\alpha\beta)_{22} + \frac{6}{13}(\alpha\beta)_{23} + \bar{\varepsilon}_{2\cdot\cdot}$
B totals		$9\mu + 3\alpha_1 + 6\alpha_2 + 9\beta_1 + 3(\alpha\beta)_{11} + 6(\alpha\beta)_{21} + \varepsilon_{\cdot1\cdot}$	$12\mu + 4\alpha_1 + 8\alpha_2 + 12\beta_2 + 4(\alpha\beta)_{12} + 8(\alpha\beta)_{22} + \varepsilon_{\cdot2\cdot}$	$18\mu + 6\alpha_1 + 12\alpha_2 + 18\beta_3 + 6(\alpha\beta)_{13} + 12(\alpha\beta)_{23} + \varepsilon_{\cdot3\cdot}$	$39\mu + 13\alpha_1 + 26\alpha_2 + 9\beta_1 + 12\beta_2 + 18\beta_3 + 3(\alpha\beta)_{11} + 4(\alpha\beta)_{12} + 6(\alpha\beta)_{13} + 6(\alpha\beta)_{21} + 8(\alpha\beta)_{22} + 12(\alpha\beta)_{23} + \varepsilon_{\cdots}$	
B means		$\mu + \frac{1}{3}\alpha_1 + \frac{2}{3}\alpha_2 + \beta_1 + \frac{1}{3}(\alpha\beta)_{11} + \frac{2}{3}(\alpha\beta)_{21} + \bar{\varepsilon}_{\cdot1\cdot}$	$\mu + \frac{1}{3}\alpha_1 + \frac{2}{3}\alpha_2 + \beta_2 + \frac{1}{3}(\alpha\beta)_{12} + \frac{2}{3}(\alpha\beta)_{22} + \bar{\varepsilon}_{\cdot2\cdot}$	$\mu + \frac{1}{3}\alpha_1 + \frac{2}{3}\alpha_2 + \beta_3 + \frac{1}{3}(\alpha\beta)_{13} + \frac{2}{3}(\alpha\beta)_{23} + \varepsilon_{\cdot3\cdot}$		$\mu + \frac{1}{3}\alpha_1 + \frac{2}{3}\alpha_2 + \frac{3}{13}\beta_1 + \frac{4}{13}\beta_2 + \frac{6}{13}\beta_3 + \frac{3}{39}(\alpha\beta)_{11} + \frac{4}{39}(\alpha\beta)_{12} + \frac{6}{39}(\alpha\beta)_{13} + \frac{6}{39}(\alpha\beta)_{21} + \frac{8}{39}(\alpha\beta)_{22} + \frac{12}{39}(\alpha\beta)_{23} + \bar{\varepsilon}_{\cdots}$

$$\text{Unweighted mean} = \tfrac{1}{6}[(\mu + \alpha_1 + \beta_1 + (\alpha\beta)_{11} + \bar{\varepsilon}_{11\cdot}) + (\mu + \alpha_1 + \beta_2 + (\alpha\beta)_{12} + \bar{\varepsilon}_{12\cdot}) + (\mu + \alpha_1 + \beta_3 + (\alpha\beta)_{13} + \bar{\varepsilon}_{13\cdot}) + (\mu + \alpha_2 + \beta_1 + (\alpha\beta)_{21} + \bar{\varepsilon}_{21\cdot}) + (\mu + \alpha_2 + \beta_2 + (\alpha\beta)_{22} + \bar{\varepsilon}_{22\cdot}) + (\mu + \alpha_2 + \beta_3 + (\alpha\beta)_{23} + \bar{\varepsilon}_{23\cdot})] = \mu + [3\,\Sigma\,\alpha_i + 2\sum \beta_j + \Sigma\,(\alpha\beta)_{ij} + (\sum \bar{\varepsilon}_{ij\cdot})]/6$$

For these restrictions, the experimental mean $\bar{Y}...$, a *weighted* mean of the cell means, is an unbiased estimate of μ. Examination of the treatment totals and means of Table 18.2 shows that this is a reasonable set of restrictions from a purely computational point of view. For example, to estimate the variance among, or the sum of squares of, the β's, we must eliminate the $(\alpha\beta)$'s in the B means since they differ from mean to mean and, consequently, would contribute to the variance among the B means. On the other hand, the restrictions hopefully imply the relative frequencies with which various α's, β's, and $(\alpha\beta)$'s are present in their respective populations. This is information about the model and determines computing procedure.

Other restrictions may result in an analysis of a different form. Consider the alternative set of restrictions

$$\sum \hat{\alpha}_i = 0 \qquad \sum \hat{\beta}_j = 0 \qquad \sum_i \widehat{(\alpha\beta)}_{ij} = 0 \qquad \text{for all } j$$

$$\sum_j \widehat{(\alpha\beta)}_{ij} = 0 \qquad \text{for all } i$$

Now the *unweighted* mean of the cell means is an unbiased estimate of μ, as can be seen from Table 18.2. For these restrictions, the analysis is different and more involved than that outlined at the beginning of this section.

Now suppose that the model does not include an interaction. By crossing out the $(\alpha\beta)$'s in Table 18.2, we see that all B means contain the same weighted sum of the α's. Hence they contribute nothing to the variance among the B means. Any reasonable restrictions on the $\hat{\alpha}$'s would not affect our estimate of the variance among, or the sum of squares of, the β's.

Thus it becomes clear that the choice of a set of restrictions, on the estimates of the various effects, has a real effect on the analysis of variance when there is interaction and this choice should be made on the basis of assumptions which are a part of the model.

Exercise 18.3.1 In Exercise 15.3.3, a balanced set of data is given. To this set, add the following observations for students who preferred print to braille.

Data:	Pretest		Posttest	
Treatment:	1	2	1	2
	98,64	87,89	93,80	87,88

Analyze all the pretest data using the method of this section.
Analyze all the posttest data using the method of this section.

18.4 Disproportionate Subclass Number Analysis

First, the model and analysis for the one-way classification with unequal numbers of observations per treatment were discussed in Chap. 7. The error sum of squares is an SS(within treatments), and SS(treatments) is a weighted sum of squares among means with weights dependent on the variance of each mean.

For the analysis of data in a two-way classification with disproportionate subclass numbers, first observe Table 18.3. It is apparent that we cannot compute a variance among the weighted A means that will be free from the B effect. No restriction on the β's can eliminate this difficulty since the ratio of the coefficient of β_1 to the coefficient of β_2 varies with the A level. One possibility is to obtain row and column means as unweighted averages of cell means and use the restriction that $\sum \hat{\beta}_j = 0$, provided that there is at least one entry in every cell. This raises the question of efficiency, since the means have different variances. A similar difficulty arises in connection with a sum of squares for factor B.

The inability to obtain a sum of squares for A or for B that is free of the other factor is summed up by saying that the data are *nonorthogonal*. As a result we resort to the basic method of least squares. This method was once called the *method of fitting constants* and was recommended when the model did not include interaction, although a test of interaction could be made with little additional effort. At that time, computing was less sophisticated and fitting the additional interaction constants was difficult.

The method is applicable when some cells have no observations. It may be used with covariates. For the techniques, we rely on the discussion of regression as given in Chaps. 13 and 14.

We illustrate by first setting up a problem with $n_{11} = 3$, $n_{12} = 1$,

Table 18.3 Numbers of observations and row and column means for a disproportionate subclass numbers illustration

Model: $Y_{ijk} = \mu + \alpha_i + \beta_j + \varepsilon_{ijk}$, no interaction

		Numbers				
		b_1	b_2	b_3	Total	A means
Numbers	a_1	3	5	12	20	$\mu + \alpha_1 + \frac{3}{20}\beta_1 + \frac{5}{20}\beta_2 + \frac{12}{20}\beta_3 + \bar{\varepsilon}_{1..}$
	a_2	6	7	8	21	$\mu + \alpha_2 + \frac{6}{21}\beta_1 + \frac{7}{21}\beta_2 + \frac{8}{21}\beta_3 + \bar{\varepsilon}_{2..}$
	Total	9	12	20	41	
B means		$\mu + \frac{3}{9}\alpha_1 + \frac{6}{9}\alpha_2 + \beta_1 + \bar{\varepsilon}_{.1.}$	$\mu + \frac{5}{12}\alpha_1 + \frac{7}{12}\alpha_2 + \beta_2 + \bar{\varepsilon}_{.2.}$	$\mu + \frac{12}{20}\alpha_1 + \frac{8}{20}\alpha_2 + \beta_3 + \bar{\varepsilon}_{.3.}$		

$n_{21} = 4$, and $n_{22} = 2$. With Eq. (18.1) in mind, the set of observations is written as

$$
\begin{pmatrix} Y_{111} \\ Y_{112} \\ Y_{113} \\ Y_{121} \\ Y_{211} \\ Y_{212} \\ Y_{213} \\ Y_{214} \\ Y_{221} \\ Y_{222} \end{pmatrix}
=
\begin{array}{c}
\begin{array}{ccccccccc} \mu & \alpha_1 & \alpha_2 & \beta_1 & \beta_2 & (\alpha\beta)_{11} & (\alpha\beta)_{12} & (\alpha\beta)_{21} & (\alpha\beta)_{22} \end{array} \\
\begin{pmatrix}
1 & 1 & 0 & 1 & 0 & 1 & 0 & 0 & 0 \\
1 & 1 & 0 & 1 & 0 & 1 & 0 & 0 & 0 \\
1 & 1 & 0 & 1 & 0 & 1 & 0 & 0 & 0 \\
1 & 1 & 0 & 0 & 1 & 0 & 1 & 0 & 0 \\
1 & 0 & 1 & 1 & 0 & 0 & 0 & 1 & 0 \\
1 & 0 & 1 & 1 & 0 & 0 & 0 & 1 & 0 \\
1 & 0 & 1 & 1 & 0 & 0 & 0 & 1 & 0 \\
1 & 0 & 1 & 1 & 0 & 0 & 0 & 1 & 0 \\
1 & 0 & 1 & 0 & 1 & 0 & 0 & 0 & 1 \\
1 & 0 & 1 & 0 & 1 & 0 & 0 & 0 & 1
\end{pmatrix}
\end{array}
\begin{pmatrix} \mu \\ \alpha_1 \\ \alpha_2 \\ \beta_1 \\ \beta_2 \\ (\alpha\beta)_{11} \\ (\alpha\beta)_{12} \\ (\alpha\beta)_{21} \\ (\alpha\beta)_{22} \end{pmatrix}
+
\begin{pmatrix} \varepsilon_{111} \\ \varepsilon_{112} \\ \varepsilon_{113} \\ \varepsilon_{121} \\ \varepsilon_{211} \\ \varepsilon_{212} \\ \varepsilon_{213} \\ \varepsilon_{214} \\ \varepsilon_{221} \\ \varepsilon_{222} \end{pmatrix}
\tag{18.3}
$$

Equation (18.3) is simply the statement $\mathbf{Y} = \mathbf{X\beta} + \boldsymbol{\varepsilon}$. The parameters above the $\mathbf{X}$ matrix are a convenient repetition of the elements in the $\boldsymbol{\beta}$ vector. All nine X's are dummy or indicator variables registering presence (1) or absence (0) of the parameter. Thus, the first equation states: $Y_{111} = \mu + \alpha_1 + \beta_1 + (\alpha\beta)_{11} + \varepsilon_{111}$.

The least-squares equations are $\mathbf{X'X\hat{\beta}} = \mathbf{X'Y}$, where

$$
\mathbf{X'X} = \left(\begin{array}{c|cc|cc|cccc}
10 & 4 & 6 & 7 & 3 & 3 & 1 & 4 & 2 \\
\hline
4 & 4 & 0 & 3 & 1 & 3 & 1 & 0 & 0 \\
6 & 0 & 6 & 4 & 2 & 0 & 0 & 4 & 2 \\
\hline
7 & 3 & 4 & 7 & 0 & 3 & 0 & 4 & 0 \\
3 & 1 & 2 & 0 & 3 & 0 & 1 & 0 & 2 \\
\hline
3 & 3 & 0 & 3 & 0 & 3 & 0 & 0 & 0 \\
1 & 1 & 0 & 0 & 1 & 0 & 1 & 0 & 0 \\
4 & 0 & 4 & 4 & 0 & 0 & 0 & 4 & 0 \\
2 & 0 & 2 & 0 & 2 & 0 & 0 & 0 & 2
\end{array}\right)
\tag{18.4}
$$

and

$$
\mathbf{X'Y} = \begin{pmatrix} Y_{\cdots} \\ Y_{1\cdot\cdot} \\ Y_{2\cdot\cdot} \\ Y_{\cdot1\cdot} \\ Y_{\cdot2\cdot} \\ Y_{11\cdot} \\ Y_{12\cdot} \\ Y_{21\cdot} \\ Y_{22\cdot} \end{pmatrix}
$$

Solution of these equations calls for $(\mathbf{X}'\mathbf{X})^{-1}$ if it exists. However, we note that the coefficients in rows 2 and 3 sum to those in row 1, those in rows 4 and 5 sum to those in row 1, those in rows 6 and 7 sum to those in row 2, those in rows 6 and 8 sum to those in row 4, those in rows 7 and 9 sum to those in row 5, and those in rows 8 and 9 sum to those in row 3. The model is overparametrized and $\mathbf{X}'\mathbf{X}$ is singular.

When $\mathbf{X}'\mathbf{X}$ is singular, the normal equations have many solutions. To get a unique solution, restrictions on the model or constraints on the solution are needed. We assume that you will use high-speed computers and their printouts.

An experiment with mice was conducted by Eugene J. Eisen at North Carolina State University. Among the characteristics studied was litter size. This is a discrete variable, but the numbers run from 1 to 25. It is analyzed here as a continuous variable for which the assumptions of normality and independence and homogeneity of error are valid.

Litter size may be affected by the selection history of the population and by the size of the litter in which the mother was raised. These are the sources of variation studied here. The data are from five lines:

11. Selected for high litter size L
12. Selected for high six-week body weight W
14. Selected for an index combining low L and high W
15. An unselected control
16. Selected for an index combining high L and low W

The number reared, NREAR in the printout tables, refers to the litter size in which the females were reared. These had been artificially adjusted as needed at day of birth to be 8, 12, or 16. When mature, the females had, in turn, produced litters the size of which is the observation considered.

The numbers in the cells ranged from 44 to 50. This disproportionality is far from severe, but the numbers are still neither equal nor proportional.

The SAS (14.13) printout available to us provides, for each cell, n_{ij}, $Y_{ij\cdot}$, $\bar{Y}_{ij\cdot}$, min Y_{ijk}, max Y_{ijk}, s_{ij}^2, $s_{ij}/\sqrt{n_{ij}}$, and the coefficient of variation. All this is useful information. Table 18.4 gives $\bar{Y}_{ij\cdot}$'s and n_{ij}'s only.

Table 18.5 is a printout of the analysis of variance. There were 717 observations, so there are 716 df for the corrected, or adjusted, total sum of squares. The SS(model) is

$$\hat{\boldsymbol{\beta}}'\mathbf{X}'\mathbf{Y} - Y_{\cdots}^2/n_{\cdot\cdot} = \sum\left(\frac{Y_{ij\cdot}^2}{n_{ij}}\right) - \frac{Y_{\cdots}^2}{n_{\cdot\cdot}} = \text{SS(among cells)}$$

SS(model) is further partitioned into main effect and interaction sums of squares. The TYPE I SS entries have been computed sequentially so that only the interaction has been adjusted for all other elements in the model. The TYPE III SS entries are sums of squares for reductions attributable to

Table 18.4 Mean litter size and number of litters observed, $Y_{ij\cdot}(n_{ij})$, for selected populations according to litter size in which female was reared

		Female reared in litter size		
		8	12	16
	11	18.23(48)	17.55(47)	16.48(48)
Population	12	14.53(49)	14.00(49)	13.74(47)
= line	14	10.87(47)	11.17(47)	10.29(48)
	15	12.16(49)	11.84(49)	11.96(50)
	16	14.40(50)	14.80(44)	13.67(45)

Source: Data obtained through the courtesy of Eugene J. Eisen, North Carolina State University, Raleigh, North Carolina.

including elements corresponding to the named source, last in the model. The null hypotheses being tested are, in terms of cell means, described by the full model:

$$H_0(\text{populations}): \mu_{11} + \mu_{12} + \mu_{13} = \mu_{21} + \mu_{22} + \mu_{23} = \mu_{31} + \mu_{32} + \mu_{33}$$
$$= \mu_{41} + \mu_{42} + \mu_{43} = \mu_{51} + \mu_{52} + \mu_{53}$$

$$H_0(\text{number reared}): \mu_{11} + \mu_{21} + \mu_{31} + \mu_{41} + \mu_{51}$$
$$= \mu_{12} + \mu_{22} + \mu_{32} + \mu_{42} + \mu_{52}$$
$$= \mu_{13} + \mu_{23} + \mu_{33} + \mu_{43} + \mu_{53}$$

For these data, interaction is not significant. Interpret this as saying that the sets of five line (POP) means run nearly parallel for the three litter sizes in which the females were reared (NREAR), or that the differences among line means are not dependent on number reared.

Table 18.6 is another part of the SAS printout. This gives least-squares means for the lines and the litter sizes in which the females were reared. These are computed from least-squares estimates of the parameters as $(\hat{\mu} + \hat{\alpha}_i)$'s and $(\hat{\mu} + \hat{\beta}_j)$'s. Standard errors are given. Null hypotheses, H_0: $\mu = 0$, are tested for each mean given. This part of the program is meaningless here. Means within each set are tested pairwise. If these were reasonable planned comparisons, they would be preferred. Note the warning against blindly accepting these results. The fifteen least-squares means were also provided and similarly tested. These are the cell means when the model includes interaction. They already appear in Table 18.4.

Since interaction is of about the same order of magnitude as error, there is no need to propose a model with interaction. This is the case for which the

Table 18.5 Analysis of variance of mice data

GENERAL LINEAR MODELS PROCEDURE

Model: $Y_{ijk} = \mu + \alpha_i + \beta_j + (\alpha\beta)_{ij} + \varepsilon_{ijk}$

DEPENDENT VARIABLE: Y

SOURCE	DF	SUM OF SQUARES	MEAN SQUARE	F VALUE	PR > F	R-SQUARE	C.V.
MODEL	14	3840.25238981	274.30374213	29.06	0.0001	0.366936	22.4195
ERROR	702	6625.47145956	9.43799353		STD DEV		MEAN
CORRECTED TOTAL	716	10465.72384937			3.07213176		13.70292887

SOURCE	DF	TYPE I SS	F VALUE	PR > F	DF	TYPE III SS	F VALUE	PR > F
POP	4	3698.99948468	97.98	0.0001	4	3695.93018099	97.90	0.0001
NREAR	2	85.66916501	4.54	0.0110	2	87.53206237	4.64	0.0100
POP*NREAR	8	55.58374012	0.74	0.6596	8	55.58374012	0.74	0.6596

Table 18.6 Least-squares means for main effects

General Linear Models Procedure

Model: $Y_{ijk} = \mu + \alpha_i + \beta_j + (\alpha\beta)_{ij} + \varepsilon_{ijk}$

POP	LSMEAN	STD ERR LSMEAN	PROB > |T| HO:LSMEAN = 0	PROB > |T| I/J	HO: LSMEAN(I) = LSMEAN(J) 1	2	3	4	5
11	17.4205083	0.2569172	0.0001	1	.	0.0001	0.0001	0.0001	0.0001
12	14.0917644	0.2551759	0.0001	2	0.0001	.	0.0001	0.0001	0.5922
14	10.7780733	0.2578203	0.0001	3	0.0001	0.0001	.	0.0009	0.0001
15	11.9866667	0.2525391	0.0001	4	0.0001	0.0001	0.0009	.	0.0001
16	14.2873737	0.2609795	0.0001	5	0.0001	0.5922	0.0001	0.0001	.

NOTE: TO ENSURE OVERALL PROTECTION LEVEL, ONLY PROBABILITIES ASSOCIATED WITH PRE-PLANNED COMPARISONS SHOULD BE USED.

NREAR	LSMEAN	STD ERR LSMEAN	PROB > |T| HO:LSMEAN = 0	PROB > |T| I/J	HO: LSMEAN(I) = LSMEAN(J) 1	2	3
8	14.0390769	0.1971210	0.0001	1	.	0.5501	0.0039
12	13.8711187	0.2001340	0.0001	2	0.5501	.	0.0232
16	13.2284362	0.1992537	0.0001	3	0.0039	0.0232	.

NOTE: TO ENSURE OVERALL PROTECTION LEVEL, ONLY PROBABILITIES ASSOCIATED WITH PRE-PLANNED COMPARISONS SHOULD BE USED.

method of fitting constants or of least squares was originally proposed. Suppose that we propose such a model.

For the illustration, the **X** matrix of Eq. (18.3) no longer needs the last four columns. The upper left 5×5 corner of **X′X** in Eq. (18.4) becomes the required **X′X** matrix. No $Y_{ij\cdot}$'s are needed in **X′Y**. There are four fewer normal equations and what was earlier called interaction is now a part of error. However, the new **X′X** matrix is still singular.

For the mice data, **X** has only $1 + 5 + 3 = 9$ columns. The last $5 \times 3 = 15$ columns and 15 rows of the original **X′X** are no longer needed, and the upper left 9×9 corner is the new **X′X** matrix. Table 18.7 gives the new analysis.

Type I sums of squares are identical with those in Table 18.5 except that there is no interaction term. The same sequence of fitting parameters is being followed as far as this model calls for. Type III sums of squares are different because fewer parameters are fitted. Again, both main effects are declared significant; both null hypotheses are rejected.

Since there is no interaction in the model, the only interest is in main effects. The appropriate means are those for lines and numbers reared. Least-squares means are included in Table 18.7. These are not the same as those in Table 18.6 because a different set of equations has been solved. Since interaction was small enough to be left out of the model and disproportionality is not great, the differences are small. Again, note the warning concerning the use of the program tests.

Table 18.7 Analysis of variance for mice data

General Linear Models Procedure

Model: $Y_{ijk} = \mu + \alpha_i + \beta_j + \varepsilon_{ijk}$

DEPENDENT VARIABLE: Y

SOURCE	DF	SUM OF SQUARES	MEAN SQUARE	F VALUE	PR > F	R-SQUARE	C.V.
MODEL	6	3784.66864969	630.77810828	67.03	0.0001	0.361625	22.3862
ERROR	710	6681.05519968	9.40993690		STD DEV		MEAN
CORRECTED TOTAL	716	10465.72384937			3.06756205		13.70292887

SOURCE	DF	TYPE I SS	F VALUE	PR > F	DF	TYPE III SS	F VALUE	PR > F
POP	4	3698.99948468	98.27	0.0001	4	3693.04715859	98.12	0.0001
NREAR	2	85.66916501	4.55	0.0109	2	85.66916501	4.55	0.0109

LEAST SQUARES MEANS

POP	LSMEAN	STD ERR LSMEAN	PROB > |T| HO:LSMEAN = 0	PROB > |T| I/J	HO: LSMEAN(I) = LSMEAN(J) 1	2	3	4	5
11	17.4206343	0.2565249	0.0001	1	.	0.0001	0.0001	0.0001	0.0001
12	14.0899613	0.2547570	0.0001	2	0.0001	.	0.0001	0.0001	0.6075
14	10.7780127	0.2574266	0.0001	3	0.0001	0.0001	.	0.0008	0.0001
15	11.9897149	0.2521544	0.0001	4	0.0001	0.0001	0.0008	.	0.0001
16	14.2770880	0.2602676	0.0001	5	0.0001	0.6075	0.0001	0.0001	.

NOTE: TO ENSURE OVERALL PROTECTION LEVEL, ONLY PROBABILITIES ASSOCIATED WITH PRE-PLANNED COMPARISONS SHOULD BE USED.

NREAR	LSMEAN	STD ERR LSMEAN	PROB > |T| HO:LSMEAN = 0	PROB > |T| I/J	HO: LSMEAN(I) = LSMEAN(J) 1	2	3
8	14.0381786	0.1967991	0.0001	1	.	0.5295	0.0041
12	13.8617923	0.1997314	0.0001	2	0.5295	.	0.0260
16	13.2332758	0.1988791	0.0001	3	0.0041	0.0260	.

NOTE: TO ENSURE OVERALL PROTECTION LEVEL, ONLY PROBABILITIES ASSOCIATED WITH PRE-PLANNED COMPARISONS SHOULD BE USED.

Exercise 18.4.1 In Sec. 2.15, a recommendation was made about the relative sizes of the standard deviation and the unit of measurement.

What was the recommendation and how does it apply here?

Exercise 18.4.2 What might have been an appropriate transformation of the data prior to an analysis of variance? Why did you choose this transformation?

Exercise 18.4.3 Suggest an alternative approach to the analysis of the original mice data such that Chaps. 9 and 15 can be applied. (*Hint:* Disproportionality is not great.)

Exercise 18.4.4 The Rawls (15.21) data given in Exercise 15.3.3 are incomplete. There were additional observations on the same treatment and two additional treatments. The latter were:

3. Five lessons on efficient listening techniques prior to listening-practice training and
4. A control group

The additional data follow:

Pretest data

	Treatment 1	Treatment 2
Braille	87	
Print	98, 64	87, 89, 82, 91

Posttest data

	Treatment 1	Treatment 2
Braille	92	
Print	93, 80	87, 88, 90, 86

Pretest data

	Treatment 3	Treatment 4
Braille	97, 86, 73	92, 91
Print	94, 77, 97, 90, 64, 86, 83, 85	80, 66, 80, 86, 95, 75, 96, 86, 91

Posttest data

	Treatment 3	Treatment 4
Braille	96, 79, 75	93, 97
Print	90, 68, 98, 95, 73, 78, 78, 92	73, 48, 86, 78, 93, 85, 95, 88, 95

Using all the posttest data, obtain an analysis where braille and print are the categories of one direction of classification and treatments are those of the other.

Exercise 18.4.5 Analyze the posttest data as above but use the pretest data as values of a covariate.

18.5 Other Analytical Techniques

Yates (18.5) proposed analyses using cell means. These are the *method of unweighted means* and the *method of weighted squares of means*. The former method is approximate in that it proceeds as though the means had equal variances. Since $\sigma_{\bar{Y}}^2 = \sigma^2/n_{ij}$, the variances are unequal when n_{ij} is not constant, the basis of this chapter.

The method of weighted squares of means uses linear functions of means and, in the analysis, weights these according to the variance of the linear function. For this method, the hypotheses tested are those given in Sec. 18.4 for the method of least squares.

These methods and others are considered by Gosslee and Lucas (18.2). They are concerned with effects on tabulated significance levels and with the computation of power.

Searle (18.3, Chap. 8) also discusses these methods and the hypotheses being tested.

Steel and Torrie (18.4, Chap. 13) illustrate methods for $r \times 2$ and 2×2 tables. At one time, these methods were popular, but modern computers have made them almost obsolete.

References

18.1. Addelman, S.: "The generalized randomized block design," *Amer. Statist.*, **23(4):** 35–36 (1969).

18.2. Gosslee, D. G., and H. L. Lucas: "Analysis of variance of disproportionate data when interaction is present," *Biom.*, **21:**115–133 (1965).

18.3. Searle, S. R.: *Linear Models*, 1st ed., Wiley, New York, 1971.

18.4. Steel, R. G. D., and J. H. Torrie: *Principles and Procedures of Statistics*, 1st ed., McGraw-Hill, New York, 1960.

18.5. Yates, F.: "The analysis of multiple classifications with unequal numbers in the different subclasses," *J. Amer. Statist. Ass.*, **29:**51–66 (1934).

CHAPTER

NINETEEN

CURVE FITTING

19.1 Introduction

The simplest and most common type of curve fitting is for the straight line. However, when pairs of observations are plotted, they often fall on a curved line; biological or some other theory may even call for a curve of specified form. This chapter considers such regression. In addition, there is a brief discussion of the construction and use of orthogonal polynomials.

19.2 Regression that Is Not Linear

A relation between two variables may be approximately linear when studied over a limited range but markedly curvilinear when a broader range is considered. For example, the relation between maturity and yield of canning peas is usually linear over the maturity range acceptable to the canning trade. However, as maturity increases, the rate of increase in yield decreases, that is, becomes curvilinear. Similarly, the rate of increase in yield tends to improve throughout the immature stages. A linear equation is inadequate to describe the relation over the entire range.

In addition to the desirability of using an appropriately descriptive curve, it is sound procedure to remove from error any component that measures curvilinear regression. Thus, if an observation is properly described as $Y = \beta_0 + \beta_1 X + \beta_2 X^2 + \varepsilon$, and we use $Y = \beta_0 + \beta X + \varepsilon$ as the model, then we assign a part of the variation among population means, namely, that associated with $\beta_2 X^2$, to the measurement of error. Clearly this inflates our measure of error.

The selection of the form of the regression equation which best expresses a curvilinear relation is not always a simple problem. There is practically no limit to the number of kinds of curves that can be expressed by mathematical equations. Among the possible equations, many may exist which do about equally well in terms of minimizing SS(residuals). Hence, in choosing the form of curve, it is desirable to have some theory relative to the form, the theory being provided by specialists working in the subject matter area. In addition, it may be well to consider the work involved in fitting the regression and whether the customary assumptions necessary for the validity of estimation and testing procedures will be valid.

Such considerations lead us to classify curvilinear relations into two types: linear or nonlinear in the parameters. Models which are *linear in the parameters* are ones for which multiple regression techniques are available. They include polynomial models. Models which are *nonlinear in the parameters* are *intrinsically linear* if a transformation will make them linear. Logarithmic and exponential curves are typical examples. Models which cannot be linearized by a transformation are not intrinsically linear and associated analyses are referred to as *nonlinear regressions*. This problem is not discussed here, but an introduction is given in Draper and Smith (19.3, Chap. 10) and Gallant (19.6) furnishes an expository article.

Transformations are intended to provide an easier fitting procedure and/or valid estimation and testing procedures. For example, we may agree that the equation $E(Y) = \beta_0 X^{\beta_1}$ is based on sound biological reasoning. Then $\log E(Y) = \log \beta_0 + \beta_1 \log X$ is a linear equation if the pair of observations is considered to be $(\log Y, \log X)$. The procedures in Chaps. 10 and 17 apply. With such data as these, it is not uncommon to find that assumptions concerning normality are more nearly appropriate on the transformed scale than on the original.

We now consider two general types of curves: polynomials and exponential or logarithmic curves. Examples follow, for which general forms are shown in Fig. 19.1. For the exponential equations, e may be replaced by any other constant without affecting the form of the curve being fitted. For the equation $E(Y) = \beta_0 X^{\beta_1}$, integral values of the exponent β_1 give special cases of polynomials. However, this type of curve is more likely to be used when a fractional exponent is desired, as is often the case in the field of economics.

Polynomial	Exponential	Logarithmic
Linear:		
$E(Y) = \beta_0 + \beta_1 X$	$e^{E(Y)} = \beta_0 X^{\beta_1}$	$E(Y) = \beta_0' + \beta_1 \log X$
Quadratic:		
$E(Y) = \beta_0 + \beta_1 X + \beta_2 X^2$	$E(Y) = \beta_0 \beta_1^X$	$\log E(Y) = \beta_0' + \beta_1' X$
Cubic:		
$E(Y) = \beta_0 + \beta_1 X + \beta_2 X^2 + \beta_3 X^3$	$E(Y) = \beta_0 X^{\beta_1}$	$\log E(Y) = \beta_0' + \beta_1 \log X$

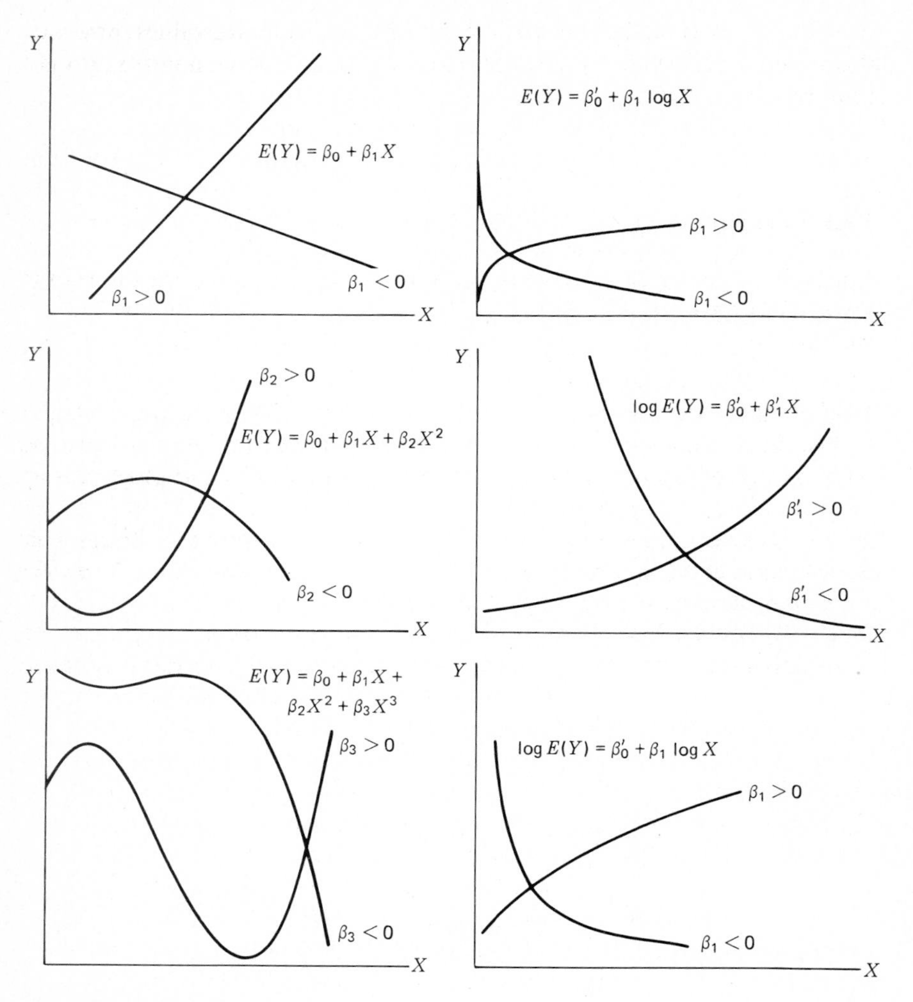

Figure 19.1 General types of curves.

Polynomials may have peaks and depressions numbering, at most, one less than the highest exponent. For example, the bottom left illustration in Fig. 19.1 has one peak and one depression, two such places for a curve where the highest exponent is 3. Peaks are called *maxima*; depressions are called *minima*. In fitting polynomial curves, the investigator is usually interested in some particular segment of the entire range represented by the equation.

The exponential or logarithmic curves, except those of the form $\log E(Y) = \beta_0' + \beta_1' \log X$ are characterized by a flattening at one end of the range. For example, the curve $E(Y) = \log X$ approaches closer and closer to

$X = 0$ as Y takes on numerically larger and larger negative values; however, this curve never crosses the vertical line $X = 0$. Negative numbers do not have real logarithms.

19.3 Logarithmic or Exponential Curves

Logarithmic, or simply log, curves are linear when plotted on the proper logarithmic paper. Referring to Fig. 19.1 (the right-hand side, top to bottom) we have:

1. $e^Y = \beta_0 X^{\beta_1}$ or $Y = \beta_0' + \beta_1 \log X$. The points (X, Y) plot as a straight line on semilog paper, where Y is plotted on the equal-interval scale and X on the log scale. Essentially, the semilog paper finds and plots the logs of X.
2. $Y = \beta_0 \beta_1^X$ or $\log Y = \beta_0' + \beta_1' X$. The points (X, Y) plot as a straight line on semilog paper, where Y is plotted on the log scale and X on the equal-interval scale (see Fig. 19.2 also).
3. $Y = \beta_0 X^{\beta_1}$ or $\log Y = \beta_0' + \beta_1 \log X$. This plots as a straight line on double-log paper. Here both scales are logarithmic. (See Fig. 19.3 also.)

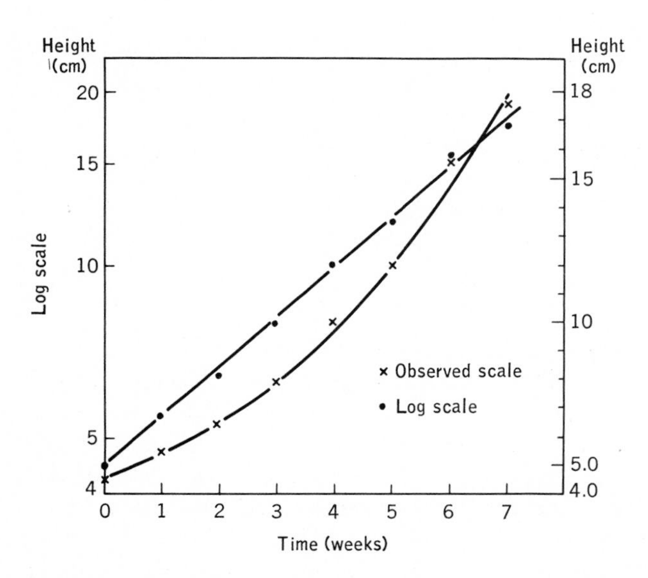

Figure 19.2 Observed points plotted on fixed-interval and log scales.

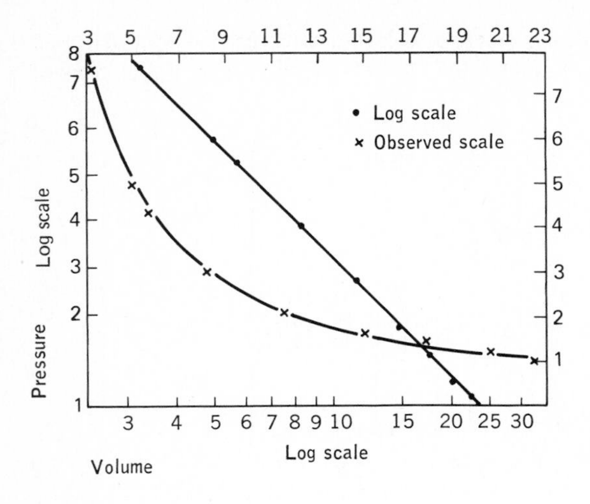

Figure 19.3 Observed points plotted on fixed-interval and log scales.

To determine whether data can be described by a log curve, it is often sufficient to plot the data on log paper. After a decision has been made about the type of log curve, the observed values of X and/or Y are transformed to logarithms before the computations can be performed. The transformed data are then handled by the methods of Chaps. 10 and 17. The usual assumptions apply to the transformed data rather than to the original.

W. J. Drapala, Mississippi State College, has supplied two sets of data for illustration. The data in Table 19.1 are heights in centimeters above the cotyledons, at weekly intervals, of Golden Acre cabbage. The data are plotted in Fig. 19.2, with X on the fixed-interval scale and Y on the log as well as the fixed-interval scale. Note how linear the set of points becomes when plotted on semilog paper.

Table 19.1 Height above the cotyledons for Golden Acre cabbage measured at weekly intervals

Weeks after first observation X	Height, cm Y	Common logarithm of height Y
0	4.5	0.653
1	5.5	0.740
2	6.5	0.813
3	8.0	0.903
4	10.0	1.000
5	12.0	1.079
6	15.5	1.190
7	17.5	1.243

Table 19.2 Analysis of cotyledon data by SAS

GENERAL LINEAR MODELS PROCEDURE

DEPENDENT VARIABLE: LOGY

SOURCE	DF	SUM OF SQUARES	MEAN SQUARE	F VALUE	PR > F	R-SQUARE	C.V.
MODEL	1	0.31497610	0.31497610	2347.62	0.0001	0.997451	1.2157
ERROR	6	0.00080501	0.00013417		STD DEV		LOGY MEAN
CORRECTED TOTAL	7	0.31578111			0.01158310		0.95276619

SOURCE	DF	TYPE I SS	F VALUE	PR > F	DF	TYPE IV SS	F VALUE	PR > F
X	1	0.31497610	2347.62	0.0001	1	0.31497610	2347.62	0.0001

PARAMETER	ESTIMATE	T FOR HO: PARAMETER = 0	PR > |T|	STD ERROR OF ESTIMATE
INTERCEPT	0.64966880	86.89	0.0001	0.00747686
X	0.08659926	48.45	0.0001	0.00178731

Table 19.3 Pressure of oxygen gas kept at 25°C when made to occupy various volumes

Volume, liters, X	Pressure, atm, Y	Common logarithm Volume X	Common logarithm Pressure Y
3.25	7.34	0.512	0.866
5.00	4.77	0.699	0.679
5.71	4.18	0.757	0.621
8.27	2.88	0.918	0.459
11.50	2.07	1.061	0.316
14.95	1.59	1.175	0.201
17.49	1.36	1.243	0.134
20.35	1.17	1.309	0.068
22.40	1.06	1.350	0.025

We now proceed with calculations on the transformed data, as in Chap. 10 or 13. Alternatively, a computer program provides information, such as in Table 19.2.

The regression equation is

$$\widehat{\log Y} = 0.6497 + 0.0866X$$

The mean of the log Y values is 0.9528.

The data in Table 19.3 are pressures, in atmospheres, of oxygen gas kept at 25°C when made to occupy various volumes, measured in liters. The data are curvilinear when plotted on the equal-interval scale and nearly linear on the double log scale (see Fig. 19.3). The relation $\widehat{\log Y} = b_0 + b_1 \log X$ is fitted. Again the procedures of Chaps. 10 and 13 are appropriate. Table 19.4 is part of a computer printout of the data analysis. The regression equation is

$$\widehat{\log Y} = 1.3790 - 1.0022 \log X$$

Note that the F value should begin with 4. However, the number is too large for the space available, so all 9's are printed by programming convention.

Exercise 19.3.1 Brockington et al. (19.2) collected the data shown in the accompanying table on the relation between moisture content and interstitial relative humidity for whole-kernel corn.

Table 19.4 Analysis of pressure data by SAS

GENERAL LINEAR MODELS PROCEDURE

DEPENDENT VARIABLE: LOGY

SOURCE	DF	SUM OF SQUARES	MEAN SQUARE	F VALUE	PR > F	R-SQUARE	C.V.
MODEL	1	0.70897285	0.70897285	99999.99	0.0000	0.999998	0.1054
ERROR	7	0.00000109	0.00000016		STD DEV		LOGY MEAN
CORRECTED TOTAL	8	0.70897394			0.00039463		0.37435348

SOURCE	DF	TYPE I SS	F VALUE	PR > F	DF	TYPE IV SS	F VALUE	PR > F
LOGX	1	0.70897285	99999.99	0.0000	1	0.70897285	99999.99	0.0000

PARAMETER	ESTIMATE	T FOR HO: PARAMETER = 0	PR > |T|	STD ERROR OF ESTIMATE
INTERCEPT	1.37899089	2820.73	0.0001	0.00048888
LOGX	−1.00219470	−2133.68	0.0001	0.00046970

Sample no.	Moisture content		Equilibrium relative humidity, percent
	Brown-Duval	Two-stage oven	
1	7.0	9.4	40.0
2	7.5	9.9	40.0
3	11.6	12.9	59.0
4	11.8	12.6	63.5
5	12.9	14.1	71.5
6	13.2	14.7	71.0
7	14.0	15.2	76.5
8	14.2	14.6	75.5
9	14.6	15.2	79.0
10	14.8	15.8	79.0
11	15.7	15.8	82.0
12	17.3	17.2	85.5
13	17.4	17.0	85.0
14	17.8	18.2	87.5
15	18.0	18.5	86.5
16	18.8	18.2	88.0
17	18.9	19.4	90.0
18	20.0	20.3	90.5
19	20.7	19.9	88.5
20	22.4	19.5	89.5
21	22.5	19.8	91.0
22	26.8	22.6	92.0

Plot Y = equilibrium relative humidity against X = moisture content (either measurement) with X on ordinary scale and log-scale graph paper. What seems to be an appropriate choice of scales to give a straight line? Compute the linear regression of equilibrium relative humidity on log of moisture content. What percentage of SS(total) is accounted for by linear regression?

Exercise 19.3.2 In a study of optimum plot size and shape, Weber and Horner (19.9) considered length of plot and variance of plot means per basic unit for yield in grams and protein percentage (among other plot shapes and characters). They obtained the data shown in the accompanying table.

Shape	Number of units	Variance	
		Yield, g	Protein, percent
8 × 1	1	949	.116
16 × 1	2	669	.080
24 × 1	3	540	.053
32 × 1	4	477	.048

Plot the two sets of variances against number of units after transforming all three variables to log scales. Do the resulting data appear to be reasonably linearly related?

19.4 The Second-degree Polynomial

Section 14.8 dealt briefly with polynomial models. Here we illustrate with a polynomial of degree 2.

Let Eq. (19.1) be the mathematical description of an observation. Clearly, linearity applies to the parameters to be estimated and not to the observable ones.

$$Y_i = \beta_0 + \beta_1 X_i + \beta_2 X_i^2 + \varepsilon_i \tag{19.1}$$

In this equation β_1 and β_2 are partial regression coefficients, as discussed in Chap. 14, but they cannot be interpreted in other than a two-dimensional space.

For least-squares estimates of the parameters, Eq. (19.2) must be satisfied.

$$\sum (Y - \hat{Y})^2 = \sum (Y_i - \hat{\beta}_0 - \hat{\beta}_1 X_i - \hat{\beta}_2 X_i^2)^2 = \min \tag{19.2}$$

The normal or least-squares equations are

$$\mathbf{X'X\hat{\beta}} = \mathbf{X'Y} \tag{19.3}$$

where

$$\mathbf{X'X} = \begin{pmatrix} n & \sum X_i & \sum X_i^2 \\ \sum X_i & \sum X_i^2 & \sum X_i^3 \\ \sum X_i^2 & \sum X_i^3 & \sum X_i^4 \end{pmatrix} \qquad \text{and} \qquad \mathbf{X'Y} = \begin{pmatrix} \sum Y_i \\ \sum X_i Y_i \\ \sum X_i^2 Y_i \end{pmatrix}$$

The data in Table 19.5 are used to illustrate. Numerical entries for **X′X** and **X′Y** are given there. Table 19.6 provides an analysis of variance, tests of hypotheses, and estimates of the necessary parameters. Approximately 91 percent ($= 100R^2$) of the variation, as measured by the total sum of squares,

Table 19.5 Yield Y, in pounds per plot, and tenderometer reading X, of Alaska peas grown at Madison, Wisconsin, 1953

Y Yield, pounds per plot:	24.0	22.0	26.5	22.0	25.0	37.5	36.0	39.5	32.0	26.5	55.5	49.5	56.0	55.5
X Tenderometer reading:	76.2	76.8	77.3	79.2	80.0	87.8	93.2	93.5	94.3	96.8	97.5	99.5	104.2	106.3

Y Yield, pounds per plot:	58.0	61.5	69.0	71.5	73.0	76.5	78.5	74.0	71.5	77.0	85.5
X Tenderometer reading:	106.7	119.0	119.7	119.8	119.8	123.5	141.0	142.3	145.5	149.0	150.0

$\sum X = 2{,}698.9$	$\sum X^2 = 305{,}148.35$	$\sum X^3 = 36{,}045{,}287.22$	$\sum X^4 = 4{,}429{,}289{,}685.23$
$\sum Y = 1{,}303.5$	$\sum Y^2 = 78{,}797.25$	$\sum XY = 152{,}129.55$	$\sum X^2Y = 18{,}424{,}791.12$

Table 19.6 Analysis of Alaska pea data by SAS

GENERAL LINEAR MODELS PROCEDURE

DEPENDENT VARIABLE: Y

SOURCE	DF	SUM OF SQUARES	MEAN SQUARE	F VALUE	PR > F	R-SQUARE	C.V.
MODEL	2	9888.85463514	4944.42731757	115.24	0.0001	0.912866	12.5627
ERROR	22	943.90536486	42.90478931		STD DEV		Y MEAN
CORRECTED TOTAL	24	10832.76000000			6.55017475		52.14000000

SOURCE	DF	TYPE I SS	F VALUE	PR > F	DF	TYPE IV SS	F VALUE	PR > F
X	1	9441.75392063	220.06	0.0001	1	917.28607392	21.38	0.0001
X*X	1	447.10071451	10.42	0.0039	1	447.10071451	10.42	0.0039

PARAMETER	ESTIMATE	T FOR HO: PARAMETER = 0	PR > |T|	STD ERROR OF ESTIMATE
INTERCEPT	−138.50680942	−4.33	0.0003	31.98150177
X	2.71328314	4.62	0.0001	0.58680743
X*X	−0.00837858	−3.23	0.0039	0.00259550

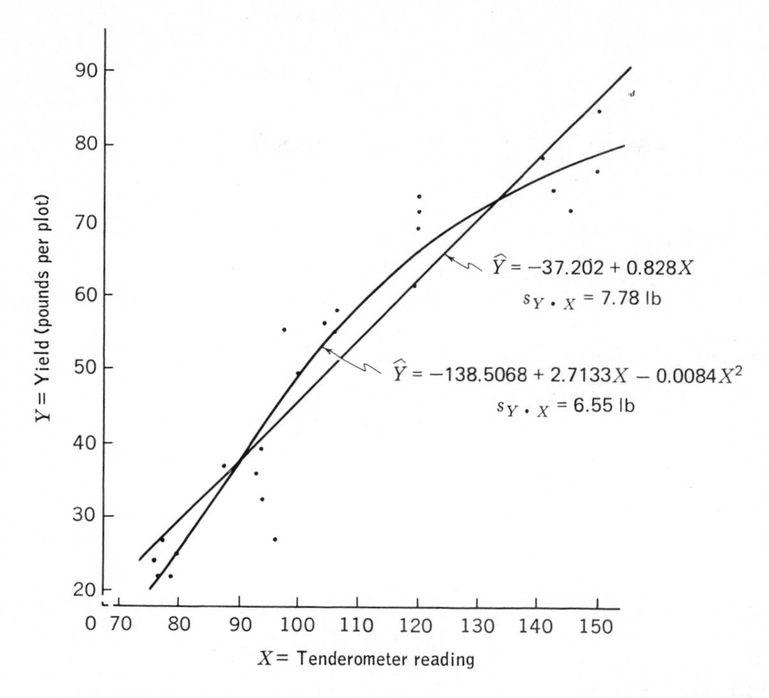

Figure 19.4 Relationship between yield and tenderometer reading for data in Table 19.5

can be explained by a quadratic equation in X. The sample regression equation is

$$\hat{Y} = -138.5068 + 2.7133X - 0.0084X^2$$

Figure 19.4 shows both linear and quadratic equations. Computations for the linear regression were available on printout but are not shown here.

Exercise 19.4.1 To Table 10.5 add the pair of observations (1,949, 1,796). Compute the quadratic regression of number of horses on year. Would you want to include X^2 in the regression equation? Why?

19.5 Orthogonal Polynomials

When increments between successive levels of X are equal and the Y values have a common variance, tables of values of orthogonal polynomials can be used in computations leading to tests of hypotheses about the goodness of fit of polynomials of various degrees. With the orthogonal polynomials themselves, one can also find regression equations. Both procedures were illustrated in Sec. 15.7.

Orthogonal polynomials can be used in situations where the X's are not equally spaced and/or observations have unequal but known variances. Successive polynomials are independent of one another and enable us to compute additional sums of squares attributable to the various powers of X.

For unequally spaced X's and/or Y means based on unequal numbers, Robson (19.8) uses what is essentially Fisher's (19.4, 19.5) argument to obtain a recursion formula for computing coefficients. (A recursion formula is one which is applied over and over again, each new application making use of the previous application.) Robson proceeds as follows:

Any least-squares regression equation may be expressed in the form

$$\hat{Y}_i = b_0 f_0(X_i) + b_1 f_1(X_i) + \cdots + b_r f_r(X_i) \tag{19.4}$$

$i = 1, \ldots, n > r$, where $\hat{Y}_i$ is the estimated population mean of the Y's at $X = X_i$. The polynomial $f_j(X_i)$ is of degree j and will provide the orthogonal polynomial values, one for each X, required to determine the regression coefficients. The coefficients are

$$b_j = \sum_i Y_i f_j(X_i) \tag{19.5}$$

Each regression coefficient represents a contrast or comparison, as defined in Sec. 8.3. These contrasts are orthogonal and give additional sums of squares attributable to including X to the jth power in the regression equation. Thus b_0 is the zero degree or mean (not main) effect, b_1 is the first degree or linear effect, and so on. Finally

$$\sum_i Y_i^2 = b_0^2 + \cdots + b_{n-1}^2$$

if we carry r out to $n - 1$ so that all df $= n$ are individually accounted for.

The recursion formula given by Robson is Eq. (19.6) with c_h defined by Eq. (19.7).

$$f_h(X_i) = \frac{1}{c_h}\left[X_i^h - \sum_{j=0}^{h-1} f_j(X_i) \sum_{g=1}^{n} X_g^h f_j(X_g)\right] \tag{19.6}$$

$$c_h^2 = \sum_i \left[X_i^h - \sum_{j=0}^{h-1} f_j(X_i) \sum_{g=1}^{n} X_g^h f_j(X_g)\right]^2 \tag{19.7}$$

Notice that c_h^2 is the sum of the squares of quantities like that in the bracket of Eq. (19.6).

We shall now illustrate the use of the recursion formula. Suppose that we have means for the percentage of digestion of cellulose at 6, 12, 18, 24, 36, 48, and 72 h. Application of Eqs. (19.6) and (19.7) gives

$$f_0(X_i) = \frac{1}{c_0}(X_i^0) = \frac{1}{c_0}$$

$$c_0^2 = X_1^0 + \cdots + X_n^0 = n$$

(A quantity raised to the zero power equals 1.) Now

$$f_0(X_1) = \frac{1}{\sqrt{n}} = f_0(X_2) = \cdots = f_0(X_n)$$

From Eq. (19.5),

$$b_0 = \sum Y_i \frac{1}{\sqrt{n}}$$

and the reduction attributable to this polynomial is

$$b_0^2 = \frac{(\sum Y)^2}{n}$$

This is the correction term as we might have expected. The remaining $n - 1$ regression coefficients are concerned with the partitioning of the $n - 1$ degrees of freedom for treatment means.

Next,

$$\begin{aligned} f_1(X_i) &= \frac{1}{c_1}\left[X_i - f_0(X_i) \sum_{g=1}^{n} X_g f_0(X_g)\right] \\ &= \frac{1}{c_1}\left(X_i - \frac{1}{\sqrt{n}} \sum_{g=1}^{n} X_g \frac{1}{\sqrt{n}}\right) \\ &= \frac{1}{c_1}(X_i - \bar{X}) \\ c_1^2 &= \sum (X_i - \bar{X})^2 \end{aligned}$$

Now

$$\bar{X} = 216/7 = 30.86 \qquad \text{and} \qquad \sum (X_i - \bar{X})^2 = 3{,}198.86$$

$$f_1(X_1) = \frac{(6 - 30.86)}{\sqrt{3{,}198.86}}, \ldots, f_1(X_n) = \frac{(72 - 30.86)}{\sqrt{3{,}198.86}}$$

Finally

$$b_1 = \sum Y_i \frac{(X_i - \bar{X})}{\sqrt{\sum (X_i - \bar{X})^2}}$$

and the reduction attributable to linear regression is

$$b_1^2 = \frac{[\sum Y_i(X_i - \bar{X})]^2}{\sum (X_i - \bar{X})^2}$$

Again, this result was expected. The quantity in the brackets of the numerator is usually written in the form $\sum (Y_i - \bar{Y})(X_i - \bar{X})$, but the two forms are equivalent. Note that for $r = 1$, Eq. (19.4) becomes

$$\hat{Y} = \frac{(\sum Y_i)}{\sqrt{n}}\frac{1}{\sqrt{n}} + \frac{\sum Y_i(X_i - \bar{X})}{\sqrt{\sum (X_i - \bar{X})^2}}\frac{(X - \bar{X})}{\sqrt{\sum (X_i - \bar{X})^2}}$$

$$= \bar{Y} + \frac{\sum (X_i - \bar{X})(Y_i - \bar{Y})}{\sum (X_i - \bar{X})^2}(X - \bar{X})$$

For the second-degree equation,

$$f_2(X_i) = \frac{1}{c_2}\left[X_i^2 - \frac{1}{\sqrt{n}}\left(\sum_{g=1}^{n} X_g^2 \frac{1}{\sqrt{n}}\right) - \frac{X_i - \bar{X}}{\sqrt{\sum_i (X_i - \bar{X})^2}}\sum_{g=1}^{n} X_g^2 \frac{X_g - \bar{X}}{\sqrt{\sum_i (X_i - \bar{X})^2}}\right]$$

$$= \frac{1}{c_2}\left[X_i^2 - \frac{1}{n}\sum_g X_g^2 - \frac{(X_i - \bar{X})\sum_g X_g^2(X_g - \bar{X})}{\sum_i (X_i - \bar{X})^2}\right]$$

Again, we must find c_2^2 by Eq. (19.7). Note that $f_2(X_i)$ is a polynomial of degree 2; it has an X_i^2, an X_i as an $X_i - \bar{X}$ times a constant, and a constant term, namely, $-\sum X_g^2/n$. The fact that there is an X_i shows that the complete quadratic equation will have a coefficient of X that differs from the coefficient of X in the linear equation; the coefficient of X_i in $f_2(X_i)$ supplies the adjustment.

Note that we have computed the orthogonal functions for the general case. Then, for our example, we have used the X's of the experiment to get the coefficients of the Y's for the linear function of the Y's which gives us the additional reduction attributable to the highest power of X that has been introduced.

Exercise 19.5.1 A. van Tienhoven, Cornell University, conducted a 5×5 factorial experiment to study the effects of thyroid hormone (TH) and thyroid stimulating hormone (TSH) on follicular epithelium heights (among other responses) in chicks. TH is measured in γ units, TSH in Junkmann-Schoeller units, and the response in micrometer units. Treatment totals are shown in the accompanying table. Each total is of five observations.

		TSH				
		.00	.03	.09	.27	.81
	.00	3.42	6.21	11.21	14.40	19.40
	.04	5.64	5.85	9.16	18.30	19.65
TH	.16	5.13	8.39	12.74	15.20	15.07
	.64	5.37	5.24	9.14	17.66	16.30
	2.56	4.54	6.49	8.37	14.23	16.90

Source: Unpublished data used with permission of A. van Tienhoven, Cornell University, Ithaca, New York.

The response as measured by epithelium heights is supposed to follow a logarithmic curve. The first levels of TH and TSH are not in equally spaced log sequences with the other levels. However, information was wanted for this particular treatment.

A preliminary analysis follows.

Ignore treatments TSH = .00 and TH = .00. Plot the response to TH, for each level of TSH, on log paper with treatment on the log scale. Does the response appear to be linear on this scale? Repeat for the response to TSH.

Use orthogonal polynomials to compute sums of squares for the overall linear, quadratic, and cubic responses to TSH for the four nonzero levels. Choose the log scale for treatments so that the table of coefficients may be used directly. Test each response for significance.

Consider how you would test the homogeneity of these various responses over levels of TH. Test the homogeneity of the cubic responses since they measure deviations from quadratic responses and might be considered as candidates for an error term.

Compute sums of squares for overall linear, quadratic, and cubic responses to TH.

How do you find coefficients for measuring TSH(linear) times TH(linear), TSH(linear) times TH(quadratic), and TSH(quadratic) times TH(linear)? Find and test these components.

Preliminary analysis

Source	df	SS
Total	123	1,378.85
TSH	4	540.33
TH	4	48.09
TSH × TH	16	154.67
Error	99†	635.76

† There was one missing observation.

Exercise 19.5.2 Use Eq. (19.6) to compute the cubic orthogonal polynomial.

Exercise 19.5.3 From the results in the text and of Exercise 19.5.2, compute your own table of orthogonal polynomial coefficients for four and five equally spaced and equally replicated treatments. Comment.

References

19.1. Anderson, R. L., and E. E. Houseman: "Tables of orthogonal polynomial values extended to $n = 104$," *Iowa Agr. Exp. Sta. Res. Bull.* 297, 1942.

19.2. Brockington, S. F., H. C. Dorin, and H. K. Howerton: "Hygroscopic equilibria of whole kernel corn," *Cereal Chem.*, **26:**166–173 (1949).

19.3. Draper, N. R., and H. Smith, Jr.: *Applied Regression Analysis*, 1st ed., Wiley, New York, 1966.

19.4. Fisher, R. A.: "The influence of rainfall on the yield of wheat at Rothamsted," *Phil. Trans. Roy. Soc.*, B. **213:**89–142 (1925).

19.5. Fisher, R. A.: *Statistical Methods for Research Workers*, 11th ed., rev., Hafner, New York, 1950.

19.6. Gallant, A. R.: "Nonlinear regression," *Amer. Statist.*, **29:** 73–81 (1975).
19.7. Pearson, E. S., and H. O. Hartley (eds): *Biometrika Tables for Statisticians*, vol. 1, Cambridge, New York, 1954.
19.8. Robson, D. S.: "A simple method for constructing orthogonal polynomials when the independent variable is unequally spaced," *Biom.*, **15:** 187–191 (1959).
19.9. Weber, C. R., and T. W. Horner: "Estimation of cost and optimum plot size and shape for measuring yield and chemical characters in soybeans," *Agron. J.*, **49:** 444–449 (1957).

CHAPTER

TWENTY

SOME USES OF CHI-SQUARE

20.1 Introduction

The chi-square test criterion is most commonly associated with enumeration data. However, the chi-square distribution is a continuous distribution based upon an underlying normal distribution. At this point, we introduce a chapter on chi-square to stress, to some degree, its true nature by associating it with data from continuous distributions in several useful situations. We then proceed in two subsequent chapters to illustrate its use with enumeration data.

Chi-square is defined in Sec. 3.9 as the sum of squares of independent, normally distributed variables with zero mean and unit variance, as illustrated in Eqs. (3.13) and (3.14). In this chapter, we show how to compute a confidence interval for σ^2 using the χ^2 distribution. This is an exact procedure. The test criterion χ^2 is also used where it is an obvious approximation; for example, see Sec. 11.5 on testing the homogeneity of correlation coefficients. We also discuss two similar uses, tests of the homogeneity of variances and of the goodness of fit of observed continuous data to theoretical distributions.

20.2 Confidence Interval for σ^2

Consider the statement

$$P(\chi_0^2 \leq \chi^2 \leq \chi_1^2) = .95$$

This is a statement about the random variable χ^2. An obvious choice of χ_0^2 and χ_1^2 would be the values $\chi^2_{.975}$ and $\chi^2_{.025}$, values such that

$$P(\chi^2 \leq \chi^2_{.975}) = .025 \qquad \text{and} \qquad P(\chi^2 \geq \chi^2_{.025}) = .025$$

These two values are convenient to use when computing a confidence interval for σ^2. However, they do not give the shortest possible confidence interval.

The customary procedure for computing a 95 percent confidence interval for σ^2 starts by combining the pair of probability statements above. We obtain

$$P(\chi^2_{.975} \leq \chi^2 \leq \chi^2_{.025}) = .95$$

where $\chi^2 = (n-1)s^2/\sigma^2$ by definition. (For a 99 percent confidence interval, use $\chi^2_{.995}$ and $\chi^2_{.005}$; and so on.) This formula leads to

$$P\left[\frac{(n-1)s^2}{\chi^2_{.025}} \leq \sigma^2 \leq \frac{(n-1)s^2}{\chi^2_{.975}}\right] = .95 \tag{20.1}$$

This equation is still an equation about the random variable χ^2 or about s^2, though it is now made to sound like an equation about σ^2. From a particular sample, we compute $(n-1)s^2/\chi^2_{.025}$ and $(n-1)s^2/\chi^2_{.975}$ as the endpoints of the 95 percent confidence interval for σ^2.

For example, Table 4.3, sample 1, has $SS = (n-1)s^2 = 2{,}376.40$ for $n = 10$. (We know that $\sigma^2 = 144$.) For a confidence interval for σ^2, compute

$$\frac{2{,}376.40}{\chi^2_{.025}} = \frac{2{,}376.40}{19.0} = 125.07$$

and

$$\frac{2{,}376.40}{\chi^2_{.975}} = \frac{2{,}376.40}{2.70} = 880.15$$

We now say that σ^2 lies between 125.07 and 880.15 unless the sample was an unusual one. In this case, we know that σ^2 does lie in the confidence interval because we sampled a known population.

Exercise 20.2.1 Compute a 90 percent confidence interval for σ^2 for the second sample in Table 4.3. A 95 percent confidence interval for the third sample. A 99 percent confidence interval for the fourth sample.

Exercise 20.2.2 Compute 95 percent confidence intervals for σ^2 for each soil type sampled in Table 5.6. Do the confidence intervals overlap? Compare this result with the result of the F-test of H_0: $\sigma_1^2 = \sigma_2^2$ versus H_1: $\sigma_1^2 \neq \sigma_2^2$. Comment.

Exercise 20.2.3 Begin with the statement $P(\chi^2 \leq \chi^2_{.05}) = .95$ and show how this leads to a lower bound on the size of σ^2.

Exercise 20.2.4 Begin with the statement $P(\chi^2 \geq \chi^2_{.95}) = .95$ and show how this leads to an upper bound on the size of σ^2.

Note: Exercises 20.2.3 and 20.2.4 provide techniques for constructing one-sided confidence intervals.

Exercise 20.2.5 Construct a 90 percent one-sided confidence interval for σ^2 for the second sample in Table 4.3. Let it be open to the right.

Exercise 20.2.6 Construct a 95 percent one-sided confidence interval for σ^2 for the third sample in Table 4.3. Let zero be the left endpoint.

20.3 Homogeneity of Variance

In a study including the inheritance of seed size in flax, Myers (20.8) obtained the variances among weights per 50 seeds from individual plants for parents and the F_1 generation. These are given in Table 20.1.

One might wish to test the homogeneity of such variances for the same reasons one tests the homogeneity of means or to establish whether or not an assumption of homogeneity, required for a valid analysis of variance of the data, is met. A discussion of such assumptions was given in Sec. 7.10. If the hypothesis of homogeneity of variance is rejected, then an analysis of variance of the data would likely be done on transformed data. Transformations were discussed in Sec. 9.16.

The test procedure, an approximate one, is due to Bartlett (20.1, 20.2) and is a modification of the Neyman-Pearson likelihood ratio test. It is carried out in Table 20.1. If natural logarithms (base e) are used, the multiplier 2.3026 is not required; this is used only with common logarithms (base 10).

Table 20.1 Test of the homogeneity of k variances

Class	df	$\sum (Y - \bar{Y})^2$	s^2	$\log s^2$	$(n-1) \log s^2$	$1/(n-1)$
Redwing	81	4,744.17	58.57	1.76768	143.18208	.01235
Ottawa 770B	44	3,380.96	76.84	1.88559	82.96596	.02273
F_1	13	1,035.71	79.67	1.90129	24.71677	.07692
Totals	138	9,160.84			250.86481	.11200
Pooling			66.38	1.82204	251.44152	

$$\chi^2 = 2.3026\{[\sum (n_i - 1)] \log \bar{s^2} - \sum (n_i - 1) \log s_i^2\}$$

$$= 2.3026(251.44152 - 250.86481) = 1.3279 \quad \text{with 2 df}$$

$$\text{Correction factor} = 1 + \frac{1}{3(k-1)}\left[\sum \frac{1}{n_i - 1} - \frac{1}{\sum (n_i - 1)}\right]$$

$$= 1 + \frac{1}{3(2)}\left[.11200 - \frac{1}{138}\right] = 1.01746$$

$$\text{Corrected } \chi^2 = \frac{1.3279}{1.01746} = 1.305 \quad \text{not significant}$$

The correction factor should improve the approximation to χ^2 when sample sizes are small. It is always greater than 1 and its use decreases the crude χ^2. Thus, we generally compute the corrected χ^2 only when the crude χ^2 is significant but near the critical value.

An assumption for the appropriate use of this test is that the underlying distributions be normal. When this is not so, the test may detect anormality rather than heterogeneity of variance. This test is more sensitive to anormality than is the use of F in the analysis of variance.

Independent χ^2 values are additive, that is, the distribution of such a sum is also distributed as χ^2 with degrees of freedom equal to the sum of those for the individuals. This is true only for the crude χ^2's and not for the corrected ones. Thus, if variances were available for several years, it might be informative to make within- and among-year comparisons. Also, if variances were available for several segregating generations, one might compare among parents and F_1 (as here), among segregating generations, and between the two groups. The total χ^2 can be used as an arithmetic check, at least.

Exercise 20.3.1 Variances for the data of Table 7.1 vary from 1.28 to 33.64. While this is quite a range, each has only 4 degrees of freedom. Test the homogeneity of these variances. Can you see how to reduce the computations when all variances are based on the same number of degrees of freedom?

Note: Pearson and Hartley (20.9) have provided tables of critical values of the test criterion s^2_{max}/s^2_{min} and of Cochran's (20.3) $s^2_{max}/\sum s^2_i$ test. Tables for the former test are also available in Rohlf and Sokal (20.12) and for the latter in Dixon and Massey (20.11). These tests require that sample sizes be equal. Like Bartlett's test, they are also sensitive to anormality.

Exercise 20.3.2 Check the homogeneity of the variances in Exercise 7.3.1.

Exercise 20.3.3 The variances in Exercise 7.4.1 are based on different numbers of degrees of freedom. Check their homogeneity.

20.4 Goodness of Fit for Continuous Distributions

It is often desired to know whether or not a given set of data approximates a given distribution such as the normal or chi-square. As an example of this, consider the data of Table 20.2, earlier presented in Table 2.5. Let us test the observed distribution against the normal distribution.

To compare an observed distribution with a normal distribution, expected cell frequencies are required. The yield value of 3 g includes yields to 5.5 g, of 8 g includes yields greater than 5.5 and up to 10.5 g, etc. To compute expected frequencies, the probabilities associated with each interval are necessary. These are found from Table A.4. Values for μ and σ must be estimated from our data. We find $\bar{Y} = 31.93$ and $s = 12.80$ and consider

Table 20.2 Observed and expected values of yield, in grams, of 229 spaced plants of Richland soybeans

Yield	3	8	13	18	23	28	33	38	43	48	53	58	63	68
Observed frequency	7	5	7	18	32	41	37	25	22	19	6	6	3	1
End point	5.5	10.5	15.5	20.5	25.5	30.5	35.5	40.5	45.5	50.5	55.5	60.5	65.5	
Deviation from mean	−26.43	−21.43	−16.43	−11.43	−6.43	−1.43	3.57	8.57	13.57	18.57	23.57	28.57	33.57	
Standard deviations from mean	−2.065	−1.674	−1.284	−0.893	−0.502	−0.112	0.279	0.670	1.060	1.451	1.841	2.232	2.623	
Probability	.0194	.0277	.0525	.0863	.1219	.1477	.1545	.1386	.1068	.0712	.0405	.0201	.0084	.0044
Expected frequency	4.4	6.3	12.0	19.8	27.9	33.8	35.4	31.7	24.5	16.3	9.3	4.6	1.9	1.0
Contribution to χ^2	1.54	0.27	2.08	0.16	0.60	1.53	0.07	1.42	0.26	0.45	1.17	0.43	0.64	0.00

$\bar{Y} = 31.93$ $s = 12.80$ $\chi^2 = 10.62$ with $14 - 3 = 11$ df

them to be μ and σ. Now,

$$P(Y < 5.5) = P\left(Z < \frac{5.5 - 31.93}{12.80}\right)$$

$$= P(Z < -2.065) = .0194$$

$$P(5.5 < Y < 10.5) = P\left(\frac{5.5 - 31.93}{12.80} < Z < \frac{10.5 - 31.93}{12.80}\right)$$

$$= P(-2.065 < Z < -1.674) = .0471 - .0194$$

$$= .0277$$

and so on. Each probability times the total frequency 229 gives an expected frequency. The probability associated with the last cell is the probability of a value greater than 65.5 and is not the probability of a value greater than 65.5 but not more than 70.5. The computations are shown in Table 20.2. The sum of the probabilities should differ from 1 by rounding errors only. The sum of the expected frequencies should differ from 229 by rounding errors only.

Compute the value of the test criterion

$$\chi^2 = \sum \frac{(\text{observed} - \text{expected})^2}{\text{expected}} \tag{20.2}$$

$$= 10.62 \qquad \text{with } (14 - 1 - 2) = 11 \text{ df} \qquad \text{not significant.}$$

In general, the number of degrees of freedom for χ^2 is the number of cells decreased by the number of restrictions imposed on the sampling and the number of independent parameters estimated. Here, we have 14 cells, are restricted to tests of samples of size 229, and must estimate the two parameters of the normal distribution, namely, μ and σ^2. The test criterion is distributed approximately as χ^2, provided that expected frequencies are not too small.

Expected frequencies begin at 1.0. This is a small expectation. Some writers have suggested five to ten as minimum and would have us pool the first two cells as a new first and the last three or four as a new last. This would improve the approximation to χ^2. However, since the tails of a distribution often offer the best source of evidence for distinguishing among hypothesized distributions, the improvement has been at the expense of the power of the test. Cochran (20.4 to 20.6) has shown that there is little disturbance to the 5 percent level when a single expectation is as low as .5 and two expectations may be as low as 1 for fewer degrees of freedom than for our example. The 1 percent level shows a somewhat greater disturbance than the 5 percent. For Table 20.2, no pooling would seem to be necessary. There is no evidence to suggest that the normal distribution does not provide an adequate fit.

Exercise 20.4.1 Fit a normal distribution to the table of butterfat data given as Table 4.1 assuming $\mu = 40$ and $\sigma = 12$ lb. Test the goodness of fit.

Exercise 20.4.2 Fit a normal distribution to the 500 means of Table 4.4, assuming no knowledge of the population mean and variance. Test the goodness of fit.

20.5 Combining Probabilities from Tests of Significance

Fisher (20.7) has shown that $-2 \log P$, where logs are to the base e and P is the probability of obtaining a value of the test criterion as extreme or more extreme than that obtained in a particular test, is distributed as χ^2 with two degrees of freedom. Such values may be added. In practice, it is customary to use logs to the base 10 and multiply the result by 2.3026 to give logs to the base e. Multiplication is conveniently done after addition rather than for the separate values.

This relation between P and χ^2 may be used when it is desired to pool information available from data not suitable for pooling. Such data must be from independent trials.

For example, we may have information on the difference in response to a check or standard treatment and a particular experimental treatment from several quite different experiments. These treatments may be the only ones common to the experiments, which may include different experimental designs. Each experiment may show the probability of a larger value of the test criterion, not necessarily the same criterion for all tests, to be between .15 and .05 for the particular comparison. Probabilities are computed on the assumption that the null hypothesis is true. No one value may be significant yet each may suggest the possibility of a real difference. The test would be applied to the combined probabilities, combination being carried out by adding the values of $-2 \log P$.

The use of this pooling procedure requires that the tables of the original test criteria be reasonably complete with respect to probability levels; interpolation must then be used. Next refer the sum of the $-2 \log P$ values to the χ^2 table, Table A.5, where the value of P for the pooled information is obtained. This pooled χ^2 has $2k$ degrees of freedom when k probabilities are being combined.

Wallis (20.10) suggests that this test is rarely or never ideal but is likely to be highly satisfactory in practice.

References

20.1. Bartlett, M. S.: "Properties of sufficiency and statistical tests," *Proc. Roy. Soc.*, **A160:**268–282 (1937).

20.2. Bartlett, M. S.: "Some examples of statistical methods of research in agriculture and applied biology," *J. Roy. Statist. Soc. Suppl.*, **4:**137–183 (1937).

20.3. Cochran, W. G.: "The distribution of the largest of a set of estimated variances as a fraction of their total," *Ann. Eugen.*, **11:**47–52, (1941).

20.4. Cochran, W. G.: "The χ^2 correction for continuity," *Iowa State Coll. J. Sci.*, **16:**421–436 (1942).
20.5. Cochran, W. G.: "The χ^2 test of goodness of fit," *Ann. Math. Statist.*, **23:**315–345 (1952).
20.6. Cochran, W. G.: "Some methods for strengthening the common χ^2 tests," *Biom.*, **10:**417–451 (1954).
20.7. Fisher, R. A.: *Statistical Methods for Research Workers*, 11 ed., rev., Hafner, New York, 1950.
20.8. Myers, W. M.: "A correlated study of the inheritance of seed size and botanical characters in the flax cross, Redwing × Ottawa 770B," *J. Amer. Soc. Agron.*, **28:**623–635 (1936).
20.9. Pearson, E. S., and H. O. Hartley (eds.): *Biometrika Tables for Statisticians*, 3d ed. Cambridge, New York, 1966.
20.10. Wallis, W. A.: "Compounding probabilities from independent significance tests," *Econ.*, **10:**229–248 (1942).
20.11. Dixon, W. J., and F. J. Massey, Jr.: *Introduction to Statistical Analysis*, 3d ed., McGraw-Hill, New York, 1969.
20.12. Rohlf, F. J., and R. R. Sokal: *Statistical Tables*. Freeman, San Francisco, 1969.

CHAPTER

TWENTY-ONE

ENUMERATION DATA I: ONE-WAY CLASSIFICATIONS

21.1 Introduction

This chapter is concerned with *enumeration data* classified according to a single criterion.

Enumeration data generally involve a discrete variable, that is, a qualitative rather than a quantitative characteristic. Thus, they consist of the numbers of individuals falling into well-defined classes. For example, a population is sampled and the numbers of males and females in the sample are observed, or the numbers of affirmatives, negatives, and maybes in response to a question on a questionnaire are counted, and so on.

21.2 The χ^2 Test Criterion

In Sec. 3.9, Eq. (3.13), the statistic chi-square with n degrees of freedom is defined as the sum of squares of n independent, normally distributed variates with zero means and unit variances. In other words,

$$\chi^2 = \sum_i \frac{(Y_i - \mu_i)^2}{\sigma_i^2} \tag{21.1}$$

where the Y_i are independent.

Except for Chap. 20, χ^2 has been mentioned infrequently and only when it was involved in other distributions; for example, F is a ratio of two χ^2's divided by their degrees of freedom. In this chapter, test criteria called χ^2 are frequently used. However, we are now dealing with discrete data so that the test criteria are not χ^2 quantities as defined in Eq. (21.1), even when the null hypothesis is true. This means that the test criteria can be distributed only approximately as χ^2 quantities.

The χ^2 distribution, when associated with discrete data, is usually in conjunction with a test of *goodness of fit*. The test criterion is

$$\chi^2 = \sum \frac{(\text{observed} - \text{expected})^2}{\text{expected}} \tag{21.2}$$

The sum is taken over all cells in the classification system. *Observed* refers to the numbers observed in the cells; *expected* refers to the average numbers or expected values when the hypothesis is true, that is, to the theoretical values. The sum of such deviations, namely, values of (observed − expected), will equal zero within rounding errors. The number of degrees of freedom involved will be discussed for several situations as they arise.

21.3 Two-cell Tables, Confidence Limits for a Proportion or Percentage

Many sampling situations allow only two possible outcomes, for example, the numbers of yeses and noes in response to a question, or the numbers of individuals showing the presence or absence of a qualitative characteristic. An estimate of a population proportion or a test of hypothesis about a proportion is often required. Consider the following example. In studying *Dentaria* in an area near Ithaca, New York, a class in taxonomy and ecology observed the numbers of plants which did or did not flower. This was done for a number of samples. In one sample, there were 42 flowering and 337 nonflowering plants. Let us set a confidence interval on the proportion of flowering plants in the population.

Assume that sampling has been random and from a stable population. Since there are only two possible outcomes associated with an individual, we have a so-called *binomial population*, as discussed in Chap. 3. The parameter to be estimated by a confidence interval is the proportion of flowering plants in the population of plants or the probability that a randomly selected plant will be a flowering plant. The parameter is generally denoted by p and its estimate, the observed proportion by $\hat{p}$. The expected value or mean of all possible $\hat{p}$ values is p, that is, $\hat{p}$ is an unbiased estimator of p, the population mean. The variance of the statistic $\hat{p}$ is $p(1 - p)/n$, where n is the total number of observations in the sample; it is estimated by $\hat{p}(1 - \hat{p})/n$ when necessary. Note that the variance is computed from the mean. Often, $1 - p$ and $1 - \hat{p}$ are written as q and $\hat{q}$, respectively.

We now proceed to use the normal distribution as an approximation to the binomial distribution, knowing that a basic assumption is false.

1. The normal approximation As an approximation, we say $\hat{p}$ is normally distributed with mean p and variance $p(1-p)/n$, estimated by $\hat{p}(1-\hat{p})/n$. Hence the 95 percent confidence interval for p is

$$\hat{p} \pm Z_{.05}(\text{normal})\sqrt{\frac{\hat{p}(1-\hat{p})}{n}}$$

$$= \frac{42}{379} \pm 1.96\sqrt{\frac{42}{379}\frac{337}{379}\frac{1}{379}} = .111 \pm .032 = (.079, .143) \quad (21.3)$$

This approximation is not the only possible one based on the normal distribution but it is convenient and should differ little from any other based on reasonable sample size. Suggested lower limits for sample sizes are given in Table 21.1 and are due to Cochran (21.2). The table suggests that our approximation may be a poor one since we should have close to $n = 600$.

2. The exact distribution When it is decided that an approximation is inadequate, tables of the binomial distribution are required. Many such tables are available, for example, *Tables of the Cumulative Binomial Probability Distribution* by the Computation Laboratory, Harvard University (21.7), contain sums of the probabilities of k terms for $k = 1, 2, \ldots, n+1$ for $n = 1, 2, \ldots, 1{,}000$ observations in the sample, and for $p = 0.01[.01]0.50$. The National Bureau of Standards Applied Mathematics Series 6 (21.11) gives probabilities for individual terms as well. Confidence intervals computed from these tables will rarely be symmetric about $\hat{p}$, since they associate about half of the probability of a Type I error with each tail of the distribution.

Essentially we choose two values of p, say p_1 and p_2, with the property that they are the lowest and highest values of p that can be hypothesized and found acceptable on the basis of the observed data. In practice, it will usually be impossible to find probabilities exactly equal to half the probability of a

Table 21.1 Binomial sample size for normal approximation to apply

$\hat{p}$	$n\hat{p}$ = number observed in *smaller* class	n = sample size
0.5	15	30
0.4	20	50
0.3	24	80
0.2	40	200
0.1	60	600
0.05	70	1,400

Source: Reprinted with permission from W. G. Cochran, "Sampling Techniques," Table 3.3, page 41, John Wiley & Sons, Inc., New York, 1953.

Type I error. In some cases, it may be necessary to put the full probability in one tail, for example, if all or very nearly all observations fall in one of the two classes. In this case one confidence limit will be .00 or 1.00.

Tables A.14 give 95 and 99 percent confidence intervals for the binomial distribution. These are obtained from more extensive tables by Mainland et al. (21.3). To illustrate their use, a coin was tossed 30 times and 13 heads and 17 tails observed. From the tables, the 95 and 99 percent confidence intervals for the probability p, of obtaining a head in a single toss, are given as $.2546 < p < .6256$ and $.2107 < p < .6772$, respectively. The confidence limits for the probability of a tail may be found in the table or by subtracting each of the above limits from 1.00.

If we wish to use Table A.14B for the *Dentaria* data, then we must interpolate between $n = 300$ and $n = 500$. For $\hat{p} = .11$, the lower bound on the 95 percent confidence interval lies between .0771 and .0841 and the upper bound between .1508 and .1406. A rough approximation places the required endpoints midway between the paired values at .0806 and .1457. The interval is not very different from the normal approximation, especially when we consider that we are not likely to want more than two decimal points.

3. Clopper and Pearson charts Alternative to computing a confidence interval, one may use a chart entitled *Confidence Belts for p*, as given in Clopper and Pearson (21.1), or a similar chart. Table A.15 is one such chart. For the *Dentaria* data, compute $\hat{p} = 42/379 = .111$ and locate it on the $\hat{p} = Y/n$ scale; vertically above this axis find two lines marked for sample size near 379 (400 is the closest value); now move horizontally over to the p scale where the confidence interval values are found. For the 95 percent confidence interval, we obtain (.08, .15) without attempting to do any real interpolation for the observed sample size of 379.

Such charts as in Table A.15 are computed by an approximate method of interpolation, which gives a more accurate result than the normal approximation. Confidence intervals will not be symmetric about $\hat{p}$.

4. Binomial probability paper Another procedure makes use of binomial probability paper, designed by Mosteller and Tukey (21.4). This paper and the results obtained from it are based on transforming the data to a scale upon which the resulting numbers are approximately normally distributed with nearly constant variance; the implication is that the mean and variance are nearly independent.

Table A.16 is binomial paper (see also Fig. 21.1, where an example is worked). For the *Dentaria* data, plot the point (42, 337) or (337, 42). Because of the dimensions of the paper, we plot the latter. A line through this point to the origin cuts the quarter circle at the point whose coordinates are the two percentages of the problem. We read .89 and .11 as proportions. Obtaining the confidence interval involves a triangle whose long side or hypotenuse

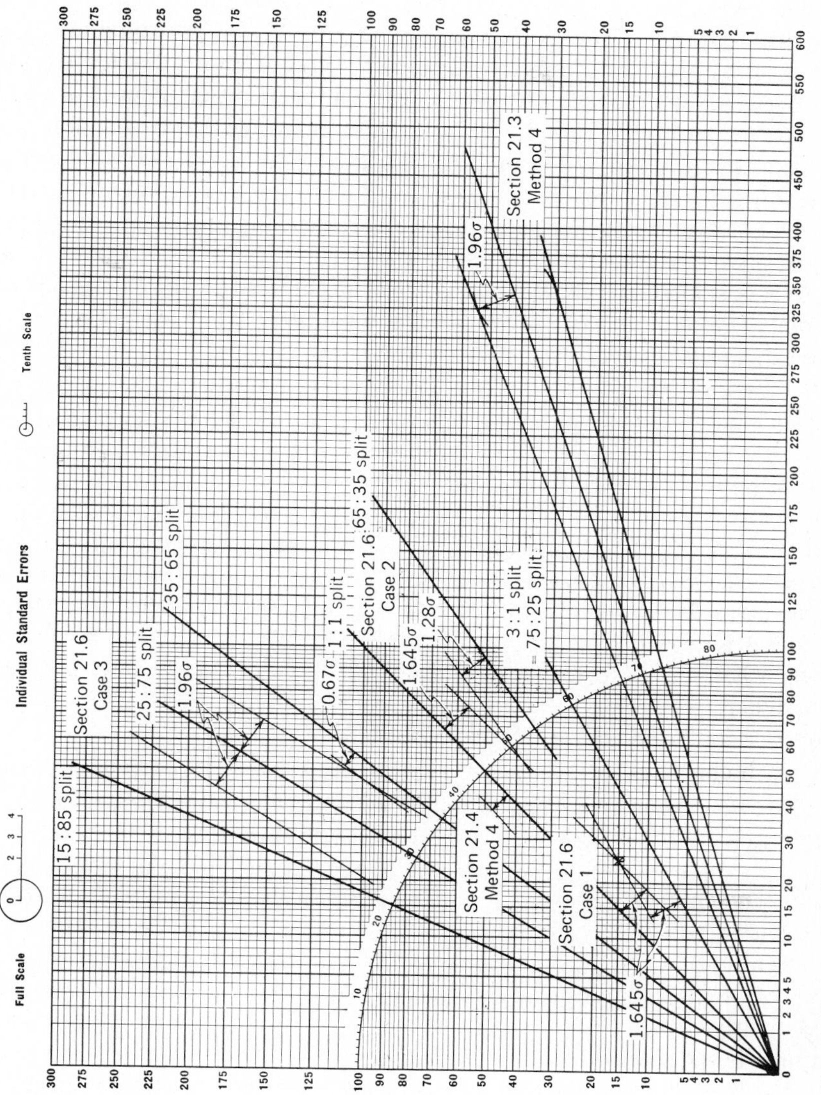

Figure 21.1 Some examples of the use of binomial probability paper.

faces away from the origin and with coordinates (337, 43), (337, 42), and (338, 42). Note that one number of the observed pair is increased by 1 to give the first coordinate, then the other to give the third; only one number is increased to give each new coordinate. Our triangle cannot be distinguished from a point. About this point, draw a circle of radius 1.96 Full Scale standard deviations. These are given on the paper. Tangents from the origin to this circle will cut the quarter circle at points whose ordinates are the confidence limits. We read .08 and .14. If we had wished a confidence interval for the proportion of nonflowering plants, we would have read the two abscissas. If the point had been distinguishable as a triangle, we would have measured two standard deviations upward from the upper acute angle and downward from the lower acute angle before drawing tangents through the quarter circle to the origin.

All our methods are seen to give virtual agreement for this problem. This depends on both the sample size and the p value. Change to percentages involves multiplication by 100.

Exercise 21.3.1 Two other samples of *Dentaria* from the same area yielded 6 flowering to 20 nonflowering and 29 flowering to 485 nonflowering plants. Obtain 95 percent confidence intervals in each case for the proportion of flowering plants in the population. Comment on the validity of each procedure.

Exercise 21.3.2 From a 30 × 10 m transect through the *Dentaria* area, all plants were enumerated and consisted of 296 flowering and 987 nonflowering plants. Assuming that these plants are a random sample from the *Dentaria* population, obtain a 95 percent confidence interval for the proportion of flowering plants in the population. Use binomial probability paper for this purpose. [You will have to change scales by plotting (296, 987) as (29.6, 98.7) and using the Tenth Scale of standard errors.]

21.4 Two-cell Tables, Tests of Hypotheses

A confidence interval procedure, as covered in Sec. 21.3, includes a test of hypothesis against two-sided alternatives. However, where it is desired to test a hypothesis, it may be more convenient to compute a test criterion than to compute a confidence interval. In general, the binomial model states that $P(\text{random observation falls in } i\text{th cell}) = p_{io}$, $i = 1, 2$ with $p_{10} + p_{20} = 1$.

Consider a certain F_1 generation of *Drosophila melanogaster* with 35 males and 46 females. It is required to test the hypothesis of a 1 : 1 sex ratio, that is, $H_0: p_{i0} = .5$.

1. The normal approximation Using the normal approximation, we test the hypothesis $\mu = p = .5$, the 1 : 1 ratio, using variance $\sigma_{\bar{Y}}^2 = \sigma^2/n = p(1-p)/n = (.5)(.5)/81$, where $81 = 35 + 46$. Compute

$$Z = \frac{35/81 - .5}{\sqrt{(.5)(.5)/81}} = -1.22$$

From Table A.4, a Z value of ± 1.96 is required for significance at the 5 percent level. Also from Table A.4, $P(|Z| \geq 1.22) = 2(.1112) = .2224$. There is no evidence to deny the null hypothesis.

A test against one-sided alternatives can also be made. For example, the 5 percent significance point is at $Z = 1.645$ if we are looking for a p that is larger than .5; it is at $Z = -1.645$ if we are looking for a p that is less than .5. For other significance levels, see Sec. 3.6, Cases 1, 1*a*, and 1*b*.

2. The χ^2 criterion Applying Eq. (21.2) to the *Drosophila* example, we compute

$$\chi^2 = \sum \frac{(\text{observed} - \text{expected})^2}{\text{expected}}$$

$$= \frac{(35 - 40.5)^2}{40.5} + \frac{(46 - 40.5)^2}{40.5} = 1.49 \qquad \text{with 1 df}$$

Here we have used the numbers observed and expected rather than a proportion as in Z. From Table A.5, we find $.25 > P$ (larger χ^2 by chance if ratio is $1:1) > .10$. Since a single degree of freedom is involved, we have the square of a single normal deviate. The single normal deviate was just computed as $Z = 1.22$ and $P(|Z| \geq 1.22) = .2224$. Now $Z^2 = 1.49 = \chi^2$. This relation between Z and χ^2 holds only for a single degree of freedom. The equivalence of these tests is easily shown by elementary algebra. The χ^2 test is against two-sided alternatives. Interpretation of the sample evidence is unchanged.

For two-celled tables, the deviations are always equal in magnitude but opposite in sign. This allows us to write Eq. (21.2) with 1 df as

$$\chi^2 = \frac{(Y - \mu)^2}{np(1 - p)} \tag{21.4}$$

where Y is one of the observed cell numbers, n_1 or n_2, and μ is the expected value for that cell, namely, np or $n(1 - p)$. Equation (21.4) is sometimes written with p and $1 - p$ replaced by their sample estimates. This gives $\chi^2 = n(Y - \mu)^2/n_1 n_2$. Values computed by the two criteria will not ordinarily be equal.

One may also use

$$\chi^2 = \frac{(r_2 n_1 - r_1 n_2)^2}{r_1 r_2 (n_1 + n_2)} \tag{21.5}$$

for a ratio $r_1 : r_2$ with observed numbers n_1 and n_2. If the ratio is expressed as $r : 1$, with $r \geq 1$, then

$$\chi^2 = \frac{(n_1 - r n_2)^2}{r(n_1 + n_2)} \tag{21.6}$$

where n_2 is the observed number in the cell with the smaller expected value. Equations (21.5) and (21.6) give the same result as Eq. (21.2).

To improve the approximation to the χ^2 distribution and thus be able to obtain a more exact probability value from the χ^2 table, Yates (21.9) has proposed a *correction for continuity*, applicable when the criterion has a single degree of freedom. This correction is intended to make the actual distribution of the criterion, as calculated from discrete data, more nearly like the χ^2 distribution based on normal deviations. The approximation calls for the absolute value of each deviation to be decreased by $\frac{1}{2}$. Thus,

$$\text{Adjusted } \chi^2 = \sum \frac{(|\text{observed} - \text{expected}| - .5)^2}{\text{expected}} \tag{21.7}$$

$$= \frac{(|35 - 40.5| - .5)^2}{40.5} + \frac{(|46 - 40.5| - .5)^2}{40.5}$$

$$= 1.23 \qquad \text{for the } \textit{Drosophila} \text{ data}$$

Adjustment results in a lower chi-square. Consequently, in testing hypotheses, it is worthwhile only when the unadjusted χ^2 is larger than the tabulated χ^2 at the desired probability level.

3. The exact distribution When the sample size is small, it is advisable to use the exact distribution, namely, the binomial. "Small" may be defined as a number less than the appropriate number in Table 21.1. Tables of the binomial distribution can be used for testing hypotheses about p without computing confidence limits. In view of the work involved, computation of such limits or the use of existing tables of confidence limits may be the more profitable procedure. Use Tables A.14 or Mainland's (21.3) tables for two-sided alternatives. If the alternatives are one-sided, obtain the confidence interval for double the probability of a Type I error acceptable for test purposes or put all the probability in the appropriate tail.

4. Binomial probability paper Binomial probability paper may also be used to test the null hypothesis. For the *Drosophila* data, plot the triangle (35, 46), (35, 47), (36, 46). This triangle is distinguishable from a point. The hypothesized probability is obtained as a *split*, here 1 : 1 or 50 : 50 and so on, which is plotted as a line through the origin and any pair of values which describe the split (see Fig. 21.1). The shortest distance from the triangle to the split, in this case from (36, 46), is compared with the standard error scale and is seen to be a little more than one standard deviation (compare $Z = 1.22$).

Exercise 21.4.1 Woodward and Rasmussen (21.8) studied hood and awn development in barley. They conclude that this development is determined by two gene pairs. Four of the nine possible F_2 genotypes should segregate in the F_3 generation. Expected ratios are 3 : 1

for the characters listed with the data below. (Correct awn classification was difficult for the third data set.)

2,376 hoods to 814 short awns
1,927 hoods to 642 long awns
1,685 long awns to 636 short awns
623 long awns to 195 short awns

Test $H_0 : p = \frac{3}{4}$ for the appropriate character in each of the four cases. Comment on the appropriateness of the test(s) you use.

21.5 Tests of Hypotheses for a Limited Set of Alternatives

When data have been obtained and a hypothesis tested, the value of the test criterion may lead us to accept the hypothesis. Acceptance of the null hypothesis means that it and chance offer a reasonable explanation of the existing data. However, chance and any value of p within the confidence interval will not lead us to deny the null hypothesis. Thus, acceptance of the null hypothesis, precisely as stated, would be a very strong statement. On the other hand, the type of alternative hypothesis discussed so far has been a set of alternatives. Hence acceptance of the alternative hypothesis is a general but somewhat indefinite statement. It is strong with respect to the null hypothesis only, since it rejects that hypothesis.

In certain genetic problems, there may be a limited number of possible null hypotheses to choose among and no one of them may be an obvious choice for the null hypothesis. For example, the experimenter may have to choose between the ratios 1 : 1 and 3 : 1. Which ratio should be tested as the null hypothesis, and how do we test against a single alternative as opposed to a set of alternatives? If both hypotheses are tested, one may be led to the conclusion that either hypothesis is satisfactory. In this case, it is clear that the sample size has been insufficient to distinguish between ratios at the chosen significance level. When more than two ratios are possible, the results of testing each ratio as a null hypothesis may be more confusing.

Problems such as those of the previous paragraph are a special class of problems and require a special solution. Thus, in the analysis of variance, an F-test is a correct general solution. However, if the experimenter wishes to test differences between all possible pairs of means, procedures such as those of Chap. 8 are advised; if treatments are a factorial set, then a test of main effects and interactions is advised. Here also, where there is a finite number of possible ratios, an alternative to the methods so far presented in this chapter is advised.

A partial solution to the problem of choosing between two or among more binomial ratios is given in Tables A.17, constructed by NaNagara (21.5). These tables give regions of acceptance for the various ratios, together with the probabilities of making a wrong decision according to which hypothesis is true. This solution begins with the premise that it is not always desirable to fix the probability of a Type I error in advance at one of the customary levels and to disregard the probability of a Type II error. This premise is particularly valid when no hypothesis is obviously the null hypothesis. Here, the probabilities of the possible errors are best fixed in advance and the sample size is then chosen so that the probabilities are not exceeded.

The method of solution, called *minimax*, is to minimize the maximum probability of an error of any kind. For example, suppose that an individual falls into one of two distinct classes and we have only two hypotheses about the ratio involved, namely, that it is 1 : 1 or 3 : 1. Suppose that the sample size is 20. If we observe 0 : 20, then we must logically accept the 1 : 1 hypothesis. The same is true if we observe 1 : 19, 2 : 18, ..., 10 : 10. Let us now jump to 15 : 5; here we must logically accept the 3 : 1 hypothesis. The same is true if we observe 16 : 4, ..., 20 : 0. The most difficult decisions will be for the observed values 11 : 9, ..., 14 : 6.

Let us now consider each of these possible cases, associate a rule for deciding between the two ratios in each case, examine the performance of each rule, and finally decide which rule is best.

Proposed rule 1 If we observe 0, 1, ..., 11 in the first class (the first 1 of 1 : 1 or the 3 of 3 : 1), accept the 1 : 1 hypothesis and reject the 3 : 1 hypothesis; if we observe 12, ..., 20 in the first class, reject the 1 : 1 hypothesis and accept the 3 : 1 hypothesis.

Performance of proposed rule 1 To judge this rule, either solely on its own merit or relative to other rules, we have to know what it will do for us if the true ratio is 1 : 1 and what it will do if the true ratio is 3 : 1.

Performance when the true ratio is 1 : 1 With this rule and a true ratio of 1 : 1, we make a wrong decision if we observe 12, ..., 20 in the first class, because the rule requires us to accept the 3 : 1 hypothesis. Let us compute the probability of making a wrong decision. To do this, add the probabilities associated with 12, ..., 20 in the first class when the true ratio is 1 : 1. This requires a table of the binomial distribution for $n = 20$ and $p = .5$. The probability is 0.2517.

Performance when the true ratio is 3 : 1 With the same rule but a true ratio of 3 : 1, we make a wrong decision if we observe 0, ..., 11 in the first class, because the rule requires us to accept the 1 : 1 hypothesis. The probability of a wrong decision is found by adding the probabilities associated with 0, ..., 11 in the first class when 3 : 1 is the true ratio. For these probabilities, we need a binomial probability table for $n = 20$ and $p = .75$ (or .25). The total probability is 0.0409.

If we now examine the performance of the proposed rule, we see that it is not too satisfactory if the true ratio is 1 : 1 but is satisfactory if the true ratio is 3 : 1. We would certainly like to have a better balance between the two probabilities. Hence, let us consider other rules.

Proposed rule 2 If we observe 0, ..., 12 in the first class, accept the 1 : 1 hypothesis and reject the 3 : 1 hypothesis; if we observe 13, ..., 20 in the first class, reject the 1 : 1 hypothesis and accept the 3 : 1 hypothesis.

Performance of proposed rule 2 if 1 : 1 is the true ratio Now we make a wrong decision if we observe 13, ..., 20 in the first class, because the rule requires us to accept the 3 : 1 hypothesis. Again we refer to the binomial probability table for $n = 20$ and $p = .5$ and find the sum of the probabilities associated with 13, ..., 20 in the first class. This is 0.1316.

Performance of proposed rule 2 if 3 : 1 is the true ratio Now we make a wrong decision if we observe 0, ..., 12 in the first class. We refer to the binomial probability table for $n = 20$ and $p = .75$ (or $p = .25$) and find the sum of the probabilities associated with 0, ..., 12 in the first class. The sum is 0.1018.

This rule has better performance than the previous one if we are trying to have the probabilities of a wrong decision about equal, regardless of which hypothesis is true. We may consider that both probabilities are too high.

Other proposed rules The other rules to be considered are: (3) to accept the 1 : 1 hypothesis and reject the 3 : 1 hypothesis if we observe 0, ..., 13 in the first class; to reject the 1 : 1 hypothesis and accept the 3 : 1 hypothesis if we observe 14, ..., 20 in the first class; and (4) to accept the 1 : 1 hypothesis and reject the 3 : 1 hypothesis if we observe 0, ..., 14 in the first class; to reject the 1 : 1 hypothesis and accept the 3 : 1 hypothesis if we observe 15, ..., 20 in the first class.

The probabilities of making wrong decisions are given in Table 21.2 for three of the four rules just discussed. The numbers under the heading "Acceptance regions for ratios" refer to the numbers observed in the first class.

Deciding among possible rules We must now decide which rule is the best. Our criterion of "best" is that the worst possible situation into which we can get ourselves should be kept within reasonable bounds. In Table 21.2, we observe that rule 1 can lead us to wrong decisions about 25 percent of the time; rule 2 about 13 percent of the time; rule 3 about 21 percent of the time. These values, underlined in Table 21.2, are from the group which contains the worst possible situation. The smallest of these values, the minimum of

Table 21.2 Probabilities of making wrong decisions for ratios 1 : 1 and 3 : 1, $n = 20$

	Acceptance regions for ratios		Probability of making a wrong decision when the true ratio is	
Rule	1 : 1	3 : 1	1 : 1	3 : 1
1	0–11	12–20	.2517	.0409
2	0–12	13–20	.1316	.1018
3	0–13	14–20	.0577	.2142

the maximum probabilities of making a wrong decision, is 0.1316. This is the best we can do and the best rule is the corresponding rule, rule 2.

In review, with Table 21.2 in mind: for a sample size of 20, suppose that the 1 : 1 ratio is accepted when there are 11 or fewer in the potentially larger group and the 3 : 1 ratio is accepted when the number is 12 or more. Then the wrong decision is made with probability .0409 if 3 : 1 is the true ratio and with probability .2517 if 1 : 1 is the true ratio. This is essentially what happens if 3 : 1 is made the ratio for the null hypothesis, if the alternative hypothesis is appropriately one-sided, and if the Type I error is fixed at 5 percent; 4.09 percent is as close as we can get to 5 percent. On the other hand, if the acceptance region for the 1 : 1 ratio calls for 13 or fewer in the potentially larger class and for the 3 : 1 ratio for 14 or more in that class, the wrong decision is made with probability .0577 if the true ratio is 1 : 1 and with probability .2142 if the true ratio is 3 : 1. This is roughly equivalent to testing the null hypothesis of a 1 : 1 ratio against appropriately one-sided alternatives and with a fixed Type I error of .05, 5.77 percent is as close as we can get to 5 percent. With the division point between 12 and 13, the probabilities of a wrong decision are more nearly equal regardless of which hypothesis is true. For the three situations, the maximum probabilities of error are .2517, .1316, and .2142. In choosing 0–12 for the first class, we choose the solution for which the maximum probability of a wrong decision is a minimum, namely, .1316.

To visualize the situation which exists when the acceptance region for the 1 : 1 ratio is 0–13, refer to Fig. 21.2. Suppose that the true ratio is 1 : 1. If we obtain 14 or more individuals in the first class, we wrongly accept the 3 : 1 ratio. The probability associated with this error is the sum of the probabilities of observing exactly 14, exactly 15, ..., exactly 20, namely, $P = .0577$, computed for the 1 : 1 ratio. This is the probability of a Type I error if the null hypothesis is that the ratio is 1 : 1. Now suppose that the true ratio is 3 : 1. If we obtain 13 or fewer individuals in the first class, we wrongly accept the ratio 1 : 1. The probability of this kind of error is the sum of the probabilities of observing exactly 13, exactly 12, ..., exactly zero,

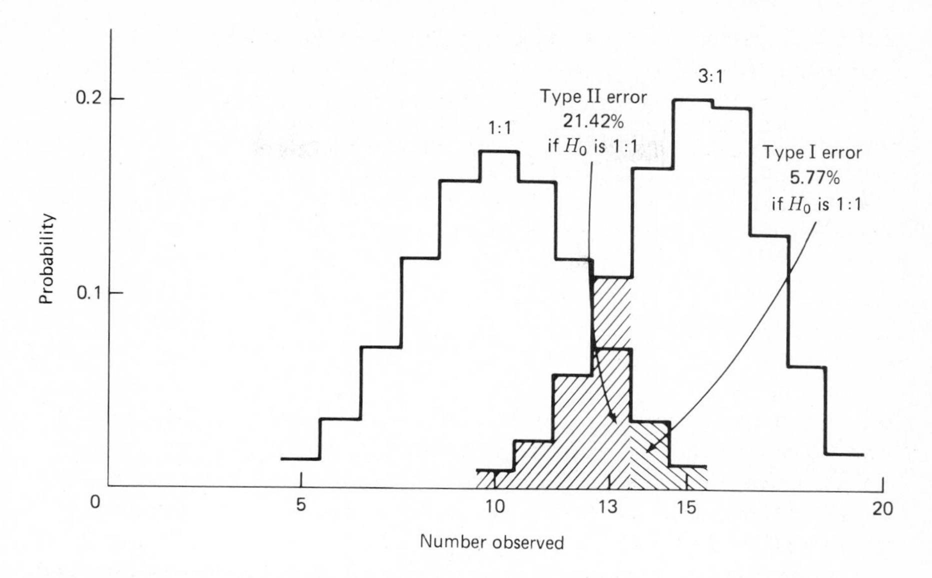

Figure 21.2 Binomial probability distributions for ratios 1 : 1 and 3 : 1 and $n = 20$.

namely, $P = .2142$, computed for the 3 : 1 ratio. This is the probability of a Type II error for the null hypothesis that the ratio is 1 : 1. Probabilities in Fig. 21.2 are shown as solid columns rather than vertical lines for reasons of clarity.

Tables A.17 contain only minimax solutions. To illustrate their use, consider Table A.17*A* for sample size 44. Accept the 1 : 1 hypothesis if 0 to 27 observations fall in the potentially larger group; if this group contains 28 to 44 observations, accept the 3 : 1 hypothesis. At worst, one would be in error 4.81 percent of the time on the average; this would be the case if data were always from a distribution with a 1 : 1 ratio. If one were never presented with data from other than a distribution with a 3 : 1 ratio, then one would be wrong 3.18 percent of the time on the average.

Since the binomial distribution is used in obtaining the tabled probabilities, it is virtually impossible to find the exact probabilities of .05 and .01 in these tables. The remaining tables of this group give rules for acceptance of various alternative hypotheses for given sample sizes, and the probabilities of making wrong decisions.

Mather (21.10) discusses a somewhat different criterion, called the *ambiguous ratio*, for distinguishing between two ratios. First, express these as $l_1 : 1$ and $l_2 : 1$, where $l_i \geq 1$. Then the ambiguous ratio is $\sqrt{l_1 l_2} : 1$, a value which determines the dividing point between regions. This leads to the *ambiguous segregation* such that χ^2 will be the same value, regardless of which ratio is proposed as the null hypothesis.

Suppose that we need to distinguish between the ratios 1 : 1 and 3 : 1 on the basis of a sample size of 20. The ambiguous ratio is $\sqrt{1(3)} : 1 = 1.732 : 1$. The dividing point is then at $[1.732/(1 + 1.732)]20 = .63397(20) = 12.7$. Consequently, we accept the 1 : 1 ratio if the potentially larger class has 12 or fewer individuals and the 3 : 1 ratio if it has 13 or more individuals.

The two regions are the same as for the minimax criterion although the ratios .63397 and .63091 are slightly different.

Exercise 21.5.1 In a genetics problem, it is required to have sufficient data to distinguish between test cross ratios 3 : 1 and 7 : 1. How many offspring should be observed if the experimenter will be satisfied with a 10 percent error regardless of which ratio is the true one?

Exercise 21.5.2 An experimenter has 727 F_2 plants to classify and knows that she will have to distinguish between the ratios 9 : 7, 13 : 3, and 15 : 1. What should her rule be to distinguish among these ratios if she wishes to have maximum protection against the worst possible situation with which nature may present her?

Exercise 21.5.3 If we try to use the ambiguous ratio technique on the problem of distinguishing among three ratios, how many dividing points can be found? How many are needed? What would be your solution?

21.6 Sample Size

Suppose that we wish to test the null hypothesis that the unknown parameter p, of a binomial population, is a specified value. In testing, we should require that we be able to detect some alternative with reasonable frequency. In the previous section, we discussed the minimax procedure for choosing acceptance and rejection regions when we are confronted with a limited set of possible p values. The associated tables, Tables A.17, may be used when it is desired to see what sort of protection is available for the rules given there; they may also be used to some extent in choosing sample size.

Let us consider the use of binomial probability paper for choosing sample size for a number of cases.

Case 1 Suppose that only two ratios are considered to be possible. It is desired to know the sample size required to distinguish between the two ratios.

For example, let the ratios 1 : 1 and 3 : 1 be the only possible ratios. Further, no matter which ratio is the true value, the seriousness of a wrong decision is about the same. In other words, no matter which ratio is true, we wish to have about the same probability of making a wrong decision. Let us set this probability at .05.

The procedure we present is based on the use of binomial probability paper. First, draw the 1 : 1 and 3 : 1 splits on the paper (see Fig. 21.1). On the side of each split nearer the other split, draw a parallel line 1.645 Full Scale units (about $1.645 \times 5 = 8.2$ mm on the commercial graph paper) from the former split. The value 1.645 is such that $P(Z \geq 1.645) = .05$ and is chosen because we are looking for an essentially one-sided test procedure regardless of which hypothesis is true. These two lines, one parallel to each split, intersect at the point (25, 15) approximately. This point is at the lower right corner of the right-angled triangle with right angle at (24, 15), and at the upper left corner for the one with right angle at (25, 14). In other words, the triangle with right angle at (25, 15) has its other angles outside both of the one-sided 95 percent confidence limits. Essentially, it provides a critical value for rejecting H_0 at $\alpha = .05$, regardless of whether a 1 : 1 or a 3 : 1 ratio has been specified. Hence we require $25 + 15 - 1 = 39$ observations in our sample. A sample of size 39 will permit us to make a decision in every case; a larger sample size will give us greater protection than desired. For the larger sample size, we will have to alter our probabilities in order to obtain a rule for deciding between alternatives that will cover all possible sample results.

If we can compare this result with that obtained from Tables A.17, we find a slight difference. The appropriate table says that 44 is the required number to guarantee the desired protection but that it actually does slightly better than required. The table also shows that 40 observations will give almost the desired protection. We must recall that binomial probability paper relies on a transformation which gives a nearly normally distributed variable and that it can give us only an approximate sample size. This accounts for the discrepancy.

Case 2 Suppose that we have only one candidate for the null hypothesis but wish to have reasonable assurance that we can detect an alternative value of a specified size.

For example, suppose that we are doing public opinion sampling using a question which requires a yes or no for an answer. We wish to test $H_0 : p = .5$ but want to detect $p = .65$ if it is in a specified direction. We decide to test H_0 at the 5 percent level using a one-sided test and to detect $p = .65$, if it is the true ratio, 90 percent of the time.

Draw the 1 : 1 and 65 : 35 splits (see Fig. 21.1). Draw a line parallel to the 1 : 1 split and 1.645 Full Scale standard deviations from it. This line will be between the two splits and represents a one-tailed test of $H_0 : p = .5$ at the 5 percent level. Also between the two splits, draw a line parallel to the 65 : 35 one and 1.28 Full Scale (about $1.28 \times 5 = 6.4$ mm) standard deviations from it. This line corresponds to a one-tailed test of $H_0 : p = .65$ at the 10 percent level. We read the point (52, 38) at the intersection of the parallel lines. The appropriate sample size should be approximately 90. In some cases, such as this, it becomes very difficult to read the scale and the paper exactly. If more accuracy is desired use the fact that $\sigma = 5.080$ mm on the Full Scale of the commercial paper.

Case 3 Suppose that we have only one candidate for the null hypothesis but wish to have a reasonable chance of detecting an alternative if it differs by as much as 10 percentage points.

For example, suppose that $H_0 : p = .25$. We wish to test this null hypothesis using a two-tailed test at the 5 percent level of significance. We wish to detect a proportion of 15 or 35 percent, if such is the true proportion, about 75 percent of the time.

Draw the 25 : 75 split. In addition, draw the 35 : 65 and 15 : 85 splits (see Fig. 21.1). On each side of the 25 : 75 split, draw a line parallel to the split and 1.96 Full Scale standard deviations from it. These correspond to the two-sided test procedure. If you simply look at the sums of the coordinates of the points where the parallel lines intersect the 35 : 65 and 15 : 85 splits, you will realize that there is no test that will guarantee us precisely some stated probability of detection for each alternative. (The points referred to are such that they give us 50 percent detection.) We will be cautious and ask for 75 percent protection in the less favorable case, namely, when $p = .35$. Now draw a line parallel to the 35 : 65 split and .67 units from it. [$P(Z \geq .67) = .25$ for the normal distribution.] The two lines intersect at approximately (46, 98). Hence the required sample size is approximately 144.

Exercise 21.6.1 Use binomial probability paper to determine the sample size necessary for distinguishing between the following ratios: 3 : 1 and 7 : 1; 9 : 7 and 15 : 1; 27 : 37 and 3 : 1. Assume that we are prepared to reject any ratio falsely about 5 percent of the time but not more frequently.

Exercise 21.6.2 For a sampling problem with discrete data, it has been decided to test $H_0 : p = .40$. A one-tailed test at the 1 percent level is to be used. It is required to detect $H_1 : p = .65$, if it is the true hypothesis, about 80 percent of the time. What is the necessary sample size?

Exercise 21.6.3 Suppose that we must distinguish between the ratios 1 : 1, 3 : 1, and 7 : 1. We would like to set the probability of rejecting each hypothesis, when true, at about .05 but will obviously have to arrange things so that this is the maximum probability of a wrong decision. Can you construct a procedure for finding the necessary sample size, using binomial probability paper? Compare your result with that obtained from Table A.17.

21.7 One-way Tables with *n* Cells

Robertson (21.6) gives data which include the F_2 progeny of a barley cross. The observed characters are non-two-row versus two-row and normal or green versus chlorina plant color. These data are given in Table 21.3. It is desired to test the hypothesis of a 9 : 3 : 3 : 1 ratio, normal dihybrid segregation. Expected values are given by np where $n = 1{,}898$ and $p = 9/16$, $3/16$, $3/16$, and $1/16$, respectively.

Table 21.3 Observed and expected values for an F_2 progeny

	Green		Chlorina		
	Non-two-row	Two-row	Non-two-row	Two-row	Totals
Observed	1,178	291	273	156	1,898
Expected	1,067.6	355.9	355.9	118.6	1,898
$(\text{Diff})^2/\text{expected}$	11.416	11.835	19.310	11.794	54.36

Calculate χ^2 as

$$\chi^2 = \sum \frac{(\text{observed} - \text{expected})^2}{\text{expected}}$$

$$= 54.36^{**} \qquad \text{with 3 df}$$

The degrees of freedom are one less than the number of cells since only the sample size is fixed and no parameters are estimated. The evidence is against the theoretical ratio of 9 : 3 : 3 : 1. The geneticist would probably conclude that linkage caused such a poor fit. (These data will be discussed further in Chap. 22.)

What was our alternative hypothesis? Simply that the ratio was other than 9 : 3 : 3 : 1. When an alternative hypothesis is specified, we would like a more efficient method of making a decision among the possible alternatives. Although a multinomial distribution is indicated as the exact distribution, it is difficult to define regions of acceptance and rejection. Table A.17 is available for choosing among a few sets of three-outcome ratios.

Exercise 21.7.1 Woodward and Rasmussen (21.8) hypothesized a 9 hooded to 3 long-awned to 4 short-awned types in the F_2 generation. The observed data were 348 : 115 : 157. Test their hypothesis. How many degrees of freedom are there for the χ^2 criterion?

References

21.1. Clopper, C. J., and E. S. Pearson: "The use of confidence or fiducial limits illustrated in the case of the binomial," *Biometrika* **26**:404 (1934).

21.2. Cochran, W. G.: *Sampling Techniques*, Wiley, New York, 1953.

21.3. Mainland, D., L. Herrera, and M. I. Sutcliffe: *Tables for Use with Binomial Samples*, published by the authors, New York, 1956.

21.4. Mosteller, F., and J. W. Tukey: "The uses and usefulness of binomial probability paper," *J. Amer. Statist. Ass.*, **44**:174–212 (1949).

21.5. NaNagara, P.: "Testing Mendelian ratios," M.S. thesis, Cornell University, Ithaca, N.Y., 1953.

21.6. Robertson, D. W.: "Maternal inheritance in barley," *Genetics* **22**:104–113 (1937).

21.7. *Tables of the Cumulative Binomial Probability Distribution*, Ann. Computation Lab. of Harvard Univ., vol. 35, Harvard University Press, Cambridge, Mass., 1955.

21.8. Woodward, R. W., and D. C. Rasmussen: "Hood and awn development in barley determined by two gene pairs," *Agron. J.*, **49**:92–94 (1957).
21.9. Yates, F.: "Contingency tables involving small numbers and the χ^2 test," *J. Roy. Statist. Soc. Suppl.*, **1**:217–235 (1934).
21.10. Mather, K. *Measurement of Linkage in Heredity*, 2d ed., Methuen, London, 1951.
21.11. *Tables of the Binomial Probability Distribution*, National Bureau of Standards Applied Mathematics Series 6, 1949.

CHAPTER

TWENTY-TWO

ENUMERATION DATA II: CONTINGENCY TABLES

22.1 Introduction

Individuals are often classified according to several variables. For example, a person may be classified as a smoker or a nonsmoker and, at the same time, as an individual with or without coronary disease; a fruit fly may be classified as male or female and according to parent mating; and so on. There are two variables of classification in each case.

In other cases, individuals may be assigned to groups and then classified within each group according to some variable. For example, an individual may be assigned to a treatment or a control group and later classified according to response to a stimulus.

For both illustrations, the data are conveniently recorded in a two-way table. This chapter deals with the analysis of enumeration data in such tables, often called contingency tables.

22.2 The Random Sampling Model

Weir (22.25) provided the data in Table 22.1, an $r \times c = 6 \times 6$ contingency table. Here, $n_{..} = 4{,}396$ individuals from a barley population have been classified simultaneously according to an A and a B esterase locus. An electrophoretic technique was used to determine the genotype or genetic makeup of each individual. The total $n_{..} = 4{,}396$ is considered to be fixed. No marginal totals are fixed but can vary from sample to sample of 4,396 observations.

Table 22.1 A 6 × 6 table of genetic frequencies

	A_1A_1	A_2A_2	A_3A_3	A_1A_2	A_1A_3	A_2A_3	
B_1B_1	311	5	205	2	103	9	$635 = n_{1\cdot}$
B_2B_2	63	954	2,172	2	3	175	$3{,}369 = n_{2\cdot}$
B_3B_3	13	275	7	1	0	4	$300 = n_{3\cdot}$
B_1B_2	1	34	12	1	1	15	$64 = n_{4\cdot}$
B_1B_3	0	1	0	0	1	1	$3 = n_{5\cdot}$
B_2B_3	2	6	1	5	1	10	$25 = n_{6\cdot}$
	390	1,275	2,397	11	109	214	4,396
	$= n_{\cdot 1}$	$= n_{\cdot 2}$	$= n_{\cdot 3}$	$= n_{\cdot 4}$	$= n_{\cdot 5}$	$= n_{\cdot 6}$	$= n_{\cdot\cdot}$

Source: Data obtained through the courtesy of Bruce Weir, North Carolina State University, Raleigh, North Carolina. See also Ref. 22.25.

An uncomplicated probability model says that the probability of a randomly selected individual being classified in the i, jth cell is p_{ij}, i, $j = 1, \ldots, 6$ with

$$\sum_{i,j} p_{ij} = 1$$

A more restricted model calls for the probability of being a particular A genotype to be independent of that for the B genotype. This means that if the probabilities for the A classes and for the B classes are known, then their products give the cell probabilities. This statement describing the model is symmetric in A and B. *Independence* and nonindependence or *interaction* are illustrated in Table 22.2.

The usual null hypothesis for such data is one of independence, namely,

$$H_0\colon p_{ij} = p_{i\cdot}p_{\cdot j} \qquad (22.1)$$

Here, p_{ij} is the probability of a randomly selected individual being classified in the i, jth cell. The $p_{i\cdot}$'s and $p_{\cdot j}$'s are row and column probabilities, respectively, with

$$\sum_i p_{i\cdot} = 1 = \sum_j p_{\cdot j}$$

The alternative hypothesis is

$$H_1\colon p_{ij} \neq p_{i\cdot}p_{\cdot j}$$

The test criterion is

$$\chi^2 = \sum \frac{(\text{observed} - \text{expected})^2}{\text{expected}} \qquad (r-1)(c-1) \text{ df} \qquad (22.2)$$

Table 22.2 Probabilities in two-way contingency tables

Independent

	A_1	A_2	Sum
B_1	$\frac{3}{4}\left(\frac{3}{4}\right) = \frac{9}{16}$	$\frac{3}{4}\left(\frac{1}{4}\right) = \frac{3}{16}$	$\frac{3}{4}$
B_2	$\frac{3}{4}\left(\frac{1}{4}\right) = \frac{3}{16}$	$\frac{1}{4}\left(\frac{1}{4}\right) = \frac{1}{16}$	$\frac{1}{4}$
Sum	$\frac{3}{4}$	$\frac{1}{4}$	1

Marginal probabilities given; independence allows computation of cell probabilities

Dependent

	A_1	A_2	Sum
B_1	$\frac{5}{8}$	$\frac{1}{8}$	$\frac{3}{4}$
B_2	$\frac{1}{8}$	$\frac{1}{8}$	$\frac{1}{4}$
Sum	$\frac{3}{4}$	$\frac{1}{4}$	1

Marginal probabilities given; dependence disallows computation of cell probabilities

Note: Cell probabilities must sum to marginal probabilities by rows and columns.

This test criterion is also called X^2, since it is distributed only approximately as χ^2. For a good approximation, expected values should not be too small.

Expected values are computed under the assumption that the null hypothesis is true. Since the $p_{i\cdot}$'s and $p_{\cdot j}$'s are not given, they must be estimated. For these, we use marginal totals to give appropriate sample proportions.

$$\hat{p}_{i\cdot} = \frac{n_{i\cdot}}{n_{\cdot\cdot}} \qquad i = 1, \ldots, r \qquad \hat{p}_{\cdot j} = \frac{n_{\cdot j}}{n_{\cdot\cdot}} \qquad j = 1, \ldots, c$$

Now $\hat{p}_{ij} = \hat{p}_{i\cdot}\hat{p}_{\cdot j}$ and the expected values are given by

$$E_{ij} = \hat{p}_{ij} n_{\cdot\cdot} = \frac{n_{i\cdot} n_{\cdot j}}{n_{\cdot\cdot}} \tag{22.3}$$

For example,

$$E_{54} = \frac{3(11)}{4{,}396} = .0075$$

The value .0075 is far below the acceptable minimum suggested by Cochran (Sec. 20.4). Hence, we collapse the table by pooling A_1 and A_2. In terms of the table, $A_1 A_1$, $A_2 A_2$, and $A_1 A_2$ become $A_1^* A_1^*$, whereas $A_1 A_3$ and $A_2 A_3$ become $A_1^* A_3$. Pool similarly for B. Table 22.3 is the result.

Again, expected values are computed. The smallest is 2.06 and should cause no difficulty. Sums of expected values by rows and columns should

Table 22.3 Calculation of χ^2 for an $r \times c$ table

		$A_1^* A_1^*$	$A_3 A_3$	$A_1^* A_3$	Totals
	Observed	1373	2389	306	4,068
$B_1^* B_1^*$	Expected	1,550.95	2,218.15	298.90	4,068.00
	Deviation	−177.95	170.85	7.10	.00
	χ^2	20.42	13.16	.17	
	Observed	289	7	4	300
$B_3 B_3$	Expected	114.38	163.58	22.04	300.00
	Deviation	174.62	−156.58	−18.04	.00
	χ^2	266.60	149.88	14.77	
	Observed	14	1	13	28
$B_1^* B_3$	Expected	10.68	15.27	2.06	28.01
	Deviation	3.32	−14.27	10.94	−.01
	χ^2	1.04	13.33	58.13	
	Observed	1,676	2,397	323	4,396
Totals	Expected	1,676.01	2,397.00	323.00	4,396.01
	Deviation	−.01	.00	.00	−.01

equal the corresponding sums of observations. Similar sums of deviations should equal zero. Small departures of these sums can be attributed to rounding errors.

Chi-square values in Table 22.3 are really contributions to the overall χ^2. Note that each is measured relative to the cell E_{ij} as $(n_{ij} - E_{ij})^2/E_{ij}$. Thus a large deviation where E_{ij} is large and a small one where E_{ij} is small can contribute about equally to χ^2. When overall χ^2 is significant, the sizes of the contributions may be helpful in interpreting the data.

Degrees of freedom for this $r \times c$ table are $(r - 1)(c - 1)$. Here, $\text{df} = 2(2) = 4$. A reasonable argument says that $n = 4{,}396$ is a restriction on the sampling and that we have had to estimate two independent row and two independent column probabilities since no assumptions were made about their values. Recall that

$$\sum \hat{p}_{i\cdot} = 1 = \sum_j \hat{p}_{\cdot j}$$

Consequently, $\text{df} = 3(3) - 1 - 2 - 2 = 4$.

Here, $\chi_4^2 = 539.50$, where $\chi_{.01}^2 = 13.3$. The data and chance do not support the null hypothesis. We conclude that row and column probabilities are not independent and that there is interaction. A single set of probabilities does not apply to each and every row; the same is true for columns. If it is now necessary to estimate cell probabilities, use $\hat{p}_{ij} = n_{ij}/n_{..}$.

A large chi-square indicates lack of independence of the variables of classification but gives little information about the degree of dependence. A measure of dependence is given by

$$\frac{\chi^2}{n(t-1)} \tag{22.4}$$

t is the smaller of r and c, and n is the total number of observations in the table. This criterion lies between 0 and 1. Its distribution is obviously related to χ^2 by a simple change of variable. Here, the value is $539.50/4{,}396(2) = 0.06$, not a very large value, in part, because of the large sample size.

There are other coefficients of contingency.

Exercise 22.2.1 Weir provides additional frequency data on two esterase loci in a barley population. The data follow.

C genotype	*B* genotype 1, 1	2, 2	1, 2
1, 1	2,172	1,019	178
2, 2	212	608	118
1, 2	13	49	27

Source: Data used with permission of Bruce Weir, North Carolina State University, Raleigh, North Carolina. See also Ref. 22.25.

Use χ^2 to test the null hypothesis that the probability of being a particular *B* genotype is independent of the probability of being a particular *C* genotype.

Exercise 22.2.2 A number of white pine trees were classified according to age class and reaction to grafts of blister rust. The data follow.

Reaction	Age of parent tree, years: 4	10	20	≥ 40
Healthy	7	6	11	15
Diseased	14	11	5	8

Use χ^2 to test the null hypothesis that the probability of a healthy reaction is independent of the probability of being selected from a particular age-class. (These data are analyzed further in Sec. 22.10.)

22.3 The Stratified Random Sampling Model

Consider the data of Di Raimondo (22.2) in Table 22.4 on mice. The mice were untreated with penicillin but injected with bacterial inoculum (*Staphylococcus aureus*) cultured in a broth enriched with the vitamins niacinamide (NA), folic acid (FA), *p*-aminobenzoic acid (Paba), and B_6 as pyridoxin, each in excess of 10 μg/ml.

It is clear that the size of each treatment group was specified. These are *independent samples* where the assignment of the mice to the groups was at random. The only probabilities involved are those of $P(A)$ and $P(\text{not } A) = P(\not{A})$; these may vary with the inoculum.

The usual null hypothesis states that p_A, the binomial parameter, is constant for all inocula, as is $p_{\not{A}}$, or

$$H_0: \begin{cases} p_{Ai} = p_A \\ p_{\not{A}i} = 1 - p_A \end{cases} \qquad \text{all } i, \text{ with } p_{Ai} + p_{\not{A}i} = 1$$

This is a hypothesis of *homogeneity*.

The alternative hypothesis, that of heterogeneity, is

$$H_1: p_{Ai} \neq p_{Ai'} \qquad \text{some } i, i'$$

The test criterion is, again, Eq. (22.2).

Expected values are computed under the assumption that the null hypothesis is true. Since p_A is not given, it must be estimated. For this, pool all the data to give

$$\hat{p}_A = \frac{n_{\cdot 1}}{n_{\cdot\cdot}} \qquad \text{and} \qquad \hat{p}_{\not{A}} = \frac{n_{\cdot 2}}{n_{\cdot\cdot}}$$

To find expected values, multiply these probabilities by each sample size as in the following:

$$E_{ij} = \hat{p}_A n_{i\cdot} \qquad (\text{or } \hat{p}_{\not{A}} n_{i\cdot})$$

$$= \frac{n_{i\cdot} n_{\cdot j}}{n_{\cdot\cdot}} \tag{22.5}$$

This is the same as Eq. (22.3).

Table 22.4 Observed and expected values for mice data

	Alive = A		Dead		Totals	
Inoculum	Observed	Expected	Observed	Expected	Observed	Expected
NA	10	9.65	30	30.35	40	40
FA	9	9.65	31	30.35	40	40
Paba	9	12.06	41	37.94	50	50
B_6	13	9.65	27	30.35	40	40
Totals	41	41.01	129	128.99	170	170

A reasonable argument to justify the degrees of freedom says that each of the r row totals has been fixed but that only $c - 1$ independent probabilities have to be estimated; here $c - 1 = 1$. Consequently, $\text{df} = rc - r - (c - 1) = (r - 1)(c - 1)$.

Here, $\chi_3^2 = 2.63$, where $\chi_{.05}^2 = 7.81$. In fact, $.50 > P(\chi_3^2 > 2.63) > .25$. On the basis of this sample, we conclude that the ratio of live to dead mice does not vary by more than chance, from inoculum to inoculum. If there are real differences in the population ratios, then our sample has not been large enough to detect these differences.

The terms independence and homogeneity tend to be used interchangeably. Lack of independence, dependence, interaction, and heterogeneity are also used interchangeably.

Alternative computational techniques are available; some are given in Steel and Torrie (22.21).

Exercise 22.3.1 In a study of the inheritance of combining ability in maize, Green (22.5) obtained three frequency distributions. The evidence favored a common variance. It then became of interest to see if the distributions had the same form regardless of the location of the distributions. The frequency distributions used to compare the forms are shown in the accompanying table.

	Class centers: Standard errors above or below the mean							
F_2 sample	-3	-2	-1	0	1	2	3	Total
High × high	1	5	28	19	22	8	—	83
High × low	2	5	19	28	23	6	—	83
Low × low	3	9	18	24	18	9	2	83

Test the hypothesis of homogeneity of form. (Recall that much information concerning the form of a distribution is associated with the tails, as was shown in Sec. 20.4. Hence, pool only the $+2$ and $+3$ classes.)

Do you think it appropriate to consider the stratified model as correct for these data? Explain.

Exercise 22.3.2 In a study of the inheritance of coumarin in sweet clover, Rinke (22.18) observed the data in the accompanying table.

	Coumarin classes in 1/100 of 1 percent			
Classes for growth habit	0–14	15–29	Above 30	Total
Standard	8	24	7	39
Intermediate standard	11	28	17	56
Intermediate alpha	9	31	11	51
Alpha	1	14	11	26
Total	29	97	46	172

What is the evidence for the independence of growth habit and coumarin content? Which sampling model do you consider appropriate for these data? Explain.

Exercise 22.3.3 Compute the coefficient of contingency for the data in Exercises 22.3.1 and 22.3.2. Comment on its applicability to these data.

22.4 The 2 × 2 or Fourfold Table

The data in Table 21.3 fall naturally in a two-way table, namely Table 22.5. Here the random sampling model is appropriate. Let us test the hypothesis of independence assuming nothing about true ratios. Whereas Eq. (22.2) is appropriate, Eq. (22.6) gives a convenient alternative for χ_1^2, regardless of which model applies.

$$\chi_1^2 = \frac{(n_{11}n_{22} - n_{12}n_{21})^2 n_{..}}{n_{1.}n_{2.}n_{.1}n_{.2}} \qquad (22.6)$$

$$= 50.54^{**} \qquad \text{for these data}$$

These data lead us to reject the null hypothesis.

Grizzle (22.6) considered the correction for continuity (see Sec. 22.5) for 2 × 2 tables by generating them under H_0, computing both corrected and uncorrected χ^2's, and comparing the empirical results with the χ_1^2 distribution at the 5 and 1 percent levels. His conclusions were that uncorrected χ^2 performs best and corrected χ^2 is too conservative, that is, rejects H_0 too few times. Also, for expectations less than 5, uncorrected χ^2 is conservative and corrected χ^2 is even more conservative.

Normal approximation Equation (22.6) is equivalent to the normal approximation given by

$$Z = \chi = \frac{\hat{p}_1 - \hat{p}_2}{\sqrt{\hat{\bar{p}}(1 - \hat{\bar{p}})(1/n_{1.} + 1/n_{2.})}} \qquad (22.7)$$

where $\hat{p}_i = n_{i1}/n_{i.}$ estimates the population parameter in the ith sample, which is of size $n_{i.}$, and $\hat{\bar{p}}$ is obtained by pooling the data.

Clearly this equation compares two sample proportions, so that it relates to the stratified model for independent samples.

The variance of $\hat{p}_1 - \hat{p}_2$ may also be estimated by $\hat{p}_1(1 - \hat{p}_1)/n_1 +$

Table 22.5 Barley data in a 2 × 2 table

	Non-two-row	Two-row	Totals
Green	1,178	291	1,469
Chlorina	273	156	429
Totals	1,451	447	1,898

$\hat{p}_2(1 - \hat{p}_2)/n_2$. Recent interest in which variance is better in the denominator of Z has led Eberhardt and Fligner (22.22), Petkau (22.23), and Conover (22.24) to make some recommendations. It would seem that Eq. (22.7) is generally satisfactory, especially for smaller sample sizes.

Binomial paper Two sample probabilities can be compared on binomial probability paper, Table A.16 (Ref. 22.15). To do so,

1. Plot each paired count and the total paired count.
2. Sum the middle distances, that is, from the center of each hypotenuse, from the two paired counts to the line through the total paired count.
3. Compare this sum with $1.96\sqrt{2} = 2.77$ or $2.57\sqrt{2} = 3.64$ Full Scale units for 5 and 1 percent levels, respectively.

Exercise 22.4.1 Di Raimondo (22.2) used two control broths in the experiment mentioned in Sec. 22.3. They were (1) a simple broth referred to as standard and (2) one with 0.15U of penicillin per milliliter. The pooled data for experiments with untreated mice were as shown in the table.

Treatment	Alive	Dead	Totals
Standard	8	12	20
Penicillin	48	62	110
Totals	56	74	130

Does the evidence support the hypothesis that P(alive) is the same for the two treatments?

What test criterion did you use and what was the probability of finding a larger value than that observed? Now try the other criterion. Again find the probability of a larger value than observed. Did you find $\chi^2 = Z^2$? Were your two probabilities of a more extreme value equal?

Exercise 22.4.2 C. A. Perrotta, University of Wisconsin, observed the frequency of visitation of mice to traps (small pieces of board) previously urinated on by mice as compared with others which were clean. The following results were obtained in 1954.

Trap was	Urinated	Clean
Visited	17	3
Not visited	9	23

Test the null hypothesis that frequency of visitation is not affected by treatment. For this, compute interaction χ^2. Compare the result with that read from binomial probability paper.

Which of the proposed models is more appropriate for these data?

Exercise 22.4.3 Smith and Nielsen (22.19) have studied clonal isolations of Kentucky bluegrass from a variety of pastures. Their observations include the data shown in the accompanying table. Is there evidence of heterogeneity in response to mildew?

No.	Character of pasture	Mildewed	Not mildewed	Total
1	Good lowland, moderately grazed	107	289	396
5	Good lowland, moderately grazed	291	81	372

Which of the proposed models is more appropriate for these data?

Exercise 22.4.4 Smith and Nielsen (22.19) observed the same fields for rust and obtained the data shown in the table. Is there evidence of heterogeneity in response to rust?

Field	Rust	No rust	Total
1	372	24	396
5	330	48	378

Which of the proposed models is more appropriate for these data?

22.5 Fisher's "Exact Test"

Occasionally it is possible to obtain only limited amounts of data, if, for example, it is necessary to destroy expensive or hard-to-obtain experimental units to get the data. When the numbers in a 2×2 table are small (all row and column totals less than 15), it may be best to compute exact probabilities rather than to rely upon an approximation. This test is usually made against one-sided alternatives for either probability model discussed, or when all marginal totals are fixed. This last type may be called the *quota sampling model*. In computing probabilities, the only tables considered are those with marginal totals the same as observed.

Consider the following data:

	Have	Have not	Total
Standard	5	2	7
Treatment	3	3	6
Total	8	5	13

When it is required to test homogeneity, we compute the probability of obtaining the observed distribution or a more extreme one, the more extreme ones being:

6	1	7
2	4	6
8	5	13

and

7	0	7
1	5	6
8	5	13

Thus, we require the sum of the probabilities associated with the three distributions given. Marginal totals are the same for all three tables. The sum of the probabilities will be used in judging significance.

The probability associated with the distribution

n_{11}	n_{12}	$n_{1\cdot}$
n_{21}	n_{22}	$n_{2\cdot}$
$n_{\cdot 1}$	$n_{\cdot 2}$	$n_{\cdot\cdot}$

is

$$P = \frac{n_{1\cdot}!\,n_{2\cdot}!\,n_{\cdot 1}!\,n_{\cdot 2}!}{n_{11}!\,n_{12}!\,n_{21}!\,n_{22}!\,n_{\cdot\cdot}!} \tag{22.8}$$

where $n_{ij}!$ is defined by

$$n! = n(n-1)\cdots 1 \text{ and } 0! = 1 \tag{22.9}$$

Read $n!$ as n factorial.

The probabilities for our three tables are

$$P = \frac{7!6!8!5!}{5!2!3!3!13!} = .3263$$

$$P = \frac{7!6!8!5!}{6!1!2!4!13!} = .0816$$

$$P = \frac{7!6!8!5!}{7!0!1!5!13!} = .0047$$

The sum of the probabilities is .4126. It is clear that computation of the first or second probability alone was sufficient to answer the question of significance. In practice, one uses this approach by computing the largest individual probability first, and so on. Note that the probabilities computed concern more extreme events in one direction. Presumably, this is the sort of test we require in a comparison of a standard and a treatment, namely, a one-sided test. If the alternatives are two-sided, the 5 and 1 percent significance levels call for probabilities of .025 and .005.

Pearson and Hartley (22.17) note that this test is nearly always conservative, and when the test is two-tailed, the probabilities are more accurately approximated by corrected χ^2. To compute this, replace $(n_{11}n_{22} - n_{12}n_{21})$ by $(|n_{11}n_{22} - n_{12}n_{21}| - n_{..}/2)$ in the numerator of Eq. (22.6).

Even though the computation of probabilities is relatively simple, Mainland (22.12, 22.13) furnishes convenient tables that eliminate the necessity of computing. The first reference includes exact probabilities for each term for equal and unequal size samples of up to 20 observations and a tabulation of those 2 × 2 tables which show significance together with the exact level of significance. The second reference includes minimum contrasts required for significance for a selection of sample sizes up to 500. Significance tables are also given by Pearson and Hartley (22.17, Table 38).

Exercise 22.5.1 For the data in this section, set down the remaining possible tables for fixed marginal totals. Compute the exact probability for each remaining table and show that the sum of the probabilities for all possible tables is unity. Are the probabilities in the set symmetrical?

Exercise 22.5.2 Test the hypothesis of homogeneity for the data of Exercise 22.4.2. Use the exact procedure of Sec. 22.5 and assume that the alternatives are two-sided. Compare the result with that previously obtained.

Exercise 22.5.3 Compute corrected χ^2 for the data in this section and in Exercise 22.5.2. From Table A.5 find the approximate probability of obtaining a larger value of χ^2 than that observed. How does this probability compare with the exact test versus two-sided alternatives?

22.6 Nonindependent Samples in 2 × 2 Tables

Suppose that we have a number of pairs of matched individuals, such as twins, available for evaluating two treatments. For example, we might wish to compare headache remedies or seasickness preventives. It makes sense to assign to a randomly selected individual from each pair a particular treatment and to the other individual, the other treatment. The resulting experiment is like a randomized block design. Sometimes it will be possible to use the same individual for both treatments but at different times. The order of assignment will be random in this case.

Here the samples are not independent, so previous analytic procedures of this chapter do not apply. However, if the paired observations are considered as bivariate observations, two-entry vectors, then the problem is readily solved. The possible vectors are (1, 1), (1, 0), (0, 1), and (0, 0), where 1 represents success and 0 failure, and the first entry is the observation on the individual receiving the first treatment, and the second is that on the one receiving the second treatment. A covariance can now be computed from these bivariate observations for inclusion in the denominator of Eq. (22.7), or Table 22.6 may be used in the simple manner described below.

Table 22.6 Presentation of data for $n_{..}$ dependent paired observations

		Second treatment was		
		S†	F	Totals
First treatment was	S	1, 1 / n_{11}	1, 0 / n_{12}	$n_{1.}$
	F	0, 1 / n_{21}	0, 0 / n_{22}	$n_{2.}$
Totals		$n_{.1}$	$n_{.2}$	$n_{..}$

† S = success; F = failure.

In the model, the probabilities are those of a random bivariate observation falling in the i, jth cell;

$$\sum_{i,j} p_{ij} = 1$$

The null hypothesis is that P(success for first treatment) = P(success for second treatment), or

$$H_0: p_{1.} = p_{.1} \qquad \text{or} \qquad p_{11} + p_{12} = p_{11} + p_{21}$$

This reduces to

$$H_0: p_{12} = p_{21}$$

$$H_1: p_{12} \neq p_{21}$$

As a consequence, we need deal only with the n_{12} and n_{21} entries, asking if they are equal within random sampling. An appropriate test criterion is Eq. (21.5) with $r = 1$, that is,

$$\chi_1^2 = \frac{(n_{12} - n_{21})^2}{n_{12} + n_{21}} \qquad 1 \text{ df} \tag{22.10}$$

As an alternative, the exact binomial distribution may be used with $p = .5$. Compute the probability for the observed $n_{12} : n_{21}$ split and for more extreme splits with fixed $n = n_{12} + n_{21}$, and finally double this probability if the test is two-sided.

Exercise 22.6.1 Suppose that an experiment is run with 150 pairs of individuals. Relief of pain is under study where an alleged painkiller is being compared with a placebo or dummy pill, often made of milk sugar. None of the patients knows which pill he or she receives.

Let the results show that 40 percent obtain relief using the dummy pill and 70 percent receive it using the real painkiller. These percentages fix all marginal totals. Fill in a value for the number of pairs where both individuals are benefited by their treatment. How many other values can you fill in by choice for these fixed marginal totals?

For your table, test H_0: $p_{1\cdot} = p_{\cdot 1}$

22.7 Homogeneity of Two-cell Samples

The two-cell table is probably the most common tabular presentation for discrete data. In other words, most discrete data are concerned with the presence or absence of a character, that is, with a *dichotomy*. Often many samples with similar information are available and it is desired to pool them to obtain a better estimate of the population proportion. Pooling is appropriate when the samples are homogeneous. It then becomes important to test the hypothesis of homogeneity.

Whereas Eq. (22.2) is appropriate, Eq. (22.11) provides a different insight.

$$\chi^2 = \frac{\sum \hat{p}_i n_{i1} - \hat{\hat{p}} n_{\cdot 1}}{\hat{\hat{p}}(1 - \hat{\hat{p}})} \tag{22.11}$$

(The subscript 1 may be replaced by the subscript 2.) Here $\hat{p}_i$ is the estimate of p for the ith sample and $\hat{\hat{p}}$ is that for the pooled data. Thus $\hat{p}_i = n_{i1}/n_{i\cdot}$. Using this estimate, we obtain the alternative

$$\chi^2 = \frac{\sum (n_{ij}^2/n_{i\cdot}) - n_{\cdot j}^2/n_{\cdot\cdot}}{n_{\cdot 1} n_{\cdot 2}/n_{\cdot\cdot}^2} \qquad j = 1 \text{ or } 2 \tag{22.12}$$

Now we can observe that the numerator is a weighted sum of squares of $\hat{p}$'s since $n_{ij}^2/n_{i\cdot} = n_{i\cdot}(n_{ij}/n_{i\cdot})^2$. This relates the computation to a weighted analysis of variance.

Consider the following example. Smith (22.20) observed annual versus biennial growth habit and its inheritance in sweet clover. He examined 38 segregating progenies, of which the results from the first six appear in Table 22.7. Applying the test of homogeneity given by Eq. (22.12), we obtain

$$\chi^2 = \frac{\sum (n_{i2}^2/n_{i\cdot}) - n_{\cdot 2}^2/n_{\cdot\cdot}}{n_{\cdot 1} n_{\cdot 2}/n_{\cdot\cdot}^2} = \frac{8.711885 - 8.404545}{.157252}$$

$$= 1.95 \qquad \text{with 5 df, ns}$$

There is no evidence from which to conclude that the cultures differ in the proportion of annual to biennial habit. One would estimate the common proportion of biennial habit plants to be $\hat{\hat{p}} = 43/220 = .195$ for the segregating progenies of these six cultures.

Table 22.7 Segregating progenies of sweet clover

	Observed values			Expected (3 : 1) values		
Culture	Annual	Biennial	Total	Annual	Biennial	χ^2(1 df)
4–3	18	6	24	18.00	6.00	0.0000
4–11	33	7	40	30.00	10.00	1.2000
4–14	38	12	50	37.50	12.50	0.0267
4–15	19	5	24	18.00	6.00	0.2222
4–16	39	7	46	34.50	11.50	2.3478
4–21	30	6	36	27.00	9.00	1.3333
Totals	177	43	220	165.00	55.00	5.1300 (6 df)

In some cases, there will be sound biological or other reasons to hypothesize the common ratio. In this particular case, there is the null hypothesis of a 3 : 1 ratio of annual to biennial habit. When the population proportion is known or hypothesized, Eq. (22.12) is modified to give

$$\chi^2 = \frac{\sum_i (n_{ij}^2/n_{i\cdot}) - n_{\cdot j}^2/n_{\cdot\cdot}}{p(1-p)} \qquad j = 1 \text{ or } 2 \tag{22.13}$$

Here, p is the population proportion, and $p = \frac{1}{4}$ or $\frac{3}{4}$. For our example,

$$\chi^2 = \frac{8.711885 - 8.404545}{.25(.75)} = 1.64 \qquad \text{with 5 df}$$

Equations (22.12) and (22.13) have the same numerator. Equation (22.13) gives a lower χ^2 than Eq. (22.12) whenever the population proportion is nearer .5 than is the observed proportion.

Exercise 22.7.1 Mendel (22.14), in his classic genetic study, observed plant to plant variation. In a series of experiments on form of seed, the first ten plants gave the following results:

Plant	1	2	3	4	5	6	7	8	9	10
Round seed	45	27	24	19	32	26	88	22	28	25
Angular seed	12	8	7	10	11	6	24	10	6	7

Test the null hypothesis H_0: 3 round: 1 angular, using totals. Test the homogeneity of the 3 : 1 ratio for the 10 plants, using the assumption that the 3 : 1 ratio is the true ratio. What is the value of the homogeneity χ^2 when the 3 : 1 ratio is not assumed?

Exercise 22.7.2 Mendel (22.14) also observed plant to plant variation in an experiment on the color of the seed albumen. The results for the first 10 plants follow:

Plant	1	2	3	4	5	6	7	8	9	10
Yellow albumen	25	32	14	70	24	20	32	44	50	44
Green albumen	11	7	5	27	13	6	13	9	14	18

Repeat Exercise 22.7.1 for this set of data.

Note: A brief but interesting commentary on Mendel, with a presentation of his findings and their reception, is given by Eisenhart (22.3).

22.8 Additivity of χ^2

The information in the data of tables such as 22.7 is not completely extracted by a homogeneity χ^2 when the investigator has a hypothesis about the population proportion. For example, a χ^2 can be computed to test the null hypothesis for each culture (row). For Table 22.7, these are shown in the last column. No individual χ^2 is significant.

Independent χ^2's can be added. We obtain a total χ^2 based on 6 degrees of freedom. The value is 5.1300 and is not significant. (Only unadjusted χ^2 values may be added.)

Also, we may compute a χ^2 based on the totals 177 and 43. Here $\chi^2 = 3.4909$ with 1 degree of freedom and is not significant though it is approaching the 5 percent point; $\chi^2_{.05} = 3.841$ for 1 degree of freedom.

Finally, the difference between the sum of the χ^2's and the overall χ^2 measures interaction. Thus, $5.1300 - 3.4909 = 1.6391$ with 5 degrees of freedom as compared with 1.64 by direct computation. This is far from significant; about two-thirds of the sum of the χ^2's is associated with a test of the ratio of the observation totals.

Now consider the χ^2's computed for this example.

*1. **Individual** χ^2**'s*** Each gives information about a particular sample. When each sample is small, it will be difficult to detect any but large departures from the null hypothesis. Also, if there are many samples and the null hypothesis is true, we expect the occasional one, about 1 in 20, to show significance falsely.

*2. **The sum of the individual** χ^2**'s*** Here we have a pooling of the information in the samples. For example, suppose that the true population was such that χ^2 was 2.000, on the average; we find $.20 > P > .10$. The individual χ^2's would be distributed about this value, some being larger and others smaller;

some χ^2's would be significant, others not. This makes the information somewhat difficult to evaluate unless we sum the χ^2's. If we have 20 samples, then the sum should be about $20(2.000) = 40.000$ with 20 degrees of freedom; this is highly significant.

One obvious difficulty arises in the interpretation of a sum of χ^2's. Suppose that the population ratios differ from sample to sample, from that of the null hypothesis. This tends to make all individual χ^2's too large. A significant sum may be attributable to more than one alternative hypothesis, that is, to heterogeneous samples.

3. χ^2 on totals Here we pool the samples and compute χ^2 with 1 degree of freedom. If the samples are homogeneous but the null hypothesis is false, then we have one large sample and are able to detect a smaller departure from the null hypothesis. For example, suppose that we sample from a population in which the hypothesis is 3 : 1 and observe 17 : 3 individuals. Here, $\chi^2 = 1.07$ and is not significant. However, if we have four times as many individuals and observe exactly the same ratio, namely, if we observe $(17 \times 4) : (3 \times 4) = 68 : 12$, then $\chi^2 = 4.27$ and is significant.

If the samples are heterogeneous, some with higher and others with lower ratios than that hypothesized, then pooling the samples can lead to a low χ^2 and acceptance of the null hypothesis. For example, if 3 : 1 is the ratio of the null hypothesis, then a sample of 67 : 13 gives $\chi^2 = 3.27$, near the tabulated 5 percent point. Also, a sample of 53 : 27 has $\chi^2 = 3.27$. This sample departs from the null hypothesis in the other direction. Pooling the samples, we have an observed ratio of 120 : 40, which fits the null hypothesis perfectly.

4. Homogeneity χ^2 It is now apparent just how important homogeneity is; it is a measure of the likeness or unlikeness of the samples. It is independent of the ratio of the null hypothesis in that the individual samples can depart from this ratio without increasing heterogeneity χ^2, provided that they depart in the same direction and to about the same extent.

In summary, χ^2 on totals and homogeneity χ^2 are a reasonably adequate analysis of the data. If homogeneity χ^2 is significant, then it may be wise to consider the individual χ^2's. The sum of the individual χ^2's may be difficult to interpret by itself.

Exercise 22.8.1 For the data of Exercise 22.7.1, compute χ^2 for each plant to test $H_0: 3:1$ ratio. Sum these χ^2's and show that the sum is equal to the sum of the two χ^2's computed for Exercise 22.7.1. Note also that the degrees of freedom are additive.

Exercise 22.8.2 Repeat Exercise 22.8.1 for the data in Exercise 22.7.2.

Exercise 22.8.3 Discuss the results obtained in Exercises 22.7.1 and 22.8.1. In 22.7.2 and 22.8.2.

22.9 More on the Additivity of χ^2

The data in Table 22.4 are homogeneous; $\chi^2(3 \text{ df}) = 2.63$. The data in Exercise 22.4.1 are also homogeneous; $\chi^2(1 \text{ df}) = .0913$. Hence, it seems appropriate to pool the data in each table and see if the treatment and control data are homogeneous. Pooling the data gives Table 22.8.

The evidence in Table 22.8 is against a common probability of death for untreated mice injected with *Staphylococcus aureus* cultured under the two sets of conditions.

The handling of the Di Raimondo data up to this point must suggest additivity of χ^2. Thus we ask the question, "Does χ^2 (within vitamins) + χ^2 (within controls) + χ^2 (vitamins versus controls) = χ^2 (vitamins and controls)?" The answer is no. In this case, the sum of the χ^2's is $2.63 + .09 + 12.10 = 14.82$ with $3 + 1 + 1 = 5$ df; χ^2 (vitamins and controls) = 14.41 with 5 degrees of freedom (see Table 22.9). The difference between the two χ^2's, each with 5 degrees of freedom, is small but is not due to rounding errors.

If the three comparisons, within vitamins, within controls, between vitamins and controls, had been in an analysis of variance, then they would clearly have been independent and the sum of their sums of squares would have been the same as that for among treatments, including both vitamins and controls. The same is not true of discrete data and χ^2 values.

Probably few people would object to the three nonindependent comparisons made if the investigator regarded them as meaningful. However, independent comparisons can be made and will now be illustrated. Situations will be pointed out where such comparisons are meaningful and, because of their independence, are to be preferred. Our illustration will be seen to be somewhat artificial.

Consider the data of Table 22.9, for which independent comparisons will now be made. Independent comparisons and their computations are due to Irwin (22.7), Lancaster (22.10, 22.11), and Kimball (22.9). Equation (22.2) was applied to give $\chi^2 = 14.41^{**}$ with 5 degrees of freedom. This value is to be partitioned into independent χ^2's with single degrees of freedom. We begin by applying Eq. (22.14). This equation is very similar to Eq. (22.6), but

Table 22.8 Pooled data from Table 22.4 and Exercise 22.4.1

Treatment	Alive	Dead	Total
Vitamins	41	129	170
Controls	56	74	130
Total	97	203	300

$$\chi^2 = \frac{[129(56) - 41(74)]^2 300}{97(203)170(130)} = 12.10^{**} \text{ with 1 df}$$

Table 22.9 Data from Table 22.4 and Exercise 22.4.1

Treatment	Alive	Dead	Total
Standard	8	12	20
Penicillin	48	62	110
NA	10	30	40
FA	9	31	40
Paba	9	41	50
B_6	13	27	40
Total	97	203	300

$\chi^2 = 14.41$** with 5 df

if you examine it carefully, you will find that it differs in both numerator and denominator. The remaining equations are obvious modifications of Eq. (22.14). Their application yields

$$\chi_1^2 = \frac{n_{..}^2(n_{11}n_{22} - n_{12}n_{21})^2}{n_{.1}n_{.2}n_{2.}n_{1.}(n_{1.} + n_{2.})} \tag{22.14}$$

$$= \frac{300^2[8(62) - 12(48)]^2}{97(203)20(110)130} = .1023, \textit{ ns}$$

$$\chi_2^2 = \frac{n_{..}^2[(n_{11} + n_{21})n_{32} - (n_{12} + n_{22})n_{31}]^2}{n_{.1}n_{.2}n_{3.}(n_{1.} + n_{2.})(n_{1.} + n_{2.} + n_{3.})} \tag{22.15}$$

$$= \frac{300^2[56(30) - 74(10)]^2}{97(203)40(130)170} = 4.5686^*$$

$$\chi_3^2 = \frac{n_{..}^2[(n_{11} + n_{21} + n_{31})n_{42} - (n_{12} + n_{22} + n_{32})n_{41}]^2}{n_{.1}n_{.2}n_{4.}(n_{1.} + n_{2.} + n_{3.})(n_{1.} + n_{2.} + n_{3.} + n_{4.})} \tag{22.16}$$

$$= \frac{300^2[66(31) - 104(9)]^2}{97(203)40(170)210} = 3.9436^*$$

$$\chi_4^2 = \frac{n_{..}^2[(n_{11} + n_{21} + n_{31} + n_{41})n_{52} - (n_{12} + n_{22} + n_{32} + n_{42})n_{51}]^2}{n_{.1}n_{.2}n_{5.}(n_{1.} + n_{2.} + n_{3.} + n_{4.})(n_{1.} + \cdots + n_{5.})} \tag{22.17}$$

$$= \frac{300^2[75(41) - 135(9)]^2}{97(203)50(210)260} = 5.7921^*$$

$$\chi_5^2 = \frac{n_{..}^2[(n_{11} + \cdots + n_{51})n_{62} - (n_{12} + \cdots + n_{52})n_{61}]^2}{n_{.1}n_{.2}n_{6.}(n_{1.} + \cdots + n_{5.})n_{..}} \tag{22.18}$$

$$= \frac{300^2[84(27) - 176(13)]^2}{97(203)40(260)300} = .0006$$

The sum of these χ^2's is 14.41 with 5 degrees of freedom, the same as that for the overall table.

The general formulas for independent χ^2's in any $r \times 2$ table are apparent from the particular cases shown.

In reviewing this illustration, we see that χ_1^2 is meaningful in that it compares two standards. Also, χ_2^2 is meaningful in that we compare the average of the responses to two standards, for which there is no evidence of a different response, with the response to a treatment. Since significance is found at this stage, there is little meaning in averaging the responses of three treatments, one of which is apparently different from the other two, for comparison with the response to a fourth treatment. For this reason, we have referred to our illustration as artificial.

The use of independent χ^2's as computed here seems to have real applicability in the case of two treatments and a standard or two standards and a treatment. If the two treatments or two checks appear to differ, the value in averaging them and comparing them with the remaining entries is doubtful. Having found significance, one might well proceed to make the nonindependent tests which seemed most profitable.

Exercise 22.9.1 In what way do Eqs. (22.6) and (22.14) differ?

Exercise 22.9.2 To the mildew data of Exercise 22.4.3, add the following:

No.	Character of pasture	Mildewed	Not mildewed	Total
9	Good upland, moderately grazed	280	144	424

To the rust data of Exercise 22.4.4, add:

Field	Rust	No rust	Total
9	371	54	425

If you feel that the methods of this section apply to either 3×2 contingency table, proceed with the application. In either case, justify your position.

22.10 Linear Regression, $r \times 2$ Tables

Cochran (22.1) gives a method for determining linear regression in $r \times 2$ tables, where rows fall in a natural order. Scores, Z_i, are assigned to rows in an attempt to convert them to values on a continuous scale. The regression coefficient b of the estimate of the row probability $\hat{p}_i$ regressed on Z_i is a weighted regression given by Eq. (22.19); $\hat{p}_i$ is given weighted $n_{i\cdot}/\bar{\hat{p}}(1 - \bar{\hat{p}})$

where $\hat{\bar{p}} = \sum_i n_{i2} / \sum_i n_{i\cdot}$.

$$b = \frac{\sum_i n_{i\cdot}(\hat{p}_i - \hat{\bar{p}})(Z_i - \bar{Z}_w)}{\sum_i n_{i\cdot}(Z_i - \bar{Z}_w)^2} \qquad \text{definition formula} \qquad (22.19)$$

$\bar{Z}_w$ is the weighted mean of Z_i defined by

$$\bar{Z}_w = \sum_i n_{i\cdot} Z_i / \sum_i n_{i\cdot}$$

The criterion for testing b is given by Eq. (22.20), though distributed only approximately as χ^2, and has one degree of freedom.

$$\chi^2 = \frac{\left[\sum_i n_{i\cdot}(\hat{p}_i - \hat{\bar{p}})(Z_i - \bar{Z}_w)\right]^2}{\hat{\bar{p}}(1 - \hat{\bar{p}}) \sum_i n_{i\cdot}(Z_i - \bar{Z}_w)^2} \qquad (22.20)$$

An experiment performed with white pine by R. F. Patton of the University of Wisconsin compared the effect of age of parent tree, from which scions were taken, upon susceptibility of grafts to blister rust, as shown in Table 22.10. All grafts were made on 4-year-old transplants.

Compute χ^2 by Eq. (22.21), a working formula for Eq. (22.20).

$$\chi^2 = \frac{\left[\sum_i n_{i2} Z_i - n_{\cdot 2}\left(\sum n_{i\cdot} Z_i / n_{\cdot\cdot}\right)\right]^2}{\left[\sum_i n_{i\cdot} Z_i^2 - \left(\sum_i n_{i\cdot} Z_i\right)^2 \Big/ n_{\cdot\cdot}\right](\hat{\bar{p}})(1 - \hat{\bar{p}})} \qquad (22.21)$$

$$= \frac{[14(1) + \cdots + 8(8) - (38)(303)/77]^2}{[21(1) + \cdots + 184(8) - 303^2/77](.4935)(.5065)}$$

$$= \frac{29.53^2}{156.17} = 5.58^* \qquad \text{with 1 df.}$$

Table 22.10 Age of parent tree and reaction of grafts to blister rust

Age of parent tree, years	Score Z_i	Healthy n_{i1}	Diseased n_{i2}	Total $n_{i\cdot}$	$\hat{p}_i = n_{i2}/n_{i\cdot}$ percent	$n_{i\cdot} Z_i$
4	1	7	14	21	67	21
10	2	6	11	17	65	34
20	4	11	5	16	31	64
40 and greater	8	15	8	23	35	184
Total		39 $= n_{\cdot 1}$	38 $= n_{\cdot 2}$	77 $= n_{\cdot\cdot}$	0.4935 $= \hat{\bar{p}}$	303

Source: Data used with permission of R. F. Patton, University of Wisconsin, Madison, Wisconsin.

The total χ^2, calculated by Eq. (22.12), can be partitioned as below.

	df	χ^2
Regression of $\hat{p}_i$ on Z_i	1	5.58*
Deviations from regression	2	2.58
Total	3	8.16*

22.11 Sample Size in 2 × 2 Tables

The problem of sample size in two-cell tables is discussed in Secs. 21.5 and 21.6. We now turn our attention to the problem of the sample size necessary to detect differences in 2 × 2 tables.

Consider the data in Table 22.8. The treatment "vitamins" consists of a homogeneous set of treatments; the treatment "controls" consists of a homogeneous pair. It is conceivable that an investigator might wish to experiment further with one of the treatments and one of the standards, or might wish to continue with a different but similar experiment where the only related information was that available from this experiment. Since the controls give a higher proportion of "alives," it is reasonable to assume that this will continue to be the case and to test only for a one-sided set of alternatives.

Paulson and Wallis (22.16) give Eq. (22.22) for determining sample size.

$$n = 1{,}641.6\left(\frac{Z_\alpha + Z_\beta}{\arcsin\sqrt{p_S} - \arcsin\sqrt{p_E}}\right)^2 \tag{22.22}$$

In this equation, angles (arcsin means "the *angle* whose sine is") are in degrees as in Table A.10, n is the number of observations in each sample, Z_α is the normal deviation such that $P(Z \geq Z_\alpha) = \alpha$, Z_β is the normal deviation such that $P(Z \geq Z_\beta) = \beta$, p_S is the population probability or proportion associated with the standard or control treatment, and p_E is that for the experimental treatment. The quantities Z_α and Z_β are obtained from Table A.4. Since p_S and p_E are never available, they must be estimated; this applies particularly to p_S whereas p_E may be chosen quite arbitrarily. Reasonably good estimates should not seriously affect the result unless at least one of the p's is very small or very large. The test procedure implied by Eq. (22.22) is χ^2 against one-sided alternatives and adjusted for continuity; the null hypothesis is that of homogeneity. If the null hypothesis is true, then it will be rejected with probability α; if the alternative that p_S is as large as stated is true, then it will be rejected with probability β. If the true p_S is closer to p_E than stated, then we fail to detect this fact more than 100β percent of the time; if the true p_S is farther from p_E than stated, then we fail to detect this fact less than 100β percent of the time, that is, we detect it with probability greater than $1 - \beta$. (If radians rather than degrees are used for angles, replace 1,641.6 by 0.5.)

We now illustrate the use of Eq. (22.22). Suppose that we plan to conduct an experiment much like that summarized in Table 22.8 but with only one standard or control and one treatment. If the null hypothesis of homogeneity is true, we are prepared to reject it only 1 percent of the time; hence $\alpha = .01$. We do not know p_S but can estimate it from Table 22.8 as $\hat{p}_S = 56/130 = .43$. We wish to detect p_E, when it is about the size observed in Table 22.8, namely, $p_E = 41/170 = .24$, with probability .75. In other words, $1 - \beta = .75$ and $\beta = .25$.

Using Eq. (22.22), we obtain

$$n = 1{,}641.6\left(\frac{2.327 + 0.675}{40.98 - 29.33}\right)^2 = 109 \text{ mice per treatment}$$

If only one method is involved in the experiment, in other words, if we must decide which of two theoretical ratios applies to a single sample, then Eq. (22.22) may be used but gives double the required sample size.

Reference (22.16) gives a nomograph based on Eq. (22.22) which may be used to determine sample size. A straightedge is the only additional equipment required. Kermack and McKendrick (22.8) also give a solution to this problem, including a table of values of n.

Exercise 22.11.1 Suppose that a standard procedure gives a response of about 65 percent kill in a binomial situation, but that the response is sufficiently variable that the standard is usually included in any experiment. It is decided to consider a proposed treatment for which it is claimed that 80 percent kill will result. A one-sided Z (or χ^2) is to be the test criterion with a 5 percent significance level; it is desired to detect an 80 percent kill in the alternative with a probability of .90. What is the necessary sample size for each treatment?

22.12 *n*-way Classification

Binomial data in tables of more than two dimensions present problems of statistics and interpretation. In Sec. 23.5, we discuss the use of a transformation for some such problems. For the present, we consider only the $2 \times 2 \times 2$ table.

In Fig. 22.1, the letters might be numbers of germinating seeds which damp off and which do not damp off (the response), according to variety and treatment. We may hypothesize that whatever treatment times response interaction there is, it differs from variety to variety by no more than random variation. In testing this hypothesis, we test a *three-factor* or *second-order interaction*.

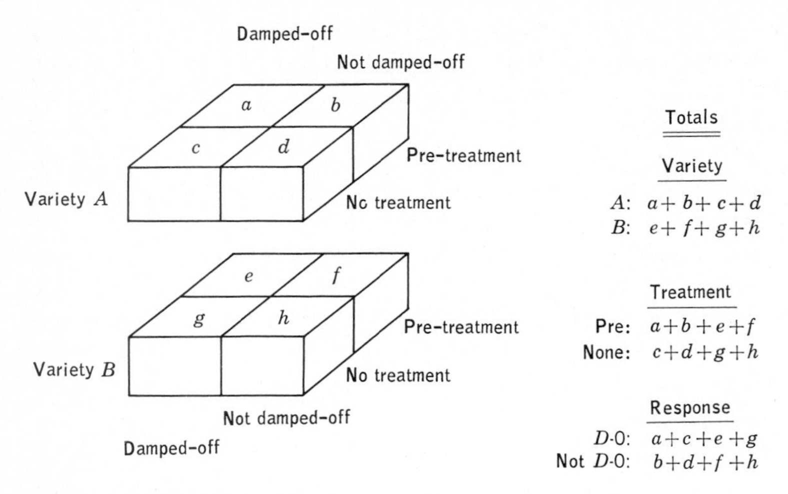

Figure 22.1 Representation of a 2 × 2 × 2 table.

Let $p_1, \ldots, p_8$ be the true relative frequencies or probabilities, not generally known, of an observation falling in cells with entries $a, \ldots, h$, respectively. If there is no treatment times response interaction for variety A, then $p_1/p_2 = p_3/p_4$ and $p_1 p_4 = p_2 p_3$. Similarly for variety B, $p_5/p_6 = p_7/p_8$ and $p_5 p_8 = p_6 p_7$. If there is interaction, the equalities do not hold. In any case, the ratios $p_1 p_4/p_2 p_3$ and $p_5 p_8/p_6 p_7$ are directly related to interaction in each table.

The null hypothesis for a three-factor interaction is that the treatment times response interaction, whether present or absent, is equal for the two varieties. This is equivalent to the hypothesis $p_1 p_4/p_2 p_3 = p_5 p_8/p_6 p_7$, or

$$H_0\colon p_1 p_4 p_6 p_7 = p_2 p_3 p_5 p_8 \tag{22.23}$$

This hypothesis involves a single degree of freedom and hence a single deviation. This can be obtained by solving the cubic equation

$$(a + X)(d + X)(f + X)(g + X) = (b - X)(c - X)(e - X)(h - X) \tag{22.24}$$

The test criterion for H_0 is given by

$$\chi^2 = X^2 \sum_i \frac{1}{E_i} \tag{22.25}$$

E_i is the expected value for the ith cell.

Example Galton obtained the data of Table 22.11 from 78 families. Offspring were classified as light-eyed or not, according to whether or not they had a light-eyed parent and whether or not they had a light-eyed grandparent.

Table 22.11 Numbers of children according to a light-eyed characteristic in child, parent, and grandparent

Grandparent		Light		Not	
Parent		Light	Not	Light	Not
Child	Light	1,928	552	596	508
	Not	303	395	225	501

The cubic equation is

$$(1{,}928 + X)(395 + X)(508 + X)(225 + X) = (552 - X)(303 - X)(596 - X)(501 - X)$$

which becomes

$$5{,}008X^3 + 1{,}174{,}832X^2 + 1{,}262{,}521{,}792X + 37{,}104{,}335{,}424 = 0$$

The solution of this equation may be obtained by trial and error. We recommend multiples of 10 as initial trial values. In this case, they must obviously be negative multiples. Once two values are obtained such that the left side of the equation changes sign, the location of the solution is reasonably well established. The final solution should involve very few additional trial values. For our equation, the solution is $X = -30.1$. From Eq. (22.25),

$$\chi^2 = (-30.1)^2\left(\frac{1}{1{,}928 - 30.1} + \cdots + \frac{1}{501 + 30.1}\right) = 16.93 \qquad \text{with 1 df}$$

The data leave little doubt about a second-order interaction. Alternately, the two first-order interactions are not homogeneous. The test is symmetric in that a comparison of any pair of first-order interactions, that is, the two variety times response, the two variety times treatment, or the two response times treatment interactions, lead to the same null hypothesis, namely, Eq. (22.23).

References

22.1. Cochran, W. G.: "Some methods for strengthening the common χ^2 tests," *Biom.*, **10:**417–451 (1954).

22.2. Di Raimondo, F.: "In vitro and in vivo antagonism between vitamins and antibiotics," *Int. Rev. Vitamin Res.*, **23:**1–12 (1951).

22.3. Eisenhart, C.: "Anniversaries in 1965 of interest to statisticians," *Amer. Statist.*, **19:**21–29 (1965).

22.4. Federer, W. T.: "Variability of certain seed, seedling, and young-plant characters of guayule," *U.S. Dept. Agr. Tech. Bull.* 919, 1946.

22.5. Green, J. M.: "Inheritance of combining ability in maize hybrids," *J. Amer. Soc. Agron.*, **40**:58–63 (1948).
22.6. Grizzle, J.: "Continuity correction in the χ^2-test for 2 × 2 tables," *The Amer. Statist.*, **21**(4):28–32 (1967).
22.7. Irwin, J. O.: "A note on the subdivision of χ^2 into components," *Biometrika*, **36**:130–134 (1949).
22.8. Kermack, W. O., and A. G. McKendrick: "The design and interpretation of experiments based on a four-fold table: The statistical assessment of the effects of treatment," *Proc. Roy. Soc. Edinburgh*, **60**:362–375 (1940).
22.9. Kimball, A. W.: "Short-cut formulas for the exact partition of χ^2 in contingency tables," *Biom.*, **10**:452–458 (1954).
22.10. Lancaster, H. O.: "The derivation and partition of χ^2 in certain discrete distributions," *Biometrika*, **36**:117–129 (1949).
22.11. Lancaster, H. O.: "The exact partition of χ^2 and its application to the problem of pooling of small expectations," *Biometrika*, **37**:267–270 (1950).
22.12. Mainland, D.: "Statistical methods in medical research. I. Qualitative Statistics (Enumeration Data)." *Can. J. Res., sect. E, Med. Sci.*, **26**:1–166 (1948).
22.13. Mainland, D., L. Herrera, and M. I. Sutcliffe: *Tables for Use with Binomial Samples*, published by the authors, New York, 1956.
22.14. Mendel, G.: *Versuche über Pflanzen Hybriden*, 1866, English translation from the Harvard University Press, Cambridge, Mass., 1948.
22.15. Mosteller, F., and J. W. Tukey: "The uses and usefulness of binomial probability paper," *J. Amer. Statist. Ass.*, **44**:174–212 (1949).
22.16. Paulson, E., and W. A. Wallis: Chap. 7 in C. Eisenhart, M. W. Hastay, and W. A. Wallis (eds.), *Techniques of Statistical Analysis*, McGraw-Hill, New York, 1947.
22.17. Pearson, E. S., and H. O. Hartley (eds.): *Biometrika Tables for Statisticians*, vol. 1, Cambridge University Press, New York, 1954.
22.18. Rinke, E. H.: "Inheritance of coumarin in sweet clover," *J. Amer. Soc. Agron.*, **37**:635–642 (1945).
22.19. Smith, D. C., and E. L. Nielsen: "Comparisons of clonal isolations of *Poa pratensis L.*, etc." *Agron. J.*, **43**:214–218 (1951).
22.20. Smith, H. B.: "Annual versus biennial growth habit and its inheritance in *Melilotus alba*," *Amer. J. Bot.*, **14**:129–146 (1927).
22.21. Steel, R. G. D., and J. H. Torrie: *Principles and Procedures of Statistics*, 1st ed., McGraw Hill, New York, 1960.
22.22. Eberhardt, K. R., and M. A. Fligner: "A comparison of two tests for equality of two proportions," *Amer. Statist.*, **31**(4):151–155 (1977).
22.23. Petkau, J.: "A fundamental question of practical statistics," letter to the Editor, *Amer. Statist.*, **32**(3):114 (1978).
22.24. Conover, W. J.: "A fundamental question of practical statistics," letter to the Editor, *Amer. Statist.*, **32**(3):114 (1978).
22.25. Weir, B. S., R. W. Allard, and A. L. Kahler: "Analysis of complex allozyme polymorphisms in a barley population," *Genetics*, **72**:505–523 (1972).

CHAPTER

TWENTY-THREE

SOME DISCRETE DISTRIBUTIONS

23.1 Introduction

Chapters 21 and 22 dealt with enumeration data. Enumeration data arise from discrete distributions. However, in discussing enumeration data, we rarely commented on the type of discrete distribution unless we stated specifically that we were assuming an underlying binomial or multinomial distribution and wished to test a null hypothesis concerning population ratios.

In this chapter, a brief discussion of several useful discrete distributions is given. The discussion includes some of the uses found for the distributions and some of the tests associated with them.

23.2 The Hypergeometric Distribution

Suppose that we have a finite population of 25 birds threatened with extinction. Of these, 20 are adult and 5 are juvenile. If we draw one at random, then the probability that it will be adult is 20/25 and that it will be juvenile is 5/25. If we draw an adult, then the probabilities at the next draw are 19/24 and 5/24; if we draw a juvenile, the probabilities are 20/24 and 4/24. In either case, they are no longer 20/25 and 5/25 because sampling has been *without replacement*. This is quite different from a binomial problem where the probability associated with a specified event is constant from trial to trial. Here, the occurrence of one event does not affect the occurrence of any other. In tossing coins, the binomial distribution applies, so we state this independence-of-events property by saying that a coin has no memory.

The bird population problem serves to introduce the *hypergeometric distribution.* A more general hypergeometric problem may be stated as follows: Given N elements consisting of N_1 with property A and $N - N_1$ with property not-A, what is the probability that a sample of n elements, drawn without replacement, will consist of n_1 with property A and $n - n_1$ with property not-A? The probability associated with this event is

$$P(n_1) = \frac{\binom{N_1}{n_1}\binom{N - N_1}{n - n_1}}{\binom{N}{n}} \tag{23.1}$$

where

$$\binom{N_1}{n_1} = \frac{N_1!}{n_1!(N_1 - n_1)!} \tag{23.2}$$

for $N_1!$ defined by Eq. (22.9). The system of probabilities is called the *hypergeometric distribution.* Note that we must say that sampling is without replacement; that is, once a sample element is drawn, it is permanently removed from the population. If sampling were with replacement, its return to the population would result in independent probabilities being associated with each draw, and we would have a binomial population.

Two common statistical problems involve the hypergeometric distribution. They are (1) quality inspection or acceptance sampling and (2) tag-recapture or mark-recapture problems.

Quality inspection or acceptance sampling The problem here is to estimate the proportion of defectives. A defective may be a punctured dry-yeast container which should be airtight, a bridge hand without a face card, or a parrot with parrot fever at the zoo. Here the population size N is known and the number of defectives N_1 is to be estimated. If a sample of n observations contains Y defectives, then N_1 may be estimated by

$$\hat{N}_1 = \frac{Y}{n} N \tag{23.3}$$

The variance of the estimate, $\hat{N}_1$, is estimated by

$$s^2_{\hat{N}1} = \frac{N(N - n)}{n} \frac{Y}{n}\left(1 - \frac{Y}{n}\right)\frac{n}{n - 1} \tag{23.4}$$

Tag-recapture problems Here we have a problem that is fairly common with respect to wildlife populations. A known number of birds, fish, or animals are captured, tagged, or otherwise marked and returned to the population. A second sample is captured and the number of recaptured individuals is observed. Here the problem is one of estimating the size of the population. An estimate is given by

$$\hat{N} = \frac{N_1 n}{Y} \tag{23.5}$$

Here N_1 is the number of tagged individuals in the population and Y is the number of tagged individuals in the sample of size n.

Hypergeometric distributions may be further generalized to include more than two classes of elements.

Exercise 23.2.1 If you have any facility with algebra, you will find it easy to rearrange Eq. (22.8) and show that it is a probability from a hypergeometric distribution.

23.3 The Binomial Distribution

Sampling a hypergeometric distribution is like drawing beans from a bag without replacement, whereas sampling a binomial distribution is like drawing beans from a bag *with replacement*. In other words, the probability associated with an event, such as drawing a specially marked bean, is constant from trial to trial. The events are said to be *mutually independent*, or simply *independent*.

The binomial distribution was discussed in Chap. 3. There the following computation of probabilities for multiple trials was given. Again,

$$P(Y = n_1 \mid n) = \binom{n}{n_1} p^{n_1}(1 - p)^{n-n_1} \qquad Y = 0, 1, \ldots, n \tag{23.6}$$

In Chaps. 21 and 22, tests of null hypotheses about binomial parameters were included. In this chapter, we will be more concerned with the assumption of a binomial distribution and will make it a part of our hypothesis and thus subject to testing.

The binomial distribution may be generalized to give the multinomial distribution where there are more than two possible outcomes for each trial. Of the possible outcomes, only one will occur at each trial.

23.4 Fitting a Binomial Distribution

What is the probability that in a family of six children, all will be girls? Assume that the binomial distribution applies and that $P(\text{girl}) = 1/2$ prior to each birth. Then $P(6 \text{ girls}) = 1/2^6 = .015625$. Obviously this is an unusual event. However, there are many families of six children. If we think of 1,000 such families, then the expected value is $np = 1{,}000(.015625) = 15.625$. In other words, if we observe a great many families of six children, we will almost certainly observe families of six girls. It is of interest to know whether they occur more or less frequently than they ought if their probabilities are binomial. In other words, do we have a binomial distribution with the required independence of events and a constant probability from event to event?

To determine if we have a binomial distribution, we must observe many families of size six. The results of our observations will be recorded as six girls and no boys, five girls and one boy, ..., no girls and six boys—seven possible outcome groups in all. Since each outcome group supplies information relative to the true distribution, we must avoid pooling groups if at all possible.

This common type of problem may involve the number of animals with a certain genetic attribute in litters of equal size, or the number responding to some stimulus where the same number of plants or animals is used from trial to trial. The answer may concern the effect of environment on a genetic character, the ability to get a constant response (within binomial sampling

Table 23.1 Fitting a binomial distribution

Data		Probability	Computations				
Y	Frequency, f	$P(Y = n_1 \mid 5)$	Coefficient	$.4^Y$	$.6^{5-Y}$	P	Expected frequency
0	13	$\binom{5}{0}$ $.4^0$ $.6^5$	1	1	.07776	.07776	6.2208
1	18	$\binom{5}{1}$ $.4$ $.6^4$	5	.4	.1296	.25920	20.7360
2	20	$\binom{5}{2}$ $.4^2$ $.6^3$	10	.16	.216	.34560	27.6480
3	18	$\binom{5}{3}$ $.4^3$ $.6^2$	10	.064	.36	.23040	18.4320
4	6	$\binom{5}{4}$ $.4^4$ $.6$	5	.0256	.6	.07680	6.1440
5	5	$\binom{5}{5}$ $.4^5$ $.6^0$	1	.01024	1	.01024	.8192
Totals	80	1.00				1.00	80.0000

All data:

$$p = .4$$
$$\hat{p} = \sum Yf(Y)/5(80) = 161/400 = .4025$$
$$\hat{\sigma}_{\hat{p}}^2 = p(1 - p)/n = .4(.6)/400 = .0006$$
$$\sigma_{\hat{p}}^2 = \hat{p}(1 - \hat{p})/n = .4025(.5975)/400 = .0006$$

Set of five samples:

$$p = .4$$
$$\hat{p} = (80 \text{ values from } 0\ [.2]\ 1)$$
$$\sigma_{\hat{p}}^2 = .4(.6)/5 = .048$$
$$\mu_Y = np = 5(.4) = 2,\ \sigma_Y^2 = np(1 - p) = 5(.4)(.6) = 1.2$$
$$\bar{Y} = \sum Yf(Y)/\sum f(Y) = 161/80 = 2.0125$$

variation) to a technique, or simply the ability to determine if the analysis of a set of data should be based on the assumption of a binomial distribution.

To illustrate the procedure of fitting a binomial distribution, consider the data of Table 23.1. They were obtained as follows: each student in a class of 80 was assigned the problem of drawing 10 random samples of 10 observations from Table 4.1. The 10 samples were randomly paired and the differences were computed. For the 5 samples of 10 random differences, $t = \bar{D}/s_{\bar{D}}$ was computed. The results should follow the t distribution, since the true mean of the differences is zero and the parent population is normal. However, computing machines and statistics were new to all students and this introduced the possibility of error.

Since we first wish to illustrate the binomial distribution *for known p*, let us arbitrarily choose $t_{.20}(9 \text{ df}) = .883$ and observe the number of t values greater in absolute value than .883 for each of the 80 sets of five samples. Denote this number by Y. We now have to see how well our data fit a binomial distribution with $p = .4$ since $P(|t| > t_{.20}) = .40$. From Eq. (23.6),

$$P(Y = n_1 | 5) = \binom{5}{n_1} .4^{n_1} \, .6^{5-n_1} \qquad \text{for } n_1 = 0, 1, \ldots, 5$$

Each probability when multiplied by 80 gives the expected frequency. These frequencies and the necessary computations are shown in Table 23.1. Note that the observed frequencies are not necessary for the computations. Additional population and sample information is given at the foot of the table.

While the coefficients are easy to obtain from Eq. (23.2), they may also be found from Pascal's triangle. Construction of the triangle is simple when you observe that each number is the sum of the two numbers in the preceding line which are above it immediately to the right and left; the first and last numbers are always 1s.

Number observed = n	Binomial coefficients										
1					1		1				
2				1		2		1			
3			1		3		3		1		
4		1		4		6		4		1	
5	1		5		10		10		5		1
⋮						⋮					

We are now ready to test the null hypothesis that we have a binomial distribution with $p = .4$. This is a goodness-of-fit test, as described in Chap. 20; the test criterion is χ^2. The computations are carried out in Table 23.2 and give $\chi^2 = 31.215^{**}$ with 5 degrees of freedom. The null hypothesis of a binomial distribution with $p = .4$ is not supported. Since we did not have to estimate p, we lose only one degree of freedom, which is associated with the restriction that the number of observations is $n = 80$.

Table 23.2 Test of the binomial distribution with $p = .4$

Y	Observed frequency	Expected frequency	Deviation	$\frac{(\text{Deviation})^2}{\text{Expected frequency}}$
0	13	6.2208	6.7792	7.388
1	18	20.7360	−2.7360	.361
2	20	27.6480	−7.6480	2.116
3	18	18.4320	−.4320	.010
4	6	6.1440	−.1440	.003
5	5	.8192	4.1808	21.337
Totals	80	80	0.0	31.215

When the data do not support the null hypothesis, we may look for the cause in the value chosen for p, in the nature of the distribution apart from the value of p, or in both. The observed proportion does not differ appreciably from the hypothetical one, so we conclude that the data are not binomially distributed. The cells with $Y = 0$ and $Y = 5$ are the only cells with positive deviations; also, they are the biggest contributors to χ^2. It seems advisable to check the computational procedures of those students obtaining consistently high or consistently low values of t.

Let us now compare the procedure of fitting the binomial distribution with the summary of procedures, Sec. 22.8, used for the data of Table 22.7. These procedures, applied to the present data, would call for an 80×2 table. Individual χ^2's would be of little use until we found out whether or not the results of the 80 trials were homogeneous. The sum of the individual χ^2's would normally be partitioned to test a hypothesis about p and one of homogeneity. The χ^2 value for totals would be a test of H_0: $p = .4$, and we would accept the null hypothesis ($\hat{p} = .4025$). Homogeneity χ^2 tests the hypothesis of a constant p from trial to trial. We hope that it would show significance. For this example, the two procedures might well lead to the same conclusions.

Can the procedures lead to different conclusions? Answer: yes. Suppose that of the 5 values in each of our 80 trials, three are less than and two are greater than .883. The observed ratio is the hypothesized one and the data are homogeneous. In other words, we could have less than binomial variation and not be able to determine so by the methods of Chap. 22. The methods of this chapter are designed expressly for detecting departures from the binomial distribution.

One other problem of fitting a binomial distribution arises. This is the problem of fitting a binomial distribution when there is not a known or hypothesized value of p. *For an unknown* p, testing the fit of a binomial distribution tests the binomial nature of the variation, including the constancy of p from trial to trial. It is necessary to estimate p, which accounts for a degree of freedom. Thus, for the data in Table 23.1, we would estimate p as $\hat{p} = .4025$, complete the fitting process of Table 23.1 using .4025 as the value of p, and proceed to the test procedure of Table 23.2. The resulting χ^2 has $6 - 2 = 4$ degrees of freedom rather than 5.

Exercise 23.4.1 Complete Pascal's triangle to $n = 10$. How many coefficients are there for $n = 7$? How many are there in general?

Exercise 23.4.2 For the data in Table 23.1, test the null hypothesis that $p = .4$, assuming a binomial distribution.

Exercise 23.4.3 Compute the theoretical mean and variance of the number of successes in five trials, using the columns headed Y and Expected frequency. Observe that they equal 5(.4) and 5(.4)(.6) as computed by formula. (See Sec. 2.17; it is hardly necessary to code.)

Exercise 23.4.4 For each of the 80 sets of five samples, the number of t's in absolute value greater than 1.833 was also observed. The data follow:

Number of $\lvert t \rvert$'s less than 1.833:	5	4	3	2	1	0
Number of samples:	51	18	6	2	2	1

What is the theoretical value of p for this binomial distribution? Fit a binomial distribution for the theoretical value of p. In testing the goodness of fit of your data, will you want to pool any of the results? Test the goodness of fit, being sure to state the number of degrees of freedom for the test criterion.

Exercise 23.4.5 The same 80 sets of five absolute values of t were observed with respect to another tabulated value of t. Whereas the results are available and given below, the value of $\lvert t \rvert$ is no longer available.

Number of $\lvert t \rvert$'s less than unstated value:	5	4	3	2	1	0
Number of samples:	23	30	16	5	4	2

Fit a binomial distribution to these data and test the goodness of fit. How many degrees of freedom does your test criterion have? Estimate the binomial p, using all the data, by means of a 95 percent confidence interval. In the light of the goodness-of-fit test, do you believe your interval is too wide, too narrow, just right?

23.5 Transformation for the Binomial Distribution

In Sec. 9.16, the arcsin $\sqrt{Y}$ transformation was recommended for binomial data. Table A.10 is used for this purpose and resulting angles are given in degrees. The variance of an observation is approximately $821/n$.

When an investigator is confident that the variation in the data is purely binomial, this transformation and the theoretical variance may be very useful. For example, many $r \times c \times 2$ *contingency tables* may be presented as $r \times c$ tables of proportions. If these proportions are transformed according to the arcsin transformation, standard analysis-of-variance procedures may be used for obtaining main effect and interaction sums of squares. The transformed proportions give a two-way table with only one observation per cell. Thus it is not possible to compute a within-cells variance. We must use the theoretical variance.

To test any null hypothesis, the procedure is as follows. Compute the appropriate sum of squares using the transformed proportions and standard analysis-of-variance procedures. *If the denominators of the proportions are the same*, then the computations are such that all sums of squares are on a per-observation basis, where per-observation refers to the common denominator. The variance to be used for each sum of squares is then $821/n$, where n is the common denominator. *If the denominators are disproportionate*, then the computations are carried out by methods implied in Sec. 22.7, with the weights based on these denominators. Now per-observation refers to the single binomial trial and the variance to be used for each sum of squares is $821/n$, where $n = 1$.

Since χ^2 equals a sum of squares divided by σ^2, mean squares are not computed. Instead, each sum of squares to be tested is divided by $821/n$ to give a χ^2 based on the number of degrees of freedom associated with the sum of squares in the numerator. The resulting χ^2's are referred to Table A.5 for judging significance. In the case of unequal denominators, values of χ^2 will not be additive.

Exercise 23.5.1 Review Exercise 9.16.2 in the light of your new knowledge of the arcsin transformation. Was the error term you used at that time a reasonable error? Are the χ^2's additive in this exercise? Why?

23.6 The Poisson Distribution

This discrete distribution is sometimes related to the binomial distribution with small p and large n. However, it is a distribution in its own right and random sampling of organisms in some medium, insect counts in field plots, noxious weed seeds in seed samples, numbers of various types of radiation particles emitted, may yield data which follow a Poisson distribution.

Probabilities for a Poisson distribution are given by

$$P(Y = k) = \frac{e^{-\mu}\mu^k}{k!} \tag{23.7}$$

This is read as "the probability that the random variable Y takes the value k is equal to . . . ." The value of k may be 0, 1, 2, . . . ; there is no stopping point. The mean of the distribution is μ; the variance is also μ. It is customary to make a number of observations and the mean of these, $\bar{Y}$, provides an estimate of both μ and σ^2.

An exact procedure for obtaining a confidence interval for the mean of a Poisson distribution (including a table) is given by Fisher and Yates (23.3). Blischke also discusses the problem (23.1).

To illustrate *fitting a Poisson distribution*, we have chosen a sample giving the actual distribution of yeast cells over 400 squares of a haemacytometer. These data were obtained by Student (23.6) and are presented in Table 23.3.

Since the parameter μ is unknown, it will be estimated from the data. Computations proceed as in Table 23.3. We have chosen to rewrite Eq. (23.7) as a recursion formula, Eq. (23.8), and to make use of this formula in obtaining probabilities.

$$P(Y = k) = \frac{\mu}{k} P(Y = k - 1) \tag{23.8}$$

The first step is to find P_0, as indicated at the foot of the table. This requires that we find the antilog of $\bar{1}.703594$—the only time that the log table is required. If a table of e^μ is available, even this single use of a log table becomes unnecessary ($e^{-\mu} = 1/e^\mu$). From here on, computing is done sequentially, with the probabilities recorded as they appear on the computer. The final step in fitting is to multiply each probability by the total frequency; in this case, 400.

To test the goodness of fit, χ^2 is an appropriate test criterion. The method is shown in Table 23.4; expected frequencies are from Table 23.3. For this test, we have five classes, the last two observed being pooled because one of the expected frequencies is less than 1. In addition, it was necessary to

Table 23.3 Fitting a Poisson distribution

Y	Observed frequency	Probability, Eq. (23.7)	Computation†	Probability	Expected frequency
0	213	$P_0 = e^{-\mu}$	.5054	.5054	202.16
1	128	$P_1 = \mu P_0$	.6825(.5054)	.3449	137.96
2	37	$P_2 = \frac{\mu}{2} P_1$	.34125 P_1	.1177	47.08
3	18	$P_3 = \frac{\mu}{3} P_2$	.2275 P_2	.0268	10.72
4	3	$P_4 = \frac{\mu}{4} P_3$	.170625 P_3	.0046	1.84
5	1	$P_5 = \frac{\mu}{5} P_4$	.1365 P_4	.0006	.24
> 5	0	$1 - \sum_{i=0}^{5} P_i$	1-1.0000	.0000	.00
$\bar{Y} = 273/400 = 0.6825$				1.0000	400.00

† $\log P_0 = -\mu \log e = -.6825(.434295) = -.296406 = \bar{1}.703594$; $P_0 = .5054$

Table 23.4 Testing the goodness of fit to a Poisson distribution

Y	Observed frequency	Expected frequency	Deviation	$\frac{(O-E)^2}{E}$
0	213	202.16	10.84	.581
1	128	137.96	−9.96	.719
2	37	47.08	−10.08	2.158
3	18	10.72	7.28	4.944
4	3 } 4	1.84 } 2.08	1.92	1.772
5	1	.24		
Totals	400	400.00	0.00	10.174

estimate μ. Hence, the degrees of freedom are $5 - 1 - 1 = 3$ df. There is evidence that these data do not fit a Poisson distribution. If there is sound reason to believe that such data arise with Poisson probabilities, then we have an unusual sample or the mean of the distribution is not stable.

Fisher (23.2) has proposed an alternative measure to χ^2 for testing goodness of fit to Poisson distributions. This test is intended more particularly for observed distributions when expected frequencies are small. Rao and Chakravarti (23.4) have considered the problem further.

Exercise 23.6.1 Student also observed the accompanying distributions. Fit a Poisson distribution to one or more of these samples.

	Y												
Sample	0	1	2	3	4	5	6	7	8	9	10	11	12
2	103	143	98	42	8	4	2						
3	75	103	121	54	30	13	2	1	0	1			
4	0	20	43	53	86	70	54	37	18	10	5	2	2

Test the goodness of fit.

23.7 Other Tests with Poisson Distributions

The fact that the mean and variance of a Poisson distribution are equal suggests that their ratio should provide a test of significance. The ratio usually used is

$$\chi^2_{n-1} = \frac{\sum (Y_i - \bar{Y})^2}{\bar{Y}} = \frac{(n-1)s^2}{\bar{Y}} \tag{23.9}$$

Note that it is the ratio of the sum of squares, rather than the variance, to the mean. It is the equation $\chi^2 = \sum [(0 - E)^2/E]$ expressed in different terms. Rejecting H_0: $\mu = \sigma^2$ is equivalent to rejecting the hypothesis that the underlying distribution is Poisson, or that μ is stable.

Let us apply this test criterion to sample 2, Exercise 23.6.1. We obtain

$$\chi^2_{399} = \frac{513.40}{1.3225} = 388.20$$

Note that the degrees of freedom are 400 − 1 = 399 df. The Y values are 0, 1, ..., 6. Since Table A.5 does not give χ^2 values for 399 degrees of freedom, we rely on the fact that $\sqrt{2\chi^2} - \sqrt{2n - 1}$ is approximately normally distributed with zero mean and unit variance. Hence, we can use Table A.4. However, a glance at Table A.5 shows that the median ($P = .5$) χ^2 value is approximately equal to the degrees of freedom. There seems little use in completing the computations.

This test criterion may be used in experimental situations such as that of Student or in more general situations. Thus, we may have t treatments and make n observations on each treatment. The experimental design may be a completely random one with equal replications, a randomized complete block design, or a Latin square. The sum of Poisson variables is also a Poisson variable. Hence, if the null hypothesis of no treatment differences is valid, the treatment totals will follow a Poisson distribution even though there are real block differences. Equation (23.9) with $t - 1$ degrees of freedom is appropriate for testing the null hypothesis of no differences among treatment means.

A somewhat special situation arises when extremely small binomial probabilities are present, for example, when numbers of mutants are being observed. If the samples are large and the numbers are small, we may assume a Poisson distribution. For example, two lines of corn were observed and the following data resulted.

	Nonmutants	Mutants	Total (approx.)
A	5×10^5	10	5×10^5
B	6×10^5	4	6×10^5

We would like to test the null hypothesis that the probability of a mutation is the same for each line. A test may be based on determining whether the 10 : 4 split is improbable in sampling a population where the true proportions are $5 \times 10^5 : 6 \times 10^5$ and we stop after 14 mutants have been observed. This problem involves a conditional Poisson distribution which can be related to a binomial distribution.

If we use the binomial distribution, the appropriate p value is $5(10^5)/[5(10^5) + 6(10^5)] = \frac{5}{11}$, which lies between .45 and .46. We now use Eq. (23.6) and find

$$P(Y \geq 10 \mid n = 14) = \sum_{n_1=10}^{14} \binom{14}{n_1} p^{n_1}(1-p)^{14-n_1}$$

This equals .0426 for $p = .45$ and .0500 for $p = .46$, as discussed in Ref. 21.7.

Since the probability of obtaining a 10 : 4 or more extreme split, under the null hypothesis, is small (very nearly .05), we reject the null hypothesis that the probability of mutation is the same for each line. Other test criteria for this example are discussed by Steel (23.5).

Exercise 23.7.1 Use Eq. (23.9) to test the null hypothesis of a stable μ for the data in Table 23.3. Repeat for any sample you may have used in completing Exercise 23.6.1. Compare the results obtained from the two criteria.

Exercise 23.7.2 Visualize a situation where the procedures of Secs. 23.6 and 23.7 would lead to different conclusions. Explain why this happens in terms of assumptions, null hypotheses, and alternative hypotheses.

Exercise 23.7.3 Apply the χ^2 test criterion to the data used in this section. Compare your result with that given in the text.

References

23.1. Blischke, W. R.: "A comparison of equal-tailed, shortest, and unbiased confidence intervals for the chi-square distribution," M.Sc. thesis, Cornell University, Ithaca, N.Y., 1958.

23.2. Fisher, R. A.: "The significance of deviations from expectation in a Poisson series," *Biom.*, **6**:17–24 (1950).

23.3. Fisher, R. A., and F. Yates: *Statistical Tables for Biological, Agricultural and Medical Research*, 5th ed., Hafner, New York, 1957.

23.4. Rao, C. R., and I. M. Chakravarti: "Some small sample tests of significance for a Poisson distribution," *Biom.*, **12**:264–282 (1956).

23.5. Steel, R. G. D.: "A problem involving minuscule probabilities," *Mimeo Series* BU-81-M, Biometrics Unit, Cornell University, Ithaca, N.Y., 1957.

23.6. Student: "On the error of counting with a haemacytometer," *Biometrika*, **5**:351–360 (1907).

CHAPTER

TWENTY-FOUR

NONPARAMETRIC STATISTICS

24.1 Introduction

The techniques so far discussed, especially those involving continuous distributions, have stressed the underlying assumptions for which the techniques are valid. These techniques are for the estimation of parameters and for testing hypotheses concerning them. They are called *parametric* statistics. The assumptions generally specify the form of the distribution and Chaps. 1 to 17 are concerned largely with data where the underlying distribution is normal.

A considerable amount of collected data is such that the underlying distribution is not easily specified. To handle such data, we need *distribution-free* statistics, that is, we need procedures that are not dependent on a specific parent distribution. If we do not specify the nature of the parent distribution, then we will not ordinarily deal with parameters. *Nonparametric* statistics compare distributions rather than parameters. These statistics may be sensitive to changes in location, in spread, or in both. We will not try to maintain a distinction between distribution-free and nonparametric statistics, but rather will call them all nonparametric statistics.

Nonparametric statistics have a number of advantages.

1. When it is possible to make only weak assumptions about the nature of the distributions underlying data, then nonparametric statistics are appropriate. Nonparametric statistics are intended to apply to a large class of distributions rather than a single distribution or all possible distributions.

2. At times, it will be possible to do little more than categorize data because of the lack of an adequate scale of measurement. In this case, a nonparametric test may be the best we can do. At other times, categorization may be a way of collecting a lot of data in a hurry—so much data that the power of a nonparametric test will be adequate for the needs of the investigator.
3. When it is possible to rank data, nonparametric procedures are available. For example, food products may be ranked for texture or flavor; plants may be scored for virus infection or plots for insect infestation; in a variety trial involving many locations, variances may be heterogeneous in violation of the usual assumptions for a valid analysis of variance, and ranks may be the best measures for an analysis.
4. Since nonparametric statistics use counts, ranks, or the signs of differences for paired observations, they are often, though not always, quick and easy to apply and to learn.

Nonparametric procedures also have disadvantages. If the form of the parent population is known to be reasonably close to a distribution for which there is standard theory, or if the data can be transformed so that such is the case, then nonparametric procedures extract less information than is available in the data. If all an investigator's experiments result in data such that the null hypothesis is true, then nonparametric procedures are as good as any others, since the investigator sets the error rate. However, if the null hypothesis is false, then the usual problem is to detect differences among means. Nonparametric procedures are not as good for this purpose, as are classical procedures provided that the assumptions about the parent distribution are valid. In particular, the efficiency of nonparametric procedures relative to parametric ones is quite high for small samples, say for $n \leq 10$; it decreases as n increases. On the other hand, efficiency may not be important for very large samples.

24.2 The χ^2 Test of Goodness of Fit

Often we wish to know not about the parameters of an assumed distribution but about its form. In other words, we wish to test the hypothesis that sample data have come from a specified distribution. The χ^2 test criterion is defined by Eqs. (20.2) and (21.2). It is appropriate for data that fall in categories. No scale is needed to define categories, though a scale may exist and be used. Probabilities are required to compute expected values for each category or cell. Cochran (20.4–20.6) proposes that none of these be less than 1. The probabilities may be provided entirely by theory or may be, in part, estimated from the data.

The use of χ^2 has already been illustrated. In Sec. 21.7, a goodness-of-fit test of a 9 : 3 : 3 : 1 distribution was made using χ^2. Categories were purely nominal and the data were not used to determine the ratio and, hence, the probabilities. In Sec. 20.4, we tested the null hypothesis that a normal distribution was involved. The original observations were measured and the scale used to determine categories. The normal parameters had to be estimated before cell probabilities could be computed. In Secs. 23.4 and 23.6, binomial and Poisson distributions were the models for goodness-of-fit tests. The data were counts.

24.3 The Kolmogorov-Smirnov One-Sample Test

This goodness-of-fit test was developed by Kolmogorov (24.10) for testing hypotheses about continuous distributions with specified parameters. It is considered to be conservative, that is, $P(\text{reject } H_0 \mid H_0 \text{ true}) <$ tabulated α, when the parameters are estimated. It is also used for testing hypotheses about discrete distributions.

In Sec. 24.6, the Kolmogorov-Smirnov two-sample test is presented. This was developed by Smirnov (24.11). Similarities between the tests have resulted in associating both names with both tests.

Suppose that we wish to test the null hypothesis that the original data of Table 2.4 follow a normal distribution. Since we have no reason to specify values of the parameters for this distribution, we estimate them by $\bar{Y} = 75.943$ and $s = 1.227$.

For the test, we require the sample cumulative distribution and the hypothesized cumulative distribution. The test statistic against two-sided alternatives is

$$D = \sup_{Y} |F_n(Y) - F_0(Y)| \tag{24.1}$$

where $F_n(Y)$ is the sample cumulative distribution and $F_0(Y)$ is the cumulative distribution under H_0. We are told to "take the supremum (sup), over all Y, of the absolute value of the difference."

Table 24.1 and Fig. 24.1 illustrate how D is computed. In Table 24.1, the ranked observations and cumulative frequencies are recorded. Note that 76.0 occurs three times whereas all other values occur only once. $F_n(Y)$ is the cumulative relative frequency or the sample cumulative distribution. In Fig. 24.1, note that $F_n(Y) = 0$ until $Y = 73.9$; here, it jumps to $F_n(Y) = \frac{1}{14} = .0714$ and remains constant until the next Y is observed at $Y = 74.2$, and so on. At $Y = 77.7$, $F_n(Y) = 1$ and continues so for $Y > 77.7$. Z values are computed at each observed Y. These are referred to Table A.4 to compute $F_0(Y) = P(Y \leq Y_i)$. Linear interpolation was used. The $F_0(Y)$ values were plotted and the smooth S-shaped $F_0(Y)$ curve was drawn.

To find D, look for the largest vertical distance between F_n and F_0. This does not necessarily occur at an observed Y. In particular, it is not sufficient to observe $|F_n(Y) - F_0(Y)|$ in Table 24.1. In Fig. 24.1, it is seen that D

Table 24.1 Computation of $F_n(Y)$ and $F_0(Y)$

Y	Cumulative frequency	$F_n(Y)$	$Z = \frac{Y - 75.943}{1.227}$	$F_0(Y)$	$\lvert F_n(Y_i) - F_0(Y_i)\rvert$	$\lvert F_n(Y_{i-1}) - F_0(Y_i)\rvert$
73.9	1	.0714	−1.6648	.0480	.0234	.0480
74.2	2	.1429	−1.4203	.0778	.0651	.0064
74.6	3	.2143	−1.0944	.1369	.0774	.0060
74.7	4	.2857	−1.0129	.1555	.1302	.0588
75.4	5	.3571	−.4424	.3291	.0280	.0434
76.0	8	.5714	.0466	.5186	.0528	.1615
76.5	9	.6429	.4540	.6750	.0321	.1036
76.6	10	.7143	.5355	.7038	.0105	.0609
76.9	11	.7857	.7800	.7823	.0034	.0680
77.3	12	.8571	1.1060	.8656	.0085	.0799
77.4	13	.9286	1.1875	.8825	.0461	.0254
77.7	14	1.0000	1.4320	.9239	.0761	.1047

occurs at the right endpoint of the interval (75.4, 76.0), where $D = \lvert F_n(75.4) - F_0(76.0)\rvert = .1615$. You might say that we need $F_n(Y)$ and $F_0(Y)$ just before Y reaches 76.0. Thus, in addition to looking at all $\lvert F_n(Y_i) - F_0(Y_i)\rvert$, it is also necessary to observe all $\lvert F_n(Y_{i-1}) - F_0(Y_i)\rvert$. These values are also shown in Table 24.1. The value $\lvert F_n(74.7) - F_0(74.7)\rvert = .1302$ was also a candidate for D; in this case, the distance is computed at the left endpoint of the interval (74.7, 75.4).

To test the null hypothesis H_0: $F(Y) = F_0(Y)$, all Y, where F_0 is the

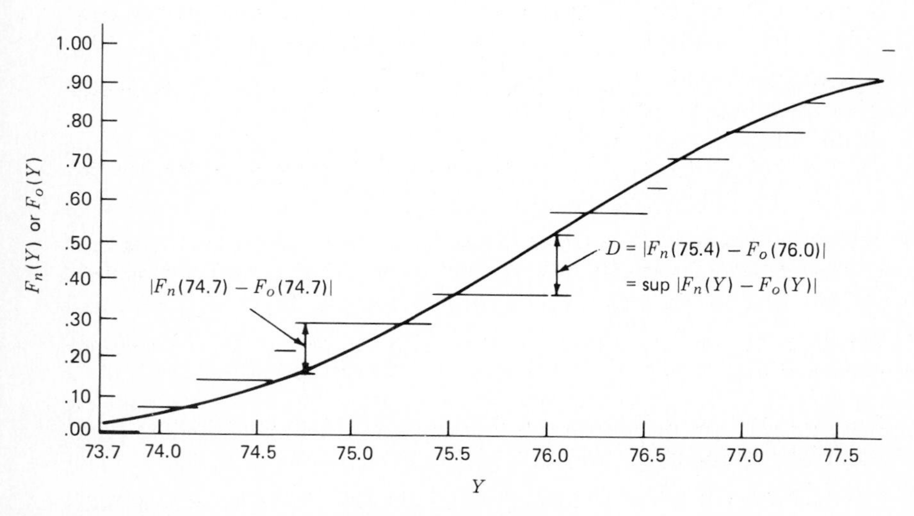

Figure 24.1 Plot for Kolmogorov-Smirnov one-sample test.

cumulative normal distribution with $\mu = 75.943$ and $\sigma = 1.227$ against the alternative H_1: $F(Y) \neq F_0(Y)$, at least one Y, refer $D = .1615$ to Table A.22. For $\alpha = .05$ and $n = 14$, the critical value is .349. There is no evidence to reject the null hypothesis.

Tests against one-sided alternatives may also be made. In this case, test H_0: $F(Y) \geq F_0(Y)$ against H_1: $F(Y) < F_0(Y)$ or H_0: $F(Y) \leq F_0(Y)$ against H_1: $F(Y) > F_0(Y)$. The test criterion is

$$D^+ = \sup_Y [F_0(Y) - F_n(Y)] \qquad \text{or} \qquad D^- = \sup_Y [F_n(Y) - F_0(Y)]$$

In other words, to find D^+, check that $F_0(Y)$ is above $F_n(Y)$ when the alternative is that $F(Y) < F_0(Y)$; and to find D^-, check that $F_0(Y)$ is below $F_n(Y)$ when the alternative is that $F(Y) > F_0(Y)$.

This test is also used in testing goodness of fit for discrete and grouped continuous data. For discrete data, H_0: $p_i = p_{io}$ for all i, that is, the null hypothesis supplies the probability that a random observation falls in the ith cell, all i. Grouping of cells is permitted here also. For grouped continuous data, $F_n(Y)$ in Eq. (24.1) is the accumulated histogram at the end of each interval and $F_0(Y)$ is the probability under H_0 accumulated similarly.

For discrete and grouped continuous data, this test is considered conservative, that is, tabulated values of D are larger than need be. Hence, the true α is smaller than the tabulated value. For more accurate critical values, see Pettit and Stephens (24.13).

Exercise 24.3.1 The data of Table 2.3 were analyzed on the assumption that they followed a normal distribution. However, there was one very large deviation. Was the assumption of normality justified?

Exercise 24.3.2 In Table 5.4, two samples of weight gains were considered. For each sample, was the assumption of an underlying normal distribution justified?

Exercise 24.3.3 In Table 5.5, it was assumed that 10 differences were normally distributed. Test the null hypothesis that this is the case.

Exercise 24.3.4 Table 2.1 contains grouped data from a continuous distribution. Test the null hypothesis that the distribution is normal. (See also Sec. 20.4.)

Exercise 24.3.5 Section 2.5 includes data concerning the distribution of a set of digits. Test the null hypothesis that these follow a uniform distribution, that is, test H_0: P(a random observation $= i) = 1/10$, $i = 0[1]9$.

Exercise 24.3.6 Test the null hypothesis that the data in Table 2.2 follow a binomial distribution with $p = .5$.

Exercise 24.3.7 Test the null hypothesis that the data in the first two columns of Table 23.1 follow a binomial distribution with $p = .4$.

Exercise 24.3.8 Test the null hypothesis that the data in the first two columns of Table 23.3 follow a Poisson distribution.

24.4 The Sign Test

In this test, we consider medians rather than means. The median is the value such that half the probability lies on each side. It is clear that the mean and median will be the same for symmetric distributions.

The sign test is based on the signs of the differences between paired values. This means that it can also be used when the paired observations are simply ranked.

To illustrate the test procedure, consider the data of Exercise 5.7.1. These data are cooling constants of freshly killed mice and of the same mice reheated to body temperature. The differences, freshly killed minus reheated, are: +92, +139, −6, +10, +81, −11, +45, −25, −4, +22, +2, +41, +13, +8, +33, +45, −33, −45, and −12. There are 12 pluses and 7 minuses. These numbers serve to test the null hypothesis that each difference has a median of zero—in other words, that pluses and minuses occur with equal probability.

To test the null hypothesis that each difference is from a probability distribution with median 0, any one of the test criteria of Sec. 21.4 is applicable. Equation (24.2) is appropriate to test H_0: $p = .5$, as is the case here.

$$\chi^2 = \frac{(n_1 - n_2)^2}{n_1 + n_2} \tag{24.2}$$

The values n_1 and n_2 are the numbers of pluses and minuses. For our example, $\chi^2 = (12 - 7)^2/19 = 25/19 = 1.32$ and is clearly not significant.

An adjustment for continuity may be made by changing the numerator of Eq. (24.2) to $(|n_1 - n_2| - 1)^2$, but this makes little difference near the critical values for $\alpha = .05$ and .01. Critical values, based on the binomial distribution, are given by Dixon and Massey (24.14).

This test is easy to apply and if we plan to use it, collection of data can be simplified. We do not need homogeneity of variance in the usual sense, since each difference may be from a different continuous distribution, provided that all distributions have zero as median. Differences must, of course, be independent. In addition, the test is not very sensitive to gross recording errors. This may be of some importance when reviewing work of other years and other investigators.

The test has the disadvantage of throwing away a lot of information in the magnitude of the differences. Thus, it is impossible to detect a departure from the null hypothesis with fewer than six pairs of observations. With 20 or more pairs of observations, it becomes more useful. When ties occur, as they do in practice, they may be assigned in equal numbers to the plus and minus categories or simply discarded along with the information they contain.

The sign test can be modified to handle a number of other situations. For example,

1. For a sample from a single population, we can test the null hypothesis that the median is a specified value. Observe the numbers of observations that lie above or below the hypothesized value and use Eq. (24.2) as test criterion.
2. For paired observations, we may ask if treatment A gives a response that is C units better than that for B. This is the usual linear model without the customary restrictions. Observe the signs of differences $Y_{1i} - (Y_{2i} + C)$ and apply the sign test.
3. For paired observations, we may ask if treatment A gives a response that is k percent better than that given by B. This is a nonadditive model that would call for a transformation if the procedures of the analysis of variance chapters were to be used. Observe the signs of differences $Y_{1i} - (1 + K)Y_{2i}$, where K is the decimal fraction corresponding to k percent, and use the sign test.

Exercise 24.4.1 Apply the sign test to the data of Table 5.5. Do you draw the same conclusion as was drawn earlier?

Exercise 24.4.2 Apply the sign test to the data in Exercise 5.7.1. In Exercise 5.7.2. In Exercise 5.7.3. In Exercise 5.7.4. What null hypothesis is being tested in each case?

24.5 Wilcoxon's Signed Rank Test

This test (Refs. 21.7 to 21.9) is an improvement on the sign test in the matter of detecting real differences with paired treatments. The improvement is attributable to the use of the magnitudes of the differences.

The steps in the procedure are

1. Rank the differences between paired values from smallest to largest without regard to sign.
2. Assign to the ranks the signs of the original differences.
3. Compute the sum of the positive ranks T_+ and the sum of the negative ranks T_-. These are related by the equation $T_+ + T_- = n(n+1)/2$. Choose the numerically smaller of T_+ and T_- and call it T. Only the smaller sum need be computed if it is apparent which one this is to be.
4. Compare the sum obtained at step 3 with the critical value.

Applying the above procedure to the mouse data of Sec. 24.4, we obtain the following.

Difference:	+2,	−4,	−6,	+8,	+10,	−11,	−12,	+13,	+22,	−25
Signed rank:	+1,	−2,	−3,	+4,	+5,	−6,	−7,	+8,	+9,	−10

Difference:	−33,	+33,	+41,	−45,	+45,	+45,	+81,	+92,	+139,
Signed rank:	$-11\frac{1}{2}$,	$+11\frac{1}{2}$,	+13,	−15,	+15,	+15,	+17,	+18,	+19

The sum of the negative ranks is $T_- = T = 54.5$.

This value, disregarding sign, is referred to Table A.18 to judge significance. The critical value at the 5 percent level is 46, so we conclude that the evidence is not sufficient to deny the null hypothesis. Note that small values of T are significant ones. For Z, t, χ^2, and F, it is the large values which generally supply evidence against the null hypothesis.

Beyond the range of Table A.18, Z and Table A.4 may be used to test significance. For $Z = (T - \mu_T)/\sigma_T$, μ_T and σ_T are given by Eqs. (24.3) for n equal to the number of pairs.

$$\mu_T = \frac{n(n+1)}{4} \quad \text{and} \quad \sigma_T = \sqrt{\frac{n(n+1)(2n+1)}{24}} \tag{24.3}$$

Note how ties are handled in the example. The average value is given to each rank. This is necessary when the tied ranks include both signs but not otherwise. In improving the sign test to give the signed rank test, it has been necessary to introduce an assumption. The assumption is that each difference is from some symmetric distribution. Thus if this assumption is valid, an inference about the median will also apply to the mean. It is not necessary that each difference have the same distribution. This test may also be used with a single sample where it is desired to test a null hypothesis about the median. Here the hypothesized value is subtracted from each observation and the resulting members are processed as in the preceding instructions.

Exercise 24.5.1 Apply Wilcoxon's signed rank test to the data of Table 5.5. Compare your conclusion with those drawn in the text and in Exercise 24.4.1.

Exercise 24.5.2 Apply Wilcoxon's signed rank test to the data in Exercise 5.7.1. In Exercise 5.7.2. In Exercise 5.7.3. In Exercise 5.7.4. Compare your present conclusions with those drawn in the exercises of Secs. 5.7 and 24.4. What null hypothesis is being tested in each case?

24.6 The Kolmogorov-Smirnov Two-Sample Test

The test calls for two independent samples and tests the null hypothesis that they come from identical distributions. If the samples are $Y_{11}, \ldots, Y_{1n_1}$ and $Y_{21}, \ldots, Y_{2n_2}$, then we have H_0: $F_1(Y) = F_2(Y)$, where F_i is the true but unspecified cumulative distribution function. The test criterion requires that the two sample distribution functions be compared. In particular, we look at the maximum numerical difference between them. Tables of critical values are provided by Birnbaum and Hall (24.15) for $n_1 = n_2$ and by Massey (24.16) for $n_1 \neq n_2$.

We illustrate the procedure using the data of Table 5.2. Table 24.2 will help clarify the instructions.

1. Rank all observations together.
2. Determine the sample cumulative distribution functions, $F_n(Y_1)$ and $F_n(Y_2)$.

Table 24.2 Computations for a Kolmogorov-Smirnov two-sample test

Y_1	$F_n(Y_1)$	Y_2	$F_n(Y_2)$	$\lvert F_n(Y_1) - F_n(Y_2)\rvert$
53.2	1/7			$\lvert 1/7 - 0\rvert = 1/7$
53.6	2/7			$\lvert 2/7 - 0\rvert = 2/7$
54.4	3/7			$\lvert 3/7 - 0\rvert = 3/7$
56.2	4/7			$\lvert 4/7 - 0\rvert = 4/7$
56.4	5/7			$\lvert 5/7 - 0\rvert = 5/7$
57.8	6/7			$\lvert 6/7 - 0\rvert = 6/7 = D$
		58.7	1/6	$\lvert 6/7 - 1/6\rvert = 29/42$
		59.2	2/6	$\lvert 6/7 - 2/6\rvert = 22/42$
		59.8	3/6	$\lvert 6/7 - 3/6\rvert = 15/42$
61.9	7/7			$\lvert 1 - 3/6\rvert = 1/2$
		62.5	4/6	$\lvert 1 - 4/6\rvert = 1/3$
		63.1	5/6	$\lvert 1 - 5/6\rvert = 1/6$
		64.2	6/6	$\lvert 1 - 1\rvert = 0$

3. Compute $|F_n(Y_1) - F_n(Y_2)|$ at each of the $n_1 + n_2$ values of Y.
4. Find D and compare with the critical value in Tables A.23*A* and A.23*B* in order to draw a conclusion.

In the example, $D = 6/7 = 36/42$ and the critical value at $\alpha = .01$ is $5/6 = 35/42$ from Table A.23*B*. The data do not support the null hypothesis, so it is rejected. We conclude that the two samples are from different populations. The ranking in Table 24.2 would certainly suggest that the distributions differ in location. However, the test is also sensitive to differences in variance, since it is a test of the equality of distributions rather than of specific parameters.

Tests against one-sided alternatives are easily made. If H_1: $F_1(Y) > F_2(Y)$, then the criterion is $D^+ = |F_n(Y_1) - F_n(Y_2)|$ for $F_n(Y_1) > F_n(Y_2)$. If H_1: $F_1(Y) < F_2(Y)$, then the criterion is $D^- = |F_n(Y_1) - F_n(Y_2)|$ for $F_n(Y_1) < F_n(Y_2)$.

The test is also used to test the equality of discrete distributions. It is not an exact test here, but it is conservative, as previously defined.

Exercise 24.6.1 The data of Table 5.6 gave some trouble in that the assumption of homogeneous variance was questionable. Test the null hypothesis that the two parent populations are identical.

Exercise 24.6.2 Apply the Kolmogorov-Smirnov test to the data of Exercise 5.5.1. Just what is the null hypothesis? What do you think is the most suitable alternative hypothesis? Is this the alternative you tested against? What test criterion should you use to detect this alternative? What is your conclusion?

Exercise 24.6.3 Repeat Exercise 24.6.2 for the data of Exercise 5.5.2.

Exercise 24.6.4 Apply the Kolmogorov-Smirnov test to the data of Exercise 5.5.5. Use a two-sided alternative hypothesis.

Exercise 24.6.5 Repeat Exercise 24.6.2 for the data of Exercise 5.5.6. (Male pheasants should be heavier, on the average, than female pheasants.)

Exercise 24.6.6 Repeat Exercise 24.6.2 for the data of Table 5.4.

24.7 The Wilcoxon-Mann-Whitney Two-Sample Test

Wilcoxon (24.7) developed this test of location for two independent samples of equal size. The test was extended to deal with unequal-sized samples by Mann and Whitney (24.3).

The test for unpaired observations is as follows, where $n_1 \leq n_2$.

1. Rank the observations for both samples together from smallest to largest.
2. Add ranks for the smaller sample. Call this T.
3. Compute $T' = n_1(n_1 + n_2 + 1) - T$, the value that you would get for the smaller sample if the observations had been ranked largest to smallest. (It is not the sum of the ranks for the other sample.)
4. Compare the smaller rank sum with tabulated values.

We now apply the test to the data of Table 5.2 on coefficients of digestibility for sheep (S) and steers (C). The observations are ordered and ranked as: 53.2 (S), 1; 53.6 (S), 2; 54.4 (S), 3; 56.2 (S), 4; 56.4 (S), 5; 57.8 (S), 6; 58.7 (C), 7; 59.2 (C), 8; 59.8 (C), 9; 61.9 (S), 10; 62.5 (C), 11; 63.1 (C), 12; 64.2 (C), 13. Tied observations, when they occur, are given the mean rank. The sums of the ranks for steers (C), the smaller sample, is $T = 60$. We also compute $T' = 6(6 + 7 + 1) - 60 = 24$.

The observed value of the test criterion is compared with the values in Table A.19, prepared by White (24.6). White also gives a table for $P = .001$. Again note that small values of this test criterion lead to rejection of the null hypothesis. Since the 5 percent value of the lesser rank sum is 27, we reject the null hypothesis. The analysis of variance gave a value of F which is just beyond the 1 percent level.

The difference between the two conclusions may result from one or more of several causes. First, if the assumptions underlying the analysis of variance are true, then we would expect it to be better able to detect real departures from the null hypothesis. Second, if the underlying assumptions are false, we may be detecting false assumptions rather than real differences. Tukey's test of additivity and the F-test of homogeneity of variance (two-tailed F) may be used to examine the validity of the assumptions. In our example, the difference between conclusions seems trivial.

If the tables are inadequate, we may make use of the mean and standard deviation of T as given in

$$\mu_T = \frac{n_1(n_1 + n_2 + 1)}{2} \quad \text{and} \quad \sigma_T = \sqrt{\frac{n_1 n_2(n_1 + n_2 + 1)}{12}} \tag{24.4}$$

With these and T, we may compute the quantity $Z = (T - \mu_T)/\sigma_T$, which is approximately normally distributed. Table A.4 may be used to judge significance.

Exercise 24.7.1 Apply the Wilcoxon-Mann-Whitney test to the data of Table 5.4. What null hypothesis are you testing? What was your alternative hypothesis? Is your conclusion different from that in the text?

Exercise 24.7.2 Apply the Wilcoxon-Mann-Whitney test to the data of Table 5.6. Do you think the test is appropriate here?

Exercise 24.7.3 Apply the Wilcoxon-Mann-Whitney test to the data of Exercise 5.5.1. What is your null hypothesis? What alternative are you using? What is your conclusion?

Exercise 24.7.4 Repeat Exercise 24.7.3 for the data of Exercise 5.5.2.

Exercise 24.7.5 Repeat Exercise 24.7.3 for the data of Exercise 5.5.5.

Exercise 24.7.6 Repeat Exercise 24.7.3 for the data of Exercise 5.5.6.

24.8 The Median Test

This test is given by Mood (24.4) for use with two independent samples. It tests the null hypothesis that two sampled continuous distributions have a common median. It is easy to use when the alternatives are two-sided, the case considered here. The procedure follows.

1. Order the two samples as one from smallest to largest. Ties are given the average of the ranks that would have been assigned.
2. Find the median.
3. For each sample, observe the number of observations greater than the median.
4. Use these two numbers and the two sample sizes to complete a 2×2 contingency table.
5. Test significance by χ^2 with one degree of freedom if both sample sizes exceed 10; otherwise, Eq. (22.8) is appropriate, especially if the sum of the two sample sizes is small. This is a term from the hypergeometric distribution.

For the coefficients of digestibility, 58.7 is the median. There is 1 S greater than the median, and 5 Cs. The 2 × 2 table is as follows.

	S	C	
Above	1	5	6
n_i − above	6	1	7
	7	6	13

The total of the "n_i − above" row will equal $(n_1 + n_2 + 1)/2$ if $n_1 + n_2$ is odd, and $(n_1 + n_2)/2$ if $n_1 + n_2$ is even.

Exercise 24.8.1 Test the null hypothesis that the sampled distributions providing the table above have the same median. Compute the probability of a table as extreme or more extreme than that observed using Eq. (22.8.) Compare your result with that from the analysis of variance and from the Wilcoxon-Mann-Whitney test. Have you used the same alternative hypothesis each time?

Exercise 24.8.2 Apply the median test to the data of Table 5.4. Of Table 5.6. Of Exercise 5.5.1. Of Exercise 5.5.2. Of Exercise 5.5.5. Of Exercise 5.5.6.

Exercise 24.8.3 Summarize the results of your application of parametric and nonparametric test procedures to the data referred to in Exercise 24.8.2. Have your alternative hypotheses always been the same?

24.9 Kruskal-Wallis *k*-Sample Test

Kruskal and Wallis (24.2) have developed a test criterion based on ranks which is appropriate for the completely random design. For $k = 2$, it is equivalent to the Wilcoxon-Mann-Whitney test. As for the other rank tests, we assume that all populations sampled are continuous and identical, except possibly for location. The null hypothesis is that the populations all have the same location.

The procedure for applying the test follows.

1. Rank all observations together from smallest to largest.
2. Sum the ranks for each sample.
3. Compute the test criterion and compare with tabulated values.

The test criterion is

$$H = \frac{12}{n(n+1)} \sum_i \frac{R_i^2}{n_i} - 3(n+1) \qquad (24.5)$$

Here n_i is the number of observations in the ith sample, $i = 1, \ldots, k$, $n = \sum n_i$, and R_i is the sum of the ranks for the ith sample. H is distributed as χ^2 with $k - 1$ degrees of freedom if the n_i are not too small. For $k = 2$, use the Wilcoxon-Mann-Whitney test and critical values given in Table A.18. For $k = 3$ and all combinations of the n_i's up to 5, 5, 5, a table of exact probabilities is given by Kruskal and Wallis (24.2). Ties are given the mean rank and, when in different treatments, a correction in H may be made. This correction will not ordinarily change the value of H appreciably. It is

$$\text{Divisor} = 1 - \frac{\sum T}{(n-1)n(n+1)} \tag{24.6}$$

where $T = (t-1)t(t+1)$ for each group of ties and t is the number of tied observations in the group. This number is used as a divisor of H to give a corrected H.

We now apply the procedure to the data of Table 7.1. The observations and their ranks are (number or letter in parentheses refers to treatment): 9.1 (4), 1; 11.6 (13), 2; 11.8 (13) 3; 11.9 (4), 4; 14.2 (13), 5; 14.3 (13), 6; 14.4 (13), 7; 15.8 (4), 8; 16.9 (C), 9; 17.0 (4), 10; 17.3 (C), 11; 17.7 (5), 12; 18.6 (7), 13; 18.8 (7), 14; 19.1 (C), 15; 19.4 (4), 17; 19.4 (1), 17; 19.4 (C), 17; 20.5 (7), 19; 20.7 (7), 20; 20.8 (C), 21; 21.0 (7), 22; 24.3 (5), 23; 24.8 (5), 24; 25.2 (5), 25; 27.0 (1), 26; 27.9 (5), 27; 32.1 (1), 28; 32.6 (1), 29; 33.0 (1), 30. The sums of the ranks for each sample are: R(1) = 130, R(5) = 111, R(4) = 40, R(7) = 88, R(13) = 23, and R(C) = 73. Now

$$H = \frac{12}{30(31)} \frac{130^2 + \cdots + 73^2}{5} - 3(31) = 21.64 \qquad \text{with } 6 - 1 = 5 \text{ df}$$

Since 21.64 is beyond the .005 probability, we reject the null hypothesis. The same conclusion was drawn when the analysis of variance was used.

Exercise 24.9.1 Apply the Kruskal-Wallis test to the data in Exercise 7.3.1. What null hypothesis are you testing? Against what alternative? What assumptions have been made?

Exercise 24.9.2 Repeat the previous exercise for the data of Exercise 7.3.3, using both the pre and post data, but separately.

Exercise 24.9.3 Repeat Exercise 24.9.1 for the data of Exercise 7.4.1.

Exercise 24.9.4 Repeat Exercise 24.9.1 for the data of Exercise 7.4.2.

24.10 The Median Test for k Samples

The *median test* may also be applied to data from a completely random design. The procedure follows.

1. Rank all observations together from smallest to largest.
2. Find the median.
3. Find the number of observations above the median for each treatment.

4. Complete a $2 \times k$ table using the numbers obtained at step 3 and the differences between the n_i's and these numbers. (See the two-sample median test of Sec. 24.8.)
5. Compute χ^2 with $k - 1$ degrees of freedom for the contingency table obtained at step 4.

Exercise 24.10.1 Apply the median test to the data of Exercise 7.3.1. What null hypothesis are you testing? Against what alternatives? What are the assumptions underlying this test procedure?

Exercise 24.10.2 Repeat Exercise 24.10.1 for the data of Exercise 7.3.3. Of Exercise 7.4.1. Of Exercise 7.4.2.

Exercise 24.10.3 Summarize the results of the analysis of variance, of the Kruskal-Wallis test, and of the median test, for the sets of data where all three tests have been used.

24.11 Friedman's Test for the Two-Way Classification

Probably the most common experimental design is the randomized complete block design with more than two treatments. Friedman (24.1) has proposed the following test for such designs:

1. Rank the treatments within each block from lowest to highest.
2. Obtain the sum of the ranks for each treatment.
3. Test the null hypothesis that the populations within a block are identical against the alternative that at least one treatment comes from populations which have a different location in one direction. The test criterion is

$$\chi_r^2 = \frac{12}{bt(t+1)} \sum_i r_{i\cdot}^2 - 3b(t+1) \qquad (24.7)$$

with $t - 1$ degrees of freedom, where t is the number of treatments, b is the number of blocks, and $r_{i\cdot}$ is the sum of the ranks for the ith treatment. Note that 12 and 3 are constants, not dependent on the size of the experiment. Definition of $r_{i\cdot}$ implies that r_{ij} is the rank of the ith treatment in the jth block. This test criterion measures the homogeneity of the t sums and is distributed approximately as χ^2. The approximation is poorest for small values of t and b. Friedman has prepared tables of the exact distribution of χ_r^2 for some pairs of small values of t and b.

Let us now apply Friedman's procedure to the data of Table 9.2, presented again in Table 24.3. Treatment responses are given opposite block numbers, and ranks below. Tied treatments are given the average rank within the block where they occur. The value of the test criterion is right at the 5 percent value for this example; the F value was beyond the 1 percent point.

Table 24.3 Oil content of Redwing flaxseed†

Block	Treatment					
	S	EB	FB	$FB(1/100)$	R	U
1	4.4(−) 2.5	3.3(−) 1	4.4(−) 2.5	6.8(+) 6	6.3(+) 4	6.4(+) 5
2	5.9(+) 4	1.9(−) 1	4.0(−) 2	6.6(+) 5	4.9(−) 3	7.3(+) 6
3	6.0(+) 4	4.9(−) 2	4.5(−) 1	7.0(+) 5	5.9(−) 3	7.7(+) 6
4	4.1(−) 2	7.1(+) 5.5	3.1(−) 1	6.4(−) 3	7.1(+) 5.5	6.7(+) 4
Rank totals	12.5	9.5	6.5	19	15.5	21

$\chi_r^2 = \frac{12}{4(6)7}(12.5^2 + \cdots + 21^2) - 3(4)7 = 11.07$ with 5 df; $\chi^2_{.05}(5 \text{ df}) = 11.1$

† See Table 9.2.

The test statistic may be adjusted for ties by dividing by the value

$$\text{Divisor} = \frac{1 - \sum_{i=1}^{b} T_i}{bt(t^2 - 1)} \tag{24.8}$$

where $T_i = \sum_h t_{ih}^3 - \sum_h t_{ih}$ and t_{ih} = the number of observations tied for a given rank in the ith block. Here h is the index of summation for the sets of ties in the block. For example, if there are three observations out of 8 tieing for ranks 4, 5, and 6 in the ith block and no other ties here, then there is only one t_i, namely 3; so $h = 1$ only and $T_i = 3^3 - 3 = 24$.

Exercise 24.11.1 Apply Friedman's procedure to the data of Exercise 9.3.1. What null hypothesis are you testing? Against what alternatives? What assumptions have been made?

Exercise 24.11.2 Repeat Exercise 24.11.1 using the data of Exercise 9.3.2.

Exercise 24.11.3 Repeat Exercise 24.11.1 using the data of Exercise 9.3.5.

24.12 A Median Test for the Two-Way Classification

An alternative procedure is given by Mood (24.4). This test assumes that the distributions are continuous and identical except for location. Note that this requires homogeneity of variance. We test whether the treatment contributions to the cell medians are all zero. The contributions are such that if they are real, their median is zero. For the random or mixed model, no assumption about interaction is necessary; for the fixed model, zero interaction is assumed.

The test procedure for treatments follows.

1. Find the median of the observations in each block.
2. Replace each observation by a plus or a minus sign, according to whether it is above or below the median of the observations in the block. (See Table 24.3.)
3. Record the numbers of plus and minus signs, by treatments, in a $2 \times t$ table.
4. Test the result as for an ordinary contingency table.

We now apply the procedure to the data of Table 24.3. It will not generally be necessary to compute medians. For example, in block 1 the median is between 4.4 and 6.3; this is sufficient for assigning pluses and minuses. The signs given in Table 24.3 are for this test. The two-way contingency table is shown below. It is now only necessary to compute χ^2 and compare with tabulated values for $t - 1 = 5$ degrees of freedom.

Treatment	*S*	*EB*	*FB*	*FB*(1/100)	*R*	*U*
Above	2	1	0	3	2	4
Not above	2	3	4	1	2	0

Exercise 24.12.1 Complete the test begun just above. What is your conclusion?

Exercise 24.12.2 Apply the median test to the data of Exercise 9.3.1. Of Exercise 9.3.2. Of Exercise 9.3.5.

Exercise 24.12.3 Summarize the results of your test procedures and conclusions for the *F*-test, Friedman's test, and the median test.

24.13 Chebyshev's Inequality

This inequality states

$$P(|Y - \mu| > k\sigma) \leq \frac{1}{k^2} \qquad (24.9)$$

Since Y is simply a random variable, we may substitute $\bar{Y}$ provided that we replace σ by $\sigma_{\bar{Y}}$. Other substitutions are also possible. Since μ and σ are a part of the probability statement, it may be better described as distribution-free rather than nonparametric. The inequality is valid for any distribution with a finite variance.

Let us apply the inequality to the problem of determining if the corn lines of Sec. 23.7 differ in mutation rate. The distribution may be binomial; in order to estimate a variance for the difference between the proportions, we will assume that to be the case. The standard deviation is

$$\hat{\sigma} = \sqrt{\frac{14}{11(10^5)}\frac{11(10^5) - 14}{11(10^5)}\left[\frac{1}{5(10^5)} + \frac{1}{6(10)^5}\right]} = \sqrt{\frac{14}{11(10^5)}\frac{11}{30(10^5)}} \text{ (approx)}$$

The null hypothesis is that μ, the difference between proportions, is zero. The observed value of Y to be used in Eq. (24.9) is

$$Y = \frac{10}{5(10^5)} - \frac{4}{6(10^5)} = \frac{40}{30(10^5)}$$

Now from the part of Eq. (24.9) in parentheses, we have

$$\frac{40}{30(10^5)} > k\sqrt{\frac{14}{11(10^5)}\frac{11}{30(10^5)}}$$

If we solve for k, we get $k = 1.95$ and $1/k^2 = .26$. Hence, the probability of obtaining a difference in proportions larger than that obtained is less than .26.

If we had been prepared to assume a normal distribution, then k would have been a normal deviation and this two-tailed procedure would call for a corresponding probability of .05, a long way from .26. We see the importance of using a nonparametric procedure when it is impossible to put much reliance on any assumptions concerning an underlying distribution, and, at the same time, the importance of taking advantage of any reasonable assumptions. In addition, it appears that we will often have to rely upon an estimate of σ.

Chebyshev's inequality may also be used to determine sample size. Suppose that we wish to estimate the mean number of colonies of a certain bacterium on a unit area of ham stored under normal conditions for a specified length of time. We wish our estimate to be within $\sigma/4$ of the true μ. How many samples are required if we wish to obtain this result with a probability of .90?

In terms of a probability statement, we want

$$P\left(|\bar{Y} - \mu| > \frac{\sigma}{4}\right) \leq .10$$

Relate this to Eq. (24.9) and we have

$$P\left(|\bar{Y} - \mu| > \frac{\sqrt{n}}{4}\frac{\sigma}{\sqrt{n}}\right) \leq .10 = \frac{4^2}{n}$$

(Clearly $k = \sqrt{n}/4$ and $1/k^2 = 4^2/n$.) We must solve the right-hand equality for n. We obtain

$$n = \frac{4^2}{.10} = 160$$

The necessary sample size is 160. Here, we did not have to specify σ.

24.14 Spearman's Coefficient of Rank Correlation

The correlation coefficient r is applicable to the bivariate normal distribution, a distribution which is not too common. Several coefficients have been proposed that do not require the assumption of a bivariate normal distribution.

Spearman's coefficient of rank correlation applies to data in the form of ranks. The data may be collected as ranks or may be ranked after observation on some other scale. It measures correspondence between ranks, so is not necessarily a measure of linear correlation. The procedure follows.

1. Rank the observations for each variable.
2. Obtain the differences in ranks for the paired observations. Let d_i = the difference for the ith pair.
3. Estimate ρ by Eq. (24.10).
4. If the number of pairs is large, the estimate may be tested using the criterion given in Eq. (24.11).

Equations (24.10) and (24.11) follow.

$$r_s = 1 - \frac{6 \sum_i d_i^2}{(n-1)n(n+1)} \tag{24.10}$$

where r_s is Spearman's rank correlation coefficient and n is the number of d's. The criterion

$$t = r_s \sqrt{\frac{n-2}{1-r_s^2}} \tag{24.11}$$

is distributed as Student's t with $n - 2$ degrees of freedom.

We now apply the procedure to the data of Exercise 11.2.1 for the characters T = tube length and L = limb length. Ties will be given the mean rank.

T:	49,	44,	32,	42,	32,	53,	36,	39,	37,	45,	41,	48,	45,	39,	40,	34,	37,	35
Rank:	17,	13,	1.5,	12,	1.5,	18,	5,	8.5,	6.5,	14.5,	11,	16,	14.5,	8.5,	10,	3,	6.5,	4
L:	27,	24,	12,	22,	13,	29,	14,	20,	16,	21,	22,	25,	23,	13,	20,	15,	20,	13
Rank:	17,	15,	1,	12.5,	2.5,	18,	4,	9,	6,	11,	12.5,	16,	14,	7,	9,	5,	9,	2.5
Difference:	0,	−2,	.5,	−.5,	−1,	0,	1,	−.5,	.6,	3.5,	−1.5,	0,	.5,	1.5,	1,	−2,	−2.5,	1.5

From Eq. (24.10),

$$r_s = 1 - \frac{6(37.50)}{17(18)19} = .9613$$

As a check, $\sum d_i = 0$. Also, r_s must lie between -1 and $+1$.

This value of r_s is obviously highly significant.

Another application is also available. In some instances, a set of objects may have a "true" order. For example, a set of paint chips may have an increasing amount of some color or a set of taste samples may have increasing amounts of a flavoring compound. If we ask a color or taste panelist to rank the set, we have a true standard with which to compare the rankings. Spearman's rank correlation is valid for rating competence.

Exercise 24.14.1 Compute t by Eq. (24.11). What null hypothesis would you be testing when comparing this t with tabulated t's in Table A.3?

Exercise 24.14.2 Compute values of r_s and t for T and N, and L and N for the data in Exercise 11.2.1. Compare your sample t with corresponding values of tabulated t. What conclusions do you draw?

Exercise 24.14.3 Compute r_s and t for the data in Exercise 11.2.2. What conclusions do you draw?

24.15 The Olmstead-Tukey Corner Test of Association

Olmstead and Tukey (24.5) have developed the following nonparametric test for the association of two continuous variables. They have called it the *quadrant sum* test. Extreme values are often the best indicators of an association between variables and this test gives them special weight. It is computed as follows:

1. Plot the paired observations.
2. Draw the medians for each variable.
3. Beginning at the top, count down the number of observations (using the Y axis) which appear, until it is necessary to cross the vertical median. Record this number together with the sign of the quadrant.
4. Repeat as in step 3 from the right, using the horizontal median.
5. Repeat from the bottom and from the left.
6. Compute the quadrant sum and compare with tabulated values.

Table A.20 is appropriate for judging the significance of any quadrant sum.

An *even number of pairs* poses no problem in drawing medians and applying the test. For an *odd number of pairs*, each median passes through a point, presumably different. Call these points (X_m, Y) and (X, Y_m). For purposes of computing the quadrant sum, replace these two pairs by the single pair (X, Y). This leaves an even number of pairs.

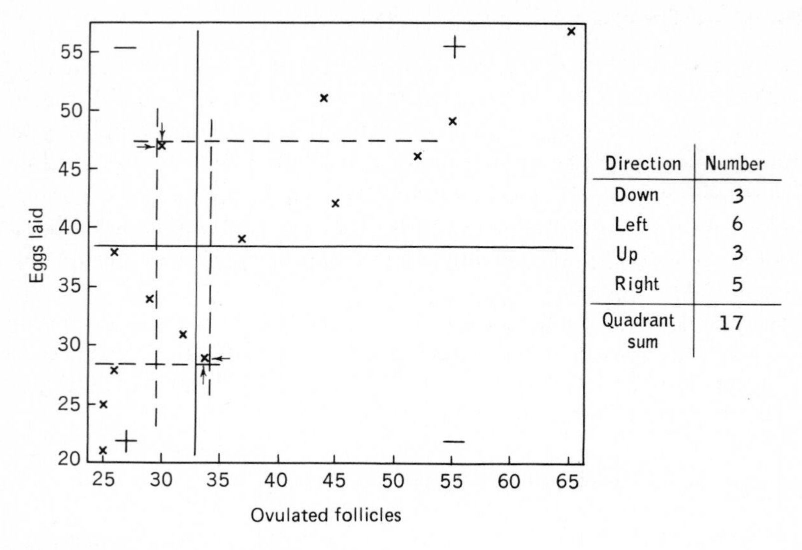

Figure 24.2 The corner test of association.

We now apply the procedure to the data of Exercise 11.2.2. These data are plotted in Fig. 24.2 where the quadrant sum is also computed. We have used arrows in our figure to show each point arrived at as the result of first crossing a median when counting in the four directions. The quadrant sum is 17 and highly significant.

Ties occur under situations like the following. If we count down to the first observation that requires us to cross the vertical median, this point may have a Y value which is common to points on the other side. For this Y value, we thus have points which are favorable for inclusion in the quadrant sum and points which are not. Olmstead and Tukey (24.5) suggest that such tied groups be treated as if the number of points before crossing the median were

$$\frac{\text{Number favorable for inclusion}}{1 + \text{number unfavorable}}$$

It is now seen that the quadrant sum test is easy to apply and places special weight on extreme values of the variables.

Exercise 24.15.1 Apply the Olmstead-Tukey test to the data used for illustration in Sec. 24.14.

Exercise 24.15.2 Apply the Olmstead-Tukey test to look for an association between T and N, and between L and N, for the data in Exercise 11.2.1.

Exercise 24.15.3 Apply the Olmstead-Tukey test to look for an association between the variables in the data of Exercise 11.2.2.

24.16 A Randomization Test for Regression

If we hypothesize that $\beta = 0$ in a linear regression problem, then this is equivalent to saying that pairings are random. In turn, all possible pairings are equally likely. Suppose that we construct all $n!$ possible pairings and compute a value of b from each. We now have an empirical distribution of b's for which we can obtain percentiles and critical values.

The data as originally observed provided a specific value of b. This can be compared with the empirical distribution to conclude whether or not to accept the null hypothesis.

To obtain the pairings, it is convenient to order the set of values of one variable and randomize the other set of values. The number $n!$ increases very fast, so that sampling the whole set of randomizations may be sufficient. In any case, high-speed computing equipment is essential.

References

24.1. Friedman, M.: "The use of ranks to avoid the assumption of normality implicit in the analysis of variance," *J. Amer. Statist. Ass.*, **32**:675–701 (1937).

24.2. Kruskal, W. H., and W. A. Wallis: "Use of ranks in one-criterion variance analysis," *J. Amer. Statist. Ass.*, **47**:583–621 (1952).

24.3. Mann, H. B., and D. R. Whitney: "On a test of whether one of two random variables is stochastically larger than the other," *Ann. Math. Statist.*, **18**:50–60 (1947).

24.4. Mood, A. M.: *Introduction to the Theory of Statistics*, McGraw-Hill, New York, 1950.

24.5. Olmstead, P. S., and J. W. Tukey: "A corner test for association," *Ann. Math. Statist.*, **18**:495–513 (1947).

24.6. White, C.: "The use of ranks in a test of significance for comparing two treatments," *Biom.*, **8**:33–41 (1952).

24.7. Wilcoxon, F.: "Individual comparisons by ranking methods," *Biom. Bull.*, **1**:80–83 (1945).

24.8. Wilcoxon, F.: "Probability tables for individual comparisons by ranking methods," *Biom. Bull.*, **3**:119–122 (1947).

24.9. Wilcoxon, F.: *Some Rapid Approximate Statistical Procedures*, American Cyanamid Company, Stamford, Conn., 1949.

24.10. Kolmogorov, A. N.: "Sulla determinazione empirica di una legge di distribuizione," *Giorn. 1st Ital. Attuari*, **4**:83–91 (1933).

24.11. Smirnov, N. V.: "Estimate of deviation between empirical distribution functions in two independent samples" (in Russian), *Bull. Moscow Univ.*, **2**:3–16 (1939).

24.12. Miller, L. H.: "Table of percentage points of Kolmogorov statistics," *J. Amer. Statist. Ass.*, **51**:111–121 (1956).

24.13. Pettit, A. N., and M. A. Stephens: "The Kolmogorov-Smirnov goodness-of-fit statistic with discrete and grouped data," *Technometrics*, **19**:205–210 (1977).

24.14. Dixon, W. J., and F. J. Massey, Jr.: *Introduction to Statistical Analysis*, 3d ed., McGraw-Hill, New York, 1969.

24.15. Birnbaum, Z. W., and R. A. Hall: "Small sample distribution for multi-sample statistics of the Smirnov type," *Ann. Math. Statist.*, **31**:710–720 (1960).

24.16. Massey, F. J., Jr., "Distribution table for the deviation between two sample cumulatives," *Ann. Math. Statist.*, **23**:435–441 (1952).

24.17. Davis, L. S., "Table Errata 266," *Math. Comput.*, **12**:262–263 (1958).

CHAPTER

TWENTY-FIVE

SAMPLING FINITE POPULATIONS

25.1 Introduction

The sampling discussed so far has been concerned with experiments in which the experimental units were not generally obtained by random procedures. Randomization was used to assign treatments to units and the populations were hypothetical ones, the units differing by random errors. We now turn our attention to populations which are no longer theoretical, but ones for which the experimental units can be enumerated and, consequently, randomly sampled. For example, silos are sampled for insecticide residues, soils for chemical analyses, plant populations for taxonomic purposes, fruit for quality, wheat fields for preharvest estimates of yield and quality, primitive races for many characteristics, people for opinions, and so on. In all these examples, populations of interest are finite populations.

A new problem arises in sampling finite populations. For example, if we want information from a sample of wholesale seed dealers in the state, we will be sampling a finite population. If our sample is large, say 25 percent of the wholesale seed dealers, we need to know if existing techniques are applicable or if it will be necessary to develop new ones.

In sampling *finite populations*, there are three fairly distinct ways in which selection may be made. These are

1. Random sampling
2, Systematic sampling
3. Authoritative sampling

Random sampling will be our chief concern. Randomness may be introduced into the sampling procedure in a number of ways to give us various sample designs. Because of randomization, valid estimates of error are possible. Probability theory can be applied and objective conclusions drawn.

Systematic sampling is used when every kth individual in the population is included in the sample. Such a procedure is always very simple but clearly unsatisfactory if unrecognized trends or cycles are present in the population. Since populations must be listed before sampling, some relation between one or more of the characters being investigated and the order of listing may be introduced unconsciously. It is not generally safe to assume that there is no such relation.

Systematic sampling can be conducted in such a way that an unbiased estimate of the sampling error may be obtained. This requires more than one systematic sample. For a single systematic sample, available formulas for estimating the variance of a mean require knowledge of the form of the population.

Authoritative sampling requires that some individual, who is well acquainted with the material to be sampled, draw the sample without regard to randomization. Such a procedure is completely dependent on the knowledge and skill of the sampler. It may produce good results in some instances but is rarely recommended.

25.2 Organizing the Survey

A considerable amount of effort must go into the planning and execution of a sample survey, quite apart from the actual sampling. We shall arbitrarily list five steps in the conduct of a survey.

1. Clarifying the objectives
2. Defining the sampling unit and population
3. Choosing the sample
4. Conducting the survey
5. Analyzing the data

These steps will now be discussed briefly.

1. Clarifying the objectives This consists primarily of stating objectives as concisely as possible, each objective being stated as a hypothesis to be tested, a confidence interval to be computed, or a decision to be made.

With the primary objective in mind, we consider what data are to be collected. When there are several objectives in mind, we may have to modify our ideas about what data are to be collected in order to accomplish all objectives. We may even have to modify our objectives so that the survey will not become too complex and costly.

Usually, the survey group will have a fixed budget and will wish to maximize the amount of information per dollar spent. Alternatively, the objectives will include a statement of the amount of information desired, generally in the form of the size of a confidence interval, and we will have to minimize the cost.

2. Defining the sampling unit and population This has been done to some degree in step 1. For sampling, the population must be divided into distinct *sampling units* which together constitute the population. There may be a number of choices for sampling units. The final choice may be somewhat arbitrary, but it must be usable. If we are sampling people, we may choose the individual, the family, or the occupants of some specified living area as the sampling unit. Whatever the choice, it will be necessary to locate and identify the unit in the field.

For random sampling, we must be able to *list* all sampling units; we may even have to list all units. Existing units, for example, lists of school children, farmers, etc., may need to be revised or new lists made, whichever seems more feasible and economical. Grids may be superimposed on maps of fields, forests, or other land areas when it is necessary to obtain crop samples or information about wildlife cover. Here we may need both ingenuity and arbitrariness, especially if we have an irregularly shaped area to sample.

While the sampling unit is being decided upon, it will be necessary to consider what is to be measured and what methods of measurement are to be used. Are we measuring height, weight, or opinion? If so, how? Can a questionnaire be used to measure emotional stresses? If so, can interviewers be obtained from university students seeking part-time employment? Can these be trained in several days? Will a prospective engineer be as useful as a premed student?

3. Choosing the sample Ways in which the sample may be drawn are termed *sample designs*. Sample designs will be discussed in later sections of this chapter.

The choice of sample size is related, in part, to available funds; if they are inadequate to permit a sample large enough to accomplish the stated objectives, the objectives should be revised or the survey delayed until adequate funds are available.

The sample design and size will give a fair idea of the extent and nature of the necessary tables and computations.

4. Conducting the survey Probably, it will be necessary to train some of the personnel in order to have uniformity in locating and identifying the sampling units and in recording responses to questionnaires or other data. A time schedule will be necessary. Some scheme is generally required for early checking on the validity of the data recorded on the various forms. Provision must be made for making quick decisions when unforeseen events arise.

5. ***Analyzing the data*** First, it will be necessary to edit the data for recording errors and invalidity. Finally, the survey should be reviewed for possible means of improving future surveys.

25.3 Probability Sampling

Suppose that our population is clearly defined and a listing of sampling units has been made. Now we can also list all possible samples. We use the term *probability sampling* when

1. Each sampling unit has or is assigned a known probability of being in the sample.
2. There is random selection at some stage of the sampling procedure and it is directly related to the known probabilities. Random selection will involve a mechanical procedure for choosing the units to be included in the sample.
3. The method for computing any estimate of a mean is clearly stated and will lead to a single value of the estimate. This is a part of the analysis of the data. In estimating any mean, we use the selection probabilities assigned to the sampling units. These will provide weights, each of which will be some constant multiple of the reciprocal of the probability.

When these criteria are satisfied, a probability of selection can be assigned to each sample and to each estimate. Hence, we can construct a probability distribution of the estimates given by our sampling plan. In this way, we can evaluate the worth of our plan and compare it with other probability sampling plans. Evaluation consists of measuring the accuracy of any estimate by the size of its standard deviation.

When the probabilities assigned to each sampling unit are all equal, then the weights to be used in computing estimates of means are all equal. We do not need to think consciously of the weights, because the sample is *self-weighting*. Whereas such samples are easy to analyze, they lack certain advantages possessed by other probability sampling plans, advantages such as ease and low cost of administration per unit of information and the ability to obtain estimates for individual strata (see Sec. 25.5).

A probability sample does not ensure that all our estimates will be unbiased. We have already seen that, in random sampling from a normal population, we choose to use $s = \sqrt{\sum (Y - \bar{Y})^2/(n - 1)}$ although it is a biased estimate of σ. Biased estimates are also used in sample surveys. They must, of course, be used with care, since they may introduce distortion into probability statements. In particular, when biased estimates are averaged (not necessarily arithmetically), the effect on the average and its ultimate use may not be apparent. Several types of probability sampling will now be discussed.

25.4 Simple Random Sampling

For random sampling, the population is listed and the plan and sample size fixed. For *simple random sampling*, each possible sample has the same probability of being selected. This is the important criterion.

In the actual process of selecting the sampling units from a finite population, a table of random numbers is used and sampling is *without replacement*. Apart from this, the sampling units are drawn independently.

Notation and definitions Because we are now dealing mainly with finite populations, some new notation and definitions are required. Notation and definitions will not be found to be completely consistent in sampling literature. We will attempt to use capital letters for population quantities and lowercase letters for sample quantities; σ^2 is also used.

To begin, let Y_i be the ith observation in the population. We also use Y_i as the ith sample observation when there is not likely to be confusion.

Population size: N

Sample size: n

Population mean:

$$\bar{Y} = \frac{\sum_i Y_i}{N} = \frac{Y.}{N}, \qquad \text{continous variable}$$

$$P = \frac{A}{N} \qquad \text{proportion}$$

For a proportion, $Y_i = 0$ or 1; $\sum Y_i/N$ is the proportion of individuals possessing a specified characteristic, so it can also serve as a definition of the population mean. It is more common to replace $\sum_i Y_i$ by A. For a percentage, $100P$ is the appropriate mean.

Sample mean:

$$\hat{\bar{Y}} = \bar{y} = \frac{\sum_i Y_i}{n} = \frac{y}{n}, \qquad \text{continous variable}$$

$$\hat{P} = p = \frac{a}{n}, \qquad \text{proportion}$$

For a proportion, a replaces $\sum_i Y_i$. Since population totals and their estimates are often of interest, the quantities Y, A, $Y.$, a are fairly common.

Population variance:

$$\sigma^2 = \frac{\sum_i (Y_i - \bar{Y})^2}{N}$$

$$S^2 = \frac{\sum_i (Y_i - \bar{Y})^2}{N - 1} \qquad (25.1)$$

We use Eq. (25.1) to define the population variance, because our definition of s^2, Eq. (25.4), gives an unbiased estimate of S^2.

Population variance of a mean:

$$S_{\bar{y}}^2 = \frac{S^2}{n}\left(\frac{N-n}{N}\right) \tag{25.2}$$

$$S_p^2 = \frac{PQ}{n}\left(\frac{N-n}{N-1}\right) \quad \text{where } Q = 1 - P \tag{25.3}$$

Sample variance:

$$s^2 = \frac{\sum_i (Y_i - \bar{y})^2}{n-1} \quad \text{an unbiased estimate of } S^2 \tag{25.4}$$

The numerator will be computed as $\sum Y_i^2 - (\sum Y_i)^2/n$.

Sample variance of a mean:

$$s_{\bar{y}}^2 = \frac{s^2}{n}\left(\frac{N-n}{N}\right) \tag{25.5}$$

$$s_p^2 = \frac{pq}{n-1}\,\frac{N-n}{N} \quad \text{where } q = 1 - p \tag{25.6}$$

Equation (25.6) gives an unbiased estimate of S_p^2 but is not generally used when computing confidence intervals. The more familiar form is implied in Eq. (25.8).

The quantity $(N - n)/N$ is known as the *finite population correction* or fpc. It may also be written as $1 - n/N$ and n/N is called the *sampling fraction.* If the sampling fraction is small, say less than 5 percent, it may be neglected. It is of interest to note that $pq/(n - 1)$ is an unbiased estimate of the population variance regardless of whether or not the population is finite. In other words, we use a biased estimate of the population variance in Chaps. 20 to 23 when we use $\hat{p}(1 - \hat{p})/n$. (Recall that in Chaps. 20 to 23 p is used as the parameter, $\hat{p}$ as the estimate.)

The confidence interval for a mean is given by Eq. (25.7). Note that it makes use of the fpc.

$$\text{CI} = \bar{y} \pm t\left[\frac{s}{\sqrt{n}}\sqrt{\frac{N-n}{N}}\right] \tag{25.7}$$

Obviously, we are assuming that $\bar{y}$ is normally distributed, knowing that the population of Y's is not normal since it is a finite population. Moreover, it is sampled without replacement.

The confidence interval for a proportion requires use of the hypergeometric distribution, Sec. 23.2, if it is to be completely valid. The interested investigator is referred to charts by Chung and DeLury (25.3). A common approximation is

$$\text{CI} = p \pm t\sqrt{\frac{pq}{n}\frac{N-n}{N-1}} \tag{25.8}$$

Note that the estimated standard deviation is not that given by Eq. (25.6) but is comparable to the population quantity given as Eq. (25.3). The estimate used in Eq. (25.8) is the more common. Table 21.1 may be used to judge the appropriateness of Eq. (25.8).

Simple random sampling is used when the population is known to be not highly variable or when the true proportion lies between 20 and 80 percent. When there is considerable variation, the sampling units should be grouped into strata in such a way that variation within strata can be expected to be less than variation among strata. This leads to stratified sampling. Much the same idea leads to an among-groups and within-groups analysis of variance.

Exercise 25.4.1 Consider the finite population consisting of the numbers 1, 2, ..., 6. Compute the mean and variance. Consider all possible samples of two observations when this population is sampled without replacement. Make a table of sample means and variances and the frequency with which each value occurs. Show that the sample mean and variance of Eq. (25.5) are unbiased estimates of the population mean and variance of Eq. (25.1). If the exercise had said "sample with replacement," what changes would be necessary in the computations?

Exercise 25.4.2 A buying population consisting of 6,000 furniture buyers is to be sampled, by mailed questionnaire, concerning an appliance preference. A random sample of 250 individuals is drawn and the questionnaire is mailed. Since the preference involves an inexpensive attachment, provision is made for yes and no responses only. All questionnaires are returned and 187 yeses counted. Estimate the true proportion of yeses in the population by means of a 95 percent confidence interval.

Exercise 25.4.3 For the same population as in Exercise 25.4.2, a lengthy questionnaire was sent to a random sample of 750 buyers. Only 469 questionnaires were returned. Estimate the true proportion of *respondents* in the population by means of a 90 percent confidence interval.

25.5 Stratified Sampling

The estimated variance of a population mean is given by Eq. (25.5) and, for a proportion, by Eq. (25.6) or the more frequent alternative implied by Eq. (25.8). To decrease the length of the confidence interval which estimates the population mean, we may increase n or decrease the population variance. Obviously, both possibilities must be considered.

The obvious way to decrease a population variance is to construct *strata* from the sampling units, the total variation being partitioned in such a way that as much as possible is assigned to differences among strata. In this way, variation within strata is kept small. Variation among the strata means in the population does not contribute to the sampling error of the estimate of the population mean. See Eq. (25.15).

Reduction in the variation of the estimate of the population mean is a very important reason for stratification. However, many surveys involve several variables and good stratification for one variable may not be so for another. Thus we find that strata are often constructed on a purely geographical basis. This generally works out well and we find that townships, counties, and land resource areas are often used as strata. This kind of stratification is often convenient for administrative reasons, since it may be possible to obtain the cooperation of town, county, or other conveniently located agencies.

In addition to increasing the precision with which means are measured, stratification permits an efficient job of allocating resources since we may use any method for deciding how many sampling units are to be taken from each stratum. It is assumed that each stratum will be sampled. Estimates of strata means are often desired and, in such cases, stratification is essential.

Notation and definitions. Notation and definitions for stratified random sampling are obviously relatives and extensions of what was given in Sec. 25.4 under the same heading.

Let Y_{ki} be the ith observation in the kth stratum, $k = 1, \ldots, s$. Strata sizes, means, and variances will be designated by N_k, $\bar{Y}_k$, or P_k, and S_k^2 with corresponding sample values of n_k, $\bar{y}_k$ or p_k, and s_k^2.

Stratum mean and variance:

$$\bar{Y}_k = \frac{\sum_{i=1}^{N_k} Y_{ki}}{N_k} = \frac{Y_k}{N_k}$$

$$P_k = \frac{A_k}{N_k}$$

$$S_k^2 = \frac{\sum_{i=1}^{N_k} (Y_{ki} - \bar{Y}_k)^2}{N_k - 1}$$

from Eq. (25.1).

Sample mean and variance for kth stratum:

$$\hat{\bar{Y}}_k = \bar{y}_k = \frac{\sum_{i=1}^{n_k} Y_{ki}}{n_k} = \frac{y_{k\cdot}}{n_k}$$

$$\hat{P}_k = p_k = \frac{a_k}{n_k}$$

$$s_k^2 = \frac{\sum_{i=1}^{n_k} (Y_{ki} - \bar{y}_k)^2}{n_k - 1}$$

from Eq. (25.4).

Parameters and statistics for the complete population are also required. Let

$$N = \sum_k N_k \qquad \text{and} \qquad n = \sum_k n_k$$

The ratio N_k/N occurs frequently enough that we give it the symbol W_k, that is, $W_k = N_k/N$, where W stands for weight.

Population mean (st means stratified):

$$\bar{Y}_{st} = \frac{\sum_k N_k \bar{Y}_k}{N} = \sum_k W_k \bar{Y}_k \tag{25.9}$$

$$P_{st} = \frac{\sum_k N_k P_k}{N} = \sum_k W_k P_k \tag{25.10}$$

Estimate of population mean:

$$\hat{\bar{Y}}_{st} = \bar{y}_{st} = \frac{\sum_k N_k \bar{y}_k}{N} = \sum_k W_k \bar{y}_k \tag{25.11}$$

$$\hat{P}_{st} = p_{st} = \frac{\sum_k N_k p_k}{N} = \sum_k W_k p_k \tag{25.12}$$

(Sample means are $\bar{y} = \sum n_k \bar{y}_k/n$ and $p = \sum_k n_k p_k/n$.)

Variance of the estimate of the population mean:

$$\begin{aligned} \sigma^2(\bar{y}_{st}) &= \sum_k \left(\frac{N_k}{N}\right)^2 \frac{S_k^2}{n_k} \frac{N_k - n_k}{N_k} \\ &= \frac{1}{N^2} \sum N_k(N_k - n_k)\frac{S_k^2}{n_k} \end{aligned} \tag{25.13}$$

Compare Eq. (25.5) with the first expression for $\sigma^2(\bar{y}_{st})$.

$$\sigma^2(p_{st}) = \sum_k \frac{N_k^2}{N^2} \frac{P_k Q_k}{n_k} \frac{N_k - n_k}{N_k - 1} \tag{25.14}$$

Compare the variance given in Eq. (25.3) with $\sigma^2(p_{st})$.

Sample variance of the estimate of the population mean:

$$\begin{aligned} s^2(\bar{y}_{st}) &= \frac{1}{N^2} \sum_k N_k(N_k - n_k)\frac{s_k^2}{n_k} \\ &= \sum_k W_k^2 \frac{s_k^2}{n_k} - \frac{1}{N} \sum_k W_k s_k^2 \end{aligned} \tag{25.15}$$

The first form is obtained from Eq. (25.13) by substituting estimates for parameters. It is an unbiased estimate of $\sigma^2(\bar{y}_{st})$. The second form may be used for computing.

$$s^2(p_{st}) = \sum_k W_k^2 \frac{p_k q_k}{n_k} \frac{N_k - n_k}{N_k - 1} \tag{25.16}$$

This equation is obtained from Eq. (25.14). It gives a biased estimate of $\sigma^2(p_{st})$ but is commonly used.

The finite population correction, if small, is ignored when computing confidence intervals.

In estimating the population mean, weights are used. For this reason, the estimate of the population mean and the sample mean, $\bar{y}_{st}$ and $\bar{y}$, respectively, need not be the same. However, when $n_1/N_1 = \cdots = n_s/N_s = n/N$, then $\bar{y}_{st} = \bar{y}$. This is called *proportional allocation* and the sample is said to be *self-weighting.*

When proportional allocation is used and the *within strata* variances are homogeneous, the results relative to variances may be summarized in an analysis-of-variance table with sources of variation for total, among strata, and within strata. The value of the particular stratification can be estimated by comparing the standard deviation of $\bar{y}_{st}$, as computed from the within-strata mean square, with that of $\bar{y}$, as computed from the total mean square. Sound procedures are given by Cochran (25.2) and by Hansen et al. (25.4).

Exercise 25.5.1 The problem of *nonrespondents* plagues users of mailed questionnaires and even interviewers. Suppose that 900 buyers are chosen randomly from a population of 6,000. Replies are received from 250 and, of these, 195 favor one suggestion. Estimate the proportion of "favorables" in the population consisting of respondents; do this by means of a 95 percent confidence interval.

From the known nonrespondents, a random sample of 50 is drawn and interviewed. These show 30 "favorables" in the sample from the population of nonrespondents. Estimate, by means of a 95 percent confidence interval, the proportion of "favorables" in this population.

Response and nonresponse to mailed questionnaires are sometimes used as a criterion for stratification. Suppose that the results above are considered to be from such strata. Estimate the population proportion of "favorables" and the standard deviation of the estimate. Give one practical and two theoretical criticisms of your procedure.

How might you use the sample results to test whether or not the two strata differed in response to the suggestion?

25.6 Optimum Allocation

Stratification generally results in decreasing the variance of the estimate of the population mean. However, proportional allocation is not always *optimum allocation* and, for this, a *variable sampling fraction* may be necessary.

Fixed cost In some sampling experiments, the cost of obtaining an observation from a sampling unit does not vary to any extent from one stratum to another and can be ignored when determining sampling fractions for the various strata. The problem is to minimize $\sigma^2(\bar{y}_{st})$ as given by Eq. (25.13) or $\sigma^2(p_{st})$ as given by Eq. (25.14). Sampling fractions are determined by the size of the strata and their variability and it is fairly clear that a larger stratum will call for a larger number of observations, as will a stratum with a high variability. It has been shown that the optimum allocation is obtained when the number of observations made in any stratum is determined by

$$n_k = n \frac{N_k S_k}{\sum_k N_k S_k} \tag{25.17}$$

Note that the denominator is the sum over all strata.

While application of this formula calls for the parameters S_k, $k = 1, \ldots, s$, it will often be necessary to use estimates. Thus, if sample information is desired for the years between censuses, standard deviations from the nearest preceding census can be used. In other cases, it may be necessary to make use of information from related sample surveys. When no estimates of the S_k's are available, proportional allocation is recommended.

Occasionally, Eq. (25.17) will give one or more n_k values greater than their corresponding N_k's. In such cases, 100 percent sampling is done in these strata and the remaining sampling fractions are adjusted so that the total sample is of the size originally planned. For example, if $n_s > N_s$ on application of Eq. (25.17), then we set $n_s = N_s$ for sampling purposes and recompute the remaining n_k's by the equation

$$n_k = \frac{(n - N_s)N_k S_k}{\sum_{k=1}^{s-1} N_k S_k} \qquad k = 1, \ldots, s - 1$$

When stratified sampling is for *proportions*, the n_k may be determined by

$$n_k = n \frac{N_k \sqrt{P_k Q_k}}{\sum_k N_k \sqrt{P_k Q_k}} \tag{25.18}$$

This equation is an approximation; it is similar to Eq. (25.17), although the former is not an approximation.

Gains in precision as a result of using optimum rather than proportional allocation are not likely to be as great for estimating proportions as for estimating means of continuous variables. Since proportional allocation gives the convenience of self-weighting samples, it is usually recommended when proportions are to be estimated.

Variable cost When the cost of obtaining an observation varies from stratum to stratum, some *cost function* is needed to give the total cost. A simple cost function is given by

$$\text{Cost} = C = a + \sum c_k n_k \tag{25.19}$$

where a is a fixed cost, regardless of the allocation of the sampling to the strata, and c_k represents the cost per observation in the kth stratum. For this cost function, the minimum $\sigma^2(\bar{y}_{st})$ is obtained if we take a large sample in a large stratum, a large sample when the stratum variance is high, and a small sample when the stratum cost is high. In other words, the sample size for any stratum is proportional to $N_k S_k/\sqrt{c_k}$.

In the actual survey, we may have to work with a fixed budget or may be required to estimate the variance of the population mean with a specified precision. The latter requirement determines the sample size and, in turn, the budget.

For a *fixed budget*, the optimum sample size for each stratum is

$$n_k = \frac{N_k S_k/\sqrt{c_k}(C - a)}{\sum_k N_k S_k \sqrt{c_k}} \tag{25.20}$$

For a *fixed variance*, Eq. (25.21) gives the optimum sample size for each stratum. Here, we minimize the cost for a fixed or predetermined variance.

$$\begin{aligned} n_k &= \frac{N_k S_k}{\sqrt{c_k}} \frac{\sum_k N_k S_k \sqrt{c_k}}{N^2\sigma^2(\bar{y}_{st}) + \sum_k N_k S_k^2} \\ &= \frac{W_k S_k}{\sqrt{c_k}} \frac{\sum_k W_k S_k \sqrt{c_k}}{\sigma^2(\bar{y}_{st}) + \sum_k W_k S_k^2/N} \end{aligned} \tag{25.21}$$

where $W_k = N_k/N$.

Rough estimates of the S_k^2's and c_k's are usually quite adequate for estimating optimum sample sizes for the strata. When sampling is to estimate *proportions*, S_k may be replaced by $\sqrt{P_k Q_k}$ in Eqs. (25.20) and (25.21) to give approximately optimum n_k's.

Exercise 25.6.1 Show that Eqs. (25.17) and (25.20) give the same results as proportional allocation when the strata variances are homogeneous and the cost c_k does not vary.

Exercise 25.6.2 The following data are from R. J. Jessen (25.5). The strata are types of farming areas, N_k is number of rural farms, $S_k^2(1)$ is a variance for number of swine, and $S_k^2(2)$ is a variance for number of sheep. The N_k's are 1939 census data whereas the S_k^2's are obtained from a 1939 sample and are estimates only.

For each set of data, compute sample sizes using proportional and optimum allocation for a total sample size of 800. Compare the results.

Stratum	1	2	3	4	5	State
N_k	39,574	38,412	44,017	36,935	41,832	200,770
$S_k^2(1)$	1,926	2,352	2,767	1,967	2,235	2,303
$S_k^2(2)$	764	20	618	209	87	235

25.7 Multistage or Cluster Sampling

In some sampling schemes, the sampling units are in groups of equal or unequal sizes and the groups, rather than the units, are randomly sampled. Such groups are called *primary sampling units*, or psu's. Observations may be obtained on all elementary units or these, in turn, may be sampled. For example, we may be interested in individuals, the elementary units, and may obtain them by drawing a random sample of families, the primary sampling unit, and observing all units within. This would be a *simple cluster sampling* plan or a *single-stage* sampling plan. In sampling the soil in a field to be used for an experiment, we might divide the field into experimental plots, place a grid over each plot to define the sampling units, then obtain several observations from each plot. This would be *two-stage* sampling or *subsampling* where the first stage was essentially a census.

Many types of cluster sampling can obviously be devised. Most will have some obvious advantages related to cost or practicability, since the cost of getting from one psu to another is likely to be larger than that of getting from one subunit to another and since identifying the psu may be simpler than identifying the subunit. When a cluster is defined by association with an area, we have *area sampling*. For example, we might sample quarter sections of land, the cluster or psu, and enumerate all farms in the psu.

Suppose that a population consists of N psu's from which we draw a random sample of size n; each psu consists of M subunits from which we draw a sample of size m for each of the n psu's. (The letters M and N, and m and n are often interchanged in sampling literature.) Now there are MN *elements* in the population and mn in the sample. The plan is two-stage sampling or subsampling.

Computations are usually carried out on a per-element basis just as we are accustomed to in the analysis of variance. An observation is denoted by Y_{ij}, where j refers to the element and i to the psu. The mean of all elements in a psu is designated by $\bar{Y}_{i\cdot}$ or simply $\bar{Y}_i$, and the population mean by $\bar{Y}_{\cdot\cdot}$ or simply $\bar{\bar{Y}}$. Corresponding sample means are given the symbols $\bar{y}_{i\cdot}$ or $\bar{y}_i$ and $\bar{y}_{\cdot\cdot}$ or $\bar{\bar{y}}$.

Let us now assume that N and M are infinite and define an element by

$$Y_{ij} = \bar{\bar{Y}} + \delta_i + \varepsilon_{ij} \tag{25.22}$$

This is a linear model such as was discussed in Secs. 7.6 and 7.7 with slightly different notation. If we denote the variance of the δ's by S_a^2 and that of the ε's by S_w^2, then sample mean squares defined as in Table 25.1 are estimates of the quantities given in the expected value column. Note that s_a^2 is not intended to be an estimate of S_a^2.

The sums of squares are usually computed from the following computation formulas rather than from the definition formulas of Table 25.1.

Among psu's: $$(n-1)s_a^2 = \frac{\sum_i Y_{i\cdot}^2}{m} - \frac{Y_{\cdot\cdot}^2}{nm}$$

Table 25.1 Analysis of variance and expected values in two-stage sampling

Source of variation	df	Mean square	Expected value of mean square
Among psu's	$n-1$	$s_a^2 = \dfrac{m \sum_i (\bar{y}_i - \bar{\bar{y}})^2}{n-1}$	$S_w^2 + mS_a^2$
Within psu's	$n(m-1)$	$s_w^2 = \dfrac{\sum_i \sum_j (Y_{ij} - \bar{y}_i)^2}{n(m-1)}$	S_w^2
Total	$nm-1$	$\dfrac{\sum_{i,j} (Y_{ij} - \bar{\bar{y}})^2}{nm-1}$	

Within psu's: $$n(m-1)s_w^2 = \sum_i \left(\sum_{j=1}^{m} Y_{ij}^2 - \frac{Y_{i\cdot}^2}{m} \right)$$

or $$= \text{SS (total)} - \text{SS (among psu's)}$$

$$\text{Total SS} = \sum_{i,j} Y_{ij}^2 - \frac{Y_{\cdot\cdot}^2}{nm}$$

If we relate the analysis of variance given in Table 25.1 to Secs. 7.6 and 7.8, we see that the mean square within psu's may be called the *sampling error* and the mean square among psu's may be called the *experimental error*.

Experimental error rather than sampling error is appropriate in terms of estimating $\bar{\bar{Y}}$ by means of a confidence interval. Experimental error is based on the unit chosen at random at the first stage of sampling and corresponds to the plot to which a treatment is applied at random in a field or laboratory experiment. In the usual course of events, we might expect sampling error to be smaller than experimental error because we expect more homogeneity within psu's than among psu's. Hence, sampling error would not be appropriate for computing a confidence interval for $\bar{\bar{Y}}$.

The variance of the sampling mean, $s^2(\bar{\bar{y}})$, is estimated by s_a^2/nm, an unbiased estimate of the true variance. We can now estimate both S_w^2 and S_a^2 and construct estimates of the variances of treatment means for different allocations of our efforts. Thus, for the present scheme,

$$\sigma^2(\bar{\bar{y}}) = \frac{S_w^2}{nm} + \frac{S_a^2}{n}$$

We do not decrease S_a^2/n by taking more subsamples, yet S_a^2 is likely to be the larger contributor to $\sigma^2(\bar{\bar{y}})$. If we were to increase n, we would decrease both contributions. Hence, in theory, the best allocation of our effort is to take as many psu's as possible and very few elements within each psu if they require an appreciable effort; of course, we require two such elements from each psu if we have to estimate either S_w^2 or S_a^2 and retain computational ease.

Theory is also available for finite populations and when the psu's differ in the number of elements they contain. The interested reader is referred to Cochran (25.2) and to Hansen et al. (25.4).

In sampling for proportions with N clusters and M elements per cluster, draw n clusters and completely enumerate them. Then an observed proportion is a true proportion P_i for the ith cluster and is not subject to sampling variation. We estimate the population proportion by

$$\hat{P} = p_{nM} = \frac{\sum_i P_i}{n}$$

and its variance by

$$s^2(p_{nM}) = \frac{N-n}{N}\frac{1}{n}\frac{\sum_i (P_i - p_{nM})^2}{n-1}$$

When the sampling scheme involves taking only m of the M elements in a cluster, then the P_i are only estimated and a term for sampling variation within clusters must be introduced into the variance of the estimate of the population proportion P. We now have

$$\hat{P} = p_{nm} = \bar{p} = \frac{\sum_i p_i}{n}$$

and

$$s^2(\bar{p}) = \frac{M-m}{M-1}\frac{m}{m-1}\frac{1}{Nnm}\sum_i p_i q_i + \frac{N-n}{N}\frac{1}{n}\frac{\sum_i (p_i - \bar{p})^2}{n-1}$$

Ladell (25.6) and Cochran (25.1) describe an interesting sampling experiment where local control, in the form of a restriction on the subsampling, was imposed. The particular example involved superimposing a Latin square design, initially without treatments, on an experimental area and then obtaining six soil samples from each plot. Wireworm counts were made on the soil samples. It was so arranged that three samples were obtained from each of the north and south halves of the plot. Consequently, nonrandom differences in numbers of wireworms between halves do not influence treatment comparisons or experimental error. The results are shown in Table 25.2; the usual "experimental error" and "treatments" are pooled here because there were no true treatments. It is readily apparent that "local control" greatly increased the precision of the experiment.

Table 25.2 Analysis of variance of wireworm data

Source	df	Sum of squares	Mean square
Rows	4	515.44	128.86
Columns	4	523.44	130.86
Experimental error	16	712.16	44.51
Between half plots	25	2,269.00	90.76
Sampling error	100	3,844.00	38.44
Totals	149	7,864.04	

Exercise 25.7.1 Suppose that we wish to have a preharvest estimate of the wheat yield for a wheat-growing state. The area in wheat is divided, for sampling purposes, into 1-acre plots. A random sample of 250 plots is drawn and two subsamples are obtained from each of the 250 plots. Each subsample is 2 ft square, approximately 1/10,000 acre, so that finite sampling theory need not be applied.

The analysis of variance gives a sampling error of 20 (within psu's) and an experimental error of 70 (among psu's). (Yields were converted to bushels per acre.) Write out the analysis of variance. Estimate components of variance. Compute the variance of a treatment mean. Estimate the variance of a treatment mean assuming that the rate of subsampling is doubled (four subsamples instead of two). Does this give an appreciable gain in precision? (Express the estimated variance as a percentage of that observed.)

Exercise 25.7.2 Use the data of Table 25.2 to compute the experimental error as if no design has been superimposed on the plots. (Use a weighted average of row, column, and experimental error mean squares.) What would sampling error have been if no local control had been used? (Use a weighted average of between half plots and sampling error mean squares.) What would experimental error have been without the design and without local control? (Add the values just computed for experimental and sampling errors. This includes sampling error without local control twice so that sampling error with local control must now be subtracted.) Compute standard deviations from each of the three variances you have just computed.

Exercise 25.7.3 What is the minimum number of subsamples per half plot with local control if it is required to estimate sampling error and, at the same time, not destroy computational ease?

References

25.1. Cochran, W. G.: "The information supplied by the sampling results," *Ann. Appl. Biol.*, **25:**383–389 (1938).
25.2. Cochran, W. G.: *Sampling Techniques*, Wiley, New York, 1953.
25.3. Chung, J. H., and D. B. DeLury: *Confidence Limits for the Hypergeometric Distribution*, University of Toronto Press, Toronto, Ontario, 1950.
25.4. Hansen, M. H., W. N. Hurwitz, and W. G. Madow: *Sample Survey Methods and Theory*, 2 vols., Wiley, New York, 1953.
25.5. Jessen, R. J.: "Statistical investigation of a sample survey for obtaining farm facts," *Iowa Agr. Exp. Sta. Res. Bull.* 304, 1942.
25.6. Ladell, W. R. S.: "Field experiments on the control of wireworms," *Ann. Appl. Biol.*, **25:**341–382 (1938).

APPENDIX

TABLES

Table A.1 Ten thousand random digits

	00–04	05–09	10–14	15–19	20–24	25–29	30–34	35–39	40–44	45–49
00	88758	66605	33843	43623	62774	25517	09560	41880	85126	60755
01	35661	42832	16240	77410	20686	26656	59698	86241	13152	49187
02	26335	03771	46115	88133	40721	06787	95962	60841	91788	86386
03	60826	74718	56527	29508	91975	13695	25215	72237	06337	73439
04	95044	99896	13763	31764	93970	60987	14692	71039	34165	21297
05	83746	47694	06143	42741	38338	97694	69300	99864	19641	15083
06	27998	42562	63402	10056	81668	48744	08400	83124	19896	18805
07	82685	32323	74625	14510	85927	28017	80588	14756	54937	76379
08	18386	13862	10988	04197	18770	72757	71418	81133	69503	44037
09	21717	13141	22707	68165	58440	19187	08421	23872	03036	34208
10	18446	83052	31842	08634	11887	86070	08464	20565	74390	36541
11	66027	75177	47398	66423	70160	16232	67343	36205	50036	59411
12	51420	96779	54309	87456	78967	79638	68869	49062	02196	55109
13	27045	62626	73159	91149	96509	44204	92237	29969	49315	11804
14	13094	17725	14103	00067	68843	63565	93578	24756	10814	15185
15	92382	62518	17752	53163	63852	44840	02592	88572	03107	90169
16	16215	50809	49326	77232	90155	69955	93892	70445	00906	57002
17	09342	14528	64727	71403	84156	34083	35613	35670	10549	07468
18	38148	79001	03509	79424	39625	73315	18811	86230	99682	82896
19	23689	19997	72382	15247	80205	58090	43804	94548	82693	22799
20	25407	37726	73099	51057	68733	75768	77991	72641	95386	70138
21	25349	69456	19693	85568	93876	18661	69018	10332	83137	88257
22	02322	77491	56095	03055	37738	18216	81781	32245	84081	18436
23	15072	33261	99219	43307	39239	79712	94753	41450	30944	53912
24	27002	31036	85278	74547	84809	36252	09373	69471	15606	77209
25	66181	83316	40386	54316	29505	86032	34563	93204	72973	90760
26	09779	01822	45537	13128	51128	82703	75350	25179	86104	40638
27	10791	07706	87481	26107	24857	27805	42710	63471	08804	23455
28	74833	55767	31312	76611	67389	04691	39687	13596	88730	86850
29	17583	24038	83701	28570	63561	00098	60784	76098	84217	34997
30	45601	46977	39325	09286	41133	34031	94867	11849	75171	57682
31	60683	33112	65995	64203	18070	65437	13624	90896	80945	71987
32	29956	81169	18877	15296	94368	16317	34239	03643	66081	12242
33	91713	84235	75296	69875	82414	05197	66596	13083	46278	73498
34	85704	86588	82837	67822	95963	83021	90732	32661	64751	83903
35	17921	26111	35373	86494	48266	01888	65735	05315	79328	13367
36	13929	71341	80488	89827	48277	07229	71953	16128	65074	28782
37	03248	18880	21667	01311	61806	80201	47889	83052	31029	06023
38	50583	17972	12690	00452	93766	16414	01212	27964	02766	28786
39	10636	46975	09449	45986	34672	46916	63881	83117	53947	95218
40	43896	41278	42205	10425	66560	59967	90139	73563	29875	79033
41	76714	80963	74907	16890	15492	27489	06067	22287	19760	13056
42	22393	46719	02083	62428	45177	57562	49243	31748	64278	05731
43	70942	92042	22776	47761	13503	16037	30875	80754	47491	96012
44	92011	60326	86346	26738	01983	04186	41388	03848	78354	14964
45	66456	00126	45685	67607	70796	04889	98128	13599	93710	23974
46	96292	44348	20898	02227	76512	53185	03057	61375	10760	26889
47	19680	07146	53951	10935	23333	76233	13706	20502	60405	09745
48	67347	51442	24536	60151	05498	64678	87569	65066	17790	55413
49	95888	59255	06898	99137	50871	81265	42223	83303	48694	81953

Table A.1 Ten thousand random digits (*Continued*)

	50–54	55–59	60–64	65–69	70–74	75–79	80–84	85–89	90–94	95–99
00	70896	44520	64720	49898	78088	76740	47460	83150	78905	59870
01	56809	42909	25853	47624	29486	14196	75841	00393	42390	24847
02	66109	84775	07515	49949	61482	91836	48126	80778	21302	24975
03	18071	36263	14053	52526	44347	04923	68100	57805	19521	15345
04	98732	15120	91754	12657	74675	78500	01247	49719	47635	55514
05	36075	83967	22268	77971	31169	68584	21336	72541	66959	39708
06	04110	45061	78062	18911	27855	09419	56459	00695	70323	04538
07	75658	58509	24479	10202	13150	95946	55087	38398	18718	95561
08	87403	19142	27208	35149	34889	27003	14181	44813	17784	41036
09	00005	52142	65021	64438	69610	12154	98422	65320	79996	01935
10	43674	47103	48614	70823	78252	82403	93424	05236	54588	27757
11	68597	68874	35567	98463	99671	05634	81533	47406	17228	44455
12	91874	70208	06308	40719	02772	69589	79936	07514	44950	35190
13	73854	19470	53014	29375	62256	77488	74388	53949	49607	19816
14	65926	34117	55344	68155	38099	56009	03513	05926	35584	42328
15	40005	35246	49440	40295	44390	83043	26090	80201	02934	49260
16	46686	29890	14821	69783	34733	11803	64845	32065	14527	38702
17	02717	61518	39583	72863	50707	96115	07416	05041	36756	61065
18	17048	22281	35573	28944	96889	51823	57268	03866	27658	91950
19	75304	53248	42151	93928	17343	88322	28683	11252	10355	65175
20	97844	62947	62230	30500	92816	85232	27222	91701	11057	83257
21	07611	71163	82212	20653	21499	51496	40715	78952	33029	64207
22	47744	04603	44522	62783	39347	72310	41460	31052	40814	94297
23	54293	43576	88116	67416	34908	15238	40561	73940	56850	31078
24	67556	93979	73363	00300	11217	74405	18937	79000	68834	48307
25	86581	73041	95809	73986	49408	53316	90841	73808	53421	82315
26	28020	86282	83365	76600	11261	74354	20968	60770	12141	09539
27	42578	32471	37840	30872	75074	79027	57813	62831	54715	26693
28	47290	15997	86163	10571	81911	92124	92971	80860	41012	58666
29	24856	63911	13221	77028	06573	33667	30732	47280	12926	67276
30	16352	24836	60799	76281	83402	44709	78930	82969	84468	36910
31	89060	79852	97854	28324	39638	86936	06702	74304	39873	19496
32	07637	30412	04921	26471	09605	07355	20466	49793	40539	21077
33	37711	47786	37468	31963	16908	50283	80884	08252	72655	58926
34	82994	53232	58202	73318	62471	49650	15888	73370	98748	69181
35	31722	67288	12110	04776	15168	68862	92347	90789	66961	04162
36	93819	78050	19364	38037	25706	90879	05215	00260	14426	88207
37	65557	24496	04713	23688	26623	41356	47049	60676	72236	01214
38	88001	91382	05129	36041	10257	55558	89979	58061	28957	10701
39	96648	70303	18191	62404	26558	92804	15415	02865	52449	78509
40	04118	51573	59356	02426	35010	37104	98316	44602	96478	08433
41	19317	27753	39431	26996	04465	69695	61374	06317	42225	62025
42	37182	91221	17307	68507	85725	81898	22588	22241	80337	89033
43	82990	03607	29560	60413	59743	75000	03806	13741	79671	25416
44	97294	21991	11217	98087	79124	52275	31088	32085	23089	21498
45	86771	69504	13345	42544	59616	07867	78717	82840	74669	21515
46	26046	55559	12200	95106	56496	76662	44880	89457	84209	01332
47	39689	05999	92290	79024	70271	93352	90272	94495	26842	54477
48	83265	89573	01437	43786	52986	49041	17952	35035	88985	84671
49	15128	35791	11296	45319	06330	82027	90808	54351	43091	30387

Table A.1 Ten thousand random digits (*Continued*)

	00–04	05–09	10–14	15–19	20–24	25–29	30–34	35–39	40–44	45–49
50	54441	64681	93190	00993	62130	44484	46293	60717	50239	76319
51	08573	52937	84274	95106	89117	65849	41356	65549	78787	50442
52	81067	68052	14270	19718	88499	63303	13533	91882	51136	60828
53	39737	58891	75278	98046	52284	40164	72442	77824	72900	14886
54	34958	76090	08827	61623	31114	86952	83645	91786	29633	78294
55	61417	72424	92626	71952	69709	81259	58472	43409	84454	88648
56	99187	14149	57474	32268	85424	90378	34682	47606	89295	02420
57	13130	13064	36485	48133	35319	05720	76317	70953	50823	06793
58	65563	11831	82402	46929	91446	72037	17205	89600	59084	55718
59	28737	49502	06060	52100	43704	50839	22538	56768	83467	19313
60	50353	74022	59767	49927	45882	74099	18758	57510	58560	07050
61	65208	96466	29917	22862	69972	35178	32911	08172	06277	62795
62	21323	38148	26696	81741	25131	20087	67452	19670	35898	50636
63	67875	29831	59330	46570	69768	36671	01031	95995	68417	68665
64	82631	26260	86554	31881	70512	37899	38851	40568	54284	24056
65	91989	39633	59039	12526	37730	68848	71399	28513	69018	10289
66	12950	31418	93425	69756	34036	55097	97241	92480	49745	42461
67	00328	27427	95474	97217	05034	26676	49629	13594	50525	13485
68	63986	16698	82804	04524	39919	32381	67488	05223	89537	59490
69	55775	75005	57912	20977	35722	51931	89565	77579	93085	06467
70	24761	56877	56357	78809	40748	69727	56652	12462	40528	75269
71	43820	80926	26795	57553	28319	25376	51795	26123	51102	89853
72	66669	02880	02987	33615	54206	20013	75872	88678	17726	60640
73	49944	66725	19779	50416	42800	71733	82052	28504	15593	51799
74	71003	87598	61296	95019	21568	86134	66096	65403	47166	78638
75	52715	04593	69484	93411	38046	13000	04293	60830	03914	75357
76	21998	31729	89963	11573	49442	69467	40265	56066	36024	25705
77	58970	96827	18377	31564	23555	86338	79250	43168	96929	97732
78	67592	59149	42554	42719	13553	48560	81167	10747	92552	19867
79	18298	18429	09357	96436	11237	88039	81020	00428	75731	37779
80	88420	28841	42628	84647	59024	52032	31251	72017	43875	48320
81	07627	88424	23381	29680	14027	75905	27037	22113	77873	78711
82	37917	93581	04979	21041	95252	62450	05937	81670	44894	47262
83	14783	95119	68464	08726	74818	91700	05961	23554	74649	50540
84	05378	32640	64562	15303	13168	23189	88198	63617	58566	56047
85	19640	96709	22047	07825	40583	99500	39989	96593	32254	37158
86	20514	11081	51131	56469	33947	77703	35679	45774	06776	67062
87	96763	56249	81243	62416	84451	14696	38195	70435	45948	67690
88	49439	61075	31558	59740	52759	55323	95226	01385	20158	54054
89	16294	50548	71317	32168	86071	47314	65393	56367	46910	51269
90	31381	94301	79273	32843	05862	36211	93960	00671	67631	23952
91	98032	87203	03227	66021	99666	98368	39222	36056	81992	20121
92	40700	31826	94774	11366	81391	33602	69608	84119	93204	26825
93	68692	66849	29366	77540	14978	06508	10824	65416	23629	63029
94	19047	10784	19607	20296	31804	72984	60060	50353	23260	58909
95	82867	69266	50733	62630	00956	61500	89913	30049	82321	62367
96	26528	28928	52600	72997	80943	04084	86662	90025	14360	64867
97	51166	00607	49962	30724	81707	14548	25844	47336	57492	02207
98	97245	15440	55182	15368	85136	98869	33712	95152	50973	98658
99	54998	88830	95639	45104	72676	28220	82576	57381	34438	24565

Source: Prepared by Fred Gruenberger, Numerical Analysis Laboratory, University of Wisconsin, Madison, Wisconsin, 1952.

Table A.1 Ten thousand random digits (*Continued*)

	50–54	55–59	60–64	65–69	70–74	75–79	80–84	85–89	90–94	95–99
50	58649	85086	16502	97541	76611	94229	34987	86718	87208	05426
51	97306	52449	55596	66739	36525	97563	29469	31235	79276	10831
52	09942	79344	78160	11015	55777	22047	57615	15717	86239	36578
53	83842	28631	74893	47911	92170	38181	30416	54860	44120	73031
54	73778	30395	20163	76111	13712	33449	99224	18206	51418	70006
55	88381	56550	47467	59663	61117	39716	32927	06168	06217	45477
56	31044	21404	15968	21357	30772	81482	38807	67231	84283	63552
57	00909	63837	91328	81106	11740	50193	86806	21931	18054	49601
58	69882	37028	41732	37425	80832	03320	20690	32653	90145	03029
59	26059	78324	22501	73825	16927	31545	15695	74216	98372	28547
60	38573	98078	38982	33078	93524	45606	53463	20391	81637	37269
61	70624	00063	81455	16924	12848	23801	55481	78978	26795	10553
62	49806	23976	05640	29804	38988	25024	76951	02341	63219	75864
63	05461	67523	48316	14613	08541	35231	38312	14969	67279	50502
64	76582	62153	53801	51219	30424	32599	49099	83959	68408	20147
65	16660	80470	75062	75588	24384	27874	20018	11428	32265	07692
66	60166	42424	97470	88451	81270	80070	72959	26220	59939	31127
67	28953	03272	31460	41691	57736	72052	22762	96323	27616	53123
68	47536	86439	95210	96386	38704	15484	07426	70675	06888	81203
69	73457	26657	36983	72410	30244	97711	25652	09373	66218	64077
70	11190	66193	66287	09116	48140	37669	02932	50799	17255	06181
71	57062	78964	44455	14036	36098	40773	11688	33150	07459	36127
72	99624	67254	67302	18991	97687	54099	94884	42283	63258	50651
73	97521	83669	85968	16135	30133	51312	17831	75016	80278	68953
74	40273	04838	13661	64757	17461	78085	60094	27010	80945	66439
75	57260	06176	49963	29760	69546	61336	39429	41985	18572	98128
76	03451	47098	63495	71227	79304	29753	99131	18419	71791	81515
77	62331	20492	15393	84270	24396	32962	21632	92965	38670	44923
78	32290	51079	06512	38806	93327	80086	19088	59887	98416	24918
79	28014	80428	92853	31333	32648	16734	43418	90124	15086	48444
80	18950	16091	29543	65817	07002	73115	94115	20271	50250	25061
81	17403	69503	01866	13049	07263	13039	83844	80143	39048	62654
82	27999	50489	66613	21843	71746	65868	16208	46781	93402	12323
83	87076	53174	12165	84495	47947	60706	64034	31635	65169	93070
84	89044	45974	14524	46906	26052	51851	84197	61694	57429	63395
85	98048	64400	24705	75711	36232	57624	41424	77366	52790	84705
86	09345	12956	49770	80311	32319	48238	16952	92088	51222	82865
87	07086	77628	76195	47584	62411	40397	71857	54823	26536	56792
88	93128	25657	46872	11206	06831	87944	97914	64670	45760	34353
89	85137	70964	29947	27795	25547	37682	96105	26848	09389	64326
90	32798	39024	13814	98546	46585	84108	74603	94812	73968	68766
91	62496	26371	89880	52078	47781	95260	83464	65942	91761	53727
92	62707	81825	40987	97656	89714	52177	23778	07482	91678	40128
93	05500	28982	86124	19554	80818	94935	61924	31828	79369	23507
94	79476	31445	59498	85132	24582	26024	24002	63718	79164	43556
95	10653	29954	97568	91541	33139	84525	72271	02546	64818	14381
96	30524	06495	00886	40666	68574	49574	19705	16429	90981	08103
97	69050	22019	74066	14500	14506	06423	38332	34191	82663	85323
98	27908	78802	63446	07674	98871	63831	72449	42705	26513	19883
99	64520	16618	47409	19574	78136	46047	01277	79146	95759	36781

Table A.2 Values of the ratio, range divided by the standard deviation σ, for sample sizes from 20 to 1,000

Number in sample	Range/σ	Number in sample	Range/σ
20	3.7	200	5.5
30	4.1	300	5.8
50	4.5	400	5.9
70	4.8	500	6.1
100	5.0	700	6.3
150	5.3	1,000	6.5

SOURCE: Abridged, with permission of the *Biometrika* trustees and the editors, from E. S. Pearson and H. O. Hartley, *Biometrika Tables for Statisticians*, vol. 1, Cambridge University Press, 1954. Original table by L. H. C. Tippett, "On the extreme individuals and the range of samples taken from a normal population," *Biometrika*, **17:** pp. 364–387, (1925).

Table A.3 Values of t

df	Probability of a numerically larger value of t								
	0.5	0.4	0.3	0.2	0.1	0.05	0.02	0.01	0.001
1	1.000	1.376	1.963	3.078	6.314	12.706	31.821	63.657	636.619
2	.816	1.061	1.386	1.886	2.920	4.303	6.965	9.925	31.598
3	.765	.978	1.250	1.638	2.353	3.182	4.541	5.841	12.941
4	.741	.941	1.190	1.533	2.132	2.776	3.747	4.604	8.610
5	.727	.920	1.156	1.476	2.015	2.571	3.365	4.032	6.859
6	.718	.906	1.134	1.440	1.943	2.447	3.143	3.707	5.959
7	.711	.896	1.119	1.415	1.895	2.365	2.998	3.499	5.405
8	.706	.889	1.108	1.397	1.860	2.306	2.896	3.355	5.041
9	.703	.883	1.100	1.383	1.833	2.262	2.821	3.250	4.781
10	.700	.879	1.093	1.372	1.812	2.228	2.764	3.169	4.587
11	.697	.876	1.088	1.363	1.796	2.201	2.718	3.106	4.437
12	.695	.873	1.083	1.356	1.782	2.179	2.681	3.055	4.318
13	.694	.870	1.079	1.350	1.771	2.160	2.650	3.012	4.221
14	.692	.868	1.076	1.345	1.761	2.145	2.624	2.977	4.140
15	.691	.866	1.074	1.341	1.753	2.131	2.602	2.947	4.073
16	.690	.865	1.071	1.337	1.746	2.120	2.583	2.921	4.015
17	.689	.863	1.069	1.333	1.740	2.110	2.567	2.898	3.965
18	.688	.862	1.067	1.330	1.734	2.101	2.552	2.878	3.922
19	.688	.861	1.066	1.328	1.729	2.093	2.539	2.861	3.883
20	.687	.860	1.064	1.325	1.725	2.086	2.528	2.845	3.850
21	.686	.859	1.063	1.323	1.721	2.080	2.518	2.831	3.819
22	.686	.858	1.061	1.321	1.717	2.074	2.508	2.819	3.792
23	.685	.858	1.060	1.319	1.714	2.069	2.500	2.807	3.767
24	.685	.857	1.059	1.318	1.711	2.064	2.492	2.797	3.745
25	.684	.856	1.058	1.316	1.708	2.060	2.485	2.787	3.725
26	.684	.856	1.058	1.315	1.706	2.056	2.479	2.779	3.707
27	.684	.855	1.057	1.314	1.703	2.052	2.473	2.771	3.690
28	.683	.855	1.056	1.313	1.701	2.048	2.467	2.763	3.674
29	.683	.854	1.055	1.311	1.699	2.045	2.462	2.756	3.659
30	.683	.854	1.055	1.310	1.697	2.042	2.457	2.750	3.646
40	.681	.851	1.050	1.303	1.684	2.021	2.423	2.704	3.551
60	.679	.848	1.046	1.296	1.671	2.000	2.390	2.660	3.460
120	.677	.845	1.041	1.289	1.658	1.980	2.358	2.617	3.373
∞	.674	.842	1.036	1.282	1.645	1.960	2.326	2.576	3.291
	0.25	0.2	0.15	0.1	0.05	0.025	0.01	0.005	0.0005
df	Probability of a larger positive value of t								

SOURCE: This table is abridged from Table III of Fisher and Yates, *Statistical Tables for Biological, Agricultural, and Medical Research*, published by Oliver and Boyd Ltd., Edinburgh, 1949, by permission of the authors and publishers.

Use 1- when crossing the middle

Table A.4 Probability of a random value of $Z = (Y - \mu)/\sigma$ being greater than the values tabulated in the margins

z	.00	.01	.02	.03	.04	.05	.06	.07	.08	.09
.0	.5000	.4960	.4920	.4880	.4840	.4801	.4761	.4721	.4681	.4641
.1	.4602	.4562	.4522	.4483	.4443	.4404	.4364	.4325	.4286	.4247
.2	.4207	.4168	.4129	.4090	.4052	.4013	.3974	.3936	.3897	.3859
.3	.3821	.3783	.3745	.3707	.3669	.3632	.3594	.3557	.3520	.3483
.4	.3446	.3409	.3372	.3336	.3300	.3264	.3228	.3192	.3156	.3121
.5	.3085	.3050	.3015	.2981	.2946	.2912	.2877	.2843	.2810	.2776
.6	.2743	.2709	.2676	.2643	.2611	.2578	.2546	.2514	.2483	.2451
.7	.2420	.2389	.2358	.2327	.2296	.2266	.2236	.2206	.2177	.2148
.8	.2119	.2090	.2061	.2033	.2005	.1977	.1949	.1922	.1894	.1867
.9	.1841	.1814	.1788	.1762	.1736	.1711	.1685	.1660	.1635	.1611
1.0	.1587	.1562	.1539	.1515	.1492	.1469	.1446	.1423	.1401	.1379
1.1	.1357	.1335	.1314	.1292	.1271	.1251	.1230	.1210	.1190	.1170
1.2	.1151	.1131	.1112	.1093	.1075	.1056	.1038	.1020	.1003	.0985
1.3	.0968	.0951	.0934	.0918	.0901	.0885	.0869	.0853	.0838	.0823
1.4	.0808	.0793	.0778	.0764	.0749	.0735	.0721	.0708	.0694	.0681
1.5	.0668	.0655	.0643	.0630	.0618	.0606	.0594	.0582	.0571	.0559
1.6	.0548	.0537	.0526	.0516	.0505	.0495	.0485	.0475	.0465	.0455
1.7	.0446	.0436	.0427	.0418	.0409	.0401	.0392	.0384	.0375	.0367
1.8	.0359	.0351	.0344	.0336	.0329	.0322	.0314	.0307	.0301	.0294
1.9	.0287	.0281	.0274	.0268	.0262	.0256	.0250	.0244	.0239	.0233
2.0	.0228	.0222	.0217	.0212	.0207	.0202	.0197	.0192	.0188	.0183
2.1	.0179	.0174	.0170	.0166	.0162	.0158	.0154	.0150	.0146	.0143
2.2	.0139	.0136	.0132	.0129	.0125	.0122	.0119	.0116	.0113	.0110
2.3	.0107	.0104	.0102	.0099	.0096	.0094	.0091	.0089	.0087	.0084
2.4	.0082	.0080	.0078	.0075	.0073	.0071	.0069	.0068	.0066	.0064
2.5	.0062	.0060	.0059	.0057	.0055	.0054	.0052	.0051	.0049	.0048
2.6	.0047	.0045	.0044	.0043	.0041	.0040	.0039	.0038	.0037	.0036
2.7	.0035	.0034	.0033	.0032	.0031	.0030	.0029	.0028	.0027	.0026
2.8	.0026	.0025	.0024	.0023	.0023	.0022	.0021	.0021	.0020	.0019
2.9	.0019	.0018	.0018	.0017	.0016	.0016	.0015	.0015	.0014	.0014
3.0	.0013	.0013	.0013	.0012	.0012	.0011	.0011	.0011	.0010	.0010
3.1	.0010	.0009	.0009	.0009	.0008	.0008	.0008	.0008	.0007	.0007
3.2	.0007	.0007	.0006	.0006	.0006	.0006	.0006	.0005	.0005	.0005
3.3	.0005	.0005	.0005	.0004	.0004	.0004	.0004	.0004	.0004	.0003
3.4	.0003	.0003	.0003	.0003	.0003	.0003	.0003	.0003	.0003	.0002
3.6	.0002	.0002	.0001	.0001	.0001	.0001	.0001	.0001	.0001	.0001
3.9	.0000									

Table A.5 Values of χ^2

df	Probability of a larger value of χ^2												
	.995	.990	.975	.950	.900	.750	.500	.250	.100	.050	.025	.010	.005
1	$.0^4393$	$.0^3157$	$.0^3982$	$.0^2393$	.0158	.102	.455	1.32	2.71	3.84	5.02	6.63	7.88
2	.0100	.0201	.0506	.103	.211	.575	1.39	2.77	4.61	5.99	7.38	9.21	10.6
3	.0717	.115	.216	.352	.584	1.21	2.37	4.11	6.25	7.81	9.35	11.3	12.8
4	.207	.297	.484	.711	1.06	1.92	3.36	5.39	7.78	9.49	11.1	13.3	14.9
5	.412	.554	.831	1.15	1.61	2.67	4.35	6.63	9.24	11.1	12.8	15.1	16.7
6	.676	.872	1.24	1.64	2.20	3.45	5.35	7.84	10.6	12.6	14.4	16.8	18.5
7	.989	1.24	1.69	2.17	2.83	4.25	6.35	9.04	12.0	14.1	16.0	18.5	20.3
8	1.34	1.65	2.18	2.73	3.49	5.07	7.34	10.2	13.4	15.5	17.5	20.1	22.0
9	1.73	2.09	2.70	3.33	4.17	5.90	8.34	11.4	14.7	16.9	19.0	21.7	23.6
10	2.16	2.56	3.25	3.94	4.87	6.74	9.34	12.5	16.0	18.3	20.5	23.2	25.2
11	2.60	3.05	3.82	4.57	5.58	7.58	10.3	13.7	17.3	19.7	21.9	24.7	26.8
12	3.07	3.57	4.40	5.23	6.30	8.44	11.3	14.8	18.5	21.0	23.3	26.2	28.3
13	3.57	4.11	5.01	5.89	7.04	9.30	12.3	16.0	19.8	22.4	24.7	27.7	29.8
14	4.07	4.66	5.63	6.57	7.79	10.2	13.3	17.1	21.1	23.7	26.1	29.1	31.3
15	4.60	5.23	6.26	7.26	8.55	11.0	14.3	18.2	22.3	25.0	27.5	30.6	32.8
16	5.14	5.81	6.91	7.96	9.31	11.9	15.3	19.4	23.5	26.3	28.8	32.0	34.3
17	5.70	6.41	7.56	8.67	10.1	12.8	16.3	20.5	24.8	27.6	30.2	33.4	35.7
18	6.26	7.01	8.23	9.39	10.9	13.7	17.3	21.6	26.0	28.9	31.5	34.8	37.2
19	6.84	7.63	8.91	10.1	11.7	14.6	18.3	22.7	27.2	30.1	32.9	36.2	38.6
20	7.43	8.26	9.59	10.9	12.4	15.5	19.3	23.8	28.4	31.4	34.2	37.6	40.0
21	8.03	8.90	10.3	11.6	13.2	16.3	20.3	24.9	29.6	32.7	35.5	38.9	41.4
22	8.64	9.54	11.0	12.3	14.0	17.2	21.3	26.0	30.8	33.9	36.8	40.3	42.8
23	9.26	10.2	11.7	13.1	14.8	18.1	22.3	27.1	32.0	35.2	38.1	41.6	44.2
24	9.89	10.9	12.4	13.8	15.7	19.0	23.3	28.2	33.2	36.4	39.4	43.0	45.6
25	10.5	11.5	13.1	14.6	16.5	19.9	24.3	29.3	34.4	37.7	40.6	44.3	46.9
26	11.2	12.2	13.8	15.4	17.3	20.8	25.3	30.4	35.6	38.9	41.9	45.6	48.3
27	11.8	12.9	14.6	16.2	18.1	21.7	26.3	31.5	36.7	40.1	43.2	47.0	49.6
28	12.5	13.6	15.3	16.9	18.9	22.7	27.3	32.6	37.9	41.3	44.5	48.3	51.0
29	13.1	14.3	16.0	17.7	19.8	23.6	28.3	33.7	39.1	42.6	45.7	49.6	52.3
30	13.8	15.0	16.8	18.5	20.6	24.5	29.3	34.8	40.3	43.8	47.0	50.9	53.7
40	20.7	22.2	24.4	26.5	29.1	33.7	39.3	45.6	51.8	55.8	59.3	63.7	66.8
50	28.0	29.7	32.4	34.8	37.7	42.9	49.3	56.3	63.2	67.5	71.4	76.2	79.5
60	35.5	37.5	40.5	43.2	46.5	52.3	59.3	67.0	74.4	79.1	83.3	88.4	92.0

SOURCE: This table is abridged from "Table of percentage points of the χ^2 distribution," *Biometrika*, **32:** 188–189 (1941), by Catherine M. Thompson. It is published here with kind permission of the author and the editor of *Biometrika*.

Table A.6 Values of F

Denominator df	Probability of a larger F	Numerator df								
		1	2	3	4	5	6	7	8	9
1	.100	39.86	49.50	53.59	55.83	57.24	58.20	58.91	59.44	59.86
	.050	161.4	199.5	215.7	224.6	230.2	234.0	236.8	238.9	240.5
	.025	647.8	799.5	864.2	899.6	921.8	937.1	948.2	956.7	963.3
	.010	4052	4999.5	5403	5625	5764	5859	5928	5982	6022
	.005	16211	20000	21615	22500	23056	23437	23715	23925	24091
2	.100	8.53	9.00	9.16	9.24	9.29	9.33	9.35	9.37	9.38
	.050	18.51	19.00	19.16	19.25	19.30	19.33	19.35	19.37	19.38
	.025	38.51	39.00	39.17	39.25	39.30	39.33	39.36	39.37	39.39
	.010	98.50	99.00	99.17	99.25	99.30	99.33	99.36	99.37	99.39
	.005	198.5	199.0	199.2	199.2	199.3	199.3	199.4	199.4	199.4
3	.100	5.54	5.46	5.39	5.34	5.31	5.28	5.27	5.25	5.24
	.050	10.13	9.55	9.28	9.12	9.01	8.94	8.89	8.85	8.81
	.025	17.44	16.04	15.44	15.10	14.88	14.73	14.62	14.54	14.47
	.010	34.12	30.82	29.46	28.71	28.24	27.91	27.67	27.49	27.35
	.005	55.55	49.80	47.47	46.19	45.39	44.84	44.43	44.13	43.88
4	.100	4.54	4.32	4.19	4.11	4.05	4.01	3.98	3.95	3.94
	.050	7.71	6.94	6.59	6.39	6.26	6.16	6.09	6.04	6.00
	.025	12.22	10.65	9.98	9.60	9.36	9.20	9.07	8.98	8.90
	.010	21.20	18.00	16.69	15.98	15.52	15.21	14.98	14.80	14.66
	.005	31.33	26.28	24.26	23.15	22.46	21.97	21.62	21.35	21.14
5	.100	4.06	3.78	3.62	3.52	3.45	3.40	3.37	3.34	3.32
	.050	6.61	5.79	5.41	5.19	5.05	4.95	4.88	4.82	4.77
	.025	10.01	8.43	7.76	7.39	7.15	6.98	6.85	6.76	6.68
	.010	16.26	13.27	12.06	11.39	10.97	10.67	10.46	10.29	10.16
	.005	22.78	18.31	16.53	15.56	14.94	14.51	14.20	13.96	13.77
6	.100	3.78	3.46	3.29	3.18	3.11	3.05	3.01	2.98	2.96
	.050	5.99	5.14	4.76	4.53	4.39	4.28	4.21	4.15	4.10
	.025	8.81	7.26	6.60	6.23	5.99	5.82	5.70	5.60	5.52
	.010	13.75	10.92	9.78	9.15	8.75	8.47	8.26	8.10	7.98
	.005	18.63	14.54	12.92	12.03	11.46	11.07	10.79	10.57	10.39
7	.100	3.59	3.26	3.07	2.96	2.88	2.83	2.78	2.75	2.72
	.050	5.59	4.74	4.35	4.12	3.97	3.87	3.79	3.73	3.68
	.025	8.07	6.54	5.89	5.52	5.29	5.12	4.99	4.90	4.82
	.010	12.25	9.55	8.45	7.85	7.46	7.19	6.99	6.84	6.72
	.005	16.24	12.40	10.88	10.05	9.52	9.16	8.89	8.68	8.51
8	.100	3.46	3.11	2.92	2.81	2.73	2.67	2.62	2.59	2.56
	.050	5.32	4.46	4.07	3.84	3.69	3.58	3.50	3.44	3.39
	.025	7.57	6.06	5.42	5.05	4.82	4.65	4.53	4.43	4.36
	.010	11.26	8.65	7.59	7.01	6.63	6.37	6.18	6.03	5.91
	.005	14.69	11.04	9.60	8.81	8.30	7.95	7.69	7.50	7.34
9	.100	3.36	3.01	2.81	2.69	2.61	2.55	2.51	2.47	2.44
	.050	5.12	4.26	3.86	3.63	3.48	3.37	3.29	3.23	3.18
	.025	7.21	5.71	5.08	4.72	4.48	4.32	4.20	4.10	4.03
	.010	10.56	8.02	6.99	6.42	6.06	5.80	5.61	5.47	5.35
	.005	13.61	10.11	8.72	7.96	7.47	7.13	6.88	6.69	6.54
10	.100	3.29	2.92	2.73	2.61	2.52	2.46	2.41	2.38	2.35
	.050	4.96	4.10	3.71	3.48	3.33	3.22	3.14	3.07	3.02
	.025	6.94	5.46	4.83	4.47	4.24	4.07	3.95	3.85	3.78
	.010	10.04	7.56	6.55	5.99	5.64	5.39	5.20	5.06	4.94
	.005	12.83	9.43	8.08	7.34	6.87	6.54	6.30	6.12	5.97
11	.100	3.23	2.86	2.66	2.54	2.45	2.39	2.34	2.30	2.27
	.050	4.84	3.98	3.59	3.36	3.20	3.09	3.01	2.95	2.90
	.025	6.72	5.26	4.63	4.28	4.04	3.88	3.76	3.66	3.59
	.010	9.65	7.21	6.22	5.67	5.32	5.07	4.89	4.74	4.63
	.005	12.23	8.91	7.60	6.88	6.42	6.10	5.86	5.68	5.54
12	.100	3.18	2.81	2.61	2.48	2.39	2.33	2.28	2.24	2.21
	.050	4.75	3.89	3.49	3.26	3.11	3.00	2.91	2.85	2.80
	.025	6.55	5.10	4.47	4.12	3.89	3.73	3.61	3.51	3.44
	.010	9.33	6.93	5.95	5.41	5.06	4.82	4.64	4.50	4.39
	.005	11.75	8.51	7.23	6.52	6.07	5.76	5.52	5.35	5.20
13	.100	3.14	2.76	2.56	2.43	2.35	2.28	2.23	2.20	2.16
	.050	4.67	3.81	3.41	3.18	3.03	2.92	2.83	2.77	2.71
	.025	6.41	4.97	4.35	4.00	3.77	3.60	3.48	3.39	3.31
	.010	9.07	6.70	5.74	5.21	4.86	4.62	4.44	4.30	4.19
	.005	11.37	8.19	6.93	6.23	5.79	5.48	5.25	5.08	4.94
14	.100	3.10	2.73	2.52	2.39	2.31	2.24	2.19	2.15	2.12
	.050	4.60	3.74	3.34	3.11	2.96	2.85	2.76	2.70	2.65
	.025	6.30	4.86	4.24	3.89	3.66	3.50	3.38	3.29	3.21
	.010	8.86	6.51	5.56	5.04	4.69	4.46	4.28	4.14	4.03
	.005	11.06	7.92	6.68	6.00	5.56	5.26	5.03	4.86	4.72

Table A.6 Values of F (*Continued*)

Numerator *df*											
10	12	15	20	24	30	40	60	120	∞	*P*	*df*
60.19	60.71	61.22	61.74	62.00	62.26	62.53	62.79	63.06	63.33	.100	1
241.9	243.9	245.9	248.0	249.1	250.1	251.1	252.2	253.3	254.3	.050	
968.6	976.7	984.9	993.1	997.2	1001	1006	1010	1014	1018	.025	
6056	6106	6157	6209	6235	6261	6287	6313	6339	6366	.010	
24224	24426	24630	24836	24940	25044	25148	25253	25359	25465	.005	
9.39	9.41	9.42	9.44	9.45	9.46	9.47	9.47	9.48	9.49	.100	2
19.40	19.41	19.43	19.45	19.45	19.46	19.47	19.48	19.49	19.50	.050	
39.40	39.41	39.43	39.45	39.46	39.46	39.47	39.48	39.49	39.50	.025	
99.40	99.42	99.43	99.45	99.46	99.47	99.47	99.48	99.49	99.50	.010	
199.4	199.4	199.4	199.4	199.5	199.5	199.5	199.5	199.5	199.5	.005	
5.23	5.22	5.20	5.18	5.18	5.17	5.16	5.15	5.14	5.13	.100	3
8.79	8.74	8.70	8.66	8.64	8.62	8.59	8.57	8.55	8.53	.050	
14.42	14.34	14.25	14.17	14.12	14.08	14.04	13.99	13.95	13.90	.025	
27.23	27.05	26.87	26.69	26.60	26.50	26.41	26.32	26.22	26.13	.010	
43.69	43.39	43.08	42.78	42.62	42.47	42.31	42.15	41.99	41.83	.005	
3.92	3.90	3.87	3.84	3.83	3.82	3.80	3.79	3.78	3.76	.100	4
5.96	5.91	5.86	5.80	5.77	5.75	5.72	5.69	5.66	5.63	.050	
8.84	8.75	8.66	8.56	8.51	8.46	8.41	8.36	8.31	8.26	.025	
14.55	14.37	14.20	14.02	13.93	13.84	13.75	13.65	13.56	13.46	.010	
20.97	20.70	20.44	20.17	20.03	19.89	19.75	19.61	19.47	19.32	.005	
3.30	3.27	3.24	3.21	3.19	3.17	3.16	3.14	3.12	3.10	.100	5
4.74	4.68	4.62	4.56	4.53	4.50	4.46	4.43	4.40	4.36	.050	
6.62	6.52	6.43	6.33	6.28	6.23	6.18	6.12	6.07	6.02	.025	
10.05	9.89	9.72	9.55	9.47	9.38	9.29	9.20	9.11	9.02	.010	
13.62	13.38	13.15	12.90	12.78	12.66	12.53	12.40	12.27	12.14	.005	
2.94	2.90	2.87	2.84	2.82	2.80	2.78	2.76	2.74	2.72	.100	6
4.06	4.00	3.94	3.87	3.84	3.81	3.77	3.74	3.70	3.67	.050	
5.46	5.37	5.27	5.17	5.12	5.07	5.01	4.96	4.90	4.85	.025	
7.87	7.72	7.56	7.40	7.31	7.23	7.14	7.06	6.97	6.88	.010	
10.25	10.03	9.81	9.59	9.47	9.36	9.24	9.12	9.00	8.88	.005	
2.70	2.67	2.63	2.59	2.58	2.56	2.54	2.51	2.49	2.47	.100	7
3.64	3.57	3.51	3.44	3.41	3.38	3.34	3.30	3.27	3.23	.050	
4.76	4.67	4.57	4.47	4.42	4.36	4.31	4.25	4.20	4.14	.025	
6.62	6.47	6.31	6.16	6.07	5.99	5.91	5.82	5.74	5.65	.010	
8.38	8.18	7.97	7.75	7.65	7.53	7.42	7.31	7.19	7.08	.005	
2.54	2.50	2.46	2.42	2.40	2.38	2.36	2.34	2.32	2.29	.100	8
3.35	3.28	3.22	3.15	3.12	3.08	3.04	3.01	2.97	2.93	.050	
4.30	4.20	4.10	4.00	3.95	3.89	3.84	3.78	3.73	3.67	.025	
5.81	5.67	5.52	5.36	5.28	5.20	5.12	5.03	4.95	4.86	.010	
7.21	7.01	6.81	6.61	6.50	6.40	6.29	6.18	6.06	5.95	.005	
2.42	2.38	2.34	2.30	2.28	2.25	2.23	2.21	2.18	2.16	.100	9
3.14	3.07	3.01	2.94	2.90	2.86	2.83	2.79	2.75	2.71	.050	
3.96	3.87	3.77	3.67	3.61	3.56	3.51	3.45	3.39	3.33	.025	
5.26	5.11	4.96	4.81	4.73	4.65	4.57	4.48	4.40	4.31	.010	
6.42	6.23	6.03	5.83	5.73	5.62	5.52	5.41	5.30	5.19	.005	
2.32	2.28	2.24	2.20	2.18	2.16	2.13	2.11	2.08	2.06	.100	10
2.98	2.91	2.85	2.77	2.74	2.70	2.66	2.62	2.58	2.54	.050	
3.72	3.62	3.52	3.42	3.37	3.31	3.26	3.20	3.14	3.08	.025	
4.85	4.71	4.56	4.41	4.33	4.25	4.17	4.08	4.00	3.91	.010	
5.85	5.66	5.47	5.27	5.17	5.07	4.97	4.86	4.75	4.64	.005	
2.25	2.21	2.17	2.12	2.10	2.08	2.05	2.03	2.00	1.97	.100	11
2.85	2.79	2.72	2.65	2.61	2.57	2.53	2.49	2.45	2.40	.050	
3.53	3.43	3.33	3.23	3.17	3.12	3.06	3.00	2.94	2.88	.025	
4.54	4.40	4.25	4.10	4.02	3.94	3.86	3.78	3.69	3.60	.010	
5.42	5.24	5.05	4.86	4.76	4.65	4.55	4.44	4.34	4.23	.005	
2.19	2.15	2.10	2.06	2.04	2.01	1.99	1.96	1.93	1.90	.100	12
2.75	2.69	2.62	2.54	2.51	2.47	2.43	2.38	2.34	2.30	.050	
3.37	3.28	3.18	3.07	3.02	2.96	2.91	2.85	2.79	2.72	.025	
4.30	4.16	4.01	3.86	3.78	3.70	3.62	3.54	3.45	3.36	.010	
5.09	4.91	4.72	4.53	4.43	4.33	4.23	4.12	4.01	3.90	.005	
2.14	2.10	2.05	2.01	1.98	1.96	1.93	1.90	1.88	1.85	.100	13
2.67	2.60	2.53	2.46	2.42	2.38	2.34	2.30	2.25	2.21	.050	
3.25	3.15	3.05	2.95	2.89	2.84	2.78	2.72	2.66	2.60	.025	
4.10	3.96	3.82	3.66	3.59	3.51	3.43	3.34	3.25	3.17	.010	
4.82	4.64	4.46	4.27	4.17	4.07	3.97	3.87	3.76	3.65	.005	
2.10	2.05	2.01	1.96	1.94	1.91	1.89	1.86	1.83	1.80	.100	14
2.60	2.53	2.46	2.39	2.35	2.31	2.27	2.22	2.18	2.13	.050	
3.15	3.05	2.95	2.84	2.79	2.73	2.67	2.61	2.55	2.49	.025	
3.94	3.80	3.66	3.51	3.43	3.35	3.27	3.18	3.09	3.00	.010	
4.60	4.43	4.25	4.06	3.96	3.86	3.76	3.66	3.55	3.44	.005	

Table A.6 Values of *F* (*Continued*)

Denominator *df*	Probability of a larger *F*	Numerator *df* 1	2	3	4	5	6	7	8	9
15	.100	3.07	2.70	2.49	2.36	2.27	2.21	2.16	2.12	2.09
	.050	4.54	3.68	3.29	3.06	2.90	2.79	2.71	2.64	2.59
	.025	6.20	4.77	4.15	3.80	3.58	3.41	3.29	3.20	3.12
	.010	8.68	6.36	5.42	4.89	4.56	4.32	4.14	4.00	3.89
	.005	10.80	7.70	6.48	5.80	5.37	5.07	4.85	4.67	4.54
16	.100	3.05	2.67	2.46	2.33	2.24	2.18	2.13	2.09	2.06
	.050	4.49	3.63	3.24	3.01	2.85	2.74	2.66	2.59	2.54
	.025	6.12	4.69	4.08	3.73	3.50	3.34	3.22	3.12	3.05
	.010	8.53	6.23	5.29	4.77	4.44	4.20	4.03	3.89	3.78
	.005	10.58	7.51	6.30	5.64	5.21	4.91	4.69	4.52	4.38
17	.100	3.03	2.64	2.44	2.31	2.22	2.15	2.10	2.06	2.03
	.050	4.45	3.59	3.20	2.96	2.81	2.70	2.61	2.55	2.49
	.025	6.04	4.62	4.01	3.66	3.44	3.28	3.16	3.06	2.98
	.010	8.40	6.11	5.18	4.67	4.34	4.10	3.93	3.79	3.68
	.005	10.38	7.35	6.16	5.50	5.07	4.78	4.56	4.39	4.25
18	.100	3.01	2.62	2.42	2.29	2.20	2.13	2.08	2.04	2.00
	.050	4.41	3.55	3.16	2.93	2.77	2.66	2.58	2.51	2.46
	.025	5.98	4.56	3.95	3.61	3.38	3.22	3.10	3.01	2.93
	.010	8.29	6.01	5.09	4.58	4.25	4.01	3.84	3.71	3.60
	.005	10.22	7.21	6.03	5.37	4.96	4.66	4.44	4.28	4.14
19	.100	2.99	2.61	2.40	2.27	2.18	2.11	2.06	2.02	1.98
	.050	4.38	3.52	3.13	2.90	2.74	2.63	2.54	2.48	2.42
	.025	5.92	4.51	3.90	3.56	3.33	3.17	3.05	2.96	2.88
	.010	8.18	5.93	5.01	4.50	4.17	3.94	3.77	3.63	3.52
	.005	10.07	7.09	5.92	5.27	4.85	4.56	4.34	4.18	4.04
20	.100	2.97	2.59	2.38	2.25	2.16	2.09	2.04	2.00	1.96
	.050	4.35	3.49	3.10	2.87	2.71	2.60	2.51	2.45	2.39
	.025	5.87	4.46	3.86	3.51	3.29	3.13	3.01	2.91	2.84
	.010	8.10	5.85	4.94	4.43	4.10	3.87	3.70	3.56	3.46
	.005	9.94	6.99	5.82	5.17	4.76	4.47	4.26	4.09	3.96
21	.100	2.96	2.57	2.36	2.23	2.14	2.08	2.02	1.98	1.95
	.050	4.32	3.47	3.07	2.84	2.68	2.57	2.49	2.42	2.37
	.025	5.83	4.42	3.82	3.48	3.25	3.09	2.97	2.87	2.80
	.010	8.02	5.78	4.87	4.37	4.04	3.81	3.64	3.51	3.40
	.005	9.83	6.89	5.73	5.09	4.68	4.39	4.18	4.01	3.88
22	.100	2.95	2.56	2.35	2.22	2.13	2.06	2.01	1.97	1.93
	.050	4.30	3.44	3.05	2.82	2.66	2.55	2.46	2.40	2.34
	.025	5.79	4.38	3.78	3.44	3.22	3.05	2.93	2.84	2.76
	.010	7.95	5.72	4.82	4.31	3.99	3.76	3.59	3.45	3.35
	.005	9.73	6.81	5.65	5.02	4.61	4.32	4.11	3.94	3.81
23	.100	2.94	2.55	2.34	2.21	2.11	2.05	1.99	1.95	1.92
	.050	4.28	3.42	3.03	2.80	2.64	2.53	2.44	2.37	2.32
	.025	5.75	4.35	3.75	3.41	3.18	3.02	2.90	2.81	2.73
	.010	7.88	5.66	4.76	4.26	3.94	3.71	3.54	3.41	3.30
	.005	9.63	6.73	5.58	4.95	4.54	4.26	4.05	3.88	3.75
24	.100	2.93	2.54	2.33	2.19	2.10	2.04	1.98	1.94	1.91
	.050	4.26	3.40	3.01	2.78	2.62	2.51	2.42	2.36	2.30
	.025	5.72	4.32	3.72	3.38	3.15	2.99	2.87	2.78	2.70
	.010	7.82	5.61	4.72	4.22	3.90	3.67	3.50	3.36	3.26
	.005	9.55	6.66	5.52	4.89	4.49	4.20	3.99	3.83	3.69
25	.100	2.92	2.53	2.32	2.18	2.09	2.02	1.97	1.93	1.89
	.050	4.24	3.39	2.99	2.76	2.60	2.49	2.40	2.34	2.28
	.025	5.69	4.29	3.69	3.35	3.13	2.97	2.85	2.75	2.68
	.010	7.77	5.57	4.68	4.18	3.85	3.63	3.46	3.32	3.22
	.005	9.48	6.60	5.46	4.84	4.43	4.15	3.94	3.78	3.64
26	.100	2.91	2.52	2.31	2.17	2.08	2.01	1.96	1.92	1.88
	.050	4.23	3.37	2.98	2.74	2.59	2.47	2.39	2.32	2.27
	.025	5.66	4.27	3.67	3.33	3.10	2.94	2.82	2.73	2.65
	.010	7.72	5.53	4.64	4.14	3.82	3.59	3.42	3.29	3.18
	.005	9.41	6.54	5.41	4.79	4.38	4.10	3.89	3.73	3.60
27	.100	2.90	2.51	2.30	2.17	2.07	2.00	1.95	1.91	1.87
	.050	4.21	3.35	2.96	2.73	2.57	2.46	2.37	2.31	2.25
	.025	5.63	4.24	3.65	3.31	3.08	2.92	2.80	2.71	2.63
	.010	7.68	5.49	4.60	4.11	3.78	3.56	3.39	3.26	3.15
	.005	9.34	6.49	5.36	4.74	4.34	4.06	3.85	3.69	3.56
28	.100	2.89	2.50	2.29	2.16	2.06	2.00	1.94	1.90	1.87
	.050	4.20	3.34	2.95	2.71	2.56	2.45	2.36	2.29	2.24
	.025	5.61	4.22	3.63	3.29	3.06	2.90	2.78	2.69	2.61
	.010	7.64	5.45	4.57	4.07	3.75	3.53	3.36	3.23	3.12
	.005	9.28	6.44	5.32	4.70	4.30	4.02	3.81	3.65	3.52

Table A.6 Values of F (*Continued*)

Numerator df											
10	12	15	20	24	30	40	60	120	∞	P	df
2.06	2.02	1.97	1.92	1.90	1.87	1.85	1.82	1.79	1.76	.100	15
2.54	2.48	2.40	2.33	2.29	2.25	2.20	2.16	2.11	2.07	.050	
3.06	2.96	2.86	2.76	2.70	2.64	2.59	2.52	2.46	2.40	.025	
3.80	3.67	3.52	3.37	3.29	3.21	3.13	3.05	2.96	2.87	.010	
4.42	4.25	4.07	3.88	3.79	3.69	3.58	3.48	3.37	3.26	.005	
2.03	1.99	1.94	1.89	1.87	1.84	1.81	1.78	1.75	1.72	.100	16
2.49	2.42	2.35	2.28	2.24	2.19	2.15	2.11	2.06	2.01	.050	
2.99	2.89	2.79	2.68	2.63	2.57	2.51	2.45	2.38	2.32	.025	
3.69	3.55	3.41	3.26	3.18	3.10	3.02	2.93	2.84	2.75	.010	
4.27	4.10	3.92	3.73	3.64	3.54	3.44	3.33	3.22	3.11	.005	
2.00	1.96	1.91	1.86	1.84	1.81	1.78	1.75	1.72	1.69	.100	17
2.45	2.38	2.31	2.23	2.19	2.15	2.10	2.06	2.01	1.96	.050	
2.92	2.82	2.72	2.62	2.56	2.50	2.44	2.38	2.32	2.25	.025	
3.59	3.46	3.31	3.16	3.08	3.00	2.92	2.83	2.75	2.65	.010	
4.14	3.97	3.79	3.61	3.51	3.41	3.31	3.21	3.10	2.98	.005	
1.98	1.93	1.89	1.84	1.81	1.78	1.75	1.72	1.69	1.66	.100	18
2.41	2.34	2.27	2.19	2.15	2.11	2.06	2.02	1.97	1.92	.050	
2.87	2.77	2.67	2.56	2.50	2.44	2.38	2.32	2.26	2.19	.025	
3.51	3.37	3.23	3.08	3.00	2.92	2.84	2.75	2.66	2.57	.010	
4.03	3.86	3.68	3.50	3.40	3.30	3.20	3.10	2.99	2.87	.005	
1.96	1.91	1.86	1.81	1.79	1.76	1.73	1.70	1.67	1.63	.100	19
2.38	2.31	2.23	2.16	2.11	2.07	2.03	1.98	1.93	1.88	.050	
2.82	2.72	2.62	2.51	2.45	2.39	2.33	2.27	2.20	2.13	.025	
3.43	3.30	3.15	3.00	2.92	2.84	2.76	2.67	2.58	2.49	.010	
3.93	3.76	3.59	3.40	3.31	3.21	3.11	3.00	2.89	2.78	.005	
1.94	1.89	1.84	1.79	1.77	1.74	1.71	1.68	1.64	1.61	.100	20
2.35	2.28	2.20	2.12	2.08	2.04	1.99	1.95	1.90	1.84	.050	
2.77	2.68	2.57	2.46	2.41	2.35	2.29	2.22	2.16	2.09	.025	
3.37	3.23	3.09	2.94	2.86	2.78	2.69	2.61	2.52	2.42	010	
3.85	3.68	3.50	3.32	3.22	3.12	3.02	2.92	2.81	2.69	.005	
1.92	1.87	1.83	1.78	1.75	1.72	1.69	1.66	1.62	1.59	.100	21
2.32	2.25	2.18	2.10	2.05	2.01	1.96	1.92	1.87	1.81	.050	
2.73	2.64	2.53	2.42	2.37	2.31	2.25	2.18	2.11	2.04	.025	
3.31	3.17	3.03	2.88	2.80	2.72	2.64	2.55	2.46	2.36	.010	
3.77	3.60	3.43	3.24	3.15	3.05	2.95	2.84	2.73	2.61	.005	
1.90	1.86	1.81	1.76	1.73	1.70	1.67	1.64	1.60	1.57	.100	22
2.30	2.23	2.15	2.07	2.03	1.98	1.94	1.89	1.84	1.78	.050	
2.70	2.60	2.50	2.39	2.33	2.27	2.21	2.14	2.08	2.00	.025	
3.26	3.12	2.98	2.83	2.75	2.67	2.58	2.50	2.40	2.31	.010	
3.70	3.54	3.36	3.18	3.08	2.98	2.88	2.77	2.66	2.55	.005	
1.89	1.84	1.80	1.74	1.72	1.69	1.66	1.62	1.59	1.55	.100	23
2.27	2.20	2.13	2.05	2.01	1.96	1.91	1.86	1.81	1.76	.050	
2.67	2.57	2.47	2.36	2.30	2.24	2.18	2.11	2.04	1.97	.025	
3.21	3.07	2.93	2.78	2.70	2.62	2.54	2.45	2.35	2.26	.010	
3.64	3.47	3.30	3.12	3.02	2.92	2.82	2.71	2.60	2.48	.005	
1.88	1.83	1.78	1.73	1.70	1.67	1.64	1.61	1.57	1.53	.100	24
2.25	2.18	2.11	2.03	1.98	1.94	1.89	1.84	1.79	1.73	.050	
2.64	2.54	2.44	2.33	2.27	2.21	2.15	2.08	2.01	1.94	.025	
3.17	3.03	2.89	2.74	2.66	2.58	2.49	2.40	2.31	2.21	.010	
3.59	3.42	3.25	3.06	2.97	2.87	2.77	2.66	2.55	2.43	.005	
1.87	1.82	1.77	1.72	1.69	1.66	1.63	1.59	1.56	1.52	.100	25
2.24	2.16	2.09	2.01	1.96	1.92	1.87	1.82	1.77	1.71	.050	
2.61	2.51	2.41	2.30	2.24	2.18	2.12	2.05	1.98	1.91	.025	
3.13	2.99	2.85	2.70	2.62	2.54	2.45	2.36	2.27	2.17	.010	
3.54	3.37	3.20	3.01	2.92	2.82	2.72	2.61	2.50	2.38	.005	
1.86	1.81	1.76	1.71	1.68	1.65	1.61	1.58	1.54	1.50	.100	26
2.22	2.15	2.07	1.99	1.95	1.90	1.85	1.80	1.75	1.69	.050	
2.59	2.49	2.39	2.28	2.22	2.16	2.09	2.03	1.95	1.88	.025	
3.09	2.96	2.81	2.66	2.58	2.50	2.42	2.33	2.23	2.13	.010	
3.49	3.33	3.15	2.97	2.87	2.77	2.67	2.56	2.45	2.33	.005	
1.85	1.80	1.75	1.70	1.67	1.64	1.60	1.57	1.53	1.49	.100	27
2.20	2.13	2.06	1.97	1.93	1.88	1.84	1.79	1.73	1.67	.050	
2.57	2.47	2.36	2.25	2.19	2.13	2.07	2.00	1.93	1.85	.025	
3.06	2.93	2.78	2.63	2.55	2.47	2.38	2.29	2.20	2.10	.010	
3.45	3.28	3.11	2.93	2.83	2.73	2.63	2.52	2.41	2.29	.005	
1.84	1.79	1.74	1.69	1.66	1.63	1.59	1.56	1.52	1.48	.100	28
2.19	2.12	2.04	1.96	1.91	1.87	1.82	1.77	1.71	1.65	.050	
2.55	2.45	2.34	2.23	2.17	2.11	2.05	1.98	1.91	1.83	.025	
3.03	2.90	2.75	2.60	2.52	2.44	2.35	2.26	2.17	2.06	.010	
3.41	3.25	3.07	2.89	2.79	2.69	2.59	2.48	2.37	2.25	.005	

Table A.6 Values of *F* (*Continued*)

Denominator *df*	Probability of a larger *F*	Numerator *df* 1	2	3	4	5	6	7	8	9
29	.100	2.89	2.50	2.28	2.15	2.06	1.99	1.93	1.89	1.86
	.050	4.18	3.33	2.93	2.70	2.55	2.43	2.35	2.28	2.22
	.025	5.59	4.20	3.61	3.27	3.04	2.88	2.76	2.67	2.59
	.010	7.60	5.42	4.54	4.04	3.73	3.50	3.33	3.20	3.09
	.005	9.23	6.40	5.28	4.66	4.26	3.98	3.77	3.61	3.48
30	.100	2.88	2.49	2.28	2.14	2.05	1.98	1.93	1.88	1.85
	.050	4.17	3.32	2.92	2.69	2.53	2.42	2.33	2.27	2.21
	.025	5.57	4.18	3.59	3.25	3.03	2.87	2.75	2.65	2.57
	.010	7.56	5.39	4.51	4.02	3.70	3.47	3.30	3.17	3.07
	.005	9.18	6.35	5.24	4.62	4.23	3.95	3.74	3.58	3.45
40	.100	2.84	2.44	2.23	2.09	2.00	1.93	1.87	1.83	1.79
	.050	4.08	3.23	2.84	2.61	2.45	2.34	2.25	2.18	2.12
	.025	5.42	4.05	3.46	3.13	2.90	2.74	2.62	2.53	2.45
	.010	7.31	5.18	4.31	3.83	3.51	3.29	3.12	2.99	2.89
	.005	8.83	6.07	4.98	4.37	3.99	3.71	3.51	3.35	3.22
60	.100	2.79	2.39	2.18	2.04	1.95	1.87	1.82	1.77	1.74
	.050	4.00	3.15	2.76	2.53	2.37	2.25	2.17	2.10	2.04
	.025	5.29	3.93	3.34	3.01	2.79	2.63	2.51	2.41	2.33
	.010	7.08	4.98	4.13	3.65	3.34	3.12	2.95	2.82	2.72
	.005	8.49	5.79	4.73	4.14	3.76	3.49	3.29	3.13	3.01
120	.100	2.75	2.35	2.13	1.99	1.90	1.82	1.77	1.72	1.68
	.050	3.92	3.07	2.68	2.45	2.29	2.17	2.09	2.02	1.96
	.025	5.15	3.80	3.23	2.89	2.67	2.52	2.39	2.30	2.22
	.010	6.85	4.79	3.95	3.48	3.17	2.96	2.79	2.66	2.56
	.005	8.18	5.54	4.50	3.92	3.55	3.28	3.09	2.93	2.81
∞	.100	2.71	2.30	2.08	1.94	1.85	1.77	1.72	1.67	1.63
	.050	3.84	3.00	2.60	2.37	2.21	2.10	2.01	1.94	1.88
	.025	5.02	3.69	3.12	2.79	2.57	2.41	2.29	2.19	2.11
	.010	6.63	4.61	3.78	3.32	3.02	2.80	2.64	2.51	2.41
	.005	7.88	5.30	4.28	3.72	3.35	3.09	2.90	2.74	2.62

SOURCE: A portion of "Tables of percentage points of the inverted beta (*F*) distribution," *Biometrika*, vol. 33 (1943) by M. Merrington and C. M. Thompson and from Table 18 of *Biometrika Tables for Statisticians*, vol. 1, Cambridge University Press, 1954, edited by E. S. Pearson and H. O. Hartley. Reproduced with permission of the authors, editors, and *Biometrika* trustees.

Table A.6 Values of F (*Continued*)

Numerator *df*											
10	12	15	20	24	30	40	60	120	∞	*P*	*df*
1.83	1.78	1.73	1.68	1.65	1.62	1.58	1.55	1.51	1.47	.100	29
2.18	2.10	2.03	1.94	1.90	1.85	1.81	1.75	1.70	1.64	.050	
2.53	2.43	2.32	2.21	2.15	2.09	2.03	1.96	1.89	1.81	.025	
3.00	2.87	2.73	2.57	2.49	2.41	2.33	2.23	2.14	2.03	.010	
3.38	3.21	3.04	2.86	2.76	2.66	2.56	2.45	2.33	2.21	.005	
1.82	1.77	1.72	1.67	1.64	1.61	1.57	1.54	1.50	1.46	.100	30
2.16	2.09	2.01	1.93	1.89	1.84	1.79	1.74	1.68	1.62	.050	
2.51	2.41	2.31	2.20	2.14	2.07	2.01	1.94	1.87	1.79	.025	
2.98	2.84	2.70	2.55	2.47	2.39	2.30	2.21	2.11	2.01	.010	
3.34	3.18	3.01	2.82	2.73	2.63	2.52	2.42	2.30	2.18	.005	
1.76	1.71	1.66	1.61	1.57	1.54	1.51	1.47	1.42	1.38	.100	40
2.08	2.00	1.92	1.84	1.79	1.74	1.69	1.64	1.58	1.51	.050	
2.39	2.29	2.18	2.07	2.01	1.94	1.88	1.80	1.72	1.64	.025	
2.80	2.66	2.52	2.37	2.29	2.20	2.11	2.02	1.92	1.80	.010	
3.12	2.95	2.78	2.60	2.50	2.40	2.30	2.18	2.06	1.93	.005	
1.71	1.66	1.60	1.54	1.51	1.48	1.44	1.40	1.35	1.29	.100	60
1.99	1.92	1.84	1.75	1.70	1.65	1.59	1.53	1.47	1.39	.050	
2.27	2.17	2.06	1.94	1.88	1.82	1.74	1.67	1.58	1.48	.025	
2.63	2.50	2.35	2.20	2.12	2.03	1.94	1.84	1.73	1.60	.010	
2.90	2.74	2.57	2.39	2.29	2.19	2.08	1.96	1.83	1.69	.005	
1.65	1.60	1.55	1.48	1.45	1.41	1.37	1.32	1.26	1.19	.100	120
1.91	1.83	1.75	1.66	1.61	1.55	1.50	1.43	1.35	1.25	.050	
2.16	2.05	1.94	1.82	1.76	1.69	1.61	1.53	1.43	1.31	.025	
2.47	2.34	2.19	2.03	1.95	1.86	1.76	1.66	1.53	1.38	.010	
2.71	2.54	2.37	2.19	2.09	1.98	1.87	1.75	1.61	1.43	.005	
1.60	1.55	1.49	1.42	1.38	1.34	1.30	1.24	1.17	1.00	.100	∞
1.83	1.75	1.67	1.57	1.52	1.46	1.39	1.32	1.22	1.00	.050	
2.05	1.94	1.83	1.71	1.64	1.57	1.48	1.39	1.27	1.00	.025	
2.32	2.18	2.04	1.88	1.79	1.70	1.59	1.47	1.32	1.00	.010	
2.52	2.36	2.19	2.00	1.90	1.79	1.67	1.53	1.36	1.00	.005	

Table A.7 Significant studentized ranges for 5 percent and 1 percent level new multiple-range test

Error *df*	Significance level	p = number of means for range being tested													
		2	3	4	5	6	7	8	9	10	12	14	16	18	20
1	.05	18.0	18.0	18.0	18.0	18.0	18.0	18.0	18.0	18.0	18.0	18.0	18.0	18.0	18.0
	.01	90.0	90.0	90.0	90.0	90.0	90.0	90.0	90.0	90.0	90.0	90.0	90.0	90.0	90.0
2	.05	6.09	6.09	6.09	6.09	6.09	6.09	6.09	6.09	6.09	6.09	6.09	6.09	6.09	6.09
	.01	14.0	14.0	14.0	14.0	14.0	14.0	14.0	14.0	14.0	14.0	14.0	14.0	14.0	14.0
3	.05	4.50	4.50	4.50	4.50	4.50	4.50	4.50	4.50	4.50	4.50	4.50	4.50	4.50	4.50
	.01	8.26	8.5	8.6	8.7	8.8	8.9	8.9	9.0	9.0	9.0	9.1	9.2	9.3	9.3
4	.05	3.93	4.01	4.02	4.02	4.02	4.02	4.02	4.02	4.02	4.02	4.02	4.02	4.02	4.02
	.01	6.51	6.8	6.9	7.0	7.1	7.1	7.2	7.2	7.3	7.3	7.4	7.4	7.5	7.5
5	.05	3.64	3.74	3.79	3.83	3.83	3.83	3.83	3.83	3.83	3.83	3.83	3.83	3.83	3.83
	.01	5.70	5.96	6.11	6.18	6.26	6.33	6.40	6.44	6.5	6.6	6.6	6.7	6.7	6.8
6	.05	3.46	3.58	3.64	3.68	3.68	3.68	3.68	3.68	3.68	3.68	3.68	3.68	3.68	3.68
	.01	5.24	5.51	5.65	5.73	5.81	5.88	5.95	6.00	6.0	6.1	6.2	6.2	6.3	6.3
7	.05	3.35	3.47	3.54	3.58	3.60	3.61	3.61	3.61	3.61	3.61	3.61	3.61	3.61	3.61
	.01	4.95	5.22	5.37	5.45	5.53	5.61	5.69	5.73	5.8	5.8	5.9	5.9	6.0	6.0
8	.05	3.26	3.39	3.47	3.52	3.55	3.56	3.56	3.56	3.56	3.56	3.56	3.56	3.56	3.56
	.01	4.74	5.00	5.14	5.23	5.32	5.40	5.47	5.51	5.5	5.6	5.7	5.7	5.8	5.8
9	.05	3.20	3.34	3.41	3.47	3.50	3.52	3.52	3.52	3.52	3.52	3.52	3.52	3.52	3.52
	.01	4.60	4.86	4.99	5.08	5.17	5.25	5.32	5.36	5.4	5.5	5.5	5.6	5.7	5.7
10	.05	3.15	3.30	3.37	3.43	3.46	3.47	3.47	3.47	3.47	3.47	3.47	3.47	3.47	3.48
	.01	4.48	4.73	4.88	4.96	5.06	5.13	5.20	5.24	5.28	5.36	5.42	5.48	5.54	5.55
11	.05	3.11	3.27	3.35	3.39	3.43	3.44	3.45	3.46	4.46	3.46	3.46	3.46	3.47	3.48
	.01	4.39	4.63	4.77	4.86	4.94	5.01	5.06	5.12	5.15	5.24	5.28	5.34	5.38	5.39
12	.05	3.08	3.23	3.33	3.36	3.40	3.42	3.44	3.44	3.46	3.46	3.46	3.46	3.47	3.48
	.01	4.32	4.55	4.68	4.76	4.84	4.92	4.96	5.02	5.07	5.13	5.17	5.22	5.24	5.26
13	.05	3.06	3.21	3.30	3.35	3.38	3.41	3.42	3.44	3.45	3.45	3.46	3.46	3.47	3.47
	.01	4.26	4.48	4.62	4.69	4.74	4.84	4.88	4.94	4.98	5.04	5.08	5.13	5.14	5.15
14	.05	3.03	3.18	3.27	3.33	3.37	3.39	3.41	3.42	3.44	3.45	3.46	3.46	3.47	3.47
	.01	4.21	4.42	4.55	4.63	4.70	4.78	4.83	4.87	4.91	4.96	5.00	5.04	5.06	5.07
15	.05	3.01	3.16	3.25	3.31	3.36	3.38	3.40	3.42	3.43	3.44	3.45	3.46	3.47	3.47
	.01	4.17	4.37	4.50	4.58	4.64	4.72	4.77	4.81	4.84	4.90	4.94	4.97	4.99	5.00

Table A.7 Significant studentized ranges for 5 percent and 1 percent level new multiple-range test (*Continued*)

Error *df*	Significance level	p = number of means for range being tested													
		2	3	4	5	6	7	8	9	10	12	14	16	18	20
16	.05	3.00	3.15	3.23	3.30	3.34	3.37	3.39	3.41	3.43	3.44	3.45	3.46	3.47	3.47
	.01	4.13	4.34	4.45	4.54	4.60	4.67	4.72	4.76	4.79	4.84	4.88	4.91	4.93	4.94
17	.05	2.98	3.13	3.22	3.28	3.33	3.36	3.38	3.40	3.42	3.44	3.45	3.46	3.47	3.47
	.01	4.10	4.30	4.41	4.50	4.56	4.63	4.68	4.72	4.75	4.80	4.83	4.86	4.88	4.89
18	.05	2.97	3.12	3.21	3.27	3.32	3.35	3.37	3.39	3.41	3.43	3.45	3.46	3.47	3.47
	.01	4.07	4.27	4.38	4.46	4.53	4.59	4.64	4.68	4.71	4.76	4.79	4.82	4.84	4.85
19	.05	2.96	3.11	3.19	3.26	3.31	3.35	3.37	3.39	3.41	3.43	3.44	3.46	3.47	3.47
	.01	4.05	4.24	4.35	4.43	4.50	4.56	4.61	4.64	4.67	4.72	4.76	4.79	4.81	4.82
20	.05	2.95	3.10	3.18	3.25	3.30	3.34	3.36	3.38	3.40	3.43	3.44	3.46	3.46	3.47
	.01	4.02	4.22	4.33	4.40	4.47	4.53	4.58	4.61	4.65	4.69	4.73	4.76	4.78	4.79
22	.05	2.93	3.08	3.17	3.24	3.29	3.32	3.35	3.37	3.39	3.42	3.44	3.45	3.46	3.47
	.01	3.99	4.17	4.28	4.36	4.42	4.48	4.53	4.57	4.60	4.65	4.68	4.71	4.74	4.75
24	.05	2.92	3.07	3.15	3.22	3.28	3.31	3.34	3.37	3.38	3.41	3.44	3.45	3.46	3.47
	.01	3.96	4.14	4.24	4.33	4.39	4.44	4.49	4.53	4.57	4.62	4.64	4.67	4.70	4.72
26	.05	2.91	3.06	3.14	3.21	3.27	3.30	3.34	3.36	3.38	3.41	3.43	3.45	3.46	3.47
	.01	3.93	4.11	4.21	4.30	4.36	4.41	4.46	4.50	4.53	4.58	4.62	4.65	4.67	4.69
28	.05	2.90	3.04	3.13	3.20	3.26	3.30	3.33	3.35	3.37	3.40	3.43	3.45	3.46	3.47
	.01	3.91	4.08	4.18	4.28	4.34	4.39	4.43	4.47	4.51	4.56	4.60	4.62	4.65	4.67
30	.05	2.89	3.04	3.12	3.20	3.25	3.29	3.32	3.35	3.37	3.40	3.43	3.44	3.46	3.47
	.01	3.89	4.06	4.16	4.22	4.32	4.36	4.41	4.45	4.48	4.54	4.58	4.61	4.63	4.65
40	.05	2.86	3.01	3.10	3.17	3.22	3.27	3.30	3.33	3.35	3.39	3.42	3.44	3.46	3.47
	.01	3.82	3.99	4.10	4.17	4.24	4.30	4.34	4.37	4.41	4.46	4.51	4.54	4.57	4.59
60	.05	2.83	2.98	3.08	3.14	3.20	3.24	3.28	3.31	3.33	3.37	3.40	3.43	3.45	3.47
	.01	3.76	3.92	4.03	4.12	4.17	4.23	4.27	4.31	4.34	4.39	4.44	4.47	4.50	4.53
100	.05	2.80	2.95	3.05	3.12	3.18	3.22	3.26	3.29	3.32	3.36	3.40	3.42	3.45	3.47
	.01	3.71	3.86	3.98	4.06	4.11	4.17	4.21	4.25	4.29	4.35	4.38	4.42	4.45	4.48
∞	.05	2.77	2.92	3.02	3.09	3.15	3.19	3.23	3.26	3.29	3.34	3.38	3.41	3.44	3.47
	.01	3.64	3.80	3.90	3.98	4.04	4.09	4.14	4.17	4.20	4.26	4.31	4.34	4.38	4.41

SOURCE: Abridged from D. B. Duncan, "Multiple range and multiple F tests," *Biometrics*, **11:** 1–42 (1955), with the permission of the editor and the author.

Table A.8 Upper percentage points of the studentized range, $q_\alpha = (\bar{Y}_{max} - \bar{Y}_{min})/s_{\bar{Y}}$

Error df	α	p = number of									
		2	3	4	5	6	7	8	9	10	11
5	.05	3.64	4.60	5.22	5.67	6.03	6.33	6.58	6.80	6.99	7.17
	.01	5.70	6.97	7.80	8.42	8.91	9.32	9.67	9.97	10.24	10.48
6	.05	3.46	4.34	4.90	5.31	5.63	5.89	6.12	6.32	6.49	6.65
	.01	5.24	6.33	7.03	7.56	7.97	8.32	8.61	8.87	9.10	9.30
7	.05	3.34	4.16	4.68	5.06	5.36	5.61	5.82	6.00	6.16	6.30
	.01	4.95	5.92	6.54	7.01	7.37	7.68	7.94	8.17	8.37	8.55
8	.05	3.26	4.04	4.53	4.89	5.17	5.40	5.60	5.77	5.92	6.05
	.01	4.74	5.63	6.20	6.63	6.96	7.24	7.47	7.68	7.87	8.03
9	.05	3.20	3.95	4.42	4.76	5.02	5.24	5.43	5.60	5.74	5.87
	.01	4.60	5.43	5.96	6.35	6.66	6.91	7.13	7.32	7.49	7.65
10	.05	3.15	3.88	4.33	4.65	4.91	5.12	5.30	5.46	5.60	5.72
	.01	4.48	5.27	5.77	6.14	6.43	6.67	6.87	7.05	7.21	7.36
11	.05	3.11	3.82	4.26	4.57	4.82	5.03	5.20	5.35	5.49	5.61
	.01	4.39	5.14	5.62	5.97	6.25	6.48	6.67	6.84	6.99	7.13
12	.05	3.08	3.77	4.20	4.51	4.75	4.95	5.12	5.27	5.40	5.51
	.01	4.32	5.04	5.50	5.84	6.10	6.32	6.51	6.67	6.81	6.94
13	.05	3.06	3.73	4.15	4.45	4.69	4.88	5.05	5.19	5.32	5.43
	.01	4.26	4.96	5.40	5.73	5.98	6.19	6.37	6.53	6.67	6.79
14	.05	3.03	3.70	4.11	4.41	4.64	4.83	4.99	5.13	5.25	5.36
	.01	4.21	4.89	5.32	5.63	5.88	6.08	6.26	6.41	6.54	6.66
15	.05	3.01	3.67	4.08	4.37	4.60	4.78	4.94	5.08	5.20	5.31
	.01	4.17	4.83	5.25	5.56	5.80	5.99	6.16	6.31	6.44	6.55
16	.05	3.00	3.65	4.05	4.33	4.56	4.74	4.90	5.03	5.15	5.26
	.01	4.13	4.78	5.19	5.49	5.72	5.92	6.08	6.22	6.35	6.46
17	.05	2.98	3.63	4.02	4.30	4.52	4.71	4.86	4.99	5.11	5.21
	.01	4.10	4.74	5.14	5.43	5.66	5.85	6.01	6.15	6.27	6.38
18	.05	2.97	3.61	4.00	4.28	4.49	4.67	4.82	4.96	5.07	5.17
	.01	4.07	4.70	5.09	5.38	5.60	5.79	5.94	6.08	6.20	6.31
19	.05	2.96	3.59	3.98	4.25	4.47	4.65	4.79	4.92	5.04	5.14
	.01	4.05	4.67	5.05	5.33	5.55	5.73	5.89	6.02	6.14	6.25
20	.05	2.95	3.58	3.96	4.23	4.45	4.62	4.77	4.90	5.01	5.11
	.01	4.02	4.64	5.02	5.29	5.51	5.69	5.84	5.97	6.09	6.19
24	.05	2.92	3.53	3.90	4.17	4.37	4.54	4.68	4.81	4.92	5.01
	.01	3.96	4.54	4.91	5.17	5.37	5.54	5.69	5.81	5.92	6.02
30	.05	2.89	3.49	3.84	4.10	4.30	4.46	4.60	4.72	4.83	4.92
	.01	3.89	4.45	4.80	5.05	5.24	5.40	5.54	5.65	5.76	5.85
40	.05	2.86	3.44	3.79	4.04	4.23	4.39	4.52	4.63	4.74	4.82
	.01	3.82	4.37	4.70	4.93	5.11	5.27	5.39	5.50	5.60	5.69
60	.05	2.83	3.40	3.74	3.98	4.16	4.31	4.44	4.55	4.65	4.73
	.01	3.76	4.28	4.60	4.82	4.99	5.13	5.25	5.36	5.45	5.53
120	.05	2.80	3.36	3.69	3.92	4.10	4.24	4.36	4.48	4.56	4.64
	.01	3.70	4.20	4.50	4.71	4.87	5.01	5.12	5.21	5.30	5.38
∞	.05	2.77	3.31	3.63	3.86	4.03	4.17	4.29	4.39	4.47	4.55
	.01	3.64	4.12	4.40	4.60	4.76	4.88	4.99	5.08	5.16	5.23

SOURCE: This table is abridged from Table 29, *Biometrika Tables for Statisticians*, vol. 1, Cambridge University Press, 1954. It is reproduced with permission of the *Biometrika* trustees and the editors, E. S. Pearson and H. O. Hartley. The original work appeared in a paper by J. M. May, "Extended and corrected tables of the upper percentage points of the 'Studentized' range," *Biometrika*, **39**: 192–193 (1952).

Table A.8 Upper percentage points of the studentized range, $q_\alpha = (\bar{Y}_{max} - \bar{Y}_{min})/s_{\bar{Y}}$ (*Continued*)

treatment means									α	Error *df*
12	13	14	15	16	17	18	19	20		
7.32	7.47	7.60	7.72	7.83	7.93	8.03	8.12	8.21	.05	5
10.70	10.89	11.08	11.24	11.40	11.55	11.68	11.81	11.93	.01	
6.79	6.92	7.03	7.14	7.24	7.34	7.43	7.51	7.59	.05	6
9.49	9.65	9.81	9.95	10.08	10.21	10.32	10.43	10.54	.01	
6.43	6.55	6.66	6.76	6.85	6.94	7.02	7.09	7.17	.05	7
8.71	8.86	9.00	9.12	9.24	9.35	9.46	9.55	9.65	.01	
6.18	6.29	6.39	6.48	6.57	6.65	6.73	6.80	6.87	.05	8
8.18	8.31	8.44	8.55	8.66	8.76	8.85	8.94	9.03	.01	
5.98	6.09	6.19	6.28	6.36	6.44	6.51	6.58	6.64	.05	9
7.78	7.91	8.03	8.13	8.23	8.32	8.41	8.49	8.57	.01	
5.83	5.93	6.03	6.11	6.20	6.27	6.34	6.40	6.47	.05	10
7.48	7.60	7.71	7.81	7.91	7.99	8.07	8.15	8.22	.01	
5.71	5.81	5.90	5.99	6.06	6.14	6.20	6.26	6.33	.05	11
7.25	7.36	7.46	7.56	7.65	7.73	7.81	7.88	7.95	.01	
5.62	5.71	5.80	5.88	5.95	6.03	6.09	6.15	6.21	.05	12
7.06	7.17	7.26	7.36	7.44	7.52	7.59	7.66	7.73	.01	
5.53	5.63	5.71	5.79	5.86	5.93	6.00	6.05	6.11	.05	13
6.90	7.01	7.10	7.19	7.27	7.34	7.42	7.48	7.55	.01	
5.46	5.55	5.64	5.72	5.79	5.85	5.92	5.97	6.03	.05	14
6.77	6.87	6.96	7.05	7.12	7.20	7.27	7.33	7.39	.01	
5.40	5.49	5.58	5.65	5.72	5.79	5.85	5.90	5.96	.05	15
6.66	6.76	6.84	6.93	7.00	7.07	7.14	7.20	7.26	.01	
5.35	5.44	5.52	5.59	5.66	5.72	5.79	5.84	5.90	05	16
6.56	6.66	6.74	6.82	6.90	6.97	7.03	7.09	7.15	.01	
5.31	5.39	5.47	5.55	5.61	5.68	5.74	5.79	5.84	.05	17
6.48	6.57	6.66	6.73	6.80	6.87	6.94	7.00	7.05	.01	
5.27	5.35	5.43	5.50	5.57	5.63	5.69	5.74	5.79	.05	18
6.41	6.50	6.58	6.65	6.72	6.79	6.85	6.91	6.96	.01	
5.23	5.32	5.39	5.46	5.53	5.59	5.65	5.70	5.75	.05	19
6.34	6.43	6.51	6.58	6.65	6.72	6.78	6.84	6.89	.01	
5.20	5.28	5.36	5.43	5.49	5.55	5.61	5.66	5.71	.05	20
6.29	6.37	6.45	6.52	6.59	6.65	6.71	6.76	6.82	.01	
5.10	5.18	5.25	5.32	5.38	5.44	5.50	5.54	5.59	.05	24
6.11	6.19	6.26	6.33	6.39	6.45	6.51	6.56	6.61	.01	
5.00	5.08	5.15	5.21	5.27	5.33	5.38	5.43	5.48	.05	30
5.93	6.01	6.08	6.14	6.20	6.26	6.31	6.36	6.41	.01	
4.91	4.98	5.05	5.11	5.16	5.22	5.27	5.31	5.36	.05	40
5.77	5.84	5.90	5.96	6.02	6.07	6.12	6.17	6.21	.01	
4.81	4.88	4.94	5.00	5.06	5.11	5.16	5.20	5.24	.05	60
5.60	5.67	5.73	5.79	5.84	5.89	5.93	5.98	6.02	.01	
4.72	4.78	4.84	4.90	4.95	5.00	5.05	5.09	5.13	.05	120
5.44	5.51	5.56	5.61	5.66	5.71	5.75	5.79	5.83	.01	
4.62	4.68	4.74	4.80	4.85	4.89	4.93	4.97	5.01	.05	∞
5.29	5.35	5.40	5.45	5.49	5.54	5.57	5.61	5.65	.01	

Table A.9*A* Table of t for one-sided comparisons between p treatment means and a control for a joint confidence coefficient of $P = .95$ and $P = .99$

Error *df*	P	p = number of treatment means, excluding control								
		1	2	3	4	5	6	7	8	9
5	.95	2.02	2.44	2.68	2.85	2.98	3.08	3.16	3.24	3.30
	.99	3.37	3.90	4.21	4.43	4.60	4.73	4.85	4.94	5.03
6	.95	1.94	2.34	2.56	2.71	2.83	2.92	3.00	3.07	3.12
	.99	3.14	3.61	3.88	4.07	4.21	4.33	4.43	4.51	4.59
7	.95	1.89	2.27	2.48	2.62	2.73	2.82	2.89	2.95	3.01
	.99	3.00	3.42	3.66	3.83	3.96	4.07	4.15	4.23	4.30
8	.95	1.86	2.22	2.42	2.55	2.66	2.74	2.81	2.87	2.92
	.99	2.90	3.29	3.51	3.67	3.79	3.88	3.96	4.03	4.09
9	.95	1.83	2.18	2.37	2.50	2.60	2.68	2.75	2.81	2.86
	.99	2.82	3.19	3.40	3.55	3.66	3.75	3.82	3.89	3.94
10	.95	1.81	2.15	2.34	2.47	2.56	2.64	2.70	2.76	2.81
	.99	2.76	3.11	3.31	3.45	3.56	3.64	3.71	3.78	3.83
11	.95	1.80	2.13	2.31	2.44	2.53	2.60	2.67	2.72	2.77
	.99	2.72	3.06	3.25	3.38	3.48	3.56	3.63	3.69	3.74
12	.95	1.78	2.11	2.29	2.41	2.50	2.58	2.64	2.69	2.74
	.99	2.68	3.01	3.19	3.32	3.42	3.50	3.56	3.62	3.67
13	.95	1.77	2.09	2.27	2.39	2.48	2.55	2.61	2.66	2.71
	.99	2.65	2.97	3.15	3.27	3.37	3.44	3.51	3.56	3.61
14	.95	1.76	2.08	2.25	2.37	2.46	2.53	2.59	2.64	2.69
	.99	2.62	2.94	3.11	3.23	3.32	3.40	3.46	3.51	3.56
15	.95	1.75	2.07	2.24	2.36	2.44	2.51	2.57	2.62	2.67
	.99	2.60	2.91	3.08	3.20	3.29	3.36	3.42	3.47	3.52
16	.95	1.75	2.06	2.23	2.34	2.43	2.50	2.56	2.61	2.65
	.99	2.58	2.88	3.05	3.17	3.26	3.33	3.39	3.44	3.48
17	.95	1.74	2.05	2.22	2.33	2.42	2.49	2.54	2.59	2.64
	.99	2.57	2.86	3.03	3.14	3.23	3.30	3.36	3.41	3.45
18	.95	1.73	2.04	2.21	2.32	2.41	2.48	2.53	2.58	2.62
	.99	2.55	2.84	3.01	3.12	3.21	3.27	3.33	3.38	3.42
19	.95	1.73	2.03	2.20	2.31	2.40	2.47	2.52	2.57	2.61
	.99	2.54	2.83	2.99	3.10	3.18	3.25	3.31	3.36	3.40
20	.95	1.72	2.03	2.19	2.30	2.39	2.46	2.51	2.56	2.60
	.99	2.53	2.81	2.97	3.08	3.17	3.23	3.29	3.34	3.38
24	.95	1.71	2.01	2.17	2.28	2.36	2.43	2.48	2.53	2.57
	.99	2.49	2.77	2.92	3.03	3.11	3.17	3.22	3.27	3.31
30	.95	1.70	1.99	2.15	2.25	2.33	2.40	2.45	2.50	2.54
	.99	2.46	2.72	2.87	2.97	3.05	3.11	3.16	3.21	3.24
40	.95	1.68	1.97	2.13	2.23	2.31	2.37	2.42	2.47	2.51
	.99	2.42	2.68	2.82	2.92	2.99	3.05	3.10	3.14	3.18
60	.95	1.67	1.95	2.10	2.21	2.28	2.35	2.39	2.44	2.48
	.99	2.39	2.64	2.78	2.87	2.94	3.00	3.04	3.08	3.12
120	.95	1.66	1.93	2.08	2.18	2.26	2.32	2.37	2.41	2.45
	.99	2.36	2.60	2.73	2.82	2.89	2.94	2.99	3.03	3.06
∞	.95	1.64	1.92	2.06	2.16	2.23	2.29	2.34	2.38	2.42
	.99	2.33	2.56	2.68	2.77	2.84	2.89	2.93	2.97	3.00

SOURCE: This table is reproduced from "A multiple comparison procedure for comparing several treatments with a control," *J. Am. Stat. Assn.*, **50:** 1096–1121 (1955), with permission of the author, C. W. Dunnett, and the editor.

Table A.9*B* Table of t for two-sided comparisons between p treatment means and a control for a joint confidence coefficient of $P = .95$ and $P = .99$

Error *df*	*P*	p = number of treatment means, excluding control								
		1	2	3	4	5	6	7	8	9
5	.95	2.57	3.03	3.39	3.66	3.88	4.06	4.22	4.36	4.49
	.99	4.03	4.63	5.09	5.44	5.73	5.97	6.18	6.36	6.53
6	.95	2.45	2.86	3.18	3.41	3.60	3.75	3.88	4.00	4.11
	.99	3.71	4.22	4.60	4.88	5.11	5.30	5.47	5.61	5.74
7	.95	2.36	2.75	3.04	3.24	3.41	3.54	3.66	3.76	3.86
	.99	3.50	3.95	4.28	4.52	4.71	4.87	5.01	5.13	5.24
8	.95	2.31	2.67	2.94	3.13	3.28	3.40	3.51	3.60	3.68
	.99	3.36	3.77	4.06	4.27	4.44	4.58	4.70	4.81	4.90
9	.95	2.26	2.61	2.86	3.04	3.18	3.29	3.39	3.48	3.55
	.99	3.25	3.63	3.90	4.09	4.24	4.37	4.48	4.57	4.65
10	.95	2.23	2.57	2.81	2.97	3.11	3.21	3.31	3.39	3.46
	.99	3.17	3.53	3.78	3.95	4.10	4.21	4.31	4.40	4.47
11	.95	2.20	2.53	2.76	2.92	3.05	3.15	3.24	3.31	3.38
	.99	3.11	3.45	3.68	3.85	3.98	4.09	4.18	4.26	4.33
12	.95	2.18	2.50	2.72	2.88	3.00	3.10	3.18	3.25	3.32
	.99	3.05	3.39	3.61	3.76	3.89	3.99	4.08	4.15	4.22
13	.95	2.16	2.48	2.69	2.84	2.96	3.06	3.14	3.21	3.27
	.99	3.01	3.33	3.54	3.69	3.81	3.91	3.99	4.06	4.13
14	.95	2.14	2.46	2.67	2.81	2.93	3.02	3.10	3.17	3.23
	.99	2.98	3.29	3.49	3.64	3.75	3.84	3.92	3.99	4.05
15	.95	2.13	2.44	2.64	2.79	2.90	2.99	3.07	3.13	3.19
	.99	2.95	3.25	3.45	3.59	3.70	3.79	3.86	3.93	3.99
16	.95	2.12	2.42	2.63	2.77	2.88	2.96	3.04	3.10	3.16
	.99	2.92	3.22	3.41	3.55	3.65	3.74	3.82	3.88	3.93
17	.95	2.11	2.41	2.61	2.75	2.85	2.94	3.01	3.08	3.13
	.99	2.90	3.19	3.38	3.51	3.62	3.70	3.77	3.83	3.89
18	.95	2.10	2.40	2.59	2.73	2.84	2.92	2.99	3.05	3.11
	.99	2.88	3.17	3.35	3.48	3.58	3.67	3.74	3.80	3.85
19	.95	2.09	2.39	2.58	2.72	2.82	2.90	2.97	3.04	3.09
	.99	2.86	3.15	3.33	3.46	3.55	3.64	3.70	3.76	3.81
20	.95	2.09	2.38	2.57	2.70	2.81	2.89	2.96	3.02	3.07
	.99	2.85	3.13	3.31	3.43	3.53	3.61	3.67	3.73	3.78
24	.95	2.06	2.35	2.53	2.66	2.76	2.84	2.91	2.96	3.01
	.99	2.80	3.07	3.24	3.36	3.45	3.52	3.58	3.64	3.69
30	.95	2.04	2.32	2.50	2.62	2.72	2.79	2.86	2.91	2.96
	.99	2.75	3.01	3.17	3.28	3.37	3.44	3.50	3.55	3.59
40	.95	2.02	2.29	2.47	2.58	2.67	2.75	2.81	2.86	2.90
	.99	2.70	2.95	3.10	3.21	3.29	3.36	3.41	3.46	3.50
60	.95	2.00	2.27	2.43	2.55	2.63	2.70	2.76	2.81	2.85
	.99	2.66	2.90	3.04	3.14	3.22	3.28	3.33	3.38	3.42
120	.95	1.98	2.24	2.40	2.51	2.59	2.66	2.71	2.76	2.80
	.99	2.62	2.84	2.98	3.08	3.15	3.21	3.25	3.30	3.33
∞	.95	1.96	2.21	2.37	2.47	2.55	2.62	2.67	2.71	2.75
	.99	2.58	2.79	2.92	3.01	3.08	3.14	3.18	3.22	3.25

SOURCE: This table is reproduced from "A multiple comparison procedure for comparing several treatments with a control," *J. Am. Stat. Assn.*, **50:** 1096–1121 (1955), with permission of the author, C. W. Dunnett, and the editor.

Table A.10 The arcsin $\sqrt{\text{percentage}}$ transformation

Transformation of binomial percentages, in the margins, to angles of equal information in degrees. The + or − signs following angles ending in 5 are for guidance in rounding to one decimal.

%	0	1	2	3	4	5	6	7	8	9
0.0	0	0.57	0.81	0.99	1.15−	1.28	1.40	1.52	1.62	1.72
0.1	1.81	1.90	1.99	2.07	2.14	2.22	2.29	2.36	2.43	2.50
0.2	2.56	2.63	2.69	2.75−	2.81	2.87	2.92	2.98	3.03	3.09
0.3	3.14	3.19	3.24	3.29	3.34	3.39	3.44	3.49	3.53	3.58
0.4	3.63	3.67	3.72	3.76	3.80	3.85−	3.89	3.93	3.97	4.01
0.5	4.05+	4.09	4.13	4.17	4.21	4.25+	4.29	4.33	4.37	4.40
0.6	4.44	4.48	4.52	4.55+	4.59	4.62	4.66	4.69	4.73	4.76
0.7	4.80	4.83	4.87	4.90	4.93	4.97	5.00	5.03	5.07	5.10
0.8	5.13	5.16	5.20	5.23	5.26	5.29	5.32	5.35+	5.38	5.41
0.9	5.44	5.47	5.50	5.53	5.56	5.59	5.62	5.65+	5.68	5.71
1	5.74	6.02	6.29	6.55−	6.80	7.04	7.27	7.49	7.71	7.92
2	8.13	8.33	8.53	8.72	8.91	9.10	9.28	9.46	9.63	9.81
3	9.98	10.14	10.31	10.47	10.63	10.78	10.94	11.09	11.24	11.39
4	11.54	11.68	11.83	11.97	12.11	12.25−	12.39	12.52	12.66	12.79
5	12.92	13.05+	13.18	13.31	13.44	13.56	13.69	13.81	13.94	14.06
6	14.18	14.30	14.42	14.54	14.65+	14.77	14.89	15.00	15.12	15.23
7	15.34	15.45+	15.56	15.68	15.79	15.89	16.00	16.11	16.22	16.32
8	16.43	16.54	16.64	16.74	16.85−	16.95+	17.05+	17.16	17.26	17.36
9	17.46	17.56	17.66	17.76	17.85+	17.95+	18.05−	18.15−	18.24	18.34
10	18.44	18.53	18.63	18.72	18.81	18.91	19.00	19.09	19.19	19.28
11	19.37	19.46	19.55+	19.64	19.73	19.82	19.91	20.00	20.09	20.18
12	20.27	20.36	20.44	20 53	20.62	20.70	20.79	20.88	20.96	21.05−
13	21.13	21.22	21.30	21.39	21.47	21.56	21.64	21.72	21.81	21.89
14	21.97	22.06	22.14	22.22	22.30	22.38	22.46	22.55−	22.63	22.71
15	22.79	22.87	22.95−	23.03	23.11	23.19	23.26	23.34	23.42	23.50
16	23.58	23.66	23.73	23.81	23.89	23.97	24.04	24.12	24.20	24.27
17	24.35+	24.43	24.50	24.58	24.65+	24.73	24.80	24.88	24.95+	25.03
18	25.10	25.18	25.25+	25.33	25.40	25.48	25.55−	25.62	25.70	25.77
19	25.84	25.92	25.99	26.06	26.13	26.21	26.28	26.35−	26.42	26.49
20	26.56	26.64	26.71	26.78	26.85+	26.92	26.99	27.06	27.13	27.20
21	27.28	27.35−	27.42	27.49	27.56	27.63	27.69	27.76	27.83	27.90
22	27.97	28.04	28.11	28.18	28.25−	28.32	28.38	28.45+	28.52	28.59
23	28.66	28.73	28.79	28.86	28.93	29.00	29.06	29.13	29.20	29.27
24	29.33	29.40	29.47	29.53	29.60	29.67	29.73	29.80	29.87	29.93
25	30.00	30.07	30.13	30.20	30.26	30.33	30.40	30.46	30.53	30.59
26	30.66	30.72	30.79	30.85+	30.92	30.98	31.05−	31.11	31.18	31.24
27	31.31	31.37	31.44	31.50	31.56	31.63	31.69	31.76	31.82	31.88
28	31.95−	32.01	32.08	32.14	32.20	32.27	32.33	32.39	32.46	32.52
29	32.58	32.65−	32.71	32.77	32.83	32.90	32.96	33.02	33.09	33.15−
30	33.21	33.27	33.34	33.40	33.46	33.52	33.58	33.65−	33.71	33.77
31	33.83	33.89	33.96	34.02	34.08	34.14	34.20	34.27	34.33	34.39
32	34.45−	34.51	34.57	34.63	34.70	34.76	34.82	34.88	34.94	35.00
33	35.06	35.12	35.18	35.24	35.30	35.37	35.43	35.49	35.55−	35.61
34	35.67	35.73	35.79	35.85−	35.91	35.97	36.03	36.09	36.15+	36.21
35	36.27	36.33	36.39	36.45+	36.51	36.57	36.63	36.69	36.75+	36.81
36	36.87	36.93	36.99	37.05−	37.11	37.17	37.23	37.29	37.35−	37.41
37	37.47	37.52	37.58	37.64	37.70	37.76	37.82	37.88	37.94	38.00
38	38.06	38.12	38.17	38.23	38.29	38.35+	38.41	38.47	38.53	38.59
39	38.65−	38.70	38.76	38.82	38.88	38.94	39.00	39.06	39.11	39.17
40	39.23	39.29	39.35−	39.41	39.47	39.52	39.58	39.64	39.70	39.76
41	39.82	39.87	39.93	39.99	40.05−	40.11	40.16	40.22	40.28	40.34
42	40.40	40.46	40.51	40.57	40.63	40.69	40.74	40.80	40.86	40.92
43	40.98	41.03	41.09	41.15−	41.21	41.27	41.32	41.38	41.44	41.50
44	41.55+	41.61	41.67	41.73	41.78	41.84	41.90	41.96	42.02	42.07
45	42.13	42.19	42.25−	42.30	42.36	42.42	42.48	42.53	42.59	42.65−
46	42.71	42.76	42.82	42.88	42.94	42.99	43.05−	43.11	43.17	43.22
47	43.28	43.34	43.39	43.45+	43.51	43.57	43.62	43.68	43.74	43.80
48	43.85+	43.91	43.97	44.03	44.08	44.14	44.20	44.25+	44.31	44.37
49	44.43	44.48	44.54	44.60	44.66	44.71	44.77	44.83	44.89	44.94

SOURCE: This table appeared in *Plant Protection* (Leningrad), **12:** 67 (1937), and is reproduced with permission of the author, C. I. Bliss.

Table A.10 The arcsin $\sqrt{\text{percentage}}$ transformation (*Continued*)

%	0	1	2	3	4	5	6	7	8	9
50	45.00	45.06	45.11	45.17	45.23	45.29	45.34	45.40	45.46	45.52
51	45.57	45.63	45.69	45.75 −	45.80	45.86	45.92	45.97	46.03	46.09
52	46.15 −	46.20	46.26	46.32	46.38	46.43	46.49	46.55 −	46.61	46.66
53	46.72	46.78	46.83	46.89	46.95 +	47.01	47.06	47.12	47.18	47.24
54	47.29	47.35 +	47.41	47.47	47.52	47.58	47.64	47.70	47.75 +	47.81
55	47.87	47.93	47.98	48.04	48.10	48.16	48.22	48.27	48.33	48.39
56	48.45 −	48.50	48.56	48.62	48.68	48.73	48.79	48.85 +	48.91	48.97
57	49.02	49.08	49.14	49.20	49.26	49.31	49.37	49.43	49.49	49.54
58	49.60	49.66	49.72	49.78	49.84	49.89	49.95 +	50.01	50.07	50.13
59	50.18	50.24	50.30	50.36	50.42	50.48	50.53	50.59	50.65 +	50.71
60	50.77	50.83	50.89	50.94	51.00	51.06	51.12	51.18	51.24	51.30
61	51.35 +	51.41	51.47	51.53	51.59	51.65 −	51.71	51.77	51.83	51.88
62	51.94	52.00	52.06	52.12	52.18	52.24	52.30	52.36	52.42	52.48
63	52.53	52.59	52.65 +	52.71	52.77	52.83	52.89	52.95 +	53.01	53.07
64	53.13	53.19	53.25 −	53.31	53.37	53.43	53.49	53.55 −	53.61	53.67
65	53.73	53.79	53.85 −	53.91	53.97	54.03	54.09	54.15 +	54.21	54.27
66	54.33	54.39	54.45 +	54.51	54.57	54.63	54.70	54.76	54.82	54.88
67	54.94	55.00	55.06	55.12	55.18	55.24	55.30	55.37	55.43	55.49
68	55.55 +	55.61	55.67	55.73	55.80	55.86	55.92	55.98	56.04	56.11
69	56.17	56.23	56.29	56.35 +	56.42	56.48	56.54	56.60	56.66	56.73
70	56.79	56.85 +	56.91	56.98	57.04	57.10	57.17	57.23	57.29	57.35 +
71	57.42	57.48	57.54	57.61	57.67	57.73	57.80	57.86	57.92	57.99
72	58.05 +	58.12	58.18	58.24	58.31	58.37	58.44	58.50	58.56	58.63
73	58.69	58.76	58.82	58.89	58.95 +	59.02	59.08	59.15 −	59.21	59.28
74	59.34	59.41	59.47	59.54	59.60	59.67	59.74	59.80	59.87	59.93
75	60.00	60.07	60.13	60.20	60.27	60.33	60.40	60.47	60.53	60.60
76	60.67	60.73	60.80	60.87	60.94	61.00	61.07	61.14	61.21	61.27
77	61.34	61.41	61.48	61.55 −	61.62	61.68	61.75 +	61.82	61.89	61.96
78	62.03	62.10	62.17	62.24	62.31	62.37	62.44	62.51	62.58	62.65 +
79	62.72	62.80	62.87	62.94	63.01	63.08	63.15 −	63.22	63.29	63.36
80	63.44	63.51	63.58	63.65 +	63.72	63.79	63.87	63.94	64.01	64.08
81	64.16	64.23	64.30	64.38	64.45 +	64.52	64.60	64.67	64.75 −	64.82
82	64.90	64.97	65.05 −	65.12	65.20	65.27	65.35 −	65.42	65.50	65.57
83	65.65 −	65.73	65.80	65.88	65.96	66.03	66.11	66.19	66.27	66.34
84	66.42	66.50	66.58	66.66	66.74	66.81	66.89	66.97	67.05 +	67.13
85	67.21	67.29	67.37	67.45 +	67.54	67.62	67.70	67.78	67.86	67.94
86	68.03	68.11	68.19	68.28	68.36	68.44	68.53	68.61	68.70	68.78
87	68.87	68.95 +	69.04	69.12	69.21	69.30	69.38	69.47	69.56	69.64
88	69.73	69.82	69.91	70.00	70.09	70.18	70.27	70.36	70.45 −	70.54
89	70.63	70.72	70.81	70.91	71.00	71.09	71.19	71.28	71.37	71.47
90	71.56	71.66	71.76	71.85 +	71.95 +	72.05 −	72.15 −	72.24	72.34	72.44
91	72.54	72.64	72.74	72.84	72.95 −	73.05 −	73.15 +	73.26	73.36	73.46
92	73.57	73.68	73.78	73.89	74.00	74.11	74.21	74.32	74.44	74.55 −
93	74.66	74.77	74.88	75.00	75.11	75.23	75.35 −	75.46	75.58	75.70
94	75.82	75.94	76.06	76.19	76.31	76.44	76.56	76.69	76.82	76.95 −
95	77.08	77.21	77.34	77.48	77.61	77.75 +	77.89	78.03	78.17	78.32
96	78.46	78.61	78.76	78.91	79.06	79.22	79.37	79.53	79.69	79.86
97	80.02	80.19	80.37	80.54	80.72	80.90	81.09	81.28	81.47	81.67
98	81.87	82.08	82.29	82.51	82.73	82.96	83.20	83.45 +	83.71	83.98
99.0	84.26	84.29	84.32	84.35 −	84.38	84.41	84.44	84.47	84.50	84.53
99.1	84.56	84.59	84.62	84.65 −	74.68	84.71	84.74	84.77	84.80	84.84
99.2	84.87	84.90	84.93	84.97	85.00	85.03	85.07	85.10	85.13	85.17
99.3	85.20	85.24	85.27	85.31	85.34	85.38	85.41	85.45 −	85.48	85.52
99.4	85.56	85.60	85.63	85.67	85.71	85.75 −	85.79	85.83	85.87	85.91
99.5	85.95 −	85.99	86.03	86.07	86.11	86.15 −	86.20	86.24	86.28	86.33
99.6	86.37	86.42	86.47	86.51	86.56	86.61	86.66	86.71	86.76	86.81
99.7	86.86	86.91	86.97	87.02	87.08	87.13	87.19	87.25 +	87.31	87.37
99.8	87.44	87.50	87.57	87.64	87.71	87.78	87.86	87.93	88.01	88.10
99.9	88.19	88.28	88.38	88.48	88.60	88.72	88.85 +	89.01	89.19	89.43
100.0	90.00									

Table A.11A Confidence belts for the correlation coefficient ρ: $P = .95$

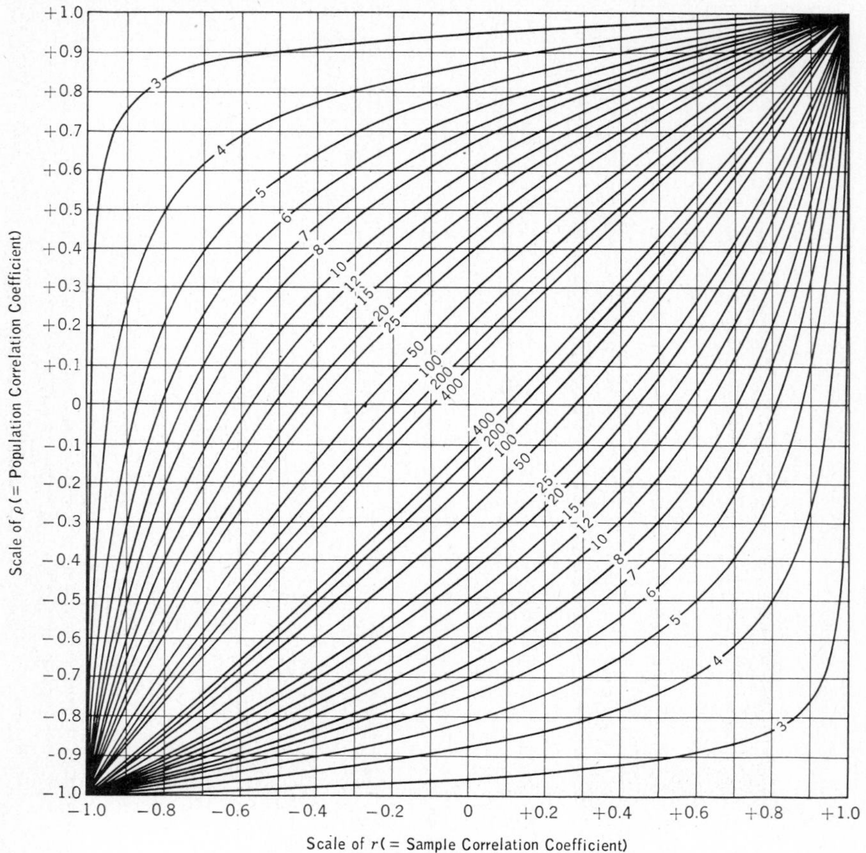

The numbers on the curves indicate sample size

SOURCE: This table is reproduced with the permission of E. S. Pearson, from F. N. David, *Tables of the Ordinates and Probability Integral of the Distribution of the Correlation Coefficient in Small Samples*, Cambridge University Press for the *Biometrika* trustees, 1938.

Table A.11*B* Confidence belts for the correlation coefficient ρ: $P = .99$

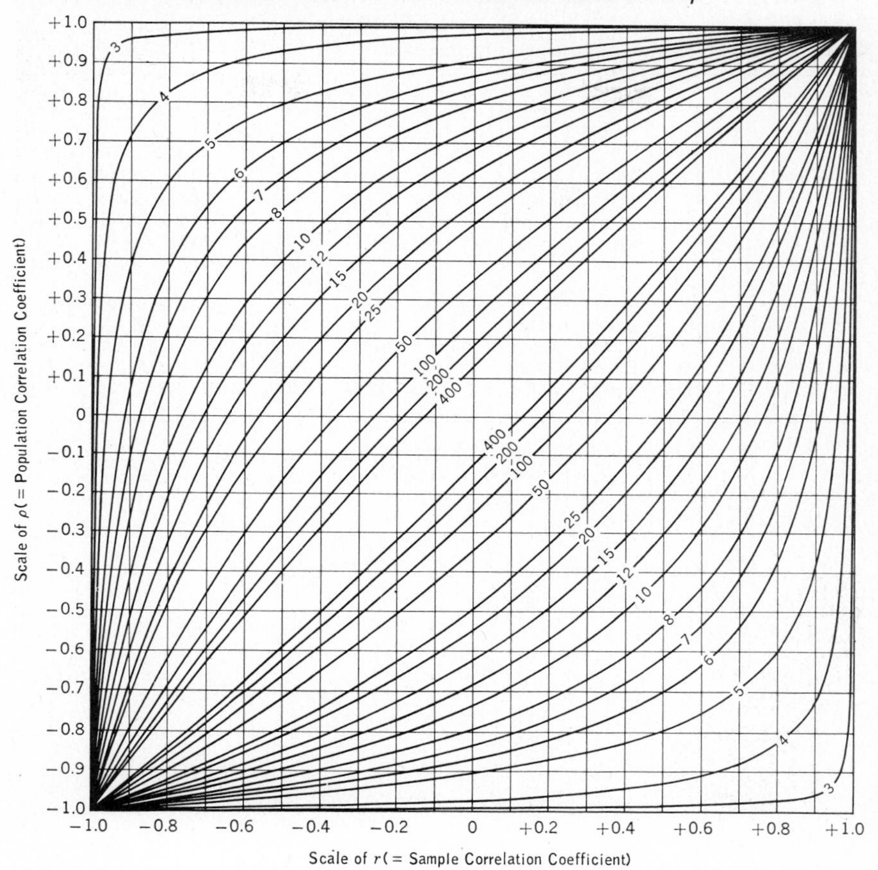

The numbers on the curves indicate sample size

SOURCE: This table is reproduced with the permission of E. S. Pearson, from F. N. David, *Tables of the Ordinates and Probability Integral of the Distribution of the Correlation Coefficient in Small Samples*, Cambridge University Press for the *Biometrika* trustees, 1938.

Table A.12 Transformation of r to Z

Values of $Z = .5 \ln (1 + r)/(1 - r) = \tanh^{-1} r$ appear in the body of the table for corresponding values of r, the correlation coefficient, in the margins.

r	.00	.01	.02	.03	.04	.05	.06	.07	.08	.09
.0	.00000	.01000	.02000	.03001	.04002	.05004	.06007	.07012	.08017	.09024
.1	.10034	.11045	.12058	.13074	.14093	.15114	.16139	.17167	.18198	.19234
.2	.20273	.21317	.22366	.23419	.24477	.25541	.26611	.27686	.28768	.29857
.3	.30952	.32055	.33165	.34283	.35409	.36544	.37689	.38842	.40006	.41180
.4	.42365	.43561	.44769	.45990	.47223	.48470	.49731	.51007	.52298	.53606
.5	.54931	.56273	.57634	.59014	.60415	.61838	.63283	.64752	.66246	.67767
.6	.69315	.70892	.72500	.74142	.75817	.77530	.79281	.81074	.82911	.84795
.7	.86730	.88718	.90764	.92873	.95048	.97295	.99621	1.02033	1.04537	1.07143
.8	1.09861	1.12703	1.15682	1.18813	1.22117	1.25615	1.29334	1.33308	1.37577	1.42192
.9	1.47222	1.52752	1.58902	1.65839	1.73805	1.83178	1.94591	2.09229	2.29756	2.64665

SOURCE: This table is abridged from Table XII of *Standard Four-figure Mathematical Tables*, 1931, by L. M. Milne-Thomson and L. J. Comrie, with permission of the authors and the publishers, Macmillan and Company, London.

Table A.13 Significant values of r and R

Error *df*	*P*	Independent variables				Error *df*	*P*	Independent variables			
		1	2	3	4			1	2	3	4
1	.05	.997	.999	.999	.999	24	.05	.388	.470	.523	.562
	.01	1.000	1.000	1.000	1.000		.01	.496	.565	.609	.642
2	.05	.950	.975	.983	.987	25	.05	.381	.462	.514	.553
	.01	.990	.995	.997	.998		.01	.487	.555	.600	.633
3	.05	.878	.930	.950	.961	26	.05	.374	.454	.506	.545
	.01	.959	.976	.983	.987		.01	.478	.546	.590	.624
4	.05	.811	.881	.912	.930	27	.05	.367	.446	.498	.536
	.01	.917	.949	.962	.970		.01	.470	.538	.582	.615
5	.05	.754	.836	.874	.898	28	.05	.361	.439	.490	.529
	.01	.874	.917	.937	.949		.01	.463	.530	.573	.606
6	.05	.707	.795	.839	.867	29	.05	.355	.432	.482	.521
	.01	.834	.886	.911	.927		.01	.456	.522	.565	.598
7	.05	.666	.758	.807	.838	30	.05	.349	.426	.476	.514
	.01	.798	.855	.885	.904		.01	.449	.514	.558	.591
8	.05	.632	.726	.777	.811	35	.05	.325	.397	.445	.482
	.01	.765	.827	.860	.882		.01	.418	.481	.523	.556
9	.05	.602	.697	.750	.786	40	.05	.304	.373	.419	.455
	.01	.735	800	.836	.861		.01	.393	.454	.494	.526
10	.05	.576	.671	.726	.763	45	.05	.288	.353	.397	.432
	.01	.708	.776	.814	.840		.01	.372	.430	.470	.501
11	.05	.553	.648	.703	.741	50	.05	.273	.336	.379	.412
	.01	.684	.753	.793	.821		.01	.354	.410	.449	.479
12	.05	.532	.627	.683	.722	60	.05	.250	.308	.348	.380
	.01	.661	.732	.773	.802		.01	.325	.377	.414	.442
13	.05	.514	.608	.664	.703	70	.05	.232	.286	.324	.354
	.01	.641	.712	.755	.785		.01	.302	.351	.386	.413
14	.05	.497	.590	.646	.686	80	.05	.217	.269	.304	.332
	.01	.623	.694	.737	.768		.01	.283	.330	.362	.389
15	.05	.482	.574	.630	.670	90	.05	.205	.254	.288	.315
	.01	.606	.677	.721	.752		.01	.267	.312	.343	.368
16	.05	.468	.559	.615	.655	100	.05	.195	.241	.274	.300
	.01	.590	.662	.706	.738		.01	.254	.297	.327	.351
17	.05	.456	.545	.601	.641	125	.05	.174	.216	.246	.269
	.01	.575	.647	.691	.724		.01	.228	.266	.294	.316
18	.05	.444	.532	.587	.628	150	.05	.159	.198	.225	.247
	.01	.561	.633	.678	.710		.01	.208	.244	.270	.290
19	.05	.433	.520	.575	.615	200	.05	.138	.172	.196	.215
	.01	.549	.620	.665	.698		.01	.181	.212	.234	.253
20	.05	.423	.509	.563	.604	300	.05	.113	.141	.160	.176
	.01	.537	.608	.652	.685		.01	.148	.174	.192	.208
21	.05	.413	.498	.522	.592	400	.05	.098	.122	.139	.153
	.01	.526	.596	.641	.674		.01	.128	.151	.167	.180
22	.05	.404	.488	.542	.582	500	.05	.088	.109	.124	.137
	.01	.515	.585	.630	.663		.01	.115	.135	.150	.162
23	.05	.396	.479	.532	.572	1,000	.05	.062	.077	.088	.097
	.01	.505	.574	.619	.652		.01	.081	.096	.106	.115

SOURCE: Reproduced from G. W. Snedecor, *Statistical Methods*, 4th ed, The Iowa State College Press, Ames, Iowa, 1946, with permission of the author and publisher.

Table A.14*A* Binomial confidence limits†

Number with characteristic	*P*	Sample size			
		10	15	20	25
0	.95	.0000–.3085	.0000–.2180	.0000–.1685	.0000–.1372
	.99	.0000–.4113	.0000–.2976	.0000–.2327	.0000–.1910
1	.95	.0025–.4450	.0017–.3200	.0013–.2485	.0010–.2036
	.99	.0005–.5440	.0003–.4027	.0002–.3170	.0002–.2624
2	.95	.0252–.5560	.0166–.4049	.0124–.3170	.0098–.2605
	.99	.0108–.6480	.0071–.4871	.0053–.3870	.0042–.3208
3	.95	.0667–.6520	.0433–.4807	.0321–.3793	.0255–.3124
	.99	.0370–.7350	.0239–.5607	.0177–.4505	.0140–.3748
4	.95	.1220–.7380	.0780–.5514	.0575–.4365	.0455–.3610
	.99	.0768–.8091	.0488–.6278	.0358–.5065	.0283–.4241
5	.95	.1870–.8130	.1185–.6162	.0868–.4913	.0684–.4072
	.99	.1280–.8720	.0803–.6889	.0585–.5605	.0460–.4700
6	.95		.1633–.6774	.1190–.5430	.0935–.4514
	.99		.1167–.7440	.0845–.6095	.0662–.5138
7	.95		.2129–.7338	.1538–.5920	.1206–.4938
	.99		.1587–.7954	.1140–.6570	.0890–.5556
8	.95			.1910–.6395	.1496–.5350
	.99			.1460–.7010	.1136–.5954
9	.95			.2305–.6848	.1797–.5748
	.99			.1808–.7430	.1401–.6336
10	.95			.2720–.7280	.2112–.6132
	.99			.2175–.7825	.1680–.6704
11	.95				.2441–.6506
	.99				.1975–.7055
12	.95				.2781–.6869
	.99				.2284–.7393
13	.95				
	.99				
14	.95				
	.99				

† Confidence intervals found from these tables are such that probabilities of approximately .025 and .005 are associated with unusual events at each extreme. Hence, the confidence probabilities are at least .95 and .99 and are .975 and .995 when the number possessing the characteristic is zero.

To interpolate in this table, use the formula $CI(T)n(T)/n$, where $CI(T)$ and $n(T)$ are the

Table A.14A Binomial confidence limits (*Continued*)

Sample size					P	Number with characteristic
30	50	100	500	1,000		
.0000–.1157	.0000–.0711	.0000–.0362	.0000–.0074	.0000–.0037	.95	0
.0000–.1619	.0000–.1005	.0000–.0516	.0000–.0105	.0000–.0053	.99	
.0009–.1779	.0005–.1066	.0002–.0545	.0001–.0111	.0000–.0056	.95	1
.0002–.2233	.0001–.1398	.0000–.0721	.0000–.0148	.0000–.0074	.99	
.0082–.2209	.0049–.1372	.0024–.0704	.0005–.0144	.0002–.0072	.95	2
.0035–.2735	.0021–.1721	.0010–.0894	.0002–.0184	.0001–.0092	.99	
.0211–.2653	.0126–.1657	.0062–.0853	.0012–.0174	.0006–.0087	.95	3
.0116–.3203	.0069–.2032	.0034–.1057	.0007–.0218	.0003–.0109	.99	
.0377–.3074	.0223–.1925	.0110–.0993	.0022–.0204	.0011–.0102	.95	4
.0234–.3639	.0138–.2313	.0068–.1208	.0013–.0250	.0007–.0125	.99	
.0564–.3474	.0332–.2182	.0164–.1129	.0032–.0232	.0016–.0116	.95	5
.0379–.4044	.0222–.2580	.0110–.1353	.0022–.0281	.0011–.0141	.99	
.0770–.3856	.0454–.2431	.0224–.1260	.0044–.0259	.0022–.0130	.95	6
.0543–.4426	.0318–.2842	.0156–.1493	.0031–.0310	.0015–.0156	.99	
.0992–.4229	.0582–.2675	.0286–.1390	.0056–.0286	.0028–.0144	.95	7
.0729–.4801	.0425–.3092	.0208–.1628	.0041–.0339	.0020–.0170	.99	
.1229–.4589	.0717–.2912	.0351–.1516	.0069–.0313	.0035–.0157	.95	8
.0930–.5158	.0540–.3336	.0263–.1761	.0052–.0368	.0026–.0185	.99	
.1473–.4940	.0858–.3144	.0420–.1640	.0083–.0339	.0041–.0170	.95	9
.1143–.5500	.0660–.3573	.0321–.1892	.0063–.0396	.0031–.0199	.99	
.1729–.5280	.1004–.3372	.0490–.1762	.0096–.0365	.0048–.0183	.95	10
.1369–.5835	.0786–.3804	.0382–.2020	.0075–.0423	.0037–.0213	.99	
.1993–.5613	.1154–.3595	.0562–.1883	.0110–.0390	.0050–.0196	.95	11
.1606–.6157	.0920–.4032	.0445–.2145	.0087–.0450	.0043–.0226	.99	
.2266–.5939	.1307–.3817	.0636–.2002	.0125–.0416	.0062–.0209	.95	12
.1850–.6469	.1056–.4256	.0510–.2269	.0099–.0477	.0050–.0240	.99	
.2546–.6256	.1463–.4034	.0711–.2120	.0139–.0441	.0069–.0221	.95	13
.2107–.6772	.1198–.4473	.0577–.2392	.0112–.0504	.0056–.0253	.99	
.2835–.6566	.1623–.4248	.0787–.2237	.0154–.0465	.0077–.0234	.95	14
.2373–.7066	.1342–.4688	.0646–.2513	.0126–.0530	.0063–.0267	.99	

tabled confidence interval and sample size next below that for the observed sample size n. For example, if three individuals out of 40 possess the characteristic, then the lower value of the 99% confidence interval is calculated as $.0116(30)/40 = .0087$.

SOURCE: Abridged from *Statistical Tables for Use with Binomial Samples,* published bv D. Mainland, L. Herrera, and M. I. Sutcliffe, New York, 1956, with permission of the authors.

Table A.14B Binomial confidence limits

Observed fraction	P	Sample size 50	75	150	300	500	1,000
.01	.95				.0021–.0289	.0032–.0232	.0048–.0183
	.99				.0011–.0361	.0022–.0280	.0037–.0213
.02	.95				.0086–.0420	.0106–.0356	.0129–.0301
	.99				.0067–.0500	.0087–.0412	.0113–.0336
.03	.95				.0152–.0550	.0179–.0481	.0211–.0419
	.99				.0122–.0640	.0152–.0544	.0188–.0459
.04	.95				.0217–.0681	.0253–.0605	.0292–.0536
	.99				.0177–.0779	.0217–.0675	.0264–.0582
.05	.95			.0211–.0981	.0283–.0811	.0326–.0729	.0373–.0654
	.99			.0156–.1150	.0232–.0918	.0283–.0807	.0339–.0705
.06	.95			.0283–.1104	.0363–.0928	.0411–.0843	.0463–.0764
	.99			.0219–.1279	.0307–.1040	.0363–.0924	.0425–.0818
.07	.95			.0355–.1227	.0444–.1045	.0496–.0956	.0552–.0873
	.99			.0282–.1408	.0381–.1162	.0443–.1042	.0512–.0931
.08	.95			.0427–.1350	.0524–.1162	.0581–.1070	.0642–.0983
	.99			.0345–.1537	.0455–.1284	.0523–.1160	.0598–.1043
.09	.95			.0499–.1473	.0605–.1280	.0666–.1183	.0732–.1093
	.99			.0408–.1666	.0529–.1406	.0604–.1277	.0684–.1156
.10	.95			.0571–.1595	.0685–.1397	.0751–.1297	.0821–.1203
	.99			.0471–.1796	.0604–.1528	.0684–.1395	.0770–.1269
.11	.95			.0651–.1711	.0771–.1508	.0841–.1406	.0914–.1310
	.99			.0544–.1915	.0685–.1643	.0770–.1507	.0860–.1378
.12	.95			.0730–.1827	.0857–.1620	.0930–.1516	.1006–.1416
	.99			.0617–.2035	.0767–.1758	.0856–.1619	.0951–.1486
.13	.95			.0810–.1942	.0943–.1732	.1020–.1625	.1099–.1523
	.99			.0690–.2155	.0848–.1873	.0942–.1731	.1041–.1595
.14	.95			.0890–.2058	.1030–.1843	.1109–.1734	.1192–.1630
	.99			.0764–.2274	.0930–.1988	.1028–.1843	.1131–.1704
.15	.95		.0780–.2512	.0970–.2174	.1116–.1955	.1198–.1844	.1284–.1737
	.99		.0628–.2844	.0837–.2394	.1012–.2103	.1114–.1955	.1221–.1813
.16	.95		.0857–.2626	.1054–.2285	.1205–.2064	.1290–.1950	.1379–.1842
	.99		.0690–.2961	.0916–.2508	.1097–.2214	.1203–.2063	.1314–.1919
.17	.95		.0934–.2741	.1139–.2396	.1294–.2172	.1382–.2057	.1473–.1947
	.99		.0759–.3078	.0995–.2622	.1183–.2325	.1292–.2172	.1407–.2025
.18	.95		.1011–.2855	.1223–.2508	.1384–.2281	.1474–.2164	.1567–.2052
	.99		.0829–.3195	.1074–.2736	.1269–.2436	.1381–.2281	.1499–.2132
.19	.95		.1088–.2969	.1307–.2619	.1473–.2390	.1566–.2271	.1662–.2157
	.99		.0898–.3312	.1153–.2850	.1355–.2547	.1471–.2390	.1592–.2238
.20	.95		.1165–.3084	.1392–.2731	.1562–.2498	.1658–.2378	.1756–.2262
	.99		.0967–.3429	.1232–.2964	.1440–.2657	.1560–.2499	.1684–.2345
.21	.95		.1246–.3194	.1479–.2839	.1654–.2604	.1752–.2483	.1852–.2365
	.99		.1042–.3541	.1316–.3075	.1529–.2765	.1651–.2605	.1778–.2450
.22	.95		.1327–.3304	.1567–.2947	.1745–.2711	.1845–.2588	.1947–.2469
	.99		.1116–.3652	.1399–.3185	.1618–.2874	.1743–.2712	.1872–.2555
.23	.95		.1409–.3414	.1654–.3055	.1837–.2817	.1939–.2693	.2043–.2573
	.99		.1191–.3764	.1482–.3295	.1706–.2982	.1834–.2818	.1967–.2659
.24	.95		.1490–.3524	.1742–.3164	.1929–.2924	.2033–.2799	.2139–.2677
	.99		.1265–.3876	.1565–.3405	.1795–.3090	.1926–.2925	.2061–.2764
.25	.95	.1384–.3927	.1572–.3634	.1830–.3272	.2020–.3030	.2126–.2904	.2234–.2781
	.99	.1125–.4365	.1340–.3988	.1648–.3516	.1884–.3198	.2017–.3031	.2155–.2869

Table A.14*B* Binomial confidence limits (*Continued*)

Observed fraction	*P*	Sample size 50	75	150	300	500	1,000
.26	.95	.1465–.4034	.1656–.3741	.1920–.3378	.2113–.3135	.2221–.3008	.2331–.2883
	.99	.1198–.4472	.1419–.4095	.1734–.3623	.1975–.3303	.2110–.3136	.2250–.2973
.27	.95	.1545–.4140	.1741–.3848	.2010–.3484	.2207–.3239	.2316–.3111	.2427–.2986
	.99	.1271–.4579	.1498–.4203	.1821–.3729	.2066–.3409	.2204–.3241	.2346–.3076
.28	.95	.1626–.4247	.1826–.3955	.2100–.3590	.2300–.3344	.2411–.3215	.2524–.3089
	.99	.1344–.4686	.1577–.4310	.1907–.3836	.2157–.3515	.2297–.3346	.2441–.3180
.29	.95	.1706–.4354	.1911–.4061	.2190–.3695	.2393–.3449	.2506–.3319	.2621–.3192
	.99	.1408–.4792	.1656–.4418	.1994–.3943	.2247–.3621	.2390–.3451	.2537–.3284
.30	.95	.1787–.4461	.1996–.4168	.2280–.3801	.2487–.3553	.2601–.3423	.2717–.3295
	.99	.1491–.4899	.1735–.4525	.2080–.4050	.2338–.3726	.2483–.3555	.2632–.3387
.31	.95	.1871–.4565	.2083–.4272	.2372–.3905	.2582–.3656	.2697–.3525	.2815–.3397
	.99	.1568–.5002	.1818–.4629	.2169–.4155	.2431–.3830	.2578–.3659	.2729–.3490
.32	.95	.1955–.4668	.2171–.4376	.2464–.4009	.2676–.3760	.2793–.3628	.2912–.3499
	.99	.1646–.5105	.1901–.4733	.2258–.4259	.2524–.3934	.2673–.3762	.2825–.3592
.33	.95	.2038–.4772	.2259–.4481	.2556–.4113	.2771–.3863	.2890–.3731	.3009–.3601
	.99	.1723–.5208	.1984–.4838	.2347–.4364	.2617–.4038	.2768–.3865	.2922–.3695
.34	.95	.2122–.4876	.2346–.4585	.2648–.4217	.2866–.3966	.2986–.3833	.3107–.3703
	.99	.1801–.5311	.2067–.4942	.2436–.4468	.2710–.4142	.2862–.3969	.3018–.3797
.35	.95	.2206–.4980	.2434–.4689	.2740–.4320	.2961–.4069	.3082–.3936	.3204–.3805
	.99	.1878–.5414	.2150–.5046	.2525–.4572	.2803–.4246	.2957–.4072	.3114–.3900
.36	.95	.2293–.5080	.2524–.4790	.2834–.4422	.3057–.4171	.3179–.4038	.3302–.3906
	.99	.1960–.5513	.2236–.5147	.2617–.4674	.2897–.4348	.3053–.4174	.3212–.4002
.37	.95	.2380–.5181	.2615–.4892	.2928–.4524	.3153–.4273	.3276–.4139	.3400–.4007
	.99	.2042–.5612	.2322–.5247	.2708–.4776	.2992–.4450	.3149–.4276	.3309–.4103
.38	.95	.2467–.5281	.2705–.4993	.3022–.4626	.3249–.4375	.3373–.4241	.3498–.4109
	.99	.2123–.5710	.2409–.5348	.2800–.4879	.3087–.4552	.3245–.4378	.3407–.4205
.39	.95	.2554–.5382	.2795–.5095	.3116–.4728	.3345–.4477	.3470–.4343	.3597–.4210
	.99	.2205–.5809	.2495–.5449	.2891–.4981	.3181–.4655	.3342–.4480	.3504–.4306
.40	.95	.2641–.5482	.2885–.5196	.3210–.4830	.3441–.4579	.3568–.4444	.3695–.4311
	.99	.2287–.5908	.2581–.5549	.2983–.5083	.3276–.4757	.3438–.4582	.3602–.4408
.41	.95	.2731–.5580	.2978–.5296	.3305–.4931	.3539–.4679	.3666–.4545	.3793–.4412
	.99	.2372–.6004	.2670–.5647	.3076–.5182	.3372–.4857	.3535–.4683	.3700–.4509
.42	.95	.2821–.5678	.3070–.5395	.3401–.5031	.3636–.4780	.3764–.4646	.3892–.4512
	.99	.2457–.6099	.2759–.5745	.3170–.5282	.3468–.4958	.3632–.4783	.3798–.4610
.43	.95	.2910–.5776	.3163–.5494	.3496–.5132	.3733–.4881	.3862–.4746	.3991–.4613
	.99	.2542–.6195	.2849–.5843	.3264–.5382	.3564–.5059	.3729–.4884	.3896–.4710
.44	.95	.3000–.5874	.3256–.5593	.3592–.5232	.3830–.4981	.3960–.4847	.4090–.4714
	.99	.2627–.6290	.2938–.5941	.3357–.5482	.3660–.5159	.3827–.4985	.3995–.4811
.45	.95	.3090–.5971	.3348–.5693	.3687–.5333	.3928–.5082	.4058–.4948	.4189–.4814
	.99	.2712–.6386	.3027–.6038	.3451–.5582	.3756–.5260	.3924–.5086	.4093–.4912
.46	.95	.3183–.6067	.3443–.5790	.3785–.5431	.4026–.5182	.4157–.5048	.4288–.4914
	.99	.2800–.6478	.3119–.6133	.3547–.5680	.3854–.5359	.4022–.5185	.4192–.5012
.47	.95	.3275–.6162	.3538–.5886	.3882–.5530	.4125–.5281	.4256–.5148	.4387–.5014
	.99	.2889–.6569	.3211–.6228	.3642–.5777	.3952–.5458	.4121–.5285	.4291–.5112
.48	.95	.3368–.6257	.3633–.5983	.3979–.5625	.4223–.5381	.4355–.5247	.4487–.5114
	.99	.2978–.6661	.3304–.6323	.3738–.5875	.4049–.5557	.4219–.5385	.4390–.5212
.49	.95	.3461–.6352	.3728–.6080	.4076–.5728	.4321–.5481	.4454–.5347	.4586–.5214
	.99	.3067–.6753	.3396–.6417	.3834–.5973	.4147–.5656	.4318–.5484	.4489–.5312
.50	.95	.3553–.6447	.3823–.6177	.4173–.5827	.4420–.5580	.4553–.5447	.4685–.5315
	.99	.3155–.6845	.3488–.6512	.3929–.6071	.4245–.5755	.4416–.5584	.4589–.5411

SOURCE: Abridged from *Statistical Tables for Use with Binomial Samples*, published by D. Mainland, L. Herrera, and M. I. Sutcliffe, New York, 1956, with permission of the authors.

Table A.15*A* Confidence belts for proportions: confidence coefficient of .95

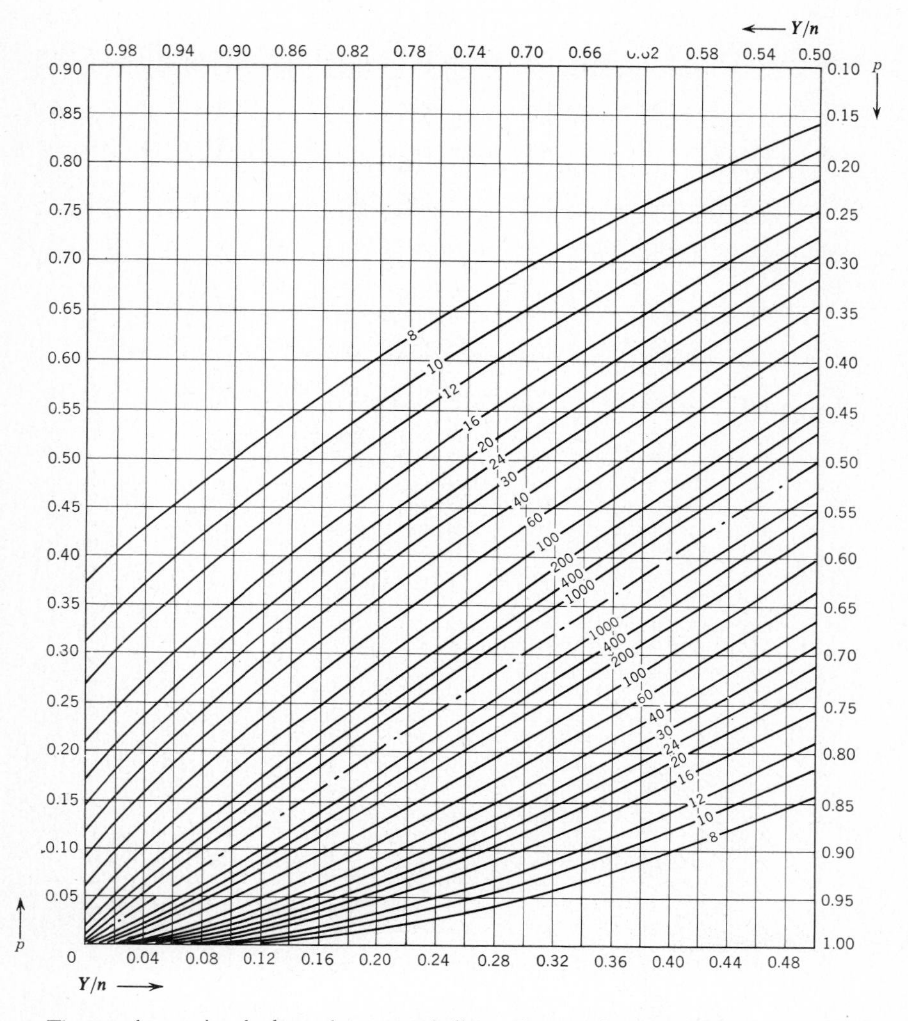

The numbers printed along the curves indicate the sample size n. For a given value of the abscissa Y/n, p_A and p_B are the ordinates read from (or interpolated between) the appropriate lower and upper curves, and $\Pr\,(p_A \leq p \leq p_B) \leq 1 - 2\alpha$.

SOURCE: Reproduced with permission of the *Biometrika* trustees and the editors, from E. S. Pearson and H. O. Hartley, *Biometrika Tables for Statisticians*, vol. 1, Cambridge University Press, 1954.

Table A.15*B* Confidence belts for proportions: confidence coefficient of .99

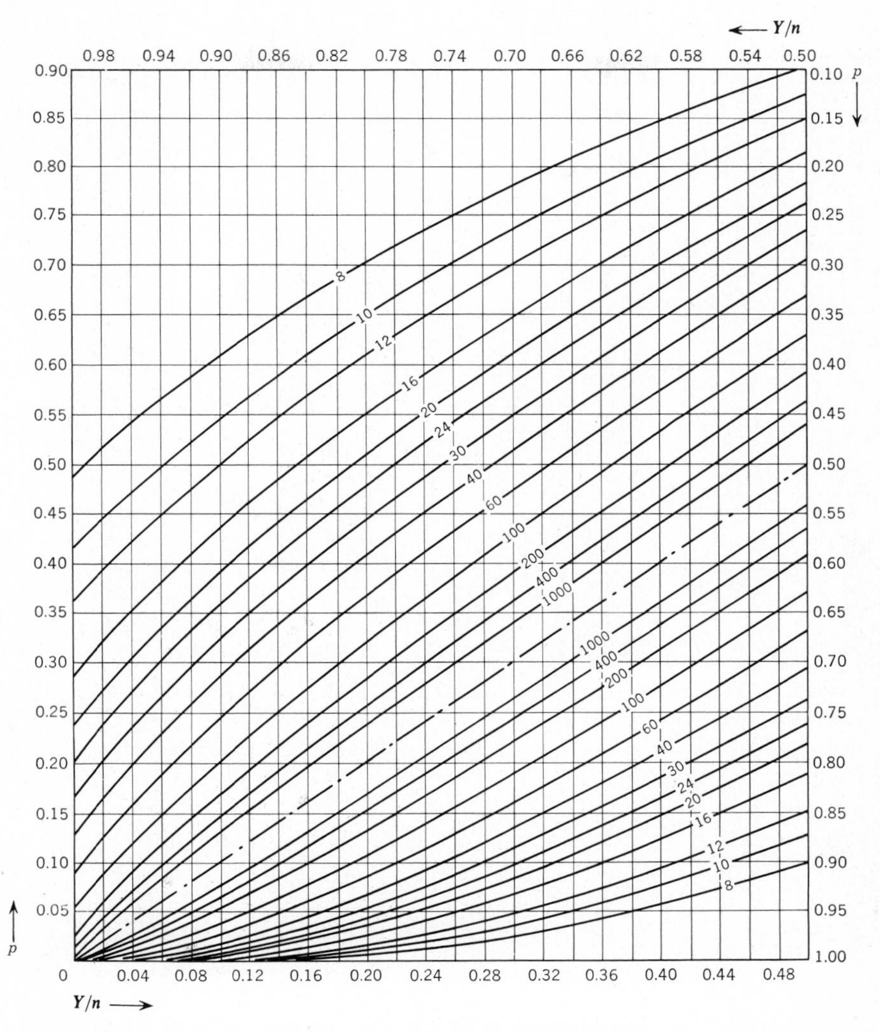

The numbers printed along the curves indicate the sample size n. Note: The process of reading from the curve can be simplified with the help of the right-angled corner of a loose sheet of paper or thin card, along the edges of which are marked off the scales shown in the top left-hand corner of the chart.

Source: Reproduced with permission of the *Biometrika* trustees and the editors, from E. S. Pearson and H. O. Hartley, *Biometrika Tables for Statisticians* vol. 1, Cambridge University Press, 1954.

Table A.16 Mosteller-Tukey binomial probability paper

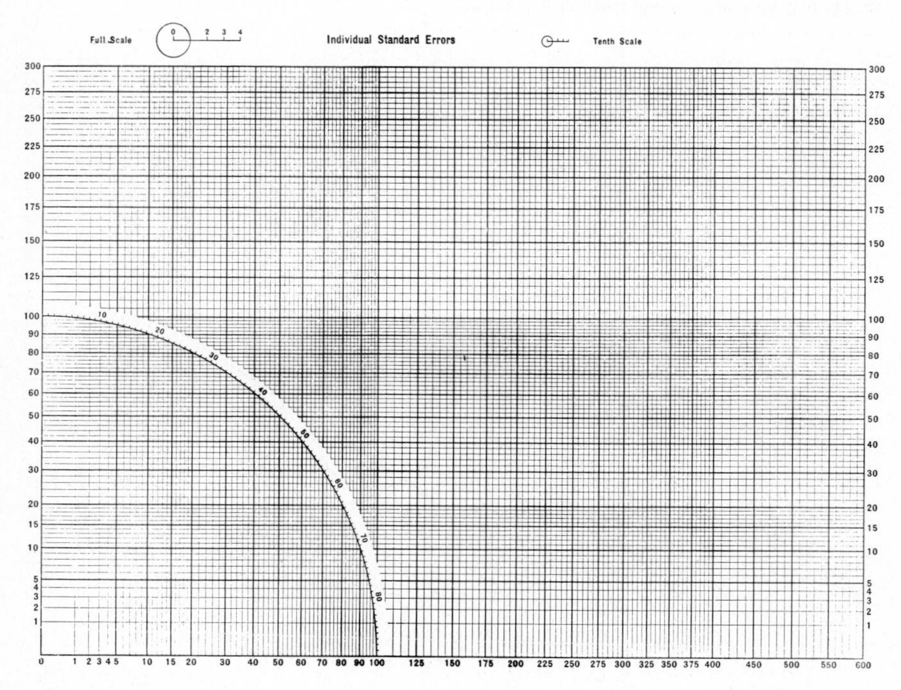

SOURCE: This chart first appeared in F. Mosteller and J. W. Tukey, "The uses and usefulness of binomial probability paper," *J. Am. Stat. Assn.*, **44**: 174–212 (1949). It is reproduced with permission of the authors, editor, and the Codex Book Company, Inc.

Table A.17*A* Sample size and the probability of making a wrong decision between the test cross ratios 1 : 1 and 3 : 1

Sample size n	Ratio accepted	Classes in regions of acceptance	Probability of making a wrong decision
20	1:1	0–12	.1316
	3:1	13–20	.1018
30	1:1	0–18	.1002
	3:1	19–30	.0507
40	1:1	0–25	.0403
	3:1	26–40	.0544
44	1:1	0–27	.0481
	3:1	28–44	.0318
50	1:1	0–31	.0325
	3:1	32–50	.0287
60	1:1	0–37	.0259
	3:1	38–60	.0154
70	1:1	0–44	.0112
	3:1	45–70	.0163
80	1:1	0–50	.0092
	3:1	51–80	.0089

$$\left.\begin{matrix} 1:1 = .5: & .5 \\ 3:1 = .75: & .25 \end{matrix}\right\} \text{The dividing line } R/n \doteq .63091$$

SOURCE: Reprinted from Prasert NaNagara, *Testing Mendelian Ratios,* M.S. Thesis, 1953, Cornell University, Ithaca, N.Y.

Table A.17*B* Sample size and the probability of making a wrong decision between the test cross ratios 3 : 1 and 7 : 1†

Sample size n	Ratio accepted	Classes in regions of acceptance	Probability of making a wrong decision
20	3:1	0–16	.2252
	7:1	17–20	.2347
30	3:1	0–24	.2026
	7:1	25–30	.1644
40	3:1	0–32	.1820
	7:1	33–40	.1190
50	3:1	0–40	.1637
	7:1	41–50	.0879
60	3:1	0–49	.0859
	7:1	50–60	.1231
70	3:1	0–57	.08
	7:1	58–70	.09
80	3:1	0–65	.08
	7:1	66–80	.06
90	3:1	0–73	.07
	7:1	74–90	.05
100	3:1	0–82	.04
	7:1	83–100	.07
110	3:1	0–90	.04
	7:1	91–110	.05
200	3:1	0–164	.01
	7:1	165–200	.01+
210	3:1	0–171	.011
	7:1	172–210	.006

$\left.\begin{array}{l}3:1 = .75:\ .25 \\ 7:1 = .875:\ .125\end{array}\right\}$ The dividing line $R/n \doteq .81786$

† See Table A.17*A*.

Table A.17*C* Sample size and the probability of making a wrong decision among the test cross ratios 1 : 1, 3 : 1, and 7 : 1†

Sample size n	Ratio accepted	Classes in regions of acceptance	Probability of making a wrong decision
20	1:1	0–11	.2517
	3:1	12–16	.2661*
	7:1	17–20	.2347
30	1:1	0–17	.1808
	3:1	18–24	.2242*
	7:1	25–30	.1644
40	1:1	0–23	.1341
	3:1	24–32	.1936*
	7:1	33–40	.1190
50	1:1	0–31	.0325
	3:1	32–41	.1203
	7:1	42–50	.1660*
60	1:1	0–37	.0259
	3:1	38–49	.1013
	7:1	50–60	.1231*
80	1:1	0–50	.01
	3:1	51–65	.08*
	7:1	66–80	.06
100	1:1	0–63	.00
	3:1	64–82	.04
	7:1	83–100	.07*
110	1:1	0–69	.00
	3:1	70–90	.04
	7:1	91–110	.05*
200	1:1	0–126	.00
	3:1	127–164	.01
	7:1	165–200	.01+*
210	1:1	0–132	.000
	3:1	133–171	.011*
	7:1	172–210	.006

1:1 = .5: .5
3:1 = .75: .25
7:1 = .875: .125

(1:1, 3:1) The dividing line $R/n \doteq .63091$
(3:1, 7:1) The dividing line $R^1/n \doteq .81786$

† See Table A.17*A*.

Table A.17*D* Sample size and the probability of making a wrong decision among the F_2 ratios 9 : 7, 13 : 3, and 15 : 1†

Sample size n	Ratio accepted	Classes in regions of acceptance	Probability of making a wrong decision
	9:7	0–12	.29
20	13:3	13–17	.34*
	15:1	18–20	.15
	9:7	0–19	.17
30	13:3	20–26	.18*
	15:1	27–30	.12
	9:7	0–34	.03
50	13:3	35–44	.09*
	15:1	45–50	.09
	9:7	0–51	.020
75	13:3	52–66	.048*
	15:1	67–75	.044
	9:7	0–104	.000
150	13:3	105–132	.010*
	15:1	133–150	.006

9:7 = .5625: .4375
13:3 = .8125: .1875
15:1 = .9375: .0625

The dividing line $R/n \doteq .69736$
The dividing line $R^1/n \doteq .88478$

† See Table A.17*A*.

Table A.17E Sample size and the probability of making a wrong decision among the F_2 ratios 27 : 37, 55 : 9, and 63 : 1†

Sample size n	Ratio accepted	Classes in regions of acceptance	Probability of making a wrong decision
	27:37	0–12	.03
20	55:9	13–18	.21*
	63:1	19–20	.04
	27:37	0–19	.01
30	55:9	20–28	.06
	63:1	29–30	.08*
	27:37	0–26	.00
40	55:9	27–37	.07*
	63:1	38–40	.03
	27:37	0–33	.00
50	55:9	34–47	.02
	63:1	48–50	.04*
	27:37	0–49	.000
75	55:9	50–70	.014*
	63:1	71–75	.007
	27:37	0–59	.000
90	55:9	60–84	.008*
	63:1	85–90	.003
	27:37	0–63	.000
95	55:9	64–89	.005*
	63:1	90–95	.004
	27:37	0–66	.000
100	55:9	67–94	.003
	63:1	95–100	.005*

27:37 = .421875: .578125
55:9 = .859375: .140625 } The dividing line $R/n \doteq .665214$
63:1 = .984375:. 015625 } The dividing line $R^1/n \doteq .94178$

† See Table A.17A.

Table A.17*F* Sample size and the probability of making a wrong decision among the F_2 ratios 27 : 37, 9 : 7, 3 : 1, 13 : 3, 55 : 9, 15 : 1, and 63 : 1†

Sample size *n*	Ratio accepted	Classes in regions of acceptance	Probability of making a wrong decision
	27:37	0–22	.342
	9:7	23–29	.405
	3:1	30–37	.517
50	13:3	38–41	.521*
	55:9	42–45	.415
	15:1	46–48	.372
	63:1	49–50	.177
	27:37	0–33	.330
	9:7	34–44	.319
	3:1	45–57	.379
75	13:3	58–63	.383
	55:9	64–69	.400*
	15:1	70–73	.375
	63:1	74–75	.328
	27:37	0–49	.059
	9:7	50–66	.096
	3:1	67–77	.314
100	13:3	78–84	.372*
	55:9	85–92	.352
	15:1	93–97	.334
	63:1	98–100	.206
	27:37	0–246	.00
	9:7	247–330	.00
	3:1	331–387	.10
500	13:3	388–418	.10*
	55:9	419–451	.09
	15:1	452–483	.01
	63:1	484–500	.00
	27:37	0–393	.00
	9:7	394–528	.00
	3:1	529–625	.02
800	13:3	626–670	.04+*
	55:9	671–722	.04
	15:1	723–772	.00
	63:1	773–800	.00
	27:37	0–676	.00
	9:7	677–908	.00
	3:1	909–1075	.00
1375	13:3	1076–1151	.01
	55:9	1152–1241	.01
	15:1	1242–1328	.00
	63:1	1329–1375	.00

27 : 37 } 9 : 7 — The dividing line $R/n \doteq .4921$
9 : 7 } 3 : 1 — The dividing line $R/n \doteq .6605$
3 : 1 } 13 : 3 — The dividing line $R/n \doteq .7823$
13 : 3 } 55 : 9 — The dividing line $R/n \doteq .8368$
55 : 9 } 15 : 1 — The dividing line $R/n \doteq .9031$
15 : 1 } 63 : 1 — The dividing line $R/n \doteq .9660$

† See Table A.17*A*.

Table A.17*G* Sample size and the probability of making a wrong decision among the test cross ratios 2 : 1 : 1, 1 : 2 : 1, and 1 : 1 : 2†

Sample size, n	*Probability of making a wrong decision*
20	.1890
40	.0645
45	.0501
50	.0394
70	.0147
75	.0113
80	.0099

Accept 2:1:1 when the first group is larger than the other two; accept 1:2:1 when the second group is larger than the other two; and accept 1:1:2 when the third group is the largest group.

† See Table A.17*A*.

Table A.17*H* Sample size and the probability of making a wrong decision among the test cross ratios 1 : 1 : 2, 1 : 1 : 4, and 1 : 1 : 6†

Sample size n	Ratio accepted	Classes in regions of acceptance	Probability of making a wrong decision
	1:1:2	0–27	.240
50	1:1:4	28–35	.305*
	1:1:6	36–50	.252
	1:1:2	0–54	.18
100	1:1:4	55–71	.16
	1:1:6	72–100	.21*
	1:1:2	0–117	.01
200	1:1:4	118–142	.10
	1:1:6	143–200	.11*
	1:1:2	0–193	.00
330	1:1:4	194–234	.05*
	1:1:6	235–330	.04
	1:1:2	0–377	.000
646	1:1:4	378–458	.008
	1:1:6	459–646	.010*

Accept 1:1:2 when the number of individuals in the third group z is less than $.5850n$; accept 1:1:4 when z is between $.5850n$ and $.7095n$; accept 1:1:6 when z is greater than $.7095n$.

† See Table A.17*A*.

Table A.17I Sample size and the probability of making a wrong decision among the F_2 ratios 9 : 6 : 1, 9 : 3 : 4, and 12 : 3 : 1†

Sample size n	Ratio accepted	Classes in regions of acceptance	Probability of making a wrong decision
20	9:6:1	$y \geq 6$ and $x < 14$	.213
	9:3:4	$y < 6$ and $x < 14$	.312*
	12:3:1	$x \geq 14$	.214
50	9:6:1	$y \geq 14$ and $x < 34$	.084
	9:3:4	$y < 14$ and $x < 34$	.134*
	12:3:1	$x \geq 34$	.098
75	9:6:1	$y \geq 21$ and $x < 50$	.054
	9:3:4	$y < 21$ and $x < 50$	.075*
	12:3:1	$x \geq 50$	.039
90	9:6:1	$y \geq 25$ and $x < 60$	.035
	9:3:4	$y < 25$ and $x < 60$	.051*
	12:3:1	$x \geq 60$	.028
150	9:6:1	$y \geq 42$ and $x < 100$	.008
	9:3:4	$y < 42$ and $x < 100$	.009*
	12:3:1	$x \geq 100$	.008

x and y are the numbers of individuals in the first and the second groups of the sample, respectively.

Accept 9 : 6 : 1 when $y \geq .27457n$ and $x < .6605n$
Accept 9 : 3 : 4 when $y < .27457n$ and $x < .6605n$
Accept 12 : 3 : 1 when $x \geq .6605n$

† See Table A.17A.

Table A.17*J* Sample size and the probability of making a wrong decision between the F_2 ratios 27 : 9 : 28 and 81 : 27 : 148†

Sample size *n*	Ratio accepted	Classes of *z* in regions of acceptance	Probability of making a wrong decision
20	27 : 9 : 28 81 : 27 : 148	0–10 11–20	.2144 .3125
40	27 : 9 : 28 81 : 27 : 148	0–20 21–40	.1694 .1998
60	27 : 9 : 28 81 : 27 : 148	0–30 31–60	.1345 .1370
100	27 : 9 : 28 81 : 27 : 148	0–50 51–100	.09 .07
135	27 : 9 : 28 81 : 27 : 148	0–68 69–135	.05+ .05−
200	27 : 9 : 28 81 : 27 : 148	0–101 102–200	.02 .02
269	27 : 9 : 28 81 : 27 : 148	0–136 137–269	.010 .009

z is the number of individuals in the third group of the sample. The dividing line $R/n \doteq .50788$.

† See Table A.17*A*.

Table A.18 Wilcoxon's signed rank test

Tabulated values of T are such that numerically smaller values occur by chance with stated probability†

Pairs *n*	Probability .05	.02	.01	Pairs *n*	Probability .05	.02	.01
6	0	—	—	16	30	24	20
7	2	0	—	17	35	28	23
8	4	2	0	18	40	33	28
9	6	3	2	19	46	38	32
10	8	5	3	20	52	43	38
11	11	7	5	21	59	49	43
12	14	10	7	22	66	56	49
13	17	13	10	23	73	62	55
14	21	16	13	24	81	69	61
15	25	20	16	25	89	77	68

† Probabilities are for two-tailed tests. For one-tailed tests, the above probabilities become .025, .01, and .005.

SOURCE: Reproduced from F. Wilcoxon, *Some Rapid Approximate Statistical Procedures*, American Cyanamid Company, Stamford, Conn., 1949, with permission of the author and the American Cyanamid Company. The values in this table were obtained by rounding off values given by Tukey in Memorandum Rept. 17, "The simplest signed rank tests," Stat. Research Group, Princeton Univ., 1949.

Table A.19 Critical points of rank sums

(Two-tailed alternatives)

n_2 = larger n	P	n_1 = smaller n													
		2	3	4	5	6	7	8	9	10	11	12	13	14	15
4	.05			10											
	.01			—											
5	.05		6	11	17										
	.01		—	—	15										
6	.05		7	12	18	26									
	.01		—	10	16	23									
7	.05		7	13	20	27	36								
	.01		—	10	17	24	32								
8	.05	3	8	14	21	29	38	49							
	.01	—	—	11	17	25	34	43							
9	.05	3	8	15	22	31	40	51	63						
	.01	—	6	11	18	26	35	45	56						
10	.05	3	9	15	23	32	42	53	65	78					
	.01	—	6	12	19	27	37	47	58	71					
11	.05	4	9	16	24	34	44	55	68	81	96				
	.01	—	6	12	20	28	38	49	61	74	87				
12	.05	4	10	17	26	35	46	58	71	85	99	115			
	.01	—	7	13	21	30	40	51	63	76	90	106			
13	.05	4	10	18	27	37	48	60	73	88	103	119	137		
	.01	—	7	14	22	31	41	53	65	79	93	109	125		
14	.05	4	11	19	28	38	50	63	76	91	106	123	141	160	
	.01	—	7	14	22	32	43	54	67	81	96	112	129	147	
15	.05	4	11	20	29	40	52	65	79	94	110	127	145	164	185
	.01	—	8	15	23	33	44	56	70	84	99	115	133	151	171
16	.05	4	12	21	31	42	54	67	82	97	114	131	150	169	
	.01	—	8	15	24	34	46	58	72	86	102	119	137	155	
17	.05	5	12	21	32	43	56	70	84	100	117	135	154		
	.01	—	8	16	25	36	47	60	74	89	105	122	140		
18	.05	5	13	22	33	45	58	72	87	103	121	139			
	.01	—	8	16	26	37	49	62	76	92	108	125			
19	.05	5	13	23	34	46	60	74	90	107	124				
	.01	3	9	17	27	38	50	64	78	94	111				
20	.05	5	14	24	35	48	62	77	93	110					
	.01	3	9	18	28	39	52	66	81	97					
21	.05	6	14	25	37	50	64	79	95						
	.01	3	9	18	29	40	53	68	83						
22	.05	6	15	26	38	51	66	82							
	.01	3	10	19	29	42	55	70							
23	.05	6	15	27	39	53	68								
	.01	3	10	19	30	43	57								
24	.05	6	16	28	40	55									
	.01	3	10	20	31	44									
25	.05	6	16	28	42										
	.01	3	11	20	32										
26	.05	7	17	29											
	.01	3	11	21											
27	.05	7	17												
	.01	4	11												
28	.05	7													
	.01	4													

SOURCE: Reprinted from Colin White, "The use of ranks in a test of significance for comparing two treatments," *Biometrics*, **8:** 33–41 (1950), with permission of the editor and the author.

Table A.20 Working significance levels for magnitudes of quadrant sums

Significance level	*Magnitude of quadrant sum*†
.10	9
.05	11
.02	13
.01	14–15
.005	15–17
.002	17–19
.001	18–21

† The smaller magnitude applies for large sample size, the larger magnitude for small sample size. Magnitude equal to or greater than twice the sample size less 6 should not be used.

SOURCE: Reprinted from P. S. Olmstead and J. W. Tukey, "A corner test for association," *Annals Math. Stat.*, **18:** 495–513 (1947), with permission of the authors, editor, and courtesy of Bell Telephone Laboratories, Inc.

Table A.21 Duncan-Waller minimum-average-risk t values ($k = 100$)

q	*f* = 4	6	8	10	12	14	16	18	20	24	30	40	60	120	∞
							†$F = 1.2$ ($a = .913$, $b = 2.449$)								
2–6	*	*	*	*	*	*	*	*	*	*	*	*	*	*	2.85
8	2.85	2.91	2.94	2.96	2.97	2.98	2.99	2.99	2.99	3.00	3.00	3.00	3.00	3.00	3.00
10	2.85	2.93	2.98	3.01	3.04	3.05	3.06	3.07	3.08	3.09	3.10	3.10	3.11	3.12	3.12
12	2.85	2.95	3.01	3.05	3.08	3.10	3.12	3.13	3.14	3.16	3.17	3.19	3.20	3.21	3.22
14	2.85	2.96	3.03	3.08	3.12	3.14	3.16	3.18	3.19	3.21	3.23	3.25	3.27	3.29	3.31
16	2.85	2.97	3.05	3.11	3.15	3.18	3.20	3.22	3.24	3.26	3.28	3.31	3.33	3.36	3.38
20	2.85	2.99	3.08	3.14	3.19	3.23	3.26	3.28	3.30	3.33	3.37	3.40	3.44	3.47	3.50
40	2.85	3.02	3.13	3.22	3.29	3.35	3.39	3.43	3.47	3.52	3.58	3.64	3.72	3.79	3.87
100	2.85	3.04	3.17	3.28	3.36	3.44	3.50	3.55	3.59	3.67	3.76	3.86	3.98	4.11	4.23
∞	2.85	3.05	3.20	3.32	3.42	3.50	3.58	3.64	3.70	3.80	3.91	4.06	4.24	4.45	4.22
							†$F = 1.4$ ($a = .845$, $b = 1.871$)								
2–4	*	*	*	*	*	*	*	*	*	*	*	*	*	*	2.57
6	2.85	2.85	2.84	2.83	2.82	2.82	2.81	2.80	2.80	2.79	2.78	2.77	2.75	2.74	2.72
8	2.85	2.88	2.89	2.90	2.90	2.90	2.89	2.89	2.89	2.88	2.88	2.87	2.86	2.85	2.83
10	2.85	2.90	2.93	2.94	2.95	2.95	2.96	2.96	2.96	2.96	2.96	2.95	2.94	2.93	2.92
12	2.85	2.92	2.95	2.98	2.99	3.00	3.00	3.01	3.01	3.01	3.01	3.01	3.00	2.99	2.98
14	2.85	2.93	2.97	3.00	3.02	3.03	3.04	3.04	3.05	3.05	3.06	3.06	3.05	3.05	3.03
16	2.85	2.94	2.99	3.02	3.04	3.06	3.07	3.08	3.08	3.09	3.09	3.10	3.10	3.09	3.08
20	2.85	2.95	3.01	3.05	3.08	3.10	3.11	3.12	3.13	3.14	3.15	3.16	3.16	3.16	3.14
40	2.85	2.98	3.06	3.12	3.16	3.19	3.22	3.24	3.25	3.28	3.30	3.31	3.32	3.32	3.28
100	2.85	2.99	3.09	3.16	3.22	3.26	3.29	3.32	3.34	3.38	3.41	3.43	3.45	3.42	3.31
∞	2.85	3.01	3.12	3.20	3.26	3.31	3.35	3.39	3.42	3.46	3.50	3.53	3.54	3.46	3.22

† *Boundary conditions for Table A.21:*

For $F \leq 2.4$, interpolate on $a = 1/F^{1/2}$ unless both $q > 100$ and $f < 10$, then use $b = [F/(F-1)]^{1/2}$.

For $F > 2.4$, interpolate on b unless both $q \leq 20$ and $f \leq 20$, then use a.

SOURCE: Personal communication from David B. Duncan.

†$F = 1.7$ ($a = .767$, $b = 1.558$)

2	*	*	*	*	*	*	*	*	*	*	*	*	*	2.26
4	*	*	*	*	*	2.61	2.59	2.58	2.56	2.54	2.52	2.50	2.48	2.45
6	2.85	2.82	2.79	2.76	2.74	2.72	2.71	2.70	2.69	2.67	2.65	2.63	2.61	2.58	2.56
8	2.85	2.84	2.83	2.81	2.80	2.78	2.77	2.76	2.75	2.74	2.72	2.70	2.68	2.65	2.62
10	2.85	2.86	2.86	2.85	2.84	2.83	2.82	2.81	2.80	2.79	2.77	2.75	2.73	2.70	2.66
12	2.85	2.87	2.88	2.88	2.87	2.86	2.85	2.84	2.84	2.82	2.81	2.79	2.76	2.73	2.69
14	2.85	2.88	2.90	2.90	2.89	2.89	2.88	2.87	2.86	2.85	2.83	2.81	2.79	2.75	2.71
16	2.85	2.89	2.91	2.91	2.91	2.90	2.90	2.89	2.89	2.87	2.86	2.84	2.81	2.77	2.73
20	2.85	2.90	2.93	2.93	2.94	2.93	2.93	2.92	2.92	2.91	2.89	2.87	2.84	2.80	2.74
40	2.85	2.93	2.97	2.99	3.00	3.00	3.00	3.00	2.99	2.98	2.97	2.94	2.89	2.83	2.74
100	2.85	2.94	2.99	3.02	3.04	3.05	3.05	3.05	3.05	3.04	3.02	2.98	2.92	2.83	2.71
∞	2.85	2.95	3.01	3.05	3.07	3.08	3.09	3.09	3.08	3.07	3.05	3.01	2.93	2.81	2.68

†$F = 2.0$ ($a = .707$, $b = 1.414$)

2	*	*	*	*	*	*	*	*	*	*	*	*	*	*	2.21
4	*	2.74	2.67	2.63	2.59	2.56	2.54	2.52	2.51	2.49	2.46	2.44	2.41	2.39	2.36
6	2.85	2.79	2.74	2.70	2.67	2.64	2.62	2.60	2.59	2.57	2.54	2.52	2.49	2.46	2.42
8	2.85	2.81	2.77	2.74	2.71	2.69	2.67	2.65	2.64	2.62	2.59	2.56	2.53	2.49	2.46
10	2.85	2.83	2.80	2.77	2.74	2.72	2.70	2.69	2.67	2.65	2.62	2.59	2.56	2.52	2.47
12	2.85	2.84	2.82	2.79	2.77	2.75	2.73	2.71	2.70	2.67	2.64	2.61	2.57	2.53	2.48
14	2.85	2.85	2.83	2.81	2.79	2.77	2.75	2.73	2.72	2.69	2.66	2.63	2.59	2.54	2.49
16	2.85	2.85	2.84	2.82	2.80	2.78	2.76	2.74	2.73	2.70	2.67	2.64	2.59	2.54	2.49
20	2.85	2.86	2.85	2.84	2.82	2.80	2.78	2.77	2.75	2.72	2.69	2.65	2.61	2.55	2.48
40	2.85	2.88	2.89	2.88	2.86	2.85	2.83	2.81	2.80	2.77	2.73	2.68	2.62	2.55	2.46
100	2.85	2.89	2.91	2.90	2.89	2.88	2.86	2.84	2.82	2.79	2.75	2.69	2.62	2.53	2.45
∞	2.85	2.90	2.92	2.92	2.91	2.90	2.88	2.86	2.85	2.81	2.76	2.69	2.61	2.52	2.43

* All differences not significant.

† See boundary conditions on page 615.

Table A.21 Duncan-Waller minimum-average-risk t values ($k = 100$) (*Continued*)

q	f: 4	6	8	10	12	14	16	18	20	24	30	40	60	120	∞
							†$F = 2.4$ ($a = .645$, $b = 1.309$)								
2	*	*	*	*	*	*	*	*	*	*	*	*	*	2.18	2.16
4	2.85	2.71	2.63	2.57	2.53	2.49	2.47	2.44	2.43	2.40	2.37	2.34	2.31	2.28	2.25
6	2.85	2.75	2.68	2.63	2.58	2.55	2.52	2.50	2.48	2.46	2.42	2.39	2.36	2.32	2.28
8	2.85	2.77	2.71	2.66	2.62	2.59	2.56	2.54	2.52	2.49	2.45	2.42	2.38	2.34	2.29
10	2.85	2.79	2.73	2.68	2.64	2.61	2.58	2.56	2.54	2.50	2.47	2.43	2.39	2.34	2.30
12	2.85	2.79	2.74	2.70	2.66	2.62	2.60	2.57	2.55	2.52	2.48	2.44	2.39	2.35	2.29
14	2.85	2.80	2.75	2.71	2.67	2.64	2.61	2.58	2.56	2.53	2.49	2.44	2.40	2.35	2.29
16	2.85	2.81	2.76	2.72	2.68	2.65	2.62	2.59	2.57	2.53	2.49	2.45	2.40	2.34	2.29
20	2.85	2.82	2.77	2.73	2.69	2.66	2.63	2.60	2.58	2.54	2.50	2.45	2.40	2.34	2.28
40	2.85	2.83	2.80	2.76	2.72	2.69	2.66	2.63	2.60	2.56	2.51	2.46	2.39	2.33	2.27
100	2.85	2.84	2.81	2.78	2.74	2.71	2.67	2.64	2.62	2.57	2.51	2.45	2.39	2.32	2.26
∞	2.85	2.85	2.83	2.79	2.76	2.72	2.68	2.65	2.62	2.57	2.51	2.45	2.38	2.31	2.25
							†$F = 3.0$ ($a = .577$, $b = 1.225$)								
2	*	*	*	2.41	2.36	2.32	2.29	2.27	2.25	2.22	2.20	2.17	2.14	2.11	2.09
4	2.85	2.68	2.57	2.50	2.45	2.41	2.38	2.35	2.33	2.30	2.27	2.24	2.20	2.17	2.13
6	2.85	2.71	2.61	2.54	2.49	2.44	2.41	2.39	2.36	2.33	2.29	2.26	2.22	2.18	2.14
8	2.85	2.72	2.63	2.56	2.51	2.47	2.43	2.40	2.38	2.34	2.31	2.27	2.22	2.18	2.14
10	2.85	2.74	2.65	2.58	2.52	2.48	2.44	2.41	2.39	2.35	2.31	2.27	2.22	2.18	2.13
12	2.85	2.74	2.66	2.59	2.53	2.49	2.45	2.42	2.40	2.36	2.31	2.27	2.22	2.18	2.13
14	2.85	2.75	2.66	2.60	2.54	2.49	2.46	2.43	2.40	2.36	2.32	2.27	2.22	2.17	2.13
16	2.85	2.75	2.67	2.60	2.55	2.50	2.46	2.43	2.40	2.36	2.32	2.27	2.22	2.17	2.12
20	2.85	2.76	2.68	2.61	2.55	2.51	2.47	2.43	2.41	2.36	2.32	2.27	2.22	2.17	2.12
40	2.85	2.77	2.70	2.63	2.57	2.52	2.48	2.44	2.41	2.37	2.32	2.26	2.21	2.16	2.11
100	2.85	2.78	2.71	2.64	2.58	2.53	2.49	2.45	2.42	2.37	2.31	2.26	2.21	2.16	2.11
∞	2.85	2.79	2.71	2.65	2.59	2.53	2.49	2.45	2.42	2.37	2.31	2.26	2.20	2.15	2.11

							$\dagger F = 4.0$ ($a = .500$, $b = 1.155$)								
2	*	2.58	2.44	2.35	2.29	2.25	2.22	2.20	2.18	2.15	2.12	2.09	2.06	2.03	2.00
4	2.85	2.63	2.50	2.41	2.35	2.30	2.27	2.24	2.22	2.18	2.15	2.12	2.08	2.05	2.01
6	2.85	2.65	2.52	2.43	2.37	2.32	2.28	2.25	2.23	2.19	2.16	2.12	2.08	2.04	2.01
10	2.85	2.67	2.55	2.46	2.39	2.34	2.30	2.26	2.24	2.20	2.16	2.12	2.08	2.04	2.00
20	2.85	2.69	2.57	2.47	2.40	2.35	2.30	2.27	2.24	2.20	2.15	2.11	2.07	2.03	1.99
∞	2.85	2.71	2.59	2.49	2.42	2.36	2.31	2.27	2.24	2.19	2.15	2.11	2.06	2.02	1.99
							$\dagger F = 6.0$ ($a = .408$, $b = 1.095$)								
2	2.85	2.53	2.37	2.27	2.21	2.16	2.13	2.10	2.08	2.04	2.02	1.99	1.96	1.93	1.90
4	2.85	2.56	2.40	2.30	2.23	2.18	2.14	2.12	2.09	2.06	2.02	1.99	1.96	1.93	1.90
6	2.85	2.58	2.42	2.31	2.24	2.19	2.15	2.12	2.09	2.06	2.02	1.99	1.95	1.92	1.89
10	2.85	2.59	2.43	2.32	2.24	2.19	2.15	2.12	2.09	2.06	2.02	1.99	1.95	1.92	1.89
20	2.85	2.60	2.44	2.32	2.25	2.19	2.15	2.12	2.09	2.05	2.02	1.98	1.95	1.92	1.89
∞	2.85	2.61	2.44	2.33	2.25	2.19	2.15	2.12	2.09	2.05	2.02	1.98	1.95	1.92	1.89
							$\dagger F = 10.0$ ($a = .316$, $b = 1.054$)								
2	2.85	2.48	2.30	2.19	2.12	2.07	2.04	2.01	1.99	1.96	1.93	1.90	1.87	1.85	1.82
4	2.85	2.49	2.31	2.20	2.13	2.08	2.04	2.01	1.99	1.96	1.93	1.90	1.87	1.84	1.82
6	2.85	2.50	2.31	2.20	2.13	2.08	2.04	2.01	1.99	1.96	1.93	1.90	1.87	1.84	1.82
10–∞	2.85	2.51	2.32	2.20	2.13	2.08	2.04	2.01	1.99	1.96	1.93	1.90	1.87	1.84	1.82
							$\dagger F = 25.0$ ($a = .200$, $b = 1.021$)								
2–4	2.85	2.40	2.20	2.10	2.03	1.99	1.95	1.93	1.91	1.88	1.86	1.83	1.80	1.78	1.76
10–∞	2.85	2.41	2.21	2.10	2.03	1.99	1.95	1.93	1.91	1.88	1.86	1.83	1.80	1.78	1.76
							$\dagger F = \infty$ ($a = 0$, $b = 1$)								
2–∞	2.85	2.33	2.13	2.03	1.97	1.93	1.90	1.88	1.86	1.84	1.81	1.79	1.76	1.74	1.72

* All differences not significant.

† See boundary conditions on page 615.

Table A.22 Critical values for the Kolmogorov-Smirnov one-sample test

One-sided test, α =	.10	.05	.025	.01	.005
Two-sided test, α =	.20	.10	.05	.02	.01
n = 1	.900	.950	.975	.990	.995
2	.684	.776	.842	.900	.929
3	.565	.636	.708	.785	.829
4	.493	.565	.624	.689	.734
5	.447	.509	.563	.627	.669
6	.410	.468	.519	.577	.617
7	.381	.436	.483	.538	.576
8	.358	.410	.454	.507	.542
9	.339	.387	.430	.480	.513
10	.323	.369	.409	.457	.489
11	.308	.352	.391	.437	.468
12	.296	.338	.375	.419	.449
13	.285	.325	.361	.404	.432
14	.275	.314	.349	.390	.418
15	.266	.304	.338	.377	.404
16	.258	.295	.327	.366	.392
17	.250	.286	.318	.355	.381
18	.244	.279	.309	.346	.371
19	.237	.271	.301	.337	.361
20	.232	.265	.294	.329	.352
21	.226	.259	.287	.321	.344
22	.221	.253	.281	.314	.337
23	.216	.247	.275	.307	.330
24	.212	.242	.269	.301	.323
25	.208	.238	.264	.295	.317
26	.204	.233	.259	.290	.311
27	.200	.229	.254	.284	.305
28	.197	.225	.250	.279	.300
29	.193	.221	.246	.275	.295
30	.190	.218	.242	.270	.290
31	.187	.214	.238	.266	.285
32	.184	.211	.234	.262	.281
33	.182	.208	.231	.258	.277
34	.179	.205	.227	.254	.273
35	.177	.202	.224	.251	.269
36	.174	.199	.221	.247	.265
37	.172	.196	.218	.244	.262
38	.170	.194	.215	.241	.258
39	.168	.191	.213	.238	.255
40	.165	.189	.210	.235	.252
Approximation for $n > 40$:	$\frac{1.0730}{\sqrt{n}}$	$\frac{1.2239}{\sqrt{n}}$	$\frac{1.3581}{\sqrt{n}}$	$\frac{1.5174}{\sqrt{n}}$	$\frac{1.6276}{\sqrt{n}}$

Source: This table is extracted from "Table of percentage points of Kolmgorov statistics," *J. Amer. Statist. Assoc.*, **51**:111–121 (1956), with permission of the author, L. H. Miller, and the editor.

Table A.23*A* Critical values for the Kolmogorov-Smirnov two-sample test, $n_1 = n_2$

One-sided test	$1 - \alpha = 0.90$	0.95	0.975	0.99	0.995
Two-sided test	$1 - \alpha = 0.80$	0.90	0.95	0.98	0.99
$n =$ 3	2/3	2/3			
4	3/4	3/4	3/4		
5	3/5	3/5	4/5	4/5	4/5
6	3/6	4/6	4/6	5/6	5/6
7	4/7	4/7	5/7	5/7	5/7
8	4/8	4/8	5/8	5/8	6/8
9	4/9	5/9	5/9	6/9	6/9
10	4/10	5/10	6/10	6/10	7/10
11	5/11	5/11	6/11	7/11	7/11
12	5/12	5/12	6/12	7/12	7/12
13	5/13	6/13	6/13	7/13	8/13
14	5/14	6/14	7/14	7/14	8/14
15	5/15	6/15	7/15	8/15	8/15
16	6/16	6/16	7/16	8/16	9/16
17	6/17	7/17	7/17	8/17	9/17
18	6/18	7/18	8/18	9/18	9/18
19	6/19	7/19	8/19	9/19	9/19
20	6/20	7/20	8/20	9/20	10/20
21	6/21	7/21	8/21	9/21	10/21
22	7/22	8/22	8/22	10/22	10/22
23	7/23	8/23	9/23	10/23	10/23
24	7/24	8/24	9/24	10/24	11/24
25	7/25	8/25	9/25	10/25	11/25
26	7/26	8/26	9/26	10/26	11/26
27	7/27	8/27	9/27	11/27	11/27
28	8/28	9/28	10/28	11/28	12/28
29	8/29	9/29	10/29	11/29	12/29
30	8/30	9/30	10/30	11/30	12/30
31	8/31	9/31	10/31	11/31	12/31
32	8/32	9/32	10/32	12/32	12/32
33	8/33	9/33	11/33	12/33	13/33
34	8/34	10/34	11/34	12/34	13/34
35	8/35	10/35	11/35	12/35	13/35
36	9/36	10/36	11/36	12/36	13/36
37	9/37	10/37	11/37	13/37	13/37
38	9/38	10/38	11/38	13/38	14/38
39	9/39	10/39	11/39	13/39	14/39
40	9/40	10/40	12/40	13/40	14/40
Approximation for $n > 40$:	$\frac{1.5174}{\sqrt{n}}$	$\frac{1.7308}{\sqrt{n}}$	$\frac{1.9206}{\sqrt{n}}$	$\frac{2.1460}{\sqrt{n}}$	$\frac{2.3018}{\sqrt{n}}$

Source: This table is extracted from "Small-sample distribution for multi-sample statistics of the Smirnov type," *Ann. Math. Statist.*, **31**:710–720 (1960), with permission of the authors, Z. W. Birnbaum and R. A. Hall, and the editor.

Table A.23B Critical values for the Kolmogorov-Smirnov two-sample test, $n_1 \neq n_2$

One-sided test		$1 - \alpha = 0.90$	0.95	0.975	0.99	0.995
Two-sided test		$1 - \alpha = 0.80$	0.90	0.95	0.98	0.99
$n_1 = 3$	$n_2 =$ 4	3/4	3/4			
	5	2/3	4/5	4/5		
	6	2/3	2/3	5/6		
	7	2/3	5/7	6/7	6/7	
	8	5/8	3/4	3/4	7/8	
	9	2/3	2/3	7/9	8/9	8/9
	10	3/5	7/10	4/5	9/10	9/10
	12	7/12	2/3	3/4	5/6	11/12
$n_1 = 4$	$n_2 =$ 5	3/5	3/4	4/5	4/5	
	6	7/12	2/3	3/4	5/6	5/6
	7	17/28	5/7	3/4	6/7	6/7
	8	5/8	5/8	3/4	7/8	7/8
	9	5/9	2/3	3/4	7/9	8/9
	10	11/20	13/20	7/10	4/5	4/5
	12	7/12	2/3	2/3	3/4	5/6
	16	9/16	5/8	11/16	3/4	13/16
$n_1 = 5$	$n_2 =$ 6	3/5	2/3	2/3	5/6	5/6
	7	4/7	23/35	5/7	29/35	6/7
	8	11/20	5/8	27/40	4/5	4/5
	9	5/9	3/5	31/45	7/9	4/5
	10	1/2	3/5	7/10	7/10	4/5
	15	8/15	3/5	2/3	11/15	11/15
	20	1/2	11/20	3/5	7/10	3/4
$n_1 = 6$	$n_2 =$ 7	23/42	4/7	29/42	5/7	5/6
	8	1/2	7/12	2/3	3/4	3/4
	9	1/2	5/9	2/3	13/18	7/9
	10	1/2	17/30	19/30	7/10	11/15
	12	1/2	7/12	7/12	2/3	3/4
	18	4/9	5/9	11/18	2/3	13/18
	24	11/24	1/2	7/12	5/8	2/3
$n_1 = 7$	$n_2 =$ 8	1/2	33/56	5/8	41/56	3/4
	9	31/63	5/9	40/63	5/7	47/63
	10	33/70	39/70	43/70	7/10	53/70
	14	3/7	1/2	4/7	9/14	5/7
	28	3/7	13/28	15/28	17/28	9/14
$n_1 = 8$	$n_2 =$ 9	4/9	13/24	5/8	2/3	3/4
	10	19/40	21/40	23/40	27/40	7/10
	12	11/24	1/2	7/12	5/8	2/3
	16	7/16	1/2	9/16	5/8	5/8
	32	13/32	7/16	1/2	9/16	19/32

Table A.23*B* Critical values for the Kolmogorov-Smirnov two-sample test, $n_1 \neq n_2$ (*Continued*)

One-sided test		$1-\alpha = 0.90$	0.95	0.975	0.99	0.995
Two-sided test		$1-\alpha = 0.80$	0.90	0.95	0.98	0.99
$n_1 = 9$	$n_2 = 10$	7/15	1/2	26/45	2/3	31/45
	12	4/9	1/2	5/9	11/18	2/3
	15	19/45	22/45	8/15	3/5	29/45
	18	7/18	4/9	1/2	5/9	11/18
	36	13/36	5/12	17/36	19/36	5/9
$n_1 = 10$	$n_2 = 15$	2/5	7/15	1/2	17/30	19/30
	20	2/5	9/20	1/2	11/20	3/5
	40	7/20	2/5	9/20	1/2	
$n_1 = 12$	$n_2 = 15$	23/60	9/20	1/2	11/20	7/12
	16	3/8	7/16	23/48	13/24	7/12
	18	13/36	5/12	17/36	19/36	5/9
	20	11/30	5/12	7/15	31/60	17/30
$n_1 = 15$	$n_2 = 20$	7/20	2/5	13/30	29/60	31/60
$n_1 = 16$	$n_2 = 20$	27/80	31/80	17/40	19/40	41/80
Approximation for large samples:	$\sqrt{\frac{n_1+n_2}{n_1 n_2}} \times$	1.0730	1.2239	1.3581	1.5174	1.6276

Source: This table is extracted from "Distribution table for the deviation between two sample cumulatives," *Ann. Math. Statist.*, **23:**435–441 (1952), with permission of the author, F. J. Massey, Jr., and the editor.

Table A.24 Greek alphabet

(Letter and name)

A α	Alpha	H η	Eta	N ν	Nu	T τ	Tau
B β	Beta	Θ θ	Theta	Ξ ξ	Xi	Υ υ	Upsilon
Γ γ	Gamma	I ι	Iota	O o	Omicron	Φ ϕ	Phi
Δ δ	Delta	K κ	Kappa	Π π	Pi	X χ	Chi
E ε	Epsilon	Λ λ	Lambda	P ρ	Rho	Ψ ψ	Psi
Z ζ	Zeta	M μ	Mu	Σ σ	Sigma	Ω ω	Omega

INDEX